Lecture Notes in Computer Science 9109

More information about this series at http://www.springer.com/series/7408

Nikolaj Bjørner · Frank de Boer (Eds.)

FM 2015: Formal Methods

20th International Symposium Oslo, Norway, June 24–26, 2015 Proceedings

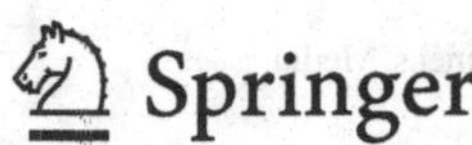

Springer

Editors
Nikolaj Bjørner
Microsoft Research
Redmond
Washington
USA

Frank de Boer
Centrum voor Wiskunde en Informatica
Amsterdam
The Netherlands

ISSN 0302-9743 ISSN 1611-3349 (electronic)
Lecture Notes in Computer Science
ISBN 978-3-319-19248-2 ISBN 978-3-319-19249-9 (eBook)
DOI 10.1007/978-3-319-19249-9

Library of Congress Control Number: 2015939719

LNCS Sublibrary: SL2 – Programming and Software Engineering

Springer Cham Heidelberg New York Dordrecht London

Printed on acid-free paper

Springer International Publishing AG Switzerland is part of Springer Science+Business Media (www.springer.com)

In Memoriam

Peter Lucas (1935–2015)

Chairman of Formal Methods Europe 1995–2000

Sadly, Peter Lucas passed away February 2nd, 2015 peacefully after a lengthy illness. He is remembered by many for his important contributions to the development of computer languages, and to those connected with FME as the chairman who established the association as a free and independent organisation. Colleagues will remember him as a computer scientist whose technical passion and skill were matched by a wise, balanced, and cheerful outlook.

Preface

This year we celebrate the 20th anniversary of the International Symposium on Formal Methods in Oslo, during June 24–26. FM 2015 attracted 124 submissions to the main track. Each submission was reviewed by at least three Program Committee members. The committee decided to accept 32 papers, resulting in an acceptance rate of 0.26. These conference proceedings further contain nine papers selected by the Program Committee of the Industry Track, which was chaired by Ralf Huuck (NICTA, Australia), Peter Gorm Larsen (Aarhus University, Denmark), and Andreas Roth (SAP, Germany).

The program includes four invited talks by Elvira Albert (Complutense University of Madrid, Spain), Werner Damm (Carl von Ossietzky Universität Oldenburg, DE), Valérie Issarny (Inria, France), and Leslie Lamport (Microsoft Research, USA). Furthermore, the overall program includes 11 workshops selected by the Workshop Chairs Marieke Huisman (Twente University, The Netherlands) and Volker Stolz (University of Oslo, Norway), four tutorials selected by the Tutorial Chairs Ferruccio Damiani (University of Torino, Italy) and Cristian Prisacariu (University of Oslo, Norway), a Doctoral Symposium organized by Bernhard Aichernig (TU Graz, Austria) and Alessandro Rossini (Sintef, Norway) with a keynote by Stijn de Gouw (CWI, The Netherlands), and a tool exhibition organized by Richard Bubel (TU Darmstadt, Germany) and Rudolf Schlatte (University of Oslo, Norway). The resulting program covers a wide spectrum of all the different aspects of the use of, and research on, formal methods for software development.

Thanks to all involved, i.e., all the Program Committee members, subreviewers, and the different chairs. Special thanks are due to the excellent local organization by Einar Broch Johnsen (University of Oslo, Norway) who was professionally supported by the Local Organization Chairs Violet Pun (University of Oslo, Norway) and Lizeth Tapia (University of Oslo, Norway), the Financial Chairs Arnaud Gotlieb (Simula Research Labs, Norway) and Ingrid Chieh Yu (University of Oslo, Norway), and the Publicity Chair Martin Steffen (University of Oslo, Norway).

Of particular interest to note here is that because of the very special occasion of the 20th anniversary Formal Methods Europe decided this year on a FME Fellowship Award.

Finally, FM 2015 gratefully recognizes the support of our sponsors: the Research Council of Norway, the City of Oslo, the Norwegian Centre for Software Verification and Validation (CERTUS), the Dutch Centre for Mathematics and Computer Science (CWI), and Microsoft Research.

April 2015

Nikolaj Bjørner
Frank de Boer
Peter Gorm Larsen

Organization

Program Committee

Erika Ábrahám	RWTH Aachen University, Germany
Bernhard K. Aichernig	TU Graz, Austria
Gilles Barthe	IMDEA Software Institute, Spain
Marcello Bonsangue	Leiden University, The Netherlands
Michael Butler	University of Southampton, UK
Andrew Butterfield	Trinity College, Dublin, Ireland
Ana Cavalcanti	University of York, UK
David Clark	University College London, UK
Jin Song Dong	National University of Singapore, Singapore
Michael Emmi	IMDEA Software Institute, Spain
John Fitzgerald	Newcastle University, UK
Nate Foster	Cornell University, USA
Vijay Ganesh	University of Waterloo, Canada
Diego Garbervetsky	Universidad de Buenos Aires
Dimitra Giannakopoulou	NASA Ames, USA
Stefania Gnesi	ISTI-CNR, Italy
Ganesh Gopalakrishnan	University of Utah, USA
Orna Grumberg	Technion - Israel Institute of Technology, Israel
Arie Gurfinkel	Software Engineering Institute, Carnegie Mellon University, USA
Klaus Havelund	Jet Propulsion Laboratory, California Institute of Technology, USA
Anne E. Haxthausen	Technical University of Denmark, Denmark
Ian J. Hayes	University of Queensland, Australia
Gerard Holzmann	Jet Propulsion Laboratory, California Institute of Technology, USA
Reiner Hähnle	Technical University of Darmstadt, Germany
Daniel Jackson	MIT, USA
Cliff Jones	Newcastle University, UK
Gerwin Klein	NICTA and University of New South Wales, Australia
Laura Kovacs	Chalmers University of Technology, Sweden
Marta Kwiatkowska	University of Oxford, UK
Peter Gorm Larsen	Aarhus University, Denmark
Yves Ledru	Laboratoire d'Informatique de Grenoble - Université Joseph Fourier, France

K. Rustan M. Leino	Microsoft Research, USA
Martin Leucker	University of Lübeck, Germany
Shaoying Liu	Hosei University, Japan
Tom Maibaum	McMaster University, Canada
Dominique Mery	Université de Lorraine, France
César Muñoz	NASA, USA
Peter Müller	ETH Zürich, Switzerland
David Naumann	Stevens Institute of Technology, USA
Tobias Nipkow	Technische Universität München, Germany
Jose Oliveira	Universidade do Minho, Portugal
Olaf Owe	University of Oslo, Norway
Sam Owre	SRI International, USA
Andrei Paskevich	Université Paris-Sud, France
Grigore Rosu	University of Illinois at Urbana-Champaign, USA
Kristin Yvonne Rozier	NASA Ames Research Center, USA
Sanjit A. Seshia	University of California, Berkeley, USA
Natasha Sharygina	Universita' della Svizzera Italiana, Switzerland
Viorica Sofronie-Stokkermans	University Koblenz-Landau, Germany
Jun Sun	Singapore University of Technology and Design, Singapore
Kenji Taguchi	AIST, Japan
Margus Veanes	Microsoft Research, USA
Ji Wang	National Laboratory for Parallel and Distributed Processing, China
Alan Wassyng	McMaster University, Canada
Heike Wehrheim	University of Paderborn, Germany
Michael Whalen	University of Minnesota, USA
Jim Woodcock	University of York, UK
Gianluigi Zavattaro	University of Bologna, Italy
Pamela Zave	AT&T Laboratories-Research, USA

Additional Reviewers

Abdelkader, Karam
Alberti, Francesco
Alt, Leonardo
Andre, Etiene
Andronick, June
Bai, Guandong
Barbosa, Luis
Barnat, Jiri
Basset, Nicolas
Berger, Christian
Bonakdarpour, Borzoo
Bornat, Richard
Brazdil, Tomas
Bryans, Jeremy W.
Bubel, Richard
Castano, Rodrigo
Cerone, Andrea
Ceska, Milan
Chatterjee, Krishnendu
Chen, Liqian
Christakis, Maria
Ciancia, Vincenzo
Ciolek, Daniel
Clarkson, Michael
Cohen, Ernie
Coleman, Joey
Colley, John
Daniel, Holcomb
Decker, Normann
Delahaye, Benoit
Delzanno, Giorgio
Demasi, Ramiro
Desai, Ankush
Din, Crystal Chang
Dodds, Mike
Donzé, Alexandre
Duan, Lian
Duflot, Marie
Dupressoir, François
Enea, Constantin
Fedyukovich, Grigory
Fernandez, Matthew
Ferrari, Alessio
Fontaine, Pascal
Ghassabani, Elaheh
Girard, Antoine
Golden, Bat-Chen
Grall, Herve
Gui, Lin
Hahn, Ernst Moritz
Harder, Jannis
Helvensteijn, Michiel
Hyvärinen, Antti
Immler, Fabian
Isenberg, Tobias
Jacob, Jeremy
Jacobs, Bart
Jansen, Nils
Jeannin, Jean-Baptiste
Ji, Ran
Joshi, Rajeev
Jovanovic, Aleksandra
Kahsai, Temesghen
Kinder, Johannes
Kini, Dileep
Kong, Weiqiang
Kotelnikov, Evgenii
Kremer, Gereon
Kremer, Steve
Kromodimoeljo, Sentot
Kumar Singh, Neeraj
Kuraj, Ivan
Kuruma, Hironobu
Külahçioğlu Özkan, Burcu
Lammich, Peter
Latella, Diego
Lewis, Corey
Li, Li
Li, Liyi
Li, Yi
Liang, Jia
Lopez Pombo, Carlos
Lorber, Florian
Loreti, Michele
Malik, Avinash
Mamouras, Konstantinos
Melgratti, Hernan
Meller, Yael

Melquiond, Guillaume
Miyazawa, Alvaro
Moore, Brandon
Mosses, Peter
Murray, Toby
Muschevici, Radu
Mödersheim, Sebastian A.
Nakata, Keiko
Navas, Jorge A.
Near, Joseph
Newsham, Zack
Nguyen, Kim
Parker, David
Parkinson, Matthew
Passmore, Grant
Pavese, Esteban
Pek, Edgar
Rabe, Markus N.
Ranzato, Francesco
Regis, German
Remke, Anne
Rossi, Matteo
Rozier, Eric
Sadigh, Dorsa
Salehi Fathabadi, Asieh
Sankaranarayanan, Sriram
Scheffel, Torben
Schmitz, Malte
Schumi, Richard
Schupp, Stefan
Sewell, Thomas
Shi, Ling
Shimakawa, Masaya
Shoaei, Mohammad Reza
Singh, Neeraj
Sinha, Rohit
Smith, Andrew
Snook, Colin
Solin, Kim
Stefanescu, Andrei
Stork, Sven
Stümpel, Annette
Summers, Alexander J.
Talbot, Jean-Marc
Tarrach, Thorsten
Thoma, Daniel
Tiezzi, Francesco
Tiwari, Ashish
Travkin, Oleg
Turrini, Andrea
Vu, Linh H.
Wang, Chen-Wei
Wasser, Nathan
Whiteside, Iain
Wiltsche, Clemens
Xiao, He
Zhang, Yi
Zhao, Yang
Zheng, Yunhui
Zoppi, Edgardo
Zulkoski, Edward

Contents

Invited Presentations

Main Track

Industry Track

Invited Presentations

Resource Analysis: From Sequential to Concurrent and Distributed Programs

Elvira Albert[1], Puri Arenas[1], Jesús Correas[1], Samir Genaim[1], Miguel Gómez-Zamalloa[1], Enrique Martin-Martin[1], Germán Puebla[2], and Guillermo Román-Díez[2](✉)

[1] DSIC, Complutense University of Madrid, Madrid, Spain
[2] DLSIIS, Technical University of Madrid, Madrid, Spain
groman@fi.upm.es

Abstract. Resource analysis aims at automatically inferring *upper/lower bounds* on the worst/best-case cost of executing programs. Ideally, a resource analyzer should be parametric on the *cost model*, i.e., the type of cost that the user wants infer (e.g., number of steps, amount of memory allocated, amount of data transmitted, etc.). The inferred upper bounds have important applications in the fields of program optimization, verification and certification. In this talk, we will review the basic techniques used in resource analysis of sequential programs and the new extensions needed to handle concurrent and distributed systems.

1 Introduction

One of the most important characteristics of a program is the amount of resources that its execution will require, i.e., its *resource consumption*. Resource analysis (a.k.a. cost analysis [23]) aims at *statically* bounding the cost of executing programs for any possible input data value. Typical examples of resources include execution time, memory watermark, amount of data transmitted over the net, etc. Resource usage information has many applications, both during program development and deployment. *Upper bounds* on the worst-case cost are useful because they provide *resource guarantees*, i.e., it is ensured that the execution of the program will never exceed the amount of resources inferred by the analysis. *Lower bounds* on the best-case cost have applications in program parallelization, they can be used to decide if it is worth executing locally a task or requesting remote execution. Therefore, automated ways of estimating resource usage are quite useful and the general area of resource analysis has received [23,14,22] and is nowadays receiving [6,15,16,17] considerable attention. In this paper, we describe the main components underlying resource analysis of a today's imperative programming language, e.g., such techniques have been applied to analyze the resource consumption of sequential Java and Java bytecode [19]. In a next step, we describe the extension of the sequential framework to handle concurrent programs and overview the new notions of cost that arise in these contexts.

N. Bjørner and F. de Boer (Eds.): FM 2015, LNCS 9109, pp. 3–17, 2015.
DOI: 10.1007/978-3-319-19249-9_1

The rest of the paper is organized in four sections as follows:

- *Sequential.* Section 2 considers a minimalistic imperative language and summarizes the process of, from a program, generating *upper bounds* on the worst-case cost of executing the program in terms of the input data sizes. We also discuss relevant extensions of the basic framework to handle object-oriented programs and non-cumulative resources.
- *Distribution and Concurrency.* Section 3 describes the extension of such techniques to analyze distributed and concurrent programs. First, in Section 3.1, we introduce the basic instructions for *distribution*, namely to create distributed locations and to spawn an asynchronous task in a remote location; and for concurrency, in particular an instruction to synchronize with the termination of an asynchronous task and be able to release the processor if the task has not terminated yet (in this case, another task waiting in this location can take the processor). In Sections 3.2 and 3.3, we consider the distribution aspects from the point of view of resource consumption. Here our main concern is to be able to infer the resource consumption distributed among the locations of the system rather than producing a monolithic expression that amalgamates the whole cost. For this purpose, we present the notion of *cost centers* and describe an underlying analysis to obtain them. In Section 3.4, we consider the inference of the cost in the presence of tasks with concurrent interleavings. This is challenging because the global variables can be modified between the time a task suspends until it resumes, and this can affect its resource consumption (e.g., the size of the data structure that a loop traverses can be increased during its suspension). We sketch a novel technique to infer the resource consumption in these cases.
- *New notions.* In this context of distributed systems, new notions of cost arise. In first place, there are new cost models that can be considered to estimate the performance of a distributed system, namely it is particularly interesting to predict the load balance of the distributed locations, the amount of data transferred among them and the parallelism achieved. Moreover, it is relevant to obtain the *peak* of the resource usage of each distributed location rather than the total amount of resources allocated in it. In order to infer such peak cost, one needs first to estimate the *queue configuration* of each distributed location, i.e., the tasks that might be simultaneously in such location queue and then we can accumulate their resource consumption together. This notion of peak is especially relevant in the context of *non-cumulative* resources that might increase and decrease along the execution. Finally, we introduce the notion of *parallel cost* which aims at overviewing the resource consumption of the overall distributed system by exploiting the parallelism among their nodes such that when tasks execute in parallel we only consider the duration of the longest among them.
- *Conclusions.* Finally, in Section 5 we conclude and point out open problems in this setting and our directions for future research.

2 Resource Analysis of Sequential Code

In this section we consider a sequential language which is deliberately simple to describe the analysis in a clear way. Distributed/concurrent operations are introduced later in Section 3. A program is a collection of methods of the form $T\ m(\textsf{int}\ x_1,\ldots,\textsf{int}\ x_k)\{s_1; s_2;\ldots,s_n;\}$, where x_i, $1 \leq i \leq k$, denote variables names and $T \in \{\textsf{int},\textsf{void}\}$. Each instruction $s_i \in \mathit{Instr}$, $1 \leq i \leq n$, adheres to the following grammar:

$$s ::= x = e \mid \textbf{if}\ b\ \textbf{then}\ s\ \textbf{else}\ s \mid \textbf{while}\ b\ \textbf{do}\ s \mid x = m(\bar{y}) \mid \textbf{return}\ x$$

where x, y denote variables names. For the sake of generality, the syntax of expressions e and Boolean conditions b is not specified. As notation, for any entity A, we use $\bar{A}$ as a shorthand for $A_1,\ldots,A_n$.

A common way to rigorously represent an execution is by means of a state transition system, which is an abstract machine that consists of a set Σ of states and a binary relation $\leadsto \subseteq \Sigma \times \Sigma$, which represents transitions between states. An execution $\mathcal{E}$ starts from an initial state $\mathcal{S}_0$ containing a method call. We use $\mathcal{S}_i \leadsto_s \mathcal{S}_j$, with $\mathcal{S}_i, \mathcal{S}_j \in \Sigma$, to denote that there is a transition from $\mathcal{S}_i$ to $\mathcal{S}_j$ in which instruction s has been executed. A state is *final* iff it has no successors. Similarly, an execution is final if it finishes in a final state. Note that for our sequential language, executions consist of only one branch. However, as we will see in Section 3, for distributed and concurrent languages, multiple results for an initial call can be computed.

2.1 Cost Models

The notion of cost model for a program specifies how the resource consumption of a program is calculated, given a resource of interest. It basically defines how to measure the resource consumption, i.e., the cost, associated to each execution step and, by extension, to an entire execution. Thus, a *cost model* $\mathcal{M}$ is a function defined as $\mathcal{M} : \mathit{Instr} \mapsto \mathbb{R}$ and the *cost of an execution step* is defined as $\mathcal{M}(\mathcal{S}\leadsto_s\mathcal{S}')=\mathcal{M}(s)$. For instance, a cost model which counts the number of execution steps can be defined as $\mathcal{M}_{\textsf{ninst}}(s) = 1$ for any $s \in \mathit{Instr}$ and a cost model counting the number of times that a concrete method m is executed can be defined as:

$$\mathcal{M}_{\textsf{calls}}(s) = \begin{cases} 1 \text{ if } s \text{ is a call } m(\bar{x}) \\ 0 \text{ otherwise} \end{cases}$$

Now, given a cost model $\mathcal{M}$ and an execution $\mathcal{E}$, the *cost* of $\mathcal{E}$ w.r.t. $\mathcal{M}$, denoted as $\mathit{Cost}(\mathcal{E},\mathcal{M})$ is defined as the sum of the costs of all execution steps in $\mathcal{E}$.

2.2 Upper Bounds

An upper bound for $m(\bar{x})$ w.r.t. a cost model $\mathcal{M}$, is a function $f(\bar{x}) = \textsf{cexp}$ on $\bar{x}$ which guarantees that for all $\bar{u} \in \mathbb{Z}$, and for any final execution $\mathcal{E}$ starting from

$m(\bar{u})$ it holds that $Cost(\mathcal{E}, \mathcal{M}) \leq f(\bar{u})$. The *cost expressions* cexp that can be handled in our framework follow the grammar below:

$$\mathsf{cexp} ::= r \mid \mathsf{nat}(l) \mid \mathsf{cexp}\ op\ \mathsf{cexp} \mid \log_n(\mathsf{nat}(l)+1) \mid n^{\mathsf{nat}(l)} \mid \max(S)$$

where $op \in \{+, *\}$, $r \in \mathbb{R}^+$, $n > 1 \in \mathbb{Z}^+$, $\mathsf{nat}(l)$ is defined as $\mathsf{nat}(l) = \max(\{l, 0\})$, $\max(S)$ stands for the maximum of the set of cost expressions S and l denotes a *linear expression* of the form $u_0 + u_1x_1 + \ldots u_nx_n$. The use of the nat-operator ensures that cost expressions are always evaluated to non-negative values. For instance the expression $\mathsf{nat}(x-1)$ is a valid cost expression which returns 0 for all $x \leq 1$.

The cost analysis framework that we follow [3] is based on transforming the original program in a set of cost equations by applying different static analyses and transformations on the source program. In particular, the main two steps to produce cost equations are: the transformation of the program into direct recursive form, and a size analysis which infers how the sizes of data change along the execution. From the equations, the upper bound is computed by (1) bounding the number of iterations of each recursive equation using linear ranking functions [21] and (2) by maximizing the local cost of each equation. As an example, consider the cost model which counts the number of executed instructions together with the program:

```
int m(int x, int y) {
  int r = 0, a;
  while (x < y) {
    a = p(x);
    r = r + a;
    x = x + 1;
  }
  return r;
}
```

```
int p(int x) {
  x = x + 1;
  return x;
}
```

Considering that the cost of $\mathsf{x} = \mathsf{x} + 1$ is 2 (the addition plus the assignment), an upper bound for p is 3. For the case of m, first we bound the number of iterations in the while loop by means of the linear ranking function $\mathsf{nat}(y - x)$. Secondly, we multiply the bound on the number of iterations by the cost inside the loop (8, which results from the 4 instructions in the loop, 1 method call, and the 3 instructions of the method) and the cost of executing the condition (1). Thus $\mathsf{nat}(y - x) * 9$ is an upper bound for the while loop. Finally, we add 3 due to the costs of the instructions outside the loop and the final evaluation of the guard, and the upper bound for m results in $m^+(x, y) = 3 + \mathsf{nat}(y - x) * 9$.

Suppose now that method p has an upper bound $p^+(x) = \mathsf{nat}(x)$. Then the cost of the instruction $\mathsf{a} = \mathsf{p(x)}$ is obtained by maximizing $p^+(x)$ in the context of its execution, namely $\mathsf{x} < \mathsf{y}$, which results in $\mathsf{nat}(y)$. Hence now the upper bound for m would be $m^+(x, y) = 3 + \mathsf{nat}(y - x) * (\mathsf{nat}(y) + 6)$.

2.3 Extensions of Sequential Resource Analysis

The language we have used along this section does not contain a global memory, instead all variables in a method are local to it. In the presence of global variables, the computation of upper bounds becomes harder since when bounding the number of iterations of a loop we must take into account if the condition of the loop depends on a shared variable. For example, suppose we extend the language in Section 2 to support classes and objects in the standard way, where a class may contain integer fields shared by all objects of the class. Consider the following implementation of method m:

```
int m(A o1, A o2, int y) {
   int r = 0;
   while (o1.x < y) {
      a = p(o2);
      r = r + a;
      o1.x = o1.x + 1;
   }
   return r;
}

int p(A o2) {
   // read and write field o2.x
   return o2.x;
}
```

where o_1, o_2 are objects of a class A which contains a field x. The termination of the while loop depends clearly on the call $p(o_2)$ in the following sense: If o_1 and o_2 points to the same memory location, then field x is always accessed by the same reference, say o_1, and it can be treated as a local variable, what allows to apply the same techniques than in Section 2.2 in order to compute an upper bound. Otherwise, we will not be able to infer the cost as it will depend on the calling context of method m. Our approach [2] consists in computing the sequence of (*access path*) used to access each field in the program. Then, if the field is not written or its written by a unique access path, such a field is considered as *trackable*, i.e., the field can be treated as a local variable for the method. For our example at hand, it holds that in method m, the field x is read and written by two different references, o_1 and o_2 and hence the field is not trackable and the termination of the loop can not be proven. However suppose that, after the instruction int $r = 0$, we add $o_1 = o_2$. Now field x is written only using o_1 and thus the field is considered trackable, what allows us to compute an upper bound for method m similarly as done in Section 2.2 but in terms of o_1.x. More sophisticated approaches to deal with shared memory can be found in [4] and [5], where reference fields and array fields are also considered.

Another extension to sequential resource analysis is the inference of non-cumulative resources [9]. Existing cost analysis frameworks have been defined for cumulative resources which keep on increasing along the computation. In contrast, non-cumulative resources are acquired and (possibly) released along the execution. Examples of non-cumulative cost are memory usage in the presence of garbage collection, number of connections established that are later closed, or resources requested to a virtual host which are released after using them.

It is recognized that non-cumulative resources introduce new challenges in resource analysis [12,18]. This is because the resource consumption can increase and decrease along the computation, and it is not enough to reason on the final state of the execution, but rather the upper bound on the cost can happen at any intermediate step. The analysis of non-cumulative resources is defined in two steps: (1) We first infer the sets of resources which can be in use simultaneously (i.e., they have been both acquired and none of them released at some point of the execution). This process is formalized as a static analysis that (over-)approximates the sets of acquire instructions that can be in use simultaneously, allowing us to capture the simultaneous use of resources in the execution. (2) We then perform a *program-point* resource analysis which infers an upper bound on the cost at the points of interest, namely the points at which the resources are acquired. From such upper bounds, we can obtain the *peak* cost by just eliminating the cost due to acquire instructions that do not happen simultaneously with the others (according to the analysis information gathered at step 1).

3 Resource Analysis of Distributed Concurrent Systems

This section describes the basic extensions to resource analysis of distributed and concurrent systems.

3.1 The Language

We consider a distributed concurrent programming model with explicit locations and cooperative concurrency between the tasks at each location. Each location represents a processor with a procedure stack and an unordered buffer of pending tasks. Initially all processors are idle. When an idle processor's task buffer is non-empty, some task is selected for execution. Besides accessing its own processor's global storage, each task can post tasks to the buffers of any processor, including its own, or synchronize with the reception of other tasks. When a task completes, its processor becomes idle again, chooses the next pending task, and so on. The number of locations need not be known a priory (e.g., locations may be virtual). Syntactically, a location will therefore be similar to an *object* and can be dynamically created using the instruction **newLoc**. The new set of instructions of the language, extended with distributed operations from that of Section 2, is as follows:

$$s' ::= s \mid x = \textbf{newLoc} \mid x = \textbf{newDC} \mid f = x.m(\bar{y}) \mid \textbf{await}\ f? \mid x = f.\textbf{get}$$

Let us observe that now variables can hold locations and therefore the set of types is extended to {**void**, **int**, **loc**}, being **loc** the set of locations and distributed components. The special location identifier *this* denotes the current location. We can achieve different ways of distributing an application by creating new locations with **newLoc** or new distributed components by means of **newDC**. When we use **newDC**, a new distributed component is created, whereas when we use **newLoc**, the created location (and its resource consumption) belongs to the current distributed component.

The language is also extended with *future variables*, denoted by f in the grammar, which are used to check if the execution of an asynchronous task has finished. Method calls on locations are asynchronous and are associated with a future variable that will hold their result. The instruction **await** f? allows synchronizing the execution of the current task with the task which the future variable f is pointing to; and instruction $x = f$.**get** is used to retrieve the value stored in f.

3.2 Cost Models

In Section 2.1 we presented some important cost models for sequential programs. However, other interesting cost models can be defined in distributed and concurrent systems, as shown in [1]. For instance, a cost model that counts the total *number of distributed components* (*number of locations*), created along the execution can be defined as $\mathcal{M}_{\mathsf{loc}}(s) = 1$ if $s \equiv x =$ **newDC** (**newLoc**) and $\mathcal{M}_{\mathsf{loc}}(s) = 0$ otherwise. Since distributed components are the distribution units, this cost model provides an indication on the amount of parallelism that might be achieved.

A cost model that counts instructions of the form $x.m(\bar{y})$ can be used to infer the *number of tasks* that are spawned along an execution. This cost model can be refined to count the number of calls to specific methods, locations or distributed components by focusing on specific method and object names.

Communications play a fundamental role in the design of a distributed system, because they influence their performance. A cost model that counts the *number of communications* or the amount of *transmitted data* is very useful when designing distributed systems. The goal of such cost models is to infer, not only the number of communications between locations or distributed components, but also the sizes of the arguments in the task invocation and of the returned values. This cost model that over-approximates the amount of data transmitted uses size analysis [13] to infer upper bounds on the data sizes at the points in which tasks are spawned. In particular, given an instruction $x.m(\bar{y})$ it over-approximates the size of $\bar{y}$ and also of the returned value.

3.3 Distribution: Cost Centers

In a distributed setting, the above notion of cost model has to be extended because, rather than considering a single component in which all steps are performed, we have in general multiple locations and distributed components possibly running concurrently and/or distributively on different CPUs. Thus, rather than aggregating the cost of all executing steps, it is required to treat execution steps which occur on different locations or components separately. With this aim, we adopt the notion of *cost centers* [20], proposed for profiling functional programs. The upper bounds will use cost centers in order to keep the resource usage assigned to the different components separate.

Ideally, one would like to have a different cost center for each different location or distributed component created along the execution of the program.

However this cannot be determined statically and has to be approximated. For this aim, we rely on points-to analysis in order to approximate the set of locations or distributed components which each reference variable may point to during program execution. This allows us to make the analysis object-sensitive and separate the cost that corresponds to different instances of locations and/or distributed components that are created at the same program point but that correspond to different object names and may belong to different distributed components.

3.4 Concurrency: MHP-based Analysis

Resource consumption inference in concurrent and distributed systems is more difficult than in the sequential case, since different tasks can interleave their executions and therefore change the value of shared variables. This situation becomes clearer in the following example from [11], where g is a shared variable and x is a variable local to S_2:

S_1:
```
1 while (g > 0){
2   g = g - 1;
3   await *?
4 }
```

S_2:
```
5 while (x > 0){
6   x = x -1;
7   g = *;
8 }
```

The instruction at L7, that updates the field g, may interleave with **await** *? at L3 in S_1. Therefore the number of iterations of the loop S_1 may differ from the original value of g, as the value of that shared variable can change between iterations. To infer the number of iterations of S_1 we use the following approach [11]:

1. Locate those instructions that update shared variables and can interleave with the loop. In the example, the only interleaving instruction that updates g is L7. To obtain this information we use a *may-happen-in-parallel* analysis [10]. This analysis over-approximates the pairs of program instructions that can execute in parallel or in an interleaved way.
2. Find an upper-bound on the number of times that those interleaving instructions are executed. This computation may require the recursive calculation of upper bounds for other loops. In the example above, a sound and precise bound on the number of executions of L7 is x, since x is a local variable.
3. Finally, the upper bound for S_1 is the maximum number of iterations ignoring the instruction **await** *? , but assuming that at this point g can take its maximum value g^+, multiplied by the maximum number of visits to L7. Thus, $g^+ * x$ is a sound upper bound.

Once we have computed an upper bound on the iterations of the loop, we can easily infer the concrete resource consumption by using a concrete cost model. Notice that the may-happen-in-parallel analysis is crucial, since it will be able to discard some spurious interleavings that will lead to imprecise upper bounds. Otherwise, we will be forced to consider that every updating instruction could interleave with every loop. Note also that the may-happen-in-parallel analysis is independent and it is used as a *black-box*, so any improvement on it will enhance the upper bounds automatically.

4 New Notions of Cost in Distributed Systems

Building upon the basic analysis presented in the previous section, in this section we describe new cost models and notions of cost that appear in distributed systems.

4.1 Advanced Cost Models

By building upon the cost models described in Section 3.2, we have defined several advanced cost models that provide indicators to assess the level of distribution in the system [7], the amount of communication among distributed nodes that it requires, and how balanced the load of the distributed nodes that compose the system is. Our indicators are given as functions on the input data sizes, and they can be used to automate the comparison of different distributed settings and guide towards finding the optimal configuration. Let us see an example to explain these issues:

```
1  void m(int n){
2    loc a = newLoc | newDC;
3    while (n > 0) {
4      loc b = newLoc | newDC;
5      b.p(n,a);
6      n = n − 1;
7    }
8  }
9  void p(int n, loc a) {
10   while (n > 0) {
11     a.q();
12     n = n − 1;
13   }
14 }
15 q() { 10 instr }
```

Method m creates one location using **newLoc**(or distributed component using **newDC**) at L2 pointed by variable a and it contains a loop that creates n locations (or distributed components) at L4. Such loop also spawns n tasks executing method p (L5). Method p contains a loop that calls q n times (L11). Those program points where locations are created, L2 and L4, are crucial for determining the behaviour of the system. Depending on the creation of a distributed component (**newDC**) or a location (**newLoc**), we obtain a different setting whose performance could be radically different from the others. To evaluate which setting has a better performance, we define the notion of *performance indicator*. A performance indicator is a function, expressed in terms of the input arguments of the program, that evaluates to a number in the range [0–1], such that the closer to one the better the performance. We define three different indicators:

1. The *distribution function* ($\mathcal{D}$) measures how much distributed the application is. It is defined as the relation between the number of distributed components that are created for this particular setting with respect to the maximum number of potential distributed components that could be created if all location instances were distributed components, i.e., the optimal setting from a distribution perspective in which we have as many distributed components as possible.
2. The *communication function* ($\mathcal{K}$) aims at measuring the level of external communications performed (i.e., calls to locations that belong to other distributed components). The motivation is that calls to other distributed components are potentially more expensive (as they require communications costs) and thus one wants to minimize them as much as possible. It is defined as one minus the ratio between the number of communications that the program performs in the current setting, and the maximum number of communications when using a setting in which all locations are created as distributed components and thus every asynchronous call (on a location different from the one executing) is external.
3. The *balance function* ($\mathcal{B}$) measures the balance level of the distributed system. We consider that the system is optimally balanced when all its components execute the same number of instructions. The *balance function* makes use of the upper bounds on the number of instructions and the upper bounds on the number of distributed components (and locations) to measure the standard deviation of the number of instructions executed by each distributed component. As we want to measure the balance level by means of a number in the interval [0–1] as in the other indicators, we divide the standard deviation by the maximum dispersion of the distributed components from the average.

Figure 1 shows the graphical representation of the functions $\mathcal{D}$, $\mathcal{K}$ and $\mathcal{B}$ for two possible settings by using **newLoc** or **newDC** at L2 and L4 of the program shown above. By means of the evaluation of the performance indicators we can observe that for Setting 1 higher values of n lead to a better distribution behaviour because a new distributed component is created at each iteration of the loop in m. Regarding communications, Setting 2 behaves better for lower values of n, but for higher values of n, both settings behave badly (close to 0). In addition, the evaluation of the balance function indicates that the load of the system is better balanced with Setting 1. The information obtained from the performance indicators could be extremely useful in the deployment process of a distributed system. In order to find the optimal setting for a distributed system, we should be able to: (1) generate all possible settings automatically, (2) generate performance indicators for each of them and (3) be able to compare such indicators for the different settings.

4.2 Peak Cost

The framework presented so far allows us to infer the total number of instructions that it needs to execute, the total amount of memory that it will need

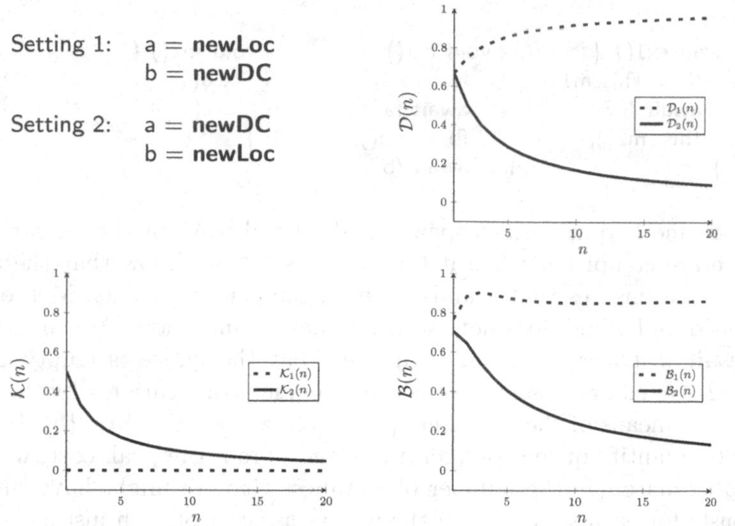

Fig. 1. Graphical representation of the functions $\mathcal{D}$, $\mathcal{K}$ and $\mathcal{B}$

to allocate, or the total number of tasks that will be added to its queue. This is a too pessimistic estimation of the amount of resources actually required in the real execution. The amount of work that each location has to perform can greatly vary along the execution depending on: (1) the amount of tasks posted to its queue, (2) their respective costs, and (3) the fact that they may be posted in parallel and thus be pending to execute *simultaneously*. In order to obtain a more accurate measure of the resources required by a location, the *peak* of the resource consumption can be inferred instead [8], which captures the maximum amount of resources that the location might require along any execution. In addition to its application to verification, this information is crucial to dimensioning the distributed system: it will allow us to determine the size of each location *task queue*; the required size of the location's memory; and the processor execution speed required to execute the peak of instructions and provide a certain response time. It is also of great relevance in the context of software *virtualization* as used in cloud computing, as the peak cost allows estimating how much processing/storage capacity one needs to buy in the host machine, and thus can greatly reduce costs.

Inferring the peak cost is challenging because it increases and decreases along the execution, unlike the standard notion of *total cost* which is cumulative. To this end, it is very relevant to infer, for each distributed component, its *abstract queue configuration*, which captures all possible configurations that its queue can take along the execution. A particular queue configuration is given as the sets of tasks that the location may have pending to execute at a moment of time. For instance, let us see the following example program, which has as entry method ex1:

```
1 void ex1() {
2   ff = this.m1();
3   await ff ?;
4   this . m2();
5 }
6 void m1() {
7   fa = x.a();
8   await fa ?;
9   fb = x.b();
10  await fb ?;
11 }
12 void m2() {
13  x. d();
14  x. e();
15 }
```

It first invokes method m1, which spawns tasks a and b. Method m1 guarantees that a and b are completed when it finishes. Besides, we know that the **await** instruction in L8 ensures that a and b cannot happen in parallel. Method m2 spawns tasks d and e and does not await for their termination. We can observe that the **await** instructions in m1 guarantee that the queue is empty before launching m2. We can represent the tasks in the queue of location x by the tasks queue graph by means of the following queue configurations: $\{\{a\}, \{b\}, \{d, e\}\}$.

In order to quantify queue configurations and obtain the peak cost, we need to over-approximate: (1) the number of instances that we might have running simultaneously for each task and (2) the worst-case cost of such instances. The main extension is to define cost centers of the form $c(o{:}m)$ which contain the location name o and the task m running on it. Now, using the upper bounds on the total cost in Section 3.3 we already gather both types of information. This is because the cost attached to the cost center $c(o{:}m)$ accounts for the accumulation of the resource consumption of *all* tasks running method m at location o. We therefore can safely use the total cost of the entry method $p(\bar{x})$ restricted to $o{:}m$, denoted $p^+(\bar{x})|_{\{o:m\}}$, as the upper bound of the cost associated with the execution of method m at location o which sets up to 0 the cost centers different from $c(o{:}m)$. The key idea to infer the *quantified queue configuration*, or simply *peak cost*, of each location is to compute the total cost for each element in the set of abstract configurations and stay with the maximum of all of them. In the previous example, the peak cost of location x in ex1 is $max\{ex_1^+(n)|_{c_1}, ex_1^+(n)|_{c_2}, ex_1^+(n)|_{c_3}\}$, where $c_1 = \{x{:}a\}$, $c_2 = \{x{:}b\}$ and $c_3 = \{x{:}d, x{:}e\}$.

4.3 Parallel Cost

Parallel cost differs from the standard notion of *serial cost* by exploiting the truly concurrent execution model of distributed processing to capture the cost of synchronized tasks executing in parallel. It is also different to the peak cost since this one is still serial; i.e., it accumulates the resource consumption in each component and does not exploit the overall parallelism as it is required for inferring the parallel cost. It is challenging to infer parallel cost because one needs to soundly infer the parallelism between tasks while accounting for waiting and idle processor times at the different locations. We are currently developing a static analysis to obtain the parallel cost.

5 Conclusions and Future Research

Inferring the resource consumption (a.k.a cost) of computer programs, which is a general form of complexity, is one of the most fundamental tasks in computer science, and its automation has been the subject of voluminous research in the last decade.

Research in this area resulted in several cost analysis frameworks for sequential low- and high-level modern programming languages, such as the sequential fragments of Java and its corresponding low-level bytecode. These frameworks have been enhanced overtime to scale for large programs, and to handle programs with complex control-flow and sophisticated heap data-structures. They have also been extended to support non-cumulative cost models in which resources can be released as well, e.g., memory consumption in the presence of garbage collection. The underlying complexity analyses employed by these frameworks range from the classical worst/best case approach to more advanced ones such as the amortised analysis approach, and thus they offer users a wide range of performance/precision trade-offs. Some of these frameworks also provide support for certification and verification of resource consumption.

Research in recent years has concentrated on extending the sequential cost analysis frameworks to handle concurrency and distribution. The main challenge was to handle new notions of cost that are more suitable for such programming paradigms. This includes the peak cost, that refers to the maximal amount of resources that can be used simultaneously (by different tasks), and the parallel cost, that do not accumulate the cost of tasks that are executing in parallel on different computing units. The underlying techniques for these notions of cost rely on the use of MHP analysis, which provides information on which tasks might interleave or execute in parallel. Another important functionality that was introduced is the ability to attribute cost to particular nodes of a distributed system, which is of utmost importance for optimizing the resource usage of such systems or balancing the load of their nodes.

In spite of the remarkable achievements in the field of cost analysis, there are still several directions that need to be considered in the future: (1) exploring new applications for cost analysis. A promising direction is the use of cost analysis to identify security vulnerabilities that are related to resource consumption; (2) current techniques for cost analysis of concurrent programs predict the cost at the algorithmic level, more work is required to leverage these techniques to take the underlying (multi-core) architecture into account. This would require supporting more sophisticated concurrency models; (3) in the context of parallelism, cost analysis of massive parallel programs has not been investigated yet, more attentions should be paid to such programming paradigms as they are popular in scientific communities; (4) support for probabilistic information is probably the most important and appealing direction. Probabilistic distributions can be used to describe a cost model, which allows constructing platform dependent cost models (e.g., energy) using profiling tools. Probabilistic distributions can be also used to describe the distribution of the input data, which can then be used to infer notions such average cost and distribution of cost.

Acknowledgments. This work was funded partially by the EU project FP7-ICT-610582 ENVISAGE: Engineering Virtualized Services (http://www.envisage-project.eu), by the Spanish MINECO project TIN2012-38137, and by the CM project S2013/ICE-3006.

References

1. Albert, E., Arenas, P., Correas, J., Genaim, S., Gómez-Zamalloa, M., Puebla, G., Román-Díez, G.: Object-Sensitive Cost Analysis for Concurrent Objects. Software Testing, Verification and Reliability (2015), http://dx.doi.org/10.1002/stvr.1569
2. Albert, E., Arenas, P., Genaim, S., Puebla, G.: Field-Sensitive Value Analysis by Field-Insensitive Analysis. In: Cavalcanti, A., Dams, D.R. (eds.) FM 2009. LNCS, vol. 5850, pp. 370–386. Springer, Heidelberg (2009)
3. Albert, E., Arenas, P., Genaim, S., Puebla, G.: Closed-Form Upper Bounds in Static Cost Analysis. Journal of Automated Reasoning 46(2), 161–203 (2011)
4. Amato, G., Parton, M., Scozzari, F.: From Object Fields to Local Variables: A Practical Approach to Field-Sensitive Analysis. In: Cousot, R., Martel, M. (eds.) SAS 2010. LNCS, vol. 6337, pp. 100–116. Springer, Heidelberg (2010)
5. Albert, E., Arenas, P., Genaim, S., Puebla, G., Román-Díez, G.: Conditional Termination of Loops over Heap-allocated Data. Science of Computer Programming 92, 2–24 (2014)
6. Albert, E., Arenas, P., Genaim, S., Puebla, G., Zanardini, D.: Cost Analysis of Object-Oriented Bytecode Programs. Theoretical Computer Science 413(1), 142–159 (2012)
7. Albert, E., Correas, J., Puebla, G., Román-Díez, G.: Quantified Abstract Configurations of Distributed Systems. Formal Aspects of Computing (2015), http://dx.doi.org/10.1007/s00165-014-0321-z
8. Albert, E., Correas, J., Román-Díez, G.: Peak Cost Analysis of Distributed Systems. In: Müller-Olm, M., Seidl, H. (eds.) Static Analysis. LNCS, vol. 8723, pp. 18–33. Springer, Heidelberg (2014)
9. Albert, E., Fernández, J.C., Román-Díez, G.: Non-Cumulative Resource Analysis. In: Baier, C., Tinelli, C. (eds.) TACAS 2015. LNCS, vol. 9035, pp. 85–100. Springer, Heidelberg (2015)
10. Albert, E., Flores-Montoya, A.E., Genaim, S.: Analysis of May-Happen-in-Parallel in Concurrent Objects. In: Giese, H., Rosu, G. (eds.) FORTE 2012 and FMOODS 2012. LNCS, vol. 7273, pp. 35–51. Springer, Heidelberg (2012)
11. Albert, E., Flores-Montoya, A., Genaim, S., Martin-Martin, E.: Termination and Cost Analysis of Loops with Concurrent Interleavings. In: Van Hung, D., Ogawa, M. (eds.) ATVA 2013. LNCS, vol. 8172, pp. 349–364. Springer, Heidelberg (2013)
12. Albert, E., Genaim, S., Gómez-Zamalloa, M.: Parametric Inference of Memory Requirements for Garbage Collected Languages. In: Proc. of ISMM 2010, pp. 121–130. ACM (2010)
13. Cousot, P., Halbwachs, N.: Automatic discovery of linear restraints among variables of a program. In: POPL, pp. 84–96 (1978)
14. Debray, S.K., Lin, N.W.: Cost Analysis of Logic Programs. ACM Transactions on Programming Languages and Systems 15(5), 826–875 (1993)
15. Gulwani, S., Mehra, K.K., Chilimbi, T.M.: Speed: Precise and Efficient Static Estimation of Program Computational Complexity. In: Proc. of POPL 2009, pp. 127–139. ACM (2009)
16. Hoffmann, J., Aehlig, K., Hofmann, M.: Multivariate Amortized Resource Analysis. In: Proc. of POPL 2011, pp. 357–370. ACM (2011)

17. Hoffmann, J., Shao, Z.: Type-Based Amortized Resource Analysis with Integers and Arrays. In: Codish, M., Sumii, E. (eds.) FLOPS 2014. LNCS, vol. 8475, pp. 152–168. Springer, Heidelberg (2014)
18. Hofmann, M., Jost, S.: Static prediction of heap space usage for first-order functional programs. In: Proc. of POPL 2013, pp. 185–197. ACM (2003)
19. Lindholm, T., Yellin, F.: The Java Virtual Machine Specification. Addison-Wesley (1996)
20. Morgan, R.G., Jarvis, S.A.: Profiling Large-Scale Lazy Functional Programs. Journal of Functional Programing 8(3), 201–237 (1998)
21. Podelski, A., Rybalchenko, A.: A Complete Method for the Synthesis of Linear Ranking Functions. In: Steffen, B., Levi, G. (eds.) VMCAI 2004. LNCS, vol. 2937, pp. 239–251. Springer, Heidelberg (2004)
22. Sands, D.: A Naïve Time Analysis and its Theory of Cost Equivalence. Journal of Logic and Computation 5(4), 495–541 (1995)
23. Wegbreit, B.: Mechanical Program Analysis. Communications of the ACM 18(9), 528–539 (1975)

AVACS: Automatic Verification and Analysis of Complex Systems Highlights and Lessons Learned

Werner Damm(✉)

AVACS Coordinator,
Carl von Ossietzky Universität Oldenburg, Oldenburg, Germany
werner.damm@offis.de

This talk presents highlights and lessons learned from the Transregional Collaborative Research Center AVACS, funded by the German Science Foundation under contract SFB-TR 14 from January 1, 2004 to December 31, 2015 with a total funding of about 30 Million €, involving between 18 to 22 principal investigators at the three AVACS sites Freiburg, Oldenburg and Saarbrücken. Through this funding the German Science Foundation provided an excellent environment for foundational cross-site research in the highly relevant and challenging research are of Automatic Verification and Analysis of Complex Systems.

The AVACS project (see www.avacs.org) addresses the rigorous mathematical verification and analysis of models and realizations of complex safety-critical computerized systems, such as aircraft, trains, cars, or networked systems of these, whose failure can endanger human life. Our aim is to raise the state of the art in automatic verification and analysis techniques (V&A) from a level, where it is applicable only to isolated facets of the underlying space of mathematical models, to a level allowing a comprehensive and holistic verification of such systems:

1. We investigate the mathematical models and their interrelationship, as they arise at the various levels of design of safety-critical computerized systems. Behavioral models range from classical nondeterministic transition systems to probabilistic, real-time, and hybrid system models, to models reflecting the dynamic evolution of the system communication structure.
2. The investigated classes of models cover all typical system structures in this application domain, describing how to build models of complex systems hierarchically from such classes of models. These include distributed target architectures (such as hierarchical bus structures connecting multiple electronic control units), task models (task structures coming with communication and timing requirements), specification models of electronic control units (such as captured in Matlab/Simulink), system models (e.g., of vehicles), and models of systems of systems (e.g., for coordinated vehicle maneuvers).
3. The investigated classes of time models are expressive enough to cover all layers of the design space of such applications, including physical latencies of vehicles in performing coordinated maneuvers, system-level timing requirements such as response times to external events and timeliness requirements for protocols,

N. Bjørner and F. de Boer (Eds.): FM 2015, LNCS 9109, pp. 18–19, 2015.
DOI: 10.1007/978-3-319-19249-9_2

dense-time closed-loop models of controllers and plants, discrete-time design models of controllers, end-to-end deadlines on task chains, and worst-case execution times of tasks on modern processor architectures.

4. We provide largely automatic techniques to verify or falsify the compliance of models expressed in this rich model space against classes of requirements subsuming timeliness, safety, probabilistic reachability, stability and other classes of requirements, formalized in suitable logics.
5. We provide methods and tools for building such formal proofs for complete systems from guarantees of subsystems, ultimately striving to relate top-level requirements, such as for performing coordinated vehicle maneuvers to avoid collisions, to worst-case execution times of the tasks implementing control functions for such maneuvers.

Main Track

Automated Circular Assume-Guarantee Reasoning

Karam Abd Elkader[1], Orna Grumberg[1], Corina S. Păsăreanu[2], and Sharon Shoham[3(✉)]

[1] Technion – Israel Institute of Technology, Haifa, Israel
[2] CMU/NASA Ames Research Center, USA
[3] The Academic College of Tel aviv Yaffo, Tel Aviv, Israel
sharon.shoham@gmail.com

Abstract. Compositional verification techniques aim to decompose the verification of a large system into the more manageable verification of its components. In recent years, compositional techniques have gained significant successes following a breakthrough in the ability to automate assume-guarantee reasoning. However, automation is still restricted to simple acyclic assume-guarantee rules.

In this work, we focus on automating *circular* assume-guarantee reasoning in which the verification of individual components mutually depends on each other. We use a sound and complete circular assume-guarantee rule and we describe how to automatically build the assumptions needed for using the rule. Our algorithm accumulates *joint* constraints on the assumptions based on (spurious) counterexamples obtained from checking the premises of the rule, and uses a SAT solver to synthesize minimal assumptions that satisfy these constraints.

We implemented our approach and compared it with an established learning-based method that uses an acyclic rule. In all cases, the assumptions generated for the circular rule were significantly smaller, leading to smaller verification problems. Further, on larger examples, we obtained a significant speedup as well.

1 Introduction

Compositional verification techniques aim to break up the global verification of a program into local, more manageable, verification of its individual components. The environment for each component, consisting of the other program's components, is replaced by a "small" *assumption*, making each verification task easier. This style of reasoning is often referred to as *Assume-Guarantee* (AG) reasoning [17,20].

Progress has been made on automating compositional reasoning using learning and abstraction-refinement techniques for iterative building of the necessary assumptions [7,19,3,4,2,5,6]. This work has been done mostly in the context of applying a simple compositional assume-guarantee rule, where assumptions and properties are related in an *acyclic* manner. For example, in a two component program, suppose component M_1 guarantees property P under assumption A on its environment. Further suppose that M_2 unconditionally guarantees A. Then it follows that the composition $M_1||M_2$ also satisfies P (denoted here as rule **NonCIRC-AG**).

However, there is another important category of rules that involve *circular reasoning*. These rules use inductive arguments, over time, formulas to be checked, or both, e.g. [17,14,15,1], which makes automation challenging. Circular assume-guarantee rules have been successfully used in scaling model checking, and have often been found to

N. Bjørner and F. de Boer (Eds.): FM 2015, LNCS 9109, pp. 23–39, 2015.
DOI: 10.1007/978-3-319-19249-9_3

be more effective than non-circular rules [14,15,16,21,12,11]. Further, they could naturally exploit the inherent circular dependency exhibited by the verified systems, but their applicability has been hindered by the manual effort involved in defining assumptions.

In this work we propose a novel *circular* compositional verification technique that is fully *automated*. The technique uses the following assume-guarantee circular rule **CIRC-AG**, for proving that $M_1||M_2 \models P$, based on assumptions g_1 and g_2. Components, properties and assumptions are Labeled Transition Systems (LTSs).

$$\begin{array}{ll} \text{(Premise 1)} & M_1 \models g_2 \triangleright g_1 \\ \text{(Premise 2)} & M_2 \models g_1 \triangleright g_2 \\ \text{(Premise 3)} & g_1||g_2 \models P \\ \hline & M_1||M_2 \models P \end{array}$$

Similar rules have been studied before [15,18,9]. The rule is both *sound* and *complete*. Premises 1 and 2 of the rule use inductive arguments to ensure soundness and have the form $M \models A \triangleright P$, which means that for every trace σ of size k, if σ is in the language of M, and its prefix of size $k-1$ is in the language of A then σ is also in the language of P. Intuitively, premises 1 and 2 prove, in a *compositional and inductive* manner, that every trace in the language of $M_1||M_2$ is also included in the language of $g_1||g_2$. Premise 3 ensures that every trace in the language of $g_1||g_2$ is also included in the language of P, thus the consequence of the rule is obtained. Completeness of the rule stems from the fact that M_1 and M_2 (restricted to appropriate alphabets) can be used for g_1 and g_2 in a successful application of the rule.

Coming up manually with assumptions g_1 and g_2 that are small and also satisfy the premises of the rule is difficult. We propose an algorithm, Automated Circular Reasoning (ACR), for the automated generation of the assumptions. In ACR the assumptions are initially approximate and are iteratively refined based on counterexamples obtained from checking the rule premises and found to be spurious (i.e. do not indicate real errors). Refinement is performed using a SAT solver over a set of constraints that determine how the assumptions should be refined in order to avoid producing the same counterexample in subsequent iterations. The algorithm is guaranteed to terminate, returning either minimal assumptions that satisfy the rule premises (meaning that the property holds) or a real counterexample (indicating a property violation).

Our search for minimal assumptions using SAT is inspired by [10]. However, in [10] a single (separating) assumption is generated, with the goal of automating non-circular reasoning. ACR, on the other hand, searches for two mutually dependent assumptions to be used with circular reasoning. Finding such assumptions poses unusual challenges since they need to be generated in a tightly related manner. We achieve this by constraining the assumption refinement with boolean combinations of requirements that certain traces must or must not be included in the language of the updated assumptions. For example, we may require "trace σ_1 must not be in g_1 **or** trace σ_2 must be in g_2". The SAT encoding of this constraint makes sure that at least one of its disjuncts will be satisfied. Solving the constraints for increasing number of states in $|g_1|+|g_2|$, yields the minimal candidate assumptions to be used in the next iteration of ACR. We establish the correctness of our ACR algorithm (proofs are omitted due to space constraints).

To the best of our knowledge, our work is the first to fully automate circular assume-guarantee reasoning. We implemented our algorithm and compared it with an established learning-based method that uses the acyclic rule NonCIRC-AG [7]. Our experiments indicate that the assumptions generated using the circular rule can be much smaller, leading to smaller verification problems, both in the number of explored states and the analysis time.

2 Preliminaries

Let *Act* be the universal set of observable actions and let τ denote a local action, unobservable to a component's environment.

Definition 1. *A* Labeled Transition System *(LTS) M is a quadruple* $(Q, \alpha M, \delta, q_0)$ *where Q is a finite set of states, $\alpha M \subseteq Act$ is a finite set of observable actions called the alphabet of M, $\delta \subseteq Q \times (\alpha M \cup \tau) \times Q$ is a transition relation, and $q_0 \in Q$ is the initial state.*

M is *nondeterministic* if it contains a τ transition or if there exist $(q, a, q'), (q, a, q'') \in \delta$ such that $q' \neq q''$. Otherwise, M is *deterministic* (denoted as DLTS). We write $\delta(q, a) = \perp$ if there is no q' such that $(q, a, q') \in \delta$. For a DLTS, we write $\delta(q, a) = q'$ to denote that $(q, a, q') \in \delta$.

Note. A non-deterministic LTS can be converted to a deterministic LTS that accepts the same language. However the deterministic LTS might have exponentially many more states than the non-deterministic LTS.

Paths and Traces. A *trace* σ is a sequence of observable actions. We use σ_i to denote the prefix of σ of length i. A *path* in an LTS $M = (Q, \alpha M, \delta, q_0)$ is a sequence $p = q_0, a_0, q_1, a_1 \cdots, a_{n-1}, q_n$ of alternating states and observable or unobservable actions of M, such that for every $k \in \{0, \ldots, n-1\}$ we have $(q_k, a_k, q_{k+1}) \in \delta$. The *trace* of p is the sequence $b_0 b_1 \cdots b_l$ of actions along p, obtained by removing from $a_0 \cdots a_{n-1}$ all occurrences of τ. The set of all traces of paths in M is called the *language* of M, denoted $L(M)$. A trace σ is *accepted* by M if $\sigma \in L(M)$. Note that $L(M)$ is prefix-closed and that the empty trace, denoted by ϵ, is accepted by any LTS.

Projections. For $\Sigma \subseteq Act$, we use $\sigma{\downarrow_\Sigma}$ to denote the trace obtained by removing from σ all occurrences of actions $a \notin \Sigma$. $M{\downarrow_\Sigma}$ is defined to be the LTS over alphabet Σ obtained by renaming to τ all the transitions labeled with actions that are not in Σ. Note that $L(M{\downarrow_\Sigma}) = \{\sigma{\downarrow_\Sigma} \mid \sigma \in L(M)\}$.

Parallel Composition. Given two LTSs M_1 and M_2 over alphabet αM_1 and αM_2, respectively, their *interface alphabet* αI consists of their common alphabet. That is, $\alpha I = \alpha M_1 \cap \alpha M_2$. The parallel composition operator $||$ is a commutative and associative operator that combines the behavior of two components by synchronizing on the actions in their interface and interleaving the remaining actions.

Let $M_1 = (Q_1, \alpha M_1, \delta_1, q_{0_1})$ and $M_2 = (Q_2, \alpha M_2, \delta_2, q_{0_2})$ be two LTSs. Then $M_1 || M_2$ is an LTS $M = (Q, \alpha M, \delta, q_0)$, where $Q = Q_1 \times Q_2$, $q_0 = (q_{0_1}, q_{0_2})$, $\alpha M = \alpha M_1 \cup \alpha M_2$, and δ is defined as follows where $a \in \alpha M \cup \{\tau\}$:

- if $(q_1, a, q_1') \in \delta_1$ for $a \notin \alpha M_2$, then $((q_1, q_2), a, (q_1', q_2)) \in \delta$ for every $q_2 \in Q_2$,
- if $(q_2, a, q_2') \in \delta_2$ for $a \notin \alpha M_1$, then $((q_1, q_2), a, (q_1, q_2')) \in \delta$ for every $q_1 \in Q_1$,
- if $(q_1, a, q_1') \in \delta_1$ and $(q_2, a, q_2') \in \delta_2$ for $a \neq \tau$, then $((q_1, q_2), a, (q_1', q_2')) \in \delta$.

Lemma 1. *[7] For every $t \in (\alpha M_1 \cup \alpha M_2)^*$, $t \in L(M_1||M_2)$ if and only if $t{\downarrow}_{\alpha M_1} \in L(M_1)$ and $t{\downarrow}_{\alpha M_2} \in L(M_2)$.*

Example 1. Consider the example in Figure 1. This is a variation of the example of [7] modified to illustrate circular dependencies. LTSs In and Out have interface alphabet $\{send, ack\}$. Their composition $In||Out$ is an LTS where the transition from state 0 to 1 in component In (labeled with *ack*) never takes place, since there is no corresponding matching transition in component Out. Similarly the transition from state 2 to 3 in component Out (labeled with *send*) never takes place. As a result, $In||Out$ simply repeats the trace $\langle in, send, out, ack\rangle$.

Properties and Satisfiability. A *safety property* is defined as an LTS P, whose language $L(P)$ defines the set of acceptable behaviors over the alphabet αP of P. An LTS M over $\alpha M \supseteq \alpha P$ satisfies P, denoted $M \models P$, if $\forall \sigma \in L(M).\sigma{\downarrow}_{\alpha P} \in L(P)$. To check a safety property P, its LTS is transformed into a deterministic LTS, which is also completed by adding an error state π and adding transitions from every state q in the deterministic LTS into π for all the missing outgoing actions of q; the resulting LTS is called an *error LTS*, denoted by P_{err}. Checking that $M \models P$ is done by checking that π is not reachable in $M||P_{err}$.

A trace $\sigma \in \alpha M^*$ is a *counterexample* for $M \models P$ if $\sigma \in L(M)$ but $\sigma{\downarrow}_{\alpha P} \notin L(P)$.

The *Order* LTS from Figure 1 depicts a safety property satisfied by $In||Out$. Note that neither In, nor Out, satisfy this property individually. For example, the trace $\langle in, send, ack, ack\rangle$ of In is a counterexample for $In \models Order$.

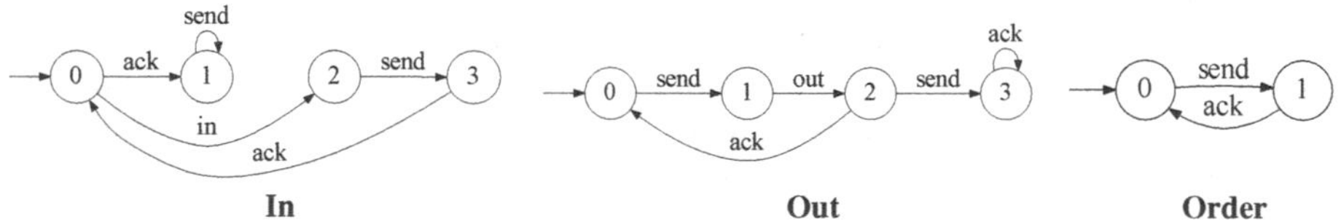

Fig. 1. LTSs describing the In and Out components and the $Order$ property

3 Circular Assume-Guarantee Reasoning

In this section we formally establish the soundness and completeness of the circular rule CIRC-AG introduced in Section 1 (proofs are omitted due to space constraints). We start by defining inductive properties. CIRC-AG uses formulas of the form $M \models A \triangleright P$, where M is a component, P is a property, and A is an assumption about M's environment. To ensure soundness of the circular rule the assume-guarantee formula is defined using induction over finite traces.

Definition 2. *Let M, A and P be LTSs over $\alpha M, \alpha A$ and αP respectively, such that $\alpha P \subseteq \alpha M$. We say that $M \models A \triangleright P$ holds if $\forall k \geq 1$ $\forall \sigma \in (\alpha M \cup \alpha A)^*$ of length k such that $\sigma{\downarrow_{\alpha M}} \in L(M)$, if $\sigma_{k-1}{\downarrow_{\alpha A}} \in L(A)$ then $\sigma{\downarrow_{\alpha P}} \in L(P)$.*

Intuitively, the formula states that if a trace in M satisfies the assumption A up to step $k-1$, it should guarantee P up to step k. As an example consider the LTSs In from Figure 1 and g_1 and g_2 from Figure 2. Then $In \models g_2 \triangleright g_1$. On the other hand, $In \not\models g_1 \triangleright g_2$ since the trace $\sigma = \langle in, send, ack, ack\rangle \in L(In)$ is such that $\sigma_{k-1}{\downarrow_{\alpha g_1}} = \langle send, ack\rangle \in L(g_1)$, but $\sigma{\downarrow_{\alpha g_2}} = \langle send, ack, ack\rangle \notin L(g_2)$. σ is therefore a counterexample for $In \models g_1 \triangleright g_2$.

Definition 3. *A trace $\sigma \in (\alpha M \cup \alpha A)^*$ of length k is a* counterexample *for $M \models A \triangleright P$ if $\sigma{\downarrow_{\alpha M}} \in L(M)$ and $\sigma_{k-1}{\downarrow_{\alpha A}} \in L(A)$ but $\sigma{\downarrow_{\alpha P}} \notin L(P)$.*

Soundness and Completeness of Rule CIRC-AG. To establish the soundness of rule CIRC-AG we have the following requirements. M_1, M_2 and P are LTSs where $\alpha P \subseteq \alpha M_1 \cup \alpha M_2$. Moreover, g_1, g_2 are LTSs, used as *assumptions* in the rule, such that $\alpha M_1 \cap \alpha P \subseteq \alpha g_1$ and $\alpha M_2 \cap \alpha P \subseteq \alpha g_2$.

The following lemmas include several observations that are useful both in the soundness and completeness proofs and in the algorithm for automatic generation of assumptions g_1 and g_2, needed for the rule.

Lemma 2. *Let g_1 and g_2 be LTS assumptions successfully used in CIRC-AG, such that $\alpha M_i \cap \alpha P \subseteq \alpha g_i$. Then* **(1)** *$M_1||M_2 \models g_1||g_2$.* **(2)** *$M_1||g_2 \models P$ and $M_2||g_1 \models P$.*

Lemma 3. *Let M_1, M_2, P be LTSs over $\alpha M_1, \alpha M_2, \alpha P$ respectively. Let $\alpha g_1 \supseteq \alpha I \cup (\alpha M_1 \cap \alpha P)$ and $\alpha g_2 \supseteq \alpha I \cup (\alpha M_2 \cap \alpha P)$. Then $M_1||M_2 \models P$ if and only if $M_1{\downarrow_{\alpha g_1}}||M_2{\downarrow_{\alpha g_2}} \models P$.*

Theorem 1. *The Rule CIRC-AG is sound and complete.*

Soundness states that if there exist LTS assumptions g_1 and g_2 that satisfy all premises of CIRC-AG, then $M_1||M_2 \models P$. This result follows from Lemma 2, Item (1). Completeness states that if $M_1||M_2 \models P$ holds we can always find g_1 and g_2 such that the premises of the rule hold. Indeed completeness is established by showing that if $M_1||M_2 \models P$, then $g_1 = M_1{\downarrow_{\alpha g_1}}$ and $g_2 = M_2{\downarrow_{\alpha g_2}}$ where $\alpha g_1 = \alpha M_1 \cap (\alpha M_2 \cup \alpha P)$ and $\alpha g_2 = \alpha M_2 \cap (\alpha M_1 \cup \alpha P)$, satisfy the premises of the rule.

Example 2. Consider our running example (Figure 1), and consider the assumptions g_1 and g_2 depicted in Figure 2, over alphabet $\alpha g_1 = \alpha In \cap (\alpha Out \cup \alpha Order)$ and $\alpha g_2 = \alpha Out \cap (\alpha In \cup \alpha Order)$. In both cases $\alpha g_i = \{send, ack\}$. As stated above, $In \models g_2 \triangleright g_1$. Similarly, $Out \models g_1 \triangleright g_2$. Moreover, $g_1||g_2 \models Order$. It follows that $In||Out \models Order$ can be verified using CIRC-AG with g_1 and g_2 as assumptions.

4 Automatic Reasoning with CIRC-AG

We describe an iterative algorithm to automate the application of rule CIRC-AG by automating the assumption generation.

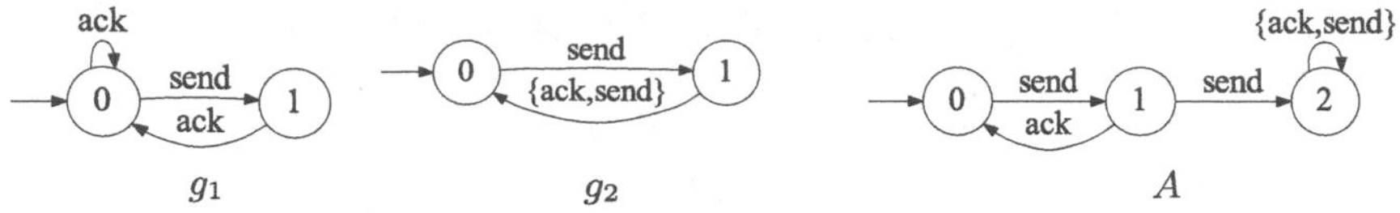

Fig. 2. LTSs describing the assumptions g_1 and g_2 generated by ACR, and the assumption A generated with L*. $\alpha g_1 = \alpha g_2 = \alpha A = \{send, ack\}$

Checking Inductive Properties. We first introduce a simple algorithm that checks if an inductive property of the form $M \models A \triangleright P$, where $\alpha P \subseteq \alpha M$, holds and if it does not, it returns a counterexample. To do so, we consider the LTS $M||A||P_{err}$. We label its states by (parameterized) propositions err_a, where $a \in \alpha P$. (s_M, s_A, s_P) is labeled by err_a if s_M has an outgoing transition in M labeled by a, but the corresponding transition (labelled by a) leads to π in P_{err}. We then check if a state q labeled by err_a is reachable in $M||A||P_{err}$. If so, then the algorithm returns the trace of a path from q_0 to q extended with action a as a counterexample. Intuitively, such a path to q represents a trace in M that satisfies A (because it is a trace in $M||A$) such that if we extend it by a we get a trace in M violating P.

Overview of the Main Algorithm. We propose an iterative algorithm to automate the application of the rule CIRC-AG by automating the assumption generation. Previous work used approximate iterative techniques based on automata learning or abstraction refinement to automate the assumption generation in the context of *acyclic* rules [7,19,3,4,2,5,6]. A different approach [10] used a SAT solver over a set of constraints encoding how the assumptions should be updated to find minimal assumptions; the method was shown to work well in practice, in the context of the same *acyclic* rule. We follow the latter approach here and we adapt it to reasoning for *cyclic* rules and checking inductive assume-guarantee properties. As mentioned, this is challenging due to the mutual dependencies between the two assumptions that we need to generate. We achieve this by constraining the assumptions with boolean combinations of requirements that certain traces must or must not be included in the language of the updated assumptions.

Algorithm 1 describes our Automated Circular Reasoning (ACR) algorithm for checking $M_1||M_2 \models P$ using the rule CIRC-AG.

We fix the alphabet of the assumptions g_1 and g_2 to be $\alpha g_1 = \alpha M_1 \cap (\alpha M_2 \cup \alpha P)$ and $\alpha g_2 = \alpha M_2 \cap (\alpha M_1 \cup \alpha P)$. By the completeness proof of the rule, this suffices.

ACR maintains a set C of *membership* constraints on g_1 and g_2. At each iteration it calls GENASSMP (described in Section 6) to synthesize, using a SAT solver, new minimal assumptions g_1 and g_2 that satisfy all the constraints in C. GENASSMP also receives as input a parameter k which provides a lower bound on the total number of states in the assumptions we look for. This avoids searching for smaller assumptions that cannot satisfy C. The algorithm then invokes APPLYAG (described in Section 5) to check the three premises of rule CIRC-AG using the obtained assumptions g_1 and g_2. APPLYAG may return a conclusive result: either "$M_1||M_2 \models P$" or "$M_1||M_2 \not\models P$",

Algorithm 1. Main algorithm for automating rule CIRC-AG for checking $M_1||M_2 \models P$

```
1: procedure ACR(M1, M2, P)
2:     Initialize: C = ∅, k = 2
3:     repeat
4:         (g1, g2) = GENASSMP(C, k)
5:         (C', Result) = APPLYAG(M1, M2, P, g1, g2)
6:         C = C ∪ C', k = |g1| + |g2|
7:     until (Result ≠ "continue")
8:     return Result
9: end procedure
```

in which case ACR terminates. If no conclusive result is obtained, it means that g_1 and g_2 do not satisfy the premises of the rule. Further, the counterexamples demonstrating the falsification of the premises are not suitable for concluding $M_1||M_2 \not\models P$, i.e. they are spurious. In this case APPLYAG returns "continue" together with new membership constraints that determine how the assumptions should be refined. The new constraints are added to C. Note that since the set C of constraints is monotonically increasing, any new pair (g_1', g_2') that satisfies it also satisfies previous sets of constraints. The previous set was satisfied by assumptions whose total size is $|g_1| + |g_2|$ but not smaller. Thus, we should start our search for new (g_1', g_2') from $k = |g_1| + |g_2|$ number of states. k is updated accordingly (line 6).

Example 3. The assumptions g_1 and g_2 from Figure 2 used to verify $In||Out \models Order$ with CIRC-AG were obtained by ACR in the 7th iteration. The LTS A from Figure 2 describes the assumption obtained with the algorithm of [7], which is based on acyclic rule NonCIRC-AG and uses L* for assumption generation. Notice that both g_1 and g_2 are smaller than A (and our experiments show that they can be much smaller in practice). The reason is that, after a successful application of CIRC-AG, $g_1||g_2$ overapproximates $M_1||M_2$. This means that each g_i overapproximates the part of M_i restricted to the composition with the other component. For example g_1 does not include the traces leading to state 1 from *In* since they do not participate in the composition. Similarly g_2 does not include the traces leading to state 3 in *Out*. In contrast, for the acyclic rule, the assumption A has to overapproximate M_2 (*Out*) as a whole. Therefore, CIRC-AG can result in substantially smaller assumptions, as also demonstrated by our experiments.

Membership Constraints. Membership constraints are used by our algorithm to gather information about traces that need to be in $L(g_i)$ or must not be in $L(g_i)$, for $i = 1, 2$. Thus they allow us to encode dependencies between the languages of the two assumptions $L(g_1)$ and $L(g_2)$. The constraints are defined by formulas with a special syntax and semantics, as defined below.

Definition 4. *Membership constraints formulas over* $(\alpha g_1, \alpha g_2)$ *are defined inductively as follows: For every* $\sigma_1 \in \alpha g_1^*$ *and* $\sigma_2 \in \alpha g_2^*$ *the formulas* $+(\sigma_1, 1)$, $-(\sigma_1, 1)$, $+(\sigma_2, 2)$, $-(\sigma_2, 2)$ *are* atomic *membership constraints formulas. Further, if* c_1 *and* c_2 *are membership constraints formulas, then so are* $(c_1 \wedge c_2)$ *and* $(c_1 \vee c_2)$.

Given a membership constraints formula c, $Strings(c, i)$ is the set of prefixes of all $\sigma \in \alpha g_i{}^*$ such that $+(\sigma, i)$ or $-(\sigma, i)$ is an atomic formula in c.

Definition 5. *Let c be a membership constraints formula over $(\alpha g_1, \alpha g_2)$, and let A_1 and A_2 be two LTSs. The satisfaction of c by (A_1, A_2) is defined inductively. $(A_1, A_2) \models c$ if and only if $\alpha A_1 = \alpha g_1$ and $\alpha A_2 = \alpha g_2$, and:*

- *if c is an atomic formula of the form $+(\sigma, i)$ then $\sigma \in L(A_i)$.*
- *if c is an atomic formula of the form $-(\sigma, i)$ then $\sigma \notin L(A_i)$.*
- *if c is of the form $(c_1 \wedge c_2)$ then $(A_1, A_2) \models c_1$ and $(A_1, A_2) \models c_2$.*
- *if c is of the form $(c_1 \vee c_2)$ then $(A_1, A_2) \models c_1$ or $(A_1, A_2) \models c_2$.*

For a set C of membership constraints formulas over $(\alpha g_1, \alpha g_2)$, we say that A_1 and A_2 satisfy C if and only if for every $c \in C$, $(A_1, A_2) \models c$.

For example, a membership constraint of the form $+(\sigma_1, 1) \vee -(\sigma_2, 2)$ requires that $\sigma_1 \in L(g_1)$ or $\sigma_2 \notin L(g_2)$ (or both).

5 ApplyAG Algorithm

Given assumptions g_1,g_2, ApplyAG (see Algorithm 2) applies assume-guarantee reasoning by checking the three premises of rule CIRC-AG using g_1 and g_2. In the algorithm we check premises 1, 2, 3 in this order but in fact the order of the checks does not matter and the checks can be done in parallel. If all three premises are satisfied, then, since the rule is sound, it follows that $M_1||M_2 \models P$ holds (and this is returned to the user). Otherwise, at least one of the premises does not hold. Hence a counterexample σ for (at least) one of the premises is found. ApplyAG then checks if the counterexample indicates a real violation for $M_1||M_2 \models P$, as described below. If this is the case, then ApplyAG returns $M_1||M_2 \not\models P$. Otherwise ApplyAG uses the counterexample to compute a set of new membership constraints C and returns "continue" (note that in the first two cases an empty constraint set is returned).

Notation. For readability, in ApplyAG (and UpdateConstraints) we use $\sigma\!\downarrow \in L(A)$ and $\sigma\!\downarrow \notin L(A)$ as a shorthand for $\sigma\!\downarrow_{\alpha A} \in L(A)$ and $\sigma\!\downarrow_{\alpha A} \notin L(A)$, respectively.

Checking Validity of a Counterexample. Given a counterexample σ for one of the premises of the CIRC-AG rule, ApplyAG checks if σ can be extended into a trace in $L(M_1||M_2)$ which does not satisfy P. This check is performed either by ApplyAG directly (if premise 3 fails: in lines 9-16 of ApplyAG) or by algorithm UpdateConstraints (if one of the first two premises fails). In essence, a counterexample σ is real if $\sigma\!\downarrow_{\alpha g_1} \in L(M_1\!\downarrow_{\alpha g_1})$, $\sigma\!\downarrow_{\alpha g_2} \in L(M_2\!\downarrow_{\alpha g_2})$ and $\sigma\!\downarrow_{\alpha P} \notin L(P)$. This is also stated by the following lemma, which follows from Lemma 1 and Lemma 3.

Lemma 4. *If $\sigma\!\downarrow_{\alpha g_1} \in L(M_1\!\downarrow_{\alpha g_1})$, $\sigma\!\downarrow_{\alpha g_2} \in L(M_2\!\downarrow_{\alpha g_2})$ and $\sigma\!\downarrow_{\alpha P} \notin L(P)$, then $M_1||M_2 \not\models P$. Moreover, σ can be extended into a counterexample for $M_1||M_2 \models P$.*

For example, in line 9 of Algorithm 2, $\sigma \in (\alpha g_1 \cup \alpha g_2)^*$ is a counterexample for premise 3, hence $\sigma{\downarrow_{\alpha P}} \notin L(P)$. It therefore suffices to check if $\sigma{\downarrow_{\alpha g_1}} \in L(M_1{\downarrow_{\alpha g_1}})$ and $\sigma{\downarrow_{\alpha g_2}} \in L(M_2{\downarrow_{\alpha g_2}})$ in order to conclude that a real counterexample exists (line 11). Similarly, in Algorithm 3, $\sigma a \in (\alpha M_i \cup \alpha g_j)^*$ is a counterexample for premise i for $i \in \{1, 2\}$, hence $\sigma a{\downarrow_{\alpha M_i}} \in L(M_i)$, and since $\alpha g_i \subseteq \alpha M_i$, also $\sigma a{\downarrow_{\alpha g_i}} \in L(M_i{\downarrow_{\alpha g_i}})$. In line 3, the algorithm then checks if, in addition, $\sigma a{\downarrow_{\alpha g_j}} \in L(M_j{\downarrow_{\alpha g_j}})$ and $\sigma a{\downarrow_{\alpha P}} \notin L(P)$. If these conditions hold then by Lemma 4 the counterexample is real (line 5).

Computation of New Membership Constraints based on Counterexamples. When the counterexample found for one of the premises does not produce a real counterexample for $M_1 || M_2 \models P$, then APPLYAG (or UPDATECONSTRAINTS) analyzes the counterexample and computes new membership constraints to *refine* the assumptions. In essence, these constraints encode whether the counterexample trace (or a restriction of it) should be added to or removed from the languages of the two assumptions such that future checks will not produce the same counterexample again.

If premise 3 does not hold, i.e. $g_1 || g_2 \not\models P$ and the reported counterexample σ is found not to be real then it should be removed from $L(g_1)$ or from $L(g_2)$ (in this way the trace will no longer be present in the composition $g_1 || g_2$ for the assumptions computed in subsequent iterations). Therefore in line 14, APPLYAG adds the corresponding constraint $(-(\sigma{\downarrow_{\alpha g_1}}, 1) \vee -(\sigma{\downarrow_{\alpha g_2}}, 2))$ to C.

If either premise 1 or 2 does not hold, i.e. $M_i \not\models g_j \triangleright g_i$, then the analysis of the counterexample $\sigma_i a_i$ (for i=1 or 2) and the addition of constraints (if needed) are performed by UPDATECONSTRAINTS (see Algorithm 3). Specifically, in this case $\sigma_i a_i$ should be added to $L(g_i)$ or its prefix σ_i should be removed from $L(g_j)$ (where $j \neq i$). In both cases, this ensures that checking $M_i \not\models g_j \triangleright g_i$ in subsequent iterations will no longer produce the same counterexample (see Definition 2).

We add this constraint in line 11 of Algorithm 3, where C is updated with $(-(\sigma{\downarrow_{\alpha g_j}}, j) \vee +(\sigma a{\downarrow_{\alpha g_i}}, i)$. Although this simple refinement would work for all cases, note that Algorithm 3, uses a more involved refinement. The reason is that we exploit the properties stated in Lemma 2, Items (1) and (2), to detect more elaborate constraints; using the lemma and analyzing both σ and σa allows us to *accelerate* the refinement process.

For example, in line 18, the subconstraint $+(\sigma a{\downarrow_{\alpha g_i}}, i)$ is conjoined with $-(\sigma a{\downarrow_{\alpha g_j}}, j)$. This is because Lemma 2, Item (2) establishes that $M_i || g_j \models P$ is a necessary condition for a successful application of CIRC-AG. Therefore since $\sigma a{\downarrow_{\alpha g_i}} \in L(M_i{\downarrow_{\alpha g_i}})$ and $\sigma a{\downarrow_{\alpha P}} \notin L(P)$, then $\sigma a{\downarrow_{\alpha g_j}}$ must not be in $L(g_j)$. Explanations of other cases appear as comments in the pseudocode. Note that there are more cases that we do not show in order to simplify the presentation.

Example 4. Consider the LTSs from Figure 3, produced in the 6th iteration of ACR. When trying to apply CIRC-AG with these assumptions, APPLYAG obtains the trace $\langle send, out, send \rangle$ as a counterexample for $Out \models g_1^{(6)} \triangleright g_2^{(6)}$ (premise 2). Since $\langle send, out, send \rangle{\downarrow_{\alpha g_1}} \notin L(In{\downarrow_{\alpha g_1}})$, the counterexample turns out to be spurious, and after checking the additional conditions in UPDATECONSTRAINTS, $-(\langle send \rangle, 1) \vee (+(\langle send, send \rangle, 2) \wedge -(\langle send, send \rangle, 1))$ is produced in line 18 as a membership constraint in order to eliminate it in the following iterations.

Algorithm 2. Applying CIRC-AG with g_1 and g_2, and constraint updating

procedure APPLYAG(M_1, M_2, P, g_1, g_2)
    if $M_1 \not\models g_2 \triangleright g_1$ **then**
        Let $\sigma_1 a_1$ be a counterexample for $M_1 \not\models g_2 \triangleright g_1$
        return UPDATECONSTRAINTS($1, 2, M_1, M_2, P, \sigma_1 a_1$)
    else if $M_2 \not\models g_1 \triangleright g_2$ **then**
        Let $\sigma_2 a_2$ be a counterexample for $M_2 \not\models g_1 \triangleright g_2$
        return UPDATECONSTRAINTS($2, 1, M_2, M_1, P, \sigma_2 a_2$)
    else if $g_1 || g_2 \not\models P$ **then**
        Let σ be a counterexample for $g_1 || g_2 \not\models P$
        if ($\sigma\!\downarrow\, \in L(M_1 \downarrow \alpha g_1)$ && $\sigma \downarrow\in L(M_2 \downarrow \alpha g_2)$) **then**
            return ($\emptyset$, "$M_1 || M_2 \not\models P$")
        else // $\sigma \notin L(M_1\!\downarrow_{\alpha g_1} || M_2\!\downarrow_{\alpha g_2}), \sigma\!\downarrow\, \notin L(P)$
            // Remove σ from g_1 or remove σ from g_2
            $C = \{(-(\sigma\!\downarrow_{\alpha g_1}, 1) \vee -(\sigma\!\downarrow_{\alpha g_2}, 2))\}$
            return (C, "continue")
        end if
    else
        return ($\emptyset$, "$M_1 || M_2 \models P$")
    end if
end procedure

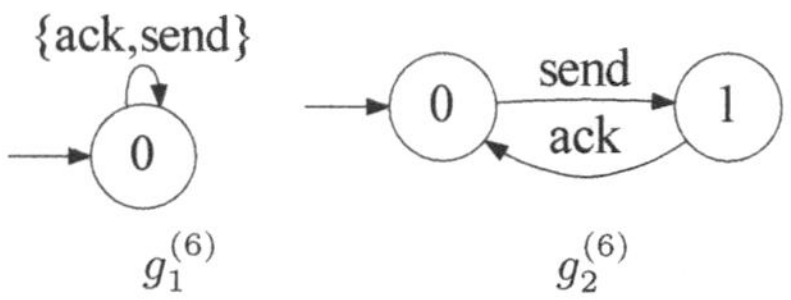

Fig. 3. LTSs produced in the 6th iteration of ACR

In the following we state the progress of assumption refinement based on spurious counterexamples.

Lemma 5. *Let σ be a spurious counterexample obtained for premise $i \in \{1, 2, 3\}$ of CIRC-AG with respect to assumptions g_1, g_2 and let C be the updated set of constraints. Then any pair of LTSs g_1' and g_2' such that $(g_1', g_2') \models C$ will no longer exhibit σ as a counterexample for premise i of CIRC-AG.*

Corollary 1. *Any pair of LTSs g_1' and g_2' such that $(g_1', g_2') \models C$ is different from every previous pair of LTSs considered by the algorithm.*

The following two lemmas state that the added membership constraints do not over-constrain the assumptions. They ensure that the "desired" assumptions that enable to verify (Lemma 6) or falsify (Lemma 7) the property are always within reach.

Lemma 6. *Suppose $M_1 || M_2 \models P$ and let g_1 and g_2 be LTSs that satisfy the premises of rule CIRC-AG. Then (g_1, g_2) satisfy every set of constraints C produced by* APPLYAG.

Lemma 7. *Let $g_1 = M_1\!\downarrow_{\alpha g_1}$ and $g_2 = M_2\!\downarrow_{\alpha g_2}$. Then (g_1, g_2) satisfy every set of constraints C produced by* APPLYAG.

Algorithm 3. Computation of constraints based on a counterexample for $M_i \models g_j \triangleright g_i$

// σa is a counterexample for $M_i \models g_j \triangleright g_i$, i.e. $\sigma a\!\downarrow \in L(M_i), \sigma\!\downarrow \in L(g_j), \sigma a\!\downarrow \notin L(g_i)$
procedure UPDATECONSTRAINTS($i, j, M_i, M_j, P, \sigma a$)
  if $\sigma a\!\downarrow \in L(M_j\!\downarrow_{\alpha g_j})$ and $\sigma a\!\downarrow \notin L(P)$ **then**
    // $\sigma a\!\downarrow \in L(M_i\!\downarrow_{\alpha g_i} || M_j\!\downarrow_{\alpha g_j})$ and $\sigma a\!\downarrow \notin L(P)$
    return ($\emptyset$, "$M_i || M_j \not\models P$")
  if $\sigma a\!\downarrow \in L(M_j\!\downarrow_{\alpha g_j})$ and $\sigma a\!\downarrow \in L(P)$ **then**
    // Add σa to both g_i and g_j to ensure $M_1\!\downarrow_{\alpha g_1} || M_2\!\downarrow_{\alpha g_2} \models g_1 || g_2$ (Lemma 2 (1))
    $C = \{+(\sigma a\!\downarrow_{\alpha g_i}, i), +(\sigma a\!\downarrow_{\alpha g_j}, j)\}$
  if $\sigma a\!\downarrow \notin L(M_j\!\downarrow_{\alpha g_j})$ and $\sigma\!\downarrow \notin L(M_j\!\downarrow_{\alpha g_j})$ and $\sigma a\!\downarrow \in L(P)$ **then**
    // Remove σ from g_j or add σa to g_i
    $C = \{(-(\sigma\!\downarrow_{\alpha g_j}, j) \vee +(\sigma a\!\downarrow_{\alpha g_i}, i)\}$
  if $\sigma a\!\downarrow \notin L(M_j\!\downarrow_{\alpha g_j})$ and $\sigma\!\downarrow \notin L(M_j\!\downarrow_{\alpha g_j})$ and $\sigma a\!\downarrow \notin L(P)$ and $\sigma\!\downarrow \notin L(P)$ **then**
    // Remove σ from g_j (Because of Lemma 2 (2))
    $C = \{-(\sigma\!\downarrow_{\alpha g_j}, j)\}$
  if $\sigma a\!\downarrow \notin L(M_j\!\downarrow_{\alpha g_j})$ and $\sigma\!\downarrow \notin L(M_j\!\downarrow_{\alpha g_j})$ and $\sigma a\!\downarrow \notin L(P)$ and $\sigma\!\downarrow \in L(P)$ **then**
    // Remove σ from g_j or (add σa to g_i and remove it from g_j)
    // In the latter case removal of σa from g_j is due to Lemma 2 (2)
    $C = \{(-(\sigma\!\downarrow_{\alpha g_j}, j) \vee (+(\sigma a\!\downarrow_{\alpha g_i}, i) \wedge -(\sigma a\!\downarrow_{\alpha g_j}, j)))\}$
  return (C, "continue")
end procedure

6 GENASSMP Algorithm

Given a set of membership constraints C, and a lower bound k on the total number of states in $|g_1| + |g_2|$, we compute assumptions g_1 and g_2 that satisfy C. Similarly to previous work [10] we build assumptions as deterministic LTSs (even though APPLYAG is not restricted to deterministic LTSs). Technically, for each value of k starting from the given k, GENASSMP encodes the structure of the desired DLTSs g_1 and g_2 with $|g_1| + |g_2| \leq k$, as well as the membership constraints, as a SAT instance $SatEnc_k(C)$. It then searches for a satisfying assignment and obtains DLTSs g_1 and g_2 based on this assignment. k is increased only when $SatEnc_k(C)$ is unsatisfiable, hence minimal DLTSs that satisfy C are obtained.

We use the following encoding of the problem of finding whether there are DLTSs g_1 and g_2 with k states in total such that $(g_1, g_2) \models C$.

Variables used for Encoding the LTSs Structure. Let $n = \lceil \log_2(k+2) \rceil$. We use boolean vectors of length n to encode the states of g_1 and g_2, where for each of them we add a special "error" state. For each $0 \leq m \leq k+1$ we use $\overline{m}$ to denote the n-bit vector that represents the number m. We fix the vector $\overline{0}$ to represent the error state of g_1, and the vector $\overline{k+1}$ to represent the error state of g_2. We explicitly add the error states in order to distinguish between traces that are rejected by the DLTS and traces for which the behavior is unspecified. For every $i \in \{1, 2\}$:

- Let S_i include the prefixes of all traces over αg_i which are constrained in C with respect to i. That is, $S_i = \bigcup_{c \in C} Strings(c, i)$.
- For every $\sigma \in S_i$, we introduce a set of boolean variables $Var(\sigma, i) = \{v^j_{(\sigma,i)} \mid 0 \leq j \leq n-1\}$. We denote by $\overline{v}_{(\sigma,i)}$ the vector $(v^0_{(\sigma,i)} \cdots v^{n-1}_{(\sigma,i)})$ of boolean variables. $\overline{v}_{(\sigma,i)}$ represents the state of g_i reached when traversing σ.

We define $V_{g_i} = \bigcup_{\sigma \in S_i} Var(\sigma, i)$. In addition to V_{g_1} and V_{g_2}, we introduce a set V_{aux} of boolean variables which consist of the following variables:

- To guarantee that the LTSs we produce are indeed deterministic, we add a set of boolean variables which are used to enumerate the (non error) states in the DLTSs. For this we use $k \times |\alpha g_1 \cup \alpha g_2|$ vectors of boolean variables, each of size n: For every $1 \leq m \leq k$ and $a \in (\alpha g_1 \cup \alpha g_2)$, we introduce a set of boolean variables $Var(m, a) = \{u^j_{(m,a)} \mid 0 \leq j \leq n-1\}$. We denote by $\overline{u}_{(m,a)}$ the vector $(u^0_{(m,a)} \cdots u^{n-1}_{(m,a)})$ of boolean variables. $\overline{u}_{(m,a)}$ represents the state (of either g_1 or g_2) reached from state m after seeing action a.
- To guarantee that the states of the DLTSs are disjoint, we introduce another vector $\overline{u} = (u^0 \cdots u^{n-1})$ of boolean variables, used to represent the number l such that all states of g_1 are smaller or equal l and all states of g_2 are larger than l.

Variables used for Encoding Membership Constraints. For every disjunctive membership constraint formula $c \in C$ we introduce a boolean "selector" variable en_c that determines which of the disjuncts of *c must* be satisfied (the other disjunct might be satisfied as well). Technically, let $En_c = \{en_c \mid c \in C\}$, and let $A = En_c \cup \{\neg en_c \mid en_c \in En_c\} \cup \{true\}$. We define $\theta^{add}_{g_1}, \theta^{rem}_{g_1} : S_1 \rightarrow 2^A$ and $\theta^{add}_{g_2}, \theta^{rem}_{g_2} : S_2 \rightarrow 2^A$ such that for every $\sigma \in S_i$, $\theta^{add}_{g_i}(\sigma)$ and $\theta^{rem}_{g_i}(\sigma)$ are the smallest sets such that $true \in \theta^{add}_{g_1}(\epsilon)$ and $true \in \theta^{add}_{g_2}(\epsilon)$, and for every $c \in C$:

- if $c = (-(\sigma{\downarrow_{\alpha g_i}}, i) \vee -(\sigma{\downarrow_{\alpha g_j}}, j))$ then $en_c \in \theta^{rem}_{g_i}(\sigma{\downarrow_{\alpha g_i}})$ and $\neg en_c \in \theta^{rem}_{g_j}(\sigma{\downarrow_{\alpha g_j}})$.
- if $c = +(\sigma{\downarrow_{\alpha g_i}}, i)$ then $true \in \theta^{add}_{g_i}(\sigma{\downarrow_{\alpha g_i}})$.
- if $c = -(\sigma{\downarrow_{\alpha g_i}}, i)$ then $true \in \theta^{rem}_{g_i}(\sigma{\downarrow_{\alpha g_i}})$.
- if $c = (-(\sigma{\downarrow_{\alpha g_j}}, j) \vee +(\sigma a{\downarrow_{\alpha g_i}}, i))$ then $en_c \in \theta^{rem}_{g_j}(\sigma{\downarrow_{\alpha g_j}})$ and $\neg en_c \in \theta^{add}_{g_i}(\sigma a{\downarrow_{\alpha g_i}})$.
- if $c = (-(\sigma{\downarrow_{\alpha g_j}}, j) \vee (+(\sigma a{\downarrow_{\alpha g_i}}, i) \wedge -(\sigma a{\downarrow_{\alpha g_j}}, j)))$ then $en_c \in \theta^{rem}_{g_j}(\sigma{\downarrow_{\alpha g_j}})$, $\neg en_c \in \theta^{add}_{g_i}(\sigma a{\downarrow_{\alpha g_i}})$ and $\neg en_c \in \theta^{rem}_{g_j}(\sigma a{\downarrow_{\alpha g_j}})$.

Intuitively, if at least one of the literals in $\theta^{add}_{g_i}(\sigma)$ is satisfied then σ must be added to the language of g_i, and similarly for $\theta^{rem}_{g_i}(\sigma)$ with removal. These sets are therefore interpreted as disjunctions. Formally, let $Bool(A)$ be the set of boolean formulas over A. For $\theta^{ac}_{g_i} : S_i \rightarrow 2^A$ (where $ac \in \{rem, add\}$), we define $\tilde{\theta}^{ac}_{g_i} : S_i \rightarrow Bool(A)$ as follows: $\tilde{\theta}^{ac}_{g_i}(\sigma) = \begin{cases} false & \theta^{ac}_{g_i}(\sigma) = \emptyset \\ \bigvee \theta^{ac}_{g_i}(\sigma) & \text{otherwise} \end{cases}$

SAT Constraints. $SatEnc_k(C)$ is a set of constraints (with the meaning of conjunction) over the variables $En_c \cup V_{g_1} \cup V_{g_2} \cup V_{aux}$ defined as follows:

- Encoding the LTSs structures into SAT constraints:
  1. For every trace $\sigma_1 \in S_1$ we add the constraint $\overline{v}_{(\sigma_1,1)} \leq \overline{u}$, and for every trace $\sigma_2 \in S_2$ we add the constraint $\overline{u} < \overline{v}_{(\sigma_2,2)}$ (separating states of the DLTSs). We also add a constraint $\overline{1} \leq \overline{u} \leq \overline{k-1}$ to restrict the range of $\overline{u}$.
  2. For every $\sigma \in S_2$ we add the following constraint $\overline{v}_{(\sigma,2)} \leq \overline{k+1}$ (every trace is mapped to a valid state in the DLTSs).
  3. For every $i \in \{1,2\}$, every trace $\sigma \in S_i$, every action $a \in \alpha g_i$ such that $\sigma a \in S_i$, and for every $1 \leq m \leq k$, we add the following constraint: $(\overline{v}_{(\sigma,i)} = \overline{m} \Rightarrow \overline{v}_{(\sigma a,i)} = \overline{u}_{(m,a)}$ (the DLTSs are deterministic).
  4. For every trace $\sigma \in S_1$ and action $a \in \alpha g_1$, if $\sigma a \in S_1$ then we add the following constraint: $\overline{v}_{(\sigma,1)} = \overline{0} \Rightarrow \overline{v}_{(\sigma a,1)} = \overline{0}$ (the error state of g_1 is a sink state; DLTSs are prefix closed).
  5. For every string $\sigma \in S_2$ and action $a \in \alpha g_2$, if $\sigma a \in S_2$ then we add the following constraint: $\overline{v}_{(\sigma,2)} = \overline{k+1} \Rightarrow \overline{v}_{(\sigma a,2)} = \overline{k+1}$ (the error state of g_2 is a sink state; DLTSs are prefix closed).
- Encoding the membership constraints formulas into SAT constraints:
  6. For every trace $\sigma \in S_1$ we add the constraint: $\tilde{\theta}_{g_1}^{rem}(\sigma) \Rightarrow \overline{v}_{(\sigma,1)} = \overline{0}$.
  7. For every trace $\sigma \in S_2$ we add the constraint: $\tilde{\theta}_{g_2}^{rem}(\sigma) \Rightarrow \overline{v}_{(\sigma,2)} = \overline{k+1}$.
  8. For every trace $\sigma \in S_1$ we add the constraint: $\tilde{\theta}_{g_1}^{add}(\sigma) \Rightarrow \overline{v}_{(\sigma,1)} \neq \overline{0}$.
  9. For every trace $\sigma \in S_2$ we add the constraint: $\tilde{\theta}_{g_2}^{add}(\sigma) \Rightarrow \overline{v}_{(\sigma,2)} \neq \overline{k+1}$.

Note that the implications in constraints 6-9 guarantee that a trace is accepted by g_i (leads to a non-error state) whenever it is required to be added to g_i (as encoded by $\theta_{g_i}^{add}(\sigma{\downarrow_{\alpha g_i}})$). However, it may be accepted also in other cases, provided it is not required to be removed by other constraints. The same holds for removal of traces.

Lemma 8. *$SatEnc_k(C)$ is satisfiable if and only if there exist DLTSs g_1 and g_2 that satisfy C such that $|g_1| + |g_2| = k$.*

Due to Lemma 7 which ensures that (the nondeterministic) LTSs $M_1{\downarrow_{\alpha g_1}}$ and $M_2{\downarrow_{\alpha g_2}}$ satisfy C, we get the following corollary, which ensures termination of GENASSMP:

Corollary 2. *At every iteration of* ACR, *there exists $k \leq O(2^{|M_1|} + 2^{|M_2|})$ where $SatEnc_k(C)$ is satisfiable.*

In fact, since the minimal k is found, minimal assumptions that satisfy C are obtained. In particular, together with Lemma 6, this ensures that when $M_1||M_2 \models P$, then minimal assumptions for which CIRC-AG is applicable are eventually obtained.

From SAT Assignment to LTS Assumptions. Given a satisfying assignment ψ to $SatEnc_k(C)$, we use ψ to generate assumptions g_1 and g_2 that satisfy C.

First, we extract DLTSs $A_1(\psi)$ and $A_2(\psi)$ extended with error states: $A_i(\psi) = (Q_i, \alpha g_i, \delta_i, q_0^i, \pi_i)$ where $Q_i = \{\overline{m} \in \{0,1\}^n \mid \exists \sigma \in S_i$ such that $\psi(\overline{v}_{(\sigma,i)}) = \overline{m}\}$, $q_0^i = \psi(\overline{v}_{(\epsilon,i)})$, $\pi_1 = \overline{0}$, $\pi_2 = \overline{k+1}$, and $\delta_i(\overline{m}, a) = \overline{m}'$ if there exists $\sigma \in S_i$ such that $\psi(\overline{v}_{(\sigma,i)}) = \overline{m} \wedge \sigma a \in S_i \wedge \psi(\overline{v}_{(\sigma a,i)}) = \overline{m}'$, and otherwise $\delta_i(\overline{m}, a) = \perp$ (undefined).

Note that δ_i is deterministic and it is well defined, since constraint 3 of $SatEnc_k(C)$ ensures that if there exist $\sigma, \sigma' \in S_i$ such that $\psi(\overline{v}_{(\sigma,i)}) = \psi(\overline{v}_{(\sigma',i)})$ and both σa and $\sigma' a$ are in S_i, then also $\psi(\overline{v}_{(\sigma a,i)}) = \psi(\overline{v}_{(\sigma' a,i)})$. Further, by constraint 1, $Q_1 \cap Q_2 = \emptyset$.

$A_1(\psi)$ and $A_2(\psi)$ can be thought of as error LTSs, except that they might be incomplete: δ_i is a partial function. As in an error LTS, traces leading to an error state in $A_i(\psi)$ are rejected. Traces for which δ_i is undefined are unspecified (recall that such traces do not exist in an error LTS, which is complete, and in a DLTS, in contrast, such traces are rejected). The latter represent traces that do not affect the satisfaction of C.

We transform $A_1(\psi)$ and $A_2(\psi)$ into (complete) error LTSs by extending δ_i to total functions. Since unspecified traces do not affect satisfaction of C, any completion results in DLTSs that satisfy C. In practice, if $\delta_i(\overline{m}, a) = \bot$, we define $\delta_i(\overline{m}, a) = \overline{m}$.

To obtain DLTSs, we remove the error states. We denote the result by $LTS(A_i(\psi))$.

Lemma 9. *Let $g_1 = LTS(A_1(\psi))$ and $g_2 = LTS(A_2(\psi))$, where ψ satisfies $SatEnc_k(C)$. Then g_1 and g_2 are DLTSs such that (1) $(g_1, g_2) \models C$ and (2) $|g_1| + |g_2| \leq k$.*

Example 5. Consider the 7th (and final) iteration of ACR. Since the assumptions from the 6th iteration (Figure 3) have a total of 3 states, the search performed by GENASSMP at the 7th iteration starts with $k = 3$, and since $SatEnc_3(C)$ is unsatisfiable, k is increased to 4, yielding (the final) g_1 and g_2 with a total of 4 states (Figure 2). Note that (g_1, g_2) indeed satisfy the membership constraint $-(\langle send \rangle, 1) \vee (+(\langle send, send \rangle, 2) \wedge -(\langle send, send \rangle, 1)) \in C$ from the previous iteration (due to the right disjunct). In particular, they do not exhibit the counterexample from Example 4.

7 Correctness, Termination and Minimality

In this section we argue that our main algorithm ACR is correct, it terminates and produces minimal assumptions.

Theorem 2 (Correctness and Termination). *Given components M_1 and M_2, and property P,* ACR *terminates and returns "$M_1||M_2 \models P$" if P holds on $M_1||M_2$ and "$M_1||M_2 \not\models P$", otherwise.*

Proof (sketch). ACR returns "$M_1||M_2 \models P$" if and only if all premises of CIRC-AG hold, in which case correctness follows from the soundness of CIRC-AG. On the other hand, if ACR returns "$M_1||M_2 \not\models P$", then correctness is ensured by Lemma 4. It remains to prove that ACR terminates. First, Corollary 2 ensures that at every iteration of ACR, $SatEnc_k(C)$ is satisfiable for some $k = O(2^{|M_1|} + 2^{|M_2|})$. Therefore, each iteration terminates. Moreover, by Corollary 1, the pair of DLTSs generated at each iteration is different from all pairs considered in previous iterations, which ensures progress of ACR. Finally, by Lemma 7, $g_1 = M_1{\downarrow_{\alpha g_1}}$ and $g_2 = M_2{\downarrow_{\alpha g_2}}$ always satisfy C. Therefore ACR terminates at the latest when $g_1 = M_1{\downarrow_{\alpha g_1}}$ and $g_2 = M_2{\downarrow_{\alpha g_2}}$, in which case premises 1 and 2 of CIRC-AG necessarily hold and premise 3 amounts to $M_1{\downarrow_{\alpha g_1}}||M_2{\downarrow_{\alpha g_2}} \models P$, hence either all premises hold or a real counterexample is obtained. □

Theorem 3 (Minimality). *If* $M_1||M_2 \models P$ *then* ACR *terminates with DLTSs* g_1 *and* g_2 *whose total number of states is minimal among all pairs of DLTSs that satisfy the CIRC-AG rule.*

Proof (sketch). Termination follows from Theorem 2. Let n be the minimal total number of states of DLTSs that satisfy rule CIRC-AG. By Lemma 6, the corresponding DLTSs satisfy C at any iteration of ACR. Therefore by Lemma 8, $SatEnc_n(C)$ is satisfiable at any iteration and in particular in the last one, where Lemma 9 ensures that the obtained DLTSs $g_1 = LTS(A_1(\psi))$, $g_2 = LTS(A_2(\psi))$ are such that $|g_1| + |g_2| \leq n$. □

8 Evaluation and Concluding Remarks

We implemented ACR in the LTSA (Labelled Transition System Analyser) tool [13]; we use MiniSAT [8] for SAT solving. We optimized our implementation to perform incremental SAT encoding using the ability of MiniSAT to solve CNF formulas under a set of unit clause assumptions. We also made ACR return (at each iteration) k counterexamples for the three premises where, k is $|g_1| + |g_2|$.

We compared ACR with learning-based assume guarantee reasoning (based on rule NonCIRC-AG), on the following examples [19]: *Gas Station* (3 to 5 customers), *Chiron* – a model of a GUI (2 to 5 event handlers), *Client Server* – a client-server application (6 to 9 clients), and a NASA rover model: *MER* (2 to 4 users competing for two common resources). We used the same two-way decompositions reported in previous experiments. Experiments were performed on a MacBook Pro with a 2.3 GHz Intel Core i7 CPU and with 16 GB RAM running OS X 10.9.4 and a Suns JDK version 7.

Table 1 summarizes our results. For both approaches, we report the analysis time (in seconds) and the assumption sizes. Measuring memory is unreliable due to the garbage collection and the interfacing with MiniSAT via native method calls (our measurements indicate that memory consumption is stable and does not increase dramatically for larger cases). We instead report the maximum numbers of states observed for checking the premises of the two rules. We put a limit of 1800 seconds for each experiment; "–" indicates that the time for that case exceeds this limit.

In all the experiments ACR generates smaller assumptions and in the majority of cases this results in smaller analysis time and state space explored. For larger cases the assumptions generated by ACR are *significantly* smaller. For the Gas Station, ACR significantly outperforms learning in terms of analysis time and states explored, while for all other cases the two approaches are comparable, at smaller sizes. However at larger configurations (Client Server 8 and 9, MER 4) ACR again significantly outperforms the learning-based approach. In all but one case (Chiron 5) the smaller assumptions generated with ACR lead to smaller state spaces for checking the rule premises. Case Chiron 5 is still comparable in terms of running time but it may indicate that the two-way decomposition that we used (found to be optimal for learning in previous studies) may not be optimal for ACR. We plan to investigate this further in future work.

Future Work. ACR can be optimized in many ways. Currently we are checking the three premises one after the other at each iteration and get k different counterexamples for each one of them. We can check them in parallel on different machines. We

Table 1. Comparison of ACR (rule CIRC-AG) and learning (rule NonCIRC-AG). Best results are shown in bold.

Case	ACR Time	$\lvert g_1 \rvert$	$\lvert g_2 \rvert$	Premise1	Premise2	Premise3	L^* Time	$\lvert A \rvert$	Premise1	Premise2
GasSt 3	**26**	**3**	**3**	2588	1093	6	–	>351	>8243	>4045
GasSt 4	**48**	**3**	**3**	19503	2196	4	–	>381	>165836	>47360
GasSt 5	**309**	**3**	**3**	132608	6995	6	–	>207	>560000	>61058
Chiron 2	1.257	**2**	**2**	134	204	5	**0.5**	9	256	198
Chiron 3	**2.013**	**2**	**2**	341	2244	5	2.121	25	492	2736
Chiron 4	**3.149**	**2**	**2**	449	6681	5	6.341	45	860	18370
Chiron 5	34	**2**	**2**	1152	258456	5	**33**	122	2101	138537
ClServ 6	11	**7**	**2**	256	16	10	**8**	256	256	2505
ClServ 7	33	**8**	**2**	576	17	10	33	576	576	6455
ClServ 8	**53**	**9**	**2**	1280	17	9	138	1280	1280	16199
ClServ 9	**249.839**	**10**	**2**	2816	23	14	725	2816	2816	39769
MER 2	**4.397**	**5**	**2**	30	147	6	4.54	46	313	79
MER 3	**35**	**7**	**2**	83	1198	13	50	274	3146	250
MER 4	**1220.649**	**9**	**2**	97	7109	9	–	>1210	>128883	>549

further plan to investigate alphabet refinement and generalization to n-way decompositions (for $n > 2$) – both these techniques significantly enhanced the performance of compositional acyclic techniques [19]. For the n-way decompositions we can either consider a recursive application of our current approach to the system decomposed in two components, each decomposed in two sub-components etc. or a more involved approach that synthesizes directly n assumptions, one for each component. We leave this for future work. We also plan to explore learning and abstraction-refinement for discovering suitable assumptions. Although these techniques might not guarantee minimal assumptions, they can be less computationally demanding than our current approach.

Acknowledgements. This research was partially supported by BSF grant no. 2012259 and NSF grant no. 1329278.

References

1. Alur, R., Henzinger, T.A.: Reactive modules. Formal Methods in System Design 15(1), 7–48 (1999)
2. Alur, R., Madhusudan, P., Nam, W.: Symbolic compositional verification by learning assumptions. In: Etessami, K., Rajamani, S.K. (eds.) CAV 2005. LNCS, vol. 3576, pp. 548–562. Springer, Heidelberg (2005)
3. Gheorghiu Bobaru, M., Păsăreanu, C.S., Giannakopoulou, D.: Automated assume-guarantee reasoning by abstraction refinement. In: Gupta, A., Malik, S. (eds.) CAV 2008. LNCS, vol. 5123, pp. 135–148. Springer, Heidelberg (2008)
4. Chaki, S., Clarke, E., Sinha, N., Thati, P.: Automated assume-guarantee reasoning for simulation conformance. In: Etessami, K., Rajamani, S.K. (eds.) CAV 2005. LNCS, vol. 3576, pp. 534–547. Springer, Heidelberg (2005)
5. Chen, Y.-F., Clarke, E.M., Farzan, A., Tsai, M.-H., Tsay, Y.-K., Wang, B.-Y.: Automated assume-guarantee reasoning through implicit learning. In: Touili, T., Cook, B., Jackson, P. (eds.) CAV 2010. LNCS, vol. 6174, pp. 511–526. Springer, Heidelberg (2010)

6. Chen, Y.-F., Farzan, A., Clarke, E.M., Tsay, Y.-K., Wang, B.-Y.: Learning minimal separating DFA's for compositional verification. In: Kowalewski, S., Philippou, A. (eds.) TACAS 2009. LNCS, vol. 5505, pp. 31–45. Springer, Heidelberg (2009)
7. Cobleigh, J.M., Giannakopoulou, D., Păsăreanu, C.S.: Learning assumptions for compositional verification. In: Garavel, H., Hatcliff, J. (eds.) TACAS 2003. LNCS, vol. 2619, pp. 331–346. Springer, Heidelberg (2003)
8. Een, N., Šorensson, N.: The minisat, http://minisat.se
9. Graf, S., Passerone, R., Quinton, S.: Contract-based reasoning for component systems with rich interactions. In: Sangiovanni-Vincentelli, A., Zeng, H., Di Natale, M., Marwedel, P. (eds.) Embedded Systems Development. Embedded Systems, vol. 20, pp. 139–154. Springer, New York (2014)
10. Gupta, A., McMillan, K.L., Fu, Z.: Automated assumption generation for compositional verification. Formal Methods in System Design 32(3), 285–301 (2008)
11. Henzinger, T.A., Liu, X., Qadeer, S., Rajamani, S.K.: Formal specification and verification of a dataflow processor array. In: ICCAD, pp. 494–499 (1999)
12. Henzinger, T.A., Qadeer, S., Rajamani, S.K.: You assume, we guarantee: Methodology and case studies. In: Hu, A.J., Vardi, M.Y. (eds.) CAV 1998. LNCS, vol. 1427, pp. 440–451. Springer, Heidelberg (1998)
13. Magee, J., Kramer, J.: Concurrency: State Models and Java Programs. John Wiley & Sons (1999)
14. McMillan, K.L.: Verification of an implementation of Tomasulo's algorithm by compositional model checking. In: Hu, A.J., Vardi, M.Y. (eds.) CAV 1998. LNCS, vol. 1427, pp. 110–121. Springer, Heidelberg (1998)
15. McMillan, K.L.: Circular compositional reasoning about liveness. In: Pierre, L., Kropf, T. (eds.) CHARME 1999. LNCS, vol. 1703, pp. 342–346. Springer, Heidelberg (1999)
16. McMillan, K.L.: Verification of infinite state systems by compositional model checking. In: Pierre, L., Kropf, T. (eds.) CHARME 1999. LNCS, vol. 1703, pp. 219–237. Springer, Heidelberg (1999)
17. Misra, J., Chandy, K.M.: Proofs of networks of processes. IEEE Trans. Software Eng. 7(4), 417–426 (1981)
18. Namjoshi, K.S., Trefler, R.J.: On the competeness of compositional reasoning. In: Emerson, E.A., Sistla, A.P. (eds.) CAV 2000. LNCS, vol. 1855, pp. 139–153. Springer, Heidelberg (2000)
19. Pasareanu, C.S., Giannakopoulou, D., Bobaru, M.G., Cobleigh, J.M., Barringer, H.: Learning to divide and conquer: applying the L* algorithm to automate assume-guarantee reasoning. Formal Methods in System Design 32(3), 175–205 (2008)
20. Pnueli, A.: In transition from global to modular temporal reasoning about programs. In: Logics and Models of Concurrent Systems. NATO ASI Series (1985)
21. Rushby, J.: Formal verification of mcmillan's compositional assume-guarantee rule. In: CSL Technical Report, SRI (2001)

Towards Formal Verification of Orchestration Computations Using the $\mathbb{K}$ Framework

Musab A. AlTurki(✉) and Omar Alzuhaibi

King Fahd University of Petroleum and Minerals Dhahran,
Dhahran, Saudi Arabia
musab@kfupm.edu.sa, omar.zud@gmail.com

Abstract. Orchestration provides a general model of concurrent computations. A minimal yet expressive theory of orchestration is provided by Orc, in which computations are modeled by site calls and their orchestrations through a few combinators. Using Orc, formal verification of correctness of orchestrations amounts to devising an executable formal semantics of Orc and leveraging existing tool support. Despite its simplicity and elegance, giving formal semantics to Orc capturing precisely its intended behaviors is far from trivial primarily due to the challenges posed by concurrency, timing and the distinction between internal and external actions. This paper presents a semantics-based approach for formally verifying Orc orchestrations using the $\mathbb{K}$ framework. Unlike previously developed operational semantics of Orc, the $\mathbb{K}$ semantics is not directly based on the interleaving semantics given by Orc's SOS specification. Instead, it is based on concurrent rewriting enabled by $\mathbb{K}$. It also utilizes various $\mathbb{K}$ facilities to arrive at a clean, minimal and elegant semantic specification. To demonstrate the usefulness of the proposed approach, we describe a specification for a simple robotics case study and provide initial formal verification results.

Keywords: Formal semantics · Orc · $\mathbb{K}$ framework · Concurrency · Program verification

1 Introduction

Orchestration provides a general model of concurrent computations, although it is more often referred to in the context of service orchestrations describing the composition and management of (web) services. A minimal yet expressive theory of orchestration is provided by the Orc calculus [20,22,21], in which computations are modeled by site calls and their orchestrations through four semantically rich combinators: the "parallel", "sequential", "pruning" and "otherwise" combinators. Orc provides an elegant yet expressive programming model for concurrent and real-time computations. While Orc's simplicity and mathematical elegance enable formal reasoning about its constructs and programs, its programming model is very versatile and easily applicable to a very wide range of programming domains, including web-based programming, business processes, and distributed cyber-physical system applications, as amply demonstrated in [22,21].

N. Bjørner and F. de Boer (Eds.): FM 2015, LNCS 9109, pp. 40–56, 2015.
DOI: 10.1007/978-3-319-19249-9_4

As for other theories and programming models, devising formal semantics for Orc is of fundamental importance for several reasons, including theoretical advancements and refinements to its underlying theory, formal verification of its programs, building formally verifiable implementations, and also for unambiguous documentation. Furthermore, to better satisfy these goals, the semantics has to be *executable*, enabling quick prototyping and simulation of Orc programs through a formally defined interpreter induced by the executable specification. The rewriting logic semantics project [17,18,8,19] has been advocating this approach of formal executable semantics and has proved its value for many programming models and languages, including widely used general-purpose languages like Java [10,11] and C [9].

Giving formal executable semantics to Orc constructs capturing precisely its intended behaviors has been of interest since Orc's inception due mainly to the challenges posed by concurrency, timing and the distinction between internal and external actions. A simple computation in Orc is modeled by a site call, representing a request for a service, and more complex computations can be achieved by combining site calls into expressions using one or more of Orc's four sequential and parallel combinators. A complete formal executable semantics elegantly capturing its semantic subtleties, including its real-time behaviors and transition priorities, was given in rewriting logic [16] and implemented in the Maude tool [1,2]. This semantics is based on the original reference SOS semantic specification of the instantaneous (untimed) semantics of Orc [22].

In what can be considered as a continuation of these efforts, this paper presents a formal, executable semantics of Orc using the $\mathbb{K}$ framework [24,15], which is a derivative of the rewriting logic framework, towards providing a $\mathbb{K}$ -based framework for formally specifying and verifying Orc orchestrations. Unlike previously developed operational semantics of Orc, the $\mathbb{K}$ semantics described here is not directly based on the interleaving semantics given by the reference SOS specification of Orc. Instead, the $\mathbb{K}$ semantics provides the advantage of true concurrency enabled by $\mathbb{K}$, where two (or more) concurrent transitions are allowed to fire even in the presence of (read-access) resource sharing. It also utilizes $\mathbb{K}$'s specialized notations and facilities to arrive at a clean, minimal and elegant semantic specification. Moreover, the semantics is executable in the associated $\mathbb{K}$ tool [6,14], enabling rapid prototyping and formal analysis of Orc programs. Furthermore, the semantics implicitly presents a generic methodology through which concurrency combinators are mapped to threads and computations in $\mathbb{K}$, which can be instantiated to other concurrency calculi. Finally, to demonstrate the usefulness and applicability of the proposed approach, we describe a specification for a simple robotics case study and provide initial formal verification results.

The paper is organized as follows. In Section 2 below, we overview the $\mathbb{K}$ framework and Orc. Then, in Section 3, we present the $\mathbb{K}$ semantics of Orc. This is followed by a discussion of some sample Orc programs in Section 4. The paper concludes in Section 5 with a summary and a discussion of future work.

2 Background

This section presents some preliminaries on the $\mathbb{K}$ framework and the $\mathbb{K}$ tool, and introduces the Orc calculus along with some simple examples.

2.1 The $\mathbb{K}$ Framework

$\mathbb{K}$ [24,25] is a framework for formally defining the syntax and semantics of programming languages. It includes several specialized syntactic notations and semantic innovations that make it easy to write concise and modular definitions of programming languages. $\mathbb{K}$ is based on context-insensitive term rewriting, and builds upon three main concepts inspired by existing semantic frameworks:

- *Computational Structures (or Computations)*: A computation is a task that is represented by a component of the abstract syntax of the language or by an internal structure with a specific semantic purpose. Computations enable a natural mechanism for flattening the (abstract) syntax of a program into a sequence of tasks to be performed.
- *Configurations*: A configuration is a representation of the static state of a program in execution. $\mathbb{K}$ models a configuration as a possibly nested cell structure. Cells are labeled and represent fundamental semantic components, such as environments, stores, threads, locks, stacks, etc., that are needed for defining the semantics.
- *Rules*: Rules give semantics to language constructs. They apply to configurations, or fragments of configurations, to transform them into other configurations. There are two types of rules in $\mathbb{K}$: *structural rules*, which rearrange the structure of a configuration into a behaviorally equivalent configuration, and *computational rules*, which define externally observable transitions across different configurations. This distinction is similar to that of equations and rules in Rewriting Logic [16], and to that of heating/cooling rules and reaction rules in CHAM [3].

To briefly introduce the notations used in $\mathbb{K}$ rules, we present a $\mathbb{K}$ rule used for variable lookup (Fig. 1).

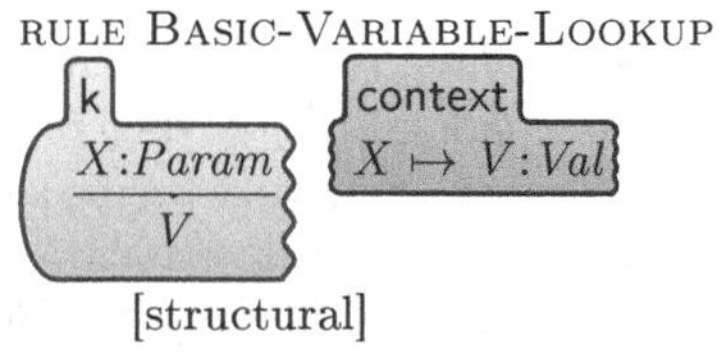

Fig. 1. Variable lookup rule as defined in $\mathbb{K}$

The illustrated rule shows two bubbles, each representing a cell predefined in the configuration. `k` is the computation cell, while `context` is the cell that holds variable mappings. Each bubble can be smooth or torn from the left, right, or both sides. A both-side-smooth cell means that the matched cell should contain only the content specified in the rule. A right-side-torn cell means that the matching should occur at the beginning of the cell; this allows for matching when more contents are at the end of the matched cell. Similarly, a left-side-torn cell means that the matching should occur at the end of the cell, so that unspecified content can be on left of the specified term. A both-sides-torn cell means that the matching can occur anywhere in the matched cell. Furthermore, Upper-case identifiers such as X and V are variables to be referenced inside the rule only; they can be followed by a colon meaning "of type". Finally, the horizontal line means that the top term rewrites to the bottom term. What this rule does is that it matches a *Param* X at the beginning of a `k` cell, matches the same X in the context cell mapped to a *Value* V, and then rewrites the X in the `k` cell to the value V.

$\mathbb{K}$ combines many of the desirable features of existing semantics frameworks, including expressiveness, modularity, convenient notations, intuitive concepts, conformance to standards, etc. One very useful facility of $\mathbb{K}$ when defining programming languages is the ability to tag rules with built-in attributes, e.g. `strict`, for specifying evaluation strategies, which are essentially notational conveniences for a special category of structural rules (called heating/cooling rules) that rearrange a computation to the desired evaluation strategy. Using attributes, instead of explicitly writing down these rules protects against potential specification errors and avoids going into unwanted non-termination. In general, these attributes constitute a very useful feature of $\mathbb{K}$ that makes defining complex evaluation strategies quite easy and flexible.

Furthermore, $\mathbb{K}$ is unique in that it allows for true concurrency even with shared reads, since rules are treated as transactions. In particular, instances of possibly the same or different computational rules can match overlapping fragments of a configuration and concurrently fire if the overlap is not being rewritten by the rules. Truly concurrent semantics of $\mathbb{K}$ is formally specified by graph rewriting [7]. For more details about the $\mathbb{K}$ framework and its features and semantics, the reader is referred to [24,25].

An implementation of the $\mathbb{K}$ framework is given by the $\mathbb{K}$ tool [6,14], which is based on Maude [4], a high-performance rewriting logic engine. Using the underlying facilities of Maude, the $\mathbb{K}$ tool can interpret and run $\mathbb{K}$ semantic specifications providing a practical mechanism to simulate programs in the language being specified and verify their correctness. In addition, the $\mathbb{K}$ tool includes a state-space search tool and a model checker (based, respectively, on Maude's search and LTL model-checking tools), as well as a deductive program verifier for the targeted language. This allows for dynamic formal verification of Orc programs in our case.

The $\mathbb{K}$ tool can compile definitions into a Maude definition using the `kompile` command. It can then do several operations on the compiled definition using its Maude backend. `krun` can execute programs and display the final configuration. `krun` with the `--search` option displays all different solutions that can be reached through any non-deterministic choices introduced by the definition. An option `--pattern` can be specified to only display configurations that match a certain pattern. Moreover, `--ltlmc` directly uses Maude's LTL model checker[1].

The $\mathbb{K}$ tool effectively combines the simplicity and suitability of the $\mathbb{K}$ framework to defining programming languages with the power and features of Maude. A fairly recent reference on the $\mathbb{K}$ tool that gently introduces its most commonly useful features can be found in [6].

2.2 The Orc Calculus

Orc [20,22] is a theory for orchestration of services that provides an expressive and elegant programming model for timed, concurrent computations. A *site* in Orc represents a service (computation) provider, which, when called, may produce, or *publish*, at most one value. Site calls are *strict*, i.e., they have a call-by-value semantics. Moreover, different site calls in Orc may occur at different times. For effective programming in Orc, a few *internal* sites are assumed, namely (1) the *if* (b) site, which publishes a signal if b is true and remains silent otherwise, (2) *Clock*, which publishes the current time value, and (3) $Rtimer(t)$, which publishes a signal after t time units.

Syntax of Orc. An Orc program $\tilde{d}; f$ is a list of expression definitions $\tilde{d}$ followed by an expression f. An Orc *expression* describes how site calls (and responses) are combined in order to perform a useful computation. The abstract syntax of Orc expressions is shown in Fig. 2. We assume a special site response value **stop**, which may be used to indicate termination of a site call without necessarily publishing a standard Orc value.

$$\begin{array}{rl} f, g \in \text{Expression} ::= & \mathbf{0} \;\mid\; p(\tilde{p}) \;\mid\; f \mid g \;\mid\; f > x > g \;\mid\; g < x < f \;\mid\; f\, ;\, g \\ p \in \text{Parameter} ::= & x \;\mid\; w \\ & x \in \mathit{Variable} \qquad w \in \mathit{Value} \cup \{\mathbf{stop}\} \end{array}$$

Fig. 2. Abstract syntax of Orc expressions

An Orc *expression* can be: (1) the silent expression ($\mathbf{0}$), which represents a site that never responds; (2) a parameter or an expression call having an optional list of actual parameters as arguments; or (3) the composition of two expressions by one of four composition operators. These are: (1) the "parallel" combinator, $f \mid g$, which models concurrent execution of independent threads of computation; (2) the "sequential" combinator, $f > x > g$, which executes f, and for each value w published by f creates a fresh instance of g, with x bound to w, and runs that

[1] The latest release of $\mathbb{K}$ 3.5 depends on Maude as well as Java as backends. It is the last version to support the Maude backend. Developments are running on the Java backend to incorporate all of Maude's features.

instance in parallel with the current evaluation of $f >x> g$; (3) the "pruning" combinator, $f <x< g$, which executes f and g concurrently but terminates g once g has published its first value, which is then bound to x in f; finally (4) the "otherwise" combinator, $f \,;\, g$, which attempts to execute f to completion, and then executes g only if f terminates without ever publishing a value.

A variable x occurs *bound* in an expression g when g is the right (resp. left) subexpression of a sequential composition $f >x> g$ (resp. a pruning composition $g <x< f$). If a variable is not bound in either of the two above ways, it is said to be *free*. We use the syntactic sugar $f \gg g$ (resp. $g \ll f$) for sequential composition (resp. pruning composition) when x is *not* free in g. To minimize use of parentheses, we assume the following precedence order (from highest to lowest): $\gg$, $|$, $\ll$, $;$.

To illustrate the informal meaning of the combinators, we list some examples here. Many more examples and larger programs can be found in [22,12,5,13,21].

Example 1. Suppose we want to get the current price of gold, and that we have three sites that provide this service: GoldSeek, GoldPrice, and Kitco. In such a case, we only care about receiving an answer as soon as possible. So, it would make sense to call these three sites in parallel. The expression would be: $(\mathit{GoldSeek}() \mid \mathit{GoldPrice}() \mid \mathit{Kitco}())$. Now, suppose we want the price in a different unit, say Euro/gram instead of USD/Oz. We need only one of these three sites to publish a value. Observe the following Orc expression:

$\mathit{Converter}(x, \mathit{USD/Oz}, \mathit{EUR/gram}) < x < (\mathit{GoldSeek}() \mid \mathit{GoldPrice}() \mid \mathit{Kitco}())$.

The pruning combinator tells the parallel expression to give it only the first value it publishes. As soon as it receives a value, it prunes the whole right-side expression and passes the value to the left side, and binds it to x.

Example 2. Suppose we have a site called *FireAlarm* that when called, remains silent unless a fire has been detected, in which case it publishes the fire's location. That information is sent to the fire department which needs to make a decision to dispatch a fire engine. The fire department calls a site *CalcNearestStation* and gives it the location of the fire to locate the nearest fire station. The response is then passed on to a site *Dispatch* which will dispatch a fire truck from the given station to the given location. The Orc expression would be:

$$\begin{aligned} &\mathit{FireAlarm}() > \mathit{fireLoc} > \mathit{CalcNearestStation}(\mathit{fireLoc}) \\ &\qquad > \mathit{station} > \mathit{Dispatch}(\mathit{station}, \mathit{fireLoc}) \end{aligned}$$

After detailing our semantics of Orc in Section 3, we show the output of executing some sample expressions in Section 4.

Operational Semantics of Orc. The reference semantics of Orc is the informal but detailed semantics of Orc given by Misra and illustrated by many examples in [20]. A structural operational semantics (SOS) for the instantaneous (untimed) behaviors of Orc was also developed by Misra and Cook in [22]. An updated SOS listing that includes rules for the semantics of the *otherwise* combinator and **stop** site responses is given in [2].

The SOS semantics specifies an interleaving semantics of the possible behaviors of an Orc expression as a labeled transition system with four types of actions an Orc expression may take: (1) publishing a value, (2) calling a site, (3) making an unobservable transition τ, and (4) consuming a site response. As discussed by Misra and Cook in [22], the SOS semantics is highly non-deterministic, allowing *internal* transitions within an Orc expression (value publishing, site calls, and τ transitions) and the *external* interaction with sites in the environment (through site return events) to be interleaved in any order. Therefore, a *synchronous semantics* was proposed in [22] by placing further constraints on the application of SOS semantic rules, effectively giving internal transitions higher priority over the external action of consuming a site response.

A timed SOS specification extending the original SOS with timing was also proposed [26]. The timed SOS refines the SOS transition relation into a relation on time-shifted Orc expressions and timed labels of the form (l, t), where t is the amount of time taken by a transition. In this extended relation, a transition step of the form $f \overset{(l,t)}{\hookrightarrow} f'$ states that f may take an action l to evolve to f' in time t, and, if $t \neq 0$, no other transition could have taken place during the t time period. To properly reflect the effects of time elapse, parts of the expression f may also have to be time-shifted by t. The semantics described in [26] abstracted away the non-publishing events as unobservable transitions, which is the level of abstraction we assume in the $\mathbb{K}$ semantics we describe next.

3 $\mathbb{K}$-Semantics of Orc

The semantics of Orc in $\mathbb{K}$ is specified in two modules: (1) the syntax module, which defines the abstract syntax of Orc in a BNF-like style along with any relevant evaluation strategy annotations, and (2) the semantics module, which defines the structure of a configuration and the rules (both structural and computational) that define Orc program behaviors. These modules are explained in some detail in this section. The full $\mathbb{K}$ specification of Orc can be found at (http://www.ccse.kfupm.edu.sa/~musab/orc-k).

3.1 Syntax Module

Orc is based on execution of expressions, which can be simple values or site calls, or more complex compositions of simpler subexpressions using one or more of its combinators. Looking at Fig. 2 showing the abstract syntax of the Orc calculus, the following grammar defined in $\mathbb{K}$ syntax is almost identical (with *Pgm* and *Exp* as syntactic categories for Orc programs and expressions, respectively):

An Orc value, which could be an integer, a string, a boolean, or the `signal` value, is syntactic sugar for a site call that publishes that value and halts.

A site call looks like a function call, having the site name and a list of actual parameters we call *Arguments*. A site, when called, may publish a standard Orc value or a special value `stop`, which indicates termination with no value being published. A site call can result in publishing at most one value.

```
SYNTAX Pgm ::= ExpDefs Exp

SYNTAX Arg ::= Val
             | Identifier

SYNTAX Call ::= ExpId(Params)
              | SiteId(Args) [strict(2)]

SYNTAX Exp ::= Arg
             | Call
             > Exp > Param > Exp [right]
             > Exp | Exp [right]
             > Exp < Param < Exp [left]
             > Exp ; Exp [left]
```

Fig. 3. Syntax of Orc as defined in $\mathbb{K}$

There are a few semantic elements, which appear in Fig. 3, that $\mathbb{K}$ allows to define within the syntax module. The first is precedence, denoted by the $>$ operator. As mentioned in Section 2.2, the order of precedence of the four combinators from highest to lowest is: the sequential, the parallel, the pruning, and then the otherwise combinator. In addition, we prefer for simpler expressions to be matched before complex ones; so, on top, we put *Arg* and *Call*.

The second semantic element that is defined within the syntax module of $\mathbb{K}$ is `right`- or `left`-associativity. It is important to note that the parallel operator is defined as right-associative, rather than fully-associative because $\mathbb{K}$'s parser does not yet support full associativity. However, this is resolved in the semantics by transforming the tree of parallel composition into a fully-associative soup of threads as discussed in Section 3.2.

The third is strictness. `strict(i)` means that the ith term in the right hand side of the production must be evaluated before the production is matched.

3.2 Semantics Module

This module specifies the semantics of the language using $\mathbb{K}$ rules. Each rule specifies one or more *rewrites*, that take place in different parts of the *configuration*. We first explain the structure of the configuration, followed by key rules.

Configuration. A configuration in $\mathbb{K}$ is a representation of a state consisting of possibly nested cells. Fig. 4 shows the structure of our configuration. A cell `thread` is declared with multiplicity *, i.e., zero, one, or more threads. Enclosed in `thread` is the main cell `k`. `k` is the computation cell where we execute our program. We handle Orc productions from inside the `k` cell.

The `context` cell is for mapping variables to values. The `publish` cell keeps the published values of each thread, and `gPublish` is for globally published values. `props` holds thread management flags. `varReqs` helps manage context sharing. `gVars` holds environment control and synchronization variables. The `in` and `out` cells are respectively the standard input and output streams. And finally, `defs` holds the expressions defined at the beginning of an Orc program.

Each cell is declared with an initial value. The `$PGM` variable, which is the initial value of the `k` cell, tells 𝕂 that this is where we want our program to go (after it is parsed). So by default, the initial configuration, shown in Fig. 4, would hold a single thread with the `k` cell holding the whole Orc program as the `Pgm` non-terminal defined in the syntax above.

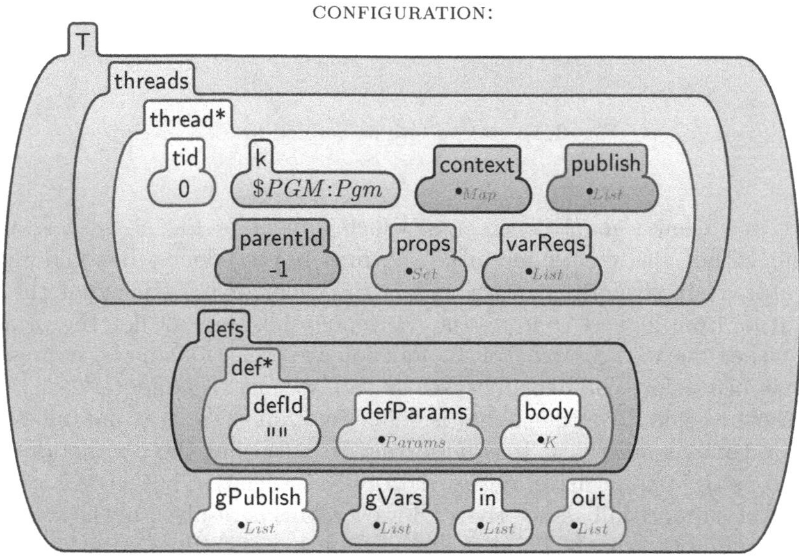

Fig. 4. Structure of the configuration

𝕂 **Rules.** For clarity and convenience, we first illustrate the essence of the rules as transformations in schematic diagrams. Then we show some representative rules exactly as they are defined in 𝕂 . Our schematic diagrams use the following notations. Each box represents a thread while lines are drawn between boxes to link a parent thread to child threads, where a parent thread appears above its child threads. The positioning of a child thread indicates whether that thread is a left-side child or a right-side child (which is needed by the sequential and pruning compositions). Note that in the specification, this information is maintained through meta thread properties. The center of a box holds the expression the thread is executing. A letter v at the lower right corner of the box represents a value which the thread has published. A letter P at the lower left corner denotes the `publishUp` flag which basically tells the thread to move its published values to its parent thread. Variable mappings such as $x \to v$ mapping a variable x to a value v are displayed at the bottom of the box. Finally, the symbol $\Rightarrow$ denotes a rewrite.

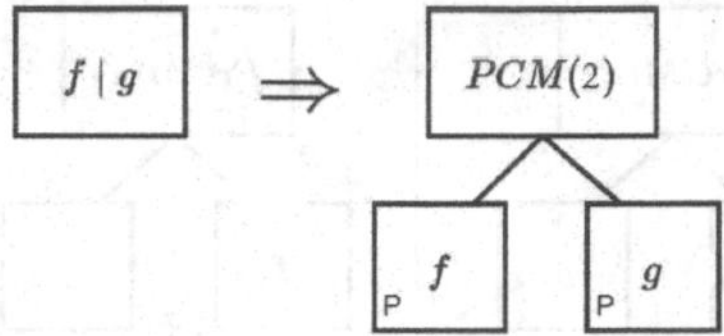

Fig. 5. Transformation rule of the parallel combinator

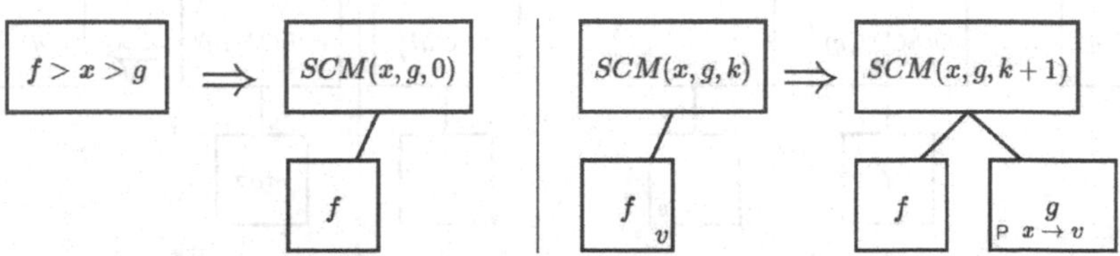

Fig. 6. Transformation rules of the sequential combinator

Combinators. Orc has four combinators, which combine subexpressions according to four distinct patterns of concurrent execution, *parallel*, *sequential*, *pruning* and *otherwise*.

Parallel Combinator. Given an expression $f \mid g$ as shown in Fig. 5, the rule creates a manager thread carrying a meta-function called *PCM*(x), short for Parallel Composition Manager, where x is the count of sub-threads it is managing. Child threads are created as well for each of the expressions f, and g. This of course extends to any number of subexpressions in the initial expression. For example, $f \mid g \mid h$ will transform to *PCM*(3) and so on, as each subexpression will be matched in turn.

Sequential Combinator. The first rule of the sequential combinator, shown in Fig. 6, creates a manager called *SCM*, short for Sequential Composition Manager; and it creates one child that will execute f. The manager keeps three pieces of information: x, the parameter through which values are passed to instances of g; g, the right-side expression; and k, a count of active instances of g which is initially 0.

Every time f publishes a value, the second rule in Fig. 6 creates an instance of g with its x parameter mapped to the published value. The new instance will work independently of all of f, the manager, and any other instance that was created before. So in effect, it is working in parallel with the whole composition, as is meant by the informal semantics [20].

Pruning Combinator. The idea of the pruning expression is to pass the first value published by g to f as a variable x defined in the context of f. Regardless, f should start execution anyway. If it needed a value for x to continue its execution,

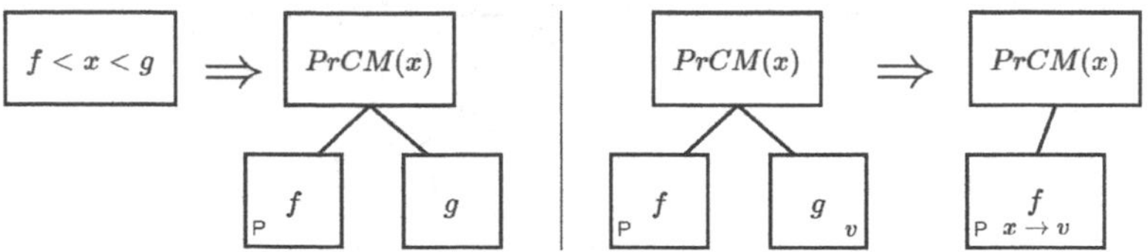

Fig. 7. Transformation rules of the pruning combinator

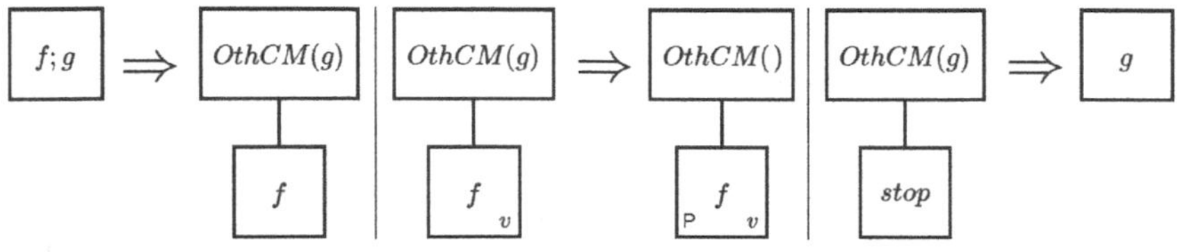

Fig. 8. Transformation rules of the otherwise combinator

it would wait for it. So, the first rule of the pruning combinator creates a manager *PrCM* (short for Pruning Composition Manager), a thread executing f, and another thread executing g. See Fig. 7. The second rule is responsible for passing the published value from g to f and terminating (pruning) g. These two rules are shown in Figures 10 and 11 as they are defined in $\mathbb{K}$.

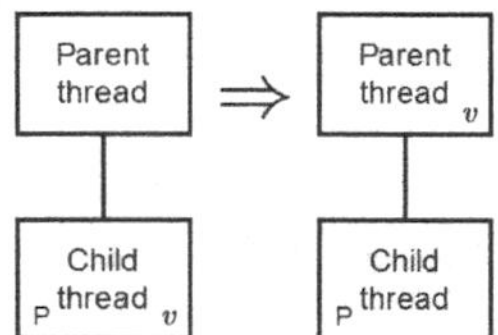

Fig. 9. Transformation rule of publishing values

Otherwise Combinator. The otherwise combinator is implemented in three rules shown in Fig. 8. It starts by creating a manager called *OthCM* (short for Otherwise Composition Manager) and a child thread to execute f. Then if f publishes its first value, g is discarded and f may continue to execute and is given permission to publish. However, if f halts without publishing anything, the third rule applies and the whole otherwise expression is replaced by g. As mentioned in Section 2.2, *stop* is a special value that indicates that an expression has halted.

Publishing and Variable Lookup. Due to the uniform structure of thread hierarchy common in the productions of all four combinators, defining general operations like publishing and variable lookup become compositional.

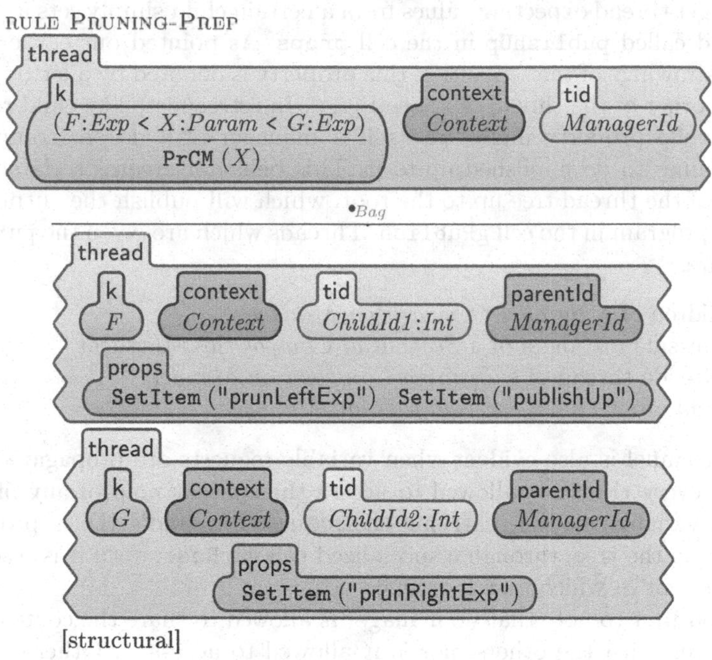

Fig. 10. First 𝕂 rule of the Pruning Combinator

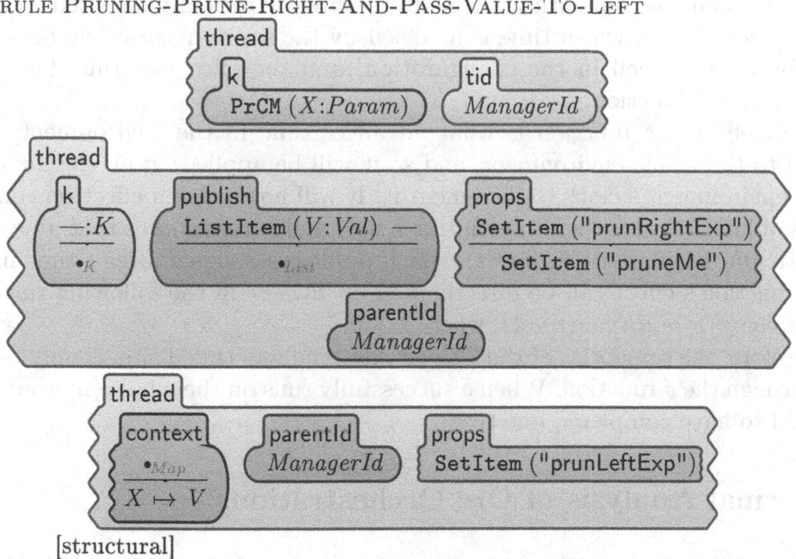

Fig. 11. Second 𝕂 rule of the Pruning Combinator

A manager thread expecting values from a certain child simply sets a property in the child called `publishUp` in the cell `props`. As pointed out earlier, in our schematic drawings of the semantics, this property is denoted by a letter P in the lower left corner of the thread box. See Fig. 9. In retrospect, The child receiving the `publishUp` property might be itself a manager of a deeper composition, awaiting values to be published up to it. This behavior creates a channel from the leaves of the thread tree up to the root, which will publish the output of the whole Orc program in the cell `gPublish`. Threads which are given the `publishUp` property are:

- All children of a *Parallel Composition Manager.*
- All right-side instances of a *Sequential Composition Manager*
- The left-side thread of a *Pruning Composition Manager*
- The child of an *Otherwise Composition Manager.*

Such a channel is also evident when variable requests are propagated up the tree, since every thread is allowed to access the context map of any of its ancestors. A variable request, carrying the requester thread's ID, is propagated recursively up the tree, through a specialized cell `varReqs`, until it is resolved or reaches the root in which case it resets.

It is important to note that no manager is allowed to share the context of any of its children with the others, nor is it allowed to access it. Otherwise, some values could be accidentally overwritten if copied from one scope to another.

Synchronization and Time. The semantics of our (discrete) timing model follows the standard semantics of time in rewrite theories implemented in Real-Time Maude [23], in which time is modeled by the set of natural numbers captured by a `clock` cell in the configuration, and the effects of time lapse are modeled by a δ function.

Effectively, the δ function is what advances time in the environment. It is applied to the whole environment, and so it will be applied on all threads, and on the environment's clock to increment it. It will not have an effect on computations of internal sites, but only on timer sites and external sites that are yet to respond. One such site is $Rtimer(t)$, which publishes a signal after t time units. The δ function's effect can be directly seen on *Rtimer* in the following rule:

$\delta(Rtimer(t)) \Rightarrow Rtimer(t-1)$, where $t > 0$.

Therefore, the semantics of the *Rtimer* site, and any timed site, is only realizable through the δ function. When δ successfully runs on the whole environment, it is said to have completed one tick.

4 Formal Analysis of Orc Orchestrations

In this section, we present an example showing the formal analysis that can be done on Orc programs using the $\mathbb{K}$ tool. We defined external Orc sites to simulate a robot moving around a room with obstacles. A layout of the room we will be working with is shown in Fig. 12. We could of course work with a

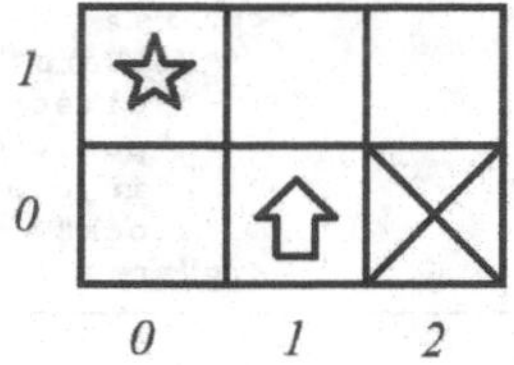

Fig. 12. Initial configuration of the robot environment

more complex environment, but the purpose here is a simple demonstration and a proof of the concept. We first simulate the movement of the robot, and then show an example of formal verification.

Robot Sites' Semantics. Before running any example, we explain our semantics of these robot sites. *MoveFwd* will cause the robot to move a distance of one block in its direction. *turnRight* and *turnLeft* will rotate the robot, while standing on the same block, 90 degrees clockwise and counterclockwise respectively. We also made each of these sites takes a certain amount of time to respond. *MoveFwd* takes three time units while each of *turnRight* and *turnLeft* take one time unit. Hitting an obstacle while trying to move forward will still consume three time units but will turn on a flag called *isBumperHit* which will reset on the next action.

4.1 Simulation

The robot starts at (1,0) facing north. Suppose that we want to move it towards the star at (0,1). The following Orc program will do just that:
MoveFwd() $\gg$ *TurnLeft*() $\gg$ *MoveFwd*()

Running **krun** on the expression outputs the final configuration as shown in Fig. 13. Some parts were omitted for space convenience. However, the important parts are the position, direction and the *isBumperHit* flag. We can see that they ended up as expected: the robot is at (1,0) facing west, and the bumper is not hit. Notice also that the clock is at seven time units, the time it takes for two *MoveFwd*'s and one *turnLeft*.

Writing the same program again but this time adding another *MoveFwd* to the end of the sequence makes the expression:
MoveFwd() $\gg$ *TurnLeft*() $\gg$ *MoveFwd*() $\gg$ *MoveFwd*()

Running this will cause the robot to hit the wall. That will turn on the *isBumperHit* flag as in Fig. 13. This time, the clock is at 10 time units, three units more consumed by the additional *MoveFwd*.

4.2 Verification

Here, we show a simplistic example that demonstrates the formal verification capabilities of $\mathbb{K}$. First we introduce an element of nondeterminism. Consider

```
<gVars>
  "BotVars" |->
    "direction" |-> (-1,0)
    "position" |-> (0,1)
    "is_bumper_hit" |-> false
  "clock" |-> 7
</gVars>
```

```
<gVars>
  "BotVars" |->
    "direction" |-> (-1,0)
    "position" |-> (0,1)
    "is_bumper_hit" |-> true
  "clock" |-> 10
</gVars>
```

Fig. 13. selected output of running simulations: example 1 (left), example 2 (right)

the Orc expression *RandomMove*() that is defined as:

MoveFwd() | *TurnLeft*() $\gg$ *MoveFwd*() | *TurnRight*() $\gg$ *MoveFwd*()

Executing this expression, the robot should nondeterministically choose between one of the paths separated by the parallel operator. Suppose we need to know whether this program will cause the robot to hit an obstacle or not. Running the program with `krun --search --pattern` and specifying *isBumperHit* $\rightarrow$ *true* as the pattern will show all configurations where the robot hits. The full command looks like this:

```
krun bot.orc --search --pattern "<gVars>... \"BotVars\" |->
  (M:Map \"is_bumper_hit\" |-> B) </gVars> when B ==K true"
```

The output of that command shows only one solution; it shows a configuration where the position is $(1,0)$, the initial position, and the direction is east. Obviously, the robot reached there by picking the third choice, *TurnRight*() $\gg$ *MoveFwd*().

Now consider making two random moves in sequence: *RandomMove*() $\gg$ *RandomMove*(). Checking for all possible configurations where the robot hits reveals five solutions while checking for when the robot reaches the star at (0,1) shows two solutions. Searching in more complex environments with more complex expressions reveals many more solutions.

We demonstrated the potential of exploiting $\mathbb{K}$'s state search capabilities for purposes of formal verification. Other methods that $\mathbb{K}$ provides such as Maude's LTL model checker and Maude's proof environment are sure to deliver more in-depth verification.

5 Conclusion and Future Developments

In this paper, we have presented a first attempt at devising a formal executable semantics for Orc in the $\mathbb{K}$ framework and how it may be used for verifying Orc programs. The semantics is distinguished from other operational semantics by the fact that it is not directly based on Orc's original interleaving SOS semantics. The semantics takes advantage of concurrent rewriting facilitated by the underlying $\mathbb{K}$ formalism to capture its concurrent semantics and makes use of $\mathbb{K}$'s innovative notation to document the meaning of its various combinators.

Due to subtleties related to timing and transition priorities, faithfully capturing the Orc semantics is a nontrivial challenge for any semantic framework.

We plan to continue extending and refining the semantics so that all such subtleties are appropriately handled. Furthermore, executability of the semantics does not just mean the ability to interpret Orc programs using the semantics specification; it also means that dynamic formal verification, such as model checking, of Orc programs can be performed, which is something that we plan to demonstrate using the 𝕂 tool with its Maude model checker. Moreover, an investigation of how the resulting semantics relates to the existing rewriting logic semantics would be an interesting future direction.

Acknowledgments. We thank José Meseguer and Grigore Roşu for their very helpful discussions, suggestions and comments on the work presented here. We also thank the anonymous reviewers for their valuable comments. This work was partially supported by King Fahd University of Petroleum and Minerals through Grant JF121005.

References

1. AlTurki, M.: Rewriting-based Formal Modeling, Analysis and Implementation of Real-Time Distributed Services. PhD thesis, University of Illinois at Urbana-Champaign (August 2011), http://hdl.handle.net/2142/26231
2. AlTurki, M.A., Meseguer, J.: Executable rewriting logic semantics of Orc and formal analysis of Orc programs. Journal of Logical and Algebraic Methods in Programming (to appear, 2015)
3. Berry, G., Boudol, G.: The chemical abstract machine. Theor. Comput. Sci. 96(1), 217–248 (1992)
4. Clavel, M., Durán, F., Eker, S., Lincoln, P., Martí-Oliet, N., Meseguer, J., Talcott, C.: All About Maude - A High-Performance Logical Framework. LNCS, vol. 4350. Springer, Heidelberg (2007)
5. Cook, W.R., Patwardhan, S., Misra, J.: Workflow patterns in Orc. In: Ciancarini, P., Wiklicky, H. (eds.) COORDINATION 2006. LNCS, vol. 4038, pp. 82–96. Springer, Heidelberg (2006)
6. Şerbănuţă, T.F., Arusoaie, A., Lazar, D., Ellison, C., Lucanu, D., Roşu, G.: The 𝕂 primer (version 3.3). In: Hills, M. (ed.) Proceedings of the Second International Workshop on the 𝕂 Framework and its Applications (𝕂 2011), vol. 304, pp. 57–80. Elsevier (2014)
7. Şerbănuţă, T.F., Roşu, G.: A truly concurrent semantics for the 𝕂 framework based on graph transformations. In: Ehrig, H., Engels, G., Kreowski, H.-J., Rozenberg, G. (eds.) ICGT 2012. LNCS, vol. 7562, pp. 294–310. Springer, Heidelberg (2012)
8. Şerbănuţă, T.F., Roşu, G., Meseguer, J.: A rewriting logic approach to operational semantics. Information and Computation 207(2), 305–340 (2009); Special issue on Structural Operational Semantics (SOS)
9. Ellison, C., Roşu, G.: An executable formal semantics of C with applications. In: Field, J., Hicks, M. (eds.) Proceedings of the 39th ACM SIGPLAN-SIGACT Symposium on Principles of Programming Languages, POPL 2012, pp. 533–544. ACM, Philadelphia (2012)
10. Farzan, A., Chen, F., Meseguer, J., Roşu, G.: Formal analysis of Java programs in JavaFAN. In: Alur, R., Peled, D.A. (eds.) CAV 2004. LNCS, vol. 3114, pp. 501–505. Springer, Heidelberg (2004)

11. Farzan, A., Meseguer, J., Roşu, G.: Formal JVM code analysis in JavaFAN. In: Rattray, C., Maharaj, S., Shankland, C. (eds.) AMAST 2004. LNCS, vol. 3116, pp. 132–147. Springer, Heidelberg (2004)
12. Kitchin, D., Powell, E., Misra, J.: Simulation using orchestration. In: Meseguer, J., Roşu, G. (eds.) AMAST 2008. LNCS, vol. 5140, pp. 2–15. Springer, Heidelberg (2008)
13. Kitchin, D., Quark, A., Misra, J.: Quicksort: Combining concurrency, recursion, and mutable data structures. In: Roscoe, A.W., Jones, C.B., Wood, K.R. (eds.) Reflections on the Work of C.A.R. Hoare, History of Computing, pp. 229–254. Springer, London (2010)
14. Lazar, D., Arusoaie, A., Şerbănuţă, T.F., Ellison, C., Mereuta, R., Lucanu, D., Roşu, G.: Executing formal semantics with the $\mathbb{K}$ tool. In: Giannakopoulou, D., Méry, D. (eds.) FM 2012. LNCS, vol. 7436, pp. 267–271. Springer, Heidelberg (2012)
15. Lucanu, D., Şerbănuţă, T.F., Roşu, G.: $\mathbb{K}$ framework distilled. In: Durán, F. (ed.) WRLA 2012. LNCS, vol. 7571, pp. 31–53. Springer, Heidelberg (2012)
16. Meseguer, J.: Conditional rewriting logic as a unified model of concurrency. Theoretical Computer Science 96(1), 73–155 (1992)
17. Meseguer, J., Roşu, G.: Rewriting logic semantics: From language specifications to formal analysis tools. In: Basin, D., Rusinowitch, M. (eds.) IJCAR 2004. LNCS (LNAI), vol. 3097, pp. 1–44. Springer, Heidelberg (2004)
18. Meseguer, J., Roşu, G.: The rewriting logic semantics project. Theoretical Computer Science 373(3), 213–237 (2007)
19. Meseguer, J., Roşu, G.: The rewriting logic semantics project: A progress report. In: Owe, O., Steffen, M., Telle, J.A. (eds.) FCT 2011. LNCS, vol. 6914, pp. 1–37. Springer, Heidelberg (2011)
20. Misra, J.: Computation orchestration: A basis for wide-area computing. In: Broy, M. (ed.) Proc. of the NATO Advanced Study Institute, Engineering Theories of Software Intensive Systems. NATO ASI Series, Marktoberdorf, Germany (2004)
21. Misra, J.: Structured concurrent programming. Manuscript, University of Texas at Austin (December 2014), http://www.cs.utexas.edu/users/misra/temporaryFiles.dir/Orc.pdf
22. Misra, J., Cook, W.R.: Computation orchestration. Software and Systems Modeling 6(1), 83–110 (2007)
23. Ölveczky, P.C., Meseguer, J.: Semantics and pragmatics of Real-Time Maude. Higher-Order and Symbolic Computation 20(1-2), 161–196 (2007)
24. Roşu, G., Şerbănuţă, T.F.: An overview of the $\mathbb{K}$ semantic framework. Journal of Logic and Algebraic Programming 79(6), 397–434 (2010); Membrane computing and programming
25. Roşu, G., Şerbănuţă, T.F.: $\mathbb{K}$ overview and SIMPLE case study. In: Hills, M. (ed.) Proceedings of the Second International Workshop on the $\mathbb{K}$ Framework and its Applications ($\mathbb{K}$ 2011). Electronic Notes in Theoretical Computer Science, vol. 304, pp. 3–56. Elsevier (2014)
26. Wehrman, I., Kitchin, D., Cook, W.R., Misra, J.: A timed semantics of Orc. Theoretical Computer Science 402(2-3), 234–248 (2008); Trustworthy Global Computing

Narrowing Operators on Template Abstract Domains

Gianluca Amato(✉), Simone Di Nardo Di Maio, Maria Chiara Meo, and Francesca Scozzari

Dipartimento di Economia, Università di Chieti-Pescara, Pescara, Italy
g.amato@unich.it

Abstract. In the theory of abstract interpretation, a descending phase may be used to improve the precision of the analysis after a post-fixpoint has been reached. Termination is often guaranteed by using narrowing operators. This is especially true on numerical domains, since they are generally endowed with infinite descending chains which may lead to a non-terminating descending phase in the absence of narrowing. We provide an abstract semantics which improves the analysis precision and shows that, for a large class of numerical abstract domains over integer variables (such as intervals, octagons and template polyhedra), it is possible to avoid infinite descending chains and omit narrowing. Moreover, we propose a new family of narrowing operators for real variables which improves the analysis precision.

1 Introduction

Computing a static analysis in the framework of *abstract interpretation* [6,7] typically amounts to solve a set of equations describing the program behavior. Given a program to be analyzed, we associate to each control point i of the program an unknown[1] x_i and an equation $x_i = \Phi_i(x_1, \ldots, x_n)$, where Φ_i is a monotone, state-transition operator. The unknowns $x_1, \ldots, x_n$ range over an *abstract domain* A, which encodes the property we want to analyze. An element of A is called *abstract object* and represents a set of concrete states.

We are interested in finding the (least) solution, over the domain A, of the set of equations $\Phi = (\Phi_1, \ldots, \Phi_n)$ associated to the program to be analyzed. The abstract interpretation framework ensures that any solution of the set of equation correctly approximates the concrete behavior of the program, and the smaller the solution, the more precise is the result of the analysis. In theory, the least solution of the system can be exactly computed as the limit of a Kleene iteration, starting from the least element of A^n. In practice, such a method can be unfeasible, since many abstract domains exhibit infinite ascending chains, and thus the computation may not terminate. Moreover, even for finite abstract domains, it may happen that the ascending chains are very long, and this method would result impractical.

[1] We use the terms *variable* to denote a variable in the program, and *unknown* to denote a variable in the data-flow equations.

N. Bjørner and F. de Boer (Eds.): FM 2015, LNCS 9109, pp. 57–72, 2015.
DOI: 10.1007/978-3-319-19249-9_5

The standard method to perform the analysis is to compute an approximation of the least solution of the system of equations using widening and narrowing operators [5,8]. For specific abstract domains or for restricted classes of programs, we may find in the literature alternatives, such as acceleration operators [12] and strategy/policy iteration [4,10,11], but these methods are not generally applicable and their complexity may be impractical.

A widening, generally denoted by ∇, is a binary operator over the abstract domain A such that:

- it is an upper bound;
- when used in equations of the kind $x_i = x_i \nabla \Phi_i(x_1, \ldots, x_n)$, it precludes the insurgence of infinite ascending chains for x_i.

The widening operator compares the value of x_i in the previous iteration with its value in the current iteration and, in some cases, returns an approximated value. Widening is used to ensure the termination of the analysis, while introducing a loss in precision. This is realized by replacing some of the original equations $x_i = \Phi_i(x_1, \ldots, x_n)$ with $x_i = x_i \nabla \Phi_i(x_1, \ldots, x_n)$. The replacement may involve all unknowns or, more commonly, only the ones corresponding to loop heads. Applying widening in this way ensures the termination of a Kleene iteration, but we only get a post-fixpoint of the function $\Phi = (\Phi_1, \ldots, \Phi_n)$, instead of the least one.

Once we reach a post-fixpoint, we can start a new Kleene iteration, giving origin to a descending chain which improves the result of the analysis. However, due to infinite descending chains in the abstract domain, the descending iteration might not terminate. The next example[2] shows this phenomenon using the abstract domain $\mathsf{Int}_{\mathbb{Z}}$ of intervals over integer numbers [5], defined as:

$$\mathsf{Int}_{\mathbb{Z}} = \{[l, u] \subseteq \mathbb{Z} \mid l \leq u \in \mathbb{Z} \cup \{-\infty, \infty\}\} \cup \{\emptyset\},$$

where $\emptyset$ denotes the empty set of concrete states, i.e., an unreachable control point. The standard widening on intervals [5] is defined as follows:

$$\begin{aligned} \emptyset \nabla I &= I \\ I \nabla \emptyset &= I \\ [l_1, u_1] \nabla [l_2, u_2] &= [l', u'] \end{aligned}$$

where

$$l' = \begin{cases} l_1 & \text{if } l_1 \leq l_2 \\ -\infty & \text{otherwise} \end{cases} \qquad u' = \begin{cases} u_1 & \text{if } u_1 \geq u_2 \\ +\infty & \text{otherwise} \end{cases}$$

Essentially, it works by preserving stable bounds and removing unstable ones. For instance, $[0, 3] \nabla [0, 4] = [0, \infty]$. In this way, infinite ascending chains are precluded.

---

[2] To the best of our knowledge, this is the first example in the literature which shows a program analysis iterating over an infinite descending sequence in an integer numerical domain.

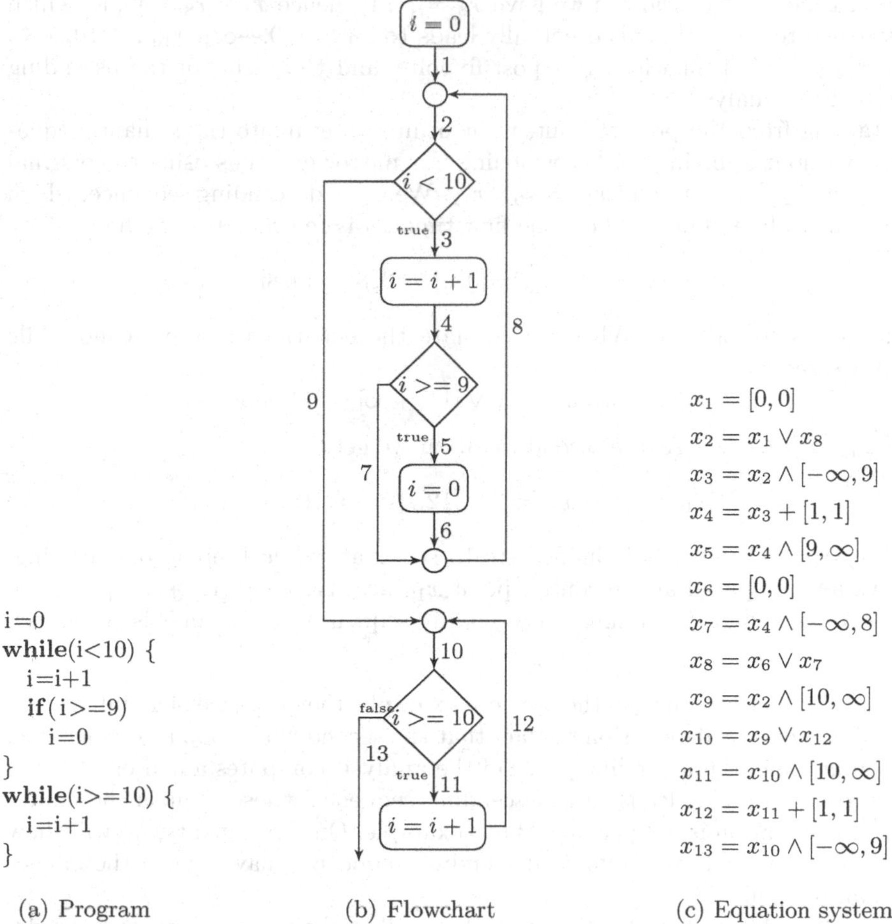

(a) Program (b) Flowchart (c) Equation system

Fig. 1. The example program doubleLoop

Example 1. Consider the example program doubleLoop in Fig. 1(a), and the corresponding flowchart and set of equations in Fig. 1(b) and 1(c). We perform the analysis using the integer interval domain $\mathsf{Int}_{\mathbb{Z}}$ with the standard widening. Therefore, we replace the second and the tenth equation in Fig.1(c) with

$$x_2 = x_2 \nabla (x_1 \vee x_8)$$
$$x_{10} = x_{10} \nabla (x_9 \vee x_{12}) \ .$$

Note that these two equations correspond to the loop joins. We assume to follow a work-list based iteration sequence, although the result is analogous with other standard two-phases iteration schemas.

The first time x_2 is considered, we have $x_1 = [0, 0]$ and $x_2 = x_8 = \emptyset$. Widening does not trigger and x_2 gets updated to $x_2 := x_1 \vee x_8 = [0, 0]$. However, the second time x_2 is considered we have $x_8 = [1, 1]$, hence $x_1 \vee x_8 = [0, 1]$, which is widened to $[0, +\infty]$. This eventually leads to $x_9 := [10, +\infty]$, $x_{10} := [10, +\infty]$ and $x_{12} := [11, +\infty]$ which is a post-fixpoint and the result of the ascending phase of the analysis.

Starting from the post-fixpoint, we continue to evaluate the semantic equations, without applying neither widening nor narrowing, thus using the original equations $x_2 = x_1 \vee x_8$ and $x_{10} = x_9 \vee x_{12}$. We get a descending sequence, which turns out to be infinite. In fact, the first time x_2 is re-evaluated, we have

$$x_2 := x_1 \vee x_8 = [0, 0] \vee [0, 8] = [0, 8]$$

which leads to $x_9 := \emptyset$. When we evaluate the equations in the second while loop, we get

$$x_{10} := x_9 \vee x_{12} = \emptyset \vee [11, +\infty] = [11, +\infty]$$

and $x_{12} = [12, +\infty]$. At the second iteration we get

$$x_{10} := x_9 \vee x_{12} = \emptyset \vee [12, +\infty] = [12, +\infty]$$

and $x_{12} := [13, +\infty]$. It is immediate to see that, while keeping on iterating, the values computed at the control point x_{10} are $[11, +\infty]$, $[12, +\infty]$, $[13, +\infty]$, $[14, +\infty]$, ... which is an infinite descending sequence, whose limit is the empty set. □

It is worth noting that, in the previous example, the existence of an infinite descending sequence depends on the fact that the second while loop is unreachable, although the initial ascending phase of the analysis computes a non-empty over approximation. This leads to a descending sequence whose limit is the empty set. This situation is not peculiar of our example. On the contrary, we will show that this is the only way infinite descending sequences may arise in the integer interval domain.

To avoid the insurgence of infinite descending chains, we may stop the descending iteration at an arbitrary step, still obtaining a post-fixpoint, or we may use a narrowing operator. Narrowing, generally denoted by $\triangle$, is a binary operator on a abstract domain A such that:

- $a_1 \triangle a_2$ is only defined when $a_2 \leq a_1$;
- it holds that $a_2 \leq a_1 \triangle a_2 \leq a_1$;
- when used in equations of the kind $x_i = x_i \triangle \Phi_i(x_1, \ldots, x_n)$, it precludes the insurgence of infinite descending chains for x_i.

The standard narrowing for intervals [5], for example, is defined as:

$$I \triangle \emptyset = \emptyset$$
$$[l_1, u_1] \triangle [l_2, u_2] = [l', u']$$

where

$$l' = \begin{cases} l_2 & \text{if } l_1 = -\infty \\ l_1 & \text{otherwise} \end{cases} \qquad u' = \begin{cases} u_2 & \text{if } u_1 = +\infty \\ u_1 & \text{otherwise} \end{cases}$$

Essentially, it works by refining only unbounded extremes. For instance, $[0,\infty] \vartriangle [0,10] = [0,10]$ but $[0,10] \vartriangle [0,9] = [0,10]$. Let us reconsider Example 1 and show what happens when we use narrowing in the descending phase.

Example 2. Consider the same program, flowchart and equations of Example 1, together with the result of the analysis after the ascending phase. We now replace the equations for x_2 and x_{10} with $x_2 = x_2 \vartriangle (x_1 \vee x_8)$ and $x_{10} = x_{10} \vartriangle (x_9 \vee x_{12})$ and start a descending iteration.

When the second equation is first re-evaluated, the current value for x_2 is $[0,+\infty]$, hence the standard narrowing allows to change $+\infty$ into 8, and we have $x_2 := [0,8]$ as for the case without narrowing. However, when x_{10} is evaluated for the first time in the decreasing sequence, we have $x_{10} := [10,+\infty] \vartriangle [11,+\infty] = [10,+\infty]$: the standard narrowing precludes further improvements on the second loop. The descending sequence terminates at the cost of a big loss of precision, since we are not able to detect anymore that control points 10–12 are unreachable. □

In the rest of the paper, we will show that narrowing for the integer interval domain is superfluous, and may be removed upon adopting a slightly different semantic operator for loop joins which preserves unreachability. Moreover, we generalize this result to all the template abstract domains over integer variables.

Furthermore, we show that such a result can be used to design a more precise narrowing on template abstract domain over reals, exploiting the fact that we never get infinite descending chains of integer intervals.

2 Narrowing on Intervals of Integers

Example 1 shows an analysis which leads to an infinite descending chain of intervals. In particular, the chain is $[11,+\infty]$, $[12,+\infty]$, $[13,+\infty]$,... and its limit is the empty set. It turns out that the only infinite descending chains of intervals are of the kind

$$[n_0,+\infty],[n_1,+\infty],[n_2,+\infty],\ldots$$

or

$$[-\infty,-n_0],[-\infty,-n_1],[-\infty,-n_2],\ldots$$

where $\{n_i\}_{i\in\mathbb{N}}$ is an infinite ascending chain of integers. The limit of all these chains is the empty set.

Proposition 3. *Let $\{I_i\}_{i\in\mathbb{N}}$ be an infinite descending chain of integer intervals. Then $\wedge_{i\in\mathbb{N}} I_i = \emptyset$.*

In the rest of the paper we assume to deal only with structured programs, whose flowchart is *reducible*. Intuitively, this means that every loop has a single well defined entry point.

Assume *loop* is the entry point of a loop and its corresponding equation is $x_{loop} = x_{in} \vee x_{back}$, where *in* is the edge in the flowchart which comes from outside the loop and *back* the back edge. Since in a reducible flowchart the entry point of a loop dominates all the nodes inside the loop, if control point *in* is unreachable (i.e., $x_{in} = \emptyset$ in the interval domain) the same holds for control point *loop*.

Therefore, we may change the abstract semantics of the program by replacing each equation corresponding to a loop join $x_{loop} = x_{in} \vee x_{back}$ with $x_{loop} = x_{in} \vee^{\emptyset} x_{back}$, where $\vee^{\emptyset}$ is a left-strict variant of the join operator defined as:

$$I_1 \vee^{\emptyset} I_2 = \begin{cases} \emptyset & \text{if } I_1 = \emptyset \\ I_1 \vee I_2 & \text{otherwise} \end{cases} \tag{1}$$

The new set of equations is correct (again, only on reducible flowcharts) and more precise. Moreover, during the descending phase of the analysis, narrowing is not required to achieve termination. Actually, assume that an infinite descending chain arises during the descending phase. Let *loop* be one of the outermost loop heads whose variable x_{loop} infinitely decreases. In the presence of left-strict joins, this leads to a contradiction. The equation of x_{loop} is $x_{loop} = x_{in} \vee^{\emptyset} x_{back}$. The value of x_{in} is definitively constant. Once it reaches its definitive value $\bar{x}_{in}$, we may have only two cases:

- if $\bar{x}_{in} = \emptyset$, then the first time x_{loop} is re-evaluated we have $x_{loop} := \emptyset$ and x_{loop} cannot descend anymore, contradicting our hypothesis;
- if $\bar{x}_{in} \neq \emptyset$, then $x_{loop} \geq \bar{x}_{in}$ always, and therefore it cannot descend infinitely, due to Proposition 3.

The considerations above hold for any numerical abstract domain A with a distinguished value denoting unreachability. In the following, we will refer to such a distinguished value as $\emptyset$, which is the common notation in all the numerical domains in the literature.

This discussion leads therefore to the following results.

Theorem 4. *Assume given a numerical abstract domain A with a distinguished value $\emptyset$ denoting unreachability. Assume we have a system of data-flow equations Φ generated by a structured program whose loop head nodes are of the form $x_{loop} = x_{in} \vee x_{back}$. Then, replacing $\vee$ with $\vee^{\emptyset}$ in all the loop heads, the new set of data-flow equations is still correct.*

Theorem 5. *In the hypothesis of Theorem 4, assume A is the abstract domain of integer intervals. Then every iteration strategy on the equations in Φ starting from a post-fixpoint of Φ leads to a finite sequence.*

Note that a descending sequence without narrowing always leads to a fixpoint of the equation system, instead of a post-fixpoint.

Some of the restrictions of Theorem 4 may be easily lifted. For example, if a loop join node has equation

$$x_{loop} = x_{in_1} \vee \cdots \vee x_{in_u} \vee x_{back_1} \vee \cdots \vee x_{back_v} ,$$

where all the edges in_i come from outside the loop and all the $back_j$'s are back edges, we may use left-strict join in this way:

$$x_{loop} = (x_{in_1} \vee \cdots \vee x_{in_u}) \vee^{\emptyset} (x_{back_1} \vee \cdots \vee x_{back_v}) .$$

Moreover, it is possible to extend Theorem 4 to non reducible flowcharts, provided we only apply the left-strict join to the loop heads that dominate the sources of the back edges.

When avoiding narrowing, we may find programs whose descending chain is arbitrarily long, but finite. The next example shows this phenomenon.

Example 6. Consider the example program doubleLoop2 in Fig. 2(a), and the corresponding flowchart and set of equations in Fig. 2(b) and 2(c). We first perform the analysis using the integer interval domain $\mathsf{Int}_{\mathbb{Z}}$ with the standard widening and narrowing and then we recompute the analysis without narrowing.

In the ascending phase we use widening on the join loops: $x_2 = x_2 \nabla (x_1 \vee^{\emptyset} x_4)$ and $x_6 = x_6 \nabla (x_5 \vee^{\emptyset} x_8)$. The post-fixpoint is:

$$\begin{array}{lll} x_1 = [0,0] & x_4 = [1,11] & x_7 = [-\infty,100] \\ x_2 = [0,\infty] & x_5 = [11,\infty] & x_8 = [-\infty,99] \\ x_3 = [0,10] & x_6 = [-\infty,\infty] & x_9 = [101,\infty] \end{array}$$

Now we start the descending phase with the standard narrowing, using the equations $x_2 = x_2 \Delta (x_1 \vee^{\emptyset} x_4)$ and $x_6 = x_6 \Delta (x_5 \vee^{\emptyset} x_8)$. When we first apply narrowing in the second equation, we get:

$$x_2 = x_2 \Delta (x_1 \vee^{\emptyset} x_4) = [0,\infty] \Delta [0,11] = [0,11]$$

and therefore $x_5 = [11,11]$. We now apply narrowing in the sixth equation:

$$x_6 = x_6 \Delta (x_5 \vee^{\emptyset} x_8) = [-\infty,\infty] \Delta [-\infty,99] = [-\infty,99]$$

and therefore we have $x_7 = [-\infty,99]$, $x_8 = [-\infty,98]$ and $x_9 = \emptyset$, which is the fixpoint.

We now recompute the descending phase without narrowing, using the equations

$$\begin{aligned} x_2 &= x_1 \vee^{\emptyset} x_4 \\ x_6 &= x_5 \vee^{\emptyset} x_8 . \end{aligned}$$

The first while loop behaves as before with $x_5 = [11,11]$. Now we enter the second while loop. The first iteration is the same as before using narrowing, and we get:

$$\begin{array}{ll} x_6 = [-\infty,99] & x_8 = [-\infty,98] \\ x_7 = [-\infty,99] & x_9 = \emptyset \end{array}$$

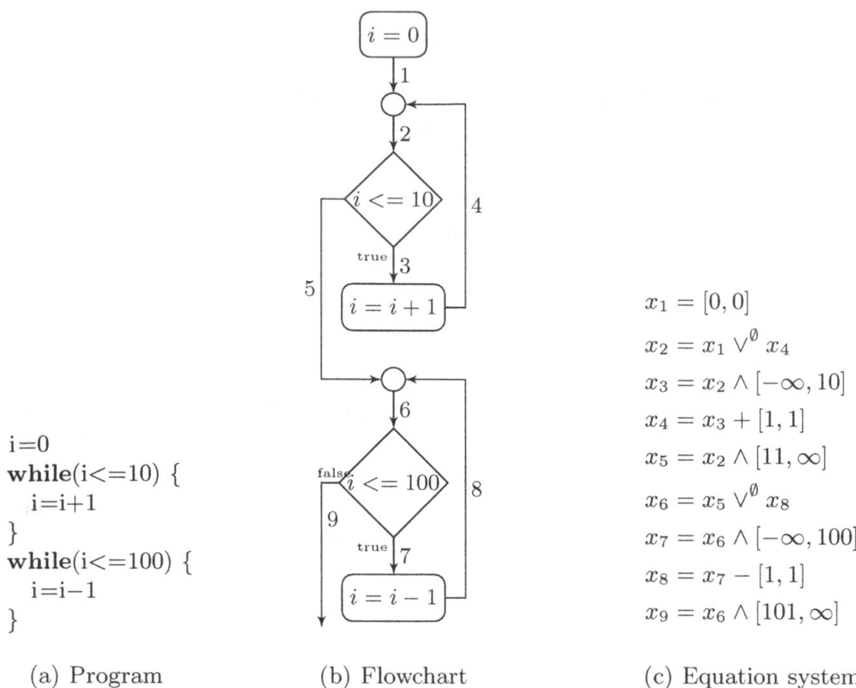

Fig. 2. The example program doubleLoop2

But now we are able to continue the descending phase, which is:

	2^{ns} descending iteration	3rd d. i.	4th d. i.	...	last d. i.
x_6	$[-\infty, 98]$	$[-\infty, 97]$	$[-\infty, 96]$	...	$[-\infty, 11]$
x_7	$[-\infty, 98]$	$[-\infty, 97]$	$[-\infty, 96]$	...	$[-\infty, 11]$
x_8	$[-\infty, 97]$	$[-\infty, 96]$	$[-\infty, 95]$	...	$[-\infty, 10]$

Note that, by continuing the descending phase till the fixpoint, we are able to detect that the guard in the second while loop is over dimensioned, since the variable i never reaches the value 100. □

2.1 Template Abstract Domains

The above result on intervals can be extended to the whole family of template abstract domains. We call template abstract domains those numerical domains where the coefficients of the allowed constraints are fixed in advance, before starting the analysis. Most important template abstract domains are the domain of intervals (also called box domain) [5], octagons [14] and template polyhedra [15]. Non-template abstract domains are, among others, polyhedra [9] and two-variable for linear inequality [16].

All the template abstract domains may be described using a fixed matrix which describes the constraints and any abstract object o is a subset of $\mathbb{R}^n$ (or $\mathbb{Z}^n$ if working with integer variables) of the form $o = \{\boldsymbol{x} \in \mathbb{R}^n \mid \boldsymbol{l} \leq A\boldsymbol{x} \leq \boldsymbol{u}\}$ where A is the constraint matrix, $\boldsymbol{l}$ and $\boldsymbol{u}$ are, respectively, the lower and upper bounds.

A box is an abstract object where A is the identity matrix. Octagons are those objects where the coefficient matrix A allows constrains of the form $\pm x \pm y \leq c$. Finally, template polyhedra are those objects where the coefficient matrix A is arbitrary but fixed a priori.

Under the hypothesis of Theorem 4, it is possible to extend Theorem 5 to all the template abstract domains. In fact, given a narrowing operator on intervals, we can immediately define a corresponding component-wise narrowing operator on any template abstract domain. We first show that template abstract domains over integers enjoy a property similar to Prop. 3. Note that a template domain over integers only needs to have integer bounds, while the coefficients of the constraint matrix may be reals.

Proposition 7. *Let A be a template abstract domain over integers and $\{I_i\}_{i\in\mathbb{N}}$ be an infinite descending chain of objects $I_i \in A$. Then $\wedge_{i\in\mathbb{N}} I_i = \emptyset$, where $\emptyset$ is a distinguished value of A denoting unreachability.*

Exploiting the above proposition and Theorem 4, we can prove a result analogue to Theorem 5 which, in presence of a left-strict join, allows us to avoid narrowing, still guaranteeing termination.

Theorem 8. *In the hypothesis of Theorem 4, assume A is a template abstract domain over integers. Then every iteration strategy on the equations in Φ starting from a post-fixpoint of Φ leads to a finite sequence.*

3 Narrowing on Reals

The left-strict join we have introduced for integer domains may also be used with abstract domains over real variables. This improves the precision of the analysis, but does not ensure that the descending phase will terminate. This depends on the fact that, once we admit real variables, we can have infinite descending chains whose limit is not the empty set. Nonetheless, in this case the left-strict join may be exploited to define a narrowing more precise than the standard one.

The next example shows that on the standard interval domain $\mathsf{Int}_{\mathbb{R}}$ for real variables, the descending phase of the analysis may lead to an infinite descending chain whose limit is not the empty set. We recall that

$$\mathsf{Int}_{\mathbb{R}} = \{[l, u] \subseteq \mathbb{R} \mid l \leq u \in \mathbb{R} \cup \{-\infty, \infty\}\} \cup \{\emptyset\}.$$

Example 9. Consider the example program realLoop in Fig. 3(a), and the corresponding flowchart and equations in Fig. 3(b) and 3(c). The ascending phase

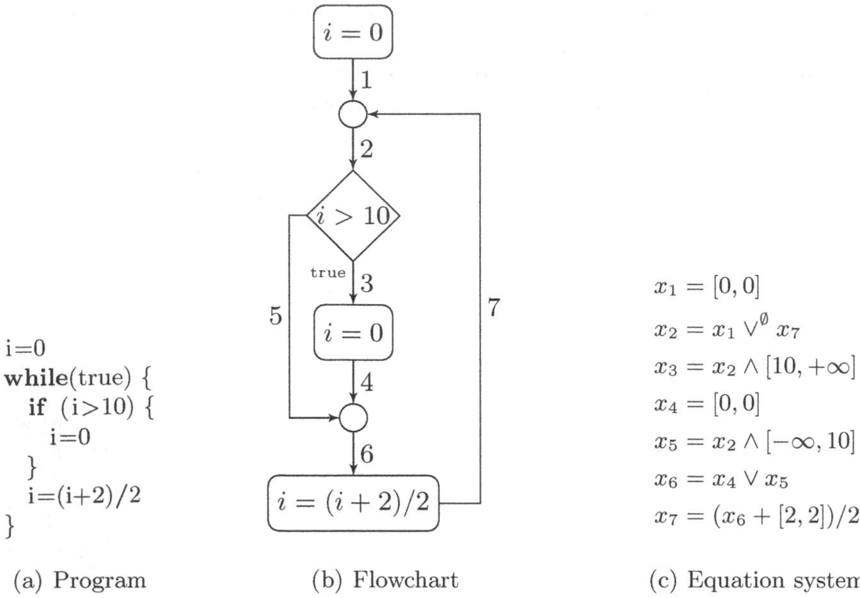
i=0
while(true) {
if (i>10) {
i=0
}
i=(i+2)/2
}
$i = 0$
1
2
$i > 10$
true
3
5
$i = 0$
4
6
7
$i = (i + 2)/2$
$x_1 = [0, 0]$
$x_2 = x_1 \vee^{\emptyset} x_7$
$x_3 = x_2 \wedge [10, +\infty]$
$x_4 = [0, 0]$
$x_5 = x_2 \wedge [-\infty, 10]$
$x_6 = x_4 \vee x_5$
$x_7 = (x_6 + [2, 2])/2$

(a) Program (b) Flowchart (c) Equation system

Fig. 3. The example program realLoop

using left-strict join and standard widening, i.e., $x_2 = x_2 \nabla (x_1 \vee^{\emptyset} x_7)$, reaches a post-fixpoint in two iterations.

	1st ascending iteration	2nd ascending iteration
x_1	$[0, 0]$	$[0, 0]$
x_2	$[0, 0]$	$[0, 0] \nabla [0, 1] = [0, +\infty]$
x_3	$\emptyset$	$[10, +\infty]$
x_4	$[0, 0]$	$[0, 0]$
x_5	$[0, 0]$	$[0, 10]$
x_6	$[0, 0]$	$[0, 10]$
x_7	$[1, 1]$	$[1, 6]$

We now start from the post fixpoint a descending iteration without applying narrowing, using the original equation $x_2 = x_1 \vee^{\emptyset} x_7$.

	1st descending iteration	2nd descending iteration
x_1	$[0, 0]$	$[0, 0]$
x_2	$[0, 0] \vee^{\emptyset} [1, 6] = [0, 6]$	$[0, 0] \vee^{\emptyset} [1, 4] = [0, 4]$
x_3	$\emptyset$	$\emptyset$
x_4	$[0, 0]$	$[0, 0]$
x_5	$[0, 6]$	$[0, 4]$
x_6	$[0, 6]$	$[0, 4]$
x_7	$[1, 4]$	$[1, 3]$

At the next iterations, we obtain:

$$x_2 = [0,3] \qquad\qquad x_7 = \left[1, \frac{5}{2}\right]$$

$$x_2 = \left[0, \frac{5}{2}\right] \qquad\qquad x_7 = \left[1, \frac{9}{4}\right]$$

and so on, without terminating. The fixpoint, which is $x_2 = [0, 2]$ and $x_7 = [1, 2]$, is not the empty set. □

Exploiting Proposition 3, we can define a new narrowing operator on intervals for real variables which refines successive descending iterations at the nearest integer, since we cannot have an infinite descending chain whose bounds are all integers.

Definition 10 (Narrowing on reals). *We define a narrowing operator* Δ^1 *on* $Int_{\mathbb{R}}$ *as follows:*

$$I \,\Delta^1\, \emptyset = \emptyset$$

$$[l_1, u_1] \,\Delta^1\, [l_2, u_2] = [l', u']$$

where

$$l' = \begin{cases} l_2 & \text{if } l_1 = -\infty \\ \max(l_1, \lfloor l_2 \rfloor) & \text{otherwise} \end{cases}$$

$$u' = \begin{cases} u_2 & \text{if } u_1 = +\infty \\ \min(u_1, \lceil u_2 \rceil) & \text{otherwise} \end{cases}$$

The new narrowing Δ^1 refines infinite bounds to finite values, as the standard one, and refines finite bounds only to new integer values. Since infinite descending sequences on integer template domains are precluded by the use of left-strict joins, the descending sequence terminates.

Theorem 11. *The operator* Δ^1 *is a narrowing operator on template domains when the loop join is left-strict.*

In the next example we compare the standard narrowing with the new narrowing on reals Δ^1.

Example 12. We compute the descending chain of Example 9 using the standard narrowing on intervals. We start from the post fixpoint and use the equation $x_2 = x_2 \,\Delta\, (x_1 \vee^{\emptyset} x_7)$. At the first descending iteration we get

$$x_2 = [0, +\infty] \,\Delta\, ([0,0] \vee^{\emptyset} [1,6]) = [0, +\infty] \,\Delta\, [0,6] = [0,6] \ .$$

Note that we get exactly the same value as in the first descending iteration without narrowing. Therefore, we compute for the other unknowns exactly the same values, in particular $x_7 = [1, 4]$. It is immediate to see that this is a fixpoint for the computation using the standard narrowing, since no more unbounded values appear. In fact, we have that

$$x_2 = x_2 \vartriangle (x_1 \vee^{\emptyset} x_7) = [0, 6] \vartriangle [0, 4] = [0, 6] \ .$$

We now recompute the descending chain of Example 9 using the narrowing on reals $\vartriangle^1$ in Def. 10. The first descending iteration is the same as for the standard narrowing, and we get $x_2 = [0, 6]$ and $x_7 = [1, 4]$. In the second descending iteration we have

$$x_2 = x_2 \vartriangle^1 (x_1 \vee^{\emptyset} x_7) = [0, 6] \vartriangle^1 [0, 4] = [0, 4]$$

and $x_7 = [1, 3]$. In the third descending iteration we have

$$x_2 = [0, 4] \vartriangle^1 [0, 3] = [0, 3]$$

and $x_7 = [1, \frac{5}{2}]$. This is the fixpoint, since

$$x_2 = [0, 3] \vartriangle^1 \left[0, \frac{5}{2}\right] = [0, 3] \ .$$

In this case, we get a result strictly more precise than with the standard narrowing. □

It is worth noting that $\vartriangle^1$ could be easily generalized by rounding numbers at the multiple of any strictly positive constant value $\delta \in \mathbb{R}$.

Definition 13 (δ-narrowing). *Let $\delta \in \mathbb{R}$ such that $\delta > 0$. We define a new narrowing on intervals of reals:*

$$I \vartriangle^{\delta} \emptyset = \emptyset$$
$$[l_1, u_1] \vartriangle^{\delta} [l_2, u_2] = [l', u']$$

where

$$l' = \begin{cases} l_2 & \text{if } l_1 = -\infty \\ \max(l_1, \delta \lfloor l_2/\delta \rfloor) & \text{otherwise} \end{cases}$$

$$u' = \begin{cases} u_2 & \text{if } u_1 = +\infty \\ \min(u_1, \delta \lceil u_2/\delta \rceil) & \text{otherwise} \end{cases}$$

The above narrowing produces a descending chain whose elements differ for a multiple of δ, which is fixed in advance. Since the limit of these chains is still the empty set, it is immediate to see that $\vartriangle^{\delta}$ in the above definition is a narrowing operator on intervals of reals. It generalizes $\vartriangle^1$ given in Definition 10. In fact, Def. 13 boils down to Def. 10 when $\delta = 1$. Moreover, it can be easily generalized to template abstract domains.

Theorem 14. *For any $\delta \in \mathbb{R}$ such that $\delta > 0$, the operator Δ^δ is a narrowing operators on template abstract domains when the loop join is left-strict.*

The next example applies the new narrowing Δ^δ to the program realLoop.

Example 15. We compute the descending chain for the example program realLoop in Fig. 3(a) using δ-narrowing with $\delta = \frac{1}{100}$. We get the following values for x_2:

$$[0,6],[0,4],[0,3],\left[0,\frac{5}{2}\right],\left[0,\frac{9}{4}\right],\left[0,\frac{213}{100}\right],\left[0,\frac{207}{100}\right],\left[0,\frac{204}{100}\right],\left[0,\frac{202}{100}\right],\left[0,\frac{201}{100}\right]$$

where the last one is the fixpoint. □

As an alternative, instead of rounding bounds to a multiple of δ, we may refine bounds with the new value only if the difference w.r.t. the previous value is greater than a given δ. We call this δ*-narrowing.

Definition 16 (δ*-narrowing). *Let $\delta \in \mathbb{R}$ such that $\delta > 0$. We define a new narrowing on intervals of reals:*

$$I \,\Delta^{\delta*}\, \emptyset = \emptyset$$

$$[l_1, u_1] \,\Delta^{\delta*}\, [l_2, u_2] = [l', u']$$

where

$$l' = \begin{cases} l_2 & \text{if } l_1 = -\infty \text{ or } l_2 - l_1 \geq \delta \\ l_1 & \text{otherwise} \end{cases}$$

$$u' = \begin{cases} u_2 & \text{if } u_1 = +\infty \text{ or } u_1 - u_2 \geq \delta \\ u_1 & \text{otherwise} \end{cases}$$

The above narrowing keeps iterating while the difference between two successive iterations is greater than δ. Since the limit of any such descending chain is still the empty set, we can prove that $\Delta^{\delta*}$ is a narrowing operator under the same hypothesis of Th. 14

Theorem 17. *For any $\delta \in \mathbb{R}$ such that $\delta > 0$, the operator $\Delta^{\delta*}$ is a narrowing operator on template domains when the loop join is left-strict.*

The next example shows the narrowing $\Delta^{\delta*}$ in the program realLoop.

Example 18. We compute the descending chain for the example program realLoop in Fig. 3(a) using δ*-narrowing with $\delta = \frac{1}{100}$. We get the following values for x_2:

$$[0,6],[0,4],[0,3],\left[0,\frac{5}{2}\right],\left[0,\frac{9}{4}\right],\left[0,\frac{17}{8}\right],\left[0,\frac{33}{16}\right],\left[0,\frac{65}{32}\right],\left[0,\frac{129}{64}\right]$$

where the last one is the fixpoint. □

4 Conclusion and Related Work

We believe the main contribution of this paper is a deeper theoretical understanding of termination issues during descending iterations within the framework of static analysis by abstract interpretation. In details, we have:

- introduced a refined join operator for loop heads which improves precision by preserving unreachability;
- shown that, when using the new join operator with an integer template abstract domain, the descending phase of the analysis terminates even without using a narrowing operator;
- presented several improved (more precise) narrowings for template abstract domains over reals, to be used with the new join operator;
- shown, for the first time, examples of programs over integers and reals where the descending phase of the analysis is either infinite or arbitrarily long.

Both the new join and the improved narrowings may be easily applied to existent analyzers with little effort. In the case of structured program, they only require a single check in the abstract join in order to make it strict.

The new join operator may be used systematically with structured programs, since it improves both precision and speed at the same time. The same cannot be said for the new narrowings over reals or for the idea of not using narrowing at all with integer domains. In this case, we may get better precision, as shown in Example 9, but at the expense of a greater computational cost, since the analysis of the loops might be repeated several times. The good point is that we increase the computational cost only when we improve precision w.r.t. the standard narrowing.

The impact of the repeated computations of loops might be probably reduced by delaying analysis of the inner loops until outer loops are stabilized, so that a long descending sequence in a loop does not force to repeatedly analyze the inner loops. However the impact of the new narrowing on the precision and performance of the analysis on realistic test cases will be the topic of a future work.

Only a few papers in the literature deal with narrowing and the descending phase of the analysis. In [13], the authors try to recover precision by restarting the analysis after that a post-fixpoint has been reached. In [1,3,2] the authors propose to combine widening and narrowing during the analysis, resulting in multiple intertwined ascending and descending phases. Moreover, [1] also proposes to restart (part of) the analysis when the abstract value associated to the exit node of a loop is refined during the descending phase. Our left-strict join operator may be viewed as a variant of the restarting policy in [1], where restart is triggered only when unreachability is detected. For instance, in the example program doubleLoop in Fig. 1(a), the restarting policy triggers a full analysis (widening and narrowing phases) of the second loop with an initial assignment which maps every unknown of the second loop to bottom. However, while in the previous work restarting is a feature of the equation solver, here it is realized directly at the semantic level.

Mostly, our work is orthogonal to the ones cited above: the new operators we have defined may be used within these frameworks to get more precise results.

The idea of avoiding narrowing in the descending phase is used in many papers, with the proviso of bounding the number of descending iterations to ensure termination. In this paper we show that, under certain conditions and ignoring performance issues, we do not need to bound the number of iterations.

References

1. Amato, G., Scozzari, F.: Localizing widening and narrowing. In: Logozzo, F., Fähndrich, M. (eds.) Static Analysis. LNCS, vol. 7935, pp. 25–42. Springer, Heidelberg (2013)
2. Amato, G., Scozzari, F., Seidl, H., Apinis, K., Vojdani, V.: Efficiently intertwining widening and narrowing. ArXiv e-prints, 1503.00883 (2015)
3. Apinis, K., Seidl, H., Vojdani, V.: How to combine widening and narrowing for non-monotonic systems of equations. In: Proceedings of the 34th ACM SIGPLAN Conference on Programming Language Design and Implementation, PLDI 2013, pp. 377–386. ACM, New York (2013)
4. Costan, A., Gaubert, S., Goubault, É., Martel, M., Putot, S.: A policy iteration algorithm for computing fixed points in static analysis of programs. In: Etessami, K., Rajamani, S.K. (eds.) CAV 2005. LNCS, vol. 3576, pp. 462–475. Springer, Heidelberg (2005)
5. Cousot, P., Cousot, R.: Static determination of dynamic properties of programs. In: Proceedings of the Second International Symposium on Programming, pp. 106–130, Paris, France, Dunod (1976)
6. Cousot, P., Cousot, R.: Abstract interpretation: A unified lattice model for static analysis of programs by construction or approximation of fixpoints. In: POPL 1977: Proceedings of the 4th ACM SIGACT-SIGPLAN Symposium on Principles of Programming Languages, pp. 238–252. ACM Press, New York (1977)
7. Cousot, P., Cousot, R.: Systematic design of program analysis frameworks. In: POPL 1979: Proceedings of the 6th ACM SIGACT-SIGPLAN Symposium on Principles of Programming Languages, pp. 269–282. ACM Press, New York (1979)
8. Cousot, P., Cousot, R.: Comparing the Galois connection and widening/narrowing approaches to abstract interpretation. In: Bruynooghe, M., Wirsing, M. (eds.) PLILP 1992. LNCS, vol. 631, pp. 269–295. Springer, Heidelberg (1992)
9. Cousot, P., Halbwachs, N.: Automatic discovery of linear restraints among variables of a program. In: POPL 1978: Proceedings of the 5th ACM SIGACT-SIGPLAN Symposium on Principles of Programming Languages, pp. 84–97. ACM Press, New York (1978)
10. Gawlitza, T.M., Monniaux, D.: Invariant generation through strategy iteration in succinctly represented control flow graphs. Logical Methods in Computer Science 8(3) (2012)
11. Gawlitza, T.M., Seidl, H.: Solving systems of rational equations through strategy iteration. ACM Transactions on Programming Languages and Systems 33(3), 1–48 (2011)
12. Gonnord, L., Halbwachs, N.: Combining widening and acceleration in linear relation analysis. In: Yi, K. (ed.) SAS 2006. LNCS, vol. 4134, pp. 144–160. Springer, Heidelberg (2006)

13. Halbwachs, N., Henry, J.: When the decreasing sequence fails. In: Miné, A., Schmidt, D. (eds.) SAS 2012. LNCS, vol. 7460, pp. 198–213. Springer, Heidelberg (2012)
14. Miné, A.: The octagon abstract domain. Higher-Order and Symbolic Computation 19(1), 31–100 (2006)
15. Sankaranarayanan, S., Sipma, H.B., Manna, Z.: Scalable analysis of linear systems using mathematical programming. In: Cousot, R. (ed.) VMCAI 2005. LNCS, vol. 3385, pp. 25–41. Springer, Heidelberg (2005)
16. Simon, A., King, A., Howe, J.M.: Two variables per linear inequality as an abstract domain. In: Leuschel, M. (ed.) LOPSTR 2002. LNCS, vol. 2664, pp. 71–89. Springer, Heidelberg (2003)

Detection of Design Flaws in the Android Permission Protocol Through Bounded Verification

Hamid Bagheri[1,2(✉)], Eunsuk Kang[1], Sam Malek[2], and Daniel Jackson[1]

[1] Computer Science and Artificial Intelligence Laboratory, Massachusetts Institute of Technology, Cambridge, USA
hbagheri@mit.edu

[2] Department of Computer Science, George Mason University, Fairfax, USA

Abstract. The ever increasing expansion of mobile applications into nearly every aspect of modern life, from banking to healthcare systems, is making their security more important than ever. Modern smartphone operating systems (OS) rely substantially on the permission-based security model to enforce restrictions on the operations that each application can perform. In this paper, we perform an analysis of the permission protocol implemented in Android, a popular OS for smartphones. We propose a formal model of the Android permission protocol in Alloy, and describe a fully automatic analysis that identifies potential flaws in the protocol. A study of real-world Android applications corroborates our finding that the flaws in the Android permission protocol can have severe security implications, in some cases allowing the attacker to bypass the permission checks entirely.

1 Introduction

Modern mobile devices provide a framework for multiple applications to interact with each other by exporting and invoking APIs. From a security and privacy perspective, some of the resources shared through the APIs may be considered more critical than others; for example, an ability to send a text message is more dangerous than an ability to change the ringtone on the phone. Therefore, a mechanism that can be used by the developer to control access to critical resources is essential.

Popular operating systems such as Android, iOS, and Windows Phone implement a *permission-based* model for controlling the types of resources that each application is allowed to access. In this model, a developer protects a critical resource inside an application by assigning an explicit permission, which must be obtained by any application that wishes to access the resource. Permissions are typically granted to an application at the discretion of the end user, who makes a decision based on the perceived trustworthiness of the application.

In recent years, researchers have identified a number of flaws in the permission mechanisms that lead to serious security and privacy breaches [1,2,3,4,5,6]. The typical manner in which these problems are discovered involves a careful scrutiny

N. Bjørner and F. de Boer (Eds.): FM 2015, LNCS 9109, pp. 73–89, 2015.
DOI: 10.1007/978-3-319-19249-9_6

by security experts, sometimes long after these devices are released. Many issues are overarching design flaws that require system-wide reasoning—not easily attainable through conventional analysis methods such as testing and static analysis, which are more suited for detecting bugs in individual parts of the system.

Just as techniques in formal methods have proven practical in assessing the security of network protocols [7], we believe that building a formal model of a permission protocol and performing a rigorous analysis can identify potential vulnerabilities and candidate fixes. This paper, unlike prior studies of Android security (including ours [8]) that leverage code analyses to check a particular application for vulnerabilities, instead focuses on modeling and analyzing the Android permission protocol for design flaws. Our model is written in Alloy [9], a language based on a first-order relational logic, with an analysis engine that performs bounded verification of models. As far as we are aware, our work is the first that describes an *automated* analysis of the Android permission protocol.

Through an analysis of our model, we identified a number of vulnerabilities in the protocol that allow a malicious application to entirely bypass permission checks. In particular, we performed a study of a vulnerability that has not been studied in the security literature before—called the *custom permission vulnerability*. To confirm that an abstract attack scenario identified during the analysis is indeed realistic, we demonstrated the attack on concrete Android applications across different versions of Android. Through our study, we show that the custom permission vulnerability is widespread, and that many popular applications are, in fact, susceptible to this type of attacks.

The rest of the paper is structured in the following way. We begin by giving a brief background on Android and motivating why securing its permission protocol can be a challenging task (Section 2). We then describe a formal model of the permission protocol in Alloy (Section 3) and an automated security analysis of the model (Section 4). We present an experiment to demonstrate the feasibility and prevalence of the custom permission vulnerability in existing Android applications (Section 5). Finally, we discuss the related work (Section 6) and conclude with future work (Section 7).

2 Background and Motivation

An *application* is the primary unit of functionality in Android: A typical device is constantly running numerous applications to support the user's needs, such as a messaging service, a mail client, a navigation application, just to name a few.

The success of Android is in part due to its flexible framework for cross-application communication and sharing. Each application is organized into a set of *components*, which export APIs to other applications, thus enabling reuse of functionality across multiple project and software vendors. For example, the developer of a navigation application may encapsulate its map search functionality into an individual component, and provide it as a service to the rest of the device. There are four types of components: *service*, *activity*, *broadcast receiver*, and *content provider*, each serving a different purpose.

A potential downside to the open-ended nature of the Android framework is an increased risk for security and privacy breaches. Some components handle information that is considered particularly critical, and so freely sharing these components without discretion may lead to undesirable consequences for the user. For example, the navigation application may not want to release map search histories as part of a component API, since a rogue application could use these data to extrapolate the user's travel pattern for a malicious purpose.

Android uses a permission-based mechanism to control how applications interact with each other. Before an application can access a component, it must be granted an explicit *permission* to do so by the user. Each permission is associated with a *protection level*, which indicates the trustworthiness of an application that may be granted this permission. There are three types of protection levels: (1) *normal*, meaning the permission is granted to every application, (2) *dangerous*, granted only at the discretion of the device user, and (3) *signature*, granted only to applications from the same developer[1]. A runtime engine monitors every invocation of an API operation and ensures that the calling application has the permission to perform that operation.

An Android device contains a number of built-in permissions for basic features, such as sending a text message, turning on GPS, and accessing the Internet. In addition, Android allows a third-party application to define *custom permissions* and selectively control access to its components. Typically, permissions are granted to an application at the time of its installation; however, a special type of permissions called *URI permissions* may be temporarily granted and revoked during the lifetime of an application.

The goal of the Android permission protocol is to prevent any *unauthorized access*; that is, each application should be able to access only those components that it is granted permissions for, and no more. Ensuring that the system achieves this goal, however, is a challenging task, especially since it can be difficult to predict all the ways in which a malicious application may attempt to misuse the system. An attack may involve performing a complex but obscure sequence of operations that would unlikely be encountered during normal usage scenarios. Identifying such attacks requires system-wide reasoning, and cannot be easily achieved by conventional analysis methods such as testing and static analysis, which are more suited at detecting defects in individual parts of the system.

Motivated by this challenge, we explored an approach to analyzing the security of the Android permission protocol by constructing a formal model and performing an automated analysis of the model. Two key elements that distinguish our approach from previous studies of Android security are as follows:

- **System-wide Dynamic Reasoning:** By modeling the behavior of Android in terms of architectural-level operations (such as installing or removing an application) executed over a sequence of discrete time steps, we are able to perform system-wide reasoning that would be difficult to achieve using static analysis or testing. For example, our analysis can explore all possible orders

[1] A fourth protection level, *signature/system*, also exists but is rarely used, and so, for the purpose of our discussion, will be grouped into *signature*.

in which applications are installed and check whether a particular ordering could be exploited by an attacker (which, in fact, turned out to be the key to an actual attack that involved custom permissions).
- **Concretization:** The result of the analysis, performed on an *abstract* model, is used to guide an implementation-level analysis that checks a *concrete* Android application for the presence of a vulnerability.

This approach demonstrates a potential synergy between model-based and code analysis techniques for an *end-to-end* security analysis: A system-level reasoning is first performed on a high-level model of the system, generating information about potential vulnerabilities, each of which can be confirmed for presence in the implementation using techniques such as static analysis, testing, or inspection.

3 Android Permission Model

In this section, we describe a formal model of the Android permission protocol in Alloy [9], a specification language based on a first-order relational logic. Alloy is suitable for this modeling task because (1) its flexible core allows one to model and integrate different aspects of a system, and (2) its backend tool, the Alloy Analyzer, provides an automated analysis for checking assertions and generating counterexamples. However, our approach does not prescribe the use of a particular formalism, and other languages may well be suitable.

Our model is based on the official documentation on Android permissions from Google [10]. Android is a large and complex operating system, and modeling it in its entirety would be infeasible. Thus, we focused on the parts of Android that are relevant to the permission mechanism—how permissions are granted and maintained, and how they constrain the behavior of an application. As a result, other aspects of Android (such as intents) are omitted from this model.

One of the challenges that we encountered during our modeling task was due to the fact that some of the key aspects of the Android permission protocol are *under-specified* in the official documentation. For example, the document fails to describe what happens to the permissions that have already been granted when the application that defines those permissions is uninstalled. To avoid over-specification (and possibly ruling out counterexamples), we deliberately left the corresponding parts of the model under-specified. This was possible because Alloy supports *partial* modeling: It allows parts of the system to be left unspecified, allowing the Alloy Analyzer to explore all alternative behaviors.

Figure 1 shows an abridged version of the model in Alloy[2], divided into three parts: (1) the architecture of an Android device (lines 4-19), (2) the Android

[2] The Alloy keyword sig introduces a *signature*, which defines a set of elements in the universe. A signature may contain one or more *fields*, each introducing a relation that maps the elements of the signature to the field expression; for example, field protectionLevel in Permission is a binary relation that maps each Permission object to its protection level (line 25). The keyword extends creates a subtyping relationship between two signatures; an abstract signature has no elements except those belonging to its extensions, and one sig introduces a signature that contains only one element.

permission scheme (lines 21-26), and (3) system operations that modify or depend on the permissions (lines 28-66).

3.1 Permissions

An Android *device* consists of a number of interacting *applications*, each containing zero or more *components* that may export services to other applications. The set of applications running on a device may change over time as new applications are installed and existing ones are removed. We model the dynamic aspect of the system by using a standard Alloy idiom in which an execution is represented as a sequence of time steps, and each mutable object is associated with a different state in each time step [9]. To do this, we introduce a set of totally ordered elements as signature Time, and add it as the last column of relations that are considered mutable[3]; for example, the field apps uses Time to keep track of the installed applications at each time step (line 6).

An application may use permissions to control access to its components by other applications. Each permission object, shown on line 25, is associated with a name and a protection level, which can take one of the three values: Normal, Dangerous, and Signature (in order of increasing criticality). Permissions can be assigned to an application at two different levels. Each component may be guarded by at most one permission (represented by the field guard on line 17), which must be acquired by an application before being able to access the component. In addition, an application may be assigned its own guard (line 13), which is imposed on every one of its components; when both the application and one of its components have a guard, the component-specific permission takes the priority.

Note that the type of the field guard in both Application and Component is PermName. In other words, the guard does not contain information about the protection level that is intended for the component being accessed. As discussed later in the section, this turns out to be a design flaw in Android that can be exploited by a malicious application for unauthorized access.

In addition to a set of built-in permissions that are available by default on Android, an application developer may create one or more *custom permissions* to protect an application-specific component (lines 7-8). For example, each Android device contains a built-in permission called android.permission.INTERNET, controlling which applications are allowed to use the built-in component that provides Internet access. A third-party navigation application may provide its map search capability as a service to other applications, and define a custom permission called com.myapp.perm.SEARCH_MAP to control its access.

A *content provider* is a type of storage component containing one or more database tables that are identified by *URIs* (line 19)[4]. By default, obtaining a permission on a content provider grants access to all of its tables. To allow more

[3] The ordering library in Alloy imposes a total order on an input signature (line 1).

[4] Other types of components—service, activity, and broadcast receiver—can be treated equally as far as permissions are concerned, and are omitted from Figure 1.

```
open util/ordering[Time]
sig Time {}

/* Android architecture */
one sig Device {
  apps: Application -> Time,          // currently installed applications
  builtinPerms: set Permission,       // permissions built into Android
  customPerms: Permission -> Time }   // currently active custom permissions
sig Application {
  declaredPerms: set Permission,      // custom permission declarations
  usesPerms: set PermName,            // permissions it intends to use
  grantedPerms: Permission -> Time,   // permissions currently granted
  guard: lone PermName,
  components: set Component }
sig Component {
  app: Application,
  guard: lone PermName }
sig URI {} // points to a table inside a content provider
sig ContentProvider in Component { paths: set URI }

/* Permission objects */
sig PermName {}  -- permission name
abstract sig ProtectionLevel {}
one sig Normal, Dangerous, Signature extends ProtectionLevel {}
sig Permission { name: PermName, protectionLevel: ProtectionLevel }
sig URIPermission in Permission { uri: URI }

/* Invocation operation */
pred invoke[t, t': Time, caller, callee: Component] {
  caller.app + callee.app in Device.apps.t
  canCall[caller, callee, t]
  noChanges[t, t'] }
pred canCall[caller, callee: Component, t: Time] {
  guardedBy[callee] in (caller.app.grantedPerms.t).name }
fun guardedBy[c: Component]: PermName {
  {p: PermName | (p = c.guard) or (no c.guard and p = c.app.guard) } }
pred noChanges[t, t': Time] {
  Device.apps.t' = Device.apps.t
  Device.customPerms.t' = Device.customPerms.t
  all a : Application | a.grantedPerms.t' = a.grantedPerms.t }

/* Install operation */
pred install[t, t': Time, app: Application] {
  app not in Device.apps.t
  Device.customPerms.t' = Device.customPerms.t + newCustomPerms[t,app]
  grantPermissions[t', app]
  all a : Application - app | a.grantedPerms.t' = a.grantedPerms.t
  Device.apps.t' = Device.apps.t + app }
fun newCustomPerms[t: Time, app: Application]: set Permission {
  {p: app.declaredPerms | p.name not in (Device.customPerms.t).name} }
pred grantPermissions[t: Time, app: Application] {
  app.grantedPerms.t.name = app.usesPerms
  app.grantedPerms.t in Device.customPerms.t + Device.builtinPerms }

/* Uninstall operation */
pred uninstall[t, t': Time, app: Application] {
  app in Device.apps.t
  Device.apps.t' = Device.apps.t - app
  Device.customPerms.t' = Device.customPerms.t - app.declaredPerms
  all a : Application - app | a.grantedPerms.t' = a.grantedPerms.t }

/* Event trace definition */
fact traces {
  all t: Time - last | let t' = t.next |
    some app: Application, c1,c2: Component |
      install[t, t', app] or uninstall[t, t', app] or invoke[t, c1, c2] }
```

Fig. 1. A snippet of the Alloy model of the Android permission protocol

fine-grained control, Android provides a special type of permissions called *URI permissions* (line 26), which can be used to grant access to a particular URI inside a content provider.

Finally, an application specifies its intent to access a component by including the name of the associated permission as one of its *uses-permissions* (line 11). When an application is installed, the device determines the set of permissions that should be granted to the application using usesPerms.

3.2 System Behavior

Three types of operations relevant to the Android permission scheme are described in the Alloy model: invoking a component, which succeeds only when the calling application has the appropriate permission, and installing and uninstalling an application, which may modify the custom permissions on the device.

Invoke Operation. The operation of a component invoking another component is expressed as predicate invoke (lines 29-32), which evaluates to true if and only if caller successfully invokes callee between time steps t and t'. The predicate is, in turn, defined as a conjunction of three constraints: both caller and callee must belong to some application on the device (line 30), caller must have the permission to access callee (31), and no changes are made to the active permissions during the invocation (32).

The predicate canCall defines what it means for caller to be able to invoke callee at time step t (lines 33-34); that is, caller must possess the permission that guards callee[5]. Note that callee may be guarded by no permission at all (i.e., guardedBy may return an empty set), in which case canCall is trivially satisfied; in other words, a component without a guard can be accessed by any other component.

Recall that a component's guard is simply the name of a permission, and so its protection level, by design, plays no role in determining whether caller should be allowed to invoke callee. While not explicitly stated in the Android documentation, this design decision relies on one critical assumption: If an application possesses a permission to access a component with a certain protection level, then it must have been authorized by the user to do so during its installation. However, as our analysis will reveal, this assumption is false: It is possible for a malicious application to obtain a permission to a component with a high protection level (e.g., dangerous), even though the authorization was intended for a lower protection level (e.g., normal). Section 4 describes this attack in detail.

Install Operation. The first constraint in install describes the precondition for the operation: app must not already exist on the device at time t (line 44). The four constraints that follow describe the effect of the operation on the device:

– If app declares its own custom permissions, they are added to the device, except those that already exist on the device at time t; function newCustomPerms describes exactly those new permissions to be added (lines 49-50).

[5] Keywords + and in are union and subset operators, respectively.

- Every permission that app requests in its usesPerms is granted to the new application by the device (lines 51-53).
- The permissions granted to other applications on the device are unaffected.
- Finally, app is added to the set of existing applications on the device.

Note that the process of granting a permission through the user's approval is implicit in this model; grantPermissions simply sets the granted permissions to those in the application's usesPerms (line 52), without describing how a decision about each permission is made. This modeling choice reflects the rather coarse-grained nature of Android permissions: Unless an application is granted *every* one of its uses-permissions, it will not be installed on the device (i.e., the user has no ability to selectively grant permissions[6].). In other words, the details of how permissions are granted are not relevant to our analysis, because the effect of installation is always the same: Each installed application will possess all of the permissions that it requests.

Uninstall Operation. This operation removes the specified application app from the device, as well as all of its associated custom permissions. The permissions granted to every other application remains the same during the operation.

Trace Definition. The fact[7] traces defines the behavior of the system as a set of traces that it may produce (lines 62-66). Conceptually, a trace is a sequence of time steps, where between each pair of adjacent steps, t and t', one or more of the system operations takes place[8]. Given this definition, a satisfying instance of the model found by the Alloy Analyzer will correspond to exactly one of the possible traces of the system.

Other Parts. Due to limited space, Figure 1 omits details about other aspects of the permission protocol that are present in the full Alloy model, including: different types of components (beside content providers), dynamic allocation and checking of URI permissions, and application signatures. The complete model is available online at our project site[9].

4 Analysis

In this section, we describe an automated analysis to check whether the Android permission protocol, as specified in our model, satisfies its goal of preventing unauthorized access.

An Alloy *assertion* is used to state a property that the model is expected to satisfy. When prompted to check an assertion, the Alloy Analyzer explores all

[6] While outside the scope of our analysis, previous studies have pointed this out as a major source of usability and privacy issues in Android [1].

[7] An Alloy *fact* is a constraint that holds for every satisfying instance of the model.

[8] This trace definition precludes stuttering, as we did not deem it necessary for this model; however, an operation that represents *noop* could be added to allow it.

[9] http://sdg.csail.mit.edu/projects/android

```
assert NoUnauthorizedAccess {
  all t, t' : Time, callee, caller : Component |
    invoke[t, t', caller, callee] implies authorized[caller,callee,t] }

// True iff caller is authorized to invoke callee
pred authorized[caller,callee: Component, t: Time] {
  let pname = guardedBy[callee],
    grantedPerm = caller.app.grantedPerms.t & name.pname,
    requiredPerm =
      (callee.app.declaredPerms + Device.builtinPerms) & name.pname |
        some pname implies
          equalOrHigher[grantedPerm.protectionLevel,
                        requiredPerm.protectionLevel] }
```

Fig. 2. Assertions on the Android permission protocol

possible behaviors of the system and finds a counterexample, if any, that corresponds to a violation of the assertion. The analysis is *exhaustive but bounded* up to a user-specified scope on the size of the domains: If there is a counterexample within the scope, the analyzer is guaranteed to find it, but absence of a counterexample does not imply the validity of the assertion. In practice, many system flaws can be demonstrated with a small number of objects [11], and if desired, the user can iteratively re-analyze the model with larger scopes to gain further confidence.

An important security property of Android is that every component invocation is *authorized*; that is, when a component invokes another component, the caller must have been granted the permission that was declared by the developer to protect the callee.

This property is formally specified as Alloy assertion NoUnauthorizedAccess in Figure 2. Predicate authorized describes what it means for component caller to be authorized to invoke callee. Its definition relies on two different types of permission: grantedPerm represents the permission that is granted to caller during its installation; requiredPerm, on the other hand, represents the custom permission that was declared specifically to guard callee. Then, caller is considered authorized to invoke callee only if the protection level of grantedPerm is equal to or higher than that of requiredPerm.

4.1 Custom Permission Vulnerability

Analysis. When prompted to check the assertion, the Alloy Analyzer returns a counterexample trace that demonstrates how a design flaw in Android may lead to a violation of the property. The analysis was performed with a scope of 5 on the size of each domain, and took approximately 4 seconds to complete[10].

[10] The analysis was performed on a Mac OS X machine with 1.8 GHz Intel Dual Cores and 4GB of RAM.

A visualization of the counterexample is shown in Figure 3. In this trace, Application0 declares a custom permission (Permission1) to guard its component (labeled victim) with the protection level of Signature, meaning that only those applications that share the same signature should be able to access it. A separate, malicious application, Application1, bypasses the signature requirement by exploiting a design oversight in Android: Namely, it allows multiple applications to define custom permissions with the same name, but without a clear specification of which one should take precedence when they have different protection levels.

To carry out this type of attack, Application1 declares its own custom permission (Permission0) with the same name as Permission1 but with the lowest protection level, Normal. The attack comprises of the following three operations:

- Step (a): Application1 is installed before Application0, activating its custom permission (Permission0) with the Normal protection level on the device.
- Step (b): Application0 is installed, but a custom permission with the same name is already active, and so Permission1 is ignored. As a result, Application1 continues to hold the same permission that it was granted in Step (a).
- Step (c): The malicious component inside Application1 is able to access victim, despite not having the same signature as Application0.

(a)

Component (victim) app: Application0 guardedBy: PermName
components
Application0
declaredPerms
Permission1 name: PermName protectionLevel: Signature
Component (malicious) app: Application1
components
Application1 (being installed) usesPerms: PermName
declaredPerms
Permission0 name: PermName protectionLevel: Normal

(b)

Component (victim) app: Application0 guardedBy: PermName
components
Application0 (being installed)
declaredPerms
Permission1 name: PermName protectionLevel: Signature
Component (malicious) app: Application1
Device customPerms: Permission0
apps
components
Application1 usesPerms: PermName
grantedPerms
declaredPerms
Permission0 name: PermName protectionLevel: Normal

(c)

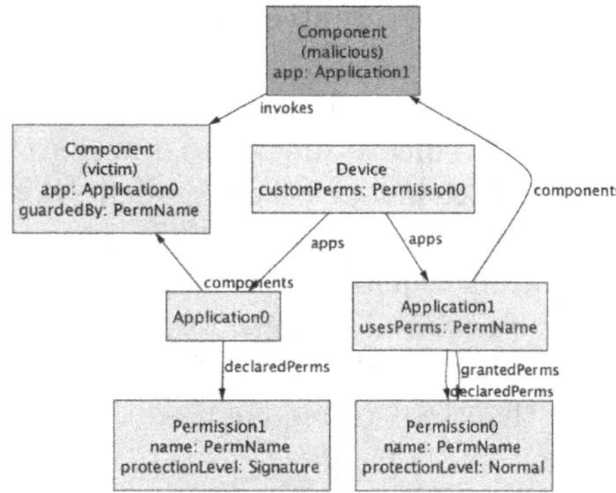

Fig. 3. A counterexample showing an unauthorized access of component victim by malicious Application1 through a custom permission misuse

Evaluating a Fix. One potential fix to this flaw is to disallow multiple applications that define a custom permission with the same name from simultaneously existing on the device. In our Alloy model, this fix can be expressed by adding the following constraint to the install operation from Figure 1:

```
// can't install if a declared perm is named the same as existing one
no p : app.declaredPerms | p.name in (Device.customPerms.t).name
```

Re-analyzing the assertion NoUnauthorizedAccess, however, reveals another counterexample. This scenario begins in the same way as the one in Figure 3, where a malicious application (App1) defines its own custom permission with the same name as another permission, but with a lower protection level. Furthermore, another malicious application (App2) that uses this permission is installed. In the next step, App1 is uninstalled, and its associated custom permission is removed from the device. However, Android fails to revoke the same permission from applications that use it (namely, App2), resulting in a dangling permission. When the victim application (App0) is installed, App2 is still able to access the victim component, but with the lower protection level that was defined by App1.

This demonstrates that simply disallowing an installation of applications with duplicate permissions is not sufficient. The uninstall operation must also be amended to ensure that granted permissions are revoked when an application that declares those permissions is uninstalled. This can be done by modifying the constraint on line 60 in Figure 1 as follows:

```
all a: Application - app |
   a.grantedPerms.t' = a.grantedPerms.t - app.declaredPerms
```

4.2 Other Vulnerabilities Found

Our analysis revealed two other types of vulnerabilities in the permission protocol. Due to limited space, we only briefly discuss them here, and refer the reader to our project site for more detail.

URI Permission Flaw. A malicious application can obtain a URI permission to a part of a content provider that it is not authorized to access. This vulnerability is due to another flaw in the Android permission protocol: granted URI permissions are not revoked when the associated content provider is uninstalled, leaving dangling permissions that can be exploited for a similar type of attack as in Section 4.1.

To our knowledge, this vulnerability with URI permissions is a previously unknown one. However, further study revealed that the vulnerability exists up to Android version 2.3.7; in newer devices, the URI permissions are revoked during uninstallation, disallowing the attack. Our analysis detected this as a counterexample because the model, reflecting the current Android documentation, was deliberately under-specified with respect to the effect of uninstallation on URI permissions.

Improper Delegation. A malicious application may be able to *indirectly* invoke a component, without having a permission to do so, by interacting with a third component that possess the permission. This vulnerability has been identified as the *permission re-delegation* attack in previous work by Felt and her colleagues [12]; our analysis was able to automatically rediscover it.

5 Experiments

A rigorous analysis of a formal model, such as the one described in Section 4, can be used to identify potential flaws at the design level, but by itself does not form a complete security analysis of the system. Instead, the formal analysis must be complemented with a systematic analysis of the concrete system to confirm whether those flaws can lead to *realistic* vulnerabilities, and subsequently attacks.

In this section, we present an experimental study to answer the following two research questions:

- **RQ1:** Can the flaws identified in our formal analysis of Android permission protocol cause an actual attack with serious security consequences?
- **RQ2:** How susceptible are real-world Android applications to security attacks that are due to these flaws in Android permission protocol?

In particular, we focus on the custom permission vulnerability in Section 4.1, as it has not been previously studied in the literature[11]. To address RQ1, we developed demonstrative applications that represent postulated malicious behaviors in the generated counterexample in Figure 3, and observe whether the permission requirement could be bypassed as in the scenario. For RQ2, we performed a study on hundreds of real-world Android applications and quantitatively measured the prevalence of the security vulnerability due to the flaws found in Android permission protocol.

5.1 Demonstration of the Attack

To test the feasibility of the Alloy counterexample in Figure 3, we developed a skeletal address book application that corresponds to the victim application in the trace (cf. Application0 in Fig. 3). Figure 4(a) partially shows an Android manifest file[12] for this application. It defines a custom permission, named ADBOOK_READ, with the *signature* protection level (lines 2–3). This permission is then specified as a guard (in line 7) to protect access to the AddrBookProvider component (lines 4–9), which stores the content of the address book.

As declared in its manifest, the AddrBook application does not grant access to its data to any other application. It is thus expected that only applications that explicitly request the ADBOOK_READ permission and are signed with the same signature will be allowed to read the address book contents.

Next, we developed an application that represents postulated malicious behaviors in the Alloy counterexample. Figure 4(b) shows part of the manifest file implementation for MalApp (corresponding to Application1 in Fig. 3). Similar to the address book application, it declares the ADBOOK_READ permission, albeit with

[11] The URI permission vulnerability is omitted since it exists only on an outdated version of Android, and the improper delegation flow has already been studied in [12].

[12] A manifest file contains, among other things, declarations of uses and custom permissions for an application.

a lower protection level, *normal*. It further includes a *uses-permission* element to declare that it requires the self-declared custom permission (lines 15–16). The MalActivity component, which represents the malicious component in the counterexample, then simply sends a query to the AddrBookProvider component.

The two applications were signed with different keys to reflect a real scenario, where they would be from different developers. We then installed and executed them, according to the counterexample, on two versions of the Android SDK—2.3.7 and 4.4.4—under the Genymotion[13] emulator. We repeated the experiments with different combinations of protection levels for AddressBook and MalApp. In all cases, we observed that MalApp was successfully able to access the content of the address book, confirming the feasibility of the attack.

```
1  //(a) Address book -------------------------------
2  <permission android:name="com.example.ADBOOK_READ"
3    android:protectionLevel="signature" />
4  <application android:label="AddressBook">
5    <provider android:name=".AddressBookProvider"
6     android:authorities=".AddressBookProvider"
7     android:readPermission="com.example.ADBOOK_READ"
8     <!--android:grantUriPermissions="true"-->
9     >
10   </provider>
11 </application>
12 //(b) Custom permission vulnerability-------------
13 <permission android:name="com.example.ADBOOK_READ"
14   android:protectionLevel="normal" />
15 <uses-permission android:name=
16   "com.example.ADBOOK_READ" />
17 <application android:label="MalApp">
18   <activity
19    android:name=".MalActivity"
20    android:label="MalApp" >
21    <intent-filter>
22     <action android:name="MAIN" />
23     <category android:name="LAUNCHER" />
24    </intent-filter>
25   </activity>
26 </application>
```

Fig. 4. Snippets of the demonstrative applications that represent the counterexample scenarios shown in Fig. 3

5.2 Prevalence of the Vulnerability

To estimate the prevalence of this vulnerability among real Android applications, we examined 1,500 applications collected from two repositories: (1) popular free applications from Google's Play Store[14] and (2) open-source applications from the F-Droid repository[15].

An application is at risk of containing a custom permission vulnerability if (1) it defines a custom permission used to protect a component API and (2) it does not implement an *additional*, dynamic check to ensure that the calling application is authorized to access the API. We constructed a custom static analysis tool to check these two conditions. For each application, our tool decompiles the related Android package file to extract its manifest file. It then pairs the manifest file with the corresponding application's bytecode to perform the following checks:

[13] www.genymotion.com
[14] http://play.google.com/store/apps
[15] https://f-droid.org/

- **Permission:** The tool checks the manifest file for any declaration of custom permissions, and whether those permissions are actually used to guard components.
- **Dynamic enforcement:** There is a programmatic but limited method for an application to protect itself against the custom permission attack. If it knows a whitelist of trusted calling applications, then it can implement a dynamic check to reject calls from unknown applications (however, it may not be possible to construct such a list for an open-ended application that is designed to interact with many applications). The tool analyzes the bytecode for the presence of this optional check by searching for the use of built-in Android functions such as *getCallingUid*, which returns the caller's information.

Results. The total numbers of custom permissions defined within the apps for our Google Play and F-Droid test sets are 536 and 171, respectively. 201 (47.26%) of the apps in our Google Play test set define at least one custom permission, whereas this number is just 67 (6.42%) for the F-Droid repository. The average number of custom permissions per app for those that define at least one custom permission is 2.64. Out of the apps that define custom permissions, 116 (57.71%) apps in the case of Google Play and 45 (67.16%) in the case of F-Droid use those permissions to protect their components. Just under 5% of all the apps in our test set perform the dynamic check.

According to Figure 5(a), about 61% of the components protected by custom permissions are of type Service or Broadcast Receiver. This is important because the lack of a visible user interface in these types of components promotes possibilities for a stealthy permission re-delegation attack [12]. More than 85% of custom permissions are defined at signature or dangerous protection levels that regulate access to critical APIs, as shown in Figure 5(b).

The results show that custom permissions are widely used by real-world Android applications to guard critical APIs. Most developers do not perform any additional check to ensure that incoming APIs are from trusted callers, suggesting that they may be unaware of the custom permission vulnerability, despite its potential for security breaches.

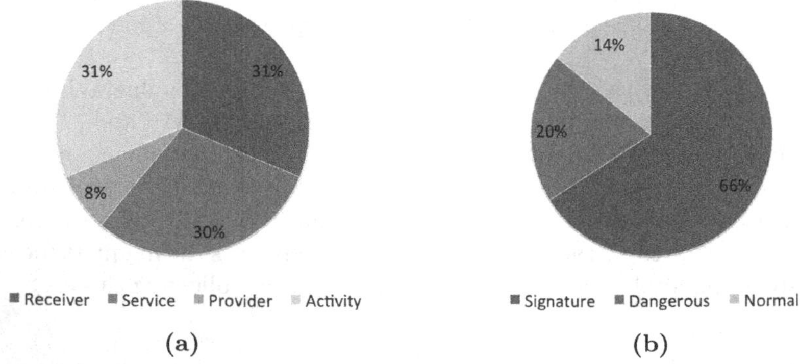

Fig. 5. (a) Frequency of component types protected by custom permissions; (b) Categorization of custom permissions based on their protection levels

6 Related Work

The custom permission vulnerability in Section 4.1 was first described in a blog post by an independent security researcher [13]. However, despite its potential security consequences, the vulnerability has not received widespread attention among Android developers; as revealed by our study in Section 5, a significant number of Android applications are still vulnerable to this attack. To our knowledge, the vulnerability has not been studied in the academic literature.

We are aware of two previous works that describe a formalization of the Android permission protocol. Shin and his colleagues encoded a formal model of the protocol in Coq and proved a set of security properties using its interactive theorem proving facility [14]. The main difference between their work and ours is in the kind of analysis performed. A successful Coq proof provides a stronger theoretical guarantee than an Alloy analysis, which is bounded to finite domains in the universe. On the other hand, the Alloy Analyzer is capable of generating counterexamples, which we found tremendously helpful for identifying the vulnerabilities in the system. Even though the properties proven were similar to ours, their analysis failed to identify the custom permission vulnerability, because the definition of the installation operation in their model is over-constrained — their model prevents an application from being installed if it declares a permission that already exists on the device, ruling out behavior that would have revealed the attack.

Fragkaki et al. describe a logical formalization of a permission model similar to the one used in Android [15]. However, they only performed an informal analysis of the model, and did not identify the custom permission vulnerability.

Most of the previous works in Android security involve performing manual inspection or program analysis to identify a particular vulnerability in Android applications [2,4,6,8,16,17,18,19]. Two previous projects deal specifically with permission vulnerabilities in Android. Felt and her colleagues performed a study of existing applications for permission usage and discovered that many of them are "overprivileged" (i.e., given more permissions than they need) [1]. However, their study does not consider custom permissions. In a separate work, Felt et al. describe a type of attack called *permission re-delegation*, and show that many existing Android applications are vulnerable to this type of attack [12].

A number of static analysis tools, such as ComDroid [16], Epicc [17], FlowDroid [19], have been developed to detect a flow of malicious data within an application or between multiple applications. However, these tools do not deal with permission-related vulnerabilities.

More recently, we developed COVERT [8], an approach for compositional analysis of Android inter-application vulnerabilities. COVERT uses static analysis techniques to extract a formal model of Android apps. It then performs the analysis for inter-application vulnerabilities in a modular way, permitting the results of such analyses to be composed to support incremental verification of apps as they are installed, updated, and removed.

These research efforts are mainly focused on analyzing a *particular* application (or a set of apps, in case of COVERT) by extracting relevant security behaviors from it. In contrast, our work focuses on analyzing the *general* underlying Android permission protocol itself, and identifying *design flaws* that may be applicable to all Android applications.

7 Conclusion

In this paper, we presented a formal model of the Android permission protocol in Alloy, and an automated analysis that identified a number of flaws in the protocol that cause serious security vulnerabilities. We also performed a study of one of the vulnerabilities and showed that it is prevalent among many existing Android applications.

It is notable that *underspecification* of the Android permission protocol was essential; it allowed us to avoid specifying aspects of behavior that were not clear in the documentation, and led to the discovery of vulnerabilities that had eluded an earlier analysis of the very same protocol by others (which, due to the use of a theorem prover based on a functional language, had not supported underspecification).

While this paper has focused on the analysis of Android, we believe that our approach can be applied to other types of mobile devices that rely on permissions, such as iOS and Windows Phone. By building a precise model of the permission mechanism and subjecting it to exhaustive analysis, the device designer may be able to discover potential vulnerabilities, instead of relying solely on manual scrutiny by security experts.

We plan to further explore the synergy between formal analysis of a high-level system model and implementation-level techniques, as mentioned in Section 2. We are currently working on an end-to-end security analysis framework that combines a model-based detection of system-level attacks with a suite of static analysis tools that can identify particular types of vulnerabilities; our target domains include web security, mobile devices, and system-of-systems. We believe that our work in this paper presents a first step towards this goal.

Acknowledgment. This work was supported in part by awards D11AP00282 from the US Defense Advanced Research Projects Agency, H98230-14-C-0140 from the US National Security Agency, HSHQDC-14-C-B0040 from the US Department of Homeland Security, and CCF-1252644 from the US National Science Foundation.

References

1. Felt, A.P., Chin, E., Hanna, S., Song, D., Wagner, D.: Android permissions demystified. In: 18th ACM Conference on Computer and Communications Security (CCS), pp. 627–638 (2011)
2. Davi, L., Dmitrienko, A., Sadeghi, A.-R., Winandy, M.: Privilege escalation attacks on android. In: Burmester, M., Tsudik, G., Magliveras, S., Ilić, I. (eds.) ISC 2010. LNCS, vol. 6531, pp. 346–360. Springer, Heidelberg (2011)

3. Pandita, R., Xiao, X., Yang, W., Enck, W., Xie, T.: Whyper: Towards automating risk assessment of mobile applications. In: Proceedings of the 22nd USENIX Conference on Security, SEC 2013, pp. 527–542. USENIX Association, Berkeley (2013)
4. Grace, M., Zhou, Y., Wang, Z., Jiang, X.: Systematic detection of capability leaks in stock android smartphones. In: Proceedings of the 19th Annual Symposium on Network and Distributed System Security (2012)
5. Schlegel, R., Zhang, K., Zhou, X., Intwala, M., Kapadia, A., Wang, X.: Soundcomber: A stealthy and context-aware sound trojan for smartphones. In: Proc. of 18th Annual Network and Distributed System Security Symposium, NDSS (2011)
6. Enck, W., Octeau, D., McDaniel, P., Chaudhuri, S.: A study of android application security. In: Proc. of USENIX (2011)
7. Woodcock, J., Larsen, P.G., Bicarregui, J., Fitzgerald, J.: Formal methods: Practice and experience. ACM Comput. Surv. 41(4), 19:1–19:36 (2009)
8. Bagheri, H., Sadeghi, A., Garcia, J., Malek, S.: Covert: Compositional analysis of android inter-app permission leakage. IEEE Transactions on Software Engineering (2015)
9. Jackson, D.: Software Abstractions: Logic, Language, and Analysis, 2nd edn. MIT Press (2012)
10. Google: Android system permissions, http://developer.android.com/guide/topics/security/permissions.html
11. Andoni, A., Daniliuc, D., Khurshid, S., Marinov, D.: Evaluating the small scope hypothesis, http://sdg.csail.mit.edu/pubs/2002/SSH.pdf
12. Felt, A.P., Wang, H.J., Moshchuk, A., Hanna, S., Chin, E.: Permission re-delegation: Attacks and defenses. In: 20th USENIX Security Symposium (2011)
13. Mark Murphy: Vulnerabilities with custom permissions (2014), http://commonsware.com/blog/2014/02/12/vulnerabilities-custom-permissions.html
14. Shin, W., Kiyomoto, S., Fukushima, K., Tanaka, T.: A formal model to analyze the permission authorization and enforcement in the android framework. In: IEEE International Conference on Privacy, Security, Risk and Trust, pp. 944–951 (2010)
15. Fragkaki, E., Bauer, L., Jia, L., Swasey, D.: Modeling and enhancing android's permission system. In: 17th European Symposium on Research in Computer Security (ESORICS), pp. 1–18 (2012)
16. Chin, E., Felt, A.P., Greenwood, K., Wagner, D.: Analyzing inter-application communication in android. In: Proceedings of the 9th International Conference on Mobile Systems, Applications, and Services, MobiSys 2011. ACM, New York, pp. 239–252 (2011)
17. Octeau, D., McDaniel, P., Jha, S., Bartel, A., Bodden, E., Klein, J., Traon, Y.L.: Effective Inter-Component Communication Mapping in Android with Epicc: An Essential Step Towards Holistic Security Analysis. In: Proceedings of the 22nd USENIX Security Symposium, Washington, DC (August 2013)
18. Enck, W., Gilbert, P., Chun, B.G., Cox, L.P., Jung, J., McDaniel, P., Sheth, A.N.: Taintdroid: An information-flow tracking system for realtime privacy monitoring on smartphones. In: Proc. of USENIX OSDI (2011)
19. Arzt, S., Rasthofer, S., Bodden, E., Bartel, A., Klein, J., Le Traon, Y., Octeau, D., McDaniel, P.: Flowdroid: Precise context, flow, field, object-sensitive and lifecycle-aware taint analysis for android apps. In: Proceedings of the 35th Annual ACM SIGPLAN Conference on Programming Language Design and Implementation, PLDI 2014 (2014)

Privacy by Design in Practice: Reasoning about Privacy Properties of Biometric System Architectures

Julien Bringer[1], Hervé Chabanne[1,2], Daniel Le Métayer[3], and Roch Lescuyer[1(✉)]

[1] Morpho, Issy-Les-Moulineaux, France
roch.lescuyer@morpho.com
[2] Télécom ParisTech, Paris, France
[3] Inria, Université de Lyon, France

Abstract. The work presented in this paper is the result of a collaboration between academics, industry and lawyers to show the applicability of the privacy by design approach to biometric systems and the benefit of formal methods to this end. The choice of particular techniques and the role of the components (central server, secure module, terminal, smart card, etc.) in the architecture have a strong impact on the privacy guarantees provided by a biometric system. However, existing proposals were made on a case by case basis, which makes it difficult to compare them and to provide a rationale for the choice of specific options. In this paper, we show that a general framework for the definition of privacy architectures can be used to specify these options and to reason about them in a formal way.

1 Introduction

Biometric recognition [19] is an efficient way to identify or to authenticate a person. Biometric systems involve two main phases: enrolment and verification (either authentication or identification) [19]. Enrolment is the registration phase, in which the biometric traits of a person are collected and recorded within the system. In the *authentication* mode, a fresh biometric trait is collected and compared with the registered one by the system to check that it corresponds to the claimed identity. In the *identification* mode, a fresh biometric data is collected and the corresponding identity is searched in a database of enrolled biometric references.

Biometric characteristics, such as fingerprints or iris, are stable over time and highly discriminating, which are key advantages for applications such as access control. However, from a privacy point of view, these advantages turn into drawbacks: because of their stability over time, and because an individual cannot easily change his biometrics, the leak of biometric traits to a malicious entity may give rise to serious privacy risks, including tracking and identity theft.

A wide array of techniques (encryption, homomorphic encryption, secure multi-party computation, etc.) and architectures have been proposed to take

N. Bjørner and F. de Boer (Eds.): FM 2015, LNCS 9109, pp. 90–107, 2015.
DOI: 10.1007/978-3-319-19249-9_7

into account privacy requirements in the implementation of privacy preserving biometric systems. Some solutions involve dedicated cryptographic primitives such as secure sketches [9] and fuzzy vaults [20,38], others rely on adaptations of existing cryptographic tools [25] or the use of secure hardware solutions [31]. The choice of particular techniques and the role of the components (central server, secure module, terminal, smart card, etc.) in the architecture have a strong impact on the privacy guarantees provided by a solution. However, existing proposals were made on a case by case basis, which makes it difficult to compare them, to provide a rationale for the choice of specific options and to capitalize on past experience. In this paper, we show that a general framework for the definition of privacy architectures can be used to specify these options, to reason about them in a formal way and to justify their design in terms of trust assumptions. This work, which has been conducted in an interdisciplinary project involving lawyers and computer scientists, can be seen as an illustration of the feasibility of the *privacy-by-design* approach in an industrial environment.

The privacy by design approach is often praised by lawyers as well as computer scientists as an essential step towards a better privacy protection. It will even become a legal obligation in the European Community if the current draft of the Data Protection Regulation [11] eventually gets adopted. However, it is one thing to impose by law the adoption of privacy by design, quite another to define precisely what it is intended to mean and to ensure that it is put into practice. Its general philosophy is that privacy should not be treated as an afterthought but rather as a first-class requirement in the design of IT systems: in other words, designers should have privacy in mind from the start when they define the features and architecture of a system. However, the practical application of this philosophy raises a number of challenges: first of all the privacy requirements must be defined precisely; then it must be possible to reason about potential tensions between privacy and other requirements and to explore different combinations of privacy enhancing technologies to build systems meeting all these requirements.

A first step in this direction is described in [2] which introduces a system for defining privacy architectures and reasoning about their properties. In this paper, we show how this framework can be used to apply a privacy by design approach for the implementation of biometric systems. In Section 2 we provide an outline of the framework defined in [2]. In Sections 3 to 6, we describe several architectures for biometric systems, considering both existing systems and more advanced solutions, and show that they can be defined in this framework. This makes it possible to highlight their commonalities and differences especially with regard to their underlying trust assumptions. Section 7 sketches related works and Section 8 concludes the paper with suggestions of avenues for further work.

2 General Approach

The objective of the work presented in [2] was precisely to address the needs identified in the introduction, that is to say to provide a formal and systematic approach to privacy by design. In practice, this framework makes it possible to express privacy and integrity requirements (typically the fact that an entity must obtain guarantees about the correctness of a value), to analyse their potential tensions and to make reasoned architectural choices based on explicit trust assumptions. The motivations for the approach come from the following observations:

- First, one of the key decisions that has to be taken in the design of a privacy compliant system is the location of the data and the computations: for example, a centralized system in which all data is collected and all results computed brings strong integrity guarantees to the operator at the price of a loss of privacy for data subjects. Decentralized solutions may provide better privacy protections but weaker guarantees for the operator. The use of privacy enhancing technologies such as homomorphic encryption or secure multi-party computation can in some cases reconcile both objectives.
- The choice among the architectural options should be guided by the assumptions that can be placed by the actors on the other actors and on the components of the architecture. This trust itself can be justified in different ways (security protocol, secure or certified hardware, accredited third party, etc.).

As far as the formal model is concerned, the framework proposed in [2] relies on a dedicated epistemic logic. Indeed, because privacy is closely connected with the notion of knowledge, epistemic logics [12] form an ideal basis to reason about privacy properties but standard epistemic logics based on possible worlds semantics suffer from a weakness (called "logical omniscience" [17]) which makes them unsuitable in the context of privacy by design.

We assume that the functionality of the system is expressed as the computation of a set of equations $\Omega := \{X = T\}$ over a language $Term$ of terms T defined as follows, where C represents constants ($Cx \in Const$), X variables ($X \in Var$) and F functions ($F \in Fun$):

$$T ::= X \mid Cx \mid F(T_1, \ldots, T_n)$$

An *architecture* is defined by a set of components C_i, for $i \in [1, n]$, and a set A of relations. The relations define the capacities of the components and the trust assumptions. In this paper, we use the following language to define the relations:

$$\begin{aligned} A &::= \{R\} \\ R &::= Has_i(X) \mid Receive_{i,j}(\{S\}, \{X\}) \mid Compute_i(X = T) \\ &\quad\;\; \mid Verify_i^{Attest}(S) \qquad\; \mid Trust_{i,j} \\ S &::= Attest_i(\{Eq\}) \\ Eq &::= Pred(T_1, \ldots, T_n) \end{aligned}$$

The notation $\{Z\}$ denotes a set of terms of category Z. $Has_i(X)$ denotes the fact that component C_i possesses (or is the origin of) the value of X, which may correspond to situations in which X is stored on C_i or C_i is a sensor collecting the value of X. $Receive_{i,j}(\{S\},\{X\})$ means that C_i can receive the values of variables in $\{X\}$ together with the statements in $\{S\}$ from C_j . We consider only one type of statements here, namely attestations: $Attest_i(\{Eq\})$ is the declaration by C_i that the properties in $\{Eq\}$ hold. $Verify_i^{Attest}(S)$ is the verification by component C_i of the authenticity[1] of the S statement. In this paper we use the set of predicates $Pred := \{=, \in\}$. $Compute_i(X = T)$ means that component C_i can compute the term T and assign its value to X and $Trust_{i,j}$ represents the fact that component C_i trusts component C_j. Graphical data flow representations can be derived from architectures expressed in this language. For the sake of readability, we use both notations in the next sections.

The subset of the privacy logic used in this paper is the following dedicated epistemic logic:

$$\begin{aligned} \varphi &::= Has_i^{all}(X) \mid Has_i^{none}(X) \mid K_i(Prop) \mid \varphi_1 \ \wedge \ \varphi_2 \\ Prop &::= Pred(T_1, \ldots, T_n) \mid Prop_1 \ \wedge \ Prop_2 \end{aligned}$$

$Has_i^{all}(X)$ and $Has_i^{none}(X)$ denote the facts that component C_i respectively can or cannot get the value of X. K_i denotes the epistemic knowledge following the "deductive algorithmic knowledge" philosophy [12,33] that makes it possible to avoid the logical omniscience problem. In this approach, the knowledge of a component C_i is defined as the set of properties that this component can actually derive using its own information and the deductive system $\triangleright_i$.

Another relation, Dep_i, is used to take into account dependencies between variables. $Dep_i(X, \{X^1, \ldots X^n\})$ means that if C_i can obtain the values of variables $X^1, \ldots X^n$ then it may be able to derive the value of X. The absence of such a relation is an assumption that C_i cannot derive the value of X from the values of $X^1, \ldots, X^n$. It should be noted that this dependency relation is associated with a given component: different components may have different capacities. For example, if component C_i is the only component able to decrypt a variable ev to get the clear text v, then $Dep_i(v, \{ev\})$ holds but $Dep_j(v, \{ev\})$ does not hold for any $j \neq i$.

The semantics $\mathcal{S}(A)$ of an architecture A is defined as the set of states of the components C_i of A resulting from compliant execution traces [2]. A compliant execution trace contains only events that are instantiations of relations (e.g. $Receive_{i,j}$, $Compute_i$, etc.) of A. The semantics $S(\varphi)$ of a property φ is defined as the set of architectures meeting φ. For example, $A \in S(Has_i^{none}(X))$ if for all states $\sigma \in \mathcal{S}(A)$, the state σ_i is such that $\sigma_i(X) = \perp$, which expresses the fact that the component C_i cannot assign a value to the variable X.

To make it possible to reason about privacy properties, an axiomatisation of this logic is presented and is proven sound and complete. The soundness theorem states that for all A, if $A \vdash \varphi$, then $A \in S(\varphi)$. Completeness means that for all A, if $A \in S(\varphi)$ then $A \vdash \varphi$. Finally, a decidability property ensures that if

[1] This verification concerns the authenticity of the statement only, not its truth that C_i may even not be able to carry out itself. In practice, it could be the verification of a digital signature. But here, at the architecture level, we do not detail how such a verification is done.

$$\textbf{H1}\ \frac{Has_i(X) \in A}{A \vdash Has_i^{all}(X)} \qquad \textbf{H2}\ \frac{Receive_{i,j}(S,E) \in A \qquad X \in E}{A \vdash Has_i^{all}(X)}$$

$$\textbf{H3}\ \frac{Compute_i(X = T) \in A}{A \vdash Has_i^{all}(X)}$$

$$\textbf{H5}\ \frac{Dep_i(X, \{X^1, \ldots, X^n\}) \qquad \forall l \in [1,n], A \vdash Has_i^{all}(X^l)}{A \vdash Has_i^{all}(X)}$$

$$\textbf{H6}\ \frac{\text{None of the pre-conditions of } \textbf{H1} \text{ to } \textbf{H5} \text{ holds for } X}{A \vdash Has_i^{none}(X)}$$

$$\textbf{K1}\ \frac{Compute_i(X = T) \in A}{A \vdash K_i(X = T)} \qquad \textbf{K}\triangleright\ \frac{E \triangleright_i Eq_0 \qquad \forall Eq \in E : A \vdash K_i(Eq)}{A \vdash K_i(Eq_0)}$$

$$\textbf{K5}\ \frac{Verif_i^{Attest}(Attest_j(E)) \in A \qquad Trust_{i,j} \in A \qquad Eq \in E}{A \vdash K_i(Eq)}$$

Fig. 1. A subset of rules from the axiomatics of [2]

the deductive systems $\triangleright_i$ are decidable, then the axiomatics is also decidable. A subset of the axiomatics useful for this paper are presented in Figure 1.

3 Biometric Systems Architectures

Before starting the presentation of the different biometric architectures in the next sections, we introduce in this section the basic terminology used in this paper and the common features of the architectures. For the sake of readability, we use upper case sans serif letters S, T, *etc.* rather than indexed variables C_i to denote components. By abuse of notation, we will use component names instead of indices and write, for example, $Receive_{\mathsf{U},\mathsf{T}}(\{\}, \{\mathtt{dec}\})$. Type letters `dec`, `br`, *etc.* denote variables. The set of components of an architecture is denoted by $\mathcal{J}$.

The variables used in biometric system architectures are the following:

- A biometric reference template `br` built during the enrolment phase.
- A raw biometric data `rd` provided by the user during the verification phase.
- A fresh template `bs` derived from `rd` during the verification phase.
- A threshold `thr` which is used during the verification phase as a closeness criterion for the biometric templates.
- The output `dec` of the verification which is the result of the matching between the fresh template `bs` and the enrolled templates `br`, considering the threshold `thr`.

Two components appear in all biometric architectures: a component U representing the user, and the terminal T which is equipped with a sensor used to acquire biometric traits. In addition, biometric architectures may involve an explicit issuer I, enrolling users and certifying their templates, a server S managing a database containing enrolled templates, a module (which can be a hardware security module, denoted HSM) to perform the matching and eventually to take the decision, and a smart card C to store the enrolled templates (and in some cases to perform the matching). Figure 2 introduces some graphical representations used in the figures of this paper.

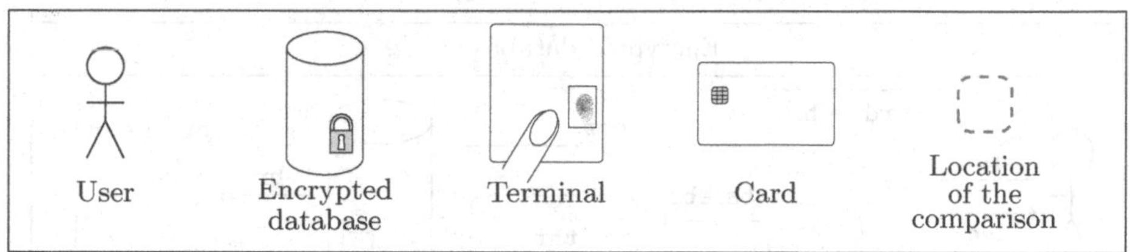

Fig. 2. Graphical representations

In this paper, we focus on the verification phase and assume that enrolment has already been done. Therefore the biometric reference templates are stored on a component which can be either the issuer ($Has_{\mathsf{I}}(\texttt{br})$) or a smart card ($Has_{\mathsf{C}}(\texttt{br})$). A verification process is initiated by the terminal T receiving as input a raw biometric data rd from the user T. T extracts the fresh biometric template bs from rd using the function $Extract \in Fun$. All architectures A therefore include $Receive_{\mathsf{T},\mathsf{U}}(\{\}, \{\texttt{rd}\})$ and $Compute_{\mathsf{T}}(\texttt{bs} = Extract(\texttt{rd}))$ and the Dep_{T} relation is such that $(\texttt{bs}, \{\texttt{rd}\}) \in Dep_{\mathsf{T}}$. In all architectures A, the user receives the final decision dec (which can typically be positive or negative) from the terminal: $Receive_{\mathsf{U},\mathsf{T}}(\{\}, \{\texttt{dec}\}) \in A$. The matching itself, which can be performed by different components depending on the architecture, is expressed by the function $\mu \in Fun$ which takes as arguments two biometric templates and the threshold thr.

4 Protecting the Reference Templates with Encryption

Let us consider first the most common architecture deployed for protecting biometric data. When a user is enrolled his reference template is stored encrypted, either in a terminal with an embedded database, or in a central database. During the identification process, the user supplies a fresh template, the reference templates are decrypted by a component (which can be typically the terminal or a dedicated hardware security module) and the comparison is done inside this component. The first part of Figure 3 shows an architecture A_{ed} in which reference templates are stored in a central database and the decryption of the references and the matching are done inside the terminal. The second part of the figure shows an architecture A_{hsm} in which the decryption of the references and the matching are done on a dedicated hardware security module. Both architectures are considered in turn in Subsections 4.1 and 4.2.

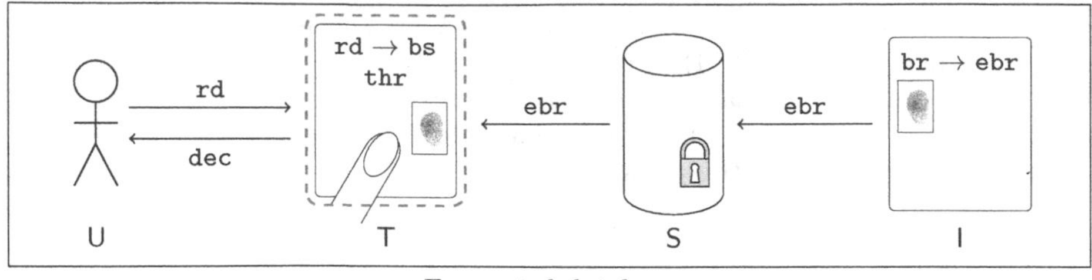

Encrypted database

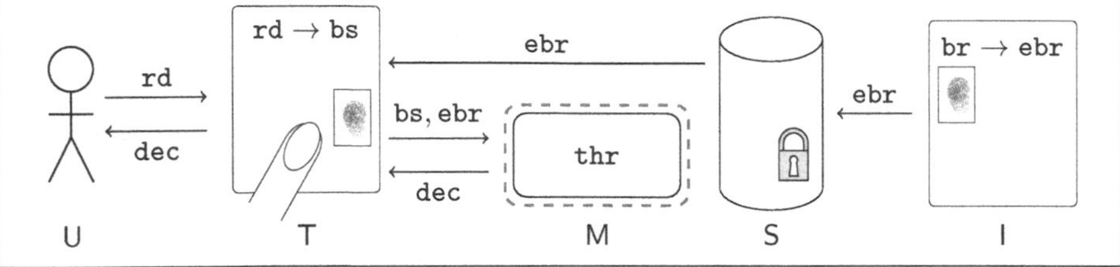

Encrypted database with a hardware security module (HSM)

Fig. 3. Classical architectures with an encrypted database

4.1 Use of an Encrypted Database

The first architecture A_{ed} is composed of a user U, a terminal T, a server S managing an encrypted database ebr and an issuer I enrolling users and generating the encrypted database ebr. The set *Fun* includes the encryption and decryption functions *Enc* and *Dec*. When applied to an array, *Enc* is assumed to encrypt each entry of the array. At this stage, for the sake of conciseness, we consider only biometric data in the context of an identification phase. The same types of architectures can be used to deal with authentication, which does not raise any specific issue. The functionality of the architecture is $\Omega := \{\mathtt{ebr} = Enc(\mathtt{br}), \mathtt{br}' = Dec(\mathtt{ebr}), \mathtt{bs} = Extract(\mathtt{rd}), \mathtt{dec} = \mu(\mathtt{br}', \mathtt{bs}, \mathtt{thr})\}$, and the architecture is defined as:

$$\begin{aligned} A_{\mathsf{ed}} := \big\{ & Has_{\mathsf{I}}(\mathtt{br}), Has_{\mathsf{U}}(\mathtt{rd}), Has_{\mathsf{T}}(\mathtt{thr}), Compute_{\mathsf{I}}(\mathtt{ebr} = Enc(\mathtt{br})), \\ & Receive_{\mathsf{S},\mathsf{I}}(\{Attest_{\mathsf{I}}(\mathtt{ebr} = Enc(\mathtt{br}))\}, \{\mathtt{ebr}\}), \\ & Receive_{\mathsf{T},\mathsf{S}}(\{Attest_{\mathsf{I}}(\mathtt{ebr} = Enc(\mathtt{br}))\}, \{\mathtt{ebr}\}), Trust_{\mathsf{T},\mathsf{I}}, \\ & Verify_{\mathsf{T}}^{Attest}(Attest_{\mathsf{I}}(\mathtt{ebr} = Enc(\mathtt{br}))), Receive_{\mathsf{T},\mathsf{U}}(\{\}, \{\mathtt{rd}\}), \\ & Compute_{\mathsf{T}}(\mathtt{bs} = Extract(\mathtt{rd})), Compute_{\mathsf{T}}(\mathtt{br}' = Dec(\mathtt{ebr})), \\ & Compute_{\mathsf{T}}(\mathtt{dec} = \mu(\mathtt{br}', \mathtt{bs}, \mathtt{thr})), Receive_{\mathsf{U},\mathsf{T}}(\{\}, \{\mathtt{dec}\}) \big\} \end{aligned}$$

The properties of the encryption scheme are captured by the dependence and deductive relations. The dependence relations are: $(\mathtt{ebr}, \{\mathtt{br}\}) \in Dep_{\mathsf{I}}$, and $\{(\mathtt{bs}, \{\mathtt{rd}\}), (\mathtt{dec}, \{\mathtt{br}', \mathtt{bs}, \mathtt{thr}\}), (\mathtt{br}', \{\mathtt{ebr}\}), (\mathtt{br}, \{\mathtt{ebr}\})\} \subseteq Dep_{\mathsf{T}}$. Moreover the deductive algorithm relation contains: $\{\mathtt{ebr} = Enc(\mathtt{br})\} \rhd \{\mathtt{br} = Dec(\mathtt{ebr})\}$.

From the point of view of biometric data protection, the property that this architecture is meant to ensure is the fact that the server should not have access to the reference template, that is to say: $Has_{\mathsf{S}}^{none}(\mathtt{br})$, which can be proven using Rule **H6** (the same property holds for $\mathtt{br}'$):

$$\textbf{H6}\ \frac{Has_{\mathsf{S}}(\mathtt{br}) \notin A_{\mathsf{ed}} \quad \nexists \overrightarrow{X} : (\mathtt{br}, \overrightarrow{X}) \in Deps_{\mathsf{S}} \quad \nexists T : Compute_{\mathsf{S}}(\mathtt{br} = T) \in A_{\mathsf{ed}} \quad \nexists j \in \mathcal{J}, \nexists S, \nexists E, Receive_{\mathsf{S},j}(S, E) \in A_{\mathsf{ed}} \wedge \mathtt{br} \in E}{A_{\mathsf{ed}} \vdash Has_{\mathsf{S}}^{none}(\mathtt{br})}$$

It is also easy to prove, using **H2** and **H5**, that the terminal has access to $\mathtt{br}'$: $Has_{\mathsf{T}}^{all}(\mathtt{br}')$.

As far as integrity is concerned, the terminal should be convinced that the matching is correct. The proof relies on the trust placed by the terminal in the issuer (about the correctness of $\mathtt{ebr}$) and the computations that the terminal can perform by itself (through $Compute_{\mathsf{T}}$ and the application of $\triangleright$):

$$\textbf{K5}\ \frac{Verify_{\mathsf{T}}^{Attest}(\{Attest_{\mathsf{I}}(\mathtt{ebr} = Enc(\mathtt{br}))\}) \in A_{\mathsf{ed}} \qquad Trust_{\mathsf{T},\mathsf{I}} \in A_{\mathsf{ed}}}{A_{\mathsf{ed}} \vdash K_{\mathsf{T}}(\mathtt{ebr} = Enc(\mathtt{br}))}$$

$$\textbf{K}\triangleright\ \frac{\{\mathtt{ebr} = Enc(\mathtt{br})\} \triangleright \{\mathtt{br} = Dec(\mathtt{ebr})\} \qquad A_{\mathsf{ed}} \vdash K_{\mathsf{T}}(\mathtt{ebr} = Enc(\mathtt{br}))}{A_{\mathsf{ed}} \vdash K_{\mathsf{T}}(\mathtt{br} = Dec(\mathtt{ebr}))}$$

$$\textbf{K1}\ \frac{Compute_{\mathsf{T}}(\mathtt{br}' = Dec(\mathtt{ebr})) \in A_{\mathsf{ed}}}{A_{\mathsf{ed}} \vdash K_{\mathsf{T}}(\mathtt{br}' = Dec(\mathtt{ebr}))}$$

Assuming that all deductive relations include the properties (commutativity and transitivity) of the equality, **K**$\triangleright$ can be used to derive: $A_{\mathsf{ed}} \vdash K_{\mathsf{T}}(\mathtt{br} = \mathtt{br}')$. A further application of **K1** with another transitivity rule for the equality allows us to obtain the desired integrity property:

$$\textbf{K}\triangleright\ \frac{A_{\mathsf{ed}} \vdash K_{\mathsf{T}}(\mathtt{br} = \mathtt{br}') \qquad \textbf{K1}\ \dfrac{Compute_{\mathsf{T}}(\mathtt{dec} = \mu(\mathtt{br}', \mathtt{bs}, \mathtt{thr})) \in A_{\mathsf{ed}}}{A_{\mathsf{ed}} \vdash K_{\mathsf{T}}(\mathtt{dec} = \mu(\mathtt{br}', \mathtt{bs}, \mathtt{thr}))}}{A_{\mathsf{ed}} \vdash K_{\mathsf{T}}(\mathtt{dec} = \mu(\mathtt{br}, \mathtt{bs}, \mathtt{thr}))}$$

4.2 Encrypted Database with a Hardware Security Module

The architecture presented in the previous subsection relies on the terminal to decrypt the reference template and to perform the matching operation. As a result, the clear reference template is known by the terminal and the only component that has to be trusted by the terminal is the issuer. If it does not seem sensible to entrust the terminal with this central role, another option is to delegate the decryption of the reference template and computation of the matching to a hardware security module so that the terminal itself never stores any clear reference template. This strategy leads to architecture A_{hsm} pictured in the second part of Figure 3.

In addition to the user U, the issuer I, the terminal T, and the server S, the set of components contains a hardware security module M. The terminal does not perform the matching, but has to trust M. This trust can be justified in practice by the level of security provided by the HSM M (which can also be endorsed by an official security certification scheme). The architecture is described as follows in our framework:

$$\begin{aligned}A_{\mathsf{hsm}} := \{&Has_{\mathsf{I}}(\mathtt{br}), Has_{\mathsf{U}}(\mathtt{rd}), Has_{\mathsf{M}}(\mathtt{thr}), Compute_{\mathsf{I}}(\mathtt{ebr} = Enc(\mathtt{br})),\\ &Receive_{\mathsf{S,I}}(\{Attest_{\mathsf{I}}(\mathtt{ebr} = Enc(\mathtt{br}))\}, \{\mathtt{ebr}\}),\\ &Receive_{\mathsf{T,S}}(\{Attest_{\mathsf{I}}(\mathtt{ebr} = Enc(\mathtt{br}))\}, \{\mathtt{ebr}\}), Trust_{\mathsf{T,I}},\\ &Verify_{\mathsf{T}}^{Attest}(Attest_{\mathsf{I}}(\mathtt{ebr} = Enc(\mathtt{br}))), Receive_{\mathsf{T,U}}(\{\}, \{\mathtt{rd}\}),\\ &Compute_{\mathsf{T}}(\mathtt{bs} = Extract(\mathtt{rd})), Receive_{\mathsf{M,T}}(\{\}, \{\mathtt{bs}, \mathtt{ebr}\}),\\ &Compute_{\mathsf{M}}(\mathtt{br}' = Dec(\mathtt{ebr})), Compute_{\mathsf{M}}(\mathtt{dec} = \mu(\mathtt{br}', \mathtt{bs}, \mathtt{thr})),\\ &Verify_{\mathsf{T}}^{Attest}(\{Attest_{\mathsf{M}}(\mathtt{dec} = \mu(\mathtt{br}', \mathtt{bs}, \mathtt{thr}))\}), Trust_{\mathsf{T,M}},\\ &Receive_{\mathsf{T,M}}(\mathcal{A}, \{\mathtt{dec}\}), Verify_{\mathsf{T}}^{Attest}(\{Attest_{\mathsf{M}}(\mathtt{br}' = Dec(\mathtt{ebr}))\})\}\end{aligned}$$

where the set of attestations $\mathcal{A}$ received by the terminal from the module is $\mathcal{A} := \{Attest_{\mathsf{M}}(\mathtt{dec} = \mu(\mathtt{br}', \mathtt{bs}, \mathtt{thr})), Attest_{\mathsf{M}}(\mathtt{br}' = Dec(\mathtt{ebr}))\}$.

The trust relation between the terminal and the module makes it possible to apply rule **K5** twice:

$$\frac{Verify_{\mathsf{T}}^{Attest}(\{Attest_{\mathsf{M}}(\mathtt{dec} = \mu(\mathtt{br}', \mathtt{bs}, \mathtt{thr}))\}) \in A_{\mathsf{hsm}} \qquad Trust_{\mathsf{T,M}} \in A_{\mathsf{hsm}}}{A_{\mathsf{hsm}} \vdash K_{\mathsf{T}}(\mathtt{dec} = \mu(\mathtt{br}', \mathtt{bs}, \mathtt{thr}))}$$

$$\mathbf{K5}\ \frac{Verify_{\mathsf{T}}^{Attest}(\{Attest_{\mathsf{M}}(\mathtt{br}' = Dec(\mathtt{ebr}))\}) \in A_{\mathsf{hsm}} \qquad Trust_{\mathsf{T,M}} \in A_{\mathsf{hsm}}}{A_{\mathsf{hsm}} \vdash K_{\mathsf{T}}(\mathtt{br}' = Dec(\mathtt{ebr}))}$$

The same proof as in the previous subsection can be applied to establish the integrity of the matching. The trust relation between the terminal and the issuer and the rules **K5**, **K**$\triangleright$ make it possible to derive: $A_{\mathsf{hsm}} \vdash K_{\mathsf{T}}(\mathsf{br} = Dec(\mathsf{ebr}))$. Then two successive applications of **K**$\triangleright$ regarding the transitivity of the equality lead to: $A_{\mathsf{hsm}} \vdash K_{\mathsf{T}}(\mathtt{dec} = \mu(\mathtt{br}, \mathtt{bs}, \mathtt{thr}))$.

As in architecture A_{ed}, the biometric references are never disclosed to the server. However, in contrast with A_{ed}, they are not disclosed either to the terminal, as shown by rule **H6**:

$$\mathbf{H6}\ \frac{\begin{array}{c}Has_{\mathsf{T}}(\mathtt{br}) \notin A_{\mathsf{hsm}} \quad \nexists \overrightarrow{X} : (\mathtt{br}, \overrightarrow{X}) \in Dep_{\mathsf{T}} \quad \nexists T : Compute_{\mathsf{T}}(\mathtt{br} = T) \in A_{\mathsf{hsm}}\\ \nexists j \in \mathcal{J}, \nexists S, \nexists E, Receive_{\mathsf{T},j}(S, E) \in A_{\mathsf{hsm}} \wedge \mathtt{br} \in E\end{array}}{A_{\mathsf{hsm}} \vdash Has_{\mathsf{T}}^{none}(\mathtt{br})}$$

5 Enhancing Protection with Homomorphic Encryption

In both architectures of Section 4, biometric templates are protected, but the component performing the matching (either the terminal or the secure module) gets access to the reference templates. In this section, we show how homomorphic encryption can be used to ensure that no component gets access to the biometric reference templates during the verification.

Homomorphic encryption schemes [14] makes it possible to compute certain functions over encrypted data. For example, if *Enc* is a homomorphic encryption scheme for multiplication then there is an operation $\otimes$ such that:

$$c_1 = Enc(m_1) \wedge c_2 = Enc(m_2) \Rightarrow c_1 \otimes c_2 = Enc(m_1 \times m_2).$$

Figure 4 presents an architecture A_{hom} derived from A_{hsm} in which the server performs the whole matching computation over encrypted data. The user supplies a template that is sent encrypted to the server. The server also owns an encrypted reference template. The comparison, i.e. the computation of the distance between the templates, is done by the server but the server does not get access to the biometric data or to the result. This is made possible through the use a homomorphic encryption scheme. On the other hand, the module gets the result, but does not get access to the templates. Let us note that A_{hom} is just one of the possible ways to use homomorphic encryption in this context: the homomorphic computation of the distance could actually be made by another component (for example the terminal itself) since it does not lead to any leak of biometric data.

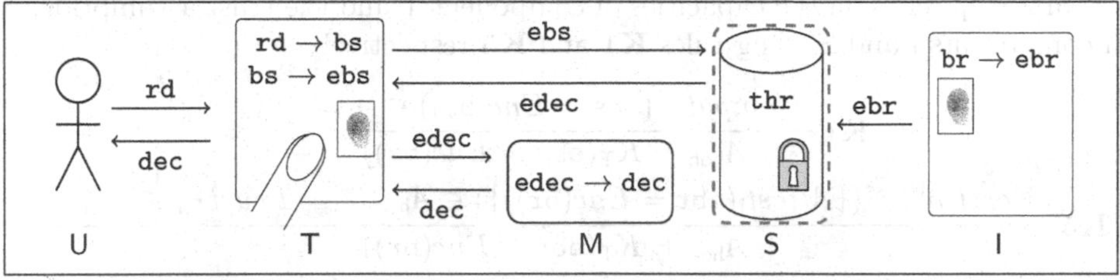

Fig. 4. Comparison over encrypted data with homomorphic encryption

The homomorphic property of the encryption scheme needed for this application depends on the matching algorithm. An option is to resort to a fully homomorphic encryption scheme (FHE) [14] as in the solution described in [37] which uses a variant of a FHE scheme for face-recognition. However, schemes with simpler homomorphic functionalities can also be sufficient (examples can be found in [7,6]). Since we describe our solutions at the architecture level, we do not need to enter into details regarding the chosen homomorphic scheme. We just need to assume the existence of a homomorphic matching function $Hom\text{-}\mu$ with the following properties captured by the algorithmic knowledge relations:

$$\{\mathtt{ebr} = Enc(\mathtt{br}), \mathtt{ebs} = Enc(\mathtt{bs}), \mathtt{edec} = Hom\text{-}\mu(\mathtt{ebr}, \mathtt{ebs}, \mathtt{thr})\} \triangleright \{Dec(\mathtt{edec}) = \mu(\mathtt{br}, \mathtt{bs}, \mathtt{thr})\} \quad (1)$$

The dependence relations include the following: $\{(\mathtt{bs}, \{\mathtt{rd}\}), (\mathtt{ebs}, \{\mathtt{bs}\})\} \subseteq Dep_{\mathsf{T}}$; $(\mathtt{ebr}, \{\mathtt{br}\}) \in Dep_{\mathsf{I}}$; $\{(\mathtt{br}, \{\mathtt{ebr}\}), (\mathtt{bs}, \{\mathtt{ebs}\}), (\mathtt{dec}, \{\mathtt{edec}\})\} \subseteq Dep_{\mathsf{M}}$.

Architecture A_{hom} is defined as follows:

$$\begin{aligned}A_{\mathsf{hom}} := \{&Has_{\mathsf{I}}(\mathtt{br}), Has_{\mathsf{U}}(\mathtt{rd}), Has_{\mathsf{S}}(\mathtt{thr}), Compute_{\mathsf{I}}(\mathtt{ebr} = Enc(\mathtt{br})),\\ &Receive_{\mathsf{S,I}}(\{Attest_{\mathsf{I}}(\{\mathtt{ebr} = Enc(\mathtt{br})\})\}, \{\mathtt{ebr}\}), Receive_{\mathsf{T,U}}(\{\}, \{\mathtt{rd}\}),\\ &Compute_{\mathsf{T}}(\mathtt{bs} = Extract(\mathtt{rd})), Compute_{\mathsf{T}}(\mathtt{ebs} = Enc(\mathtt{bs})),\\ &Receive_{\mathsf{S,T}}(\{\}, \{\mathtt{ebs}\}), Compute_{\mathsf{S}}(\mathtt{edec} = Hom\text{-}\mu(\mathtt{ebr}, \mathtt{ebs}, \mathtt{thr})),\\ &Receive_{\mathsf{T,S}}(\mathcal{A}, \{\mathtt{edec}\}), Verify_{\mathsf{T}}^{Attest}(Attest_{\mathsf{I}}(\{\mathtt{ebr} = Enc(\mathtt{br})\})),\\ &Verify_{\mathsf{T}}^{Attest}(Attest_{\mathsf{S}}(\{\mathtt{edec} = Hom\text{-}\mu(\mathtt{ebr}, \mathtt{ebs}, \mathtt{thr})\})), Trust_{\mathsf{T,S}},\\ &Trust_{\mathsf{T,I}}, Receive_{\mathsf{M,T}}(\{\}, \{\mathtt{edec}\}), Compute_{\mathsf{M}}(\mathtt{dec} = Dec(\mathtt{edec})),\\ &Receive_{\mathsf{T,M}}(\{Attest_{\mathsf{M}}(\{\mathtt{dec} = Dec(\mathtt{edec})\})\}, \{\mathtt{dec}\}), Trust_{\mathsf{T,M}},\\ &Verify_{\mathsf{T}}^{Attest}(Attest_{\mathsf{M}}(\{\mathtt{dec} = Dec(\mathtt{edec})\})), Receive_{\mathsf{U,T}}(\{\}, \{\mathtt{dec}\})\}\end{aligned}$$

where the set $\mathcal{A}$ of attestations received by the terminal from the server is: $\mathcal{A} := \{Attest_{\mathsf{I}}(\{\mathtt{ebr} = Enc(\mathtt{br})\}), Attest_{\mathsf{S}}(\{\mathtt{edec} = Hom\text{-}\mu(\mathtt{ebr}, \mathtt{ebs}, \mathtt{thr})\})\}$.

In order to prove that the terminal can establish the integrity of the result dec, we can proceed in two steps, proving first the correctness of edec and then deriving the correctness of edec using the properties of homomorphic encryption. The first step relies on the capacities of component T and the trust assumptions on components I and S using rules **K1** and **K5** respectively.

$$\textbf{K1}\ \frac{Compute_{\mathsf{T}}(\mathtt{ebs} = Enc(\mathtt{bs})) \in A_{\mathsf{hom}}}{A_{\mathsf{hom}} \vdash K_{\mathsf{T}}(\mathtt{ebs} = Enc(\mathtt{bs}))}$$

$$\textbf{K5}\ \frac{Verify_{\mathsf{T}}^{Attest}(\{Attest_{\mathsf{I}}(\mathtt{ebr} = Enc(\mathtt{br}))\}) \in A_{\mathsf{hom}} \qquad Trust_{\mathsf{T,I}} \in A_{\mathsf{hom}}}{A_{\mathsf{hom}} \vdash K_{\mathsf{T}}(\mathtt{ebr} = Enc(\mathtt{br}))}$$

$$\textbf{K5}\ \frac{Verify_{\mathsf{T}}^{Attest}(\{Attest_{\mathsf{S}}(\mathtt{edec} = Hom\text{-}\mu(\mathtt{br}, \mathtt{bs}, \mathtt{thr}))\}),\ \ Trust_{\mathsf{T,S}} \in A_{\mathsf{hom}}}{A_{\mathsf{hom}} \vdash K_{\mathsf{T}}(\mathtt{edec} = Hom\text{-}\mu(\mathtt{br}, \mathtt{bs}, \mathtt{thr}))}$$

The second step can be done through the application of the deductive algorithmic knowledge regarding the homomorphic encryption property (with LHS_1 the left hand-side of equation (1)) :

$$\textbf{K}\triangleright\ \frac{LHS_1 \triangleright \{Dec(\mathtt{edec}) = \mu(\mathtt{br}, \mathtt{bs}, \mathtt{thr})\} \qquad \forall Eq \in LHS_1 : A_{\mathsf{hom}} \vdash K_{\mathsf{T}}(Eq)}{A_{\mathsf{hom}} \vdash K_{\mathsf{T}}(Dec(\mathtt{edec}) = \mu(\mathtt{br}, \mathtt{bs}, \mathtt{thr}))}$$

The desired property is obtained through the application of rules **K5** and **K**$\triangleright$ exploiting the trust relation between T and M and the transitivity of equality.

$$\textbf{K5}\ \frac{Verify_{\mathsf{T}}^{Attest}(\{Attest_{\mathsf{M}}(\mathtt{dec} = Dec(\mathtt{edec}))\}) \in A_{\mathsf{hom}} \qquad Trust_{\mathsf{T,M}} \in A_{\mathsf{hom}}}{A_{\mathsf{hom}} \vdash K_{\mathsf{T}}(\mathtt{dec} = Dec(\mathtt{edec}))}$$

$$\textbf{K}\triangleright\ \frac{A_{\mathsf{hom}} \vdash K_{\mathsf{T}}(Dec(\mathtt{edec}) = \mu(\mathtt{br}, \mathtt{bs}, \mathtt{thr})) \quad A_{\mathsf{hom}} \vdash K_{\mathsf{T}}(\mathtt{dec} = Dec(\mathtt{edec}))}{A_{\mathsf{hom}} \vdash K_{\mathsf{T}}(\mathtt{dec} = \mu(\mathtt{br}, \mathtt{bs}, \mathtt{thr}))}$$

As far as privacy is concerned, the main property that A_{hom} is meant to ensure is that no component (except the issuer) has access to the biometric references.

Rule **H6** makes it possible to prove that U, T, and S never get access to br, as in Section 4. The same rule can be applied here to prove $A_{\mathsf{hom}} \nvdash Has_{\mathsf{M}}^{all}(\mathtt{ebr})$ exploiting the fact that neither $(\mathtt{br}, \{\mathtt{edec}\})$ nor $(\mathtt{br}, \{\mathtt{dec}\})$ belong to Dep_{M}.

6 The Match-On-Card Technology

Another solution can be considered when the purpose of the system is identification rather than authentication. In this case, it is not necessary to store a database of biometric reference templates and a (usually unique) reference template can be stored on a smart card. A smart card based privacy preserving architecture has been proposed recently which relies on the idea of using the card not only to store the reference template but also to perform the matching itself. Since the comparison is done inside the card the reference template never leaves the card. In this *Match-On-Card* (MOC) technology [31,30,15] (also called *comparison-on-card*), the smart card receives the fresh biometric template, carries out the comparison with its reference template, and sends the decision back (as illustrated in Figure 5).

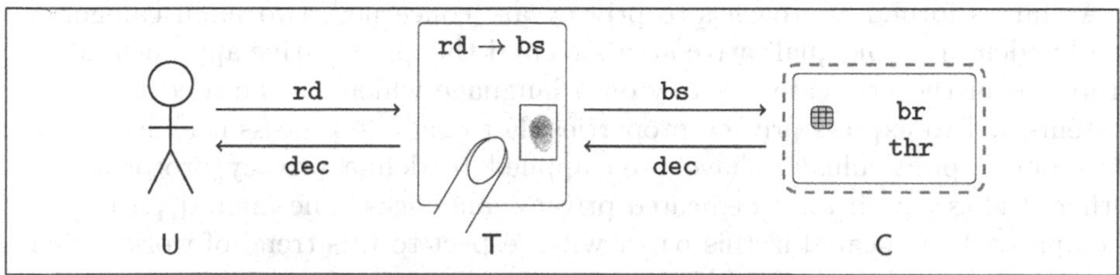

Fig. 5. Biometric verification using the Match-On-Card technology

In this architecture, the terminal is assumed to trust the smart card. This trust assumption is justified by the fact that the card is a tamper-resistant hardware element. This architecture is simpler than the previous ones but not always possible in practice (for a combination of technical and economic reasons) and may represent a shift in terms of trust if the smart card is under the control of the user.

More formally, the MOC architecture is composed of a user U, a terminal T, and a card C. The card C attests that the templates br and bs are close (with respect to the threshold thr):

$$\begin{aligned} A_{\mathsf{moc}} := \{ & Has_{\mathsf{C}}(\mathtt{br}), Has_{\mathsf{U}}(\mathtt{rd}), Has_{\mathsf{C}}(\mathtt{thr}), Receive_{\mathsf{T},\mathsf{U}}(\{\}, \{\mathtt{rd}\}), \\ & Compute_{\mathsf{T}}(\mathtt{bs} = Extract(\mathtt{rd})), Receive_{\mathsf{C},\mathsf{T}}(\{\}, \{\mathtt{bs}\}), \\ & Compute_{\mathsf{C}}(\mathtt{dec} = \mu(\mathtt{br}, \mathtt{bs}, \mathtt{thr})), Receive_{\mathsf{U},\mathsf{T}}(\{\}, \{\mathtt{dec}\}), \\ & Receive_{\mathsf{T},\mathsf{C}}(\{Attest_{\mathsf{C}}(\mathtt{dec} = \mu(\mathtt{br}, \mathtt{bs}, \mathtt{thr}))\}, \{\mathtt{dec}\}), \end{aligned}$$

$$Verify_{\mathsf{T}}^{Attest}(\{Attest_{\mathsf{C}}(\mathtt{dec} = \mu(\mathtt{br}, \mathtt{bs}, \mathtt{thr}))\}), Trust_{\mathsf{T},\mathsf{C}}\}$$

Using rule **H6**, it is easy to show that no component apart from C gets access to br. The proof of the integrity property relies on the capacities of component T and the trust assumption on component C using rules **K1** and **K5** respectively.

7 Related Works

Generally speaking, while the privacy of biometric data has attracted a lot of attention in the news (for instance, with the introduction of a fingerprint sensor in the new iphone) and among lawyers and policy makers[2], it has not triggered such a strong interest in the computer science community so far. Most studies in this area are done on a case by case basis and at a lower level than the architectures described here. For example,[36] proposes a security model for biometric-based authentication taking into account privacy properties[3] and applies it to biometric authentication. The underlying proofs rely on cryptographic techniques related to the ElGamal public key encryption scheme. [21,23,24] develop formal models from an information theoretic perspective relying on specific representations of biometric templates close to error correcting codes.

As far as formal approaches to privacy are concerned, two main categories can be identified: the qualitative approach and the quantitative approach. Most proposals of the first category rely on a language which can be used to define systems and to express privacy properties. For example process calculi such as the applied pi-calculus [1] have been applied to define privacy protocols [8]. Other studies [4,5] involve dedicated privacy languages. The main departure of the approach advocated in this paper with respect to this trend of work is that we reason at the level of architectures, providing ways to express properties without entering into the details of specific protocols. Proposals of the second category rely on privacy metrics such as k-anonymity, l-diversity, or ϵ-differential privacy [10] which can be seen as ways to measure the level of privacy provided by an algorithm. Methods [27] have been proposed to design algorithms achieving privacy metrics or to verify that a system achieves a given level of privacy. These contributions on privacy metrics are complementary to the work described in this paper. We follow a qualitative (or logical) approach here, proving that a given privacy property is met (or not) by an architecture. As suggested in the next section, an avenue for further research would be to cope with quantitative reasoning as well, using inference systems to derive properties expressed in terms of privacy metrics.

Several authors [16,22,28,29,34] have already pointed out the complexity of "privacy engineering" as well as the "richness of the data space"[16] calling for the development of more general and systematic methodologies for privacy by design. [22,26] point out the complexity of the implementation of privacy and

[2] For example with a proposal adopted by the French Senate in May 2014 to introduce stronger requirements for the use of biometrics.

[3] Including impersonation resilience, identity privacy or transaction anonymity.

the large number of options that designers have to face. To address this issue and favour the adoption of these tools, [22] proposes a number of guidelines for the design of compilers for secure computation and zero-knowledge proofs whereas [13] provides a language and a compiler to perform computations on private data by synthesising zero-knowledge protocols. None of these proposals addresses the architectural level and makes it possible to get a global view of a system and to reason about its underlying trust assumption.

8 Conclusion

The work presented in this paper is the result of a collaboration between academics, industry and lawyers to show the applicability of the privacy by design approach to biometric systems and the benefit of formal methods to this end. Indeed, even if privacy by design should soon become a legal obligation in the European Community [11] its application to real systems is far from obvious. We have presented in the same formal framework a variety of architectural options for privacy preserving biometric systems. One of the main benefits of the approach is to provide formal justifications for the architectural choices and a rigorous basis for their comparison. Table 1 is a recap chart of the architectures reviewed in this paper. One of the most interesting pieces of information is the trust assumptions which are highlighted by the model. The first line shows that A_{ed} is the architecture in which the strongest trust in put in the terminal that does not have to trust any other component apart from the issuer and is able to get access to `br`. Architecture A_{hsm} is a variant of A_{ed}; it places less trust in the terminal that has to trust the hardware security module to perform the matching. A_{hom} is the architecture in which the terminal is less trusted: it has to trust the issuer, the hardware security module and the server for all sensitive operations and its role is limited to the collection of the fresh biometric trait and the computation of the fresh template. Architecture A_{moc} is similar to this respect but all sensitive operations are gathered into a single component, namely the smart card. It should be clear that no solution is inherently better than the others and, depending on the context of deployment and the technology used, some trust assumptions may be more reasonable than others. In any case, it is of prime importance to understand the consequences of a particular choice in terms of trust.

For the sake of conciseness, we have presented only four architectures in the body of this paper but more complex architectures can be described in the same framework. Generally speaking, the privacy logic used here can be extended with new privacy enhancing technologies with the associated properties. For example, [2] uses zero-knowledge proofs and commitments to define privacy preserving smart metering architectures.

Another benefit of the formal approach followed in this paper is that it can provide the foundations for a systematic approach to privacy by design. We have proposed a proof of concept implementation of a system to support designers in their task (see [3]). In this system, the user can introduce his privacy and

Table 1. Comparison between architectures

Arch.	Computations	Template protection		Trust relations
	Location of the matching	Components accessing the references br	Components accessing the query bs	
A_{ed}	T	I, T	T	(T, I)
A_{hsm}	M	I, M	T, M	(T, I), (T, M)
A_{hom}	S	I	T	(T, I), (T, M), (T, S)
A_{moc}	M	M	T, M	(T, M)

Components are: user U, terminal T, server S, secure module M (used as a generic name for a hardware security module or a card C), issuer I.
A trust relation (i, j) means that component i trusts component j.

integrity requirements (as well as any requirements imposed by the environment such as the location of a given operation on a designated component) and choose different options for the distribution of the operations and the trust assumptions. When an architecture has been built, the system can try to verify the required properties with or without the help of the designer.

As stated above, we have focused on the architectural level here. As a result, we do not cover the full development cycle. Preliminary work has been done to address the mapping from the architecture level to the protocol level to ensure that a given implementation, expressed as an applied pi-calculus protocol, is consistent with an architecture [35].

As far as the formal approach is concerned, it would also be interesting to study how it could be used in the context of future privacy certification schemes. This would be especially interesting in the context of the future European Data Protection Regulation [11] which promotes not only privacy by design but also privacy seals.

In this paper, we have considered only the verification phase and all databases are static (all users are supposed to be enrolled before any verification step). We leave for future work the integration of dynamic databases. This integration requires the treatment of user revocation, which is an important feature of biometric systems.

We are currently working on other architectures such as biometric systems based on secure multi-party computation (SMC) [32,18] or using *a posteriori* verifications. For example, to reduce the amount of trust placed in the terminal in architecture A_{ed}, the computations of terminal could be sporadically checked following a trust by accountability approach [2]. Last, but not least, the most challenging aspect that is not addressed here is the inherent leakage of the matching result. This potential leakage should be expressed in the dependency relations but this would require the introduction of more sophisticated domains to reason about amounts of information (rather than binary *Has* properties).

Acknowledgements. This work has been partially funded by the French ANR-12-INSE-0013 project BIOPRIV and the European FP7-ICT-2013-1.5 project PRIPARE.

References

1. Abadi, M., Fournet, C.: Mobile values, new names, and secure communication. In: ACM Symposium on Principles of Programming Languages, POPL 2001, pp. 104–115. ACM Press (2001)
2. Antignac, T., Le Métayer, D.: Privacy architectures: Reasoning about data minimisation and integrity. In: Mauw, S., Jensen, C.D. (eds.) STM 2014. LNCS, vol. 8743, pp. 17–32. Springer, Heidelberg (2014)
3. Antignac, T., Le Métayer, D.: Trust driven strategies for privacy by design. In: Damsgaard Jensen, C., Marsh, S., Dimitrakos, T., Murayama, Y. (eds.) IFIPTM 2015. IFIP AICT, vol. 454, pp. 60–75. Springer, Heidelberg (2015)
4. Barth, A., Datta, A., Mitchell, J.C., Nissenbaum, H.: Privacy and contextual integrity: Framework and applications. In: IEEE Symposium on Security and Privacy, S&P 2006, pp. 184–198. IEEE Computer Society (2006)
5. Becker, M.Y., Malkis, A., Bussard, L.: S4P: A generic language for specifying privacy preferences and policies. Technical report, Microsoft Research / IMDEA Software / EMIC (2010)
6. Blanton, M., Gasti, P.: Secure and efficient protocols for iris and fingerprint identification. In: Atluri, V., Diaz, C. (eds.) ESORICS 2011. LNCS, vol. 6879, pp. 190–209. Springer, Heidelberg (2011)
7. Bringer, J., Chabanne, H., Izabachène, M., Pointcheval, D., Tang, Q., Zimmer, S.: An application of the Goldwasser–Micali cryptosystem to biometric authentication. In: Pieprzyk, J., Ghodosi, H., Dawson, E. (eds.) ACISP 2007. LNCS, vol. 4586, pp. 96–106. Springer, Heidelberg (2007)
8. Delaune, S., Kremer, S., Ryan, M.: Verifying privacy-type properties of electronic voting protocols: A taster. In: Chaum, D., Jakobsson, M., Rivest, R.L., Ryan, P.Y.A., Benaloh, J., Kutylowski, M., Adida, B. (eds.) Towards Trustworthy Elections. LNCS, vol. 6000, pp. 289–309. Springer, Heidelberg (2010)
9. Dodis, Y., Reyzin, L., Smith, A.: Fuzzy extractors: How to generate strong keys from biometrics and other noisy data. In: Cachin, C., Camenisch, J.L. (eds.) EUROCRYPT 2004. LNCS, vol. 3027, pp. 523–540. Springer, Heidelberg (2004)
10. Dwork, C.: Differential privacy. In: Bugliesi, M., Preneel, B., Sassone, V., Wegener, I. (eds.) ICALP 2006. LNCS, vol. 4052, pp. 1–12. Springer, Heidelberg (2006)
11. European Parliament. European Parliament legislative resolution of 12 March 2014 on the proposal for a regulation of the European Parliament and of the Council on the protection of individuals with regard to the processing of personal data and on the free movement of such data. General Data Protection Regulation, Ordinary legislative procedure: first reading (2014)
12. Fagin, R., Halpern, J., Moses, Y., Vardi, M.: Reasoning About Knowledge. MIT Press (2004)
13. Fournet, C., Kohlweiss, M., Danezis, G., Luo, Z.: ZQL: A compiler for privacy-preserving data processing. In: USENIX 2013 Security Symposium, pp. 163–178. USENIX Association (2013)
14. Gentry, C.: Fully homomorphic encryption using ideal lattices. In: ACM Symposium on Theory of Computing, STOC 2009, pp. 169–178. ACM Press (2009)

15. Govan, M., Buggy, T.: A computationally efficient fingerprint matching algorithm for implementation on smartcards. In: Biometrics: Theory, Applications, and Systems, BTAS 2007, pp. 1–6. IEEE Computer Society (2007)
16. Gürses, S., Troncoso, C., Díaz, C.: Engineering Privacy by Design. Presented at the Computers, Privacy & Data Protection Conference (2011)
17. Halpern, J.Y., Pucella, R.: Dealing with logical omniscience. In: Conference on Theoretical Aspects of Rationality and Knowledge, TARK 2007, pp. 169–176 (2007)
18. Huang, Y., Malka, L., Evans, D., Katz, J.: Efficient privacy–preserving biometric identification. In: Network and Distributed System Security Symposium, NDSS 2011. The Internet Society (2011)
19. Jain, A.K., Ross, A., Prabhakar, S.: An introduction to biometric recognition. IEEE Trans. Circuits Syst. Video Techn. 14(1), 4–20 (2004)
20. Juels, A., Sudan, M.: A fuzzy vault scheme. Des. Codes Cryptography 38(2), 237–257 (2006)
21. Kanak, A., Sogukpinar, I.: BioPSTM: a formal model for privacy, security, and trust in template-protecting biometric authentication. Security and Communication Networks 7(1), 123–138 (2014)
22. Kerschbaum, F.: Privacy-preserving computation (position paper). In: Preneel, B., Ikonomou, D. (eds.) APF 2012. LNCS, vol. 8319, pp. 41–54. Springer, Heidelberg (2014)
23. Lai, L., Ho, S.-W., Poor, H.V.: Privacy-security trade-offs in biometric security systems – Part I: single use case. IEEE Transactions on Information Forensics and Security 6(1), 122–139 (2011)
24. Lai, L., Ho, S.-W., Poor, H.V.: Privacy-security trade-offs in biometric security systems – Part II: multiple use case. IEEE Transactions on Information Forensics and Security 6(1), 140–151 (2011)
25. Li, H., Pang, L.: A novel biometric–based authentication scheme with privacy protection. In: Conference on Information Assurance and Security, IAS 2009, pp. 295–298. IEEE Computer Society (2009)
26. Maffei, M., Pecina, K., Reinert, M.: Security and privacy by declarative design. In: IEEE Symposium on Computer Security Foundations, CSF 2013, pp. 81–96. IEEE Computer Society (2013)
27. McSherry, F.: Privacy integrated queries: an extensible platform for privacy-preserving data analysis. In: ACM Conference on Management of Data, SIGMOD 2009, pp. 19–30. ACM Press (2009)
28. Le Métayer, D.: Privacy by design: A formal framework for the analysis of architectural choices. In: ACM Conference on Data and Application Security and Privacy, CODASPY 2013, pp. 95–104. ACM Press (2013)
29. Mulligan, D.K., King, J.: Bridging the gap between privacy and design. University of Pennsylvania Journal of Constitutional Law 14, 989–1034 (2012)
30. National Institute of Standards and Technology (NIST). MINEXII – an assessment of Match–On–Card technology (2011), http://www.nist.gov/itl/iad/ig/minexii.cfm
31. International Standard Organization. International standard iso/iec 24787:2010, information technology – identification cards – on-card biometric comparison (2010)
32. Osadchy, M., Pinkas, B., Jarrous, A., Moskovich, B.: SCiFI – A system for secure face identification. In: IEEE Symposium on Security and Privacy, S&P 2010, pp. 239–254. IEEE Computer Society (2010)
33. Pucella, R.: Deductive algorithmic knowledge. J. Log. Comput. 16(2), 287–309 (2006)

34. Spiekermann, S., Cranor, L.F.: Engineering privacy. IEEE Trans. Software Eng. 35(1), 67–82 (2009)
35. Ta, V.-T., Antignac, T.: Privacy by design: On the conformance between protocols and architectures. In: Cuppens, F., Garcia-Alfaro, J., Zincir Heywood, N., Fong, P.W.L. (eds.) FPS 2014. LNCS, vol. 8930, pp. 65–81. Springer, Heidelberg (2015)
36. Tang, Q., Bringer, J., Chabanne, H., Pointcheval, D.: A formal study of the privacy concerns in biometric-based remote authentication schemes. In: Chen, L., Mu, Y., Susilo, W. (eds.) ISPEC 2008. LNCS, vol. 4991, pp. 56–70. Springer, Heidelberg (2008)
37. Troncoso-Pastoriza, J.R., Pérez-González, F.: Fully homomorphic faces. In: International Conference on Image Processing, ICIP 2012, pp. 2657–2660. IEEE Computer Society (2012)
38. Uludag, U., Pankanti, S., Jain, A.K.: Fuzzy vault for fingerprints. In: Kanade, T., Jain, A., Ratha, N.K. (eds.) AVBPA 2005. LNCS, vol. 3546, pp. 310–319. Springer, Heidelberg (2005)

A Specification Language for Static and Runtime Verification of Data and Control Properties

Wolfgang Ahrendt[1(✉)], Jesús Mauricio Chimento[1], Gordon J. Pace[2], and Gerardo Schneider[3]

[1] Chalmers University of Technology, Gothenburg, Sweden
{ahrendt,chimento}@chalmers.se
[2] University of Malta, Msida, Malta
gordon.pace@um.edu.mt
[3] University of Gothenburg, Gothenburg, Sweden
gerardo@cse.gu.se

Abstract. Static verification techniques can verify properties across all executions of a program, but powerful judgements are hard to achieve automatically. In contrast, runtime verification enjoys full automation, but cannot judge future and alternative runs. In this paper we present a novel approach in which data-centric and control-oriented properties may be stated in a single formalism, amenable to both static and dynamic verification techniques. We develop and formalise a specification notation, *ppDATE*, extending the control-flow property language used in the runtime verification tool LARVA with pre/post-conditions and show how specifications written in this notation can be analysed both using the deductive theorem prover KeY and the runtime verification tool LARVA. Verification is performed in two steps: KeY first partially proves the data-oriented part of the specification, simplifying the specification which is then passed on to LARVA to check at runtime for the remaining parts of the specification including the control-centric aspects. We apply the approach to Mondex, an electronic purse application.

1 Introduction

Runtime verification and static verification are widely used verification techniques. *Runtime verification* is concerned with the monitoring of software, providing guarantees that observed executions of a program comply with specified properties. This approach can be used on systems of a complexity that is difficult to address by *static verification* such as systems with numerous interacting sub-units, heavy usage of mainstream libraries, and real world deployments. On the other hand, with runtime verification it is not possible to extrapolate about all possible execution paths. Furthermore, monitoring incurs runtime overheads which may be prohibitive in certain systems.

In this paper we present a way of addressing these issues by combining runtime verification with static verification. We start by statically verifying the

N. Bjørner and F. de Boer (Eds.): FM 2015, LNCS 9109, pp. 108–125, 2015.
DOI: 10.1007/978-3-319-19249-9_8

system against a specification, identifying parts which can either be verified automatically or partially resolved, thus leaving a simpler specification to check at runtime, in turn reducing the overheads induced by monitoring.

As observed, static and dynamic verification have largely disjoint strengths — whereas the former excels in data-oriented properties and struggles to handle complex control-flow logic, the latter handles control-flow properties with substantially lower overheads than data-oriented ones. Combining the two approaches can thus allow the verification process to deal with richer properties with greater ease. However, one of the challenges is to identify a specification notation in which properties which refer to both the data- and control-flow of a system can not only be expressed, but also decomposed to ensure applicability of the different verification techniques. In order to address this issue we have, in a previous paper [3], proposed the StaRVOOrS framework. One key part of that framework was the proposal of a specification notation, called *ppDATE*, and a verification methodology, to specify and verify both *control-oriented* properties and *data-oriented* properties.

Our contributions are: i) A formal definition of *ppDATE* (Sec. 3.3); ii) An algorithm to translate *ppDATE* into *DATE* [10], the formalism used in the runtime verification tool Larva [11] (Sec. 3.4); iii) Application of our approach to Mondex [21], an electronic purse application (Sec 4); iv) A description of the results of the case study including an analysis of the verification process providing evidence that our approach substantially reduces the overhead of the runtime monitoring (Sec. 5).

2 The StaRVOOrS Framework

The StaRVOOrS framework (STAtic and Runtime Verification of Object-ORiented Software), which we originally suggested in [3], combines the use of the deductive source code verifier KeY [7] with that of the runtime monitoring tool Larva [11]. KeY is a deductive verification system for data-centric *functional correctness* properties of Java source code, which generates, from JML and Java, proof obligations in *dynamic logic* (a modal logic for reasoning about programs) and attempts to prove them. Larva (*Logical Automata for Runtime Verification and Analysis*) [11] is an automata-based Runtime Verification tool for Java programs which automatically generates a runtime monitor from a property using an automaton-based specification notation *DATE*. Larva transforms the specification into monitoring code together with AspectJ code to link the system with the monitors.

Fig. 1 gives an abstract view of the framework workflow. Given a Java program P and a specification S of the properties to be verified (given in the language *ppDATE*, see Sec. 3), these are transformed into suitable input for the *Deductive Verifier* module which, in principle, might statically fully verify the properties related to pre/post-conditions. What is not proved statically will then be left to be checked at runtime. Here, not only the completed but also the *partial* proofs are used to generate path conditions for not statically verified executions. The

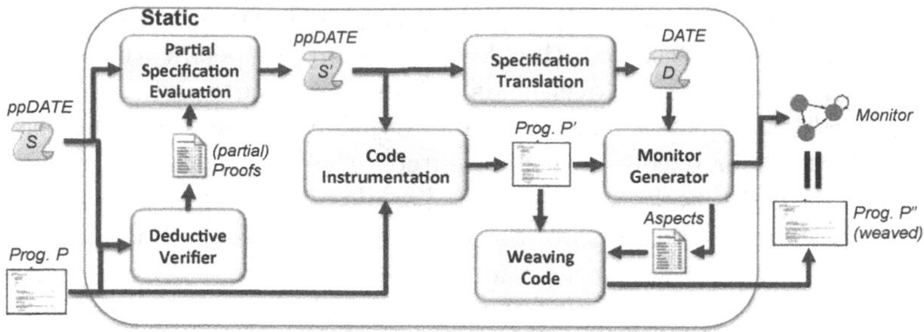

Fig. 1. High-level description of the StaRVOOrS framework workflow

Partial Specification Evaluator module then rewrites the original specification S into S', refining the original pre-conditions with the aforementioned path conditions. Note that S' is no longer a full specification of the desired behaviour. Instead, it only specifies executions that are not covered by the static verification.

In a next step, the resulting *ppDATE* specification S' is, via *Specification Translation*, turned into a specification in *DATE* format (D), suitable for the runtime verifier. As *DATE* has no native support for pre/post-conditions, these are simulated by pure *DATE* concepts (see Sec. 3.4). This also requires changes to the code base (done by the *Code Instrumentation* module), like adding counters to distinguish different executions of the same code unit, or adding methods which operationalise pre/post-condition evaluation. The instrumented program P' and the *DATE* specification D are given to the *Monitor Generator*, which uses aspect-oriented programming techniques to capture relevant system events. Later on, the generated aspects are weaved (*Weaving Code*) into P'. The final step in the workflow is the actual runtime verification, which executes the weaved program P'' — running the original program in parallel with a monitor of the simplified property. In case of a runtime error, a trace is produced to be analysed.

3 *ppDATE*: A Specification Language for Data- and Control-oriented Properties

In general, formalisms for specifying software fall into two very different categories. *Data-oriented* properties may be written in expressive formalisms (like first-order logic), but they only talk about specific points in the execution, rather than traces. One instance of this is the *Java Modelling Language* (JML) [16], which mainly allows for the specification of pre/post-conditions of method calls, and class invariants. Such formalisms are not well suited for specifying legal sequences of events or states. The other category, which we call *control-oriented*, offers great flexibility in specifying legal sequences of events or states, using automata or temporal logics, but supports only simple constraints on data. One instance of this is *Dynamic Automata with Timers and Events* (*DATE*) [10].

In real scenarios, there is often a need to specify both, rich data constraints and legal execution sequences. Still, when formalising such scenarios, traditionally a formalism from either of the two categories is chosen. This leads to *coding* the aspects that are less supported in the respective formalism, like, e.g., coding legal execution traces via model/ghost fields in JML, or coding richer data constraints in *DATE* by extending the code basis with checkers for specific constraints. Even if such codings might be necessary somewhere in the process, we claim that they should not be the duty of the user when formulating properties. Instead, we propose a language which natively supports both types of properties, and let the machinery do necessary codings automatically (as is performed in the modules *Specification Translation* and *Code Instrumentation* in Fig. 1). The language we propose combines features from *DATE* and (very basic) JML, and is called *ppDATE* (*pre*/*post DATE*), which allows to annotate states with Hoare triples. This also enables us to employ two verification tools in the workflow: KeY, which offers static verification of Java source code annotated with JML, and LARVA, which supports runtime verification of *DATE* properties.

3.1 Events

Both *DATE*s and *ppDATE*s use system events to trigger transitions, which typically correspond to the entering or leaving a method or a code block.

Definition 1. *Given an alphabet Σ of named code (typically the union of named functions Φ and named code blocks Λ), we will denote the event marking the entry into $\sigma \in \Sigma$ as $\sigma^{\downarrow}$, and the exit as $\sigma^{\uparrow}$. The set of all such events over alphabet Σ will be written as $\Sigma^{\updownarrow}$.*

For instance, in Java, Φ are methods, and Λ are labelled statements — a singleton statement, whether elementary or structured, can be labelled directly, whereas a sequence of statements, to be named, is put into a labelled block. In addition, we will assume that the system events are indexed by an identifier unique to each execution of a function or block, as in $\sigma^{\downarrow}_{id}$ and $\sigma^{\uparrow}_{id}$. These identifiers can be created automatically using techniques as those presented in [13] or through stack frame references.

3.2 DATE

DATE [10] is an automaton-based control-flow formalism used in LARVA. At their simplest level, *DATE*s are finite state automata, whose transitions are triggered by system events (primarily entry points and exit points of methods) and timers, but augmented with a symbolic state which may be used in conditions guarding transitions and can be modified via actions also specified as part of the transition.

As an example of a *DATE*, consider the automaton depicted in Fig. 2, but ignoring the information given in the states. Transitions are tagged as $e \mid c \mapsto a$, where e is the event which triggers the transition, c is the condition which has to hold when event e happens for the transition to be taken, and a is an action

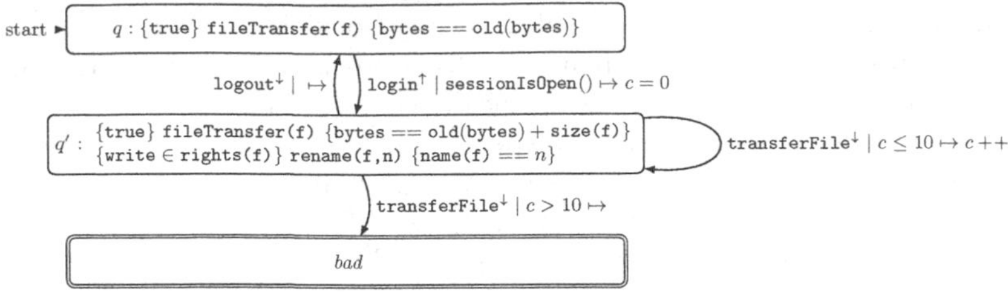

Fig. 2. A *ppDATE* limiting file transfers

to be executed upon taking the transition. Some states (one in the example) are marked as bad states, which indicate that a property violation has taken place when they are reached. The *DATE* component of the property shown (i.e. everything in the diagram except for the information in the states of the automaton) in the example ensures that no more than 10 file transfers take place in a single login session. Note that the specification also uses a new variable as part of the monitor (variable c) which keeps count of the number of files transferred in a single session.

*DATE*s may refer to *valuations* θ of *program variables*. In addition, they also feature another type of variables, called *monitor variables* which do not belong to the program under scrutiny, but instead are local to an automaton, and can be used, for instance, for counting visits to a state (among others). The values of those variables are stored in *valuations* ν of *monitor variables*, and changed only in actions a of transitions. Both actions and conditions in transitions can depend on program variables as well as on monitor variables. Given a condition c, we write $(\theta, \nu) \models c$ to denote that c is satisfied by valuations θ and ν. In the following, Θ denotes the set of all valuations of program variables for a given program under scrutiny.

Definition 2. *A DATE M on a system with program variable valuations over Θ is a tuple $\langle Q, \mathcal{V}, \Sigma, t, B, q_0, \nu_0 \rangle$:*

- *Q is the set of automaton states.*
- *$\mathcal{V}$ is the set of valuations of monitor variables.*
- *Σ is the alphabet, made up of function names Φ and block names Λ.*
- *t is the transition relation among states in Q, where each transition is tagged with (i) the event in $\Sigma^{\updownarrow}$ which will trigger it; (ii) a condition on program and monitor variables; (iii) an action which may change the valuation of monitor variables: $t \subseteq Q \times \Sigma^{\updownarrow} \times \mathcal{P}(\Theta \times \mathcal{V}) \times (\Theta \times \mathcal{V} \longrightarrow \mathcal{V}) \times Q$.*
- *$B \subseteq Q$ is the set of bad states.*
- *$q_0 \in Q$ is the initial state.*
- *$\nu_0 \in \mathcal{V}$ is the initial valuation of monitor variables.*

We will write $q \xrightarrow{e|c \mapsto a}_M q'$ to mean that $(q, e, c, a, q') \in t$. The subscript M is omitted if it is clear from the context. We say that a DATE is deterministic *whenever the following hold: if* $q \xrightarrow{e|c\mapsto a} q'$ *and* $q \xrightarrow{e|c'\mapsto a'} q''$ *and* $q' \neq q''$*, then* c *and* c' *are mutually exclusive, i.e.* $c \cap c' = \emptyset$.

Consider once again, the *DATE* shown in Fig. 2. This can be formalised as follows: $M = \langle Q, \mathcal{V}, \Sigma, t, B, q_0, \nu_0 \rangle$ over program variable valuations Θ, where: $Q = \{q, q', \mathtt{bad}\}$, $\mathcal{V} = \{(c, n) \mid n \in \mathbb{Z}\}$, $\Sigma = \{\mathtt{fileTransfer}, \mathtt{login}, \mathtt{logout}\}$, $B = \{\mathtt{bad}\}$, $q_0 = q$, $\nu_0 = (c, 0)$. Furthermore, the transition relation t consists of four elements, including $q' \xrightarrow{\mathtt{fileTransfer}^{\downarrow}|c\leq 10 \mapsto c{+}{+}} q'$ and $q' \xrightarrow{\mathtt{fileTransfer}^{\downarrow}|c>10 \mapsto \mathtt{skip}} \mathtt{bad}$.

We can now define the semantics of *DATE*s by identifying how a trace generated by the system changes the states of the *DATE*.

Definition 3. *We define that a* trace $w \in (\Sigma^{\updownarrow} \times \Theta)^*$ shifts a monitor from configuration $(q,\nu) \in Q \times \mathcal{V}$ to configuration $(q',\nu') \in Q \times \mathcal{V}$*, written* $(q,\nu) \overset{w}{\Rightarrow} (q',\nu')$*, by induction over* w*:*

$$\begin{aligned}
&(q,\nu) \overset{\varepsilon}{\Rightarrow} (q',\nu') \overset{df}{=} q = q' \wedge \nu = \nu';\\
&(q,\nu) \overset{(e,\theta):w}{\Longrightarrow} (q',\nu') \overset{df}{=} \exists\, q'',\nu'' \cdot \ \exists\, c, a \cdot\\
&\qquad q \xrightarrow{e|c\mapsto a} q'' \wedge ((\theta,\nu) \models c) \wedge \nu'' = a(\theta,\nu) \wedge (q'',\nu'') \overset{w}{\Rightarrow} (q',\nu');\\
&(q,\nu) \overset{(e,\theta):w}{\Longrightarrow} (q',\nu') \overset{df}{=} (q,\nu) \overset{w}{\Rightarrow} (q',\nu') \wedge \nexists\, q'', c, a \cdot q \xrightarrow{e|c\mapsto a} q'' \wedge ((\theta,\nu) \models c).
\end{aligned}$$

Given a DATE M*, a trace* $w \in (\Sigma^{\updownarrow} \times \Theta)^*$ *is said to be a* counter example *if both* $(q_0,\nu_0) \overset{w}{\Rightarrow} (q,\nu)$ *and* $q \in B$.

The set of *violating traces of a DATE* M, written $\mathcal{VT}(M)$ is defined to be traces which have a counter example of M as a prefix.

What we have given here is a subset of the full expressive power of *DATE*s. *DATE*s support further features, including: (i) timers which may be used in the transition conditions or as events to trigger transitions; (ii) communication between *DATE* automata using standard CCS-like channels with $c!$ acting as a broadcast on channel c and which can be read by another automaton matching on event $c?$; and (iii) replication of automata through which every time a particular event in some way distinct from earlier ones (e.g. using a method's parameters or the target object) is received a new automaton is created (e.g. used to replicate a property for each instance of a class). We use the latter two features of *DATE*s when translating *ppDATE*s into *DATE*s. Refer to [10] for the semantics of *DATE*s.

3.3 ppDATE

ppDATE extends *DATE* with elements of data-oriented specification, by assigning (zero or more) Hoare triples to each state. Intuitively, upon entering the code unit $\sigma \in \Sigma$ while in a state which contains a Hoare triple $\{\pi\}\sigma\{\pi'\}$, and given that pre-condition π was satisfied, one should ensure that post-condition π' is satisfied upon exit of σ.

Let us reconsider the property shown in Fig. 2, this time also looking at the information given in the states. Some states are tagged with Hoare triples which should hold when the automaton lies in that state. In addition to ensuring no more than 10 transfers per login session, the Hoare triples also ensure that: (i) the number of bytes transferred increases when a file transfer is done while logged in, (ii) but not when an attempt to transfer a file is done when logged out; and (iii) renaming a file works as expected if the user has the sufficient rights and is logged in.

In *ppDATE*s pre/post-conditions are evaluated over *valuations* θ of *program variables* (defined as for *DATE*s, cf. Sec. 3.2). For instance, $\theta \models \pi$ may or may not hold, where θ is a mapping from program locations like object fields, array fields, and method parameters, to values of the right type.

Definition 4. *A ppDATE (pre/post-condition DATE) M_p on a system with program variable valuations over Θ consist of (i) a DATE $M = \langle Q, \mathcal{V}, \Sigma, t, B, q_0, \nu_0 \rangle$ and (ii) a function τ which tags each state of the automaton with Hoare triples for particular function and block names: $\tau \in Q \longrightarrow \mathcal{P}(\mathcal{P}(Q) \times \Sigma \times \mathcal{P}(Q))$.*

Notation for transitions, and definition of configuration changes over strings of system behaviour are carried over unchanged from *DATE*s. We use the usual Hoare triple notation $\{\pi\}\,\sigma\,\{\pi'\} \in \tau(q)$ to denote $(\pi, \sigma, \pi') \in \tau(q)$. Although determinism on the Hoare triples' preconditions is not problematic in itself, we choose to extend the determinism condition to ensure that for any two Hoare triples in a single state over the same function have disjoint precondition so as to have a more effective monitoring algorithm of these triples: for any $\{\pi_1\}\,\sigma\,\{\pi_1'\}$ and $\{\pi_2\}\,\sigma\,\{\pi_2'\}$ in $\tau(q)$, $\pi_1 \cap \pi_2 = \emptyset$.

To formalise the *ppDATE* shown in Fig. 2 we use the *DATE* defined earlier, and add a function τ mapping states to sets of Hoare triples, such as:

$$\begin{aligned}\tau(q') = \{\ &\{\texttt{true}\}\ \texttt{fileTransfer(f)}\ \{\texttt{bytes} == \texttt{old(bytes)} + \texttt{size(f)}\},\\ &\{\texttt{write} \in \texttt{rights(f)}\}\ \texttt{rename(f,n)}\ \{\texttt{name(f)} == \texttt{n}\} \quad \}\end{aligned}$$

We can now define the semantics of *ppDATE*s by extending the notion of counter-examples to include violations of postconditions.

Definition 5. *Given a ppDATE $M_p = \langle M, \tau \rangle$, a trace $w \in (\Sigma^{\updownarrow} \times \Theta)^*$ is said to be a* counter example *if either (i) w is a counter example of M; or (ii) w can be decomposed into four parts $w = w_1 +\!\!+ \langle(\sigma_{id}^{\downarrow}, \theta_1)\rangle +\!\!+ w_2 +\!\!+ \langle(\sigma_{id}^{\uparrow}, \theta_2)\rangle$ such that the following conditions hold:*

(a) Trace w_1 takes M from the initial configuration to some configuration (q, ν): $(q_0, \nu_0) \stackrel{w_1}{\Longrightarrow} (q, \nu)$;
(b) There is a Hoare triple of σ enforced in state q: $\{\pi\}\,\sigma\,\{\pi'\} \in \tau(q)$;
(c) Valuation θ_1 satisfies the precondition: $\theta_1 \models \pi$;
(d) Valuation θ_2 does not satisfy the postcondition: $\theta_2 \not\models \pi'$.

Recall that each event in a trace is annotated with an identifier, unique per entry-exit pair — therefore, the $\sigma_{id}^{\downarrow}$ and $\sigma_{id}^{\uparrow}$ appearing in the trace (i) match the method named σ in the Hoare triples; and (ii) ensures (by construction of the identifiers) that v_{id} does not appear in w_2.

As before, the set of *violating traces of a ppDATE* M_p, written $\mathcal{VT}(M_P)$ is defined to be traces which have a counter example of M_P as a prefix.

Note that Definition 5 allows for the inclusion of events corresponding to calls to the methods specified in the states (part of the Hoare triples). This is natural as concrete traces in *ppDATE*s do not necessarily coincide with "paths" of the DATE component of the *ppDATE*. For instance, in Fig. 2 a call to `rename(·)` when in state q' is a valid one and a corresponding event $\texttt{rename}^{\downarrow}$ will be present in the trace of the *ppDATE*.

3.4 Translation from *ppDATE* to *DATE*

In our architecture, KeY first tries to prove all data-oriented parts of a *ppDATE* S, and the partial proofs are used to get an optimised *ppDATE* S'. To make the property S' runtime-checkable, we further translate away the (remaining/optimised) Hoare triples, to arrive at a set of parallel[1], pure *DATE*s D that can be processed by LARVA. One complication in the translation is the possibility that a Hoare triple in a state may 'clash' with an outgoing event. This would for instance be the case if we added to Fig. 2 a transition from q to q' with $\texttt{fileTransfer}^{\downarrow}$ as a triggering event. For clarity of presentation we give two algorithms, one for the case when no such clashes arise, and then for the full case. Formally, we define a clashing Hoare triple as follows.

Definition 6. *Given a ppDATE* $M_p = \langle M, \tau \rangle$ *with* $M = \langle Q, \mathcal{V}, \Sigma, t, q_0, \nu_0 \rangle$, *a Hoare triple* $\{\pi\}\,\sigma\,\{\pi'\} \in \tau(q)$, *for some* $q \in Q$, *is called* clashing *if an outgoing transition from* q *is guarded by event* $\sigma^{\downarrow}$ *(i.e.,* $\exists\ c, a, q' \ \cdot\ q \xrightarrow{\sigma^{\downarrow}|c \mapsto a} q'$*). A* clash-free *ppDATE is a ppDATE with no clashing Hoare triple.*

We now present the algorithm to translate a clash-free *ppDATE* into *DATE*s. The translation works by replacing each Hoare triple $\{\pi\}\,\sigma\,\{\pi'\}$ in a state q by a new reflexive transition (from q to q) triggered by an entry into function σ such that the precondition π holds, and sending a message which is used to replicate a parallel post-condition checking *DATE* automaton.

Algorithm 1 *Given a* clash-free *ppDATE* $M_p = \langle M, \tau \rangle$, *we can construct a set of parallel DATEs equivalent to* M_p *in the following manner:*

1. *Give each Hoare triple in* M_p *a unique name* h, *to be interpreted as a channel name in the DATEs to be constructed.*
2. *For each Hoare triple* h, *construct a replicated DATE automaton* M_h *(called* the post-condition checker*), parameterised over identifier id, as shown below[2]:*

[1] Multiple, parallel *DATE*s define behaviour of a sequential application in the sense that each event in the application may trigger transitions in a number of *DATE*s. In addition, the *DATE*s can synchronise with each other by means of channels.

[2] Following the semantics of *DATE*s, whenever a message is received on channel h with a new identifier, this automaton is replicated and the first transition is taken.

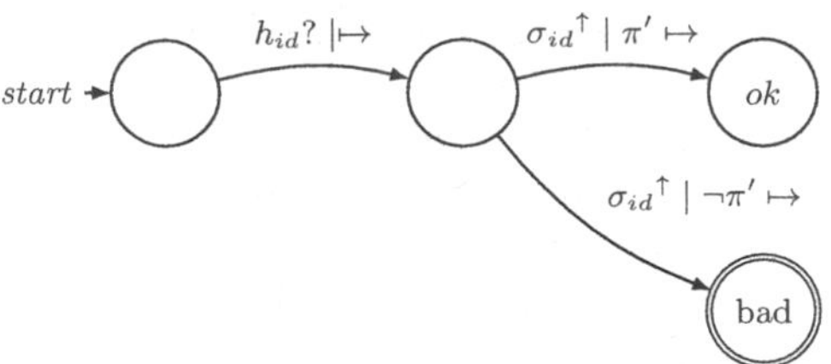

3. *Turn M, the DATE component of M_p, into the DATE M' such that, for each Hoare triple $\{\pi\}\,\sigma\,\{\pi'\}$ named h in $\tau(q)$ is replaced by a transition $q \xrightarrow{\sigma_{id}{}^{\downarrow} \mid \pi \mapsto h_{id}!}_{M'} q$.*
4. *The resulting set of parallel DATEs is defined to be: $\{M'\} \cup \{M_h \mid h$ is a Hoare triple identifier from $M\}$.*

This translation works well except that it would introduce non-determinism when the *ppDATE* includes clashes. To extend the translation to work in the presence of clashes, we transform Hoare triples clashing with a transition into a family of disjoint transitions each of which performs the transition but also checks whether the post-condition checker should be triggered.

Algorithm 2 *Given a general ppDATE M_p, we can construct a set of parallel DATEs equivalent to M_p by following Algorithm 1 except that we replace Step 3., by the following rule:*

3a. Each non-clashing Hoare triple h: $\{\pi\}\,\sigma\,\{\pi'\}$ in $\tau(q)$ is turned into a transition $q \xrightarrow{\sigma_{id}{}^{\downarrow} \mid \pi \mapsto h_{id}!}_{M'} q$.

3b. For each clashing Hoare triple h: $\{\pi\}\,\sigma\,\{\pi'\} \in \tau(q)$, clashing with n outgoing transitions, $q \xrightarrow{\sigma^{\downarrow} \mid c_i \mapsto a_i} q_i$ $(0 \leq i < n)$:
- *Replace $q \xrightarrow{\sigma^{\downarrow} \mid c_i \mapsto a_i}_{M} q_i$ with $q \xrightarrow{\sigma_{id}{}^{\downarrow} \mid c_i \mapsto \{a_i;\ if\, \pi\ \mathbf{then}\, h_{id}!\}}_{M'} q_i$;*
- *Add the following transition $q \xrightarrow{\sigma_{id}{}^{\downarrow} \mid (\neg c_0 \wedge \ldots \wedge \neg c_n \wedge \pi) \mapsto h_{id}!}_{M'} q$.*

4 Case Study: Mondex

Mondex is an electronic purse application used by smart cards products [1], and it has been used as a benchmark problem within the Verified Software Grand Challenge context [21]. Mondex's original sanitised specification written in Z, together with hand-written proofs of different properties, can be found in [17]. Our variant is strongly inspired by a JML formalisation given in [19]. However, *ppDATE* has native (automata) states, unlike Z or JML. This allowed us to naturally represent the overall status of the observed system by states (see the nodes of the graph in Fig. 3), instead of representing the status by additional data like in Z or JML.

Mondex essentially provides a financial transaction system supporting transferring of funds between accounts, or 'purses'. We focus on analysing the transactions taking place between these purses, which follow a multi-step message exchange protocol: whenever a transaction between two purses is to take place, (i) the source and destination purses should (independently) register with the central fund transferring manager; (ii) then a request to deduct funds from the source purse may arrive, followed by (iii) a request to add the funds to the destination purse; and (iv) finally, there should be an acknowledgement that the transfer took place, before the transaction ends.

The original version of Mondex works on Java Card, and all controls in relation to security properties have to be handled on the card, rather than being monitored on an external source. In our case study, we have verified a version of the protocol which works using a server, rather than a smart card. The only principal difference in the protocol implementation is that the server version uses return values to control the protocol rather than raising Java Card exceptions. The full specification and code of the case study can be found in [2]. The specification consists on a *ppDATE* automaton with 10 states, 25 transitions and a total of 26 different Hoare triples. The implementation consists on 514 lines of code (without comments) which are distributed over 8 files.

4.1 *ppDATE* Property

As typical in transaction-based systems, the Mondex case study illustrates how complexity can arise from accessing different purses concurrently and in a manner not predicted by the system developer. Specifications of such systems have to reflect this emerging complexity and include (i) constraints as to the control flow of the system — the order in which different components are accessed; and (ii) constraints on how these components behave when accessed both when access is expected and when it is not. Our formalism, *ppDATE*, addresses both these orthogonal issues in a structured manner.

The top-level specification of the Mondex purse-management systems can be found in Fig. 3. For space reasons, the Hoare triples populating the states are not depicted in this figure, but instead, we will show them for specific states further on. At the automaton level, the *ppDATE* (which we will call S) expresses the protocol governing how the purses are to be accessed, by specifying the order in which the components (in this case methods used to access the purses) can be called. For instance, after the parties are initialised (encoded in S's state named Parties Initialised), a request to deduct more money than what is found in the source purse should fail, while a request to deduct an amount of money which is available should take us to a state (named Money deducted) in which the protocol now allows for the money to be transferred to the destination purse. The ordering is crucial and appears in practically all financial transaction systems so as to ensure that no money will be created at any point in the transaction. Similarly, access to any unregistered purse takes us to a bad state[3] since the system should never allow these methods to be accessed. Notice that comparing

[3] These transitions are not drawn in the diagram (but are mentioned in the note underneath) so as to avoid confusion. Note that LARVA will not take any explicit action when reaching a bad state: the corresponding automaton will stay in that

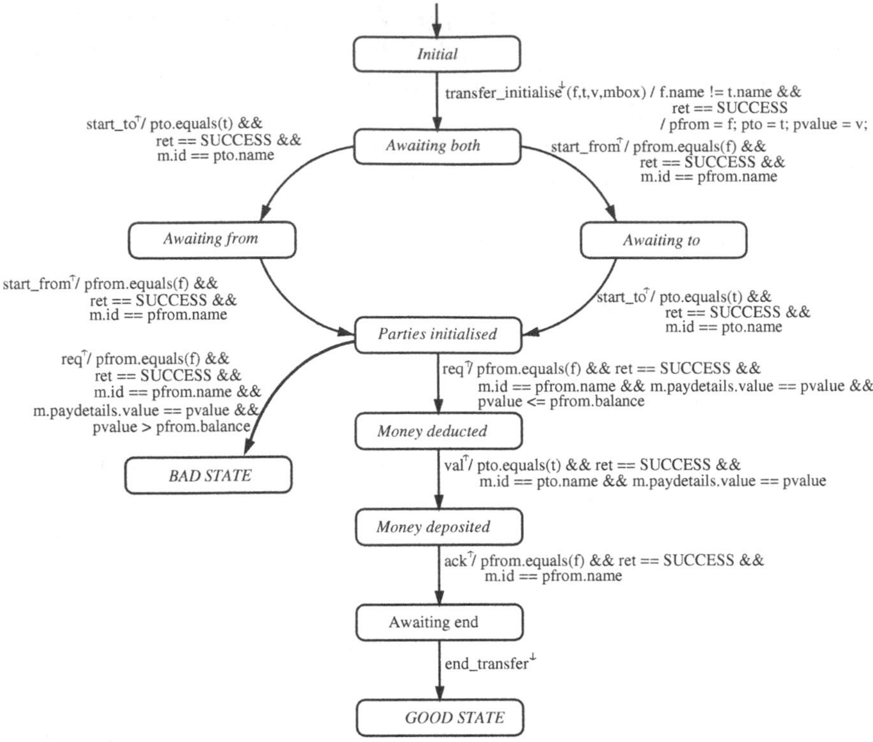

Fig. 3. *ppDATE* to monitor the behaviour of the transaction protocol

`m.paydetails.value` and `pvalue` is needed in order to check that the message received is part of the ongoing transaction.

Over and above the specification of the protocol, one has to specify the behaviour of the involved methods, which obviously changes together with the status of the protocol. For instance, transfer of funds from a purse to another should succeed once both purses have been registered, but should fail if attempted before registration or if an attempt is made to perform the transfer multiple times. This behaviour is encoded by different Hoare triples assigned to different S states. For instance, just after the registration of two purses (in S's state Parties initialised), the method `val_operation` which requests money from

state until the whole monitor is restarted (unless it is explicitly specified on the monitor what action to take when reaching a bad state). A log is kept indicating this.

the source purse should succeed and deduct the money from the purse (provided enough money is available) as shown in the Hoare triple[4] below:

```
{ checkSameTransaction() == SUCCESS
  && transaction.value <= (ShortMaxValue - balance); }
val_operation
{ \result == SUCCESS
  && (balance == \old(balance) + transaction.value); }
```

On the other hand, if the same method is accessed after the funds have already been deducted (S's state Money deducted) then the purse content should remain unchanged, and the request should be ignored:

```
{ checkSameTransaction() == SUCCESS
  && transaction.value <= (ShortMaxValue - balance); }
val_operation
{ \result == IGNORED; }
```

Note that both Hoare triples above have the same pre-condition, but the different *ppDATE* states they belong to demand different behaviour (i.e., post-conditions) of `val_operation`.

The control-oriented properties basically ensure that the message exchange goes as expected. In contrast, the pre/post-conditions (in total, there are 26 Hoare triples in the states of the *ppDATE*) ensure the well-behaviour of the individual steps.

4.2 Combined Static and Runtime Verification

Following the verification approach from Fig. 1, we start by extracting the Hoare triples from the *ppDATE* which are translated to JML annotations in the source code. KeY then generates corresponding proof obligations in dynamic logic and starts a proof attempt. Note that, in this work, we use KeY only fully automatically, not using its rich support for interactive theorem proving, neither assuming user provided proof-hinting annotations (like loop invariants).

When trying to prove these formulae, KeY creates proof branches corresponding to case distinctions in the code. Usually, KeY manages to automatically close the proofs of the simpler branches, but may not (automatically) close more difficult branches. Still, the open goals contain path conditions, i.e., conditions on the valuation of program variables *before* the method was entered. We use this information to refine the pre-condition to the cases where KeY cannot close the proof.

For instance, consider the part of the specification already discussed in the previous section — the JML pre/post-condition from the the state Parties initialised, when a request for a money transfer is received:

```
requires checkSameTransaction() == SUCCESS
         && transaction.value <= (ShortMaxValue - balance);
ensures \result == SUCCESS
```

[4] In the pre- and post-conditions, we use basic JML expression syntax [16].

```
        && (balance == \old(balance) + transaction.value);
```

The code (and consequently KeY) branches on the status of the transaction, and one of the branches, when the transaction is not awaiting a money deduction request, is closed successfully. The other branch is left open. From the open goal, we can read off the path condition `status == ProtocolStatus.Epv` (i.e. the receiver purse is expecting to receive the requested value). Only if this condition holds upon entry of `val_operation`, the post-condition will need to be checked at runtime. All other cases are proved correct statically, by KeY. Before generating the runtime monitor, we therefore refine the corresponding Hoare triple in *ppDATE* to include this path condition:

```
{ checkSameTransaction() == SUCCESS
  && transaction.value <= (ShortMaxValue - balance)
  && status == ProtocolStatus.Epv; }
val_operation
{ \result == SUCCESS
        && (balance == \old(balance) + transaction.value); }
```

In our case study, except for two Hoare triples related to the initialisation and termination of a transaction which were fully proven by KeY, all the other 24 triples were refined in this manner.

The resulting *ppDATE* specification can now be transformed into an equivalent *DATE*, and the runtime verification tool LARVA is used to monitor the system for possible violations.

The implementation of Mondex we describe in this section has been fully verified with our technique, albeit in an iterative manner since verification revealed some errors we made in our original implementation of Mondex (see next section).

5 Experimentation

Here, we summarise the experimental results of applying our approach to the Mondex case study. In particular, we compare execution times of (a) the unmonitored implementation, (b) the monitored implementation using the original specification S, and (c) the monitored implementation using specification S', obtained from S via static (partial) proof analysis. The table below shows the average execution time, on a PC Intel Core i7 using a single core, for these three scenarios when the system is ran performing different numbers of transactions. Statically analysing all the Hoare triples took KeY around 2.15 minutes. However, the real gain is that this analysis is done once and for all prior to deployment, and the gains reported in the table below improves performance for all executions once the system is deployed.

Transactions	(a) no monitoring	(b) monitoring S	(c) monitoring S'
10	8 ms	120 ms	15 ms
100	50 ms	3500 ms	90 ms
1000	250 ms	330000 ms	375 ms

As expected, adding a monitor caused overhead on the execution time (b). However, this overhead is substantially reduced by using our approach (c). The relative difference is quite remarkable: at least 10 times faster for low number of transactions, and increasing up to 900 times faster as the number of transactions increases. This large reduction in execution time overheads when optimising the monitor is primarily due to the fact that data-oriented monitoring can be prohibitively expensive in the first place. In fact, using our approach, each function with a satisfied precondition fires an additional automaton being traversed in parallel. This results in the large overheads in the case study. However, by pruning away many of these checks through the typical case of a strengthening of the precondition results in the gains we obtain. This indicates that using static analysis to pare down the data-oriented aspect of the properties is ideal in this situation, in that we are attacking directly the overlap between a strength of static analysis and a weakness of dynamic analysis.

Note that it is usually impossible to get a full proof when using a static verifier like KeY in the simple way we do, i.e., without user interaction, and without poof supporting annotations (like loop invariants). But the missing proving power is only one aspect. The other is that branches may be open because the corresponding execution path is actually erroneous. KeY cannot *per se* distinguish these two cases, but LARVA can detect the erroneous case when it appears at runtime. Note that the above table does not say anything about errors revealed by applying our approach to the case study. It only shows execution times of the various scenarios *after* errors were revealed and removed. However, finding errors is the one of the most important purposes of verification, so we briefly discuss some errors in the following.

In our variant of Mondex, in order to scale the transaction count, several purses are iteratively generated, using the index for the name of the purse created in each iteration. Executing the application with the monitor generated by StaRVOOrS led to a runtime failure. Inspecting the monitor-generated (failing) execution trace allowed us to spot the problem. Originally, the index of the loop was initialised with 0, but the names of the purses were assumed to be greater than 0. This lead to a purse with an invalid name, causing a failure which was detected by StaRVOOrS.

We have also intentionally injected errors into the Mondex case study, to test whether the approach would detect them. All of them were successfully detected with StaRVOOrS. We have also considered incomplete or wrong specifications. This can mean very different things. In a case where the specification is too weak, such that the implementation fulfils it for wrong reasons, we may not catch that. This is a common issue for practically all verification approaches. At least, in our approach of combined data- and control-oriented verification, we have some chance that a problem propagates to a state where the specification is strong enough to catch it. If on the other hand a Hoare triple accidentally puts wrong demands on the implementation, KeY will naturally not be able to prove it. Thereby, the StaRVOOrS methodology ensures that the property is checked at runtime. Even there, verification will fail (if only that part is executed), but this time, we get a failing trace. Analysing it will show that, actually, the computation was fine, suggesting that the specification was wrong in the first place. For example, the post-condition used for static analysis (see Sec. 4.2) of the method initialising the sender purse during a transaction used a wrong variable, and KeY was not able to prove it. At runtime, the replicated automaton checking the post-condition shifted to a bad state, even if the computation lead to the expected results, allowing us to spot, and correct, the failing post-condition.

6 Related Work

The combination of different verification techniques is gaining more and more popularity. One active area of research is the combination of static analysis and testing, e.g. [4,9,12,14,15,18]. A direct comparison of our work with those would not be fully fair as we have different objectives. We are not aiming at generating test cases, but at monitoring the actual post-deployment runs of the system. What we have in common is that static analysis/verification is used to limit the dynamic efforts, there by filtering test cases, here by filtering checks at runtime.

A different line of research is the combination of testing and runtime verification, as done by Falzon and Pace in [13] where QuickCheck and LARVA are combined. Similar to *ppDATE*s, QuickCheck automata employ pre-postconditions but as part of the transitions as opposed to the states as used in *ppDATE*s.

The work by Wonisch *et al.* in [20] is concerned with the use of program transformation to avoid unsafe program executions. Their main objective is the optimisation of runtime monitoring by using static analysis (rather than full-blown static *verification*) techniques.

In [8] static analysis is used to improve the performance of runtime monitoring based on tracematches. The paper presents a static analysis technique to speed up trace matching by reducing the runtime instrumentation needed. The static analysis part is based on three stages: ruling out some tracematches, eliminating inconsistent instrumentation points, and finally further refinement of the analysis taking into account execution order.

In [22], Zee *et al.* explore the combination of static and runtime verification, aiming at a specification language whose specifications can be both statically analysed and runtime checked. They extend the static verifier Jahob with techniques to verify specifications at runtime, and can execute specifications using quantifiers, set comprehensions, integer and object expressions amongst other constructs. Most of the properties they can verify are data-centric, whereas we also cover control-centric properties. We could benefit from incorporating some of their solutions for complex data structures in our approach.

Several specification approaches, like SPARK [5], JML and SPEC# [6] are supported by both static and runtime verification tools. However, to the best of our knowledge, static verification is not used for optimising runtime verification.

7 Conclusions

In this paper we have presented the StaRVOOrS framework combining (partial) static and (optimised) runtime verification. As a first step, we have instantiated our approach with the tools KeY and Larva. We have presented and formalised a notation, *ppDATE*, which allows us to arbitrarily combine control-oriented (based on automata with event-triggered transitions) and data-oriented (relating final and initial data values) properties in a single formalism, and thereby to describe a larger variety of applications. An additional interesting aspect of this combination is that data-oriented properties formulated in a pre/post style can be made dependent on the history of previous events.

To illustrate how this framework works, we have applied it to a variant of the Mondex case study [19,21]. In this case study, we analyse the behaviour of the transaction protocol for transferring money between electronic purses, and we demonstrate how this protocol can be partly statically, partly dynamically verified using our framework. Apart from this case study, we have also applied our framework on a different case study — a simple system, in which users may login and perform different operations (see [2] for the sources of this case study).

The difference in performance between the fully monitored and the version with simplified monitors is, in itself, motivation to look further into how we can extend our approach. The huge gains are primarily a side-effect of the large costs of data-oriented property monitoring, meaning that any reduction in the magnitude of the monitored properties can lead to large reductions in overheads. Our approach may thus be a way of dealing with this class of properties which one typically shies away from monitoring due to the large overheads involved.

The exact gain of optimising runtime monitoring by static results will vary depending on the application, but in our approach, it will be substantial whenever there are enough paths through the computation which are simple enough for automated (static) verification, and yet appear frequently during runtime, which arguably is common in many applications. In addition, we want to highlight that the combination of static and runtime verification does not only speed up the execution time of a monitored system, but moreover increases confidence, as parts of the system are proved to be correct once and for all.

Both, the efficiency gain for monitoring and the confidence gain, will only increase along with future improvements in the used static verifier. For instance, if ongoing work on loop invariant generation in KeY will lead to closing some more branches in typical proofs, then this will have an immediate effect that is proportional to the frequency of executing those loops at runtime.

We are currently proving the soundness of the transformation of *ppDATE*s to *DATE*s, and automating the verification process to use KeY and Larva with *ppDATE*s. Finally, an interesting question is whether static verification could be used to (partially) prove the control-oriented part of *ppDATE*s. This is an open question left for future work.

Acknowledgements. We would like to thank Christian Colombo and Martin Henschel for their support concerning implementation issues about Larva and KeY respectively.

We also thank the anonymous reviewers for their valuable comments to improve the presentation of the paper.

References

1. MasterCard International Inc. Mondex, http://www.mondexusa.com/
2. StaRVOOrS, http://www.cse.chalmers.se/~chimento/starvoors/files.html
3. Ahrendt, W., Pace, G., Schneider, G.: A Unified Approach for Static and Runtime Verification: Framework and Applications. In: Margaria, T., Steffen, B. (eds.) ISoLA 2012, Part I. LNCS, vol. 7609, pp. 312–326. Springer, Heidelberg (2012)
4. Artho, C., Biere, A.: Combined static and dynamic analysis. In: AIOOL 2005. ENTCS, vol. 131, pp. 3–14 (2005)
5. Barnes, J.: SPARK: The Proven Approach to High Integrity Software. Altran Praxis, UK (2012), http://www.altran.co.uk
6. Barnett, M., Leino, K.R.M., Schulte, W.: The Spec# programming system: An overview. In: Barthe, G., Burdy, L., Huisman, M., Lanet, J.-L., Muntean, T. (eds.) CASSIS 2004. LNCS, vol. 3362, pp. 49–69. Springer, Heidelberg (2005)
7. Beckert, B., Hähnle, R., Schmitt, P.H. (eds.): Verification of Object-Oriented Software. LNCS, vol. 4334. Springer, Heidelberg (2007)
8. Bodden, E., Hendren, L., Lhoták, O.: A staged static program analysis to improve the performance of runtime monitoring. In: Ernst, E. (ed.) ECOOP 2007. LNCS, vol. 4609, pp. 525–549. Springer, Heidelberg (2007)
9. Christakis, M., Müller, P., Wüstholz, V.: Collaborative verification and testing with explicit assumptions. In: Proceedings of the FM2012: Formal Methods - 18th International Symposium, Paris, France, August 27-31, pp. 132–146 (2012)
10. Colombo, C., Pace, G.J., Schneider, G.: Dynamic Event-Based Runtime Monitoring of Real-Time and Contextual Properties. In: Cofer, D., Fantechi, A. (eds.) FMICS 2008. LNCS, vol. 5596, pp. 135–149. Springer, Heidelberg (2009)
11. Colombo, C., Pace, G.J., Schneider, G.: LARVA - A Tool for Runtime Monitoring of Java Programs. In: SEFM 2009, pp. 33–37. IEEE Computer Society (2009)
12. Csallner, C., Smaragdakis, Y.: Check 'n' crash: combining static checking and testing. In: 27th International Conference on Software Engineering, ICSE 2005, May 15-21, St. Louis, Missouri, USA, pp. 422–431 (2005)
13. Falzon, K., Pace, G.: Combining testing and runtime verification techniques. In: Machado, R.J., Maciel, R.S.P., Rubin, J., Botterweck, G. (eds.) MOMPES 2012. LNCS, vol. 7706, pp. 38–57. Springer, Heidelberg (2013)
14. Flanagan, C., Leino, K.R.M., Lillibridge, M., Nelson, G., Saxe, J.B., Stata, R.: Extended Static Checking for Java. In: Knoop, J., Hendren, L.J. (eds.) PLDI 2002, pp. 234–245. ACM (2002)
15. Ge, X., Taneja, K., Xie, T., Tillmann, N.: Dyta: dynamic symbolic execution guided with static verification results. In: Proceedings of the 33rd International Conference on Software Engineering, ICSE 2011, Waikiki, Honolulu, HI, USA, May 21-28, pp. 992–994 (2011)
16. Leavens, G.T., Poll, E., Clifton, C., Cheon, Y., Ruby, C., Cok, D., Müller, P., Kiniry, J., Chalin, P.: JML Reference Manual. Draft 1.200 (2007)
17. Stepney, S., Cooper, D., Woodcock, J.: An Electronic Purse: Specification, Refinement and Proof. Technical monograph PRG-126, Oxford University Computing Laboratory (2000)
18. Tillmann, N., de Halleux, J.: Pex-White Box Test Generation for.NET.. In: Beckert, B. (ed.) TAP. LNCS, vol. 4966, pp. 134–153. Springer, Heidelberg (2008)

19. Tonin, I.: Verifying the Mondex case study. The KeY approach. Technical Report 2007-4, Universität Karlsruhe (2007)
20. Wonisch, D., Schremmer, A., Wehrheim, H.: Zero Overhead Runtime Monitoring. In: Hierons, R.M., Merayo, M.G., Bravetti, M. (eds.) SEFM 2013. LNCS, vol. 8137, pp. 244–258. Springer, Heidelberg (2013)
21. Woodcock, J.: First Steps in the Verified Software Grand Challenge. In: SEW 2006, pp. 203–206. IEEE Computer Society (2006)
22. Zee, K., Kuncak, V., Taylor, M., Rinard, M.C.: Runtime Checking for Program Verification.. In: Sokolsky, O., Taşıran, S. (eds.) RV 2007. LNCS, vol. 4839, pp. 202–213. Springer, Heidelberg (2007)

Certificates for Parameterized Model Checking

Sylvain Conchon[1,2], Alain Mebsout[2,3], and Fatiha Zaïdi[1](✉)

[1] LRI, Université Paris-Sud, CNRS, F-91405, Orsay, France
fatiha.zaidi@lri.fr
[2] INRIA Saclay – Île-de-France, F-91893, Orsay cedex, France
[3] The University of Iowa, Iowa City, IA, United States

Abstract. This paper presents a technique for the certification of Cubicle, a model checker for proving safety properties of parameterized systems. To increase the confidence in its results, Cubicle now produces a proof object (or certificate) that, if proven valid, guarantees that the answer for this specific input is correct. The main challenges addressed in this paper are (1) the production of such certificates without degrading the performances of the model checker and (2) the construction of these proof objects so that they can be independently and efficiently verified by an SMT solver. Since the burden of correctness insurance now relies on this external solver, a stronger guarantee is obtained by the use of multiple backend automatic provers for redundancy. Experiments show that our approach does not impact Cubicle's performances and that we were able to verify certificates for challenging parameterized problems. As a byproduct, these certificates allowed us to find subtle and critical implementation bugs in Cubicle.

1 Introduction

Multi-core architectures or distributed systems usually rely on protocols (such as mutual exclusion, cache coherence or fault-tolerance) which are designed for an arbitrary number of components. These protocols are critical and known as being notoriously difficult to design essentially because of their highly asynchronous and fine-grained concurrent nature. As a result, their validation by simulation is risky because some race conditions appear scarcely and are unlikely to be reproduced. Consequently, the formal verification of these protocols is a necessity.

One of the most successful formal technique for verifying concurrent systems is model checking which automatically determines if a model, usually described by a transition system, meets a specification expressed as temporal properties. When the model is defined independently of the number of components, its verification is known as the *parameterized model checking problem.*

Being parameterized or not, the answer produced by a model checker is usually simply "yes" or "no". When the result is negative, a counterexample (in the form of a sequence of transitions) can also be easily returned (and checked by the user). On the contrary, model checkers rarely return a proof evidence for a positive answer. So, should we trust a model checker when it simply returns "yes"? From our experience, given the high complexity of the implementation of these tools, the answer is clearly no.

N. Bjørner and F. de Boer (Eds.): FM 2015, LNCS 9109, pp. 126–142, 2015.
DOI: 10.1007/978-3-319-19249-9_9

To be sure of the correctness of these answers, we can either use a certified model checker [12] or a model checker that produces in addition a proof of its result, also called a *certificate* [21]. The advantage of the first approach is that the model checker is verified correct once and for all. However, this is a very heavy task since model checkers are profoundly optimized programs with a large number of components. In the second approach, certificates have to be checked after each run. Its advantage is to be far less intrusive, the only necessity is to instrument an already existing model checker. However, this approach is only applicable if certificates or proof objects are small and simple enough to be checked in a reasonable time after the fact.

The aim of this work is to bring a higher level of confidence in the results produced by Cubicle [6], an SMT-based model checker for proving safety properties of parameterized systems[1]. Cubicle represents states as logical formulas (expressed in a fragment of first-order logic) and checks that unsafe states are not reachable using a backward analysis. In that framework, it is far simpler to produce and check a certificate than to certify the model checker itself. Indeed, Cubicle is a very complex piece of software combining higher order functional programming style with efficient imperative data structures and concurrency. As far as we know, there are no framework for certifying such a program as is. Furthermore, we demonstrate through a set of experiments that checking proof objects can be done efficiently, even for industrial size protocols.

The content of the paper, our contributions and the originality of our approach are as follows:

- Extract an inductive invariant ϕ from the backward reachability loop and generate proof obligations (POs) whose validity guarantees that ϕ is an inductive invariant subsuming the original safety property (Section 3). These POs are first order formulas which are sent to an automatic theorem prover (Section 4).
- A set of algorithmic techniques to enrich and simplify the certificates in order to handle more complex and larger problems (Section 5). A stronger guarantee on the certification process is achieved by redundancy: each PO is independently proven by several tools (SMT solvers, automatic theorem provers, *etc.*).

We illustrate the general approach with a running example: a simple cache coherence protocol. We show the merit of our approach in Section 5.2 through a set of benchmarks for which the certification process is conducted entirely automatically. These notably include two industrial parameterized cache coherence protocols: FLASH and a new protocol developed at Intel and Duke.

Last but not least, the certificates allowed us to find several bugs in Cubicle whose severity can be classified as harmless to critical with a direct impact on its correctness. Some of these bugs have been found by testing but others have escaped all traditional debugging techniques because they only appear very rarely and are related to tricky implementation details.

[1] Developed conjointly between Université Paris-Sud and Intel.

2 Array Based Transition Systems

Cubicle is based on the theoretical foundation of *Model Checking Modulo Theories* (MCMT) [14] by Ghilardi and Ranise. This is a declarative framework for parameterized systems in which transitions and properties are expressed in a particular fragment of first order logic. Systems expressible in this framework are called array based transition systems because their state can be seen as a set of unbounded arrays whose indexes range over elements of the parameterized domain.

Definition 1. *An* array based transition system *is a tuple* $\mathcal{S} = (Q, I, \tau)$ *where* Q *is a set of function symbols (also called arrays) representing the state variables,* I *is a formula which characterizes the* initial states *of the system (in which variables of* Q *can appear free) and* τ *is a transition relation.*

In the following, the formula I is universally quantified. The relation τ is expressed in the form of a disjunction of existentially quantified (by zero, one, or several variables of the parameterized domain) formulas. Each component of this disjunction is called a transition and is said to be parameterized by its existential variables. Following usual notations, we note x' the value of $x \in Q$ after executing the transition. Transitions relate values of primed and un-primed variables and arrays, and are of the form:

$$t(Q, Q') \equiv \exists \bar{i}.\ \underbrace{\gamma(\bar{i}, Q)}_{\text{guard}} \wedge \underbrace{\bigwedge_{x \in Q} \forall \bar{j}.x'(\bar{j}) = \delta_x(\bar{i}, \bar{j}, Q)}_{\text{action}}$$

where γ is a quantifier free formula called the *guard* of t and δ_x is a quantifier free formula called the *update* of x.

Safety properties are expressed by characterizing unsafe states. An unsafe formula must be in a special form called a *cube*, *i.e.* a conjunction of literals existentially quantified by distinct variables:

$$\Theta \equiv \exists (\bar{i}).\ distinct(\bar{i}) \wedge l_1(\bar{i}) \wedge \ldots \wedge l_n(\bar{i}).$$

Running Example. We illustrate this framework on a simplified version of the directory based cache coherence protocol proposed by German [24]. In Figure 1, we give a high-level view of the evolution of a single cache as a state diagram. The protocol consists of a global directory which maintains the consistency of a shared memory between a parameterized number of cache clients. The status of each cache i is indicated by a variable `Cache`[i] which can be in one of the three states: (E)xclusive (read and write accesses), (S)hared (read access only) or (I)nvalid (no access to the memory). Clients send requests to the directory when cache misses occur: `rs` for a shared access (read miss), `re` for an exclusive access (write miss). The directory has four variables: a boolean flag `Exg` indicates whether a client has an exclusive access to the main memory, a boolean array `Shr`, such that `Shr`[i] is true when a client i is granted (read or write) access to the memory, `Cmd` stores the current request (ϵ stands for the absence of request), and `Ptr` contains the emitter of the current request.

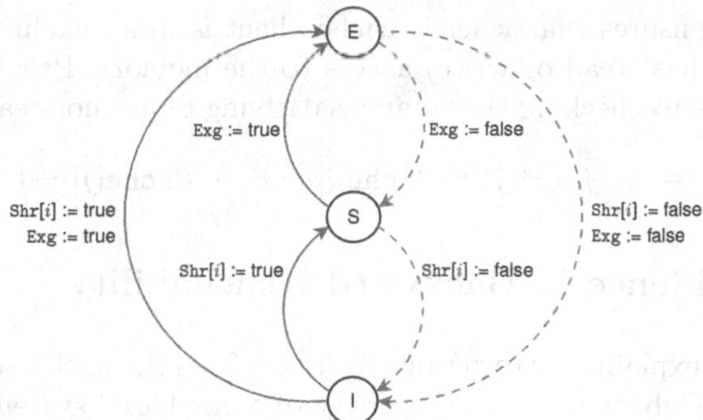

Fig. 1. High level overview of German-*esque*

The array based transition system for this protocol is described by its initial states, represented by the following logical formula (caches are invalid, no access has been given and there is no request to be processed)

$$I \equiv \forall i.\ \mathsf{Cache}[i] = \mathsf{I} \wedge \mathsf{Shr}[i] = \mathsf{false} \wedge \mathsf{Exg} = \mathsf{false} \wedge \mathsf{Cmd} = \epsilon$$

and by its transition relation given below (an horizontal line separates guards from actions, depicted in blue when they modify variables while the ones that don't change values are light gray). For instance, transition t_6 should read as: if there exists a process i such that the current pointer ($\mathtt{Ptr}$) is i, the command to be processed is a request to exclusive access (re), the flag Exg is not set and the array Shr contains false for *all processes*, then erase the command, set the flag Exg, register the process i in Shr and change the cache state of i to exclusive (E).

$$\tau \equiv t_1 \vee t_2 \vee t_3 \vee t_4 \vee t_5 \vee t_6$$

$$t_1 : \exists i.\ \begin{array}{l} \mathsf{Cache}[i] = \mathsf{I} \wedge \mathsf{Cmd} = \epsilon \wedge \\ \hline \mathtt{Ptr}' = i \wedge \mathsf{Cmd}' = \mathsf{rs} \wedge \\ \mathsf{Exg}' = \mathsf{Exg} \wedge \\ \forall j.\ \mathsf{Shr}[j] = \mathsf{Shr}'[j] \wedge \\ \quad \mathsf{Cache}[j] = \mathsf{Cache}'[j] \end{array}$$

$$t_2 : \exists i.\ \begin{array}{l} \mathsf{Cache}[i] \neq \mathsf{E} \wedge \mathsf{Cmd} = \epsilon \wedge \\ \hline \mathtt{Ptr}' = i \wedge \mathsf{Cmd}' = \mathsf{re} \wedge \\ \mathsf{Exg}' = \mathsf{Exg} \wedge \\ \forall j.\ \mathsf{Shr}[j] = \mathsf{Shr}'[j] \wedge \\ \quad \mathsf{Cache}[j] = \mathsf{Cache}'[j] \end{array}$$

$$t_3 : \exists i.\ \begin{array}{l} \mathsf{Shr}[i] = \mathsf{true} \wedge \mathsf{Cmd} = \mathsf{re} \wedge \\ \hline \mathtt{Ptr}' = \mathtt{Ptr} \wedge \mathsf{Cmd}' = \mathsf{Cmd} \wedge \\ \mathsf{Exg}' = \mathsf{false} \wedge \\ \forall j.\ ite(i = j, \neg\mathsf{Shr}'[j], \\ \qquad \mathsf{Shr}'[j] = \mathsf{Shr}[j]) \wedge \\ \forall j.\ ite(i = j, \mathsf{Cache}'[j] = \mathsf{I}, \\ \qquad \mathsf{Cache}'[j] = \mathsf{Cache}'[j]) \end{array}$$

$$t_4 : \exists i.\ \begin{array}{l} \mathsf{Shr}[i] = \mathsf{true} \wedge \mathsf{Cmd} = \mathsf{rs} \wedge \mathsf{Exg} \wedge \\ \hline \mathtt{Ptr}' = \mathtt{Ptr} \wedge \mathsf{Cmd}' = \mathsf{Cmd} \wedge \\ \mathsf{Exg}' = \mathsf{false} \wedge \forall j.\mathsf{Shr}'[j] = \mathsf{Shr}[j] \wedge \\ \forall j.\ ite(i = j, \mathsf{Cache}'[j] = \mathsf{S}, \\ \qquad \mathsf{Cache}'[j] = \mathsf{Cache}'[j]) \end{array}$$

$$t_5 : \exists i.\ \begin{array}{l} \mathtt{Ptr} = i \wedge \mathsf{Cmd} = \mathsf{rs} \wedge \neg\mathsf{Exg} \wedge \\ \hline \mathtt{Ptr}' = \mathtt{Ptr} \wedge \mathsf{Cmd}' = \epsilon \wedge \\ \mathsf{Exg}' = \mathsf{Exg} \wedge \\ \forall j.\ ite(i = j, \mathsf{Shr}'[j], \\ \qquad \mathsf{Shr}'[j] = \mathsf{Shr}[j]) \wedge \\ \forall j.\ ite(i = j, \mathsf{Cache}'[j] = \mathsf{S}, \\ \qquad \mathsf{Cache}'[j] = \mathsf{Cache}'[j]) \end{array}$$

$$t_6 : \exists i.\ \begin{array}{l} \mathtt{Ptr} = i \wedge \mathsf{Cmd} = \mathsf{re} \wedge \neg\mathsf{Exg} \wedge \\ \forall j.\ \neg\mathsf{Shr}[j] \wedge \\ \hline \mathtt{Ptr}' = \mathtt{Ptr} \wedge \\ \mathsf{Cmd}' = \epsilon \wedge \mathsf{Exg}' = \mathsf{true} \wedge \\ \forall j.\ ite(i = j, \mathsf{Shr}'[j], \\ \qquad \mathsf{Shr}'[j] = \mathsf{Shr}[j]) \wedge \\ \forall j.\ ite(i = j, \mathsf{Cache}'[j] = \mathsf{E}, \\ \qquad \mathsf{Cache}'[j] = \mathsf{Cache}'[j]) \end{array}$$

This protocol ensures that when a cache client is in an exclusive state then no other process has (read or write) access to the memory. Proving this safety property amounts to checking that states satisfying Θ are not reachable:

$$\Theta \equiv \exists i, j.\ i \neq j \wedge \texttt{Cache}[i] = \mathsf{E} \wedge \texttt{Cache}[j] \neq \mathsf{I}$$

3 Proof Evidence in Backward Reachability

In this section we explain how to get proof objects from the backward reachability analysis used by Cubicle to prove the safety of array based systems.

For a state formula φ and a transition $\tau \in \mathcal{T}$, let $pre(\tau, \varphi)$ be the formula describing the set of states from which a state satisfying φ can be reached in one τ-step. The pre-image *closure* of φ, denoted by $\textsc{Pre}^*(\varphi)$, is defined as follows

$$\begin{cases} \textsc{Pre}^0(\varphi) \triangleq \varphi \\ \textsc{Pre}^n(\varphi) \triangleq pre(\tau, \textsc{Pre}^{n-1}(\varphi)) \\ \textsc{Pre}^*(\varphi) \triangleq \bigvee_{k \in \mathbb{N}} \textsc{Pre}^k(\varphi) \end{cases}$$

and the pre-image of a set of formulas V is defined by $\textsc{Pre}^*(V) = \bigcup_{\varphi \in V} \textsc{Pre}^*(\varphi)$. We also write $\textsc{Pre}(\varphi)$ for $\textsc{Pre}^1(\varphi)$.

Definition 2. *A formula φ is said to be* reachable *iff* $\textsc{Pre}^*(\varphi) \wedge I$ *satisfiable. It is* unreachable *otherwise.*

The framework of MCMT gives sufficient conditions for which the reachability problem (Is the unsafe formula Θ reachable in the system $\mathcal{S}$?) is decidable. In particular, we consider that the pre-image of a cube by the transition relation τ ($\textsc{Pre}_\tau$) is effectively computable. The interested reader is referred to [14] for more details. Under these conditions, safety can be checked by backward reachability analysis.

We give a standard backward reachability algorithm for this framework, as defined by the function BWD in Algorithm 1. Starting with an empty formula $\mathcal{V}$ of *visited nodes* (*i.e.* false) and a queue $\mathcal{Q}$ of *pending nodes* initialized with a formula Θ, BWD iteratively computes the backward reachability graph of $\textsc{Pre}^*_\tau(\Theta)$. The algorithm terminates when a node fails the *safety check* (consistency with the initial condition — line 6), or when all nodes in $\mathcal{Q}$ are *subsumed* by $\mathcal{V}$ (line 8). These logical checks are performed by an SMT solver.

In the case where the return value of the algorithm is ***unsafe***, it is easy to expose an error trace — from the initial states to one of the violated property — to the user. This trace can then be replayed afterwards to ensure the system is indeed unsafe with respect to its specification. In the case where the return value is ***safe***, a certificate can be produced. Because of the nature of the program at hand, any instrumentation for certification purposes could either diminish efficiency (in the worst case, prevent the verification of industrial size systems) or even badly interfere and compromise the correctness (this is however not

Algorithm 1. Backward reachability analysis

Input: an array based system $\mathcal{S} = (Q, I, \tau)$ and a cube Θ
Variables:
$\mathcal{V}$: visited cubes
$\mathcal{Q}$: work queue

```
function BWD(𝒮,Θ) : begin
    𝒱 := ∅;
    push(𝒬, Θ);
    while not_empty(𝒬) do
        φ := pop(𝒬);
        if φ ∧ I satisfiable then
            return unsafe
        else if φ ⊭ 𝒱 then
            𝒱 := 𝒱 ∨ φ;
            push(𝒬, PRE_τ(φ));
    return safe
```

problematic from a certification standpoint if the results are to be independently checked, but it would nonetheless render the tool ineffective). In fact, there is no need for this certificate to contain or reflect all reasoning steps taken by the model checker, such as pre-images, fixpoint and safety checks, because $\mathcal{V}$ already contains enough information to guarantee the correctness.

Definition 3. *An* invariant *of a system is any property that holds in all reachable states of the system.*

The notion of safety is very closely related to the one of invariance. Checking the safety of a system essentially amounts to ensuring that a given property is an invariant of this system. In reality, for a system, the set of all *reachable* states constitutes the *strongest inductive invariant* (green-shaded area of Figure 2(a)). Dually, the set of states that *cannot reach* an unsafe state of the system constitutes

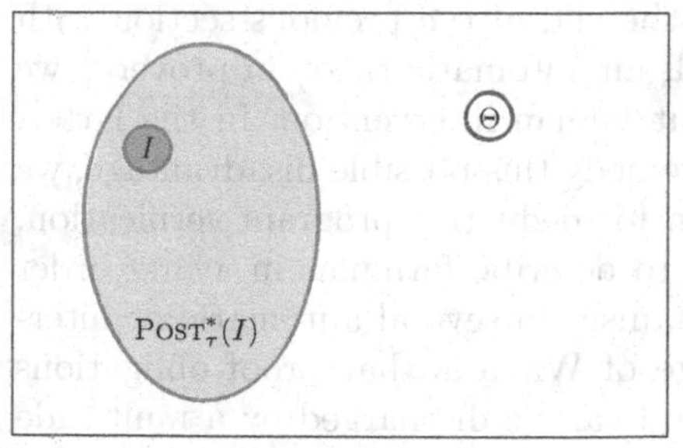

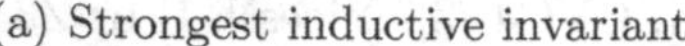
(a) Strongest inductive invariant

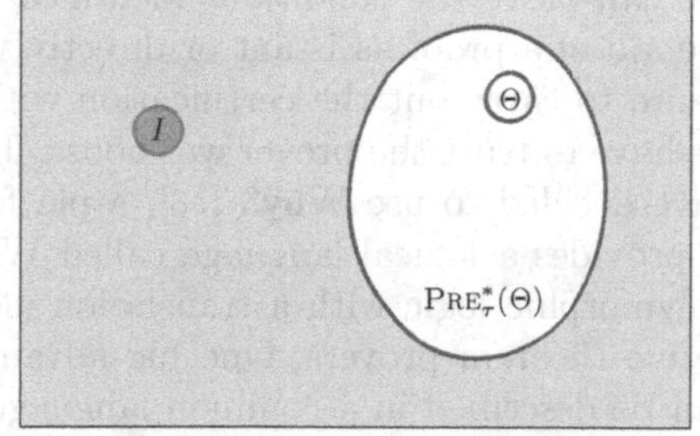

(b) Weakest inductive invariant

Fig. 2. Inductive invariants computed by forward and backward reachability analyses

the *weakest inductive invariant* (*w.r.t.* the unsafe states) of the system (green part of Figure 2(b)).

The set $\mathcal{V}$ computed by Cubicle (in Algorithm 1) is really the negation of this weakest inductive invariant. It forms in itself a proof or a certificate of safety of the system. Moreover, it is very simple to establish that a formula ϕ is an inductive invariant of a system $\mathcal{S} = (Q, I, \tau)$. All that is necessary is for it to verify the two following conditions:

$$I(X) \models \phi(X) \tag{1}$$

initialization

$$\phi(X) \wedge \tau(X, X') \models \phi(X'). \tag{2}$$

preservation

The base case (1) says that the invariant ϕ must be true in the initial states of the system and the inductive case (2) says that the invariant must be preserved by the transition relation. If additionally, we have

$$\phi(X) \models P(X) \tag{3}$$

property

then the property P is an invariant (not necessarily inductive) of the system.

If we take $\phi = \neg\mathcal{V}$ and $P = \neg\Theta$, where $\mathcal{V}$ is the disjunction of visited cubes in Algorithm 1 and Θ is the unsafe formula for the system, then these three conditions are verified. Indeed, we have by construction that $\mathcal{V} \models \text{PRE}^*_\tau(\Theta)$, $\mathcal{V}$ is closed by pre-image, *i.e.* $\mathcal{V}(X') \wedge \tau(X, X') \models \mathcal{V}(X)$ so $\neg\mathcal{V}(X) \wedge \tau(X, X') \models \neg\mathcal{V}(X')$. Because $\mathcal{V}$ contains Θ, the final condition (3) is also verified.

To certify that the result of Algorithm 1 implemented by Cubicle is correct, it suffices to independently make sure that $\phi = \neg\mathcal{V}$ and $P = \neg\Theta$ satisfy the three conditions (1), (2) and (3). In the sequel, we show how to do this automatically and efficiently.

4 A Certification Framework for Cubicle

We can prove the conditions identified at the end of the previous section with the aid of a proof assistant or directly with an automatic theorem prover if we desire to carry out the certification without human intervention. In the latter, we have to trust the prover we choose. To remedy this possible disadvantage, we have decided to use Why3 [13], a platform for deductive program verification. It provides a logical language called Why to describe formulas in a first order polymorphic logic with a translation mechanism to several automatic or interactive theorem provers. One big advantage of Why3 is that proof obligations can be described in a common language and can be discharged by a multitude of backend tools: SMT solvers like Alt-Ergo [5], CVC4 [3], Yices [11] or Z3 [8]; resolution based solvers like E [27], iProver [17], SPASS [30], Vampire [25]; or when necessary, even proof assistants like Coq [9] or PVS [23].

Redundancy as a tool is used in multiple contexts. For instance, control systems of avionics are physical entities which can fail (with known probabilities), and higher fault tolerance is achieved by having several identical redundant components and voting mechanisms. In formal methods, the use of different tools to independently corroborate results is a way to achieve a higher level of confidence. In our case, we trust our certification process when at least two independent solvers confirm the validity of our certificates.

Our certification process follows the diagram of Figure 3. The inductive invariant ϕ constitutes the essence of the certificate produced by Cubicle. It can then be fed directly to the checker (here Why3) or can be simplified and enriched with a set L of lemmas (box Simpl described in Section 5). Once the solvers used by the checker redundantly prove the conditions (1)–(3), the certificate is declared valid.

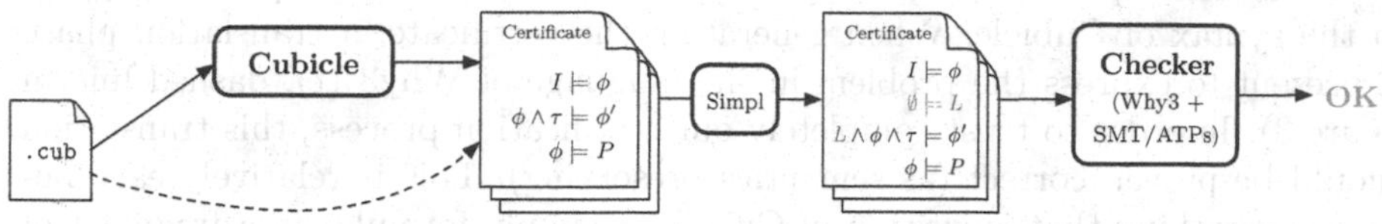

Fig. 3. Certification schema

Running Example. When Cubicle is executed (without any options) on the small protocol of Section 2, the certificate ϕ produced is composed of 15 quantified clauses. Now, proofs obligations are generated in Why3's input language to ensure that ϕ is indeed inductive.

$$\phi \equiv \phi_1 \wedge \phi_2 \wedge \phi_3 \wedge \phi_4 \wedge \phi_5 \wedge \phi_6 \wedge \phi_7 \wedge \phi_8 \wedge \phi_9 \wedge \phi_{10} \wedge \phi_{11} \wedge \phi_{12} \wedge \phi_{13} \wedge \phi_{14} \wedge \phi_{15}$$

$$\begin{aligned}
\phi_1 &\equiv \neg(\exists z_1, z_2.\ z_1 \neq z_2 \wedge \texttt{Exg} \wedge \texttt{Cmd} = \texttt{rs} \wedge \texttt{Ptr} = z_1 \wedge \texttt{Cache}[z_2] \neq \texttt{I} \wedge \texttt{Shr}[z_1] \wedge \neg\texttt{Shr}[z_2])\\
\phi_2 &\equiv \neg(\exists z_1, z_2.\ z_1 \neq z_2 \wedge \texttt{Cache}[z_1] = \texttt{E} \wedge \texttt{Cache}[z_2] \neq \texttt{I})\\
\phi_3 &\equiv \neg(\exists z_1, z_2, z_3.\ z_2 \neq z_3 \wedge z_1 \neq z_3 \wedge z_1 \neq z_2 \wedge\\
&\quad \texttt{Exg} \wedge \texttt{Cmd} = \texttt{rs} \wedge \texttt{Ptr} = z_1 \wedge \texttt{Cache}[z_2] \neq \texttt{I} \wedge \neg\texttt{Shr}[z_2] \wedge \texttt{Shr}[z_3])\\
\phi_4 &\equiv \neg(\exists z_1, z_2.\ z_1 \neq z_2 \wedge \texttt{Cmd} = \texttt{re} \wedge \texttt{Ptr} = z_2 \wedge \texttt{Cache}[z_1] = \texttt{E} \wedge \neg\texttt{Shr}[z_1] \wedge \texttt{Shr}[z_2])\\
\phi_5 &\equiv \neg(\exists z_1, z_2.\ z_1 \neq z_2 \wedge \neg\texttt{Exg} \wedge \texttt{Cmd} = \epsilon \wedge \texttt{Cache}[z_1] \neq \texttt{E} \wedge \texttt{Cache}[z_2] \neq \texttt{I} \wedge \neg\texttt{Shr}[z_1] \wedge \neg\texttt{Shr}[z_2])\\
\phi_6 &\equiv \neg(\exists z_1, z_2.\ z_1 \neq z_2 \wedge \texttt{Cmd} = \texttt{re} \wedge \texttt{Ptr} = z_1 \wedge \texttt{Cache}[z_2] \neq \texttt{I} \wedge \texttt{Shr}[z_1] \wedge \neg\texttt{Shr}[z_2])\\
\phi_7 &\equiv \neg(\exists z_1, z_2.\ z_1 \neq z_2 \wedge \texttt{Exg} \wedge \texttt{Cmd} = \texttt{rs} \wedge \texttt{Cache}[z_1] = \texttt{E} \wedge \texttt{Shr}[z_2])\\
\phi_8 &\equiv \neg(\exists z_1, z_2, z_3.\ z_2 \neq z_3 \wedge z_1 \neq z_3 \wedge z_1 \neq z_2 \wedge\\
&\quad \texttt{Cmd} = \texttt{re} \wedge \texttt{Ptr} = z_1 \wedge \texttt{Cache}[z_2] \neq \texttt{I} \wedge \neg\texttt{Shr}[z_1] \wedge \neg\texttt{Shr}[z_2] \wedge \texttt{Shr}[z_3])\\
\phi_9 &\equiv \neg(\exists z_1, z_2.\ z_1 \neq z_2 \wedge \neg\texttt{Exg} \wedge \texttt{Cmd} = \texttt{rs} \wedge \texttt{Ptr} = z_2 \wedge \texttt{Cache}[z_1] = \texttt{E})\\
\phi_{10} &\equiv \neg(\exists z_1, z_2.\ z_1 \neq z_2 \wedge \neg\texttt{Exg} \wedge \texttt{Cmd} = \texttt{re} \wedge \texttt{Ptr} = z_2 \wedge \texttt{Cache}[z_1] = \texttt{E} \wedge \neg\texttt{Shr}[z_1] \wedge \neg\texttt{Shr}[z_2])\\
\phi_{11} &\equiv \neg(\exists z_1, z_2.\ z_1 \neq z_2 \wedge \neg\texttt{Exg} \wedge \texttt{Cmd} = \texttt{re} \wedge \texttt{Ptr} = z_1 \wedge \texttt{Cache}[z_2] \neq \texttt{I} \wedge \neg\texttt{Shr}[z_1] \wedge \neg\texttt{Shr}[z_2])\\
\phi_{12} &\equiv \neg(\exists z_1, z_2.\ z_1 \neq z_2 \wedge \texttt{Cmd} = \epsilon \wedge \texttt{Cache}[z_1] \neq \texttt{E} \wedge \texttt{Cache}[z_2] \neq \texttt{I} \wedge \texttt{Shr}[z_1] \wedge \neg\texttt{Shr}[z_2])\\
\phi_{13} &\equiv \neg(\exists z_1, z_2.\ z_1 \neq z_2 \wedge \texttt{Exg} \wedge \texttt{Cmd} = \epsilon \wedge \texttt{Cache}[z_1] = \texttt{E} \wedge \texttt{Cache}[z_2] = \texttt{I} \wedge \texttt{Shr}[z_2])\\
\phi_{14} &\equiv \neg(\exists z_1, z_2.\ z_1 \neq z_2 \wedge \neg\texttt{Exg} \wedge \texttt{Cmd} = \texttt{rs} \wedge \texttt{Ptr} = z_1 \wedge \texttt{Cache}[z_2] \neq \texttt{I} \wedge \neg\texttt{Shr}[z_2])\\
\phi_{15} &\equiv \neg(\exists z_1, z_2.\ z_1 \neq z_2 \wedge \neg\texttt{Exg} \wedge \texttt{Cmd} = \epsilon \wedge \texttt{Cache}[z_1] = \texttt{E} \wedge \texttt{Cache}[z_2] = \texttt{I})
\end{aligned}$$

This certificate is immediate to extract from the set $\mathcal{V}$ computed by Cubicle so there is zero overhead. It is then fed directly to Why3 which in turn calls several automated theorem provers. The certificate contains quantifiers (both universal and existential) so we are limited to solvers that natively support them. Here we chose to have Why3 call seven different backend provers to discharge the proof obligations of our certificate. The results of this certificate's verification are given in table 1. Each prover was run with a timeout of five seconds. Times are given in seconds and bold numbers stand for a "valid" answer, barred text in red cells is for the answer "unkown" while T.O. denotes executions that did not end in the allocated time (120s). The PO for preservation is split in 15 subgoals (one for each conjunct of ϕ') and we can notice that each goal is discharged by at least three provers.

Remark. The input file describing both the system and the properties is given in the syntax of Cubicle. When generating the certificate, a translation phase is present to express the problem in the language of Why3 (*cf.* dashed line in figure 3). In order to trust completely our certification process, this translation should be proven correct (as semantics preserving). This is relatively easy because everything that is written in Cubicle is simply formulas in a fragment of first order logic, so there exists a one-to-one correspondence and the translation essentially consists in a pretty printing step. Ideally, we could even adopt the same input language (*i.e.* Why3's) to describe parameterized systems and thus dissipate all remaining doubts.

Table 1. Why3's output on certificate for German-*esque*

Proof obligations		Alt-Ergo (0.96)	CVC3 (2.4.1)	CVC4 (1.3)	Eprover (1.8-001)	Spass (3.5)	Yices (1.0.40)	Z3 (4.3.2)
initialisation	1.	**0.02**	**0.02**	**0.01**	**0.01**	**0.05**	**0.13**	**0.01**
property	1.	**0.01**	**0.01**	**0.01**	**0.01**	**0.02**	**0.00**	**0.00**
preservation	1.	~~0.01~~	~~0.85~~	**0.03**	**0.03**	**0.03**	~~1.01~~	**0.02**
	2.	~~0.01~~	~~0.69~~	**0.04**	**0.20**	T.O.	~~0.97~~	**0.02**
	3.	**0.02**	**0.03**	**0.03**	**0.02**	**0.04**	**0.35**	**0.01**
	4.	~~0.01~~	~~1.18~~	**0.03**	**0.03**	**0.36**	~~0.67~~	**0.02**
	5.	**0.03**	~~0.99~~	**0.04**	T.O.	T.O.	**1.08**	**0.01**
	6.	**0.03**	~~1.24~~	**0.04**	**0.04**	**3.65**	**0.91**	**0.01**
	7.	**0.02**	**0.03**	**0.03**	**0.04**	**0.05**	**0.61**	**0.01**
	8.	**0.06**	~~1.18~~	**0.03**	**0.07**	**59.6**	~~0.82~~	**0.01**
	9.	**0.02**	~~1.17~~	**0.03**	**0.01**	**0.06**	~~1.33~~	**0.01**
	10.	**0.03**	**0.03**	**0.02**	**0.04**	**0.81**	~~1.49~~	**0.01**
	11.	~~0.01~~	~~0.58~~	**0.02**	**0.03**	**0.18**	~~0.99~~	**0.02**
	12.	**0.03**	**0.03**	**0.03**	**0.05**	**0.45**	**0.78**	**0.01**
	13.	**0.03**	~~0.93~~	**0.02**	**0.01**	**0.08**	~~0.95~~	**0.01**
	14.	~~0.01~~	~~0.82~~	**0.20**	**0.21**	**4.60**	~~2.12~~	**0.01**
	15.	**0.02**	**0.03**	**0.02**	**0.02**	**0.07**	**0.83**	**0.01**

Certificates for toy examples like a simple atomic mutex can be verified by all seven provers, but here the protocol German-*esque*, while simply expressed, is far from trivial. POs related to the initialization (1) and property (3) conditions are easily and almost instantly discharged by all solvers. However POs that concern preservation are usually a lot more difficult. These rather disappointing performances can be attributed to the ubiquitous quantifiers of these goals, in particular in the representation of the transition relation. Most of these solvers use very sensitive heuristics for quantifiers so performances are often uneven and hard to predict. However results for this (small) benchmark are still satisfactory because all goals are proven independently several times.

This is an efficient and unintrusive way of generating correctness certificates. The remaining challenge is now to be able to automatically verify these certificates for problems whose size and complexity are orders of magnitude larger.

5 Simpler *and* Richer Certificates

One nice feature of extracting certificates in this manner is that the certification phase becomes completely independent of the model checking phase. In particular certificates are completely oblivious to any optimization — that preserves the transitive closure property of $\mathcal{V}$— used inside Cubicle. For instance, running a parallel reachability loop or changing the search strategy does not impair the ability to produce correct certificates. Even if one optimization was incorrect, a certificate could still be produced the same way, but would likely[2] not be verified by external solvers.

5.1 Invariants Inference

One crucial optimization used in Cubicle is a mechanism for automatically inferring quantified invariants [7]. Invariants found this way are particularly valuable because they allow our technique for parameterized verification to scale up effectively on industrial size protocols. Inevitably, it also speeds up the verification for small and medium size problems. It is a well known fact that invariants, if given or when found, will prune the search space and directly impact the time and space used by model checking algorithms. The number of visited nodes (in $\mathcal{V}$) is thus immediately diminished so this constitutes an effective way of *reducing the size* of the certificate. One particularity of the algorithm BRAB (Backward Reachability with Approximations and Backtracking) described in [7] and implemented in Cubicle is that inferred invariants are inserted and proved by the same backward reachability loop. From a certification standpoint, this ensures that $\neg\mathcal{V}$ will remain inductive at the

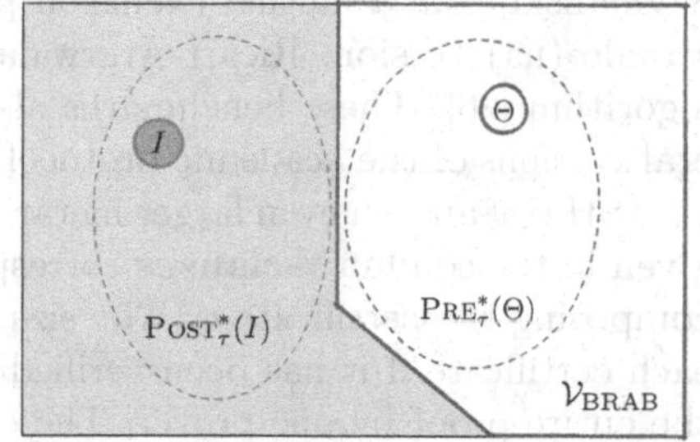

Fig. 4. Inductive invariant computed by BRAB

[2] If one optimization is incorrect but the resulting certificate is verified for one particular benchmark then it simply means that the model checker gave a correct answer by incorrect means.

end of the search, meaning that the technique described in section 3 is still applicable.

In fact the inductive invariant computed by BRAB is halfway between the strongest and the weakest invariant (see Figure 4). $\phi \equiv \neg\mathcal{V}_{\text{BRAB}}$ is a good candidate for a certificate, being expressible more easily that either of those extremes. The underlying reason is that the "internal proof" constructed by the model checker is much shorter.

Running Example. By now running BRAB instead of traditional backward reachability, the certificate extracted at the end of the search is only composed of *four* quantified clauses (*cf.* below) and Table 2 shows that it is proved in totality by all seven solvers we used.

$$\begin{aligned}
\phi &\equiv \phi_1 \;\wedge\; \phi_2 \;\wedge\; \phi_3 \;\wedge\; \phi_4 \\
\phi_1 &\equiv \neg(\exists z_1, z_2.\ z_1 \neq z_2 \wedge \\
&\qquad \mathtt{Cache}[z_1] = \mathsf{E} \wedge \mathtt{Cache}[z_2] \neq \mathsf{I}) \\
\phi_2 &\equiv \neg(\exists z_1.\ \neg\mathbf{Exg} \wedge \mathtt{Cache}[z_1] = \mathsf{E}) \\
\phi_3 &\equiv \neg(\exists z_1, z_2.\ z_1 \neq z_2 \wedge \\
&\qquad \mathtt{Cache}[z_1] = \mathsf{E} \wedge \mathtt{Shr}[z_2]) \\
\phi_4 &\equiv \neg(\exists z_1.\ \mathtt{Cache}[z_1] \neq \mathsf{I} \wedge \\
&\qquad\qquad \neg\mathtt{Shr}[z_1])
\end{aligned}$$

Table 2. Why3's output on certificate generated by BRAB for German-*esque*

Proof obligations		Alt-Ergo (0.96)	CVC3 (2.4.1)	CVC4 (1.3)	Eprover (1.8-001)	Spass (3.5)	Yices (1.0.40)	Z3 (4.3.2)
initialisation	1.	0.01	0.01	0.03	0.01	0.02	0.00	0.00
property	1.	0.01	0.00	0.01	0.01	0.02	0.00	0.00
preservation	1.	0.02	0.02	0.03	0.08	0.12	0.01	0.00
	2.	0.02	0.02	0.04	0.11	0.11	0.05	0.01
	3.	0.02	0.02	0.03	0.04	0.07	0.01	0.01
	4.	0.03	0.02	0.03	0.13	0.08	0.26	0.01

Experiments. By running Cubicle with the BRAB algorithm we are able to prove the safety of a selected set of benchmarks and we are able to generate certificates small enough for most of them so that they can be verified automatically and independently. To obtain the results depicted in Table 3 we executed Cubicle version 1.0.2 and Why3 0.83 (with the backend solvers used previously) on a laptop with a dual core Intel i7 processor (1.7 GHz) and 8GB of memory. Szymanski_* is a mutual exclusion protocol given in an atomic (at) and non-atomic (na) version. Ricart-Argrwala is a distributed timed mutual exclusion algorithm [26]. These benchmarks also include cache coherence protocols: several versions of the academic protocol German and two industrial size problems: FLASH [18] and an even larger hierarchical protocol Hirr_PV [20]. The numbers given in the column **∀-clauses** correspond to the number of quantified formulas composing the certificate ϕ. The size is for the resulting Why3 file. We say for each certificate if it has been verified and the shortest amount of time to carry the entire proof by one prover. The column **Level** denotes the minimum number of solvers that were able to independently discharge each proof obligation. It morally depicts the level of confidence we get with this certificate.

We can see that the certificates for academic problems can be verified in just a couple seconds but larger certificates are out of reach of all solvers, mostly due to their size.

Table 3. Result for the verification of certificates generated with BRAB

Benchmark	∀-clauses	Size	Verified	Level	Time
Szymanski_at	31	18 kB	Yes	3	0.96s
Szymanski_na	38	28 kB	Yes	2	1.45s
Ricart_Agrawala	30	39 kB	Yes	2	1.26s
German_Baukus	48	44 kB	Yes	2	1.58s
German.CTC	69	83 kB	Yes	2	2.73s
German_pfs	51	50 kB	Yes	3	1.79s
Flash_nodata	41	123 kB	Yes	2	2.99s
Flash	733	650 kB	No	0	-
Hirr_PV_nodata	2704	1.9 MB	No	0	-
Hirr_PV	2815	1.9 MB	No	0	-

5.2 Intermediate Lemmas

While certificates can be simplified, they can also be enriched to ease the tasks of the automated solvers. The hardest part for these solvers to handle preservation proof obligations is to find good instances of the quantified formulas that appear in their context. If we take a look at the PO (4.) of preservation in the previous table 2, it takes the form $\phi_1 \wedge \phi_2 \wedge \phi_3 \wedge \phi_4 \wedge \tau \models \phi'_4$. With a closer inspection we can remark that we already have $\phi_4 \wedge \tau \models \phi'_4$ which directly implies the PO we want to prove. We call these pieces of additional information *intermediate lemmas* and show in the following how to enrich our certificates with them.

The information we need to infer these lemmas is actually already computed by Cubicle during fixpoint checks. Every time a cube φ_0 is added to $\mathcal{V}$, its pre-image $\text{Pre}_\tau(\varphi_0)$ is added to $\mathcal{Q}$. When part of this pre-image passes the fixpoint check, we can retrieve the necessary information of which elements of $\mathcal{V}$ were really useful. This can be done by asking for the *unsat core*[3] of this particular SMT check. The union of the unsat cores, for the fixpoints of all $\text{Pre}_\tau(\varphi_0)$, makes up the part of $\mathcal{V}$ that is sufficient to prove the preservation of $\neg\varphi_0$ by τ.

Some extra bookkeeping can be added to the reachability loop to gather this information during runtime. However it can also be reconstructed after the fact simply with $\mathcal{V}$. This has two advantages. First, it allows to keep the model checking phase and the certification phase separated and independent. Second, computing the reasons for the inductiveness of $\mathcal{V}$ once $\mathcal{V}$ is complete yields possibly smaller and simpler intermediate lemmas.

We denote by UC a function that returns the unsat core for a satisfiability check in the form of a set of formulas[4]. Our algorithm to extract intermediate lemmas is given by Algorithm 2. It uses the fact that at the end of the search $\mathcal{V}$ is closed under pre-image as shown in Figure 5. For each node φ of $\mathcal{V}$ uc is the

[3] The quality of the unsat core depends on the solver we use, but our goal here is only to trim the context. Because only a small portion of the context is necessary for the proof, most solvers will reflect this in their unsat cores.

[4] If the check is satisfiable then UC fails, though in our case, if the certificate is correct this should never happen. This amounts to a pre-verification of inductiveness of the certificate by Cubicle itself.

subset of $\mathcal{V}$ that makes the pre-image of φ be in $\mathcal{V}$. Now, going the other way around, if we start in a state of the conjunction Γ, then we necessarily end up in φ after one step of τ. This is what is stated by the lemma added to $\mathcal{L}$ line **6**.

When the intermediate lemmas are assumed by the solvers, the proof of preservation is trivial by a simple propositional reasoning. The burden of verification is shifted to the proof of these intermediate lemmas instead but they are much smaller than the original POs arising from the proof of preservation. For instance, the largest premise of a lemma for the protocol FLASH (see section 5.2) is composed of 41 quantified formulas while the majority has less than 20 (instead of 742 originally). Because the lemmas extraction shown in algorithm 2 is only a series of fixpoint checks, the time spent for the construction of the certificate is always strictly less that the time spent for the model checking phase. This overhead is in our sense acceptable.

Algorithm 2. Intermediate lemmas extraction

Input: $\mathcal{V}$: visited cubes
Variables: $\mathcal{L}$: a set of intermediate lemmas
1 $\mathcal{L} := \emptyset$;
2 **foreach** $\varphi \in \mathcal{V}$ **do**
3   **let** uc = $\mathtt{UC}(\mathrm{PRE}_\tau(\varphi) \models \mathcal{V}) \setminus \mathrm{PRE}_\tau(\varphi)$ **in**
4   (* uc *is a subset of* $\mathcal{V}$ *)
5   **let** $\Gamma = \bigwedge_{\psi \in \mathrm{uc}} \psi$ **in**
6     $\mathcal{L}$:= "$\Gamma \wedge \tau \models \varphi'$" $\cup\ \mathcal{L}$;
7 **return** $\mathcal{L}$

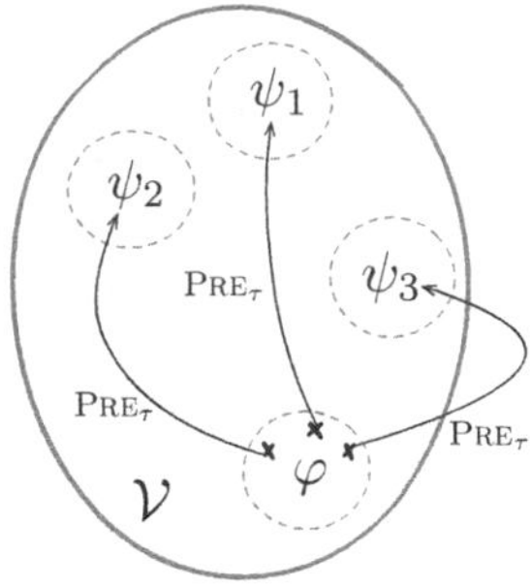

Fig. 5. Finding intermediate lemmas

Table 4. Result for the verification of certificates with intermediate lemmas

Benchmark	MC.	Gen.	∀-clauses	Size	Verified	Level	Time
Szymanski_at	0.04s	0.01s	31	21 kB	Yes	3	0.66s
Szymanski_na	0.06s	0.03s	38	30 kB	Yes	2	1.79s
Ricart_Agrawala	0.05s	0.02s	16	36 kB	Yes	2	0.52s
German_Baukus	0.10s	0.03s	48	40 kB	Yes	**3**	1.16s
German.CTC	0.14s	0.07s	69	62 kB	Yes	**4**	1.98s
German_pfs	0.11s	0.04s	48	43 kB	Yes	3	1.42s
Flash_nodata	0.11s	0.09s	41	133 kB	Yes	**3**	2.68s
Flash	1m09s	35.8s	733	1.1 MB	**Yes**	**1**	4m7s
Hirr_PV_nodata	4m51s	1m13s	2704	3.4 MB	**Yes**	**1**	42m
Hirr_PV	4m54s	1m25s	2815	3.5 MB	**Yes**	**1**	53m

Experiments. We give experimental results in Table 4 for certificates enriched with intermediate lemmas. The Cubicle systems and corresponding Why3 certificates are available at http://cubicle.lri.fr/certificates. We use the same set of benchmarks as in the previous section. The column **MC.** gives the time spent by Cubicle for model checking the problem, whereas the column **Gen.** gives the time that was necessary to generate the certificate (essentially compute the intermediate lemmas). We can see that it is always faster to generate the certificate than to do the model checking phase. The number of clauses does not change compared to Table 3 but the files are now larger because they include all the extra intermediate lemmas. We can see that it is far more advantageous to pay the price for including these hints in the certificate. Some of the certificates for easier (academic) protocols are now entirely proven by more solvers independently and in a shorter time. Notably, we are now able to verify (albeit only with confidence level 1) the certificates for industrial size protocols FLASH and Hirr_PV. They are significantly larger – a few megabytes instead of kilobytes – and only one SMT solver (Z3) was able to completely discharge all POs. Only a few subgoals are problematic for other solvers, likely due to some inappropriate heuristic for quantifiers instantiation. For instance, 718 of the 736 POs for FLASH were proven by at least two solvers. We would still like to increase the level of confidence brought by the certificates for these large problems.

Exposing Bugs in Cubicle. Cubicle has itself directly benefited from the generation of certificates. During our experiments on our various benchmarks, we were at first not able to verify the certificates for Hirr_PV_nodata and Hirr_PV but only a few (approximately a dozen) of obligations for the intermediate lemmas failed to prove. This allowed us to uncover a bug of Cubicle that was present in its optimized *ad-hoc* instantiation mechanism. Some substitutions were ill-formed in the computation of relevant permutations which would cause the fixpoint check (line 8 of Algorithm 1) to answer incorrectly in some specific cases when multiply nested if-then-else constructs were present in the original system. The Hirr_PV benchmarks are some of the only ones that triggered this bug which had escaped our testing process so far.

6 Related Work

Two different lines of work coexist for the certification of verification tools. One approach focuses on verifying the program correct once and for all. In this category, there exists several different approaches for proving a program correct. For some programming languages, it is possible to prove the code directly (*e.g.* using ESC Java, Frama-C, VCC, F* etc.), though this is a very tough job because such programs are often very complex, the proofs rapidly become convoluted and are unlikely to be automated. One advantage is that the performances of such programs can be close to the ones of their non certified counterparts. One example of this kind of certification effort is the modern SAT solver `versat` which was developed and verified using the programming language GURU [22]. We are however not aware of similar results for model checkers.

Another possibility is to prove the algorithm correct in a descriptive language adapted to verification (*e.g.* interactive proof assistants like Coq, PVS or Isabelle) and obtain an executable program through a refinement process or a code extraction mechanism. In the recent years, certified software of this category have gained interest. Worth mentioning is the C compiler CompCert [19] or the operating system micro-kernel seL4 [16]. CompCert is written entirely in Coq and uses external oracles in some of the compilation passes. These oracles provide solutions (*e.g.* a coloring of a graph) that can be verified by a certified checker. Our oracles, on the other hand, do not even need to provide correct results because they only suggest potential invariants.

Although the first formal verification of a model checker in Coq for the modal μ-calculus [28] goes back to 1998, only recently have *certified verification tools* started to emerge. Blazy *et al.* have verified a static analyzer for C programs [4] to be used inside CompCert. Although this static analyzer is not on par with the performances of commercial tools, it is sufficient to enable safely some of the optimizations of a compiler. The most relevant works concerning model checking are probably [1] and [12]. Amjad [1] shows how to embed BDD based symbolic model checking algorithms in the HOL theorem prover so that results are returned as theorems. This approach relies on the correctness of the backend BDD package. Esparza *et al.* [12] have fully verified a version of the Spin model checker with the Isabelle theorem prover. Using successive refinements, they built a correct by construction model checker from high level specifications down to functional (SML) code.

Usually in these approaches, a trade-off exists between an efficient program from a precise algorithm working on complex data structures, and a less concrete program from an algorithm where some data structures and operations are abstracted.

The other approach consists in relying on tools that produce traces or certificates to be checked afterwards. This is the approach which is adopted in our work. An approach for the certification of SAT and SMT solvers is the work by Keller *et al.* [2] whose idea consists in having the solver produce a detailed certificate in which each rule is read and verified by the composition of several small certified (in Coq) checkers. CVC4 is also able to produce full proof trees in a variant of the Edinburgh Logical Framework extended with side conditions [29].

One recent of such application to model checking is Slab [10] which produces certificates in the form of inductive verification diagrams to be checked by SMT solvers.

7 Conclusion

We have presented a technique for certifying the parameterized model checker Cubicle. We showed how to extract certificates from runs of backward reachability analysis in the form of inductive invariants. This approach is minimally intrusive and works with most optimizations. It even directly benefits from the algorithm BRAB to reduce the size and complexity of these certificates. The aim of this work was to bring a higher level of confidence in the results of a parameterized model checker such as Cubicle. We think this is a success because we were able to automatically verify large certificates for industrial size cache coherence protocols. This progress was made possible essentially by computing intermediate lemmas to help and guide the automated theorem provers.

So far our certification framework demands that we trust three of its components:

1. Our translation of Cubicle's systems in Why3's first order logic. An immediate next step for our work would be to unify these two input specification languages.

2. The logic part of the deductive platform Why3. We don't use any advanced programming features of Why3 so this reduces our trust base. A possibility would be to use a certified version of Why3 [15].
3. The automated theorem provers. It would not be unreasonable to place our trust in *e.g.* one of the SMT solvers, but our technique makes use of redundancy by using multiple solvers. This allows to not trust any single prover.

To further this effort, an interesting approach would be to remove all quantifiers from the certificates. This is feasible because the unsat cores of Algorithm 2 can be easily refined to include useful instances. It would allow to use solvers that do not support quantifiers and reduce the burden on the ones who do.

Acknowledgment. This work was partially supported by the French ANR project ANR-12-INSE-0007 Cafein.

References

1. Amjad, H.: Programming a symbolic model checker in a fully expansive theorem prover. In: Basin, D., Wolff, B. (eds.) TPHOLs 2003. LNCS, vol. 2758, pp. 171–187. Springer, Heidelberg (2003)
2. Armand, M., Faure, G., Grégoire, B., Keller, C., Théry, L., Wener, B.: Verifying sat and smt in coq for a fully automated decision procedure. In: PSATTT 2011: International Workshop on Proof-Search in Axiomatic Theories and Type Theories (2011)
3. Barrett, C., Conway, C.L., Deters, M., Hadarean, L., Jovanović, D., King, T., Reynolds, A., Tinelli, C.: CVC4. In: Gopalakrishnan, G., Qadeer, S. (eds.) CAV 2011. LNCS, vol. 6806, pp. 171–177. Springer, Heidelberg (2011)
4. Blazy, S., Laporte, V., Maroneze, A., Pichardie, D.: Formal verification of a C value analysis based on abstract interpretation. In: Logozzo, F., Fähndrich, M. (eds.) SAS 2013. LNCS, vol. 7935, pp. 324–344. Springer, Heidelberg (2013)
5. Bobot, F., Conchon, S., Contejean, É., Iguernelala, M., Lescuyer, S., Mebsout, A.: The alt-ergo automated theorem prover (2008)
6. Conchon, S., Goel, A., Krstić, S., Mebsout, A., Zaïdi, F.: Cubicle: A Parallel SMT-Based Model Checker for Parameterized Systems - Tool Paper. In: Madhusudan, P., Seshia, S.A. (eds.) CAV 2012. LNCS, vol. 7358, pp. 718–724. Springer, Heidelberg (2012)
7. Conchon, S., Goel, A., Krstić, S., Mebsout, A., Zaïdi, F.: Invariants for finite instances and beyond. In: FMCAD, pp. 61–68. IEEE (2013)
8. de Moura, L., Bjørner, N.S.: Z3: An efficient SMT solver. In: Ramakrishnan, C.R., Rehof, J. (eds.) TACAS 2008. LNCS, vol. 4963, pp. 337–340. Springer, Heidelberg (2008)
9. Dowek, G., Felty, A., Herbelin, H., Huet, G., Werner, B., Paulin-Mohring, C., et al.: The coq proof assistant user's guide: Version 5.6 (1991)
10. Dräger, K., Kupriyanov, A., Finkbeiner, B., Wehrheim, H.: SLAB: A certifying model checker for infinite-state concurrent systems. In: Esparza, J., Majumdar, R. (eds.) TACAS 2010. LNCS, vol. 6015, pp. 271–274. Springer, Heidelberg (2010)
11. Dutertre, B., de Moura, L.: The Yices SMT solver. Technical report, SRI International (2006)

12. Esparza, J., Lammich, P., Neumann, R., Nipkow, T., Schimpf, A., Smaus, J.-G.: A fully verified executable LTL model checker. In: Sharygina, N., Veith, H. (eds.) CAV 2013. LNCS, vol. 8044, pp. 463–478. Springer, Heidelberg (2013)
13. Filliâtre, J.-C., Paskevich, A.: Why3 — where programs meet provers. In: Felleisen, M., Gardner, P. (eds.) ESOP 2013. LNCS, vol. 7792, pp. 125–128. Springer, Heidelberg (2013)
14. Ghilardi, S., Ranise, S.: Backward reachability of array-based systems by SMT solving: Termination and invariant synthesis. LMCS 6(4) (2010)
15. Herms, P., Marché, C., Monate, B.: A certified multi-prover verification condition generator. In: Joshi, R., Müller, P., Podelski, A. (eds.) VSTTE 2012. LNCS, vol. 7152, pp. 2–17. Springer, Heidelberg (2012)
16. Klein, G., Elphinstone, K., Heiser, G., Andronick, J., Cock, D., Derrin, P., Elkaduwe, D., Engelhardt, K., Kolanski, R., Norrish, M., Sewell, T., Tuch, H., Winwood, S.: sel4: Formal verification of an os kernel. In: ACM SIGOPS, SOSP, pp. 207–220. ACM, New York (2009)
17. Korovin, K.: iProver – an instantiation-based theorem prover for first-order logic (System description). In: Armando, A., Baumgartner, P., Dowek, G. (eds.) IJCAR 2008. LNCS (LNAI), vol. 5195, pp. 292–298. Springer, Heidelberg (2008)
18. Kuskin, J., Ofelt, D., Heinrich, M., Heinlein, J., Simoni, R., Gharachorloo, K., Chapin, J., Nakahira, D., Baxter, J., Horowitz, M., Gupta, A., Rosenblum, M., Hennessy, J.: The Stanford FLASH multiprocessor. In: Computer Architecture, pp. 302–313 (April 1994)
19. Leroy, X.: A formally verified compiler back-end. J. Autom. Reason. 43(4), 363–446 (2009)
20. Matthews, L.: Personal communication
21. Namjoshi, K.S.: Certifying model checkers. In: Berry, G., Comon, H., Finkel, A. (eds.) CAV 2001. LNCS, vol. 2102, pp. 2–13. Springer, Heidelberg (2001)
22. Oe, D., Stump, A., Oliver, C., Clancy, K.: `versat`: A verified modern SAT solver. In: Kuncak, V., Rybalchenko, A. (eds.) VMCAI 2012. LNCS, vol. 7148, pp. 363–378. Springer, Heidelberg (2012)
23. Owre, S., Rushby, J.M., Shankar, N.: Pvs: A prototype verification system. In: Kapur, D. (ed.) CADE 1992. LNCS, vol. 607, pp. 748–752. Springer, Heidelberg (1992)
24. Pnueli, A., Ruah, S., Zuck, L.D.: Automatic deductive verification with invisible invariants. In: Margaria, T., Yi, W. (eds.) TACAS 2001. LNCS, vol. 2031, pp. 82–97. Springer, Heidelberg (2001)
25. Riazanov, A., Voronkov, A.: Vampire. In: Ganzinger, H. (ed.) CADE 1999. LNCS (LNAI), vol. 1632, pp. 292–296. Springer, Heidelberg (1999)
26. Ricart, G., Agrawala, A.K.: An optimal algorithm for mutual exclusion in computer networks. Communications of the ACM 24(1), 9–17 (1981)
27. Schulz, S.: System description: E 1.8. In: McMillan, K., Middeldorp, A., Voronkov, A. (eds.) LPAR-19 2013. LNCS, vol. 8312, pp. 735–743. Springer, Heidelberg (2013)
28. Sprenger, C.: A verified model checker for the modal mgr-calculus in coq. In: Steffen, B. (ed.) TACAS 1998. LNCS, vol. 1384, pp. 167–183. Springer, Heidelberg (1998)
29. Stump, A.: Proof checking technology for satisfiability modulo theories. Electronic Notes in Theoretical Computer Science 228, 121–133 (2009)
30. Weidenbach, C., Dimova, D., Fietzke, A., Kumar, R., Suda, M., Wischnewski, P.: SPASS version 3.5. In: Schmidt, R.A. (ed.) CADE-22. LNCS, vol. 5663, pp. 140–145. Springer, Heidelberg (2009)

Safety, Liveness and Run-Time Refinement for Modular Process-Aware Information Systems with Dynamic Sub Processes

Søren Debois[1(✉)], Thomas Hildebrandt[1], and Tijs Slaats[1,2]

[1] IT University of Copenhagen, København S, Denmark
{debois,hilde,tslaats}@itu.dk
[2] Exformatics A/S, København S, Denmark

Abstract. We study modularity, run-time adaptation and refinement under safety and liveness constraints in event-based process models with dynamic sub-process instantiation. The study is part of a larger programme to provide semantically well-founded technologies for modelling, implementation and verification of flexible, run-time adaptable process-aware information systems, moved into practice via the Dynamic Condition Response (DCR) Graphs notation co-developed with our industrial partner. Our key contributions are: (1) A formal theory of dynamic sub-process instantiation for declarative, event-based processes under safety and liveness constraints, given as the DCR* process language, equipped with a compositional operational semantics and conservatively extending the DCR Graphs notation; (2) an expressiveness analysis revealing that the DCR* process language is Turing-complete, while the fragment corresponding to DCR Graphs (without dynamic sub-process instantiation) characterises exactly the languages that are the union of a regular and an omega-regular language; (3) a formalisation of run-time refinement and adaptation by composition for DCR* processes and a proof that such refinement is undecidable in general; and finally (4) a decidable and practically useful sub-class of run-time refinements. Our results are illustrated by a running example inspired by a recent Electronic Case Management solution based on DCR Graphs and delivered by our industrial partner. An online prototype implementation of the DCR* language (including examples from the paper) and its visualisation as DCR Graphs can be found at http://tiger.itu.dk:8020/.

1 Introduction

Many software systems today control critical and increasingly complex long-running processes, often operating in unpredictable contexts. This is particularly the case for *Process-aware Information Systems* (PAIS) [32] and *Business Process Management Systems* (BPMS) [2], which constitute the practical context of the present work. The research in these fields deals with studying systems

Supported by the Velux foundation (grant 33295) and Innovation Fund Denmark.

N. Bjørner and F. de Boer (Eds.): FM 2015, LNCS 9109, pp. 143–160, 2015.
DOI: 10.1007/978-3-319-19249-9_10

driven by explicit process designs for the enactment and management of business processes and human workflows, and the study of formalisms for describing the process designs has always played a central role. Particularly popular models tend to specify explicit sequencing of business activities as flow graphs, e.g., Petri Nets and Workflow Nets [1], which are the closest formal counterpart to the industrial standard Business Process Model and Notation (BPMN) [30].

However, an approach to process implementation based on flow graphs implicitly assumes the initial design of a *pre-specified* process graph, that implements the believed best practice given the initial required set of business rules and legal constraints. This is problematic in several ways: Firstly, the explicit flow graph often imposes more constraints than necessary. Secondly, procedures, rules and regulations change or the process graph turns out not to be the desired practice anyway. For longer running processes, such as the management of mortgages of a credit institution, such changes need to be reflected in *running* processes. Moreover, while the flow graph may be initially verified to be compliant with the given business rules and legal constraints, only some of the rules are explicitly represented in decision points, others are implemented implicitly in the sequencing of actions. Thus, it is typically difficult to determine how a flow graph should be changed if some of the business rules or legal constraints not explicitly represented in decision points are changed.

Declarative process languages [3,17] address this deficiency by leaving the exact sequencing of activities undefined, yet specifying the constraints processes must respect. This gives a workflow system the maximum flexibility available under the rules and regulations of the process. In practice, the caseworker or process engine is empowered to take what is considered the appropriate steps (e.g. considering resource usage) for the process and situation at hand, subject only to the constraints expressed in the process model. If the constraint language is well designed, the constraints can directly represent the business and legal regulations, making it easy to add or update constraints if the regulations change. If the constraints are compiled to e.g. an automaton before execution (as in e.g. [3]), adaptations will only take effect on new instances of the process and not the running processes. However, run-time adaptations become a possibility if the constraints are interpreted at run-time. This is the case for the *Dynamic Condition Response (DCR) Graphs* notation, introduced in [17,28] and further co-developed with our industrial partner Exformatics in [18,7,29,19,12].

As we shall see, DCR Graphs represent any behaviour that can be described as the union of a regular and an ω-regular language. Conversely, it has been shown that a DCR Graph can be mapped to a Büchi-automaton, and so DCR Graphs can be analysed by standard automata-based model-checking techniques.

However, a workflow process may involve dynamic creation of an *a priori* unbounded number of new (sub) processes at run-time, as captured by the workflow patterns for creation of multiple instances in [33]. While it is of course possible to spawn new processes at run-time in any sensible electronic case management system, the compound behaviour of old and new processes is not explicitly represented by the formal model, and thus eludes formal analysis. Hence the central motivation for the present paper: We need to formally understand the dynamic creation of sub-processes, and we need to understand and control its interaction with run-time adaptation.

Tentative steps towards such an understanding were taken in [12], where we presented an extension of DCR Graphs to so-called *hierarchical DCR Graphs*, supporting dynamic creation of sub-processes. However, the graphical representation and formalisation of DCR Graphs is hard to manage and reason about for complex hierarchical processes composed of many parts, in particular when the different parts are dynamically created. Also, the expressive power of hierarchical DCR Graphs was left open in [12], as were the computational complexity of their refinements.

In the present paper, we contribute the following:

1. a formal theory of dynamic sub-process instantiation in declarative process models as a conservative extension of DCR Graphs,
2. an expressiveness analysis of the formal theory, revealing that dynamic sub-processes makes it Turing complete,
3. a notion of run-time adaptation by composition and a notion of refinement,
4. a proof that refinement is in general undecidable for processes with dynamic sub-processes
5. a practically useful and decidable sub class of run-time refinements defined as non-invasive adaptations

We illustrate our findings with a running example: a grant application process of a funding agency, which was recently implemented by our industry partner Exformatics in a DCR Graph-based commercial solution [10].

Overview of the paper: In Sec. 2 we present the DCR process language corresponding to the DCR Graphs notation and state its expressiveness, corresponding exactly to languages being the union of regular and ω-regular languages. We then extend the DCR language in Sec. 3 to DCR*, supporting dynamic creation of sub-processes with fresh (local) events and prove that DCR* is Turing complete. We address run-time adaptation by composition and refinement in Sec. 4, proving undecidability of refinement in general for DCR* and providing a practically useful, decidable sub-class of refinements referred to as non-invasive adaptations. Finally, in Sec. 5, we discuss related work and conclude. For want of space, most proofs and some examples have been relegated to the full version of this paper [11]. An online prototype implementation of the process language (and all examples of the paper), with a mapping to DCR Graphs, can be found at http://tiger.itu.dk:8020/.

2 Dynamic Condition Response (DCR) Processes

We now introduce the Dynamic Condition Response (DCR) process language. We shall see later that this language corresponds to the DCR Graph model [28,17]. Assume fixed universes of *events* $\mathcal{E}$ and *labels* $\mathcal{L}$; each event $e \in \mathcal{E}$ has an associated label $\ell(e) \in \mathcal{L}$. [1] Labels will be used as a (finite) alphabet for defining

[1] Unless explicitly stated, in all examples the label of an event is the event.

the language recognized by a DCR process. A DCR process $[M]\ T$ comprises a *marking* M and a *term* T. The syntax of both are given in Fig. 1 below.

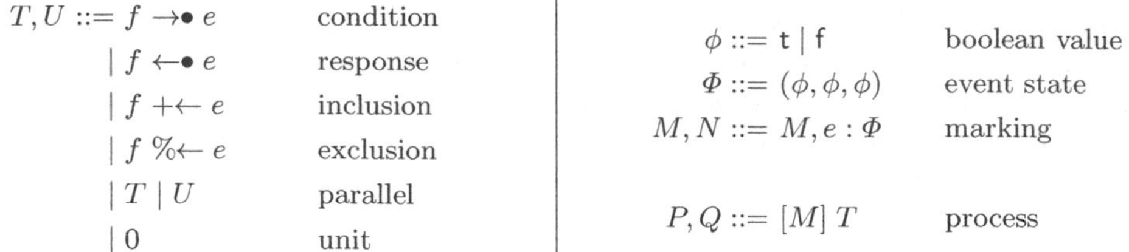

Fig. 1. DCR Processes Syntax

A term is a parallel composition of *constraint and effect relations* between *events*:

1. A *condition* $f \rightarrow\bullet e$ imposes the *constraint* that for event e to happen, the event f must either previously have happened or currently be excluded.
2. A *response* $f \leftarrow\bullet e$ imposes the *effect* that when e happens, f becomes restless and must eventually happen or be excluded.
3. An *exclusion* $f \,\%\!\!\leftarrow e$ imposes the *effect* that when e happens, it *excludes* f. An excluded event cannot happen; it is ignored as a condition; and it need not happen if restless, unless it is re-included by the final relation:
4. An *inclusion* $f +\!\!\leftarrow e$ imposes the *effect* that when the event e happens, it re-includes the event f.

All four relations refer to a marking M, a finite map from events to triples of booleans (h, i, r), referred to as the *event state* and indicating whether or not the event previously (h)appened, is currently (i)ncluded, and/or is (r)estless. A restless event represents an unfulfilled obligation: once it happens, it ceases to be restless. As commonly done for environments, we write markings as finite lists of pairs of events and event states, e.g. $e_1 : \Phi_1, \ldots, e_k : \Phi_k$ but treat them as maps, writing $\mathsf{dom}(M)$ and $M(e)$, and understand $M, e : \Phi$ to be undefined when $e \in \mathsf{dom}(M)$. The *free events* $\mathsf{fe}(T)$ of a term T is (for now) simply the set of events appearing in it. (This changes when we introduce local events in Sec. 3 below.) We require of a process $P = [M]\ T$ that $\mathsf{fe}(T) \subseteq \mathsf{dom}(M)$, and so define $\mathsf{fe}(P) = \mathsf{dom}(M)$. The *alphabet* $\mathsf{alph}(P)$ is the set of labels of its free events.

Example 1 (Grant process term). The grant application process implementation described in [10] involves at a high-level only four events: recv(an application is received), deadline(the current deadline for the current round has been reached), round(the application round is (re)opened for applications), and bm(a board meeting is held). Hereto come three constraints: 1) Applications can only be received after a round is opened and until the deadline has been reached. 2) After a round is opened, a board meeting must eventually be held. 3) If a round is open, and the deadline has not yet been met, a board meeting can not be held unless at least one application has been received. The events and constraints can be modelled by the following term:

$$T_0 = \mathsf{recv}\ \%\!\leftarrow \mathsf{deadline} \mid \mathsf{recv} +\!\leftarrow \mathsf{round} \mid \mathsf{bm} \leftarrow\!\bullet\ \mathsf{round} \mid \mathsf{recv} \rightarrow\!\bullet\ \mathsf{bm}$$

The first constraint is that the event deadline *excludes* the event recv, representing that applications can not be received after the deadline. The second constraint is that the event round *includes* the event recv, representing that applications can (again) be received if the round is (re)opened. The third constraint is that the event bm is a *response* to the event round, representing that a board meeting must happen eventually if the round is opened. The last constraint is that the event recv is a condition for bm, representing that, if the event recv is included, an application must have been received before the board meeting can be held. The initial state of the process is then defined by declaring that no event has happened and no event is restless (i.e. required to happen) and every event but recv is included. This is represented by the marking:

$$M_0 = \mathsf{round} : (\mathsf{f},\mathsf{t},\mathsf{f}), \mathsf{deadline} : (\mathsf{f},\mathsf{t},\mathsf{f}), \mathsf{recv} : (\mathsf{f},\mathsf{f},\mathsf{f}), \mathsf{bm} : (\mathsf{f},\mathsf{t},\mathsf{f})\ .$$

We give semantics to DCR processes incrementally. First, the notion of an event being *enabled* and what *effects* it has. The judgement $[M]\ T \vdash e : E, I, R$, defined (for atomic terms, parallel will be dealt with later) in Fig. 2. It should be read: "in the marking M, the (atomic) term T allows the event e to happen with the effects of excluding events E, including events I, and making events R restless."

$$[M, f : (h, i, \_), e : (\_, \mathsf{t}, \_)]\ f \rightarrow\!\bullet\ e \vdash e : \emptyset, \emptyset, \emptyset \qquad \text{(when } i \Rightarrow h\text{)}$$
$$[M, e : (\_, \mathsf{t}, \_)]\ f \leftarrow\!\bullet\ e \vdash e : \emptyset, \emptyset, \{f\}$$
$$[M, e : (\_, \mathsf{t}, \_)]\ f +\!\leftarrow e \vdash e : \emptyset, \{f\}, \emptyset$$
$$[M, e : (\_, \mathsf{t}, \_)]\ f\ \%\!\leftarrow e \vdash e : \{f\}, \emptyset, \emptyset$$
$$[M, e : (\_, \mathsf{t}, \_)]\ 0 \vdash e : \emptyset, \emptyset, \emptyset$$
$$[M, e : (\_, \mathsf{t}, \_)]\ f'\ \mathcal{R}\ f \vdash e : \emptyset, \emptyset, \emptyset \qquad \text{(when } e \neq f\text{)}$$

Fig. 2. Enabling & effects. We write "_" for "don't care", i.e., either true t or false f, and write $\mathcal{R}$ for any of the relations $\rightarrow\!\bullet$, $\leftarrow\!\bullet$, $+\!\leftarrow$, $\%\!\leftarrow$.

The first rule says that if f is a condition for e, then e can happen only if (1) it is itself included, and (2) if f is included, then f previously happened. The second rule says that if f is a response to e and e is included, then e can happen with the effect of making f restless. The third (fourth) rule says that if f is included (excluded) by e and e is included, then e can happen with the effect of including (excluding) f. The fifth rule says that the completely unconstrained process 0, an event e can happen if it is currently included. The last rule says that a relation allows any included event e to happen without effects when e is not the relation's right-hand–side event.

Given enabling and effects of events, we define the *action* of respectively an *event* e and an *effect* $\delta = (E, I, R)$ on a marking M pointwise by the action on individual event states $f : (h, i, r)$ as follows.

(Event action) $e \cdot (f : (h, i, r))) \stackrel{\text{def}}{=} f : (\underbrace{h \vee (f{=}e)}_{\text{happened?}},\ i,\ \underbrace{r \wedge (f{\neq}e)}_{\text{restless?}})$

(Effect action) $\delta \cdot (f : (h, i, r)) \stackrel{\text{def}}{=} f : (h,\ \underbrace{(i \wedge f{\notin}E) \vee f{\in}I}_{\text{included?}},\ \underbrace{r \vee f{\in}R}_{\text{restless?}})$

That is, for the event action, if $f = e$, the event is marked "happened" (first component becomes t) and it ceases to be restless (last component becomes f). For the effect action, the event only stays included (second component) if $f \notin E$ (it is not excluded) or $f \in I$ (it is included). This also means that if an event is both excluded and included by the effect, inclusion takes precedence. Finally, f is marked restless (third component) if either it was already restless or it became restless ($f \in R$). We then define the combined action of an event and effect by $(e : \delta) \cdot M = \delta \cdot (e \cdot M)$.

With these mechanics in place, we give transition semantics of processes in Fig. 3 below, where the *merge of effects* $\delta_1 \oplus \delta_2$ is simply defined as the pointwise union: $(E_1, I_1, R_1) \oplus (E_2, I_2, R_2) = (E_1 \cup E_2, I_1 \cup I_2, R_1 \cup R_2)$.

$$\frac{[M]\ T \vdash e : \delta}{[M]\ T \xrightarrow{e:\delta} T}\ [\text{INTRO}] \qquad \frac{[M]\ T_1 \xrightarrow{e:\delta_1} T_1' \qquad [M]\ T_2 \xrightarrow{e:\delta_2} T_2'}{[M]\ T_1 \mid T_2 \xrightarrow{e:\delta_1 \oplus \delta_2} T_1' \mid T_2'}\ [\text{PAR}]$$

$$\frac{[M]\ T \xrightarrow{e:\delta} T'}{[M]\ T \xrightarrow{e} [e : \delta \cdot M]\ T'}\ [\text{EFFECT}]$$

Fig. 3. Basic transition semantics

We use two forms of transitions: the *effect transition* $[M]\ T \xrightarrow{e:\delta} T'$ says that $[M]\ T$ may exhibit event e with effect δ, in the process updating the term T to become T'. (At this stage we will always have $T = T'$; we will need updates only when we extend the calculus in Section 3 below.) The *process transition* $[M]\ T \xrightarrow{e} [N]\ U$ takes a process to another process, applying the effect of e to the marking M, and thus only exhibiting the event e. The [INTRO] rule elevates an enabled event with an effect to an effect transition. The [PAR] rule merges the effects of transitions from the two sides of a parallel; note that markings on either side must be the same. The [EFFECT] rule lifts an effect transition to a process transition by applying the effect to the marking.

Process transitions gives rise to an LTS, which we equip with a notion of *acceptance* defined below a run is accepting if every restless event eventually either happens or is excluded.

Definition 2. *A DCR process defines an LTS with states* $[M]\ T$ *and (process) transitions* $[M]\ T \xrightarrow{e} [N]\ U$*. A run of* $[M]\ T$ *is a finite or infinite sequence of transitions* $[M]\ T = [M_0]\ T_0 \xrightarrow{e_0} \cdots$ *. A run is* accepting *iff for every state*

$[M_i]\ T_i$, *if whenever an event* e *is restless in* M_i, *i.e.* $M_i(e) = (\_, \_, \mathsf{t})$, *then there exists some* $j \geq i$ *s.t. either* $[M_j]\ T_j \xrightarrow{e:\delta} [M_{j+1}]\ T_{j+1}$ *or* e *is excluded in* M_j, *i.e.* $M_j(e) = (\_, \mathsf{f}, \_)$. *A* trace *of a process* $[M]\ T$ *is a possibly infinite string* $s = (s_i)_{i \in I}$ *s.t.* $[M]\ T$ *has an accepting run* $[M_i]\ T_i \xrightarrow{e_i} [M_{i+1}]\ T_{i+1}$ *with* $s_i = \ell(e_i)$. *The* language $\mathsf{lang}(P)$ *of a process* P *is the set of traces of* P.

Example 3 (Grant process transitions). As transitions change only marking, not terms, we show a run by showing changes in the marking. In the table below, rows indicate changes to the marking as the event on the left happens. Columns "h,i,r" indicate whether an event is marked (h)appened, (i)ncluded, and/or (r)estless. The column "Accepts?" indicates whether the current marking is accepting or not and the final column "Enabled" indicates which events are enabled after executing the event on the left.

Event	round			deadline			recv			bm			Accepts?	Enabled
happening	h	i	r	h	i	r	h	i	r	h	i	r		
(none)	f	t	f	f	t	f	f	f	f	f	t	f	t	{round, deadline, bm}
round	t							t				t	f	{round, deadline, recv}
deadline				t				f					f	{round, deadline, bm}
bm										t		f	t	{round, deadline, bm}
round								t		t		t	f	{round, deadline, recv}
recv							t						f	{round, deadline, recv, bm}
bm												f	t	{round, deadline, recv, bm}

After the first round event, bm cannot happen because of recv $\rightarrow\!\bullet$ bm. When deadline happens, it excludes recv because of recv $\%\!\leftarrow$ deadline, and exclusion of recv voids the condition recv $\rightarrow\!\bullet$ bm; so after deadline, bm may again happen. When round subsequently re-includes recv, bm is again disabled. Acceptance of the processes changes throughout. Because of bm $\leftarrow\!\bullet$ round, whenever round executes it makes bm restless, preventing the process from accepting until bm later happens, ceasing to be restless. In our examples, we identify events and labels, so the above table indicates an accepting trace ⟨round, deadline, bm, round, recv, bm⟩.

Finally, we note the connection of DCR processes to DCR Graphs [28,35,12] and their expressiveness; proof of the latter is included in the full version [11].

Theorem 4. *There exists a language-preserving bijection between DCR processes and finite DCR graphs.*

Theorem 5. *DCR processes characterise exactly the languages that are the union of a regular and an* ω*-regular language.*

3 DCR* Processes: Local Events and Reproduction

Below we extend the DCR process language to support dynamic creation of sub processes. We do this by extending the syntax with *local* and *reproductive* events as shown in Fig. 4, giving rise to the DCR* process language.

The *local event* $(\nu e : \Phi)\ T$ asserts that e with state Φ is local to the term T. Here, e is binding in Φ and T; for reasons which will be clear when we define accepting runs below, we will follow the Barendregt-convention and assume that all such local events are distinct. A *reproductive event* $e\{T\}$ creates, whenever the event e happens, a copy of T in parallel (to maintain the Barendrecht-convention, every local event in the copy is α-converted to a fresh, *but identically labelled* event).[2]

$$
\begin{array}{rlll}
T, U ::= & \ldots & & \\
 & \mid (\nu e : \Phi)\ T & & \text{local event} \\
 & \mid e\{T\} & & \text{reproductive event}
\end{array}
$$

Fig. 4. DCR* syntax

Example 6 (Grant process with reproductive and local events). We now consider three extra requirements: 1) When an application is received, a committee must recommend either *approval* or *rejection* to the board. 2) The committee might withdraw an approval, by later rejecting the application, but cannot reverse a rejection. 3) The board cannot make a final decision until it has a recommendation for every received application. We again use events recv and bm for receiving an application and convening a board meeting. We declare recv to be reproductive by adding the reproductive event recv{A}, where

$$A = (\nu \mathsf{approve} : (\mathsf{f},\mathsf{t},\mathsf{t}))\ (\nu \mathsf{reject} : (\mathsf{f},\mathsf{t},\mathsf{f}))\ \big(\mathsf{approve}\ \%\!\!\leftarrow \mathsf{reject} \mid \mathsf{approve} \rightarrow\!\bullet\ \mathsf{bm}\big)$$

Because approve and reject are local, each dynamically created sub-process A will have distinct decision events (all with the labels approve and reject though) that cannot be constrained further outside the scope. But, approve has a condition relation to the non-local bm, which means that each distinct approve event will become a condition for the (global) event bm. The exclude relation from reject to approve model that it is not possible to approve after a rejection, but nothing disallows rejection after approval. Both events have initially the local state "not-happened" and "included". We make the approve event initially restless in its local state, which will mean that in order for the process to be accepting either approve must happen or be excluded (because reject happens).

The transition rules for the new constructs are given in Fig. 5. Only terms and transition rules are extended; markings are the same.

Rule [LOCAL] gives semantics to events happening in the scope of a local event binder. An effect on the local event is recorded in the marking in the binder of that event. The event might have effects on non-local events, e.g., in $(\nu f : M)\ e \mathrel{+\!\!\leftarrow} f$, the local f has effects on the non-local e. Thus the effects are preserved in the conclusion, except that part of the effect which pertain only to f. Rule [PAR-2] propagates a local effect through a parallel composition. It's possible that the effect δ mentions events in U; however, it cannot mention events *local* to U. So the effects of δ on U are fully expressed in the (eventual) effect of δ on M. Rule [EFFECT-2] lifts effect transitions with local events to process transitions. Finally, the rule [REP] implements reproductive events: If

[2] We assume an infinite number of events in $\mathcal{E}$ for each label in $\mathcal{L}$.

$$\frac{[M, f:\Phi]\ T \xrightarrow{e:\delta} T' \quad f:\Phi' = (e:\delta)\cdot(f:\Phi) \quad \gamma = \nu e \text{ if } e = f, \text{ o.w. } \gamma = e}{[M]\ (\nu f:\Phi)\ T \xrightarrow{\gamma:(\delta\backslash f)} (\nu f:\Phi')\ T'}\ [\text{LOCAL}]$$

$$\frac{[M]\ T \xrightarrow{\nu e:\delta} T'}{[M]\ T \mid U \xrightarrow{\nu e:\delta} T' \mid U}\ [\text{PAR-2}] \qquad \frac{[M]\ T'' \xrightarrow{e:\delta} T' \quad T \cong_\alpha T''}{[M]\ e\{T\} \xrightarrow{e:\delta} e\{T\} \mid T'}\ [\text{REP}]$$

$$\frac{[M]\ T \xrightarrow{\nu e:\delta} T'}{[M]\ T \xrightarrow{\nu e} [\delta\cdot M]\ T'}\ [\text{EFFECT-2}]$$

Here $\delta\backslash f = (E\backslash\{f\}, I\backslash\{f\}, R\backslash\{f\})$. We omit the obvious rule symmetric to [PAR-2].

Fig. 5. Transition semantics for local and reproductive events

the guarding event e happening would update the body T to become T', then e can unfold to such a T'. In DCR*, the term *does* change as the process evolves.

To define accepting runs we need to track local restless events across transitions. For this reason we assume the unique local events and maintain this by α-conversion (denoted by $\cong_\alpha$) of local events when a reproductive event happens, i.e., local events duplicated by [REP] are chosen globally fresh.

Definition 7. *A run of a DCR* process $[M]\ T$ is a finite or infinite sequence $[M_i]\ N_i \xrightarrow{\lambda_i} [M_{i+1}]\ N_{i+1}$ with $\lambda = e_i$ or $\lambda = \nu e_i$. The trace of a run is the sequence of labels of its events, i.e., the string given by $\ell(\lambda_i)$ where $\ell(\nu e) \stackrel{def}{=} \ell(e)$. A run is* accepting *if whenever an event e is marked as restless in M_i respectively a local event νe is marked as restless by its binder in T_i, then there exists some $j \geq i$ s.t. either $[M_j]\ T_j \xrightarrow{\lambda_i} [M_{j+1}]\ T_{j+1}$ with $\lambda_i = e$ respectively $\lambda_i = \nu e$; or the event state of e in M_j respectively T_j has e excluded.*

Example 8. A possible transition sequence for the reproductive $\mathsf{recv}\{A\}$ event defined above in the marking $M_1 = \mathsf{recv} : (\mathsf{f},\mathsf{t},\mathsf{f}), \mathsf{bm} : (\mathsf{f},\mathsf{t},\mathsf{f})$ is as follows.

$$[M_1]\ \mathsf{recv}\{A\} \xrightarrow{\mathsf{recv}} [M_2]\ \mathsf{recv}\{A\} \mid A_1$$

$$\xrightarrow{\mathsf{recv}} [M_2]\ \mathsf{recv}\{A\} \mid A_1 \mid A_2 \tag{1}$$

$$\xrightarrow{\nu\mathsf{approve}_1} [M_2]\ \mathsf{recv}\{A\} \mid ((\nu\mathsf{approve}_1 : (\mathsf{t},\mathsf{t},\mathsf{f}))\ (\nu\mathsf{reject}_1 : (\mathsf{f},\mathsf{t},\mathsf{f})) \tag{2}$$

$$\mathsf{approve}_1 \%\!\leftarrow \mathsf{reject}_1 \mid \mathsf{approve}_1 \rightarrow\!\bullet\ \mathsf{bm}) \mid A_2$$

$$\xrightarrow{\nu\mathsf{reject}_2} [M_2]\ \mathsf{recv}\{A\} \mid ((\nu\mathsf{approve}_1 : (\mathsf{t},\mathsf{t},\mathsf{f}))\ (\nu\mathsf{reject}_1 : (\mathsf{f},\mathsf{t},\mathsf{f})) \tag{3}$$

$$\mathsf{approve}_1 \%\!\leftarrow \mathsf{reject}_1 \mid \mathsf{approve}_1 \rightarrow\!\bullet\ \mathsf{bm})$$

$$((\nu\mathsf{approve}_2 : (\mathsf{f},\mathsf{f},\mathsf{t}))\ (\nu\mathsf{reject}_2 : (\mathsf{t},\mathsf{t},\mathsf{f}))$$

$$\mathsf{approve}_2 \%\!\leftarrow \mathsf{reject}_2 \mid \mathsf{approve}_2 \rightarrow\!\bullet\ \mathsf{bm})$$

$$\xrightarrow{\mathsf{bm}} [M_3]\ \mathsf{recv}\{A\} \mid \cdots \tag{4}$$

Here $M_2 = \mathsf{recv} : (\mathsf{t},\mathsf{t},\mathsf{f}), \mathsf{bm} : (\mathsf{f},\mathsf{t},\mathsf{f})$ and $M_3 = \mathsf{recv} : (\mathsf{t},\mathsf{t},\mathsf{f}), \mathsf{bm} : (\mathsf{t},\mathsf{t},\mathsf{f})$.

At (1), the processes A_1 and A_2 are copies of A where the local events $\mathsf{approve}$ and reject have been α-converted to $\mathsf{approve}_1, \mathsf{approve}_2$ (but still labelled $\mathsf{approve}$) and $\mathsf{reject}_1, \mathsf{reject}_2$ (but still labelled reject) respectively, following the convention of unique local events. Moreover, because they have not happened in the local markings under the binders, bm cannot happen. To see this, observe that by the [PAR]-rule, for the whole process to exhibit bm, every part of it must also exhibit bm. But $(\nu \mathsf{approve}_1 : (\mathsf{f}, \mathsf{t}, \mathsf{t})) \ldots \mathsf{approve}_1 \rightarrow\!\bullet\ \mathsf{bm}$ cannot: the hypothesis of rule [LOCAL], that bm could happen if $\mathsf{approve}_1$ is considered global with marking $(\mathsf{f}, \mathsf{t}, \mathsf{t})$, cannot be established.

When a local $\mathsf{approve}_i$ event happens, its local marking changes to reflect that the event happened and is no longer restless, as indicated with grey background in (2). However, $\mathsf{approve}_1$ happening is not enough to enable bm; it is still disabled by the other copy. Also, the entire process is not in an accepting state, since $\mathsf{approve}_2$ is still restless and included. Once reject happens in the second copy (3), excluding $\mathsf{approve}$ in that copy, bm is enabled and the process is in an accepting state: of the two local $\mathsf{approve}$ events bm is conditional upon, one has happened (and thus also no longer restless), and the other is excluded (and thus also no longer required for acceptance).

3.1 Encoding of Minsky Machines

We now show that DCR* has the full power of Turing machines by reduction from the Halting Problem for Minsky machines [26].

A Minsky machine $m = (R_1, R_2, P, c)$ comprises two unbounded *registers* R_1, R_2; a *program* P, which is a list of pairs of addresses and instructions; and a *program counter* c, giving the address of the current instruction. It has the following instruction set.

$\texttt{inc}(i, a)$	Add 1 to the contents of register i. Proceed to a.
$\texttt{decjz}(i, a, b)$	If register i is zero, proceed to a. Otherwise subtract 1 from register i and proceed to b.
$\texttt{halt}$	Halt execution (w.l.o.g. assumed to appear exactly once).

We construct, given a Minsky machine m, a term $\mathsf{t}(m)$ and a marking $\mathsf{m}(m)$. We model machine instructions as events. To maintain execution order, we model program addresses explicitly as events a. These events serve only to constrain the execution of other events; they should not themselves happen, and we prevent them from doing so with a condition $a \rightarrow\!\bullet\ a$ for each a. By making each instruction event e conditional on its program point a, $a \rightarrow\!\bullet\ e$, we ensure that e *may happen only if* a *is excluded*. To move the program counter from a to b, we re-include a and exclude b. We define a shorthand $\mathsf{insn}(e, a, b)$ for an instruction event e at program point a proceeding to program point b as follows:

$$\mathsf{insn}(e, a, b) = a \rightarrow\!\bullet\ e \mid a \,+\!\!\leftarrow e \mid b \,\%\!\!\leftarrow e$$

Now, registers. We model each $a : \texttt{decjz}(i, b, c)$ by two events: one, $\texttt{decjz}^a$, which can happen only when the register is zero, and a second, $\texttt{decjn}^a$, which can happen only when it is not. Then we model increments by making each increment reproductive, replicating a new copy of $\texttt{decjn}^a$ for every decrement instruction $a : \texttt{decjz}(i, b, c)$ in P. The copies produced by a single increment represents the *opportunity* for exactly one of these instructions to decrement. Thus, we make the copies in a single increment exclude each other. To make sure that $\texttt{decjz}^a$ cannot happen if the register is non-zero, that is, if no $\texttt{decjn}^a$ is present, we make the latter a condition of the former: $\texttt{decjn}^a \rightarrow\!\bullet\ \texttt{decjz}^a$. Altogether, the term for one increment is constructed by the following function. (We write $(N_{i \in I} x_i : M)$ for $(\nu x_{i_1} : M) \ldots (\nu x_{i_n} : M)$ when $I = \{i_1, \ldots, i_n\}$.)

$$\mathsf{one}(i) = \Big(\mathop{\mathsf{N}}_{a:\texttt{decjz}(i,c,d)} \texttt{decjn}^a : (\mathsf{f},\mathsf{t},\mathsf{f}) \Big) \prod_{a:\texttt{decjz}(i,c,d)} \Big(\mathsf{insn}(\texttt{decjn}^a, a, d) \mid \texttt{decjn}^a \rightarrow\!\bullet\ \texttt{decjz}^a \mid \prod_{a':\texttt{decjz}(i,b',c')} \texttt{decjn}^{a'} \ \%\!\leftarrow \texttt{decjn}^a \Big)$$

Adding one to a register i is accomplished by making a new copy of $\mathsf{one}(i)$.

$$\mathsf{inc}(a, i, b) = \mathsf{insn}(\texttt{inc}^a, a, b) \mid \texttt{inc}^a\{\mathsf{one}(i)\}$$

We put it all together and define $\mathsf{t}(m)$ for a Minsky machine $m = (R_1, R_2, P, c)$.

$$\mathsf{t}(m) = \prod_{a:\texttt{inc}(i,b)\in P} \mathsf{inc}(a, i, b) \mid \prod_{a:\texttt{decjz}(i,b,c)\in P} \mathsf{insn}(\texttt{decjz}^a, a, b) \mid \prod_{a:\texttt{halt}\in P} a \rightarrow\!\bullet\ \texttt{halt} \mid \prod_{a:I\in P} a \rightarrow\!\bullet\ a \mid \prod_{i<R_1} \mathsf{one}(1) \mid \prod_{i<R_2} \mathsf{one}(2)$$

Finally, the marking $\mathsf{m}(m)$ is given below. (Recall that c is the program counter.)

	c	a when $a \neq c$	$\texttt{decjz}^a$	$\texttt{inc}^a$	$\texttt{halt}$
Happened	f	f	f	f	f
Included	f	t	t	t	t
Restless	f	f	f	f	t

This encodes a Minsky machine as a DCR*-process:

Theorem 9. *A Minsky machine m halts iff $[\mathsf{m}(m)]\ \mathsf{t}(m)$ has an accepting run.*

Proof. (outline) The proof is based on a bisimulation relation between finite execution traces of the Minsky machine m and reachable markings of the encoding $[\mathsf{m}(m)]\ \mathsf{t}(m)$. First we observe that in every reachable marking of $[\mathsf{m}(m)]\ \mathsf{t}(m)$ exactly one of the program address events will be included and exactly one event is enabled. The bisimulation relation will relate an execution trace of the Minsky machine ending in address j to a marking in which that event is excluded. Next we prove that for every pair, the machine can perform an instruction iff the encoding can execute the corresponding event, and that the form of the process $t(m)$ is preserved as well as the global marking $m(m)$, except that instruction events are being recorded as executed (and excluded in the case of `decjn`) is preserved by steps. It follows that the restless **halt** event can be eventually executed if and only if the machine can execute the halt command.

Example 10. As an example, let us consider a Minsky machine adding the contents of register 2 to register 1. We'll consider the machine $(0, 1, P, 1)$, where P is the program:

$1 : \texttt{decjz}(2, 3, 2)$
$2 : \texttt{inc}(1, 1)$
$3 : \texttt{halt}$

Applying the above construction, we get the following term (split out in a table for readability).

$\prod_{a:\texttt{inc}(i,b)\in P} \mathsf{inc}(a, i, b)$	$\prod_{a:\texttt{decjz}(i,b,c)\in P} \mathsf{insn}(\texttt{decjz}^a, a, b)$
$2 \rightarrow\!\bullet\ \texttt{inc}^2$ $2\ \%\!\leftarrow \texttt{inc}^2$ $1 +\!\leftarrow \texttt{inc}^2$ $\texttt{inc}^2\{0\}$	$1 \rightarrow\!\bullet\ \texttt{decjz}^1$ $1 +\!\leftarrow \texttt{decjz}^1$ $3\ \%\!\leftarrow \texttt{decjz}^1$

$\prod_{a:\texttt{halt}\in P} a \rightarrow\!\bullet\ \texttt{halt}$	$\prod_{a:I\in P} a \rightarrow\!\bullet\ a$	$\prod_{i<R_1} \mathsf{one}(1)$	$\prod_{i<R_2} \mathsf{one}(2)$
$3 \rightarrow\!\bullet\ \texttt{halt}$	$1 \rightarrow\!\bullet\ 1$ $2 \rightarrow\!\bullet\ 2$ $3 \rightarrow\!\bullet\ 3$	0	$(\nu\texttt{decjn}^1 : (\mathsf{f},\mathsf{t},\mathsf{f}))$ $1 \rightarrow\!\bullet\ \texttt{decjn}^1$ $1 +\!\leftarrow \texttt{decjn}^1$ $2\ \%\!\leftarrow \texttt{decjn}^1$ $\texttt{decjn}^1 \rightarrow\!\bullet\ \texttt{decjz}^1$ $\texttt{decjn}^1\ \%\!\leftarrow \texttt{decjn}^1$

We emphasise that in the column $\Pi_{i<R_2}\mathsf{one}(2)$, all instances of $\texttt{decjn}^1$ are within the scope of the binder and thus local.

4 Run-time Adaptations by Composition and Refinement

We now turn to investigating run-time refinement and adaptations of DCR* processes by composition. We shall find that, as a consequence of the Turing-completeness of DCR*, refinement is in general undecidable. We however identify and exemplify a practically useful, decidable sub-class of refinements, which we call *non-invasive adaptations.*

To define composition of processes, we need to define merge of markings:

$$(M_1, e : m) \oplus (M_2, e : m) = (M_1 \oplus M_2), e : m$$
$$(M_1, e : m) \oplus M_2 = (M_1 \oplus M_2), e : m \quad \text{when } e \notin \mathsf{dom}(M_2)$$

Note that merge on markings is *partial,* since it is only defined on markings that agree on their overlap. When the merge of the markings of two processes is defined, we say that the processes are *marking compatible.*

Definition 11. *Given marking compatible DCR* processes* $[M]\ T$ *and* $[N]\ S$ *their* composition *is defined as* $[M]\ T \oplus [N]\ S = [M \oplus N]\ T \mid S$.

Example 12. Suppose that *as the grant process of Example 1 runs*, e.g. just after the round has been opened, a new requirement comes up: For regulatory reasons, a board meeting must eventually be followed by an audit. We model this constraint by a new event, audit, which must be a response to bm. As we are introducing a new event, we must also introduce additional marking. The following process R_1 embodies the adaptation we wish to achieve.

$$R_1 = [\mathsf{bm} : (\mathsf{f}, \mathsf{t}, \mathsf{t}), \mathsf{audit}(\mathsf{f}, \mathsf{t}, \mathsf{f})]\ \mathsf{audit} \leftarrow\!\bullet\ \mathsf{bm}$$

Assume the process $P = [M_1]\ T_1$ is the process reached after the first step of Example 3, i.e. $[M_0]\ T_1 \xrightarrow{\mathsf{round}} P$. We can then adapt P to include R_1 simply by composing the two processes:

$$P_1 = P \oplus R_1 = [M_1, \mathsf{audit} : (\mathsf{f}, \mathsf{t}, \mathsf{f})]\ T_1 \mid \mathsf{audit} \leftarrow\!\bullet\ \mathsf{bm}$$

As a second example, suppose further that it is also decreed that *during* an audit, no further applications can be received. We adapt P_1 with R_2 as follows:

$$\begin{aligned} R_2 &= [\mathsf{recv} : (\mathsf{f}, \mathsf{t}, \mathsf{f}), \mathsf{audit} : (\mathsf{f}, \mathsf{t}, \mathsf{f}), \mathsf{pass} : (\mathsf{f}, \mathsf{t}, \mathsf{f})]\ \mathsf{recv}\ \%\!\leftarrow \mathsf{audit} \mid \mathsf{recv} +\!\leftarrow \mathsf{pass} \\ P_2 &= P_1 \oplus R_2 \\ &= [M_1, \mathsf{audit} : (\mathsf{f}, \mathsf{t}, \mathsf{f}), \mathsf{pass} : (\mathsf{f}, \mathsf{t}, \mathsf{f})]\ T_1 \mid \mathsf{audit} \leftarrow\!\bullet\ \mathsf{bm} \\ &\quad \mid \mathsf{recv}\ \%\!\leftarrow \mathsf{audit} \mid \mathsf{recv} +\!\leftarrow \mathsf{pass} \end{aligned}$$

When we extend the set of requirements by a (run-time) adaptation of P to P', we often want to ensure that the results is a refinement of the existing requirements, meaning that the old set of requirements is upheld. Informally, the adapted process does not exhibit behaviour disallowed by P. We cannot simply formulate refinement by language inclusion $\mathsf{lang}(P') \subseteq \mathsf{lang}(P)$, since we may not only add new constraints, but also new *events* (and thus new labels), like audit in the above example. Instead, we define refinement as language inclusion only w.r.t. the alphabet of P. In doing so we employ the following notation.

Notation. Given a sequence s, write $s|_\Sigma$ for the largest sub-sequence s' of s s.t. $s'_i \in \Sigma$; e.g, if $s = AABC$ then $s|_{A,C} = AAC$.

Definition 13. *Given DCR* processes* P *and* P', *we say that* P' is a refinement of P *iff* $\mathsf{lang}(P')|_{\mathsf{alph}(P)} \subseteq \mathsf{lang}(P)$.

When merging in new constraints P' to a process P gives rise to a refinement we will say P' is conservative for P, as defined formally below.

Definition 14. *Given marking compatible DCR* processes* P *and* Q, *we say that* Q *is* conservative *for* P *iff* $P \oplus Q$ *is a refinement of* P.

Example 15. Continuing the above example, we now see a fundamental distinction between the adaptation by R_1 and R_2: the former refines P, whereas the latter does not refine P_1. To see this, observe for R_1 that it only makes P_2 *less* accepting (because of the potential restlessness of the new event audit). For R_2, observe that $P_1 \oplus R_2$ has the following accepting execution:

$$P_1 \oplus R_2 \xrightarrow{\mathsf{audit}} \xrightarrow{\mathsf{bm}} \xrightarrow{\mathsf{audit}}$$

Here audit excludes recv, and so enables bm to execute; bm in turn makes audit restless, so after a second audit, we have an accepting trace $t = \langle \mathsf{audit},\ \mathsf{bm},\ \mathsf{audit} \rangle$. However, bm cannot be the first event of a trace of P_1, because it is conditional on the non-executed recv. Formally, we found a counter-example to refinement:

$$\langle \mathsf{audit},\ \mathsf{bm},\ \mathsf{audit} \rangle|_{\mathsf{alph}(P_1)} = \langle \mathsf{bm} \rangle \notin \mathsf{lang}(P_1)$$

Inspecting the adaptation R_2 more closely, one see that the problem comes from the dynamic exclusion of the recv event, since it not only makes the reception of applications impossible, but also enables events such as bm that are conditional on recv. A better way is to block recv by introducing a new condition:

$$R_2' = [\mathsf{recv} : (\mathsf{f},\mathsf{t},\mathsf{f}), \mathsf{audit} : (\mathsf{f},\mathsf{t},\mathsf{f})]\ \mathsf{audit}\{(\nu \mathsf{pass} : (\mathsf{f},\mathsf{t},\mathsf{f}))\ \mathsf{pass} \to\!\bullet\ \mathsf{recv}\}$$

Here, once audit happens, recv is barred from executing until the local event pass has happened. The corresponding adaptation $P_2 \oplus R_2$ *is* a refinement.

Unfortunately the property of one process being conservative for another is undecidable:

Theorem 16. *It is undecidable whether a DCR*-process P is conservative for a DCR*-process Q.*

Proof. Let m be a Minsky machine, and take $M = [\mathsf{m}(m)]\ \mathsf{m}(t)$ to be the encoding of m as a DCR* process following Theorem 9. Take P to be the process $P = []\ (\nu e : (\mathsf{f},\mathsf{t},\mathsf{f}))\ e \to\!\bullet\ e$, with e labelled `halt`. We show that m is terminating iff M is not conservative for P. Clearly $\mathsf{lang}(P) = \epsilon$, that is, the only trace of P is the empty trace. By Theorem 9, the encoding M of m has a trace exhibiting the label `halt` iff m terminates, so $\mathsf{lang}(P \oplus M)|_{\mathsf{alph}(P)}$ has a non-empty trace iff m terminates. It follows that $\mathsf{lang}(P \oplus M)|_{\mathsf{alph}(P)} \subseteq \mathsf{lang}(P)$ iff m does not terminate, and so M is conservative for P iff m does not terminate.

Fortunately, we have identified a large class of practically useful refinements, which we dub *non-invasive* adaptations.

Definition 17 (Non-invasive adaptation). *Let $P_1 = [M_1]\ T_1$ and $P_2 = [M_2]\ T_2$ be processes. We say that P_1* non-invasive *for P_2 iff*

1. *For every context $C(-)$, such that $T_1 = C(e \to\!\%\ f)$ or $T_1 = C(e \to\!+\ f)$, either f is bound in $C(-)$ or $f \notin \mathsf{fe}(P_2)$; and*
2. *For every label $l \in \mathsf{alph}(P_1) \cap \mathsf{alph}(P_2)$, no bound event of T_1 is labelled l, and if $e \in \mathsf{fe}(P_1)$ is labelled l, then $e \in \mathsf{fe}(P_2)$.*

It's straightforward to verify that non-invasiveness is decidable, and that R_1 and R'_2 are non-invasive adaptations for P and P_1 respectively, whereas R_2 is not for P_1 (because of the exclusion of bm).

Moreover, we can indeed prove that non-invasive adaptations are conservative, and thus gives rise to refinements (proof in the full version [11]):

Theorem 18. *If P is non-invasive for Q then P is conservative for Q.*

Non-invasiveness adaptations admits a large class of practically important refinements. As illustrated by the adaptations given by R_1 and R'_2, the permitted adaptations correspond to dynamically adding an arbitrary new process to the running process, and adding arbitrary condition and response relations between events of the composed process. Even though existing events can not be excluded by new events, it is possible to arbitrarily block events of the original process.

Within the application area of business process modelling, it is a common change to add such possibility/requirement of taking additional actions interleaved between existing actions. Indeed, the need for a non-invasive, run-time adaptation showed up in the implementation of the grant application process [10]. After the start of an application round, a forgotten requirement was realised: If the account number of a grant holder is changed, then the accountant must verify, that the account belongs to the grant holder before the next payment. The adaptation was made to the DCR Graph representing the run-time state of the grant application system *without terminating or restarting any systems.*

5 Conclusion, Related and Future Work

We studied the interplay of dynamic process instantiation, run-time adaptation and refinement in the context of a declarative event-based process language, generalising our prior work on DCR Graphs co-developed and implemented by our industrial partner. Specifically, we proved that dynamic process instantiation makes the language Turing-complete, and as a consequence, refinement undecidable. We then identified a large, decidable and practically useful class of refinements referred to as non-invasive adaptations. All findings and problems were illustrated by a running example extracted from a real case.

Related Work. The DCR language is as we have seen closely related to DCR Graphs [28,35,17], which descend from event structures, and thus have relations to Petri Nets. Petri Nets have been extended to allow modular definition (e.g. via shared transitions [25]) and to represent infinite computations and ω-regular languages (e.g., Büchi Nets [14]). However, Petri nets introduce the intentional construct of *places* marked with *tokens*, as opposed to event structures and DCR* processes, which only rely on causal and conflict relations between events. Variants of event structures with asymmetric conflict relation relates to the asymmetric exclude relation of DCR processes, including extended bundle event structures [23,16], dual event structures [22,24], asymmetric event structures [6], and precursor event structures [15]. Automata based models like Event automata [31] and local event structures [20] also allow asymmetric conflicts, but use explicit states and do not express causality and conflicts as relations between events. Besides the early work on restless events in [36], we are not aware of other published work generalising event-structures to be able to express liveness properties, nor to distinguish between events that *may* and events that *must eventually be executed.* Reproductive events of the DCR* process language relate to replication in process calculi and higher-order Petri nets [21]. We believe to be the first to combine higher-order features and liveness.

Run-time adaptation has been studied also for Petri nets [34] and process calculi [5,8,9], but tends to require predefined adaptation points, and often deal with adaptations via higher-order primitives. In contrast, adaptation in DCR* is dealt with by composition, which due to the declarative nature allow for cross-cutting adaptations without the need for pre-specified adaptation points.

In the BPM community, the seminal declarative process language is Declare [3,4]. As Declare is based on mapping primitives to LTL, which are then mapped to automata, it necessarily distinguishes between run-time and design-time. In contrast, in DCR processes, design-time and run-time representation is literally the same. Declare has a relatively large set of basic constraints, the formal expressiveness of which is clearly limited by that of LTL, while DCR processes with only 4 basic constraints offers the full expressiveness of regular and ω-regular languages. A different approach is [27], which provides a mapping from Declare to the CLIMB, which allows the use of its reasoning techniques for support and verification of Declare processes at both design- and run-time.

Imperative process models such as BPMN [30] have supported dynamic sub-processes for some time now, they are only recently being studied for declarative languages [37]. Here, sub-processes do not have independent life cycles, that is, when a sub-process is spawned, it must run to completion before its super-process may resume. Interestingly, it is noted in *ibid.* that extending the model with sub-processes seems to increase its expressive power; we formally confirm that supposition here, finding DCR graphs with sub-processes to be Turing complete.

Future Work. DCR* processes as defined here only interact via shared events. We are currently working on adding interaction between concurrent events, labelled with send and receive labels as found e.g. in the π-calculus, thereby lifting the results of the present paper to π-like languages. Towards better analysis of the infinite-state DCR* language, we have initiated work on exploiting the idea of responses and restless events in the domain of behavioural types [13] and run-time monitoring [28]. The DCR* process language would benefit from a closer investigation of its relation to modular [25] and higher-order Petri Nets [21]. Finally, time constraints and more general adaptations as initiated in [19,29], e.g. allowing to remove constraints and events should be further investigated.

Acknowledgments. We thank the anonymous reviewers for helpful comments.

References

1. van der Aalst, W.M.P.: The application of petri nets to workflow management. Journal of Circuits, Systems, and Computers 8(1), 21–66 (1998)
2. van der Aalst, W.M.P., ter Hofstede, A.H.M., Weske, M.: Business process management: A survey. In: van der Aalst, W.M.P., ter Hofstede, A.H.M., Weske, M. (eds.) BPM 2003. LNCS, vol. 2678, pp. 1–12. Springer, Heidelberg (2003)
3. van der Aalst, W.M.P., Pesic, M.: DecSerFlow: Towards a truly declarative service flow language. In: Bravetti, M., Núñez, M., Zavattaro, G. (eds.) WS-FM 2006. LNCS, vol. 4184, pp. 1–23. Springer, Heidelberg (2006)
4. van der Aalst, W.M.P., Pesic, M., Schonenberg, H., Westergaard, M., Maggi, F.M.: Declare. Webpage (2010), http://www.win.tue.nl/declare/
5. Anderson, G., Rathke, J.: Dynamic software update for message passing programs. In: Jhala, R., Igarashi, A. (eds.) APLAS 2012. LNCS, vol. 7705, pp. 207–222. Springer, Heidelberg (2012)
6. Baldan, P., Corradini, A., Montanari, U.: Contextual petri nets, asymmetric event structures, and processes. Information and Computation 171, 1–49 (2001)
7. Barthe, G., Pardo, A., Schneider, G. (eds.): SEFM 2011. LNCS, vol. 7041. Springer, Heidelberg (2011)
8. Bravetti, M., Giusto, C.D., Pérez, J.A., Zavattaro, G.: Steps on the road to component evolvability. In: Proceedings of the 7th International Conference on Formal Aspects of Component Software, FACS 2010, pp. 295–299 (2012), http://dx.doi.org/10.1007/978-3-642-27269-1_19
9. Bravetti, M., Giusto, C.D., Pérez, J.A., Zavattaro, G.: Adaptable processes. Logical Methods in Computer Science 8(4) (2012)
10. Debois, S., Hildebrandt, T., Marquard, M., Slaats, T.: A case for declarative process modelling: Agile development of a grant application system. In: EDOCW/AdaptiveCM 2014, pp. 126 - 133. IEEE (September 2014)
11. Debois, S., Hildebrandt, T., Slaats, T.: Safety, liveness and run-time refinement for modular process-aware information systems with dynamic sub processes (full version) (2015), http://www.itu.dk/~debois/dcrstar-tr.pdf
12. Debois, S., Hildebrandt, T.T., Slaats, T.: Hierarchical declarative modelling with refinement and sub-processes. In: Sadiq, S., Soffer, P., Völzer, H. (eds.) BPM 2014. LNCS, vol. 8659, pp. 18–33. Springer, Heidelberg (2014), http://dx.doi.org/10.1007/978-3-319-10172-9
13. Debois, S., Hildebrandt, T.T., Slaats, T., Yoshida, N.: Type checking liveness for collaborative processes with bounded and unbounded recursion. In: Ábrahám, E., Palamidessi, C. (eds.) FORTE 2014. LNCS, vol. 8461, pp. 1–16. Springer, Heidelberg (2014)
14. Esparza, J., Melzer, S.: Model checking LTL using constraint programming. In: Azéma, P., Balbo, G. (eds.) ICATPN 1997. LNCS, vol. 1248, pp. 1–20. Springer, Heidelberg (1997)
15. Fecher, H., Majster-Cederbaum, M.: Event structures for arbitrary disruption. Fundam. Inf. 68(1-2), 103–130 (2005)
16. van Glabbeek, R.J., Vaandrager, F.W.: Bundle event structures and CCSP. In: Amadio, R.M., Lugiez, D. (eds.) CONCUR 2003. LNCS, vol. 2761, pp. 57–71. Springer, Heidelberg (2003)
17. Hildebrandt, T.T., Mukkamala, R.R.: Declarative event-based workflow as distributed dynamic condition response graphs. In: PLACES. EPTCS. EPTCS, vol. 69, pp. 59–73 (2010)

18. Hildebrandt, T.T., Mukkamala, R.R., Slaats, T.: Nested dynamic condition response graphs. In: Arbab, F., Sirjani, M. (eds.) FSEN 2011. LNCS, vol. 7141, pp. 343–350. Springer, Heidelberg (2012)
19. Hildebrandt, T.T., Mukkamala, R.R., Slaats, T., Zanitti, F.: Contracts for cross-organizational workflows as timed dynamic condition response graphs. J. Log. Algebr. Program. 82(5-7), 164–185 (2013)
20. Hoogers, P.W., Kleijn, H.C.M., Thiagarajan, P.S.: An event structure semantics for general petri nets. Theoretical Computer Science 153(1-2), 129–170 (1996)
21. Janneck, J.W., Esser, R.: Higher-order petri net modelling: Techniques and applications. In: Proceedings of the Conference on Application and Theory of Petri Nets: Formal Methods in Software Engineering and Defence Systems, CRPIT 2002, pp. 17–25 (2002)
22. Katoen, J.P.: Quantitative and qualitative extensions of event structures. Ph.D. thesis, University of Twente, Enschede (April 1996)
23. Langerak, R.: Transformations and Semantics for LOTOS. Universiteit Twente (1992)
24. Langerak, R., Brinksma, E., Katoen, J.-P.: Causal ambiguity and partial orders in event structures. In: Mazurkiewicz, A., Winkowski, J. (eds.) CONCUR 1997. LNCS, vol. 1243, pp. 317–331. Springer, Heidelberg (1997)
25. Latvala, T., Mäkelä, M.: LTL model checking for modular petri nets. In: Cortadella, J., Reisig, W. (eds.) ICATPN 2004. LNCS, vol. 3099, pp. 298–311. Springer, Heidelberg (2004)
26. Minsky, M.L.: Computation: Finite and Infinite Machines. Prentice-Hall (1967)
27. Montali, M.: Specification and Verification of Declarative Open Interaction Models - A Logic-Based Approach, LNBIP, vol. 56. Springer, Heidelberg (2010)
28. Mukkamala, R.R.: A Formal Model For Declarative Workflows: Dynamic Condition Response Graphs. Ph.D. thesis, IT University of Copenhagen (June 2012)
29. Mukkamala, R.R., Hildebrandt, T., Slaats, T.: Towards trustworthy adaptive case management with dynamic condition response graphs. In: EDOC, pp. 127–136. IEEE (2013)
30. Object Management Group BPMN Technical Committee: Business Process Model and Notation, version 2.0, http://www.omg.org/spec/BPMN/2.0/PDF
31. Pinna, G., Poign, A.: On the nature of events: another perspective in concurrency. Theoretical Computer Science 138(2), 425–454 (1995), meeting on the mathematical foundation of programing semantics
32. Reichert, M., Weber, B.: Enabling Flexibility in Process-Aware Information Systems - Challenges, Methods, Technologies. Springer (2012)
33. Russell, N., ter Hofstede, A., van der Aalst, W., Mulyar, N.: Workflow control-flow patterns: A revised view (2006), http://BPMcenter.org
34. Sibertin-Blanc, C., Mauran, P., Padiou, G.: Safe Adaptation of Component Coordination. In: Proceedings of the Third International Workshop on Coordination and Adaption Techniques for Software Entities, vol. 189, pp. 69–85 (juillet 2007)
35. Slaats, T., Mukkamala, R.R., Hildebrandt, T., Marquard, M.: Exformatics declarative case management workflows as DCR graphs. In: Daniel, F., Wang, J., Weber, B. (eds.) BPM 2013. LNCS, vol. 8094, pp. 339–354. Springer, Heidelberg (2013)
36. Winskel, G.: Events in Computation. Ph.D. thesis, University of Edinburgh (1980)
37. Zugal, S., Soffer, P., Pinggera, J., Weber, B.: Expressiveness and understandability considerations of hierarchy in declarative business process models. In: Bider, I., et al. (eds.) EMMSAD 2012 and BPMDS 2012. LNBIP, vol. 113, pp. 167–181. Springer, Heidelberg (2012)

Verifying Opacity of a Transactional Mutex Lock

John Derrick[1(✉)], Brijesh Dongol[2], Gerhard Schellhorn[3], Oleg Travkin[4], and Heike Wehrheim[4]

[1] Department of Computing, University of Sheffield, Sheffield, UK
j.derrick@dcs.shef.ac.uk
[2] Department of Computer Science, Brunel University, London, UK
[3] Universität Augsburg, Institut für Informatik, 86135, Augsburg, Germany
[4] Universität Paderborn, Institut für Informatik, 33098, Paderborn, Germany

Abstract. Software transactional memory (STM) provides programmers with a high-level programming abstraction for synchronization of parallel processes, allowing blocks of codes that execute in an interleaved manner to be treated as an atomic block. This atomicity property is captured by a correctness criterion called *opacity*. Opacity relates histories of a sequential atomic specification with that of STM implementations.

In this paper we prove opacity of a recently proposed STM implementation (a Transactional Mutex Lock) by Dalessandro et al.. The proof is carried out within the interactive verifier KIV and proceeds via the construction of an intermediate level in between sequential specification and implementation, leveraging existing proof techniques for linearizability.

1 Introduction

Software transactional memory (STM) is a mechanism that provides an illusion of atomicity in concurrent programs and thus aims to reduce the burden of implementing synchronization mechanisms on a programmer. The analogy of STMs is with database transactions, which perform a series of updates to data atomically in an all-or-nothing manner. If a transaction succeeds, all its operations succeed, and otherwise, all its operations fail. Since the first proposal of an STM [20], a number of STM implementations have been presented (e.g. [11,3]). Intuitively, an STM should behave like a lock mechanism for critical sections: transactions appear to be executed sequentially, but – unlike conventional locking mechanisms – STMs should (and do) allow for concurrency between transactions. The locking mechanism of Transactional Mutex Locks [4] which we study in this paper implements an optimistic locking scheme. These currently find their way into standard programming languages, for instance via the new class `StampedLock` of the Java 8 release.

As STM implementations allow several operations to execute simultaneously, what one means by "correctness" is open to interpretation. Several notions of correctness have been defined, e.g., strict serializability [17], opacity [8,2], TMS1 and TMS2 [6], and virtual world consistency [13]. A number of researchers have already considered methods for verifying correctness of transactional memory implementations; a comprehensive survey may be found in [14]. Formal verification is clearly needed as STM

N. Bjørner and F. de Boer (Eds.): FM 2015, LNCS 9109, pp. 161–177, 2015.
DOI: 10.1007/978-3-319-19249-9_11

implementations employ fine-grained operations allowing interleavings between concurrent transactions, and subtle errors are therefore likely to arise but difficult to detect via e.g. testing.

In this paper, we provide the first formal, mechanised proof of correctness of the Transactional Mutex Lock (TML). As correctness criterion we employ the recently given definition of opacity of Attiya et al. [2]. It provides strong guarantees to programmers in the form of *observational refinement* allowing programmers to reason about programs using opaque STMs in terms of atomic transactions. Our proof technique is fully mechanised within the interactive prover KIV [18] and leverages existing proof techniques [5] for linearizability [12].

More specifically, our approach consists of two steps: we (1) show that all runs of TML are linearizable to runs in which first of all reads and writes to memory occur atomically, and (2) establish an invariant about such runs stating that they all have "matching" runs in which whole transactions are executed atomically. These two steps are necessary for covering the two sorts of non-atomicity in STMs: STMs decompose (atomic) transactions into several operations (begin, read, write etc.), but also further decompose these operations into several steps (accessing and manipulating so-called meta-data) as to allow for a maximum of concurrency. The former decomposition is accounted for in step (2), the latter in step (1).

The paper is structured as follows: Section 2 gives an introduction to software transactional memory, presents our case study and defines the correctness criterion of opacity. Our general proof approach with steps (1) and (2) is described in Section 3; Section 4 explains both steps for our case study, the Transactional Mutex Lock. Section 5 concludes and discusses related work.

2 Software Transactional Memory and Opacity

Software Transactional Memory (STM) provides programmers with an easy-to-use synchronisation mechanism for concurrent access to shared data. The basic mechanism is a programming construct that allows one to specify blocks of code as *transactions*, with properties of database transactions (e.g., atomicity, consistency and isolation) [10]. All statements inside a transaction execute *as though they were atomic*. However – like database transactions – software transactions need not successfully terminate, i.e., might abort.

To support the concept of software transactions, STMs usually provide a number of operations to programmers: operations to start (`TMBegin`) or to end a transaction (`TMEnd`), and operations to read or write shared data (`TMRead`, `TMWrite`)[1]. These operations can be called (invoked) from within a program (possibly with some arguments, e.g., the variable to be read) and then will return with a response. Except for starting transactions, all other operations might potentially respond with `abort`, thereby aborting the whole transaction. STMs expect the programmer to always start with `TMBegin`, then a number of reads and writes can follow, and eventually the transaction is ended by calling `TMEnd` unless one of the other operations has already aborted.

[1] In general, arbitrary operations can be used here; for simplicity we use reads and writes to variables.

```
Init: glb = 0

TMBegin:
// B1 is LP if even glb
B1 do loc := glb
B2 while (loc & 1)
B3 return ok;

TMEnd:
// E1 is LP if even loc
E1 if (loc & 1)
E2   glb++;  // LP
E3 return commit;

TMRead(addr):
R1 tmp := *addr;
R2 if (glb = loc) // LP
R3    return tmp;
R4 else return abort;

TMWrite(addr,val):
W1 if (loc & 0)
// W2 is LP when glb ≠ loc
W2  if (!cas(&glb, loc, loc+1))
W3      return abort;
W4    else loc++;
W5 *addr := val; // LP
W6 return ok;
```

Fig. 1. The Transactional Mutex Lock (TML)

2.1 Example: Transactional Mutex Lock

In this paper, we will study a particular implementation of STM, namely the Transactional Mutex Lock (TML) of Dalessandro *et al.* [4]. It provides exactly the four types of operations, but operation TMEnd will never respond with abort. See Fig. 1 (the references in the comments to LP are explained later).

The TML uses a global counter *glb* (initially 0) shared by all processes, and local variables *tmp* (temporarily storing the value read from an address) and *loc* (storing a copy of *glb*). Variable *glb* records whether there is a live writing transaction. Namely, *glb* is odd if there is a live writing transaction, and even otherwise. Initially, *glb* is 0 and hence even.

Operation TMBegin copies the value of *glb* into its local variable *loc* and checks whether *glb* is even. If so, the transaction is started, and otherwise, the process attempts to start again by rereading *glb*. A TMRead operation succeeds as long as *glb* equals *loc* (meaning no writes have occurred since the transaction began), otherwise it aborts the current transaction. The first execution of TMWrite attempts to increment *glb* using a *cas* (compare-and-swap), which atomically compares the first and second parameters, and sets the first parameter to the third if the comparison succeeds. If the *cas* attempt fails, a write by another transaction must have occured, and hence, the current transaction aborts. Otherwise *loc* is incremented (making its value odd) and the write is performed. Note that because *loc* becomes odd after the first successful write, all successive writes that are part of the same transaction will perform the write directly after testing *loc* at line 1. Further note that if the *cas* succeeds, *glb* becomes odd, which prevents other transactions from starting, and causes all concurrent live transactions still wanting to read or write to abort. Thus a writing transaction that successfully updates *glb* effectively locks shared memory. Operation TMEnd checks to see if a write has occurred by testing whether *loc* is odd. If the test succeeds, *glb* is incremented (to an even value), allowing other transactions to begin.

Table 1. Events appearing in the histories of TML

invocations	possible matching responses
$inv_p(\texttt{TMBegin})$	$res_p(\texttt{TMBegin(ok)})$
$inv_p(\texttt{TMEnd})$	$res_p(\texttt{TMEnd(commit)})$, $res_p(\texttt{TMEnd(abort)})$
$inv_p(\texttt{TMRead}(x))$	$res_p(\texttt{TMRead}(v))$, $res_p(\texttt{TMRead(abort)})$
$inv_p(\texttt{TMWrite}(x, v))$	$res_p(\texttt{TMWrite(ok)})$, $res_p(\texttt{TMWrite(abort)})$

The key question we want to answer in this paper is: "Does the TML correctly implement an STM", i.e., does TML guarantee that transactions look as though they were executed atomically, even when a large number of transactions are running concurrently. Concurrently here means that the individual lines in the operations (i.e., B1, B2, etc) can be interleaved by different calling processes. We start by first fixing the meaning of a "correctness" for an STM implementation as *opacity* [8]. We formalise this via a series of definitions leading up to the definition of an opaque history in Definition 5 below.

2.2 Opacity

There are numerous formalizations of opacity in the literature; our definition mainly follows Attiya et al. [2]. We model shared memory by a set *Addr* of addresses or locations. For simplicity we assume addresses hold integer, denoted $\mathbb{Z}$, values only, hence $State == Addr \rightarrow \mathbb{Z}$ describes the possible states of the shared memory. Initially, all addresses hold the value 0. As standard in the literature, opacity is defined on the *histories* of an implementation. Histories are sequences of *events* that record all interactions between the implementation and its clients. Histories form an abstraction of the actual interleaving of individual lines of code, and thus an event is either an invocation (*inv*) or a response (*res*). For the TML implementation, the possible invocation and matching response events are given in Table 1. In the table, p is a process identifier from a set of processes P (and is given as a subscript to an invocation or response), x is an address of a variable and v a value.

Example 1. The following history h_1 is a possible execution of the TML. It accesses the address x by two processes 2 and 3 running concurrently.

$$\begin{aligned} h_1 \mathrel{\widehat{=}} \langle & inv_3(\texttt{TMBegin});\ inv_2(\texttt{TMBegin});\ res_3(\texttt{TMBegin(ok)});\ res_2(\texttt{TMBegin(ok)}); \\ & inv_3(\texttt{TMWrite}(x, 4));\ inv_2(\texttt{TMRead}(x));\ res_2(\texttt{TMRead}(0)); \\ & res_3(\texttt{TMWrite(ok)});\ inv_3(\texttt{TMEnd});\ res_3(\texttt{TMEnd(commit)})\rangle \end{aligned}$$ □

Notation. We use the following notation on histories: for a history h, $h \upharpoonright p$ is the projection onto the events of process p only and $h[i..j]$ the subsequence of from $h(i)$ to $h(j)$ inclusive. For a response event e, we let $rval(e)$ denote the value returned by e; for instance $rval(\texttt{TMBegin(ok)}) = \texttt{ok}$. If e is not a response event, then we let $rval(e) = \bot$.

Histories. We're interested in three different types of histories. At the concrete level the TML implementation produces histories where the events are interleaved. h_1 above is an example of such a history. At the abstract level we're interested in *sequential histories* which are ones where there is no interleaving at any level - transactions are atomic: completed transactions end before the next transaction starts. As part of the proof we use an intermediate specification which has *alternating histories*, which we define now.

A history h is *alternating* if $h = \langle\rangle$ or h is an alternating sequence of invocation and matching response events starting with an invocation. For the rest of this paper, we assume each process invokes at most one operation at a time and hence assume that $h \upharpoonright p$ is alternating for any history h and process p. Note that this does not necessarily mean h is alternating itself. Opacity is defined for well-formed histories, which formalises the allowable interaction between an STM implementation and its clients. Given a projection $h \upharpoonright p$ of a history h onto a process p, a consecutive subsequence $t = \langle s_0, \ldots, s_m\rangle$ of $h \upharpoonright p$ is a *transaction* of process p if $s_0 = inv_p(\mathtt{TMBegin})$ and

- either $rval(s_m) \in \{\mathtt{commit}, \mathtt{abort}\}$ or s_m is the last event of process p in $h \upharpoonright p$, and
- for all $0 < i < m$, event s_i is not a transaction invocation, i.e., $s_i \neq inv_p(\mathtt{TMBegin})$ and not a transaction completion, i.e., $rval(s_i) \notin \{\mathtt{commit}, \mathtt{abort}\}$.

Furthermore, t is *committing* whenever $rval(s_m) = \mathtt{commit}$ and *aborting* whenever $rval(s_m) = \mathtt{abort}$. In these cases, the transaction t is *finishing*, otherwise t is *live*. A history is *well-formed* if it consists of transactions only and at most one live transaction per process.

Example 2. The history h_1 given above is well-formed, and contains a committing transaction of process 3 and a live transaction of process 2. □

The basic principle behind the definition of opacity (and similar definitions) is the comparison of a given concurrent history against a sequential one. The matching sequential history has to (a) consist of the same events, and (b) preserve the real-time order of transactions.

Sequential histories. We now define formally the notion of sequentiality, noting that sequentiality refers to transactions: a sequential history is alternating and does not interleave events of different transactions. We first define non-interleaved histories.

Definition 1 (Non-interleaved history). *A well-formed history h is* non-interleaved *if transactions of different processes do not overlap. That is, for any processes p and q and histories h_1, h_2 and h_3, if $h = h_1 \frown \langle inv_p(\mathtt{TMBegin})\rangle \frown h_2 \frown \langle inv_q(\mathtt{TMBegin})\rangle \frown h_3$ and h_2 contains no* TMBegin *operations, then either h_2 contains a response event e such that $rval(e) \in \{\mathtt{abort}, \mathtt{ok}\}$, or h_3 contains no operations of process p.* □

In addition to being non-interleaved, a sequential history has to ensure that the behaviour is meaningful with respect to the reads and writes of the transactions. For this, we look at each address in isolation and define what a valid sequential behaviour on a single address is.

Definition 2 (Valid history). *Let $h = \langle ev_0, \ldots, ev_{2n-1}\rangle$ be a sequence of alternating invocation and response events starting with an invocation and ending with a response.*

We say h is valid *if there exists a sequence of states $\sigma_0, \ldots, \sigma_n$ such that $\sigma_0(x) = 0$ for all $x \in Addr$ and, for all i such that $0 \leq i < n$ and $p \in P$:*

1. *if* $ev_{2i} = inv_p(\mathtt{TMWrite}(x, v))$ *and* $ev_{2i+1} = res_p(\mathtt{TMWrite}(\mathtt{ok}))$ *then* $\sigma_{i+1} = \sigma_i[x := v]$
2. *if* $ev_{2i} = inv_p(\mathtt{TMRead}(x))$ *and* $ev_{2i+1} = res_p(\mathtt{TMRead}(v))$ *then* $\sigma_i(x) = v$ *and* $\sigma_{i+1} = \sigma_i$.
3. *for all other pairs of events (reads and writes with an abort response, as well as begins and ends)* $\sigma_{i+1} = \sigma_i$.

We write $[\![h]\!](\sigma)$ *if* σ *is a sequence of states that makes h valid (since the sequence is unique, if it exists, it can be viewed as the semantics of h).* □

The point of STMs is that the effect of the writes only takes place when the transaction commits. Writes in a transaction that abort don't effect the memory. However, all reads must be consistent with previously committed writes. Therefore, only some histories of an object reflect ones that could be produced by an STM. We call these the *legal* histories, and they are defined as follows.

Definition 3 (Legal histories). *Let hs be a non-interleaved history and i an index of hs. Let* hs' *be the projection of* $hs[0..(i-1)]$ *onto all events of committed transactions plus the events of the transaction to which* $hs(i)$ *belongs. Then we say hs* is legal at *i whenever* hs' *is valid. We say hs* is legal *iff it is legal at each index i.* □

This allows us to define sequentiality for a single history, which we lift to the level of specifications.

Definition 4 (Sequential history). *A well-formed history hs is* sequential *if it is non-interleaved and legal. We denote by* $\mathcal{S}$ *the set of all possible well-formed sequential histories.*

Opaque histories. Opacity relates concurrent histories that an implementation generates to sequential histories. We say a history h is *equivalent* to a history h', denoted $h \equiv h'$, if for all processes $p \in P$, $h \upharpoonright p = h' \upharpoonright p$. Further, the *real-time order* on transactions t_1 and t_2 in a history h is defined as $t_1 \prec_h t_2$ if t_1 is a finished transaction and the last event of t_1 in h occurs before the first event of t_2.

A given concrete history may be incomplete, i.e., consist of pending operation calls, which may be distinguished in a history as an invocation that has no matching response. As some of these pending calls may have taken effect, pending operation calls may be completed by adding matching responses. There may also be incomplete operation calls that have not taken effect; it is safe to remove the pending invocations. It is however not possible to determine whether or not a pending operation call has taken effect from the history only; therefore, we define a function *complete*(h) that constructs all possible completions of h by appending matching responses and removing pending invocations.

Definition 5 (Opaque history). *A history h is* opaque *iff for some* $hc \in complete(h)$, *there exists a sequential history* $hs \in \mathcal{S}$ *such that* $hc \equiv hs$ *and* $\prec_{hc} \subseteq \prec_{hs}$; *a set of histories* $\mathcal{H}$ *is* opaque *iff each* $h \in \mathcal{H}$ *is opaque; and an STM implementation is* opaque *iff its set of histories is opaque.* □

Example 3. The above history h_1 is opaque; the corresponding sequential history is

$$\begin{aligned} hs \mathrel{\widehat{=}} \langle & inv_2(\texttt{TMBegin});\ res_2(\texttt{TMBegin(ok)});\ inv_2(\texttt{TMRead}(x);\ res_2(\texttt{TMRead}(0)); \\ & inv_3(\texttt{TMBegin});\ res_3(\texttt{TMBegin(ok)});\ inv_3(\texttt{TMWrite}(x,4)); \\ & res_3(\texttt{TMWrite(ok)});\ inv_3(\texttt{TMEnd});\ res_3(\texttt{TMEnd(commit)})\rangle \end{aligned}$$

However, a history may not be opaque for several reasons. A very simple example is h_2, which violates memory semantics, since it reads a value 4, that has not been written:

$$h_2 \mathrel{\widehat{=}} \langle inv_1(\texttt{TMBegin});\ res_1(\texttt{TMBegin(ok)});\ inv_1(\texttt{TMRead}(x));\ res_1(\texttt{TMRead}(4))\rangle$$

A second more complex example is h_3.

$$\begin{aligned} h_3 \mathrel{\widehat{=}} \langle & inv_1(\texttt{TMBegin});\ res_1(\texttt{TMBegin(ok)});\ inv_2(\texttt{TMBegin});\ res_2(\texttt{TMBegin(ok)}); \\ & inv_1(\texttt{TMWrite}(x,3));\ res_1(\texttt{TMWrite(ok)});\ inv_2(\texttt{TMRead}(x));\ res_2(\texttt{TMRead}(3))\rangle \end{aligned}$$

Transaction 2 reads value 3 written by transaction 1, which is still live. This is disallowed by opacity, since all values read must from a state where only the effects of transactions that have already committed are visible.

$$\begin{aligned} h_4 \mathrel{\widehat{=}} \langle & inv_1(\texttt{TMBegin});\ res_1(\texttt{TMBegin(ok)});\ inv_1(\texttt{TMRead}(x));\ res_1(\texttt{TMRead}(0)); \\ & inv_2(\texttt{TMBegin});\ res_2(\texttt{TMBegin(ok)});\ inv_2(\texttt{TMWrite}(x,4)); \\ & res_2(\texttt{TMWrite(ok)});\ inv_2(\texttt{TMWrite}(y,4));\ res_2(\texttt{TMWrite(ok)}); \\ & inv_2(\texttt{TMEnd});\ res_2(\texttt{TMEnd(commit)});\ inv_1(\texttt{TMRead}(y));\ res_1(\texttt{TMRead}(4))\rangle \end{aligned}$$

In h_4 transaction 1 reads $x = 0$ from initial memory, then transaction 2 runs, which writes $x = y = 4$ and commits. Finally transaction 1 reads $y = 4$. This also violates opacity, since it is not possible to order the transactions sequentially: either transaction 1 runs first (and reads $x = y = 0$), or transaction 2 runs first (in which case transaction 1 should read $x = y = 4$). The TML will prevent h_4 — the second read of transaction 1 will abort because its *loc* value is smaller than *glb*, which was incremented by the first write of transaction 2. However, in general an implementation could allow transaction 2 to read $y = 0$, i.e., if we replace the last event in h_4 by $res_2(\texttt{TMRead}(0))$, the modified history is still opaque.

Thus our question of implementation correctness of the TML can now be rephrased as: *Are all the well-formed histories generated by TML opaque?* Having provided the necessary formalism to pose this question, we now explain our general proof method for showing opacity of TML.

Aside. Neither h_3 nor h_4 violate strict serializability [17]. To satisfy strict serializability, for h_3 we must guarantee that transaction 1 always commits, while for h_4 we require that transaction 1 detects the inconsistent reads when attempting a commit, and to abort.

Strict serializability is too weak, and histories such as h_4 are problematic for implementations in which reading and writing transaction variables is alternated with computations that use these values. To see this, suppose all committing transactions are required to preserve the invariant $x = y$ (the transactions in h_4 satisfy this invariant). Then, assuming all transactions act as if they are atomic, transaction 1 could rely on

```
ABegin:                     AEnd:
  return ok                  return commit

ARead(addr):                AWrite(addr,val):
  atomic {                    atomic {
    return addr                 addr := val ; return ok
    or                          or
    return abort }              return abort }
```

Fig. 2. Atomic specification of an STM

reading equal values for x and y. Even though transaction 1 will not be able to successfully commit, it could attempt to compute $x/(y+4-x)$ after reading x and y, which would give an unexpected division by zero.

3 A Proof Method for Opacity

Proving opacity of an STM object is difficult, as it determines a relationship between a fine-grained implementation in which individual statements (and hence, operations) may be interleaved, in terms of a sequential specification in which unbounded (but finite) sequences of transactional memory operations are considered atomic. The operations of STM implementations are however simple: there are operations to begin and end a transaction and operations to read and write from memory. The majority of these leave memory unchanged; for our TML example, the only operation that modifies memory is a write operation that does not abort. Note that this is not the only possibility — there are STM implementations that use *deferred updates*, where write operations leave memory unchanged and writes are only performed when transactions end.

Our proof method uses an intermediate specification which is an *atomic specification* of an STM implementation (with non deferred updates) where each operation is atomic, thus interleaving of statements within an operation does not occur.

The proof method works by (a) showing that every history in the TML implementation can be linearized by an alternating history of this intermediate specification, and (b) these alternating histories are themselves opaque. We describe the proof method using TML as a running example. Our proofs have been fully automated in KIV [18], the resulting development may be viewed online(https://swt.informatik.uni-augsburg.de/swt/projects/TML.html). The link also contains additional notes on our KIV proof.

3.1 Defining an Atomic Specification of an STM

The definition of the intermediate specification is simple, and the atomic specification of an STM is given in Fig. 2. For example, the `ARead(x)` operation is an abstraction of `TMRead(x)` that reads and returns the value of x in a single atomic step or it aborts. (We assume that `or` defines a non-deterministic choice.)

3.2 Linearizability and Opacity

Correctness of the TML implementation is shown using *linearizability* [12], which is the standard correctness criterion for concurrent objects. The idea of linearizability is:

Linearizability provides the illusion that each operation applied by concurrent processes takes effect instantaneously at some point between its invocation and its return. This point is known as the *linearization point.*

In other words, if two operations overlap, then they may take effect in any order from an abstract perspective, but otherwise they must take effect in the order in which they are invoked. This provides a meaning for fine-grained concurrent objects with overlapped operation calls in terms of the abstract object, whose operation calls do not overlap.

As with opacity, the formal definition of linearizability is given in terms of histories (of invocation/response events); for every concurrent history we have to find an equivalent alternating (invocations immediately followed by the matching response) history that preserves real time order of operations. The *real-time order* on operation calls[2] o_1 and o_2 in a history h is defined as $o_1 \lll_h o_2$ if the return of o_1 precedes the invocation of o_2 in h.

Linearizability differs from opacity in that it does not deal with transactions; thus transactions may still be interleaved in a matched alternating history. As with opacity, the given concurrent history may be incomplete. Thus the definition of linearizability uses a function *complete* that adds matching returns to pending invocations to a history h, then removes any remaining pending invocations.

Definition 6 (Linearizability). *A history h is* linearized *by alternating history ha, if there exists a history $hc \in complete(h)$ such that $hc \equiv ha$ and $\lll_{hc} \subseteq \lll_{ha}$. A concurrent object is linearizable with respect to a specification if for each concurrent history h, there is an alternating history ha of the specification that linearizes it.* □

With linearizability formalised, we now present the main theorem for our proof method, which enables opacity to be proved via histories of the atomic specification of an STM.

Theorem 1. *A concrete history h is opaque if there exists an alternating history ha such that h is linearizable with respect to ha and ha is opaque.*

Proof. Suppose (a) h is linearizable with respect to ha and (b) ha is opaque with respect to hs. Then, by (a), there exists a history $hc \in complete(h)$ such that $hc \equiv ha$ and $\lll_{hc} \subseteq \lll_{ha}$ and by (b), there exists a well-formed sequential history hs such that $ha \equiv hs$ and $\prec_{ha} \subseteq \prec_{hs}$. We must show that $hc \equiv hs$ and $\prec_{hc} \subseteq \prec_{hs}$ holds. Clearly, $hc \equiv hs$ because $\equiv$ is transitive, and if $\lll_{hc} \subseteq \lll_{ha}$ and $\prec_{ha} \subseteq \prec_{hs}$, then $\prec_{hc} \subseteq \prec_{hs}$ because preserving the real-time order of operations also preserves the real-time order of transactions. □

In applying this to TML, we show that every concurrent history h will be linearized by an alternating history ha of the intermediate specification given in Figure 2, and that every such ha is opaque.

Because the histories of the atomic specification of an STM are alternating, i.e., each operation invocation is immediately followed by its response, we further simplify reasoning by reasoning about *runs*, which abstractly represent alternating histories. Thus we specifically show that the run r corresponding to ha is opaque.

A *run* is a sequence of run events (see column 1 of Table 2), representing a matching invocation/response event pair; *Begin*(p) denotes a `TMBegin` operation by process p; run

[2] Note: this is different from the real time order on transactions defined in Section 2.2

Table 2. Run events abstracting matching invocation/return pairs

run events	possible sequential invocation/response pairs
$Begin(p)$	$\langle inv_p(\texttt{TMBegin}), res_p(\texttt{TMBegin(ok)})\rangle$
$Read(p, x, v)$	$\langle inv_p(\texttt{TMRead}(x)), res_p(\texttt{TMRead}(v))\rangle$
$Write(p, x, v)$	$\langle inv_p(\texttt{TMWrite}(x, v)), res_p(\texttt{TMWrite(ok)})\rangle$
$Commit(p)$	$\langle inv_p(\texttt{TMEnd}), res_p(\texttt{TMEnd(commit)})\rangle$
$Abort(p)$	$\langle inv_p(\texttt{TMRead}(x)), res_p(\texttt{TMRead(abort)})\rangle$, $\langle inv_p(\texttt{TMWrite}(x, v)), res_p(\texttt{TMWrite(abort)})\rangle$, $\langle inv_p(\texttt{TMEnd}), res_p(\texttt{TMEnd(abort)})\rangle$

events $Read(p, x, v)$ and *Write(p,x,v)* denote successful read and write operations by process p on address x with value v; run event $Commit(p)$ denotes a successful TMBegin operation by process p; and $Abort(p)$ denotes an operation invocation that aborts.

Example 4. The run corresponding to the history

$$\begin{aligned} ha \mathrel{\widehat=} \langle & inv_2(\texttt{TMBegin});\ res_2(\texttt{TMBegin(ok)});\ inv_2(\texttt{TMRead}(x);\ res_2(\texttt{TMRead}(0)); \\ & inv_3(\texttt{TMBegin});\ res_3(\texttt{TMBegin(ok)});\ inv_3(\texttt{TMWrite}(x, 4)); \\ & res_3(\texttt{TMWrite(ok)});\ inv_3(\texttt{TMEnd});\ res_3(\texttt{TMEnd(commit)}), \\ & inv_2(\texttt{TMRead}(x);\ res_2(\texttt{TMRead(abort)})\rangle \end{aligned}$$

is $\langle Begin(2);\ Read(2, x, 0);\ Begin(3);\ Write(3, x, 4);\ Commit(3);\ Abort(2)\rangle$. □

Because Abort(p) relates to several possible pairs, a run is more abstract than a history. Although it is possible to obtain a 1-1 correspondence between runs and histories by defining other types of run events, the encoding in this paper simplifies the mechanisation of the proof.

4 Proving Opacity of TML

In this section we apply the theory from the previous section and show how opacity of the TML may be proved. Section 4.1 describes how the TML may be modelled in KIV, Section 4.2 presents the linearizability proof and Section 4.3 the opacity of the runs recorded as part of this proof.

4.1 Modelling TML in KIV

Before we discuss the proof steps, we first describe how the different specifications are modelled in KIV.

The concrete specification: To model the concrete state of the TML, we use KIV's record type, which is used to define a constructor mkcs (make concrete state cs) containing a list of fields of some type. Field glb represents the global variable glb, and mem represents the memory state and hence maps addresses to values (in this case integers). Local variables are mappings from processes (of type Proc) to values; for the TML, we have local variable pc for the program counter, loc for the local copy of glb, as well as variable a and v storing the input/output addresses and values, respectively. We thus use the following state:

```
CState =
mkcs(. .glb : nat, . .mem : address → int, . .pc : Proc → PC,
     . .loc : Proc → nat, . .a : Proc → address, . .v : Proc → int)
```

Modelling atomic statements: Modelling an atomic statement of the TML as a KIV state transition is also straightforward; for example, consider statement labelled W2, which is modelled by write2-def below. Here, COP is used to denote that the step is internal (i.e., neither an invocation nor a response; such steps have an additional input resp. output parameter) and write2 is the index of the operation. Modifications to glb and pc are conditional, denoted by ⊃, on the test loc = glb. Thus, if loc = glb, then pc' is set to W3, otherwise pc' is set to W6. The transitions alter the concrete state, the after state is denoted by dashed variables.

```
write2-def:
⊢ COP(write2)(glb, mem, pc, loc, a, v, glb', mem', pc', loc', a', v')
↔
( pc = W2 ∧ loc' = loc ∧ mem' = mem ∧ a' = a ∧ v' = v
    ∧ glb' = (loc = glb ⊃ loc + 1;glb) ∧ pc' = (loc = glb ⊃ W3;W6) );
```

Promotion to system wide steps: Local specifications must now be promoted to the level of the system, where the system consists of the concrete state *cs* together with a variable *r* representing the run so far.

As promotion is a standard procedure [21], we omit the full details here. In KIV we define one generic promoted KIV state transition COp-def that gets instantiated to specific promoted transitions as necessary.

More interestingly, as part of the promotion we record run events in the run variable r, at the *linearization points* of the operations TMBegin, TMRead, TMEnd, and TMWrite.

The linearization points of these transitions are annotated in comments in the code in Figure 1. As with standard linearizability proofs, linearization points are often conditional and their locations sometimes not intuitive. An operation may either linearize the invoked operation or linearize to abort. Operation TMBegin linearizes at B1 if an even value of glb is loaded into loc; in this case the operation will definitely go on to start a transaction as the outcome of the next test is determined locally. Operation TMRead linearizes at R2 to a non-aborting Read if the value of glb is the same as the stored value in loc, and linearizes to an aborting Read if the value of glb changes. Operation TMWrite linearizes successfully when the memory is updated at W5, and linearizes to Abort if the cas at W2 fails. Finally, operation TMEnd never aborts, yet there are two linearization points depending on whether successfully executed a TMWrite. If no writes were performed, then loc must be even; such a transaction must linearize at E1, otherwise if the transaction had performed a successful write, then loc must have been set to an odd value at W4, therefore, the linearization point for TMEnd for such a transaction is is E2.

The expression on the right of "`r' =`" below is an if-then-else expression describing the value of `r'` (i.e., the value of `r` in the post state). To save space some details are omitted, and replaced by "`...`". Thus, for example, the first condition states that `r'` is set to `r + Begin(p)`, which concatenates `Begin(p)` to `r`, whenever `pc = B1 ∧ even(glb)` holds in the pre-state, i.e., whenever process p executes line `B1` where the value of `glb` is even.

```
COp-def :
⊢ COp(cj, p)(cs, r, cs', r')
↔ ( ∃ pc, loc, a, v. COP(cj)(cs.glb, cs.mem,..., cs'.glb, cs'.mem,...)
∧
      pc = cs.glb ∧ loc = cs.loc(p) ... ∧
      r' = (pc = B1 ∧ even(glb) ⊃ r + Begin(p) ;
           (pc = R2 ∧ loc = glb ⊃ r + Read(p, a, v) ;
           (pc = R2 ∧ loc ≠ glb ⊃ r + Abort(p) ;
           (pc = W2 ∧ glb ≠ loc ⊃ r + Abort(p) ;
           (pc = W5 ⊃ r + Write(p, a, v) ;
           (pc = E1 ∧ even(loc) ⊃ r + Commit(p) ;
           (pc = E2 ⊃ r + Commit(p) ;
           r ))))))));
```

4.2 Step 1: Proving Linearizability with Respect to the Intermediate Specification

Having described how we model the TML implementation in KIV, including the embedding of the linearization points in the promoted operations, the next step is to show that every history h of this TML implementation is linearized by an alternating history of the intermediate specification. To simplify the proof, the alternating histories have been represented by runs.

We thus show that h is linearized to a run r. This is done by proving two lemmas in KIV for each operation of transaction (`TMWrite` etc).

First, when executed by process p no operation ever passes more than one linearization point (LP) in any execution (regardless of other interleaved operations executed by other processes) before executing a return (so even nonterminating `TMBegin`s never execute more than one LP).

Second, if the operation reaches a return and terminates, then it has executed exactly one LP, i.e. exactly one run event of process p has been added to the run r. The arguments of this run event agree with the actual input/output of the invoking/response transition. As an example, the write operation adds $Write(p,x,v)$ to r when executing the instruction at `W5` (and therefore actually writes v to $mem(x)$), and we prove that this is possible only when the input to the invoking instruction of TMWrite is x, v and the output is empty.

Note that this encoding is recording the (more abstract) runs directly, as opposed to recording an alternating history which is abstracted to runs as a separate step. This simplified the KIV proof significantly without affecting soundness. In particular, linearizability is guaranteed because the linearization points that occur are done by steps of the operations themselves (more intricate examples where linearization points are executed by other threads need more complex techniques, see [19] for a complete proof method). The method used here is akin to the technique used in [22], where concrete states are augmented with auxiliary variables representing the abstract state together with additional modifications of the auxiliary state at the linearization points.

4.3 Step 2: Proving Opacity of Alternating Histories Using Runs

In this subsection we prove an alternating history which linearized a concurrent TML history is itself opaque. Together with the results defined above this will be sufficient to show opacity of the TML.

Firstly, we define opacity for runs, and show that proving opacity of runs is equivalent to proving opacity of alternating histories. Secondly, we discuss the KIV proof of opacity for TML runs. (Note that the descriptions below differ slight from the actual KIV proof online; as we use modified function names here to keep this paper self-contained, i.e., the proof can be understood without having to refer to the KIV specification online.)

Defining opacity for runs. Many of the definitions follow over from the definitions for histories in Section 2. We also need to define the semantics of a valid run on a sequence of states. To define opacity of a run, we first define the semantics of each run event from Table 2 on the memory state $mem \in State$ to produce the next state mem'. Notation $mem[x := v]$ denotes functional override, where $mem(x)$ is updated to v.

$$\begin{aligned} [\![Begin(p)]\!](mem, mem') &\mathrel{\widehat=} mem' = mem \\ [\![Read(p,x,v)]\!](mem, mem') &\mathrel{\widehat=} mem' = mem \wedge mem(x) = v \\ [\![Write(p,x,v)]\!](mem, mem') &\mathrel{\widehat=} mem' = mem[x := v] \\ [\![Commit(p)]\!](mem, mem') &\mathrel{\widehat=} mem' = mem \\ [\![Abort(p)]\!](mem, mem') &\mathrel{\widehat=} mem' = mem \end{aligned}$$

Semantics of individual run events are lifted to the level of runs as follows. Below, σ is a sequence of memory states and $\#\sigma$ defines the length of σ, which by the first conjunct is one more than the length of r. By the second conjunct, for each n, the transition from $\sigma(n)$ to $\sigma(n+1)$ is generated using $r(n)$. Because the memory state has been made explicit, $[\![\mathsf{r}]\!](\sigma)$ only holds for valid and legal runs.

$$[\![r]\!](\sigma) \mathrel{\widehat=} \#\sigma = \#r + 1 \wedge \forall\, n \bullet n < \#r \Rightarrow [\![r(n)]\!](\sigma(n), \sigma(n+1));$$

Finally, we define opaque runs as follows, where run r is mapped to sequential run rs. Predicate $r \equiv rs$ ensures equivalence between r and rs, predicate $\prec_r \subseteq \prec_{rs}$ ensures real-time ordering is preserved, and *interleaved* states that transactions may be overlap. The final conjuct ensures rs is both valid and legal as defined in Definitions 2 and 3, respectively, where *committed* restricts a given run to the committed runs plus the (live) transaction to which $r(n)$ belongs as defined in Definition 3.

$$\begin{aligned} opaque(r, rs) \mathrel{\widehat=} {}& r \equiv rs \wedge \prec_r \subseteq \prec_{rs} \wedge \neg interleaved(rs) \wedge \\ & \forall\, n \bullet n < \#rs \Rightarrow \exists\, \sigma \bullet \sigma(0) = (\lambda\, x \bullet 0) \wedge [\![committed(rs[0..n])]\!](\sigma) \end{aligned}$$

We must now ensure that proving opacity of runs is sufficient for proving opacity of complete alternating histories. This is established via the following theorem. We say a run r corresponds to an alternating history ha iff r can obtained from ha by replacing each pair of matching events in ha by the corresponding run event from Table 2.

Theorem 2. *An alternating history ha is opaque if there exists a run r that corresponds to ha and r is opaque.*

Proof. The proof of this theorem is straightforward as the definition of opacity of a run is built on the opacity of an alternating history. □

The invariants for opacity. The rest of the proof is now about proving that for each execution of the TML augmented with runs (cs, r), it is possible to find an rs such that $opaque(r, rs)$.

As with our work on linearizability we prove this via construction of an appropriate invariant. The main proof then shows that all augmented states (cs, r) generated by a concurrent execution of the TML implementation satisfies the predicate $\exists rs \bullet INV(cs, r, rs)$. The formula $INV(cs, r, rs)$ defines a number of invariants for a sequential history rs, which in particular imply $opaque(r, rs)$, which we now explain.

The formula $INV(cs, r, rs)$ formalizes the observation that the (legal) transaction sequences rs generated by the TML implementation always consist of three parts: a first one that alternates finished transactions and live transactions with an even value for $loc(p)$ that is already smaller than the current value of glb. The processes p executing such live transactions have only done reads. They are still able to successfully commit, but they are no longer able to successfully read or write. A second part that consists of transactions of processes p that have $loc(p) = glb$ (or $loc(p)+1 = glb$, in case a writing transaction exists). Finally, an optional live writing transaction. The process p executing this transaction either satisfies $odd(loc(p)) \wedge loc(p) = glb$ or $pc(p) = W4 \wedge odd(glb) \wedge glb = loc(p) + 1$.

That the partitioning is an invariant is established by proving some additional simpler properties of the TML implementation with respect to the corresponding sequential run rs. The most important ones are as follows, where p is assumed to be the process generating the transaction.

INV1. Transactions for which $loc(p)$ is even have not performed any writes.

INV2. Any live transaction with an odd value of $loc(p)$ is the last transaction in rs, and $loc(p) = glb$ in this case. This implicitly implies that there is at most one live transaction with an odd value for $loc(p)$.

INV3. If the sequential run rs contains a live transaction t by process p with $loc(p) = glb$ and $pc(p) = W5$, any finished transaction must occur before t.

INV4. Live transactions are ordered (non-strictly) by their local values of loc. This property is crucial for preserving real-time order, since a larger loc implies that the transaction has started later.

INV5. Strengthening $opaque(r, rs)$, the state sequence σ that is needed to ensure that the last event of rs is valid (cf. Def. 3) always ends with current memory. Formally, for any augmented state cs, r the sequential history rs is such, that for its projection rs' to events of committed transactions plus the events of the last transaction a (unique) state sequence σ with $[\![rs']\!]\sigma$ exists where the last element of σ is equal to $cs.mem$.

INV6. Aborted transactions contain no write operations.

Opacity proof in KIV. The proof proceeds by assuming $INV(cs, r, rs)$ holds for some rs, we show that the invariant holds after any step of the TML specification that generates cs', r', it must be possible to construct a new sequence rs' such that $INV(cs', r', rs')$ holds.

For all steps that do not linearize (i.e. do not modify r) this is easy, we simply choose $rs' = rs$. Therefore, each of these proofs except for the operation at `W4` (that increments loc) is trivial.

Linearization steps of a TML operation add the corresponding run event re to r, i.e. $r' = r \frown \langle re \rangle$. The proof for the LP of `TMBegin` (i.e., line `B1`) is relatively simple, the new rs' has the newly started transaction concatenated at the end. For the other LPs, we use a function $tseq(rs)$, which generates a sequence of transactions from rs in order[3]. In particular, if $ts = tseq(rs)$, then $rs = ts(0) \frown ts(1) \frown \cdots \frown ts(\#ts - 1)$. At each LP, assuming $ts = tseq(rs)$, we add a run event re at the end of some $ts(j)$ and leave all other $ts(i)$ unchanged to generate a new ts'. The sequence ts' may also reorder transactions in ts that overlap in r', however, in most cases, the order of transactions is left unchanged, i.e. the choice for ts' is $ts[j := ts(j) \frown \langle re \rangle]$. We then consider $rs' = tseq(ts')$ and we show that this new rs' preserves the memory semantics.

Because opacity holds for the transaction sequence rs before the LP step, we know from Definition 5 that for each transaction $ts(k)$ a memory sequence σ_k exists, that fits the run events of the committed transactions before k together with the run events in $ts(k)$. In the following, we refer to σ_k as *the memory sequence validating* $ts[0..k]$. There are three cases.

1. For $k = j$, we choose $\sigma' := \sigma \frown \langle mem' \rangle$, where mem' is computed from the last element $mem := last(\sigma)$ by applying the semantics of the added event re on $last(\sigma)$.
2. For $k < j$, we choose $\sigma'_k = \sigma_k$, since the extended transaction is not present.
3. For $j < k$, we choose $\sigma'_k = \sigma_k$ when re is not a commit. The difficult case remaining is the one where $ts'(j)$ is committing. However, because $ts'(j)$ is not the last transaction in the sequence, it cannot have an odd loc due to **INV2**, and by **INV1**, the transaction has not performed any writes. Therefore, the memory sequence σ'_j that validates $ts'[0..j]$ is of the form $\sigma_0 \frown \langle mem \rangle^n$, where $\langle mem \rangle^n$ is a sequence of $mems$ of length n. The memory sequence σ_k that validates $ts[0..k]$ has prefix $\sigma_0 \frown \langle mem \rangle^n$, since $j < k$. Therefore, $\sigma_k = \sigma_0 \frown \langle mem \rangle^n \frown \sigma'$ and the new memory sequence that validates $ts'(k)$ can be set to $\sigma_0 \frown \langle mem \rangle^{n+1} \frown \sigma'$.

This proves the main invariant that rs' is legal. However, there is an additional problem when (a) run event re is a *Commit* or *Abort* or (b) $loc(p)$ is incremented at `W4`. Both (a) and (b) may violate **INV3**, which is necessary to ensure that real-time order in r is preserved. For both scenarios, we must commute the transaction with current $loc(p)$ value. Case (a) must move the committing reader to the start among those whose value of loc equals $loc(p)$. In terms of the split of the transaction sequence into three parts,

[3] Technically, a transaction sequence ts is represented in KIV as a sequence of ranges $m_i..n_i$, such that m_i and n_i mark the first and last event of a transaction in r. Assuming $r[m_i] = Begin(p_i)$, the events of transaction $ts(i)$ then are specified as $ts(i) = r[m_i..n_i] \upharpoonright p_i$. The opacity predicate is therefore defined directly in terms of the range sequence instead of using rs.

the transaction was one of the transactions of part 2, and must now become the last transaction of part 1. Case (b) must move the transaction that executes `W4` to the end of *ts* (it moves from part 2 to become the single writer of part 3). Both cases can be reduced to a lemma, that says that adjacent transactions $ts(n), ts(n+1)$ executed by processes p and q, respectively, can be reordered whenever $loc(p) = loc(q)$. This is because by property **INV2**, both $loc(p)$ and $loc(q)$ must be even and by **INV1** neither may have performed any writes.

Proof statistics. Specifying and proving opacity using KIV required four weeks of work. In particular, half the time was invested to develop an elegant formalisation of transactions that does not have to refer to auxiliary data like transaction identifiers and does not have to explicitly specify permutations. The most difficult part of the proof was figuring out a good lemma that gives criteria for preserving the semantics. This proof and the proofs of the main goals for each of the 7LPs + the goal for pc=W4 are rather complex. They each have between 50 and 100 interactions. Our first guess for defining the invariant left out the two properties **INV4** and **INV6**, they were added during the proof, which also took ca. two person weeks. Streamlining these techniques in the context of a larger example (e.g., the TL2 algorithm [3]) is a topic of future work.

5 Conclusions

There are many notions of correctness for STMs [14,9]. Of these, opacity is an easy-to-understand notion that ensures all reads are consistent with committed writing transactions. We have developed a proof method for, and verified opacity of, a transactional mutex lock implementation. Many definitions of opacity in the literature require an explicit mention of the permutations on histories, which would make proofs significantly more complex. Our formalization has avoided the explicit use of permutations.

Opacity defines correctness in terms of histories generated by interleaving STM operations as well as statements within the operations. Our method simplifies proof of opacity by reformulating opacity terms of runs, and proving opacity of the runs. A run allows interleaving of operations, but each operation is treated as being atomic, and hence, the statements within an operation are not interleaved. Linearizability is used to justify replacing an interleaved history by an alternating one (Theorem 1), while Theorem 2 justifies proving opacity of an alternating history by proving opacity of the run corresponding to the history.

Although there are several works comparing and contrasting different correctness conditions for STM (including opacity) (e.g., [6,16,1]), there only a handful of papers that consider verification of the STM implementations themselves. A model checking approach is presented in [7], however, the technique only considers *conflicts* between read and write operations in different transactions. More recently, Lesani has considered opacity verification of numerous algorithms [14], which includes techniques for reducing the problem of proving opacity into one of verifying a number of simpler invariants on the orders of events [15]. However, these decomposed invariants apply directly to the interleaved histories of the implementation at hand, as opposed to our method that performs a decomposition via runs.

References

1. Attiya, H., Gotsman, A., Hans, S., Rinetzky, N.: Safety of live transactions in transactional memory: TMS is necessary and sufficient. In: Kuhn, F. (ed.) DISC 2014. LNCS, vol. 8784, pp. 376–390. Springer, Heidelberg (2014)
2. Attiya, H., Gotsman, A., Hans, S., Rinetzky, N.: A programming language perspective on transactional memory consistency. In: Fatourou, P., Taubenfeld, G. (eds.) PODC 2013, pp. 309–318. ACM (2013)
3. Dice, D., Shalev, O., Shavit, N.: Transactional locking II. In: Dolev, S. (ed.) DISC 2006. LNCS, vol. 4167, pp. 194–208. Springer, Heidelberg (2006)
4. Dalessandro, L., Dice, D., Scott, M.L., Shavit, N., Spear, M.F.: Transactional mutex locks. In: D'Ambra, P., Guarracino, M., Talia, D. (eds.) Euro-Par 2010, Part II. LNCS, vol. 6272, pp. 2–13. Springer, Heidelberg (2010)
5. Derrick, J., Schellhorn, G., Wehrheim, H.: Verifying linearisability with potential linearisation points. In: Butler, M., Schulte, W. (eds.) FM 2011. LNCS, vol. 6664, pp. 323–337. Springer, Heidelberg (2011)
6. Doherty, S., Groves, L., Luchangco, V., Moir, M.: Towards formally specifying and verifying transactional memory. Formal Asp. Comput. 25(5), 769–799 (2013)
7. Guerraoui, R., Henzinger, T.A., Singh, V.: Model checking transactional memories. Distributed Computing 22(3), 129–145 (2010)
8. Guerraoui, R., Kapalka, M.: On the correctness of transactional memory. In: Chatterjee, S., Scott, M.L. (eds.) PPOPP, pp. 175–184. ACM (2008)
9. Guerraoui, R., Kapalka, M.: Principles of Transactional Memory. Synthesis Lectures on Distributed Computing Theory. Morgan & Claypool Publishers (2010)
10. Harris, T., Larus, J.R., Rajwar, R.: Transactional Memory, 2nd edition. Synthesis Lectures on Computer Architecture. Morgan & Claypool Publishers (2010)
11. Harris, T.L., Fraser, K.: Language support for lightweight transactions. In: Crocker, R., Steele Jr., G.L. (eds.) OOPSLA, pp. 388–402. ACM (2003)
12. Herlihy, M., Wing, J.M.: Linearizability: A correctness condition for concurrent objects. ACM TOPLAS 12(3), 463–492 (1990)
13. Imbs, D., Raynal, M.: Virtual world consistency: A condition for STM systems (with a versatile protocol with invisible read operations). Theor. Comput. Sci. 444, 113–127 (2012)
14. Lesani, M.: On the Correctness of Transactional Memory Algorithms. PhD thesis, UCLA (2014)
15. Lesani, M., Palsberg, J.: Decomposing opacity. In: Kuhn, F. (ed.) DISC 2014. LNCS, vol. 8784, pp. 391–405. Springer, Heidelberg (2014)
16. Luchangco, V., Lesani, M., Moir, M.: Putting opacity in its place. In: Workshop on the Theory of Transactional Memory (2012)
17. Papadimitriou, C.H.: The serializability of concurrent database updates. J. ACM 26(4), 631–653 (1979)
18. Reif, W., Schellhorn, G., Stenzel, K., Balser, M.: Structured specifications and interactive proofs with KIV. In: Automated Deduction—A Basis for Applications. Interactive Theorem Proving, vol. II, ch.1, pp. 13–39. Kluwer (1998)
19. Schellhorn, G., Derrick., J., Wehrheim, H.: A Sound and Complete Proof Technique for Linearizability of Concurrent Data Structures. ACM Trans. Comput. Logic, 15 (2014)
20. Shavit, N., Touitou, D.: Software transactional memory. Distributed Computing 10(2), 99–116 (1997)
21. Spivey, J.M.: The Z Notation: A Reference Manual. Prentice Hall (1992)
22. Vafeiadis, V.: Modular fine-grained concurrency verification. PhD thesis, University of Cambridge (2007)

A Framework for Correctness Criteria on Weak Memory Models

John Derrick[1(✉)] and Graeme Smith[2]

[1] Department of Computing, University of Sheffield, Sheffield, UK
j.derrick@dcs.shef.ac.uk
[2] School of Information Technology and Electrical Engineering,
The University of Queensland, Brisbane, Australia

Abstract. The implementation of weak (or relaxed) memory models is standard practice in modern multiprocessor hardware. For efficiency, these memory models allow operations to take effect in shared memory in a different order from that which they occur in a program. A number of correctness criteria have been proposed for concurrent objects operating on such memory models, each reflecting different constraints on the objects which can be proved correct. In this paper, we provide a framework in which correctness criteria are defined in terms of two components: the first defining the particular criterion (as it would be defined in the absence of a weak memory model), and the second defining the particular weak memory model. The framework facilitates the definition and comparison of correctness criteria, and encourages reuse of existing definitions. The latter enables properties of the criteria to be proved using existing proofs. We illustrate the framework via the definition of correctness criteria on the TSO (Total Store Order) weak memory model.

1 Introduction

Modern multiprocessor architectures support *weak* (or *relaxed*) memory models [19]. Architectures implementing weak memory models are now ubiquitous. An example is the TSO (Total Store Order) memory model that is implemented by the x86 architecture [16,19] and is used by the major chip manufacturers Intel and AMD. Weak memory models are also implemented by the Power architecture [1] used by IBM, and ARM [1] which is claimed to be the most widely used architecture in mobile devices [8]. For efficiency, writes to variables in weak memory models do not take effect in shared memory immediately. For example, in TSO, writes are buffered and written to memory at a time determined by the hardware or, if required, by the software employing a *fence* (or *memory barrier*) instruction. Such instructions flush the entire contents of the buffer to memory.

While fences (and other constructs available to programmers in weak memory models) can be used to ensure writes to shared memory occur immediately, they are expensive and reduce the efficiency gains the hardware was designed to achieve. For this reason, fences are used sparingly, programmers relying instead on an understanding of the subtleties of their algorithms to ensure correctness.

N. Bjørner and F. de Boer (Eds.): FM 2015, LNCS 9109, pp. 178–194, 2015.
DOI: 10.1007/978-3-319-19249-9_12

As a result there has been a growing interest in formal approaches to verifying algorithms on weak memory models, in particular on TSO, in recent years [3,9,5,18,20,21].

There are a number of notions of correctness for concurrent objects (i.e., objects designed to be accessed simultaneously by multiple threads), the most important ones being *linearizability* [11], *sequential consistency* [13] and *quiescent consistency* [2,17]. We shall largely concentrate on linearizability here. This requires that given an abstract specification and a proposed implementation of a concurrent object, there exists a sequential execution of the abstract specification for every concurrent execution of the implementation such that the abstract and concrete executions produce the same results. The sequential execution is usually obtained by identifying *linearization points* at which the potentially overlapping concurrent operations are deemed to take effect instantaneously.

There has been a wealth of work on verifying linearizability for standard architectures, and recently attention has turned to its verification on weak memory models. For example, two approaches have emerged for adapting linearizability to TSO. The first involves modifying the abstract specification to take into account the effects of buffering. For example, Burckhardt et al. [3] do this directly by supplementing the abstract specification with buffers and operations for flushing the buffer. Alternatively, Gotsman et al. [9] add nondeterminism to the abstract specification to capture the effects of buffering.

The second approach to adapting linearizability to TSO does not involve such modification of the abstract specification. Instead, it involves fundamental changes to the definition of linearizability to account for the effects of buffering. We have defined such an approach in [5]. The motivation for this approach is to allow implementations on TSO to be proved correct with respect to standard specifications (or interfaces) which may appear in a software library. While the modified specifications defined in [3] and [9] correctly capture the modified behaviour of an object due to TSO, they do not reflect the expected specification of such an object be it a software lock, or a data structure such as a queue or stack. The advantage of the approach given in [5] is that we enable the verification of implementations running on TSO against specifications naturally appearing in software libraries.

Our definition of TSO linearizability in [5] is one of a range of possible definitions. For example, it does not ensure sequential consistency, i.e., that instructions performed by a single thread occur in the order they are invoked. This restricts its application to certain objects and contexts in which those objects are used; in general, a correctness criterion only ensures refinement under certain assumptions on objects and their contexts [7]. Stronger definitions ensuring sequential consistency are also possible.

In this paper we provide a general framework for defining correctness criteria on weak memory models in general, and illustrate its use on TSO in particular. The framework is inspired by the work of Kogan and Herlihy on the correctness of futures in parallel computing [12]. Following our motivation above, our framework specifically targets criteria which can be used to verify an implementation against the expected specification of an object appearing in a library. Correctness criteria such as linearizability, sequential consistency etc. are usually defined in terms of *histories*, i.e., allowable sequences of operation invocations and responses, of the specification and implementation. Here we provide a natural generalisation of such definitions to define a framework where a correctness criteria comprises two parts:

1. a transformation on the histories of the implementation (representing the memory model), and
2. a partial order on the range of the histories of the implementation (representing the particular correctness criterion).

The partial order captures a correctness criterion by constraining which operations in an implementation history can be reordered in order to match a corresponding specification history. The framework allows us to more easily define correctness criteria as well as compare correctness criteria and their properties.

Section 2 introduces our running example, the Linux reader-writer mechanism *seqlock*, and provides partial order–based formal definitions of established correctness criteria such as linearizability as the basis for our framework. Section 3 provides the necessary background on TSO and in Section 4 we introduce the framework and illustrate it by defining a range of definitions of linearizability on TSO and discuss their application to *seqlock*. We investigate the properties of definitions within the framework in Section 5 before concluding in Section 6.

2 A Framework for Consistency Conditions

2.1 Case Study: *seqlock*

To illustrate correctness criteria and the subsequent effects of TSO on them, consider the Linux reader-writer mechanism *seqlock*, which allows reading of shared variables without locking the global memory, thus supporting fast write access. First consider it running on a standard architecture. A process wishing to *write* to the shared variables `x1` and `x2` acquires a software lock (by atomically setting a variable `lock` to 1 when it is 0[1]) and increments a counter `c`. It then proceeds to write to the variables, and finally increments `c` again before releasing the lock (by setting `lock` to 0). The lock ensures synchronisation between writers, and the counter `c` ensures the consistency of values read by other processes. The two increments of `c` ensure that it is odd when a process is writing to the variables, and even otherwise. Hence, when a process wishes to *read* the shared variables, it waits in a loop until `c` is even before reading them. Also, before returning it checks that the value of `c` has not changed (i.e., another write has not begun). If it has changed, the process starts over.

An abstract specification of *seqlock*, in which operations are regarded as atomic, is given in Figure 1. A typical implementation, in which the statements of operations may be interleaved, is given in Figure 2. In the implementation, a local variable `c0` is used by the `read` operation to record the (even) value of

[1] This can be implemented, for example, using a spin lock [10].

```
word x1 = 0, x2 = 0;
                                      read(out word d1,d2) {
write(in word d1,d2) {                   d1 = x1;
   x1 = d1;                              d2 = x2;
   x2 = d2;                           }
}
```

Fig. 1. *seqlock* specification

```
word x1 = 0, x2 = 0;
word c = 0, lock = 0;                 read(out word d1,d2) {
                                         word c0;
write(in word d1,d2) {                   do {
   acquire;                                  do {
   c++;                                         c0 = c;
   x1 = d1;                                  } while (c0 % 2 != 0);
   x2 = d2;                                  d1 = x1;
   c++;                                      d2 = x2;
   release;                              } while (c != c0);
}                                     }
```

Fig. 2. *seqlock* implementation [3]

c before the operation begins updating local variables d1 and d2. The natural question to ask is whether this implementation is *correct* in some sense.

2.2 Formal Definitions of Correctness Criteria

Linearizability [11] is widely regarded as the standard correctness criterion for concurrent objects, and can be used to check whether the implementation of *seqlock* is correct with respect to the abstract specification given above. The idea of linearizability is that:

> Linearizability provides the illusion that each operation applied by concurrent processes takes effect instantaneously at some point between its invocation and its return. This point is known as the *linearization point.*

In other words, if two operations overlap, then they may take effect in any order from an abstract perspective, but otherwise they must take effect in the order in which they are invoked.

Formally, linearizability is defined in terms of *histories* which are sequences of *events* which can be invocations or returns of operations from a set I and performed by a particular process from a set P. Invocations have an associated input from domain In, and returns an output from domain Out. Both domains contain the value $\perp$ indicating no input or output.

$$\begin{aligned} Event &\mathrel{\widehat{=}} inv\langle\langle P \times I \times In\rangle\rangle \mid ret\langle\langle P \times I \times Out\rangle\rangle \\ History &\mathrel{\widehat{=}} \operatorname{seq} Event \end{aligned}$$

For example, the following is a possible history of *seqlock*, where p and q are processes.

$$h = \langle inv(p, \mathtt{write}, (1,2)), inv(q, \mathtt{read}, \bot), ret(p, \mathtt{write}, \bot), ret(q, \mathtt{read}, (1,2))\rangle$$

Notation: For a history h, $h = \langle head\ h\rangle \frown tail\ h$ (where $\frown$ is sequence concatenation), $\#h$ is the *length* of the sequence, and $h(n)$ its nth element (for $n : 1..\#h$). Furthermore, $h \oplus \{n \mapsto e\}$ replaces the nth element of history h with event e when $n \leq \#h$. Predicates $inv?(e)$ and $ret?(e)$ determine whether an event $e \in Event$ is an invoke or return, respectively. We let $e.i \in I$ denote the operation of an event. We let $e.\pi \in P$ denote the process which performs event e. □

We assume each event in a history can be uniquely identified by its operation. In practice, we could annotate operation names with additional information, e.g., an integer value, to distinguish different occurrences of the same operation. For example, the above history h, could be extended with a second write operation as follows.

$$h' = \langle inv(p, \mathtt{write}_0, (1,2)), inv(q, \mathtt{read}, \bot), ret(p, \mathtt{write}_0, \bot), ret(q, \mathtt{read}, (1,2)),$$
$$inv(q, \mathtt{write}_1, (3,4)), ret(q, \mathtt{write}_1, \bot)\rangle$$

A history h then defines a partial order $<_h$ on its operations denoting whether an operation *precedes* another. An operation o_1 precedes an operation o_2 iff o_1's return event occurs before the invocation event of o_2.

$$o_1 <_h o_2 \ \widehat{=}\ \exists\, m, n : 1 \mathrel{..} \#h \bullet m < n \land$$
$$ret?(h(m)) \land h(m).i = o_1 \land inv?(h(n)) \land h(n).i = o_2$$

In history h', $\mathtt{write}_0 <_{h'} \mathtt{write}_1$ and $\mathtt{read} <_{h'} \mathtt{write}_1$, but $\mathtt{write}_0$ and $\mathtt{read}$ are not related by $<_{h'}$ since they overlap.

Since operations are atomic in an abstract specification, its histories are *sequential*, i.e., each operation invocation will be followed immediately by its return. In this case, $<_h$ will be a total order. The histories of a concurrent implementation, however, may have overlapping operations and hence have the invocations and returns of operations separated. However to be *legal*, a history should not have returns for which there has not been an invocation.

$$legal(h) \ \widehat{=}\ \forall\, n : 1 \mathrel{..} \#h \bullet ret?(h(n)) \Rightarrow$$
$$(\exists\, m : 1 \mathrel{..} n-1 \bullet inv?(h(m)) \land h(m).i = h(n).i)$$

The histories of specifications are also *complete*, i.e., they have a return for each invocation. This is not necessarily the case for implementation histories. For example, the subhistory of h', $\langle inv(p, \mathtt{write}_0, (1,2)), inv(q, \mathtt{read}, \bot)\rangle$, is also a history. To make an implementation history complete, it is necessary to add additional returns for those operations which have been invoked and are deemed to have occurred, and to remove the remaining invocations without matching returns. We define a function *complete* to do the latter.

$$complete(h) \mathrel{\widehat{=}} \begin{cases} \langle\rangle & \text{if } h = \langle\rangle \\ complete(tail\ h) & \text{if } inv?(head\ h) \wedge NoRet(h) \\ \langle head\ h\rangle \frown complete(tail\ h) & \text{otherwise} \end{cases}$$

where $NoRet(h) \mathrel{\widehat{=}} \nexists n : 2 \mathrel{..} \#h \bullet ret?(h(n)) \wedge h(n).i = (head\ h).i$.

Definition 1 (Linearizability). *An implementation of a concurrent object is linearizable with respect to a specification of the object when for each history h of the implementation, there is a (sequential) history hs of the specification such that*

EqSeq *the operations of a legal completion of h are identical to those of hs, i.e.,*

$$\begin{aligned} &\exists\, hr, hc : History \bullet \\ &\quad (\forall\, n : 1 \mathrel{..} \#hr \bullet ret?(hr(n)) \wedge hc = complete(h \frown hr)) \wedge \\ &\quad legal(hc) \wedge \\ &\quad (\forall\, o : I \bullet \\ &\qquad (\exists\, n : 1 \mathrel{..} \#hc \bullet hc(n).i = o) \Leftrightarrow (\exists\, m : 1 \mathrel{..} \#hs \bullet hs(m).i = o)) \end{aligned}$$

Ord *the precedence ordering of h is preserved by that of hs, i.e., only overlapping operations of h may be reordered with respect to each other in hs, i.e.,*

$$<_h \;\subseteq\; <_{hs}$$ □

As an example, *seqlock* can be shown to be linearizable. Definition 1 generalises the original definition of linearizability of Herlihy and Wing [11] since in the original formulation, condition (EqSeq) of Definition 1 was stronger requiring that the operations performed by a particular process have the same order in the specification and implementation histories. This additional restriction is not necessary, however, since it is implied by condition (Ord) when we do not have a weak memory model. In that case, there is a total order between operations performed by a single process in any implementation history (and condition (Ord) preserves that total order in the corresponding specification history). The weaker condition in Definition 1 enables us to use the definition for other correctness criteria simply by changing the partial order $<_h$. This is illustrated in Section 2.3. It also allows us to define alternative definitions of linearizability for weak memory models including those such as that in [5] which allow overlapping, and hence reorderable, operations performed by a single process. We return to this point in Section 4.

2.3 Sequential Consistency and Quiescent Consistency

The formulation of linearizability in Definition 1 provides a general approach for defining correctness criteria for concurrent objects. *EqSeq* states that a concurrent implementation history can be viewed as a sequential specification history, and is common to all correctness criteria. *Ord* restricts the possible reordering of concurrent operations, and distinguishes one correctness criterion from another.

After linearizability, the dominant correctness criteria are *sequential consistency* [13] and *quiescent consistency* [2,17]. Sequential consistency requires that the operations performed by any given process occur in *program order*, i.e., they occur in the implementation in the same order that they occur in the specification. Quiescent consistency requires the order of operations in the implementation separated by *quiescent states*, i.e., states in which no operations are being performed, occur in the same order as in the specification. These criteria are defined in terms of Definition 1 as follows.

Definition 2 (Sequential consistency). *An implementation of a concurrent object is sequentially consistent with respect to a specification of the object when for each history h of the implementation, there is a (sequential) history hs of the specification such that* EqSeq *of Definition 1 holds, and*

$$<_h^{sc} \;\subseteq\; <_{hs}$$

where

$$o_1 <_h^{sc} o_2 \;\widehat{=}\; \exists\, m, n : 1 \,..\, \#h \bullet m < n \wedge h(m).\pi = h(n).\pi \wedge \\ inv?(h(m)) \wedge h(m).i = o_1 \wedge inv?(h(n)) \wedge h(n).i = o_2 \quad \Box$$

The definition of $<_h^{sc}$ ensures that events performed by the same process occur in the implementation in the order that they are invoked. As discussed above, this property is ensured by linearizability when we do not have a weak memory model (since operations performed by a single process will not overlap). Hence from Definitions 1 and 2, we can show that sequential consistency is weaker than linearizability, as is well known [10].

Definition 3 (Quiescent consistency). *An implementation of a concurrent object is quiescent consistent with respect to a specification of the object when for each history h of the implementation, there is a (sequential) history hs of the specification such that* EqSeq *of Definition 1 holds, and*

$$<_h^{qc} \;\subseteq\; <_{hs}$$

where

$$o_1 <_h^{qc} o_2 \;\widehat{=}\; \exists\, l, m, n : 1 \,..\, \#h \bullet l \leq m < n \wedge \\ ret?(h(l)) \wedge h(l).i = o_1 \wedge inv?(h(n)) \wedge h(n).i = o_2 \wedge \\ (\forall\, j : 1 \,..\, m \bullet inv?(h(j)) \Rightarrow \\ (\exists\, k : j+1 \,..\, m \bullet ret?(h(k)) \wedge h(k).i = h(j).i)) \quad \Box$$

The definition of $<_h^{qc}$ ensures that events separated by a quiescent state, i.e., a point in the history up to which all invocations have a matching return, occur in the implementation in the order they are invoked. It implies $o_1 <_h o_2$ and hence the order is more restrictive than that for linearizability. As a consequence, quiescent consistency is weaker than linearizability, as is well known [10].

3 The TSO Memory Model

The standard definitions of linearizability and other correctness criteria assume the concurrent object being verified is not running on a weak memory model. Thus, while *seqlock* can be proved linearizable on a standard architecture, when run on TSO the behavior cannot be matched to an abstract history using the standard definition of linearizability given in Definition 1.

Due to its relative simplicity, the TSO (Total Store Order) memory model [16,19] has received more attention from the verification community than other weaker memory models such as Power and ARM [1]. In TSO, each processor core uses a write buffer (as shown in Figure 3), which is a FIFO queue that stores pending writes to memory. A processor core (from this point on referred to as a *process*) performing a *write* to a memory location enqueues the write to the buffer and continues computation without waiting for the write to be committed to memory. Pending writes do not become visible to other processes until the buffer is *flushed* committing (some or all) pending writes to memory.

In general, flushes are controlled by the hardware. However, a programmer may explicitly include a *fence*, or *memory barrier*, instruction in a program's code to force the contents of the write buffer to be flushed. Therefore, although TSO allows non-sequentially consistent executions, it is used in many modern architectures on the basis that these can be prevented, where necessary, by programmers using fence instructions.

The value of a memory location *read* by a process is the most recent in the processor's local buffer. This is known as *Intra-Process Forwarding* (IPF). If there is no such value (e.g., initially or when all writes corresponding to the location have been flushed), the value of the location is fetched from memory. The use of local buffers allows a read by one process, occurring after a write by another, to return an older value as if it occurred before the write. This is called *Write* → *Read* reordering. It is this combination of IPF and *Write* → *Read* reordering that defines the TSO memory model.

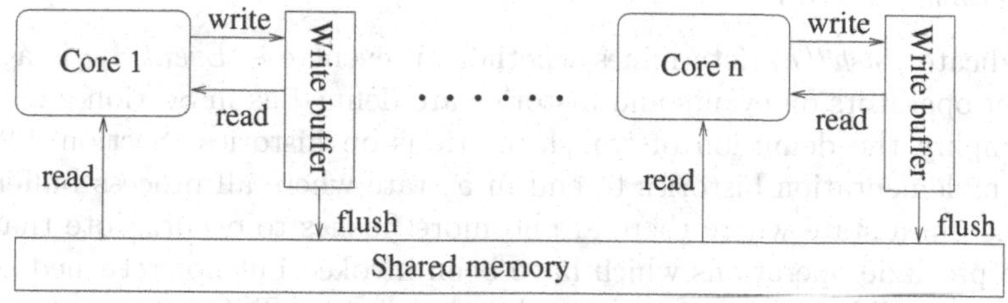

Fig. 3. The TSO memory model

As an example, consider running *seqlock* on TSO. In TSO the `acquire` operation of the software lock necessarily has a fence to ensure synchronization between writer threads, however a fence is not required by the `release` operation, the effect of which may be delayed. This can lead to unexpected behaviour on TSO. For example, if a process p writes the values 1 and 2 to `x1` and `x2`, and then performs a read before its buffer is flushed, it will return 1 and 2 due to IPF. However, another process performing a read immediately after the read by p will return the values of `x1` and `x2` before p's write which are not necessarily 1 and 2. This is a case of *Write* $\rightarrow$ *Read* reordering and results in a sequence of `write` and `read` operations which is not possible according to the specification of Figure 1.

4 Framework for Weak Memory Models

It is necessary therefore to adapt definitions of correctness criteria to weak memory models. In particular, it is necessary to take into account the behaviour allowed by these models in the implementation histories, and how these histories relate to the specification histories. In this section we describe how this can be done.

4.1 Extending the Definition of Implementation Histories

We begin by extending implementation histories to explicitly include flushes. As such histories are usually generated from a formal model of the implementation, this is easily achieved by including an additional flush operation in the model (and capturing fence instructions by a sequence of flushes). An example of such an approach can be found in [5].

In this paper, we associate a flush with a pair: the process whose buffer is flushed, and either an operation, if the flush is of the last value written by the operation, or $\bot$ otherwise. Again, determining the flush of the last value written by an operation can be deduced from a suitable formal model of the implementation as, for example, in [5]. Events and histories of implementations are then defined as follows.

$$\begin{array}{lcl} \mathit{Event}_{\mathit{Impl}} & \widehat{=} & \mathit{inv}\langle\langle P \times I \times \mathit{In}\rangle\rangle \mid \mathit{ret}\langle\langle P \times I \times \mathit{Out}\rangle\rangle \mid \mathit{flush}\langle\langle P \times (I \cup \{\bot\})\rangle\rangle \\ \mathit{History}_{\mathit{Impl}} & \widehat{=} & \mathrm{seq}\, \mathit{Event}_{\mathit{Impl}} \end{array}$$

The predicate $\mathit{flush?}(e)$ determines whether an event $e \in \mathit{Event}_{\mathit{Impl}}$ is a flush, and other operators on events and histories are defined as in Section 2.2.

To simplify the definition of transformations on histories (Section 4.2), we require implementation histories to end in a state where all process buffers are empty, i.e., in a state where there are no more flushes to occur. Note that this does not preclude operations which have been invoked but not returned. As an example, a possible history of *seqlock* when running on TSO is

$$\begin{array}{ll} h_{TSO} = & \langle \mathit{inv}(p, \mathtt{write}, (1,2)), \mathit{flush}(p, \bot), \mathit{flush}(p, \bot), \mathit{ret}(p, \mathtt{write}, \bot), \\ & \mathit{flush}(p, \bot), \mathit{inv}(q, \mathtt{read}, \bot), \mathit{flush}(p, \bot), \mathit{flush}(p, \bot), \mathit{ret}(q, \mathtt{read}, (1,2)), \\ & \mathit{flush}(p, \mathtt{write})\rangle \end{array}$$

where the first 5 flushes correspond, respectively, to the first value written to `lock`, the first value written to `c`, the values written to `x1` and `x2`, and the second value written to `c`, and the final flush corresponds to the second value written to `lock` (which is the final value written by the `write` operation). Note that q's read can return any time after the second value of `c` is written, including before the software lock is released.

4.2 Transforming Implementation Histories

In the absence of a weak memory model, an operation by a process is deemed to take effect (and hence be able to influence other processes) at some point between its invocation and return. Hence as seen in Section 2.2, the partial orders used to define correctness criteria are based on the relative ordering of invocations and returns of operations in implementation histories. On a weak memory model, however, the effect of an operation may be delayed until some, or all, of its writes have been flushed. For example, in h_{TSO} the effect of the `write` operation is not visible to the reader process q until the flush of the second value written to `c`, despite the fact that the `write` operation returns earlier.

In general on TSO, an operation's effect may take effect at any time up to the flush of the last value written by the operation. We therefore transform our implementation histories to extend operations which perform writes. The effective return of an operation in a TSO history is either the flush of the final value written by the operation or the return of the operation, whichever occurs later in the history. Hence, a history is transformed by

- moving the return of an operation to replace the final flush for the operation when such a flush occurs after the return, and
- removing all other flushes.

This is formalised in the following definition.

Definition 4 (TSO transformation *trans*). *We define* trans *as follows:*

$$trans(h) \;\widehat{=}\; \begin{cases} \langle\rangle & \textit{if } h = \langle\rangle \\ trans(tail\ h) & \textit{if } flush?(head\ h) \\ trans(tail(h \oplus \{n \mapsto head\ h\})) & \textit{if } DelayedRet(h) \textit{ with } n \leq \#h \\ \langle head\ h\rangle \frown trans(tail\ h) & \textit{otherwise} \end{cases}$$

where $DelayedRet(h) \;\widehat{=}\; ret?(head\ h) \wedge flush?(h(n)) \wedge (head\ h).i = h(n).i.$ □

For example, for h_{TSO} given above, $trans(h_{TSO})$ is

$$\langle inv(p, \texttt{write}, (1,2)), inv(q, \texttt{read}, \bot), ret(q, \texttt{read}, (1,2)), ret(p, \texttt{write}, \bot)\rangle$$

where the `write` and `read` operations now overlap. This history intuitively captures the behaviour on TSO and can be compared to histories of the abstract specification using the definitions of correctness criteria of Section 2.2.

Definition 5 (Linearizability on TSO). *An implementation of a concurrent object is linearizable on TSO with respect to a specification of the object when for each history h_{TSO} of the implementation, there exists a (sequential) history hs of the the specification such that conditions* EqSeq *and* Ord *of Definition 1 hold with $h = trans(h_{TSO})$.* □

Similarly, sequential consistency and quiescent consistency can be defined on TSO using *trans* and Definitions 2 and 3, respectively. In fact, any correctness criterion defined in terms of a partial order as in Section 2.2 can be adapted to TSO following Definition 5. Furthermore, such correctness criteria can be adapted to other weak memory models by defining a suitable history transformation function capturing their behaviour.

This approach defines our framework for correctness criteria on weak memory models.

Definition 6 (Correctness criteria framework). *Given a correctness criterion C and a (weak) memory model M, correctness is defined in terms of*

- *a partial order $<_h^C$ constraining the allowed reordering of operations in an implementation history h to match a specification history, and*
- *a transformation $trans_M$ for modifying implementation histories to incorporate the effects of M and remove implementation level details, such as flushes.*

A concrete object is correct with respect to a specification when Definition 1 holds with h replaced by $trans_M(h)$ and $<_h$ replaced by $<^C_{trans_M(h)}$. □

Investigating the full use of the framework for a range of correctness criteria and weak memory models is beyond the scope of this paper. In the remainder of this section, we focus on alternative definitions of linearizability on TSO. Definition 5 is equivalent to the definition of TSO linearizability in [5] and thus does not imply sequential consistency. This is because operations on a single process can overlap when the return of at least one of them is moved to a future flush, one occurring after the invocation of the other operation. For example, the history

$$\langle inv(p, \texttt{write}, (1,2)), ret(p, \texttt{write}, \bot), inv(p, \texttt{read}, \bot), ret(p, \texttt{read}, (1,2)), \ldots, flush(p, \texttt{write})\rangle$$

(where ... elides a sequence of flushes) is transformed to

$$\langle inv(p, \texttt{write}, (1,2)), inv(p, \texttt{read}, \bot), ret(p, \texttt{read}, (1,2)), ret(p, \texttt{write}, \bot)\rangle$$

The operations in the transformed history are no longer ordered by $<_h$ and so can occur in an order different to their invocation order in a matching specification history. While this is sufficient for verifying a range of concurrent objects, e.g., those where sequential consistency is ensured due to fence instructions (the *spinlock* case study in [5] is such an example), more widely applicable definitions of TSO linearizability can also be readily defined.

We illustrate the use of the framework below to provide two alternative definitions of linearizability on TSO which preserve invocation order on a single process and hence imply sequential consistency. The first modifies the partial order defining linearizability, and the second modifies both the partial order and *trans*, and hence adopts a different understanding of behaviour on the TSO memory model. The framework allows these alternatives to be easily defined and compared.

4.3 Modifying the Partial Order

The simplest way to add sequential consistency to the TSO definition of linearizability is to weaken the partial order (and hence strengthen the reordering constraints). This can be done using the existing partial orders as follows.

$$o_1 <'_h o_2 \;\widehat{=}\; o_1 <_h o_2 \vee o_1 <_h^{sc} o_2$$

It follows directly from the definition that if $<'_h \subseteq <_{hs}$, for some implementation history h and specification history hs, then $<_h \subseteq <_{hs}$ and $<_h^{sc} \subseteq <_{hs}$. Therefore, if an object is correct with respect to a specification using the partial order $<'_h$, it is also linearizable and sequentially consistent with respect to the specification.

As with Definition 5, it is not possible to prove *seqlock* correct using the correctness criterion defined using this weakened partial order. For both criteria, this can be shown using the following history corresponding to the example TSO behaviour:

$$\begin{aligned}&\langle inv(p, \mathtt{write}, (1,2)), ret(p, \mathtt{write}, \bot), inv(p, \mathtt{read}_0, \bot), ret(p, \mathtt{read}_0, (1,2)),\\ &\quad inv(q, \mathtt{read}_1, \bot), ret(q, \mathtt{read}_1, (0,0)), \ldots, \mathit{flush}(p, \mathtt{write})\rangle\end{aligned}$$

The only specification history that can be associated with the above is

$$\begin{aligned}&\langle inv(q, \mathtt{read}_1, \bot), ret(q, \mathtt{read}_1, (0,0)), inv(p, \mathtt{write}, (1,2)), ret(p, \mathtt{write}, \bot),\\ &\quad inv(p, \mathtt{read}_0, \bot), ret(p, \mathtt{read}_0, (1,2))\rangle\end{aligned}$$

i.e., where the `read` operation of q returning the older values of `x1` and `x2` occurs before the `write` operation which in turn occurs before the `read` operation of p returning the newer values. This reordering is forbidden by the criteria, however, because the two `read` operations do not overlap, and hence cannot be reordered.

4.4 Modifying the History Transformation

The history transformation of Definition 4 accurately captures the effective delay of operations performing writes to shared memory under TSO. However, it does not consider the possibility of delay to operations which do not perform such writes. The operation `read` of *seqlock* is such an operation. Although it writes to variables `c0`, `d1` and `d2`, these are not shared by other processes and hence reside on a local processor stack for the duration of the operation. Consequently, the effect of a **read** is not visible to other processes and we only require that it occurs before the next operation of the same process takes effect (to ensure sequential consistency).

In fact, all operations of a process which do not perform writes to shared memory can occur (in order) at any time up to the return of the next operation of the process which does perform such a write. To help specify the required history transformation, we first specify a function τ which moves an event e to just before the next flush of the last value written by an operation by the same process in a history h. If there is no such flush, e is moved to the end of the history.

$$\tau(e,h) \mathrel{\widehat{=}} \begin{cases} \langle e\rangle & \text{if } h = \langle\,\rangle \\ \langle e\rangle \frown h & \text{if } \mathit{flush?}(\mathit{head}\ h) \text{ and } \mathit{LastWrite}(h) \\ \langle \mathit{head}\ h\rangle \frown \tau(e, \mathit{tail}\ h) & \text{otherwise} \end{cases}$$

where $\mathit{LastWrite}(h) \mathrel{\widehat{=}} (\mathit{head}\ h).\pi = e.\pi \wedge \mathit{head}\ h.i \neq \bot$.

The required definition can then be given using the existing definition of *trans* as follows. In addition to the transformations of Definition 5, the returns of operations which do not write values to global variables are moved to just before the next flush of the last variable written by an operation by the same process, or to the end of the history if there is no such flush.

Definition 7 (Extended TSO transformation $trans_{ext}$). *The extended TSO transformation $trans_{ext}$ is defined as:*

$$\mathit{trans}_{ext}(h) \mathrel{\widehat{=}} \begin{cases} \tau(\mathit{head}\ h, \mathit{tail}\ h) & \textit{if } \mathit{ret?}(\mathit{head}\ h) \textit{ and } \mathit{NoFlush}(h) \\ \mathit{trans}(h) & \textit{otherwise} \end{cases}$$

where $\mathit{NoFlush}(h) \mathrel{\widehat{=}} \nexists n : 2 \mathinner{..} \#h \bullet \mathit{flush?}(h(n)) \wedge (\mathit{head}\ h).i = h(n).i.$ □

Applying $trans_{ext}$ to the implementation history of Section 4.3 we get

$$\langle \mathit{inv}(p, \mathtt{write}, (1,2)), \mathit{inv}(p, \mathtt{read}_0, \bot), \mathit{inv}(q, \mathtt{read}_1, \bot), \mathit{ret}(q, \mathtt{read}_1, (0,0)), \\ \mathit{ret}(p, \mathtt{write}, \bot), \mathit{ret}(p, \mathtt{read}_0, (1,2))\rangle$$

which under either $<_h$ or $<'_h$ can be reordered to give the specification history of Section 4.3. (Note that the recursive definition of $trans_{ext}$ will move the return of p's `write` before moving the return of p's `read` resulting in the latter being moved to the end of the history.)

5 Properties of Correctness Criteria

As we have seen in Section 4, our framework facilitates reuse in the definition of new correctness criteria. In this section, we look at how it also facilitates reuse of proofs of properties of those criteria.

Two important properties of linearizability are that the criterion is *non-blocking* and *compositional* [11]. A non-blocking criterion is one where a pending invocation, i.e., one for which there is no return, is never required to wait for another pending invocation to complete in order to satisfy the criterion. In other words, if h is an implementation history of an object satisfying the criterion and has a pending invocation $inv(p, op, -)$ then $h \frown \langle ret(p, op, -)\rangle$ also satisfies the criterion (where $-$ stands for arbitrary input or output).

To prove this for TSO linearizability (Definition 5), we use the following theorem from Herlihy and Wing [11], where *linearizable* refers to the fact that the history can be related to a specification history by satisfying conditions *EqSeq* and *Ord* of Definition 1.

Theorem 1. *If $inv(p, op, -)$ is a pending invocation in a linearizable implementation history h, then $h \frown \langle ret(p, op, -)\rangle$ is also linearizable.* □

To state the equivalent theorem in the context of TSO, we need to ensure that when we extend h with the return event, the history still ends in a state with all buffers empty. In general, additional write statements may need to occur before the return, and hence additional flushes will be required.

Theorem 2. *If $inv(p, op, -)$ is a pending invocation in a TSO linearizable implementation history h, then $h \frown f \frown \langle ret(p, op, -)\rangle$ is also TSO linearizable, where f is a sequence of flush events required to ensure all buffers are empty at the end of the history.*

Proof. If h is TSO linearizable then $trans(h)$ is linearizable by Definition 5. Therefore, $trans(h) \frown \langle ret(p, op, -)\rangle$ is linearizable by Theorem 1. Since we can find a sequence of flush events f such that

$$trans(h) \frown \langle ret(p, op, -)\rangle = trans(h \frown f \frown \langle ret(p, op, -)\rangle)$$

by Definition 4, $h \frown f \frown \langle ret(p, op, -)\rangle$ is also TSO linearizable (by Definition 5). □

The non-blocking property can similarly be proved for the alternative definitions of TSO linearizability in Section 4.

A compositional correctness criterion is one where a system composed of several objects satisfies the criterion if and only if each object does. To prove this for TSO linearizability, we use the following theorem from Herlihy and Wing [11], where $h|_x$ is the subsequence of h of all events on object x.

Theorem 3. *An implementation history h is linearizable if and only if, for each object x, $h|_x$ is linearizable.* □

In the context of TSO, we interpret $h|_x$ to include flushes of values written by operations on object x.

Theorem 4. *An implementation history h is TSO linearizable if and only if, for each object x, $h|_x$ is TSO linearizable.*

Proof. We prove the "if" direction, then the "only if" direction.

(i) If $h|_x$ is TSO linearizable then $trans(h|_x)$ is linearizable by Definition 5. Since $trans(h)|_x = trans(h|_x)$ by Definition 4, $trans(h)|_x$ is also linearizable. Therefore, if for all objects x, $h|_x$ is TSO linearizable then $trans(h)$ is linearizable by Theorem 3. Hence, h is TSO linearizable (by Definition 5).

(ii) If h is TSO linearizable then $trans(h)$ is linearizable by Definition 5. Therefore, for all objects x, $trans(h)|_x$ is linearizable by Theorem 3. Since $trans(h)|_x = trans(h|_x)$ by Definition 4, for each x, $trans(h|_x)$ is also linearizable. Hence, for all objects x, $h|_x$ is TSO linearizable (by Definition 5). □

Compositionality can be proved similarly for the alternative definitions of TSO linearizability in Section 4. The key point with each of the proofs in this section is that they take advantage of the framework's reuse of definitions from standard linearizability to reuse the proofs of Theorems 1 and 3 where the difficult proof work is done.

6 Conclusion

This paper has presented a framework for the definition of correctness criteria for concurrent objects operating on weak memory models. The key to this framework is that such a definition comprises two parts: one defining the particular criterion, and one the weak memory model. For the former, we followed the work of Herlihy and Wing [11] who defined linearizability in terms of a partial order on the operations within the history of a concurrent object. We showed how other well known criteria, sequential consistency and quiescent consistency, can similarly be defined in terms of a partial order. To define a particular weak memory model we used transformations on implementation histories which move the return points of operations to the point in the history where they take effect in shared memory. The approach was illustrated via two interpretations of the TSO (Total Store Order) weak memory model [16,19].

As well as making the definition of correctness criteria more systematic, the framework facilitates the reuse of existing definitions. The definition of a particular criterion can be reused across different memory models, or modified slightly for use on a single memory model. Similarly, slight modifications to the definitions of a memory model can be made to reflect different interpretations of it. Examples were given for variations of the definition of linearizability on TSO. This reuse of definitions also enables the reuse of proofs simplifying the verification of properties of the new correctness criteria.

An alternative framework of definitions of consistency including linearizability is given in [6]. Although this is similar in spirit to what we try and achieve here, our use of transformations above means that we have one definition of each consistency criteria (linearizabiltiy, sequential consistency etc.) that can be used on any memory model. To change between memory models we just need to change the transformation. Indeed that was one of the motivations of the framework that we developed here. This is in contrast to the framework defined in [6] that defines linearizability and quiescent consistency on TSO from scratch since the definitions in that paper encode both the consistency condition and the necessary transformation in one definition together. Another advantage of our use of transformations is that it enables us to reuse both criteria definitions and their associated proofs of non-blocking and compositionality. In [6] it is necessary to redo these proofs from scratch as well.

Future work on our framework will include defining transformations for other weak memory models, as well as proof techniques for proving concurrent objects correct with respect to defined criteria. The latter will build on the sound and complete proof techniques for linearizabilty by Derrick et al. [4,15] (which are defined in terms of simulations for non-atomic refinement) which have been implemented in the theorem prover KIV [14].

References

1. Alglave, J., Fox, A., Ishtiaq, S., Myreen, M.O., Sarkar, S., Sewell, P., Nardelli, F.Z.: The Semantics of Power and ARM Multiprocessor Machine Code. In: Petersen, L., Chakravarty, M.M.T. (eds.) DAMP 2009, pp. 13–24. ACM (2008)
2. Aspnes, J., Herlihy, M., Shavit, N.: Counting networks. J. ACM 41(5), 1020–1048 (1994)
3. Burckhardt, S., Gotsman, A., Musuvathi, M., Yang, H.: Concurrent library correctness on the TSO memory model. In: Seidl, H. (ed.) Programming Languages and Systems. LNCS, vol. 7211, pp. 87–107. Springer, Heidelberg (2012)
4. Derrick, J., Schellhorn, G., Wehrheim, H.: Mechanically verified proof obligations for linearizability. ACM Trans. Program. Lang. Syst. 33(1), 4 (2011)
5. Derrick, J., Smith, G., Dongol, B.: Verifying linearizability on TSO architectures. In: Albert, E., Sekerinski, E. (eds.) IFM 2014. LNCS, vol. 8739, pp. 341–356. Springer, Heidelberg (2014)
6. Dongol, B., Derrick, J., Groves, L., Smith, G.: Defining correctness conditions for concurrent objects in multicore architectures. In: ECOOP 2015, LNCS. Springer (2015)
7. Filipovic, I., O'Hearn, P.W., Rinetzky, N., Yang, H.: Abstraction for concurrent objects. Theoretical Computer Science 411(51-52), 4379–4398 (2010)
8. Fitzpatrick, J.: An interview with Steve Furber. Commun. ACM 54(5), 34–39 (2011)
9. Gotsman, A., Musuvathi, M., Yang, H.: Show no weakness: Sequentially consistent specifications of TSO libraries. In: Aguilera, M.K. (ed.) DISC 2012. LNCS, vol. 7611, pp. 31–45. Springer, Heidelberg (2012)
10. Herlihy, M., Shavit, N.: The Art of Multiprocessor Programming. Morgan Kaufmann (2008)
11. Herlihy, M., Wing, J.M.: Linearizability: A correctness condition for concurrent objects. ACM Trans. Program. Lang. Syst. 12(3), 463–492 (1990)
12. Kogan, A., Herlihy, M.: The future(s) of shared data structures. In: PODC 2014, pp. 30–39. ACM (2014)
13. Lamport, L.: How to make a multiprocessor computer that correctly executes multiprocess programs. IEEE Trans. Computers 28(9), 690–691 (1979)
14. Reif, W., Schellhorn, G., Stenzel, K., Balser, M.: Structured specifications and interactive proofs with KIV. In: Automated Deduction, pp. 13–39. Kluwer (1998)

15. Schellhorn, G., Wehrheim, H., Derrick, J.: A sound and complete proof technique for linearizability of concurrent data structures. ACM Trans. on Computational Logic, 15(4), 31:1–31:37 (2014)
16. Sewell, P., Sarkar, S., Owens, S., Nardelli, F.Z., Myreen, M.O.: x86-TSO: a rigorous and usable programmer's model for x86 multiprocessors. Commun. ACM 53(7), 89–97 (2010)
17. Shavit, N., Zemach, A.: Diffracting trees. ACM Trans. Comput. Syst. 14(4), 385–428 (1996)
18. Smith, G., Derrick, J., Dongol, B.: Admit your weakness: Verifying correctness on TSO architectures. In: Lanese, I., Madelaine, E. (eds.) FACS 2014. LNCS, vol. 8997, pp. 364–383. Springer, Heidelberg (2015)
19. Sorin, D.J., Hill, M.D., Wood, D.A.: A Primer on Memory Consistency and Cache Coherence. Synthesis Lectures on Computer Architecture. Morgan & Claypool Publishers (2011)
20. Travkin, O., Mütze, A., Wehrheim, H.: SPIN as a linearizability checker under weak memory models. In: Bertacco, V., Legay, A. (eds.) HVC 2013. LNCS, vol. 8244, pp. 311–326. Springer, Heidelberg (2013)
21. Travkin, O., Wehrheim, H.: Handling TSO in mechanized linearizability proofs. In: Yahav, E. (ed.) HVC 2014. LNCS, vol. 8855, pp. 132–147. Springer, Heidelberg (2014)

Semantics-Preserving Simplification of Real-World Firewall Rule Sets

Cornelius Diekmann(✉), Lars Hupel, and Georg Carle

Technische Universität München, München, Germany
diekmann@net.in.tum.de

Abstract. The security provided by a firewall for a computer network almost completely depends on the rules it enforces. For over a decade, it has been a well-known and unsolved problem that the quality of many firewall rule sets is insufficient. Therefore, there are many tools to analyze them. However, we found that none of the available tools could handle typical, real-world *iptables* rulesets. This is due to the complex chain model used by *iptables*, but also to the vast amount of possible match conditions that occur in real-world firewalls, many of which are not understood by academic and open source tools.

In this paper, we provide algorithms to transform firewall rulesets. We reduce the execution model to a simple list model and use ternary logic to abstract over all unknown match conditions. These transformations enable existing tools to understand real-world firewall rules, which we demonstrate on four decently-sized rulesets. Using the Isabelle theorem prover, we formally show that all our algorithms preserve the firewall's filtering behavior.

Keywords: Computer networks · Firewalls · Isabelle · Netfilter Iptables · Semantics

1 Introduction

Firewalls are a fundamental security mechanism for computer networks. Several firewall solutions, ranging from open source [2,28,29] to commercial [3,13], exist. Operating and managing firewalls is challenging as rulesets are usually written manually. While vulnerabilities in the firewall software itself are comparatively rare, it has been known for over a decade [32] that many firewalls enforce poorly written rulesets. However, the prevalent methodology for configuring firewalls has not changed. Consequently, studies regularly report insufficient quality of firewall rulesets [7,12,18,21,27,31,33,34].

Therefore, several tools [18–22, 25, 30, 33] have been developed to ease firewall management and reveal configuration errors. However, when we tried to analyze real-world firewalls with the publicly available tools, none of them could handle our firewall rules. We found that the firewall model of the available tools is too simplistic.

In this paper, we address the following fundamental problem: Many tools do not understand real-world firewall rules. To solve the problem, we transform and simplify the rules such that they are understood by the respective tools.

N. Bjørner and F. de Boer (Eds.): FM 2015, LNCS 9109, pp. 195–212, 2015.
DOI: 10.1007/978-3-319-19249-9_13

```
Chain INPUT (policy ACCEPT)
target      prot source          destination
DOS_PROTECT all  0.0.0.0/0       0.0.0.0/0
ACCEPT      all  0.0.0.0/0       0.0.0.0/0    state RELATED,ESTABLISHED
DROP        tcp  0.0.0.0/0       0.0.0.0/0    tcp dpt:22
DROP        tcp  0.0.0.0/0       0.0.0.0/0    multiport dports ↩
                                   21,873,5005,5006,80,548,111,2049,892
DROP        udp  0.0.0.0/0       0.0.0.0/0    multiport dports ↩
                                                123,111,2049,892,5353
ACCEPT      all  192.168.0.0/16 0.0.0.0/0
DROP        all  0.0.0.0/0       0.0.0.0/0

Chain DOS_PROTECT (1 references)
target      prot source          destination
RETURN      icmp 0.0.0.0/0       0.0.0.0/0    icmptype 8 limit: ↩
                                                     avg 1/sec burst 5
DROP        icmp 0.0.0.0/0       0.0.0.0/0    icmptype 8
RETURN      tcp  0.0.0.0/0       0.0.0.0/0    tcp flags:0x17/0x04 ↩
                                                limit: avg 1/sec burst 5
DROP        tcp  0.0.0.0/0       0.0.0.0/0    tcp flags:0x17/0x04
RETURN      tcp  0.0.0.0/0       0.0.0.0/0    tcp flags:0x17/0x02 ↩
                                           limit: avg 10000/sec burst 100
DROP        tcp  0.0.0.0/0       0.0.0.0/0    tcp flags:0x17/0x02
```

Fig. 1. Linux *iptables* ruleset of a Synology NAS (network attached storage) device

To demonstrate the problem by example, we decided to use *ITVal* [19] because it natively supports *iptables* [28], is open source, and supports calls to user-defined chains. However, ITVal's firewall model is representative of the model used by the majority of tools; therefore, the problems described here also apply to a vast range of other tools. Firewall models used in related work are surveyed in Sect. 2. For this example, we use the firewall rules in Fig. 1, taken from an NAS device. The ruleset reads as follows: First, incoming packets are sent to the user-defined `DOS_PROTECT` chain, where some rate limiting is applied. Afterwards, the firewall allows all packets which belong to already established connections. This is generally considered good practice. Then, some services, identified by their ports, are blocked. Finally, the firewall allows all packets from the local network 192.168.0.0/16 and discards all other packets. We used ITVal to partition the IP space into equivalence classes (i.e. ranges with the same access rights) [20]. The expected result is a set of two IP ranges: the local network 192.168.0.0/16 and the "rest". However, ITVal erroneously only reports one IP range: the universe. Removing the first two rules (in particular the call in the `DOS_PROTECT` chain) lets ITVal compute the expected result.

We identified two main problems which prevent tools from "understanding" real-world firewalls. First, calling and returning from custom chains, due to the possibility of complex nested chain calls. Second, more seriously, most tools do not understand the firewall's match conditions. In the above example, the rate limiting is not understood. The problem of unknown match conditions cannot simply be solved by implementing the rate limiting feature for the respective tool. The major reason is that the underlying algorithm might not be capable of dealing with this special case. Additionally, firewalls, such as *iptables*, support numerous match conditions and several new ones are added in every release.[1] We expect even more match conditions for nftables [29] in the future since they can be written as simple userspace programs [17]. Therefore, it is virtually impossible to write a tool which understands all possible match conditions.

In this paper, we build a fundamental prerequisite to enable tool-supported analysis of *real-world* firewalls: We present several steps of semantics-preserving ruleset simplification, which lead to a ruleset that is "understandable" to subsequent analysis tools: First, we unfold all calls to and returns from user-defined chains. This process is exact and valid for arbitrary match conditions. Afterwards, we process unknown match conditions. For that, we embed a ternary-logic semantics into the firewall's semantics. Due to ternary logic, all match conditions not understood by subsequent analysis tools can be treated as always yielding an unknown result. In a next step, all unknown conditions can be removed. This introduces an over- and underapproximation ruleset, called upper/lower closure. Guarantees about the original ruleset dropping/allowing a packet can be given by using the respective closure ruleset.

To summarize, we provide the following contributions:

1. a formal semantics of *iptables* packet filtering (Sect. 4),
2. chain unfolding: transforming a ruleset in the complex chain model to a ruleset in the simple list model (Sect. 5),
3. an embedded semantics with ternary logic, supporting arbitrary match conditions, introducing a lower/upper closure of accepted packets (Sect. 6), and
4. normalization and translation of complex logical expressions to an *iptables*-compatible format, discovering a meta-logical firewall algebra (Sect. 7).

We evaluate applicability on large real-world firewalls in Sect. 8. All proofs are machine-verified with Isabelle [24] (Sect. 3). Therefore, the correctness of all obtained results only depends on a small and well-established mathematical kernel and the *iptables* semantics (Fig. 2).

2 Firewall Models in the Literature and Related Work

Packets are routed through the firewall and the firewall needs to decide whether to allow or deny a packet. A firewall ruleset determines the firewall's filtering behavior. The firewall inspects its ruleset for each single, arbitrary packet to determine the action to apply to the packet. The ruleset can be viewed as a list of rules; usually it is processed sequentially and the first matching rule is applied.

[1] As of version 1.4.21 (Linux kernel 3.13), *iptables* supports more than 50 match conditions.

The literature agrees on the definition of a single firewall rule. It consists of a predicate (the match expression) and an action. If the match expression applies to a packet, the action is performed. Usually, a packet is scrutinized by several rules. Zhang et al. [34] specify a common format for packet filtering rules. The action is either "allow" or "deny", which directly corresponds to the firewall's filtering decision. The ruleset is processed strictly sequentially. Yuan et al. [33] call this the *simple list model.* ITVal also supports calls to user-defined chains as an action. This allows "jumping" within the ruleset without having a final filtering decision yet. This is called the *complex chain model* [33].

In general, a packet header is a bitstring which can be matched against [35]. Zhang et al. [34] support matching on the following packet header fields: IP source and destination address, protocol, and port on layer 4. This model is commonly found in the literature [4,5,25,33,34]. ITVal extends these match conditions with flags (e.g. `TCP SYN`) and connection states (`INVALID, NEW, ESTABLISHED, RELATED`). The state matching is treated as just another match condition.[2] This model is similar to Margrave's model for IOS [21]. When comparing these features to the simple firewall in Fig. 1, it becomes obvious that none of these tools supports that firewall.

We are not aware of any tool which uses a model fundamentally different than those described in the previous paragraph. Our model enhances existing work in that we use ternary logic to support arbitrary match conditions. To analyze a large *iptables* firewall, the authors of Margrave [21] translated it to basic Cisco IOS access lists [3] by hand. With our simplification, we can automatically remove all features not understood by basic Cisco IOS. This enables translation of any *iptables* firewall to a basic Cisco access lists which is guaranteed to drop no more packets than the original *iptables* firewall. This opens up all tools available only for Cisco IOS access lists, e.g. Margrave [21] and Header Space Analysis [15].[3]

3 Formal Verification with Isabelle

We verified all proofs with Isabelle, using its standard Higher-Order Logic (HOL). The corresponding theory files are publicly available. An interested reader may consult the detailed (100+ pages) proof document.

[2] Firewalls can be stateful or stateless. Most firewalls nowadays are stateful, which means the firewall remembers and tracks information of previously seen packets, e.g. the TCP connection a packet belongs to and the state of this connection. ITVal does not track the state of connections. Match conditions on connection states are treated exactly the same as matches on a packet header. In general, focusing on rulesets and not firewall implementation, matching on *iptables* conntrack states is exactly as matching on any other (stateless) condition. However, internally, not only the packet header is consulted but also the current connection tables. Note that existing firewall analysis tools also largely ignore state [21]. In our semantics, we also model stateless matching.

[3] Note that the other direction is considered easy [26], because basic Cisco IOS access lists have "no nice features" [11]. Note that there also are *Advanced* Access Lists.

Notation. We use pseudo code close to SML and Isabelle. Function application is written without parentheses, e. g. $f\ a$ denotes function f applied to parameter a. We write :: for prepending a single element to a list, e. g. a::b::$[c, d] = [a, b, c, d]$, and ::: for appending lists, e. g. $[a, b]$:::$[c, d] = [a, b, c, d]$. The empty list is written as []. $[f\ a.\ a \leftarrow l]$ denotes a list comprehension, i. e. applying f to every element a of list l. $[f\ x\ y.\ \ x \leftarrow l_1,\ y \leftarrow l_2]$ denotes the list comprehension where f is applied to each combination of elements of the lists l_1 and l_2. For $f\ x\ y = (x, y)$, this returns the cartesian product of l_1 and l_2.

4 Semantics of *iptables*

We formalized the semantics of a subset of *iptables*. The semantics focuses on access control, which is done in the `INPUT`, `OUTUT`, and `FORWARD` chain. Thus packet modification (e. g. NAT) is not considered (and also not allowed in these chains).

Match conditions, e. g. `source 192.168.0.0/24` and `protocol TCP`, are called *primitives*. A primitive matcher γ decides whether a packet matches a primitive. Formally, based on a set X of primitives and a set of packets P, a primitive matcher γ is a binary relation over X and P. The semantics supports arbitrary packet models and match conditions, hence both remain abstract in our definition.

In one firewall rule, several primitives can be specified. Their logical connective is conjunction, for example `src 192.168.0.0/24` *and* `tcp`. Disjunction is omitted because it is neither needed for the formalization nor supported by *iptables*; this is consistent with the model by Jeffrey and Samak [14]. Primitives can be combined in an algebra of *match expressions* M_X:

$$mexpr \quad = \quad x \quad \text{for } x \in X \quad | \quad \neg\, mexpr \quad | \quad mexpr \wedge mexpr \quad | \quad \texttt{True}$$

For a primitive matcher γ and a match expression $m \in M_X$, we write $m \rhd_\gamma p$ if a packet $p \in P$ matches m, essentially lifting γ to a relation over M_X and P, with the connectives defined as usual. With completely generic P, X, and γ, the semantics can be considered to have access to an oracle which understands all possible match conditions.

Furthermore, we support the following *actions*, modeled closely after *iptables*: `Accept`, `Reject`, `Drop`, `Log`, `Empty`, `Call` c for a chain c, and `Return`. A *rule* can be defined as a tuple (m, a) for a match expression m and an action a. A list (or sequence) of rules is called a *chain*. For example, the beginning of the `DOS_PROTECT` chain in Fig. 1 is [(`icmp` ∧ `icmptype 8 limit: ...`, `Return`), ...].

A set of chains associated with a name is called a *ruleset*. Let Γ denote the mapping from chain names to chains. For example, Γ `DOS_PROTECT` returns the contents of the `DOS_PROTECT` chain. We assume that Γ is well-formed that means, if a `Call` c action occurs in a ruleset, then the chain named c is defined in Γ. This assumption is justified as the Linux kernel only accepts well-formed rulesets.

The semantics of a firewall w.r.t. to a given packet p, a background ruleset Γ, and a primitive matcher γ can be defined as a relation over the currently

$$\textsc{Skip}\ \frac{}{p \vdash \langle [],\ t\rangle \Rightarrow t} \qquad \textsc{Accept}\ \frac{m\ \rhd_\gamma p}{p \vdash \langle [(m,\ \texttt{Accept})],\ ?\rangle \Rightarrow \checkmark}$$

$$\textsc{Drop}\ \frac{m\ \rhd_\gamma p}{p \vdash \langle [(m,\ \texttt{Drop})],\ ?\rangle \Rightarrow \times} \qquad \textsc{Reject}\ \frac{m\ \rhd_\gamma p}{p \vdash \langle [(m,\ \texttt{Reject})],\ ?\rangle \Rightarrow \times}$$

$$\textsc{NoMatch}\ \frac{\neg\, m\ \rhd_\gamma p}{p \vdash \langle [(m,\ a)],\ ?\rangle \Rightarrow ?} \qquad \textsc{Decision}\ \frac{t \neq ?}{p \vdash \langle rs,\ t\rangle \Rightarrow t}$$

$$\textsc{Seq}\ \frac{p \vdash \langle rs_1,\ ?\rangle \Rightarrow t \qquad p \vdash \langle rs_2,\ t\rangle \Rightarrow t'}{p \vdash \langle rs_1 ::: rs_2,\ ?\rangle \Rightarrow t'}$$

$$\textsc{CallResult}\ \frac{m\ \rhd_\gamma p \qquad p \vdash \langle \Gamma\ c,\ ?\rangle \Rightarrow t}{p \vdash \langle [(m,\ \texttt{Call}\ c)],\ ?\rangle \Rightarrow t}$$

$$\textsc{CallReturn}\ \frac{m\ \rhd_\gamma p \qquad \Gamma\ c = rs_1 ::: (m',\ \texttt{Return}) :: rs_2 \qquad m'\ \rhd_\gamma p \qquad p \vdash \langle rs_1,\ ?\rangle \Rightarrow ?}{p \vdash \langle [(m,\ \texttt{Call}\ c)],\ ?\rangle \Rightarrow ?}$$

$$\textsc{Log}\ \frac{m\ \rhd_\gamma p}{p \vdash \langle [(m,\ \texttt{Log})],\ ?\rangle \Rightarrow ?} \qquad \textsc{Empty}\ \frac{m\ \rhd_\gamma p}{p \vdash \langle [(m,\ \texttt{Empty})],\ ?\rangle \Rightarrow ?}$$

(for any primitive matcher γ and any well-formed ruleset Γ)

Fig. 2. Big Step semantics for *iptables*

active chain and the state before and the state after processing this chain. The semantics is specified in Fig. 2. The expression $p \vdash \langle rs,\ t\rangle \Rightarrow t'$ states that starting with state t, after processing the chain rs, the resulting state is t'. For a packet p, our semantics focuses on firewall filtering decisions. Therefore, only the following three states are necessary: The firewall may allow (✓) or deny (✗) the packet, or it may not have come to a decision yet (?).

We will now discuss the most important rules. The Accept rule describes the following: if the packet p matches the match expression m, then the firewall with no filtering decision (?) processes the singleton chain $[(m, \texttt{Accept})]$ by switching to the allow state. Both the Drop and Reject rules deny a packet; the difference is only in whether the firewall generates some informational message, which does not influence filtering. The NoMatch rule specifies that if the firewall has not come to a filtering decision yet, it can process any non-matching rule without changing its state. The Decision rule specifies that as soon as the firewall made a filtering decision, it does not change its decision. The Seq rule specifies that if the firewall has not come to a filtering decision and it processes the chain rs_1 which results in state t and starting from t processes the chain rs_2 which results in state t', then both chains can be processed sequentially, ending in state t'. The CallResult rule specifies that if a matching `Call` to a chain named "c" occurs, the resulting state t is the result of processing the chain $\Gamma\ c$. Likewise, the CallReturn rule specifies that if processing a prefix rs_1 of the called chain does not lead to a filtering decision and directly afterwards, a matching `Return` rule occurs, the called chain is processed without result.[4] The Log rule does not influence the filtering behavior. Similarly, the Empty rule does not result in a filtering decision. An Empty rule, i.e. a rule without an action, occurs if *iptables* only updates its internal state, e.g. updating packet counters.[5]

The subsequent parts of this paper are all based on these semantics. Whenever we provide a procedure P to operate on chains, we proved that the firewall's filtering behavior is preserved, formally:

$$p \vdash \langle P\ rs,\ t\rangle \Rightarrow t' \quad \textit{iff} \quad p \vdash \langle rs,\ t\rangle \Rightarrow t'$$

All our proofs are machine-verified with Isabelle. Therefore, once the reader is convinced of the semantics as specified in Fig. 2, the correctness of all subsequent theorems follows automatically – without any hidden assumptions or limitations.

The rules in Fig. 2 are designed such that every rule can be inspected individually. However, considering all of them together, it is not immediately clear whether the result depends on the order of their application to a concrete ruleset and packet. Theorem 1 states that the semantics is deterministic, i.e. only one uniquely defined outcome is possible.

Theorem 1 (Determinism).

$$\textit{If} \quad p \vdash \langle rs,\ s\rangle \Rightarrow t \quad \textit{and} \quad p \vdash \langle rs,\ s\rangle \Rightarrow t' \quad \textit{then} \quad t = t'$$

5 Custom Chain Unfolding

In this section, we present algorithms to convert a ruleset from the complex chain model to the simple list model.

[4] The semantics gets stuck if a `Return` occurs on top-level. However, this is not a problem since we make sure that this cannot happen. *iptables* specifies that a `Return` on top-level in a built-in chain is allowed and in this corner case, the chain's default policy is executed. To comply with this behavior, we always start analysis of a ruleset as follows: [(`True`, `Call` *start-chain*), (`True`, *default-policy*)], where the start chain is one of *iptables*' built-in `INPUT`, `FORWARD`, or `OUTPUT` chains with a default policy of either `Accept` or `Drop`.

[5] A rule without an action can also be used to mark a packet for later handling. This marking may influence the filtering decision. Since our primitive matchers and packets are completely generic, this case can be represented within our model: Instead of updating the firewall's internal state, an additional "ghost field" must be introduced in the packet model. Since packets are immutable, this field cannot be set by a rule but the packet must be given to the firewall with the final value of the ghost field already set. Hence, an analysis must be carried out with an arbitrary value of the ghost fields. We admit that this model is very unwieldy. However, when later embedding the more practical ternary semantics, we want to mention that all primitives which mark a packet for later processing can be considered "unknown" and are correctly abstracted by these semantics.

The function pr ("process return") iterates over a chain. If a Return rule is encountered, all subsequent rules are amended by adding the Return rule's negated match expression as a conjunct. Intuitively, if a Return rule occurs in a chain, all following rules of this chain can only be reached if the Return rule does not match.

$$\begin{aligned}
&\texttt{add-match}\; m'\; rs &&= [(m \wedge m', a).\ (m, a) \leftarrow rs]\\
&\texttt{pr}\; [] &&= []\\
&\texttt{pr}\; ((m, \texttt{Return}) :: rs) &&= \texttt{add-match}\; (\neg m)\; (\texttt{pr}\; rs)\\
&\texttt{pr}\; ((m, a) :: rs) &&= (m, a) :: \texttt{pr}\; rs
\end{aligned}$$

The function pc ("process call") iterates over a chain, unfolding one level of Call rules. If a Call to the chain c occurs, the chain itself (i.e. $\Gamma\ c$) is inserted instead of the Call. However, Returns in the chain need to be processed and the match expression for the original Call needs to be added to the inserted chain.

$$\begin{aligned}
&\texttt{pc}\; [] &&= []\\
&\texttt{pc}\; ((m, \texttt{Call}\; c) :: rs) &&= \texttt{add-match}\; m\; (\texttt{pr}\; (\Gamma\ c)) ::: \texttt{pc}\; rs\\
&\texttt{pc}\; ((m, a) :: rs) &&= (m, a) :: \texttt{pc}\; rs
\end{aligned}$$

The procedure pc can be applied arbitrarily many times and preserves the semantics. It is sound and complete.

Theorem 2 (Soundness and Completeness).

$$p \vdash \langle \texttt{pc}^n\ rs,\ t\rangle \Rightarrow t' \quad \textit{iff} \quad p \vdash \langle rs,\ t\rangle \Rightarrow t'$$

In each iteration, the algorithm unfolds one level of Calls. The algorithm needs to be applied until the result no longer changes. Note that the semantics allows non-terminating rulesets; however, the only rulesets that are interesting for analysis are the ones actually accepted by the Linux kernel.[6] Since it rejects rulesets with loops, both our algorithm and the resulting ruleset are guaranteed to terminate.

Corollary 1. *Every ruleset (with only* Accept, Drop, Reject, Log, Empty, Call, Return *actions) accepted by the Linux kernel can be unfolded completely while preserving its filtering behavior.*

In addition to unfolding calls, the following transformations applied to any ruleset preserve the semantics:

- Replacing Reject actions with Drop actions,
- Removing Empty and Log rules,
- Simplifying match expressions which contain True or ¬ True.
- For some given primitive matcher, specific optimizations may also be performed, e.g. rewriting src 0.0.0.0/0 to True.

[6] The relevant check is in mark_source_chains, file source/net/ipv4/netfilter/ip_tables.c of the Linux kernel version 3.2.

[(¬ (icmp ∧ icmptype 8 limit: ...) ∧ icmp ∧ icmptype 8, Drop),
(¬ (icmp ∧ icmptype 8 limit: ...) ∧ ¬ (tcp ∧ tcp flags:0x17/0x04 limit: ...) ∧
tcp ∧ tcp flags:0x17/0x04, Drop), ..., (src 192.168.0.0/16, Accept), ...]

Fig. 3. Unfolded Synology Firewall

Therefore, after unfolding and optimizing, a chain which only contains Allow or Drop actions is left. In the subsequent sections, we require this as a precondition. As an example, recall the firewall in Fig. 1. Its INPUT chain after unfolding and optimizing is listed in Fig. 3. Observe that the computed match expressions are beyond iptable's expressiveness. An algorithm to normalize the rules to an *iptables*-compatible format will be described in Sect. 7.

6 Unknown Primitives

As we argued earlier, it is infeasible to support all possible primitives of a firewall. Suppose a new firewall module is created which provides the ssh_blacklisted and ssh_innocent primitives. The former applies if an IP address has had too many invalid SSH login attempts in the past; the latter is the opposite of the former. Since we made up these primitives, no existing tool will support them. However, a new version of *iptables* could implement them or they can be provided as third-party kernel modules. Therefore, our ruleset transformations must take unknown primitives into account. To achieve this, we lift the primitive matcher γ to ternary logic, adding Unknown as matching outcome. We embed this new "approximate" semantics into the semantics described in the previous sections. Thus, it becomes easier to construct matchers tailored to the primitives supported by a particular tool.

6.1 Ternary Matching

Logical conjunction and negation on ternary values are as before, with these additional rules for Unknown operands (commutative cases omitted):

True ∧ Unknown = Unknown   False ∧ Unknown = False   ¬ Unknown = Unknown

These rules correspond to Kleene's 3-valued logic [16] and are well-suited for firewall semantics: The first equation states that, if one condition matches, the final result only depends on the other condition. The next equation states that a rule cannot match if one of its conditions does not match. Finally, by negating an unknown value, no additional information can be inferred.

We demonstrate this by example: the two rulesets [(ssh_blacklisted, Drop)] and [(True, Call c)] where $\Gamma\, c$ = [(ssh_innocent, Return), (True, Drop)] have exactly the same filtering behavior. After unfolding, the second ruleset collapses to [(¬ ssh_innocent, Drop)]. Both the ssh_blacklisted and the ssh_innocent primitives are `Unknown` to our matcher. Thus, since both rulesets have the same filtering behavior, a packet matching `Unknown` in the first ruleset should also match ¬ `Unknown` in the second ruleset matches.

6.2 Closures

In the ternary semantics, it may be unknown whether a rule applies to a packet. Therefore, the matching semantics are extended with an *"in-doubt"-tactic*. This tactic is consulted if the result of a match expression is `Unknown`. It decides whether a rule applies.

We introduce the *in-doubt-allow* and *in-doubt-deny* tactics. The first tactic forces a match if the rule's action is `Accept` and a mismatch if it is `Drop`. The second tactic behaves in the opposite manner. Note that an unfolded ruleset is necessary, since no behavior can be specified for `Call` and `Return` actions.[7]

We denote the exact Boolean semantics with "$\Rightarrow$" and embedded ternary semantics with an arbitrary tactic α with "$\Rightarrow_\alpha$". In particular, $\alpha = allow$ for *in-doubt-allow* and $\alpha = deny$ analogously.

"$\Rightarrow$" and "$\Rightarrow_\alpha$" are related to the in-doubt-tactics as follows: considering the set of all accepted packets, *in-doubt-allow* is an overapproximation, whereas *in-doubt-deny* is an underapproximation. In other words, if "$\Rightarrow$" accepts a packet, then "$\Rightarrow_{\mathrm{allow}}$" also accepts the packet. Thus, from the opposite perspective, the *in-doubt-allow* tactic can be used to guarantee that a packet is certainly dropped. Likewise, if "$\Rightarrow$" denies a packet, then "$\Rightarrow_{\mathrm{deny}}$" also denies this packet. Thus, the *in-doubt-deny* tactic can be used to guarantee that a packet is certainly accepted.

For example, the unfolded firewall of Fig. 1 contains rules which drop a packet if a limit is exceeded. If this rate limiting is not understood by γ, the *in-doubt-allow* tactic will never apply this rule, while with the *in-doubt-deny* tactic, it is applied universally.

We say that the Boolean and the ternary matchers agree iff they return the same result or the ternary matcher returns `Unknown`. Interpreting this definition, the ternary matcher may always return `Unknown` and the Boolean matcher serves as an oracle which knows the correct result. Note that we never explicitly specify anything about the Boolean matcher; therefore the model is universally valid, i.e. the proof holds for an arbitrary oracle.

If the exact and ternary matcher agree, then the set of all packets allowed by the *in-doubt-deny* tactic is a subset of the packets allowed by the exact semantics, which in turn is a subset of the packets allowed by the *in-doubt-allow* tactic. Therefore, we call all packets accepted by $\Rightarrow_{\mathrm{deny}}$ the *lower closure*, i.e. the semantics which accepts at most the packets that the exact semantics accepts. Likewise, we call all packets accepted by $\Rightarrow_{\mathrm{allow}}$ the *upper closure*, i.e. the semantics which accepts at least the packets that the exact semantics accepts. Every packet which is not in the upper closure is guaranteed to be dropped by the firewall.

[7] The final decision (✓ or ✗) for `Call` and `Return` rules depends on the called/calling chain.

Theorem 3 (Lower and Upper Closure of Allowed Packets).

$$\{p.\ p \vdash \langle rs,\ ⓘ \rangle \Rightarrow_{\text{deny}} \oslash\} \subseteq \{p.\ p \vdash \langle rs,\ ⓘ \rangle \Rightarrow \oslash\} \subseteq \{p.\ p \vdash \langle rs,\ ⓘ \rangle \Rightarrow_{\text{allow}} \oslash\}$$

The opposite holds for the set of denied packets.

For the example in Fig. 1, we computed the closures (without the `RELATED, ESTABLISHED` rule, see Sect. 6.4) and a ternary matcher which only understands IP addresses and layer 4 protocols. The lower closure is the empty set since rate limiting could apply to any packet. The upper closure is the set of packets originating from 192.168.0.0/16.

6.3 Removing Unknown Matches

In this section, as a final optimization, we remove all unknown primitives. We call this algorithm `pu` ("process unknowns"). For this step, the specific ternary matcher and the choice for the in-doubt-tactic must be known.

In every rule, top-level unknown primitives can be rewritten to `True` or $\neg$ `True`. For example, let m_u be a primitive which is unknown to γ. Then, for in-doubt-allow, (m_u, `Accept`) is equal to (`True`, `Accept`) and (m_u, `Drop`) is equal to ($\neg$ `True`, `Drop`). Similarly, negated unknown primitives and conjunctions of (negated) unknown primitives can be rewritten.

Hence, the base cases of `pu` are straightforward. However, the case of a negated conjunction of match expressions requires some care.The following equation represents the De Morgan rule, specialized to the in-doubt-allow tactic.

$$\texttt{pu}\ (\neg (m_1 \wedge m_2),\ a) \quad = \begin{cases} \texttt{True} & \text{if } \texttt{pu}\ (\neg m_1,\ a) = \texttt{True} \\ \texttt{True} & \text{if } \texttt{pu}\ (\neg m_2,\ a) = \texttt{True} \\ \texttt{pu}\ (\neg m_2,\ a) & \text{if } \texttt{pu}\ (\neg m_1,\ a) = \neg\, \texttt{True} \\ \texttt{pu}\ (\neg m_1,\ a) & \text{if } \texttt{pu}\ (\neg m_2,\ a) = \neg\, \texttt{True} \\ \neg (\neg\, \texttt{pu}\ (\neg m_1,\ a) \wedge \neg\, \texttt{pu}\ (\neg m_2,\ a)) & \text{otherwise} \end{cases}$$

The $\neg$ `Unknown` = `Unknown` equation is responsible for the complicated nature of the De Morgan rule. Fortunately, we machine-verified all our algorithms. For example, during our research, we wrote a seemingly simple (but incorrect) version of `pu` and everybody agreed that the algorithm looks correct. In the early empirical evaluation, with yet unfinished proofs, we did not observe our bug. Only because of the failed correctness proof did we realize that we introduced an equation that only holds in Boolean logic.

Theorem 4 (Soundness and Completeness).

$$p \vdash \langle [\texttt{pu}\ r.\ \ r \leftarrow\ rs],\ t \rangle \Rightarrow_{\text{allow}} t' \quad \textit{iff} \quad p \vdash \langle rs,\ t \rangle \Rightarrow_{\text{allow}} t'$$

Theorem 5. *Algorithm* `pu` *removes all unknown primitive match expressions.*

An algorithm for the in-doubt-deny tactic (with the same equation for the De Morgan case) can be specified in a similar way. Thus, $\Rightarrow_\alpha$ can be treated as if it were defined only on Boolean logic with only known match expressions.

As an example, we examine the ruleset of the upper closure of Fig. 1 (without the `RELATED,ESTABLISHED` rule, see Sect. 6.4) for a ternary matcher which only understands IP addresses and layer 4 protocols. The ruleset is simplified to [(`src 192.168.0.0/16`, `Accept`), (`True`, `Drop`)]. ITVal can now directly compute the correct results on this ruleset.

6.4 The RELATED,ESTABLISHED Rule

Since firewalls process rules sequentially, the first rule has no dependency on any previous rules. Similarly, rules at the beginning have very low dependencies on other rules. Therefore, firewall rules in the beginning can be inspected manually, whereas the complexity of manual inspection increases with every additional preceding rule.

It is good practice [9] to start a firewall with an `ESTABLISHED` (and sometimes `RELATED`) rule. This also happens in Fig. 1 after the rate limiting. The `ESTABLISHED` rule usually matches most of the packets [9],[8] which is important for performance; however, when analyzing the filtering behavior of a firewall, it is important to consider how a connection can be brought to this state. Therefore, we remove this rule and only focus on the connection setup.

The `ESTABLISHED` rule essentially allows packet flows in the opposite direction of all subsequent rules [6]. Unless there are special security requirements (which is not the case in any of our analyzed scenarios), the `ESTABLISHED` rule can be excluded when analyzing the connection setup [6, Corollary 1].[9] If the `ESTABLISHED` rule is removed and in the subsequent rules, for example, a primitive `state NEW` occurs, our ternary matcher returns `Unknown`. The closure procedures handle these cases automatically, without the need for any additional knowledge.

7 Normalization

Ruleset unfolding may result in non-atomic match expressions, e.g. $\neg (a \wedge b)$. *iptables* only supports match expressions in *Negation Normal Form* (NNF).[10] There, a negation may only occur before a primitive, not before compound expressions. For example, $\neg$ (`src` *ip*) $\wedge$ `tcp` is a valid NNF formula, whereas $\neg$ ((`src` *ip*) $\wedge$ `tcp`) is not. We normalize match expressions to NNF, using the following observations:

The De Morgan rule can be applied to match expressions, splitting one rule into two. For example, [($\neg$ (`src` *ip* $\wedge$ `tcp`), `Allow`)] and [($\neg$ `src` *ip*, `Allow`), ($\neg$ `tcp`, `Allow`)] are equivalent. This introduces a "meta-logical" disjunction consisting of a sequence of consecutive rules with a shared action. For example, $[(m_1, a), (m_2, a)]$ is equivalent to $[(m_1 \vee m_2, a)]$.

[8] We revalidated this observation in September 2014 and found that in our firewall, which has seen more than 15 billion packets (19+ Terabyte data) since the last reboot, more than 95% of all packets matched the first `RELATED,ESTABLISHED` rule.

[9] The same can be concluded for reflexive ACLs in Cisco's IOS Firewall [3].

[10] Since match expressions do not contain disjunctions, any match expression in NNF is trivially also in *Disjunctive Normal Form* (DNF).

For sequences of rules with the same action, a distributive law akin to common Boolean logic holds. For example, the conjunction of the two rulesets $[(m_1, a), (m_2, a)]$ and $[(m_3, a), (m_4, a)]$ is equivalent to the ruleset $[(m_1 \wedge m_3, a), (m_1 \wedge m_4, a), (m_2 \wedge m_3, a), (m_2 \wedge m_4, a)]$. This can be illustrated with a situation where $a = \texttt{Accept}$ and a packet needs to pass two firewalls in a row.

We can now construct a procedure which converts a rule with a complex match expression to a sequence of rules with match expressions in NNF. It is independent of the particular primitive matcher and the in-doubt tactic used. The algorithm n ("normalize") of type $M_X \to \text{List}(M_X)$ is defined as follows:

$$
\begin{aligned}
&\texttt{n True} &&= [\texttt{True}] \\
&\texttt{n}\ (m_1 \wedge m_2) &&= [x \wedge y.\ x \leftarrow \texttt{n}\ m_1,\ y \leftarrow \texttt{n}\ m_2] \\
&\texttt{n}\ (\neg\,(m_1 \wedge m_2)) &&= \texttt{n}\ (\neg m_1)\ ::: \ \texttt{n}\ (\neg m_2) \\
&\texttt{n}\ (\neg\neg m) &&= \texttt{n}\ m \\
&\texttt{n}\ (\neg\texttt{True}) &&= [] \\
&\left.\begin{aligned}&\texttt{n}\ x &&= [x] \\ &\texttt{n}\ (\neg x) &&= [\neg x]\end{aligned}\right\} && \text{for } x \in X
\end{aligned}
$$

The second equation corresponds to the distributive law, the third to the De Morgan rule. For example, $\texttt{n}\ (\neg\,(\texttt{src}\ ip \wedge \texttt{tcp})) = [\neg\,\texttt{src}\ ip, \neg\,\texttt{tcp}]$. The fifth rule states that non-matching rules can be removed completely.

The unfolded ruleset of Fig. 3, which consists of 9 rules, can be normalized to a ruleset of 20 rules (due to distributivity). In the worst case, normalization can cause an exponential blowup. Our evaluation shows that this is not a problem in practice, even for large rulesets. This is because rulesets are usually managed manually, which naturally limits their complexity to a level processible by state-of-the-art hardware.

Theorem 6. n *always terminates, all match expressions in the returned list are in NNF, and their conjunction is equivalent to the original expression.*

We show soundness and completeness w.r.t. arbitrary γ, α, and primitives. Hence, it also holds for the Boolean semantics. In general, proofs about the ternary semantics are stronger (the ternary primitive matcher can simulate the Boolean matcher).

Theorem 7 (Soundness and Completeness).

$$p \vdash \langle [(m', a).\ m' \leftarrow \texttt{n}\ m],\ t\rangle \Rightarrow_\alpha t' \quad \textit{iff} \quad p \vdash \langle [(m, a)],\ t\rangle \Rightarrow_\alpha t'$$

After having been normalized by n, the rules can mostly be fed back to *iptables*. For some specific primitives, *iptables* imposes additional restrictions, e.g. that at most one primitive of a type may be present in a single rule. For our evaluation, we only need to solve this issue for IP address ranges in CIDR notation [10]. We introduced and verified another transformation which computes intersection of IP address ranges, which returns at most one range. This is sufficient to process all rulesets we encountered during evaluation.

8 Evaluation

In this section, we demonstrate the applicability of our ruleset preprocessing. Usually, network administrators are not inclined towards publishing their firewall ruleset because of potential negative security implications. For this evaluation, we have obtained approximately 20k real-world rules and the permission to publish them. In addition to the running example in Fig. 1 (a small real-world firewall), we tested our algorithms on four other real-world firewalls. We put focus on the third ruleset, because it is one of the largest and the most interesting one.

For our analysis, we wanted to know how the firewall partitions the IPv4 space. Therefore, we used a matcher γ which only understands source/destination IP addresses and the layer 4 protocols TCP and UDP. Our algorithms do not require special processing capabilities, they can be executed within seconds on a common off-the-shelf 4 GB RAM laptop.

Ruleset 1 is taken from a Shorewall [8] firewall, running on a home router, with around 500 rules. We verified that our algorithms correctly unfold, preprocess, and simplify this ruleset. We expected to see, in both the upper and lower closure, that the firewall drops packets from private IP ranges. However, we could not see this in the upper closure and verified that the firewall does indeed not block such packets if their connection is in a certain state. The administrator of the firewall confirmed this issue and is currently investigating it.

Ruleset 2 is taken from a small firewall script found online [1]. Although it only contains about 50 rules, we found that it contains a serious mistake. We assume the author accidentally confused *iptables*' `-I` (insert at top) and `-A` (append at tail) options. We saw this after unfolding, as the firewall allows nearly all packets at the beginning. Subsequent rules are shadowed and cannot apply. However, these rules come with a documentation of their intended purpose, such as "drop reserved addresses", which highlights the error. We verified the erroneous behavior by installing the firewall on our systems. The author is currently investigating this issue. Thus, our unfolding algorithm alone can provide valuable insights.

Ruleset 3 & 4 are taken from the main firewall of our lab (Chair for Network Architectures and Services). One snapshot was taken 2013 with 2800 rules and one snapshot was taken 2014, containing around 4000 rules. It is obvious that these rulesets have historically grown. About ten years ago, these two rulesets would have been the largest real-world rulesets ever analyzed in academia [32].

We present the analysis results of the 2013 version of the firewall. Details can be found in the additional material. We removed the first three rules. The first rule was the `ESTABLISHED` rule, as discussed in Sect. 6.4. Our focus was put on the second rule when we calculated the lower closure: this rule was responsible for the lower closure being the empty set. Upon closer inspection of this rule, we realized that it was 'dead', i.e. it can never apply. We confirmed this observation by changing the target to a `Log` action on the real firewall and could never see a hit of this rule for months. Due to our analysis, this rule could be removed.

The third rule performed SSH rate limiting (a `Drop` rule). We removed this rule because we had a very good understanding of it. Keeping it would not influence correctness of the upper closure, but lead to a smaller lower closure than necessary.

First, we tested the ruleset with the well-maintained Firewall Builder [22]. The original ruleset could not be imported by Firewall Builder due to 22 errors, caused by unknown match expressions. Using the calculated upper closure, Firewall Builder could import this ruleset without any problems.

Next, we tested ITVal's IP space partitioning query [20]. On our original ruleset with 2800 rules, ITVal completed the query with around 3 GB of RAM in around 1 min. Analyzing ITVal's debug output, we found that most of the rules were not understood correctly due to unknown primitives. Thus, the results were spurious. We could verify this as 127.0.0.0/8, obviously dropped by our firewall, was grouped into the same class as the rest of the Internet. In contrast, using the upper and lower closure ruleset, ITVal correctly identifies 127.0.0.0/8 as its own class.

We found another interesting result about the ITVal tool: The (optimized) upper closure ruleset only contains around 1000 rules and the lower closure only around 500 rules. Thus, we expected that ITVal could process these rulesets significantly faster. However, the opposite is the case: ITVal requires more than 10 times the resources (both CPU and RAM, we had to move the analysis to a $>$ 40 GB RAM cluster) to finish the analysis of the closures. We assume that this is due to the fact that ITVal now understands *all* rules.

9 Conclusion

This work was motivated by the fact that we could not find any tool which helped analyzing our lab's and other firewall rulesets. Though much related work about firewall analysis exists, all academic firewall models are too simplistic to be applicable to those real-world rulesets. With the transformations presented in this paper, they became processable by existing tools. With only a small amount of manual inspection, we found previously unknown issues in four real-world firewalls.

We introduced an approximation to reduce even further the complexity of real-world firewalls for subsequent analysis. In our evaluation, we found that the approximation is good enough to provide meaningful results. In particular, using further tools, we were finally able to provide our administrator with a meaningful answer to the question of how our firewall partitions the IP space.

Our transformations can be extended for different firewall configurations. A user must only provide a primitive matcher for the firewall match conditions she wishes to support. Since we use ternary logic, a user can specify "unknown" as matching outcome, which makes definition of new primitive matchers very easy. The resulting firewall ruleset conforms to the simple list model in Boolean logic (i.e. the common model found in the literature).

Future work includes increasing the accuracy of the approximation by providing more feature-rich primitive matchers and directly implementing firewall analysis algorithms in Isabelle to formally verify them. Another planned application is to assist firewall migration between different vendors and migrating legacy firewall systems to new technologies. In particular, such a migration can be easily prototyped by installing a new firewall in chain with the legacy firewall such that packets need to pass both systems: with the assumption that users only complain if services no longer work, the formal argument in this paper proves that the new firewall with an upper closure ruleset operates without user complaints. A new fast firewall with a lower closure ruleset allows bypassing a slow legacy firewall, probably removing a network bottleneck, without security concerns.

Availability

The analyzed firewall rulesets can be found at

https://github.com/diekmann/net-network

Our Isabelle formalization can be obtained from

https://github.com/diekmann/Iptables_Semantics

Acknowledgments. A special thanks goes to Andreas Korsten for valuable discussions. We thank Julius Michaelis for contributing his Shorewall firewall. We express our gratitude to both for agreeing to publish their firewalls. In addition, Julius and Lars Noschinski contributed proofs to the formalization of the IP address space. Manuel Eberl, Lukas Schwaighofer, and Fabian Immler commented on early drafts of this paper. This work was greatly inspired by Tobias Nipkow's and Gerwin Klein's book on semantics in Isabelle [23].

This work has been supported by the German Federal Ministry of Education and Research (BMBF), EUREKA project SASER, grant 16BP12304, and by the European Commission, FP7 project EINS, grant 288021.

References

1. IPTables Example Config, http://networking.ringofsaturn.com/Unix/iptables.php (retrieved September 2014)
2. PF: The OpenBSD packet filter, http://www.openbsd.org/faq/pf/
3. Cisco IOS firewall - configuring IP access lists. Document ID: 23602 (December 2007), http://www.cisco.com/c/en/us/support/docs/security/ios-firewall/23602-confaccesslists.html
4. Bartal, Y., Mayer, A., Nissim, K., Wool, A.: Firmato: A novel firewall management toolkit. In: Symposium on Security and Privacy, pp. 17–31. IEEE (1999)
5. Brucker, A.D., Brügger, L., Wolff, B.: Model-based firewall conformance testing. In: Suzuki, K., Higashino, T., Ulrich, A., Hasegawa, T. (eds.) TestCom/FATES 2008. LNCS, vol. 5047, pp. 103–118. Springer, Heidelberg (2008)
6. Diekmann, C., Hupel, L., Carle, G.: Directed security policies: A stateful network implementation. In: Third International Workshop on Engineering Safety and Security Systems. EPTCS, vol. 150, pp. 20–34 (May 2014)

7. Diekmann, C., Posselt, S.-A., Niedermayer, H., Kinkelin, H., Hanka, O., Carle, G.: Verifying security policies using host attributes. In: Ábrahám, E., Palamidessi, C. (eds.) FORTE 2014. LNCS, vol. 8461, pp. 133–148. Springer, Heidelberg (2014)
8. Eastep, T.M.: iptables made easy – shorewall (2014), http://shorewall.net/
9. Engelhardt, J.: Towards the perfect ruleset (May 2011), http://inai.de/documents/Perfect_Ruleset.pdf
10. Fuller, V., Li, T.: Classless Inter-domain Routing (CIDR): The Internet Address Assignment and Aggregation Plan. RFC 4632 (Best Current Practice) (August 2006), http://www.ietf.org/rfc/rfc4632.txt
11. Gartenmeister, M.: Iptables vs. Cisco PIX (April 2005), http://lists.netfilter.org/pipermail/netfilter/2005-April/059714.html
12. Hamed, H., Al-Shaer, E.: Taxonomy of conflicts in network security policies. IEEE Communications Magazine 44(3), 134–141 (2006)
13. Hewlett Packard: IP firewall configuration guide (2005), ftp://ftp.hp.com/pub/networking/software/ProCurve-SR-IP-Firewall-Config-Guide.pdf
14. Jeffrey, A., Samak, T.: Model checking firewall policy configurations. In: Policies for Distributed Systems and Networks, pp. 60–67. IEEE (July 2009)
15. Kazemian, P., Varghese, G., McKeown, N.: Header space analysis: static checking for networks. In: Networked Systems Design and Implementation, pp. 113–126. USENIX (April 2012)
16. Kleene, S.C.: Introduction to Metamathematics. Bibliotheca Mathematica. North-Holland, Amsterdam (1952)
17. Leblond, E.: Why you will love nftables (January 2014), https://home.regit.org/2014/01/why-you-will-love-nftables/
18. Mansmann, F., Göbel, T., Cheswick, W.: Visual analysis of complex firewall configurations. In: Proceedings of the Ninth International Symposium on Visualization for Cyber Security, VizSec 2012, pp. 1–8. ACM (2012)
19. Marmorstein, R.M., Kearns, P.: A tool for automated iptables firewall analysis. In: USENIX Annual Technical Conference, FREENIX Track, pp. 71–81 (2005)
20. Marmorstein, R.M., Kearns, P.: Firewall analysis with policy-based host classification. In: Large Installation System Administration Conference, vol. 6, p. 4. USENIX (December 2006)
21. Nelson, T., Barratt, C., Dougherty, D.J., Fisler, K., Krishnamurthi, S.: The margrave tool for firewall analysis. In: Large Installation System Administration Conference. USENIX (November 2010)
22. NetCitadel, Inc.: FirewallBuilder ver. 5.1, http://www.fwbuilder.org
23. Nipkow, T., Klein, G.: Concrete Semantics. Springer (2014)
24. Nipkow, T., Paulson, L.C., Wenzel, M.: Isabelle/HOL: A Proof Assistant for Higher-Order Logic. LNCS, vol. 2283. Springer, Heidelberg (2002), http://isabelle.in.tum.de/doc/tutorial.pdf (last updated 2014)
25. Pozo, S., Ceballos, R., Gasca, R.M.: CSP-based firewall rule set diagnosis using security policies, pp. 723–729. IEEE (April 2007)
26. Renard, B.: cisco-acl-to-iptables (2013), http://git.zionetrix.net/?a=summary&p=cisco-acl-to-iptables (retrieved September 2014)
27. Sherry, J., Hasan, S., Scott, C., Krishnamurthy, A., Ratnasamy, S., Sekar, V.: Making middleboxes someone else's problem: Network processing as a cloud service. ACM SIGCOMM Computer Communication Review 42(4), 13–24 (2012)
28. The netfilter.org project: netfilter/iptables project, http://www.netfilter.org/
29. The netfilter.org project: netfilter/nftables project, http://www.netfilter.org/

30. Tongaonkar, A., Inamdar, N., Sekar, R.: Inferring higher level policies from firewall rules. In: Large Installation System Administration Conference, vol. 7, pp. 1–10. USENIX (2007)
31. Verizon Business RISK team, United States Secret Service: 2010 data breach investigations report (2010), http://www.verizonenterprise.com/resources/reports/rp_2010-DBIR-combined-reports_en_xg.pdf
32. Wool, A.: A quantitative study of firewall configuration errors. IEEE Computer 37(6), 62–67 (2004)
33. Yuan, L., Chen, H., Mai, J., Chuah, C.N., Su, Z., Mohapatra, P.: FIREMAN: a toolkit for firewall modeling and analysis. In: Symposium on Security and Privacy, pp. 199–213. IEEE (May 2006)
34. Zhang, B., Al-Shaer, E., Jagadeesan, R., Riely, J., Pitcher, C.: Specifications of a high-level conflict-free firewall policy language for multi-domain networks. In: Symposium on Access Control Models and Technologies, pp. 185–194. ACM (2007)
35. Zhang, S., Mahmoud, A., Malik, S., Narain, S.: Verification and synthesis of firewalls using SAT and QBF. In: Network Protocols (ICNP), pp. 1–6 (October 2012)

Parameter Synthesis Through Temporal Logic Specifications

Thao Dang[1], Tommaso Dreossi[1,2(✉)], and Carla Piazza[2]

[1] VERIMAG, 2 avenue de Vignate, 38610, Gieres, France
{thao.dang,tommaso.dreossi}@imag.fr
[2] University of Udine, via delle Scienze, 206 33100, Udine, Italy
carla.piazza@uniud.it

Abstract. Parameters are often used to tune mathematical models and capture nondeterminism and uncertainty in physical and engineering systems. This paper is concerned with parametric nonlinear dynamical systems and the problem of determining the parameter values that are consistent with some expected properties. In our previous works, we proposed a parameter synthesis algorithm limited to safety properties and demonstrated its applications for biological systems. Here we consider more general properties specified by a fragment of STL (Signal Temporal Logic), which allows us to deal with complex behavioral patterns that biological processes exhibit. We propose an algorithm for parameter synthesis w.r.t. a property specified using the considered logic. It exploits reachable set computations and forward refinements. We instantiate our algorithm in the case of polynomial dynamical systems exploiting Bernstein coefficients and we illustrate it on an epidemic model.

Keywords: Parameter synthesis · STL · Biological systems · Reachability

1 Introduction

Temporal logic [1] is a formalism used to specify and reason on properties that involve time. It is typically adopted in the context of formal verification, where a temporal logic formula specifies the acceptable behaviors of a system and an algorithm is used to check whether all the behaviors of the system satisfy the formula. Such a procedure is commonly known as model checking [2]. Recently, temporal logic has found applications outside formal verification, for instance *monitoring*. In this case, a formal model is not necessary, since the system can be treated as a black box whose observable behaviors can be monitored by evaluating the satisfaction of the desired temporal property. *Signal Temporal Logic* (STL [3, 4]) is a recently developed logic that allows specifying properties of dense-time real-valued signals. It is particularly suitable for monitoring both industrial case studies (see, e.g., [5, 6]) and biological systems (see, e.g., [7, 8]). It has also been used in the study of parametric systems, (see, e.g., [9])

This work has been partially supported by GNCS-INDAM project "Algoritmica per il model checking e la sintesi di sistemi safety-critical".

N. Bjørner and F. de Boer (Eds.): FM 2015, LNCS 9109, pp. 213–230, 2015.
DOI: 10.1007/978-3-319-19249-9_14

where parametric disturbance rejection properties are formalized in STL and then verified. One of its interesting aspects is its semantics. In addition to the classical semantics, where the result of the evaluation of a formula is a truth value, STL offers a quantitative semantics that gives the idea of "how robustly" a property is satisfied [10, 11].

In this work we propose an application of STL in the context of parameter synthesis for dynamical systems. More concretely, given a parametric nonlinear dynamical system and an STL property, we want to find a set of parameter values that guarantees that all the possible runs of the model satisfy the property. The parameter synthesis is an important problem, since it allows the designer to fine-tune the model so that it captures and retains only the behaviors of interest.

Dealing with nonlinear dynamical systems is not easy. If reasoning on single trajectory can be efficiently done by standard techniques, the problem of verifying sets of trajectories remains difficult despite a number of existing methods (see, e.g., [12–14]). Adding parameter synthesis to such a context makes the problem even more challenging. Indeed, in addition to computing the trajectories of a parametric system, one needs to determine sets of parameter values such that the corresponding trajectories satisfy a given specification.

STL and its monitoring algorithms have been conceived to evaluate logic formulas on single continuous signals [3, 4]. In order to adapt STL to our synthesis problem, we need to introduce a new semantics defined on sets of traces rather than on a single one. This semantical definition requires then a new algorithm, since it is not easy to adapt the existing ones. In fact, available algorithms compute the truth values of a formula in a bottom-up approach, where atomic predicates are evaluated on the full-length signal and the final result is obtained by combining the logical operators. This approach does not suit our case, since the system traces are affected by the eventual dynamical parameter restriction in order to satisfy the property. This means that we cannot know precisely the complete system evolution until the valid parameter values are determined. For this reason we propose a new algorithm that operates in a forward way where, at each step, valid parameter sets are identified and the system evolves in the next steps under the on-the-fly synthesized parameters. We defer a discussion on related work in parameter synthesis to the final section, after our approach is described.

The paper begins with the preliminaries introducing the STL logic, the new semantics, and the parameter synthesis problem. In Section 3 we describe the abstract synthesis algorithm, we discuss its correctness and computational complexity.[1] Section 4 is dedicated to the concretization of our synthesis algorithm for nonlinear discrete-time polynomial dynamical systems. To show the effectiveness of the proposed approach, we apply our algorithm on an epidemic model describing the transmission of diseases through a population. We provide some experimental results and scalability evaluations obtained from a prototype C++

[1] All the proofs can be found at http://www-verimag.imag.fr/~dreossi/docs/papers/parasynth.pdf

tool. These results are reported in Section 5. Finally, the paper ends with related works, a summary of our results, and possible future developments.

2 Preliminaries and Problem Statement

2.1 Parametric Dynamical Systems

Let $\mathbb{R}$ denote the set of reals. We consider a discrete-time parametric dynamical system

$$\mathbf{x}(k+1) = \mathbf{f}(\mathbf{x}(k), \mathbf{p}) \qquad \mathbf{x}(0) \in X^{-}, \mathbf{p} \in P, \tag{1}$$

where $\mathbf{x} \in \mathbb{R}^n$ is the vector of state variables, $\mathbf{p} \in P \subseteq \mathbb{R}^m$ is the vector of parameters, $\mathbf{f}$ is a vector of functions $f_i : \mathbb{R}^n \times \mathbb{R}^m \to \mathbb{R}$ for $i = 1, \ldots, n$. The set $X^{-} \subseteq \mathbb{R}^n$ is called *pre-initial set*, and the set P is called *parameter set.* We use $X^0 = \mathbf{f}(X^{-}, P)$ to denote the initial set of starting states at time 0. The distinction between pre-initial and initial sets is introduced to overcome a technical issue, i.e., the pre-initial set may not satisfy the specification of interest, while the initial one does.

Given $\mathbf{x} \in X^{-}$ and $\mathbf{p} \in P$, let

$$tr_{\mathbf{p}}^{K}(\mathbf{x}) = \langle \mathbf{x}(0) = \mathbf{f}(\mathbf{x}, \mathbf{p}), \ldots, \mathbf{x}(j-1) = \mathbf{f}^{j}(\mathbf{x}, \mathbf{p}), \ldots, \mathbf{x}(K) = \mathbf{f}^{K+1}(\mathbf{x}, \mathbf{p})\rangle$$

be the trace of length $K \in \mathbb{N}$ of the system originating from $\mathbf{x}$ with parameter values $\mathbf{p}$. The set of all possible traces of the dynamical system (1) can be denoted as $Tr_{\mathbf{p}}^{K}(X^{-}) = \{tr_{\mathbf{p}}^{K}(\mathbf{x}) \mid \mathbf{x} \in X^{-}\}$ and $Tr_{P}^{K}(X^{-}) = \{Tr_{\mathbf{p}}^{K}(X^{-}) \mid \mathbf{p} \in P\}$.

2.2 Logic

Let $\mathbb{B} = \{true, false\}$ be the set of Boolean values and $\Sigma = \{\sigma_1, \ldots, \sigma_k\}$ be a finite set of predicates mapping $\mathbb{R}^n$ to $\mathbb{B}$. For a given $j \in \{1, \ldots, k\}$, the predicate σ_j is of the form $\sigma_j \equiv s_j(x_1, \ldots, x_n) \sim 0$ where $\sim \in \{<, \geq\}$ and $s_j : \mathbb{R}^n \to \mathbb{R}$ is a function over the state variables.

We consider *Signal Temporal Logic* (STL) [3, 15] formulas in positive normal form, *i.e.*, formulas generated through the following grammar:

$$\varphi := \sigma \mid \varphi \wedge \varphi \mid \varphi \vee \varphi \mid \varphi\, \mathcal{U}_{\mathcal{I}}\, \varphi \tag{2}$$

where $\sigma \in \Sigma$ and $\mathcal{I} \subset \mathbb{N}$ denotes the interval $\mathcal{I} = [a, b]$ with $a \leq b$ in $\mathbb{N}$. For $t \in \mathbb{N}$, $t + \mathcal{I}$ is the set $\{t + t' \mid t' \in \mathcal{I}\}$. We can define in the usual way other common operators, such as $\top, \bot, \mathcal{R}_{\mathcal{I}}, \Diamond_{\mathcal{I}}, \Box_{\mathcal{I}}$. Note that the negation operator is not included in the presented grammar. However, a given STL formula including some negations, can be rewritten in positive normal form by pushing the negations down to the predicates and reversing their inequalities. Finally, the horizon $h(\varphi)$ of a formula φ is the last time instant to which φ refers, i.e.:

$$h(\sigma) = 0 \qquad h(\varphi_1 \wedge \varphi_2) = h(\varphi_1 \vee \varphi_2) = max(h(\varphi_1), h(\varphi_2))$$
$$h(\varphi_1 \mathcal{U}_{[a,b]} \varphi_2) = max(h(\varphi_1) + b - 1, h(\varphi_2) + b).$$

Given $\mathbf{x} \in X^-$ and $\mathbf{p} \in P$ we can consider the standard Boolean semantics of STL formulas over the trace $tr_{\mathbf{p}}^K(\mathbf{x})$. Let φ be a formula such that $t+h(\varphi) \leq K$, we define:

$$\begin{aligned}
tr_{\mathbf{p}}^K(\mathbf{x}), t \models \sigma \quad & \text{iff } \sigma(\mathbf{x}(t)) \text{ is true} \\
tr_{\mathbf{p}}^K(\mathbf{x}), t \models \varphi_1 \wedge \varphi_2 \quad & \text{iff } tr_{\mathbf{p}}^K(\mathbf{x}), t \models \varphi_1 \text{ and } tr_{\mathbf{p}}^K(\mathbf{x}), t \models \varphi_2 \\
tr_{\mathbf{p}}^K(\mathbf{x}), t \models \varphi_1 \vee \varphi_2 \quad & \text{iff } tr_{\mathbf{p}}^K(\mathbf{x}), t \models \varphi_1 \text{ or } tr_{\mathbf{p}}^K(\mathbf{x}), t \models \varphi_2 \\
tr_{\mathbf{p}}^K(\mathbf{x}), t \models \varphi_1 \mathcal{U}_{\mathcal{I}} \varphi_2 \quad & \text{iff } \exists t' \in t+\mathcal{I}\ tr_{\mathbf{p}}^K(\mathbf{x}), t' \models \varphi_2 \text{ and } \forall t'' \in [t,t')\ tr_{\mathbf{p}}^K(\mathbf{x}), t'' \models \varphi_1
\end{aligned}$$

We use the notation $tr_{\mathbf{p}}^K(\mathbf{x}) \models \varphi$ for $tr_{\mathbf{p}}^K(\mathbf{x}), 0 \models \varphi$. We say that $Tr_P^K(X^-)$ *satisfies* a formula φ, denoted as $Tr_P^K(X^-) \models \varphi$ if and only if

$$\forall \mathbf{p} \in P\ \forall tr_{\mathbf{p}}^K(\mathbf{x}) \in Tr_{\mathbf{p}}^K(X^-) : tr_{\mathbf{p}}^K(\mathbf{x}) \models \varphi.$$

Note that we consider discrete-time systems over a finite horizon; our formulas can thus be encoded in LTL formulas involving Boolean and next operators interpreted over finite traces [16]. However, STL offers us some advantages. First, to express the bounded until operator using LTL, the corresponding formula may be long. Furthermore, STL has both a quantitative discrete-time and a continuous-time semantics. For some classes of systems, the quantitative analysis on a time-discretized system gives complete information also on its continuous-time version [10].

2.3 Parameter Synthesis Problem

Our parameter synthesis problem can now be stated as follows. Let X^- be a pre-initial set, P be a parameter set, and φ a logical formula, find the largest subset $P_\varphi \subseteq P$ such that starting from X^-, the behaviors of the system satisfy φ up to time K, that is $Tr_{P_\varphi}^K(X^-) \models \varphi$.

The above problem requires handling sets of parametric traces, which is hard especially when the solution of the dynamical system can only be approximated, as in the case of polynomial systems that we will specifically treat later. Therefore, we consider a variant of this problem for approximated sets of traces. The set $Tr_P^K(X^-)$ of traces can be over-approximated by considering the sets $X^{j+1} = \{\mathbf{f}(\mathbf{x}, \mathbf{p}) \mid \mathbf{x} \in X^j, \mathbf{p} \in P\}$, for $j = 0, \ldots, K$, where X^- acts as X^{-1}, and the *behaviors* defined as $\mathcal{W}_P^K(X^-) = \langle X^0, X^1, \ldots, X^K \rangle$. It is important to note that this over-approximation does not keep the relation between a trace and its corresponding parameter value.

On behaviors we can define a semantics that reflects the parameter refinement problem we are interested in. In particular, we consider the function $\mathcal{X}(\varphi, \mathcal{W}_P^K(X^-), t)$ defined by structural induction on formulas as follows:

$$\mathcal{X}(\sigma, \mathcal{W}_P^K(X^-), t) = P_\sigma^t, \text{ where } P_\sigma^t \text{ is the largest subset } P_\sigma^t \subseteq P \text{ such that}$$
$$\forall \mathbf{x} \in X^{t-1}, \forall \mathbf{p} \in P_\sigma^t, \sigma(\mathbf{f}(\mathbf{x}, \mathbf{p})) \text{ is true}$$
$$\mathcal{X}(\varphi_1 \wedge \varphi_2, \mathcal{W}_P^K(X^-), t) = \mathcal{X}(\varphi_1, \mathcal{W}_P^K(X^-), t) \cap \mathcal{X}(\varphi_2, \mathcal{W}_P^K(X^-), t)$$
$$\mathcal{X}(\varphi_1 \vee \varphi_2, \mathcal{W}_P^K(X^-), t) = \mathcal{X}(\varphi_1, \mathcal{W}_P^K(X^-), t) \cup \mathcal{X}(\varphi_2, \mathcal{W}_P^K(X^-), t)$$
$$\mathcal{X}(\varphi_1 \mathcal{U}_\mathcal{I} \varphi_2, \mathcal{W}_P^K(X^-), t) = \bigcup_{t' \in t+\mathcal{I}} (\mathcal{X}(\varphi_2, \mathcal{W}_P^K(X^-), t') \cap \bigcap_{t'' \in [t,t')} \mathcal{X}(\varphi_1, \mathcal{W}_P^K(X^-), t''))$$

Intuitively, $\mathcal{X}(\varphi, \mathcal{W}_P^K(X^-), t)$ returns a subset P_φ^t of parameters that ensures that φ is satisfied at time t starting from any point in X^{t-1} and assigning to the parameters any value in P_φ^t. We say that a behavior $\mathcal{W}_P^K(X^-)$ *satisfies* a formula φ, denoted with $\mathcal{W}_P^K(X^-) \models \varphi$, if and only if $\mathcal{X}(\varphi, \mathcal{W}_P^K(X^-), 0) = P$.

We can prove that $\mathcal{X}(\varphi, \mathcal{W}_P^K(X^-), t)$ reverse the order of inclusions between parameter sets and it is idempotent. This implies that the refined set of parameter values satisfies the formula φ, as stated by the following theorem.

Theorem 1. *If $\mathcal{X}(\varphi, \mathcal{W}_P^K(X^-), 0) = P_\varphi$, then $\mathcal{W}_{P_\varphi}^K(X^-) \models \varphi$.*

The following results establish relationships between the two semantics. Since $\mathcal{W}_P^K(X^-)$ over-approximates $Tr_P^K(X^-)$, if a formula φ is satisfied by $\mathcal{W}_P^K(X^-)$, then it is satisfied also by $Tr_P^K(X^-)$.

Theorem 2. *If $\mathcal{X}(\varphi, \mathcal{W}_P^K(X^-), 0) = P_\varphi$, then $Tr_{P_\varphi}^K(X^-) \models \varphi$.*

If we compute $P_\varphi = \mathcal{X}(\varphi, \mathcal{W}_P^K(X^-), 0)$ then we have an under-approximation of the solution of the original parameter synthesis problem. Moreover, P_φ is nothing but the solution of a parameter synthesis problem over behaviors. In this approach we introduce three main sources of approximation error.

First, in the semantics of disjunction over behaviors we impose that for a value $\mathbf{p}$ either all the points $\mathbf{x}$ satisfy the first disjunct or they all satisfy the second one. In a more general setting, this would correspond to approximating a property of the form $\forall y(A(y) \vee B(y))$ with $\forall y(A(y)) \vee \forall y(B(y))$.

Second, $\mathcal{W}_P^K(X^-)$ represents a set of traces that is larger than $Tr_P^K(X^-)$, since from each point in X^j we can reach each point in X^{j+1}. This influences the semantics of the until operator. In fact, we need to require that there exists a time point t' at which φ_2 is satisfied from all the points.

Third, $\mathcal{W}_P^K(X^-)$ is a-priori computed using P, so we also propagate points of X^j that are not necessarily reachable if we replace P with a proper subset.

In the next sections we present an algorithm that computes an under-approximation of the solution to the original parameter synthesis problem. Our algorithm is inspired by $\mathcal{X}(\varphi, \mathcal{W}_P^K(X^-), 0)$, but it produces a better approximation since the parameter set is dynamically refined and the above-mentioned third source of approximation is avoided as at each step only the refined parameter set is used to determine the next states.

3 Parameter Synthesis Algorithm

An intuitive way to solve our synthesis problem is to express the behavior set X^j at each time instant j, up to time K. Then by examining the sets from time K back to time 0 we can derive the conditions on the parameters for the satisfaction of the temporal property, as in the standard monitoring approaches [3]. In other terms, we could use such backward analysis for the semantics defined by (2.3). However, while in monitoring only a single trace is considered at a time and furthermore the trace is already given, in our parameter synthesis problem the behavior set needs to be approximated (since exact reachability computation for nonlinear systems is often impossible). When approximations are used, a major drawback of such a backward procedure is that the approximation error depends on the size of the parameter set and is accumulated step after step. The more spurious behaviors are included in the computed set, the more restricted the parameter set is. In order to gain more accuracy, it is thus important to be able to remove, as early as possible, the parameter values that make the system violate the property. This is the reason we opt for a forward procedure.

We describe our top-down algorithm ParaSynth(X, P, φ) (Algorithm 1), that takes as input a set of states X, a set of parameters P, and a formula φ, and refines P through a series of recursions driven by the structure of φ. At each step, we let the system evolve under the parameter set synthesized up to that step. It is structured in four main blocks, one for each type of subformulæ: predicate, conjunction, disjunction, and until. It uses the following two basic functions. Given a set X, a parameter set P and a predicate σ,

- ReachStep(X, P) computes the image $\mathbf{f}(X, P)$ of X under P;
- RefPredicate(X, P, σ) computes the largest subset $P_\sigma \subseteq P$ such that all states in $\mathbf{f}(X, P_\sigma)$ (computed by ReachStep) satisfy σ, that is $P_\sigma = \{\mathbf{p} \mid \mathbf{p} \in P \ \wedge\ \forall \mathbf{x} \in X\, \sigma(\mathbf{f}(\mathbf{x}, \mathbf{p})) = \mathit{true}\}$. We call the computation of RefPredicate a basic refinement, since it is a refinement of the parameter set w.r.t. a predicate.

The base case is when the formula φ is a predicate σ (Line 2). In this case, the algorithm simply calls the function RefPredicate(X, P, σ) that refines the parameter set P w.r.t. the predicate σ and returns the result.

If φ is the conjunction of two formulas $\varphi_1 \wedge \varphi_2$ (Line 5), from P the algorithm, with two recursive calls, produces two refined parameter sets P_{φ_1} and P_{φ_2}, w.r.t. the subformulas φ_1 and φ_2, respectively, and then returns the intersection $P_{\varphi_1} \cap P_{\varphi_2}$. Similarly, if φ is a disjunction $\varphi_1 \vee \varphi_2$ (Line 8), the algorithm returns the union $P_{\varphi_1} \cup P_{\varphi_2}$.

The case where φ is $\varphi_1 \mathcal{U}_\mathcal{I} \varphi_2$ (Line 11) is slightly more complicated and requires a specific function UntilSynth (Algorithm 2). The function UntilSynth$(X, P, \varphi_1 \mathcal{U}_{[a,b]} \varphi_2)$ is structured in three main blocks, depending on the values a, b: (1) $a > 0$ and $b > 0$; (2) $a = 0$ and $b > 0$; (3) $a = 0$ and $b = 0$. Intuitively, the function recursively transforms the cases (1) and (2) into the base case (3). Notice that a single until formula $\varphi_1 \mathcal{U}_{[a,b]} \varphi_2$ may require several basic refinements. Consider for instance the case where φ_1 always holds and φ_2

Algorithm 1 Parameter synthesis.

```
function ParaSynth(X, P, φ)
    if φ = σ then                                              ▷ Predicate
        return RefPredicate(X, P, σ)
    end if
    if φ = φ_1 ∧ φ_2 then                                      ▷ Conjunction
        return ParaSynth(X, P, φ_1) ∩ ParaSynth(X, P, φ_2)
    end if
    if φ = φ_1 ∨ φ_2 then                                      ▷ Disjunction
        return ParaSynth(X, P, φ_1) ∪ ParaSynth(X, P, φ_2)
    end if
    if φ = φ_1 U_I φ_2 then                                    ▷ Until
        return UntilSynth(X, P, φ_1 U_I φ_2)
    end if
end function
```

Algorithm 2 Until synthesis.

```
function UntilSynth(X, P, φ_1 U_[a,b] φ_2)
    if a > 0 and b > 0 then                                    ▷ Outside interval
        P_φ1 ← ParaSynth(X, P, φ_1)                            ▷ Check φ_1
        if P_φ1 = ∅ then
            return ∅
        else
            X' ← ReachStep(X, P_φ1)
            return UntilSynth(X', P_φ1, φ_1 U_[a-1,b-1] φ_2)
        end if
    end if
    if a = 0 and b > 0 then                                    ▷ In interval
        P_φ1 ← ParaSynth(X, P, φ_1)                            ▷ Check φ_1
        P_φ2 ← ParaSynth(X, P, φ_2)                            ▷ Check φ_2
        if P_φ1 = ∅ then
            return P_φ2                                        ▷ Until unsatisfied
        else
            X' ← ReachStep(X, P_φ1)
            return P_φ2 ∪ UntilSynth(X', P_φ1, φ_1 U_[a,b-1] φ_2)
        end if
    end if
    if a = 0 and b = 0 then                                    ▷ Base
        return ParaSynth(X, P, φ_2)
    end if
end function
```

holds at several time points inside $[a, b]$. Here the number of basic refinements that $\varphi_1 \mathcal{U}_{[a,b]} \varphi_2$ requires is exactly the number of time points at which φ_2 holds. We now analyze the three cases in UntilSynth reported:

(1) $a > 0$ and $b > 0$: the until formula is satisfied if φ_1 holds until φ_2 is true inside the interval $[a, b]$. We first refine the parameters at time 0 over φ_1,

obtaining the subset P_{φ_1} (Line 3). If P_{φ_1} is empty, the until formula cannot be satisfied, and the algorithm returns the empty set. If P_{φ_1} is not empty, the algorithm performs a reachability step using the valid parameter set P_{φ_1} to produce the new set X' (Line 7). Now the algorithm proceeds with the recursive call UNTILSYNTH$(X', P_{\varphi_1}, \varphi_1 \mathcal{U}_{[a,b]-1} \varphi_2)$ (Line 8). This can be seen as making a step towards the interval $[a, b]$, except that instead of restoring the synthesis from time 1, we shift the interval backwards by 1. Hence, the next refinement is computed always at time 0.

(2) $a = 0$ and $b > 0$: there are two ways to satisfy the until formula: (1) φ_2 is satisfied right now at time 0, or (2) φ_1 holds until φ_2 is satisfied before the time instant b. In the first case, we need to refine the parameter set w.r.t. φ_2. If the resulting P_{φ_2} is not empty, it is a valid parameter set that satisfies the until formula. In the second case, the algorithm refines w.r.t. φ_1 and checks whether the result P_{φ_1} is empty (Line 12). If so, the until formula cannot be satisfied in the future. Hence the algorithm returns the refined set P_{φ_2} previously computed. If P_{φ_1} is not empty, the procedure performs a reachability step under the refined parameters P_{φ_1}, obtaining the new set X'. Similarly to the previous case, we execute a step forward by shortening the interval by one (Line 18). The procedure then returns the union of P_{φ_2} and the result provided by the recursive call;

(3) $a = 0$ and $b = 0$: this is the base case of the recursive calls. It suffices to refine w.r.t. φ_2 and return P_{φ_2}.

Example 1. We illustrate PARASYNTH in the case $\phi = (\phi_1 \vee \phi_2)\mathcal{U}_{[1,2]}(\phi_3 \wedge \phi_4)$.

With the call PARASYNTH$(X^-, P, (\phi_1 \vee \phi_2)\mathcal{U}_{[1,2]}(\phi_3 \wedge \phi_4))$ the algorithm enters the until section and calls UNTILSYNTH. The first synthesis is performed inside the ($a > 0$ and $b > 0$) case w.r.t. to the sub-formula $\phi_1 \vee \phi_2$. PARASYNTH computes the refined sets $P^0_{\phi_1}$ and $P^0_{\phi_2}$ w.r.t. ϕ_1 and ϕ_2, and returns the union $P^0_{\phi_1 \vee \phi_2} = P^0_{\phi_1} \cup P^0_{\phi_2}$. Back to the until synthesis, supposing that $P^0_{\phi_1 \vee \phi_2}$ is not empty, the algorithm computes X^0 through a reachability step from X^- under the parameter set $P^0_{\phi_1 \vee \phi_2}$, and calling itself with the updated reachability set, the refined parameter set, and the shifted until interval, i.e., UNTILSYNTH$(X^0, P^0_{\phi_1 \vee \phi_2}, (\phi_1 \vee \phi_2)\mathcal{U}_{[0,1]}(\phi_3 \wedge \phi_4))$.

At this point UNTILSYNTH enters the ($a = 0$ and $b > 0$) section. It first refines w.r.t. $(\phi_3 \wedge \phi_4)$, trying to find the first final solution. To do so, it calls PARASYNTH$(X^0, P^0_{\phi_1 \vee \phi_2}, \phi_3 \wedge \phi_4)$ that produces the parameter set $P^1_{\phi_3 \wedge \phi_4} = P^1_{\phi_3} \cap P^1_{\phi_4}$, result of the intersection of the two refinements of $P^0_{\phi_1 \vee \phi_2}$ w.r.t. ϕ_3 and ϕ_4. This set $P^1_{\phi_3 \wedge \phi_4}$, if not empty, represents the first valid parameter set.

Trying to find other possible solutions, the algorithm proceeds by computing the parameter set $P^1_{\phi_1 \vee \phi_2}$ through the refinement of $P^0_{\phi_1 \vee \phi_2}$ w.r.t. $\phi_1 \vee \phi_2$ and performing a reachability step to the new set $X^1_{\prime\prime}$. It then calls itself reducing the until interval to $[0, 0]$. This is the base case ($a = 0$ and $b = 0$): the algorithm refines w.r.t. $\phi_3 \wedge \phi_4$ and returns the refined parameter set $P^2_{\phi_3 \wedge \phi_4}$. The synthesis process is shown in Figure 1a. The figure depicts the series of refinements and reachable sets that lead to the final result $P^2_{\phi_3 \wedge \phi_4} \cup P^1_{\phi_3 \wedge \phi_4}$.

In the following, we prove the correctness of the presented algorithm and determine its computational complexity.

Theorem 3. *If* PARASYNTH (X^-, P, φ) *returns* P_φ, *then* $\mathcal{X}(\varphi, \mathcal{W}_P^K(X^-), 0) \subseteq P_\varphi$ *and* $Tr_{P_\varphi}^K(X^-) \models \varphi$.

We remark that the above theorem has been proved under the assumption that the function REACHSTEP(X, P) computes exactly the image $\mathbf{f}(X, P)$ and the function REFPREDICATE(X, P, σ) the largest valid parameter set for the predicate σ. However, it is not hard to see that, for Theorem 3 to hold, it suffices to provide an over-approximation of the image $\mathbf{f}(X, P)$ and an under-approximation of the valid parameter set.

As far as the computational complexity of our algorithm is concerned, let us refer to REFPREDICATE, REACHSTEP, $\cup$, and $\cap$ as symbolic operations. If we have a formula without until operators our procedure performs a number of symbolic operations that is linear in the length of the formula. In the case of formulas with possibly nested until operators in the worst case we could perform an exponential number of symbolic operations w.r.t. the minimum between the length of the formula and its time horizon. Let us consider the case of formulas using only predicates and $\mathcal{U}_{[0,1]}$ operators. Let the length of a formulas φ be defined as the maximum number of nested until operators. For a formula $\varphi_1 \mathcal{U}_{[0,1]} \varphi_2$ having length m and horizon k our recursive procedure has a recursive complexity equation in term of symbolic operations of the form

$$T(m,k) = \begin{cases} \Theta(1) & \text{if } m = 1 \text{ or } k = 0 \\ T(m_2, k_2) + T(m_1, k_1) + T(m, k-1) + \Theta(1) & \text{otherwise} \end{cases}$$

where m_i and k_i are the length and horizon of φ_i. In the worst case we could have $m_2 = m - 2$ and $k_2 = k - 1$. In this case we obtain $T(m,k) \geq 2T(m-2, k-1) + \Theta(1)$, which tells us that in the worst case $T(m,k) = \Omega(2^{min(m,k)})$ (number of symbolic operations). If we were interested in monitoring a formula over a finite set of traces, we could have reduced such complexity to a polynomial one (see, e.g., [3, 15]). As we already pointed out, since we are interested in refining sets of parameters and we do not use a precomputed set of traces to avoid rough approximations, we do not see an easy way to reduce such complexity. Finally, it is important to notice that the worst case complexity occurs only in very pathological cases, which are not typical in real case studies.

4 The Case of Polynomial Systems

In Section 3 we presented an abstract algorithm that synthesizes a parameter set under which the behavior of a system satisfies a given formula. A concrete application depends on the ability to represent the parameter set, to implement the function REACHSTEP for computing the behavior set, and the function REFPREDICATE for refining the parameter set. We now propose a concretization of the algorithm for nonlinear polynomial dynamical systems with polytopic parameter sets. The implementation that we present extends the synthesis procedures developed in our previous works for safety specifications [17, 18]. Notice that the abstract algorithm exposed in Section 3 can be used for more general systems as long as an implementation of the required procedures are provided. An example might be continuous-time piecewise-linear dynamical systems, for which reachability techniques and tools have been developed [19, 20].

From now on, we work with polynomial discrete-time dynamical systems of the form $\mathbf{x}(k+1) = \mathbf{f}(\mathbf{x}(k), \mathbf{p})$, where $\mathbf{x} \in \mathbb{R}^n$ and $\mathbf{p} \in P$. The parameter set P is a bounded polytope in $\mathbb{R}^m$ and the polynomial function $\mathbf{f}$ is linear in $\mathbf{p}$.

To compute the functions $\text{RefPredicate}(X, P, \sigma)$ and $\text{ReachStep}(X, P)$, we extend our reachability computation method based on the Bernstein form of polynomials proposed in [17, 18] which we briefly recall in the following.

The sets of states are represented with template parallelotopes, that is the n-dimensional generalization of the parallelograms. In order to exploit linear programming, we require the predicates σ to be non-strict linear inequalities over the state variables $\mathbf{x}$[2]. In [17, 18] we developed a technique that, under these assumptions, converts the parameter synthesis problem into a linear program. In particular, if the predicate σ is of the from $s(\mathbf{x}) \leq 0$ and the parameter set $P \subset \mathbb{R}^m$ is a convex polytope, to find a subset $P_s \subseteq P$ such that the image $\mathbf{f}(\mathbf{x}, \mathbf{p})$ satisfies $\sigma(\mathbf{x})$ for all $\mathbf{x} \in X$ and $\mathbf{p} \in P_s$, it suffices to require $s(\mathbf{f}(\mathbf{x}, \mathbf{p})) \leq 0$ to hold for all $\mathbf{x} \in X$ and $\mathbf{p} \in P_s$. We call P_s the valid parameter set w.r.t. the predicate σ. Note that $s(\mathbf{f}(\mathbf{x}, \mathbf{p}))$ is a polynomial in $\mathbf{x}$ and is linear in $\mathbf{p}$. To find P_s, we take advantage of the geometric properties of the coefficients $\mathbf{b}_1(\mathbf{p}), \ldots, \mathbf{b}_n(\mathbf{p})$ of the polynomial $s(\mathbf{f}(\mathbf{x}, \mathbf{p}))$ expressed in Bernstein form. Intuitively, these coefficients provide an upper and a lower bound of the considered polynomial. Thus, if we can restrict the parameter set P such each control point is smaller than 0, then the resulting restricted set P_s contains all the valid parameter values w.r.t. the predicate σ. The behavior set can also be over-approximated by composing the template constraints of the parallelotope with $\mathbf{f}$ and bound the resulting function by exploiting its Bernstein coefficients. Since the parameters $\mathbf{p}$ appear linearly in the dynamics, the coefficients $\mathbf{b}_1(\mathbf{p}), \ldots, \mathbf{b}_n(\mathbf{p})$ are linear functions of $\mathbf{p}$. Hence, the valid parameter set can be determined by solving a linear system where all the coefficients are constrained to be non-positive.

4.1 Parameter Set Representation

A convex polytope is the simplest form that we use to represent a parameter set. With the notation $P \equiv A\mathbf{p} \leq b$ we mean that the parameter set P corresponds to the solution of the linear system $A\mathbf{p} \leq b$. More complex parameter sets can be obtained by the intersection and the union of several basic convex polytopes.

Let $P_1 \equiv A_1\mathbf{p} \leq b_1$ and $P_2 \equiv A_2\mathbf{p} \leq b_2$ be two convex polytopes. It is not difficult to see that the intersection $P_1 \cap P_2$ is the convex polytope that corresponds to $P_1 \cap P_2 \equiv A\mathbf{p} \leq b$, where $A = \left[\begin{smallmatrix} A_1 \\ A_2 \end{smallmatrix}\right]$ and $b = \left[\begin{smallmatrix} b_1 \\ b_2 \end{smallmatrix}\right]$. Less trivial is the union of two convex polytopes since it might not be convex and consequently the

[2] Note that using only non strict inequalities, truth values $\top$ and $\bot$ can be abbreviated as $\top := z(\mathbf{x}) \leq 0$ and $\bot := o(\mathbf{x}) \leq 0$, where $z(\mathbf{x}) = 0$ and $o(\mathbf{x}) = 1$ for all $\mathbf{x} \in \mathbb{R}^n$.

representation through a linear system may not be possible. For this reason we symbolically represent the union of two polytopes P_1 and P_2 by simply keeping the list of the corresponding linear systems. Formally, with an abuse of notation, $P_1 \cup P_2$ is represented as $P_1 \cup P_2 \equiv \{A_1\mathbf{p} \leq b_1, A_2\mathbf{p} \leq b_2\}$.

If a parameter set P is in the form $P = \bigcup_{i=1}^{n} \bigcap_{j=1}^{m_i} P_{i,j} = (P_{1,1} \cap \ldots \cap P_{1,m_1}) \cup \ldots \cup (P_{n,1} \cap \ldots \cap P_{n,m_n})$ then it is said to be in *union normal form*. This form is suitable for our set representation since the intersections of sets can be collapsed in a unique linear system while the unions can be stored in single list.

4.2 Parameter Synthesis

We now discuss the implementation using the above represention of parameter sets and the behavior computation based on the Bernstein form.

The refinement REFPREDICATE(X, P, σ) where $P \equiv \{P_1, \ldots, P_n\}$ (Algorithm 1, Line 2) can be done by refining each polytope P_i w.r.t. σ (using the procedure exposed in [17]). Each function returns a set $P_{i,\sigma} \subseteq P$. The final result $P_\sigma \subseteq P$ is the union of the basic polytopes, represented as $P_\sigma \equiv \{P_{1,\sigma}, \ldots, P_{n,\sigma}\}$.

The conjunction and disjunction cases (Lines 5 and 8) involve the intersection and union of P_{φ_1} and P_{φ_1} provided in union normal form. The intersection can be obtained by intersecting each basic polytope of P_{φ_1} with each basic polytope of P_{φ_2}. This operation can be carried out by just merging the linear systems representing the considered basic polytopes. The union can be easily obtained by concatenating the lists of basic polytopes that compose P_{φ_1} and P_{φ_2}.

We now focus on Algorithm 2, in particular on the calls of the functions REACHSTEP and UNTILSYNTH (Lines 7 and 13). Here the main issue concerns the computation of REACHSTEP(X, P) whose result can be non-convex. To this end, we open several branches, one for each basic convex polytope of P. Hence, instead of computing a single behavior set, we split the computation in several reachability steps, one for each basic parameter set and refine the parameters from them w.r.t. the considered sub-formula.

Example 2. Let us consider the formula $(\phi_1 \vee \phi_2)\mathcal{U}_{[1,2]}(\phi_3 \wedge \phi_4)$ of Example 1.The algorithm starts with PARASYNTH $(X^-, P, (\phi_1 \vee \phi_2)\mathcal{U}_{[1,2]}(\phi_3 \wedge \phi_4))$ that invokes UNTILSYNTH that enters in the case ($a > 0$ and $b > 0$) and performs the first refinement of P w.r.t. the sub-formula $\phi_1 \vee \phi_2$ by calling PARASYNTH. This function synthesizes P by refining w.r.t. both the predicates ϕ_1 and ϕ_2 and merging the partial results. The result is the set $P^0_{\phi_1 \vee \phi_2} \equiv \{P^0_{\phi_1}, P^0_{\phi_2}\}$. At this point, UNTILSYNTH opens a branch from X^- for each computed refinement. We denote by X^0_1 the set reached from X^- under $P^0_{\phi_1}$ and by X^0_2 the set reached from X^- under $P^0_{\phi_2}$. UNTILSYNTH proceeds with two recursive calls, UNTILSYNTH$(X^0_1, P^0_{\phi_1}, (\phi_1 \vee \phi_2)\mathcal{U}_{[0,1]}(\phi_3 \wedge \phi_4))$ and UNTILSYNTH$(X^0_2, P^0_{\phi_2}, (\phi_1 \vee \phi_2)\mathcal{U}_{[0,1]}(\phi_3 \wedge \phi_4))$. We now consider the first recursive call. In this phase, UNTILSYNTH is in the case ($a = 0$ and $b > 0$). First, trying to satisfy the whole until, the algorithm refines the set $P^0_{\phi_1}$ w.r.t. ϕ_3 and ϕ_4. This is done by calling PARASYNTH $(X^0, P^0_{\phi_1}, \phi_3 \wedge \phi_4)$. We denote the result with $P^{1,1}_{\phi_3 \wedge \phi_4} = P^1_{\phi_3} \cap P^1_{\phi_4}$. If not empty, $P^{1,1}_{\phi_3 \wedge \phi_4}$ is the first valid parameter set. Trying to find other solutions, UNTILSYNTH refines also w.r.t. $\phi_1 \vee \phi_2$ opening two new branches, one for each disjunct. Each branch corresponds to a recursive call of the form PARASYNTH $(X^1_2, P^{1,1}_{\phi_1}, (\phi_1 \vee \phi_2)\mathcal{U}_{[0,0]}(\phi_3 \wedge \phi_4))$. The synthesis process is shown in Figure 1b.

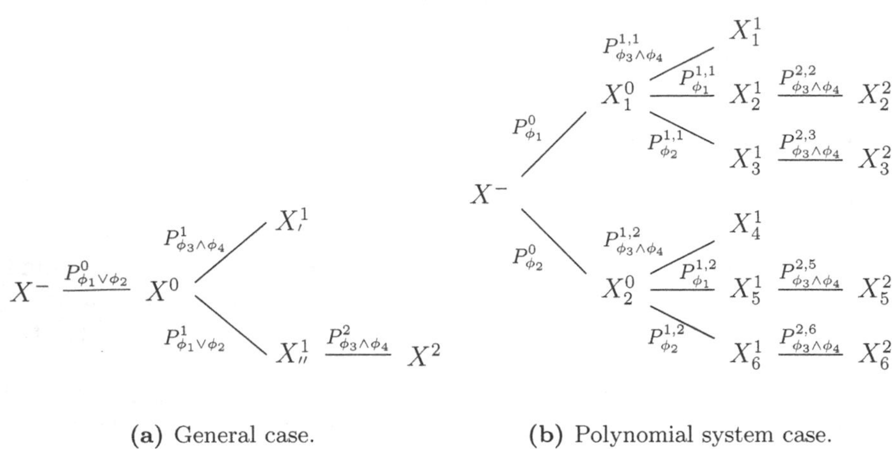

(a) General case.

(b) Polynomial system case.

Fig. 1. Parameter synthesis sequences

5 Experimental Results

We implemented a prototype tool[3] written in C++ that exploits the GiNaC library [21] to symbolically manipulate polynomials and GLPK (GNU Linear Programming Kit)[4] to solve linear programs. The experiments have been carried out on an Intel Core(TM)2 Duo (2.40 GHz, 4GB RAM) running Ubuntu 12.04.

In this final section we first apply our technique on a model of diseases transmission. The model is a variation of the system that describes the Ebola outbreak in Congo 1995 and Uganda 2000 presented in [22]. A population composed of N individuals, is classified in five compartments S, E, Q, I, and R. Each individual, at a certain time, belongs to a specific compartment accordingly with his/her relationship with the disease. All the individual displacements between compartments are regulated by the parameters $\beta, \kappa_1, \kappa_2, \gamma_1, \gamma_2$, and σ.

S contains the healthy individuals that are *susceptible* to the disease. A member of S who enters in contact with a sick person, moves to E, that is the class of individuals who have been *exposed* to the disease. The ratio I/N is the probability that a susceptible individual enters in contact with an infected one, while β is the transmission rate. An exposed individual is either moved in *quarantine* in Q, or directly in the *infected* I compartment, depending on whether the

[3] Available on line at https://github.com/tommasodreossi/parasynth

[4] http://www.gnu.org/software/glpk/glpk.html

malady was diagnosed. The controllable quarantine rate is κ_1, while $1/\kappa_2$ is the mean incubation period. A person in quarantine, if considered healthy after the isolation period, is moved back to the susceptible group. The unfortunate case is when the individual manifests symptoms and moves from the quarantine to the infected group. The reintegration with the susceptible people happens after a period of $1/\gamma_1$, while the incubation period is $1/\gamma_2$. Finally an individual is *removed* from the system by migrating in R at a recovering or death rate σ. The epidemic model is formalized through the following system:

$$
\begin{aligned}
S_{n+1} &= S_n - S_n \beta I_n / N + \gamma_1 Q_n \\
E_{n+1} &= E_n + S_n \beta I_n / N - (\kappa_1 + \kappa_2) E_n \\
Q_{n+1} &= Q_n + \kappa_1 E_n - (\gamma_1 + \gamma_2) Q_n \\
I_{n+1} &= I_n + \gamma_2 Q_n + \kappa_2 E_n - \sigma I_n \\
R_{n+1} &= R_n + \sigma I_n
\end{aligned}
$$

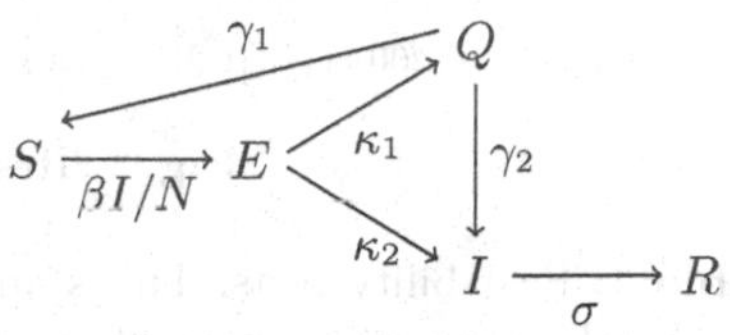

The difference between our model and the one presented in [22] is that we introduce the quarantine compartment and consider the reintegration of individual in the susceptible population. Doing so, we enrich the original model by making it more realistic and interesting. Also, our model is defined on discrete time. Note that in the literature there are various works presenting epidemic models directly with discrete-time dynamics or difference equations (see, e.g., [23, 24]).

We first considered a population of $N = 1000$ individuals, of which $S = 800$ are susceptible and $I = 200$ are infected. We fixed the parameters values as specified in [22] in the case of the Ebola outbreak in Uganda during 2000. The uncontrollable parameter values are $\beta = 0.35, \kappa_2 = 0.3, \gamma_2 = 0.6$, and $\sigma = 0.28$, while the controllable parameters are $\kappa_1 \in [0.2, 0.3]$ and $\gamma_1 \in [0.2, 0.5]$ that represent the quarantine rate and mean isolation period, respectively. We considered the specification $\phi_1 \equiv (I(t) \leq 200)\mathcal{U}_{[6,10]}(Q(t) \leq 20)$ whose meaning is to avoid the saturation of the quarantine compartment especially in the time interval between 6 and 10 when a number of infected individuals higher than 200 is expected. Our tool found five feasible parameters sets in 0.10 seconds, one of which is shown in Figure 2a.

In a second experiment, we changed the uncontrollable parameter values to $\beta = 0.9$, $\kappa_2 = 0.5$, $\gamma_2 = 0.5$, and $\sigma = 0.28$, while the controllable parameters to $\kappa_1 \in [0.2, 0.3]$ and $\gamma_1 \in [0.2, 0.5]$. Instead of imposing directly a constraint on the system, we could imagine a scenario where we have a maximum number of 40 patients in quarantine unless the number of infected patients is below 270. This means that if there are less than 270 infected individuals, then we have free resources that can be devoted to the quarantine. This property can be formalized with the formula $\phi_2 \equiv (Q(t) \leq 40)\mathcal{U}_{[10,15]}(I(t) \leq 270)$. Our tool found a valid parameter set in 0.14 seconds.

Finally, on the same system configuration, we tested a more complex until formula that involves a disjunction, that is $\phi_3 \equiv (Q(t) \leq 50)\mathcal{U}_{[5,15]}(E(t) > 100 \vee Q(t) > 25)$. Our tool found four parameter refinements in 0.14 seconds. Figure 2b depicts the union of the refined parameter sets.

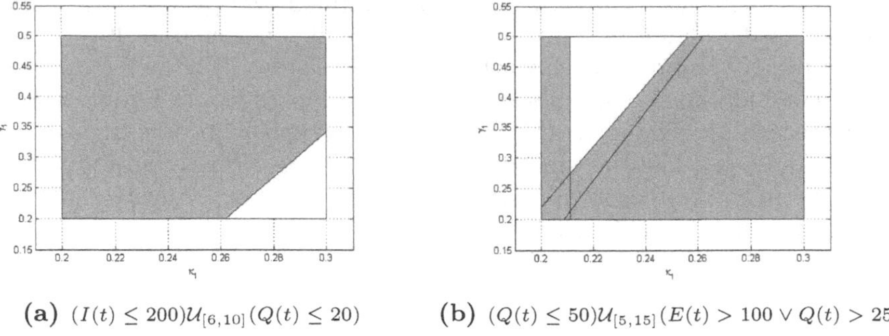

(a) $(I(t) \leq 200)\mathcal{U}_{[6,10]}(Q(t) \leq 20)$ (b) $(Q(t) \leq 50)\mathcal{U}_{[5,15]}(E(t) > 100 \vee Q(t) > 25)$

Fig. 2. Results of the refinements

Table 1. Scalability tests. Times are in seconds. Values in parenthesis are the computed polytopes per refinement. $\phi_1 \equiv (I(t) \leq 200)\mathcal{U}_{[a,b]}(Q(t) \leq 20)$, $\phi_2 \equiv (Q(t) \leq 40)\mathcal{U}_{[a,b]}(I(t) \leq 270)$, $\phi_3 \equiv (Q(t) \leq 50)\mathcal{U}_{[a,b]}(E(t) > 100 \vee Q(t) > 25)$.

a	b	ϕ_1	ϕ_2	ϕ_3
5	15	0.20 (11)	0.15 (7)	0.14 (4)
5	20	0.35 (16)	0.24 (11)	0.21 (4)
5	30	0.82 (26)	0.55 (21)	0.36 (4)
5	50	2.63 (46)	1.65 (41)	0.80 (4)
5	100	-	10.95 (91)	1.69 (4)
5	125	-	-	1.69 (4)
15	20	0.29 (6)	0.22 (4)	0.19 (0)
20	30	0.64 (11)	0.45 (11)	0.35 (0)
30	50	1.88 (21)	1.27 (21)	0.78 (0)
50	100	13.00 (51)	6.89 (51)	1.72 (0)
100	200	-	-	1.66 (0)

(a) Increasing until interval

N	ϕ_1^N	ϕ_2^N	ϕ_3^N
1	0.11 (5)	0.14 (2)	0.13 (4)
2	0.26 (9)	0.36 (7)	0.29 (3)
3	0.48 (13)	0.69 (12)	0.50 (3)
4	0.74 (17)	1.09 (17)	0.70 (3)
5	1.10 (21)	1.61 (22)	1.01 (3)
6	1.50 (25)	2.28 (27)	1.20 (3)
7	1.97 (29)	3.05 (32)	1.65 (3)
8	2.59 (33)	3.97 (37)	1.81 (3)
9	3.23 (37)	5.06 (42)	2.16 (3)
10	4.98 (42)	6.70 (47)	2.56 (3)
15	10.33 (61)	11.80 (62)	4.85 (3)
16	11.75 (65)	15.98 (67)	5.43 (3)
17	-	-	5.97 (3)

(b) Nesting until

In order to evaluate the scalability of our method, we now consider non-trivial formulas that we artificially created. First, we take the three until formulas ϕ_1, ϕ_2, and ϕ_3 previously defined and we stretch their intervals $[a, b]$. In the worst case, such growth exponentially increases the number of branches that our algorithm must open. Table 1a reports the running times for this test. For ϕ_1 we are able to stretch the interval up to $[50, 100]$, that deals to a parameter set composed by 51 convex polytopes. For ϕ_2 the maximum tractable interval was $[5, 100]$, for which a parameter set of cardinality 91 is found. Finally, we notice that enlargement of the window of ϕ_3 does not affect the parameter refinement, that is valid refinements are found only for the initial part of the interval. Not growing in the size of the results, the algorithm needs linear time in the until time horizon. As second evaluation, we nest several until on the (most critical) right hand side. For instance, the double nesting of ϕ_1 is $\phi_1^N \equiv (I(t) \leq 200)\mathcal{U}_{[6,10]}((I(t) \leq 200)\mathcal{U}_{[6,10]}(Q(t) \leq 20))$ with $N = 2$. Table 1b reports the running times for this evaluation. Our tool computes refinements of ϕ_1 and ϕ_2 nested 16 times, finding 65 and 67 convex parameter sets. As in the previous case, nesting ϕ_3 does not increase the size of the result, thus the computation times are restrained. It is interesting to notice that even if ϕ_1 and ϕ_2 are composed by less atomic formulas than ϕ_3, their running times and size of results, are sensibly larger than the latter. This suggests that it might be hard to estimate a priori the algorithm performance just by looking at the specification, since its execution time "numerically" depends on the system's behavior and mostly on the computed partial refinements. Finally, these experiments show that the weakness of our tool is memory. So far, parameter set are represented as lists of linear systems composed by collections of inequalities. To reduce memory consumption it might be interesting to introduce mechanisms to avoid the insertion of redundant constraints and polytopes included in larger ones.

6 Related Work and Conclusion

In this work we proposed a parameter synthesis algorithm for STL specifications. We extended standard STL defined on single traces to sets of traces generated by parametric dynamical systems. The whole procedure operates forwardly, that is refining the parameter sets and computing the behavior on-the-fly, in order to obtain less restrictive parameter sets. We proved the correctness of the algorithm and discussed its computational complexity. Moreover, we provided a concrete implementation of the algorithm for polynomial discrete-time dynamical systems, that produces valid parameter sets in form of sets of convex polytopes. The algorithm was implemented and illustrated on an epidemic model.

In the literature there are different approaches to the problem of finding good parameters. In [25] pure model checking is used on discrete finite structures. Parametric interaction graphs representing Genetic Regulatory Networks are analyzed through LTL in [26]. Discrete-time simulations are considered in [27], where parameters optimize the satisfaction degree of LTL formulas constrained over the reals. [28] describes stochastic approaches for parameter fitting over experimental data, and [29] parameter synthesis for CTMC w.r.t. CSL (Continuous Stochastic Logic) specifications. [30] uses simulation guided analysis to find values of the parameters that do not produce oscillating behaviors, while counterexample guided abstraction refinement over linear hybrid automata has been proposed in [31]. A parameter synthesis approach based on "good" parameters values was proposed in [32] over timed automata with respect to safety properties. Parametric temporal properties are considered in [9], where the parameters are identified to make a temporal property satisfied by experimental data. Many of the above mentioned works find applications in the study of biological systems.

The paper [33] is close to our work since it considers discrete-time systems and LTL properties; however the targeted systems are piecewise-affine (PWA) and the systems we address are polynomial. While our algorithm approximates the reachable sets of polynomial systems, the approach in this work involves computing first a discrete abstraction of the original PWA system. In the abstraction (that is a transition system), each transition is labeled with a set of parameter values that allow the transition to be feasible. LTL model checking is then used to remove some transitions so that the resulting system satisfies the property. The parameters are finally restricted to allow only the remaining transitions. Note that due to special properties of multi-affine functions, the discrete abstraction can be performed efficiently. Nevertheless, this is not possible for the polynomial functions in our problem. Another related work is [34] where STL properties and continuous-time nonlinear systems are considered; it computes the reachable set using the trajectories from a finite number of initial states and sensitivity analysis to determine the robustness of the trajectory set from the neighborhoods of those initial states. The parameter set is refined when the trajectory set violates the property. This approach requires a box discretization of the parameter set that is less compact than our polytopic set representation. A similar approach using robustness is applied to a biological system in [35].

The main novelty of our results is that our parameter synthesis method that can handle nonlinear polynomial systems and complex properties specified using STL. We are able to specify interesting temporal properties and reason on the behavior of a dynamical system and its parameters. Two directions are promising. First, we intend to extend our approach to quantitative semantics integrating a robustness metric such as in [34]. The second direction concerns the treatment of continuous-time dynamical systems and dense-time STL. This is straightforward for linear systems by using one of the available polytope-based algorithms for continuous-time reachability operations, such as [36]. For nonlinear systems, conservatively enclosing the reachable sets over time intervals could be done by exploting ideas from interval computation.

References

1. Pnueli, A.: The temporal logic of programs. In: Symposium on Foundations of Computer Science, SFCS, pp. 46–57. IEEE (1977)
2. Clarke, E.M., Grumberg, O., Peled, D.: Model checking. MIT press (1999)
3. Maler, O., Nickovic, D.: Monitoring temporal properties of continuous signals. In: Lakhnech, Y., Yovine, S. (eds.) FORMATS 2004 and FTRTFT 2004. LNCS, vol. 3253, pp. 152–166. Springer, Heidelberg (2004)
4. Maler, O., Nickovic, D., Pnueli, A.: Checking temporal properties of discrete, timed and continuous behaviors. Pillars of Computer Science, 475–505 (2008)
5. Jones, K.D., Konrad, V., Nickovic, D.: Analog property checkers: a DDR2 case study. Formal Methods in System Design 36(2), 114–130 (2010)
6. Jin, X., Donzé, A., Deshmukh, J.V., Seshia, S.A.: Mining requirements from closed-loop control models. In: Proc. of International Conference on Hybrid Systems: Computation and Control, HSCC, pp. 43–52. ACM (2013)
7. Donzé, A., Fanchon, E., Gattepaille, L.M., Maler, O., Tracqui, P.: Robustness analysis and behavior discrimination in enzymatic reaction networks. PLOS One 6(9), e24246 (2011)

8. Stoma, S., Donzé, A., Bertaux, F., Maler, O., Batt, G.: STL-based Analysis of TRAIL-induced Apoptosis Challenges the Notion of Type I/Type II Cell Line Classification. PLoS Computational Biology 9(5), e1003056 (2013)
9. Asarin, E., Donzé, A., Maler, O., Nickovic, D.: Parametric identification of temporal properties. In: Khurshid, S., Sen, K. (eds.) RV 2011. LNCS, vol. 7186, pp. 147–160. Springer, Heidelberg (2012)
10. Fainekos, G.E., Pappas, G.J.: Robustness of temporal logic specifications for continuous-time signals. Theoretical Computer Science 410(42), 4262–4291 (2009)
11. Bartocci, E., Bortolussi, L., Nenzi, L.: On the robustness of temporal properties for stochastic models. In: Hybrid Systems and Biology, HSB. EPTCS, vol. 125, pp. 3–19 (2013)
12. Chen, X., Ábrahám, E., Sankaranarayanan, S.: Flow*: An analyzer for non-linear hybrid systems. In: Sharygina, N., Veith, H. (eds.) CAV 2013. LNCS, vol. 8044, pp. 258–263. Springer, Heidelberg (2013)
13. Gao, S., Kong, S., Chen, W., Clarke, E.M.: Delta-complete analysis for bounded reachability of hybrid systems. CoRR abs/1404.7171 (2014)
14. Testylier, R., Dang, T.: NLTOOLBOX: A library for reachability computation of nonlinear dynamical systems. In: Van Hung, D., Ogawa, M. (eds.) ATVA 2013. LNCS, vol. 8172, pp. 469–473. Springer, Heidelberg (2013)
15. Donzé, A., Ferrère, T., Maler, O.: Efficient robust monitoring for STL. In: Sharygina, N., Veith, H. (eds.) CAV 2013. LNCS, vol. 8044, pp. 264–279. Springer, Heidelberg (2013)
16. De Giacomo, G., Vardi, M.Y.: Linear temporal logic and linear dynamic logic on finite traces. In: Proc. of Intenrational Joint Conference on Artificial Intelligence, IJCAI, IJCAI/AAAI (2013)
17. Dreossi, T., Dang, T.: Parameter synthesis for polynomial biological models. In: Proc. of International Conference on Hybrid Systems: Computation and Control, HSCC, pp. 233–242. ACM (2014)
18. Dang, T., Dreossi, T., Piazza, C.: Parameter synthesis using parallelotopic enclosure and applications to epidemic models (2014), http://www-verimag.imag.fr/~dreossi/docs/papers/hsb_2014.pdf
19. Asarin, E., Bournez, O., Dang, T., Maler, O.: Approximate reachability analysis of piecewise-linear dynamical systems. In: Lynch, N.A., Krogh, B.H. (eds.) HSCC 2000. LNCS, vol. 1790, pp. 20–31. Springer, Heidelberg (2000)
20. Frehse, G., Le Guernic, C., Donzé, A., Cotton, S., Ray, R., Lebeltel, O., Ripado, R., Girard, A., Dang, T., Maler, O.: SpaceEx: Scalable verification of hybrid systems. In: Gopalakrishnan, G., Qadeer, S. (eds.) CAV 2011. LNCS, vol. 6806, pp. 379–395. Springer, Heidelberg (2011)
21. Bauer, C., Frink, A., Kreckel, R.: Introduction to the GiNaC framework for symbolic computation within the C++ programming language. Journal of Symbolic Computation 33(1), 1–12 (2002)
22. Chowell, G., Hengartner, N.W., Castillo-Chavez, C., Fenimore, P.W., Hyman, J.: The basic reproductive number of Ebola and the effects of public health measures: the cases of Congo and Uganda. Journal of Theoretical Biology 229(1), 119–126 (2004)
23. Allen, L.J.: Some discrete-time SI, SIR, and SIS epidemic models. Mathematical Biosciences 124(1), 83–105 (1994)
24. Zhou, X., Li, X., Wang, W.-S.: Bifurcations for a deterministic sir epidemic model in discrete time. Advances in Difference Equations 2014(1), 1–16 (2014)

25. Barnat, J., Brim, L., Krejci, A., Streck, A., Safranek, D., Vejnar, M., Vejpustek, T.: On parameter synthesis by parallel model checking. IEEE/ACM Trans. Comput. Biol. Bioinformatics 9(3), 693–705 (2012)
26. Gallet, E., Manceny, M., Le Gall, P., Ballarini, P.: An LTL Model Checking Approach for Biological Parameter Inference. In: Merz, S., Pang, J. (eds.) ICFEM 2014. LNCS, vol. 8829, pp. 155–170. Springer, Heidelberg (2014)
27. Rizk, A., Batt, G., Fages, F., Soliman, S.: Continuous valuations of temporal logic specifications with applications to parameter optimization and robustness measures. Theoretical Computer Science 412(26), 2827–2839 (2011)
28. Gratie, D.-E., Iancu, B., Petre, I.: ODE Analysis of Biological Systems. In: Bernardo, M., de Vink, E., Di Pierro, A., Wiklicky, H. (eds.) SFM 2013. LNCS, vol. 7938, pp. 29–62. Springer, Heidelberg (2013)
29. Češka, M., Dannenberg, F., Kwiatkowska, M., Paoletti, N.: Precise parameter synthesis for stochastic biochemical systems. In: Mendes, P., Dada, J.O., Smallbone, K. (eds.) CMSB 2014. LNCS, vol. 8859, pp. 86–98. Springer, Heidelberg (2014)
30. Dreossi, T., Dang, T.: Falsifying oscillation properties of parametric biological models. In: Hybrid Systems and Biology, HSB. EPTCS, vol. 125, pp. 53–67 (2013)
31. Frehse, G., Jha, S.K., Krogh, B.H.: A counterexample-guided approach to parameter synthesis for linear hybrid automata. In: Egerstedt, M., Mishra, B. (eds.) HSCC 2008. LNCS, vol. 4981, pp. 187–200. Springer, Heidelberg (2008)
32. André, É., Soulat, R.: Synthesis of timing parameters satisfying safety properties. In: Delzanno, G., Potapov, I. (eds.) RP 2011. LNCS, vol. 6945, pp. 31–44. Springer, Heidelberg (2011)
33. Yordanov, B., Belta, C.: Parameter synthesis for piecewise affine systems from temporal logic specifications. In: Egerstedt, M., Mishra, B. (eds.) HSCC 2008. LNCS, vol. 4981, pp. 542–555. Springer, Heidelberg (2008)
34. Donzé, A.: Breach, A Toolbox for Verification and Parameter Synthesis of Hybrid Systems. In: Touili, T., Cook, B., Jackson, P. (eds.) CAV 2010. LNCS, vol. 6174, pp. 167–170. Springer, Heidelberg (2010)
35. Sankaranarayanan, S., Miller, C., Raghunathan, R., Ravanbakhsh, H., Fainekos, G.: A model-based approach to synthesizing insulin infusion pump usage parameters for diabetic patients. In: Proc. of Annual Allerton Conference on Communication, Control, and Computing. IEEE (2012)
36. Frehse, G., Le Guernic, C., Donzé, A., Cotton, S., Ray, R., Lebeltel, O., Ripado, R., Girard, A., Dang, T., Maler, O.: SpaceEx: Scalable verification of hybrid systems. In: Gopalakrishnan, G., Qadeer, S. (eds.) CAV 2011. LNCS, vol. 6806, pp. 379–395. Springer, Heidelberg (2011)

Trace-Length Independent Runtime Monitoring of Quantitative Policies in LTL

Xiaoning Du(✉), Yang Liu, and Alwen Tiu

School of Computer Engineering, Nanyang Technological University, Singapore
{xndu,yangliu,atiu}@ntu.edu.sg

Abstract. Linear temporal logic (LTL) has been widely used to specify runtime policies. Traditionally this use of LTL is to capture the qualitative aspects of the monitored systems, but recent developments in metric LTL and its extensions with aggregate operators allow some quantitative policies to be specified. Our interest in LTL-based policy languages is driven by applications in runtime Android malware detection, which requires the monitoring algorithm to be independent of the length of the system event traces so that its performance does not degrade as the traces grow. We propose a policy language based on a past-time variant of LTL, extended with an aggregate operator called the counting quantifier to specify a policy based on the number of times some sub-policies are satisfied in the past. We show that a broad class of policies, but not all policies, specified with our language can be monitored in a trace-length independent way without sacrificing completeness, and provide a concrete algorithm to do so. We implement and test our algorithm in an existing Android monitoring framework and show that our approach can effectively specify and enforce quantitative policies drawn from real-world Android malware studies.

1 Introduction

Linear temporal logic (LTL) has been widely used as a specification language to specify runtime properties of systems and languages. Traditionally, this use of LTL is concerned mainly with qualitative properties, such as relative ordering of events, or eventuality of events, etc. Our interest in the LTL-based policy languages is motivated by the demand for Android malware detection. In this setting, some attack patterns cannot be stated as pure LTL formulas as they require specifications of quantitative measures such as frequency of certain activities (e.g., sending SMS) commonly found in botnet attacks. Recent studies [22,21] indicate that Android malware is increasingly designed to turn infected phones into botnets, so to be practically useful, any monitoring framework for Android needs to take into account quantitative measures in their policy specifications.

One way to detect the kind of botnet attacks mentioned above is to count the number of certain events, such as SMS messages sent from an app, and notify the user once the count goes beyond some limit. To design a monitoring framework that can enfoce this kind of policies, one approach is to build into LTL a notion of counting of events [7], or more generally, aggregate operators [6]. The main problem is that monitoring algorithms for such extensions have not been well studied, and can be very inefficient, e.g., PSPACE complete (in the size of policy and the trace) for the extension of LTL with the

N. Bjørner and F. de Boer (Eds.): FM 2015, LNCS 9109, pp. 231–247, 2015.
DOI: 10.1007/978-3-319-19249-9_15

counting quantifier [7], and PTIME (in the size of the trace) when the policy is fixed. In the online monitoring of OS kernels, where near real-time decisions need to be made, the dependence of the monitor on the size of the trace would make it impractical even if its complexity is PTIME (assuming the policy is fixed), as its performance would degrade as the trace size grows. We attempt to address this problem in a minimal setting to demonstrate that it is possible to design a monitoring framework that is expressive enough to specify various quantitative properties and enforceable efficiently.

In this work, we propose an extension of Past Time LTL (PTLTL) [19], named PTLTL_{cnt}, to support the *counting quantifier*, which is motivated and extended from [7], and arithmetic functions and relations. PTLTL_{cnt} considers only the fragment of PTLTL with past time operators, as this is sufficient for our purpose to enforce history-sensitive access control. For our intended application of monitoring Android applications, once we fix the policy to be monitored, the monitoring algorithm space requirement and runtime should be constant, i.e., independent of the length of the system event trace. Following [8], we call this type of monitoring algorithms as trace-length independent (TLI) monitoring algorithms. Note that we require that the generated TLI algorithms to be complete with respect to the policy specifications; otherwise the problem would be trivial as one could simply make various ad hoc restrictions such as restricting the time window for the monitoring. In [19], it is shown that a trace-length independent monitor can be generated for every formula of PTLTL. For richer logics, such as those considered in [7,8] and our own PTLTL_{cnt}, this is not always possible, i.e., there are formulas for which the monitor needs to store the entire history of events. For example, in PTLTL_{cnt} one can write a formula that compares the numbers of two events, say e_1 and e_2. Let x and y denote the number of past occurrences of events of e_1 and e_2, respectively. To check the relation $x < y$ at any state, we would need to keep the counts of both e_1 and e_2; such counts would grow as the trace grows, so the space requirement for monitoring this formula is not bounded. We could only store $|x - y|$ in this case, but this absolute value can still grow infinitely.

As far as we know, there has been so far no study on trace-length independence monitoring for LTL with aggregate operators like the counting quantifier. To solve this issue, we first formally identify the precise characteristics of the class arithmetic relations that can be monitored in a trace-length independent way. Then we show that if all arithmetic relations in a PTLTL_{cnt} formula are TLI-monitorable, the formula itself is also TLI-monitorable. More importantly, we show how to construct a TLI monitoring algorithm when all relations are TLI-monitorable.

We have performed a number of case studies on Android to show the practicality of our specification language for malware detection. We have implemented the proposed language and algorithm based on an existing Android monitoring framework called LogicDroid [17]. The experimental results shows that our approach can effectively specify and enforce a range of quantitative policies drawn from real-world Android malware.

Organization. Section 2 presents the formal syntax and semantics of PTLTL_{cnt}. Section 3 proposes the trace-length independent monitoring algorithm for PTLTL_{cnt} with univariate countingparts. This is generalized this to the multivariate case in Section 4. Some Android policy examples are introduced in Section 5. Section 6 describes the implementation of our algorithms for monitoring in LogicDroid. The related works are discussed in Section 7. Section 8 concludes the paper. Due to space constraints, some proofs are omitted but they will be made available in an extended version of this paper.

2 The Policy Specification Language PTLTL$_{cnt}$

In this section, we formally introduce PTLTL$_{cnt}$ as an extension of PTLTL extended with a *counting quantifier*, which counts how many times a sub-policy has been satisfied in the past, as well as arithmetic operators and relations. Our counting quantifier has a slightly different semantics compared to that of [7] as explained later. Our language admits the usual arithmetic operators such as $+$, $-$ and $\times$, and relations $=$, $<$, $\leq$ and $\geq$. We assume a countably infinite set of constants. We use a, b, c and d to range over constant symbols of type integers. We denote with AP the set of propositional variables. Elements of AP are ranged over by P, Q and S. We assume an infinite set $\mathcal{V}$ of variables of type integers, whose elements are ranged over by x, y and z. Terms are built from constants, variables and arithmetic operators, and are denoted by s, t, u and v.

The syntax of PTLTL$_{cnt}$ is defined via the following grammar:

$$\phi := \bot \mid AP \mid (t > 0) \mid \neg\phi \mid \phi \vee \phi \mid \bullet\phi \mid \phi \,\mathbb{S}\, \phi \mid \mathcal{C}x : \langle \phi, \phi \rangle.\phi$$

The operators are those of PTLTL except for the counting quantifier $\mathcal{C}$ and the relation $t > 0$. The variable x in $\mathcal{C}x : \langle \phi_1, \phi_2 \rangle.\varphi$ is a bound variable, whose scope is over φ, so x is not free in either ϕ_1 or ϕ_2. Intuitively, the meaning of $\mathcal{C}x : \langle \phi_1, \phi_2 \rangle.\varphi$ is as follows: suppose that ϕ_2 is true at exactly n states since the latest state where ϕ_1 holds; then the instance of φ with x mapped to n must also be true. The formula ϕ_1 acts as a *counter reset* condition. We assume the reader is familiar with the notion of free and bound variables. We assume that bound variables in a formula are pairwise distinct. We write $\phi(x_1, \ldots, x_n)$ to mean that the free variables of ϕ are in $\{x_1, \ldots, x_n\}$ and we write $\phi(t_1, \ldots, t_n)$ to denote the instance of $\phi(x_1, \ldots, x_n)$ where t_i is substituted for x_i.

In the definition of formulas, we have kept a minimum number of logical operators. The omitted operators can be derived using the given operators, e.g., propositional operators such as $\top$ (truth), $\wedge$ (conjunction), $\rightarrow$ (implication), and modal operators such as $\blacklozenge$ (sometime in the past), which is defined as $\blacklozenge\phi \equiv \top \,\mathbb{S}\, \phi$, and $\blacksquare$ (globally in the past), which is defined as $\blacksquare\phi \equiv \neg\blacklozenge\neg\phi$. Note also that all other arithmetic relations can be derived from the relation of the form $(t > 0)$ and logical connectives: $s > t \equiv (s - t) > 0$, $s \leq t \equiv \neg(s > t)$, $s = t \equiv (s \leq t) \wedge (t \leq s)$, $s \geq t \equiv s > t \vee s = t$, and $s < t \equiv s \leq t \wedge \neg(s = t)$.

The semantics of PTLTL$_{cnt}$ is defined with respect to a finite trace model, as in [19]. A trace is just a sequence of states, where each state itself consists of a set of atomic propositions. These atomic propositions correspond to events of interests that are being monitored in a system. We assume an interpretation function I which maps constant symbols to integers, and arithmetic operators and relation symbols to their corresponding semantic counterparts. We assume the usual arithmetic operators, and in addition, depending on applications, we may assume a fixed set of function symbols denoting computable functions over the integer domain. Since terms and relations can contain variables, we additionally need to interpret these variables. This is done via a *valuation function*, i.e., a function from variables to integers. Formally, given an interpretation function I and a valuation function ν, the interpretation of a term t, written $t^{I,\nu}$ is defined as in first-order logic [16]. However, since we shall only work within a fixed interpretation, we shall drop the superscript I in the following semantics definition.

A *model* for PTLTL$_{cnt}$ is a triple (ρ, ν, i), where ρ is a trace, ν is a valuation function and i is a natural number. For a trace ρ, we write ρ_i to denote its i-th *state*. For a valuation ν, we write $\nu[x \mapsto n]$ to denote the function which is identical to ν except for the valuation of x, i.e., $\nu[x \mapsto n](y) = \nu(y)$, when $y \neq x$, and $\nu[x \mapsto n](x) = n$. The satisfiability relation between a model (ρ, ν, i) and a formula ϕ, written $\rho, \nu, i \models \phi$, is defined by induction on ϕ below, where $\rho, \nu, i \not\models \phi$ if $\rho, \nu, i \models \phi$ is false.

- $\rho, \nu, i \not\models \phi$ if $i < 1$ or $i > |\rho|$.
- $\rho, \nu, i \not\models \bot$.
- $\rho, \nu, i \models P$ iff $P \in \rho_i$.
- $\rho, \nu, i \models t > 0$ iff $t^\nu > 0$ is true.
- $\rho, \nu, i \models \neg\phi$ iff $\rho, \nu, i \not\models \phi$.
- $\rho, \nu, i \models \phi \vee \psi$ iff $\rho, \nu, i \models \phi$ or $\rho, \nu, i \models \psi$.
- $\rho, \nu, i \models \bullet\phi$ iff $i > 1$ and $\rho, \nu, i-1 \models \phi$.
- $\rho, \nu, i \models \phi_1 \,\mathbb{S}\, \phi_2$ iff $\rho, \nu, i \models \phi_2$, or $\rho, \nu, i \models \phi_1$ and $\rho, \nu, i-1 \models \phi_1 \,\mathbb{S}\, \phi_2$ with $i > 1$.
- $\rho, \nu, i \models \mathcal{C}x : \langle\phi, \psi\rangle.\varphi$ iff $\rho, \nu[x \mapsto n], i \models \varphi$ where $n = |\{j | r \leq j \leq i \text{ and } \rho, \nu, j \models \psi\}|$ and $r = max(\{j | \rho, \nu, j \models \phi, j \leq i\} \cup \{1\})$

We write $\rho, i \models \phi$ when $\rho, \nu, i \models \phi$ for every valuation ν.

Example 1. For an authentication server (e.g., bank) which validates a user's credential, a common login policy can be that if a user fails to enter the correct password three times in a row, then the user's account is temporarily disabled. Let us consider only two system events: a correct password was entered (*cp*), and a wrong password was entered (*wp*) by a particular user. The logic policy can be specified as follows:

$$\blacksquare[\neg(cp \wedge wp) \wedge (\mathcal{C}x : \langle cp, wp\rangle.x < 3)]. \tag{1}$$

The first conjunct expresses a consistency property, i.e., a password entered cannot be both correct and wrong at the same time. The variable x stores the number of times a wrong password was entered since the last time a correct password was entered (or since the beginning of the trace, if no correct password has been entered so far). Consider the event trace $\rho = [\{wp\}; \{cp\}; \{wp\}; \{wp\}; \{cp\}; \{wp\}]$. Then formula (1) above is true at every state. □

In general, the counting quantifier can be used to express quantitative properties within a 'session' (e.g., an authentication session, a life cycle of a process, etc). One could introduce two events: $start$ and end, to mark the beginning and the end of a session. Then to check that the number of occurrences of an event e within a session is less than n, for example, one can simply use the formula $\mathcal{C}x : \langle start, e \wedge \neg end\rangle.\ x < n$ in conjunction with other formulas expressing the well-formedness of a session (e.g., every end corresponds to a $start$, etc). If e is a simple event (e.g., the wp event in Example 1), one could encode this in LTL using standard temporal operators, but at the expense of conciseness, i.e., one needs to expand the parameter n into n instances of $e \wedge \neg end$. For example, Example 1 can be alternatively specified as

$$\blacksquare[\neg(cp \wedge wp) \wedge \neg(\bullet wp \wedge \bullet(wp \wedge \bullet wp)))].$$

That is, there cannot be three consecutive wp events any time in the past. However, this is the case only when there are no events being monitored other than cp and wp. When other events are possible, then we need to specify that events other than cp can happen in between two consecutive wp events. In general, in a formula $\mathcal{C}x : \langle\phi_1, \phi_2\rangle.\phi_3$, any of the ϕ_i could be a complicated temporal formula, e.g., it could involve nested counting quantifiers and other temporal operators. In such a case, the encoding into pure LTL becomes less obvious and less concise. We shall see more examples drawn from Android malware study in Section 5.

Our counting quantifier is a generalization of Bauer et. al.'s counting quantifier [7]. Their counting quantifier is semantically defined as follows: $\rho, \nu, i \vDash \mathcal{N}x : \psi.\varphi$ iff $\rho, \nu[x \mapsto n], i \vDash \varphi$ where $n = |\{j | 1 \leq j \leq i \text{ and } \rho, \nu, j \vDash \psi\}|$. However, in terms of expressiveness, they are actually equivalent, as shown next.

Proposition 1. *The counting quantifiers $\mathcal{C}$ and $\mathcal{N}$ are equivalent, i.e., one can be defined in terms of the other.*

Proof. (*Outline.*) The quantifier $\mathcal{N}$ can be encoded using $\mathcal{C}$ as follows: $\mathcal{N}x : \phi.\psi \equiv \mathcal{C}x : \langle\bot, \psi\rangle.\varphi$. Conversely, $\mathcal{C}$ can be encoded using $\mathcal{N}$ as follows:

$$\mathcal{C}x : \langle\phi, \psi\rangle.\varphi \equiv \mathcal{N}z : \phi.\ \mathcal{N}x : (\psi \wedge \mathcal{N}y : \phi.y = z).\ \varphi.$$

Note that the subformula $\mathcal{N}y : \phi.y = z$ acts essentially as a counter reset. It is not difficult to check from their semantics that these encodings are correct. □

Note that although $\mathcal{C}$ can be encoded using $\mathcal{N}$, the encoding introduces nested occurrences of $\mathcal{N}$ and one needs to compare at least two counting variables. In general, policies involving two or more counting variables are impossible to enforce in a trace-length independent way, as our example in the introduction shows. We could have simply used the original counting quantifier $\mathcal{N}$, but we would then have to use the encoding above, that involves comparing two or more variables, to capture the idea of a session. Such encodings would thus obscure the underlying structure of the problem, and makes it harder to systematically generate TLI monitors from a given specification. For instance, the policy described in Example 1 uses only one counting variable when expressed using $\mathcal{C}$, and results in Section 3 would guarantee the existence of TLI monitors for that particular policy. Had we chosen to encode it using $\mathcal{N}$, we would have to work harder in order to show that the policy is in fact TLI monitorable.

3 Trace-length Independent Monitoring for PTLTL$_{cnt}$

In a setting with limited storage and computation resource (e.g., an OS kernal or embedded devices), an online monitoring algorithm that requires the storage of the entire event trace is no practical, even if its complexity is PTIME. Ad hoc restrictions such as limiting the time window or enforcing bounded storage of events are not desirable as they may introduce incompleteness with respect to the policies being enforced, i.e., there may be violations to the policies that can only be detected on a trace of events longer than what could fit in the storage. In early work such as [19], monitoring algorithms are designed so that their memory requirement is constant, when one fixes the formula to be monitored, without compromising the completeness of the monitor with respect to the formula. For example, for PTLTL [19], one needs to maintain only two states of each subformula of a policy to enforce without losing completeness of the algorithms. Following [8], we call this type of monitoring algorithms as trace-length independent monitoring algorithms, and we call formulas that can be monitored in a trace-length independent way trace-length independent formulas, or *TLI-formulas* for short, and such formulas are said to be *TLI-monitorable*.

Since a main difference between PTLTL$_{cnt}$ and PTLTL is the presence of arithmetic relations, we first look at a class of relations $\phi(x_1,\ldots,x_n)$ that are TLI-monitorable (the precise definition will be given later). If all relations in a formula are all TLI-monitorable, then it is straightforward to check that the formula itself must be TLI-monitorable. In this section, we look at the univariate case, i.e., functions with arity 1. We generalize this to the multivariate case in Section 4.

In the following, all variables range over integers and the domains of functions are assumed to be tuples of integers, unless otherwise stated. Further, given a function F of arity n, we denote with $\varphi_F(x_1,\ldots,x_n)$ the relation $F(x_1,\ldots,x_n) > 0$.

Definition 1. *Given a function F, we construct a binary function F_G as follows:*

$$F_G(x_1,\ldots,x_n) = \begin{cases} 0 & \text{if } F(x_1,\ldots,x_n) \leq 0 \\ 1 & \text{otherwise} \end{cases}$$

We call F_G the *G-function* of F, which can be seen as the characteristic function of φ_F.

Definition 2. *A function F defined on domain $\mathbb{D}$ is said to be* periodic *over interval I with period T if we have*

$$F(x) = F(x+T)$$

for all values of $x \in \mathbb{D} \cap I$, with also $(x+T) \in \mathbb{D} \cap I$.

Definition 3. *A total function $F : \mathbb{N} \to \mathbb{R}$ is said to be* lower-bounded periodic, *or* lb-periodic *for short, if there is a $b \in \mathbb{N}$ such that F is periodic on interval $[b, +\infty)$.*

Definition 4. *Let $F : \mathbb{N} \to \mathbb{R}$ be a total function. Then φ_F is* TLI-monitorable *if there are two constants c and k, with $c \geq k \geq 1$ and $c, k \in \mathbb{N}$, such that*

$$\varphi_F(x) = H(\varphi_F(x-1),\ldots,\varphi_F(x-k))$$

for $x \geq c$, where H is a total computable Boolean function.

Intuitively, TLI-monitorable relations are those for which the $F(x) > 0$ can be solved incrementally, i.e., if we know the truth values of $F(y) > 0$ for a finite number of $y < x$, we would be able to compute the truth value of $F(x) > 0$. Notice that there is no need to store the actual value of the counting variable x nor $F(x)$ in this incremental computation; all that matters is the truth value of the relation $F(x) > 0$. Thus the space required for monitoring such relations remain constant irrespective of the value of x.

Example 2. Let $F(x) = x^2 - 8x + 15$, where $x \in \mathbb{N}$. The G-function of F in this case is

$$F_G(x) = \begin{cases} 0 & \text{if } 3 \leq x \leq 5 \\ 1 & \text{otherwise} \end{cases}$$

This is because $F(x) \leq 0$ is satisfied only when $3 \leq x \leq 5$. □

We now characterize precisely the class of relations which are TLI-monitorable according to Definition 4.

Lemma 1. *Let $F : \mathbb{N} \to \mathbb{R}$ be a total function. Then φ_F is TLI-monitorable if F_G is lb-periodic.*

Example 3. The function F_G in Example 2 is lb-periodic, with the lower bound 6, and period 1. So φ_F is TLI-monitorable according to Lemma 1. □

We now prove the converse: every TLI-monitorable function must be lb-periodic.

Lemma 2. *Given a total function $F : \mathbb{N} \to \mathbb{R}$, if φ_F is TLI-monitorable, then F_G is lb-periodic.*

With sufficiency and necessity proved in Lemma 1 and Lemma 2 respectively, we get the following theorem:

Theorem 1. *Given a total function $F : \mathbb{N} \to \mathbb{R}$, φ_F is TLI-monitorable iff F_G is lb-periodic.*

The abstract characterization in Theorem 1 is in a way quite obvious from the definition of TLI-monitorable relations. The important part is that monitorability is associated with periodic "relations" (F_G) rather than functions (F). That is, F may not be periodic yet still be TLI-monitorable (see Theorem 2 below). In concrete applications, since we are usually only given the function F and not F_G, the difficult problem is in deciding whether F_G is lb-periodic given F. In the following, we show some broad classes of functions for which their G-functions are lb-periodic.

Theorem 2. *Given a computable total function $F : \mathbb{N} \to \mathbb{R}$, φ_F is TLI-monitorable if F satisfies one of the following conditions:*

1. *F is lb-periodic.*
2. *F is monotonously increasing/decreasing.*
3. *F is a univariate polynomial.*

Now, we shall look at the monitoring problems for formulas in which all relations and functions are univariate and TLI-monitorable.

To monitor a formula $\mathcal{C}x : \langle \phi, \psi \rangle.\varphi(x)$, we first extract all functions involving x from φ. Suppose as $F(x)$ is one of the functions extracted. According to Theorem 1, the G-function $F_G(x)$ for $F(x)$ should be lb-periodic for $\varphi_F(x)$ to be TLI-monitorable. Then the track of $\varphi_F(x)$ can be seen as a path ended with a loop. Then the values of $\varphi_F(x)$ repeats periodically as x increases. We can thus quotient the values of x based on the period of F_G to form a finite set of equivalence classes.

Definition 5. *Given a TLI-monitorable relation φ_F with lb-periodic function F_G that is periodic over $[b, +\infty)$ with period T, we define the* equivalence class *for the domain of F as:*

$$[i] = \begin{cases} \{i\} & \text{if } i < b \\ \{a | ((a - b) \bmod T + b) \equiv i\} & \text{otherwise} \end{cases}$$

Obviously, the number of the equivalence classes should be $(b{+}T)$ and every element within an equivalence class will have the same φ_F value. To check the value of $\varphi_F(x)$ at any point x, it is sufficient to check the value of φ_F at the equivalence class of x. For simplicity, each equivalence class is indexed with the minimal element in the set. The reset condition ϕ is orthogonal to the issue of quotienting the values of x; when it is satisfied, the count for x is reset to 0. We write $\mathfrak{r}(\rho, i, Cx : \langle\phi, \psi\rangle.\varphi)$ to denote the index of equivalence class to which the counter of ψ belongs with model (ρ, ν, i).

In the following, we shall assume that, given a formula φ, every subformula of φ of the form $Cx : \langle\phi, \psi\rangle.\varphi$ has the property that x occurs exactly once in a univariate function. This is not a real limitation as the case where x is vacuous or occurs more than once (in different univariate functions) can be encoded into an equivalent formula where each quantified variable occurs exactly once. If x is vacuous in φ, then $Cx : \langle\phi, \psi\rangle.\varphi$ is logically equivalent ot φ. If x occurs twice, i.e., φ is, e.g., $\varphi_1(x) \wedge \varphi_2(x)$, then we rewrite the formula to an equivalent one: $Cx : \langle\phi, \psi\rangle.Cy : \langle\phi, \psi\rangle.\varphi_1(x) \wedge \varphi_2(y)$. This holds because x and y are bound to the same value at every state. The same technique generalizes to the cases where x occurs more than twice in φ.

Given the above restriction on the syntax of formulas, in a formula $Cx : \langle\phi, \psi\rangle.\varphi$, we can extract exactly one function F where x is used. As in the case of monitoring algorithms in [19,17], the key to get the trace-length independence property is to express the semantics of all logical operators in a recursive form, i.e., the truth value of φ at state i is a function of truth values of subformulas of φ and/or the truth value of φ at state $i-1$. All operators except the counting quantifier are already in recursive form. The next theorem shows that the semantics of the counting quantifier also admits a recursive form, when all relations in the formula to be monitored are univariate and TLI-monitorable.

Theorem 3. *Given a model (ρ, ν, i) and a closed formula $Cx : \langle\phi, \psi\rangle.\varphi(x)$ where x occurs in a function F, and $\varphi_F(x)$ is TLI-monitorable with the lb-periodic function F_G that is periodic over $[b, +\infty)$ with period T, the following holds for every $1 < i \leq |\rho|$:*

$$\begin{aligned}
&\rho, \nu, i \models Cx : \langle\phi, \psi\rangle.\varphi \textit{ iff } \rho, \nu, i \models \phi, \textit{ and } \rho, \nu, i \models \varphi(0);\\
&\textit{or } \rho, \nu, i \models \psi, \mathfrak{r}(\rho, i-1, Cx : \langle\phi, \psi\rangle.\varphi) < b, \textit{ and } \rho, \nu, i \models \varphi_F((\mathfrak{r}(\rho, i-1, Cx : \langle\phi, \psi\rangle.\varphi) + 1);\\
&\textit{or } \rho, \nu, i \models \psi, \mathfrak{r}(\rho, i-1, Cx : \langle\phi, \psi\rangle.\varphi) \geq b, \textit{ and } \rho, \nu, i \models \varphi_F((\mathfrak{r}(\rho, i-1, Cx : \langle\phi, \psi\rangle.\varphi) + 1 - b)\\
&\qquad \bmod T + b);\\
&\textit{or } \rho, \nu, i \models \neg\phi, \rho, i \models \neg\psi, \textit{ and } \rho, \nu, i-1 \models Cx : \langle\phi, \psi\rangle.\varphi(x)
\end{aligned}$$

Once we get the semantics of all logical operators of PTLTL$_{cnt}$ in a recursive form, we can use dynamic programming to design a trace-length independence algorithm for PTLTL$_{cnt}$. Following the algorithm for PTLTL [19], we compute the truth values of every subformula of a given formula φ, at exactly two successive states. However, for quantified formulas, its subformulas would contain free variables, and their truth values would thus depend on the values of x. To avoid coding valuation of variables explicitly in the monitoring algorithm, we need to instantiate x to concrete terms before computing their truth values. Given the restriction imposed on the formulas as discussed above, we can associate each quantified variable x in φ with exactly one univariate function;

```
struct CntInfo {
  int indexEC;
  int period;
  int lowerBound;
}
```

Fig. 1. CntInfo Data Structure

Algorithm 1. $Monitor(\rho, i, \phi)$

Init($\rho, \phi, prev, cur, cnt$);
for $j = 1$ *to* i **do**
  Iter($\rho, j, \phi, prev, cur, cnt$);
return $cur[idx(\phi)]$;

let us call it F_x. Since φ_{F_x} is TLI-monitorable, by Definition 5, we can compute a finite set of equivalence classes for the values of x. Suppose this set has n elements $\{e_1, \ldots, e_n\}$. Then we need to instantiate x only with these n values. So given a subformula $\mathcal{C}x : \langle\phi, \psi\rangle.\theta(x)$ of φ, we define its immediate subformulas as: ϕ, ψ and $\varphi(e_i)$, for $1 \leq i \leq n$. We let $Sub(\varphi)$ denote the set of all subformulas of φ.

Now we will describe how monitoring can be done for ϕ, given ρ and $1 \leq i \leq |\rho|$. Let $\phi_1, \phi_2, \ldots, \phi_m$ be an enumeration of $Sub(\phi)$ respecting the order that any formula has an enumeration number greater than that of all its subformulae. Following the notations in [17], we can assign to each $\psi \in Sub(\phi)$ an index i, such that $\psi = \phi_i$ in this enumeration. We refer to this index as $idx(\psi)$. We maintain two Boolean arrays $prev[1, \ldots, m]$ and $cur[1, \ldots, m]$. The intention is that given ρ and $i > 1$, the value of $prev[k]$ corresponds to the truth value of the judgment $\rho, \nu, i-1 \vDash \phi_k$ and the truth value of $cur[k]$ corresponds to the truth value of the judgment $\rho, \nu, i \vDash \phi_k$.

Recall that each quantified variable is used in exactly one univariate function. For each variable x, we keep a data structure *CntInfo*, shown in Figure 1, which stores the lower bound (*lowerBound*) and the period (*period*) of the G-function, and the index of the equivalence class induced by the G-function (*indexEC*). The initialization of an instance of *CntInfo* is conducted in *init_counter()*, which will set *lowerBound* and *period* the accordingly, and zero the *indexEC*. The array $cnt[1, \ldots, l]$ in both *Init* and *Iter* algorithm stores a list of *CntInfo* objects associated with each variables. We assign an index $idx_c(x)$ to each variable x, and $cnt[idx_c(x)]$ maintains the information associated with the counter variable x.

The main monitoring algorithm (Algorithm 1) is divided into two sub-procedures: the initialisation procedure (Algorithm 2) and the iterative procedure (Algorithm 3). In the pseudocode of the algorithms, we overload some logical symbols to denote operators on boolean values. It is straightforward to see that, once the formula to be monitored is fixed, the space required to run the algorithm does not grow with the length of traces. In particular, the values of the counter variables (the *indexEC* field) is bounded, i.e., it never grows beyond $period + lowerBound$.

4 Extension to Multivariate Relations

We now look at the case where relations can be multivariate. We shall restrict our discussions to the bivariate case; the extension to the multivariate case is straightforward and does not require any new techniques so we omit details here.

Algorithm 2. $Init(\rho, \phi, prev, cur, cnt)$

```
for k = 1 to m do
    switch φ_k do
        case ⊥ cur[k] ← false
        case P cur[k] ← P ∈ ρ_1
        case ¬ψ cur[k] ← ¬cur[idx(ψ)]
        case t > 0 cur[k] ← t^ν > 0
        case ψ_1 ∨ ψ_2 cur[k] ← cur[idx(ψ_1)] ∨ cur[idx(ψ_2)]
        case •ψ cur[k] ← false
        case ψ_1 S ψ_2 cur[k] ← cur[idx(ψ_2)]
        case Cx : ⟨ψ_1, ψ_2⟩.φ(x)
            init_counter(cnt[idx_c(x)]);
            if !cur[idx(ψ_1)] then
                if cur[idx(ψ_2)] then
                    cnt[idx_c(x)].count + +;
                    cur[k] ← cur[idx(φ(1))];
            else cur[k] ← cur[idx(φ(0))]
return cur[idx(φ)];
```

Definition 6. *Let $F : \mathbb{N} \times \mathbb{N} \to \mathbb{R}$ be a total function, then φ_F is TLI-monitorable if there are constants c_1, c_2 and k_1, k_2, with $c_1 \geq k_1 \geq 1$, $c_2 \geq k_2 \geq 1$ and $c_1, c_2, k_1, k_2 \in \mathbb{N}$, such that*

$$\varphi_F(x,y) = \begin{cases} F(x,y) > 0 & \text{if } x < c_1 \text{ and } y < c_2, \\ H\begin{pmatrix} \varphi_F(x-k_1,y), & \ldots, & \varphi_F(x-1,y), \\ \varphi_F(x-k_1,y-1), & \ldots, & \varphi_F(x,y-1), \\ \varphi_F(x-k_1,y-k_2), & \ldots, & \varphi_F(x,y-k_2) \end{pmatrix} & \text{otherwise.} \end{cases}$$

where H is a total computable Boolean function.

Theorem 4. *Given a total function $F : \mathbb{N} \times \mathbb{N} \to \mathbb{R}$, if there are constants T_x, c_x, T_y and c_y such that $F_G(x,c)$ is lb-periodic with period T_x for any $c \in \mathbb{N} \geq c_y$, and $F_G(d,y)$ is lb-periodic with period T_y for any $d \in \mathbb{N} \geq c_x$, then φ_F is TLI-monitorable.*

Essentially, Theorem 4 says that φ is TLI-monitorable if the period of a projection of F into one of its parameter is independent of the other parameter, once the value of that parameter exceeds a certain threshold. This allows us to quotation the values of each parameters into their own equivalence classes independently of each other.

The monitoring algorithm is surprisingly the same as the univariate case. We still need to adopt the same restriction regarding the occurrences of variables as in the univariate case, i.e., that each quantified variable appears exactly once in a bivariate function. The main difference between the univarite and the bivariate case is finding the right lower bound and the periods of each variables, a process which takes place outside the algorithm; once these parameters are defined, the monitoring algorithm proceeds as in the univariate case.

Algorithm 3. $Iter(\rho, i, \phi, prev, cur, cnt)$

```
prev ← cur;
for k = 1 to m do
    switch φ_k do
        case ⊥ cur[k] ← false
        case P cur[k] ← P ∈ ρ_i
        case ¬ψ cur[k] ← ¬cur[idx(ψ)]
        case t > 0 cur[k] ← t^ν > 0
        case ψ1 ∨ ψ2 cur[k] ← cur[idx(ψ1)] ∨ cur[idx(ψ2)]
        case •ψ cur[k] ← prev[idx(ψ)]
        case ψ1 S ψ2 cur[k] ← cur[idx(ψ2)] ∨ (cur[idx(ψ1)] ∧ prev[idx(ψ2)])
        case Cx : ⟨ψ1, ψ2⟩.φ(x)
            if !(cur[idx(ψ1)] ∨ cur[idx(ψ2)]) then cur[k] ← pre[k]
            else
                if cur[idx(ψ1)] then
                    cnt[idx_c(x)].indexEC ← 0;
                else
                    if cur[idx(ψ2)] then
                        n ← ++cnt[idx_c(x)].indexEC;
                        lowerBound ← cnt[idx_c(x)].lowerBound;
                        period ← cnt[idx_c(x)].period;
                        if n ≥ lowerBound + period then
                            cnt[idx_c(x)].indexEC ←
                            (n − lowerBound) mod period + lowerBound;
                cur[k] ← cur[idx(φ(cnt[idx_c(x)].indexEC))];
return cur[idx(φ)];
```

The extension to the multivariate case follows the same idea, i.e., a sufficient condition for φ_F, when F is an n-ary function, to be monitorable is that the period of any of its projection is independent of the other projections.

5 Case Studies in Android

In this section, some concrete policies in Android systems are provided as case studies for PTLTL$_{cnt}$. In the rest of this paper, we assume the following atomic propositions in Android OS. S_i (or E_i) means the application with UID i starts to run (or stops running). M_i means the application with UID i sends out a message. I_i means the application with UID i opens an Internet connection socket. F_i : the application with UID i forks a new child process. C_i means the application with UID i accesses the contact database.

The following policies refer to the malicious access patterns that are forbidden in Android systems. At any moment, if $\rho, \nu, |\rho| \not\models \phi$ holds, and when a new event P occurs, the monitor checks whether $[\rho; P], \nu, |\rho| + 1 \not\models \phi$ holds. If it does, the process forwards fluently. Otherwise, a suspicious alert will send to the user. As for the specific limit on specific counted amount, we just give a rough estimation for illustration purpose.

1. $\mathcal{C}x : \langle S_i, M_i \wedge \neg E_i \rangle.(x > 5)$
   This policy is to guarantee that an app with UID i cannot send more that 5 SMS messages during a single run, which is inspired by [3] for stopping unintended SMS transmissions. In [21], authors found that current Android botnets are exploiting SMS messages to gather money by sending SMS to premium-rate numbers. With the specified policy, it helps to make possible discovery of an Android bot.
2. $\mathcal{C}x : \langle S_i, I_i \wedge \neg E_i \rangle.(x > 200)$
   This policy says that an app cannot open Internet connection socket for more than 200 times in a single run. If an Android app aims at flooding a targeted server to launch a DDoS attack, one way to achieve this is to open massive Internet connections. This policy can help to control the amount of Internet connections, thus preventing some potential malware.
3. $\mathcal{C}x : \langle S_i, F_i \wedge \neg E_i \rangle.(x > 2^{16})$
   This policy says that during the life cycle of an application, it is not allowed to create more than 2^{16} child processes to exhaust the *pid*, i.e., the process identifier in Linux kernel. *RageAgainstTheCage* [1] is a well-known exploit in Android, which can perform unauthorized privileged actions by gaining the root access. This malware uses a vulnerability in Android kernel to get the root privilege by keeping forking the child process to 2^{16}. With this policy specified using PTLTL$_{cnt}$, constraint is set to how many child processed an application can fork in a single run, it will be much helpful to prevent this attack.

6 Implementation and Evaluation

We have implemented the monitoring algorithm for PTLTL$_{cnt}$ and evaluated it on LogicDroid platform [17], which is a modified Android system based on Android 4.1. The Android IPC (Inter-process communication) calls, like opening Internet socket, sending SMS and accessing contact database hooked by LogicDroid form the set of events against which policies in PTLTL$_{cnt}$ need to be checked. Since LogicDroid does not yet implement hooks to detect the start or end of a process or an app, the reset conditions in our example policies are not applicable. In particular, policy 3 in Section 5, which counts the child processes forked by an app, has not yet been tested due to the lack of support for process forking detection in LogicDroid.

The list of six policies adopted in our experiments is presented in Figure 2. among which the first two are that introduced in Section 5, and the others are artificial examples to evaluate the robustness of our approach. To keep the diversity of the policies, the number of counters in the six policies is 1, 1, 2, 3, 6, 10 separately. Also there are policies with complicate reset conditions. Each policy is implemented as a Linux kernel module according to the algorithm described in Section 3. For every counter variable in the tested policies, the initialization of fields *period* and *lowerBound* in *CntInfo* struct are currently done manually.

To test the practicability and efficiency of our approach, we implement a fuzzy testing app to trigger three kinds of IPC calls (M_i, I_i and C_i in Section 5) randomly. For

1. $\mathcal{C}x : \langle S_i, M_i \wedge \neg E_i \rangle.(x > 5)$
2. $\mathcal{C}x : \langle S_i, I_i \wedge \neg E_i \rangle.(x > 200)$
3. $\mathcal{C}x : \langle \bot, M_i \rangle.\mathcal{C}y : \langle \bot, I_i \rangle.K(x, y) > 0$ with the definition of function K as follows:

$$K(x,y) = \begin{cases} 3x - 4y & \text{if } x < 5 \text{ and } y < 4, \\ K(x-3, y) & \text{if } x \geq 5 \text{ and } y < 4, \\ K(x, y-2) & \text{if } x < 5 \text{ and } y \geq 4, \\ K(x-3, y-2) & \text{otherwise.} \end{cases}$$

Note that each projection of function K becomes periodic once $x > 9$ and $y > 13$, so it is easy to show that φ_K is TLI-monitorable.
4. $(I_i \, \mathbb{S} \, C_i) \wedge \mathcal{C}x : \langle \bot, M_i \rangle.\mathcal{C}y : \langle \bot, I_i \rangle.\mathcal{C}z : \langle \bot, C_j \rangle.H(x, y, z) > 0$ with function H defined as follows:

$$H(x,y,z) = \begin{cases} 3x - 4y + 2z & \text{if } x < 19 \text{ and } y < 13 \text{ and } z < 5, \\ H(x-9, y, z) & \text{if } x \geq 19 \text{ and } y < 13 \text{ and } z < 5, \\ H(x, y-2, z) & \text{if } x < 19 \text{ and } y \geq 13 \text{ and } z < 5, \\ H(x, y, z-1) & \text{if } x < 19 \text{ and } y < 13 \text{ and } z \geq 5, \\ H(x-9, y-2, z) & \text{if } x \geq 19 \text{ and } y \geq 13 \text{ and } z < 5, \\ H(x, y-2, z-1) & \text{if } x < 19 \text{ and } y \geq 13 \text{ and } z \geq 5, \\ H(x-9, y, z-1) & \text{if } x \geq 19 \text{ and } y < 13 \text{ and } z \geq 5, \\ H(x-9, y-2, z-1) & \text{otherwise.} \end{cases}$$

Each projection of function H is periodic when $x > 19$, $y > 13$ and $z > 5$, so φ_H is TLI-monitorable.
5. $\mathcal{C}x_1 : \langle \bot, \bullet C_i \rangle \wedge \mathcal{C}x_2 : \langle \bot, \neg I_i \rangle \wedge \mathcal{C}x_3 : \langle I_i, C_i \rangle \wedge \mathcal{C}x_4 : \langle \bot, \bullet I_i \rangle \wedge \mathcal{C}x_5 : \langle \bot, M_i \rangle \wedge \mathcal{C}x_6 : \langle \bot, I_i \rangle$
6. $\mathcal{C}x_1 : \langle \bot, \bullet C_i \rangle \wedge \mathcal{C}x_2 : \langle \bot, \neg I_i \rangle \wedge \mathcal{C}x_3 : \langle I_i, C_i \rangle \wedge \mathcal{C}x_4 : \langle \bot, \bullet I_i \rangle \wedge \mathcal{C}x_5 : \langle \bot, M_i \rangle \wedge \mathcal{C}x_6 : \langle \bot, I_i \rangle \wedge \mathcal{C}x_7 : \langle \bot, \neg M_i \rangle \wedge \mathcal{C}x_8 : \langle \bot, \bullet M_i \rangle \wedge \mathcal{C}x_{10} : \langle \mathcal{C}x_9 : \langle \bot, \neg C_i \rangle, M_i \rangle$

Fig. 2. Additional policies used in the experiments

the evaluation, we measure the detection time of the monitoring process (i.e., the execution time of a policy monitoring kernel module for processing a single event) and the memory used by the system with the extra policy monitoring kernel module. All the experiments are conducted in the LogicDroid emulator on 64-bit Ubuntu 14.04LTS with 16GB RAM and an Intel Xeon(R) CPU E5-1650 v2 with 3.50GHz. Our implementation and the models shown in this section are available in [2].

Figure 3 shows the time used by the monitor for a single event check. To measure the detection time, we launch the fuzzy testing app to send 1000 IPC calls continuously, therefore the monitor kernel module will be invoked 1000 times. We record the detection time in every 50 calls as shown in Figure 3. It can be seen from the figure that the time used for each policy monitoring kernel module is stable, i.e., does not increase with trace length grows. There is no obvious difference between the time cost for different policies, and the average checking time is 6 to 8 microseconds. Figure 4 shows the memory usage of the emulator with the six different kernel modules. To consider the impact of the additional kernel module on memory usage in the emulator more accurately, we measure the memory when every 1000 IPC calls are triggered for continuous

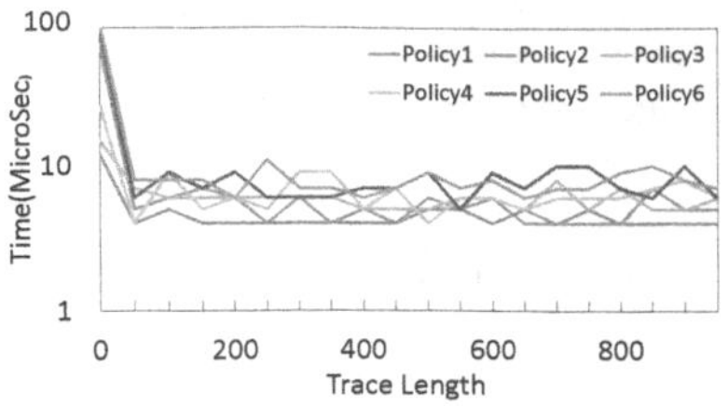

Fig. 3. Time of Single Round Checking

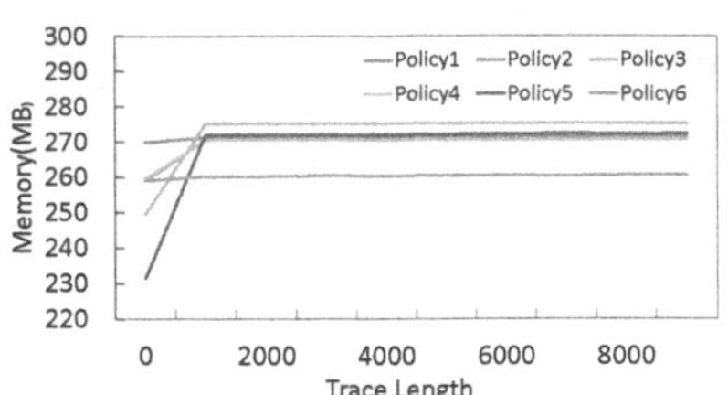

Fig. 4. Memory Usage

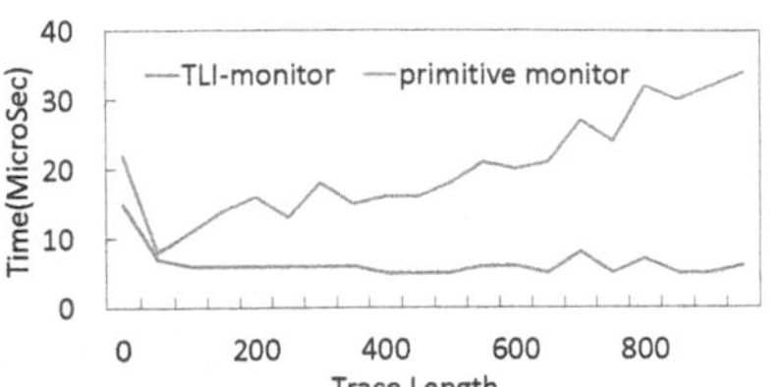

Fig. 5. Comparison of Checking Time

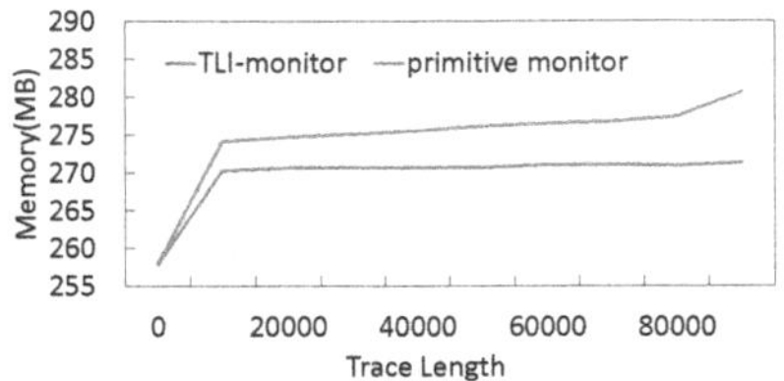

Fig. 6. Comparison of Memory Usage

10 times. Clearly, all of the memory usage measured for the emulator with different kernel module installed in turn are quite stable (i.e., does not increase with the time), which supports our claim that the proposed algorithm is trace-length independent.

Note that the six policies module tested in the experiment are with a increasing number of counters. From the results shown in Figure 3 and Figure 4, we can know that the number of counters involved in a policy has little timing and memory influence.

To give an emperical validation of the effectiveness of our monitoring algorithm, comparison experiments have been done with a direct primitive counting mechanism, where all events will be recorded and the entire history will be searched to get the statistics of count when the monitor checks the validation. The results of monitoring the policy 3 in Figure 2 are shown in Figure 5 and Figure 6. For the detection time, it is following the previous measure experiment. While the memory is measured when every 10000 IPC calls are triggered for continuous 10 times. We choose a different setting to make visible the gradually increasing tendency of memory used by the primitive monitor. As can be seen, there is obvious increase of the time and space required by the primitive monitor as the trace length grows.

7 Related Work

This section lists some recent works on counting quantifier combined with different kinds of logic theories, aiming to increase the expressiveness of the logic. A brief outline of the history of trace-length independent runtime monitoring will also be given.

Inspired by the aggregation operators in database query language like SQL, Basin *et al.* [6] extend metric first-order temporal logic (MFOTL) with aggregation operators, like SUM, CNT, MAX and AVG, and proposed a monitoring algorithm for language. The core of this work is to translate policies specified with the extended MFOTL to the corresponding extended relational algebra. For their monitoring algorithm, functions are handled similarly to Prolog. Even through some optimizations are taken to accelerate computations in monitoring, the aggregation operators are out of their consideration. Another language, SOLOIST [11], is based on a many-sorted first-order metric temporal logic and extended with new temporal modalities that support aggregate operators for events occurring in a certain time window. For its monitoring, Bianculli *et al.* [12] proposed to translate the formulae in SOLOIST to formulae of CLTLB($\mathscr{D}$) [10], and Bersani *et al.* [9] presented an approach to encode SOLOIST formulae into QF-EUFIDL formulae. Nevertheless, both approaches depend on SMT-solver to do the final satisfiability checking. The evaluations of the above two works show that increasing time and memory will be needed when the length of the trace grows.

Laroussinie *et al.* [20] presented a quantitative extension for LTL, called CLTL, allowing to specify the number of states satisfying certain sub-formulas along paths, which provided the same semantics with ours. They also showed even though CLTL formulae can be translated into classical LTL, an exponential blow-up in formula size is inevitable. As for the satisfiability and model-checking problems for CLTL, they turned out to be EXPSPACE-complete, but PSPACE-complete when restricting CLTL to a fragment. Actually this fragment just belongs to a subset of the TLI-formulas defined in our work, for which the relation function will grow monotonously with any involved count increasing.

Other monitoring approaches that provide support for different kinds of aggregations are LarvaSat [13], LOLA [14], as well as rule-based EAGLE [4], RULER [5] and LOGFIRE [18], and one based on algebraic alternating automata [15], However, all monitoring algorithms for the above languages still need to record the specific counted values, even though most of them avoided storing the entire trace history. In principle, these counters can increase indefinitely, so their space complexity is not constant unlike our monitoring algorithms.

There are some works [19,8,17] concentrate on designing trace-length independent monitoring algorithms. In particular, this work can be seen as an effort to extend the LogicDroid framework to incorporate the counting quantifier of [7]. Although the concept of trace-length independence is proposed in 2013, there are also some prior works which imply this property in their algorithm design. For the best of our knowledge, this is first work on designing trace-length independence algorithms involving counting quantifier, not even other aggregation operators. For now, we are the first one to implement a trace-length independent runtime verification algorithm for the logic language with a counting quantifier.

8 Conclusion

We have presented a formal policy specification language PTLTL_{cnt} that allows expressions of quantitative policies. We consider the questions of when a formula is trace-length independent monitorable. For univariate relations, we obtain sufficient and necessary conditions for the relations to be TLI-monitorable. We then discussed an extension to the multivariate relations. Assuming the relations are all TLI-monitorable, we construct a TLI monitoring algorithm for $PTLTL_{cnt}$. We have implemented and tested our monitoring algorithm, and the experimental results more or less confirm our theoretical results. Currently, we have not yet addressed the integration of the counting quantifier with metric operators and recursive predicates of [17]. This is a subject of immediate future work. We also plan to look to incorporate other, more expressive aggregrate operators from [6].

Acknowledgment. We thank the anonymous referees for their helpful comments. This research is supported by the National Research Foundation, Prime Ministers Office, Singapore under its National Cybersecurity R&D Program (Award No. NRF2014NCR-NCR001-30) and administered by the National Cybersecurity R&D Directorate.

References

1. Rageagainstthecage (2011), http://thesnkchrmr.wordpress.com/2011/03/24/rageagainstthecage
2. Tli monitoring of ltl extended with a counting quantifier (2015), http://pat.sce.ntu.edu.sg/xndu/fm2015
3. Arzt, S., Falzon, K., Follner, A., Rasthofer, S., Bodden, E., Stolz, V.: How useful are existing monitoring languages for securing android apps? In: ATPS, pp. 107–122 (2013)
4. Barringer, H., Goldberg, A., Havelund, K., Sen, K.: Rule-based runtime verification. In: Steffen, B., Levi, G. (eds.) VMCAI 2004. LNCS, vol. 2937, pp. 44–57. Springer, Heidelberg (2004)
5. Barringer, H., Rydeheard, D., Havelund, K.: Rule systems for run-time monitoring: from eagle to ruler. Journal of Logic and Computation 20(3), 675–706 (2010)
6. Basin, D., Klaedtke, F., Marinovic, S., Zălinescu, E.: Monitoring of temporal first-order properties with aggregations. In: Legay, A., Bensalem, S. (eds.) RV 2013. LNCS, vol. 8174, pp. 40–58. Springer, Heidelberg (2013)
7. Bauer, A., Goré, R., Tiu, A.: A first-order policy language for history-based transaction monitoring. In: Leucker, M., Morgan, C. (eds.) ICTAC 2009. LNCS, vol. 5684, pp. 96–111. Springer, Heidelberg (2009)
8. Bauer, A., Küster, J.-C., Vegliach, G.: From propositional to first-order monitoring. In: Legay, A., Bensalem, S. (eds.) RV 2013. LNCS, vol. 8174, pp. 59–75. Springer, Heidelberg (2013)
9. Bersani, M.M., Bianculli, D., Ghezzi, C., Krstić, S., San Pietro, P.: SMT-based checking of SOLOIST over sparse traces. In: Gnesi, S., Rensink, A. (eds.) FASE 2014. LNCS, vol. 8411, pp. 276–290. Springer, Heidelberg (2014)
10. Bersani, M.M., Frigeri, A., Morzenti, A., Pradella, M., Rossi, M., Pietro, P.S.: Constraint ltl satisfiability checking without automata. Journal of Applied Logic 12(4), 522–557 (2014)
11. Bianculli, D., Ghezzi, C., San Pietro, P.: The tale of SOLOIST: A specification language for service compositions interactions. In: Păsăreanu, C.S., Salaün, G. (eds.) FACS 2012. LNCS, vol. 7684, pp. 55–72. Springer, Heidelberg (2013)
12. Bianculli, D., Krstic, S., Ghezzi, C., San Pietro, P.: From soloist to cltlb (d): Checking quantitative properties of service-based applications (2013)
13. Colombo, C., Gauci, A., Pace, G.J.: LarvaStat: Monitoring of statistical properties. In: Barringer, H., et al. (eds.) RV 2010. LNCS, vol. 6418, pp. 480–484. Springer, Heidelberg (2010)
14. D'Angelo, B., Sankaranarayanan, S., Sanchez, C., Robinson, W., Finkbeiner, B., Sipma, H.B., Mehrotra, S., Manna, Z.: Lola: Runtime monitoring of synchronous systems. In: TIME, pp. 166–174 (2005)

15. Finkbeiner, B., Sankaranarayanan, S., Sipma, H.B.: Collecting statistics over runtime executions. Form. Methods Syst. Des. 27(3), 253–274 (2005)
16. Fitting, M.: First-Order Logic and Automated Theorem Proving. Springer (1996)
17. Gunadi, H., Tiu, A.: Efficient runtime monitoring with metric temporal logic: A case study in the android operating system. In: FM, pp. 296–311 (2014)
18. Havelund, K.: Rule-based runtime verification revisited. International Journal on Software Tools for Technology Transfer 17(2), 1–28 (2012)
19. Havelund, K., Roşu, G.: Synthesizing monitors for safety properties. In: Katoen, J.-P., Stevens, P. (eds.) TACAS 2002. LNCS, vol. 2280, pp. 342–356. Springer, Heidelberg (2002)
20. Laroussinie, F., Meyer, A., Petonnet, E.: Counting ltl. In: TIME, pp. 51–58 (2010)
21. Pieterse, H., Olivier, M.S.: Android botnets on the rise: Trends and characteristics. In: ISSA2, pp. 1–5 (2012)
22. Zhou, Y., Jiang, X.: Dissecting android malware: Characterization and evolution. In: SP, pp. 95–109 (2012)

Probabilistic Bisimulation for Realistic Schedulers

Christian Eisentraut[1], Jens Chr. Godskesen[2], Holger Hermanns[1], Lei Song[3(✉)], and Lijun Zhang[4]

[1] Saarland University, Saarbrücken, Germany
[2] IT University of Copenhagen, København S, Denmark
[3] University of Technology Sydney, Sydney, Australia
lei.song@uts.edu.au
[4] State Key Laboratory of Computer Science, Institute of Software, CAS, Beijing, China

Abstract. Weak distribution bisimilarity is an equivalence notion on probabilistic automata, originally proposed for Markov automata. It has gained some popularity as the coarsest behavioral equivalence enjoying valuable properties like preservation of trace distribution equivalence and compositionality. This holds in the classical context of arbitrary schedulers, but it has been argued that this class of schedulers is unrealistically powerful. This paper studies a strictly coarser notion of bisimilarity, which still enjoys these properties in the context of realistic subclasses of schedulers: Trace distribution equivalence is implied for partial information schedulers, and compositionality is preserved by distributed schedulers. The intersection of the two scheduler classes thus spans a coarser and still reasonable compositional theory of behavioral semantics.

1 Introduction

Compositional theories have been an important technique to deal with complex stochastic systems effectively. Their potential ranges from compositional minimization [6,4] approaches to component based verification [26,21]. Due to their expressiveness, Markov automata have attracted many attentions [33,13,19], since they were introduced [16]. Markov automata are a compositional behavioral model for continuous time stochastic and non-deterministic systems [15,16] subsuming interactive Markov chains (IMCs) [23] and probabilistic automata (PAs) [31] (and hence also Markov decision processes and Markov chains).

On Markov automata, weak probabilistic bisimilarity has been introduced as a powerful way for abstracting from internal computation cascades, and this is obtained by relating sub-probability distributions instead of states. In the sequel we call this relation *weak distribution bisimulation*, and focus on probabilistic automata, arguably the most widespread subclass of Markov automata. Nevertheless all the results we establish carry over to Markov automata.

On probabilistic automata, weak distribution bisimilarity is strictly coarser than weak bisimilarity, and is the coarsest congruence preserving trace distribution equivalence [8]. More precisely, it is the coarsest reduction-closed barbed

N. Bjørner and F. de Boer (Eds.): FM 2015, LNCS 9109, pp. 248–264, 2015.
DOI: 10.1007/978-3-319-19249-9_16

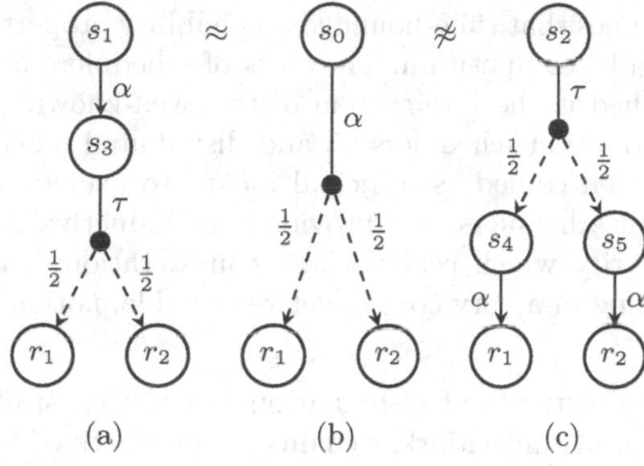

Fig. 1. Distinguishing probabilistic automata

congruence [25] with respect to parallel composition. Decision algorithms for weak distribution bisimilarity have also been proposed [14,29].

Weak distribution bisimilarity enables us to equate automata such as the ones on the left in Fig. 1, both of which exhibit the execution of action α followed by states r_1 and r_2 with probability $\frac{1}{2}$ each for an external observer. Specifically, the internal transition of the automaton on the left remains fully transparent. Standard bisimulation notions fail to equate these automata. Surprisingly, the automata on the right are not bisimilar even though the situation seems to be identical for an external observer.

The automata on the right of Fig. 1 are to be distinguished, because otherwise compositionality with respect to parallel composition would be broken. However, as observed in [31,18], the general scheduler in the parallel composition is too powerful: the decision of one component may depend on the history of other components. This is especially not desired for partially observable systems, such as multi-agent systems or distributed systems [3,32]. In distributed systems, where components only share the information they gain through explicit communication via observable actions, this behavior is unrealistic. Thus, for practically relevant models, weak distribution bisimilarity is still too fine. The need to distinguish the two automata on the right of Fig. 1 is in fact an unrealistic artifact, and this will motivate the definition of a coarser notion of equality equating them.

In this paper, we present a novel notion of weak bisimilarity on PAs, called *late distribution bisimilarity*, that is coarser than the existing notions of weak bisimilarity. It equates, for instance, all automata in Fig. 1. As weak distribution bisimilarity is the coarsest notion of equivalence that preserves observable behavior and is closed under parallel composition [8], late distribution bisimilarity cannot satisfy these properties in their entirety. However, as we will show, for a natural class of schedulers, late distribution bisimilarity preserves observable behavior, in the sense that trace distribution equivalence (*i*) is implied by late distribution bisimilarity, and (*ii*) is preserved in the context of parallel composition.

This for instance implies that time-bounded reachability properties are preserved with respect to parallel composition. The class of schedulers under which these properties are satisfied is the intersection of two well-known scheduler classes, namely partial information schedulers [7] and distributed schedulers [18]. Both these classes have been coined as principal means to exclude undesired or unrealistically powerful schedulers. We provide a co-inductive definition for late distribution bisimilarity which echoes these considerations on the automaton level, thereby resulting in a very coarse, yet reasonable, notion of equality.

Related Work. Many variants of bisimulations have been studied for different stochastic models, for instance Markov chains [1], interactive Markov chains [23], probabilistic automata [27,31,2], and alternating automata [10]. These equivalence relations are state-based, as they relate states of the corresponding models. Depending on how internal actions are handled, bisimulation relations can usually be categorized into strong bisimulations and weak bisimulations. The later is our main focus in this paper.

Markov automata arise as a combination of PAs and IMCs. In [16], a novel *distribution-based* weak bisimulation has been proposed: it is weaker than the state-based weak bisimulation in [31], and if restricted to continuous-time Markov chains, generates an equivalence established in the Petri net community [13]. Later, another weak bisimulation has been investigated in [8], which is essentially the same as [16]. In this paper, we propose a weaker bisimulation relation – late distribution bisimulation, which is coarser than both of them.

Interestingly, after the *distribution-based* weak bisimulations being introduced in [16], several *distribution-based* strong bisimulations have been proposed. In [22], it is shown that, the strong version of the relation in [16] coincides with the lifting of the classical state-based strong bisimulations. Recently, three different distribution-based strong bisimulations have been defined: paper [17] defines bisimulation relations and metrics which extend the well-known language equivalence [11] of labelled Markov chain; another definition in [24] applies to discrete systems as well as to systems with uncountable state and action spaces; in [32], for multi-agent systems, a decentralized strong bisimulation relation is proposed which is shown to be compositional with respect to partial information and distributed schedulers. All these relations enjoy some interesting properties, and they are incomparable to each other: we refer to [32] for a detailed discussion. The current paper extends the decentralized strong bisimulation in [32] to the weak case. The extension is not trivial, as internal transitions need to be handled carefully, particularly when lifting transition relations to distributions. We show that our novel weak bisimulation is weaker than that in [16], and as in [32], we show that it is compositional with respect to partial information and distributed schedulers.

Organization of the Paper Section 2 recalls some notations used in the paper. Late distribution bisimulation is proposed and discussed in Section 3, and its properties are established in Section 4 under realistic schedulers. Section 5 concludes the paper. A discussion why all results established in this paper directly carry over to Markov automata can be found in [12].

2 Preliminaries

Let S be a finite set of states ranged over by $r, s, \ldots$. A *distribution* is a function $\mu : S \to [0,1]$ satisfying $\mu(S) = \sum_{s \in S} \mu(s) = 1$. Let $Dist(S)$ to denote the set of all distributions, ranged over by $\mu, \nu, \gamma, \ldots$. Define $Supp(\mu) = \{s \mid \mu(s) > 0\}$ as the support set of μ. If $\mu(s) = 1$, then μ is called a *Dirac* distribution, written as δ_s. Let $|\mu| = \mu(S)$ denote the size of the distribution μ. Given a real number x, $x \cdot \mu$ is the distribution such that $(x \cdot \mu)(s) = x \cdot \mu(s)$ for each $s \in Supp(\mu)$ if $x \cdot |\mu| \leq 1$, while $\mu - s$ is the distribution such that $(\mu - s)(s) = 0$ and $(\mu - s)(r) = \mu(r)$ with $s \neq r$. Moreover, $\mu = \mu_1 + \mu_2$ whenever $\mu(s) = \mu_1(s) + \mu_2(s)$ for each $s \in S$ and $|\mu| \leq 1$. We often write $\{s : \mu(s) \mid s \in Supp(\mu)\}$ alternatively for a distribution μ. For instance, $\{s_1 : 0.4, s_2 : 0.6\}$ denotes a distribution μ such that $\mu(s_1) = 0.4$ and $\mu(s_2) = 0.6$.

2.1 Probabilistic Automata

Initially introduced in [31], *probabilistic automata* (PAs) have been popular models for systems with both non-deterministic choices and probabilistic dynamics. Below we give their formal definition.

Definition 1. *A PA $\mathcal{P}$ is a tuple $(S, Act_\tau, \to, \bar{s})$ where*

- *S is a finite set of states,*
- *$Act_\tau = Act \,\dot{\cup}\, \{\tau\}$ is a set of actions including the internal action τ,*
- *$\to \subset S \times Act_\tau \times Dist(S)$ is a finite set of probabilistic transitions, and*
- *$\bar{s} \in S$ is the initial state.*

Let $\alpha, \beta, \gamma, \ldots$ range over the actions in Act_τ. We write $s \xrightarrow{\alpha} \mu$ if $(s, \alpha, \mu) \in \to$. A *path* is a finite or infinite alternative sequence $\pi = s_0, \alpha_0, s_1, \alpha_1, s_2 \ldots$ of states and actions, such that for each $i \geq 0$ there exists a distribution μ with $s_i \xrightarrow{\alpha_i} \mu$ and $\mu(s_{i+1}) > 0$. Some notations are defined as follows: $|\pi|$ denotes the length of π, i.e., the number of states on π, while $\pi\downarrow$ is the last state of π, provided π is finite; $\pi[i] = s_i$ with $i \geq 0$ is the $(i+1)$-th state on π if it exists; $\pi[0..i] = s_0, \alpha_0, s_1, \alpha_1, \ldots, s_i$ is the prefix of π ending at state $\pi[i]$.

Let $Paths^\omega(\mathcal{P}) \subseteq S \times (Act_\tau \times S)^\omega$ and $Paths^*(\mathcal{P}) \subseteq S \times (Act_\tau \times S)^*$ denote the sets containing all infinite and finite paths of $\mathcal{P}$ respectively. Let $Paths(\mathcal{P}) = Paths^\omega(\mathcal{P}) \cup Paths^*(\mathcal{P})$. We will omit $\mathcal{P}$ if it is clear from the context. We also let $Paths(s)$ be the set containing all paths starting from $s \in S$, similarly for $Paths^*(s)$ and $Paths^\omega(s)$.

Due to non-deterministic choices in PAs, a probability measure cannot be defined directly. As usual, we shall introduce the definition of *schedulers* to resolve the non-determinism. Intuitively, a scheduler will decide which transition to choose at each step, based on the history execution. Formally,

Definition 2. *A scheduler is a function*

$$\xi : Paths^* \mapsto Dist(Act_\tau \times Dist(S))$$

such that $\xi(\pi)(\alpha,\mu) > 0$ *implies* $\pi\downarrow \xrightarrow{\alpha} \mu$. *A scheduler* ξ *is* deterministic *if it returns only Dirac distributions, that is,* $\xi(\pi)(\alpha,\mu) = 1$ *for some* α *and* μ. ξ *is* memoryless *if* $\pi\downarrow = \pi'\downarrow$ *implies* $\xi(\pi) = \xi(\pi')$ *for any* $\pi, \pi' \in Paths^*$, *namely, the decision of* ξ *only depends on the last state of a path.*

In this paper, we are restricted to schedulers satisfying the following condition: For any $\pi \in Paths^*$, $\xi(\pi)(\alpha,\mu) > 0$ and $\xi(\pi)(\beta,\nu) > 0$ imply $\alpha = \beta$. In other words, ξ always chooses transitions with the same label at each step. This class of schedulers suffices for our purpose.

Let $\pi \leq \pi'$ iff π is a prefix of π'. Let C_π denote the *cone* of a finite path π, which is the set of infinite paths having π as their prefix, i.e.,

$$C_\pi = \{\pi' \in Paths^\omega \mid \pi \leq \pi'\}.$$

Given a starting state s, a scheduler ξ, and a finite path $\pi = s_0, \alpha_0, s_1, \alpha_1, \ldots, s_k$, the measure $Pr_{\xi,s}$ of a cone C_π is defined inductively as:

- $Pr_{\xi,s}(C_\pi) = 0$ if $s \neq s_0$;
- $Pr_{\xi,s}(C_\pi) = 1$ if $s = s_0$ and $k = 0$;
- otherwise $Pr_{\xi,s}(C_\pi) =$

$$Pr_{\xi,s}(C_{\pi[0..k-1]}) \cdot \left(\sum_{(s_{k-1},\alpha_{k-1},\mu)\in\rightarrow} \xi(\pi[0..k-1])(\alpha_{k-1},\mu)\cdot\mu(s_k) \right).$$

Let $\mathcal{B}$ be the smallest algebra that contains all the cones and is closed under complement and countable unions. By standard measure theory [20,28], this algebra is a σ-*algebra* and all its elements are measurable sets of paths. Moreover, $Pr_{\pi,s}$ can be extended to a unique measure on $\mathcal{B}$.

Large systems are usually built from small components. This is done by using the parallel operator of PAs [31].

Definition 3. *Let* $\mathcal{P}_1 = (S_1, Act_\tau, \rightarrow_1, \bar{s}_1)$ *and* $\mathcal{P}_2 = (S_2, Act_\tau, \rightarrow_2, \bar{s}_2)$ *be two* PA*s and* $A \subseteq Act$, *then* $\mathcal{P}_1 \parallel_A \mathcal{P}_2 = (S, Act_\tau, \rightarrow, \bar{s})$ *such that*

- $S = \{s_1 \parallel_A s_2 \mid (s_1,s_2) \in S_1 \times S_2\}$,
- $s_1 \parallel_A s_2 \xrightarrow{\alpha} \mu_1 \parallel_A \mu_2$ *iff*
  - *either* $\alpha \in A$ *and* $\forall i \in \{1,2\}.s_i \xrightarrow{\alpha}_i \mu_i$,
  - *or* $\alpha \notin A$ *and* $\exists i \in \{1,2\}.(s_i \xrightarrow{\alpha}_i \mu_i$ *and* $\mu_{3-i} = \delta_{s_{3-i}})$.
- $\bar{s} = \bar{s}_1 \parallel_A \bar{s}_2$,

where $\mu_1 \parallel_A \mu_2$ *is a distribution such that* $(\mu_1 \parallel_A \mu_2)(s_1 \parallel_A s_2) = \mu_1(s_1)\cdot\mu_2(s_2)$.

2.2 Trace Distribution Equivalence

In this subsection we introduce the notion of trace distribution equivalence [30] adapted to our setting with internal actions. Let $\varsigma \in Act^*$ denote a finite trace of a PA $\mathcal{P}$, which is an ordered sequence of visible actions. Each trace ς induces a cylinder C_ς which is defined as follows:

$$C_\varsigma = \cup\{C_\pi \mid \pi \in Paths^* \wedge trace(\pi) = \varsigma\}$$

where $trace(\pi) = \epsilon$ denotes an empty trace if $|\pi| \leq 1$, and

$$trace(\pi) = \begin{cases} trace(\pi') & \pi = \pi' \circ (\tau, s') \\ trace(\pi')\alpha & \pi = \pi' \circ (\alpha, s') \wedge \alpha \neq \tau \end{cases}.$$

Since C_ς is a countable set of cylinders, it is measurable. Below we define *trace distribution equivalences*, each of which is parametrized by a certain class of schedulers.

Definition 4. *Let s_1 and s_2 be two states of a* PA*, and $\mathcal{S}$ a set of schedulers. Then, $s_1 \equiv_{\mathcal{S}} s_2$ iff for each scheduler $\xi_1 \in \mathcal{S}$ there exists a scheduler $\xi_2 \in \mathcal{S}$, such that $Pr^{\xi_1}_{s_1}(C_\varsigma) = Pr^{\xi_2}_{s_2}(C_\varsigma)$ for each finite trace ς and vice versa. If $\mathcal{S}$ is the set of all schedulers, we simply write $\equiv$.*

Different from [30,32], we abstract internal transitions when defining traces of a path. Therefore, the definition above is also a weaker version of the corresponding definition in [30,32].

2.3 Partial Information and Distributed Schedulers

In this subsection we define two prominent sub-classes of schedulers, where the power of schedulers are limited. We first introduce some notations. Let $EA : S \mapsto 2^{Act}$ such that

$$EA(s) = \{\alpha \in Act \mid \exists \mu . s \stackrel{\alpha}{\Longrightarrow} \mu\},$$

that is, the function EA returns the set of visible actions that a state is able to perform, possibly after some internal transitions. We generalize this function to paths as follows: $EA(\pi) =$

$$\begin{cases} EA(s) & \pi = s & (1) \\ EA(\pi') & \pi = \pi' \circ (\tau, s) \wedge EA(\pi'\downarrow) = EA(s) & (2) \\ EA(\pi')\alpha EA(s) & \pi = \pi' \circ (\alpha, s) \wedge (\alpha \neq \tau \vee EA(\pi'\downarrow) \neq EA(s)) & (3) \end{cases}$$

where case (2) takes care of a special situation such that internal actions do not change enabled actions. In this case EA will not see the difference. Intuitively, $EA(\pi)$ abstracts concrete states on π to their corresponding enabled actions. Whenever an invisible action does not change the enabled actions, this will simply be omitted. In other words, $EA(s)$ can be seen as the interface of s, which is observable by other components. Other components can observe the execution of s, as long as either it performs a visible action $\alpha \neq \tau$, or its interface has been changed ($EA(\pi'\downarrow) \neq EA(s)$). We are now ready to define the *partial information schedulers* [7] as follows:

Definition 5. *A scheduler ξ is a partial information scheduler of s if for any $\pi_1, \pi_2 \in Paths^*(s)$, $EA(\pi_1) = EA(\pi_2)$ implies:*

- *either $\xi(\pi_1) = (\tau, \mu)$ or $\xi(\pi_2) = (\tau, \mu)$ for some μ,*
- *or $\xi(\pi_1) = (\alpha, \mu)$ and $\xi(\pi_2) = (\alpha, \nu)$ for some μ, ν such that $\alpha \neq \tau$.*

ξ is a partial information scheduler of a PA *$\mathcal{P}$ iff it is a partial information scheduler for every state of $\mathcal{P}$.*

We denote the set of all partial information schedulers by $\mathcal{S}_P$. Intuitively a partial information scheduler can only distinguish states via different enabled visible actions. A scheduler cannot choose different transitions of states only because they have different state identities. This fits very well to a behavior-oriented rather than state-oriented view, as it is typical for process calculi. Consequently, for two different paths π_1 and π_2 with $EA(\pi_1) = EA(\pi_2)$, a partial information scheduler either chooses a transition labelled with τ action for π_i $(i = 1, 2)$, or it chooses transitions labelled with the same visible actions for both π_1 and π_2. Partial information schedulers do not impose any restriction on the execution of τ transitions, instead they can be performed spontaneously.

When composing parallel systems, general schedulers defined in Definition 2 allow one component to make decisions based on full information of other components. This may be unrealistically powerful as argued in [18]. To deal with this, another important sub-class of schedulers called *distributed schedulers* has been introduced [18]. The main idea is to assume that all parallel components run in autonomous and can only make their local scheduling decisions in isolation. In other words, each component can use only that information about other components that has been conveyed to it beforehand. We omit the formal definition of distributed schedulers, which can be found in [18] or [32]. In the sequel we let $\mathcal{S}_D$ denote the set of all distributed schedulers.

3 Weak Bisimilarities for Probabilistic Automata

In this section, we first introduce weak distribution bisimulation, which is a variant of weak bisimulation defined in [8], and then define late distribution bisimulation, which is strictly coarser than weak distribution bisimulation.

3.1 Weak Distribution Bisimulation

As usual, a standard weak transition relation is needed in the definitions of bisimulation that allows one to abstract internal actions. Intuitively, $s \stackrel{\alpha}{\Longrightarrow} \mu$ denotes that a distribution μ is reached from s by a α-transition, which may be preceded and followed by an arbitrary sequence of internal transitions. Formally, we define them as derivations [9] for PAs. In the following, let $\mu \xrightarrow{\alpha} \mu'$ iff there exists a transition $s \xrightarrow{\alpha} \mu_s$ for each $s \in \mathit{Supp}(\mu)$ such that $\mu' = \sum_{s\in \mathit{Supp}(\mu)} \mu(s) \cdot \mu_s$. Then, $s \stackrel{\tau}{\Longrightarrow} \mu$ iff there exists

$$\begin{aligned} \delta_s &= \mu_0^{\rightarrow} + \mu_0^{\times}, \\ \mu_0^{\rightarrow} &\xrightarrow{\tau} \mu_1^{\rightarrow} + \mu_1^{\times}, \\ \mu_1^{\rightarrow} &\xrightarrow{\tau} \mu_2^{\rightarrow} + \mu_2^{\times}, \\ &\dots \end{aligned}$$

where $\mu = \sum_{i\geq 0} \mu_i^{\times}$. We write $s \stackrel{\alpha}{\Longrightarrow} \mu$ iff there exists $s \stackrel{\tau}{\Longrightarrow}\xrightarrow{\alpha}\stackrel{\tau}{\Longrightarrow} \mu$.

Given a transition relation $\rightsquigarrow \subseteq S \times \mathit{Act}_\tau \times \mathit{Dist}(S)$, we let $s \stackrel{\alpha}{\rightsquigarrow}_c \mu$ iff there exists a finite number of real numbers $w_i > 0$, and transitions $s \stackrel{\alpha}{\rightsquigarrow} \mu_i$ such that $\sum_i w_i = 1$, and $\sum_i w_i \cdot \mu_i = \mu$. We call $\rightsquigarrow_c$ *combined transitions* (of $\rightsquigarrow$). In general, we lift a transition relation $\rightsquigarrow \subseteq S \times \mathit{Act}_\tau \times \mathit{Dist}(S)$ over states to a transition relation $\mathit{Dist}(S) \times \mathit{Act}_\tau \times \mathit{Dist}(S)$ over distributions by letting $\mu \stackrel{\alpha}{\rightsquigarrow} \mu'$ iff there exists a transition $s \stackrel{\alpha}{\rightsquigarrow} \mu_s$ for each $s \in \mathit{Supp}(\mu)$ such that $\mu' = \sum_{s\in \mathit{Supp}(\mu)} \mu(s) \cdot \mu_s$.

Definition 6. *$\mathcal{R} \subseteq \mathit{Dist}(S) \times \mathit{Dist}(S)$ is a* weak distribution bisimulation *iff $\mu \mathrel{\mathcal{R}} \nu$ implies:*

1. *whenever $\mu \xrightarrow{\alpha}_c \mu'$, there exists a $\nu \stackrel{\alpha}{\Longrightarrow}_c \nu'$ such that $\mu' \mathrel{\mathcal{R}} \nu'$;*
2. *whenever $\mu = \sum_{0\leq i\leq n} p_i \cdot \mu_i$, there exists a $\nu \stackrel{\tau}{\Longrightarrow}_c \sum_{0\leq i\leq n} p_i \cdot \nu_i$ such that $\mu_i \mathrel{\mathcal{R}} \nu_i$ for each $0 \leq i \leq n$ where $\sum_{0\leq i\leq n} p_i = 1$;*
3. *symmetrically for ν.*

We say that μ and ν are weak distribution bisimilar, written as $\mu \mathrel{\bullet\!\!\approx} \nu$, iff there exists a weak distribution bisimulation $\mathcal{R}$ such that $\mu \mathrel{\mathcal{R}} \nu$. Moreover $s \mathrel{\bullet\!\!\approx} r$ iff $\delta_s \mathrel{\bullet\!\!\approx} \delta_r$.

Clause 1 is standard. Clause 2 says that no matter how we split μ, there always exists a splitting of ν probably after internal transitions to simulate the splitting of μ. Definition 6 is slightly different from Definition 5 in [8], where clause 2 is missing and clause 1 is replaced by: whenever $\mu \stackrel{\alpha}{\Longrightarrow}_c \sum_{0\leq i\leq n} p_i \cdot \mu_i$, there exists $\nu \stackrel{\alpha}{\Longrightarrow}_c \sum_{0\leq i\leq n} p_i \cdot \nu_i$ such that $\mu_i \mathrel{\mathcal{R}} \nu_i$ for each $0 \leq i \leq n$. Essentially, this condition subsumes clause 2, since $\mu = \sum_{0\leq i\leq n} p_i \cdot \mu_i$ implies $\mu \stackrel{\tau}{\Longrightarrow}_c \sum_{0\leq i\leq n} p_i \cdot \mu_i$. As we prove in the following lemma, both definitions induce the same equivalence relation on PAs.

Lemma 1. *Let $\mathcal{P} = (S, \mathit{Act}_\tau, \rightarrow, \bar{s})$ be a* PA. *$\mathcal{R} \subseteq \mathit{Dist}(S) \times \mathit{Dist}(S)$ is a* weak distribution bisimulation *iff $\mu \mathrel{\mathcal{R}} \nu$ implies that*

1. *whenever $\mu \stackrel{\alpha}{\Longrightarrow}_c \mu'$, there exists $\nu \stackrel{\alpha}{\Longrightarrow}_c \nu'$ such that $\mu' \mathrel{\mathcal{R}} \nu'$,*
2. *whenever $\mu = \sum_{0\leq i\leq n} p_i \cdot \mu_i$, there exists $\nu \stackrel{\tau}{\Longrightarrow}_c \sum_{0\leq i\leq n} p_i \cdot \nu_i$ such that $\mu_i \mathrel{\mathcal{R}} \nu_i$ for each $0 \leq i \leq n$ where $\sum_{0\leq i\leq n} p_i = 1$,*
3. *symmetrically for ν.*

Proof. Let $\mathcal{R} \subseteq Dist(S) \times Dist(S)$. If $\mathcal{R}$ is a weak distribution bisimulation by Lemma 1, then trivially we can show that $\mathcal{R}$ is also a weak distribution bisimulation by Definition 6, since $\rightarrow_{\mathrm{c}} \;\subset\; \Longrightarrow_{\mathrm{c}}$. In the sequel, we let $\mathcal{R}$ be a weak distribution bisimulation by Definition 6 and we show that $\mathcal{R}$ also satisfies conditions of Lemma 1. Let $\mu\ \mathcal{R}\ \nu$. It suffices to show that whenever $\mu \stackrel{\alpha}{\Longrightarrow}_{\mathrm{c}} \mu'$, there exists a $\nu \stackrel{\alpha}{\Longrightarrow}_{\mathrm{c}} \nu'$ such that $\mu'\ \mathcal{R}\ \nu'$,

Assume $\alpha = \tau$. According to the definition of derivations (P. 255), $\mu \stackrel{\tau}{\Longrightarrow}_{\mathrm{c}} \mu'$ iff there exists

$$\begin{aligned} \mu &= \mu_0^{\rightarrow} + \mu_0^{\times}, \\ \mu_0^{\rightarrow} &\stackrel{\tau}{\rightarrow}_{\mathrm{c}} \mu_1^{\rightarrow} + \mu_1^{\times}, \\ \mu_1^{\rightarrow} &\stackrel{\tau}{\rightarrow}_{\mathrm{c}} \mu_2^{\rightarrow} + \mu_2^{\times}, \\ &\vdots \end{aligned} \tag{4}$$

such that $\mu' \equiv \sum_{i \geq 0} \mu_i^{\times}$. By Definition 6, ν can simulate such a derivation at each step, namely, there exists

$$\begin{aligned} \nu &\stackrel{\tau}{\Longrightarrow}_{\mathrm{c}} \nu_0^{\rightarrow} + \nu_0^{\times}, \\ \nu_0^{\rightarrow} &\stackrel{\tau}{\Longrightarrow}_{\mathrm{c}} \nu_1^{\rightarrow} + \nu_1^{\times}, \\ \nu_1^{\rightarrow} &\stackrel{\tau}{\Longrightarrow}_{\mathrm{c}} \nu_2^{\rightarrow} + \nu_2^{\times}, \\ &\vdots \end{aligned} \tag{5}$$

such that $\mu_i^{\rightarrow}\ \mathcal{R}\ \nu_i^{\rightarrow}$ and $\mu_i^{\times}\ \mathcal{R}\ \nu_i^{\times}$ for each $i \geq 0$. Note $\mathcal{R}$ satisfies *infinite linearity*, which can be proved in a similar way as [8, Thm. A.6]. Therefore, $(\sum_{i \geq 0} \mu_i^{\times})\ \mathcal{R}\ (\sum_{i \geq 0} \nu_i^{\times})$. Since $\Longrightarrow_{\mathrm{c}}$ is transitive [8, Thm. A.4], there exists $\nu \stackrel{\tau}{\Longrightarrow}_{\mathrm{c}} \nu'$ such that $\mu'\ \mathcal{R}\ \nu'$ as desired.

In case $\mu \stackrel{\alpha}{\Longrightarrow}_{\mathrm{c}} \mu'$ with $\alpha \neq \tau$, we have $\mu \stackrel{\tau}{\Longrightarrow}_{\mathrm{c}} \mu_1' \stackrel{\alpha}{\rightarrow}_{\mathrm{c}} \mu_2' \stackrel{\tau}{\Longrightarrow}_{\mathrm{c}} \mu'$. As shown above, there exists $\nu \stackrel{\tau}{\Longrightarrow}_{\mathrm{c}} \nu_1'$ such that $\mu_1'\ \mathcal{R}\ \nu_1'$, which indicates that there exists $\nu_1' \stackrel{\alpha}{\Longrightarrow}_{\mathrm{c}} \nu_2'$ such that $\mu_2'\ \mathcal{R}\ \nu_2'$ by Definition 6, which indicates that there exists $\nu_2' \stackrel{\tau}{\Longrightarrow}_{\mathrm{c}} \nu'$ such that $\mu'\ \mathcal{R}\ \nu'$. This completes the proof. □

The above lemma implies the transitivity of the weak distribution bisimulation, and will be useful for establishing different bisimulation relations.

3.2 Late Weak Bisimulation

Clause 2 in Definition 6 allows arbitrary splittings, which is essentially the main reason that weak distribution bisimulation is unrealistically strong. In order to establish a bisimulation relation, all possible splittings of μ must be matched by ν (possibly after some internal transitions). As splittings into Dirac distributions are also considered, the individual behaviors of each single state in $Supp(\mu)$ must be matched too. However, our bisimulation is distribution-based, thus the behaviors of distributions should be matched rather than those of states. We will fix this in the definition of late distribution bisimulation. Before that, we still need some notations.

Definition 7. *A distribution μ is* transition consistent, *written as $\overrightarrow{\mu}$, if for any $s \in Supp(\mu)$ and $\alpha \neq \tau$, $s \stackrel{\alpha}{\Longrightarrow} \gamma$ for some γ implies $\mu \stackrel{\alpha}{\Longrightarrow} \gamma'$ for some γ'.*

For a distribution being transition consistent, all states in the support of the distribution should have the same set of enabled visible actions. One of the key properties of transition consistent distributions is that $\mu \stackrel{\alpha}{\Longrightarrow}$ whenever $s \stackrel{\alpha}{\Longrightarrow}$ for some state $s \in Supp(\mu)$. In contrast, when a distribution μ is not transition consistent, there must be a weak α transition of some state in $Supp(\mu)$ being *blocked.* In the sequel, when we adopt the notion of blocked states accordingly for non-weak transition relations, also τ transitions can be blocked.

We now introduce $\hookrightarrow$, an alternative lifting of transitions of states to transitions of distributions that differs from the standard definition used in [16,8]. There, a distribution is able to perform a transition labelled with α *if and only if* all the states in its support can perform transitions with the very same label. In contrast, the transition relation $\hookrightarrow$ behaves like a weak transition, where every state in the support of μ may at most perform one transition.

Definition 8. $\mu \stackrel{\alpha}{\hookrightarrow} \mu'$ *iff*

1. *either for each $s \in Supp(\mu)$ there exists $s \stackrel{\alpha}{\rightarrow} \mu_s$ such that*

$$\mu' = \sum_{s \in Supp(\mu)} \mu(s) \cdot \mu_s,$$

2. *or $\alpha = \tau$ and there exists $s \in Supp(\mu)$ and $s \stackrel{\alpha}{\rightarrow} \mu_s$ such that*

$$\mu' = (\mu - s) + \mu(s) \cdot \mu_s.$$

In the definition of late distribution bisimulation, this extension will be used to prevent τ transitions of states from being blocked. Below follows an example:

Example 1. Let $\mu = \{s_1 : 0.4, s_2 : 0.6\}$ such that $s_1 \stackrel{\tau}{\rightarrow} \delta_{s_1'} \stackrel{\alpha}{\rightarrow} \mu_1$, $s_1 \stackrel{\beta}{\rightarrow} \mu_2$, $s_2 \stackrel{\alpha}{\rightarrow} \mu_3$, and $s_2 \stackrel{\beta}{\rightarrow} \mu_4$, where $\alpha \neq \beta$ are visible actions. According to clause 1 of Definition 8, we will have $\mu \stackrel{\beta}{\hookrightarrow} (0.4 \cdot \mu_2 + 0.6 \cdot \mu_4)$. Without clause 2, this would be the only transition of μ, since the τ transition of s_1 and the α transition of s_2 will be blocked by each other, as s_1 and s_2 cannot perform transitions with labels τ and α at the same time.

Note that the α transition is blocked by the τ transition of s_1, so according to clause 2 of Definition 8, we in addition have

$$\mu \stackrel{\tau}{\hookrightarrow} (0.4 \cdot \delta_{s_1'} + 0.6 \cdot \delta_{s_2}) \stackrel{\alpha}{\hookrightarrow} (0.4 \cdot \mu_1 + 0.6 \cdot \mu_3).$$

Note that in clause 1 of Definition 6, $\rightarrow$ can be replaced by $\hookrightarrow$ without changing the resulting equivalence relation, as the same effect can be obtained by a suitable splitting in clause 2. In this example, we could let μ be split into $0.4 \cdot \delta_{s_1} + 0.6 \cdot \delta_{s_2}$, such that no transition is blocked in the resulting distributions. □

Definition 9. *$\mathcal{R} \subseteq Dist(S) \times Dist(S)$ is a* late distribution bisimulation *iff $\mu \mathcal{R} \nu$ implies:*

1. *whenever $\mu \overset{\alpha}{\hookrightarrow}_c \mu'$, there exists a $\nu \overset{\alpha}{\Longrightarrow}_c \nu'$ such that $\mu' \mathcal{R} \nu'$;*
2. *if not $\overrightarrow{\mu}$, then there exists $\mu = \sum_{0 \leq i \leq n} p_i \cdot \mu_i$ and $\nu \overset{\tau}{\Longrightarrow}_c \sum_{0 \leq i \leq n} p_i \cdot \nu_i$ such that $\overrightarrow{\mu_i}$ and $\mu_i \mathcal{R} \nu_i$ for each $0 \leq i \leq n$ where $\sum_{0 \leq i \leq n} p_i = 1$;*
3. *symmetrically for ν.*

We say that μ and ν are late distribution bisimilar, written as $\mu \approx^{\bullet} \nu$, iff there exists a late distribution bisimulation $\mathcal{R}$ such that $\mu \mathcal{R} \nu$. Moreover $s \approx^{\bullet} r$ iff $\delta_s \approx^{\bullet} \delta_r$.

In clause 1, this definition differs from Definition 6 by the use of $\hookrightarrow$. It is straightforward to show that $\hookrightarrow$ can also be used in Definition 6 without changing the resulting bisimilarity. However, in Definition 9, using $\rightarrow$ instead of $\hookrightarrow$ will lead to a finer relation. The key difference between Definition 6 and 9, however, is clause 2. As we mentioned, in Definition 6, any split of μ should be matched by ν, while in Definition 9, we require to split μ only if it is not transition consistent. Additionally, the resulting distributions μ_i must be transition consistent as well. We do not need to require that ν_i is transition consistent, as we will show later that $\overrightarrow{\mu_i}$ and $\mu_i \mathcal{R} \nu_i$ implies $\overrightarrow{\nu_i}$. According to Definition 7, splittings to transition consistent distributions ensure that all possible transitions will be considered eventually, as no transition of individual states is blocked. Therefore, clause 1 suffices to capture every visible behavior.

By introducing transition consistent distributions, we try to group states with the same set of enabled visible actions together and do not distinguish them in a distribution. This idea is mainly motivated by the work in [7], where all states with the same enabled actions are non-distinguishable from the outside. Under this assumption, a model checking algorithm was proposed. By avoiding splitting transition consistent distributions, we essentially delay the probabilistic transitions until the transition consistent condition is broken. This explains the name "late distribution bisimulation". Further, if restricting to models without internal action τ, our notion of late distribution bisimulate agrees with the decentralized bisimulations in [32].

The following theorem shows that $\approx^{\bullet}$ is an equivalence relation and $\approx^{\bullet}$ is strictly coarser than ${}^{\bullet}\!\approx$.

Theorem 1.

1. *$\approx^{\bullet}$ is an equivalence relation;*
2. *${}^{\bullet}\!\approx \ \subset \ \approx^{\bullet}$.*

Before proving Theorem 1, we shall introduce two lemmas. The lemma below resembles Lemma 1, which can be proved similarly as Lemma 1.

Lemma 2. *Let $\mathcal{P} = (S, Act_{\tau}, \rightarrow, \bar{s})$ be a* PA. *$\mathcal{R} \subseteq Dist(S) \times Dist(S)$ is a* weak distribution bisimulation *iff $\mu \mathcal{R} \nu$ implies that*

1. *whenever $\mu \overset{\alpha}{\Longrightarrow}_c \mu'$, there exists $\nu \overset{\alpha}{\Longrightarrow}_c \nu'$ such that $\mu' \mathcal{R} \nu'$,*

2. *if not* $\overrightarrow{\mu}$, *then there exists* $\mu = \sum_{0\leq i\leq n} p_i \cdot \mu_i$ *and* $\nu \stackrel{\tau}{\Longrightarrow}_c \sum_{0\leq i\leq n} p_i \cdot \nu_i$ *such that* $\overrightarrow{\mu_i}$ *and* $\mu_i \mathrel{\mathcal{R}} \nu_i$ *for each* $0 \leq i \leq n$ *where* $\sum_{0\leq i\leq n} p_i = 1$;
3. *symmetrically for* ν.

Proof. The proof is almost the same as Lemma 1 with two exceptions related to the transition consistent requirement:

- In Eq. 4 and 5, derivations should respect the transition consistent requirement, namely, states with the same set of enable actions should be in the support of either $\mu_i^{\rightarrow}$ or $\mu_i^{\times}$, similarly for $\nu_i^{\rightarrow}$ and $\nu_i^{\times}$.
- The infinite linearity of late distribution bisimulation can be proved as follows: Let

$$\mathcal{R} = \{(\sum_{i\geq 0} p_i \cdot \mu_i, \sum_{i\geq 0} p_i \cdot \nu_i) \mid \sum_{i\geq 0} p_i = 1 \wedge \forall i \geq 0. \mu_i \approx^{\bullet} \nu_i\}.$$

  We prove that $\mathcal{R}$ is a late distribution bisimulation. Let $\mu \mathrel{\mathcal{R}} \nu$. Suppose $\mu \xrightarrow{\alpha}_c \mu'$, then for all $i \geq 0$, there exists $\mu_i \xrightarrow{\alpha}_c \mu'_i$ such that $\mu' \equiv \sum_{i\geq 0} p_i \cdot \mu'_i$. Since $\mu_i \approx^{\bullet} \nu_i$, there exists $\nu_i \stackrel{\alpha}{\Longrightarrow}_c \nu'_i$ such that $\mu'_i \approx^{\bullet} \nu'_i$, which implies that $\nu \stackrel{\alpha}{\Longrightarrow}_c \nu' \equiv \sum_{i\geq 0} p_i \cdot \nu'_i$. Therefore, $\mu' \mathrel{\mathcal{R}} \nu'$ by the definition of $\mathcal{R}$. Now assume μ is not transition consistent and $\mu \equiv \sum_{1\leq j\leq n} q_j \cdot \gamma_j$ such that $\overrightarrow{\gamma_j}$. Let $\mu_i \equiv \sum_{1\leq j\leq n} q_j^i \cdot \gamma_j^i$ where $\overrightarrow{\gamma_j^i}$, $\gamma_j = \sum_{i\geq 0} q_j^i \cdot \gamma_j^i$, and $\sum_{i\geq 0} q_j^i = q_j$ for each $1 \leq j \leq n$. Then for each $i \geq 0$, there exists $\nu_i \stackrel{\tau}{\Longrightarrow}_c \sum_{1\leq j\leq n} q_j^i \cdot \gamma'^i_j$ such that $\overrightarrow{\gamma'^i_j}$ and $\gamma_j^i \approx^{\bullet} \gamma'^i_j$. Therefore, there exists $\nu \stackrel{\tau}{\Longrightarrow}_c \sum_{1\leq j\leq n} q_j \cdot \gamma'_j$, where $\gamma'_j \equiv \sum_{i\geq 0} q_j^i \cdot \gamma'^i_j$. By construction of $\mathcal{R}$, $\gamma_j \mathrel{\mathcal{R}} \gamma'_j$ for each $1 \leq j \leq n$ as desired.

□

The following lemma states that μ and ν must be transition consistent or not at the same time, if they are late distribution bisimilar.

Lemma 3. $\mu \approx^{\bullet} \nu$ *and* $\overrightarrow{\mu}$ *imply* $\overrightarrow{\nu}$.

Proof. By contraposition. Assume $\mu \approx^{\bullet} \nu$ and $\overrightarrow{\mu}$, but not $\overrightarrow{\nu}$. Since $\mu \approx^{\bullet} \nu$, there exists a late distribution bisimulation $\mathcal{R}$ such that $\mu \mathrel{\mathcal{R}} \nu$. Moreover, $\mu \stackrel{\alpha}{\Longrightarrow}$ implies $\nu \stackrel{\alpha}{\Longrightarrow}$ and vice versa for any α. Therefore, $EA(\mu) = EA(\nu)$, where $EA(\mu) = \{\alpha \mid \exists \mu'.\mu \stackrel{\alpha}{\Longrightarrow} \mu'\}$, similarly for $EA(\nu)$. Since ν is not transition consistent, there exists $s \in Supp(\nu)$ such that $s \stackrel{\alpha}{\Longrightarrow}$ with $\alpha \notin EA(\nu)$, i.e., some transitions of states in $Supp(\mu)$ with label α are blocked. This indicates that there exists $\nu = \sum_{i\in I} p_i \cdot \nu_i$ with $\overrightarrow{\nu_i}$ for each $i \in I$ such that $\nu_j \stackrel{\alpha}{\Longrightarrow}$ for some $j \in I$. Since $\overrightarrow{\mu}$ and $\alpha \notin EA(\mu)$, there does not exist $\mu \stackrel{\tau}{\Longrightarrow} \sum_{i\in I} p_i \cdot \mu_i$ such that $\mu_i \stackrel{\alpha}{\Longrightarrow}$ for some $i \in I$. This contradicts the assumption that $\mu \approx^{\bullet} \nu$. □

Finally, we are ready to show the proof of Theorem 1.

Proof of Theorem 1. First, the second clause $^\bullet\!\approx \;\subset\; \approx^\bullet$ is easy to establish: Since the second condition of Definition 6 implies the second condition of Definition 9, but not vice versa. PA in Fig. 1 shows that the inclusion is strict.

Now we prove that $\approx^\bullet$ is an equivalence relation. We prove transitivity (other parts are easy). For any μ, ν, and γ, assume $\mu \approx^\bullet \nu$ and $\nu \approx^\bullet \gamma$, we prove that $\mu \approx^\bullet \gamma$. According to Definition 9, there exists late distribution bisimulations $\mathcal{R}_1$ and $\mathcal{R}_2$ such that $\mu\ \mathcal{R}_1\ \nu$ and $\nu\ \mathcal{R}_2\ \gamma$. Let

$$\mathcal{R} = \mathcal{R}_1 \circ \mathcal{R}_2 = \{(\mu, \gamma) \mid \exists \nu.(\mu\ \mathcal{R}_1\ \nu \wedge \nu\ \mathcal{R}_2\ \gamma)\},$$

it then suffices to prove that $\mathcal{R}$ is also a late distribution bisimulation.

Let $\mu\ \mathcal{R}\ \gamma$ such that $\mu\ \mathcal{R}_1\ \nu$ and $\nu\ \mathcal{R}_2\ \gamma$ for some ν. We shall prove:

1. Whenever $\mu \stackrel{\alpha}{\Longrightarrow}_{\mathrm{c}} \mu'$, there exists $\gamma \stackrel{\alpha}{\Longrightarrow}_{\mathrm{c}} \gamma'$ such that $\mu'\ \mathcal{R}\ \gamma'$. This is achieved by applying Lemma 3.
2. If not $\overrightarrow{\mu}$, there exists $\mu = \sum_{i \in I} p_i \cdot \mu_i$ and $\gamma \stackrel{\tau}{\Longrightarrow}_{\mathrm{c}} \sum_{i \in I} p_i \cdot \gamma_i$ such that $\mu_i\ \mathcal{R}\ \gamma_i$ for each $i \in I$, where $\sum_{i \in I} p_i = 1$. Assume μ is not transition consistent; otherwise it is easy. Since $\mu \approx^\bullet \nu$, there exists $\nu \stackrel{\tau}{\Longrightarrow}_{\mathrm{c}} \sum_{i \in I} p_i \cdot \nu_i$ such that $\overrightarrow{\mu_i}$ and $\mu_i\ \mathcal{R}_1\ \nu_i$ for each $i \in I$. By Lemma 3, $\overrightarrow{\nu_i}$ for each $i \in I$. We distinguish the following two cases:
   (a) $\nu = \sum_{i \in I} p_i \cdot \nu_i$.
   According to Lemma 3, ν is not transition consistent, and moreover, we have $\overrightarrow{\nu_i}$ for each $i \in I$. Since $\nu\ \mathcal{R}_2\ \gamma$, there exists $\gamma \stackrel{\tau}{\Longrightarrow}_{\mathrm{c}} \sum_{i \in I} \gamma_i$ such that $\nu_i\ \mathcal{R}_2\ \gamma_i$, thus we have $\mu_i\ \mathcal{R}\ \gamma_i$ by the definition of $\mathcal{R}$ for each $i \in I$.
   (b) $\nu \stackrel{\tau}{\Longrightarrow}_{\mathrm{c}} \nu' = \sum_{i \in I} p_i \cdot \nu_i$.
   Since $\nu\ \mathcal{R}_2\ \gamma$, there exists $\gamma \stackrel{\tau}{\Longrightarrow}_{\mathrm{c}} \gamma'$ such that $\nu'\ \mathcal{R}_2\ \gamma'$ according to the first clause of Definition 9. Since μ is not transition consistent, so there exists $i, j \in I$ such that $i \neq j$ and $EA(\mu_i) \neq EA(\mu_j)$, which indicates that $EA(\nu_i) \neq EA(\nu_j)$. Therefore, ν' is not transition consistent. As a result there exists $\gamma' \stackrel{\tau}{\Longrightarrow}_{\mathrm{c}} \sum_{i \in I} p_i \cdot \gamma_i$ such that $\nu_i\ \mathcal{R}_2\ \gamma_i$, thus $\mu_i\ \mathcal{R}\ \gamma_i$ for each $i \in I$.

This completes our proof. □

4 Properties of Late Distribution Bisimilarity

In this section we show that results established in [32] can be extended to the setting, where internal transitions are abstracted. We concentrate on two properties of late distribution bisimulation: compositionality and preservation of trace distributions. When general schedulers are considered, the two properties do not hold, hence we will restrict ourselves to partial information distributed schedulers. We mention that both partial information and distributed schedulers were proposed to rule out unrealistic behaviors of general schedulers; see [7] and [18] for more details.

We first define some notations. To play with schedulers, we parameterize transition relations with schedulers explicitly. A transition from s to μ with label α is induced by a scheduler ξ, written as $s \xrightarrow{\alpha}_{\xi} \mu$, iff $\mu \equiv \sum_{\mu' \in Dist(S)} \xi(s)(\alpha, \mu')\cdot\mu'$. As before, such a transition relation can be lifted to distributions: $\mu \xrightarrow{\alpha}_{\xi} \nu$ to denote that μ can evolve into ν by performing a transition with label α under the guidance of ξ, where $s \xrightarrow{\alpha}_{\xi} \nu_s$ for each $s \in Supp(\mu)$ and $\nu \equiv \sum_{s \in Supp(\mu)} \mu(s)\cdot\nu_s$. Since no a priori information is available, given a distribution μ, for each $s \in Supp(\mu)$, we simply use s as the history information for ξ to guide the execution, which correspond to *memoryless* schedulers and suffice for the purpose of defining bisimulations. Moreover, weak transitions $s \xRightarrow{\alpha}_{\xi} \mu$ and their lifting to distributions can be defined similarly; see Section 3.1.

Below we define an alternative definition of Definition 9, where schedulers are considered explicitly.

Definition 10. *Let $\xi_1, \xi_2, \xi \in \mathcal{S}$ for a given set of schedulers $\mathcal{S}$. $\mathcal{R} \subseteq Dist(S) \times Dist(S)$ is a late distribution bisimulation with respect to $\mathcal{S}$ iff $\mu\ \mathcal{R}\ \nu$ implies:*

1. *whenever $\mu \xrightarrow{\alpha}_{\xi_1} \mu'$, there exists $\nu \xRightarrow{\alpha}_{\xi_2} \nu'$ such that $\mu'\ \mathcal{R}\ \nu'$;*
2. *if not $\overrightarrow{\mu}$, then there exists $\mu = \sum_{0 \le i \le n} p_i\cdot\mu_i$ and $\nu \xRightarrow{\tau}_{\xi} \sum_{0 \le i \le n} p_i\cdot\nu_i$ such that $\overrightarrow{\mu_i}$ and $\mu_i\ \mathcal{R}\ \nu_i$ for each $0 \le i \le n$ where $\sum_{0 \le i \le n} p_i = 1$;*
3. *symmetrically for ν.*

We write $\mu \approx^{\bullet}_{\mathcal{S}} \nu$ iff there exists a late distribution bisimulation $\mathcal{R}$ with respect to $\mathcal{S}$ such that $\mu\ \mathcal{R}\ \nu$. And we write $s \approx^{\bullet}_{\mathcal{S}} r$ iff $\delta_s \approx^{\bullet}_{\mathcal{S}} \delta_r$.

Different from Definition 9, in Definition 10, every transition is induced by a scheduler in $\mathcal{S}$. Obviously, when $\mathcal{S}$ is the set of all schedulers, these two definitions coincide. Thus, $s_1 \approx^{\bullet} s_2 \Longleftrightarrow s_1 \approx^{\bullet}_{\mathcal{S}_D} s_2$, provided s_1 and s_2 contain no parallel operators, as in this case $\mathcal{S}_D$ represents the set of all schedulers.

Below is a theorem showing that distribution bisimulation and partial information schedulers are closely related. It shows that partial information schedulers are enough to discriminate late distribution bisimilarity with respect to arbitrary schedulers. Furthermore, late distribution bisimulation implies trace distribution equivalence under partial information schedulers.

Theorem 2. *For any states s_1 and s_2,*

1. *$s_1 \approx^{\bullet} s_2$ iff $s_1 \approx^{\bullet}_{\mathcal{S}_P} s_2$;*
2. *$s_1 \approx^{\bullet} s_2$ implies $s_1 \equiv_{\mathcal{S}_P} s_2$.*

If looking at the effect of parallel composition, we can establish compositionality if distributed schedulers are considered:

Theorem 3. *For any states s_1, s_2, and s_3,*

$$s_1 \approx^{\bullet}_{\mathcal{S}_D} s_2 \text{ implies } s_1 \parallel_A s_3 \approx^{\bullet}_{\mathcal{S}_D} s_2 \parallel_A s_3.$$

As in the strong setting [32], by restricting to the set of schedulers in $\mathcal{S}_P \cap \mathcal{S}_D$, late distribution bisimulation is compositional and preserves trace distribution equivalence. Furthermore, late distribution bisimulation is the coarsest congruence satisfying the two properties with respect to schedulers in $\mathcal{S}_P \cap \mathcal{S}_D$.

Theorem 4. *Let $\mathcal{S} = \mathcal{S}_P \cap \mathcal{S}_D$. $s_1 \approx^{\bullet}_{\mathcal{S}} s_2$ iff $s_1 \equiv^c_{\mathcal{S}} s_2$ for any s_1 and s_2, where $s_1 \equiv^c_{\mathcal{S}} s_2$ iff $s_1 \equiv_{\mathcal{S}} s_2$ and $s_1 \parallel_A s_3 \equiv_{\mathcal{S}} s_2 \parallel_A s_3$ for any s_1, s_2, s_3, and A.*

We mention that schedulers in $\mathcal{S}_P \cap \mathcal{S}_D$ arise very natural in practice, for instance in decentralized multiagent systems [3], where all agents are autonomous (corresponding to distributed schedulers) and states are partially observable (corresponding to partial information schedulers).

In [24] an algorithm was proposed to compute distribution-based bisimulation relations. We discuss briefly that the algorithm can also be adapted to compute late distribution bisimulation. First observe that the relation $\approx^{\bullet}$ is linear, namely, $\mu_1 \approx^{\bullet} \nu_1$ and $\mu_2 \approx^{\bullet} \nu_2$ imply $(p \cdot \mu_1 + (1-p) \cdot \mu_2) \approx^{\bullet} (p \cdot \nu_1 + (1-p) \cdot \nu_2)$ for any $p \in [0,1]$. By fixing an arbitrary order on the state space of a given PA, each distribution can be viewed as a vector in $[0,1]^n$ with n being the number of states. Then for any s and α, it is easy to see that $\{\mu \mid s \xrightarrow{\alpha} \mu\}$ constitutes a convex hull. According to [5, Prop. 3 and 4], every such convex hull has a finite number of extreme points, which can be enumerated by restricting to Dirac memoryless schedulers. For deciding $\approx^{\bullet}$, it suffices to restrict to these finitely many extreme distributions. By doing so, all weak transitions can be handled in the same way as non-deterministic strong transitions in [24]. Not surprisingly, this will cause an exponential blow-up. We refer readers to [24] for more details of the remaining procedure.

5 Conclusion and Future Work

In this paper, we proposed the notion of late distribution bisimilarity for PAs, which enjoys some interesting properties if restricted to the two well-known subclasses of schedulers: partial information schedulers and distributed schedulers. Under partial information schedulers, late distribution bisimulation implies trace distribution equivalence, while under distributed schedulers, compositionality can be derived. Furthermore, if restricted to partial information distributed schedulers, late distribution bisimulation has shown to be the coarsest relation which is compositional and preserves trace distribution equivalence.

As future work we intend to study reduction barbed congruences [8] under subclasses of schedulers, in order to pinpoint the characteristics of late distribution bisimilarity. The axiom system and logical characterization of $\approx^{\bullet}$ would be also interesting. The algorithm in [24] is exponential in the worst case. We will work out whether or not more efficient algorithms exist.

Acknowledgments. Many thanks to the anonymous referees for their valuable suggestions on an early version of this paper. This work has been supported by the DFG as part of the SFB/TR 14 "Automatic Verification and Analysis of Complex Systems" (AVACS), by the European Union Seventh Framework Programme under grant agreements 295261 (MEALS) and 318490 (SENSATION), by the National Natural Science Foundation of China (Grant Nos. 61428208, 61472473 and 61361136002), and by the CAS/SAFEA International Partnership Program for Creative Research Team. Part of this work was done while Lei

Song was at Max-Planck Institute for Informatics and Saarland University in Saarbrücken, Germany.

References

1. Baier, C., Katoen, J.-P., Hermanns, H., Wolf, V.: Comparative branching-time semantics for Markov chains. Inf. Comput. 200(2), 149–214 (2005)
2. Bernardo, M., De Nicola, R., Loreti, M.: Relating strong behavioral equivalences for processes with nondeterminism and probabilities. Theor. Comput. Sci. 546, 63–92 (2014)
3. Bernstein, D.S., Givan, R., Immerman, N., Zilberstein, S.: The complexity of decentralized control of Markov decision processes. Math. Oper. Res. 27(4), 819–840 (2002)
4. Boudali, H., Crouzen, P., Stoelinga, M.: A rigorous, compositional, and extensible framework for dynamic fault tree analysis. IEEE Trans. Dependable Sec. Comput. 7(2), 128–143 (2010)
5. Cattani, S., Segala, R.: Decision algorithms for probabilistic bisimulation. In: Brim, L., Jančar, P., Křetínský, M., Kučera, A. (eds.) CONCUR 2002. LNCS, vol. 2421, pp. 371–385. Springer, Heidelberg (2002)
6. Chehaibar, G., Garavel, H., Mounier, L., Tawbi, N., Zulian, F.: Specification and Verification of the PowerScale^{TM} bus arbitration protocol: An industrial experiment with lotos. In: FORTE, pp. 435–450 (1996)
7. De Alfaro, L.: The verification of probabilistic systems under memoryless partial-information policies is hard. Technical report, DTIC Document (1999)
8. Deng, Y., Hennessy, M.: On the semantics of Markov automata. Information and Computation 222, 139–168 (2013)
9. Deng, Y., van Glabbeek, R., Hennessy, M., Morgan, C.: Testing finitary probabilistic processes. In: Bravetti, M., Zavattaro, G. (eds.) CONCUR 2009. LNCS, vol. 5710, pp. 274–288. Springer, Heidelberg (2009)
10. Desharnais, J., Gupta, V., Jagadeesan, R., Panangaden, P.: Weak bisimulation is sound and complete for pCTL*. Inf. Comput. 208(2), 203–219 (2010)
11. Doyen, L., Henzinger, T.A., Raskin, J.: Equivalence of labeled Markov chains. Int. J. Found. Comput. Sci. 19(3), 549–563 (2008)
12. Eisentraut, C., Godskesen, J.C., Hermanns, H., Song, L., Zhang, L.: Late Weak Bisimulation for Markov Automata. CoRR, abs/1202.4116 (2014), http://arxiv.org/abs/1202.4116
13. Eisentraut, C., Hermanns, H., Katoen, J.-P., Zhang, L.: A semantics for every GSPN. In: Colom, J.-M., Desel, J. (eds.) PETRI NETS 2013. LNCS, vol. 7927, pp. 90–109. Springer, Heidelberg (2013)
14. Eisentraut, C., Hermanns, H., Krämer, J., Turrini, A., Zhang, L.: Deciding bisimilarities on distributions. In: Joshi, K., Siegle, M., Stoelinga, M., D'Argenio, P.R. (eds.) QEST 2013. LNCS, vol. 8054, pp. 72–88. Springer, Heidelberg (2013)
15. Eisentraut, C., Hermanns, H., Zhang, L.: Concurrency and composition in a stochastic world. In: Gastin, P., Laroussinie, F. (eds.) CONCUR 2010. LNCS, vol. 6269, pp. 21–39. Springer, Heidelberg (2010)
16. Eisentraut, C., Hermanns, H., Zhang, L.: On probabilistic automata in continuous time. In: LICS, pp. 342–351 (2010)
17. Feng, Y., Zhang, L.: When equivalence and bisimulation join forces in probabilistic automata. In: Jones, C., Pihlajasaari, P., Sun, J. (eds.) FM 2014. LNCS, vol. 8442, pp. 247–262. Springer, Heidelberg (2014)

18. Giro, S., D'Argenio, P.R.: Quantitative model checking revisited: neither decidable nor approximable. In: Raskin, J.-F., Thiagarajan, P.S. (eds.) FORMATS 2007. LNCS, vol. 4763, pp. 179–194. Springer, Heidelberg (2007)
19. Guck, D., Timmer, M., Hatefi, H., Ruijters, E., Stoelinga, M.: Modelling and analysis of Markov reward automata. In: Cassez, F., Raskin, J.-F. (eds.) ATVA 2014. LNCS, vol. 8837, pp. 168–184. Springer, Heidelberg (2014)
20. Halmos, P.R.: Measure theory, vol. 1950. Springer (1974)
21. He, F., Gao, X., Wang, B., Zhang, L.: Leveraging weighted automata in compositional reasoning about concurrent probabilistic systems. In: POPL, pp. 503–514. ACM (2015)
22. Hennessy, M.: Exploring probabilistic bisimulations, part I. Formal Asp. Comput. 24(4-6), 749–768 (2012)
23. Hermanns, H.: Interactive Markov chains: and the quest for quantified quality. Springer, Heidelberg (2002)
24. Hermanns, H., Krčál, J., Křetínský, J.: Probabilistic bisimulation: Naturally on distributions. In: Baldan, P., Gorla, D. (eds.) CONCUR 2014. LNCS, vol. 8704, pp. 249–265. Springer, Heidelberg (2014)
25. Honda, K., Tokoro, M.: On asynchronous communication semantics. In: Zatarain-Cabada, R., Wang, J. (eds.) ECOOP-WS 1991. LNCS, vol. 612, pp. 21–51. Springer, Heidelberg (1992)
26. Kwiatkowska, M., Norman, G., Parker, D., Qu, H.: Assume-guarantee verification for probabilistic systems. In: Esparza, J., Majumdar, R. (eds.) TACAS 2010. LNCS, vol. 6015, pp. 23–37. Springer, Heidelberg (2010)
27. Philippou, A., Lee, I., Sokolsky, O.: Weak bisimulation for probabilistic systems. In: Palamidessi, C. (ed.) CONCUR 2000. LNCS, vol. 1877, pp. 334–349. Springer, Heidelberg (2000)
28. Rudin, W.: Real and complex analysis. Tata McGraw-Hill Education (2006)
29. Schuster, J., Siegle, M.: Markov automata: Deciding weak bisimulation by means of non-navely vanishing states. Information and Computation 237, 151–173 (2014)
30. Segala, R.: A compositional trace-based semantics for probabilistic automata. In: Lee, I., Smolka, S.A. (eds.) CONCUR 1995. LNCS, vol. 962, pp. 234–248. Springer, Heidelberg (1995)
31. Segala, R.: Modeling and Verification of Randomized Distributed Realtime Systems. PhD thesis. MIT (1995)
32. Song, L., Feng, Y., Zhang, L.: Decentralized bisimulation for multiagent systems. In: AAMAS, pp. 209-217. IFAAMAS (2015)
33. Timmer, M., van de Pol, J., Stoelinga, M.I.A.: Confluence reduction for Markov automata. In: Braberman, V., Fribourg, L. (eds.) FORMATS 2013. LNCS, vol. 8053, pp. 243–257. Springer, Heidelberg (2013)

QPMC: A Model Checker for Quantum Programs and Protocols

Yuan Feng[1], Ernst Moritz Hahn[2], Andrea Turrini[2(✉)], and Lijun Zhang[2]

[1] Centre for Quantum Computation and Intelligent Systems, University of Technology Sydney, Sydney, Australia

[2] State Key Laboratory of Computer Science, Institute of Software, Chinese Academy of Sciences, Beijing, China

andrea.turrini@gmail.com

Abstract. We present QPMC *(Quantum Program/Protocol Model Checker)*, an extension of the probabilistic model checker ISCASMC to automatically verify quantum programs and quantum protocols. QPMC distinguishes itself from the previous quantum model checkers proposed in the literature in that it works for general quantum programs and protocols, not only those using Clifford operations. A command-line version of QPMC is available at http://iscasmc.ios.ac.cn/tool/qmc/.

1 Introduction and Motivation

Although commercial quantum computers are still in their infancy, rapid progress has been made in building reliable and scalable components for quantum computers. In particular, quantum cryptographic systems are already commercially available by companies such as Id Quantique, Cerberis, MagiQ Technologies, SmartQuantum, and NEC. The security of quantum cryptographic protocols is mathematically provable, based on the principles of quantum mechanics, without imposing any restrictions on the computational capacity of an attacker. In practice, however, security analysis of quantum cryptographic protocols is notoriously difficult; for example, the manual proof of BB84 in [15] contains about 50 pages. It is hard to imagine such an analysis being carried out for more sophisticated quantum protocols. Thus, techniques for automated or semi-automated verification of these protocols will be indispensable.

In the last decade, researchers started to explore the possibility of applying model checking, one of the dominant techniques for verification which has a large number of successful industrial applications, to the verification of quantum programs as well as quantum protocols. The main obstacle is that the set of all quantum states, traditionally regarded as the underlying state space of the model to be checked, is a continuum. Hence, the techniques of classical model checking, which normally work only for a finite state space, cannot be applied directly. Gay et al. [10] provided a solution to this problem by restricting the state space to a set of finitely describable states called *stabiliser states*, and restricting the quantum operations applied on them to the class of *Clifford group*. By doing this, they were able to obtain an efficient model checker [11] for quantum protocols, employing purely classical algorithms.

N. Bjørner and F. de Boer (Eds.): FM 2015, LNCS 9109, pp. 265–272, 2015.
DOI: 10.1007/978-3-319-19249-9_17

There is one limitation of the approach by Gay et al.: since only quantum protocols expressible in stabiliser formalism are considered, so that the state space can be encoded in a classical way, their model checker does not work for general protocols. To deal with this problem, one of the authors of the current paper and his colleagues proposed a novel notion of super-operator weighted Markov chain in which the state space is taken classical (and usually can be finite), while all quantum effects are encoded in the super-operators labelling the transitions [9]. This model is especially suited for verification of *classical properties* for which only the measurement outcomes as well as the probabilities of obtaining them are relevant, and the quantum effects caused by superposition, entanglement, etc., are merely employed to increase the efficiency or security of the protocol. Typical examples include super-dense coding [6], quantum coin-flipping protocol [4], and quantum key distribution protocols [3,4].

The distinct advantage of super-operator weighted Markov chains, for model checking purpose, is twofold: (1) It provides a way to check *once for all* in that once a property is verified, it holds for all input quantum states. This is especially important for the verification of quantum programs. For example, for the reachability problem we calculate the accumulated *super-operator*, say $\mathcal{E}$, along all valid paths. As a result, the reachability *probability* when the program is executed on the input quantum state ρ is simply the trace $\mathrm{tr}(\mathcal{E}(\rho))$ of $\mathcal{E}(\rho)$; (2) As the state space is usually finite, techniques from classical model checking can be adapted to verification of quantum systems.

The contribution of this paper is the development of a software tool that implements the techniques and algorithms proposed in [9]. The implementation is based on IsCASMC [12], a web-based model checker for probabilistic systems.

Other related works. Besides the model checker proposed by Gay et al. [11], recently Ardeshir-Larijani et al. developed equivalence checkers for deterministic quantum protocols [1] as well as concurrent quantum protocols that behave *functionally* [2]. As for [11], these tools work only within the stabiliser formalism, and the generalisation to general quantum protocols seems difficult.

2 The QMC Model and the Logic QCTL

In this section, we recall the notion of quantum Markov chains that serves as the semantic model of quantum programs and protocols. We assume the readers are familiar with the basic notions of quantum information theory [9, 16].

Let $\mathcal{S}(\mathcal{H})$ be the set of *super-operators* over a Hilbert space $\mathcal{H}$. Here a super-operator is a completely positive linear operator from $\mathcal{L}(\mathcal{H})$ to itself, where $\mathcal{L}(\mathcal{H})$ is the set of linear operators on $\mathcal{H}$. In particular, we denote by $\mathcal{I}_\mathcal{H}$ and $0_\mathcal{H}$ the identity and null super-operators in $\mathcal{S}(\mathcal{H})$, respectively. For any $\mathcal{E}, \mathcal{F} \in \mathcal{S}(\mathcal{H})$, let $\mathcal{E} \lesssim \mathcal{F}$ if for any quantum state ρ in $\mathcal{H}$, $\mathrm{tr}(\mathcal{E}(\rho)) \leq \mathrm{tr}(\mathcal{F}(\rho))$. Note that the trace tr of a (unnormalised) quantum state denotes the probability that the (normalised) state is reached [17]. Intuitively, $\mathcal{E} \lesssim \mathcal{F}$ means that the success probability of performing $\mathcal{E}$ is always not greater than that of performing $\mathcal{F}$, whatever the initial state is. Let $\approx$ be $\lesssim \cap \gtrsim$.

We denote by $\mathcal{S}^\mathcal{I}(\mathcal{H})$ the set of trace-nonincreasing super-operators over $\mathcal{H}$; that is, $\mathcal{S}^\mathcal{I}(\mathcal{H}) = \{\mathcal{E} \in \mathcal{S}(\mathcal{H}) \mid 0_\mathcal{H} \lesssim \mathcal{E} \lesssim \mathcal{I}_\mathcal{H}\}$. Observe that $\mathcal{E} \in \mathcal{S}^\mathcal{I}(\mathcal{H})$ if and only if for any quantum state ρ, $\mathrm{tr}(\mathcal{E}(\rho)) \in [0,1]$. It is natural to regard the set $\mathcal{S}^{\mathcal{I}}(\mathcal{H})$ as the quantum correspondence of $[0,1]$, the domain of traditional probabilities. This is exactly the key to the notion of quantum Markov chains defined in [9].

Definition 1 (Quantum Markov Chain [9]). *A super-operator weighted Markov chain, also referred to as quantum Markov chain (QMC) for simplicity, over a Hilbert space $\mathcal{H}$ is a tuple $(S, \mathbf{Q}, AP, L)$, where*

(1) S is a countable (typically finite) set of classical states;
(2) $\mathbf{Q}\colon S \times S \to \mathcal{S}^{\mathcal{I}}(\mathcal{H})$ is called the transition matrix *where for each $s \in S$, the super-operator $\sum_{t \in S} \mathbf{Q}(s,t)$ is trace-preserving;*
(3) AP is a finite set of atomic propositions; *and*
(4) $L\colon S \to 2^{AP}$ is a labelling function.

From the above definition, a QMC is simply a discrete time Markov chain (DTMC) with all traditional probabilities replaced by *quantum probabilities* from $\mathcal{S}^{\mathcal{I}}(\mathcal{H})$. The properties are expressed using the quantum computation tree logic (QCTL) proposed in [9], which is a natural extension of PCTL. The syntax of QCTL is as follows:

$$\Phi ::= a \mid \neg\Phi \mid \Phi \wedge \Phi \mid \mathbb{Q}_{\sim\mathcal{E}}[\phi]$$
$$\phi ::= \mathbf{X}\Phi \mid \Phi\, \mathbf{U}^{\leq k}\, \Phi \mid \Phi\, \mathbf{U}\, \Phi$$

where $a \in AP$ is an atomic proposition, $\sim\, \in \{\lesssim, \gtrsim, \eqsim\}$, $\mathcal{E} \in \mathcal{S}^{\mathcal{I}}(\mathcal{H})$, and $k \in \mathbb{N}$. We call Φ a *state formula* and ϕ a *path formula*. We use the following abbreviations: $\Phi_1 \vee \Phi_2 \equiv \neg(\neg\Phi_1 \wedge \neg\Phi_2)$, $\mathtt{tt} \equiv a \vee \neg a$, $\mathbf{F}\Phi \equiv \mathtt{tt}\, \mathbf{U}\, \Phi$, and $\mathbf{F}^{\leq k}\Phi \equiv \mathtt{tt}\, \mathbf{U}^{\leq k}\, \Phi$.

Note the essential difference between QCTL and the traditional PCTL:

- in PCTL we have the probabilistic operator formula $\mathbb{P}_{\sim p}[\phi]$ with $\sim\, \in \{\leq, \geq\}$, which asserts that the probability of paths from a certain state satisfying the path formula ϕ is constrained by $\sim p$ where $0 \leq p \leq 1$,
- in QCTL, $\mathbb{P}_{\sim p}[\phi]$ is replaced by $\mathbb{Q}_{\sim\mathcal{E}}[\phi]$, which asserts that the accumulated super-operators corresponding to paths from a certain state satisfying the formula ϕ is constrained by $\sim \mathcal{E}$ where $0_{\mathcal{H}} \lesssim \mathcal{E} \lesssim \mathcal{I}_{\mathcal{H}}$.

Note that $\mathbb{P}_{\sim p}[\phi]$ is a special case of $\mathbb{Q}_{\sim\mathcal{E}}[\phi]$ by taking $\mathcal{E} = p\mathcal{I}_{\mathcal{H}}$.

Example 1. A simple quantum loop program goes as follows:

$$l_0 : q := \mathcal{A}(q)$$
$$l_1 : \mathbf{while}\ M[q]\ \mathbf{do}$$
$$l_2 : \qquad q := \mathcal{G}(q)$$
$$l_3 : \mathbf{end}$$

where for $E_0 = |0\rangle\langle 0| + \frac{1}{\sqrt{2}}|1\rangle\langle 1|$ and $E_1 = \frac{1}{\sqrt{2}}|0\rangle\langle 1|$, $\mathcal{A} = \{E_0, E_1\}$ is the $\frac{1}{2}$-amplitude damping channel, $M = \lambda_0|0\rangle\langle 0| + \lambda_1|1\rangle\langle 1|$, and $\mathcal{G}$ is the Hadamard super-operator. In this program, we first apply $\mathcal{A}$ on the quantum system q for the initialisation. At line l_1, the two-outcome projective measurement M is applied. If the outcome λ_0 is observed, then the program terminates at line l_3; otherwise it proceeds to l_2 where the super-operator $\mathcal{G}$ is performed, and then the program returns to line l_1 and another iteration continues.

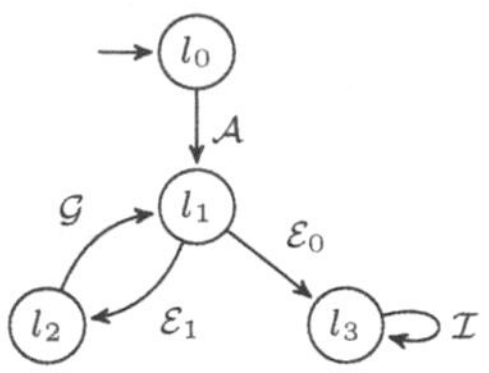

The QMC for this program, depicted on the right, is constructed as follows. Let $S = AP = \{ l_i \mid 0 \leq i \leq 3\}$, $L(l_i) = \{l_i\}$ for each i, and $\mathbf{Q}$ be defined as $\mathbf{Q}(l_0, l_1) = \mathcal{A}$, $\mathbf{Q}(l_1, l_3) = \mathcal{E}_0 = \{|0\rangle\langle 0|\}$, $\mathbf{Q}(l_1, l_2) = \mathcal{E}_1 = \{|1\rangle\langle 1|\}$, $\mathbf{Q}(l_2, l_1) = \mathcal{G}$, and $\mathbf{Q}(l_3, l_3) = \mathcal{I}$.

l_0 $\mathcal{A}$ l_1 $\mathcal{G}$ $\mathcal{E}_0$ l_2 $\mathcal{E}_1$ l_3 $\mathcal{I}$

The QCTL formula $\mathbb{Q}_{\gtrsim \mathcal{E}}[\mathbf{F}\ l_3]$ asserts the probability that the loop program terminates is lower bounded by $\mathcal{E}$, that is, for any initial quantum state ρ, the termination probability is not less than $\mathrm{tr}(\mathcal{E}(\rho))$. In particular, the property that it always terminates for any input can be described as $\mathbb{Q}_{\gtrsim \mathcal{I}}[\mathbf{F}\ l_3]$.

3 The Tool QPMC

The QPMC model checker is the extension to QMCs of the web-based model checker IscasMC [12]. In order to support quantum operations, IscasMC has been enriched with the data structures for matrices and super-operators as well as the algorithms to manipulate them. Correspondingly, we have extended the PRISM [14] language used for modelling classical MCs with new keywords and operations specific for QMCs.

Implementation Aspect. IscasMC is written in Java with a few optional parts (which are not used for QMCs) being written in C. While the syntax of models is very close to the one of PRISM, the code of IscasMC is not based on the former.

The integration of QMCs into IscasMC has been possible because the underlying algorithms integrated into our model checker work with generic values rather than, for instance, being restricted to computations with IEEE 754 double values. Thus, by defining the way of how mathematical operations are to be performed on super-operators, how they can be compared and how they can be displayed to the user, we are able to use algorithms already implemented in IscasMC. Thus, we can for instance use a variant of the well-known value iteration algorithms. Because QMCs do not behave exactly as DTMCs, some care has to be taken. Multiplication of super-operators is not commutative which needs to be taken into account in the value iteration. Also, the precomputation of states which reach target states with probability 1 has to be adapted.

Complex numbers, matrices and super-operators are stored using IEEE 754 doubles and manipulated using standard operations. QPMC could be extended to instead use representations of numbers with higher or infinite precision (using symbolic representations) e.g. for stiff models. Doing so would not affect the rest of the implementation.

IscasMC is split into several packages, to allow a clear separation between, for instance, the user interface, operations on mathematical objects, syntax trees of models and properties, etc. This way, extensions of one part are possible without interfering with the other modules. This allows for instance to quickly integrate additional operations on super-operators if they turn out to be useful for end users.

QPMC is available at http://iscasmc.ios.ac.cn/tool/qmc/ where it is possible to download the latest stable version, together with a brief summary on the required dependencies and on the usage.

```
qmc // model type

const vector |p>_2 = (|0>_2 + |1>_2)/sqrt(2);
const matrix E0 = |0>_2 <0|_2 + |1>_2 <1|_2/sqrt(2);
const matrix E1 = |0>_2 <1|_2/sqrt(2);
const superoperator(2) ampdamp = << E0, E1 >>;

module loop
  s : [0..3] init 0;
  [] (s=0) -> ampdamp: (s'=1);
  [] (s=1) -> << M1 >> : (s'=2) + << M0 >> : (s'=3);
  [] (s=2) -> << HD >> : (s'=1);
  [] (s=3) -> (s'=3);
endmodule
```

Fig. 1. Source code for the QMC in Example 1

Modeling Language. We extend the well-known PRISM [14] guarded-command based language to model QMCs. Fig. 1 depicts the source code in our language that describes the quantum loop program in Example 1:

- The keyword **qmc** specifies the model type.
- In addition to the constants definable in PRISM, one can specify constants of types **vector**, **matrix**, and **superoperator**. Notably, QPMC supports the use of *bra-ket* notation which is standard for describing quantum states in quantum mechanics. Specifically, `|v>_n` denotes a vector in $\mathcal{H}_n$, the n-dimensional Hilbert space. To ease notations, we have predefined the computational basis `|0>_n`, ..., `|n-1>_n` for $\mathcal{H}_n$; that is, for each $0 \leq i < n$,

$$\texttt{|i>\_n} = (0, \cdots, 0, 1, 0, \cdots, 0)^T$$

  where 1 appears at the $(i+1)$-th entry. These vectors can be used for free. The operations such as *inner product*, *outer product*, and *tensor product* over bra-ket vectors are denoted in the normal way. For example, `<0|1>_2` stands for $\langle 0|1\rangle$, `|0>_2 <1|_2` for $|0\rangle\langle 1|$ in $\mathcal{H}_2$, and `|0>_2 |1>_2` means $|01\rangle = |0\rangle \otimes |1\rangle$ in $\mathcal{H}_2 \otimes \mathcal{H}_2$. We use Kraus operators collected in a pair of double angle brackets to represent a super-operator. For example, the following statement

  `const superoperator(2) ampdamp = << E0, E1 >>;`

  defines a super-operator named ampdamp in the Hilbert space $\mathcal{H}_2$ with the Kraus operators $\{E0, E1\}$. For convenience of the users, we predefined some useful matrices listed below:
  - the n-dimensional *identity* matrix **ID**$(n) = diag(1, \ldots, 1)$;
  - the *Pauli* matrices **PX** $= \begin{pmatrix} 0 & 1 \\ 1 & 0 \end{pmatrix}$, **PY** $= \begin{pmatrix} 0 & -i \\ i & 0 \end{pmatrix}$, **PZ** $= \begin{pmatrix} 1 & 0 \\ 0 & -1 \end{pmatrix}$, the *Hadamard* matrix **HD** $= \frac{1}{\sqrt{2}} \begin{pmatrix} 1 & 1 \\ 1 & -1 \end{pmatrix}$, and the *phase-shift* matrix **PS**$(\theta) = \begin{pmatrix} 1 & 0 \\ 0 & e^{i\theta} \end{pmatrix}$. We also predefined the *measurement operators* with respect to the computational basis in $\mathcal{H}_2$: **M0** $= \begin{pmatrix} 1 & 0 \\ 0 & 0 \end{pmatrix}$ and **M1** $= \begin{pmatrix} 0 & 0 \\ 0 & 1 \end{pmatrix}$;

- the *control-not* matrix **CN** = **ID**(2) ⊕ **PX**, and the *swap* matrix **SW** = **ID**(1) ⊕ **PX** ⊕ **ID**(1),
- the *Toffoli* matrix **TF** = **ID**(4) ⊕ **CN**, and the *Fredkin* matrix **FK** = **ID**(4) ⊕ **SW**.

– The main behavior of the QMC is described in the **module** environment. It has a state variable s, and several guarded commands representing the system transitions. As in PRISM, each guarded command has a precondition, and a sum of updates. The only difference is that each update is associated with a super-operator instead of a probability. We always omit the identity super-operators along the updates.

Properties. To help reasoning, besides the logical operators presented in QCTL, we also support an extended operator Q=?[ϕ], where ϕ is a path formula, to calculate (the matrix representation[1] of) the super-operator of satisfying ϕ. We further provide a function qeval(Q=?[ϕ], ρ) to compute the density operator obtained from applying the resultant super-operator on a given density operator ρ, and

$$\text{qprob}(\text{Q=?}[\phi], \rho) = \text{tr}(\text{qeval}(\text{Q=?}[\phi], \rho))$$

to calculate the probability of satisfying ϕ, starting from the quantum state ρ.

Quantum loop program. For the quantum program in Example 1, we check the following properties

```
Q>=1 [ F (s=3) ]
qeval(Q=?[F (s=3)], |p>_2 <p|_2)
qeval(Q=?[F (s=3)], ID(2)/2)
```

where the first one checks if $l_0 \models \mathbb{Q}_{\gtrsim \mathcal{I}}[\mathbf{F}\ l_3]$ and the last two show the output states when the inputs of the program are the pure state $|+\rangle\langle+|$ where $|+\rangle = \frac{|0\rangle+|1\rangle}{\sqrt{2}}$ and the maximally mixed state $I/2$, respectively. QPMC returns **true** for the first property and $\begin{pmatrix} 1 & 0 \\ 0 & 0 \end{pmatrix}$ for the last two, as expected.

It is worth noting that the termination properties we checked here cannot be verified by the previous tools in [1, 2, 11] for the following two reasons: (1) the loop program employs an amplitude damping operation which does not belong to the Clifford group; (2) the program is an open system which takes an arbitrary quantum state as its input, and we are checking the termination for *any* input state.

Superdense coding protocol. Another protocol we analysed is the superdense coding protocol [6] that permits to use a single qubit to faithfully transmit two classical bits, under the hypothesis that a maximally entangled state is already shared between the

[1] The matrix representation of a super-operator $\{ E_i \mid i \in I \}$ in an n-dimensional Hilbert space $\mathcal{H}$ is an n^2 by n^2 matrix $\sum_{i \in I} E_i \otimes E_i^*$, where the complex conjugate is taken according to some orthonormal basis of $\mathcal{H}$. See [9] for more details.

sender and the receiver. As for the quantum loop example, QPMC establishes the correctness of the protocol by returning **true** for the property Q>=1 [F (succ)]. That is, the success state, where the original message has been transmitted from Alice to Bob faithfully, will be reached for sure.

Quantum key distribution protocol. The third protocol we considered is the quantum key distribution protocol [4] that allows Alice and Bob to create and share a private key between them, in a provably secure way, without interacting with a trusted third party for the exchange. For simplicity, we only consider the basic version of BB84 where the channels used are perfect, and no eavesdropper exists. Then the correctness of the protocol can be described by the properties Q<=0 [F (fail)] and Q=0.5 [F (succ)], meaning that BB84 never fails (i.e., it always generates identical keys between Alice and Bob), and with probability exactly 0.5 (the best success probability one can achieve), it successfully terminates at a shared key. QPMC returns **true** for both the properties.

Performance of the tool. Each experiment has been performed on a MacBook Pro with a 2.9 GHz Intel Core i7 processor with 8 GB 1600 MHz DDR3 RAM, taking an overall time of less than 1 second per model.

4 Conclusion and Future Work

Based on the theoretical work in [9], we have presented QPMC, a model checker aiming at verification of quantum programs and quantum protocols. Compared with the existing model checkers for the same purpose in the literature, our tool is able to verify more general programs and protocols which are beyond the stabiliser formalism.

For further studies, we are going to use qCCS, a quantum extension of CCS developed by one of the authors and his colleagues [7,8,19], as our modelling language. This will make the protocol description more intuitive and more readable. We also plan to consider analysis of LTL properties. Classical decision algorithms check acceptance of bottom strongly connected components and then compute reachability probabilities for transient states. We would like to see how this technique can be extended to QMCs.

Acknowledgments. This work is supported by Australian Research Council (Grant No. DP130102764), the National Natural Science Foundation of China (Grant Nos. 61428208, 61472473 and 61361136002), the Chinese Academy of Sciences Fellowship for International Young Scientists (Grant Nos. 2013Y1GB0006 and 2015VTC029), AMSS-UTS Joint Research Laboratory for Quantum Computation, Chinese Academy of Sciences, and the CAS/SAFEA International Partnership Program for Creative Research Team.

References

1. Ardeshir-Larijani, E., Gay, S., Nagarajan, R.: Equivalence checking of quantum protocols. In: Piterman, N., Smolka, S.A. (eds.) TACAS 2013. LNCS, vol. 7795, pp. 478–492. Springer, Heidelberg (2013)

2. Ardeshir-Larijani, E., Gay, S., Nagarajan, R.: Verification of concurrent quantum protocols by equivalence checking. In: Ábrahám, E., Havelund, K. (eds.) TACAS 2014. LNCS, vol. 8413, pp. 500–514. Springer, Heidelberg (2014)
3. Bennett, C.H.: Quantum cryptography using any two nonorthogonal states. Physical Review Letters 68, 3121 (1992)
4. Bennett, C.H., Brassard, G.: Quantum cryptography: Public-key distribution and coin tossing. In: Proceedings of the IEEE International Conference on Computer, Systems and Signal Processing, pp. 175–179 (1984)
5. Bennett, C.H., Brassard, G., Crepeau, C., Jozsa, R., Peres, A., Wootters, W.: Teleporting an unknown quantum state via dual classical and EPR channels. Physical Review Letters 70, 1895–1899 (1993)
6. Bennett, C.H., Wiesner, S.J.: Communication via one- and two-particle operators on Einstein-Podolsky-Rosen states. Physical Review Letters 69(20), 2881–2884 (1992)
7. Feng, Y., Duan, R., Ji, Z., Ying, M.: Probabilistic bisimulations for quantum processes. Information and Computation 205(11), 1608–1639 (2007)
8. Feng, Y., Duan, R., Ying, M.: Bisimulation for Quantum Processes. ACM Transactions on Programming Languages and Systems 34(4), 1–43 (2012)
9. Feng, Y., Yu, N., Ying, M.: Model checking quantum Markov chains. Journal of Computer and System Sciences 79(7), 1181–1198 (2013)
10. Gay, S., Nagarajan, R., Papanikolaou, N.: Probabilistic model-checking of quantum protocols. In: Proceedings of the 2nd International Workshop on Developments in Computational Models (2006)
11. Gay, S.J., Nagarajan, R., Papanikolaou, N.: QMC: A model checker for quantum systems. In: Gupta, A., Malik, S. (eds.) CAV 2008. LNCS, vol. 5123, pp. 543–547. Springer, Heidelberg (2008)
12. Hahn, E.M., Li, Y., Schewe, S., Turrini, A., Zhang, L.: iscasMc: A web-based probabilistic model checker. In: Jones, C., Pihlajasaari, P., Sun, J. (eds.) FM 2014. LNCS, vol. 8442, pp. 312–317. Springer, Heidelberg (2014)
13. Kraus, K.: States, Effects and Operations: Fundamental Notions of Quantum Theory. Springer, Berlin (1983)
14. Kwiatkowska, M., Norman, G., Parker, D.: PRISM 4.0: Verification of probabilistic real-time systems. In: Gopalakrishnan, G., Qadeer, S. (eds.) CAV 2011. LNCS, vol. 6806, pp. 585–591. Springer, Heidelberg (2011)
15. Mayers, D.: Unconditional security in quantum cryptography. Journal of the ACM 48(3), 351–406 (2001)
16. Nielsen, M., Chuang, I.: Quantum computation and quantum information. Cambridge university press (2000)
17. Selinger, P.: Towards a quantum programming language. Mathematical Structures in Computer Science 14(4), 527–586 (2004)
18. von Neumann, J.: Mathematical Foundations of Quantum Mechanics. Princeton University Press, Princeton (1955)
19. Ying, M., Feng, Y., Duan, R., Ji, Z.: An algebra of quantum processes. ACM Transactions on Computational Logic (TOCL) 10(3), 1–36 (2009)

Automated Verification of RPC Stub Code

Matthew Fernandez(✉), June Andronick, Gerwin Klein, and Ihor Kuz

NICTA and UNSW, Sydney, Australia
{matthew.fernandez,june.andronick,gerwin.klein,
ihor.kuz}@nicta.com.au

Abstract. Formal verification has been successfully applied to provide strong correctness guarantees of software systems, but its application to large code bases remains an open challenge. The technique of component-based software development, traditionally employed for engineering benefit, also aids reasoning about such systems. While there exist compositional verification techniques that leverage the separation implied by a component system architecture, they implicitly rely on the component platform correctly implementing the isolation and composition semantics they assume. Any property proven using these techniques is vulnerable to being invalidated by a bug in the code of the platform itself. In this paper, we show how this assumption can be eliminated by automatically generating machine-checked proofs of the correctness of a component platform's generated Remote Procedure Call (RPC) code. We demonstrate how these generated proofs can be composed with hand-written proofs to yield a system-level property with equivalent assurance to an entirely hand-written proof. This technique forms the basis of a scalable approach to formal verification of large software systems.

1 Introduction

In the design of safety- and security-critical software, it is desirable to provide the high levels of assurance that can be achieved by formal verification. State of the art code-level verification currently scales to tens of thousands of lines of code [13, 16], while high assurance software can often exceed one million lines of code. For such large systems, pervasive code-level verification still is infeasible and new techniques are required.

Component-based software engineering facilitates the design and implementation of large software systems [25]. This methodology involves specifying a system as a collection of isolated software elements that communicate via explicit connections, expressed in an architectural description. An example would be a simple system with two separate components, a client `c` and a server `s`, with a communication connection between them, allowing `c` to invoke a function implemented in `s`. The component platform would generate so-called *glue code* to perform argument marshalling and unmarshalling, and use the underlying operating system's communication mechanisms to transfer the data between components. By decomposing the problem of system verification along component boundaries, assurance of larger systems becomes tractable. A proof of system correctness chains together individual correctness proofs of the underlying operating system, component platform code, and user-provided component code.

N. Bjørner and F. de Boer (Eds.): FM 2015, LNCS 9109, pp. 273–290, 2015.
DOI: 10.1007/978-3-319-19249-9_18

Compositional verification of component systems is not a new concept, with existing techniques such as [2, 4] aiming to increase scalability through decomposition. However, all existing techniques we are aware of assume that an underlying component platform correctly implements the isolation and composition semantics they rely upon. This assumption encompasses the glue code, generated by the component platform. A defect anywhere in the glue code generation logic can falsify the implicit assumptions of a compositional reasoning framework and thereby invalidate derived properties [7].

To preserve the abstraction of a component system architecture and to aid reasoning about component systems, we aim to automate the production of functional correctness proofs for platform glue code. In this paper, we focus on generated code for *Remote Procedure Calls* (RPC) in particular. RPC is a common communication abstraction in component platforms. We refer to such generated code as RPC stubs in the context of this paper. Our generated proofs are machine-checked by the interactive theorem prover Isabelle/HOL [19], and the resulting proofs are designed to be manually composed with hand-written proofs of user-provided code. Together, the generated and hand-written proofs can yield a proof of functional correctness of a whole system. Though relying on generated proof script, the final proof carries the same level of assurance as a manually-constructed, machine-checked proof.

The main challenge of this work is in generating an Isabelle/HOL proof script that corresponds to a generated implementation. Since the implementation is derived from a system architecture description, and the existing code generator is largely string- and template-based, it is infeasible to provide a single proof for the correctness of any possible glue code (that is, to verify the generator itself). Instead, we use a translation validation approach and build on our previous work that demonstrated the absence of undefined behaviour in component platform glue code [6].

We use an existing component platform, CAmkES [14], and focus on the verification of its C backend targeting the seL4 microkernel [13]. In future work, we intend to leverage the functional correctness proof of seL4, though for now we implicitly assume the semantics of its system calls in our execution model.

We make the following novel contributions:(i) We demonstrate a technique for automatically generating functional correctness proofs of generated RPC code, removing the assumption of correct RPC stubs present in existing compositional reasoning frameworks and (ii) we present a strategy for composition of automated and manual proofs that does not require trusting the proof generator.

After describing, in Sect. 2, the runtime environment and the C verification framework we use, we elaborate the proof generation process in Sect. 3 and describe what precisely the generated proofs show. Being result verification, the approach is best demonstrated working through an example instance, which we do in Sect. 4. We discuss the trustworthiness of the resulting property and limitations of our approach in Sect. 5.

2 Background

2.1 seL4

To date, seL4 is the only general purpose operating system kernel with a code-level proof of functional correctness [13]. It contains around 9700 lines of C that have been

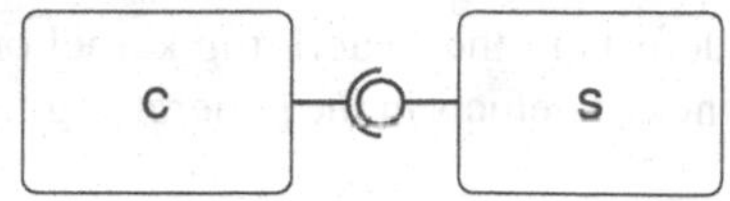

Fig. 1. Example CAmkES system architecture

proven to implement an abstract specification of the kernel's behaviour. The verification of seL4 extends to access control and information flow guarantees [17, 24].

The microkernel provides a minimal number of services to userspace processes, with abstractions for processor time (threads) and virtual memory. All authority in seL4 is provided through capabilities, kernel-administered access tokens for resources. Communication is achieved by having a capability to an endpoint object and invoking this capability. Capabilities have associated rights, with a *write* capability required to send on an endpoint and *read* capability to receive on an endpoint. The kernel provides a synchronous Inter-Process Communication (IPC) mechanism that allows a sender to transfer up to 484 bytes to a cooperative receiver from a fixed window of their address space known as their IPC buffer. The IPC buffer is accessed by a pair of utility functions, `seL4_GetMR` and `seL4_SetMR`, that are provided for reading and writing individual words at offsets into the buffer. For further information about the seL4 primitives, the reader is referred to the programmer's reference [26].

2.2 CAmkES

CAmkES is a component platform for implementing microkernel-based embedded systems [14]. A user provides a high-level architectural description of her system, and code implementing the logic of each component in the system. At compile time, CAmkES generates glue code to establish and enforce communication channels between the user's component instances, as described in her architectural description. For each component instance, its user-provided code and generated code are compiled and linked together to form an executable image. We focus on CAmkES' C backend for seL4 in this work, as representative of an environment for building high assurance systems. The correctness guarantees of seL4 present a strong foundation and C requires no implicit assumption of a correct language runtime.

CAmkES architectures are limited to static systems and all components are instantiated on system start. Three communication abstractions are available for system design: dataports, events and procedures. Procedures, which we focus on in this work, are used for representing communication in the style of synchronous function calls. Their semantics follows the well known Remote Procedure Call abstraction, so we use RPC terminology to refer to them. At compile time, CAmkES generates RPC stubs to perform argument marshalling, argument unmarshalling, and kernel invocations to transfer control and data between components. Because all communication channels are established statically and are local to a processor, communication runtime failures in CAmkES systems can only occur by defects in the underlying kernel or generated glue code. In this work, we prove the absence of defects in the generated glue code and use a formally verified kernel as substrate.

Component architectures are often represented diagrammatically as a set of boxes for the component instances and arrows for the connections between them. Fig. 1 provides an example, showing two connected component instances. Here s implements a single procedural interface, containing one or more exposed methods. An interface of the same type is expected by c. The two interfaces are connected, such that s provides the interface c is using. Though Fig. 1 only shows basic functionality, the full feature set of CAmkES is sufficient to build complex systems such as network routers and file systems. We will elaborate the example from Fig. 1 in Sect. 4.

2.3 Verification Framework

To reason about C programs, we first translate them into Isabelle/HOL. We initially use the C-to-Simpl parser [27, 29] to translate source code to a representation in the generic imperative language Simpl [23] in Isabelle/HOL. This translation is designed to be as straightforward as possible and to match the semantics of a large subset of C99 [12]. Following this, we use the AutoCorres tool [10, 11] to perform further automatically verified transformations within Isabelle/HOL that abstract the Simpl representation, resulting in a monadic functional specification that more closely resembles the programmer's intuition and facilitates reasoning on top. The C-to-Simpl parser's initial translation step can be independently validated using binary verification [24].

To reason about abstracted C programs, we adopt a variant of Hoare triples for stating the pre- and post-conditions of a potentially nondeterministic monadic function [5], which, in addition to transforming the state, may return a value or may fail. The following notation states that, if the pre-condition P holds and the function f terminates normally, then the post-condition Q will hold after f has executed.

$$\{\!|P|\!\}\ f\ \{\!|Q|\!\}$$

P is a predicate over the initial state (memory, global structures, etc.), whereas Q is a predicate over two parameters: the return value of f and the final state.

The above statement allows for the possibility that f fails or does not terminate, for example, by performing an operation with undefined behaviour in C. To express total correctness of f, we use the following variant that requires termination and absence of failure, including absence of guard violations.

$$\{\!|P|\!\}\ f\ \{\!|Q|\!\}!$$

In the remainder of this paper we use the following notation to refer to the initial state in the post-condition, for example, to express that the effect of a given C function f is to modify the state according to a specification function g, ignoring f's return value.

$$\{\!|\lambda s.\ s = s0|\!\}\ f\ \{\!|\lambda\_\ s.\ s = g\ s0|\!\}!$$

We refer to [5] for further details of this Hoare calculus for monadic functions.

3 Generating Correct RPC Stubs

Our anticipated process for verifying a component-based system is depicted in Fig. 2, where solid borders surround user-provided artefacts and dashed borders surround generated artefacts. The CAmkES platform generates a generic theorem of the correctness of RPC stub code for each procedure, alongside the generated code itself. The formal representations of the RPC stub functions in these theorems are derived by the C-to-Simpl parser directly from the generated code. The user can then instantiate the generic theorems for specific correctness properties.

In the context of RPC stubs, it is not immediately clear what "correctness" means for generated code. In this section, we explain our criteria for correct RPC stubs and elaborate on what precisely is proven in the Isabelle/HOL theories we generate.

Let `f` be the RPC stub code that provides a conduit for invoking a remote function `g`. Then, intuitively, invocation of `f` should be somehow equivalent to a direct invocation of `g`, were it colocated with the caller.

Since, by design, it is expected that the RPC code perform observable actions, we cannot expect full equivalence. However, we do expect to be able to lift suitable correctness specifications in the form of Hoare triples about `g` from the remote context into the local context. We state the correctness of glue code by specifying this lifting, and the generated glue code proofs establish that this specification lifting is indeed achieved. The generality of the specifications we allow for `g`, implies not only what the glue code must do, but also what it must *not* do (e.g. interfere with `g`'s private state or the caller's private state). We expect this form of statement and mechanism to readily generalise to the other transport mechanisms component platforms provide.

To be useful, the proofs we generate must be composable with (almost) arbitrary user-provided proofs, both of functions `g`, and of the contexts where `g` and `f` are used. We allow the proof engineer to state and prove the correctness criteria of her own functions *after* generation of the proofs of RPC stub correctness. To accomplish this, we parameterise the generated proofs within an Isabelle locale. Isabelle locales are named contexts containing fixed parameters, assumptions and definitions [28]. We show an

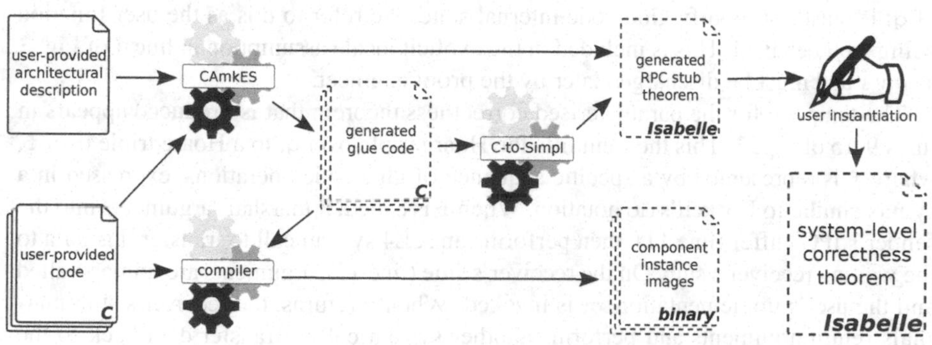

Fig. 2. Workflow for producing a proof of system correctness

```
1  locale rpcstubs =
2    fixes P_g :: lifted_globals ⇒ ... ⇒ bool
3    fixes Q_g :: lifted_globals ⇒ lifted_globals ⇒ ... ⇒ bool
4    assumes g_wp: ⦃λs. s = s0 ∧ inv s ∧ P_g s ...⦄ g ⦃λr s. inv s ∧ Q_g s0 s ...⦄!
5    assumes g_stable_setmr1: ∀ s i x. P_g (setMR s i x) = P_g s
6    assumes g_stable_setmr2: ∀ s i x. Q_g (setMR s i x) = Q_g s
7    assumes g_stable_setmr3: ∀ s0 s i x. Q_g s0 (setMR s i x) = Q_g s0 s
8
9  theorem f_wp:
10   ⦃λs. s = s0 ∧ inv s ∧ ... ∧ P_g s ...⦄
11    do f_marshal ...;
12      g_internal;
13      f_unmarshal ...
14    od
15   ⦃λr s. inv s ∧ Q_g s0 s ...⦄!
```

Fig. 3. RPC locale template

informal version of the template of the locale we generate in Fig. 3, and refer to lines from it in the following discussion.

For each user-provided function `g`, we assume locale parameters P_g and Q_g that capture the pre-condition and post-condition of `g` (lines 2-4). The generated proofs and specification for `f` then describe under which circumstances P_g and Q_g specify the behaviour of the function `f`, including the RPC stubs for `g`.

Not all P_g and Q_g are suitable. In particular, they must not make statements about glue code variables and memory. We refer to this as wellformedness of the pre- and post-condition. An example of this is shown in lines (5-7) of Fig. 3, which require that P_g and Q_g do not depend on the contents of the IPC buffer. Ideally, this would already be achieved by language scoping mechanisms, but C provides no guarantees and Isabelle no scoping. Instead we phrase these conditions as explicit locale assumptions that the proof engineer must discharge when making use of the generated proofs.

In addition to restrictions on P_g and Q_g, we also require restrictions on the behaviour of `g`: it must not modify glue-code internal state. We refer to this as the user function being well behaved. This is included in the explicit locale assumption in line 4 of Fig. 3 as *inv s* and must be discharged later by the proof engineer.

The template for the parameterised correctness theorem that is produced appears in lines 9-15 of Fig. 3. This theorem lifts the Hoare triple over `g`, to a Hoare triple over `f`, where `f` is represented by a specific sequence of glue code operations, expressed in a syntax similar to Haskell's `do` notation. When `f` is called, it marshals arguments into the sender's IPC buffer (line 11), then performs an seL4 system call to transfer this data to the waiting receiver's stub. On the receiver's side (line 12), arguments are unmarshalled and the user's implementation, `g`, is invoked. When `g` returns, the receiver's stub marshals return arguments and performs another system call to transfer data back to the sender. Finally, `f` unmarshals return arguments and returns to the caller (line 13). The seL4 system calls do not occur in this theorem; this means that for now we axiomatise

```
1  procedure Swapper {
2    unsigned int swap(inout int a, inout int b);
3  }
4
5  component Client { control; uses Swapper cs; }
6
7  component Service {  provides Swapper ss;  }
8
9  assembly {
10   composition {
11     component Client c;
12     component Service s;
13     connection seL4RPCSimple conn(from c.cs, to s.ss);
14   }
15 }
```

Fig. 4. Example system specification in CAmkES

the semantics of these seL4 system calls as a direct function call from `f` to the receiver's stub code.

To utilise the generated proofs, for instance in the context of hand-written proofs of further user-provided code, the proof engineer instantiates (*interprets* in Isabelle parlance) the generated locale by providing specific pre- and post-conditions for `g` and discharging the locale assumptions. The manual inputs are the specific pre- and post-conditions for `g`, a proof that `g` satisfies these, a proof that P_g and Q_g are wellformed, and a proof that `g` itself is well behaved. The result is a specific Hoare triple about `f` that can be used in further proofs.

Neither proving wellformedness of P_g and Q_g nor proving `g` is well behaved is onerous. They can mostly be discharged automatically once the user-code and specification are provided. The work for proving something about an RPC function `f` is reduced to proving almost the same property about `g`, pretending that it runs locally.

Sect. 4 provides a worked example of how exactly to achieve this.

4 Methodology Demonstrated on Example System

4.1 Component Architecture

The simplified example depicted previously in Fig. 1, describes an RPC interface provided by *s* and used by *c*. Fig. 4 shows the textual description of this system in CAmkES. It starts with the procedure interface definition `Swapper` (lines 1-3), comprising one method `swap`. The method takes two integer parameters that are used as both inputs and outputs, and also returns an unsigned integer value. The specification proceeds to define two component *types*, *Client* (line 5) and *Service* (line 7). *Client* has an active thread of execution, denoted by the *control* keyword and expects an instance of the *Swapper* interface under the name *cs*. *Service* is reactive, indicated by the lack of the *control* keyword, and implements an instance of the *Swapper* interface under the name *ss*.

```
static unsigned int counter;

unsigned int
ss_swap(int *a, int *b){
    int temp = *a;
    *a = *b; *b = temp;
    counter++;
    return counter;
}
```

Fig. 5. User-provided source code of *Service*

```
int run(void) {
    int x = 3;
    int y = 5;
    unsigned int i;
    i = cs_swap(&x, &y);
    return 0;
}
```

Fig. 6. User-provided source code of *Client*

The final block describes the architecture of the composed system. There is a single instance of each component type (lines 11-12) and the outgoing interface, expected by *c*, is provided by *s* via a connection *conn* of type *seL4RPCSimple*. The connection type determines the underlying transport for communication at runtime. Here, *seL4RPCSimple* is a type for RPC communication in the C language that uses the component instances' IPC buffers and an seL4 endpoint to pass arguments and return values.

The system we have just described contains a component instance *s* that exports a method for swapping the values of two integer parameters. The semantics we give to the `swap` method is not described in the architecture description. It is instead defined by user-provided code discussed in Sect. 4.2.

Component architectures would typically have many more procedures, interfaces, components, and connections. Though we have used this approach on larger systems, for simplicity of presentation we keep the system small in this example. There are few surprises and minimal manual work involved in moving to larger systems, chiefly because the lemma statements and generated proofs we go on to describe work for arbitrary numbers of components and connections, and the glue code proofs are pair-wise independent, so the proof size scales linearly in the size of the architecture.

4.2 User and Generated Code

The engineer developing a component system provides code for each component type in the system. Conceptually, she provides the contents of each of the boxes of an architectural diagram such as Fig. 1.

Fig. 5 and Fig. 6 give the C code for the components *Service* and *Client*, respectively. The code for *Service* exports a function, `ss_swap`, that swaps the value of two integer pointers and increments a global counter, returning the new value of the counter. The code for *Client* comprises a function, `run`, that acts as the component's entry point. It calls the function `cs_swap` with two local values it wishes to exchange. No code needs to be provided for `cs_swap` as this is what the component platform generates. The example demonstrates that our framework can handle bidirectional parameters, return values and manipulation of component-global state.

Note that this code is provided once per component *type* and then re-used for every instance of that type. In our example, there is only one instance of each type (*c* of type *Client* and *s* of type *Service*) so each piece of user code is only used once.

Fig. 7 and Fig. 8 show the RPC stubs automatically produced by CAmkES for this system. The first of these receives the user's call to `cs_swap`, marshals function arguments into *c*'s IPC buffer and then invokes a capability to an seL4 endpoint to transfer the data to *s*. After receiving *s*'s reply, it unmarshals the response and returns to the user. The second RPC stub operating in *s*'s address space, receives an incoming call from *c* as an invocation of the function `ss_swap_internal`. It unmarshals the call arguments, calls the user's implementation from Fig. 5, marshals the user's return values into *s*'s IPC buffer and then sends this reply message to *c*.

The stub for *s* is more complex than the stub for *c* as it has to deal with pointers that are part of the stub's private state. These pointers are accessed via the functions `get_swap_a` and `get_swap_b`, which are only expected to be called from the stub code.

Though the user designing a component system may think of her architecture as depicted in Fig. 1, the system at runtime is shown more precisely in Fig. 9. Each component instance is comprised of the code the user has provided (shown in solid boxes) and the generated stubs (shown in dashed boxes). When *c* invokes `cs_swap`, which the user thinks of as an RPC to *s*, *c*'s RPC stub runs and performs an seL4 system call. The seL4 kernel invokes the RPC stub of *s* which then calls the user's `ss_swap` function, making it seem as if this function call came directly from *c*. On return from `ss_swap`, the RPC stub returns the response via seL4 to *c*'s RPC stub, which in turn delivers this to `cs_swap`. This control flow has the effect of allowing the user to design her system and reason about it in terms of abstract RPC operations, while CAmkES and seL4 implement the underlying communication mechanism.

4.3 Generated Proofs

The aim of the generated proofs is to guarantee the correctness of the RPC code produced by the component platform, intuitively showing that using the component platform gives the same assurance as running the function locally. The verification effort required from the proof engineer should therefore be comparable to the effort that would have been required to show the correctness of a local call.

For our example, Fig. 10 shows a 'natural' correctness property for `ss_swap` that might be used if it were just a local function. The pre-condition (line 1) requires that *x* and *y* are valid pointers. More precisely, the expression *ptr_valid_s32 st p* requires that the pointer *p* is a valid reference to a signed 32-bit value in state *st*.

The post-condition states that the value of the global *counter* will be updated and returned (line 3) and that the values at the pointers *x* and *y* will be swapped (lines 4-5). The function *ptr_coerce* is analogous to type casting in C and the expression *heap_w32 st p* returns the value pointed to by *p* in the state *st*. It is straightforward to prove this property using the existing translation tools and manual reasoning. It would also be straightforward to then use the resulting lemma in proofs for functions that call `ss_swap` directly.

In order to reason about execution in our example component-based system, we wish to claim that invoking *c*'s stub, `cs_swap`, is equivalent to invoking `ss_swap` directly. In this work, we are focussing on the generated glue code. This means we do

```
static unsigned int cs_swap_marshal(int a, int b) {
  unsigned int index = 0;
  seL4_SetMR(index, 0);  index++;
  seL4_SetMR(index, (seL4_Word)a);  index++;
  seL4_SetMR(index, (seL4_Word)b);  index++;
  return index;
}

static void cs_swap_call(unsigned int length) {
  seL4_MessageInfo_t info =
    seL4_MessageInfo_new(0, 0, 0, length);
  (void)seL4_Call(6, info); /* Call the seL4 endpoint */
}

static unsigned int cs_swap_unmarshal(int *a, int *b) {
  unsigned int index = 0;
  unsigned int ret = (unsigned int)seL4_GetMR(index);  index++;
  *a = (int)seL4_GetMR(index);  index++;
  *b = (int)seL4_GetMR(index);  index++;
  return ret;
}

unsigned int cs_swap(int *a, int *b) {
  unsigned int length = cs_swap_marshal(*a, *b);
  cs_swap_call(length);
  unsigned int ret = cs_swap_unmarshal(a, b);
  return ret;
}
```

Fig. 7. Generated stub for *c*

```
/* User-provided implementation. */
extern unsigned int ss_swap(int *a, int *b);

static void ss_swap_unmarshal(int *a, int *b) {
  unsigned int index = 1;
  *a = seL4_GetMR(index);  index++;
  *b = seL4_GetMR(index);  index++;
}

static unsigned int ss_swap_invoke(int *a, int *b) {
  return ss_swap(a, b);
}

static unsigned int ss_swap_marshal(unsigned int ret, int a, int b) {
  unsigned int index = 0;
  seL4_SetMR(index, (seL4_Word)ret);  index++;
  seL4_SetMR(index, (seL4_Word)a);    index++;
  seL4_SetMR(index, (seL4_Word)b);    index++;
  return index;
}

unsigned int ss_swap_internal(void) {
  int *a = get_swap_a();
  int *b = get_swap_b();
  ss_swap_unmarshal(a, b);
  unsigned int ret = ss_swap_invoke(a, b);
  unsigned int length = ss_swap_marshal(ret, *a, *b);
  return length;
}
```

Fig. 8. Generated stub for *s*

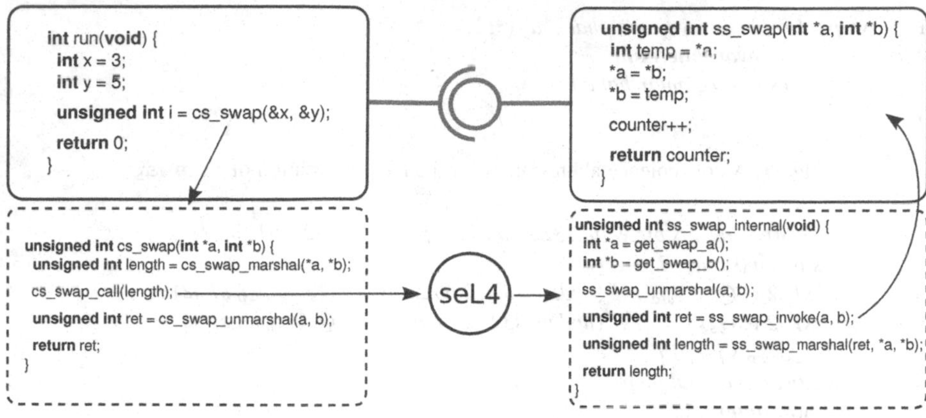

Fig. 9. Example system at runtime

$$
\begin{array}{l}
\{\!|\lambda s.\ s = s0 \wedge ptr\_valid\_s32\ s\ x \wedge ptr\_valid\_s32\ s\ y|\!\} \\
\quad ss\_swap\ x\ y \\
\{\!|\lambda r\ s.\ r = counter\ s0 + 1 \wedge counter\ s = r \wedge \\
\qquad heap\_w32\ s\ (ptr\_coerce\ x) = heap\_w32\ s0\ (ptr\_coerce\ y) \wedge \\
\qquad heap\_w32\ s\ (ptr\_coerce\ y) = heap\_w32\ s0\ (ptr\_coerce\ x)|\!\}!
\end{array}
$$

Fig. 10. A 'natural' correctness property if `ss_swap` were a local function

not yet connect to the formal seL4 specification, but instead axiomatise the `seL4_Call` as a direct invocation of `ss_swap_internal`, which is the effect of this system call. We intend to replace this axiomatisation with the seL4 specification in future work as discussed in Sect. 5.2. For now, the resulting sequence of operations that we wish to claim is equivalent to `ss_swap` is shown in Fig. 11. The steps are: marshalling in `c`, then the entire execution in `s`, including unmarshalling, executing `ss_swap`, and marshalling results, and finally unmarshalling of the result in `c` again.

The pre-condition and post-condition of `ss_swap` that the generated proofs are parameterised with are referred to as P_{ss_swap} and Q_{ss_swap}, respectively. The pre-condition is a predicate over the initial state and values of the input arguments to `ss_swap`. The post-condition is a predicate over the initial state, final state, return value, input arguments and output arguments to `ss_swap`. The types of these parameters may seem unnecessarily verbose, but they provide the user with the flexibility to state any correctness property that is expressible of a direct invocation of `ss_swap`.

Fig. 12 shows the correctness statement that the generated proof for the RPC stub provides. Though this appears larger and more dense than that in Fig. 10, it is not much more complicated. The expression *inv s*, present in both the pre- and post-conditions, captures the assumptions on user code mentioned in Sect. 3: in particular that user code does not violate the stub code's invariant which usually is easiest achieved by showing that it does not access glue code private state at all. The *ptr_valid_s32* pre-conditions (line

```
swap a b ≡ do cs_swap_marshal (*a) (*b);
              ss_swap_internal;
              cs_swap_unmarshal a b
           od
```

Fig. 11. A convenience abbreviation for the RPC invocation of `ss_swap`

```
1   {|λs. s = s0 ∧ inv s ∧ ptr_valid_s32 s p0_out ∧ ptr_valid_s32 s p1_out ∧
2       distinct [p0_out, p1_out] ∧
3       (∀ s1 s2 v. Q_ss_swap s1 (update_s32 s2 p0_out v) = Q_ss_swap s1 s2) ∧
4       (∀ s1 s2 v. Q_ss_swap s1 (update_s32 s2 p1_out v) = Q_ss_swap s1 s2) ∧
5       P_ss_swap s p0 p1|}
6    do cs_swap_marshal p0 p1;
7      ss_swap_internal;
8      cs_swap_unmarshal p0_out p1_out
9    od
10  {|λr s. inv s ∧ Q_ss_swap s0 s r p0 (ucast (heap_w32 s (ptr_coerce p0_out)))
11                        p1 (ucast (heap_w32 s (ptr_coerce p1_out)))|}!
```

Fig. 12. Generated RPC stub equivalence lemma

1) are familiar from the previous lemma. The *distinct* pre-condition (line 2) requires that the two pointers involved are not equal. While not strictly necessary in this case, the generated proofs conservatively require absence of aliasing between any user-provided pointers. This requirement, which is not an assumption of the implementation itself, is a convenience to ease the proof which we intend to remove in future.

The next two conjuncts (lines 3-4) state that the user's post-condition must not access the values of the pointer arguments through its final state parameter. This seems counter-intuitive, but we use it to allow internal stub code variables to substitute for the user's pointers when marshalling and unmarshalling arguments. That is, the user's post-condition can depend on the *values* of the arguments, but cannot depend on their *addresses*. The final conjunct (line 5) states that the user's pre-condition must hold prior to execution.

The post-condition (lines 10-11) is simpler, merely stating that the user's post-condition holds in addition to the glue code invariants. Here, *ucast* converts an unsigned 32-bit value to a signed 32-bit value.

For readability, we have omitted the proofs of the generated lemmas in this section, which themselves are also generated. However, the full CAmkES specification, user-provided code and framework for generating and validating the proofs we have described in this section are available online.[1]

4.4 User Instantiation

With the generated lemma from Fig. 12, all that remains is for the user to instantiate the locale with her specific pre- and post-condition and provide proofs for the locale

[1] https://github.com/seL4/camkes-manifest/tree/FM2015

```
1  Q_ss_swap s0 s r a b a_out b_out ≡ r = counter s0 + 1 ∧ counter s = r ∧
2                 is_valid_w32 s0 = is_valid_w32 s ∧
3                 a_out = b ∧ b_out = a
```

Fig. 13. User-instantiated post-condition

```
{|λs. s = s0 ∧ inv s ∧ ptr_valid_s32 s p0_out ∧ ptr_valid_s32 s p1_out ∧
    distinct [p0_out, p1_out]|}
  do cs_swap_marshal p0 p1;
    ss_swap_internal;
    cs_swap_unmarshal p0_out p1_out
  od
{|λr s. inv s ∧ r = counter s0 + 1 ∧ counter s = r ∧
         is_valid_w32 s0 = is_valid_w32 s ∧
         ucast (heap_w32 s (ptr_coerce p0_out)) = p1 ∧
         ucast (heap_w32 s (ptr_coerce p1_out)) = p0|}!
```

Fig. 14. Instantiated generated correctness lemma

assumptions, in particular the correctness of her `ss_swap` function. The natural pre-condition for this function is that from Fig. 10, but this is already subsumed by the generated pre-condition in Fig. 12. Therefore the user may instantiate her pre-condition to just λ *s a b. True*.

The natural post-condition, shown in Fig. 13, differs slightly from that of Fig. 10 as well. The first two conjuncts (line 1) are familiar from Fig. 10 and state the modification to, and return of, the global `counter`. The next (line 2) states that the initial state and the final state have identical sets of valid 32-bit pointers; that is, `ss_swap` does not invalidate any `int` pointers. This condition is relied upon by the generated proofs in assuming that internal pointers used for marshalling and unmarshalling are not invalidated by running user code. The final two conjuncts (line 3) are the equivalent of the final two from Fig. 10, though note that the user can now more conveniently express the property in terms of values, rather than pointer dereferences.

Having shown that this pre- and post-condition are wellformed and that the user-provided code is well behaved, the generated lemma is instantiated as shown in Fig. 14. Note that this is simpler than the generic lemma of Fig. 12 because some of the pre-conditions can be automatically discharged by simplification. The idea is that this will always be the case for well-behaved functions.

To demonstrate that this lemma can be used in further hand-written proofs, we consider a sample property of the `ss_swap` function, that swapping two pointers twice returns the pointers to their original value. This property is shown in Fig. 15 and has a straightforward proof stemming from the lemma in Fig. 14. Again, as intended, this final lemma is much simpler than the intermediate generated forms, requiring only the stub code invariant, the user's properties of the pointer arguments and inequality of the two pointers.

```
{|λs. s = s0 ∧ inv s ∧ ptr_valid_s32 s x ∧ ptr_valid_s32 s y ∧ x ≠ y|}
 do swap x y;
   swap y x
 od
{|λ_ s. inv s ∧
      ucast (heap_w32 s (ptr_coerce y)) = ucast (heap_w32 s0 (ptr_coerce y)) ∧
      ucast (heap_w32 s (ptr_coerce x)) = ucast (heap_w32 s0 (ptr_coerce x))|}!
```

Fig. 15. Applying generated proofs: swapping pointers twice returns them to their original state

5 Discussion

5.1 Trusting Generated Proofs

Having proven a system property by composing manual proofs with generated proofs, it is reasonable to ask what elements of the proof infrastructure need to be trusted. Isabelle/HOL is an LCF-style theorem prover [9], meaning that any proof within it relies only on the correctness of a small proof kernel. While we retain the assumption on the correctness of the Isabelle/HOL kernel, we would like to avoid requiring the user to trust additional tools.

We have not proven correctness of the code and proof generator itself. However, the proofs it produces are checked by Isabelle/HOL against the representation of the generated code presented by the C-to-Simpl translation. That means the proof generator does not need to be trusted, but the C-to-Simpl translation does. As mentioned in Sect. 2.3, there is separate work that reduces this trust even further and can be used to connect the Isabelle C semantics directly to binary code [24].

A fully manual proof using the same C verification infrastructure would end up with the same level of trustworthiness in the resulting property. The automation we provide saves the user the time and effort on tedious proofs, without increasing her assumptions.

5.2 Assumptions, Limitations and Future Work

Our generated proofs have limitations that we intend to lift in future work. In this section we make these explicit and discuss how they may be removed.

CAmkES supports a wide range of data types for RPC parameters, including language independent types such as `int` and `string`, C-specific types such as `uint64_t` and more general arbitrary types that are represented by a `typedef` in C. Additionally, arrays of any type from these categories are supported. The generated proofs currently only handle RPC interfaces using C-specific integer types and language independent types excluding `string`. This limitation is driven by pragmatics and is not fundamental to the system design. A future iteration of the tool will support all CAmkES data types.

The semantics of the seL4 system calls that we use is currently implicitly assumed in the generated proofs. In particular, we assume that the IPC primitives transfer the sender's IPC buffer to the receiver. This is the case in seL4. This implicit assumption could be eliminated by connecting to the existing seL4 specifications for these system calls and composing them with the RPC stub proofs. This connection to seL4 would also solve the following two limitations.

The current structure of the generated proofs would permit heap accesses that cross component boundaries. This most closely models colocating two components in a single address space. While the generated proofs do not assume or rely on this property, the framework currently does not prevent the proof engineer from making use of it. A user-provided proof written for a context where a global variable of component A is accessible in component B would be unsound in the case where the components are isolated from each other. In other words, connecting the model to the full seL4 specification with a setup where address spaces are not shared, would fail. Future versions of the framework could enforce this separation of component heaps from the outset using separation logic [22] and thereby ensure that user-provided proofs will compose correctly in a final system instance.

As a final limitation, the execution model used in our proofs relies on the seL4 kernel to be configured correctly. In particular, the proofs in this work describe the correctness of communication code in a CAmkES system. This communication is effected by operating on seL4 capabilities, unforgeable access tokens that are distributed to components on start up. Their presence is necessary to ensure the expected semantics of the system calls we assume. Furthermore, the *absence* of additional capabilities to component-private memory will guarantee isolation between components. An approach for removing this limitation would be to target the existing seL4 initialisation framework that has been verified to correctly configure userspace systems [3]. This proof can compose with our framework, but we do not yet show that the input CAmkES delivers to this initialiser implements the user's architecture description.

As far as we are aware none of these limitations are fundamental problems of the approach. The aim of this paper is to show the feasibility of automatically generating correctness proofs for glue code. The instantiation of these proofs to the seL4 execution environment can be achieved separately in future work.

6 Related Work

The proofs of generated code we have presented in this work are produced by the same tool [14] that generates the RPC stubs themselves. We do not rely on the correctness of the generator, or any implicit correspondence between the generated code and proofs as they are checked by Isabelle/HOL. In this sense, our approach is inspired by translation validation [20] and proof-carrying code [18].

Many verification frameworks have been proposed in the past for dealing with component-based systems, for example [1, 2, 8]. Our framework provides similar functionality. The work on which we report is not specifically aimed at increasing the ease of compositional reasoning. Instead, where our work differs is that we do not implicitly assume the correctness of generated RPC stubs, and instead provide an accompanying formal proof. To our knowledge, no current component-based verification framework provides such an automated code-level proof of generated platform code.

With respect to correct code generation and chained proofs, our work shares aspects with compiler verification. The CompCert verified compiler [15] and recent extensions to apply verification across translation units [21] have similarities, but work in a more controlled environment which enables more automated techniques. Our focus is on providing a compositional environment for interactive theorem proving that integrates with a larger interactive proof about the behaviour of the system, allowing the user a high degree of expressivity and control over the correctness properties they prove.

7 Conclusions

As the amount of code in high assurance systems increases, the only feasible approach to software verification is the application of compositional techniques. Existing frameworks for the verification of component-based systems all assume the correctness of the generated code of the component platform. In this work, we have demonstrated a technique for removing this assumption in the case of RPC stubs. We have shown how to compose generated RPC stub proofs with hand-written proofs to eventually yield a system-level correctness guarantee. By reducing the assumptions in component-based reasoning, we increase the reach of formal verification and raise the bar for assurance of large software systems.

Acknowledgements. NICTA is funded by the Australian Government through the Department of Communications and the Australian Research Council through the ICT Centre of Excellence Program.

This material is based on research sponsored by Air Force Research Laboratory and the Defense Advanced Research Projects Agency (DARPA) under agreement number FA8750-12-9-0179. The U.S. Government is authorized to reproduce and distribute reprints for Governmental purposes notwithstanding any copyright notation thereon. The views and conclusions contained herein are those of the authors and should not be interpreted as necessarily representing the official policies or endorsements, either expressed or implied, of Air Force Research Laboratory, the Defense Advanced Research Projects Agency or the U.S. Government.

References

[1] Adamek, J.: Static analysis of component systems using behavior protocols. In: OOPSLA, Anaheim, CA, US, pp. 116–117 (October 2003)

[2] Basu, A., Bensalem, S., Bozga, M., Combaz, J., Jaber, M., Nguyen, T.H., Sifakis, J.: Rigorous component-based system design using the BIP framework. Softw. 28(3), 41–48 (2011)

[3] Boyton, A., et al.: Formally verified system initialisation. In: Groves, L., Sun, J. (eds.) ICFEM 2013. LNCS, vol. 8144, pp. 70–85. Springer, Heidelberg (2013)

[4] Cobleigh, J.M., Giannakopoulou, D., Păsăreanu, C.S.: Learning assumptions for compositional verification. In: Garavel, H., Hatcliff, J. (eds.) TACAS 2003. LNCS, vol. 2619, pp. 331–346. Springer, Heidelberg (2003)

[5] Cock, D., Klein, G., Sewell, T.: Secure microkernels, state monads and scalable refinement. In: Mohamed, O.A., Muñoz, C., Tahar, S. (eds.) TPHOLs 2008. LNCS, vol. 5170, pp. 167–182. Springer, Heidelberg (2008)

[6] Fernandez, M., Kuz, I., Klein, G., Andronick, J.: Towards a verified component platform. In: PLOS, Farmington, PA, USA, p. 6 (November 2013)

[7] Fisler, K., Adsul, B.: Decomposing verification around end-user features. In: Meyer, B., Woodcock, J. (eds.) VSTTE 2005. LNCS, vol. 4171, pp. 74–81. Springer, Heidelberg (2008)
[8] Giannakopoulou, D., Păsăreanu, C.S., Barringer, H.: Assumption generation for software component verification. In: 17th ASE, Edinburgh, UK, pp. 3–12 (September 2002)
[9] Gordon, M.J.C., Milner, R., Wadsworth, C.P. (eds.): Edinburgh LCF. LNCS, vol. 78. Springer, Heidelberg (1979)
[10] Greenaway, D., Andronick, J., Klein, G.: Bridging the gap: Automatic verified abstraction of C. In: Beringer, L., Felty, A. (eds.) ITP 2012. LNCS, vol. 7406, pp. 99–115. Springer, Heidelberg (2012)
[11] Greenaway, D., Lim, J., Andronick, J., Klein, G.: Don't sweat the small stuff: Formal verification of C code without the pain. In: Proceedings of the 35th ACM SIGPLAN Conference on Programming Language Design and Implementation, Edinburgh, UK, pp. 429–439 (June 2014)
[12] ISO/IEC: Programming languages — C. Technical Report 9899:TC2, ISO/IEC JTC1/SC22/WG14 (May 2005)
[13] Klein, G., Elphinstone, K., Heiser, G., Andronick, J., Cock, D., Derrin, P., Elkaduwe, D., Engelhardt, K., Kolanski, R., Norrish, M., Sewell, T., Tuch, H., Winwood, S.: seL4: Formal verification of an OS kernel. In: SOSP, Big Sky, MT, USA, pp. 207–220 (October 2009)
[14] Kuz, I., Liu, Y., Gorton, I., Heiser, G.: CAmkES: A component model for secure microkernel-based embedded systems. Journal of Systems and Software Special Edition on Component-Based Software Engineering of Trustworthy Embedded Systems 80(5), 687–699 (2007)
[15] Leroy, X.: Formal certification of a compiler back-end, or: Programming a compiler with a proof assistant. In: 33rd POPL, Charleston, SC, USA, pp. 42–54 (2006)
[16] Leroy, X.: A formally verified compiler back-end. JAR 43(4), 363–446 (2009)
[17] Murray, T., Matichuk, D., Brassil, M., Gammie, P., Bourke, T., Seefried, S., Lewis, C., Gao, X., Klein, G.: seL4: from general purpose to a proof of information flow enforcement. In: IEEE Symp. Security & Privacy, San Francisco, CA, pp. 415–429 (May 2013)
[18] Necula, G.C., Lee, P.: Safe kernel extensions without run-time checking. In: 2nd OSDI, Seattle, WA, US, pp. 229–243 (October 1996)
[19] Nipkow, T., Paulson, L.C., Wenzel, M.: Isabelle/HOL — A Proof Assistant for Higher-Order Logic. LNCS, vol. 2283. Springer, Heidelberg (2002)
[20] Pnueli, A., Siegel, M.D., Singerman, E.: Translation validation. In: Steffen, B. (ed.) TACAS 1998. LNCS, vol. 1384, pp. 151–166. Springer, Heidelberg (1998)
[21] Ramananandro, T., Shao, Z., Weng, S.C., Koenig, J., Fu, Y.: A compositional semantics for verified separate compilation and linking. In: 4th CPP, Mumbai, India, pp. 3–14 (January 2015)
[22] Reynolds, J.C.: Separation logic: A logic for mutable data structures, Copenhagen, Denmark (July 2002)
[23] Schirmer, N.: Verification of Sequential Imperative Programs in Isabelle/HOL. PhD thesis, Technische Universität München (2006)
[24] Sewell, T., Myreen, M., Klein, G.: Translation validation for a verified OS kernel. In: PLDI, Seattle, Washington, USA, pp. 471–481 (June 2013)
[25] Szyperski, C.: Component Software: Beyond Object-Oriented Programming, Essex, England (1997)
[26] Trustworthy Systems Team: seL4 v1.03 (August 2014) (release August 10, 2014)
[27] Tuch, H., Klein, G., Norrish, M.: Types, bytes, and separation logic. In: 34th POPL, Nice, France, pp. 97–108 (January 2007)

[28] Wenzel, M.: The Isabelle/Isar Reference Manual (August 2014)
[29] Winwood, S., Klein, G., Sewell, T., Andronick, J., Cock, D., Norrish, M.: Mind the gap: A verification framework for low-level C. In: Berghofer, S., Nipkow, T., Urban, C., Wenzel, M. (eds.) TPHOLs 2009. LNCS, vol. 5674, pp. 500–515. Springer, Heidelberg (2009)

Property-Driven Fence Insertion Using Reorder Bounded Model Checking

Saurabh Joshi(✉) and Daniel Kroening

Department of Computer Science, University of Oxford, Oxford, UK
{saurabh.joshi,daniel.kroening}@cs.ox.ac.uk

Abstract. Modern architectures provide weaker memory consistency guarantees than sequential consistency. These weaker guarantees allow programs to exhibit behaviours where the program statements appear to have executed out of program order. Fortunately, modern architectures provide memory barriers (fences) to enforce the program order between a pair of statements if needed. Due to the intricate semantics of weak memory models, the placement of fences is challenging even for experienced programmers. Too few fences lead to bugs whereas overuse of fences results in performance degradation. This motivates automated placement of fences. Tools that restore sequential consistency in the program may insert more fences than necessary for the program to be correct. Therefore, we propose a property-driven technique that introduces *reorder-bounded exploration* to identify the smallest number of program locations for fence placement. We implemented our technique on top of CBMC; however, in principle, our technique is generic enough to be used with any model checker. Our experimental results show that our technique is faster and solves more instances of relevant benchmarks than earlier approaches.

1 Introduction

Modern multicore CPUs implement optimizations such as *store buffers* and *invalidate queues*. These features result in weaker memory consistency guarantees than sequential consistency (SC) [20]. Though such hardware optimizations offer better performance, the weaker consistency has the drawback of intricate and subtle semantics, thus making it harder for programmers to anticipate how their program might behave when run on such architectures. For example, it is possible for a pair of statements to appear to have executed out of the program order.

Consider the program given in Fig. 1a. Here, `x` and `y` are shared variables whereas `r1` and `r2` are thread-local variables. Statements s_1 and s_3 perform write operations. Owing to store buffering, these writes may not be reflected immediately in the memory. Next, both threads may proceed to perform the

This research was supported by ERC project 280053 and by the Semiconductor Research Corporation (SRC) project 2269.002.

N. Bjørner and F. de Boer (Eds.): FM 2015, LNCS 9109, pp. 291–307, 2015.
DOI: 10.1007/978-3-319-19249-9_19

read operations s_2 and s_4. Since the write operations might still not have hit the memory, stale values for `x` and `y` may be read in `r2` and `r1`, respectively. This will cause the assertion to fail. Such behaviour is possible with architectures that implement *Total Store Order (TSO)*, which allows write-read reordering. Note that on a hypothetical architecture that guarantees sequential consistency, this would never happen. However, owing to store buffering, a global observer might witness that the statements are executed in the order (s_2, s_4, s_1, s_3), which results in the assertion failure. We say that (s_1, s_2) and (s_3, s_4) have been reordered.

Fig. 1b shows how the assertion might fail on architectures that implement *Partial Store Order (PSO)*, which permits write-write and write-read reordering. Using SC, one would expect to observe `r2` == `1` if `r1` == `1` has been observed. However, reordering of the write operations (s_1, s_2) leads to the assertion failure. Architectures such as Alpha, POWER and SPARC RMO even allow read-write and read-read reorderings, amongst other behaviours. Fortunately, all modern architectures provide various kinds of *memory barriers (fences)* to prohibit unwanted weakening. Due to the intricate semantics of weak memory models and fences, an automated approach to the placement of fences is desirable.

In this paper, we make the following contributions:

- We introduce *ReOrder Bounded Model Checking (ROBMC)*. In ROBMC, the model checker is restricted to exploring only those behaviours of a program that contain at most k reorderings for a given bound k. The reorder bound is a new parameter for bounding model checking that has not been explored earlier.
- We study how the performance of the analysis is affected as the bound changes.
- We implement two ROBMC-based algorithms. In addition, we implement earlier approaches in the same framework to enable comparison with ROBMC.

The rest of the paper is organized as follows. Section 2 provides an overview and a motivating example for ROBMC. Sections 3 and 4 provide preliminaries and describe earlier approaches respectively. ROBMC is described in Section 5. Related research is discussed in Section 6. Experimental results are given in Section 7. Finally, we make concluding remarks in Section 8.

2 Motivation and Overview

There has been a substantial amount of previous research on automated fence insertion [3,4,7,11,17,23,24]. We distinguish approaches that aim to restore sequential consistency (SC) and approaches that aim to ensure that a user-provided assertion holds. Since every fence incurs a performance penalty, it is desirable to keep the number of fences to a minimum. Therefore, a property-driven approach for fence insertion can result in better performance. The downside of the property-driven approach is that it requires an explicit specification.

Consider the example given in Fig. 1c. Here, `x,y,z,w` are shared variables initialized to 0. All other variables are thread-local. A processor that implements

(a)

```
x = 0, y = 0;

s1 : x = 1;   ||  s3 : y = 1;
s2 : r1 = y;  ||  s4 : r2 = x;

assert(r1 == 1||r2 == 1);
```

(b)

```
x = 0, y = 0;

s1 : x = 1;  ||  s3 : r1 = y;
s2 : y = 1;  ||  s4 : r2 = x;

assert(r1! = 1||r2 == 1);
```

(c)

```
x = 0, y = 0, w = 0, z = 0;

s1 : z = 1;   ||  s5 : w = 1;
s2 : p1 = w;  ||  s6 : p2 = z;
s3 : x = 1;   ||  s7 : y = 1;
s4 : r1 = y;  ||  s8 : r2 = x;

assert(r1 == 1||r2 == 1);
assert(p1 + p2 >= 0);
```

Fig. 1. (a) Reordering in TSO. (b) Reordering in PSO. (c) A program with *innocent* and *culprit* reorderings.

total store ordering (TSO) permits a read of a global variable to precede a write to a different global variable when there are no dependencies between the two statements. Note that if (s_3, s_4) or (s_7, s_8) is reordered, the assertion will be violated. We shall call such pairs of statements *culprit pairs*. By contrast, the pairs (s_1, s_2) and (s_5, s_6) do not lead to an assertion violation irrespective of the order in which their statements execute. We shall call such pairs *innocent pairs*. A tool that restores SC would insert four fences, one for each pair mentioned earlier. However, only two fences (between s_3, s_4 and s_7, s_8) are necessary to avoid the assertion violation.

Some of the earlier property-driven techniques for fence insertion [3, 22] use the following approach. Consider a counterexample to the assertion. Every counterexample to the assertion must contain at least one culprit reordering. If we prevent all culprit reorderings, the program will satisfy the property. This is done in an iterative fashion. For all the counterexamples seen, a smallest set of reorderings S is selected such that S has at least one reordering in common with each of the counterexamples. Let us call such a set a *minimum-hitting-set* (*MHS*) over all the set of counterexamples C witnessed so far. All the weakenings in *MHS* are excluded from the program. Even though *MHS* may not cover all the culprit reorderings initially, it will eventually consist of culprit pairs only. Since one cannot distinguish the innocent pairs from the culprit ones a priori, such an approach may get distracted by innocent pairs, thus, taking too long to identify the culprit pairs.

To illustrate, let us revisit the example in Fig. 1c. Let us name the approach described above FI (Fence Insertion). Let the first counterexample path π^1 be $(s_2, s_1, s_6, s_5, s_4, s_7, s_8, s_3)$. The set of reorderings is $\{(s_1, s_2), (s_3, s_4), (s_5, s_6)\}$. Method FI may choose to forbid the reordering of $\{(s_1, s_2)\}$, as it is one of the choices for the *MHS*. Next, let $\pi^2 = (s_1, s_2, s_6, s_5, s_4, s_7, s_8, s_3)$. The set of reorderings for this trace is $\{(s_3, s_4), (s_5, s_6)\}$. There are multiple possible choices for *MHS*. For instance, FI may choose to forbid $\{(s_5, s_6)\}$. Let $\pi^3 = (s_2, s_1, s_5, s_6, s_8, s_3, s_4, s_7)$. As the set of reorderings is $\{(s_1, s_2), (s_7, s_8)\}$, one of the choices for the *MHS* is $\{(s_1, s_2), (s_5, s_6)\}$. Recall that (s_1, s_2) and (s_5, s_6) are innocent pairs. On the other hand, (s_3, s_4) and (s_7, s_8) are culprit pairs. FI may continue with $\pi^4 = (s_1, s_2, s_5, s_6, s_4, s_7, s_8, s_3)$. The set of reorderings in π^4 is $\{(s_3, s_4)\}$. An adversarial *MHS* would be $\{(s_1, s_2), (s_3, s_4)\}$. Let π^5 be $(s_1, s_2, s_6, s_5, s_8, s_3, s_4, s_7)$. The reorderings $\{(s_5, s_6), (s_7, s_8)\}$ will finally lead to the solution $\{(s_3, s_4), (s_7, s_8)\}$. In the 6th iteration FI will find that the program is safe with a given *MHS*. For brevity, we have not considered traces with reorderings (s_1, s_4) and (s_5, s_8). In the worst case, considering these reorderings might lead to even more traces.

As we can see, the presence of innocent pairs plays a major role in how fast FI will be able to find the culprit pairs. Consider a program with many more innocent pairs. FI will require increasingly more queries to the underlying model checker as the number of innocent pairs increases.

To address the problem caused by innocent pairs, we propose *Reorder Bounded Model Checking* (ROBMC). In ROBMC, we restrict the model checker to exploring only the behaviours of the program that have at most k reorderings for a given reordering bound k. Let us revisit the example given in Fig. 1c to see how the bounded exploration affects the performance. Assume that we start with the bound $k = 1$. Since the model checker is forced to find a counterexample with only one reordering, there is no further scope for an innocent reordering to appear in the counterexample path. Let the first trace found be $\pi^1 = (s_1, s_2, s_4, s_5, s_6, s_7, s_8, s_3)$. There is only one reordering $\{(s_3, s_4)\}$ in this trace. The resulting *MHS* will be $\{(s_3, s_4)\}$. Let the second trace be $\pi^2 = (s_1, s_2, s_5, s_6, s_8, s_3, s_4, s_7)$. As the only reordering is $\{(s_7, s_8)\}$, the *MHS* over these two traces would be $\{(s_3, s_4)(s_7, s_8)\}$. The next query would declare the program safe. Now, even with a larger bound, no further counterexamples can be produced. This example shows how a solution can be found much faster with ROBMC compared to FI. In the following sections, we describe our approach more formally.

3 Preliminaries

Let P be a concurrent program. A program execution is a sequence of events. An event e is a four-tuple

$$e \equiv \langle tid, in, var, type \rangle$$

where *tid* denotes the thread identifier associated with the event and *in* denotes the instruction that triggered the event. Instructions are dynamic instances of program statements. A program statement can give rise to multiple instructions due to loops and procedure calls. $stmt : Instr \to Stmt$ denotes a map from instructions to their corresponding program statements. The program order between any two instructions I_1 and I_2 is denoted as $I_1 <_{po} I_2$, which indicates that I_1 precedes I_2 in the program order. The component *var* denotes the global/shared variable that participated in the event e. The type of the event is represented by *type*, which can either be *read* or *write*. Without loss of generality, we assume that P only accesses one global/shared variable per statement. Therefore, given a statement $s \in Stmt$, we can uniquely identify the global variable involved as well as the type of the event that s gives rise to. Any execution of program P is a sequence of events $\pi = (e_1, \ldots, e_n)$. The ith event in the sequence π is denoted by $\pi(i)$.

Definition 1. *A pair of statements* (s_1, s_2) *of a program is said to be* reordered *in an execution* π *if:*

$$\exists_i \exists_j\, ((e_i.tid = e_j.tid) \wedge (\pi(i) = e_i) \wedge (\pi(j) = e_j) \\ \wedge (j < i) \wedge (e_i.in = I_1 \wedge e_j.in = I_2) \\ \wedge (I_1 <_{po} I_2) \wedge (stmt(I_1) = s_1 \wedge stmt(I_2) = s_2))$$

According to Defn. 1, two statements are reordered if they give rise to events that occurred out of program order.

Definition 2. *We write* $RO_A(s_1, s_2)$ *to denote that an architecture* A *allows the pair of statements* (s_1, s_2) *to be reordered.*

Different weak memory architectures permit particular reorderings of events.

- **Total Store Order (TSO)**: TSO allows a read to be reordered before a write if they access different global variables.

$$RO_{tso}(s_1, s_2) \equiv (s_1.var \neq s_2.var) \wedge (s_1.type = write \wedge s_2.type = read)$$

- **Partial Store Order (PSO)**: PSO allows a read or write to be reordered before a write if they access different global variables.

$$RO_{pso}(s_1, s_2) \equiv (s_1.var \neq s_2.var) \wedge (s_1.type = write)$$

Partial-order based models for TSO, PSO, *read memory order (RMO)* and POWER are presented in detail in [7].

Definition 3. *Let* C *be a set consisting of non-empty sets* $S_1, \ldots, S_n$*. The set* $\mathcal{H}$ *is called a* hitting-set *(HS) of* C *if:*

$$\forall_{S_i \in C} \mathcal{H} \cap S_i \neq \emptyset$$

$\mathcal{H}$ *is called a* minimal-hitting-set *(mhs) if any proper subset of* $\mathcal{H}$ *is not a hitting-set.* $\mathcal{H}$ *is a* minimum-hitting-set *(MHS) of* C *if* C *does not have a smaller hitting-set. Note that a collection* C *may have multiple minimum-hitting-sets.*

4 Property-driven Fence Insertion

4.1 Overview

In this section we will discuss two approaches that were used earlier for property-driven fence insertion. We will present our improvements in the next section.

For a program P of size $|P|$, the total number of pairs of statements is $|P|^2$. Since the goal is to find a subset of these pairs, the search space is $2^{|P|^2}$. Thus, the search space grows *exponentially* as the size of the program is increased.

An automated method for fence insertion typically includes two components: (1) a model checker M and (2) a search technique that uses M iteratively in order to find a solution. We assume that the model checker M has the following properties:

- M should be able to find counterexamples to assertions in programs given a memory model.
- M should return the counterexample π in form of a sequence of events as described in Section 3.
- For a pair of statements (s_1, s_2) for which $RO_A(s_1, s_2)$ holds, M should be able to enforce an ordering constraint $s_1 \prec s_2$ that forbids the exploration of any execution where (s_1, s_2) is reordered.

4.2 Fence Insertion Using Trace Enumeration

Alg. 1 is a very simple approach to placing fences in the program with the help of such a model checker. The algorithm is representative of the technique that is used in DFENCE [24]. Alg. 1 iteratively submits queries to M for a counterexample (Line 7). All the pairs of statements that have been reordered in π are collected in SP (Line 11). To avoid the same trace in future iterations, reordering of at least one of these pairs must be disallowed. The choice of which reorderings must be banned is left open. This process is repeated until no further error traces are found. Finally, *computeMinimalSolution*(ϕ) computes a minimal set of pairs of statements such that imposing ordering constraints on them satisfies ϕ.

Termination and Soundness. Even though the program may have unbounded loops and thus potentially contains an unbounded number of counterexamples, Alg. 1 terminates. The reason is that an ordering constraint $s_1 \prec s_2$ disallows reordering of all events that are generated by (s_1, s_2). The number of iterations is bounded above by $2^{|P|^2}$, which is the size of the search space. Soundness is a consequence of the fact that the algorithm terminates only when no counterexamples are found. A minimal-hitting-set (mhs) is computed over all these counterexamples to compute the culprit pairs that must not be reordered. Since every trace must go through one of these pairs, it cannot manifest when the reordering of these pairs is banned. The number of pairs computed is minimal, thus, Alg. 1 does not guarantee the least number of fences. One can replace the minimal-hitting-set (mhs) with a minimum-hitting-set (MHS) in order to obtain such a guarantee.

4.3 Accelerated Fence Insertion

Alg. 2 is an alternative approach to fence insertion. The differences between Alg. 1 and Alg. 2 are highlighted. Alg. 2 has been used in [22,23] and is a variant of the approach used in [3]. Alg. 2 starts with an ordering constraint ϕ (Line 5), which is initially unrestricted. A call to the model checker M is made (Line 7) to check whether the program P under the constraint ϕ has a counterexample. From a counterexample π, we collect the set of pairs of statements SP that have been reordered in π (Line 11). This set is put into a collection C.

Next, we compute a minimum-hitting-set over C. This gives us one of the smallest sets of pairs of statements that can avoid all the counterexamples seen so far. The original approach in [22] uses a minimal-hitting-set (mhs). The ordering

Algorithm 1. Trace Enumerating Fence Insertion (TE)

1. **Input:** Program P
2. **Output:** Set S of pairs of statements that must not be reordered to avoid assertion failure
3. $C := \emptyset$
4. $S := \emptyset$
5. $\phi := true$
6. **loop**
7. $\langle result, \pi \rangle := M(P_\phi)$
8.   **if** $result = SAFE$ **then**
9.   **break**
10.   **end if**
11. $SP := GetReorderedPairs(\pi)$
12.   **if** $SP = \emptyset$ **then**
13.   **print Error:** Program cannot be repaired
14.   **return errorcode**
15.   **end if**
16. $\phi := \phi \wedge \left(\bigvee_{(s_1,s_2) \in SP} s_1 \prec s_2 \right)$
17. **end loop**
18. $S := computeMinimalSolution(\phi)$
19. **return** S

Algorithm 2. Accelerated Fence Insertion (FI)

1. **Input:** Program P
2. **Output:** Set S of pairs of statements that must not be reordered to avoid assertion failure
3. $C := \emptyset$
4. $S := \emptyset$
5. $\phi := true$
6. **loop**
7. $\langle result, \pi \rangle := M(P_\phi)$
8.   **if** $result = SAFE$ **then**
9.   **break**
10.   **end if**
11. $SP := GetReorderedPairs(\pi)$
12.   **if** $SP = \emptyset$ **then**
13.   **print Error:** Program can not be repaired
14.   **return errorcode**
15.   **end if**
16. $C := C \cup \{SP\}$
17. $S := MHS(C)$
18. $\phi := \bigwedge_{(s_1,s_2) \in S} s_1 \prec s_2$
19. **end loop**
20. **return** S

constraint ϕ is updated using the minimum-hitting-set (Lines 17–18). Alg. 2 tells the model checker which reorderings from each counterexample are to be banned at every iteration, which is in contrast to Alg. 1. Alg. 2 assumes that an assertion violation in P is due to a reordering. If a counterexample is found without any reordering, the algorithm exits with an error (Lines 12–15). Finally, the algorithm terminates when no more counterexamples can be found (Lines 8–10).

Termination and Soundness. The argument that applies to Alg. 1 can also be used to prove termination and soundness of Alg. 2. In addition, the constraint ϕ generated is generally stronger (i.e. $\phi_{\text{Alg. 2}} \rightarrow \phi_{\text{Alg. 1}}$) than the constraint generated by Alg. 1. Thus, for the same sequence of traces, Alg. 2 typically converges to a solution faster than Alg. 1.

5 Reorder-Bounded Exploration

Alg. 2 can further be improved by avoiding innocent reorderings so that culprit reorderings responsible for the violation of the assertion are found faster.

As discussed in Section 2, Alg. 2 requires many iterations to converge and terminate in the presence of innocent reorderings. The reason is that the model checker may not return the simplest possible counterexample that explains the assertion violation due to reorderings. In order to address this problem, we need a model checker M' with an additional property as follows:

- M' takes P_ϕ and k as inputs. Here, P_ϕ is the program along with the ordering constraint ϕ and k is a positive integer. M' produces a counterexample π for P_ϕ such that π has at most k reorderings. If it cannot find a counterexample with at most k reorderings, then it will declare P_ϕ safe.

With a model checker M', we can employ Alg. 3 to speed up the discovery of the smallest set of culprit pairs of statements. The steps that differ from Alg. 2 in Alg. 3 are highlighted. Alg. 3 initializes the reordering bound k (Line 5) to a given lower bound K_1. The model checker M' is now called with this bound to obtain a counterexample that has at most k reorderings (Line 9). When the counterexample cannot be found, the bound k is increased according to some strategy denoted by *increaseStrategy* (Line 22). Note that collection C and the ordering constraint ϕ are preserved even when k is increased. Thus, when k is increased from k_1 to k_2, the search for culprit reorderings starts directly with the ordering constraints that repair the program for up to k_1 reorderings. Only those counterexamples that require more than k_1 and fewer than k_2 culprit reorderings will be reported. Let us assume that P does not have any counterexample with more than k_{opt} reorderings. If k_{opt} is much smaller than k, the performance of Alg. 3 might suffer due to interference from innocent reorderings. If the increase in k is too small, the algorithm might have to go through many queries to reach the given upper bound K_2. It can be beneficial to increase the bound k by a larger amount after witnessing a few successive *SAFE* queries, and by a smaller amount when a counterexample has been found recently.

Building M'. A model checker M' that supports bounded exploration can be constructed from M as follows. For every pair (s_1, s_2) that can potentially be reordered, we introduce a new auxiliary Boolean variable a_{12}. Then, a constraint $\neg a_{12} \leftrightarrow (s_1 \prec s_2)$ can be added. This allows us to enforce the ordering constraint $s_1 \prec s_2$ by manipulating values assigned to a_{12}. For a given bound k, we can enforce a reorder-bounded exploration by adding a cardinality constraint $\sum a_{ij} \leq k$. This constraint forces only up to k auxiliary variables to be set to *true*, thus, allowing only up to k reorderings.

Algorithm 3. ROBMC

```
Input: Program P, lower bound K1 and an upper bound K2
Output: Set S of pairs of statements that must not be reordered to avoid assertion failure
C := ∅
S := ∅
k := K1
φ := true
while k ≤ K2 do
    loop
        ⟨result, π⟩ := M'(P_φ, k)
        if result = SAFE then
            break
        end if
        SP := GetReorderedPairs(π)
        if SP = ∅ then
            print Error: Program cannot be repaired
            return errorcode
        end if
        C := C ∪ {SP}
        S := MHS(C)
        φ := ⋀_{(s1,s2)∈S} s1 ≺ s2
    end loop
    k := increaseStrategy(k)
end while
return S
```

Optimizing Alg. 3. Even when the correct solution for the program is found, Alg. 3 has to reach the upper bound K_2 to terminate. This can cause many further queries for which the model checker M' is going to declare the program *SAFE*. To achieve soundness with Alg. 3, K_2 should be as high as the total number of all the pairs of statements that can be potentially reordered. This leads to a very high value for K_2, which may reduce the advantage that Alg. 3 has over Alg. 2.

We can avoid these unnecessary queries if the model checker M' produces a proof whenever it declares the program P_ϕ as *SAFE*. This proof is analogous to an *unsatisfiable core* produced by many SAT/SMT solvers whenever the result of a query is *unsat.*[1] With this additional feature of M', we can check whether the cardinality constraint $\sum a_{ij} \leq k$ was the reason for declaring the program *SAFE*. If not, we know that P is safe under the ordering constraint ϕ irrespective of the bound. Therefore, Alg. 3 can terminate early as shown in Alg. 4. The difference between Alg. 3 and Alg. 4 is highlighted in Alg. 4. The model checker M' now returns ψ as a proof when P_ϕ is safe (Line 10). When M' declares P_ϕ as safe, Alg. 4 checks whether the bound k is the reason that P_ϕ is declared safe (Line 12). If not, the termination flag is set to *true* to trigger early termination (Line 13).

[1] SAT solvers such as MiniSat [13] and Lingeling [10] allow to query whether a given assumption was part of the unsatisfiable core [14].

Algorithm 4. ROBMC-ET

```
Input: Program P, lower bound K1 and an upper bound K2
Output: Set S of pairs of statements that must not be reordered to avoid assertion failure
C := ∅
S := ∅
k := K1
φ := true
terminate := false
while k ≤ K2 and terminate = false do
    loop
        ⟨result, π, ψ⟩ := M′(P_φ, k)
        if result = SAFE then
            if not safeDueToBound(k, ψ) then
                terminate := true
            end if
            break
        end if
        SP := GetReorderedPairs(π)
        if SP = ∅ then
            print Error: Program cannot be repaired
            return errorcode
        end if
        C := C ∪ {SP}
        S := MHS(C)
        φ := ⋀_{(s1,s2)∈S} s1 ≺ s2
    end loop
    k := increaseStrategy(k)
end while
return S
```

Termination and Soundness. Let the program P have counterexamples with up to k_{opt} culprit reorderings. If the value of the upper bound K_2 for Alg. 3 and Alg. 4 is smaller than k_{opt}, there might exist traces that the algorithms fail to explore. For soundness, the value of K_2 should thus be higher than k_{opt}. Since k_{opt} is generally not known a priori, a conservative value of K_2 should be equal to the total number of pairs of statements for which reordering might happen ($RO_A(s_1, s_2)$ is *true*). Termination is guaranteed due to finiteness of the number of pairs of statements and K_2.

6 Related Work

There are two principal approaches for modelling weak memory semantics. One approach is to use operational models that explicitly model the buffers and queues to mimic the hardware [1, 2, 5, 11, 18, 23, 24]. The other approach is to axiomatize the observable behaviours using partial orders [6, 7, 9]. Buffer-based modelling is closer to the hardware implementation than the partial-order based approach. However, the partial-order based approach provides an abstraction of the underlying complexity of the hardware and has been proven effective [6]. Results on complexity and decidability for various weak memory models such as TSO, PSO and RMO are given in [8].

$$[\mathtt{x_i} = 0;\ \mathtt{y_i} = 0;]^n$$
$$\mathtt{s1} = 0;\ \mathtt{s2} = 0;$$

$$\begin{bmatrix} \mathtt{x_i} = 1; \\ \mathtt{s1{+}{=}y_i}; \end{bmatrix}^n \quad || \quad \begin{bmatrix} \mathtt{y_i} = 1; \\ \mathtt{s2{+}{=}x_i}; \end{bmatrix}^n$$

$$\mathtt{assert(s1 + s2 >= 0);}$$

Fig. 2. A parameterized program. Here, $[\mathtt{st}]^n$ denotes that the statement **st** is repeated n times.

Due to the intricate and subtle semantics of weak memory consistency and the fences offered by modern architectures, there have been numerous efforts aimed at automating fence insertion [3, 4, 7, 11, 15, 17, 22–24]. These works can be divided into two categories. In one category, fences are inserted in order to restore sequential consistency [4,7,11]. The primary advantage is that no external specification is required. On the downside, the fences inferred by these methods may be unnecessary.

The second category are methods that insert only those fences that are required for a program to satisfy given properties [2, 3, 22–24]. These techniques usually require repetitive calls to a model checker or a solver. DFENCE is a dynamic analysis tool that falls into this category. Our work differs from DFENCE as ours is a fully static approach as compared to the dynamic approach used by DFENCE. A direct comparison with DFENCE cannot be made. However, we have implemented their approach in our framework and we present an experimental comparison using our re-implementation.

MEMORAX [3] and REMMEX [22, 23] also fall into the category of property-driven tools. MEMORAX [1] computes all possible minimal-hitting-set solutions. Though it computes the smallest possible solution, exhaustively searching for all possible solutions can make such an approach slow. Moreover, MEMORAX requires that the input program is written in RMM — a special purpose language. Alg. 2 captures what MEMORAX would do if it has to find only one solution. REMMEX also falls in the category of property-driven tools and their approach is given as Alg. 2.

Bounded model checking has been used for the verification of concurrent programs [6, 27]. In context-bounded model checking [19, 27], the number of interleavings in counterexamples is bounded, but executions are explored without depth limit. ROBMC is orthogonal to these ideas, as here the bound is on the number of event reorderings.

7 Implementation and Experimental Results

7.1 Experimental Setup

To enable comparison between the different approaches, we implemented all four algorithms in the same code base, using CBMC [6] as the model checker. CBMC

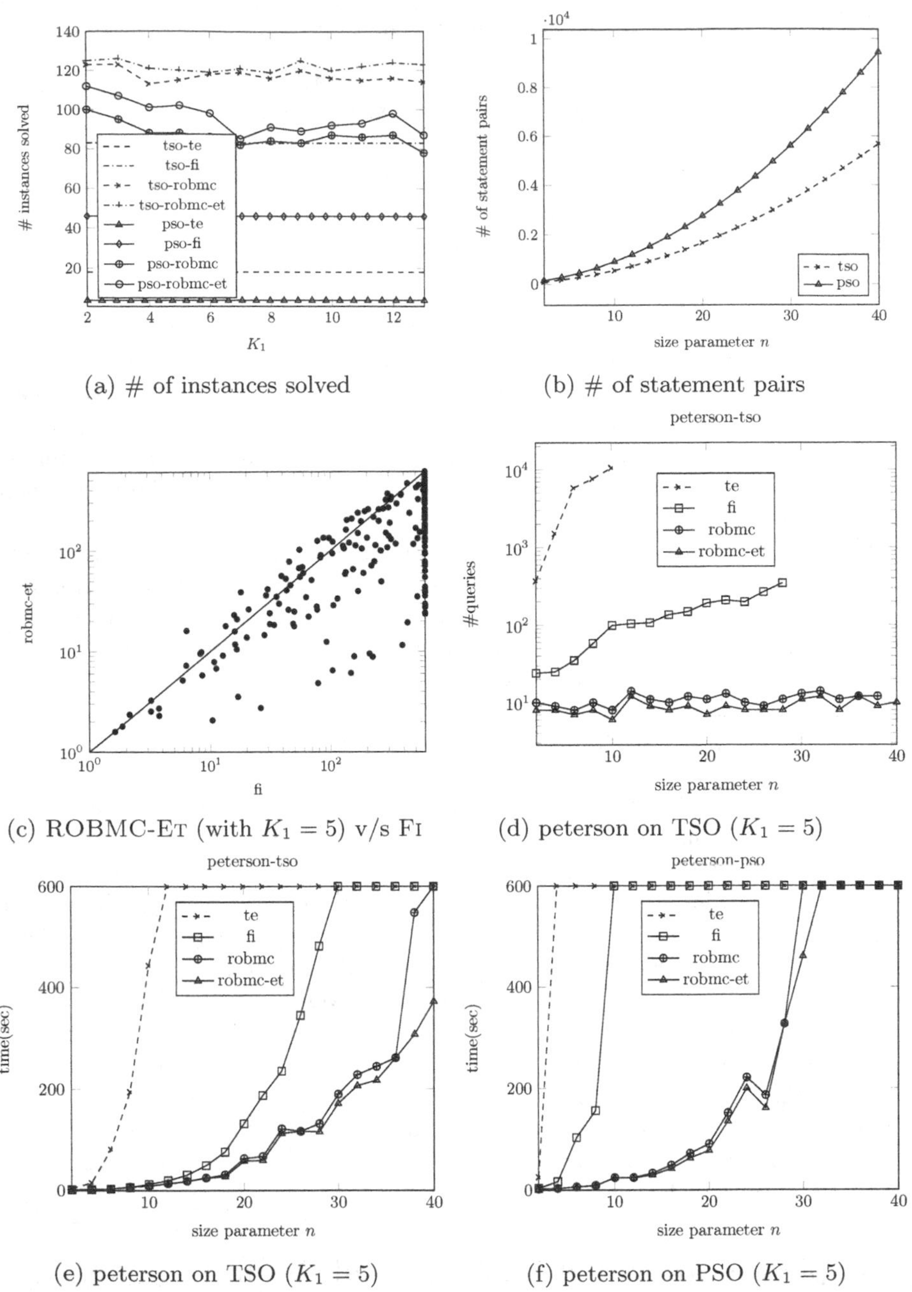

(a) # of instances solved

(b) # of statement pairs

(c) ROBMC-ET (with $K_1 = 5$) v/s FI

(d) peterson on TSO ($K_1 = 5$)

(e) peterson on TSO ($K_1 = 5$)

(f) peterson on PSO ($K_1 = 5$)

Fig. 3. For all experiments : Timeout=600 seconds, K_2=all pairs of statement (for soundness)

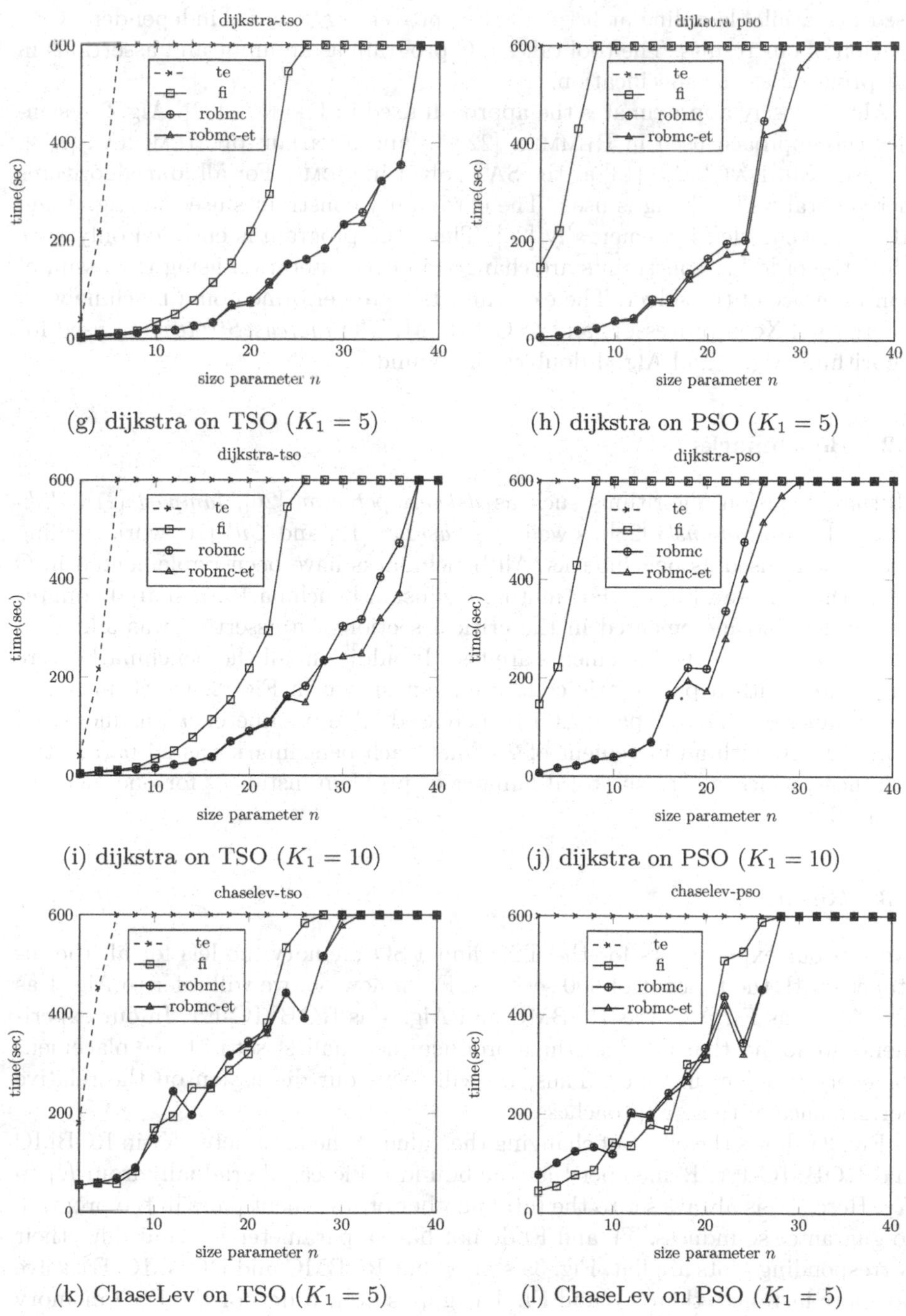

(g) dijkstra on TSO ($K_1 = 5$)

(h) dijkstra on PSO ($K_1 = 5$)

(i) dijkstra on TSO ($K_1 = 10$)

(j) dijkstra on PSO ($K_1 = 10$)

(k) ChaseLev on TSO ($K_1 = 5$)

(l) ChaseLev on PSO ($K_1 = 5$)

Fig. 3. (*continued*)

explores loops until a given bound. Our implementation and the benchmarks used are available online at http://www.cprover.org/glue for independent verification of our results. The tool takes a C program as an input and assertions in the program as the specification.

Alg. 1 closely approximates the approach used in DFENCE [24]. Alg. 2 resembles the approach used in REMMEX [22, 23] and a variant of MEMORAX [1, 3]. We used MINISAT 2.2.0 [13] as the SAT solver in CBMC. For all four algorithms incremental SAT solving is used. The cardinality constraints used in Alg. 3 and Alg. 4 are encoded incrementally [25]. Thus, the program is encoded only once while the ordering constraints are changed in every iteration using the assumption interface of the solver. The experiments were performed on a machine with 8-core Intel Xeon processors and 48 GB RAM. The *increaseStrategy*(k) used for algorithms Alg. 3 and Alg. 4 doubles the bound k.

7.2 Benchmarks

Mutual exclusion algorithms such as *dekker*, *peterson* [26], *lamport* [21], *dijkstra* [21] and *szymanski* [28] as well as *ChaseLev* [12] and *Cilk* [16] work stealing queues were used as benchmarks. All benchmarks have been implemented in C using the `pthread` library. For mutual exclusion benchmarks, a shared counter was added and incremented in the critical section. An assertion was added to check that none of the increments are lost. In addition, all the benchmarks were augmented with a parametric code fragment shown in Fig. 2, which increases the number of innocent pairs as n is increased. The parameter n was increased from 2 to 40 with an increment of 2. Thus, each benchmark has 20 parametric instances, which makes the total number of problem instances for one memory model 140.

7.3 Results

We ran our experiments for the TSO and PSO memory models for all the instances with the timeout of 600 seconds. From now on, we will refer to Alg. 1 as TE, Alg. 2 as FI, Alg. 3 as ROBMC and Alg. 4 as ROBMC-ET. In our experiments we found that all algorithms produce the smallest set of fence placement for every problem instance. Thus, we will focus our discussion on the relative performance of these approaches.

Fig. 3a shows the effect of changing the value of the parameter K_1 in ROBMC and ROBMC-ET. Remember that the bound is increased gradually from K_1 to K_2. Here, K_2 is always set to the total number of statement pairs in the program to guarantee soundness. TE and FI do not have a parameter K_1, and thus, their corresponding plots are flat. Fig. 3a shows that ROBMC and ROBMC-ET solve far more instances than TE and FI. The gap is even wider for the PSO memory model, which allows more reordering, and thus the number of innocent pairs are significantly higher compared to TSO on the same program. As expected, ROBMC-ET performs better, due to the early termination optimization. The value of K_1 barely affects the number of solved instances. The moderate downward trend for the plots as K_1 increases suggests that as K_1 increases, ROBMC tends to behave more and more like FI.

Fig. 3b shows the increase in the total number of statement pairs that can potentially be reordered as the parameter n (Fig. 2) increases for the Peterson algorithm. As expected, the number of pairs grows quadratically in n. For PSO, the increase is steeper, as PSO allows more reordering than TSO. This explains the better performance of the ROBMC approaches on PSO.

The log-scale scatter plot in Fig. 3c compares the run-time of ROBMC-ET with $K_1 = 5$ with FI over all 280 problem instances. FI times out significantly more often (data points where both time out are omitted). Even on the instances solved by both the approaches, ROBMC-ET clearly outperforms FI on all but a few instances. Those instances where FI performs better typically have very few innocent pairs. Note that the queries generated by ROBMC-ET are more expensive, as our current implementation uses cardinality constraints to enforce boundedness. Thus, it is possible for FI to sometimes perform better even though it generates a larger number of queries to the underlying model checker.

The semi-log-scale plot in Fig. 3d gives the number of queries to the model checker required by the approaches for the peterson algorithm on TSO. TE and FI generate exponentially many queries to the model checker as n increases. By contrast, the number of queries generated by ROBMC and ROBMC-ET virtually remains unaffected by n. This is expected as the search is narrow and focussed owing to the bound k.

Fig. 3e and Fig. 3f give the relative performance of all the algorithms when the size and number of innocent pairs increases with the parameter n. All plots show an exponential trajectory, indicating that ROBMC does not fundamentally reduce the complexity of the underlying problem. Even though the number of queries required remains constant (Fig. 3d), each such query becomes more expensive because of the cardinality constraints.

However, the growth rate for ROBMC and ROBMC-ET is much slower compared to TE and FI. Fig. 3e and Fig. 3f corroborate the claim that ROBMC-based approaches perform much better when there are a significant number of innocent pairs. For PSO, the performance gained by using ROBMC is even higher, as PSO allows more reordering. Similar trends are observed for dijkstra algorithm in Figs. 3g and 3h. Plots in Figs. 3g and 3i as well as Figs. 3h and 3j show that the performance of ROBMC-based approaches is not highly sensitive to the value of K_1 as it changes from 5 to 10. This is consistent with the observation made from Fig. 3a.

The performance comparision for the ChaseLev work stealing queue is given in Figs. 3k and 3l. Here it can be seen that the threshold (in terms of innocent pairs) needed for ROBMC to surpass other approaches is higher. Even for such a case, ROBMC still provides competitive performance when the number of innocent pairs are low. ROBMC regains its superiority towards the end as the number of innocent pairs increases. Thus, even when every individual query is more expensive (due to the current implementation that uses cardinality constraints to enforce the bound), ROBMC always provides almost equal or better performance for all the benchmarks.

8 Concluding Remarks

ROBMC is a new variant of Bounded Model Checking that has not been explored before. Our experimental results indicate substantial speedups when applying ROBMC for the automated placement of fences on programs with few culprit pairs and a large number of innocent pairs. In particular, we observe that the speedup obtained by using ROBMC increases when targeting a weaker architecture. Thus, ROBMC adds a new direction in bounded model checking which is worth exploring further.

Acknowledgement. The authors would like to thank Vincent Nimal for helpful discussions on the related work.

References

1. Abdulla, P.A., Atig, M.F., Chen, Y.-F., Leonardsson, C., Rezine, A.: Counterexample guided fence insertion under TSO. In: Flanagan, C., König, B. (eds.) TACAS 2012. LNCS, vol. 7214, pp. 204–219. Springer, Heidelberg (2012)
2. Abdulla, P.A., Atig, M.F., Lang, M., Ngo, T.P.: Precise and Sound Automatic Fence Insertion Procedure under PSO. In: Networked Systems (NETYS). LNCS. Springer (2015)
3. Abdulla, P.A., Atig, M.F., Chen, Y.-F., Leonardsson, C., Rezine, A.: MEMORAX, a precise and sound tool for automatic fence insertion under TSO. In: Piterman, N., Smolka, S.A. (eds.) TACAS 2013. LNCS, vol. 7795, pp. 530–536. Springer, Heidelberg (2013)
4. Alglave, J., Kroening, D., Nimal, V., Poetzl, D.: Don't sit on the fence: A static analysis approach to automatic fence insertion. In: Biere, A., Bloem, R. (eds.) CAV 2014. LNCS, vol. 8559, pp. 508–524. Springer, Heidelberg (2014)
5. Alglave, J., Kroening, D., Nimal, V., Tautschnig, M.: Software verification for weak memory via program transformation. In: Felleisen, M., Gardner, P. (eds.) ESOP 2013. LNCS, vol. 7792, pp. 512–532. Springer, Heidelberg (2013), http://dx.doi.org/10.1007/978-3-642-37036-6_28
6. Alglave, J., Kroening, D., Tautschnig, M.: Partial orders for efficient bounded model checking of concurrent software. In: Sharygina, N., Veith, H. (eds.) CAV 2013. LNCS, vol. 8044, pp. 141–157. Springer, Heidelberg (2013)
7. Alglave, J., Maranget, L., Sarkar, S., Sewell, P.: Fences in weak memory models (extended version). Formal Methods in System Design (FMSD) 40(2), 170–205 (2012)
8. Atig, M.F., Bouajjani, A., Burckhardt, S., Musuvathi, M.: On the verification problem for weak memory models. In: POPL, pp. 7–18. ACM (2010)
9. Batty, M., Owens, S., Sarkar, S., Sewell, P., Weber, T.: Mathematizing C++ concurrency. In: Principles of Programming Languages (POPL), pp. 55–66. ACM (2011)
10. Biere, A.: Lingeling, http://fmv.jku.at/lingeling/

11. Bouajjani, A., Derevenetc, E., Meyer, R.: Checking and enforcing robustness against TSO. In: Felleisen, M., Gardner, P. (eds.) ESOP 2013. LNCS, vol. 7792, pp. 533–553. Springer, Heidelberg (2013)
12. Chase, D., Lev, Y.: Dynamic circular work-stealing deque. In: Symposium on Parallelism in Algorithms and Architectures (SPAA), pp. 21–28. ACM (2005)
13. Eén, N., Sörensson, N.: MiniSatu, http://minisat.se/Main.html
14. Eén, N., Sörensson, N.: Temporal induction by incremental SAT solving. Electr. Notes Theor. Comput. Sci. 89(4), 543–560 (2003)
15. Fang, X., Lee, J., Midkiff, S.P.: Automatic fence insertion for shared memory multiprocessing. In: International Conference on Supercomputing (ICS), pp. 285–294. ACM (2003)
16. Frigo, M., Leiserson, C.E., Randall, K.H.: The implementation of the Cilk-5 multithreaded language. In: Programming Language Design and Implementation (PLDI), pp. 212–223 (1998)
17. Kuperstein, M., Vechev, M., Yahav, E.: Automatic inference of memory fences. In: Formal Methods in Computer-Aided Design (FMCAD), pp. 111–120. IEEE (2010)
18. Kuperstein, M., Vechev, M.T., Yahav, E.: Partial-coherence abstractions for relaxed memory models. In: Programming Language Design and Implementation (PLDI), pp. 187–198. ACM (2011)
19. Lal, A., Reps, T.: Reducing concurrent analysis under a context bound to sequential analysis. In: Gupta, A., Malik, S. (eds.) CAV 2008. LNCS, vol. 5123, pp. 37–51. Springer, Heidelberg (2008)
20. Lamport, L.: How to make a multiprocessor computer that correctly executes multiprocess programs. IEEE Trans. Computers 28(9), 690–691 (1979)
21. Lamport, L.: A fast mutual exclusion algorithm. ACM Trans. Comput. Syst. 5(1), 1–11 (1987)
22. Linden, A., Wolper, P.: A verification-based approach to memory fence insertion in relaxed memory systems. In: Groce, A., Musuvathi, M. (eds.) SPIN 2011. LNCS, vol. 6823, pp. 144–160. Springer, Heidelberg (2011)
23. Linden, A., Wolper, P.: A verification-based approach to memory fence insertion in PSO memory systems. In: Piterman, N., Smolka, S.A. (eds.) TACAS 2013. LNCS, vol. 7795, pp. 339–353. Springer, Heidelberg (2013)
24. Liu, F., Nedev, N., Prisadnikov, N., Vechev, M., Yahav, E.: Dynamic synthesis for relaxed memory models. In: Programming Language Design and Implementation (PLDI), pp. 429–440. ACM (2012)
25. Martins, R., Joshi, S., Manquinho, V., Lynce, I.: Incremental cardinality constraints for MaxSAT. In: O'Sullivan, B. (ed.) CP 2014. LNCS, vol. 8656, pp. 531–548. Springer, Heidelberg (2014)
26. Peterson, G.L.: Myths about the mutual exclusion problem. Inf. Process. Lett. 12(3), 115–116 (1981)
27. Qadeer, S., Rehof, J.: Context-bounded model checking of concurrent software. In: Halbwachs, N., Zuck, L.D. (eds.) TACAS 2005. LNCS, vol. 3440, pp. 93–107. Springer, Heidelberg (2005)
28. Szymanski, B.K.: A simple solution to Lamport's concurrent programming problem with linear wait. In: International Conference on Supercomputing (ICS), pp. 621–626. ACM (1988)

Verifying the Safety of a Flight-Critical System

Guillaume Brat[1], David Bushnell[2], Misty Davies[3], Dimitra Giannakopoulou[3], Falk Howar[4], and Temesghen Kahsai[1(✉)]

[1] Carnegie Mellon University, Pittsburgh, USA
[2] AerospaceComputing, Mountain View, USA
[3] NASA Ames, Mountain View, USA
[4] IPSSE, TU Clausthal, Clausthal-Zellerfeld, Germany
temesghen.kahsaiazene@nasa.gov

Abstract. This paper describes our work on demonstrating verification technologies on a flight-critical system of realistic functionality, size, and complexity. Our work targeted a commercial aircraft control system named Transport Class Model (TCM), and involved several stages: formalizing and disambiguating requirements in collaboration with domain experts; processing models for their use by formal verification tools; applying compositional techniques at the architectural and component level to scale verification. Performed in the context of a major NASA milestone, this study of formal verification in practice is one of the most challenging that our group has performed.

1 Introduction

This paper demonstrates the use of formal verification approaches on a safety-critical system of realistic functionality, size, and complexity. The work addresses a major milestone of the NASA Aviation Safety program and was performed over several months by a team involving four formal verification experts, a senior software engineer, and an aerospace engineer.

The target of our study is a Simulink model of a twin-engine aircraft simulation named Transport Class Model (TCM). The TCM was selected for a number of reasons. First, it is unclassified and can therefore be shared outside of NASA. This is important because we would like the community to benefit from our experience and to be able to use this as a common benchmark on which additional verification technologies can be applied. Second, the system was developed independently by a different NASA center and therefore we had no prior knowledge of its potential errors or its design. The setting was therefore similar to one in which a safety-critical system is handed to verification experts for analysis and certification where the experts were not involved in the system design.

As the TCM does not come with requirements, we used several sources such as pilot training manuals and the Federal Aviation Regulations for commercial aircraft, to develop the relevant requirements for our study. A significant amount

F. Howar did this work while at Carnegie Mellon University.

N. Bjørner and F. de Boer (Eds.): FM 2015, LNCS 9109, pp. 308–324, 2015.
DOI: 10.1007/978-3-319-19249-9_20

of our work involved formalizing and disambiguating requirements in collaboration with domain experts. The resulting requirements constitute verification properties, which we encoded as synchronous observers in Simulink.

The Simulink models that describe the system had to be processed in order to be usable by this study's verification tools. We used SMT-based model checking, and in particular PKind [21] to verify the properties. The Simulink models including the synchronous observers were automatically translated into the synchronous dataflow language Lustre [4], to be verified by PKind.

A major goal of this work was to experiment with compositional techniques to enable the scalable use of formal methods for systems of realistic size. Compositional verification constructs a verification argument for a complex system by composing simpler verification results at the level of the system components. There are several well-known advantages to taking such an approach. Scalability of verification is a major driver. Through the decomposition of system-level requirements into component-level ones at design time, it is easier to assign clear responsibilities to the developer of each component. Finally, as components of a system change or evolve, compositional verification enables the reuse of verification results of unchanged components.

The work described in this paper is one of the most challenging verification exercises that our team has performed. As such, it forced us to define a high-level methodology for the verification of flight-critical systems, and has enabled us to comment on advantages and limitations of verification techniques and tools in handling such systems. We found that close collaboration between verification and domain experts is required to formalize requirements and, in particular, assumptions about the physical system, without which verification would fail. Compositional verification is key in constructing scalable and meaningful proofs for complex systems in the aeronautics domain.

The remainder of the paper is organized as follows. Section 2 describes the TCM, while Section 3 discusses the process through which we obtained requirements and disambiguated and formalized them for verification. The verification effort is described in Section 4. The experience and lessons learned from this substantial effort are discussed in Section 5, with Section 6 placing this effort in the context of related work.

2 The Transport Class Model

Our target system is derived from NASA Langley's Transport Class Model (TCM) [19], a simulator of a mid-size (approximately 250,000 lb.), twin-engine, commercial transport-class aircraft. The TCM is not intended as a high-fidelity simulation of any particular transport aircraft. Rather, it is meant to be representative of the types of non-linear behaviors of this class of aircraft.

The TCM includes models for the avionics (with transport delay), actuators, engines, landing gear, nonlinear aerodynamics, sensors (including noise), aircraft parameters, equations of motion, and gravity. It is primarily implemented in Simulink, consisting of approximately 5700 Simulink blocks. The system also

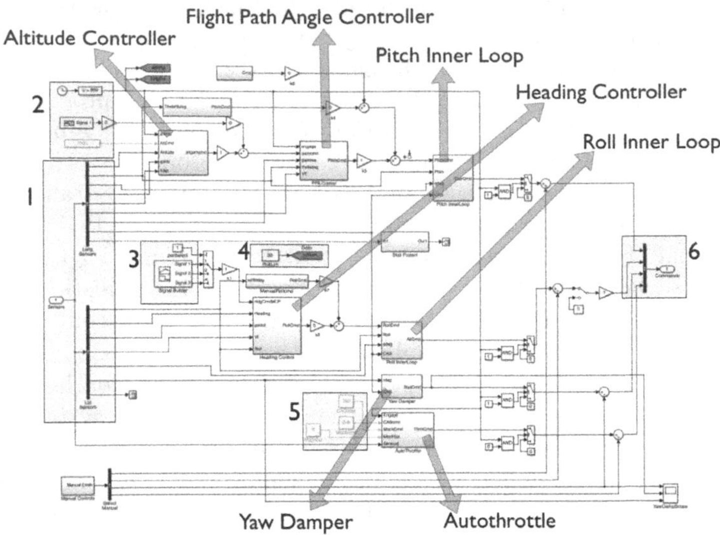

Fig. 1. The Simulink guidance and controls system for the TCM. The various numbers represents different input/output signals: (1) input from sensors, (2) input from the Mode Control Panel (MCP) and the pilot, (3) input from the pilot for yaw and roll, (4) input roll limit from MCP, (5) input from MCP for the autothrottle, (6) output command for the actuators.

includes several thousand of lines of C/C++ code in libraries, primarily used for the engines and the nonlinear aerodynamics models. Our work studies the guidance and control models and their properties within the overall context of the TCM system. These models are implemented entirely in Simulink.

Figure 1 depicts the top-level controls Simulink (data-flow) diagram. An aircraft can be controlled either manually (using a control stick and pedals), or through the mode control panel (MCP) of the flight computer (autopilot). In the diagram, pink-shaded boxes with dark outlines (to the left) highlight the inputs from the pilot and the MCP. Red arrows identify the various controls subsystems (each subsystem may itself be a complex collection of subsystems), explained below. The TCM contains inner loop proportional-integral (PI) controllers for all three angular axes of motion (roll, pitch, and yaw). These inner loop controllers function regardless of whether the pilot flies manually or the autopilot issues commands. Additionally, the TCM's autopilot can control altitude (either by flying to a directed altitude, or holding a current altitude), can reach and maintain a desired flight path angle (FPA), can reach and maintain a desired heading, and can control the airplane's speed. Finally, the blue-shaded box labeled as number 6 shows the collected outputs—the commands to the actuators.

3 Requirements: Elicitation and Formalization

Written requirements are not available for the autopilot and controls software of the TCM because it was not intended for embedded production-level code. The original implementers of the software informed us that their release process was based on a side-by-side comparison of behaviors between the simulator and an experimental aircraft. However, for the purpose of our study, we need safety properties representative of those used in the certification of civil aviation transport vehicles. For this reason, NASA's Armstrong Flight Research Center chose relevant requirements from the Federal Aviation Regulations (FARs) governing commercial aviation transport vehicles (Part 25) [9], such as the following:

> *FAR-25.672b*: The design of the stability augmentation system or of any other automatic or power operated system must permit initial counteraction of failures of the type specified in section 25.671(c) without requiring exceptional pilot skill or strength, by either the deactivation of the system, or a failed portion thereof, or by overriding the failure by movement of the flight controls in the normal sense.

FAR requirements such as the one above refer to several high-level systems, but in our study we focus on the Guidance, Navigation, and Control (GNC) system of Fig. 1. The GNC is divided into three types of components: (i) *mode logic* capturing the modes in which the autopilot can operate, how these modes are enabled and disabled, and which control systems are enabled by particular modes, (ii) components targeting *controllability* of the airplane by ensuring that the actuators can, at any instant, respond appropriately to a command, and (iii) components ensuring the *stability* and *maneuverability* of the aircraft, making the aircraft robust to state disturbances and easily controlled by the pilot.

The TCM does not contain detailed Simulink models for Navigation. Moreover, classical mathematical techniques like Lyapunov theory [22] provide well-understood ways of checking stability and maneuverability properties. The formal verification tools that our study targets are better suited for checking mode logic and simple controllability properties of type (i) and (ii) above. As a consequence, we focus on GNC-level requirements, and sub-requirements (also called "child"-requirements) that refer exclusively to Guidance. A child-requirement of the above FAR requirement, is, for example, the following:

> *GNC-150*: The Guidance Navigation and Control Function shall enable the pilot to transition the vehicle from one flight condition to another (i.e. climb to level flight) under all operating conditions including failure of a single engine.

In order to elicit such higher-level requirements into properties that can be checked on the components of our case-study, we examined pilot training materials for the Boeing 737 (B737) Automatic Flight Systems [26]. B737 is within the class of vehicles that the TCM simulator targets. Within these training materials were behavioral specifications for the B737 Altitude Acquire, Altitude

Hold, and Level Change Modes, equivalent in functionality to the TCM's Altitude Controller. We also used the specifications for the B737 Heading Select Mode as the desired properties for the TCM Heading Controller, the B737 Glide Slope Capture mode for the TCM Flight Path Angle Controller, and the B737 autothrottle for the TCM's autothrottle. We started with 88 GNC requirements, which we tried, with the help of these B737 documents, to map into safety properties of the Guidance system. This effort resulted in 20 properties, illustrated in Table 1. These 20 properties are sub-requirements of GNC-level requirements, such as the GNC-150 requirement shown above. In the rest of this paper we will use property G-120 as a running example.

3.1 Formalization

For verification, the properties shown in Table 1 must be disambiguated and formulated in terms of the signals (inputs and outputs) of the TCM model. Moreover, they have to be written in a formal language which, in our case, is Simulink (see Section 4). The requirements formalization process was performed over several iterations, and involved discussions between domain and verification experts. It included several steps, presented in this section.

1. Develop a shared understanding of the requirement. Natural language often allows for slightly different interpretations. In some cases, properties even interfered or contradicted one another. For example, what does "... to be limited by minimum and maximum engine performance ..." mean in the context of G-120? It could mean that (i) the guidance shall be capable to climb when commanded to do so, but the climb rate should be limited by engine performance and airspeed, or that (ii) the guidance is only required to be able to climb when the defined rate is within the minimum and maximum engine performance. For all such cases, we consulted with the domain expert on the team to develop a common understanding and/or we refined properties to be more precise (e.g., interpretation a. was selected for property G-120).

2. Decompose the property into a requirement on the control system and assumptions about the physics of the airplane. Since we reason formally only about controllability, we decomposed the properties into a part that can be proven formally and into corresponding assumptions about stability and physics. Such assumptions were not formally verified, but were confirmed by domain experts. For example, while G-120 specifies that the aircraft shall climb at a defined rate, the control system has got just sensors and actuators. Since we do not mathematically specify the physics behavior, we do not have a formal definition of what it means to climb at a defined rate in terms of the sensor values—instead we define climbing solely in terms of the actuator commands. Since we focus on instantaneous controllability, we require that the control system outputs a value to an actuator that moves the aircraft into the right direction (e.g., if the current climb rate is smaller than the commanded climb rate, the control system should issue a command to the ailerons that would pitch the aircraft upwards). We then assume that the inner loop controllers and physics will result in an increased climb rate.

Table 1. A summary of verified properties on the TCM

#	Property	Assumptions	Original Requirement
1	G-250	G-260	The heading control mode, when selected, sends roll commands to turn to and maintain the commanded heading.
2	G-110	G-220,G-260	The guidance system shall be capable of steering to and following a specified heading.
3	G-120	G-180,A1,A2, FPA1	The guidance shall be capable of climbing at a defined rate, to be limited by minimum and maximum engine performance and airspeed.
4	G-130	G-180,A1,A2	The guidance shall be capable of descending at a defined rate, to be limited by minimum and maximum engine performance airspeed.
5	G-140	G-120,G-200	The guidance shall be capable of climbing at a specified rate to a specified altitude, to be limited by maximum engine performance for a set airspeed
6	G-150	G-180,A1,G-120, A2,G-200	The guidance shall be capable of descending at a specified rate to a specified altitude, to be limited by maximum engine performance for a set airspeed
7	G-170 (Mode)	–	The altitude control shall engage when the altitude control mode is selected and when the FPA control mode is not selected, and when there is no manual pitch or manual roll command from the stick.
8	G-180 (Mode)	–	The FPA control shall engage when the FPA mode is selected, and when there is no manual pitch or manual roll command from the stick.
9	G-100	–	The Guidance system shall be capable of maintaining a steady speed in the normal flight envelope.
10	G-200	–	If the altitude control is engaged, once the plane is within 250 ft of the commanded altitude, the plane will remain within 250 ft of the commanded altitude.
11	G-210 (Mode)	–	If the FPA control and the altitude control are both selected, the FPA control will disengage and the altitude control will engage once the lane is within 200 ft of the commanded altitude.
12	G-220 (Mode)	–	The heading control shall engage when the heading control mode is selected, and when there is no manual pitch or manual roll command from the stick.
13	G-230	–	If the altitude control is engaged with no active speed control, the speed control shall engage and the speed command shall synchronize to the current speed, which shall become the new altitude's target speed.
14	G-240	–	The bank angle limit is established by the Bank Angle Limit Selector.
15	G-260 (Mode)	–	When the heading control mode is engaged, roll commands are given to turn in the nearest direction to the selected heading.
16	G-270 (Mode)	–	Manually positioning the thrust levers does not cause autothrottle disengagement.
17	G-290	–	The autothrottle will be limited by the max and the min throttle.
18	G-160	–	The guidance function shall be able to automatically deploy spoilers to limit speed in a descent, or when a significant reduction in airspeed is requested by the pilot, deactivating at low speed.
19	G-280	–	The FCCs shall issue a warning when the commanded altitude disagrees with the stored commanded altitude stored in the FCCs.
20	G-190	–	If any control surface actuator loses hydraulic pressure, the autopilot shall disengage.

3. Identify affected components and signals of the control model. At this stage properties are still formulated in natural language and state vague things like "The guidance shall be capable ...". Such expressions cannot be mapped to the TCM directly. The model describes sensors and signals. We therefore have to express properties in terms of the signals available in our model. In our study, we mostly relied on domain experts to help us with this step. In the case of G-120, we had to refine "being capable" as the concrete situations in which the control system is expected to act. This could be expressed as "If in FPA-control mode, and if there is no manual aileron or pitch command from the pilot ...", which can be mapped to signals in the model.

4. Decompose the requirement on the control system into sub-requirements on single components. In some cases, the formalized requirements specify behavior of the complete control system in terms of its global inputs and outputs. However, proving the requirements marked gray (7-17) in Table 1 required information about internal signals between lower level components. We therefore decomposed these requirements into sub-requirements over internal signals between components. These sub-requirements were not merely slices of the global property but actual assume/guarantee pairs that we derived manually.

Property G-120, for example, was decomposed as illustrated in Fig. 3 (the figure displays Lustre code, as translated from Simulink by our compiler). The decomposition expresses the fact that the FPA control module, when engaged, is in charge of maintaining an FPA (FPA1). The mode logic ensures that the guidance system cannot be in Altitude Control mode and FPA control mode at the same time (i.e., these modes are mutually exclusive). Based on this fact, the remaining properties express that: – in FPA control mode, the FPA control module is engaged (G-180); – if not in Altitude control mode, then the Altitude control module is not engaged (A1), and when not engaged, the Altitude control module will not send commands (A2). As a result, when in FPA control mode, the FPA will be the only mode engaged, and it will issue commands to maintain an FPA, which means that the guidance system is able to climb at a defined rate.

Property formalization helped us identify missing functionalities in the TCM model and also led us to refine many properties.

- Three requirements specify behavior for components not modeled by the TCM (e.g., spoilers). These requirements could not be formalized.
- All properties that included the behavior of the mode logic had to be made more precise. At this point, the requirements were precise enough to have a unique formal representation as (temporal) logic formulas over signals of the TCM.
- We defined five sub-requirements (e.g., A1 and A2 in Fig. 3) for properties that were verified compositionally.

All requirements except the six for the mode logic and two requirements on operational limits required making assumptions about the physics of the aircraft.

4 Verification of the TCM

This section describes our verification efforts for the TCM: how we handle Simulink models, and how we encode and verify properties. The complete TCM benchmark (Simulink models and Lustre code) can be found in http://tinyurl.com/FM15-TCM.

4.1 Handling Simulink Models

To apply SMT-based model checking, we compile the TCM Simulink model into the synchronous dataflow language Lustre [4,15]. In the following, we briefly introduce Lustre and then describe the compilation process and how safety properties are encoded and verified.

Lustre. Synchronous languages are a class of languages proposed for the design of reactive systems (i.e., systems that maintain a permanent interaction with their physical environment). Such languages are based on the theory of synchronous time, in which the system and its environment are considered to both view time with some "abstract" universal clock. Lustre combines each data stream with an associated clock as a means to discretize time. The overall system is considered to have a universal clock that represents the smallest time span the system is able to distinguish, together with additional, coarser-grained, user-defined clocks. Therefore the overall system may have different subsections that react to inputs at different frequencies. At each clock tick, the system is considered to evaluate all streams, so all values are considered stable for any actual time spent in the instant between ticks. Lustre programs and subprograms are expressed in terms of *Nodes*. Nodes directly model subsystems in a modular fashion, with an externally visible set of inputs and outputs. A *node* can be seen as a mapping of a finite set of input streams (in the form of a tuple) to a finite set of output streams (also expressed as a tuple).

Simulink to Lustre. In Matlab/Simulink from MathWorks©[1], dynamic systems are modeled as block diagrams. Simulink uses dataflow-oriented block diagram notation which consists of blocks and lines. Blocks represent either some kind of functionality, like mathematical or logical functions, or they are used for structuring the model in terms of subsystem blocks, port blocks, bus blocks etc. Every block is defined by its type and its block parameters.

We have developed a tool called GAL [7] (GeneAuto for Lustre) based on the *GeneAuto*[2] tool set. The latter is a tool for the automatic code generation of Simulink models to generate C, VHDL and Ada code. Although the development of the generator was of primary interest, the GeneAuto project also put an emphasis on the qualification of the tool-chain [28] by providing traceability information all along the code generation process.

---

1 http://www.mathworks.com/

2 http://www.geneauto.org

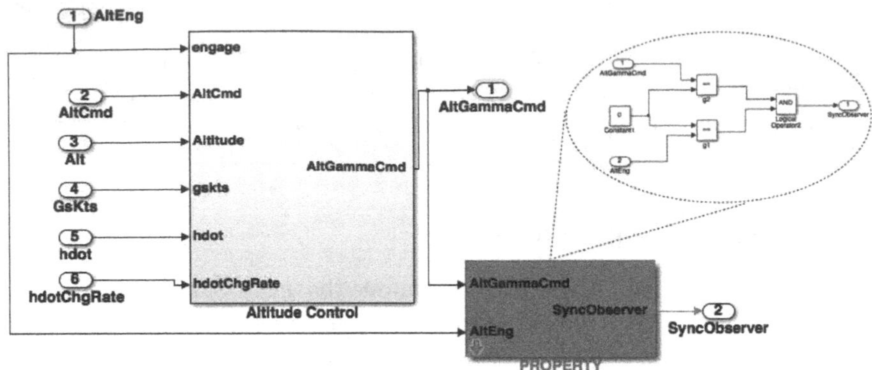

Fig. 2. Simulink model of the Altitude Controller subsystem with a safety property encoded as synchronous observer

GAL can only translate a subset of Simulink blocks. This subset can be characterized as a collection of the most basic discrete-time blocks in Simulink. In a typical controller model built by control engineers, one is likely to encounter additional blocks such as the *transfer function* block, the *saturation* blocks, the *dead-zone* block, and the *integrator* block. These blocks have to first be transformed into equivalent Simulink models that GAL can handle. We have developed an automated pre-processor for Simulink models, that transforms an arbitrary Simulink model into a model "digestible" by GAL. The pre-processor also generates an equivalence check between the original and transformed models, modulo finite-precision arithmetic and discretization. The check can be performed using standard simulation techniques supported by Matlab. Note that our pre-processor provides automated support for transformations that are standard among aerospace engineers when using the MathWorks© Simulink Coder[3].

Encoding Safety Properties. An extensively used technique to define expected behavior is *synchronous observers* [16]. Synchronous observers provide an alternative to temporal logics for specifying safety properties; the benefit of observers is that they express properties in the same notation as the system model [25]. Observers are typically used for simulation and testing purposes. A synchronous observer is a wrapper used to test observable properties of a node N with minimal modification to the node itself; it returns an error signal if the property does not hold. The task of checking the property is thus reduced to simply checking if the stream is constantly true.

Synchronous observers are expressed in Simulink using a masked subsystem block. A subsystem block is a container for a set of blocks. Masking a block means extending it with some additional parameters. An example of such synchronous observers expressed in Simulink is given in Figure 2. The red block (labeled as

[3] http://mathworks.com/products/simulink-coder/

PROPERTY) encode the safety property expressed as synchronous observer. GAL translates these blocks as a property annotation to be proven in Lustre.

Specifically, a Lustre observer is a node taking as input all the flows relevant to the safety property to be specified, and computing a Boolean flow (e.g., "Obs" in Fig. 3) which is true as long as the observed flow satisfies the property. We have used PKind [21] to prove the safety properties of Lustre programs. PKind is a parallel k-induction-based model checker [21], which includes automated invariant generation based on templates [20] and abstract interpretation [12].

4.2 Safety Verification Results

Table 1 list 20 safety properties on the TCM model. At the beginning of the verification process, we discovered several modeling errors within the TCM, which led to the falsification of some properties:

1. *Some components produced output when disabled (e.g., the altitude controller).* This happened because the TCM model given to us was incomplete: the mode logic was not implemented completely (which also affected the mode logic properties). We remedied these problems by incorporating the necessary mode logic into the model.
2. *Manual inputs from the pilot did not override the outputs of the autopilot for all three axes.* This was again due to an incompleteness in the TCM model. We added a Simulink block (before the final output of the autopilot) to reflect the fact a pilot has the ability to override the autopilot output.
3. *Some inputs were not variables but appeared as fixed constant values in the model (e.g., the bank angle limit of G-240).* This was simply a modeling error, and it was easily corrected by modifying the appropriate variables.
4. *G-180 had to be refined to resolve a conflict with G-210 and the implicit assumption that only the FPA control or the altitude control can be active at any moment in time.*

The results obtained for verification after the above changes are described in Table 1. The properties are colored according to the verification technique used. Gray properties (7-17) are the ones proved via a compositional argument. Green properties (1-6) are the ones proved with a direct (non-compositional) proof technique. Red properties (17-20) are the ones that could not be proven on this specific model of the TCM. The latter properties applied to the B737 vehicle (see Section 3), however they referenced functionalities not implemented in the TCM. It took an average of two seconds for PKind to verify the green properties.

All properties were first attempted directly, without a compositional argument. PKind was unable to verify the gray properties, despite a very high timeout setting (5 hours). Since k-induction is sound but not complete, this result has two possible interpretations: these properties are k-inductive for an extremely high k or, more plausibly, they are not k-inductive for any k. We have also tried other Lustre verification tools based on different verification techniques. Specifically, we used

Kind-2[4] and Zustre[5]. Kind-2 is a complete re-implementation of PKind that also adds a verification engine based on IC3 [2], while Zustre is a tool based on the generalized property-oriented reachability implemented in Z3 [17]. Both tools were not able to prove the gray properties.

In a second step, we decomposed the properties either in terms of component-level properties (e.g. G-120, G-130, G-140, G-150), or in "simpler" properties to deal with (e.g. G-250, G-110). We now give details of the compositional analysis of G-120 (see Section 3 for the natural language description). This property involves 3 components of the TCM longitudinal control system: the *Mode Logic*, the *Altitude* controller and the *Flight Path Angle* (FPA) controller. In order to prove G-120, we decomposed the property into 4 component-level properties: G-180 and A1 for the *Mode Logic*; A2 for the *Altitude* controller and FPA1 for the *FPA* controller. After proving the component level properties, one still needs to make a formal compositional argument that these properties imply the system-level property G-120. The latter argument is captured in Figure 3. The upper box shows the Lustre nodes of the various components involved in G-120. Each component comes with its own guarantees. Such guarantees are used as assumptions in proving G-120 (described in the lower box).

5 Lessons Learned

This section summarizes our experience and lessons learned from the application of formal verification to the TCM case study. Some findings confirmed our expectations: for example, we anticipated the fact that we would need to consult with domain experts both for requirements elicitation, and for assumption generation. We had, however, underestimated the extent to which this would be required. Others surprised us: it took an extremely long time to identify a case study that is both representative of flight-critical systems, and publicly available; the requirements elicitation and formalization phases were also much more involved than we expected. Regarding how far we would be able to go with this case study, we had no expectations to begin with, since we knew nothing about the system that we analyzed when we started our work.

1. Case studies are hard to find. It is difficult to obtain real case studies that are not proprietary and that can be shared outside an institution. The TCM is available for General Purpose Release from NASA Langley, with case number of LAR-18322-1. The process for obtaining the code is detailed in the latest NASA Software Catalog[6].

2. System description must be massaged. Despite the progress in automating verification techniques, a huge amount of effort still needs to be placed in such a task. First of all, it is rare that verification tools are able to directly handle all the features of the languages in which systems are expressed. Despite the race towards keeping verification tools up-to-date, modeling or programming

[4] http://kind2-mc.github.io/kind2/

[5] www.bitbucket.org/lememta/zustre

[6] http://technology.nasa.gov/NASA_Software_Catalog_2014.pdf

```
node AutoPilot(HeadMode, AilStick, ElevStick, AltMode: real;
   FPAMode, ATMode, AltCmd, Altitude, CAS,CASCmdMCP: real;)
returns (HeadEng, AltEng, FPAEng, ATEng: bool; CASCmd: real); let
-- G-180
 assert (FPAMode = 0.0) or (not (AilStick = 0.0)) or
        (not (ElevStick = 0.0)) or (FPAEng = true);
 -- A1
 assert (not (AltMode= 0.0)) or (AltEng = false);
tel

node AltitudeControl (AltEng: bool; AltCmd, Alt: real;
           GsKts, Hdot, HdotChgRate: real)
  returns (AltGammaCmd: real ) ;
let
 -- A2
 assert (AltEng = true) or (AltGammaCmd = 0.0);
tel

node FPAControl(Engage: bool; AltGammaCmd, Gamma: real;
              ThetaDeg, VT: real)
  returns (PitchCmd, PrePitchCmd: real);
let
-- FPA1
 assert true -> (Engage = false) or (AltGammaCmd = Gamma)
 or((AltGammaCmd > Gamma) and (PitchCmd > pre(PrePitchCmd)))
 or((AltGammaCmd < Gamma) and (PitchCmd < pre(PrePitchCmd)));
tel
```

```
node G-120 (HeadMode, AilStick, ElevStick, AltMode: real;
          FPAMode, ATMode, AltCmd, Altitude, CAS: real;
          CASCmdMCP, Gskts, Hdot, HDotChgRate, GammaCmd: real;
          Gamma, ThetaDeg, VT: real)
returns (Obs: bool); var
 AltGammaCmd, FPain, TAlt, TFpa : real;
 HeadEng, AltEng, FPAEng, ATEng : bool;
 CasCmd, PitchCmd, PrePitch : real;
let
 HeadEng,..., CasCmd = AutoPilot(HeadMode,..., CASCmdMCP);
 AltGammaCmd = AltitudeControl(AltEng,..., HDotChgRate);
 PitchCmd, PrePitch = FPAControl(FPAEng,..., VT);

 assert FPain = (AltGammaCmd + GammaCmd);
 assert (AltMode = 0.0);
 assert (not (FPAMode = 0.0));
 assert (ElevStick = 0.0);
 assert (AilStick = 0.0);
 assert (GammaCmd > 1.0 and GammaCmd < 10.0);

 Obs = true -> (GammaCmd = Gamma)
     or ((GammaCmd > Gamma) and (PitchCmd > pre(prePitch)))
     or ((GammaCmd < Gamma) and (PitchCmd < pre(PrePitch)));
 --!PROPERTY: obs = true;
tel
```

Fig. 3. Compositional argument for G-120 property

languages are typically a step ahead. There is therefore always an initial step involved, where the system description is massaged to be handled by the targeted verification tools.

3. Requirements elicitation. Requirements of flight-critical systems are often hard to identify [14,13]. Even when requirements are available, they are very often written in natural language and need to be translated into a clear notation with unambiguous semantics. We had seriously underestimated the effort that would be required in coming up with requirements that we could verify. We involved collaborators from NASA's Armstrong Flight Research Center, and still required a lot of additional effort to bridge high-level requirements with verifiable, component-level ones. It is the first time that we had to tackle requirements starting from FARs, and we appreciate the complexity of certification tasks, and the use of safety cases to organize them [6] (we used safety case tools to organize our requirements, but cannot present this work here due to limited space).

4. Incomplete requirements and assumptions. Our case study confirmed that requirements are often incomplete or even wrong. Developers often make assumptions about the physics or the environment of a system that are not explicitly expressed, and without which requirements do not hold. The capability to analyze requirements with automated tools is invaluable in identifying such problems with requirements. For example, the analysis we performed for property G-120 (see Section 4) revealed the fact that an implicit assumption needed to be formalized and become part of the requirements.

5. Scalability. The amount of progress in automating verification has been substantial. However, there will always be properties and systems on which the verification does not scale, unless more sophisticated compositional approaches are introduced to break the problem into smaller, more manageable, tasks. Compositional verification was needed to address 6 of the 20 requirements that we studied (gray properties in Figure 1). Decomposing requirements was a non-trivial, manual task. Although our tools for this type of system do not directly support automated assumption generation and compositional verification yet, we believe that such techniques could facilitate the application of our approaches [18].

6. Domain expertise. Our case study proved that we are not yet at the point where formal verification can occur in the absence of domain expertise. All of the activities in observations 2, 3, and 4 above, required extensive discussion with a domain expert that was part of the team assembled for this study.

7. Verification tools. Automated formal verification tools have made tremendous progress in recent years. They are able to cope with the growing complexities of systems. In our work, this was the key enabler in carrying out the safety analysis of TCM. Specifically, SMT-based model checking was quite effective in discharging the safety properties. In certain components of the TCM we had to deal with nonlinear arithmetic operations (e.g., trigonometric functions). While nonlinear arithmetic operations are not fully supported in current SMT solvers, we were able to cope with that by using uninterpreted functions[7]. Handling nonlinear arithmetic operations is essential for the verification of flight-critical systems; it is therefore desirable to develop tools that can robustly handle these features.

[7] The idea is to substitute nonlinear functions with uninterpreted one. This could lead to non-feasible counterexamples. In this case we add additional constraints to the uninterpreted function in order to eliminate such counterexamples.

9. Level of effort. Verifying the TCM required approximately three person months (see Table 2), with the involvement of verification and aeronautics experts. Most of our time was spent eliciting the properties, formalizing them, and creating the assumptions about the physical environment that we need for verification. We also spent several weeks working towards utilizing our verification within a future safety case effort. The actual verification process was automated, and required the least time.

Table 2. TCM verification: Approximate level-of-effort

Effort	Person Months
Implementation (Tools)	0.50
Preparation of Models	0.50
Property Elicitation	0.25
Formalization (Relation to model)	0.50
Physical Assumptions	0.50
Compositional Arguments	0.25
Verification	0.20
Safety Case Generation	0.50

6 Related Work

Our aim in designing this study was to make it as realistic, independent, and shareable as possible, and hence we targeted a system that is representative of flight-critical systems, that was developed outside our group, and that is available to the research community. It is hard to find realistic studies in the research community that are not proprietary and that can therefore be used as benchmarks.

In recent work, we have applied probabilistic verification and synthesis techniques to analyze the ACAS X onboard collision avoidance system [29]. Moreover, we have developed a testing infrastructure for the automated analysis of the AutoResolver air-traffic control system, aimed at the prediction and resolution of aircraft loss of separation [14]. A previous large study performed by our group aimed at comparing model checking, static analysis, runtime analysis and testing, through their application for finding bugs in the Executive component of an autonomous robot developed at NASA Ames [3]. These systems are not publicly available.

Several studies related to the verification of flight-critical systems have been performed by Rockwell Collins. In [23], the authors report on the use of their automated framework to verify Simulink and Stateflow designs of three aeronautics components: the ADGS-2100 Window Manager, for ensuring that data from different applications is routed to the correct aircraft display panel; two components of the operational flight program of an unmanned aerial vehicle developed by Lockheed Martin Aerospace, one involving redundancy management, and the other one in charge of generating actuator commands for the aircraft's six control surfaces. These studies confirmed the applicability and benefits of formal verification techniques in the design of flight-critical systems. The commercial components that were targeted are not publicly available.

More recently, Rockwell Collins has developed compositional techniques for scalable verification of architectural models expressed in the AADL language [5]. The Astrée static analyzer has been used to prove the absence of runtime errors from two Airbus components implemented in C [27], as well as from a C version of the automatic docking software of the Jules Vernes Automated Transfer Vehicle (ATV) enabling ESA to transport payloads to the International Space Station [1]. Galdino et al [10] used the PVS theorem prover to formally verify an air-traffic control resolution and recovery algorithm. In the domain of hybrid system verification, Platzer and Clarke [24] have applied the KeYmaera verification tool to prove properties of curved flight collision avoidance maneuvers. Esteve et al. have applied a probabilistic model checker to determine properties of an early design spacecraft model for the European Space Agency [8].

For an extensive study of success stories related to the application of formal verification in practice, we refer the reader to the technical report by Garavel and Graf [11]. Note that in this paper we focus on case studies related to avionics; several other studies of safety-critical systems have been performed, for example in the contexts of medical devices and of the automotive industry.

7 Conclusion

To summarize, we demonstrated a verification approach for the TCM controls system: a publicly available, realistic and complex flight-critical system of moderate size. This study required a significant amount of effort from a team made up of both verification and domain experts. Compositional verification was required to prove some of the safety properties of the system. The only safety properties we did not prove in this study were those in which the desired functionality had not actually been modeled. Our experience highlights the promise of compositional verification in the certification of flight-critical systems. In practice, we saw that the most significant part of our effort was in defining and formalizing the appropriate properties, starting from high-level FARs requirement, all the way down to properties of the target system.

Acknowledgment. This work was funded by the System-wide Safety Assurance Technologies project in the Aviation Safety program at NASA ARMD. T. Kahsai and F. Howar were partially supported by the NASA Contract No. NNX14AI09G. The authors wish to thank Bob Antoniewicz and his group at the NASA's Armstrong Flight Research Center for the work they did tracing the Federal Aviation Regulation requirements down to the high-level aircraft systems, and also for contributing their domain expertise towards the aircraft behavior formalization.

This research was conducted at NASA's Ames Research Center. Reference herein to any specific commercial product, process, or service by trade name, trademark, manufacturer, or otherwise, does not constitute or imply its endorsement by the United States Government.

References

1. Bouissou, O., Conquet, E., Cousot, P., Cousot, R., Feret, J., Ghorbal, K., Goubault, E., Lesens, D., Mauborgne, L., Miné, A., Putot, S., Rival, X., Turin, M.: Space software validation using abstract interpretation. In: Proc. of the Int. Space System Engineering Conf., Data Systems in Aerospace, vol. SP-669, pp. 1–7. ESA (2009)
2. Bradley, A.R.: SAT-based model checking without unrolling. In: Jhala, R., Schmidt, D. (eds.) VMCAI 2011. LNCS, vol. 6538, pp. 70–87. Springer, Heidelberg (2011)
3. Brat, G.P., Drusinsky, D., Giannakopoulou, D., Goldberg, A., Havelund, K., Lowry, M.R., Pasareanu, C.S., Venet, A., Visser, W., Washington, R.: Experimental evaluation of verification and validation tools on Martian rover software. Formal Methods in System Design 25(2-3), 167–198 (2004)
4. Caspi, P., Pilaud, D., Halbwachs, N., Plaice, J.A.: Lustre: a declarative language for real-time programming. In: Proceedings of the 14th ACM SIGACT-SIGPLAN Symposium on Principles of Programming Languages, POPL 1987, pp. 178–188. ACM (1987)
5. Cofer, D., Gacek, A., Miller, S., Whalen, M., LaValley, B., Sha, L.: Compositional verification of architectural models. In: Goodloe, A., Person, S. (eds.) NFM 2012. LNCS, vol. 7226, pp. 126–140. Springer, Heidelberg (2012)
6. Denney, E., Pai, G., Pohl, J.: AdvoCATE: An assurance case automation toolset. In: SAFECOMP Workshops, pp. 8–21 (2012)
7. Dieumegard, A., Garoche, P.-L., Kahsai, T., Taillar, A., Thirioux, X.: Compilation of synchronous observers as code contracts. In: The 30th ACM/SIGAPP Symposium on Applied Computing (2015)
8. Esteve, M., Katoen, J., Nguyen, V.Y., Postma, B., Yushtein, Y.: Formal correctness, safety, dependability, and performance analysis of a satellite. In: 34th International Conference on Software Engineering, ICSE 2012, pp. 1022–1031 (2012)
9. Federal Aviation Administration. Electronic code of federal regulations
10. Galdino, A.L., Muñoz, C., Ayala-Rincón, M.: Formal verification of an optimal air traffic conflict resolution and recovery algorithm. In: Leivant, D., de Queiroz, R. (eds.) WoLLIC 2007. LNCS, vol. 4576, pp. 177–188. Springer, Heidelberg (2007)
11. Garavel, H., Graf, S.: Formal methods for safe and secure computer systems. Technical Report BSI-Study 875, Bundesamt fuer Sicherheit in Informationstechnik (December 2013)
12. Garoche, P.-L., Kahsai, T., Tinelli, C.: Incremental invariant generation using logic-based automatic abstract transformers. In: Brat, G., Rungta, N., Venet, A. (eds.) NFM 2013. LNCS, vol. 7871, pp. 139–154. Springer, Heidelberg (2013)
13. Giannakopoulou, D., Bushnell, D.H., Schumann, J., Erzberger, H., Heere, K.: Formal testing for separation assurance. Ann. Math. Artif. Intell. 63(1), 5–30 (2011)
14. Giannakopoulou, D., Howar, F., Isberner, M., Lauderdale, T., Rakamaric, Z., Raman, V.: Taming test inputs for separation assurance. In: 19th IEEE/ACM International Conference on Automated Software Engineering (ASE 2014) (2014)
15. Halbwachs, N., Caspi, P., Raymond, P., Pilaud, D.: The synchronous dataflow programming language Lustre. In: Proceedings of the IEEE, pp. 1305–1320 (1991)
16. Halbwachs, N., Lagnier, F., Raymond, P.: Synchronous observers and the verification of reactive systems. In: AMAST, pp. 83–96 (1993)
17. Hoder, K., Bjørner, N.: Generalized property directed reachability. In: Cimatti, A., Sebastiani, R. (eds.) SAT 2012. LNCS, vol. 7317, pp. 157–171. Springer, Heidelberg (2012)

18. Howar, F., Giannakopoulou, D., Rakamaric, Z.: Hybrid learning: interface generation through static, dynamic, and symbolic analysis. In: International Symposium on Software Testing and Analysis, ISSTA, pp. 268–279 (2013)
19. Hueschen, R.M.: Development of the Transport Class Model (TCM) aircraft simulation from a sub-scale Generic Transport Model (GTM) simulation. Technical report, NASA, Langley Research Center, Hampton, VA (August 2011)
20. Kahsai, T., Ge, Y., Tinelli, C.: Instantiation-based invariant discovery. In: Bobaru, M., Havelund, K., Holzmann, G.J., Joshi, R. (eds.) NFM 2011. LNCS, vol. 6617, pp. 192–206. Springer, Heidelberg (2011)
21. Kahsai, T., Tinelli, C.: PKIND: a parallel k-induction based model checker. In: PDMC. EPTCS. EPTCS, vol. 72, pp. 55–62 (2011)
22. Lyapunov, A.: General problem of the stability of motion. PhD thesis, Univ. Kharkov (1892)
23. Miller, S.P., Whalen, M.W., Cofer, D.D.: Software model checking takes off. Commun. ACM 53(2), 58–64 (2010)
24. Platzer, A., Clarke, E.M.: Formal verification of curved flight collision avoidance maneuvers: A case study. In: Cavalcanti, A., Dams, D. (eds.) FM 2009. LNCS, vol. 5850, pp. 547–562. Springer, Heidelberg (2009)
25. Rushby, J.: The versatile synchronous observer. In: Gheyi, R., Naumann, D. (eds.) SBMF 2012. LNCS, vol. 7498, pp. 1–1. Springer, Heidelberg (2012)
26. SmartCockpit. B737 automatic flight systems summary
27. Souyris, J., Delmas, D.: Experimental assessment of Astrée on safety-critical avionics software. In: Saglietti, F., Oster, N. (eds.) SAFECOMP 2007. LNCS, vol. 4680, pp. 479–490. Springer, Heidelberg (2007)
28. Toom, A., Izerrouken, N., Naks, T., Pantel, M., Ssi-Yan-Kai, O.: Towards reliable code generation with an open tool: Evolutions of the Gene-Auto toolset. In: ERTS. Société des Ingénieurs de l'Automobile (2010), http://www.sia.fr
29. von Essen, C., Giannakopoulou, D.: Analyzing the next generation airborne collision avoidance system. In: Ábrahám, E., Havelund, K. (eds.) TACAS 2014. LNCS, vol. 8413, pp. 620–635. Springer, Heidelberg (2014)

Proving Safety with Trace Automata and Bounded Model Checking

Daniel Kroening[1], Matt Lewis[1(✉)], and Georg Weissenbacher[2]

[1] University of Oxford, Oxford, UK
[2] Vienna University of Technology, Wien, Austria
matt@cantab.net

Abstract. Loop under-approximation enriches C programs with additional branches that represent the effect of a (limited) range of loop iterations. While this technique can speed up bug detection significantly, it introduces redundant execution traces which may complicate the verification of the program. This holds particularly true for tools based on Bounded Model Checking, which incorporate simplistic heuristics to determine whether all feasible iterations of a loop have been considered.

We present a technique that uses *trace automata* to eliminate redundant executions after performing loop acceleration. The method reduces the diameter of the program under analysis, which is in certain cases sufficient to allow a safety proof using Bounded Model Checking. Our transformation is precise—it does not introduce false positives, nor does it mask any errors. We have implemented the analysis as a source-to-source transformation, and present experimental results showing the applicability of the technique.

1 Introduction

Software verification can be loosely divided into two themes: finding bugs and proving correctness. These two goals are often at odds with one another, and it is rare that a tool excels at both tasks. This tension is well illustrated by the results of the 2014 Software Verification Competition, in which several of the best-performing tools were based on Bounded Model Checking (BMC) [5]. The BMC-based tools were able to quickly find bugs in the unsafe programs, but were unable to soundly prove safety for the remaining programs. Conversely, many of the sound tools had difficulty in detecting bugs in the unsafe programs.

The reasons for this disparity are rooted in the very nature of contemporary verification tools. Tools aiming at proof typically rely on over-approximating abstractions and refinement techniques to derive the loop invariants required (e.g., [14,23]). For certain classes of programs, invariants can be found efficiently using templates [4] or theorem provers [16]. For unsafe programs, however, any

This research was supported by ERC project 280053, the Austrian National Research Network S11403-N23 (RiSE) and the LogiCS doctoral program W1255-N23 of the Austrian Science Fund (FWF) and by the Vienna Science and Technology Fund (WWTF) through grant VRG11-005.

N. Bjørner and F. de Boer (Eds.): FM 2015, LNCS 9109, pp. 325–341, 2015.
DOI: 10.1007/978-3-319-19249-9_21

attempt to construct a safety invariant must necessarily fail, triggering numerous futile refinement iterations before a valid counterexample is detected. Verifiers based on the BMC paradigm (such as CBMC [8]), on the other hand, are able to efficiently detect shallow bugs, but are unable to prove safety in most cases.

The key principle of this paper is that BMC is able to prove safety once the unwinding bound exceeds the reachability diameter of the model [5, 20]. The diameter of non-trivial programs is however in most cases unmanageably large. Furthermore, even when the diameter is small, it is often computationally expensive to determine, as the problem of computing the exact diameter is equivalent to a 2-QBF instance.

The contribution of this paper is a technique that reduces the diameter of a program in a way that the new, smaller diameter can be computed by means of a simple satisfiability check. The technique has two steps:

1. We first identify potentially deep program paths that can be replaced by a concise single-step summary called an *accelerator* [6, 7, 12].
2. We then remove those paths subsumed by the accelerators from the program using *trace automata* [13].

The resulting program preserves the reachable states of the original program, but is often very shallow, and consequently, we can obtain a sound verification result using BMC.

Our paper is organised as follows: We present a number of motivating examples and an outline of our approach in Section 2. Section 3 presents our notation, recapitulates the concept of a reachability diameter, and introduces a generalised notion of the under-approximating accelerators presented in [17, 19]. Section 4 describes the construction of accelerated programs and discusses the resulting reduction of the reachability diameter of the program. In Section 5, we introduce restricting languages and trace automata as a means to eliminate redundant transitions from accelerated programs. The experimental evaluation based on a selection of SV-COMP14 benchmarks is presented in Section 6. Finally, Section 7 briefly surveys related work.

2 Motivation

In this section we will discuss the differences between proving safety and finding bugs, with reference to some SV-COMP14 benchmarks, and informally demonstrate why our method is effective for both kinds of analyses.

The program in Figure 1, taken from the LOOPS category of SV-COMP14, proved challenging for many of the participating tools, with only 6 out of the 12 entrants solving it correctly. A proof of safety for this program using an abstract interpreter requires a relational domain to represent the invariant $\mathtt{x} + \mathtt{y} = \mathtt{N}$, which is often expensive.

The program in Figure 2 resembles the one in Figure 1, except for the negated assertion at the end. This example is very easy for Bounded Model Checkers, which are able to discover a bug in a single unwinding by assigning $\mathtt{N} = 1$.

A slight modification, however, illustrated in Figure 3, increases the number of loop iterations required to trigger the bug to 10^6, exceeding the capability of even the best BMC-based verification tools.

```
unsigned N := *;
unsigned x := N, y := 0;
while (x > 0) {
    x := x − 1;
    y := y + 1;
}
assert (y = N);
```

Fig. 1. Safe program

```
unsigned N = *;
unsigned x := N, y := 0;
while (x > 0) {
    x := x − 1;
    y := y + 1;
}
assert (y ≠ N);
```

Fig. 2. Unsafe program

```
unsigned N := 10^6;
unsigned x := N, y := 0;
while (x > 0) {
    x := x − 1;
    y := y + 1;
}
assert (y ≠ N);
```

Fig. 3. "Deep" bug

The relative simplicity of the program statements in Figures 1 to 3 makes them amenable to *acceleration* [6,7,12], a technique used to compute the effect of the repeated iteration of statements over integer linear arithmetic. Specifically, the effect of i loop iterations is that x is decreased and y is increased by i. Acceleration, however, is typically restricted to programs over fragments of linear arithmetic for which the transitive closure is effectively computable, thus restricting its applicability to programs whose semantics can be soundly modelled using unbounded integers. In reality, however, the scalar variables in Figures 1 to 3 take their values from the bounded subset $\{0, \ldots, (2^{32} - 1)\}$ of the positive integers $\mathbb{N}_0$. Traditional acceleration techniques do not account for integer overflows. To address this problem, we previously introduced *under-approximate acceleration*, bounding the acceleration to the interval in which the statements behave uniformly [17,19].

The code snippet in Figure 4 represents an under-approximating accelerator for the loop bodies in Figures 1, 2, and 3. We introduce an auxiliary variable i representing a non-deterministic number of loop iterations. The subsequent assumption guarantees that the accelerated code reflects at least one iteration (and is optional in this example). The assumption that follows warrants the feasibility of the accelerated trace (in general, this condition may contain quantifiers [17,19]). The effect of i iterations is encoded using the two assignment statements, which constitute the closed forms of the recurrence relations corresponding to the original assignments. The final assumption guarantees that i lies in the range in which the right-hand sides of the assignments behave linearly.

In general, under-approximating accelerators do not reflect all feasible iterations of the loop body. Accordingly, we cannot simply replace the original loop body. Instead, we add back the accelerator as an additional path through the loop, as illustrated in Figure 5.

The transformation preserves safety properties—that is to say, an accelerated program has a reachable, failing assertion iff the original program does. We can see that the failing assertion in Figure 5 is reachable after a single iteration of the loop, by simply choosing $i = \mathtt{N}$. Since the accelerated program contains a

```
unsigned i := *;
assume (i > 0)               } iteration counter
assume(x > 0);               } feasibility check
x := x−i;
y := y+i;                    } acceleration
assume(¬underflow (x));      } iteration bound
```

Fig. 4. Accelerated loop body

```
unsigned N := 10^6, x := N, y := 0;
while (x > 0) {
    if (*) {
        i := *; assume (i > 0);
        x := x−i; y = y+i;
        assume (x ≥ 0);
    } else {
        x := x − 1; y := y + 1;
    }
}
assert (y ≠ N);
```

Fig. 5. Accelerated unsafe program

```
unsigned N := 10^6, x := N, y := 0;
if (x > 0) {
    x := x − 1; y := y + 1;
    if (x > 0) {
        x := x − 1; y := y + 1;
        if (x > 0) {
            x := x − 1;
            y := y + 1;
            assert (x ≤ 0);
        }
    }
}
assert (y = N);
```

Fig. 6. Unwinding ($k = 3$) of safe program with $N = 10^6$

```
    unsigned N := *, x := N, y := 0;
    bool g := *;
1:  while (x > 0) {
        if (*) {
            assume (¬g);
2:          i := *; x := x−i; y = y+i;
            assume (x ≥ 0);
3:          g := T;
        } else {
            x := x − 1; y := y + 1;
            assume (underflow (x));
            g := F;
        }
    }
4:  assert (y = N);
```

Fig. 7. Accelerated and instrumented safe program

feasible trace leading to a failed assertion, we can conclude that the original program does as well, despite having only considered a single trace of length 1.

While the primary application of BMC is bug detection, contemporary Bounded Model Checkers such as CBMC are able to prove safety in some cases. CBMC unwinds loops up to a predetermined bound k (see Figure 6). *Unwinding assertions* are one possible mechanism to determine whether further unwinding is required [8, 11]. The assertion $(x \leq 0)$ in Figure 6 fails if there are feasible program executions traversing the loop more than three times. It is obvious that this assertion will fail for any $k < 10^6$.

Unfortunately, acceleration is ineffective in this setting. Since the accelerator in Figure 5 admits $i = 1$, we have to consider 10^6 unwindings before we can establish the safety of the program in Figure 1 with $N = 10^6$. For a non-deterministically assigned N, this number increases to 2^{32}.

This outcome is disappointing, since the repeated iteration of the accelerated loop body is redundant. Furthermore, there is no point in taking the unaccelerated path through the loop (unless there is an impending overflow—which can be ruled out in the given program), since the accelerator *subsumes* this execution (with $i = 1$). Thus, if we eliminate all executions that meet either of the criteria above, we do not alter the semantics of the program but may reduce the difficulty of our problem considerably.

Figure 7 shows an accelerated version of the safe program of Figure 1, but instrumented to remove redundant traces. This is achieved by introducing an auxiliary variable g which determines whether the accelerator was traversed in the previous iteration of the loop. This flag is reset in the non-accelerated branch, which, however, in our example is never feasible. It is worth noting that every feasible trace through Listing 1 has a corresponding feasible trace through Listing 7, and vice versa.

The figure to the right shows an execution of the program in Figure 7: This trace is both feasible and safe—the assertion on line 4 is not violated. It is not too difficult to see that *every* feasible trace through the program in Figure 7 has the same length, which means that we can soundly reason about its safety considering traces with a single iteration of the loop, which is a tractable (and indeed, easy) problem.

Loc.	N	x	y	i	g
1	10^4	10^4	0	0	F
2	10^4	10^4	0	0	F
3	10^4	0	10^4	10^4	F
1	10^4	0	10^4	10^4	T
4	10^4	0	10^4	10^4	T

Since the accelerated and instrumented program in Figure 7 is safe, we can conclude that the original program in Figure 1 is safe as well.

We emphasise that our approach neither introduces an over-approximation, nor requires the explicit computation of a fixed point. In addition, it is not restricted to linear integer arithmetic and bit-vectors: our prior work can generate some non-linear accelerators and also allows for the acceleration of a limited class of programs with arrays [17, 19].

3 Notation and Basic Concepts

Let Stmts be the (infinite) set of statements of a simple programming language as defined in Table 1(a), where Exprs and $\mathbb{B}$-Exprs denote expressions and predicates over the program variables Vars, respectively. Stmts* denotes the Kleene closure of Stmts. The language comprises assignments $\mathtt{x} := e$ (where $e \in$ Exprs, and $* \in$ Exprs denotes a non-deterministic value) and assumptions abbreviated by $[B]$ (with $B \in \mathbb{B}$-Exprs). Assertions are modeled using assumptions and error locations. For brevity, we omit array accesses. We assume that different occurrences of statements are distinguishable (using the program locations). The semantics is provided in Table 1(a) in terms of the weakest liberal precondition *wlp* as defined in [25]. (The weakest liberal precondition $wlp(\mathtt{stmt}, P)$ yields the weakest condition under which stmt either does not terminate or establishes P.) Programs are represented using control flow automata.

Table 1. Program Statements and Traces

(a) Syntax and Semantics

$$\texttt{stmt} ::= \texttt{x} := e \mid [B] \mid \textsf{skip}$$
$$(\texttt{x} \in \textsf{Vars},\ e \in \textsf{Exprs},\ B \in \mathbb{B}\textsf{-Exprs})$$

$$wlp(\texttt{x} := e, P) \stackrel{\text{def}}{=} P[e/\texttt{x}]$$
$$wlp(\texttt{x} := *, P) \stackrel{\text{def}}{=} \forall \texttt{x} \,.\, P$$
$$wlp([B], P) \stackrel{\text{def}}{=} B \Rightarrow P$$
$$wlp(\textsf{skip}, P) \stackrel{\text{def}}{=} P$$

(b) Transition Relations for Traces

$$[\![\textsf{stmt}]\!] \stackrel{\text{def}}{=} \neg wlp(\textsf{stmt}, \textstyle\bigvee_{\texttt{x}\in\textsf{Vars}} \texttt{x} \neq \texttt{x}')$$
$$\textsf{id} \stackrel{\text{def}}{=} [\![\textsf{skip}]\!]$$
$$[\![\textsf{stmt}_1 \cdot \textsf{stmt}_2]\!] \stackrel{\text{def}}{=} [\![\textsf{stmt}_1]\!] \circ [\![\textsf{stmt}_2]\!]$$
$$[\![\textsf{stmt}^n]\!] \stackrel{\text{def}}{=} [\![\textsf{stmt}]\!]^n,$$

where
$$\textsf{stmt}^0 \stackrel{\text{def}}{=} \varepsilon,$$
$$\textsf{stmt}^n \stackrel{\text{def}}{=} \textsf{stmt} \cdot (\textsf{stmt}^{(n-1)})$$
$$[\![\textsf{stmt}]\!]^0 \stackrel{\text{def}}{=} \textsf{id},$$
$$[\![\textsf{stmt}]\!]^n \stackrel{\text{def}}{=} [\![\textsf{stmt}]\!] \circ ([\![\textsf{stmt}]\!]^{(n-1)})$$

Definition 1 (CFA). *Let* Stmts *be as introduced above in Table 1(a).* A control flow automaton P *is a directed graph* $\langle V, E, v_0\rangle$, *where* V *is a finite set of vertices,* $\textsf{Stmts}_P \subseteq \textsf{Stmts}$ *is a finite set of statements,* $E \subseteq (V \times \textsf{Stmts}_P \times V)$ *is a set of edges, and* $v_0 \in V$ *is the initial vertex. We write* $v \xrightarrow{\textsf{stmt}} u$ *if* $\langle u, \textsf{stmt}, v\rangle \in E$.

A program state σ is a total function assigning a value to each program variable in Vars. States denotes the set of program states (not to be confused with vertices of a CFA). A transition relation $T \subseteq \textsf{States} \times \textsf{States}$ associates states with their successor states. Given Vars, let Vars′ be a corresponding set of primed variables encoding successor states. The symbolic transition relation for a statement or trace is a predicate over $\textsf{Vars} \cup \textsf{Vars}'$ and can be derived using *wlp* as indicated in Table 1(b) (cf. [9]). We write $\langle\sigma, \sigma'\rangle \in [\![\textsf{stmt}]\!]$ if $[\![\textsf{stmt}]\!]$ evaluates to true under σ and σ' (i.e., $\sigma, \sigma' \models [\![\textsf{stmt}]\!]$). The composition $[\![\pi_1]\!] \circ [\![\pi_2]\!]$ of two relations $[\![\pi_1]\!]$ and $[\![\pi_2]\!]$ is the relation $\{\langle\sigma, \sigma'\rangle \mid \exists\sigma'' \,.\, \langle\sigma, \sigma''\rangle \in [\![\pi_1]\!] \text{ and } \langle\sigma'', \sigma'\rangle \in [\![\pi_2]\!]\}$, symbolically represented as a predicate over $\textsf{Vars} \cup \textsf{Vars}'$. A trace π is *feasible* if there exist states σ, σ' such that $\langle\sigma, \sigma'\rangle \in [\![\pi]\!]$.

Given a CFA $P \stackrel{\text{def}}{=} \langle V, E, v_0\rangle$, a trace $\pi \stackrel{\text{def}}{=} \textsf{stmt}_i \cdot \textsf{stmt}_{i+1} \cdots \textsf{stmt}_n$ (where $v_{j-1} \xrightarrow{\textsf{stmt}_j} v_j$ for $i < j \leq n$ and $\pi \in \textsf{Stmts}_P^*$) of length $|\pi| = n - i + 1$ is *looping* (with head v_i) iff $v_i = v_n$, and *accepted* by the CFA iff $v_i = v_0$. We use $\mathcal{L}_P$ (where $\mathcal{L}_P \subseteq \textsf{Stmts}_P^*$) to denote the set of all traces that are accepted by the CFA P. Abusing our notation, we write $v_i \xrightarrow{\pi} v_j$ to denote path starting at v_i and ending at v_j and corresponding to the trace π.

A state σ is *reachable* from an initial state σ_0 iff there exists a trace π accepted by the CFA such that $\langle\sigma_0, \sigma\rangle \in [\![\pi]\!]$. The reachability diameter [5,20] of a transition relation is the smallest number of steps required to reach all reachable states:

Definition 2 (Reachability Diameter). *Given a CFA with initial state* σ_0, *the* reachability diameter *is the smallest* n *such that for every state* σ *reachable from* σ_0 *there exists a feasible trace* π *of length at most* n *accepted by the CFA with* $\langle\sigma_0, \sigma\rangle \in [\![\pi]\!]$.

To show that a CFA does not violate a given safety (or reachability) property, it is sufficient to explore all feasible traces whose length does not exceed the reachability diameter. In the presence of looping traces, however, the reachability diameter of a program can be infinitely large.

Acceleration [6,7,12] is a technique to compute the reflexive transitive closure $[\![\pi]\!]^* \stackrel{\text{def}}{=} \bigcup_{i=0}^{\infty}[\![\pi]\!]^i$ for a looping trace π. Equivalently, $[\![\pi]\!]^*$ can be expressed as $\exists i \in \mathbb{N}_0 \,.\, [\![\pi]\!]^i$. The aim of acceleration is to express $[\![\pi]\!]^*$ in a decidable fragment of logic. In general, this is not possible, even if $[\![\pi]\!]$ is defined in a decidable fragment of integer arithmetic such as Presburger arithmetic. For octagonal relations $[\![\pi]\!]$, however, the transitive closure is $[\![\pi]\!]^*$ is Presburger-definable and effectively computable [6, 12].

Definition 3 (Accelerated Transitions). *Given a looping trace $\pi \in \mathcal{L}_P$, we say that a trace $\hat{\pi} \in \mathsf{Stmts}^*$ is an* accelerator *for π if $[\![\hat{\pi}]\!] \equiv [\![\pi]\!]^*$.*

An accelerator $\widetilde{\pi} \in \mathsf{Stmts}^*$ is under-approximating *if the number of iterations is bounded from above by a function $\beta : \mathsf{States} \to \mathbb{N}_0$ of the starting state σ:*

$$\langle \sigma, \sigma' \rangle \in [\![\widetilde{\pi}]\!] \quad \textit{iff} \quad \exists i \in \mathbb{N}_0 \,.\, i \leq \beta(\sigma) \wedge \langle \sigma, \sigma' \rangle \in [\![\pi]\!]^i$$

We require that the function β satisfies the following monotonicity condition:

$$(i \leq \beta(\sigma) \wedge \langle \sigma, \sigma' \rangle \in [\![\pi]\!]^i) \Rightarrow (\beta(\sigma') \leq \beta(\sigma) - i) \tag{1}$$

Intuitively, β (which is not necessarily explicit in the encoding of $\widetilde{\pi}$) restricts i to the range of iterations of π which can be accelerated accurately. We say that $\widetilde{\pi}$ is strictly under-approximating if $[\![\widetilde{\pi}]\!] \subset [\![\hat{\pi}]\!]$.

We introduced under-approximating accelerators for linear integer arithmetic and the theories of bit-vectors and arrays in [17] in order to accelerate the detection of counterexamples. Under-approximations are caused by transition relations that can only be accelerated within certain intervals, e.g., the range in which no overflow occurs in the case of bit-vectors, or in which no conflicting assignments to array elements are made. The bound function β restricts this interval accordingly.

Example 1. An under-approximating accelerator for the statement $\mathtt{x} := \mathtt{x} + 1$, where $\mathtt{x}$ is a 32-bit-wide unsigned integer, can be given as the statement sequence

$$\widetilde{\pi} \stackrel{\text{def}}{=} i := *;\ [\mathtt{x} + i < 2^{32}]; \mathtt{x} := \mathtt{x} + i$$

with transition relation $\exists i \,.\, (\mathtt{x} + i < 2^{32}) \wedge (\mathtt{x}' = \mathtt{x} + i)$. Note that β is implicit here and that the alphabet of $\widetilde{\pi}$ is not restricted to Stmts_P of the CFA P.

4 Diameter Reduction via Acceleration

In this section, we introduce a reachability-preserving program transformation that reduces the reachability diameter of a CFA. While a similar transformation is used in [17] to detect counterexamples with loops, our goal here is to reduce the diameter in order to enable safety proofs (see Section 5).

Definition 4 (Accelerated CFA). *Let $P \stackrel{\text{def}}{=} \langle V, E, v_0 \rangle$ be a CFA over the alphabet* Stmts_P*, and let $\pi_1, \ldots, \pi_k$ be traces in P looping with heads $v_1, \ldots, v_k \in V$, respectively. Let $\widehat{\pi}_1, \ldots \widehat{\pi}_k$ be the (potentially under-approximating) accelerators for $\pi_1, \ldots, \pi_k$. Then the* accelerated CFA $\widehat{P} \stackrel{\text{def}}{=} \langle \widehat{V}, \widehat{E}, v_0 \rangle$ *for P is the CFA P augmented with non-branching paths $v_i \xrightarrow{\widehat{\pi}_i} v_i$ $(1 \leq i \leq k)$.*

A trace is *accelerated* if it traverses a path in $\widehat{P}$ that corresponds to an accelerator. A trace π_1 *subsumes* a trace π_2, denoted by $\pi_2 \preceq \pi_1$, if $[\![\pi_2]\!] \subseteq [\![\pi_1]\!]$. Accordingly, $\pi \preceq \widehat{\pi}$ and $\widetilde{\pi} \preceq \widehat{\pi}$ (which follows from Definition 3, since $[\![\pi]\!]^i \subseteq [\![\pi]\!]^*$ for any i). We extend the relation $\preceq$ to sets of traces: $\Pi_1 \preceq \Pi_2$ if $\left(\bigcup_{\pi \in \Pi_1} [\![\pi]\!]\right) \subseteq \left(\bigcup_{\pi \in \Pi_2} [\![\pi]\!]\right)$. A trace π is *redundant* if $\{\pi\}$ is subsumed by the set $\Pi \setminus \{\pi\}$ of other traces in the CFA.

Lemma 1. *Let $\widetilde{\pi}$ be an under-approximating accelerator for the looping trace π. Then $\widetilde{\pi} \cdot \widetilde{\pi} \preceq \widetilde{\pi}$ holds. Similarly, for an accelerator $\widehat{\pi}$ of π it holds that $\widehat{\pi} \cdot \widehat{\pi} \preceq \widehat{\pi}$.*

Proof. For accelerators that are not strictly under-approximating the claim holds trivially. Otherwise, we have

$$\begin{array}{l} \langle \sigma, \sigma'' \rangle \in [\![\widetilde{\pi} \cdot \widetilde{\pi}]\!] \qquad \Leftrightarrow \\ \exists \sigma' \,.\, \exists i, j \in \mathbb{N}_0 \,.\, \begin{pmatrix} \langle \sigma, \sigma' \rangle \in [\![\pi]\!]^i \wedge i \leq \beta(\sigma) \;\; \wedge \\ \langle \sigma', \sigma'' \rangle \in [\![\pi]\!]^j \;\wedge j \leq \beta(\sigma') \end{pmatrix} \end{array}$$

If σ' exists, Condition 1 in Definition 3 guarantees that $(\beta(\sigma') \leq \beta(\sigma) - i)$, and therefore $\langle \sigma, \sigma'' \rangle \in [\![\widetilde{\pi} \cdot \widetilde{\pi}]\!]$ implies

$$\exists i, j \in \mathbb{N}_0 \,.\, \langle \sigma, \sigma'' \rangle \in [\![\pi]\!]^{i+j} \wedge \underbrace{i \leq \beta(\sigma) \wedge j \leq \beta(\sigma) - i}_{(i+j) \leq \beta(\sigma)} \,.$$

By replacing $i + j$ with a single variable i we arrive at the definition of $[\![\widetilde{\pi}]\!]$.

We emphasize that Lemma 1 holds for accelerators $\widehat{\pi}$ as well as (strictly) under-approximating accelerators $\widetilde{\pi}$ (cf. Definition 3). In the following, we use $\widehat{\pi}$ to denote accelerators as well as under-approximating accelerators unless explicitly stated otherwise.

The following theorem states that the transformation in Definition 4 preserves the reachability of states and never increases the reachability diameter.

Theorem 1. *Let P be a CFA and $\widehat{P}$ a corresponding accelerated CFA as in Definition 4. Then the following claims hold:*

1. *Every trace in P is subsumed by at least one trace in $\widehat{P}$.*
2. *Let π_1 be an accelerated trace accepted by $\widehat{P}$, and let $\langle \sigma_0, \sigma \rangle \in [\![\pi_1]\!]$. Then there exists a trace π_2 accepted by P such that $\langle \sigma_0, \sigma \rangle \in [\![\pi_2]\!]$.*

Proof. Part 1 of the theorem holds because P is a sub-graph of $\widehat{P}$. For the second part, assume that $\widehat{\pi}_1, \ldots \widehat{\pi}_k$ are the accelerators occurring in π_1. Then there are $i_1, \ldots, i_k \in \mathbb{N}$ such that $\pi_2 \stackrel{\text{def}}{=} \pi_1[\pi_1^{i_1}/\widehat{\pi}_1] \cdots [\pi_k^{i_k}/\widehat{\pi}_k]$ and $\langle \sigma_0, \sigma \rangle \in [\![\pi_2]\!]$.

The diameter of a CFA is determined by the longest of the shortest traces from the initial state σ_0 to all reachable states [20]. Accordingly, the transformation in Definition 4 results in a reduction of the diameter if it introduces a shorter accelerated trace that results in the redundancy of this longest shortest trace. In particular, acceleration may reduce an infinite diameter to a finite one.

5 Checking Safety with Trace Automata

Bounded Model Checking owes its industrial success largely to its effectiveness as a bug-finding technique. Nonetheless, BMC can also be used to prove safety properties if the unwinding bound exceeds the reachability diameter. In practice, however, the diameter can rarely be determined statically. Instead, *unwinding assertions* are used to detect looping traces that become infeasible if expanded further [8]. Specifically, an unwinding assertion is a condition that fails for an unwinding bound k and a trace $\pi_1 \cdot \pi_2^k$ if $\pi_1 \cdot \pi_2^{k+1}$ is feasible, indicating that further iterations may be required to exhaustively explore the state space.

In the presence of accelerators, however, unwinding assertions are inefficient. Since $\widehat{\pi} \cdot \widehat{\pi} \preceq \widehat{\pi}$ (Lemma 1), repeated iterations of accelerators are redundant. The unwinding assertion for $\pi_1 \cdot \widehat{\pi}_2$, however, fails if $\pi_1 \cdot \widehat{\pi}_2 \cdot \widehat{\pi}_2$ is feasible, suggesting that further unwinding is required. Accordingly, the approximate diameter as determined by means of unwinding assertions for an accelerated program $\widehat{P}$ is the *same* as for the corresponding non-accelerated program P.

In the following, we present a technique that remedies the deficiency of unwinding assertions in the presence of accelerators by *restricting* the language accepted by a CFA.

Definition 5 (Restriction Language). *Let $\widehat{P}$ an accelerated CFA for P over the vocabulary $\mathsf{Stmts}_{\widehat{P}}$. For each accelerator $\widehat{\pi} \in \mathsf{Stmts}^+_{\widehat{P}}$, let $\pi \in \mathsf{Stmts}^+_P$ be the corresponding looping trace. The* restriction language *$\mathcal{L}_R$ for $\widehat{P}$ comprises all traces with a sub-trace characterised by the regular expression $(\pi \mid (\widehat{\pi} \cdot \widehat{\pi}))$ for all accelerators $\widehat{\pi}$ in $\widehat{P}$ with $\pi \preceq \widehat{\pi}$.*

The following lemma enables us to eliminate traces of an accelerated CFA $\widehat{P}$ that are in the restriction language $\mathcal{L}_R$.

Lemma 2. *Let $\widehat{P}$ be an accelerated CFA, and $\mathcal{L}_R$ be the corresponding restriction language. Let π_1 be a trace accepted by $\widehat{P}$ such that $\pi_1 \in \mathcal{L}_R$. Then there exists a trace π_2 which is accepted by $\widehat{P}$ such that $\pi_1 \preceq \pi_2$ and π_1 is not a sub-trace of π_2.*

Proof. The regular expression $(\pi \mid (\widehat{\pi} \cdot \widehat{\pi}))$ can match the trace π_1 for two reasons:

(a) The trace π_1 contains a sub-trace which is a looping trace π with a corresponding accelerator $\widehat{\pi}$ and $\pi \preceq \widehat{\pi}$. We obtain π_2 by replacing π with $\widehat{\pi}$.
(b) The trace π_1 contains the sub-trace $\widehat{\pi} \cdot \widehat{\pi}$ for some accelerator $\widehat{\pi}$. Since $\widehat{\pi} \cdot \widehat{\pi} \preceq \widehat{\pi}$ (Lemma 1), we replace the sub-trace with $\widehat{\pi}$ to obtain π_2.

Since the accelerator $\widehat{\pi}$ differs from the sub-trace it replaces in case (a), and $|\pi_2| < |\pi_1|$ in case (b), π_1 can not be contained in π_2.

Using Lemma 2 and induction over the number of traces and accelerators, it is admissible to eliminate all traces accepted by $\widehat{P}$ and contained in $\mathcal{L}_R$ without affecting the reachability of states:

Theorem 2. *Let $\mathcal{L}_{\widehat{P}}$ be the language comprising all traces accepted by an accelerated CFA $\widehat{P}$ and $\mathcal{L}_R$ be the corresponding restriction language. Then every trace $\pi \in \mathcal{L}_{\widehat{P}}$ is subsumed by the traces in $\mathcal{L}_{\widehat{P}} \setminus \mathcal{L}_R$.*

Notably, Definition 5 explicitly excludes accelerators $\widehat{\pi}$ that do not satisfy $\pi \preceq \widehat{\pi}$, a requirement that is therefore implicitly present in Lemma 2 as well as Theorem 2. The rationale behind this restriction is that strictly under-approximating accelerators $\widetilde{\pi}$ do not necessarily have this property. However, even if $\widetilde{\pi}$ does not subsume π in general, we can characterize the set of starting states in which it does:

$$\{\sigma \mid \langle \sigma, \sigma' \rangle \in [\![\pi]\!] \Rightarrow \langle \sigma, \sigma' \rangle \in [\![\widetilde{\pi}]\!]\} \tag{2}$$

In order to determine whether a looping path π is redundant, we presume for each accelerated looping trace π the existence of a predicate $\varphi_\pi \in \mathsf{Exprs}$ and an assumption statement $\tau_\pi \stackrel{\text{def}}{=} [\varphi_\pi]$ such that

$$[\![\, \tau_\pi \,]\!] \stackrel{\text{def}}{=} \{\langle \sigma, \sigma \rangle \mid \langle \sigma, \sigma' \rangle \in [\![\pi]\!] \Rightarrow \langle \sigma, \sigma' \rangle \in [\![\widetilde{\pi}]\!]\} \tag{3}$$

Analogously, we can define the dual statement $\overline{\tau}_\pi \stackrel{\text{def}}{=} [\neg\varphi_\pi]$. Though both $[\![\tau_\pi]\!]$ and $[\![\overline{\tau}_\pi]\!]$ are non-total transition relations, their combination $[\![\tau_\pi]\!] \cup [\![\overline{\tau}_\pi]\!]$ is total. Moreover, it does not modify the state, i.e., $[\![\tau_\pi]\!] \cup [\![\overline{\tau}_\pi]\!] \equiv [\![\mathsf{skip}]\!]$. It is therefore evident that replacing the head v of a looping trace π with the subgraph $(u)\overset{\tau_\pi}{\underset{\overline{\tau}_\pi}{\rightrightarrows}}(w)$ (and reconnecting the incoming and outgoing edges of v to u and w, respectively) preserves the reachability of states. It does, however change the traces of the CFA. After the modification, the looping traces $\tau_\pi \cdot \pi$ and $\overline{\tau}_\pi \cdot \pi$ replace π. By definition of τ_π, we have $\tau_\pi \cdot \pi \preceq \widetilde{\pi}$. Consequently, if we accelerate the newly introduced looping trace $\tau_\pi \cdot \pi$, Definition 5 and therefore Lemma 2 as well as Theorem 2 apply.

The discriminating statement $\overline{\tau}_\pi$ for the example path $\mathtt{x} := \mathtt{x} + 1$ at the end of Section 3, for instance, detects the presence of an overflow. For this specific example, $\overline{\tau}_\pi$ is the assumption $[\mathtt{x} = 2^{32} - 1]$. In practice, however, the bit-level-accurate encoding of CBMC provides a mechanism to detect an overflow *after* it happened. Therefore, we introduce statements $\overline{\tau}_\pi \stackrel{\text{def}}{=} [\mathsf{overflow}(\mathtt{x})]$ and $\tau_\pi \stackrel{\text{def}}{=} [\neg\mathsf{overflow}(\mathtt{x})]$ that determine the presence of an overflow at the end of the looping trace. The modification and correctness argument for this construction is analogous to the one above.

In order to recognize redundant traces, we use a *trace automaton* that accepts the restriction language $\mathcal{L}_R$.

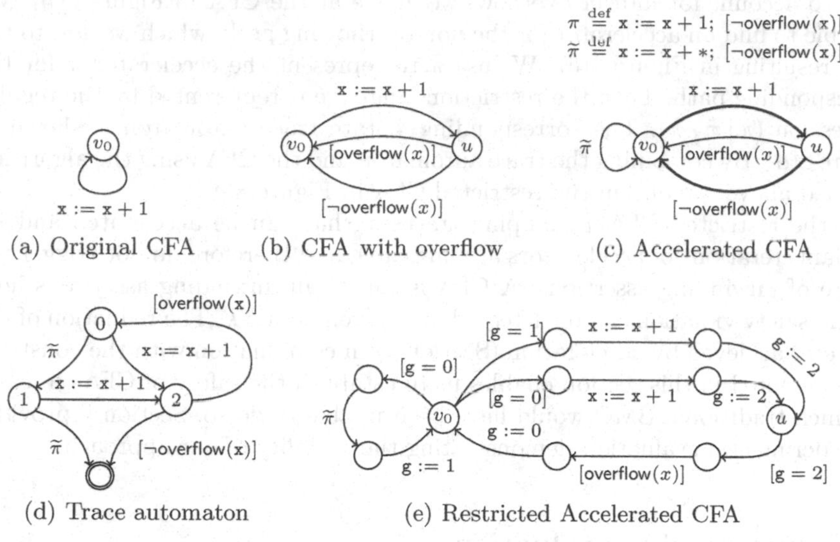

Fig. 8. Accelerating a looping path

Definition 6 (Trace Automaton). *A trace automaton T_R for $\mathcal{L}_R$ is a deterministic finite automaton (DFA) over the alphabet* $\mathsf{Stmts}_{\widehat{P}}$ *that accepts $\mathcal{L}_R$.*

Since $\mathcal{L}_R$ is regular, so is its complement $\overline{\mathcal{L}}_R$. In the following, we describe an instrumentation of a CFA $\widehat{P}$ which guarantees that every trace accepted by T_R and $\widehat{P}$ becomes infeasible. To this end, we construct a DFA T_R recognising $\mathcal{L}_R$, starting out with an ϵ-NFA which we then determinise using the subset construction [1]. While this yields (for a CFA with k statements) a DFA with $O(2^k)$ states in the worst case, in practice the DFAs generated are much smaller.

We initialise the set the vertices of the instrumented CFA $\tilde{P}$ to the vertices of $\widehat{P}$. We inline T_R by creating a fresh integer variable g in $\tilde{P}$ which encodes the state of T_R and is initialised to 0. For each edge $u \xrightarrow{s} v \in \widehat{P}$, we consider all transitions $n \xrightarrow{s} m \in T_R$. If there are no such transitions, we copy the edge $u \xrightarrow{s} v$ into $\tilde{P}$. Otherwise, we add edges as follows:

- If m is an accepting state, we do not add an edge to $\tilde{P}$.
- Otherwise, construct a new statement sequence $l \stackrel{\text{def}}{=} [\mathsf{g} = n];\ s;\ \mathsf{g} := m$ and add the path $u \xrightarrow{l} v$ to $\tilde{P}$, which simulates the transition $n \xrightarrow{s} m$.

Since we add at most a constant number of edges to $\tilde{P}$ for each transition in T_R, this construction's time and space complexity are both $\Theta(\|\widehat{P}\| + \|T_R\|)$. By construction, if a trace π accepted by CFA $\tilde{P}$ projected to $\mathsf{Stmts}_{\widehat{P}}$ is contained in the restriction language $\mathcal{L}_R$, then π is infeasible. Conceptually, our construction suppresses traces accepted by $\mathcal{L}_R$ and retains the remaining executions.

An example is shown in Figure 8. The CFA in Figure 8(a) represents an unaccelerated loop with a single path through its body. After adding an extra path to account for integer overflow, we arrive at the CFA in Figure 8(b). We are able to find an accelerator for the non-overflowing path, which we add to the CFA resulting in Figure 8(c). We use $\widetilde{\pi}$ to represent the accelerator π for the corresponding path. Then the restriction language is represented by the regular expression $(\pi \mid \widetilde{\pi} \cdot \widetilde{\pi})$. The corresponding 4-state trace automaton is shown in Figure 8(d). By combining the trace automaton and the CFA using the algorithm outlined above, we obtain the restricted CFA in Figure 8(e).

In the restricted CFA $\tilde{P}$, looping traces π that can be accelerated and redundant iterations of accelerators are infeasible and therefore do not trigger the failure of unwinding assertions. A CFA is safe if all unwinding assertions hold and no safety violation can be detected for a given bound k. The reduction of the diameter achieved by acceleration (Section 4) in combination with the construction presented in this section enables us to establish the safety of CFAs in cases in which traditional BMC would have been unable to do so. Section 6 provides an experimental evaluation demonstrating the viability of our approach.

6 Experimental Evaluation

We evaluate the effect of instrumenting accelerated programs with trace automata and determine the direct cost of constructing the automata as well as the impact of trace automata on the ability to find bugs on the one hand and prove safety on the other.

Our evaluation is based on the Loops category of the benchmarks from SV-COMP14 and a number of small but difficult hand-crafted examples[1]. Our hand-crafted examples require precise reasoning about arithmetic and arrays. The unsafe examples have deep bugs, and the safe examples feature unbounded loops. The SV-COMP14 benchmarks are largely arithmetic in nature. They often require non-trivial arithmetic invariants to be inferred, but rarely require complex reasoning about arrays. Furthermore, all bugs of the unsafe SV-COMP14 benchmarks occur within a small number of loop iterations.

In all of our experiments we used Cbmc taken from the public SVN at r3849 to perform the transformation. Since Cbmc's acceleration procedure generates assertions with quantified arrays, we used Z3 [24] version 4.3.1 as the backend decision procedure. All of the experiments were performed with a timeout of 30 s and very low unwinding limits. We used an unwinding limit of 100 for unaccelerated programs and an unwinding limit of 3 for their accelerated counterparts.

The version of Cbmc we use has incomplete acceleration support, e.g., it is unable to accelerate nested loops. As a result, there are numerous benchmarks that it cannot accelerate. We stress that our goal here is to evaluate the effect of adding trace automata to accelerated programs. Acceleration has already proven to be a useful technique for both bug-finding and proof [15,17,21,26,27] and we are interested in how well inlined trace automata can complement it.

[1] These examples have been accepted into SV-COMP15, where they can be found in the loop-acceleration directory.

Table 2. Summary of experimental results

	CBMC				CBMC + Acceleration			CBMC + Acceleration + Trace Automata		
	#Benchmarks	#Correct	Time (s)	#Benchmarks accelerated	#Correct	Acceleration Time (s)	Checking Time (s)	#Correct	Acceleration Time (s)	Checking Time (s)
SV-COMP14 safe	35	14	298.73	21	2	23.24	244.72	14	23.86	189.61
SV-COMP14 unsafe	32	20	394.96	18	11	15.79	197.94	12	16.51	173.74
Crafted safe	15	0	11.42	15	0	2.75	32.41	15	2.91	1.59
Crafted unsafe	14	0	9.03	14	14	2.85	12.24	14	2.95	2.55

Our experimental results are summarised in Table 2, and the full results are provided in our technical report [18]. We discuss the results in the remainder of this section.

Cost of Trace Automata. To evaluate the direct cost of constructing the trace automata, we direct the reader's attention to Table 2 and the columns headed "acceleration time". The first "acceleration time" column shows how long it took to generate an accelerated program without a trace automaton, whereas the second shows how long it took when a trace automaton was included. For all of these benchmarks, the additional time taken to build and insert the trace automaton is negligible. Detailed information about the size increase of the instrumented binary over the accelerated binary is provided in our technical report [18, Appendix B]. The average increase is about 15%, but the maximum increase is 77%. There is still room for optimisation, as we do not minimise the automata before inserting them.

Bug Finding. In the following, we evaluate the effectiveness of our technique for bug finding. The current state-of-the-art method for bug finding is BMC [3]. To provide a baseline for bug finding power, we start by evaluating the effect of just combining acceleration with BMC. We then evaluate the impact of adding trace automata, as compared to acceleration without trace automata. Our hypothesis is that adding trace automata has negligible impact on acceleration's ability to find bugs. The statistics we use to measure these effects are the number of bugs found and the time to find them. We measure these statistics for each of three techniques: BMC alone, acceleration with BMC, and our combination of acceleration, trace automata and BMC.

The results are summarised in Table 2. In SV-COMP14, almost all of the bugs occur after a small number of unwindings. In these cases, there are no deep loops to accelerate so just using CBMC allows the same bugs to be reached, but without the overhead of acceleration (which causes some timeouts to be hit). In the crafted set the bugs are much deeper, and we can see the effect of acceleration in discovering these bugs – none of the bugs are discovered by CBMC, but each of the configurations using acceleration finds all 14 bugs.

In both of the benchmark sets, adding trace automata does not negatively impact the bug finding ability of acceleration. Indeed, for the crafted set the addition of trace automata significantly improves bug finding performance – the total time needed to find the 14 bugs is reduced from 12.31 s to 1.85 s.

Safety Proving. We evaluate the effectiveness of our technique for proving safety *with BMC*, the key contribution of this paper. Our two benchmark sets have very different characteristics with respect to the safety proofs required for their safe examples. As can be seen from Table 2, 14 of the SV-COMP14 benchmarks can be proved safe using just BMC. That is, they can be exhaustively proved safe after a small number of loop unwindings. For the 14 cases that were provable using just BMC, none had loops that could execute for more than 10 iterations.

Of the 35 safe SV-COMP14 benchmarks, 21 contained loops that could be accelerated by our implementation. Of these 21 cases, 14 were proved safe using trace automata. These are not the same 14 cases that were proved by CBMC, and notably 8 cases with unbounded loops are included, which would be impossible to prove safe with just BMC.

Additionally we were able to solve the SUM_ARRAY_TRUE benchmark (given as Figure 9) in 1.75 s. Of all the tools entered in SV-COMP14, the only tools to claim "safe" for this benchmark were BMC-based (even though analyses able to solve this problem exist, e.g. [10]), and as such do not generate safety proofs.

```
unsigned N := *, i;
int a[M], b[M], c[M];

for (i = 0; i < M; i := i + 1) {
    c[i] := a[i] + b[i];
}

for (i = 0; i < M; i := i + 1) {
    assert (c[i] = a[i] + b[i]);
}
```

Fig. 9. The SUM_ARRAYS benchmark from SV-COMP14

For the 7 cases where accelerators were produced but we were unable to prove safety, 5 are due to timeouts, 1 is a crash in CBMC and 1 is an "incomplete". The 5 timeouts are due to the complexity of the SMT queries we produce. For these timeout cases, we generate assertions which contain non-linear multiplication and quantification over arrays, which are very difficult for Z3 to solve. The "incomplete" case (TREX03_TRUE) requires reasoning about accelerated paths that commute with each other, which we leave as future work.

7 Related Work

The diameter of a transition system was introduced in Biere et al.'s seminal paper on BMC [5] in the context of finite-state transition relations. For finite-state transition relations, approximations of the diameter can be computed symbolically by constraining the unwound transition relation to exclude executions that visit states repeatedly [20]. For software, however, this technique is ineffective. Baumgartner and Kühlmann use structural transformations of hardware designs to reduce the reachability diameter of a hardware design to obtain a complete BMC-based verification method [2]. This technique is not applicable in our context.

Trace automata are introduced in [13] as abstractions of safe traces of CFAs [14], constructed by means of interpolation. We use trace automata to recognize redundant traces.

Acceleration amounts to computing the transitive closure of a infinite state transition relation [6,7,12]. Acceleration has been successfully combined with abstract interpretation [26] as well as interpolation-based invariant construction [15]. These techniques rely on over-approximate abstractions to prove safety. We previously used acceleration and under-approximation to quickly find deep bugs [17,19,21,22]. The quantified transition relations used to encode under-approximations pose an insurmountable challenge to interpolation-based refinement techniques [17, 19], making it difficult to combine the approach with traditional software model checkers.

8 Conclusion

The reduction of the reachability diameter of a program achieved by acceleration and loop under-approximation enables the rapid detection of bugs by means of BMC. Attempts to apply under-approximation to prove safety, however, have been disappointing: the simple mechanism deployed by BMC-based tools to detect that an unwinding bound is exhaustive is not readily applicable to accelerated programs.

In this paper, we present a technique that constrains the search space of an accelerated program, enabling BMC-based tools to prove safety using a small unwinding depth. To this end, we use *trace automata* to eliminate redundant execution traces resulting from under-approximating acceleration. Unlike other safety provers, our approach does not rely on over-approximation, nor does it require the explicit computation of a fixed point. Using unwinding assertions, the smaller diameter can be computed by means of a simple satisfiability check.

References

1. Aho, A.V., Sethi, R., Ullman, J.D.: Compilers: Principles, Techniques, and Tools. Addison-Wesley Longman Publishing Co., Inc., Boston (1986)

2. Baumgartner, J., Kuehlmann, A.: Enhanced diameter bounding via structural transformations. In: Design, Automation and Test in Europe (DATE), pp. 36–41. IEEE (2004)
3. Beyer, D.: Status Report on Software Verification (Competition Summary SV-COMP 2014). In: Ábrahám, E., Havelund, K. (eds.) TACAS 2014. LNCS, vol. 8413, pp. 373–388. Springer, Heidelberg (2014)
4. Beyer, D., Henzinger, T.A., Majumdar, R., Rybalchenko, A.: Path invariants. In: Programming Language Design and Implementation (PLDI), pp. 300–309. ACM (2007)
5. Biere, A., Cimatti, A., Clarke, E., Zhu, Y.: Symbolic model checking without BDDs. In: Cleaveland, W.R. (ed.) TACAS/ETAPS 1999. LNCS, vol. 1579, pp. 193–207. Springer, Heidelberg (1999)
6. Boigelot, B.: Symbolic Methods for Exploring Infinite State Spaces. Ph.D. thesis, Université de Liège (1999)
7. Bozga, M., Iosif, R., Konečný, F.: Fast acceleration of ultimately periodic relations. In: Touili, T., Cook, B., Jackson, P. (eds.) CAV 2010. LNCS, vol. 6174, pp. 227–242. Springer, Heidelberg (2010)
8. Clarke, E., Kroning, D., Lerda, F.: A tool for checking ANSI-C programs. In: Jensen, K., Podelski, A. (eds.) TACAS 2004. LNCS, vol. 2988, pp. 168–176. Springer, Heidelberg (2004)
9. Dijkstra, E.W.: et al.: From predicate transformers to predicates, tuesday Afternoon Club Manuscript EWD821 (April 1982)
10. Dillig, I., Dillig, T., Aiken, A.: Fluid updates: Beyond strong vs. weak updates. In: Gordon, A.D. (ed.) ESOP 2010. LNCS, vol. 6012, pp. 246–266. Springer, Heidelberg (2010)
11. D'Silva, V., Kroening, D., Weissenbacher, G.: A survey of automated techniques for formal software verification. Transactions on Computer-Aided Design of Integrated Circuits and Systems (TCAD) 27(7), 1165–1178 (2008)
12. Finkel, A., Leroux, J.: How to compose Presburger-accelerations: Applications to broadcast protocols. In: Agrawal, M., Seth, A.K. (eds.) FSTTCS 2002. LNCS, vol. 2556, pp. 145–156. Springer, Heidelberg (2002)
13. Heizmann, M., Hoenicke, J., Podelski, A.: Refinement of trace abstraction. In: Palsberg, J., Su, Z. (eds.) SAS 2009. LNCS, vol. 5673, pp. 69–85. Springer, Heidelberg (2009)
14. Henzinger, T.A., Jhala, R., Majumdar, R., Sutre, G.: Lazy abstraction. In: Principles of Programming Languages (POPL), pp. 58–70. ACM (2002)
15. Hojjat, H., Iosif, R., Konečný, F., Kuncak, V., Rümmer, P.: Accelerating interpolants. In: Chakraborty, S., Mukund, M. (eds.) ATVA 2012. LNCS, vol. 7561, pp. 187–202. Springer, Heidelberg (2012)
16. Kovács, L., Voronkov, A.: Finding loop invariants for programs over arrays using a theorem prover. In: Chechik, M., Wirsing, M. (eds.) FASE 2009. LNCS, vol. 5503, pp. 470–485. Springer, Heidelberg (2009)
17. Kroening, D., Lewis, M., Weissenbacher, G.: Under-approximating loops in C programs for fast counterexample detection. In: Sharygina, N., Veith, H. (eds.) CAV 2013. LNCS, vol. 8044, pp. 381–396. Springer, Heidelberg (2013)
18. Kroening, D., Lewis, M., Weissenbacher, G.: Proving safety with trace automata and bounded model checking. CoRR abs/1410.5764 (2014), http://arxiv.org/abs/1410.5764
19. Kroening, D., Lewis, M., Weissenbacher, G.: Under-approximating loops in C programs for fast counterexample detection. Formal Methods in System Design (April 2015), http://dx.doi.org/10.1007/s10703-015-0228-1

20. Kroning, D., Strichman, O.: Efficient computation of recurrence diameters. In: Zuck, L.D., Attie, P.C., Cortesi, A., Mukhopadhyay, S. (eds.) VMCAI 2003. LNCS, vol. 2575, pp. 298–309. Springer, Heidelberg (2002)
21. Kroening, D., Weissenbacher, G.: Counterexamples with loops for predicate abstraction. In: Ball, T., Jones, R.B. (eds.) CAV 2006. LNCS, vol. 4144, pp. 152–165. Springer, Heidelberg (2006)
22. Kroening, D., Weissenbacher, G.: Verification and falsification of programs with loops using predicate abstraction. Formal Aspects of Computing 22, 105–128 (2010)
23. McMillan, K.L.: Lazy abstraction with interpolants. In: Ball, T., Jones, R.B. (eds.) CAV 2006. LNCS, vol. 4144, pp. 123–136. Springer, Heidelberg (2006)
24. de Moura, L., Bjørner, N.S.: Z3: An efficient SMT solver. In: Ramakrishnan, C.R., Rehof, J. (eds.) TACAS 2008. LNCS, vol. 4963, pp. 337–340. Springer, Heidelberg (2008)
25. Nelson, G.: A generalization of Dijkstra's calculus. ACM Transactions on Programming Languages and Systems (TOPLAS) 11(4), 517–561 (1989)
26. Schrammel, P., Jeannet, B.: Logico-numerical abstract acceleration and application to the verification of data-flow programs. In: Yahav, E. (ed.) SAS 2011. LNCS, vol. 6887, pp. 233–248. Springer, Heidelberg (2011)
27. Schrammel, P., Melham, T., Kroening, D.: Chaining test cases for reactive system testing. In: Yenigün, H., Yilmaz, C., Ulrich, A. (eds.) ICTSS 2013. LNCS, vol. 8254, pp. 133–148. Springer, Heidelberg (2013)

Verifying Parameterized Timed Security Protocols

Li Li[1(✉)], Jun Sun[2], Yang Liu[3], and Jin Song Dong[1]

[1] National University of Singapore, Singapore, Singapore
li-li@comp.nus.edu.sg
[2] Singapore University of Technology and Design, Singapore, Singapore
[3] Nanyang Technological University, Singapore, Singapore

Abstract. Quantitative timing is often explicitly used in systems for better security, e.g., the credentials for automatic website logon often has limited lifetime. Verifying timing relevant security protocols in these systems is very challenging as timing adds another dimension of complexity compared with the untimed protocol verification. In our previous work, we proposed an approach to check the correctness of the timed authentication in security protocols with fixed timing constraints. However, a more difficult question persists, i.e., given a particular protocol design, whether the protocol has security flaws in its design or it can be configured secure with proper parameter values? In this work, we answer this question by proposing a parameterized verification framework, where the quantitative parameters in the protocols can be intuitively specified as well as automatically analyzed. Given a security protocol, our verification algorithm either produces the secure constraints of the parameters, or constructs an attack that works for any parameter values. The correctness of our algorithm is formally proved. We implement our method into a tool called PTAuth and evaluate it with several security protocols. Using PTAuth, we have successfully found a timing attack in Kerberos V which is unreported before.

1 Introduction

Time could be a powerful tool in designing security protocols. For instance, distance bounding protocols rely heavily on time; session keys with limited lifetime are extensively used in practice to achieve better security. However, designing timed security protocols is more challenging than designing untimed ones because timing adds a range of attacking surface, e.g., the adversary might be able to extend the session key without proper authorization. Hence, it is important to have a formal verification framework to analyze the timed security protocols. In our previous work [20], we developed a verification algorithm to analyze whether a given protocol with fixed timing constraints is secure or not. In this work, we answer a more difficult question, i.e., given a security protocol with configurable parameters for the timing constraints, are there any parameters which could guarantee security and what are they? Having an approach to answer the question is useful in a number of ways. Firstly, it can analyze, at once, all instances

N. Bjørner and F. de Boer (Eds.): FM 2015, LNCS 9109, pp. 342–359, 2015.
DOI: 10.1007/978-3-319-19249-9_22

of the security protocols with different parameter values. Secondly, it allows the protocol designer to gain precise knowledge on the secure configuration of the parameters so as to choose the best values (e.g., in terms of minimizing the protocol execution time).

In general, parameterized timing constraints are necessary in various scenarios. First of all, they can be used to capture the general design of the protocols. For instance, since the lifetime of credentials are often related to the runtime information like network latency, it is best to keep them parameterized so that we can systematically find out their secure relations. Furthermore, parameterized timing constraints are necessary to model the properties of some special cryptographic primitives. For example, weak cryptographic functions, which are breakable by consuming extra time, may be used in the sensor networks for higher computing performance and lower power consumption. Since breaking different weak functions requires different the attack time, in order to guarantee the correctness of the protocols in these sensor networks, we need to parameterize the attack time and compute the secure configuration accordingly. Moreover, agencies often give suggestions on key crypto-period for cryptographic key management [4], so parameterized timing constraints can be used to model long term protocols.

Nevertheless, this is a highly non-trivial task. The challenges for designing timed protocol and providing proper parameter configuration are illustrated as follows. First, in the setting of timed authentication over the Internet, given the network is completely exposed to the adversary, we need to formally prove that the critical information cannot be leaked and the protocol works as intended under arbitrary attacking behaviors from the network. Second, timestamps are continuous values extracted from clocks to ensure the validity of messages and credentials. Analyzing the continuous timing constraints adds another dimension of complexity. Third, a protocol design might contain multiple timing parameters, e.g., the network latency and the session key lifetime, which could affect security of the system. Manually reasoning the least constrained and yet correct configuration for the parameters in complex protocols is extremely hard and error-prone. As a consequence, automatic analysis technique is needed for proving the correctness of the protocol and computing the parameter configurations.

Contributions. Our contributions in this work are summarized as follows. (1) We propose an intuitive method to specify parameterized timed protocols in Section 3 by extending our previous work [20] with parameterized timing constraint, secrecy query, etc. (2) Based on the specification, protocols can be verified efficiently for an unbounded number of protocol sessions in our framework as shown in Section 4. Generally, in this work, we specify the adversary's capabilities in the security protocols as a set of Horn logic rules with parameterized timing constraints. Then, we compose these rules repeatedly until a fixed-point is reached, so that we can check the intended security properties against them and compute the largest parameter configurations. The parameter configuration is represented by succinct constraints of the parameters. When the protocol could be secure with the right parameter values, our approach outputs a set of constraints on

Table 1. Syntax Hierarchy Structure

Type	Expression	
Message(m)	$f(m_1, m_2, ..., m_n)$	(function)
	$a[]$	(name)
	$[n]$	(nonce)
	v	(variable)
	t	(timestamp)
Parameter(p)	$\S p$	(parameter)
Constraint(B)	$\mathcal{C}(t_1, t_2, \ldots, t_n, \S p_1, \S p_2, \ldots, \S p_m)$	(timing constraint)
Configuration(L)	$\mathcal{C}(\S p_1, \S p_2, \ldots, \S p_m)$	(parameter configuration)
Event(e)	$know(m, t)$	(knowledge)
	$new([n], op[], \langle m_1, m_2, \ldots, m_n \rangle)$	(nonce generation)
	$init(m_1, m_2, \ldots, m_n)$	(init)
	$accept(m_1, m_2, \ldots, m_n)$	(accept)
	$leak(m)$	(leak)
Rule(R)	$[G]\ e_1, e_2, \ldots, e_n \dashv\!\![\ B\ ]\!\!\mapsto e$	(rule)
	$e \leftarrow\!\![\ B\ ]\!\!\vdash e_1, e_2, \ldots, e_n$	(query)

the parameters that are necessary for security. Otherwise, an attack is generated, which would work for any parameter values. We formally prove the correctness of our algorithm. (3) We implement our method as a tool named PTAuth. In order to handle the parameters in the timing constraints, we utilize the Parma Polyhedra Library (PPL) [3] in our tool to represent the relations between timestamps and parameters. We evaluate our approach with several security protocols in Section 5. During the experiment, we found a timing attack in the official document of Kerberos V [27] that has never been reported before.

Structure of the Paper. In Section 2, we introduce the Wide Mouthed Frog (WMF) [8] protocol and use it as a motivating example in the following paper. In Section 3, an intuitive specification method is illustrated with WMF. The detailed verification algorithms are given in Section 4. Due to the limitation of space, the complete proofs for our verification methods can be found in [1]. The experiment results are shown in Section 5, where a new attack of Kerberos V is found in RFC 4120 [27]. The related works are described in Section 6. Finally, we draw conclusions in Section 7.

2 Running Example

We use the Wide Mouthed Frog (WMF) [8] protocol as a running example to illustrate how our approach works. WMF is designed for exchanging timely fresh session keys, ensuring that the key is generated by the protocol initiator within a short time when the protocol responder accepts it.

Syntax Hierarchy. Before describing the WMF protocol, we introduce the syntax for representing the messages first as shown in Table 1. *Messages* could be defined as *functions*, *names*, *nonces*, *variables* or *timestamps*. *Functions* can be applied to a sequence of *messages*; *names* are globally shared constants; *nonces* are freshly generated random values in sessions; *variables* are memory spaces for holding *messages*; and *timestamps* are clock readings extracted during the protocol execution. In addition, we introduce *parameters* to parameterize the timing constraints. The constraint function $\mathcal{C}(\mathbb{X})$ applies succinct constraints to $\mathbb{X}$, where $\mathbb{X}$ is a set of timestamps and parameters. Each succinct constraint can be written in a general form of $l(t_1, \ldots, t_n, \S p_1, \ldots, \S p_m) \sim 0$, where $\sim \in \{<, \leq\}$ and l is a linear function. In the following paper, the symmetric encryption function is denoted as $enc_s(m, k)$, where m is the encrypted message and k is the encryption key. Furthermore, all the messages transmitted in WMF is encrypted by the shared key represented as $sk(u)$, which is only known between the user u and the server. For simplicity, the concatenation function $tuple_n(m_1, m_2, \ldots, m_n)$ is written as $\langle m_1, m_2, \ldots, m_n \rangle$ (or simply $m_1, m_2, \ldots, m_n$ when no ambiguity is introduced).

Events are constructed by attaching predicates to the message sequences. In our framework, we have five different predicates: (1) the knowledge event $know(m, t)$ means that the adversary knows the message m at the time t; (2) the nonce generation event $new([n], op[], \langle m_1, \ldots, m_n \rangle)$ means that a nonce $[n]$ is generated in the operation $op[]$ by a legitimate protocol participant with knowledge of $\langle m_1, \ldots, m_n \rangle$; (3) the event $init(m_1, \ldots, m_n)$ stands for the protocol initialization by a legitimate protocol participant with knowledge of $m_1, \ldots, m_n$; (4) similarly, the event $accept(m_1, \ldots, m_n)$ stands for the protocol acceptance by a legitimate protocol participant with knowledge of $m_1, \ldots, m_n$; (5) the event $leak(m)$ is introduced to check the leakage of the secret message m that violates the secrecy property, as shown in the example later.

Wide Mouthed Frog. The WMF protocol is a key exchange protocol consisting of three participants, i.e., the initiator *Alice*, the responder *Bob* and the server. It has the following five steps.

$$
\begin{array}{ll}
(1)\ \textit{Alice}\ \text{engages} & : new([k], alice\_gen[], \langle A[], B[], t_A \rangle) \\
 & , init_A(A[], B[], [k], t_A) \\
(2)\ \textit{Alice} \rightarrow \textit{Server} & : \langle A[], enc_s(\langle t_A, B[], [k] \rangle, sk(A[])) \rangle \\
(3)\ \textit{Server}\ \text{checks} & : t_S - t_A \leq \S p_a \\
\quad\ \textit{Server}\ \text{engages} & : init_S(A[], B[], [k], t_S) \\
(4)\ \textit{Server} \rightarrow \textit{Bob} & : enc_s(\langle t_S, A[], [k] \rangle, sk(B[])) \\
(5)\ \textit{Bob}\ \text{checks} & : t_B - t_S \leq \S p_a \\
\quad\ \textit{Bob}\ \text{engages} & : accept(A[], B[], [k], t_B)
\end{array}
$$

First, *Alice* generates a fresh key $[k]$ at time t_A with the *new* event and engages an $init_A$ event to initiate the key exchange protocol with *Bob*. Second, *Alice* sends the fresh key with the current time t_A and *Bob*'s name to the server. Third, after receiving the request from *Alice*, the server checks the freshness of the timestamp t_A and accepts *Alice*'s request by engaging an $init_S$ event. Fourth, the server sends a new message to *Bob*, informing him that the server receives a request from *Alice* at time t_S to communicate with him using the key $[k]$. Fifth, *Bob* checks the timestamp and accepts the request from *Alice* if it is timely. The transmitted messages are encrypted under the users' shared keys.

Parameters. Whether or not WMF works relies on two crucial time parameters. The first parameter is the real network latency $\S p_d$ of the network, and the second one is the message delay $\S p_a$ allowed in the message freshness checking. $\S p_d$ is initially configured as $\S p_d > 0$ because the network latency should be positive. However, the exact value of $\S p_d$ depends on the network itself and thus cannot be fixed in the protocol design. Parameter $\S p_a$ on the other hand might be related to $\S p_d$'s value, which should be answered by the verification. That is to say, the values of the parameters are better modeled as unknown parameters and we must be able to analyze the protocol without the concrete values of them. By introducing these two parameters, we want to make sure that the WMF protocol exchanges the secret session key successfully, and the correspondence between the request from Alice and the acceptance from Bob is timely. Hence, ideally a tool would automatically show us the secure configuration of $\S p_d$ and $\S p_a$. Because WMF has two message transmissions, we need to check whether $t_B - t_A \leq 2 * \S p_a$ is always satisfied.

3 Parameterized Timed Security Protocol Specification

In this section, we introduce how to model the parameterized timed security protocols. Generally, protocols as well as their underlying cryptography foundation are represented by a set of Horn logic rule variants [6] as shown in Table 1. They, denoted as $\mathbb{R}_{init}$, represent the capabilities of the adversary in the protocol.

Adversary Model. We assume that an active attacker exists in the network, extending from the Dolev-Yao model [15]. The attacker can intercept all communications, compute new messages, generate new nonces and send any message he obtained. For computation, he can use all the publicly available functions, e.g., encryption, decryption, concatenation. He can also ask the genuine protocol participants to take part in the protocol based on his needs. Comparing our attack model with the Dolev-Yao model, attacking the weak cryptographic functions and compromising legitimate protocol participant are allowed by consuming extra time, as shown later in this section.

Rule Construction. Based on the adversary model described above, the interactions available to the adversary in the protocol can be represented by Horn logic rule variants guarded by timed checking conditions. Generally, every rule consists of a set of untimed guard conditions, several premise events, some timing constraints and one conclusion event as shown in Table 1. When the guard conditions, the premise events and the timing constraints in a rule are fulfilled, its conclusion event becomes available to the adversary. We remove the brackets if the rule has no guard condition. For instance, since the symmetric encryption and decryption functions are publicly available in WMF, these capabilities of the adversary can be represented by the following two rules.

$$know(m, t_1), know(k, t_2) \dashv t_1, t_2 \leq t \mapsto know(enc_s(m, k), t) \quad (1)$$

$$know(enc_s(m, k), t_1), know(k, t_2) \dashv t_1, t_2 \leq t \mapsto know(m, t) \quad (2)$$

The rule (1) means that given a message m and a key k, the adversary can compute its encryption $enc_s(m, k)$, and the encryption can only be known after the message and the key are obtained. Similarly, the rule (2) shows the decryption capability of the adversary.

Furthermore, the adversary can register new accounts at the server, except for the existing ones of *Alice* and *Bob*. So, we have the following rule.

$$[c \neq A[] \wedge c \neq B[]]\ know(c, t_1) \dashv t_1 \leq t \mapsto know(sk(c), t) \quad (3)$$

For rules related to the protocol itself, they can be extracted from the protocol readily. For instance, the adversary can actively ask *Alice* to initiate the first step of the WMF protocol, so the messages in the second step can be intercepted from the network, which is shown by the rule (4). As Alice can initiate this protocol with any user at any time based on the adversary's needs, the constant $B[]$ is replaced with a variable R and $know(\langle R, t_A \rangle, t)$ is added to the premises of the rule, comparing with protocol description in Section 2.

$$know(\langle R, t_A \rangle, t), new([k], alice\_gen[], \langle A[], R, t_A \rangle), init_A(A[], R, [k], t_A)$$
$$\dashv t \leq t_A \mapsto know(\langle A[], enc_s(\langle t_A, R, [k] \rangle, sk(A[])) \rangle, t_A) \quad (4)$$

Similarly, based on the server's behavior (the third and fourth steps in WMF), we can construct the rule (5) shown below. Since the server provides its service to all of its users, *Alice* and *Bob*'s names are replaced by variables. The network latency and the message delay are captured by the parameterized constraints.

$$know(\langle I, enc_s(\langle t_I, R, k \rangle, sk(I)) \rangle, t), init_S(I, R, k, t_S)$$
$$\dashv t_S - t \geq \S p_d \wedge t_S - t_I \leq \S p_a \mapsto know(enc_s(\langle t_S, I, k \rangle, sk(R)), t_S) \quad (5)$$

Finally, *Bob* accepts the protocol when he receives the message from the server, indicating that the initiator is *Alice* and the request is fresh.

$$know(enc_s(\langle t_S, A[], k \rangle, sk(B[])), t)$$
$$\dashv t_B - t \geq \S p_d \wedge t_B - t_S \leq \S p_a \mapsto accept(A[], B[], k, t_B) \quad (6)$$

Additional Attack Rule. In addition to the attacker capabilities in the Dolev-Yao model, the attacker can compromise cryptographic primitives and legitimate protocol participants. For instance, we can model the brute-force attack on a weak encryption function. Given the name of the encryption function as *Crypto* and the least time of cracking *Crypto* as $\S d$, the attacking behavior can be modeled by the following rule.

$$know(Crypto(m, k), t_1) \dashv t - t_1 > \S d \mapsto know(m, t)$$

Additionally, some ciphers like RC4 which is used by WEP, key compromise on a busy network can be conducted after a short time. Given an application scenario where such attack is possible and the attacking time has a lower bound $\S d$, we can model it as follows.

$$know(RC4(m,k),t_1)\rangle \dashv t - t_1 > \S d \vdash\!\!\rightarrow know(k,t)$$

Authentication Query. Similar to our previous work [20], verifying the timely authentication is allowed in our framework. The timely authentication not only asks for the proper correspondence between the init and accept events but also requires the satisfaction of the timing constraints, formalized as follows.

Definition 1. ***Timed Authentication.*** *In a timed protocol, timed authentication holds for an event accept with some events* $\{init_1, init_2, \ldots, init_n\}$ *agreed on the event arguments and the timing constraints* B*, if and only if for every occurrence of the event accept, all of the corresponding events* $\{init_1, init_2, \ldots, init_n\}$ *are engaged before, and their timestamps should always satisfy the timing constraints* B*. We denote the* timed authentication *query as accept* $\leftarrow\!\!\dashv B \vdash init_1, init_2, \ldots, init_n$*. In order to ensure the general timed authentication, the arguments encoded in the query events should only be variables and timestamps.*

In WMF, the authentication should be accepted by the responder R only if the request is made by the initiator I within $2 * \S p_a$. Thus, we have the following authentication query.

$$accept(I,R,k,k_R) \leftarrow\!\!\dashv k_R - k_I \leq 2 * \S p_a \vdash init_A(I,R,k,t_I) \qquad (7)$$

Secrecy Query. In this work, we extend the verification algorithm developed in our previous work [20] with secrecy checking that can be relevant to timing. Secrecy checking is introduced with additional rules that lead to the leak events, representing the leakage of the secret information.

Definition 2. ***Secrecy.*** *In a security protocol, secrecy holds for a message* m *if the event leak*(m) *is unreachable when "*$new_1, new_2, \ldots, new_n, know(m,t) \dashv\!\!\vdash\!\!\rightarrow leak(m)$*" is added to* $\mathbb{R}_{init}$*, where* $new_1, new_2, \ldots, new_n$ *are the nonce generation events for all of nonces in* m*. Notice that all of the nonce generation events should have unique operation names so that they can be correctly identified.*

For instance, according to the WMF protocol, a secret session key $[k]$ is sent over the network. In order to check the secrecy property of $[k]$, we add the following rule to $\mathbb{R}_{init}$ and then check the reachability of the leak event.

$$new([k], alice\_gen[], \langle A[], B[], t_A\rangle), know([k],t) \dashv\!\!\vdash\!\!\rightarrow leak([k]) \qquad (8)$$

It means that if the session key $[k]$ generated by *Alice* for *Bob* can be known to the adversary, the secrecy property of the session key is invalid in WMF.

4 Verification Algorithm

Given a set of rules $\mathbb{R}$ and a parameter configuration L, we define $\alpha(\mathbb{R}, L) = \{[G]\ H \dashv B \cap L \mapsto f | [G]\ H \dashv B \mapsto f \in \mathbb{R}\}$, representing the rules under the parameter configuration L. Since the initial rules $\mathbb{R}_{init}$ can be extracted from the protocol as shown in Section 3, the satisfaction of an authentication query Q then depends on whether the adversary can actively guide the protocol to reach the *accept* event based on $\alpha(\mathbb{R}_{init}, L)$ without engaging the corresponding *init* events in Q or satisfying the timing constraints. Similarly, the verification of the secrecy query needs to check that the *leak* event is unreachable based on $\alpha(\mathbb{R}_{init}, L)$. In this section, we focus on computing the largest parameter configuration that ensures the correctness of the desired authentication and secrecy properties.

Given any parameter configuration L, in order to determine whether a query Q is satisfied by $\alpha(\mathbb{R}_{init}, L)$, we can adapt the verification algorithm in [20]. However, there might be infinitely many possible parameter configurations. Thus, in this work, we develop an approach to handle the parameters symbolically. Specifically, the verification is divided into two sequential phases: the rule basis construction phase and the query searching phase. In the rule base construction phase, we generate new rules by composing two rules (through unifying the conclusion of the first rule and the premise of the second rule). Our verification algorithm uses this method repeatedly to generate new rules until a fixed-point is reached. This fixed-point is called the *rule basis* if it exists. Subsequently, in the query searching phase, the query is checked against the *rule basis* to find counter examples. Generally, we need to check the event correspondence as well as the parameterized timing constraints, the verification either proves the correctness of the protocol by providing the secure configuration of the parameters (represented as succinct constraints), or reports attacks because no parameter configuration can be found. Since the verification for security protocol is generally undecidable [12], our algorithm cannot guarantee termination. However, as shown in Section 5, our algorithm can terminate on most of the evaluated security protocols. Additionally, limiting the number of protocol sessions is allowed in our framework which would guarantee the termination of our algorithm.

Rule Basis Construction. Before constructing the rule basis, we need to introduce some basic concepts first:

- If σ is a substitution for both events e_1 and e_2 such that $\sigma e_1 = \sigma e_2$, we say e_1 and e_2 are unifiable and σ is an unifier for e_1 and e_2. If e_1 and e_2 are unifiable, the most general unifier for e_1 and e_2 is an unifier σ such that for all unifiers σ' of e_1 and e_2 there exists a substitution σ'' such that $\sigma' = \sigma''\sigma$.
- Given two rules $R = [G]\ H \dashv B \mapsto e$ and $R' = [G']\ H' \dashv B' \mapsto e'$, if e and $e_0 \in H'$ can be unified with the most general unifier σ such that $\sigma G \wedge \sigma G'$ can be valid, their composition is denoted as $R \circ_{e_0} R' = \sigma([G \wedge G']\ H \cup (H' - \{e_0\})) \dashv \sigma(B \cap B') \mapsto \sigma e'$.
- Additionally, given the above two rules R and R', we define R implies R' denoted as $R \Rightarrow R'$ when $\exists \sigma, \sigma e = e' \wedge G' \Rightarrow \sigma G \wedge \sigma H \subseteq H' \wedge B' \subseteq \sigma B$.

We construct the rule basis $\beta(\mathbb{R}_{init})$ based on the initial rules $\mathbb{R}_{init}$. Firstly, we define $\mathbb{R}_v$ as follows, representing the minimal closure of the initial rules $\mathbb{R}_{init}$. (1) $\forall R \in \mathbb{R}_{init}, \exists R' \in \mathbb{R}_v, R' \Rightarrow R$, which means that every initial rule is implied by a rule in $\mathbb{R}_v$. (2) $\forall R, R' \in \mathbb{R}_v, R \not\Rightarrow R'$, which means that no duplicated rule exists in $\mathbb{R}_v$. (3) $\forall R, R' \in \mathbb{R}_v$ and $R = [G]\ H \dashv B \mapsto e$, if $\forall e' \in H, e' \in \mathbb{V}$ and $\exists e_0 \notin \mathbb{V}, S \circ_{e_0} S'$ is defined, then $\exists S'' \in \mathbb{R}_v, S'' \Rightarrow R \circ_{e_0} R'$, where $\mathbb{V}$ is a set of events that can be provided by the adversary. In this work, $\mathbb{V}$ is the *init* events, the *new* events and the $know(x,t)$ event where x is a variable. The third rule means that for any two rules in $\mathbb{R}_v$, if all premises of one rule are trivially satisfiable and their composition exists, their composition is implied by a rule in $\mathbb{R}_v$. Based on $\mathbb{R}_v$, we can calculate the rule basis as follows.

$$\beta(\mathbb{R}_{init}) = \{R \mid R = [G]\ H \dashv B \mapsto e \in \mathbb{R}_v \wedge \forall e' \in H : e' \in \mathbb{V}\}$$

Theorem 1. *For any rule R in the form of $[G]\ H \dashv B \mapsto e$ where $\forall e' \in H : e' \in \mathbb{V}$, R is derivable from $\alpha(\mathbb{R}_{init}, L)$ if and only if R is derivable from $\alpha(\beta(\mathbb{R}_{init}), L)$.*

Proof Sketch. Firstly, we need to prove that R is derivable from $\mathbb{R}_{init}$ if and only if R is derivable from $\beta(\mathbb{R}_{init})$. Then, there should exist two rule composition methods for R from $\mathbb{R}_{init}$ and $\beta(\mathbb{R}_{init})$ respectively. Then, we apply configuration L to both of the composition methods with function π. Given a rule $R = [G]\ H \dashv B \mapsto e$, we define $\pi(R, L) = [G]\ H \dashv B \cap L \mapsto e$. As L does not affect the terms but the timing constraints, we can prove that either $\pi(R, L)$ is derivable from both of $\alpha(\mathbb{R}_{init}, L)$ and $\alpha(\beta(\mathbb{R}_{init}), L)$, or it is underivable from both of them. Due to the limitation of space, the proof is presented in [1].

Query Searching. A rule is a contradiction to the authentication query if and only if its conclusion event is an *accept* event, while it does not require all the *init* events or it has looser timing constraints comparing with those in the query. Otherwise, if the rule's conclusion event is an *accept* event while this rule is not a contradiction to the authentication query, then it is an obedience. Similarly, a rule is a contradiction to the secrecy query when the *leak* event is reachable.

Definition 3. ***Authentication Contradiction and Obedience.*** *A rule $R = [G]\ H \dashv B \mapsto e$ is a contradiction to the authentication query $Q_a = e' \leftarrow\!\dashv B' \vdash H'$ denoted as $Q_a \nvdash R$ if and only if $B \neq \emptyset$, e and e' are unifiable with the most general unifier σ such that σG can be valid and $\forall \sigma', (\sigma'\sigma H' \not\subseteq \sigma H) \vee (\sigma B \not\subseteq \sigma'\sigma B')$. On the other hand, it is an obedience denoted as $Q_a \vdash R$ if and only if $B \neq \emptyset$, e and e' are unifiable with the most general unifier σ such that σG can be valid and $\exists \sigma', (\sigma'\sigma H' \subseteq \sigma H) \wedge (\sigma B \subseteq \sigma'\sigma B')$.*

Definition 4. ***Secrecy Contradiction.*** *A rule $R = [G]\ H \dashv B \mapsto e$ is a contradiction to the secrecy query Q_s of message m denoted as $Q_s \nvdash R$ if and only if G can be valid, $B \neq \emptyset$, $e = leak(m)$ and $\forall e' \in H : e' \in \mathbb{V}$.*

During the verification, our goal is to ensure that (1) no contradiction rule exists for all queries while (2) at least one obedience rule exists for every authentication query. Hence, given the authentication queries $\mathbb{Q}_A$ and the secrecy

Algorithm 1: Parameter Configuration Computation

Input : $\beta(\mathbb{R}_{init})$, L_0 - the rule basis and the initial configuration
Input : $\mathbb{Q}_A, \mathbb{Q}_S$ - the authentication and secrecy queries
Output: $\mathbb{L}$ - the set of parameter configurations

1 **Algorithm**
2 $\quad \mathbb{L} = \{L_0\}$;
3 $\quad$ **for** $Q \in \mathbb{Q}_A \cup \mathbb{Q}_S, L \in \mathbb{L}, R = [G]\ H \dashv B \mapsto f \in \alpha(\beta(\mathbb{R}_{init}), L), Q \nvdash R$ **do**
4 $\quad\quad \mathbb{L} = \mathbb{L} - \{L\}$;
5 $\quad\quad$ **for** $L' : B \cap L' = \emptyset \vee Q \vdash [G]\ H \dashv B \cap L' \mapsto f$ **do** $\mathbb{L} = \mathbb{L} \cup \{L \cap L'\}$;
6 $\quad$ **for** $L \in \mathbb{L}, Q \in \mathbb{Q}_A$ **do**
7 $\quad\quad$ **if** *cannot find* $R \in \alpha(\beta(\mathbb{R}_{init}), L), Q \vdash R$ **then** $\mathbb{L} = \mathbb{L} - \{L\}$;
8 $\quad$ **return** $\mathbb{L}$;

queries $\mathbb{Q}_S$, our goal is to compute the largest L that satisfies the following two conditions: (1) $\forall Q \in \mathbb{Q}_A \cup \mathbb{Q}_S, \{R | R \in \alpha(\beta(\mathbb{R}_{init}), L) \wedge Q \nvdash R\} = \emptyset$; (2) $\forall Q \in \mathbb{Q}_A, \{R | R \in \alpha(\beta(\mathbb{R}_{init}), L) \wedge Q \vdash R\} \neq \emptyset$. Algorithm 1 illustrates the computing process of the largest L. From line 3 to line 5, we compute the parameter configurations that remove the contradictions. From line 6 to line 7, we ensure that every authentication query has at least one obedience. In order to prove the correctness of our algorithm, we need to show that for any configuration L, a contradiction exists in $\alpha(\beta(\mathbb{R}_{init}), L)$ if and only if it exists in $\alpha(\mathbb{R}_{init}, L)$.

Theorem 2. ***Partial Correctness.*** *Let Q be the query and $\mathcal{R}_{init}$ be the initial rule set. There exists R derivable from $\alpha(\mathcal{R}_{init}, L)$ such that $Q \nvdash R$ if and only if there exists $R' \in \alpha(\beta(\mathbb{R}_{init}), L)$ such that $Q \nvdash R'$.*

Proof Sketch. **Partial Soundness.** Given Theorem 1, R' is derivable from $\alpha(\mathbb{R}_{init}, L)$. Hence, there exists R' derivable from $\alpha(\mathcal{R}_{init}, L)$ such that $Q \nvdash R'$. **Partial Completeness.** Given a rule R derivable from $\alpha(\mathcal{R}_{init}, L)$ such that $Q \nvdash R$, according to Theorem 1, there exists a rule R_0 derivable from $\alpha(\beta(\mathbb{R}_{init}), L)$ such that $Q \nvdash R_0$. So there exists a rule composition method for R_0 with rules in $\alpha(\beta(\mathbb{R}_{init}), L)$. Then, there should exist a rule R_t in the composition method with an *accept* or a *leak* event. We further prove that $Q \nvdash R_t$. Due to the limitation of space, the proof is available in [1].

Checking WMF. After checking the specification of WMF using the abovementioned algorithm, PTAuth claims an attack. The two key rules in $\beta(\mathbb{R}_{init})$ are shown below. The rule (9) represents the execution trace that the server transmits the key once from *Alice* to *Bob*. It is obedient to the query (7). However, the rule (10) is a contradiction to the query (7), because it has a weaker timing range ($t_B \leq t_A + 4 * \S p_a$) than that in the query ($t_B \leq t_A + 2 * \S p_a$). This rule stands for the execution trace that the adversary sends the message from the server back to server twice and then forwards it to *Alice*. According to the rule (5), the timestamp in the message can be updated in this method. Hence, *Bob* would not notice that the message is actually delayed when he receives it. In order to remove the contradiction, we need to configure the parameters as either $\S p_a < \S p_d$ or $\S p_a \leq 0$. However, applying any one of these constraints to the initial configuration $0 < \S p_d$ leads to the removal of the rule (9), the only obedience rule in $\alpha(\beta(\mathbb{R}_{init}), L)$. Hence, PTAuth claims that an attack is found, which means that no parameter configuration would make the protocol work.

$$\begin{aligned}
& know(t_A, t), \mathbf{new}([k], alice_gen[], \langle A[], B[], t_A \rangle) \\
& , \mathbf{init_A}(A[], B[], [k], t_A), \mathbf{init_S}(A[], B[], [k], t_S) \\
& \quad \dashv\!\{ t \leq t_A, t_B \leq t_S + \S p_a \leq t_A + 2 * \S p_a, \\
& \qquad\qquad t_A + 2 * \S p_d \leq t_S + \S p_d \leq t_B, \} \mapsto \\
& \qquad\qquad\qquad\qquad \mathbf{accept}(A[], B[], [k], t_B)
\end{aligned} \tag{9}$$

$$\begin{aligned}
& know(t_A, t), \mathbf{new}([k], alice_gen[], \langle A[], B[], t_A \rangle) \\
& , \mathbf{init_A}(A[], B[], [k], t_A), \mathbf{init_S}(A[], B[], [k], t_{S1}) \\
& , \mathbf{init_S}(B[], A[], [k], t_{S2}), \mathbf{init_S}(A[], B[], [k], t_{S3}) \\
& \quad \dashv\!\{ t \leq t_A, t_B \leq t_{S3} + \S p_a \leq t_{S2} + 2 * \S p_a \leq t_{S1} + 3 * \S p_a \leq t_A + 4 * \S p_a, \\
& \qquad\qquad t_A + 4 * \S p_d \leq t_{S1} + 3 * \S p_d \leq t_{S2} + 2 * \S p_d \leq t_{S3} + \S p_d \leq t_B \} \mapsto \\
& \qquad\qquad\qquad\qquad \mathbf{accept}(A[], B[], [k], t_B)
\end{aligned} \tag{10}$$

Corrected WMF. The WMF protocol can be fixed by inserting two different constants to the messages sent to and received from the server respectively, which breaks their symmetric structure. Using this method, the server can distinguish the messages that it sent out previously, and refuse to process them again. Our algorithm proves the correctness of this modified WMF protocol, and produces the timing constraints $0 < \S p_d \leq \S p_a$.

5 Evaluations

Based on our verification framework, we have implemented a tool named PTAuth. We encode PPL [3] in our tool to analyze the satisfaction of timing constraints. Meanwhile, in order to improve the performance, we implement an on-the-fly verification algorithm that updates the parameter configuration whenever a rule is generated. Hence, the verification process can terminate early if an attack can be found. We use PTAuth to check many security protocols as shown in Table 2. All the experiments shown in this section are conducted under Mac OS X 10.10.1 with 2.3 GHz Intel Core i5 and 16G 1333MHz DDR3. In the experiments, we have checked several timed protocols i.e., the WMF protocols [8,14], the Kerberos protocols [27], the distance bounding protocolse [7,10,28] and the CCITT protocols [11,2,8]. Additionally, we analyze the untimed protocols like the Needham-Schroeder series [26,21] and SKEME [18]. As can be seen, most of the protocols can be verified or falsified by PTAuth quickly for an unbounded number of protocol sessions. Notice that the secure configuration is given based

Table 2. Experiment Results

Protocol	Parameterized	Bounded	$\sharp\mathcal{R}^1$	Result	Time
Wide Mouthed Frog [8]	Yes	No	40	Attack [22]	39ms
Wide Mouthed Frog (c) [14]	Yes	No	35	Secure	13ms
Kerberos V [27]	Yes	No	19370	Attack	23m5s
Kerberos V (c)	Yes	Yes	438664	Secure	2h41m
Auth Range [7,10]	Yes	No	21	Secure	10ms
Ultrasound Dist Bound [28]	Yes	No	50	Attack [29]	18ms
CCITT X.509 (1) [11]	No	No	45	Attack [2]	14ms
CCITT X.509 (1c) [2]	No	No	62	Secure	37ms
CCITT X.509 (3) [11]	No	No	127	Attack [8]	84ms
CCITT X.509 (3) BAN [8]	No	No	148	Secure	131ms
NS PK [26]	No	No	68	Attack [21]	30ms
NS PK Lowe [21]	No	No	61	Secure	28ms
SKEME [18]	No	No	127	Secure	466ms

on the satisfaction of all of the queries, so we do not show the results for different queries separately in the table. The justification for the bounded verification of the corrected version of Kerberos V is presented later in this section. The PTAuth tool and the models shown in this section are available in [1]. Particularly, we have successfully found a new attack in Kerberos V [27] using PTAuth. In the following, we present the detailed findings in Kerberos V. Since Kerberos V is the latest version, we denote it as Kerberos for short unless otherwise indicated.

Kerberos Overview. Kerberos is a widely used security protocol for accessing services. For instance, Microsoft Window uses Kerberos as its default authentication method; many UNIX and UNIX-like operating systems include software for Kerberos authentication. Kerberos has a salient property such that its user can obtain accesses to a network service within a period of time using a single request. In general, this is achieved by granting an access ticket to the user, so that the user can subsequently use this ticket to authenticate himself to the server. Kerberos is complex because multiple ticket operations are supported simultaneously and many fields are optional, which are heavily relying on time. So, configuring Kerberos is hard and error-prone.

Kerberos consists of five types of entities: *User*, *Client*, *Kerberos Authentication Server* (KAS), *Ticket Granting Server* (TGS) and *Application Server* (AP). KAS and TGS together are also known as *Key Distribution Centre* (KDC). Specifically, *Users* usually are humans, and *Clients* represent their identities in the Kerberos network. KAS is the place where a *User* can initiate a logon session to the Kerberos network with a pre-registered *Client*. In return, KAS provides the *User* with (1) a *Ticket Granting Ticket* (TGT) and (2) an encrypted session key as the authorization proof to access TGS. After TGS checks the authorization from KAS, TGS issues two similar credentials (1) a *Service Ticket* (ST) and

(2) a new encrypted session key to the *User* as authorization proof to access AP. Then, the *User* can finally use them to retrieve the *Service* from AP. Additionally, both of the TGT and the ST can be postdated, validated and renewed by KDC when these operations are permitted in the Kerberos network.

Specification Highlights. Generally, by following the method described in Section 3, the specification for Kerberos itself can be extracted easily. In order to verify Kerberos comprehensively, we model several keys and timestamps (which could be optional) by following precisely its official document RFC 4120 [27].

- The user and the server are allowed to specify sub-session keys in the messages. When a sub-session key is specified, the message receiver must use it to transmit the next message rather than using the default session-key.
- Optional timestamps are allowed in the user requests and the tickets. In the following paper, *fq*, *tq* and *rq* denote the start-time, the end-time and the maximum renewable end-time requested by the users. Similarly, *sp*, *ep* and *rp* denote the start-time, the end-time and the maximum renewable end-time agreed by the servers. *sp*, *ep* and *rp* are encoded in the tickets, corresponding to *fq*, *tq* and *rq* respectively. An additional timestamp *ap* is encoded in the ticket to represent the initial authentication time of the ticket. Furthermore, *cq* represents the current-time when the request is made by the user, and *cp* stands for the current-time when the ticket is issued by the server. In Kerberos, *fq*, *rq*, *sp* and *rp* are optional. So the servers need to check their presence and construct replies accordingly.

In this work, two parameters are considered in Kerberos, i.e., the maximum lifetime $\S l$ and the maximum renewable lifetime $\S r$ of the tickets. Based on these parameters, the servers can only issue tickets whose lifetime and renewable lifetime are shorter than $\S l$ and $\S r$ respectively. Furthermore, five operations are modeled for the Kerberos servers as follows. (1) Postdated tickets can be generated for future usage. They are marked as invalid initially and they must be validated later. (2) Postdated tickets must be validated before usage. (3) Renewable tickets can be renewed before they expire. (4) Initial tickets are generated at KAS using user's client. (5) Sub-tickets are generated at TGS using existing tickets. Notice that the end-time *ep* of the sub-ticket should be no larger than the end-time of the existing ticket. Due to the space limit, we provide the complete model of Kerberos in [1].

Queries. In order to specify the queries, we define three events as follows.

- When an initial ticket is generated at KAS, an $\mathbf{init_{auth}}(k, C, S, t)$ event is engaged, where k is the fresh session key, C is the client's name, S is the **target** server's name, and t is the beginning of the ticket's lifetime.
- Whenever an new ticket is generated at KAS or TGS, an $\mathbf{init_{gen}}(k, C, S, t)$ event is engaged. Its arguments have the same meaning as those in $init_{auth}$.
- Whenever an ticket is accepted by the server, an $\mathbf{accept}(k, C, S, t)$ event is engaged, where k is the agreed session key, C is the client's name, S is the **current** server's name, and t is the acceptance time.

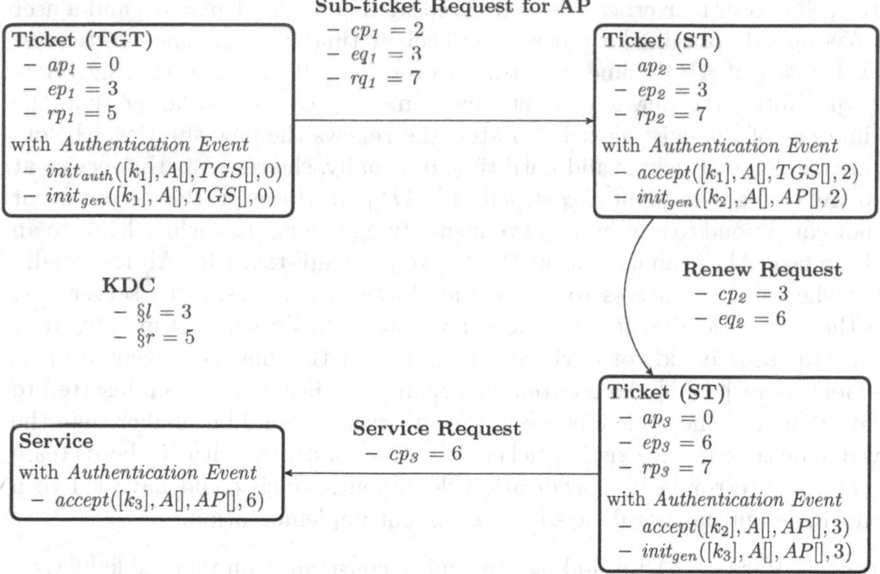

Fig. 1. Attack Found in Kerberos V

In Kerberos, we need to ensure the correctness of two timed authentications. First, whenever a server accepts a ticket, the ticket should be indeed generated within $§l$ time units using the same session key. Second, whenever a server accepts a ticket, the initial ticket should be indeed generated within $§r$ time units.

$$accept(k, C, S, t) \leftarrow\!\!\!\![\; t - t' \leq §l \;]\!\!- init_{gen}(k, C, S, t') \tag{11}$$

$$accept(k, C, S, t) \leftarrow\!\!\!\![\; t - t' \leq §r \;]\!\!- init_{auth}(k', C, S', t') \tag{12}$$

Verification Results. For the termination of the verification, we need to initially configure the parameters as $§r < n * §l$, where n can be any integer larger than 1. The requirement for this constraint is justified as follows. Algorithm 1 updates parameter configuration at line 5 to eliminate the contradiction rules. Suppose we have a rule $init_{auth}(k, C, S, t') \;-\!\![\; t - t' \leq c * §l \;]\!\!\mapsto accept(k, C, S, t)$ in the rule basis, where $c > 1$. This rule is a contradiction to the query (12) because $§r$ is not necessarily larger than $c * §l$. However, Algorithm 1 can add a new constraint $c * §l \leq §r$ to the existing configuration and then continue searching. Since we have infinitely many such rules in $\beta(\mathbb{R}_{init})$ with different values of c, the verification cannot terminate. Hence, in this work, we set the initial configuration as $§r < 2 * §l$ to avoid the non-termination. Notice that this initial configuration does not prevent us from finding attacks because it does not limit the number of sequential operations allowed in the Kerberos protocol.

After analyzing Kerberos using PTAuth, we have successfully found a security flaw in its specification document RFC 4120 [27]. The attack trace is depicted in

Figure 1. Suppose the Kerberos is configured with $\S l = 3$ and $\S r = 5$[2], and a user Alice has already obtained a renewable ticket at time 0. Then, she can request for a sub-ticket of AP at time 2 that is renewable until time 7, satisfying $rq_1 - cp_1 \leq \S r$. Notice the new sub-ticket's end-time ep_2 cannot be larger than the end-time ep_1 of the existing ticket. Later, she renews the new sub-ticket before it expires and gets a ticket valid until time 6. Finally, she requests the service at time 6 and engages an event $accept([k_3], A[], AP[], 6)$. However, this accept event does not correspond to any $init_{auth}$ event satisfying Query (12), which leads to an attack. In fact, Alice can use this method to request sub-ticket for AP repeatedly so that she can have access to the service forever. Obviously, the server who made the authentication initially does not intend to do so. Fortunately, after checking the source code of Kerberos, we find that this flaw is prevented in its implementations [24,19]. An additional checking condition[3] has been inserted to regulate that the renewable lifetime in the sub-ticket should be smaller than the renewable lifetime in the existing ticket. We later confirmed with Kerberos team that this is an error in its specification document, which could have led to a security issue but has not done so in its current implementation.

Corrected Version. After adding the timing constraints on renewable lifetime between the base-ticket and the sub-ticket, the verification cannot terminate. This is caused by an infinite dependency trace formed by tickets, as we do not limit its length. Hence, we bound the number of tickets that can be generated during the verification, which in turn bounds the number of $init_{gen}$ events in the rule. In this work, we bound the ticket number to five. This is justified as we have five different methods to generate tickets in Kerberos: the servers can postdate, validate, renew tickets, generate initial tickets and issue sub-tickets. After bounding the ticket number that can be generated, our tool proves the correctness of Kerberos and produces the configuration $0 \leq \S l \leq \S r < 2 * \S l$.

6 Related Works

As mentioned, this work is related to our previous work [20]. In this work, we additionally introduce timing parameters, secrecy queries, etc. and enhance the computation capability of the timing constraint with PPL. Furthermore, we provide the algorithm to compute the least constrained secure configuration of parameters in this work. We successfully analyze several protocols including Kerberos V and find an attack in the Kerberos V specification [27] that is unreported before. The analyzing framework closest to ours was proposed by Delzanno and Ganty [14] which applies $MSR(\mathcal{L})$ to specify unbounded crypto protocols by combining first order multiset rewriting rules and linear constraints. According to [14], the protocol specification is modified by explicitly encoding an additional timestamp, representing the initialization time, into some messages. Thus the

[2] $\S l$ and $\S r$ are represented by symbols during the verification.

[3] For krb5-1.13 from MIT, the checking is located in the file src/kdc/kdc_util.c at line 1740 - 1741. We also checked other implementations, like heimdal-1.5.2.

attack can be found by comparing the original timestamps with the new one in the messages. However, it is unclear how to verify timed protocol in general using their approach. On the other hand, our approach can be applied to protocols without any protocol modification. Many tools for verifying protocols [6,13,23] are related. However, they are not designed for timed protocols.

Kerberos has been scrutinized over years using formal methods. In [5], Bella et al. analyzed Kerberos IV using the Isabelle theorem prover. They checked various secrecy and authentication properties and took time into consideration. However, Kerberos is largely simplified in their analysis and the specification method in their work is not as intuitive as ours. Later, Kerberos V has been analyzed by Mitchell et al. [25] using state exploration tool Murφ. They claimed that an attack is found in [17] when two servers exists. However, this attack is actually prevented in Kerberos's official specification document RFC 1510 [16], which is later superseded by RFC 4120 [27] analyzed in this paper. The biggest advantages of our method is that the verification is given for an unbounded number of sessions, which is not achievable previously with the state exploration approach. For the above literatures, they did not consider alternative options supported in the protocol that may accidentally introduce attacks as we do in this work. Similar to our work, Kerberos V has been analyzed in a theorem proving context by Butler et al. [9]. They took many features into consideration, i.e., the error messages, the encryption types and the cross-realm support. These features are not cover in this work since we focus on the timestamps and timing constraint checking. Meanwhile, our framework can provide intuitive modeling and automatic verifying, while Kerberos V is analyzed manually in [9].

7 Conclusions

In this work, we developed an automatic verification framework for timed parameterized security protocols. It can verify authentication properties as well as secrecy properties for an unbounded number of protocol sessions. We have implemented our approach into a tool named PTAuth and used it to analyze a wide range of protocols shown in Section 5. In the experiments, we have found a timed attack in Kerberos V document that has never been reported before.

Since the problem of verifying security protocols is undecidable in general, we cannot guarantee the termination of our verification algorithm. When we use PTAuth to analyze the corrected version of Kerberos, PTAuth cannot terminate because of the infinite dependency chain of tickets. Hence, we have to bound the number of tickets generated in the protocol. However, in Kerberos, generating more tickets may not be helpful to break its security. Based on this observation, we want to detect and prune the non-terminable verification branches heuristically without affecting the final results in our future work. This could help us to verify large-sized and complex protocols that we cannot verify currently, as our verification algorithm only considers the general approach at present.

References

1. PTAuth extended paper, tool and experiment models, http://www.comp.nus.edu.sg/~li-li/r/time.html.
2. Abadi, M., Needham, R.M.: Prudent engineering practice for cryptographic protocols. IEEE Trans. Software Eng. 22(1), 6–15 (1996)
3. Bagnara, R., Ricci, E., Zaffanella, E., Hill, P.M.: Possibly not closed convex polyhedra and the parma polyhedra library. In: Hermenegildo, M.V., Puebla, G. (eds.) SAS 2002. LNCS, vol. 2477, pp. 213–229. Springer, Heidelberg (2002)
4. Barker, E.B., Barker, W.C., Burr, W.E., Polk, W.T., Smid, M.E.: SP 800-57. Recommendation for key management. Technical report, National Institute of Standards & Technology (2007)
5. Bella, G., Paulson, L.C.: Kerberos version IV: Inductive analysis of the secrecy goals. In: Quisquater, J.-J., Deswarte, Y., Meadows, C., Gollmann, D. (eds.) ESORICS 1998. LNCS, vol. 1485, pp. 361–375. Springer, Heidelberg (1998)
6. Blanchet, B.: An efficient cryptographic protocol verifier based on Prolog rules. In: CSFW, pp. 82–96. IEEE CS (2001)
7. Brands, S., Chaum, D.: Distance-bounding protocols (extended abstract). In: Helleseth, T. (ed.) Advances in Cryptology - EUROCRYPT 1993. LNCS, vol. 765, pp. 344–359. Springer, Heidelberg (1994)
8. Burrows, M., Abadi, M., Needham, R.M.: A logic of authentication. ACM Trans. Comput. Syst. 8(1), 18–36 (1990)
9. Butler, F., Cervesato, I., Jaggard, A.D., Scedrov, A., Walstad, C.: Formal analysis of kerberos 5. Theor. Comput. Sci. 367, 57–87 (2006)
10. Capkun, S., Hubaux, J.-P.: Secure positioning in wireless networks. IEEE Journal on Selected Areas in Communications 24(2), 221–232 (2006)
11. CCITT. The directory authentication framework - Version 7, 1987 Draft Recommendation X.509 (1987)
12. Cervesato, I., Durgin, N.A., Lincoln, P., Mitchell, J.C., Scedrov, A.: A meta-notation for protocol analysis. In: CSFW, pp. 55–69. IEEE CS (1999)
13. Cremers, C.J.F.: The Scyther tool: Verification, falsification, and analysis of security protocols. In: Gupta, A., Malik, S. (eds.) CAV 2008. LNCS, vol. 5123, pp. 414–418. Springer, Heidelberg (2008)
14. Delzanno, G., Ganty, P.: Automatic verification of time sensitive cryptographic protocols. In: Jensen, K., Podelski, A. (eds.) TACAS 2004. LNCS, vol. 2988, pp. 342–356. Springer, Heidelberg (2004)
15. Dolev, D., Yao, A.C.-C.: On the security of public key protocols. IEEE Transactions on Information Theory 29(2), 198–207 (1983)
16. Kohl, J., Neuman, B.C.: The Kerberos Network Authentication Service (Version 5). Internet Request for Comments RFC-1510. RFC Editor (1993)
17. Kohl, J.T., Neuman, B.C., T'so, T.Y.: The evolution of the kerberos authentication system. In: Distributed Open Systems, pp. 78–94. IEEE CS (1994)
18. Krawczyk, H.: Skeme: A versatile secure key exchange mechanism for internet. In: NDSS, pp. 114–127. IEEE CS (1996)
19. LDAP Account Manager. Kerberos V implementation heimdal-1.5.2 (2014), http://www.h5l.org
20. Li, L., Sun, J., Liu, Y., Dong, J.S.: Tauth: Verifying timed security protocols. In: Merz, S., Pang, J. (eds.) ICFEM 2014. LNCS, vol. 8829, pp. 300–315. Springer, Heidelberg (2014)

21. Lowe, G.: An attack on the needham-schroeder public-key authentication protocol. Information Processing Letters 56, 131–133 (1995)
22. Lowe, G.: A family of attacks upon authentication protocols. Technical report, Department of Mathematics and Computer Science, University of Leicester (1997)
23. Meier, S., Schmidt, B., Cremers, C., Basin, D.: The TAMARIN prover for the symbolic analysis of security protocols. In: Sharygina, N., Veith, H. (eds.) CAV 2013. LNCS, vol. 8044, pp. 696–701. Springer, Heidelberg (2013)
24. MIT. Kerberos V implementation krb5-1.13 (2014), http://web.mit.edu/kerberos/
25. Mitchell, J., Mitchell, M., Stern, U.: Automated analysis of cryptographic protocols using Murφ. In: S&P, pp. 141–151 (1997)
26. Needham, R.M., Schroeder, M.D.: Using encryption for authentication in large networks of computers. Commun. ACM 21(12), 993–999 (1978)
27. Neuman, C., Yu, T., Hartman, S., Raeburn, K.: The Kerberos Network Authentication Service (Version 5). RFC-4120. RFC Editor (2005)
28. Sastry, N., Shankar, U., Wagner, D.: Secure verification of location claims. In: Workshop on Wireless Security, pp. 1–10. ACM (2003)
29. Sedighpour, S., Capkun, S., Ganeriwal, S., Srivastava, M.B.: Implementation of attacks on ultrasonic ranging systems (demo). In: SenSys, p. 312. ACM (2005)

Abstraction of Elementary Hybrid Systems by Variable Transformation

Jiang Liu[1], Naijun Zhan[2], Hengjun Zhao(✉)[1], and Liang Zou[2]

[1] Chongqing Key Lab. of Automated Reasoning and Cognition, Chongqing Institute of Green and Intelligent Technology, CAS, Chongqing, China
{liujiang, zhaohengjun}@cigit.ac.cn

[2] State Key Lab. of Computer Science, Institute of Software, CAS, Beijing, China
{znj, zoul}@ios.ac.cn

Abstract. Elementary hybrid systems (EHSs) are those hybrid systems (HSs) containing elementary functions such as exp, ln, sin, cos, etc. EHSs are very common in practice, especially in safety-critical domains. Due to the non-polynomial expressions which lead to undecidable arithmetic, verification of EHSs is very hard. Existing approaches based on partition of the state space or overapproximation of reachable sets suffer from state space explosion or inflation of numerical errors. In this paper, we propose a symbolic abstraction approach that reduces EHSs to polynomial hybrid systems (PHSs), by replacing all non-polynomial terms with newly introduced variables. Thus the verification of EHSs is reduced to the one of PHSs, enabling us to apply all the well-established verification techniques and tools for PHSs to EHSs. In this way, it is possible to avoid the limitations of many existing methods. We illustrate the abstraction approach and its application in safety verification of EHSs by several real world examples.

Keywords: Hybrid system · Abstraction · Elementary function · Invariant · Verification

1 Introduction

Complex Embedded Systems (CESs) consist of software and hardware components that operate autonomous devices interacting with the physical environment. They are now part of our daily life and are used in many industrial sectors to carry out highly complex and often critical functions. The development process of CESs is widely recognized as a highly complex and challenging task. A thorough validation and verification activity is necessary to enhance the quality of CESs and, in particular, to fulfill the quality criteria mandated by the relevant standards. Hybrid systems (HSs) are mathematical models with precise mathematical semantics for CESs, wherein continuous physical dynamics are combined with discrete transitions. Based on HSs, rigorous analysis and verification

This work has been partially supported by "973 Program" under grant No. 2014CB340701, NSFC grants (Nos. 91118007, 91418204 and 61202131), the CAS/SAFEA International Partnership Program for Creative Research Teams, CAS Western Light Program and CAS Youth Innovation Promotion Association (No. 2015315), Chongqing Science and Technology Commission projects cstc2012ggB40004, cstc2014jcsfglyjs0005 and cstc2014zktjccxyyB0031.

N. Bjørner and F. de Boer (Eds.): FM 2015, LNCS 9109, pp. 360–377, 2015.
DOI: 10.1007/978-3-319-19249-9_23

of CESs become feasible, so that errors can be detected and corrected in the very early stage of design.

In practice, it is very common to model complex physical environments by ordinary differential equations (ODEs) with elementary functions such as reciprocal function $\frac{1}{x}$, exponential function e^x, logarithm function $\ln x$, trigonometric functions $\sin x$ and $\cos x$, and their compositions. We call such HSs elementary HSs (EHSs). As elementary expressions usually lead to undecidable arithmetic, the verification of EHSs becomes very hard, even intractable. Existing methods that deal with EHS verification include the level-set method [25], the hybridization method [4,15], the gridding-based abstraction refinement method [31], the interval SMT solver-based method [9,8], the Taylor model-based flowpipe approximation method [5], and so on. These methods rely either on iterative partition of the state space or on iterative computation of approximate reachable sets, which can quickly lead to explosion of state numbers or inflation of numerical errors. Moreover, most of the above mentioned methods can only do bounded model checking (BMC).

As an alternative, the constraint-based approach verifies the safety property of an HS by solving corresponding constraints symbolically or numerically, to discover a barrier (inductive invariant) that separates the reachable set from the unsafe region, which avoids exhaustive gridding or brute-force computation, and can thus overcome the limitations of the above mentioned methods. However, this method has mainly been applied to verification of polynomial hybrid systems (PHSs) [35,29,28,12,20]. Although ideas about generating invariants for EHSs appeared in [28,10], they were talked about in an ad hoc way. In [34], the author proposed a change-of-bases method to transform EHSs to PHSs, even to linear systems, but the success depends on the choice of the set of basis functions, and therefore does not apply to general EHSs.

In this paper, we investigate symbolic abstraction of general EHSs to PHSs, by extending [34] with early works on polynomialization of elementary ODEs [16,36]. Herein the abstraction is accomplished by introducing new variables to replace the non-polynomial terms. With the substitution, flows, guards and other components of the EHSs are transformed according to the chain rule of differentiation, or by the over-approximation methods proposed in the paper, so that for any trajectory of the EHSs, there always exists a corresponding trajectory of the reduced PHSs. Besides, such abstraction preserves (inductive) invariant sets, that is, any (inductive) invariant of the over-approximating PHS corresponds to an (inductive) invariant of the original EHS. Therefore, verification of the EHSs is naturally reduced to the one of the reduced PHSs. This will be shown by several real world verification problems.

The proposed abstraction applies to general EHSs. The benefit of the proposed abstraction is that it enables all the well-established verification techniques and tools for PHSs, especially the constraint-based approaches such as DAL [27] and SOS [29,18], to be applied to EHSs, and thus provides the possibility of avoiding such limitations as error inflation, state space explosion and boundedness for existing EHS verification methods. A by-product is that it also provides the possibility of generating invariants with elementary functions for PHSs, thus enhancing the power of existing PHS verification methods. In short, the proposed abstraction method can be a good alternative or complement to existing approaches.

Related Work. This work is most closely related to [34] and [16]. The abstraction in this paper is performed by systematic augmentation of the original system rather than change-of-bases, thus essentially different from [34] and generally applicable. Compared to [16], this paper gives a clearer reduction procedure for elementary ODEs and discusses the extension to hybrid systems. It was proved in [30] that safety verification of nonlinear hybrid systems is quasi-semidecidable, but to find efficient verification algorithms remains an open problem. An approximation technique for abstracting nonlinear hybrid systems to PHSs based on Taylor polynomial was proposed in [19], which requires the ODEs to have closed-form solutions to abstract the continuous flow transitions. In the recent work [7], following the line of [39], the author proposed predicate-based abstraction of general nonlinear hybrid systems by using the automated theorem prover MetiTarski [1]. In [26], the authors adopted similar recasting techniques to ours for stability analysis of non-polynomial systems. Regarding non-polynomial invariants for polynomial continuous or hybrid systems, [32] presented the first method for generating transcendental invariants using formal power series, while the more recent work [11] proposed a Darboux Polynomial-based method. Both [32] and [11] can only find non-polynomial invariants of limited forms.

Paper Organization. The rest of the paper is organized as follows. We briefly review some basic notions about hybrid systems and the theory of abstraction for hybrid systems in Section 2. Section 3 is devoted to the transformation from EDSs to PDSs, and from EHSs to PHSs. Section 4 discusses how to use the proposed abstraction approach for safety verification of EHSs. Section 5 concludes this paper.

2 Preliminary

In this section, we briefly introduce the basic knowledge of hybrid systems and define what we call *elementary hybrid systems*. Besides, we also recall the basic theory of abstraction for hybrid systems originally developed in [33,34].

Throughout this paper, we use $\mathbb{N}, \mathbb{Q}, \mathbb{R}$ to denote the set of *natural*, *rational* and *real* numbers respectively. Given a set A, the power set of A is denoted by 2^A, and the Cartesian product of n duplicates of A is denoted by A^n; for instance, $\mathbb{R}^n$ stands for the n-dimensional Euclidean space. A vector element $(a_1, a_2, \ldots, a_n) \in A^n$ is usually abbreviated by a boldface letter $\mathbf{a}$ when its dimension is clear from the context.

2.1 Elementary Continuous and Hybrid Systems

A continuous dynamical system (CDS) is modeled by first-order autonomous ordinary differential equations (ODEs)

$$\dot{\mathbf{x}} = \mathbf{f}(\mathbf{x}), \tag{1}$$

where $\mathbf{x} = (x_1, \ldots, x_n) \in \mathbb{R}^n$ and $\mathbf{f} : U \to \mathbb{R}^n$ is a vector function, called a vector field, defined on an open set $U \subseteq \mathbb{R}^n$. If $\mathbf{f}$ satisfies the *local Lipschitz condition* [17], then for any $\mathbf{x}_0 \in U$, there exists a unique differentiable vector function $\mathbf{x}(t) : (a, b) \to U$, where (a, b) is an open interval containing 0, such that $\mathbf{x}(0) = \mathbf{x}_0$ and the derivative of $\mathbf{x}(t)$ w.r.t. t satisfies $\forall t \in (a, b). \frac{\mathrm{d}\mathbf{x}(t)}{\mathrm{d}t} = \mathbf{f}(\mathbf{x}(t))$. Such $\mathbf{x}(t)$ is called the *solution* to (1) with initial value $\mathbf{x}_0$, or the *trajectory* of (1) starting from $\mathbf{x}_0$.

In many contexts, a CDS $\mathcal{C}$ may be equipped with an initial set Ξ and a domain D, represented as a triple $\mathcal{C} \widehat{=} (\Xi, \mathbf{f}, D)$.[1] If $\mathbf{f}$ is defined on $U \subseteq \mathbb{R}^n$, then Ξ and D should satisfy $\Xi \subseteq D \subseteq U$. In what follows, all CDSs will refer to the triple form unless otherwise stated. Hybrid systems (HSs) are those systems that exhibit both continuous evolutions and discrete transitions. A popular model of HSs is *hybrid automata* [2,13].

Definition 1 (Hybrid Automaton). *A hybrid automaton (HA) is a system* $\mathcal{H} \widehat{=} (Q, X, f, D, E, G, R, \Xi)$, *where*

- $Q = \{q_1, \ldots, q_m\}$ *is a finite set of modes;*
- $X = \{x_1, \ldots, x_n\}$ *is a finite set of continuous state variables, with* $\mathbf{x} = (x_1, \ldots, x_n)$ *ranging over* $\mathbb{R}^n$*;*
- $f : Q \to (U_q \to \mathbb{R}^n)$ *assigns to each mode* $q \in Q$ *a locally Lipschitz continuous vector field* $\mathbf{f}_q$ *defined on an open set* $U_q \subseteq \mathbb{R}^n$*;*
- D *assigns to each mode* $q \in Q$ *a domain* $D_q \subseteq U_q$*;*
- $E \subseteq Q \times Q$ *is a finite set of discrete transitions;*
- G *assigns to each transition* $e \in E$ *a guard* $G_e \subseteq \mathbb{R}^n$*;*
- R *assigns to each transition* $e \in E$ *a set-valued reset function* R_e*:* $G_e \to 2^{\mathbb{R}^n}$*;*
- Ξ *assigns to each* $q \in Q$ *a set of initial states* $\Xi_q \subseteq D_q$.

Actually an HA can be regarded as a composition of a finite set of CDSs $\mathcal{C}_q \widehat{=} (\Xi_q, \mathbf{f}_q, D_q)$ for $q \in Q$, together with the set of transition relations specified by (G_e, R_e) for $e \in E$. Conversely, any CDS can be regarded as a special HA with a single mode and without discrete transitions.

In this paper, we consider the class of HSs that can be defined by multivariate *elementary* functions given by the following grammar:

$$f, g ::= c \mid x \mid f + g \mid f - g \mid f \times g \mid \frac{f}{g} \mid f^a \mid e^f \mid \ln(f) \mid \sin(f) \mid \cos(f) \tag{2}$$

where $c \in \mathbb{R}$ is any real constant, $a \in \mathbb{Q}$ is any rational constant, and x can be any variable from the set of real-valued variables $\{x_1, \ldots, x_n\}$. In particular, the set of functions constructed only by the first 5 constructs are multivariate *polynomials* in $x_1, x_2, \ldots, x_n$.

The limitation of elementary functions to grammar (2) is not essential. For example, tangent and cotangent functions $\tan(f), \cot(f)$ can be easily defined. Besides, the presented approach in this paper is also applicable to other elementary functions not mentioned above, such as inverse trigonometric functions $\arcsin(f), \arccos(f)$, etc.

Definition 2 (Elementary and Polynomial HSs). *An HS or a CDS is called* elementary *(resp.* polynomial*) if it can be expressed by* elementary *(resp.* polynomial*) functions together with relational symbols* $\geqslant, >, \leqslant, <, =, \neq$ *and Boolean connectives* $\wedge, \vee, \neg, \longrightarrow, \longleftrightarrow$*, etc.*

Note that in Definition 2, the presented symbol set is complete but not minimal. Elementary (resp. polynomial) HSs or CDSs will be denoted by EHSs or EDSs (resp. PHSs or PDSs) for short.

[1] In this paper, the symbol $\widehat{=}$ is interpreted as "defined as".

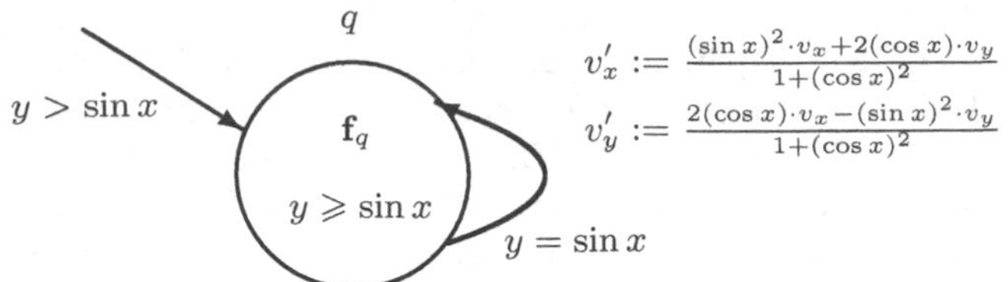

Fig. 1. The HA model of a bouncing ball on a sine-waved surface

Example 1 (Bouncing Ball). Figure 1 depicts the HA model of a bouncing ball on a sine-waved surface, adapted from a similar one in [14]. The motion of the ball stays in the two-dimensional x-y plane, with x denoting the horizontal position, y denoting the height, and v_x and v_y denoting the velocity along the two directions respectively. When the ball hits the surface given by the sine wave $y = \sin x$, its velocity changes instantaneously according to the law of perfectly elastic collision. Here, using the notation of Definition 1, we have $Q = \{q\}$, $X = \{x, y, v_x, v_y\}$, $\mathbf{f}_q$ defines the ODE

$$\begin{cases} \dot{x} &= v_x \\ \dot{y} &= v_y \\ \dot{v}_x &= 0 \\ \dot{v}_y &= -9.8 \end{cases},$$

$D_q \widehat{=} y \geqslant \sin x$, $E = \{e\}$ with $e = (q, q)$, $G_e \widehat{=} y = \sin x$, $\Xi_q \widehat{=} y > \sin x$, and $R_e(x, y, v_x, v_y) \widehat{=} \{(x, y, v'_x, v'_y)\}$ with v'_x, v'_y shown in the figure.

2.2 Semantics of Hybrid Systems

Given an HA $\mathcal{H}$, denote the state space of $\mathcal{H}$ by $\mathbb{H} \widehat{=} Q \times \mathbb{R}^n$, the domain of $\mathcal{H}$ by $D_{\mathcal{H}} \widehat{=} \bigcup_{q \in Q}(\{q\} \times D_q)$, and the set of all initial states by $\Xi_{\mathcal{H}} \widehat{=} \bigcup_{q \in Q}(\{q\} \times \Xi_q)$. The semantics of $\mathcal{H}$ can be characterized by the set of *reachable* states of $\mathcal{H}$.

Definition 3 (Reachable Set). *Given an HA $\mathcal{H}$, the* reachable set *of $\mathcal{H}$, denoted by $\mathcal{R}_{\mathcal{H}}$, consists of such $(q, \mathbf{x}) \in \mathbb{H}$ for which there exists a finite sequence*

$$(q_0, \mathbf{x}_0), (q_1, \mathbf{x}_1), \ldots, (q_l, \mathbf{x}_l)$$

such that $(q_0, \mathbf{x}_0) \in \Xi_{\mathcal{H}}$, $(q_l, \mathbf{x}_l) = (q, \mathbf{x})$, and for any $0 \leqslant i \leqslant l-1$, one of the following two conditions holds:

- *(Discrete Jump): $e = (q_i, q_{i+1}) \in E$, $\mathbf{x}_i \in G_e$ and $\mathbf{x}_{i+1} \in R_e(\mathbf{x}_i)$; or*
- *(Continuous Evolution): $q_i = q_{i+1}$, and there exists a $\delta \geqslant 0$ s.t. the trajectory $\mathbf{x}(t)$ of $\dot{\mathbf{x}} = \mathbf{f}_{q_i}$ starting from $\mathbf{x}_i$ satisfies*
  - *$\mathbf{x}(t) \in D_{q_i}$ for all $t \in [0, \delta]$; and*
  - *$\mathbf{x}(\delta) = \mathbf{x}_{i+1}$.*

Exact computation of reachable sets of hybrid systems is generally an intractable problem. For verification of safety properties, appropriate over-approximations of reachable sets will suffice.

Definition 4 (Invariant). *Given an HA $\mathcal{H}$, a set $\mathcal{I} \widehat{=} \bigcup_{q \in Q}(\{q\} \times I_q) \subseteq \mathbb{H}$ is called an* invariant *of $\mathcal{H}$, if $\mathcal{I}$ is a superset of the reachable set $\mathcal{R}_{\mathcal{H}}$, i.e. $\mathcal{R}_{\mathcal{H}} \subseteq \mathcal{I}$.*

Definition 5 (Inductive Invariant). *Given an HA $\mathcal{H}$, a set $\mathcal{I} \widehat{=} \bigcup_{q \in Q}(\{q\} \times I_q) \subseteq \mathbb{H}$ is called an* inductive invariant *of $\mathcal{H}$, if $\mathcal{I}$ satisfies the following conditions:*

- *$\Xi_q \subseteq I_q$ for all $q \in Q$;*
- *for any $e = (q, q') \in E$, if $\mathbf{x} \in I_q \cap G_e$, then $R_e(\mathbf{x}) \subseteq I_{q'}$;*
- *for any $q \in Q$ and any $\mathbf{x}_0 \in I_q$, if $\mathbf{x}(t)$ is the trajectory of $\dot{\mathbf{x}} = \mathbf{f}_q$ starting from $\mathbf{x}_0$, and there exists $T \geqslant 0$ s.t. $\mathbf{x}(t) \in D_q$ for all $t \in [0, T]$, then $\mathbf{x}(T) \in I_q$.*

It is easy to check that any inductive invariant is also an invariant.

2.3 Abstraction of Hybrid Systems

We next briefly introduce the kind of abstraction for HSs proposed in [33,34] and the significant properties about such an abstraction.

In what follows, to distinguish between the dimensions of an HS and its abstraction, we will annotate an HS $\mathcal{H}$ (a CDS $\mathcal{C}$) with the vector of its continuous state variables $\mathbf{x}$ as $\mathcal{H}_{\mathbf{x}}$ ($\mathcal{C}_{\mathbf{x}}$). We use $|\mathbf{x}|$ to denote the dimension of $\mathbf{x}$. Given a vector function Θ that maps from $D \subseteq \mathbb{R}^{|\mathbf{x}|}$ to $\mathbb{R}^{|\mathbf{y}|}$, let $\Theta(A) \widehat{=} \{\Theta(\mathbf{x}) \mid \mathbf{x} \in A\}$ for any $A \subseteq D$, and $\Theta^{-1}(B) \widehat{=} \{\mathbf{x} \in D \mid \Theta(\mathbf{x}) \in B\}$ for any $B \subseteq \mathbb{R}^{|\mathbf{y}|}$.

Definition 6 (Simulation [33]). *Given two CDSs $\mathcal{C}_{\mathbf{x}} \widehat{=} (\Xi_{\mathbf{x}}, \mathbf{f}_{\mathbf{x}}, D_{\mathbf{x}})$ and $\mathcal{C}_{\mathbf{y}} \widehat{=} (\Xi_{\mathbf{y}}, \mathbf{f}_{\mathbf{y}}, D_{\mathbf{y}})$, we say $\mathcal{C}_{\mathbf{y}}$ simulates $\mathcal{C}_{\mathbf{x}}$ or $\mathcal{C}_{\mathbf{x}}$ is simulated by $\mathcal{C}_{\mathbf{y}}$ via a continuously differentiable mapping $\Theta : D_{\mathbf{x}} \to \mathbb{R}^{|\mathbf{y}|}$, if Θ satisfies*

- *$\Theta(\Xi_{\mathbf{x}}) \subseteq \Xi_{\mathbf{y}}$, $\Theta(D_{\mathbf{x}}) \subseteq D_{\mathbf{y}}$; and*
- *for any trajectory $\mathbf{x}(t)$ of $\mathcal{C}_{\mathbf{x}}$ (i.e. a trajectory of $\dot{\mathbf{x}} = \mathbf{f}_{\mathbf{x}}(\mathbf{x})$ that starts from $\Xi_{\mathbf{x}}$ and stays in $D_{\mathbf{x}}$), $\Theta \circ \mathbf{x}(t)$ is a trajectory of $\mathcal{C}_{\mathbf{y}}$, where $\circ$ denotes composition of functions.*

We call $\mathcal{C}_{\mathbf{y}}$ an abstraction *of $\mathcal{C}_{\mathbf{x}}$ under the* simulation map *Θ.*

Abstraction of an HS can be obtained by abstracting the CDS corresponding to each mode using an individual simulation map. As argued in [34], it can be assumed without loss of generality that the collection of simulation maps for each mode all map to an Euclidean space of the same dimension, say $\mathbb{R}^{|\mathbf{y}|}$.

Definition 7 (Simulation [34]). *Given two HSs $\mathcal{H}_{\mathbf{x}} \widehat{=} (Q, X, f_{\mathbf{x}}, D_{\mathbf{x}}, E, G_{\mathbf{x}}, R_{\mathbf{x}}, \Xi_{\mathbf{x}})$ and $\mathcal{H}_{\mathbf{y}} \widehat{=} (Q, Y, f_{\mathbf{y}}, D_{\mathbf{y}}, E, G_{\mathbf{y}}, R_{\mathbf{y}}, \Xi_{\mathbf{y}})$, we say $\mathcal{H}_{\mathbf{y}}$ simulates $\mathcal{H}_{\mathbf{x}}$ via the set of maps $\{\Theta_q : D_{\mathbf{x},q} \to \mathbb{R}^{|\mathbf{y}|} \mid q \in Q\}$, if the following hold:*

- *$(\Xi_{\mathbf{y},q}, \mathbf{f}_{\mathbf{y},q}, D_{\mathbf{y},q})$ simulates $(\Xi_{\mathbf{x},q}, \mathbf{f}_{\mathbf{x},q}, D_{\mathbf{x},q})$ via Θ_q, for each $q \in Q$;*
- *$\Theta_q(G_{\mathbf{x},e}) \subseteq G_{\mathbf{y},e}$, for any $e = (q, q') \in E$;*
- *$\Theta_{q'}(R_{\mathbf{x},e}(\mathbf{x})) \subseteq R_{\mathbf{y},e}(\Theta_q(\mathbf{x}))$, for any $e = (q, q') \in E$ and any $\mathbf{x} \in G_{\mathbf{x},e}$.*

We call $\mathcal{H}_{\mathbf{y}}$ an abstraction *of $\mathcal{H}_{\mathbf{x}}$ under the set of* simulation maps *$\{\Theta_q \mid q \in Q\}$.*

Intuitively, if $\mathcal{H}_{\mathbf{y}}$ is an abstraction of $\mathcal{H}_{\mathbf{x}}$, then for any $(q, \mathbf{x})$ reachable by $\mathcal{H}_{\mathbf{x}}$, $(q, \Theta_q(\mathbf{x}))$ is a state reachable by $\mathcal{H}_{\mathbf{y}}$. Actually, we can prove the following nice property about such abstractions.

Theorem 1 (Invariant Preserving Property). *If $\mathcal{H}_{\mathbf{y}}$ is an abstraction of $\mathcal{H}_{\mathbf{x}}$ under simulation maps $\{\Theta_q \mid q \in Q\}$, and $\mathcal{I}_{\mathbf{y}} \mathrel{\widehat{=}} \bigcup_{q\in Q}(\{q\} \times I_{\mathbf{y},q})$ is an invariant (resp. inductive invariant) of $\mathcal{H}_{\mathbf{y}}$, then $\mathcal{I}_{\mathbf{x}} \mathrel{\widehat{=}} \bigcup_{q\in Q}(\{q\} \times I_{\mathbf{x},q})$ with $I_{\mathbf{x},q} \mathrel{\widehat{=}} \Theta_q^{-1}(I_{\mathbf{y},q})$ is an invariant (resp. inductive invariant) of $\mathcal{H}_{\mathbf{x}}$.*

Theorem 1 extends Theorem 3.2 of [33] in two aspects: firstly, it deals with HSs, and secondly, it applies to both invariants and inductive invariants; nevertheless, the proof of Theorem 1 can be given in a similar way and so is omitted here. The significance of Theorem 1 lies in the possibility of analyzing a complex HS by analyzing certain abstractions of it, which may be of simpler forms and thus allow the use of any available techniques and tools.

The following theorem proposed in [33] is very useful for checking or constructing simulation maps.

Theorem 2 (Simulation Checking [33]). *Let $\mathcal{C}_{\mathbf{x}}$, $\mathcal{C}_{\mathbf{y}}$, Θ be specified as in Definition 6. Suppose $|\mathbf{x}| = n$, $|\mathbf{y}| = \ell$, and $\Theta \mathrel{\widehat{=}} (\theta_1, \theta_2, \ldots, \theta_\ell)$. Then $\mathcal{C}_{\mathbf{y}}$ simulates $\mathcal{C}_{\mathbf{x}}$ if*

- *$\Theta(\Xi_{\mathbf{x}}) \subseteq \Xi_{\mathbf{y}}$, $\Theta(D_{\mathbf{x}}) \subseteq D_{\mathbf{y}}$; and*
- *$\mathbf{f}_{\mathbf{y}}(\Theta(\mathbf{x})) = \mathcal{J}_\Theta(\mathbf{x}) \cdot \mathbf{f}_{\mathbf{x}}(\mathbf{x})$, for any $\mathbf{x} \in D_{\mathbf{x}}$, where $\mathbf{f}_{\mathbf{x}}(\mathbf{x})$ is seen as a column vector, and $\mathcal{J}_\Theta(\mathbf{x})$ represents the* Jacobian matrix *of Θ at point $\mathbf{x}$.*

Example 2. Let $\mathcal{C}_{\mathbf{x}} \mathrel{\widehat{=}} \left(x \in [0,1], \dot{x} = e^x, x \in \mathbb{R}\right)$ with $\mathbf{x} = x$, $\mathcal{C}_{\mathbf{y}} \mathrel{\widehat{=}} \left(y_1 \in [0,1] \wedge y_2 \in [1,3], (\dot{y}_1, \dot{y}_2) = (y_2, y_2^2), y_1 \in \mathbb{R} \wedge y_2 > 0\right)$ with $\mathbf{y} = (y_1, y_2)$, and $\Theta \mathrel{\widehat{=}} (x, e^x)$. Then it can be checked according to Theorem 2 that $\mathcal{C}_{\mathbf{y}}$ simulates $\mathcal{C}_{\mathbf{x}}$.

We will employ Theorem 2 to prove the correctness of our abstraction of EHSs in the following section.

3 Polynomial Abstraction of EHSs

In this section, given any EHS as defined in Definition 2, we will construct a PHS that simulates the EHS in the sense of Definition 7. We will first show how elementary ODEs can be transformed into polynomial ones, and then discuss how to deal with initial sets, domains, guards, and reset maps.

3.1 Polynomialization of Elementary ODEs

In this part, we illustrate how to transform an elementary ODE equivalently into a polynomial one by introducing new variables to replace non-polynomial terms. The basic idea here is similar to [16], but we give a clearer statement of the transformation procedure and extend it from ODEs to hybrid systems.

Univariate Basic Elementary Functions. For

$$\dot{x} = f(x) \tag{3}$$

- if $f(x) = \frac{1}{x}$, then let $v = \frac{1}{x}$, and thus $\dot{v} = -\frac{\dot{x}}{x^2}$. Therefore (3) is transformed to[2]

$$\begin{cases} \dot{x} = v \\ \dot{v} = -v^3 \end{cases}$$

[2] By $v = \frac{1}{x}$, the set $\{(x, v) \mid x = 0, v \in \mathbb{R}\}$ is excluded from the domain of the transformed polynomial ODE. Such a consequence will not be explicitly mentioned in the rest of this paper.

– if $f(x) = \sqrt{x}$, then let $v = \sqrt{x}$, and thus $\dot{v} = \frac{\dot{x}}{2\sqrt{x}}$. Therefore (3) is transformed to

$$\begin{cases} \dot{x} = v \\ \dot{v} = \frac{1}{2} \end{cases}$$

– if $f(x) = e^x$, then let $v = e^x$, and thus $\dot{v} = e^x \cdot \dot{x}$. Therefore (3) is transformed to

$$\begin{cases} \dot{x} = v \\ \dot{v} = v^2 \end{cases}$$

– if $f(x) = \ln x$, then let $v = \ln x$, and thus $\dot{v} = \frac{\dot{x}}{x}$; then further let $u = \frac{1}{x}$, and thus $\dot{u} = -\frac{\dot{x}}{x^2}$. Therefore (3) is transformed to

$$\begin{cases} \dot{x} = v \\ \dot{v} = uv \\ \dot{u} = -u^2 v \end{cases}$$

– if $f(x) = \sin x$, then let $v = \sin x$, and thus $\dot{v} = \dot{x} \cdot \cos x$; then further let $u = \cos x$, and thus $\dot{u} = -\sin x \cdot \dot{x}$. Therefore (3) is transformed to

$$\begin{cases} \dot{x} = v \\ \dot{v} = uv \\ \dot{u} = -v^2 \end{cases}$$

– if $f(x) = \cos x$, then the transformation is analogous to the case of $f(x) = \sin x$.

Compositional and Multivariate Functions. Obviously, the outmost form of any compositional elementary function must be one of $f \pm g$, $f \times g$, $\frac{f}{g}$, f^a, e^f, $\ln(f)$, $\sin(f)$, $\cos(f)$. Therefore given a compositional function, we can iterate the above procedure discussed on basic cases from the innermost non-polynomial sub-term to the outside, until all the sub-expressions have been transformed into polynomials. For example,

– if $f(x) = \ln(2 + \sin x)$, we can let

$$\begin{cases} v = \sin x \\ u = \cos x \\ w = \ln(2 + v) = \ln(2 + \sin x) \\ z = \frac{1}{2+v} = \frac{1}{2+\sin x} \end{cases}, \text{ and then (3) is transformed to } \begin{cases} \dot{x} = w \\ \dot{v} = uw \\ \dot{u} = -vw \\ \dot{w} = zuw \\ \dot{z} = -z^2 uw \end{cases}.$$

Handling multivariate functions is straightforward.

In summary, we give the following assertion on polynomializing elementary ODES, the correctness of which can be given based on the formal transformation algorithms presented in the full version of this paper [22].

Proposition 1 (Polynomial Recasting). *Given an ODE* $\dot{\mathbf{x}} = \mathbf{f}(\mathbf{x})$ *with* $\mathbf{f}(\mathbf{x})$ *an elementary vector function defined on an open set* $U \subseteq \mathbb{R}^n$*, there exists a collection of variable replacement equations* $\mathbf{v} = \Gamma(\mathbf{x})$*, where* $\mathbf{v} = (v_1, v_2, \ldots, v_m)$ *is a vector of* *new variables and* $\Gamma(\mathbf{x}) = (\gamma_1(\mathbf{x}), \gamma_2(\mathbf{x}), \ldots, \gamma_m(\mathbf{x})) : U \to \mathbb{R}^m$ *is an elementary vector function, such that*

$$\begin{pmatrix} \dot{\mathbf{x}} \\ \dot{\mathbf{v}} \end{pmatrix} = \begin{pmatrix} \mathbf{f}(\mathbf{x}) \\ \mathcal{J}_\Gamma(\mathbf{x}) \cdot \mathbf{f}(\mathbf{x}) \end{pmatrix} = \begin{pmatrix} \mathbf{f}(\mathbf{x}) \\ \mathcal{J}_\Gamma(\mathbf{x}) \cdot \mathbf{f}(\mathbf{x}) \end{pmatrix} [\![\mathbf{v}/\Gamma(\mathbf{x})]\!] \mathrel{\widehat{=}} \tilde{\mathbf{f}}(\mathbf{x}, \mathbf{v}) \tag{4}$$

becomes a polynomial ODE, that is, $\tilde{\mathbf{f}}(\mathbf{x}, \mathbf{v})$ *is a polynomial vector function in variables* $\mathbf{x}$ *and* $\mathbf{v}$. *Here* $\mathsf{expr}[\![\mathbf{v}/\Gamma(\mathbf{x})]\!]$ *means replacing any occurrence of the non-polynomial term* $\gamma_i(\mathbf{x})$ *in the expression* expr *by the corresponding variable* v_i, *for all* $1 \leqslant i \leqslant m$.

It can be proved that the number of variables $\mathbf{v}$ is at most twice the number of non-polynomial terms in the original ODE, which can be a small number in practice. The transformed polynomial ODE as specified in Proposition 1 is *equivalent* to the original one in the following sense.

Theorem 3 (Trajectory Equivalence). *Let* $\mathbf{f}(\mathbf{x})$, $\Gamma(\mathbf{x})$ *and* $\tilde{\mathbf{f}}(\mathbf{x}, \mathbf{v})$ *be as specified in Proposition 1. Then for any trajectory* $\mathbf{x}(t)$ *of* $\dot{\mathbf{x}} = \mathbf{f}(\mathbf{x})$ *starting from* $\mathbf{x}_0 \in U \subseteq \mathbb{R}^n$, $\big(\mathbf{x}(t), \Gamma(\mathbf{x}(t))\big)$ *is the trajectory of* $(\dot{\mathbf{x}}, \dot{\mathbf{v}}) = \tilde{\mathbf{f}}(\mathbf{x}, \mathbf{v})$ *starting from* $(\mathbf{x}_0, \Gamma(\mathbf{x}_0))$; *conversely, for any trajectory* $(\mathbf{x}(t), \mathbf{v}(t))$ *of* $(\dot{\mathbf{x}}, \dot{\mathbf{v}}) = \tilde{\mathbf{f}}(\mathbf{x}, \mathbf{v})$ *starting from* $(\mathbf{x}_0, \mathbf{v}_0) \in \mathbb{R}^{n+m}$, *if* $\mathbf{x}_0 \in U$ *and* $\mathbf{v}_0 = \Gamma(\mathbf{x}_0)$, *then* $\mathbf{x}(t)$ *is the trajectory of* $\dot{\mathbf{x}} = \mathbf{f}(\mathbf{x})$ *starting from* $\mathbf{x}_0$.

Proof. The result can be deduced directly from (4). □

3.2 Abstracting EDSs by PDSs

In this part, given an EDS $\mathcal{C}_\mathbf{x} \mathrel{\widehat{=}} (\Xi_\mathbf{x}, \mathbf{f}_\mathbf{x}, D_\mathbf{x})$ we will construct a PDS $\mathcal{C}_\mathbf{y} \mathrel{\widehat{=}} (\Xi_\mathbf{y}, \mathbf{f}_\mathbf{y}, D_\mathbf{y})$ that simulates $\mathcal{C}_\mathbf{x}$. The construction is based on the procedure introduced in Section 3.1 on polynomial transformation of elementary ODEs. The basic idea is to construct a simulation map using the replacement equations. The difference here is that when abstracting an EDS, we need to replace non-polynomial terms occurring in not only the vector field, but also the initial set and domain. Suppose we have obtained the replacement equation $\mathbf{v} = \Gamma(\mathbf{x})$ and $\mathbf{f}_\mathbf{y}$ as defined in (4). Then we define the simulation map $\Theta : D_\mathbf{x} \to \mathbb{R}^{|\mathbf{y}|}$ as[3]

$$\Theta(\mathbf{x}) = (\mathbf{x}, \Gamma(\mathbf{x})) \; . \tag{5}$$

Now $\Xi_\mathbf{y}$ and $D_\mathbf{y}$ can be constructed using Θ, as illustrated in detail next.

To construct $\Xi_\mathbf{y}$, consider the image of $\Xi_\mathbf{x}$ under the simulation map Θ

$$\Theta(\Xi_\mathbf{x}) = \{(\mathbf{x}, \mathbf{v}) \in \mathbb{R}^{|\mathbf{y}|} \mid \mathbf{x} \in \Xi_\mathbf{x} \wedge \mathbf{v} = \Gamma(\mathbf{x})\} \, ,$$

briefly denoted by $\Theta(\Xi_\mathbf{x}) \mathrel{\widehat{=}} \Xi_\mathbf{x} \wedge \mathbf{v} = \Gamma(\mathbf{x})$, or alternatively

$$\Theta(\Xi_\mathbf{x}) \mathrel{\widehat{=}} \Xi_\mathbf{x}[\![\mathbf{v}/\Gamma(\mathbf{x})]\!] \wedge \mathbf{v} = \Gamma(\mathbf{x}) \, . \tag{6}$$

The first conjunct in (6) is of polynomial form, but the second conjunct contains elementary functions. By Definition 6, we need to get a polynomial over-approximation $\Xi_\mathbf{y}$ of $\Theta(\Xi_\mathbf{x})$, which means we need to abstract $\mathbf{v} = \Gamma(\mathbf{x})$ in (6) by polynomial expressions. We propose the following four ways to do so.

[3] Here we assume that all elementary functions in $\Xi_\mathbf{x}, \mathbf{f}_\mathbf{x}$ and $D_\mathbf{x}$ are defined on $D_\mathbf{x}$.

(W1) When $\Gamma(\mathbf{x})$ are some special kinds of elementary functions, $\mathbf{v} = \Gamma(\mathbf{x})$ can be equivalently transformed to polynomial expressions, e.g.

$$\begin{cases} v = \dfrac{1}{x} \Longleftrightarrow vx = 1 \\ v = \sqrt{x} \Longleftrightarrow v^2 = x \wedge v \geqslant 0 \end{cases} . \tag{7}$$

(W2) If $\Xi_{\mathbf{x}}$ is a bounded region and the upper/lower bounds of each component x_i of $\mathbf{x}$ can be easily obtained, then we can compute the Taylor polynomial expansion $\mathbf{p}(\mathbf{x})$ of $\Gamma(\mathbf{x})$ over the bounded region up to a certain degree, as well as an interval over-approximation $\mathbf{I}$ of the corresponding truncation error, such that $\mathbf{v} = \Gamma(\mathbf{x})$ can be approximated by $\mathbf{v} \in (\mathbf{p}(\mathbf{x}) + \mathbf{I})$.

(W3) We can also compute the range of $\Gamma(\mathbf{x})$ (over $\Xi_{\mathbf{x}}$) as an over-approximation of $\mathbf{v}$, e.g.

$$\begin{cases} v = \sin x \Longrightarrow -1 \leqslant v \leqslant 1 \\ v = e^x \Longrightarrow v > 0 \end{cases} . \tag{8}$$

(W4) The simplest way is to remove the constraint $\mathbf{v} = \Gamma(\mathbf{x})$ entirely, which means $\mathbf{v}$ is allowed to take any value from $\mathbb{R}^{|\mathbf{v}|}$.

From (W1) to (W4), the over-approximation of $\mathbf{v} = \Gamma(\mathbf{x})$ becomes more and more coarse. Usually it takes more effort to obtain a more refined abstraction, but the result would be more useful for analysis of the original system.

The construction of $D_{\mathbf{y}}$ is similar to $\Xi_{\mathbf{y}}$. Then we can give the following conclusion, the proof of which can be found in [22].

Theorem 4 (Abstracting EDS by PDS). *Given an EDS $\mathcal{C}_{\mathbf{x}} \widehat{=} (\Xi_{\mathbf{x}}, \mathbf{f}_{\mathbf{x}}, D_{\mathbf{x}})$, let $\mathcal{C}_{\mathbf{y}} \widehat{=} (\Xi_{\mathbf{y}}, \mathbf{f}_{\mathbf{y}}, D_{\mathbf{y}})$, where $\mathbf{f}_{\mathbf{y}}$ is given by (4), and $\Xi_{\mathbf{y}}, D_{\mathbf{y}}$ are given by (6) together with (W1)-(W4). Then $\mathcal{C}_{\mathbf{y}}$ is a* polynomial *abstraction of $\mathcal{C}_{\mathbf{x}}$ in the sense of Definition 6, under simulation map Θ defined by (5).*

Example 3. Consider the EDS $\mathcal{C}_{\mathbf{x}} \widehat{=} (\Xi_{\mathbf{x}}, \mathbf{f}_{\mathbf{x}}, D_{\mathbf{x}})$, where

- $\Xi_{\mathbf{x}} \widehat{=} (x + 0.5)^2 + (y - 0.5)^2 - 0.16 \leqslant 0$;
- $D_{\mathbf{x}} \widehat{=} -2 \leqslant x \leqslant 2 \wedge -2 \leqslant y \leqslant 2$; and
- $\mathbf{f}_{\mathbf{x}}$ defines the ODE

$$\begin{pmatrix} \dot{x} \\ \dot{y} \end{pmatrix} = \begin{pmatrix} e^{-x} + y - 1 \\ -\sin^2(x) \end{pmatrix} . \tag{9}$$

A PDS $\mathcal{C}_{\mathbf{y}}$ that simulates $\mathcal{C}_{\mathbf{x}}$ can be constructed as follows.

1) Noticing that $\Xi_{\mathbf{x}}$ and $D_{\mathbf{x}}$ are both in polynomial forms, we only need to replace non-polynomial terms in $\mathbf{f}_{\mathbf{x}}$. We finally obtain the replacement relations $\mathbf{v} = \Gamma(\mathbf{x})$

$$(v_1, v_2, v_3) = (\sin x, e^{-x}, \cos x) \tag{10}$$

and the transformed polynomial ODE

$$\begin{pmatrix} \dot{x} \\ \dot{y} \\ \dot{v}_1 \\ \dot{v}_2 \\ \dot{v}_3 \end{pmatrix} = \begin{pmatrix} v_2 + y - 1 \\ -v_1^2 \\ v_3(v_2 + y - 1) \\ -v_2(v_2 + y - 1) \\ -v_1(v_2 + y - 1) \end{pmatrix} , \tag{11}$$

the right-hand-side of which is defined to be $\mathbf{f_y}$.

2) The simulation map Θ is given by

$$\Theta(x, y) = (x, y, \sin x, e^{-x}, \cos x) \ . \tag{12}$$

The images of $\Xi_{\mathbf{x}}$ and $D_{\mathbf{x}}$ under Θ are

$$\Theta(\Xi_{\mathbf{x}}) \widehat{=} \Xi_{\mathbf{x}} \wedge v_1 = \sin x \wedge v_2 = e^{-x} \wedge v_3 = \cos x$$

and

$$\Theta(D_{\mathbf{x}}) \widehat{=} D_{\mathbf{x}} \wedge v_1 = \sin x \wedge v_2 = e^{-x} \wedge v_3 = \cos x$$

respectively. For the above two formulas, (W1) is not applicable, whereas we can use any of (W2)-(W4) to abstract them. Here we give one possible way adopting (W2): first, using the tool COSY INFINITY[4] for *Taylor model* [24] computation, we expand $\sin x$, e^{-x} and $\cos x$ over $x \in [-2, 2]$ at $x = 0$ up to degree 6, and obtain

$$TM_{\mathbf{x},\mathbf{v}} \widehat{=} \begin{array}{l} p_1(x) + l_1 \leqslant v_1 \leqslant p_1(x) + u_1 \\ \wedge\, p_2(x) + l_2 \leqslant v_2 \leqslant p_2(x) + u_2 \\ \wedge\, p_3(x) + l_3 \leqslant v_3 \leqslant p_3(x) + u_3 \end{array} \quad ; \tag{13}$$

then we define $D_{\mathbf{y}} \widehat{=} D_{\mathbf{x}} \wedge TM_{\mathbf{x},\mathbf{v}}$; second, from $\Xi_{\mathbf{x}}$ it can be deduced that $x \in [-0.9, -0.1]$ for any $(x, y) \in \Xi_{\mathbf{x}}$, and then we can compute the Taylor models of $\mathbf{v} = \Gamma(\mathbf{x})$ over $[-0.9, -0.1]$ and obtain $\Xi_{\mathbf{y}}$. Please see [22] for details of computed Taylor models. Thus we finally get a PDS $\mathcal{C}_{\mathbf{y}} \widehat{=} (\Xi_{\mathbf{y}}, \mathbf{f_y}, D_{\mathbf{y}})$ that simulates $\mathcal{C}_{\mathbf{x}}$.

3.3 Abstracting EHSs by PHSs

In the previous sections, we have presented a method to abstract an EDS to a PDS such that the PDS simulates the EDS. Now we show, given an EHS $\mathcal{H}_{\mathbf{x}}$, how to construct a PHS $\mathcal{H}_{\mathbf{y}}$ that simulates $\mathcal{H}_{\mathbf{x}}$. Actually, this can be easily done by just extending the previous abstraction approach a bit to take into account guard constraints and reset functions. Another difference is that we need to treat each mode of an HA separately by constructing an individual simulation map for each of them. For the details of how guards and reset maps can be abstracted, the readers can refer to the full version [22].

Example 4. Consider the EHS in Example 1 except for that the initial set is replaced by $\Xi_q \widehat{=} y \in [4.9, 5.1] \wedge x = 0 \wedge v_x = -1 \wedge v_y = 0$. Denote this EHS by $\mathcal{H}_{\mathbf{x}}$ with $\mathbf{x} = (x, y, v_x, v_y)$. By applying the proposed abstraction approach, we obtained the replacement equations $(u_1, u_2, u_3) = (\sin x, \cos x, \frac{1}{1+(\cos x)^2})$ and the corresponding polynomial abstraction $\mathcal{H}_{\mathbf{y}}$, with the polynomial guard $G_{\mathbf{y},e} \widehat{=} y = u_1$ and polynomial reset mapping $R_{\mathbf{y},e}(\mathbf{y}) \widehat{=} \{(x, y, v'_x, v'_y, u_1, u_2, u_3)\}$ where

$$\begin{cases} v'_x = u_3 \cdot (u_1^2 \cdot v_x + 2u_2 \cdot v_y) \\ v'_y = u_3 \cdot (2u_2 \cdot v_x - u_1^2 \cdot v_y) \end{cases} .$$

The complete model of $\mathcal{H}_{\mathbf{y}}$ can be found in [22].

[4] http://bt.pa.msu.edu/index_cosy.htm

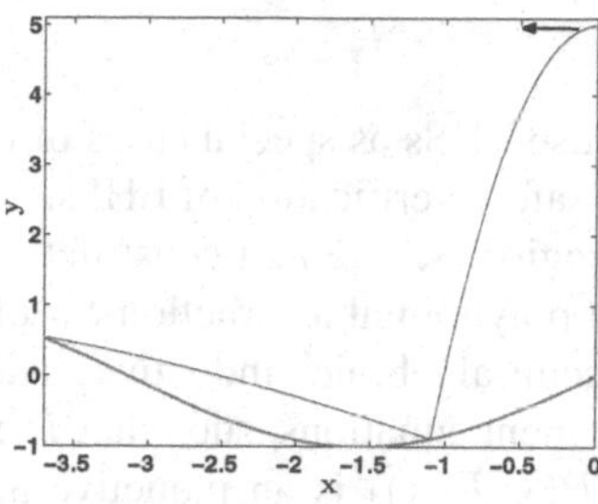
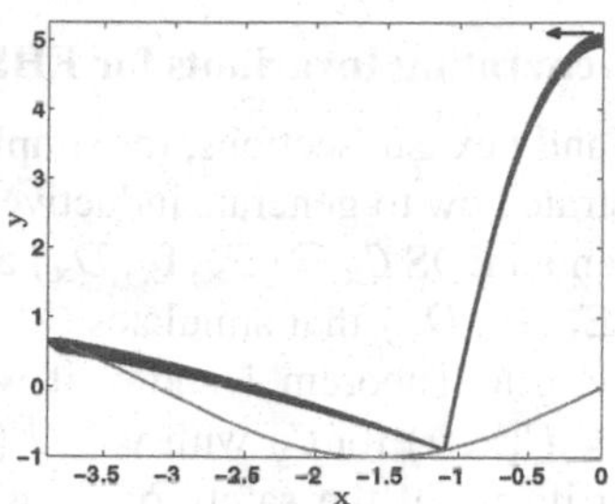

Fig. 2. Simulated trajectory with $y = 5$ and reachable set over-approximation with $y \in [4.9, 5.1]$

Then we can use existing tools for PHSs to analyze the behavior of the bouncing ball. Here we use the state-of-the-art nonlinear hybrid system analyzer Flow* [6]. The right picture in Figure 2 shows the computed reachable set over-approximation (projected to the x-y plane) of $\mathcal{H}_{\mathbf{y}}$ with the initial set $\Xi_{\mathbf{y},q}$ for the first two jumps, which is also the reachable set over-approximation of $\mathcal{H}_{\mathbf{x}}$ by Theorem 1. Note that such an analysis would NOT have been possible directly on $\mathcal{H}_{\mathbf{x}}$ in Flow* since its current version does not support elementary functions in domains, guards, or reset functions[5].

4 Application in Safety Verification of EHSs

One of the most important problems in the study of HSs is safety verification. Given an HS $\mathcal{H}$, a safety requirement for $\mathcal{H}$ can be specified as $\mathcal{S} \widehat{=} \bigcup_{q\in Q}(\{q\} \times S_q)$ with $S_q \subseteq \mathbb{R}^n$ the safe region of mode q. Alternatively, a safety property can be given as a set of unsafe regions $\mathcal{US} \widehat{=} \bigcup_{q\in Q}(\{q\} \times \bar{S}_q)$ with $\bar{S}_q$ the complement of S_q in $\mathbb{R}^n$. The safety verification problem asks whether $\mathcal{R}_{\mathcal{H}} \subseteq \mathcal{S}$, or equivalently, whether $\mathcal{R}_{\mathcal{H}} \cap \mathcal{US} = \emptyset$.

The following result relates the safety verification problem of an HS $\mathcal{H}_{\mathbf{x}}$ to that of $\mathcal{H}_{\mathbf{y}}$ which simulates $\mathcal{H}_{\mathbf{x}}$. The proof of it can be found in [22].

Theorem 5 (Safety Relation). *Let $\mathcal{US}_{\mathbf{x}} \widehat{=} \bigcup_q(\{q\} \times \bar{S}_{\mathbf{x},q})$ be a safety requirement of the HS $\mathcal{H}_{\mathbf{x}}$. Suppose $\mathcal{H}_{\mathbf{y}}$ simulates $\mathcal{H}_{\mathbf{x}}$ via simulation maps $\{\Theta_q \mid q \in Q\}$ and $\mathcal{US}_{\mathbf{y}} \widehat{=} \bigcup_q(\{q\} \times \bar{S}_{\mathbf{y},q})$ satisfies $\bar{S}_{\mathbf{y},q} \supseteq \Theta_q(\bar{S}_{\mathbf{x},q})$ for any $q \in Q$. Then $\mathcal{H}_{\mathbf{x}}$ is safe w.r.t. $\mathcal{US}_{\mathbf{x}}$, if $\mathcal{H}_{\mathbf{y}}$ is safe w.r.t. $\mathcal{US}_{\mathbf{y}}$.*

Note that if the safety properties of EHSs are not in polynomial forms but contain elementary functions, we can replace the non-polynomial terms by new variables when constructing the simulation map, as we do for the EHSs themselves.

Theorem 5 allows us to take advantage of constraint-based approaches for PHSs to verify safety properties of EHSs. In the rest of this section, we show how to perform safety verification for EHSs by combining the previous proposed polynomial abstraction method with constraint-based verification techniques for PHSs.

[5] Although Flow* does support nonlinear continuous dynamics with non-polynomial terms such as sine, cosine, square root, etc.

4.1 Generating Invariants for EHSs

In this and next subsections, for simplicity, we will use EDSs as special cases of EHSs to illustrate how to generate inductive invariants for safety verification of EHSs.

Given an EDS $\mathcal{C}_{\mathbf{x}} \,\widehat{=}\, (\Xi_{\mathbf{x}}, \mathbf{f}_{\mathbf{x}}, D_{\mathbf{x}})$ and an unsafe region $\bar{S}_{\mathbf{x}}$, we first construct a PDS $\mathcal{C}_{\mathbf{y}} \,\widehat{=}\, (\Xi_{\mathbf{y}}, \mathbf{f}_{\mathbf{y}}, D_{\mathbf{y}})$ that simulates $\mathcal{C}_{\mathbf{x}}$, as well as the polynomial abstraction $\bar{S}_{\mathbf{y}}$ of $\bar{S}_{\mathbf{x}}$. According to Theorem 1 and 5, if we can find a semi-algebraic[6] inductive invariant $P(\mathbf{y}) = P(\mathbf{x}, \mathbf{v})$ for $\mathcal{C}_{\mathbf{y}}$ with $\mathbf{v} = \Gamma(\mathbf{x})$ the replacement equations, such that $P(\mathbf{x}, \mathbf{v})$ is a certificate of the safety of $\mathcal{C}_{\mathbf{y}}$ w.r.t. $\bar{S}_{\mathbf{y}}$, then $P(\mathbf{x}, \Gamma(\mathbf{x}))$ is an inductive invariant certificate of the safety of $\mathcal{C}_{\mathbf{x}}$ w.r.t. $\bar{S}_{\mathbf{x}}$. If $P(\mathbf{x}, \mathbf{v})$ does contain variables $\mathbf{v}$, then $P(\mathbf{x}, \Gamma(\mathbf{x}))$ gives an elementary invariant of $\mathcal{C}_{\mathbf{x}}$; otherwise $P(\mathbf{x}, \Gamma(\mathbf{x}))$ is just a polynomial invariant.

Example 5. Consider the EDS $\mathcal{C}_{\mathbf{x}}$ in Example 3. We are going to verify the safety of $\mathcal{C}_{\mathbf{x}}$ w.r.t. an unsafe region $\bar{S}_{\mathbf{x}} \,\widehat{=}\, (x-0.7)^2+(y+0.7)^2-0.09 \leqslant 0$. To this end, we first verify the safety of the polynomial abstraction $\mathcal{C}_{\mathbf{y}}$ of $\mathcal{C}_{\mathbf{x}}$ obtained in Example 3, w.r.t. an unsafe region $\bar{S}_{\mathbf{y}}$ that abstracts $\bar{S}_{\mathbf{x}}$ in the way of (W2). By applying the SOS-relaxation-based invariant generation approach [29,18] with a polynomial template $p_1(\mathbf{u}, \mathbf{x}, \mathbf{v}) \leqslant 0$ of degree 3 (in $\mathbf{x}, \mathbf{v}$), where $\mathbf{v} = \Gamma(\mathbf{x})$ is defined in (10) and $\mathbf{u}$ is a vector of undetermined parameters, and using the Matlab-based tool YALMIP [23] and SeDuMi [37] (or SDPT3 [40]), we successfully generated an invariant $p_1(x, y, \sin x, e^{-x}, \cos x) \leqslant 0$ that verifies the safety of $\mathcal{C}_{\mathbf{x}}$. Please see the left part of Figure 3 for an illustration of $\mathbf{f}_{\mathbf{x}}$ (the black arrows), $D_{\mathbf{x}}$ (the outer white box), $\Xi_{\mathbf{x}}$ (the white circle), $\bar{S}_{\mathbf{x}}$ (the black circle), as well as the synthesized invariant (the grey area with curved boundary).

We next try to generate polynomial invariants for $\mathcal{C}_{\mathbf{x}}$ by constructing less accurate abstractions $\mathcal{C}_{\mathbf{y}}$ and $\bar{S}_{\mathbf{y}}$ of $\mathcal{C}_{\mathbf{x}}$ and $\bar{S}_{\mathbf{x}}$ respectively (see [22] for the details). With a polynomial template $p_2(\mathbf{u}, \mathbf{x}) \leqslant 0$ of degree 5 (in $\mathbf{x}$), we obtain an invariant $p_2(x, y) \leqslant 0$ that verifies safety of $\mathcal{C}_{\mathbf{x}}$, as shown in the right part of Figure 3. The explicit forms of both p_1 and p_2 can be found in [22].

We can see that the elementary invariant is sharper than the polynomial invariant and separates better from the unsafe region. This indicates that by allowing non-polynomial terms in templates, invariants of higher quality may be generated and thus increases the possibility of verifying safety properties of EHSs. Moreover, it also suggests that even for purely polynomial systems, one could assume any kind of elementary terms in a predefined template when generating invariants, which gives a more general method than [32,11] for generating elementary invariants for PHSs. Of course, computing elementary invariants generally takes more efforts than polynomial invariants.

4.2 More Experiments

We have implemented the proposed abstraction approach (not including the part on abstraction of replacement equations) and experimented with it on the following EHS verification examples.[7]

[6] A set $A \subseteq \mathbb{R}^n$ is called *semi-algebraic* if it can be defined by Boolean combinations of polynomial equations or inequalities.

[7] The formal abstraction algorithms can be found in [22], and all the input files for the experiments can be obtained at http://lcs.ios.ac.cn/%7Ezoul/casestudies/fm2015.zip

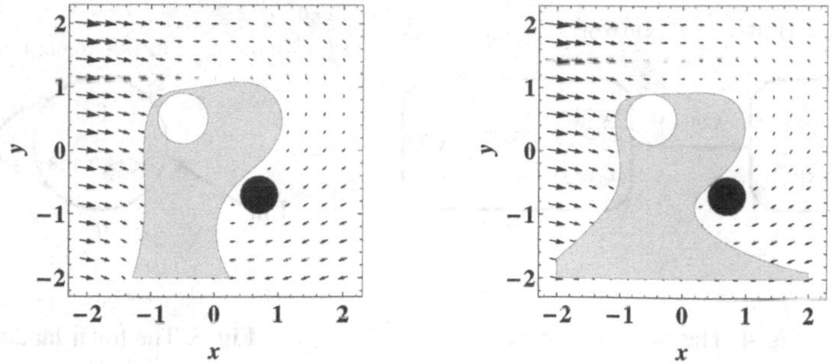

Fig. 3. Comparison of elementary and polynomial invariants generated in Example 5

Example 6 (HIV Transmission). The following continuous dynamics, with the assumption that there is no recruitment of population, has been developed to model HIV transmission [3]

$$\mathbf{f} \widehat{=} \begin{cases} \dot{u}_1 = -\frac{\beta c u_1 u_2}{u_1+u_2+u_3} - \mu u_1 \\ \dot{u}_2 = \frac{\beta c u_1 u_2}{u_1+u_2+u_3} - (\mu+\nu)u_2 \\ \dot{u}_3 = \nu u_2 - \alpha u_3 \end{cases}, \tag{14}$$

where $u_1(t), u_2(t), u_3(t)$ denote the part of population that is HIV susceptible, HIV infected, and that has AIDS respectively, β is the possibility of infection per partner contact, c is the rate of partner change, μ is the death rate of non-AIDS population, α is the death rate of AIDS patients, and ν is the rate at which HIV infected people develop AIDS. Note that the dynamics involves non-polynomial term $\frac{1}{u_1+u_2+u_3}$. In this paper, the parameters are chosen to be $\beta = 0.2, c = 10, \mu = 0.008, \alpha = 0.95$, and $\nu = 0.1$. We want to verify that with the initial set

$$\Xi \widehat{=} u_1 \in [9.985, 9.995] \wedge u_2 \in [0.005, 0.015] \wedge u_3 \in [0, 0.003],$$

the population of AIDS patients alive will always be below 1 (the population is measured in thousands). That is, the system $(\Xi, \mathbf{f}, D)$ satisfies $S \widehat{=} u_3 \leqslant 1$, where $D \widehat{=} u_1 \geqslant 0 \wedge u_2 \geqslant 0 \wedge u_3 \geqslant 0 \wedge 0 < u_1 + u_2 + u_3 \leqslant 10.013$.[8]

Example 7 (Two-Tanks). The two-tanks system shown in Figure 4 comes from [38] and has been studied in [31,14,8,7] as a benchmark for safety verification of hybrid systems. It models two connected tanks, the liquid levels of which are denoted by x_1 and x_2 respectively. The system switches between mode q_1 and q_2 when x_2 reaches 1. The system's dynamics involve non-polynomial terms such as $\sqrt{x_1}$ or $\sqrt{x_1 - x_2 + 1}$. The verification objective is to show that starting from mode q_1 with the initial set $\Xi_{q_1} \widehat{=} 5.25 \leqslant x_1 \leqslant 5.75 \wedge 0 \leqslant x_2 \leqslant 0.5$, the system will never reach the unsafe set $\bar{S}_{q_1} \widehat{=} (x_1 - 4.25)^2 + (x_2 - 0.25)^2 - 0.0625 \leqslant 0$ when staying at mode q_1.

[8] According to dynamics (14), the entire population is non-increasing, so $u_1 + u_2 + u_3$ has an upper bound.

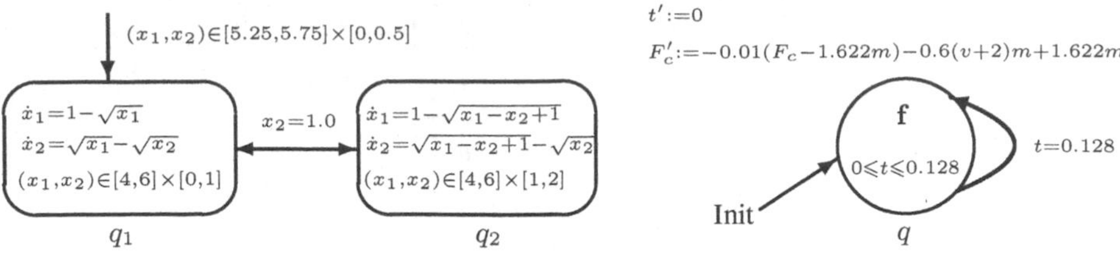

Fig. 4. The two-tanks system

Fig. 5. The lunar lander system

Example 8 (Lunar Lander). Consider a real-world example of the guidance and control of a lunar lander [41], as illustrated by Figure 5. The dynamics of the lander defined by **f** is given by

$$\begin{cases} \dot{v} &= \frac{F_c}{m} - 1.622 \\ \dot{m} &= -\frac{F_c}{2500} \\ \dot{F}_c &= 0 \\ \dot{t} &= 1 \end{cases}, \tag{15}$$

where v and m denote the vertical velocity and mass of the lunar lander; F_c denotes the thrust imposed on the lander, which is kept constant during one sampling cycle of length 0.128 seconds; at each sampling point, F_c is updated according to the guidance law shown in Figure 5. Note that the derivative of v involves non-polynomial expression $\frac{1}{m}$. We want to verify that with the initial condition $t = 0$s, $v = -2$m/s, $m = 1250$kg, $F_c = 2027.5$N, the vertical velocity of the lunar lander will be kept around the target velocity -2m/s, i.e. $|v - (-2)| \leqslant \varepsilon$, where $\varepsilon = 0.05$ is the specified bound for fluctuation of v.

Using the proposed abstraction method and the SOS-relaxation-based invariant generation method [29,18], we have successfully verified Examples 6-8. Besides, we have also compared with the performances of the EHS verification tools HSOLVER [31], Flow* [6], dReach [9] and iSAT-ODE [8] on these examples (including Example 5).[9] All the time costs are shown in Table 1. The results are obtained on the platform with Intel Core i5-3470 CPU and 4GB RAM running Windows 7 (for the proposed abstraction approach) or Ubuntu Linux 14.04 (for the other tools).

Table 1. Verification results of different methods

	EHS2PHS	HSOLVER	Flow*	dReach	iSAT-ODE
E.g. 5	1.324 or 7.994	0.739	⊖	–	⊖
E.g. 6	5.186	–	⊖	–	⊖
E.g. 7	0.977	0.477	76.742	20.351	0.949
E.g. 8	2.645	–	3.310	–	54.364

[9] Note that since Flow*, dReach and iSAT-ODE can only do BMC, we have assumed a time bound of 20s and 10s resp. for E.g. 5 and 6, and a jump bound of 40 steps and 100 steps resp. for E.g. 7 and 8.

For Table 1, we have the following remarks:

- time is measured in seconds;
- the second column (EHS2PHS) corresponds to the time costs of both abstraction and verification for the proposed approach in this paper; the time cost on E.g. 5 using the abstraction approach depends on whether we generate polynomial (1.324s) or elementary (7.994s) invariants;
- the other four tools are called on the original EHSs rather than their polynomial abstractions; – means timeout (> 1 hour); ⊖ means abnormal termination due to error inflation of continuous integration;
- all the details of inputs, experiment results, all well as options for using the tools can be obtained by investigating the aforementioned online files.

From Table 1 we can see that the time costs of the proposed abstraction approach are all acceptable, whereas there do exist examples that existing approaches cannot solve effectively.[10]

5 Conclusions

In this paper, we presented an approach to reducing an EHS to a PHS by variable transformation, and established the simulation relation between them, so that safety verification of the EHS can be reduced to that of the corresponding PHS. Thus our work enables all the well-established techniques for PHS verification to be applicable to EHSs. In particular, combined with invariant-based approach to safety verification for PHSs, it provides the possibility of overcoming the limitations of existing EHS verification approaches. Experimental results on real-world examples indicated the effectiveness of our approach.

In the future, it deserves to investigate how to reduce stability analysis of EHSs to that of PHSs using the technique developed in this paper, while stability analysis of PHSs can be well done by synthesizing (relaxed) polynomial Lyaponuv functions (e.g., cf. [21]).

Acknowledgements. We thank Prof. Martin Fränzle, Dr. Andreas Eggers, Dr. Sicun Gao and Dr. Xin Chen for their instructions on using the verification tools. We also thank the anonymous referees for their valuable comments on the earlier drafts.

References

1. Akbarpour, B., Paulson, L.: MetiTarski: An automatic theorem prover for real-valued special functions. Journal of Automated Reasoning 44(3), 175–205 (2010)
2. Alur, R., Courcoubetis, C., Henzinger, T.A., Ho, P.H.: Hybrid automata: An algorithmic approach to the specification and verification of hybrid systems. In: Grossman, R.L., Nerode, A., Ravn, A.P., Rischel, H. (eds.) Hybrid Systems, LNCS, vol. 736, pp. 209–229. Springer Berlin Heidelberg (1993)

[10] One may notice that HSOLVER is faster on the examples that it can solve, the possible reason for which is that a coarse abstraction happens to be sufficient for proving the safety of studied systems, thus saving much time for refinement.

3. Anderson, R.M.: The role of mathematical models in the study of HIV transmission and the epidemiology of AIDS. Journal of Acquired Immune Deficiency Syndromes 3(1), 241–256 (1988)
4. Asarin, E., Dang, T., Girard, A.: Hybridization methods for the analysis of nonlinear systems. Acta Informatica 43(7), 451–476 (2007)
5. Chen, X., Ábrahám, E., Sankaranarayanan, S.: Taylor model flowpipe construction for non-linear hybrid systems. In: RTSS 2012. pp. 183–192. IEEE Computer Society, Los Alamitos, CA, USA (2012)
6. Chen, X., Ábrahám, E., Sankaranarayanan, S.: Flow*: An analyzer for non-linear hybrid systems. In: Sharygina, N., Veith, H. (eds.) CAV 2013, LNCS, vol. 8044, pp. 258–263. Springer Berlin Heidelberg (2013)
7. Denman, W.: Verifying nonpolynomial hybrid systems by qualitative abstraction and automated theorem proving. In: Badger, J.M., Rozier, K.Y. (eds.) NFM 2014, LNCS, vol. 8430, pp. 203–208. Springer International Publishing (2014)
8. Eggers, A., Ramdani, N., Nedialkov, N., Fränzle, M.: Improving the SAT modulo ODE approach to hybrid systems analysis by combining different enclosure methods. Software & Systems Modeling pp. 1–28 (2012)
9. Gao, S., Kong, S., Clarke, E.: dReach: Reachability analysis for nonlinear hybrid systems (tool paper). In: HSCC 2013 (2013), http://dreal.cs.cmu.edu/#!dreach.md
10. Ghorbal, K., Platzer, A.: Characterizing algebraic invariants by differential radical invariants. In: Ábrahám, E., Havelund, K. (eds.) TACAS 2014, LNCS, vol. 8413, pp. 279–294. Springer Berlin Heidelberg (2014)
11. Goubault, E., Jourdan, J.H., Putot, S., Sankaranarayanan, S.: Finding non-polynomial positive invariants and Lyapunov functions for polynomial systems through Darboux polynomials. pp. 3571–3578. ACC 2014 (2014)
12. Gulwani, S., Tiwari, A.: Constraint-based approach for analysis of hybrid systems. In: Gupta, A., Malik, S. (eds.) CAV 2008, LNCS, vol. 5123, pp. 190–203. Springer Berlin Heidelberg (2008)
13. Henzinger, T.A.: The theory of hybrid automata. In: LICS 1996. pp. 278–292. IEEE Computer Society (Jul 1996)
14. Ishii, D., Ueda, K., Hosobe, H.: An interval-based SAT modulo ODE solver for model checking nonlinear hybrid systems. International Journal on Software Tools for Technology Transfer 13(5), 449–461 (2011)
15. Johnson, T.T., Green, J., Mitra, S., Dudley, R., Erwin, R.S.: Satellite rendezvous and conjunction avoidance: Case studies in verification of nonlinear hybrid systems. In: Giannakopoulou, D., Méry, D. (eds.) FM 2012. LNCS, vol. 7436, pp. 252–266. Springer Berlin Heidelberg (2012)
16. Kerner, E.H.: Universal formats for nonlinear ordinary differential systems. Journal of Mathematical Physics 22(7), 1366–1371 (1981)
17. Khalil, H.K.: Nonlinear Systems. Prentice Hall, third edn. (Dec 2001)
18. Kong, H., He, F., Song, X., Hung, W.N., Gu, M.: Exponential-condition-based barrier certificate generation for safety verification of hybrid systems. In: Sharygina, N., Veith, H. (eds.) CAV 2013. LNCS, vol. 8044, pp. 242–257. Springer Berlin Heidelberg (2013)
19. Lanotte, R., Tini, S.: Taylor approximation for hybrid systems. Information and Computation 205(11), 1575–1607 (Nov 2007)
20. Liu, J., Zhan, N., Zhao, H.: Computing semi-algebraic invariants for polynomial dynamical systems. In: EMSOFT 2011. pp. 97–106. ACM, New York, NY, USA (2011)
21. Liu, J., Zhan, N., Zhao, H.: Automatically discovering relaxed Lyapunov functions for polynomial dynamical systems. Mathematics in Computer Science 6(4), 395–408 (2012)
22. Liu, J., Zhan, N., Zhao, H., Zou, L.: Abstraction of elementary hybrid systems by variable transformation. CoRR abs/1403.7022 (2014), http://arxiv.org/abs/1403.7022

23. Löfberg, J.: YALMIP : A toolbox for modeling and optimization in MATLAB. In: Proc. of the CACSD Conference. Taipei, Taiwan (2004), http://users.isy.liu.se/johanl/yalmip/
24. Makino, K., Berz, M.: Taylor models and other validated functional inclusion methods. International Journal of Pure and Applied Mathematics 4(4), 379–456 (2003)
25. Mitchell, I., Tomlin, C.J.: Level set methods for computation in hybrid systems. In: Lynch, N., Krogh, B.H. (eds.) HSCC 2000, LNCS, vol. 1790, pp. 310–323. Springer Berlin Heidelberg (2000)
26. Papachristodoulou, A., Prajna, S.: Analysis of non-polynomial systems using the sum of squares decomposition. In: Henrion, D., Garulli, A. (eds.) Positive Polynomials in Control, Lecture Notes in Control and Information Science, vol. 312, pp. 23–43. Springer Berlin Heidelberg (2005)
27. Platzer, A.: Differential-algebraic dynamic logic for differential-algebraic programs. J. Log. and Comput. 20(1), 309–352 (Feb 2010)
28. Platzer, A., Clarke, E.M.: Computing differential invariants of hybrid systems as fixedpoints. In: Gupta, A., Malik, S. (eds.) CAV 2008, LNCS, vol. 5123, pp. 176–189. Springer Berlin Heidelberg (2008)
29. Prajna, S., Jadbabaie, A., Pappas, G.: A framework for worst-case and stochastic safety verification using barrier certificates. IEEE Transactions on Automatic Control 52(8), 1415–1428 (2007)
30. Ratschan, S.: Safety verification of non-linear hybrid systems is quasi-decidable. Formal Methods in System Design 44(1), 71–90 (2014)
31. Ratschan, S., She, Z.: Safety verification of hybrid systems by constraint propagation-based abstraction refinement. ACM Trans. Embed. Comput. Syst. 6(1) (Feb 2007)
32. Rebiha, R., Matringe, N., Moura, A.V.: Transcendental inductive invariants generation for non-linear differential and hybrid systems. In: HSCC 2012. pp. 25–34. ACM, New York, NY, USA (2012)
33. Sankaranarayanan, S.: Automatic abstraction of non-linear systems using change of bases transformations. In: HSCC 2011. pp. 143–152. ACM, New York, NY, USA (2011)
34. Sankaranarayanan, S.: Change-of-bases abstractions for non-linear systems. CoRR abs/1204.4347 (2012), http://arxiv.org/abs/1204.4347
35. Sankaranarayanan, S., Sipma, H.B., Manna, Z.: Constructing invariants for hybrid systems. In: Alur, R., Pappas, G.J. (eds.) HSCC 2004, LNCS, vol. 2993, pp. 539–554. Springer Berlin Heidelberg (2004)
36. Savageau, M.A., Voit, E.O.: Recasting nonlinear differential equations as S-systems: a canonical nonlinear form. Mathematical Biosciences 87(1), 83–115 (1987)
37. Sturm, J.F.: Using SeDuMi 1.02, a MATLAB toolbox for optimization over symmetric cones. Optimization Methods and Software 11-12, 625–653 (1999)
38. Stursberg, O., Kowalewski, S., Hoffmann, I., Preußig, J.: Comparing timed and hybrid automata as approximations of continuous systems. In: Antsaklis, P., Kohn, W., Nerode, A., Sastry, S. (eds.) Hybrid Systems IV, LNCS, vol. 1273, pp. 361–377. Springer Berlin Heidelberg (1997)
39. Tiwari, A.: Abstractions for hybrid systems. Formal Methods in System Design 32(1), 57–83 (2008)
40. Toh, K.C., Todd, M., Tütüncü, R.H.: SDPT3 – a MATLAB software package for semidefinite programming. Optimization Methods and Software 11, 545–581 (1999)
41. Zhao, H., Yang, M., Zhan, N., Gu, B., Zou, L., Chen, Y.: Formal verification of a descent guidance control program of a lunar lander. In: Jones, C., Pihlajasaari, P., Sun, J. (eds.) FM 2014, LNCS, vol. 8442, pp. 733–748. Springer International Publishing Switzerland (2014)

Using Real-Time Maude to Model Check Energy Consumption Behavior

Shin Nakajima(✉)

National Institute of Informatics, Tokyo, Japan
nkjm@nii.ac.jp

Abstract. Energy consumption is one of the primary non-functional concerns, especially for application programs running on systems that have limited battery capacity. A model-based analysis of energy consumption is introduced at early stages of development. As rigorous formal models of this, the power consumption automaton and a variant of linear temporal logic are proposed. Detecting unexpected energy consumption is then reduced to a model checking problem, which is unfortunately undecidable in general. This paper introduces some restrictions to the logic formulas representing energy consumption properties so that an automatic analysis is possible with Real-Time Maude.

Keywords: Android Frameworks · Weighted Timed Automaton · Linear Temporal Logic · Freeze Quantifier

1 Introduction

Modern mobile systems such as smartphones and tablet PC are powered by batteries that have limited capacity. Although the hardware components directly consume the battery power, some computer programs must be responsible for consuming the energy. Basic hardware components, the CPU and memory, are used at all times. Auxiliary functional devices, such as a WiFi or GPS component, are in operation only when they are requested by a particular application. The total energy consumption is thus attributed to a combination of the hardware and the behavior of the installed programs.

In Android-based smartphones [1], an application program, even if it is functionally correct, may suffer from unexpected energy consumption. Such energy bugs (*ebugs*) [20] originate in design flaws. Post-analysis techniques using energy profilers (cf. [21][22]) are employed to find such ebugs. A profiler is, however, a runtime monitor that checks the consumed energy of running programs. It has the same disadvantages as the program testing methods have. The profiler can only be used after all the programs have been completed, and the coverage is limited by the supplied test cases or the test environment setup. Furthermore, the measured results may contain fluctuations due to uncontrollable operation

also affiliated with SOKENDAI.

N. Bjørner and F. de Boer (Eds.): FM 2015, LNCS 9109, pp. 378–394, 2015.
DOI: 10.1007/978-3-319-19249-9_24

conditions. The energy drain caused by ebugs may be hidden within the measurement errors if the amount is comparatively small (cf. [15]).

A model-based analysis method for energy consumption is desirable to counter the disadvantages of the runtime profiler method (cf. [12]). With appropriate abstract models, it is possible to analyze the energy consumption behavior at early stages of development. The models represent both the energy consumption behavior and the specification properties that are to be checked. As rigorous formal models of this, power consumption automata (PCA) were defined as weighted timed automata (WTA) and a variant of linear temporal logic (LTL) with freeze quantifiers, called fWLTL, was introduced [14]. The energy consumption analysis problem is formulated using a method of logic model checking.

This paper focuses on model checking of fWLTL formulas. The logic formula is employed to specify flexibly the durations in which the numerical constraints on the consumed energy are checked. This duration-bounded cost constraint problem is then solved by logic model checking. However, fWLTL is expressive, and its model checking problem is undecidable in general. Accordingly, this paper proposes combining a sub-fragment of fWLTL with some approximation techniques. Specifically, the energy consumption analysis problem is translated into Real-Time Maude [16][17].

The contributions of this paper are summarized as follows; (a) the energy consumption analysis problem is encoded in fWLTL formulas, (b) two property patterns are introduced to employ a sub-fragment of fWLTL, (c) a translation method to Real-Time Maude is presented for enabling automatic analyses. The method introduces a kind of over-approximation and does not miss potential faults, which is appropriate for detecting ebugs.

2 Energy Consumption Behavior

The energy consumption of a system is represented as a state-transition system, a power consumption automaton (PCA) [12]. It keeps track of the amount of the consumed energy along its transition sequences.

2.1 Power Consumption Automaton

Figure 1 shows an example of energy consumption behavior, presented as a state-transition diagram. The example is a WiFi client device operating in a power-saving mode. It consists of four states, called power states, and several state-transition edges. In Figure 1, `DeepSleep` is the initial state, from which the system goes to `HighPower` state when it receives a beacon signal. The signal indicates that data transfer is beginning. There are then repeated transitions between `IdleListen` and `HighPower` states; in `IdleListen`, the system awaits the arrival of a new data frame. When the data transfer is over, the system goes into `LightSleep` state to prepare for a quick restart. An inactivity timer is also set, whose time-out causes the transition to `DeepSleep`. A state-transition sequence consists of many instances of each of four power states.

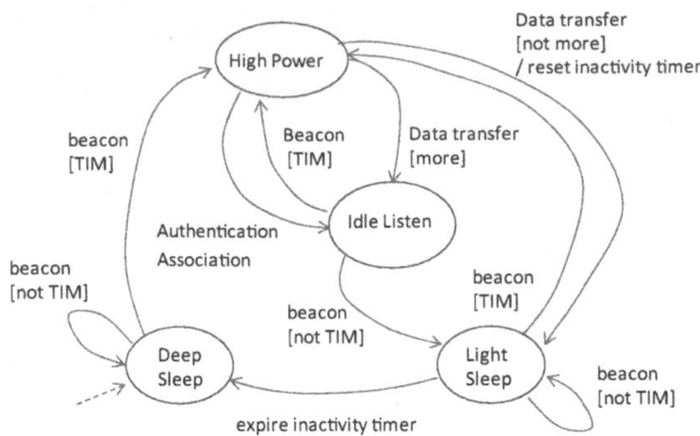

Fig. 1. An Example Diagram of Energy Consumption Behavior

The amount of consumed energy is different in each power state. `HighPower` state consumes a lot of energy in order to decode the transferred frames. In `DeepSleep` state, only power sufficient to activate a portion of the electric circuits is necessary, and thus the energy consumption rate is small. If we let $F^j(t)$ be a function of time that represents the rate of energy consumed at a state indexed by j, the total energy consumed in the time interval a to b is $E^j = \int_a^b F^j(t)dt$. Since the power states are visited many times as state transitions continue, the total energy consumption is calculated as a summation over E^js; $E = \sum_{j=0}^{n} E^j = \sum_{j=0}^{n} \int_{a^j}^{b^j} F^j(t)dt$. If we introduce a linear approximation such that $dE^j/dt = F^j(t) = M^j$ for a constant M^j at each power state, then $E = \sum_{j=0}^{n} M^j \times (b^j - a^j)$. The constant M^ℓ is an average rate of energy consumption for each power state ℓ, which is given as a specification of the hardware components.

The PCA is a subclass of linear hybrid automata (LHA) [4] since the dynamics of the energy consumption variable E take the form $dE/dt = M$, and the inactivity timer G is a clock variable such that $dG/dt = 1$ [12]. However, the PCA is simpler than the LHA in that E is an observer and does not have any effect on the state-transition behavior, while G controls the timings of the state-transition. Therefore, the PCA can be regarded as a weighted timed automaton [5][6], in which the weight is a record of the accumulated consumed energy, $\sum_{j=0}^{n} E^j$, from the initial state to the nth state.

2.2 PCA : Formal Definitions

We present a formal definition of the PCA; these will be needed for the discussion that follows. A complete definition of PCA can be found in [14].

Syntax A power consumption automaton (PCA) $\mathcal{A}$ over a set of atomic propositions *Prop* is defined as a weighted timed automaton (WTA).

$$\langle\ Loc, X, W, \Sigma \cup \{\epsilon\}, Edg, Flow, Inv, Lab\ \rangle$$

1. *Loc* is a finite set of locations. Each location corresponds to a power state.
2. X is a finite set of clock variables and W is a finite set of weight variables. X and W are disjoint ($X \cap W = \emptyset$). For a clock variable clk ($\in X$), a constant $n(\in \mathcal{N})$, and an operator $\bowtie \in \{<, \leq, =, \geq, >\}$, constraints of the form $clk \bowtie n$ and $clk_1 - clk_2 \bowtie n$ constitute a set of clock constraints $Z(X)$.
3. Σ is an alphabet, a finite set of input symbols, and ϵ is an empty symbol.
4. *Edg* represents a set of transitions. It is a finite set $Loc \times Z(X) \times \Sigma \times 2^X \times Loc$. An element of *Edg*, (l_1, g, a, r, l_2), is written as $l_1 \xrightarrow{g,a,r} l_2$, where g is a guard condition in $Z(X)$, a is an input symbol ($\in \Sigma \cup \{\epsilon\}$), and r refers to a set of clock variables ($\in 2^X$) to reset.
5. *Flow* represents the dynamics to account for the change rate of weight variables. $Flow : Loc \rightarrow (\mathcal{R}_+^W \rightarrow \mathcal{R}_+^W)$ where $\mathcal{R}_+$ is non-negative real numbers and $\mathcal{R}_+^W$ is $W \rightarrow \mathcal{R}_+$.
6. *Inv* is a mapping to clock constraints. $Inv : Loc \rightarrow Z(X)$
7. *Lab* is a mapping to a set of atomic propositions. $Lab : Loc \rightarrow 2^{Prop}$

The valuations ($\nu \in \mathcal{R}_+^{X \cup W}$) are defined in a standard way for the reset, delay, and multiplication; $\nu[r](x) = 0$ if $x \in r$ and $\nu[r](x) = \nu(x)$ otherwise, $(\nu + d)(x) = \nu(x) + d$, and $(\nu \times e)(x) = \nu(x) \times e$.

Operational Semantics. The semantics of a PCA $\mathcal{A}$ is given by a labeled transition system (LTS), $\langle S, T \rangle$. The state set S consists of tuples, (l, v, w), made of a location (a power state) l, a clock valuation v, and a weight valuation w. The set of transitions T are regular transitions, $\xrightarrow{d;e}$, as defined below.

- Regular transition : $(l_1, v_1, w_1) \xrightarrow{d;e} (l_2, v_2, w_2)$
  A delayed transition $(l_1, v_1, w_1) \xrightarrow{d} (l_1, v, w_2)$ followed by an event-trigger discrete transition $(l_1, v, w_2) \xrightarrow{e} (l_2, v_2, w_2)$. The definition agrees with an informal interpretation that a PCA stays at a particular location for a period of time before making a discrete transition to a new one.

- Event-trigger discrete transition : $(l_1, v_1, w) \xrightarrow{e} (l_2, v_2, w)$

  The transition corresponds to an edge, $l_1 \xrightarrow{g,a,r} l_2$, defined in the PCA $\mathcal{A}$. It is a state-transition from a source location l_1 to a destination l_2 with its guard g, an input symbol a, and a set of reset clocks r. The guard is satisfied at l_1 ($v_1 \models g$). For a clock variable clk, $v_2(clk) = 0$ if $clk \in r$, and $v_2 = v_1$ otherwise.

- Delayed transition : $(l, v_1, w_1) \xrightarrow{d} (l, v_1 + d, w_2)$

$$d \in \mathcal{R}_+ \wedge (d > 0) \wedge w_1 = f(0) \wedge w_2 = f(d) \wedge$$
$$\forall t \in \,]0, d[\mid v + t \models Inv(l) \wedge df/dt = Flow(l)$$

The time is advanced by an amount of the delay d, and the clock and weight are updated. In the above, $f(t)$ is a continuous function differentiable in the open time interval $]0, d[$. For an energy consumption variable E, $Flow(\ell)(E) = dE/dt = M^{\ell}$ at location ℓ, and thus $w_2(E) = M^{\ell} \times d + w_1(E)$. For a clock variable G, $Flow(\ell)(G) = dG/dt = 1$, and thus $v_2(G) = v_1(G) + d$. The valuation $w(E)$ is equal to $\sum_{j=0}^{n} E^j$ for the transition sequence.

Finally, a set of time points $\tau^j \in \mathcal{R}_+$ forms a time progression sequence, where $\tau^0 = 0$ and $\tau^{j+1} = \tau^j + d$ for a delayed transition $\xrightarrow{d}$. For a state $\sigma^j \in S$ where $\sigma^j = (l_j, v_j, w_j)$, a timed point is introduced such that $\rho^j = (\sigma^j, \tau^j)$. Then, for a sequence of timed points $\rho = \rho^0 \rho^1 \cdots$, we have a set of timed sequences $L(\mathcal{A})$ generated by a PCA $\mathcal{A}$; this is written as $\rho \in L(\mathcal{A})$.

3 Energy Consumption Properties

3.1 Duration-Bounded Cost Constraints

When considered naively, the energy consumption analysis problem simply states that the total amount of energy consumed should be less than a specified maximum. Since the consumed energy is proportional to the period during which hardware components are used and this monotonically increases, the above property is eventually violated. Therefore, the checking properties must be limited to some particular period. This results in a problem with *duration-bounded cost constraints*, in which the cost refers to the amount of energy consumed. The problem is more general than the problem of duration-bounded reachability of timed automata [2]. We need further means to specify *durations* and *cost constraints* flexibly.

For the energy consumption problem, we use a PCA to represent the energy consumption behavior. The weight (E) changes at a different rate in each state ($dE/dt = M^{\ell}$). A property to check may have three aspects; (a) specifying the period in which the check is conducted, (b) selecting appropriate paths that satisfy the condition, and (c) using numerical constraints that describe the conditions on the consumed energy. For (b), further means are needed to specify the conditions that such paths must satisfy.

The numerical constraints (c) may be more flexible than just an inequality ($\sum_j E^j \leq Max$). We consider, for example, the following constraint, where t_1, t_2 refer to time points, and u_1, u_2 are the variables referring to the weights. Let B_1 and B_2 be constants. We have a constraint $\mathcal{C}^{B_1,B_2}(t_1, t_2; u_1, u_2)$.

$$\mathcal{C}^{B_1,B_2}(t_1, t_2; u_1, u_2) \stackrel{def}{=} (t_2 - t_1 \leq B_1) \wedge (u_2 - u_1 \leq B_2)$$

The period to consider is specified by the two time points t_1 and t_2. The weights u_1 and u_2 in the constraint expression are obtained at certain states in the interval. In most cases, t_1 and u_1 (t_2 and u_2) are taken from a same state. More will be discussed in Section 4.2.

In this paper, we will use an LTL formula to express the conditions (a) and (b). If we let P_S and P_T be the state propositions to be satisfied in the start and target states respectively, the interval, depicted as $P_S \rightsquigarrow P_T$, is specified by a formula $\Diamond(P_S \wedge \Diamond P_T)$. The condition of the aspect (b) can also be specified using LTL. It may be a temporal property that is related to P_S or P_T. For example, we can choose, from the set of the paths, only those going through a particular intermediate state P_M ($P_S \rightsquigarrow P_M \wedge P_M \rightsquigarrow P_T$).

3.2 fWLTL : Formal Definitions

This section introduces fWLTL [14], a variant of LTL with freeze quantifiers.

Syntax The syntax of fWLTL is shown below.

$\phi := C$	Cost Constraints
$\mid p$	Atomic Proposition $\in Prop$
$\mid \neg\phi$	Logical Negation
$\mid \phi_1 \wedge \phi_2$	Conjunction
$\mid \phi_1 \,\mathrm{U}\, \phi_2$	Until Operator
$\mid \text{Ⅎ}^m x\ .\ \phi^x$	Freeze Quantifier over clock (X) or weight (W) variables
$\mid \text{Ⅎ}^\tau x\ .\ \phi^x$	Freeze Quantifier over time points $\{\tau^j\}$

A variable $x \in Var$, where Var is a countable set of variables, appears free in a fWLTL formula ϕ^x. A closed formula ϕ does not have any free variables. Cost constraints constitute a set $Z(X \cup W)$, where X is a finite set of clock variables and W is a finite set of weight variables (energy consumption variables). Z denotes a set of linear constraints. Furthermore, standard abbreviations are used. For example, $\Diamond\phi \equiv true \,\mathrm{U}\, \phi$ is *Eventually*, and $\Box\phi \equiv \neg(\Diamond\neg\phi)$ is *Globally*.

Semantics. We adapt the pointwise semantics for fWLTL. We use some symbols in addition to ρ^j that was introduced in Section 2.2; $\rho^j = (l_j, v_j, w_j, \tau^j)$.

- an environment $\Gamma\ :\ Var \rightarrow \mathcal{R}_+$.
  $\Gamma[x := e]$ assigns x to a value e ($e \in \mathcal{R}_+$) in the environment Γ.
- a labeling function Lab : $Loc \rightarrow 2^{Prop}$ where Loc is a finite set of locations and $Prop$ is a finite set of atomic propositions.

The following satisfiability relations $\models$, which are defined inductively, show that $\langle\, \rho,\ \Gamma\, \rangle$ satisfies an fWLTL formula ϕ; $\langle\, \rho,\ \Gamma\, \rangle \models \phi$.

$\langle\, \rho^j,\ \Gamma\, \rangle \models C$	iff $\Gamma \models C$
$\langle\, \rho^j,\ \Gamma\, \rangle \models p$	iff $p \in Lab(l_j)$
$\langle\, \rho^j,\ \Gamma\, \rangle \models \neg\phi$	iff $\langle\, \rho^j,\ \Gamma\, \rangle \not\models \phi$
$\langle\, \rho^j,\ \Gamma\, \rangle \models \phi_1 \wedge \phi_2$	iff $\langle\, \rho^j,\ \Gamma\, \rangle \models \phi_1$ and $\langle\, \rho^j,\ \Gamma\, \rangle \models \phi_2$
$\langle\, \rho^j,\ \Gamma\, \rangle \models \phi_1 \,\mathrm{U}\, \phi_2$	iff $\langle\, \rho^k,\ \Gamma\, \rangle \models \phi_2$ for some $k \geq j$ and $\langle\, \rho^i,\ \Gamma\, \rangle \models \phi_1$ for all i ($j \leq i < k$)
$\langle\, \rho^j,\ \Gamma\, \rangle \models \text{Ⅎ}^m x\ .\ \phi^x$	iff $\langle\, \rho^j,\ \Gamma[x := (v_j \cup w_j)(m)]\, \rangle \models \phi^x$
$\langle\, \rho^j,\ \Gamma\, \rangle \models \text{Ⅎ}^\tau x\ .\ \phi^x$	iff $\langle\, \rho^j,\ \Gamma[x := \tau^j]\, \rangle \models \phi^x$

An Example. We consider a simple property for the example in Figure 1. In specified intervals, both the duration and consumed energy are less than a respective maximum value. The property to check is written as

$$\Diamond \rlap{/}\mathit{I}^{\tau} x.\ \rlap{/}\mathit{I}^{P} u.\ (\texttt{IdleListen} \wedge \\ \Diamond \rlap{/}\mathit{I}^{\tau} y.\ \rlap{/}\mathit{I}^{P} v.\ (\texttt{expire} \wedge ((y - x \leq 1000) \wedge (v - u \leq 50)))) ,$$

where x and y refer to the time points while u and v record the energy consumed up to the specified states; x and u are *frozen* at a state in which the proposition `IdleListen` is *true*, and y and v are obtained in the state of `expire`.

4 Model-Based Analysis of Energy Consumption

4.1 Model Checking Problem

The duration-bounded cost constraint problem is solved by logic model checking of fWLTL. Let $L(\mathcal{A})$ be a set of timed sequences generated by a given PCA $\mathcal{A}$. Given a closed fWLTL formula ϕ, the model checking problem $(\mathcal{A},\ \Gamma \models \phi)$ is defined to ensure $\langle \rho^0, \Gamma_0 \rangle \models \phi$ with an initial empty environment Γ_0 and for all the timed sequences $\rho \in L(\mathcal{A})$. Unfortunately, the model checking problem of fWLTL is undecidable in general (see Section 6). The complexities come from various sources; (a) there are no restriction in the formula on the position of the freeze quantifier, (b) there are expressive cost constraints, (c) an infinite state space is generated by continuous time. For a practical solution to the third issue, we will adapt a method of time-bounded LTL model-checking with the sampling abstraction in continuous time. The method was originally proposed by Real-Time Maude [16][17].

4.2 Restrictions

We impose several restrictions on the property to be checked.

Guard State Proposition. We restrict the location in the formula at which the freeze quantifiers appear. Let ϕ_S be an fWLTL formula that has at least one state proposition p^g ($\phi_S = p^g \wedge \phi^x$); $p^g \in Prop$ is called a *guard state proposition*. D of $\rlap{/}\mathit{I}^D$ refers to either τ for time points or m for weights. Furthermore, b^j is τ_j for $\rlap{/}\mathit{I}^{\tau}$, and b^j is $(v_j \cup w_j)(m)$ for $\rlap{/}\mathit{I}^{m}$.

$$\langle \rho^j,\ \Gamma[x := b^j] \rangle \models\ \rlap{/}\mathit{I}^D x.\phi_S \ \text{ iff } \ \langle \rho^j,\ \Gamma \rangle \models p^g \text{ and } \langle \rho^j,\ \Gamma[x := b^j] \rangle \models \phi^x$$

A freeze quantifier operates on states that satisfy the guard state proposition.

Monotonic Constraints. A constraint $\mathcal{C}$, a condition on the consumed energy, refers to both the time points and the weight variables. It is a linear inequality defined over non-negative Real numbers R^+. We further assume that $\mathcal{C}$ is monotonic in the sense discussed below.

First, we assume, for simplicity, that a constraint $\mathcal{C}$ is decomposed into a conjunct of constituent constraints, each of which refers to either the time or weight. If we let $\mathcal{C}(t_1, t_2; u_1, u_2)$ be a constraint depending on the time points t_1 and t_2 and the weight variables u_1 and u_2, $\mathcal{C}(t_1, t_2; u_1, u_2) = \mathcal{C}^{<1>}(t_1, t_2) \wedge \mathcal{C}^{<2>}(u_1, u_2)$. The constraint C^{B_1,B_2} in Section 3.1 becomes $C^{<1>}(t_1, t_2) \wedge C^{<2>}(u_1, u_2)$ where $C^{<1>}(t_1, t_2) = (t_2 - t_1 \leq B_1)$ and $C^{<2>}(u_1, u_2) = (u_2 - u_1 \leq B_2)$. We, hereafter, consider a form of $\mathcal{C}^{<1>}(t_1, t_2)$ with $t_1 \leq t_2$.

Second, when we fix t_1 to be a particular value, the constraint $\mathcal{C}^{<1>}(t_1, t_2)$ is dependent on t_2. In general, the weight as well as the time increases monotonically because the weight refers to the total energy consumed up to a certain point. The constraint may have a similar property of monotonically increase. Formally, if a constraint is monotonic, then there is some threshold $\bar{t}$ such that $\mathcal{C}^{<1>}(t_1, t)$ is satisfied for $\forall t$ with $t < \bar{t}$ and is violated for $\bar{t} \leq \forall t$. Similarly, when we fix t_2, there is a certain threshold $\bar{t}$ such that $\mathcal{C}^{<1>}(t, t_2)$ is violated for $\forall t < \bar{t}$ and is satisfied for $\bar{t} \leq \forall t$. The constraint $(t_2 - t_1 \leq B_1)$ in Section 3.1 has this property.

The discussion above is given for $\mathcal{C}^{<1>}(t_1, t_2)$, but the monotonicity property can be generalized to the constraint of the form $\mathcal{C}(t_1, t_2; u_1, u_2)$.

Property Patterns. Although fWLTL allows us to express intervals flexibly, we will consider two practically important classes of properties. Below, we will introduce *stylized* symbols for representing these properties. $F^{\langle\tau;P\rangle}$ (or $G^{\langle\tau;P\rangle}$) is a combination of an eventuality (or a globally) operator with two freeze quantifiers. $F_{\mathcal{C}}^{\langle\tau;P\rangle}$ is $F^{\langle\tau;P\rangle}$ parameterized with the cost constraint $\mathcal{C}$, within whose quantified scope the $\mathcal{C}$ is evaluated. Q_1 and Q_2 are atomic propositions.

- Reachability :

$$\begin{aligned}\phi^{ReA} &= F^{\langle\tau;P\rangle}(Q_1 \wedge F_{\mathcal{C}}^{\langle\tau;P\rangle} Q_2) \\ &= \Diamond \text{Я}^{\tau} x. \text{Я}^{P} u. (Q_1 \wedge \Diamond \text{Я}^{\tau} y. \text{Я}^{P} v. (Q_2 \wedge \mathcal{C}(x, y; u, v)))\end{aligned}$$

- Response :

$$\begin{aligned}\phi^{ReS} &= G^{\langle\tau;P\rangle}(Q_1 \Rightarrow F_{\mathcal{C}}^{\langle\tau;P\rangle} Q_2) \\ &= \Box \text{Я}^{\tau} x. \text{Я}^{P} u. (Q_1 \Rightarrow \Diamond \text{Я}^{\tau} y. \text{Я}^{P} v. (Q_2 \wedge \mathcal{C}(x, y; u, v)))\end{aligned}$$

The intended meanings are given by the corresponding fWLTL formulas as above. Precisely, the satisfiability of the formula ϕ^{ReA} can be given as below.

$$\begin{aligned}&\langle\, \rho^0,\ \Gamma_0 \,\rangle \models \phi^{ReA} \\ \text{iff}\ \ &\exists\, i,\ j \mid (0 \leq i \leq j) \text{ and } \langle\, \rho^i,\ \Gamma[x := \tau^i; u := (v_i \cup w_i)(P)] \,\rangle \models Q_1 \\ &\qquad\qquad\qquad\quad \text{ and } \langle\, \rho^j,\ \Gamma[y := \tau^j; v := (v_j \cup w_j)(P)] \,\rangle \models Q_2 \\ &\qquad\qquad\qquad\quad \text{ and } \langle\, \rho^j,\ \Gamma \,\rangle \models \mathcal{C}\end{aligned}$$

The satisfiability of ϕ^{ReS} is similarly defined.

We will introduce an over-approximation method for enabling an automated analysis. First, we assume that $\langle\ \rho^0,\ \Gamma_0\ \rangle \models \Diamond(Q_1 \wedge \Diamond Q_2)$ and an index j is the first occurrence such that $\langle\ \rho^j,\ \Gamma\ \rangle \models Q_2$. Let k be $min^{(j)}(\ i \mid \langle\ \rho^i,\ \Gamma\ \rangle \models Q_1$ and $(i \leq j)$). Because of the monotonicity, if $C(t_k, t_j)$ is satisfied, then $C(t_i, t_j)$ is satisfied for $\forall i$ with $k{\leq}i$. In other word, if $C(t_i, t_j)$ is violated, then $C(t_k, t_j)$ is violated. Therefore, checking $C(t_k, t_j)$, if generating a counterexample, does not miss any violation of the constraint. Namely, the check is an over-approximation method, and can be used for finding potential faults.

5 Analysis with Real-Time Maude

This section explains the translation to Real-Time Maude.

5.1 A Brief Overview of Real-Time Maude

Real-Time Maude [16][17] is an extension of Maude [9] for supporting the formal specification and analysis of real-time or hybrid systems.

Real-Time Theory. A Real-Time Maude timed module specifies a real-time theory $\mathcal{R}$, which is written as (Sig, Eq, IR, TR). (Sig, Eq) is a membership equational logic theory where Sig is a signature that constitutes sort and operator declarations. Eq is a set of confluent and terminating conditional equations. (Sig, Eq) specifies the state space of the system as an algebraic data type. IR is a set of labelled instantaneous rewrite rules and TR is a set of tick rewrite rules.

Instantaneous Rewrite Rules. Instantaneous rules (IR) are inherited from Maude, and rewrite terms in a concurrent manner without any delay, that is, instantaneously. An instantaneous rewrite rule specifies one-step discrete transition. The rules are applied modulo the equations Eq.

$r : T_1(A_1) \Longrightarrow T_2(A_2)$ **if** φ .

A term $T_1(A_1)$ on the lefthand side becomes a new term $T_2(A_2)$ if the side condition φ is satisfied.

Tick Rewrite Rules. Tick rules (TR) are introduced in Real-Time Maude to be responsible for passage of time. Since time is global and proceeds uniformly, tick rules manipulate the state of the entire system. Let T_1 be a term for such a system state. T_1 represents a snapshot of the system, which is a term of sort `System` pre-defined in Real-Time Maude. A tick rule is introduced for a term of `GlobalSystem`, which takes the form, $\{\ T_1\ \}$.

$\{\ \_\ \}$: `System` $\rightarrow$ `GlobalSystem`
l : $\{\ T_1\ \} \Longrightarrow \{\ T_2\ \}$ **in time** τ_l **if** φ

The rule states the amount of the time τ_l passes when rewriting T_1 to T_2. The formula φ may refer to a condition on the time variable τ_l, and such a tick rule advances the time nondeterministically if the time value τ_l satisfies φ. The amount of time, however, is not chosen exactly, but can be any value that satisfies the condition.

Sampling Abstraction Method. Real-Time Maude adapts *sampling abstractions* for time-nondeterministic systems in which the maximum time elapsed (mte) plays an important role. Each term T_1 is accompanied by two functions δ and *mte*. The function δ returns a new term T_2, which is a modification of T_1 after the passage of time τ_l. The function *mte* returns the maximum elapsed time, during which the term T_1 is assumed not to be changed.

δ : `System Time` $\rightarrow$ `System`
mte : `System` $\rightarrow$ `TimeInf`

A tick rule takes into account these two functions. A new term is calculated with δ, and the condition φ refers to *mte* ($\tau_l \leq mte(T)$).

$$1 : \{\ T\ \} \Longrightarrow \{\ \delta(T, \tau_l)\ \}\ \textbf{in time}\ \tau_l\ \textbf{if}\ \ \tau_l \leq mte(T)$$

The $mte(T)$ is the upper limit of the time advancement. The transition is fired at least once in the time interval specified by the function $mte(T)$. Usually, the system term T is decomposed into a set of constituent terms T^j. The function $mte(T^j)$ must be defined for each T^j. In order that all $mte(T^j)$ are satisfied, their minimum value (`min(` $mte(T^j)$ `)`) is chosen. Therefore, this control strategy may result in an over-sampling for some of the components T^j, but does not miss any sampling points.

5.2 Translation to Real-Time Maude

We first consider the translation of a given power consumption automaton, which is basically encoding the labeled transition system (Section 2.2). Second, we show how freeze quantifiers are removed to obtain LTL formulas so as to employ the LTL model-checker of Real-Time Maude. In the translation, we assume the restrictions of the over-approximation method discussed in Section 4.2.

System State. We first define a term $S(l, v, w, \tau)$ of sort `System` to represent a PCA state. It has four arguments since the behavior of PCA is represented with timed states of (l, v, w, τ). For simplicity, v and w refer to the values of a clock and weight respectively here although they are valuations in the formal definitions (Section 2.2).

State Transitions. We will show how we encode state transitions. An edge of a PCA, $l_1 \xrightarrow{\varphi, E_1, r} l_2$, is interpreted as an event-trigger discrete transition,

$(l_1, v_1, w) \xrightarrow{e} (l_2, v_2, w)$. This transition is translated into an instantaneous rule of Real-Time Maude. φ is a guard condition on the transition source. For simplicity, we do not consider the invariant $Inv(l_1)$ here since it is concerned with time passage and thus needs tick rules to be encoded in Real-Time Maude.

$$E_1 \; S(l_1, v_1, w, \tau) \Longrightarrow S(l_2, v_2, w, \tau) \;\; \textbf{if} \;\; \varphi(v_1)$$

where v_2 is equal to 0 if the clock is reset or is not changed (v_1) otherwise.

A delayed transition is encoded as a tick rule of Real-Time Maude. The time-dependent behavior needs two functions δ and *mte*. The value d is chosen in a non-deterministic manner so long as $d \leq mte(S(l, v, w, \tau))$ is satisfied.

$$\delta(S(l, v, w, \tau), \; d) = S(l, v + d, M^l \times d + w, \tau + d) \; .$$

When the amount of the time that has passed is d, the clock v becomes $v + d$ and the weight is updated to be $M^l \times d + w$ for a given constant M^l.

The function *mte* just returns infinity (`INF`) for a stable state l_s, in which the system awaits an input symbol to initiate a discrete transition. For such a state l_c having a guard condition on the clock, *mte* returns the amount of time the PCA will remain in the state l_c. X_c is assumed to be a given time-out constant representing the upper limit that the system remains in the state.

$$mte(S(l_s, v, w, \tau)) = \texttt{INF} \; .$$
$$mte(S(l_c, v, w, \tau)) = X_c \; \texttt{monus} \; v \; .$$

The `monus` is a built-in operator that returns the difference $(X_c - v)$; it returns 0 if the calculated value is negative.

Variable Bindings. The encoding of the binding environment Γ is straightforward. We introduce, as a subsort of `System`, a new sort *Bindings* that has pairs of Var and `Real` as its elements. The sort Var refers to quantified variables.

$$\Gamma : Var \; \texttt{Real} \; \rightarrow \; Bindings$$

Updating the environment requires appropriate rewriting rules because *freezing* a variable is synchronized with state transitions of a PCA. We denote such an *updating* rule as $\xrightarrow{\Gamma}$.

In the operational semantics of a PCA (Section 2.2), event-trigger discrete transitions and delayed transitions are interleaving. The updating transition must be fired after a delayed transition so that the newly changed time-dependent values are accessed. A sequence of transitions is expected to be $\xrightarrow{e1}; \xrightarrow{d1}; \xrightarrow{\Gamma 1}$. In Real-Time Maude, however, the updating rule is an instantaneous rule, and thus it is enabled and fired together with the discrete transitions of the PCA. Now, imagine we have two consecutive discrete transitions where $\xrightarrow{e1}$ is followed by $\xrightarrow{e2}$. We will merge the updating rule ($\xrightarrow{\Gamma 1}$) to $\xrightarrow{e2}$ and have an instantaneous rule $\xrightarrow{\Gamma 1, e2}$. Then, the execution order will be what we intend.

Let l be a location, let τ be a time point, and let $S(l, v, w, \tau)$ represent a PCA state. The discrete transition $\xrightarrow{e2}$ is represented as a single instantaneous rule if we ignore the Γ.

$$E_2\ S(l_1, v, w, \tau) \Longrightarrow S(l_2, v, w, \tau) \quad \textbf{if}\ \varphi_2\ .$$

We consider how we define $\xrightarrow{\Gamma 1, e2}$ where Γ is updated at l_1 ($\xrightarrow{\Gamma 1}$). Since the tick rules are defined so that they are fired after $\xrightarrow{e1}$, the time-dependent values are kept in the term for which $\xrightarrow{e2}$ is fired. The above instantaneous rule must be modified to include the updates in Γ. As a concrete example, we consider the case of $\mathcal{I}^D x.(p^g \wedge \phi^x)$ where D is either m or τ. The p^g is a guard state proposition and $fresh$ is a special value denoting the variable is undefined. In the first rule, b is either $(v \cup w)(m)$ or τ.

$$\begin{aligned}
E_2\ S(l_1, v, w, \tau)\ \Gamma[x := fresh] &\Longrightarrow S(l_2, v, w, \tau)\ \Gamma[x := b] \\
&\quad \textbf{if}\ \varphi_2 \wedge (p^g \in Lab(l_1)) \\
E_2\ S(l_1, v, w, \tau)\ \Gamma[x := b] &\Longrightarrow S(l_2, v, w, \tau)\ \Gamma[x := b] \\
&\quad \textbf{if}\ \varphi_2 \wedge ((p^g \notin Lab(l_1)) \vee (b \neq fresh))
\end{aligned}$$

In addition, as the Γ is an environment for frozen variables, it is not time dependent. We define two functions δ and mte such that $\delta(\Gamma, \tau) = \Gamma$ and $mte(\Gamma) =$`INF`.

Property Language. Formulas to check are put in negation normal form.

$$\phi\ :=\ C\ \mid p \mid \neg p \mid \phi_1 \wedge \phi_2\ \mid \phi_1 \vee \phi_2\ \mid \Diamond\phi \mid \Box\phi$$

The atomic propositions that the formula ϕ refers to must be defined as equational specifications for a built-in operator $\_\models\_$. `Prop` is a sort symbol predefined in Maude to represent atomic propositions. The system state in Real-Time Maude is a `GlobalSystem` term, and state propositions are defined with respect to it.

$\_\models\_$: `GlobalSystem Prop` $\to$ `Bool`
a : $\{\ T\ \} \models$ p $=$ true **if** φ .

The atomic propositions $p \in Prop$ and the cost constraints C are defined as such equations.

$$\begin{aligned}
\{\ S(l, v, w, \tau)\ \Gamma\ \} &\models p \ \ = true \quad \textbf{if}\ \ p \in Lab(l) \\
\{\ S(l, v, w, \tau)\ \Gamma\ \} &\models \neg p = true \quad \textbf{if}\ \ p \notin Lab(l) \\
\{\ S\ \Gamma[x := b]\ \} &\models C \ \ = true \quad \textbf{if}\ \ C[b/x]
\end{aligned}$$

Correctness of Translation. After the translation to Real-Time Maude, the formula to check does not have freeze quantifiers, but the Real-Time Maude rules have the updating rules merged with discrete transitions in addition to delay transitions. We must consider properties regarding to the correctness of the translation. The property 1 was originally introduced in [11]. We followed the proof method there.

Property 1 : An instantaneous rule to encode an updating rule does not have any effect on (a) the instantaneous rules used to encode the event-trigger discrete transitions, nor on (b) the tick rules corresponding to the delayed transitions.

Proof Outline :
(a) The rule does not have any additional effect on S of the instantaneous rules (Section 5.2).

(b) Two functions ensure that Γ does not have any effect on the tick rules ($\delta(\Gamma, \tau) = \Gamma$, $mte(\Gamma) =$ `INF`).

The next property is concerned with the formula to be checked. We will first consider the reachability case ϕ^{ReA}, $F^{\langle\tau;P\rangle}(Q_1 \wedge F_C^{\langle\tau;P\rangle} Q_2)$ (Section 4.2).

Property 2 : The LTL model checking by Real-Time Maude returns a counterexample $\Longleftrightarrow$ ϕ^{ReA} in Section 4.2 returns a counterexample.

Proof Outline:
(a) the case without the constraint : ϕ^{ReA} can express $\Diamond(Q_1 \wedge \Diamond Q_2)$ because it is obtained by inserting *true* in $F_C^{\langle\tau;P\rangle}$ as $F_{true}^{\langle\tau;P\rangle}$. In the Real-Time Maude translation, the propositions Q_1 and Q_2 are defined in term of equations for an operator symbol $\_\models\_$. Therefore, both can generate counterexamples for the formula $\Diamond(Q_1 \wedge \Diamond Q_2)$ if the property is violated.

(b) the case with the constraint : We consider the case in which $\Diamond(Q_1 \wedge \Diamond Q_2)$ is satisfied because of the case (a). A counterexample of ϕ^{ReA} consists of the indices j and k such that $\langle\, \rho^j,\ \Gamma\, \rangle \models Q_2$, k $= min^{(j)}(\ i \mid \langle\, \rho^i,\ \Gamma\, \rangle \models Q_1$ and $(i \leq j)$), and C is violated for the frozen values obtained at ρ^k and ρ^j. In the Real-Time Maude translation, Γ is updated only for such j and k because of the translation of $\stackrel{\Gamma 1,e2}{\longrightarrow}$. C is also shown violated against the values obtained from such j and k by the LTL model checker of Real-Time Maude. Therefore, both can generate counterexamples that consist of the same timed state sequences.

The proof for the response property ϕ^{ReS} is essentially the same as the method for the reachability because of the following.

$$\begin{aligned}
&\Box \text{Ⅎ}^{\tau} x.\text{Ⅎ}^{P} u.(Q_1 \Rightarrow \Diamond \text{Ⅎ}^{\tau} y.\text{Ⅎ}^{P} v.(Q_2 \wedge C(x, y; u, v))) \\
&= \Box \text{Ⅎ}^{\tau} x.\text{Ⅎ}^{P} u.(\neg Q_1 \vee Q_1 \wedge \Diamond \text{Ⅎ}^{\tau} y.\text{Ⅎ}^{P} v.(Q_2 \wedge C(x, y; u, v))) \\
&= \Box(\neg Q_1 \vee \underline{\text{Ⅎ}^{\tau} x.\text{Ⅎ}^{P} u.(Q_1 \wedge \Diamond \text{Ⅎ}^{\tau} y.\text{Ⅎ}^{P} v.(Q_2 \wedge C(x, y; u, v))))}
\end{aligned}$$

Since $\neg Q_1$ is independent of any constraints, we only consider the underlined part of the sub-formula, which is similar to the formula of the reachability case.

5.3 An Example

As an initial study of the proposed method, we conducted experiments to analyze the behavior of the example PCA in Figure 1. Below, we show the cases for an instance of the property $\mathcal{C}^{B_1,B_2}$ in Section 3.1.

$$\Diamond \mathcal{I}^{\tau} x.\ \mathcal{I}^{P} u.\ (\texttt{IdleListen} \wedge \Diamond \mathcal{I}^{\tau} y.\ \mathcal{I}^{P} v.\ (\texttt{expire} \wedge \mathcal{C}^{B_1,B_2}))$$

The example PCA is defined as a term of sort *Machine*, which is a subsort of `System`. It basically consists of the timed state ρ^j, namely (l_j, v_j, w_j, τ^j). For simplicity, the term *pca* has values for clock and weight instead of valuations.

$$pca : Loc\ \texttt{Time Bool Rat Time} \rightarrow Machine$$

The first argument (of sort *Loc*) refers to a location. The next two represent the inactivity timer; the `Time` component records the timer value and the `Bool` indicates whether the timer is enabled or not. The fourth (`Rat`) is the value of the weight that records the amount of energy consumed, and the last one (`Time`) refers to the time point τ^j.

We chose concrete values M^ℓ for each state, and an expiration time X_c of the inactivity timer. We also defined a hypothetical WiFi station as the environment of the PCA being analyzed. The check was initiated by an `mc` command under the maximal tick mode (`set tick max`).

$$\texttt{mc \{ env(..) pca(..)}\ \Gamma\texttt{(..) \}}$$
$$\models^{t}\ \Diamond(\texttt{IdleListen} \wedge \Diamond(\texttt{expire} \wedge \mathcal{C}^{B_1,B_2}))\ \textbf{in time} \leq Bound$$

The experiments were conducted using Maude 2.6 and Real-Time Maude 2.3 under MacO/S 10.9.5 on 1.3 GHz Intel Core i5. When the constraint was given parameter values such that $C^{1000,30000}$ with a search bound *Bound* of 1000, the model-check was successful[1].

```
rewrites: 7910808 in 9864ms cpu (9874ms real) (801927 rewrites/second)
Result Bool : true
```

We decreased *Bound* to 590, and the check failed because the target state, in which the proposition `expire` was *true*, was not within the scope of the search. The search bound around 600 is a threshold, larger than which the search can cover the state space of this example.

A counterexample was generated for the case of $C^{600,20500}$ even when *Bound* was chosen to be larger than the threshold. The numeral constraint is violated when the upper limit of the second parameter (B_2) is small (20500 for this example). However, the constraint $C^{600,21000}$ was satisfied, and this result showed that the energy consumption was less than the specified value of 21000 in the duration of 600 ticks.

[1] The output was edited for readability.

6 Related Work

The importance of eliminating energy bugs, or *ebugs*, is dicussed in [20]. They proposed to use state-transition systems [19] for modeling the asynchronicity of the energy consumption. The model, however, was presented informally without formal definitions. Some energy profilers are developed monitoring program executions at runtime to detect potential bugs. One of the key technical points is identifying fault locations of ebugs that occur asynchronously. Eprof [21] is an energy profiler to use state tracing techniques relying on the state-transition model. ADEL [22] uses a taint-tracking method to detect asynchronous energy leaks.

The problem of model-based analysis method for energy consumption in Android smartphones is identified in [12] to counter the disadvantages of the runtime profiler method. A model-based framework for a similar problem is studied in MoVES [7], which uses a stopwatch extension of UPPAAL [8] for modeling and analyzing embedded systems such as the schedulability and energy consumption. The energy consumption model, however, is that $P(t) = C \times t$ without considering the differences in power states. PCA in this paper is defined formally and its energy consumption model is more detailed than MoVES.

Below, we show work on the model checking problems relating to our case. PCA is a kind of LHA [4]. Originally, we defined PCA as an n-rated timed system (nRTS) [12]. We used a clock variable to hold accumulated amount of consumed energy, in which a clock variable changed its rate in each power state. Our previous work [13] showed a translation to Real-Time Maude [16][17] when we regarded a PCA as an nRTS.

We now define PCA as WTA [5][6] since the energy consumption is observable and does not affect the behavior. Weights in PCA [14] are, however, defined only on states, not on transition edges. Furthermore, we introduced linear temporal logic with freeze quantifiers (fWLTL) for expressing properties to check so that the problem was solved by using the model-checking method [14].

In view of the reachability analysis, which is a basis for automatic verification methods, both nRTS and stopwatch TA are undecidable while WTA is decidable as is the timed automaton (TA). For the TA, duration-bounded reachability is decidable [2]. Furthermore, optimal or minimum-cost reachability of the WTA is also decidable [5][6]. Our logic fWLTL can encode the duration-bounded reachability problem, but it does not have any evaluation function for optimization problems.

TPTL [3] is linear temporal logic (LTL) with freeze quantifiers. Its satisfiability relation is defined by timed words generated by the TA, and the freeze quantifier refers to a time point of the binding state (*now*). Our logic fWLTL is more expressive than TPTL, since it can *freeze* weight variables as well as time points. The syntax of freeze quantifier in fWLTL [14] is introduced to express both weight variables and time points in a uniform manner . A quantified formula in TPTL, $x.\phi^x$, is expressed as $Ⅎ^{\tau} x.\phi^x$ in fWLTL. Freeze quantifiers in constraint LTL (cLTL) [10] can refer to variables other than clocks. $\downarrow_{x=m}\phi^x$ in cLTL is expressed as $Ⅎ^{m} x.\phi^x$ in fWLTL.

Model checking of metric temporal logic (MTL) for timed words is undecidable in general. It is decidable only for discrete time and undecidable for a general case of continuous time (cf. [18]). Since MTL is a proper subset of TPTL, model checking of TPTL is also undecidable for continuous time. As for the model checking of cLTL, it is decidable only for bounded discrete time and equality constraints ($\pi_1 = \pi_2$) [10]. The cost constraints to express the energy consumption properties are more complex than equality constraints. From these existing studies, we see that model checking of the fWLTL formula is undecidable in general. Therefore, we introduced a sub-fragment of fWLTL and some approximation techniques. Specifically, this paper discussed how we translated a PCA as a WTA into Real-Time Maude [16][17]. Model checking MTL properties to use Real-Time Maude is studied in [11]. We borrowed from it the idea of restricting property patterns only in specific forms, ϕ^{ReA} and ϕ^{ReS} in our case, and followed the argument on the correctness of translation (Property 1) presented there.

7 Conclusion and Future Work

This paper employed fWLTL as a property specification language used in a model-based analysis of energy consumption. Two property patterns are translated to Real-Time Maude for enabling automatic analyses. Although it is an over-approximation method, the proposed approach is effective in detecting anomalies due to energy bugs. There are some open questions that include (a) extending the class of the property patterns, and (b) developing a symbolic model-checking algorithm such as those used in [2][5][6].

Acknowledgment. The research was partially supported by JSPS KAKENHI Grant Number 26330095.

References

1. Android, http://developer.android.com
2. Alur, R., Courcoubetis, C., Henzinger, T.A.: Computing Accumulated Delays in Real-Time System. In: Courcoubetis, C. (ed.) CAV 1993. LNCS, vol. 697, pp. 181–193. Springer, Heidelberg (1993)
3. Alur, R., Henzinger, T.A.: A Really Temporal Logic. J. Assoc. Comp. Machin. 41(1), 181–204 (1994)
4. Alur, R., Courcoubetis, C., Halbwachs, N., Henzinger, T.A., Ho, P.-H., Nicollin, X., Olivero, A., Sifakis, J., Yovine, S.: The Algorithmic Analysis of Hybrid Systems. Theor. Comp. Sci. (138), 3–24 (1995)
5. Alur, R., La Torre, S., Pappas, G.J.: Optimal Paths in Weighted Timed Automata. In: Di Benedetto, M.D., Sangiovanni-Vincentelli, A. (eds.) HSCC 2001. LNCS, vol. 2034, pp. 49–62. Springer, Heidelberg (2001)
6. Behrmann, G., Fehnker, A., Hune, T., Larsen, K., Pettersson, P., Romjin, J., Vaandrager, F.: Minimum-Cost Reachability for Priced Timed Automata. In: Di Benedetto, M.D., Sangiovanni-Vincentelli, A.L. (eds.) HSCC 2001. LNCS, vol. 2034, pp. 147–161. Springer, Heidelberg (2001)

7. Brekling, A., Hansen, M.R., Madsen, J.: MoVES – A Framework for Modeling and Verifying Embedded Systems. In: Proc. ICM 2009, pp. 149–152 (2009)
8. Cassez, F., Larsen, K.G.: The Impressive Power of Stopwatches. In: Palamidessi, C. (ed.) CONCUR 2000. LNCS, vol. 1877, pp. 138–152. Springer, Heidelberg (2000)
9. Clavel, M., Duran, F., Eker, S., Lincoln, P., Marti-Oliet, N., Meseguer, J., Talcott, C. (eds.): All About Maude - A High-Performance Logical Framework. LNCS, vol. 4350. Springer, Heidelberg (2007)
10. Demri, S., Lazic, R., Nowak, D.: On the Freeze Quantifier in Constraint LTL: Decidability and Complexity. Information and Computation 205(1), 2–24 (2007)
11. Lepri, D., Olveczky, P.C., Abraham, E.: Model Checking Classes of Metric LTL Properties of Object-Oriented Real-Time Maude Specification. In: Proc. RTRTS 2010, pp. 117–136 (2010)
12. Nakajima, S.: Model-based Power Consumption Analysis of Smartphone Applications. In: Proc. ACES-MB 2013 (2013)
13. Nakajima, S.: Everlasting Challenges with the OBJ Language Family. In: Iida, S., Meseguer, J., Ogata, K. (eds.) Futatsugi Festschrift 2014. LNCS, vol. 8373, pp. 478–493. Springer, Heidelberg (2014)
14. Nakajima, S.: Model Checking of Energy Consumption Behavior. In: Proc. 1st CSDM Asia, pp. 3–14 (2014)
15. Nakajima, S., Toyoshima, M.: Behavioral Contracts for Energy Consumption. Ada User Journal 35(4), 266–271 (2014)
16. Olveczky, P.C., Meseguer, J.: Semantics and Pragmatics of Real-Time Maude. Higher-Order and Symbolic Computation 20(1-2), 161–196 (2007)
17. Olveczky, P.C., Meseguer, J.: Abstraction and Completeness for Real-Time Maude. ENTCS 176(4), 5–27 (2007)
18. Ouaknine, J., Worrell, J.: Some Recent Results in Metric Temporal Logic. In: Cassez, F., Jard, C. (eds.) FORMATS 2008. LNCS, vol. 5215, pp. 1–13. Springer, Heidelberg (2008)
19. Pathak, A., Hu, Y.C., Zhang, M., Bahl, P., Wang, Y.-M.: Fine-Grained Power Modeling for Smartphones Using System Call Tracing. In: Proc. EuroSys 2011 (2011)
20. Pathak, A., Hu, Y.C., Zhang, M.: Bootstrapping Energy Debugging on Smartphones: A First Look at Energy Bugs in Mobile Devices. In: Proc. Hotnets 2011 (2011)
21. Pathak, A., Hu, Y.C., Zhang, M.: Where is the energy spent inside my app?: Fine Grained Energy Accounting on Smartphones with Eprof. In: Proc. EuroSys 2012 (2012)
22. Zhang, L., Gordon, M.S., Dick, R.P., Mao, Z.M., Dinda, P., Yang, L.: ADEL: An Automatic Detector of Energy Leaks for Smartphone Application. In: Proc. CODES+ISSS 2012, (2012)

Static Differential Program Analysis for Software-Defined Networks

Tim Nelson(✉), Andrew D. Ferguson, and Shriram Krishnamurthi

Brown University, Providence, USA
tn@cs.brown.edu

Abstract. Networks are increasingly controlled by software, and bad updates can bring down an entire network. Network operators therefore need tools to determine the impact of changes. To address this, we present *static differential analysis* of software-defined network (SDN) controller programs. Given two versions of a controller program our tool, Chimp, builds atop Alloy to produce a set of concrete scenarios where the programs differ in their behavior. Chimp thus enables network developers to exploit the power of formal methods tools without having to be trained in formal logic or property elicitation. Furthermore, we show that there are many interesting properties that one can state about the changes themselves. Our evaluation shows that Chimp is fast, returning scenarios in under a second on several real applications.

1 Introduction

Traditional networks run individually-configured, autonomous switches that are often closed, proprietary hardware. In a software-defined network (SDN) [7], switches defer control of their behavior—and by extension, of the network—to a logically centralized server (the "controller"), which may be anything from a single commodity machine to a distributed cluster. The controller executes programs that—by updating state, interacting with other programs, and sending instructions to switches—collectively implement the network's behavior, ranging from standard network operations to novel behaviors unseen in traditional networks. SDN has been adopted by companies such as VMware (for its virtual-network products [20]) and Google (for its backbone network [15]). Programs may be written in arbitrary languages; beyond traditional languages, this is leading to a resurgence of declarative languages—like Flog [16], NLog [20] from Nicira/VMware, and Flowlog [27]—which are the focus of this work.

In this paper, we target the *evolution* of controller software. Programs evolve for many reasons: due to a bug fix, feature update, refactoring, etc. Developers need robust techniques to manage evolution because mistakes can cause an entire network to malfunction. Techniques like testing and verification are, however, only as effective as the coverage provided by their inputs; they may require a knowledge of logic that operators may not have; and most of all, they *only check what was stated.* However, when we add a new feature, we do not write

N. Bjørner and F. de Boer (Eds.): FM 2015, LNCS 9109, pp. 395–413, 2015.
DOI: 10.1007/978-3-319-19249-9_25

extensive properties or tests about parts of the system that are *unrelated*. Therefore, developers need techniques that have the ability to (perhaps unpleasantly) surprise.

We therefore present *differential analysis* for SDN controller programs, which presents the *semantic* or *behavioral* difference between two versions of a program. The core analysis only needs two versions; it does not require tests or logical properties. The output of our tool, Chimp (short for "*Ch*ange *imp*act"), is in terms of *scenarios*: concrete situations where the two programs differ. The overall goal of differential analysis is to help developers *transfer trust between versions*; if they had faith in the proper execution of an old version, the semantic differences help them focus on the only things they need to examine to extend that faith to the new version. (We contrast other forms of differential analysis in Sec. 8.)

Chimp also enables users to query differences and even verify properties of those differences. This enables many more use-cases. For instance, when a program is merely being refactored or otherwise cleaned up, there should be no behavioral change; a Chimp user can check such *differential properties*, and any counter-examples would need attention. Chimp can even contrast multiple ways of extending a program, i.e., compute the difference of differences.

This paper makes the following contributions:

1. it identifies the problem of static differential program analysis for SDNs (Sec. 2 and 3);
2. it discusses and overcomes potential challenges and pitfalls in this analysis (Sec. 2 and 5);
3. it demonstrates that this analysis can be done effectively (Sec. 6 and 7); and
4. it shows how traditional properties and differential analysis meet at *differential properties* (Sec. 2 and 4).

In short, Chimp represents a fruitful application of various formal methods to a novel and important domain.

2 Differential Analysis at Work

The work in this paper targets the class of declarative languages used to program SDNs. We focus on Flowlog [27], which is richer in expressiveness than most of the others, so that our work is most widely applicable. Beyond the details of tooling, we believe the core ideas of Chimp apply equally well to other languages (which we discuss in Sec. 8).

In an SDN, many traditional network operations are implemented entirely in software. We illustrate this with a well known networking example: Network-Address Translation (NAT), which is used widely (e.g., to multiplex multiple home machines over a shared router). Figure 1 shows two different implementations of NAT in Flowlog—an initial version without the underlined code, and a second version with it. For simplicity, this example involves a home router with only two ports (1=inside, 2=outside). The external interface uses the hardware, or MAC, address `00:00:00:00:00:FF` and is assigned the IP address `192.168.100.100`. The core ideas in this example are the same for larger devices.

```
1  TABLE nat(macaddr,ipaddr,tpport,tpport);
2  VAR nextport: tpport = 10000;
3
4  ON tcp_packet(p) WHERE p.locPt = 1 AND
5       nat(p.dlSrc,p.nwSrc,p.tpSrc,natport):
6    DO forward(new) WHERE
7       new.tpSrc = natport AND
8       new.nwSrc = 192.168.100.100 AND
9       new.locPt = 2 AND
10      new.dlSrc = 00:00:00:00:00:FF;
11
12 ON tcp_packet(p) WHERE p.locPt = 1 AND
13      NOT nat(p.dlSrc,p.nwSrc,p.tpSrc,ANY):
14   INSERT (p.dlSrc,p.nwSrc,p.tpSrc,nextport) INTO nat;
15   DO forward(new) WHERE
16      new.nwSrc = 192.168.100.100 AND
17      new.locPt = 2 AND
18      new.tpSrc = nextport AND
19      new.dlSrc = 00:00:00:00:00:FF;
20   INCREMENT nextport;
```

Packets arrive at a port (`locPt`) on a switch (`locSw`). Their headers contain a source (`dlSrc`) and destination (`dlDst`) hardware (or MAC) address. Transport Control Protocol (TCP) packets also have a source (`nwSrc`) and destination (`nwDst`) network address and a source (`tpSrc`) and destination (`tpDst`) service port.

Fig. 1. Network-address translation (NAT) in Flowlog. An initial version did not include the underlined portions, and so failed to translate MAC addresses as well as IP addresses.

Lines 1 and 2 define the controller's state schema. A database table, `nat`, stores the current NAT mappings; its first columns identify packets by source, and its final column gives an ephemeral TCP port to use in the translation. The original version identifies packets by IP address and initial TCP port; the modified version also uses MAC address. A variable (`nextport`) holds the next available TCP port for NAT to use, starting at 10000. Lines 4–10 handle outgoing packets for which a translation already exists, and lines 12–20 process outgoing packets that start new ones. We elide the code to handle return traffic, which only adds an additional 5 or 6 lines.

Each Flowlog program rule can be thought of as a database view over the program's current state and the incoming event. As in SQL or Datalog, Flowlog rule bodies constrain that view, dictating which actions the program can take. Lines 4–5 say that the forwarding action on lines 6–10 applies only for TCP packets arriving at port 1 (the internal port), where there is a matching row in the current `nat` table. It also binds the value in the final column of that row to the variable `natport`, which is used later. Lines 6–10 say to forward matching packets, but to first modify their IP source to `192.168.100.100` (the assigned IP address) and their TCP source to the value in `natport` (obtained from the `nat` table). In the modified version, the rule also sets the MAC source to `00:00:00:00:00:FF`. Lines 12–21 work similarly, but since there is no corresponding row in the `nat` table, they use the next available free port. They then insert the appropriate new row into the table and increment the `nextport` variable.

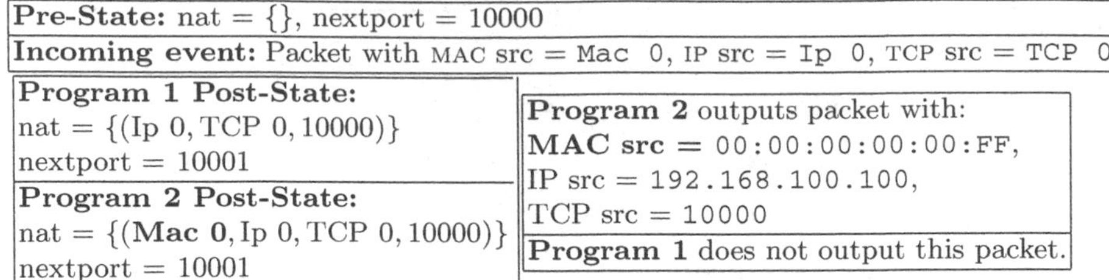
Pre-State: nat = {}, nextport = 10000
Incoming event: Packet with MAC src = Mac 0, IP src = Ip 0, TCP src = TCP 0
Program 1 Post-State:
nat = {(Ip 0, TCP 0, 10000)}
nextport = 10001
Program 2 Post-State:
nat = {(Mac 0, Ip 0, TCP 0, 10000)}
nextport = 10001
Program 2 outputs packet with:
MAC src = 00:00:00:00:00:FF,
IP src = 192.168.100.100,
TCP src = 10000
Program 1 does not output this packet.

Fig. 2. Scenarios returned by Chimp for the NAT change. In this case, both share the same pre-state and arrival event. The scenario on the left shows a *state-transition* difference caused by the new program storing the MAC source address. The scenario on the right shows that in the revised program, the packet's MAC address is modified. `Mac 0` denotes an arbitrary MAC address (and similarly for other fields).

While the original only modifies a packet's IP and TCP fields, the second version (with underlines) also changes MAC sources to reflect that the modified packet comes from the outgoing interface—standard behavior for a NAT. In order to modify addresses consistently, the new program adds a column to the `nat` table that holds the source MAC address of each NAT flow. We will now use Chimp to analyze the semantic consequences of this edit.

If we view a Flowlog program as a function that processes events, a change may have two types of semantic impact: given the same input, either the programs produce different output (e.g., forward packets differently) or they transition to different states. Chimp defines a built-in analysis for each of these: (1) `chPolOut` ("change policy output") which generates scenarios that show any differing output behavior, and (2) `chStTrans` ("change state transitions"), which shows the differences in how the two programs evolve their state. Users may select from these (and other built-in analyses, which we discuss later) or construct their own using these as a starting point.

Chimp's output provides concrete *scenarios* that show how programs can express the behavior described. When seeking semantic differences via `chPolOut` or `chStTrans`, each scenario contains a *prestate* that shows the state of the two programs before they diverge, and a *trigger event* for the divergence. Scenarios for other analyses may contain different information as requested by the user.

Figure 2 shows output scenarios for both `chPolOut` and `chStTrans` on the NAT program edit. Both show a packet arriving at the internal interface; the scenario on the left shows a state-transition difference and the scenario on the right shows a behavioral difference. The `nat` tables in these scenarios are empty because their value is immaterial for this specific behavior, and Chimp is designed to only produce *minimal* scenarios, which greatly improves the quality and brevity of output (Sec. 7).

Schema Combination. Every Flowlog program has a *schema*: a set of **TABLE** declarations, each of which includes a list of data-types that define that table's columns. A *schema clash* occurs whenever two programs declare different arities, types, or column orderings for the same table. The happens between the NAT programs (Figure 1, line 1), as the modified program adds a column to the `nat` table. This clash must be resolved in order for Chimp to have a consistent notion of "pre-state" for its analysis. To do so, Chimp creates a new version of the conflicted table for each clashing program. For the NAT example, it creates a separate three-column `nat1` table and four-column `nat2` table. Chimp then rewrites the original program to refer only to `nat1` and the modified version to `nat2`. This presents a new challenge: output scenarios will now contain both tables, and Chimp's search for scenarios will treat the two new tables independently. Since it searches all possibilities, Chimp will consider cases where (e.g.) the `nat1` table is empty but the `nat2` table is not. Scenarios where the two programs' states bear no relationship to one another may seem spurious—since the two tables were originally one, their contents should be somehow related.

Lockstep Constraints. The programmer might assert that, since the new `nat` table is just an extension of the first, the two tables should be identical in the final three columns. Formally, they would like to restrict Chimp's search to scenarios where it holds that: "Every row in `nat2` (minus its first column) is also in `nat1`; every row in `nat1` is also in `nat2` (with some MAC address in the first column)" or, in logical form:

$$\forall i, p_1, p_2\ (\exists m\ nat_2(m, i, p_1, p_2)) \iff nat_1(i, p_1, p_2)$$

We call this a *lockstep constraint* because it expresses how two programs evolve their states together. It represents an intuition about the intent of the table change. Constraints like this may be added to an analysis, analogously to adding new conditions to a SQL statement. This process lends itself to iteration, with refinements growing ever more focused as the user zeroes in on surprising behavior.

Differential Properties. Before we assert the lockstep constraint—and prevent Chimp from returning scenarios that violate it—we would like to validate the intuition it represents. To that end, we can phrase the lockstep constraint as a *differential property*, i.e., a property that spans the behavior of multiple programs, and check it in Chimp. When checking a lockstep constraint in this way, we refer to it as a lockstep property. We proceed inductively. To verify the base case, we check that the property always holds in the (empty) initial program state. The bi-implication in the above property makes this trivially true. It then suffices to check whether the programs can ever violate the property as their states evolve. To do so, we phrase the property as a custom analysis predicate (Sec. 4) and ask Chimp for counterexamples.

Perhaps surprisingly, Chimp produces a counterexample (Figure 3). This scenario shows a pre-state that respects the property (one row in each table), but a post-state that does not: a second entry, using a fresh external port, has been added to `nat2` but not to `nat1`. This means that either the revised program is wrong, or the property itself is incorrect (reflecting faulty intuition).

<table>
<tr><td colspan="5">Pre-State:</td></tr>
<tr><td>nat1 =</td><td><code>Ipaddr 0</code></td><td><code>Tpport 0</code></td><td><code>Tpport 2</code></td><td></td></tr>
<tr><td>nat2 =</td><td><code>Macaddr 0</code></td><td><code>Ipaddr 0</code></td><td><code>Tpport 0</code></td><td><code>Tpport 2</code></td></tr>
<tr><td colspan="5">Incoming event: TCP packet from:
MAC = <code>Macaddr 1</code>, IP = <code>Ipaddr 0</code>, TCP Port = <code>Tpport 0</code></td></tr>
<tr><td colspan="5">Program 1 Post-State: no change</td></tr>
<tr><td colspan="5">Program 2 Post-State:</td></tr>
<tr><td rowspan="2">nat2 =</td><td><code>Macaddr 0</code></td><td><code>Ipaddr 0</code></td><td><code>Tpport 0</code></td><td><code>Tpport 2</code></td></tr>
<tr><td><code>Macaddr 1</code></td><td><code>Ipaddr 0</code></td><td><code>Tpport 0</code></td><td><code>Tpport 0</code></td></tr>
</table>

Fig. 3. Failure of the first NAT lockstep property. Abstract values `Macaddr 0`, `Tpport 0`, ... denote disjoint arbitrary addresses, ports, etc.

The revised program correctly creates a new entry for packets with a new MAC source, even if its IP source is already in the table. This is to be expected: since the MAC sources are distinct, the packets involve separate physical machines and must be handled separately. Thus, seeing this scenario corrects the programmer's intuition and informs them that the new program has actually fixed a potential bug that they had not considered. Some reflection also leads to a more accurate constraint relating the two tables: "Every row in `nat1` is also in `nat2` (with some MAC address in the first column); for every row in `nat2` there is a row in `nat1` with the same source address and port,", or:

$$\forall i, p_1, p_2, m \; (nat_1(i, p_1, p_2) \implies \exists m' \; nat_2(m', i, p_1, p_2)) \\ \wedge (nat_2(m, i, p_1, p_2) \implies \exists p' \; nat_1(i, p_1, p'))$$

Chimp finds no counterexample to this new constraint, increasing confidence that it is correct. We now assert it in Chimp, forcing the two tables to be tightly coupled in each output scenario. As seen here, "obvious" intuitions about schema changes can be subtly wrong. Instead of assuming a standard lockstep constraint, or adding one automatically, Chimp lets users test their intuitions via analysis and then assert them explicitly. Errors revealed lead to *missing correctness properties* which can then be added to existing test- and property-suites.

3 Theory

Every Flowlog rule (an **ON** condition followed by a single action) is equivalent to a formula of first-order logic that defines the rule's meaning and enables formal reasoning. Figure 4 describes this translation in detail for rules, formulas, and terms; the translation for all rules produces the first-order theory of a Flowlog program. Flowlog's syntax is inspired by non-recursive Datalog with negation, and its logical semantics follows. Variables not explicitly quantified are interpreted universally, as in Datalog. The only exception is that the wildcard term

$$[\![\texttt{ON in}(i)\texttt{: DO out}(o)\ \texttt{WHERE}\ F]\!] = out(o) \leftarrow in(i) \wedge [\![\mathrm{F}]\!]$$
$$[\![\texttt{ON in}(i)\texttt{: INSERT}\ (o_1,...,o_k)\ \texttt{INTO R WHERE}\ F]\!] = plus_R(o_1,...o_k) \leftarrow in(i) \wedge [\![\mathrm{F}]\!])$$
$$[\![\texttt{ON in}(i)\texttt{: DELETE}\ (o_1,...,o_k)\ \texttt{FROM R WHERE}\ F]\!] = minus_R(o_1,...o_k) \leftarrow in(i) \wedge [\![\mathrm{F}]\!])$$

$$[\![\texttt{NOT f}]\!] = \neg[\![\texttt{f}]\!]$$
$$[\![\texttt{f1 AND f2}]\!] = [\![\texttt{f1}]\!] \wedge [\![\texttt{f2}]\!]$$
$$[\![\texttt{t1 = t2}]\!] = [\![\texttt{t1}]\!] = [\![\texttt{t2}]\!]$$
$$[\![\texttt{R(t1, ..., tk)}]\!] = \exists any_1, ..., any_m\ R([\![\texttt{t1}]\!], ..., [\![\texttt{tk}]\!])$$
each any_i has fresh index for every occurrence of ANY.

$$[\![\texttt{c}]\!] = c \text{ (for a constant } c)$$
$$[\![\texttt{x}]\!] = x \text{ (for a variable } v)$$
$$[\![\texttt{x.fld}]\!] = fld(x) \text{ (for a variable } x \text{ and packet field name } fld)$$
$$[\![\texttt{ANY}]\!] = any_f \text{ (where } f \text{ is a fresh index)}$$

Fig. 4. Translation of Flowlog (rules, formulas, and terms) to FOL

ANY binds tighter than other terms; the formula NOT R(ANY) means $\neg\exists\ aR(a)$ (i.e, that the relation is empty). The translation inserts quantifiers to support this. Flowlog desugars rules with OR into multiple rules in the obvious way. The **INCREMENT** keyword is syntactic sugar for relational expressions plus **INSERT** and **DELETE** rules.

For each state relation symbol R, helper relations $plus_R$ and $minus_R$ (Figure 4) describe how that relation changes for each event received. If R is the relation before an event arrives, then the new value of the relation will be:

$$(R \setminus minus_R) \cup plus_R$$

(That is, **INSERT** overrides **DELETE**.)

Flowlog disallows rule bodies that reference intensional relations (those defined by the program, e.g., `forward`, rather than stored in the program's state, e.g., `nat`). Also, rules must be *safe*: all variables (and output packet fields, in the case of a **DO** rule) in a rule's head and variables in negated body literals must appear in a non-negated literal in that rule's body.

Property-Checking. The theory of a Flowlog program, Γ, is given by taking the union of the result of Figure 4 for each rule. It contains an implication for each rule, where each rule body dictates a class of input events and program states and each head gives a corresponding program behavior. For analysis, we take the theory's *Clark completion* [1, p. 407], Γ_c, which essentially adds reverse implications that define the ways each action could be caused.

Since Γ_c defines both the consequences of arriving events and the possible triggers for a given behavior, a first-order property ϕ holds if and only if $\Gamma_c \cup \{\neg\phi\}$ is unsatisfiable. For example, the program in Figure 1 always translates TCP packets' IP source to `192.168.100.100` only if the following formula is *unsatisfiable* in conjunction with the completion of the program's theory:

$$\exists p, p'\ .\ forward(p') \wedge tcp\_packet(p) \wedge nwsrc(p') \neq 192.168.100.100$$

Models that satisfy the conjunction are counterexamples to the property.

Differential Properties. ϕ may also involve more than one program; it can express *differential* properties over multiple programs' collective behavior. The 2-program `chPolOut` analysis of Sec. 2, for example, corresponds to:

$$\exists p, p' . tcp\_packet(p) \wedge (forward_1(p') \wedge \neg forward_2(p') \vee \\ forward_2(p') \wedge \neg forward_1(p'))$$

where each $forward_i$ represents the $forward$ relation of the ith program. Chimp automatically performs this renaming for all output and state-modification relations, and we will use the notation freely when it is clear from context.

4 Flowlog to Alloy

Flowlog's runtime automatically updates the network's switches as needed; the language abstracts out the specifics of those updates and associated optimizations. Because of this *tierless* abstraction, Flowlog's first-order logic semantics can be used directly to reason about program behavior. Since Alloy supports predicate logic, producing an Alloy specification for a Flowlog program essentially involves following Figure 4. Chimp also defines several built-in analysis predicates.

Single-Program Predicates. For every action that a program can take, Chimp creates an Alloy predicate representing when that action occurs. For instance, the packet-forwarding action for each program produces a predicate with signature[1]:

```
pred forward[st: State, e: EVpacket, out: EVpacket]
```

A `State` atom represents a database over the program's schema. Events (types starting with `EV`) are generalizations of packets that also include external events or notifications from other modules. Predicates are true or false on any given input. The `forward` predicate holds on inputs consisting of a `State st`, an input `Event e`, and an output `Event out` if and only if the original program would forward `e` with the modifications expressed in `out`. Figure 5 lists other predicates that Chimp creates for each program. The higher-level predicate `outpolicy` holds any time the program will respond to event `ev` by emitting `ev2` when in state `st`, and `transition` expresses when a state-transition is taken on an event.

Cross-Program Predicates. Chimp also constructs basic cross-program differential analysis predicates (Figure 5) for each pair of programs given. To detect a difference in two programs' output (`chPolOut`), Chimp looks for an output (`outev`) that is produced by one program but not another:

[1] We have removed some machine-generated typing information and other Alloy-language foibles for brevity. Each Flowlog program produces a separate Alloy module.

Predicate	Arguments	True if the program in state s:
plus_R	$s : State, e : Event, t_0, ..., t_k$	adds $t_0, ..., t_k$ to R when receiving e
minus_R	$s : State, e : Event, t_0, ..., t_k$	removes $t_0, ..., t_k$ from R when receiving e
<action>	$s : State, e_1 : Event, e_2 : Event$	outputs e_2 (of type <action>) on e_1
outpolicy	$s : State, e_1, e_2 : Event$	outputs e_2 on receiving e_1
transition	$s : State, e : Event, s_2 : State$	transitions to s_2 on event e

Predicate	Arguments	True if the programs:
chPolOut	$s : State, e : Event$	have different output on event e in state s
chStTrans	$s : State, e : Event$	diverge in state on event e in state s
rchChPolOut	$s, s2 : State, e : Event$	chPolOut with reachability check for s
rchChStTrans	$s, s2 : State, e : Event$	chStTrans with reachability check for s

Fig. 5. Built-in predicates for each program and differential-analysis. <action> and R denote arbitrary output actions and table names.

```
pred chPolOut_1_2[st: State, ev: Event] {
  some out: Event |
   prog1/outpolicy[st,ev,out] && not prog2/outpolicy[st,ev,out] ||
   prog2/outpolicy[st,ev,out] && not prog1/outpolicy[st,ev,out] }
```

The names prog1 and prog2 denote the two programs; each has its own outpolicy. Since outpolicy is used, rather than any specific output action, this predicate is more general than the example formula in Sec. 3. chStTrans is defined similarly, checking for a mismatch in plus_R or minus_R behavior.

Custom Predicates. Users may create their own analyses in the Alloy language, usually by building atop Chimp's built-in predicates. For instance, the first differential property from Sec. 2 can be expressed as:

```
pred lockstep_nat_condition[st1, st2: State] {
  all x1, x2, x3 : univ |
    (some x4 : univ | x4 -> x1 -> x2 -> x3 in st2.nat_2) iff
    (x1 -> x2 -> x3 in st1.nat_1) }

assert lockstep_nat_assert {
  all st, st1', st2': State, ev: Event |
    (lockstep_nat_condition[st, st] and
     prog1/transition[st,ev,st1'] and prog2/transition[st,ev,st2'])
    implies
      lockstep_nat_condition[st1', st2'] }
```

using the transition predicate from Figure 5. The lockstep_nat_condition predicate identifies pairs of "safe" states that satisfy the condition. The assertion seeks a scenario where the programs transition from a "safe" to an "unsafe" state. A single pre-state suffices since the two programs' nat tables are held separately.

5 Soundness and Completeness

As is standard for such tools (including Alloy), Chimp performs *bounded* scenario finding. Along with an analysis predicate, users provide bounds for each datatype, e.g. up to 6 switches, 4 IP addresses, and so on. The search is guaranteed to be *sound* (with a caveat below); it never returns a false positive. Given its boundedness, one might reasonably inquire whether it can issue false negatives.

Every rule body is in the $\exists^*\forall^*$ fragment of first-order logic, which is well-known [5,33] to admit bounded satisfiability-checking. Positive instantiations of those bodies, as in the definition of `chPolOut`, are also in that fragment. However, negative instantiations (also used in `chPolOut` and others) are not.

A *cyclic* Flowlog program is one in which some ANY term appears together with a rule-body variable in a negated body atom. For instance, a program containing the body atom `NOT R(x, ANY)`, where `x` does not appear in the rule head, is cyclic. If a program is *acyclic*, elementary rewrites can break all $\forall\exists$ nesting in negated rule bodies. Thus, `chPolOut` and `chStTrans` over acyclic programs admit automatically-generated sufficient bounds. Acyclic Flowlog is expressive; every program in Sec. 7 is acyclic.

For cyclic programs, since both Flowlog and Alloy have a notion of types (in contrast to standard untyped first-order logic), it is possible [30] to strengthen the $\exists^*\forall^*$ condition to safely bound analysis involving limited $\forall\exists$ quantification. Chimp makes use of this information to produce bounds, and `chPolOut` and `chStTrans` are therefore complete even on many cyclic programs. Custom queries can of course introduce additional quantification that renders Chimp incomplete—e.g., as in the lockstep property of Sec. 2.

Thus, while Chimp is incomplete in general, many useful analyses have a bound under which Chimp is guaranteed to find any counterexamples; Chimp computes this bound automatically. Unlike prior work [30] on completeness in Alloy, which naively counts all well-typed ground terms, Chimp takes advantage of implicit disjunction in the analysis formulas. For instance, when seeking localized differences, there is no need to consider quantification in both `forward` and `plus_R` rules simultaneously. This produces tighter bounds that are sufficient to detect *any single semantic difference*, benefiting both performance and scenario brevity.

Where sufficient bounds cannot be established automatically, users provide bounds manually. As in Alloy, domain knowledge often eases this process. As Jackson [14] notes, even the most insidious bugs often occur on small example runs. Incomplete differential analyses can thus be viewed as a form of automated bug-finding that increases confidence in the program.

Soundness of Addition. The original Flowlog-to-Alloy translator [27] did not support Flowlog's `add` primitive. While Alloy has a notion of integers, they are bounded by a user-provided bitwidth—a fact that made using Alloy integers impractical. Instead, Chimp represents addition via a ternary relation. By default, this under-approximates true addition, sacrificing a measure of soundness for tractability. In practice, we insert additional axioms for arithmetic as needed.

Pre-State Reachability. By default, Chimp does not guarantee that prestates of scenarios it returns are reachable in real program runs. This does not render Chimp "unsound": such scenarios still witness a program state and input on which the two programs differ, and even an unreachable semantic difference can yield new insight into the programs. Nevertheless, it can be valuable to ignore unreachable scenarios and see a concrete execution trace that shows how the scenario can be reached. For these reasons, Chimp can enhance its search with full system traces. The reachability-aware analyses `rchChPolOut` ("reachable chPolOut") and `rchChStTrans` ("reachable chStTrans") behave much like their counterparts, but the scenarios they produce are augmented with separate system traces for each program. Separate traces are necessary since, if the programs' states eventually diverge, a single trace would be unable to capture behavioral differences that happen *after* divergence. Users may expect the state difference but not any subsequent deltas; a single trace could therefore conceal surprising differences. To use reachability-aware analyses, users must provide a maximum trace length to check up to. As (e.g.) a pre-state that requires 3 steps to reach will not be detected if the user-provided bound is 2 steps, reachability-awareness can cause a loss of completeness. It also negatively impacts performance, since longer traces mean a larger space of possible scenarios to search. It is up to the user to decide whether to make this tradeoff—losing completeness and performance in exchange for scenario provenance and reachability guarantees.

6 Scenario Minimization

Scenarios require user effort to understand, and needless detail increases the time taken to comprehend them as well as reducing the generality of each individual scenario. Because of this this, Chimp provably presents only minimal scenarios. Formally, let Γ be the first-order theory of a Flowlog program plus additional first-order constraints, such as the negation of properties (Sec. 3). Define the set of scenarios that satisfies Γ as $scns(\Gamma) = \{\mathbb{S} \mid \mathbb{S} \models \Gamma\}$ and the relation $\subseteq$ on scenarios to denote containment of relational facts, that is: $\mathbb{S}_1 \subseteq \mathbb{S}_2$ if and only if all facts $R(a_1, ..., a_n)$ true in $\mathbb{S}_1$ are also true in $\mathbb{S}_2$. Now the set of $\subseteq$-*minimal* scenarios for Γ is $mins(\Gamma) = \{\mathbb{S} \in scns(\Gamma) \mid \forall \mathbb{S}' \in scns(\Gamma) \,.\, \mathbb{S}' \subseteq \mathbb{S} \implies \mathbb{S} = \mathbb{S}'\}$.

In other words, minimal scenarios contain only the facts they need to satisfy the theory. For instance, removing any row in Figure 3 would either make the scenario inconsistent (i.e., not reflective of valid system behavior) or no longer satisfy the analysis predicate. Minimality also forces the use of abstract variables whenever possible. Chimp will not give a packet field or table cell a concrete value unless the scenario is contingent on that value. Otherwise, it will use an abstract value (e.g., `Macaddr 0` in Figure 3); this is key in reducing the number of scenarios given and improving the usefulness of each. To implement minimization, Chimp leverages Aluminum [28], a modified version of Alloy that iteratively removes unnecessary facts before presenting scenarios. As we will see, minimization can result in a drastic decrease in scenario size.

7 Evaluation

Our experiments include differential analyses across several programs: the NAT application from Sec. 2 (NAT); a learning-switch implementation (MAC); an address-resolution protocol (ARP) cache; a round-robin load-balancer (LB); a network-information base (NIB) that computes reachability and spanning-tree information; and a stolen-laptop detector (SL) that sends alerts if suspect addresses are seen on the network. Due to the conciseness of declarative, rule-based programming in this domain, these programs are each modest in size. Nevertheless, together they comprise a significant library of standard network functionality as well as some new behavior made possible by SDNs.

For NAT, we compare the two versions from Sec. 2 with the correct lockstep condition added, along with checking both lockstep properties. For MAC, we compare versions with and without support for host mobility. For ARP, we compare three consecutive diffs: two bugfixes (1→2 and 2→3), and a refactoring (3→4). For LB we check a bug-fix involving initialization of the controller state. The bug manifests as improper forwarding behavior after initialization, and so we enable reachability-aware analysis here. For NIB, we check a fix to how network-reachability is calculated. Originally, SL sends notifications for every suspicious packet; we compare this to a buggy new version intended to rate-limit notifications (1→2) and that version to the correct new version (2→3), as well as examine the difference-of-differences between these changes: (1→2) vs. (1→3).

Performance and Scenario Counts. Figure 6 reports the number of scenarios Chimp returns (under the corresponding bound in columns 3–7, which we discuss later), as well as Chimp's performance on each analysis. The first two columns name the program(s) and the analysis performed. The eighth column gives the number of scenarios found. It is Chimp's goal to present surprising scenarios to the user, but it cannot know ahead of time which scenarios will be most valuable. A small number of scenarios that nevertheless illustrate all potential semantic changes is therefore good in principle. Minimization plays a major role here, as even the stolen-laptop changes (with no more than 4 minimal scenarios) produce hundreds of non-minimal scenarios, many of which are (unnecessarily) as large as the bounds permit. Our experience indicates that the first scenario presented is generally interesting, especially for user-defined queries, and larger scenario-counts are to be expected when the programs differ broadly.

The final columns of Figure 6 report on runtime. Chimp first *translates* the problem to Boolean logic before *solving* to find a scenario. We report the time for both steps as the average and standard deviations of 10 runs; Chimp was started afresh each time to mitigate cache-warming effects. The solving time is the time to either produce the first scenario or complete the search without finding one. We measure performance on an Intel i5-2400 3.10 Ghz with 8GB RAM (i.e., a generic laptop). The search is largely CPU-bound, using no more than 1.5 GB of memory even on the larger analyses. Chimp returns scenarios fairly quickly—under a second, for most analyses—even when there are no results, and it must complete a search of the entire scenario-space.

Computed Bounds and Scenario Sizes. Columns 3–7 of Figure 6 report on bounds and the size of scenarios that Chimp presents. We show bounds for each datatype separately. The **B** subcolumn reflects whether Chimp was able to compute a guaranteed-sufficient bound (Sec. 5); a ✗ indicates a bound could

Programs	Analysis	MAC		IP		TCP		Events		States		Scenario	Trans (ms)		Solve (ms)	
		B	S	B	S	B	S	B	S	B	S	Count	Avg	σ	Avg	σ
NAT	`chPolOut` & Lckstp 2	✗(4)	2	✗(4)	1	✗(4)	2	2	2	1	1	>1000	438	118	112	4
	Lckstp 1	✗(3)	2	✗(3)	2	✗(3)	3	✗(1)	1	✗(3)	2	54	42	2	104	7
	Lckstp 2	✗(3)	–	✗(3)	–	✗(3)	–	✗(1)	–	✗(3)	–	0	55	4	141	4
MAC	`chPolOut`	4	–	0	–	0	–	2	–	1	–	0	6	1	1	1
	`chStTrans`	4	1	0	0	0	0	1	1	3	2	4	19	14	11	8
ARP (1→2)	`chPolOut`	13(3)	3	6(3)	1	0	0	2	2	1	1	154	33	28	20	18
ARP (2→3)	`chPolOut`	13(3)	3	6(3)	1	0	0	2	2	1	1	102	35	28	23	19
ARP (3→4)	`chPolOut`	12(3)	3	6(3)	1	0	0	2	2	1	1	324	28	24	10	11
LB	`chStTrans`	4	0	0	0	0	0	1	1	3	2	1	45	31	46	37
	`chPolOut`	4	–	0	–	0	–	2	–	1	–	0	25	2	1	1
	`rchChStTrans`	✗(4)	2	0	0	0	0	✗(3)	3	✗(3)	3	3	167	8	6011	51
	`rchChPolOut`	✗(4)	1	0	0	0	0	✗(4)	4	✗(5)	4	8	330	151	89524	555
NIB	`chStTrans`	4	0	0	0	0	0	2	2	1	1	40	242	114	2605	168
	`chPolOut`	4	–	0	–	0	–	2	–	1	–	0	3	1	1	1
Stolen Laptop (1→2)	`chPolOut`	4	0	0	0	0	0	2	2	1	1	2	14	2	11	2
	`chStTrans`	3	1	0	0	0	0	1	1	3	2	3	21	17	10	8
Stolen Laptop (2→3)	`chPolOut`	4	2	0	0	0	0	2	2	1	1	4	21	7	14	8
	`chStTrans`	2	–	0	–	0	–	1	–	3	–	0	20	13	5	4
Stolen Laptop	$\Delta(p_1, p_3) - \Delta(p_1, p_2)$	4	1	0	0	0	0	2	2	1	1	4	26	21	16	13

Fig. 6. Bounds computed, scenario sizes, number of minimal scenarios found, and performance (average and standard deviation in ms) for each analysis. For each datatype, the **B** column denotes the bounds used. A number m by itself indicates the computed sufficient bound on that datatype, which was then used in analysis. $m(n)$ says that the computed bound was m, but that we lowered it to a more reasonable n. ✗(n) denotes that a sufficient bound could not be calculated, in which case we provided a reasonable bound n. Lower numbers indicate a smaller search space. A bound of 0 means that atoms of that type were provably unnecessary in the analysis. The **S** column gives, for each datatype, the median number of atoms of that type used across all scenarios that Chimp found. A "–" indicates that the analysis found no scenarios. For reachability-aware analyses, the maximum trace-length is equal to the bound on events.

not be computed, in which case parenthetical values indicate bounds we manually provided to Chimp. Sometimes, even when a sufficient bound is available, a technical limitation in the Alloy engine—a cap on the number of potential facts value that we were unable to modify with reasonable effort—prevents us from using that bound, in which case we use a smaller number (indicated in parentheses). This is only a restriction imposed by our current toolchain, and not a fundamental limitation. As expected, Chimp is able to find a bound for each `chPolOut` and `chStTrans`, rendering its search complete on these rows.

A bound exists for the delta-of-delta analysis as well. In contrast, Chimp is unable to find sufficient bounds for checking the lockstep properties, as they use quantification in a more sophisticated way. As for reachability-aware tests, the `rchChPolOut` and `rchChStTrans` predicates admit a sufficient bound on scenario-size *per step*, thus requiring user input only to bound the number of events and states. Since the LB programs differ only in their initialization (i.e., state change, detected by `chStTrans`) `chPolOut` detects no functional differences. `rchChPolOut`, however, entails a search for the *consequences* of that change beyond its immediate effect on program state; this adds significant complexity to the search.

Scenarios, especially after minimization (Sec. 6), may not need as many elements as the bound indicates. Therefore, the **S** column presents the median number of elements across all scenarios that Chimp returned. Where available, the **B** values are quite small. However, even relative to those, the **S** values are smaller; minimal scenarios contain no irrelevant output. We see that minimizing scenarios before presenting them often reduces scenario-size by more than 50 percent. Since simpler scenarios are quicker and easier to understand, this significantly assists the user in focusing on the critical components of the change.

8 Related Work

Controller programs operate at multiple *tiers* of execution, analogous to the multi-tier nature of web programs. In particular, controller programs generate persistent instructions for switches, making this a form of metaprogramming, which can be especially hard on a static analysis. Analysis is eased in *tierless* languages like Flowlog [27], which abstract out the details of how the controller interacts with the switches. To exploit tierlessness, Chimp is specifically targeted to Flowlog, but its core ideas are not limited to one language. VMware's Nlog [20] is, like Flowlog, based in non-recursive logic-programming and has relational state, making it a prime candidate for Chimp. CSDN [4], in spite of its imperative syntax, also has relational state and a trigger-action model similar to Flowlog's. Since CSDN is not tierless, analysis would need to model switch-rule updates explicitly, yet it is amenable to relational modeling. Flog [16] is another limited-power logic-programming SDN language with relational state. Flog allows recursion, and Chimp's underlying engine assumes a non-recursive logic; Chimp is nevertheless applicable to Flog's non-recursive fragment. Chimp's methods also apply to stateless, declarative policy languages like NetCore [26].

NetKAT [3] is an SDN programming language that supports efficient [10] program differencing. NetKAT programs can express *path*-based constraints, but do not support program state. Differencing is therefore a fundamentally different problem between the two languages. NetKAT also supports host-reachability analysis that depends on the network topology; Chimp is topology-independent, and checks whether program states (not network hosts) are reachable.

Differential program analysis is well studied outside the networking space. Early work by Horwitz [13] finds which portions of two programs correspond and where they can differ. Chimp's custom predicates enable more detailed analyses, as well as providing behavioral scenarios rather than annotated code.

More recent work includes SymDiff [21], which leverages satisfiability modulo theories (SMT) technology for program comparison; Differential Assertion Checking (DAC) [22], which checks properties relative to program changes; and Differential Symbolic Execution (DSE) [31], which combines symbolic execution and SMT-solving to summarize differences between Java methods. Chimp's scenarios are analogous to the output of these tools, except that they use relational program state. Also in contrast to these tools, Chimp addresses schema clashes and differences in potential program input types, as well as reasoning about lockstep behavior. Since Chimp targets limited-power, declarative languages for network-programming, it is able to make completeness guarantees that cannot generally be made for full-featured languages, and does so without necessitating symbolic execution.

Hawblitzel, et al. [12] give a framework for comparing pairs of imperative programs via theorem provers. Like their mutual summaries, Chimp's analysis predicates describe relations over differential behavior, although mutual summaries do not assume a shared prestate by default as Chimp's basic analyses do. Unlike mutual summaries, Chimp's predicates can involve any number of Flowlog programs, as in the 3-way delta-of-deltas comparison of Sec. 7. Finally, Hawblitzel et al. do not discuss performance or brevity of output.

Chimp is partly inspired by Margrave [29], which performs differential analysis on policies such as firewalls and routing tables. Margrave accepts a limited subset of Cisco's IOS configuration language and supports additional input via an intermediate policy language; it is not designed for the SDN domain. Its policies are strictly weaker than Flowlog's: they can *read* relational state but not modify it, and they lack the ability to express even the limited universal quantification of Flowlog's ANY keyword. Margrave uses Kodkod [37], the same engine underlying Alloy and Chimp, and could thus perform some, but not all of the analyses that Chimp can—for instance, Margrave has no support for reasoning about state-reachability. Margrave bounds its analyses by naively summing all terms in a policy [30]; Chimp's focus on single-rule variations produces tighter bounds. Also in the firewall space, Liu [23] addresses change-impact analysis for firewall policies, not full SDN programs.

Dougherty et al. [9] split a program's behavior into a system automaton and a dynamic policy that filters which transitions can be taken, then give algorithms for computing the difference of multiple policies with respect to the fixed system.

These algorithms assume a common schema between policies, whereas Chimp allows for schema changes. Even more, since each Flowlog program defines its own transition system, Chimp's analysis must effectively work with multiple system automata. Finally, their work is not implemented.

Differencing techniques in the network space tend to focus on stateless forwarding policies rather than stateful programs. For instance, header-space analysis [18] could be used to compare static views of the network. In contrast, we are interested in analyzing controller *programs*, with state that changes over time.

DNA (Differential Network Analysis) [24] answers differential queries about reachability across multiple snapshots of network state (e.g., routing tables and ACLs). Chimp does not reason about network reachability, as its analysis is topology independent. Since Chimp analyzes programs, rather than snapshots of forwarding policy, it must be aware of state transitions between these snapshots, and its analysis is necessarily more complex. Like Chimp, the DNA tool minimizes its output using Boolean techniques, but Chimp's minimization also works over relational program states as well as packet headers.

Chimp is complementary to statistical tools like WISE [36], which estimates the impact of changes on response times in content-delivery-networks. Chimp's reasoning functions even in the absence of pre-existing logs, which machine-learning tools such as WISE require to train their classifiers.

In contrast to differential analysis, traditional property-verification for SDN programs is well studied. However, existing tools such as NICE [6], VeriCon [4], Verificare [34], and Flowlog's existing verification [27] lack *differential* reasoning capabilities. The same is true of recent proof-based verification efforts [8,35] for SDN languages. Many other analyses [2,11,18,19,25,32,38] work over *fixed* network policies, often accepting raw forwarding tables as input. While powerful, applying these techniques to *stateful* SDN controller programs means resorting to dynamic methods in the running system, as in the case of NetPlumber [17] and VeriFlow [19]. Chimp analyzes stateful programs statically.

9 Conclusion

Chimp was designed with several core goals in mind: to handle dynamic program state, to produce concrete scenarios and support schema changes (Sec. 2), to rule out false negatives but allow reachability-checking if desired (Sec. 5), to provide minimal, general scenario output (Sec. 6), and to support both common and user-defined queries (Sec. 4). As our evaluation shows, Chimp's performance is good enough to be used as a regular part of the development cycle. The tool currently analyzes *controller programs*, independent of the network's topology. It would also be useful to reason about network-condition changes, such as host mobility [39], and their potential impact on behavior. Improving Chimp's handling of arithmetic by incorporating SMT-solver technology would also be an interesting avenue of future work.

Acknowledgements. We are grateful to the anonymous reviewers for their helpful remarks. We thank Daniel J. Dougherty, Kathi Fisler, Rodrigo Fonseca, and Nate

Foster for useful discussions, and the Frenetic and Alloy teams for creating excellent tools we could build upon. This work is partly supported by the NSF.

References

1. Abiteboul, S., Hull, R., Vianu, V.: Foundations of Databases. Addison-Wesley (1995)
2. Al-Shaer, E., Al-Haj, S.: FlowChecker: Configuration analysis and verification of federated OpenFlow infrastructures. In: Workshop on Assurable and Usable Security Configuration (2010)
3. Anderson, C.J., Foster, N., Guha, A., Jeannin, J.B., Kozen, D., Schlesinger, C., Walker, D.: NetKAT: Semantic foundations for networks. In: Principles of Programming Languages (POPL) (2014)
4. Ball, T., Bjørner, N., Gember, A., Itzhaky, S., Karbyshev, A., Sagiv, M., Schapira, M., Valadarsky, A.: VeriCon: Towards verifying controller programs in software-defined networks. In: Programming Language Design and Implementation (PLDI) (2014)
5. Bernays, P., Schönfinkel, M.: Zum entscheidungsproblem der mathematischen Logik. Mathematische Annalen 99, 342–372 (1928)
6. Canini, M., Venzano, D., Perešíni, P., Kostić, D., Rexford, J.: A NICE way to test OpenFlow applications. In: Networked Systems Design and Implementation (2012)
7. Casado, M., Freedman, M.J., Pettit, J., Luo, J., McKeown, N., Shenker, S.: Ethane: Taking Control of the Enterprise. In: Conference on Communications Architectures, Protocols and Applications (SIGCOMM) (2007)
8. Chen, C., Jia, L., Zhou, W., Loo, B.T.: Proof-based verification of software defined networks. In: Open Networking Summit (2014)
9. Dougherty, D.J., Fisler, K., Adsul, B.: Specifying and reasoning about dynamic access-control policies. In: Furbach, U., Shankar, N. (eds.) IJCAR 2006. LNCS(LNAI), vol. 4130, pp. 632–646. Springer, Heidelberg (2006)
10. Foster, N., Kozen, D., Milano, M., Silva, A., Thompson, L.: A coalgebraic decision procedure for NetKAT. In: Principles of Programming Languages (POPL) (2015)
11. Gutz, S., Story, A., Schlesinger, C., Foster, N.: Splendid isolation: A slice abstraction for software-defined networks. In: Workshop on Hot Topics in Software Defined Networking (2012)
12. Hawblitzel, C., Kawaguchi, M., Lahiri, S.K., Rebêlo, H.: Towards modularly comparing programs using automated theorem provers. In: Bonacina, M.P. (ed.) CADE 2013. LNCS (LNAI), vol. 7898, pp. 282–299. Springer, Heidelberg (2013)
13. Horwitz, S.: Identifying the semantic and textual differences between two versions of a program. In: Programming Language Design and Implementation (PLDI) (1990)
14. Jackson, D.: Software Abstractions: Logic, Language, and Analysis, 2nd edn. MIT Press (2012)
15. Jain, S., Kumar, A., Mandal, S., Ong, J., Poutievski, L., Singh, A., Venkata, S., Wanderer, J., Zhou, J., Zhu, M., Zolla, J., Hölzle, U., Stuart, S., Vahdat, A.: B4: Experience with a globally-deployed software defined WAN. In: Conference on Communications Architectures, Protocols and Applications (SIGCOMM) (2013)
16. Katta, N.P., Rexford, J., Walker, D.: Logic programming for software-defined networks. In: Workshop on Cross-Model Design and Validation (XLDI) (2012)

17. Kazemian, P., Chang, M., Zeng, H., Varghese, G., McKeown, N., Whyte, S.: Real time network policy checking using header space analysis. In: Networked Systems Design and Implementation (2013)
18. Kazemian, P., Varghese, G., McKeown, N.: Header space analysis: Static checking for networks. In: Networked Systems Design and Implementation (2012)
19. Khurshid, A., Zou, X., Zhou, W., Caesar, M., Godfrey, P.B.: VeriFlow: Verifying network-wide invariants in real time. In: Networked Systems Design and Implementation (2013)
20. Koponen, T., Amidon, K., Balland, P., Casado, M., Chanda, A., Fulton, B., Ganichev, I., Gross, J., Gude, N., Ingram, P., Jackson, E., Lambeth, A., Lenglet, R., Li, S.H., Padmanabhan, A., Pettit, J., Pfaff, B., Ramanathan, R., Shenker, S., Shieh, A., Stribling, J., Thakkar, P., Wendlandt, D., Yip, A., Zhang, R.: Network Virtualization in Multi-tenant Datacenters. In: Networked Systems Design and Implementation (2014)
21. Lahiri, S.K., Hawblitzel, C., Kawaguchi, M., Rebêlo, H.: SYMDIFF: A language-agnostic semantic diff tool for imperative programs. In: Madhusudan, P., Seshia, S.A. (eds.) CAV 2012. LNCS, vol. 7358, pp. 712–717. Springer, Heidelberg (2012)
22. Lahiri, S.K., McMillan, K.L., Sharma, R., Hawblitzel, C.: Differential assertion checking. In: Foundations of Software Engineering (2013)
23. Liu, A.X.: Change-impact analysis of firewall policies. In: Biskup, J., López, J. (eds.) ESORICS 2007. LNCS, vol. 4734, pp. 155–170. Springer, Heidelberg (2007)
24. Lopes, N., Bjørner, N., Godefroid, P., Jayaraman, K., Varghese, G.: DNA pairing: Using differential network analysis to find reachability bugs. Tech. Rep. MSR-TR-2014-58, Microsoft Research (April 2014)
25. Mai, H., Khurshid, A., Agarwal, R., Caesar, M., Godfrey, P.B., King, S.T.: Debugging the data plane with Anteater. In: Conference on Communications Architectures, Protocols and Applications (SIGCOMM) (2011)
26. Monsanto, C., Foster, N., Harrison, R., Walker, D.: A compiler and run-time system for network programming languages. In: Principles of Programming Languages (POPL) (2012)
27. Nelson, T., Ferguson, A.D., Scheer, M.J.G., Krishnamurthi, S.: Tierless programming and reasoning for software-defined networks. In: Networked Systems Design and Implementation (2014)
28. Nelson, T., Saghafi, S., Dougherty, D.J., Fisler, K., Krishnamurthi, S.: Aluminum: Principled scenario exploration through minimality. In: International Conference on Software Engineering (2013)
29. Nelson, T., Barratt, C., Dougherty, D.J., Fisler, K., Krishnamurthi, S.: The Margrave tool for firewall analysis. In: USENIX Large Installation System Administration Conference (2010)
30. Nelson, T., Dougherty, D.J., Fisler, K., Krishnamurthi, S.: Toward a more complete Alloy. In: Derrick, J., Fitzgerald, J., Gnesi, S., Khurshid, S., Leuschel, M., Reeves, S., Riccobene, E. (eds.) ABZ 2012. LNCS, vol. 7316, pp. 136–149. Springer, Heidelberg (2012)
31. Person, S., Dwyer, M.B., Elbaum, S.G., Pasareanu, C.S.: Differential symbolic execution. In: Foundations of Software Engineering (2008)
32. Porras, P., Shin, S., Yegneswaran, V., Fong, M., Tyson, M., Gu, G.: A security enforcement kernel for OpenFlow networks. In: Workshop on Hot Topics in Software Defined Networking (2012)
33. Ramsey, F.P.: On a problem in formal logic. Proceedings of the London Mathematical Society 30, 264–286 (1930)

34. Skowyra, R., Lapets, A., Bestavros, A., Kfoury, A.: A verification platform for SDN-enabled applications. In: International Conference on Cloud Engineering (2014)
35. Stewart, G.: Computational verification of network programs in Coq. In: Gonthier, G., Norrish, M. (eds.) CPP 2013. LNCS, vol. 8307, pp. 33–49. Springer, Heidelberg (2013)
36. Tariq, M.M.B., Bhandankar, K., Valancius, V., Zeitoun, A., Feamster, N., Ammar, M.H.: Answering "what-if" deployment and configuration questions with WISE: Techniques and deployment experience. IEEE/ACM Transactions on Networking (February 2013)
37. Torlak, E., Jackson, D.: Kodkod: A relational model finder. In: Grumberg, O., Huth, M. (eds.) TACAS 2007. LNCS, vol. 4424, pp. 632–647. Springer, Heidelberg (2007)
38. Xie, G.G., Zhan, J., Maltz, D.A., Zhang, H., Greenberg, A., Hjalmtysson, G., Rexford, J.: On static reachability analysis of IP networks. In: IEEE Conference on Computer Communications (2005)
39. Zave, P., Rexford, J.: The design space of network mobility. In: Bonaventure, O., Haddadi, H. (eds.) Recent Advances in Networking. ACM SIGCOMM (2013)

A Fully Verified Container Library

Nadia Polikarpova[1(✉)], Julian Tschannen[2], and Carlo A. Furia[2]

[1] MIT CSAIL, Cambridge, USA
polikarn@csail.mit.edu
[2] Department of Computer Science, ETH Zurich, Zürich, Switzerland
{Julian.Tschannen,Carlo.Furia}@inf.ethz.ch

Abstract. The comprehensive functionality and nontrivial design of realistic general-purpose container libraries pose challenges to formal verification that go beyond those of individual benchmark problems mainly targeted by the state of the art. We present our experience verifying the full functional correctness of EiffelBase2: a container library offering all the features customary in modern language frameworks, such as external iterators, and hash tables with generic mutable keys and load balancing. Verification uses the automated deductive verifier AutoProof, which we extended as part of the present work. Our results indicate that verification of a realistic container library (135 public methods, 8,400 LOC) is possible with moderate annotation overhead (1.4 lines of specification per LOC) and good performance (0.2 seconds per method on average).

1 Introduction

The moment of truth for software verification technology comes when it is applied to realistic programs in practically relevant domains. Libraries of general-purpose data structures—called *containers*—are a prime example of such domains, given their pervasive usage as fundamental software components. Data structures are also "natural candidates for full functional verification" [63] since they have well-understood semantics and typify challenges in automated reasoning such as dealing with aliasing and the heap. This paper presents our work on verifying full functional correctness of a realistic, object-oriented container library.

Challenges. *Realistic* software has nontrivial size, a design that promotes flexibility and reuse, and an implementation that offers competitive performance. *General-purpose* software includes all the functionalities that users can reasonably expect, accessible through uniform and rich interfaces. *Full specifications* completely capture the behavior of a software component relative to the level of abstraction given by its interface. Notwithstanding the vast amount of research on functional verification of heap-manipulating programs and its applications to data structure implementations, to our knowledge, no previous work has tackled all these challenges in combination.

Rather, the focus has previously been on verifying individually chosen data structure operations, often stripped or tailored to particular reasoning techniques. Some concrete

Work partially supported by SNF grants 200021-137931 (FullContracts), 200020-134974 (LSAT), and 200021-134976 (ASII); and by ERC grant 291389 (CME).
N. Polikarpova–Work done mainly while affiliated with ETH Zurich.

N. Bjørner and F. de Boer (Eds.): FM 2015, LNCS 9109, pp. 414–434, 2015.
DOI: 10.1007/978-3-319-19249-9_26

examples from recent work in this area (see Sec. 5 for more): Zee et al. [63] verify a significant selection of complex linked data structures but not a complete container library, and they do no include certain features expected of general-purpose implementations, such as iterators or user-defined key equivalence in hash tables. Pek et al. [47] analyze realistic implementations of linked lists and trees but do not always verify full functional correctness (for example, they do not prove that reversal procedures actually reverse the elements in a list), nor can their technique handle arbitrary heap structures. Kawaguchi et al. [29] verify complex functional properties but their approach targets functional languages, where the abstraction gap between specification and implementation is narrow; hence, their specifications have a different flavor and their techniques are inapplicable to object-oriented designs. These observations do not detract from the value of these works; in fact, each challenge is formidable enough in its own right to require dedicated focused research, and all are necessary steps towards verifying realistic implementations—which has remained, however, an outstanding challenge.

Result. Going beyond the state of the art in this area, we completely verified a realistic container library, called EiffelBase2, against full functional specifications. The library, described in Sec. 4, consists of over 8,000 lines of Eiffel code in 46 classes, and offers arrays, lists, stacks, queues, sets, and tables (dictionaries). EiffelBase2's interface specifications are written in first-order logic and characterize the abstract object state using mathematical entities, such as sets and sequences. To demonstrate the usefulness of these specifications for clients, we also verified correctness properties of around 2,000 lines of client code that uses some of EiffelBase2's containers.

Techniques. A crucial feature of any verification technique is the amount of automation it provides. While some approaches, such as abstract interpretation, can offer complete "push button" automation by focusing on restricted properties, full functional verification of realistic software still largely relies on interactive theorem provers, which require massive amounts of effort from highly-trained experts [30,40]. Even data structure verification uses interactive provers, such as in [63], to discharge the most complex verification conditions. Advances in verification technology that target this class of tools have little chance of directly improving usability for *serious yet non-expert* users—as opposed to verification mavens.

In response to these concerns, an important line of research has developed verification tools that target expressive functional correctness properties, yet provide more automation and do not require interacting with back-end provers directly. Since their degree of automation is intermediate between fully automatic and interactive, such tools are called *auto-active* [36]; examples are Dafny [35], VCC [12], and VeriFast [24], as well as AutoProof, which we developed in previous work [52,56] and significantly extended as part of the work presented here.

At the core of AutoProof's verification methodology for heap-manipulating programs is *semantic collaboration* [52]: a flexible approach to reasoning about class invariants in the presence of complex inter-object dependencies. Previously, we applied the methodology only to a selection of stand-alone benchmarks; in the present work, to enable the verification of a realistic library, we extended it with support for mathematical types, abstract interface specifications, and inheritance. We also redesigned

AutoProof's encoding of verification conditions in order to achieve *predictable* performance on larger problems. These improvements directly benefit serious users of the tool by providing more automation, better user experience, and all-out support of object-oriented features as used in practice.

Contributions. This paper's work makes the following contributions:

- The first verification of full functional correctness of a *realistic general-purpose data-structure library* in a heap-based object-oriented language.
- The first verification of a significant collection of data structures carried out entirely using an *auto-active verifier.*
- The first full-fledged verification of several *advanced object-oriented patterns* that involve complex inter-object dependencies but are widely used in realistic implementations (see Sec. 2).
- A practical verification methodology and the supporting AutoProof verifier, which are suitable to reason, with *moderate annotation overhead* and *predictable performance*, about the full gamut of object-oriented language constructs.

The fully annotated source code of the EiffelBase2 container library and a web interface for the AutoProof verifier are available at:

https://github.com/nadia-polikarpova/eiffelbase2 (cite as [50])

For brevity, the paper focuses on presenting EiffelBase2's verification effort and the new features of AutoProof that we introduced to this end; our previous work [51,52,56] supplies complementary and background technical details.

2 Illustrative Examples

Using excerpts from two data structures in EiffelBase2—a linked list and a hash table—we demonstrate our approach to specifying and verifying full functional correctness of containers, and illustrate some challenges specific to realistic container libraries.

2.1 Linked List

Interface Specifications. Each class in EiffelBase2 declares its abstract state through a set of **`model`** attributes. As shown in Fig. 1, the model of class `LINKED_LIST` is a `sequence` of list elements. Its type `MML_SEQUENCE` is from the Mathematical Model Library (MML); instances of MML model classes are mathematical values that have custom logical representations in the underlying prover.

Commands—methods with observable side effects, such as `extend_back`—modify the abstract state of objects listed in their frame specification (**`modify`** clause), according to their postcondition (**`ensure`** clause). Queries—methods that return a result and have no observable side effect, such as `first`—express, in their postcondition, the return value as a function of the abstract state, which they do not modify. By referring to an explicitly declared model, interface specifications are concise, have a consistent level of

```
class LINKED_LIST [G] inherit LIST [G] model
    sequence

feature {public}
  ghost sequence: MML_SEQUENCE [G]
  ghost bag: MML_BAG [G] -- inherited from
      CONTAINER

  first: G -- First element.
    require not sequence.is_empty
    do
      assert inv
      Result := first_cell.item
    ensure Result = sequence.first

  extend_back (v: G) -- Insert 'v' at the back.
    require all o ∈ observers : not o.closed
    modify model Current [sequence]
    local cell: LINKABLE [G]
    do
      create cell.put (v)
      if first_cell = Void then
        first_cell := cell
      else
        last_cell.put_right (cell)
      end
      last_cell := cell
      cells := cells + ⟨cell⟩
      sequence := sequence + ⟨v⟩
    ensure sequence = old sequence + ⟨v⟩

feature {private}
  first_cell: LINKABLE [G]
  last_cell: LINKABLE [G]
  ghost cells: MML_SEQUENCE [LINKABLE [G]]

invariant
  cells_domain: sequence.count = cells.count
  first_cell_empty: cells.is_empty =
    (first_cell = Void)
  last_cell_empty: cells.is_empty =
    (last_cell = Void)
  owns_definition: owns = cells.range
  cells_exist: cells.non_void
  sequence_implementation: all i ∈ 1 .. cells.count
      :
    sequence [i] = cells [i].item
  cells_linked: all i, j ∈ 1 .. cells.count :
    i + 1 = j implies cells [i].right = cells [j]
  cells_first: cells.count > 0 implies
    first_cell = cells.first
  cells_last: cells.count > 0 implies
    last_cell = cells.last and last_cell.right =
      Void
  seq_refines_bag: bag = sequence.to_bag
end
```

```
class LINKED_LIST_ITERATOR [G] inherit LIST_ITERATOR
    [G]
model target, index

feature {public}
  target: LINKED_LIST [G]
  ghost index: INTEGER

  make (list: LINKED_LIST [G]) -- Constructor.
    modify Current
    modify field list [observers, closed]
    do
      target := list
      target.add_iterator (Current)
      assert target.inv_only (seq_refines_bag)
    ensure
      target = list
      index = 0
      list.observers = old list.observers + {Current
          }

  item: G -- Item at current position.
    require not off and all s ∈ subjects : s.closed
    do
      assert inv and target.inv
      Result := active.item
    ensure Result = target.sequence [index]

  forth -- Move one position forward.
    require not off and all s ∈ subjects : s.closed
    modify model Current [index]
    do ...
    ensure index = old index + 1

  remove_right -- Remove element after the current
      .
    require
      1 ≤ index ≤ target.sequence.count − 1
      target.is_wrapped -- closed and owner = Void
      all o ∈ target.observers :
        o ≠ Current implies not o.closed
    modify model target [sequence]
    do ...
    ensure target.sequence =
      old target.sequence.removed_at (index + 1)

feature {private}
  active: LINKABLE [G]

invariant
  target_exists: target ≠ Void
  subjects_definition: subjects = {target}
  index_range: 0 ≤ index ≤ target.sequence.count + 1
  cell_off: (index < 1 or target.sequence.count <
      index)
    = (active = Void)
  cell_not_off: 1 ≤ index ≤ target.sequence.count
    implies active = target.cells [index]
end
```

Fig. 1. Excerpt from EiffelBase2 classes LINKED_LIST and LINKED_LIST_ITERATOR

abstraction, and can be checked for completeness (whether they uniquely characterize the results of queries and the effect of commands on the model state [51]).

Abstract specifications are convenient for clients, which can reason about the effect of method calls in terms of the model while ignoring implementation details. Indeed, LINKED_LIST's public specification is the same as LIST's—its abstract ancestor class—and is oblivious to the fact that the sequence of elements is stored in linked nodes on the heap. While clients have it easy, verifying different implementations of the same abstract interface poses additional challenges in ensuring consistency without compromising on individual implementation features.

Connecting Abstract and Concrete State. Verifying the implementation of first in Fig. 1 requires relating the model of the list to its concrete representation. We accomplish this through the class **invariant**: the clause named sequence_implementation asserts that model attribute sequence lists the items stored in the chain of LINKABLE nodes denoted as cells; cells, in turn, is related to the concrete heap representation by invariant clauses cells_first and cells_linked.

Invariant Methodology. Reasoning based on class invariants is germane to object-oriented programming, yet the semantics of invariants is tricky. A fundamental issue is *when* (at what program points) invariants should hold. Simple syntactic approaches, which require invariants to hold at predefined points (for example, before and after every public call), are not flexible enough to reason about complex object structures. Following the approach introduced with Spec# [37,2], our methodology equips every object with a built-in ghost[1] Boolean attribute closed. Whenever an object is closed (closed is true), its invariant must hold; but when it is open (closed is false), its invariant may not hold. Built-in ghost methods unwrap and wrap mediate opening and closing objects: unwrap opens a closed object, which becomes available for modification; wrap closes an open object provided its invariant holds. To reduce manual annotations, AutoProof adds a call **Current**.unwrap[2] at the beginning of every public command; a call **Current**.wrap at the end of the command; and an assertion **Current**.closed to the command's pre- and postcondition; defaults can be overridden to implement more complex behavior.

Ownership. LINKED_LIST's invariant relies on the content of its cells. This might threaten modularity of reasoning, since an independent modification of a cell by an unknown client may break consistency of the list object. In practice, however, the cells are part of the list's internal representation, and should not be directly accessible to other clients. For such *hierarchical* object dependencies, AutoProof implements an *ownership* scheme [37,12]: each object x includes a ghost set owns of "owned" objects on which x may depend. AutoProof prevents objects in x.owns from being opened (and hence, modified) as long as x is closed; thus, x's consistency cannot be indirectly broken. LINKED_LIST's invariant clause owns_definition asserts that the list owns precisely its cells, thus allowing the following clauses to depend on the state of the cells.

Safe Iterators. Like other container libraries, EiffelBase2 offers iterator classes, which provide the most idiomatic and uniform way of manipulating containers (in particular, lists). When multiple iterators are active on the same list, consistency problems may arise: modifying the list, through its own interface or one of the iterators, may

[1] Ghost code only belongs to specifications; see Sec. 3.2 for details.

[2] In Eiffel, **Current** denotes the receiver object (**this** in Java).

invalidate the other iterators. This is not only a challenge to verification but a practical programming problem. To address it, Java's `java.util` iterators implement *fail-safe* behavior, which amounts to checking for validity at every iterator usage, raising an exception whenever the check fails. This is not a robust solution, since "the fail-fast behavior of an iterator cannot be guaranteed", and hence one cannot "write a program that [depends] on this exception for its correctness" [26]. In contrast, through complete specifications, EiffelBase2 offers robust *safe* iterators: clients reason precisely about correct usage statically, so that safe behavior will follow without runtime overhead. Fig. 1 shows excerpts from EiffelBase2's linked list iterators.

Collaborative Invariants. Object dependencies such as those arising between a list and its iterators do not quite fit hierarchical ownership schemes: an iterator's consistency depends on the list, but any one iterator cannot own the list—simply because other iterators may be active on the same list. In such cases we rely on *collaborative invariants*, introduced in our previous work [52]. In AutoProof, each object x is equipped with the ghost sets `subjects` and `observers`: x`.subjects` contains the objects x may depend on (such as an iterator's `target` list); x`.observers` contains the objects that may depend on x. AutoProof verifies that `subjects` and `observers` are consistent between dependent objects (any subject of x has x as an observer), and that any update to a subject does not affect the consistency of its observers. `LINKED_LIST_ITERATOR`'s invariant clause `subjects_definition` asserts that the iterator might depend on its `target` list; correspondingly, the list has to include all active iterators among its `observers`, which is established in the iterator's constructor by calling `target.add_iterator`. The precondition of `LINKED_LIST.extend_back` requires that all the list's `observers` be open: this way, the list can be updated without running the risk of breaking invariants of closed iterators.

2.2 Hash Table

Custom Mutable Keys. As in any realistic container library, EiffelBase2's hash tables support arbitrary objects as keys, with user-defined equivalence relations and hash functions. For example, a class `BOOK` might override the `is_equal` method (`equals` in Java) to compare two books by their ISBN, and define `hash_code` accordingly. When a table compares keys by object content rather than by reference, changing the *state* of an object used as key may break the table's consistency. Libraries without full formal specifications cannot precisely characterize such unsafe key modifications; Java's `java.util` maps, for example, generically recommend "great care [if] mutable objects are used as map keys", since "the behavior of a map is not specified if the value of an object is changed in a manner that affects equals comparisons while the object is a key in the map" [27]. In contrast, EiffelBase2's specification precisely captures which key modifications affect consistency, ensuring safe behavior without restricting usage scenarios. Fig. 2 shows excerpts from EiffelBase2's hash table and key management classes.

Shared Ownership. A table's consistency depends on its keys, but this dependency fits neither ownership nor collaboration: keys may be shared between tables, and hence any one table cannot own its keys; collaboration would require key objects to register their host tables as `observers`, thus preventing the use of independently developed classes as keys. In EiffelBase2, we address these challenges by means of a *shared ownership*

```
class HASH_TABLE [K, V]
model map, lock

feature {public}
  ghost map: MML_MAP [K, V]
  ghost lock: LOCK [K]

  extend (k: K; v: V) -- Add key-value pair.
    require
      k ∈ lock.owns
      all x ∈ map.domain : not x.is_equal (k)
      lock.is_wrapped
      observers = {}
    modify model Current [map]
    do ...
    ensure map = old map.updated (k, v)

feature {private}
  buckets: ARRAY [LINKED_LIST [PAIR [K, V]]]

invariant
  subjects_definition: subjects = {lock}
  keys_locked: map.domain ≤ lock.owns
  no_duplicates: all x, y ∈ map.domain :
    x ≠ y implies not lock.eq [x, y]
  keys_in_buckets: all x ∈ map.domain :
    buckets [index (lock.hash [x])].has (x)
end
```

```
ghost class LOCK [K]
model eq, hash

feature {public}
  eq: MML_RELATION [K, K]
  hash: MML_MAP [K, INTEGER]

  lock (key: K) -- Acquire ownership of 'key'.
    require key.is_wrapped
    modify Current
    modify field key [owner]
    do ...
    ensure owns = old owns + {key}

  unlock (key: K) -- Relinquish ownership of 'key'.
    require
      key ∈ owns
      all o ∈ observers : not key ∈ o.map.domain
    modify Current
    do ...
    ensure
      owns = old owns − {key}
      key.is_wrapped

invariant
  eq_definition: all x, y ∈ owns : eq [x, y] = x.is_equal (y)
  hash_definition: all x ∈ owns : hash [x] = x.hash_code
end
```

Fig. 2. Excerpts from classes HASH_TABLE and LOCK

specification pattern that combines ownership and collaboration. A class LOCK (outlined in Fig. 2) acts as an intermediary between tables and keys: it owns keys and maintains a summary of their properties (their hash codes and the equivalence relation induced by is_equal); multiple tables observe a single LOCK object and rely on its summary, instead of directly observing keys. Clients can also modify keys as long as the invariant of the keys' lock is maintained. Note that LOCK is a **ghost** class: its state and operations are absent from the compiled code, and thus incur no runtime overhead.

3 Verification Approach

AutoProof works by translating annotated Eiffel code into the Boogie intermediate verification language [1], and uses the Boogie verifier to generate verification conditions, which are then discharged by the SMT solver Z3. As part of verifying EiffelBase2 we extended the *verification methodology* of AutoProof (the tool's underlying logic) and substantially redesigned its *Boogie encoding*. This section presents the main new (with respect to our previous work [52]) features of both the methodology and the tool.

3.1 Specification Types

AutoProof offers a Mathematical Model Library (MML) of specification types: sets, bags (multisets), pairs, relations, maps, and sequences. Each type corresponds to a *model class* [8]: a purely applicative class whose semantics for verification is given by a collection of axioms in Boogie. Unlike verifiers that use built-in syntax for specification types, AutoProof is *extensible* with new types by providing an Eiffel wrapper class and a matching Boogie theory, which can be used like any existing MML type. The MML implementation used in EiffelBase2 relies on 228 Boogie axioms (see [49, Ch. 6] for details); most of them have been borrowed from Dafny's background theory, whose broad usage supports confidence in their consistency.

3.2 Ghost State

Auto-active verification commonly relies on *ghost state*—variables that are only mentioned in specifications and do not affect executable code—as its main mechanism for abstraction. Ghost state has to be updated inside method bodies; the overhead of such updates becomes burdensome in realistic code as ghost variables proliferate, even though their relation to physical program state mostly remains straightforward. To assuage this common problem, AutoProof offers *implicit updates* for ghost attributes: for every class invariant clause `ga = expr` that relates a ghost attribute `ga` to an expression `expr`, AutoProof implicitly adds the assignment `ga := expr` before every call to **`Current`**`.wrap`. In Fig. 1, for example, invariant clause `seq_refines_bag` gives rise to the assignment `bag := sequence.to_bag` at the end of `extend_back`; this has the effect of automatically keeping the inherited attribute `bag` in sync with its refined version, `sequence`.

3.3 Model-Based Specifications

As illustrated in Sec. 2, each class specification includes a **`model`** clause, which designates a subset of attributes of the class as the class *model*. The model precisely defines the publicly observable *abstract state* of the class, on which clients solely rely. Model attributes play a special role in frame specifications: a method annotated with the clause **`modify model`** `s[`m_1`,...,`m_n`]` can only modify attributes m_1,...,m_n in the abstract state of `s`, but has no direct restrictions on modifying the concrete state of `s` (for example, method `forth` of `LINKED_LIST_ITERATOR` in Fig. 1 can modify **`Current`**`.active` but not **`Current`**`.target`). This construct enables fine-grained, yet abstract, frame specifications, similar to data groups [38].

Declaring a model also makes it possible to reason about the *completeness* of interface specifications [51]. Informally, a command's postcondition is complete if it uniquely defines the effect of the command on the model; a query's postcondition is complete if it defines the returned result as a function of the model; the model of a class `C` is complete if it supports complete specifications of all public methods in `C`, such that different abstract states are distinguishable by public method calls. For example, a set is not a complete model for `LINKED_LIST` in Fig. 1 because the precise result of `first` cannot be defined as a function of a set; conversely, a sequence is not a complete model for a class `SET` because its interface provides no methods that discriminate element ordering. AutoProof currently does not support mechanized completeness proofs; however, we found that even reasoning informally about completeness—as we did in the design of EiffelBase2—helps provide clear guidelines for writing interface specifications and substantiates the notion of "full functional correctness".

3.4 Inheritance

Postconditions and invariants can be strengthened in descendant classes; hence, any verifier that supports inheritance has to ensure that inherited methods do not violate strengthened invariants, or are appropriately overridden [43,46].

In AutoProof, method implementations can be declared *covariant* or *nonvariant*. A nonvariant implementation cannot depend on the dynamic type of the receiver, and hence on the precise definition of its invariant; therefore, a correct nonvariant implementation remains correct in descendant classes with stronger invariants, and need not be re-verified. In contrast, a covariant implementation may depend on the dynamic type of the receiver, and hence must be re-verified when inherited. In practice, method implementations have to be covariant only if they call `Current.wrap`, which is the case for commands that directly modify attributes of `Current` (such as `extend_back` in Fig. 1): `wrap` checks that the invariant holds, a condition that may become stronger along the inheritance hierarchy. Otherwise, queries and commands that modify `Current` indirectly by calling other commands can be declared nonvariant: method `append` in `LINKED_LIST` (not shown in Fig. 1) calls `extend_back` in a loop; it then only needs to know that `Current` is `closed` but not any details of the actual invariant.

Nonvariant implementations are a prime example of how decoupling the knowledge that an object *is* consistent from the *details* of its invariant promotes modular verification. This feature is a boon of invariant-based reasoning; while a similar decoupling is achievable in separation logic through abstract predicates and predicate families [45], it is missing in other approaches such as dynamic frames [28].

3.5 Effective Boogie Encoding

The single biggest obstacle to completing the verification of EiffelBase2 has been poor verification performance on large problems: making AutoProof scale required tuning several low-level details of the Boogie translation, following a trial-and-error process. We summarize some finicky features of the translation that are crucial for performance.

Invariant Reasoning. Class invariants tend to be the most complex part of specifications in EiffelBase2; thus, their translation must avoid bogging down the prover with too much information at a time. One crucial point is when `x.wrap` is called and all of x's invariant clauses $I_1, \ldots, I_n$ are checked; the naive encoding **assert** $I_1; \ldots;$ **assert** I_n does not work well for complex invariants: for $j < k$, I_k normally does not depend on I_j, and hence the previously established fact that I_j holds just clutters the proof space. Instead, we adopt Dafny's calculational proof approach [39] and use nondeterministic branching to check each clause independently of the others.

At any program point where the scope includes a closed object x, the proof might need to make use of its invariant. AutoProof's default behavior (assume the invariants of all closed objects in scope) doesn't scale to EiffelBase2's complex specifications. Instead, we leverage once again the decoupling between the generic notion of consistency and the specifics of invariant definitions, and make the latter available to the prover selectively, by asserting AutoProof's built-in predicates: `x.inv` refers to x's whole invariant; `x.inv_only (k)` refers to `x`'s invariant clause named `k`; and `x.inv_without (k)` refers to `x`'s invariant without clause named `k` (for example, see `make`'s body in Fig. 1).

Opaque Functions are pure functions whose axiomatic definitions can be selectively introduced only when needed.[3] A function `f` declared as opaque is normally uninterpreted; but using a built-in predicate `def(f(args))` introduces `f(args)`'s definition into the proof environment. In EiffelBase2, we use opaque functions to handle complex invariant clauses that are rarely needed in proofs.

Modular Translation. AutoProof offers the choice of creating a Boogie file per class or per method to be verified. Besides the annotated implementation of the verification module, the file only includes those Boogie theories and specifications that are referenced in the module. We found that minimizing the Boogie input file can significantly impact performance, avoiding fruitless instantiations of superfluous axioms.

4 The Verified Library

EiffelBase2 was initially designed to replace EiffelBase—Eiffel's standard container library—by providing similar functionalities, a better, more modern design, and assured reliability. It originated as a case study in software development driven by strong interface specifications [51]. Library versions predating our verification effort have been used in introductory programming courses since 2011, and have been distributed with the EiffelStudio compiler since 2012.

4.1 Setup

Pre-verification EiffelBase2 included complete implementations and strong *public* functional specifications. Following the approach outlined in Sec. 2, we provided additional public specifications for dependent invariants (ownership and collaboration schemes), as well as private specifications for verification (representation invariants, ghost state and updates, loop invariants, intermediate assertions, lemmas, and so on). This effort took about 7 person-months, including extending AutoProof to support special annotations and the efficient encoding of Sec. 3.5. The most time-consuming task—making the tool scale to large examples—was a largely domain-independent, one-time effort; hence, using AutoProof in its present state to verify other similar code bases should require significantly less effort.[4]

Verified EiffelBase2 consists of 46 classes offering an API with 135 public methods; its implementation has over 8,000 lines of code and annotations in 79 abstract and 378 concrete methods. The bulk of the classes belong to one of two hierarchies: containers

[3] A similar concept was independently developed for Dafny at around the same time [11].

[4] We also have some evidence that AutoProof's usability for non-experts improved after extending it as described in this paper. Students in our "Software Verification" course used AutoProof in 2013 (pre EiffelBase2 verification) and in 2014 (post EiffelBase2 verification); working on similar projects, the students in 2014 were able to complete the verification of more advanced features and generally found the tool reasonably stable and responsive.

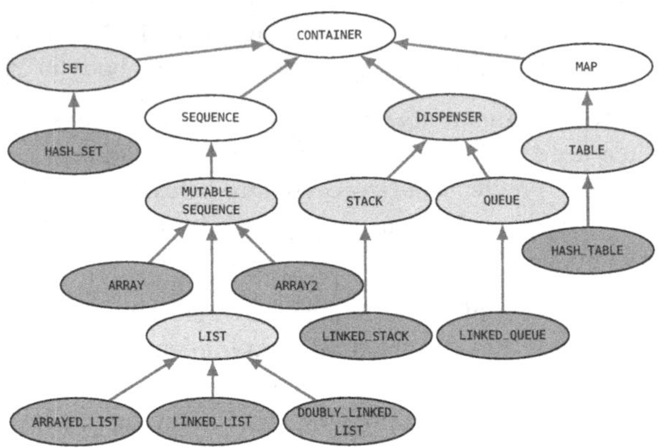

Fig. 3. EiffelBase2 containers: arrows denote inheritance; abstract classes have a lighter background (white for classes with immutable interfaces)

(Fig. 3) and iterators. Extensive usage of inheritance (including multiple inheritance) makes for uniform abstract APIs and reusable implementations.

Completeness. All 135 public methods have complete functional specifications according to the definition given in Sec. 3.3. Specifications treat integers as mathematical integers to offer nicer abstractions to clients. Pre-verification EiffelBase2 supports both object-oriented style (abstract classes) and functional style (closures or agents) definitions of object equality and hashing operators; verified EiffelBase2 covers only the object-oriented style. The library has no concurrency-related features: verification assumes sequential execution.

4.2 Verification Results

Given suitable annotations (described below), AutoProof verifies all 378 method implementations automatically.

Bugs Found. A byproduct of verification was exposing 3 subtle bugs: a division by zero resulting from conversions between machine integers of different sizes; wrong results when moving, in the same array, a range of elements to an overlapping range with a smaller offset; an incorrect implementation of subrange equality in a low-level array service class (wrapping native C arrays) used by EiffelBase2. We attribute the low number of defects in EiffelBase2 to its rigorous, specification-driven development process: designing from the start with complete model-based interface specifications forces developers to carefully consider the abstractions underlying the implementation. An earlier version of EiffelBase2 has been tested automatically against its interface specifications used as test oracles, which revealed 7 bugs [49, Ch. 4] corrected before starting the verification effort. These results confirm the intuition that lightweight formal methods, such as contract-based design and testing, can go a long way towards detecting and preventing software defects; however, full formal verification is still required to get rid of the most subtle few.

Table 1. EiffelBase2 verification statistics: for every CLASS, the number of ABStract and CONCrete methods, and the methods and well-formedness constraints that have to be VERified; the TOTAL number of non-empty non-comment lines of code, broken down into EXECutable code and SPECifications; the latter are further split into REQuirements and AUXiliary annotations; the overhead $\frac{\text{SPEC}}{\text{EXEC}}$ in both LOC (lines) and TOKens; and the verification TIME in seconds: TOTAL time per class, TRANSlation (to Boogie) time per class, and MEDian and MAXimum Boogie running times of the class's methods

CLASS	METHODS			LOC						TOK	TIME (SEC)			
	ABS	CONC	VER	TOTAL	EXEC	SPEC	REQ	AUX	$\frac{\text{SPEC}}{\text{EXEC}}$	$\frac{\text{SPEC}}{\text{EXEC}}$	TOTAL	TRANS	MED	MAX
CONTAINER	2	3	6	124	39	85	34	51	2.2	3.1	3.5	2.6	0.1	0.3
INPUT_STREAM	3	1	2	59	22	37	32	5	1.7	4.3	2.6	2.0	0.3	0.5
OUTPUT_STREAM	2	2	3	90	34	56	42	14	1.6	4.0	2.9	2.2	0.3	0.3
ITERATOR	12	4	6	241	106	135	106	29	1.3	3.6	3.8	2.6	0.2	0.3
SEQUENCE	4	9	14	182	69	113	102	11	1.6	2.5	4.8	3.0	0.1	0.3
SEQUENCE_ITERATOR	0	1	3	36	15	21	19	2	1.4	2.2	3.1	2.2	0.2	0.4
MUTABLE_SEQUENCE	3	5	8	191	83	108	74	34	1.3	3.5	7.6	3.0	0.2	2.9
IO_ITERATOR	1	1	2	58	15	43	33	10	2.9	4.9	3.1	2.2	0.4	0.5
MUTABLE_SEQUENCE_ITERATOR	1	0	1	41	19	22	11	11	1.2	1.5	2.9	2.2	0.7	0.7
ARRAY	0	16	21	275	149	126	107	19	0.8	1.6	12.5	3.4	0.2	2.1
INDEX_ITERATOR	0	13	14	91	64	27	18	9	0.4	0.3	5.0	2.9	0.1	0.2
ARRAY_ITERATOR	0	3	11	97	43	54	34	20	1.3	2.3	6.2	3.0	0.2	0.6
ARRAYED_LIST	0	20	27	389	196	193	127	66	1.0	1.9	19.5	4.5	0.2	4.3
ARRAYED_LIST_ITERATOR	0	10	18	144	81	63	34	29	0.8	1.2	9.9	3.4	0.3	1.0
ARRAY2	0	16	20	199	101	98	79	19	1.0	1.1	7.4	3.3	0.1	1.0
LIST	11	5	11	268	85	183	129	54	2.2	6.1	6.1	3.1	0.1	1.3
LIST_ITERATOR	7	0	1	118	32	86	86	0	2.7	10.2	3.0	2.3	0.7	0.7
CELL	0	1	3	23	12	11	8	3	0.9	1.1	2.7	2.1	0.1	0.3
LINKABLE	0	1	4	25	14	11	11	0	0.8	0.9	2.8	2.1	0.2	0.2
LINKED_LIST	0	23	30	558	271	287	125	162	1.1	2.1	22.3	4.2	0.3	3.3
LINKED_LIST_ITERATOR	0	28	29	402	205	197	84	113	1.0	2.0	13.6	3.9	0.2	1.4
DOUBLY_LINKABLE	0	5	10	136	37	99	85	14	2.7	3.8	4.2	2.6	0.1	0.8
DOUBLY_LINKED_LIST	0	23	30	641	291	350	147	203	1.2	2.3	31.3	4.3	0.3	10.7
DOUBLY_LINKED_LIST_ITERATOR	0	27	28	379	207	172	66	106	0.8	1.7	13.5	3.9	0.3	1.4
DISPENSER	6	0	3	68	27	41	40	1	1.5	2.9	3.0	2.4	0.1	0.4
STACK	1	0	4	25	12	13	12	1	1.1	2.1	3.2	2.3	0.2	0.3
LINKED_STACK	0	9	12	100	51	49	23	26	1.0	1.5	5.5	3.1	0.2	0.3
LINKED_STACK_ITERATOR	0	16	18	221	94	127	59	68	1.4	2.2	8.6	3.5	0.2	1.0
QUEUE	1	0	4	25	12	13	12	1	1.1	2.0	3.2	2.3	0.2	0.3
LINKED_QUEUE	0	9	12	100	51	49	23	26	1.0	1.5	5.5	3.2	0.2	0.3
LINKED_QUEUE_ITERATOR	0	16	18	221	94	127	59	68	1.4	2.2	8.6	3.5	0.2	1.0
LOCK	0	8	9	176	0	176	176	0			4.2	2.8	0.1	0.6
LOCKER	0	1	2	30	0	30	30	0			2.8	2.1	0.3	0.4
MAP	6	1	8	128	32	96	90	6	3.0	5.0	4.1	3.0	0.1	0.2
MAP_ITERATOR	2	0	4	81	19	62	44	18	3.3	7.4	3.5	2.6	0.2	0.3
TABLE	5	2	5	97	39	58	51	7	1.5	2.4	4.3	2.6	0.3	0.6
TABLE_ITERATOR	2	0	1	43	17	26	26	0	1.5	4.1	3.2	2.4	0.7	0.7
HASHABLE	1	0	1	35	9	26	21	5			2.5	1.9	0.5	0.5
HASH_LOCK	0	2	6	41	0	41	41	0			5.2	2.9	0.2	1.4
HASH_TABLE	0	26	31	695	236	459	208	251	1.9	3.6	61.4	6.5	0.4	8.7
HASH_TABLE_ITERATOR	0	23	29	572	198	374	104	270	1.9	4.1	46.9	5.8	0.8	6.3
SET	7	10	17	503	163	340	217	123	2.1	4.4	28.4	3.3	0.2	11.8
SET_ITERATOR	2	0	2	50	17	33	32	1	1.9	6.2	3.1	2.3	0.4	0.5
HASH_SET	0	10	13	146	59	87	43	44	1.5	1.9	11.1	4.1	0.4	1.1
HASH_SET_ITERATOR	0	17	18	216	91	125	42	83	1.4	2.8	18.8	4.5	0.6	2.7
RANDOM	0	11	12	100	78	22	21	1	0.3	0.3	3.4	2.6	0.1	0.1
Total	**79**	**378**	**531**	**8440**	**3489**	**4951**	**2967**	**1984**	**1.4**	**2.7**	**434.7**	**140.9**	**0.2**	**11.8**

Specification Succinctness. Tab. 1 details the size of EiffelBase2's specifications: overall, 1.4 lines of annotations per line of executable code. The same overhead in tokens—a more robust measure—is 2.7 tokens of annotation per token of executable code. The overhead is not uniform across classes: abstract classes tend to accumulate a lot of annotations which are then amortized over multiple implementations of the same abstract specification.

EiffelBase2's overhead compares favorably to the state of the art in full functional verification of heap-based data structure implementations. Pek et al's [47] verified list implementations have overheads of 0.6 (LOC) and 2.6 (tokens)[5]; given that their technique specifically targets inferring low-level annotations, EiffelBase2's specifications are generally succinct. In fact, approaches without inference or complete automation tend to require significantly more verbose annotations. Zee et al.'s [63] linked structures have overheads of 2.3 (LOC) and 8.2 (tokens); their interactive proof scripts aggravate the annotation burden. Java's `ArrayList` verified with separation logic and VeriFast [58] has overheads of 4.4 (LOC) and 10.1 (tokens).

Kinds of Specifications. [47] suggests classifying specifications according to their level of abstraction with respect to the underlying verification process. A natural classification for EiffelBase2 specifications is into *requirements* (model attributes, method pre/-post/frame specifications, class invariants, and ghost functions directly used by them) and *auxiliary* annotations (loop invariants and variants, intermediate assertions, lemmas, and ghost code not directly used in requirements). Requirements are higher level in that they must be provided independent of the verification methodology, whereas auxiliary annotations are a pure burden which could be reduced by inference. EiffelBase2 includes 3 lines of requirements for every 2 lines of auxiliary annotations. In terms of API specification, clients have to deal with 6 invariant clauses per class and 4 pre/post/frame clauses per method on average.

Auxiliary annotations can be further split into *suggestions* (`inv`, `inv_only`, and `inv_without` and opaque functions, all described in Sec. 3.5) and *structural* annotations (all other auxiliary annotations). Suggestions roughly correspond to "level-C annotations" in [47], in that they are hints to help AutoProof verify more quickly. 12% of all EiffelBase2's specifications are suggestions (mostly `inv` assertions); among structural annotations, ghost code (11%) and loop invariants (7%) are the most significant kinds. The 3/2 requirements to auxiliary annotation ratio indicates that high-level specifications prevail in EiffelBase2. The non-negligible fraction of auxiliary annotations motivates future work to automatically infer them (in particular, suggestions) when possible.

Default Annotations. help curb the annotation overhead. Default wrapping calls (Sec. 2.1) work for 83% of method bodies, and default `closed` pre-/postconditions work for 95% of method specifications; we overrode the default in the remaining cases. Implicit ghost attribute updates (Sec. 3.2) always work.

Client Reasoning. To demonstrate that EiffelBase2's interface specifications enable client reasoning, we verified parts of three gaming applications (a transportation system simulator and two board games) that were implemented to support teaching computer

[5] We counted specifications used by multiple procedures only once.

science courses and were written before verifying EiffelBase2. The applications total 37 classes and 2,040 lines of code. Their program logics rely on arrays, lists, streams, and tables from EiffelBase2; we focused on verifying correctness of the interactions between library and applications (for example, iterator safety). Annotating the clients required relatively little effort—roughly three person-days to produce around 1,700 lines of annotations—and only trifling modifications to the code. Verification of 84% of over 200 methods succeeded; the exceptions were in large classes that use up to 7 complex data structures simultaneously, where accumulated specification complexity bogs down AutoProof, which times out; verifying these complex parts would require restructuring the code to improve its modularity.

Verification Performance. In our experiments, AutoProof ran on a single core of a Windows 7 machine with a 3.5 GHz Intel i7-core CPU and 16 GB of memory, using Boogie v. 2.2.30705.1126 and Z3 v. 4.3.2 as backends. To account for noise, we ran each verification 30 times and report the mean value of the 95th percentile.

The total verification time is under 8 minutes, during which AutoProof verified 531 method implementations and well-formedness conditions, including the 378 concrete methods listed in Tab. 1, 47 ghost methods and lemmas, well-formedness of each class invariant, and 56 inherited methods that are covariant (Sec. 3.4) and hence must be re-verified; on the other hand, nonvariant annotations avoid re-verification of 343 bodies, and hence save about 30% of the total verification time.

AutoProof's behavior is not only well-performing on the whole EiffelBase2; it is also *predictable*: over 99% of the methods verify in under 10 seconds; over 89% in under 1 second; the most complex method verifies in under 12 seconds. These uniform, short verification times are a direct result of AutoProof's flexible approach to verification, and specifically of our effort to provide an effective Boogie encoding; for example, independent checking of invariant clauses (Sec. 3.5) halves the verification time of some of the most complex methods.

4.3 Challenges

Sec. 2 outlined two challenging features of realistic, general-purpose libraries (***safe iterators*** and ***custom mutable keys***); we now discuss other general challenging aspects.

General-Purpose APIs. To be general-purpose, EiffelBase2 offers feature-rich public interfaces, which amplify verification complexity. For example, lists support searching, inserting and removing elements, and merging container's content, at arbitrary positions, replacing and removing elements by value, reversing in place. Sets provide operations for subset, join, meet, (symmetric) difference, and disjointness check. All EiffelBase2's containers also offer copy constructors and object comparison—standard features in object-oriented design but routinely evaded in verification.

Object-Oriented Design. Abstract classes provide uniform, general interfaces to clients, and to this end are extensively used in EiffelBase2, but also complicate verification in different ways. First, the generality of abstract specifications may determine a wider gap between specification and implementation than if we defined specifications to individually fit each concrete implementation. For example, `ITERATOR.forth`'s precondition `all s ∈ subjects : s.closed` involves a quantification that could be avoided by replacing it with the equivalent `target.closed`. However, the quantified precondition is inherited from `INPUT_STREAM`, where `target` is not yet defined. Second, model attributes may be refined with inheritance, which requires extra invariant clauses to connect the new and the inherited specifications (e.g., `seq_refines_bag` in Fig. 1).

Realistic Implementations. Implementations in EiffelBase2 offer realistic performance, in line with standard container libraries in terms of running time and memory usage, which adds algorithmic verification complexity atop structural verification complexity. For example, `ARRAYED_LIST`'s implementation uses, like C++ STL's `Vector`, a ring buffer to offer efficient insertions and deletions at both list ends. Ring buffers were a verification challenge in a recent competition [17]; EiffelBase2's ring buffers are even more complicated as they have to support insertions and deletions inside a list, which requires a circular copy. Another example is `HASH_TABLE`, which implements transparent resizing of the bucket array to maintain a near-optimal load factor—one more feature of realistic libraries that is normally ignored in verification work.

5 Related Work

Well-defined interfaces make verifying *client* code using containers somewhat simpler than verifying container implementations. Techniques used to this end include symbolic execution [20], model checking [5], interactive provers [16], and static analysis [15].

Verification of individual data structures demonstrates that a tool or technique can address fundamental challenges; but also normally abstracts away details that are crucial in realistic general-purpose implementations such as EiffelBase2. Individual data structure challenges have been tackled using several of the major functional verification tools out there, including Why3 [59], Pangolin [53], VeriFast [58], GRASShoper [48], ACL2 [18], Dafny [14], KeY [6,19], Coq [42], and other approaches based on direct constraint solving such as [33].

Data structure collections in functional languages. Functional languages provide a higher level of abstraction than heap-based (object-oriented) ones, and their powerful type systems can naturally capture nontrivial correctness properties. Therefore, verifying data structures implemented in functional languages poses challenges largely different from those of the implementations we target in this paper. Refinement approaches [22,41] verify the correctness of a high level abstract model, which is then extended into correct-by-construction executable code. The rich type systems of functional languages support mechanisms such as recursive and polymorphic type refinements [57], which naturally capture functional correctness invariant properties of data structures. [29] applied them to verify ML implementations of lists, vectors, maps, and trees. [29]'s techniques are completely automatic and require very little annotations; but they are not directly applicable to data structures that are cyclic and allow arbitrary access patterns, or that are not defined in functional programming style.

Data structure collections in heap-based languages. Different techniques target different trade-offs between automation and expressiveness of specifications to be verified. *Simple properties* can be verified automatically with little or no annotations: absence of errors such as out of bound array accesses, null dereferences, buffer overruns, and division by zero [34], basic array properties [13], and reachability of objects in the heap (shape analysis) [54,3,4,62,7]. Within the limits of the properties they can express, these analysis techniques are applicable to realistic implementations in real programming languages. Fully automatic techniques have been gradually extended to cover some *decidable functional specification abstractions* such as sets and bags. Some works [21,9,23] are based on top of shape analysis. Others [31,32,60,25,55,61] target logic fragments amenable to SMT reasoning. These decidable abstractions capture essential traits of the interface behavior of data structures, but cannot exactly express the semantics of complex operations with arbitrary element access order.

In contrast, fully *interactive* techniques have no a priori limitations on the properties that can be reasoned upon, but require expert users who can provide low-level proof details. [44,10], for example, reason in higher-order separation logic about sharing and aliasing of data structures featuring a mix of functional and heap-based constructs; such a great flexibility brings a significant overhead in terms of proof scripts.

Auto-active verification [36] tries to provide a high degree of automation, but without sacrificing the expressiveness needed for full functional correctness. Zee et al. [63] document a landmark result in verifying full functional correctness of a significant collection of complex data structures by combining provers for various decidable fragments; however, discharging the most complex verification conditions still requires interactive proofs, which make their annotation overhead much higher than ours. Another major difference with our work is that [63] does not always consider general-purpose implementations (for example, hash tables only offer reference-based key comparison, which is too limiting in practice), nor does it target a unitarily designed library. Pek et al.'s [47] natural proofs do not require proof scripts and drastically reduce the annotation burden by inferring auxiliary (low-level) annotations; the resulting annotation overhead is slightly lower than ours (Sec. 4.2). They demonstrate their VCDryad tool on complex data structures including singly and doubly linked lists, and trees; some implementations are taken from C's `glib` and OpenBSD. Compared to EiffelBase2, their examples consist of a self-contained individual program for each functionality, and hence do not represent aspects of container libraries with uniform interfaces that contribute to verification complexity. Another difference with our work is that [47] does not always prove full functional correctness; reversal and sorting of linked lists, for example, only verify that the sets of elements are not altered but ignore their order.

6 Lessons Learned and Conclusions

We offer as conclusions the main insights into verifying realistic software and building practical verification tools that emerged from our work.

Auto-active Verification Demands Predictability. Usable auto-active verification requires predictable, moderate response time to keep users engaged in successive iterations of the feedback loop. We found timeouts a major impediment, wasting time and providing completely uninformative feedback; others report similar experiences [11]. The primary source of timeouts were futile instantiations of quantified axioms; the solution involved profiling the SMT solver's behavior and designing effective triggers.

This effort paid off as it made AutoProof's performance quite stable. However, constructing efficient axiomatizations for SMT solvers remains somewhat of a black art; automating this task is an attractive direction for future research.

Realistic Verification Calls for Flexible Tools. Verifying EiffelBase2 required a combination of effective predefined schemas (to avoid verbose, repetitive annotations of myriad run-of-the-mill cases) and full control (to tackle the challenging, idiosyncratic cases); as a result, AutoProof includes a lot of control knobs with useful defaults. This determines a different trade off than tools (such as Dafny and VeriFast) implementing bare-bones pristine methodologies, which are easier to learn but offer less support to advanced users that go the distance.

Verification Promotes Good Design. It's unsurprising that well-designed software is easier to verify; the flip-side is that developing software with verification in mind is conducive to good design. Verification commands avoiding any unnecessary complexity—a rigor which can pay off manyfold by leading to better reusability and maintainability.

It remains that the vision of "developers of data structure libraries [delivering] formally specified and fully verified implementations" [63] is still ahead of us. An important step towards achieving this vision, our work explored the major hurdles that lie in the often neglected "last mile" of verification—from challenging benchmarks to fully-specified general-purpose realistic programs—and described practical solutions to overcome them.

References

1. Barnett, M., Chang, B.-Y.E., DeLine, R., Jacobs, B., Leino, K.R.M.: Boogie: A modular reusable verifier for object-oriented programs. In: de Boer, F.S., Bonsangue, M.M., Graf, S., de Roever, W.-P. (eds.) FMCO 2005. LNCS, vol. 4111, pp. 364–387. Springer, Heidelberg (2006)
2. Barnett, M., Naumann, D.A.: Friends need a bit more: Maintaining invariants over shared state. In: Kozen, D. (ed.) MPC 2004. LNCS, vol. 3125, pp. 54–84. Springer, Heidelberg (2004)
3. Beyer, D., Henzinger, T.A., Théoduloz, G.: Lazy shape analysis. In: Ball, T., Jones, R.B. (eds.) CAV 2006. LNCS, vol. 4144, pp. 532–546. Springer, Heidelberg (2006)
4. Beyer, D., Henzinger, T.A., Théoduloz, G., Zufferey, D.: Shape refinement through explicit heap analysis. In: Rosenblum, D.S., Taentzer, G. (eds.) FASE 2010. LNCS, vol. 6013, pp. 263–277. Springer, Heidelberg (2010)
5. Blanc, N., Groce, A., Kroening, D.: Verifying C++ with STL containers via predicate abstraction. In: 22nd IEEE/ACM International Conference on Automated Software Engineering (ASE 2007), Atlanta, Georgia, USA, November 5-9, pp. 521–524 (2007)
6. Bruns, D.: Specification of red-black trees: Showcasing dynamic frames, model fields and sequences. In: Ahrendt, W., Bubel, R. (eds.) 10th KeY Symposium, Nijmegen, the Netherlands (2011), Extended Abstract
7. Calcagno, C., Distefano, D., O'Hearn, P.W., Yang, H.: Compositional shape analysis by means of bi-abduction. J. ACM 58(6), 26 (2011)
8. Charles, J.: Adding native specifications to JML. In: Workshop on Formal Techniques for Java-like Programs, (FTFJP) (2006)

9. Chin, W.-N., David, C., Nguyen, H.H., Qin, S.: Automated verification of shape, size and bag properties via user-defined predicates in separation logic. Sci. Comput. Program. 77(9), 1006–1036 (2012)
10. Chlipala, A., Gregory Malecha, J., Morrisett, G., Shinnar, A., Wisnesky, R.: Effective interactive proofs for higher-order imperative programs. In: Proceeding of the 14th ACM SIGPLAN International Conference on Functional Programming, ICFP 2009, Edinburgh, Scotland, UK, August 31- September 2, pp. 79–90. ACM (2009)
11. Christakis, M., Leino, K.R.M., Schulte, W.: Formalizing and verifying a modern build language. In: Jones, C., Pihlajasaari, P., Sun, J. (eds.) FM 2014. LNCS, vol. 8442, pp. 643–657. Springer, Heidelberg (2014)
12. Cohen, E., Dahlweid, M., Hillebrand, M., Leinenbach, D., Moskal, M., Santen, T., Schulte, W., Tobies, S.: VCC: a practical system for verifying concurrent C. In: Berghofer, S., Nipkow, T., Urban, C., Wenzel, M. (eds.) TPHOLs 2009. LNCS, vol. 5674, pp. 23–42. Springer, Heidelberg (2009)
13. Cousot, P., Cousot, R., Logozzo, F.: A parametric segmentation functor for fully automatic and scalable array content analysis. In: Proceedings of the 38th ACM SIGPLAN-SIGACT Symposium on Principles of Programming Languages, POPL 2011, Austin, TX, USA, January 26-28, pp. 105–118. ACM (2011)
14. Dafny example gallery, http://dafny.codeplex.com/SourceControl/latest (last access: November 2014)
15. Dillig, I., Dillig, T., Aiken, A.: Precise reasoning for programs using containers. In: Proceedings of the 38th Annual ACM SIGPLAN-SIGACT Symposium on Principles of Programming Languages, POPL 2011, pp. 187–200. ACM, New York (2011)
16. Dross, C., Filliâtre, J.-C., Moy, Y.: Correct code containing containers. In: Gogolla, M., Wolff, B. (eds.) TAP 2011. LNCS, vol. 6706, pp. 102–118. Springer, Heidelberg (2011)
17. Filliâtre, J.-C., Paskevich, A., Stump, A.: The 2nd verified software competition: Experience report. In: COMPARE. CEUR Workshop Proceedings, vol. 873, CEUR-WS.org (2012), https://sites.google.com/site/vstte2012/compet
18. Gamboa, R.A.: A formalization of powerlist algebra in ACL2. J. Autom. Reasoning 43(2), 139–172 (2009)
19. Gladisch, C., Tyszberowicz, S.: Specifying a linked data structure in JML for formal verification and runtime checking. In: Iyoda, J., de Moura, L. (eds.) SBMF 2013. LNCS, vol. 8195, pp. 99–114. Springer, Heidelberg (2013)
20. Gregor, D., Schupp STLlint, S.: lifting static checking from languages to libraries. Softw., Pract. Exper. 36(3), 225–254 (2006)
21. Gulwani, S., McCloskey, B., Tiwari, A.: Lifting abstract interpreters to quantified logical domains. In: Proceedings of the 35th ACM SIGPLAN-SIGACT Symposium on Principles of Programming Languages, POPL 2008, San Francisco, California, USA, January 7-12, pp. 235–246. ACM (2008)
22. Hawkins, P., Aiken, A., Fisher, K., Rinard, M., Sagiv, M.: Data representation synthesis. In: Proceedings of the 32Nd ACM SIGPLAN Conference on Programming Language Design and Implementation, PLDI 2011, pp. 38–49. ACM, New York (2011)
23. Itzhaky, S., Bjørner, N., Reps, T., Sagiv, M., Thakur, A.: Property-directed shape analysis. In: Biere, A., Bloem, R. (eds.) CAV 2014. LNCS, vol. 8559, pp. 35–51. Springer, Heidelberg (2014)
24. Jacobs, B., Smans, J., Philippaerts, P., Vogels, F., Penninckx, W., Piessens, F.: VeriFast: A powerful, sound, predictable, fast verifier for C and Java. In: Bobaru, M., Havelund, K., Holzmann, G.J., Joshi, R. (eds.) NFM 2011. LNCS, vol. 6617, pp. 41–55. Springer, Heidelberg (2011)

25. Jacobs, S., Kuncak, V.: Towards complete reasoning about axiomatic specifications. In: Jhala, R., Schmidt, D. (eds.) VMCAI 2011. LNCS, vol. 6538, pp. 278–293. Springer, Heidelberg (2011)
26. Documentation of `java.util.LinkedList`, http://docs.oracle.com/javase/8/docs/api/java/util/LinkedList.html (last access: December 2014)
27. Documentation of `java.util.Map`, http://docs.oracle.com/javase/8/docs/api/java/util/Map.html (last access: December 2014)
28. Kassios, I.T.: Dynamic frames: Support for framing, dependencies and sharing without restrictions. In: Misra, J., Nipkow, T., Sekerinski, E. (eds.) FM 2006. LNCS, vol. 4085, pp. 268–283. Springer, Heidelberg (2006)
29. Kawaguchi, M., Rondon, P.M., Jhala, R.: Type-based data structure verification. In: Proceedings of the 2009 ACM SIGPLAN Conference on Programming Language Design and Implementation, PLDI 2009, Dublin, Ireland, June 15-21, pp. 304–315 (2009)
30. Klein, G., Elphinstone, K., Heiser, G., Andronick, J., Cock, D., Derrin, P., Elkaduwe, D., Engelhardt, K., Kolanski, R., Norrish, M., Sewell, T., Tuch, H., Winwood, S.: seL4: Formal verification of an OS kernel. In: SOSP, pp. 207–220. ACM (2009)
31. Kuncak, V., Piskac, R., Suter, P.: Ordered sets in the calculus of data structures. In: Dawar, A., Veith, H. (eds.) CSL 2010. LNCS, vol. 6247, pp. 34–48. Springer, Heidelberg (2010)
32. Kuncak, V., Piskac, R., Suter, P., Wies, T.: Building a calculus of data structures. In: Barthe, G., Hermenegildo, M. (eds.) VMCAI 2010. LNCS, vol. 5944, pp. 26–44. Springer, Heidelberg (2010)
33. Lahiri, S.K., Qadeer, S.: Back to the future: revisiting precise program verification using SMT solvers. In: Proceedings of the 35th ACM SIGPLAN-SIGACT Symposium on Principles of Programming Languages, POPL 2008, San Francisco, California, USA, January 7-12, pp. 171–182. ACM (2008)
34. Laviron, V., Logozzo, F.: Subpolyhedra: a family of numerical abstract domains for the (more) scalable inference of linear inequalities. STTT 13(6), 585–601 (2011)
35. Leino, K.R.M.: Dafny: An automatic program verifier for functional correctness. In: Clarke, E.M., Voronkov, A. (eds.) LPAR-16 2010. LNCS (LNAI), vol. 6355, pp. 348–370. Springer, Heidelberg (2010)
36. Leino, K.R.M., Moskal, M.: Usable auto-active verification. In: Usable Verification Workshop (2010), http://fm.csl.sri.com/UV10/
37. M. Leino, K.R., Müller, P.: Object invariants in dynamic contexts. In: Odersky, M. (ed.) ECOOP 2004. LNCS, vol. 3086, pp. 491–515. Springer, Heidelberg (2004)
38. Leino, K.R.M., Poetzsch-Heffter, A., Zhou, Y.: Using data groups to specify and check side effects. In: Proceedings of the 2002 ACM SIGPLAN Conference on Programming Language Design and Implementation (PLDI), Berlin, Germany, June 17-19, pp. 246–257 (2002)
39. Leino, K.R.M., Polikarpova, N.: Verified calculations. In: Cohen, E., Rybalchenko, A. (eds.) VSTTE 2013. LNCS, vol. 8164, pp. 170–190. Springer, Heidelberg (2014)
40. Leroy, X.: Formal verification of a realistic compiler. Communications of the ACM 52(7), 107–115 (2009)
41. Lochbihler, A.: Light-weight containers for Isabelle: Efficient, extensible, nestable. In: Blazy, S., Paulin-Mohring, C., Pichardie, D. (eds.) ITP 2013. LNCS, vol. 7998, pp. 116–132. Springer, Heidelberg (2013)
42. Mehnert, H., Sieczkowski, F., Birkedal, L., Sestoft, P.: Formalized verification of snapshotable trees: Separation and sharing. In: Joshi, R., Müller, P., Podelski, A. (eds.) VSTTE 2012. LNCS, vol. 7152, pp. 179–195. Springer, Heidelberg (2012)
43. Müller, P., Poetzsch-Heffter, A., Leavens, G.T.: Modular invariants for layered object structures. Sci. Comput. Program. 62(3), 253–286 (2006)

44. Nanevski, A., Morrisett, G., Shinnar, A., Govereau, P., Birkedal, L.: Ynot: dependent types for imperative programs. In: Proceeding of the 13th ACM SIGPLAN International Conference on Functional Programming, ICFP 2008, Victoria, BC, Canada, September 20-28, pp. 229–240. ACM (2008)
45. Parkinson, M.J., Bierman, G.M.: Separation logic and abstraction. In: Proceedings of the 32nd ACM SIGPLAN-SIGACT Symposium on Principles of Programming Languages, POPL 2005, Long Beach, California, USA, January 12-14, pp. 247–258 (2005)
46. Parkinson, M.J., Bierman, G.M.: Separation logic, abstraction and inheritance. In: Proceedings of the 35th ACM SIGPLAN-SIGACT Symposium on Principles of Programming Languages, POPL 2008, San Francisco, California, USA, January 7-12, pp. 75–86. ACM (2008)
47. Pek, E., Qiu, X., Madhusudan, P.: Natural proofs for data structure manipulation in C using separation logic. In: ACM SIGPLAN Conference on Programming Language Design and Implementation, PLDI 2014, Edinburgh, United Kingdom, June 09-11, p. 46 (2014)
48. Piskac, R., Wies, T., Zufferey, D.: Automating separation logic with trees and data. In: Biere, A., Bloem, R. (eds.) CAV 2014. LNCS, vol. 8559, pp. 711–728. Springer, Heidelberg (2014)
49. Polikarpova, N.: Specified and Verified Reusable Components. PhD thesis, ETH Zurich (2014)
50. Nadia Polikarpova. EiffelBase2 (repository of verified code) (2015), http://dx.doi.org/10.5281/zenodo.16520
51. Polikarpova, N., Furia, C.A., Meyer, B.: Specifying reusable components. In: Leavens, G.T., O'Hearn, P., Rajamani, S.K. (eds.) VSTTE 2010. LNCS, vol. 6217, pp. 127–141. Springer, Heidelberg (2010)
52. Polikarpova, N., Tschannen, J., Furia, C.A., Meyer, B.: Flexible invariants through semantic collaboration. In: Jones, C., Pihlajasaari, P., Sun, J. (eds.) FM 2014. LNCS, vol. 8442, pp. 514–530. Springer, Heidelberg (2014)
53. Régis-Gianas, Y., Pottier, F.: A Hoare logic for call-by-value functional programs. In: Audebaud, P., Paulin-Mohring, C. (eds.) MPC 2008. LNCS, vol. 5133, pp. 305–335. Springer, Heidelberg (2008)
54. Sagiv, S., Reps, T.W., Wilhelm, R.: Parametric shape analysis via 3-valued logic. ACM Trans. Program. Lang. Syst. 24(3), 217–298 (2002)
55. Suter, P., Steiger, R., Kuncak, V.: Sets with cardinality constraints in satisfiability modulo theories. In: Jhala, R., Schmidt, D. (eds.) VMCAI 2011. LNCS, vol. 6538, pp. 403–418. Springer, Heidelberg (2011)
56. Tschannen, J., Furia, C.A., Nordio, M., Polikarpova, N.: AutoProof: Auto-active functional verification of object-oriented programs. In: Baier, C., Tinelli, C. (eds.) TACAS 2015. LNCS, vol. 9035, pp. 566–580. Springer, Heidelberg (2015)
57. Vazou, N., Seidel, E.L., Jhala, R.: LiquidHaskell: Experience with refinement types in the real world. In: Proceedings of the 2014 ACM SIGPLAN Symposium on Haskell, Haskell 2014, pp. 39–51. ACM, New York (2014)
58. Verifast example gallery, http://people.cs.kuleuven.be/~bart.jacobs/verifast/examples/ (last access: November 2014)
59. Why3 example gallery, http://toccata.lri.fr/gallery/why3.en.html (last access: November 2014)
60. Wies, T., Muñiz, M., Kuncak, V.: An efficient decision procedure for imperative tree data structures. In: Bjørner, N., Sofronie-Stokkermans, V. (eds.) CADE 2011. LNCS, vol. 6803, pp. 476–491. Springer, Heidelberg (2011)

61. Wies, T., Muñiz, M., Kuncak, V.: Deciding functional lists with sublist sets. In: Joshi, R., Müller, P., Podelski, A. (eds.) VSTTE 2012. LNCS, vol. 7152, pp. 66–81. Springer, Heidelberg (2012)
62. Yang, H., Lee, O., Berdine, J., Calcagno, C., Cook, B., Distefano, D., O'Hearn, P.W.: Scalable shape analysis for systems code. In: Gupta, A., Malik, S. (eds.) CAV 2008. LNCS, vol. 5123, pp. 385–398. Springer, Heidelberg (2008)
63. Zee, K., Kuncak, V., Rinard, M.C.: Full functional verification of linked data structures. In: Proceedings of the ACM SIGPLAN 2008 Conference on Programming Language Design and Implementation, Tucson, AZ, USA, June 7-13, pp. 349–361 (2008)

Counterexamples for Expected Rewards

Tim Quatmann[1], Nils Jansen[1], Christian Dehnert[1], Ralf Wimmer[2], Erika Ábrahám[1], Joost-Pieter Katoen[1(✉)], and Bernd Becker[2]

[1] RWTH Aachen University, Aachen, Germany
katoen@cs.rwth-aachen.de
[2] Albert-Ludwigs-Universität, Freiburg, Germany

Abstract. The computation of counterexamples for probabilistic systems has gained a lot of attention during the last few years. All of the proposed methods focus on the situation when the probabilities of certain events are too high. In this paper we investigate how counterexamples for properties concerning *expected costs* (or, equivalently, expected rewards) of events can be computed. We propose methods to extract a minimal subsystem which already leads to costs beyond the allowed bound. Besides these exact methods, we present heuristic approaches based on path search and on best-first search, which are applicable to very large systems when deriving a minimum subsystem becomes infeasible due to the system size. Experiments show that we can compute counterexamples for systems with millions of states.

1 Introduction

Probabilistic model checking. Model checking is a well-established verification technique used in software and hardware industry. One of its key features is the ability to generate *counterexamples* in case the property is refuted [1]. Probabilistic model checkers such as PRISM [2] aim at verifying models that incorporate randomness. Successful applications include randomized distributed algorithms, hardware [3], security [4], and systems biology [5]. Properties typically quantify the likelihood of reachability objectives such as "Is the probability that the protocol successfully terminates at least 0.99?". Probabilistic model checking has recently been identified as one of the three main new avenues in verification [6].

Rewards. This paper focuses on the treatment of *resource consumption* in probabilistic model checking. In addition to probabilistic reachability this allows to consider the cost – measured in terms of units of used resources – of reaching a certain set of states. Such costs can be used to keep track of memory consumption, battery usage, and heat generation, to mention a few. Treating resource consumption in verification models has resulted in extensions of timed automata with "prices" [7], games with "energy" [8] and "battery" transition systems [9]. We consider discrete-time Markov chains (DTMCs, for short) that are extended

This work was supported by the Excellence Initiative of the German federal and state government.

N. Bjørner and F. de Boer (Eds.): FM 2015, LNCS 9109, pp. 435–452, 2015.
DOI: 10.1007/978-3-319-19249-9_27

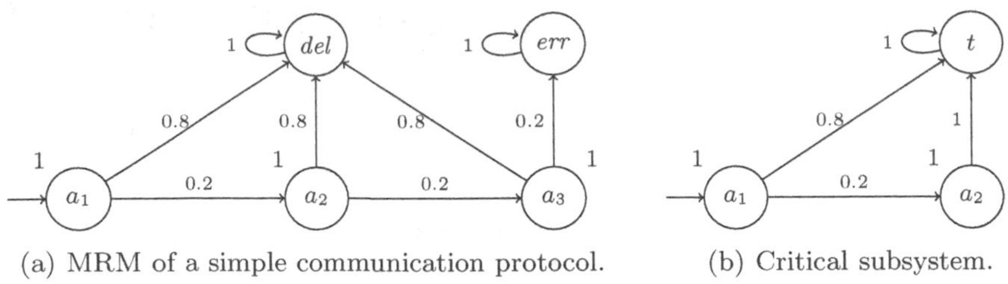

(a) MRM of a simple communication protocol. (b) Critical subsystem.

Fig. 1. Example MRM and critical subsystem

with *rewards*. These so-called Markov reward models (MRMs) [10] are pivotal in the field of *performability*, i. e., the interdependent analysis of reliability and performance of systems, as stressed in [11].

Topic of This Paper. The verification of MRMs is well-developed since more than a decade [12], and is efficiently supported by tools like PRISM. Key performability questions that can be handled are of the form "Is the expected number of steps until termination at most ten?". Although such questions can be handled efficiently (and symbolically), the feedback in case such questions are violated is limited. Typically, only the expected resource consumption is provided, but no indication is provided about the cause of property violation. This paper attempts to fill this gap by providing several algorithms to generate counterexamples to expected cost properties. That is to say, we present automated means that yield diagnostic information in case the expected accumulated resource consumption exceeds an a priori given upper bound. These counterexamples are fragments of the MRM under consideration – so-called *critical subsystems* – that already violate the expected cost property. This paper thus extends the current facilities for counterexample generation for probabilistic reachability (and ω-regular) properties, cf. a recent survey [13], with expected cost properties. We consider two possible types of counterexamples which are both natural extensions of the ones for reachability: a critical part of the original MRM that is computed *narrowing down the faulty behavior* or the MRM in which the reward of irrelevant states is set to zero while *the probabilistic behavior of the system is preserved.*

An Example. Let us illustrate this by means of a small example. Figure 1(a) presents a model of a simple communication protocol. Up to three times a message is being sent (states a_1, a_2, and a_3). The loss probability of a message is 0.2. The protocol terminates in state *del* when the message is successfully delivered or otherwise in state *err*. States a_i are equipped with reward one; all other states have reward zero. It is easy to see that the protocol refutes the property "the expected number of steps until termination is below 1.2". A fragment of the protocol model already violating the property is given in Figure 1(b).

Approach and Related Work. Our approach is based on extending the notion of *critical subsystems*, which were introduced in [14,15] to expected cost properties. This gives the first direct method for counterexamples against expected cost properties. As explained above, two types of such subsystems are considered. To compute these counterexamples, we present three different techniques. The first one is an encoding of critical subsystems by means of *mixed-integer linear programming* (MILP). Together with different optimization functions, *minimal* counterexamples can be obtained using standard MILP solvers such as GUROBI [16]. This approach is applicable to both types of counterexamples. The second algorithm is based on path searching algorithms. Intuitively, a subsystem is incrementally built by connecting path fragments of high costs with respect to their probability. This extends an approach presented in [15]. The last approach exploits *best-first* (bf) search which is in fact an on-the-fly exploration the MRM's state space [14]. The last two methods are applicable to critical subsystems and strongly depend on an appropriate *value function* that takes both the rewards and the path probabilities into account; we will discuss several different options for such functions. Note that all approaches on counterexample generation in the probabilistic setting suffer from the fact that the verification process—mostly based on the solving of linear equation systems—does not incorporate the computation of counterexamples as a by-product, see for instance [13]. We have implemented all our approaches and compare their applicability on several PRISM benchmarks. The conducted experiments show that the MILP approaches often yield a (nearly) minimal critical subsystem in just a few seconds, whereas the best-first search approach scales to models of 10^7 states and 10^8 transitions while yielding larger results than the path search.

2 Preliminaries

In this section we introduce the foundations needed for our methods.

Definition 1 (Discrete-time Markov Chain). *A* discrete-time Markov chain (DTMC) *is a tuple $\mathcal{D} = (S, s_I, P)$ with a finite set of states S, an initial state $s_I \in S$, and a transition probability matrix $P\colon S \times S \to [0,1] \subseteq \mathbb{R}$ with $\sum_{s' \in S} P(s, s') = 1$ for all $s \in S$.*[1]

Assume a DTMC $\mathcal{D}$. The *graph* of $\mathcal{D}$ is given by $\mathcal{G}_\mathcal{D} = (S, E)$ where $(s, s') \in E \Leftrightarrow P(s, s') > 0$. E is called the set of *transitions*. A state $s \in S$ is *absorbing* iff $P(s, s) = 1$.

A *path* of a DTMC $\mathcal{D}$ is a non-empty (finite or infinite) sequence $\pi = s_0 s_1 \dots$ of states $s_i \in S$ such that $P(s_i, s_{i+1}) > 0$ for all i. Let $\mathrm{Paths}^\mathcal{D}_{\mathit{fin}}$ denote all finite paths of $\mathcal{D}$ and $\mathrm{Paths}^\mathcal{D}_{\mathit{fin}}(s)$ those starting in $s \in S$. For a set $T \subseteq S$, we denote the set of finite paths starting in s and ending in the first visit of some $t \in T$ by $\mathrm{Paths}^\mathcal{D}_{\mathit{fin}}(s, \Diamond T) = \{s_0 \dots s_n \in \mathrm{Paths}^\mathcal{D}_{\mathit{fin}}(s) \mid s_n \in T \text{ and } s_i \notin T \text{ for all } i < n\}$. A state $s' \in S$ is *reachable* from s iff $\mathrm{Paths}^\mathcal{D}_{\mathit{fin}}(s, \Diamond\{s'\}) \neq \emptyset$. Let $\mathrm{Paths}^\mathcal{D}_{\mathit{fin}}(S', S'')$

[1] Note that for our methods we assume probabilities and rewards to be from $\mathbb{Q}$.

for $S', S'' \subseteq S$ denote the set of paths starting in a state from S' and ending in a state from S'' without visiting a state from $S' \cup S''$ in between.

Let $\pi = s_0 s_1 \dots s_n \in \mathrm{Paths}^{\mathcal{D}}_{\mathit{fin}}$ be a finite path. Its probability is given by $P(\pi) = \prod_{i=0}^{n-1} P(s_i, s_{i+1})$. Consider a state $s \in S$ and a set of dedicated *target states* $T \subseteq S$. The *reachability probability*, i. e., the probability to eventually reach a state $t \in T$ when starting in s is given by

$$\Pr^{\mathcal{D}}(s \models \lozenge T) := \sum_{\pi \in \mathrm{Paths}^{\mathcal{D}}_{\mathit{fin}}(s, \lozenge T)} P(\pi).$$

Note that no path $\pi \in \mathrm{Paths}^{\mathcal{D}}_{\mathit{fin}}(s, \lozenge T)$ is a proper prefix of another path $\pi' \in \mathrm{Paths}^{\mathcal{D}}_{\mathit{fin}}(s, \lozenge T)$ as these paths end at the first visit of a state in $T \subseteq S$. Therefore we can take the sum of their probabilities to obtain the reachability probability.

Definition 2 (Markov Reward Model). *A* Markov reward model (MRM) *is a tuple* $\mathcal{M} = (\mathcal{D}, \mathrm{rew})$ *with the* underlying DTMC $\mathcal{D} = (S, s_I, P)$ *and the* reward function $\mathrm{rew} \colon S \to \mathbb{R}_{\geq 0}$.

Note that for our applications only rational numbers are used as rewards. The presented notions for DTMCs are also applicable to MRMs and refer to the underlying DTMC. For instance, $\mathrm{Paths}^{\mathcal{M}}_{\mathit{fin}}$ refers to paths in the DTMC $\mathcal{D}$ of the MRM $\mathcal{M} = (\mathcal{D}, \mathrm{rew})$. Intuitively, the reward $\mathrm{rew}(s)$ is earned on leaving the state $s \in S$. The *(cumulative) reward* of a finite path $\pi = s_0 \dots s_n \in \mathrm{Paths}^{\mathcal{M}}_{\mathit{fin}}$ is given by $\mathrm{rew}^{\mathcal{M}}(\pi) = \sum_{i=0}^{n-1} \mathrm{rew}(s_i)$. The *expected reward* is the expected amount of reward that has been accumulated until a set of target states $T \subseteq S$ is reached when starting in a state s. If $\Pr^{\mathcal{D}}(s \models \lozenge T) < 1$, we follow the usual definition and set $\mathrm{ExpRew}^{\mathcal{M}}(s \models \lozenge T) := \infty$.[2] Otherwise we define

$$\mathrm{ExpRew}^{\mathcal{M}}(s \models \lozenge T) := \sum_{\pi \in \mathrm{Paths}^{\mathcal{D}}_{\mathit{fin}}(s, \lozenge T)} P(\pi) \cdot \mathrm{rew}(\pi)\,.$$

For all notations, we will in the following omit the superscript $\mathcal{M}$ (or $\mathcal{D}$) if it is clear from the context. Note that rewards can also be defined for transitions. These transition rewards can be transformed to state rewards by means of a simple transformation.

Definition 3 (Reachability Property, Expected Reward Property). *For a DTMC* $\mathcal{D} = (S, s_I, P)$ *with* $s \in S$ *and* $T \subseteq S$*, a probability bound* $\lambda \in [0, 1]$*, and a comparison operator* $\triangleleft \in \{<, \leq\}$*, the* reachability property $\mathbb{P}_{\triangleleft\lambda}(\lozenge T)$ *is satisfied in* s*, written* $s \models \mathbb{P}_{\triangleleft\lambda}(\lozenge T)$*, iff* $\Pr(s \models \lozenge T) \triangleleft \lambda$.

Given an MRM $\mathcal{M} = (\mathcal{D}, \mathrm{rew})$ *and a reward bound* $\lambda' \in \mathbb{R}_{\geq 0}$*, the* expected reward property $\mathbb{E}_{\triangleleft\lambda'}(\lozenge T)$ *is satisfied in* s*, denoted by* $s \models \mathbb{E}_{\triangleleft\lambda'}(\lozenge T)$*, iff* $\mathrm{ExpRew}(s \models \lozenge T) \triangleleft \lambda'$.

Let $\mathcal{D} \models \mathbb{P}_{\triangleleft\lambda}(\lozenge T) \Leftrightarrow s_I \models \mathbb{P}_{\triangleleft\lambda}(\lozenge T)$ *and* $\mathcal{M} \models \mathbb{E}_{\triangleleft\lambda'}(\lozenge T) \Leftrightarrow s_I \models \mathbb{E}_{\triangleleft\lambda'}(\lozenge T)$.

[2] The intuition is as follows: If a state with positive reward from which no target state is reachable is visited infinitely often, an infinite amount of reward will be collected. If this case is excluded, the definition can be generalized.

As transitions leaving a target state $t \in T$ do not affect reachability probabilities and expected rewards, we assume that all target states are absorbing. Note that we explicitly do not include properties with lower bounds here. For reachability properties with lower bounds, we can formulate equivalent properties with upper bounds by considering the probability to reach a state from which no state $t \in T$ is reachable. This transformation is, however, not applicable for expected reward properties. The standard method to check whether $s \models \mathbb{E}_{\lhd\lambda}(\lozenge T)$ (or $s \models \mathbb{P}_{\lhd\lambda}(\lozenge T)$) for a state $s \in S$ is to solve a linear equation system. For expected rewards the equation system has the following shape (assuming $\Pr^{\mathcal{M}}(s \models \lozenge T) = 1$):

$$r_s = \begin{cases} 0 & \text{for } s \in T, \\ \text{rew}(s) + \sum_{s' \in S} P(s,s') \cdot r_{s'} & \text{otherwise}. \end{cases} \tag{1}$$

The unique solution for r_s yields the values $\text{ExpRew}(s \models \lozenge T))$ for every state $s \in S$. For more details and the corresponding linear equation system for reachability probabilities we refer to [17].

We will need mixed integer linear programs (MILPs) which optimize a linear objective function under a condition specified by a conjunction of linear inequalities. A subset of the variables in the inequalities is restricted to take only integer values, which makes solving MILPs NP-hard [18, Problem MP1].

Definition 4 (Mixed Integer Linear Program). *Let $A \in \mathbb{Q}^{m \times n}$, $B \in \mathbb{Q}^{m \times k}$, $b \in \mathbb{Q}^m$, $c \in \mathbb{Q}^n$, and $d \in \mathbb{Q}^k$. A* mixed integer linear program *(MILP) consists of minimizing $c^T x + d^T y$ such that $Ax + By \leq b$ and $x \in \mathbb{R}^n$, $y \in \mathbb{Z}^k$.*

MILPs are typically solved by a combination of a branch-and-bound algorithm with the generation of so-called cutting planes. These algorithms heavily rely on the fact that relaxations of MILPs which result by removing the integrality constraints can be solved efficiently. Efficient tools are available, e. g., Gurobi [16]. We refer the reader to [19] for more information on solving MILPs.

We now briefly recall the central definitions of counterexamples for reachability properties.

Definition 5 (Evidence, Counterexample [20]). *Let $\mathcal{D} = (S, s_I, P)$ be a DTMC, $T \subseteq S$ be a set of target states, and $\mathbb{P}_{\lhd\lambda}(\lozenge T)$ be a reachability property violated by $\mathcal{D}$. Paths in $\text{Paths}^{\mathcal{D}}_{fin}(s_I, \lozenge T)$ are called* evidences. *A* counterexample *C is a set of evidences such that $P(C) := \sum_{\pi \in C} P(\pi) \not\lhd \lambda$. C is* minimal *if $|C| \leq |C'|$ holds for all counterexamples C' and* smallest *if it is minimal and $P(C) \geq P(C')$ holds for all minimal counterexamples C'.*

Smallest counterexamples can be computed using algorithms for finding the k shortest paths in a directed graph. As it is infeasible to compute smallest counterexamples for large DTMCs, numerous heuristic approaches have been proposed, based on best-first search, SAT-based bounded model checking, and BDD-based symbolic methods.

The drawback of all path-based counterexamples is that the number of paths even in a minimal counterexample can be very large; [20] presents an example where the number of paths in a minimal counterexample is doubly exponential in the system parameters – and therefore much larger than the number of system states. To obtain a more compact representation, the usage of critical subsystems has been proposed [14,15].

Definition 6 (Selection, Critical Subsystem). *Let $\mathcal{D} = (S, s_I, P)$ be a DTMC, $T \subseteq S$ a set of target states, and $\mathbb{P}_{\trianglelefteq\lambda}(\lozenge T)$ a reachability property which is violated by $\mathcal{D}$. A subset $S' \subseteq S$ of states with $s_I \in S'$ is called a* selection. *The* subsystem *of $\mathcal{D}$ induced by a selection S' is the DTMC $\mathcal{D}' = (S' \uplus \{t\}, s_I, P')$ where $t \notin S$ is a new state and P' is defined by*

$$P'(s, s') = \begin{cases} P(s, s') & \text{if } s, s' \in S' \\ \sum_{s'' \in S \setminus S'} P(s, s'') & \text{if } s \in S' \text{ and } s' = t \\ 1 & \text{if } s = s' = t \\ 0 & \text{otherwise.} \end{cases}$$

We call a selection S' and its induced subsystem critical *for $\mathbb{P}_{\trianglelefteq\lambda}(\lozenge T)$ if $\mathbb{P}_{\trianglelefteq\lambda}(\lozenge T')$ is violated in the induced subsystem with $T' = T \cap S'$.*

The additional absorbing state $t \notin S$ is only required here to ensure that the probabilities of the transitions leaving a certain state sum up to one. Critical subsystems have the property that the set of paths from the initial to a target state forms a counterexample according to Definition 5.

The computation of critical subsystems with a minimum number of states using MILP has been investigated in [21]. Heuristic approaches which typically yield small, but not necessarily minimal counterexamples are also available. They are mostly based on the path-search approaches mentioned above.

3 Critical Subsystems for Expected Rewards

Consider in the following an MRM $\mathcal{M} = (\mathcal{D}, \text{rew})$ with $\mathcal{D} = (S, s_I, P)$ and an expected reward property $\mathbb{E}_{\trianglelefteq\lambda}(\lozenge T)$ with $\trianglelefteq \in \{<, \leq\}$, $\lambda \in \mathbb{R}_{\geq 0}$ such that $\mathcal{M} \not\models \mathbb{E}_{\trianglelefteq\lambda}(\lozenge T)$. We assume all target states $t \in T$ to be absorbing.

If $\Pr(s_I \models \lozenge T) < 1$, the expected reward is infinite, and it directly follows that $\mathbb{E}_{\trianglelefteq\lambda}(\lozenge T)$ is violated for all $\lambda \in \mathbb{R}_{\geq 0}$. In this case, a path from s_I to a state from which no state in T is reachable indicates why $\Pr(s_I \models \lozenge T) < 1$ holds and can therefore serve as a counterexample. Such a path can be found via simple reachability analysis on the graph of the DTMC.

In the following, we will only consider the more interesting case where $\Pr(s_I \models \lozenge T) = 1$ and thus $\text{ExpRew}(s_I \models \lozenge T) < \infty$ holds.

To indicate why the MRM $\mathcal{M}$ violates the property $\mathbb{E}_{\trianglelefteq\lambda}(\lozenge T)$, we adjust the notion of critical subsystems for reachability properties to expected reward properties. The idea is to select states of the original system in order to form a subsystem that already refutes the property.

Definition 7 (Critical Subsystem for Expected Reachability). *Let $\mathcal{M} = (\mathcal{D}, \text{rew})$ be an MRM with $\mathcal{D} = (S, s_I, P)$. For a selection of states $S' \subseteq S$, a* subsystem *of* $\mathcal{M}$ *is given by the MRM* $\mathcal{M}' = (\mathcal{D}', \text{rew}')$ *with* $\mathcal{D}' = (S' \uplus \{t\}, s_I, P')$ *where* $t \notin S$ *is a new state,* $\text{rew}'(t) = 0$, $\text{rew}'(s) = \text{rew}(s)$ *for all* $s \in S'$ *and* P' *as in Definition 6. The subsystem* $\mathcal{M}'$ *is* critical *for a property* $\mathbb{E}_{\trianglelefteq\lambda}(\lozenge T)$ *iff* $\mathcal{M}' \not\models \mathbb{E}_{\trianglelefteq\lambda}(\lozenge T')$ *where* $T' = (T \cap S') \cup \{t\}$.

In contrast to critical subsystems for reachability properties, the new absorbing state t has to be considered as a target state. This is reasonable because in the original MRM the probability to reach a target state is one by assumption. If t were not a target state, the probability to reach a target state in the subsystem would be less than one and therefore the expected reward infinite. That means, the subsystem would be critical for every bound $\lambda \in \mathbb{R}_{\geq 0}$, even if $\mathcal{M} \models \mathbb{E}_{\trianglelefteq\lambda}(\lozenge T)$. Such a subsystem can obviously not be considered a counterexample. The definition above ensures that $\Pr^{\mathcal{M}'}(s_I \models \lozenge T') = 1$ holds for every possible subsystem $\mathcal{M}'$ of $\mathcal{M}$ by adding the new state t to the set of target states. From $\Pr^{\mathcal{M}}(s_I \models \lozenge T) = 1$, it also follows that $\Pr^{\mathcal{M}}(s \models \lozenge T) = 1$ holds for every state s that lies on a path in $\text{Paths}^{\mathcal{M}}_{\mathit{fin}}(s_I, \lozenge T)$.

This means that the reachability of target states is already given by assumption. In a subsystem $\mathcal{M}'$, the transitions leading to t can be interpreted as "shortcuts" to a target state. If $\mathcal{M}'$ is critical, then the reward collected within the subsystem is already too large, even if all other states would have reward zero. This allows us to hide the unimportant details of how a state in T will eventually be reached and we can focus on the parts of the model where reward is collected. Note that this reasoning would not be valid if we allow for states with negative rewards: Parts of the model where enough reward is collected might be followed by states with negative rewards. Hence, the details of how a state in T is reached would not be unimportant anymore. A critical subsystem can also not serve as a counterexample for an expected reward property with a *lower* bound as this would require to indicate an upper bound of the expected reward of the model.

Alternative Definition of Critical Subsystems. We discuss another notion for critical subsystem for expected reward properties. According to Definition 7, the original system was restricted with respect to its states. It is also natural to change the rewards that are assigned to states *without changing the behavior of the system.* The goal is now to only restrict the positive rewards in the system as much as possible. To avoid confusion, this is called a *critical reward subsystem.*

Definition 8 (Critical Reward Subsystem). *Let* $\mathcal{M} = (\mathcal{D}, \text{rew})$ *be an MRM with* $\mathcal{D} = (S, s_I, P)$. *For a selection* $S' \subseteq S$, *the* reward subsystem *of* $\mathcal{M}$ *induced by* S' *is defined as the MRM* $\mathcal{M}' = (\mathcal{D}, rew')$ *where*

$$rew'(s) = \begin{cases} rew(s) & \text{for } s \in S' \\ 0 & \text{otherwise.} \end{cases}$$

The reward subsystem $\mathcal{M}'$ *is* critical *for a property* $\mathbb{E}_{\trianglelefteq\lambda}(\lozenge T)$ *iff* $\mathcal{M}' \not\models \mathbb{E}_{\trianglelefteq\lambda}(\lozenge T)$.

A critical reward subsystem indicates the parts of the system that give enough reward to refute a property without ruling out possible system behavior (i. e.,

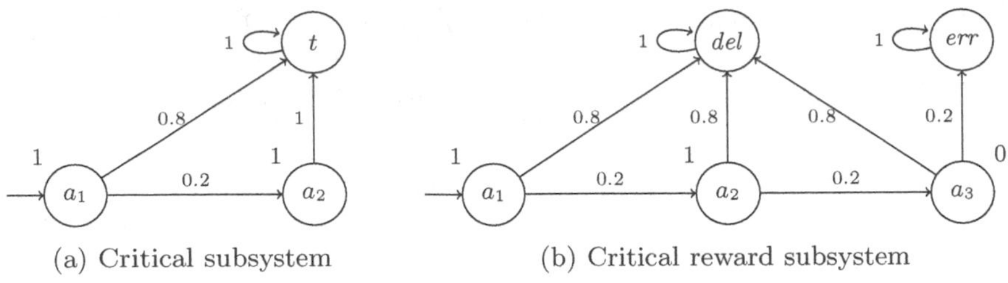

(a) Critical subsystem (b) Critical reward subsystem

Fig. 2. The different notions of critical subsystems

without disregarding states in the underlying DTMC). Depending on the particular application, this can be advantageous, although there are examples where a critical subsystem according to Definition 7 should be preferred. For instance, consider an MRM $\mathcal{M}$ with exactly one state s such that $rew(s) > 0$. Every reward subsystem of $\mathcal{M}$ is either equal to $\mathcal{M}$ or only has states with reward zero and is therefore less useful for debugging purposes.

In conclusion, we reconsider the MRM depicted in Figure 1(a). For the violated property $\mathbb{E}_{<1.2}(\Diamond\{del, err\})$, we show the two notions of critical subsystems in Figure 2. The critical subsystem according to Definition 7 in Figure 2(a) has reduced state space, while for the critical reward subsystem according to Definition 8 in Figure 2(b), a reward of zero is assigned to state a_3.

4 Generation of Critical Subsystems

We now present different approaches to generate a subsystem of the MRM $\mathcal{M} = (\mathcal{D}, \text{rew})$, $\mathcal{D} = (S, s_I, P)$, that is critical for the property $\mathbb{E}_{<\lambda}(\Diamond T)$[3]. We assume in the following that $\mathcal{M}$ violates the property, that $\Pr^{\mathcal{M}}(s \models \Diamond T) = 1$, that the target states in T are absorbing, that all states in S are reachable from the initial state $s_I \notin T$, and that $\text{ExpRew}^{\mathcal{M}}(s_I \models \Diamond T) > 0$.

4.1 Minimal Critical Subsystem Generation

We start with the problem of generating *minimal critical subsystems.* A critical subsystem is called *minimal* if it is induced by a selection $S' \subseteq S$ such that $|S'| \leq |S''|$ holds for all selections $S'' \subseteq S$ that induce critical subsystems. We fix the set of states with positive reward by $S_R := \{s \in S \mid \text{rew}(s) > 0\}$. To reduce the number of states that have to be considered, the first step is to determine the set of *contributing states*, which are given by

$$\widehat{S} = \{s \in S \setminus T \mid \text{ a state } s' \in S_R \text{ is reachable from } s\}.$$

[3] the subsequently discussed Path search and Best-first search approaches are also applicable for $\mathbb{E}_{\leq\lambda}(\Diamond T)$.

$\widehat{S}$ can be obtained via a reachability analysis in the underlying graph of the MRM. Starting from a non-contributing state $s \in S \setminus \widehat{S}$, a state with positive reward cannot be reached. Therefore, adding s to a selection S' does not have any effect on the expected reward of the subsystem induced by S' and minimal critical subsystems contain only contributing states.

In a second step we formulate an MILP to find a selection $S' \subseteq \widehat{S}$ that induces a minimal critical subsystem $\mathcal{M}'$ of $\mathcal{M}$ for $\mathbb{E}_{<\lambda}(\Diamond T)$. For all $s \in \widehat{S}$, variables $x_s \in \{0,1\}$ are used with the interpretation that $x_s = 1$ iff $s \in S'$. Furthermore, variables $r_s \in \mathbb{R}_{\geq 0}$ are used to take into account the expected reward for the states in the resulting subsystem, more precisely, $0 \leq r_s \leq \mathrm{ExpRew}^{\mathcal{M}'}(s \models \Diamond T')$ with $T' = (T \cap S') \cup \{t\}$. The MILP can be formulated as follows:

$$\text{minimize} \quad -\frac{1}{2 \cdot \mathrm{ExpRew}^{\mathcal{M}}(s_I \models \Diamond T)} \cdot r_{s_I} + \sum_{s \in \widehat{S}} x_s \tag{2a}$$

such that

$$\forall s \in \widehat{S}\colon \quad r_s \leq (\mathrm{ExpRew}^{\mathcal{M}}(s \models \Diamond T)) \cdot x_s \tag{2b}$$

$$\forall s \in \widehat{S}\colon \quad r_s \leq \mathrm{rew}(s) + \sum_{s' \in \widehat{S}} P(s,s') \cdot r_{s'} \tag{2c}$$

$$r_{s_I} \geq \lambda \tag{2d}$$

We can obtain the values $\mathrm{ExpRew}^{\mathcal{M}}(s \models \Diamond T)$ for all $s \in \widehat{S}$ as a side-product from model checking. Condition 2b ensures that, if the state is not included, i. e., $x_s = 0$, r_s is explicitly set to zero in order to avoid unwanted contribution to the expected reward of the initial state in the subsystem. For states in the selected subsystem, i. e., $x_s = 1$, Condition 2b is not a real restriction as $\mathrm{ExpRew}^{\mathcal{M}'}(s \models \Diamond T') \leq \mathrm{ExpRew}^{\mathcal{M}}(s \models \Diamond T)$ holds for all states $s \in S'$. In Constraint 2c, the value of r_s is bounded from above by the actual expected reward in the subsystem by using the linear equation system as in Equation 1. Transitions that lead to states in $S \setminus \widehat{S}$ are not considered since the expected reward of these states is always 0. Constraint 2d ensures the criticality of the subsystem by forcing the expected reward of the initial state to be at least λ. Finally, consider the objective function in (2a), which enforces a minimal critical subsystem with maximal expected reward among all minimal critical subsystems: The second summand ensures the minimality of the critical subsystem by minimizing the sum of all x_s-variables. The first summand ensures a maximal value for the r_{s_I}-variable of the initial state by minimizing its negative value. Additionally, this value needs to be in the open interval $(0,1)$ as otherwise the solver could include another state s, i. e., $x_s = 1$, and thereby break the minimality criterion. This is achieved by the factor $c \cdot 1/\mathrm{ExpRew}^{\mathcal{M}}(s_I \models \Diamond T)$ for arbitrary $0 < c < 1$ (we chose $c = 1/2$). This maximal value will be exactly the expected reward of the initial state in the minimal critical subsystem. Note that this is not necessary in order to achieve a state-minimal subsystem. In our experiments as well as in the following objective functions, we omit this summand.

Redundant constraints which prune sub-optimal solutions from the search space can be added to this MILP to assist the solver in finding an optimal solution quickly. We omit these constraints here as they have a very similar shape as for reachability properties. We refer the reader to [21] for details.

Alternative Objective Functions. Instead of a critical subsystem with a minimal number of states, other notions might be beneficial dependent on the application at hand. We discuss a few possibilities below to give an intuition on how our approach can be adapted in the desired way. For instance, we replace (2a) with one of the following objective functions:

$$\text{minimize} \quad \sum_{s\in S_R} x_s \quad (3) \qquad \sum_{s\in S_R} \text{rew}(s)\cdot x_s \quad (4) \qquad \sum_{s\in S_R} \text{rew}(s)^2\cdot x_s \quad (5)$$

To obtain a minimal *number of selected states with positive rewards*, (3) can be used. By (4), the *sum of all rewards* occurring in the subsystem is minimized, while we minimize the *norm of the rewards* occurring in the subsystem by (5).

Critical Reward Subsystems. We also give an MILP formulation to generate minimal critical reward subsystems as in Definition 8:

$$\text{minimize} \quad \sum_{s\in S_R} x_s \tag{6a}$$

such that

$$\forall s \in \widehat{S}\colon \quad r_s \leq \text{rew}(s)\cdot x_s + \sum_{s'\in\widehat{S}} P(s,s')\cdot r_{s'} \tag{6b}$$

$$r_{s_I} \geq \lambda \tag{6c}$$

The objective function (6a) only minimizes the number of states with positive reward from S_R. In Constraint 6b, the expected reward for each state $s \in \widehat{S}$ that is included in the selection is computed and assigned as upper bound to r_s. Constraint 6c ensures the criticality of the subsystem.

Note that in contrast to the MILP formulation (2a)–(2d), we do not need to explicitly assign non-selected states an expected reward of zero as it suffices to only set the contributing reward of non-selected states to zero.

4.2 Path Search Approach

The *path search approach* is an extension of the local path search presented in [15]. Originally, this heuristic approach is used to generate small critical subsystems of DTMCs for reachability properties. The algorithm can be adapted to work for MRMs and expected reward properties by taking the rewards into consideration.

For this purpose, a *value function* $V\colon S\times S \to [0,1] \subseteq \mathbb{R}$ is used to evaluate the benefit of transitions. The function should take rewards and probabilities into account such that a high value $V(s,s')$ means that it might be beneficial to include the states s and s' in the subsystem. A sequence of states $s_0 \ldots s_n$ with

$V(s_i, s_{i+1}) > 0$ for all $0 \leq i < n$ should be a valid path of $\mathcal{M}$ and vice versa. We therefore require $V(s, s') > 0$ iff $P(s, s') > 0$ for all $s, s' \in S$. For a path $\pi = s_0 \dots s_n \in \text{Paths}^{\mathcal{M}}_{fin}$ the value of a path is given by $V(\pi) = \prod_{i=0}^{n-1} V(s_i, s_{i+1})$. Given a set of paths $\Pi \subseteq \text{Paths}^{\mathcal{M}}_{fin}$, a path $\pi \in \Pi$ is called *most valuable* if $V(\pi) \geq V(\pi')$ for all $\pi' \in \Pi$. To ensure that there is always a most valuable path, we require that $0 \leq V(s, s') \leq 1$ for all $s, s' \in S$. If $V(s, s') = 1$, we additionally require $V(s, s'') = 0$ for all $s'' \neq s'$ to exclude infinitely many most valuable paths that arbitrarily often take loops with value one. Reasonable definitions for V will be discussed later.

We consider paths from $\text{Paths}^{\mathcal{M}}_{fin}(S_{\text{start}}, S_{\text{end}})$ for $S_{\text{start}}, S_{\text{end}} \subseteq S$. Furthermore, for paths of length two we require that the last state is not contained in S_{start} (note that the sets S_{start} and S_{end} do not have to be disjoint).

The first step of the path search approach is always to find a most valuable path that starts in the initial state and ends in one of the target states. A selection S' is initialized with the states visited on that path. After that, most valuable paths connecting already selected states with target states or, again, selected states are repeatedly searched. The selection S' is extended by the states visited on these paths until it induces a critical subsystem. Algorithm 1 describes the procedure. Here, the function FINDMOSTVALUABLEPATH($V, S_{\text{start}}, S_{\text{end}}$) returns a most valuable path with respect to the value function V that connects S_{start} with S_{end}. Such a function can be realized by using an adaptation of Dijkstra's shortest path algorithm where the values are multiplied (instead of summed) and paths with maximal (instead of minimal) values are chosen. The function SUBSYS($\mathcal{M}, S'$) returns the subsystem of $\mathcal{M}$ induced by S'.

Algorithm 1. Path Search Approach

Input: MRM $\mathcal{M}$, property $\mathbb{E}_{\triangleleft\lambda}(\lozenge T)$
Output: A critical subsystem of $\mathcal{M}$ for $\mathbb{E}_{\triangleleft\lambda}(\lozenge T)$

initialize value function $V\colon S \times S \to [0, 1]$
$\pi \leftarrow$ FINDMOSTVALUABLEPATH($V, \{s_I\}, T$)
$S' \leftarrow \{s \in S \mid s \text{ is visited by } \pi\}$
while SUBSYS($\mathcal{M}, S'$) is not critical for $\mathbb{E}_{\triangleleft\lambda}(\lozenge T)$ **do**
    $\pi \leftarrow$ FINDMOSTVALUABLEPATH($V, S', S' \cup T$)
    $S' \leftarrow S' \cup \{s \in S \mid s \text{ is visited by } \pi\}$
end while
return SUBSYS($\mathcal{M}, S'$)

It is not required to check in every iteration whether the current selection already induces a critical subsystem. To save computation time, the condition is checked only if at least $|S| \cdot c$ additional states have been selected since the last check (for a constant $0 < c \leq 1$).

Value Functions. We propose two different value functions. First, we want to take both the probability of a transition $(s, s') \in E$ and the reward of the state s into account by using their product:

$$V_1(s, s') = P(s, s') \cdot \frac{\text{rew}(s) + \varepsilon}{\max_{s'' \in S}(\text{rew}(s'')) + \varepsilon}$$

In order to avoid a value of zero and the division by zero, we add a constant $\varepsilon > 0$ to both the numerator and the denominator. The value is scaled by the maximal occurring reward in order to ensure it to be from $[0, 1]$.

As a second proposal, we make use of the actual expected reward of all states inside the original system:

$$V_2(s, s') = \frac{\text{ExpRew}(s \models \Diamond T) + \varepsilon}{\max_{s'' \in S}(\text{ExpRew}(s'' \models \Diamond T)) + 2\varepsilon}$$

We scale these values by the maximal occurring expected reward and add constants. For the denominator we add a larger value in order to have a value which is smaller than one. Note that $V_2(s, s')$ is independent of s'. This is not disadvantageous since the value of a path will still depend on all visited states (except the last one which is either a target state or already selected). It is also possible to just use probabilities for our computations. However, in our experiments V_2 performed best for most cases.

4.3 Best-first Search Approach

The *best-first search approach* is another heuristic approach to generate critical subsystems. It is related to the extended best first search (XBF) presented in [14]. A value function $f \colon S \to \mathbb{R}$ evaluates how beneficial it is to select a given state. For the best-first search, we denote value functions with f (instead of V) to avoid confusion with the value functions of the path search approach. In contrast to XBF, where the model is explored in an on-the-fly manner, the model is analyzed in advance. The obtained information can be used for f. On the one hand, this increases the effort to get the values of the function but, on the other hand, the provided values can be more accurate.

Algorithm 2 illustrates how a critical subsystem is generated with the help of such a value function f. It uses two sets of states: S' and S_{explore}. S' is a selection to which more and more states are added until it induces a critical subsystem. The set S_{explore} always contains the states that are considered to be explored, starting with the initial state s_I. Repeatedly a state $s \in S_{\text{explore}}$ with maximal value $f(s)$ is explored. This means that s is added to the selection S', removed from S_{explore}, and all non-selected successors of s are added to S_{explore}. Target states do not need to be explored and are therefore directly added to S' and not added to S_{explore}. The procedure stops as soon as the subsystem of $\mathcal{M}$ induced by S' (denoted by $\textsc{SubSys}(\mathcal{M}, S')$) is critical. Similar to the path search approach, computation time can be saved by only checking this condition if at least $|S| \cdot c$ states have been added to S' since the last check.

Algorithm 2. Best-first Search Approach

Input: MRM $\mathcal{M}$, property $\mathbb{E}_{\trianglelefteq\lambda}(\lozenge T)$
Output: A critical subsystem of $\mathcal{M}$ for $\mathbb{E}_{\trianglelefteq\lambda}(\lozenge T)$

initialize function $f\colon S \to \mathbb{R}$
$S' \leftarrow \emptyset$
$S_{\text{explore}} \leftarrow \{s_I\}$
repeat
  choose $s \in S_{\text{explore}}$ with $f(s) \geq f(s')$ for all $s' \in S_{\text{explore}}$
  $S' \leftarrow S' \cup \{s\} \cup \{s' \in T \mid P(s, s') > 0\}$
  $S_{\text{explore}} \leftarrow (S_{\text{explore}} \cup \{s' \in S \mid P(s, s') > 0 \text{ and } s' \notin S'\}) \setminus \{s\}$
until SUBSYS($\mathcal{M}, S'$) is critical for $\mathbb{E}_{\trianglelefteq\lambda}(\lozenge T)$
return SUBSYS($\mathcal{M}, S'$)

Possible value functions f for all $s \in S$ are:

$$f_1(s) := \text{ExpRew}(s \models \lozenge T) \qquad f_2(s) := P(\pi^{s}_{s_I}) \cdot \text{ExpRew}(s \models \lozenge T)$$

$$f_3(s) := P(\pi^{s}_{s_I}) \cdot \max_{s' \in S}(P(\pi^{s'}_{s}) \cdot \text{rew}(s'))$$

Here, $\pi^{s'}_{s}$ denotes a path from $s \in S$ to $s' \in S$ with maximal probability, i. e., $P(\pi^{s'}_{s}) \geq P(\pi)$ for all paths π from s to s'. The expected rewards of every state can be obtained as a side product from model checking. For a state $s \in S$, the value $f_1(s)$ provides information about the benefit of s itself as well as the "future" of s, i. e., the benefit of the states that are reachable via s. To also consider the "past" of s, f_2 uses the probability to reach s. Hence, the probability to reach a state s is estimated by the probability of a single path. The probabilities $P(\pi^{s}_{s_I})$ for all states $s \in S$ can be obtained by using a variant of Dijkstra's shortest path algorithm. Finally, function f_3 evaluates whether there is a state s' that is reachable from s with high probability and that has high reward.

5 Experimental Results

In this section we report on a selection of our benchmark results. We implemented all approaches presented in the previous sections in C++ using GUROBI [16] as MILP solver. All experiments were conducted on a Windows 64 bit system with a 2.66 GHz CPU and 6 GB RAM. We used the following benchmarks which are all available (partly without the reward definitions) for PRISM [2].

The aim of the *crowds protocol* [22] (crowds) is to hide the identity of the sender of a message by randomly routing the message within a group of crowd members, consisting of good and bad members, the latter ones trying to collect information about the identity of a sender. The model can be scaled in the number N of *good members* and the number K of message deliveries. The time a single crowd member requires to forward or deliver a message varies between one and five time units. We consider *the expected time needed to deliver K messages.*

Table 1. Experimental results (TO> 1 h, MO> 6 GB)

		Critical Subsystem				Crit. Rew. Subsys.
		Minimal MILP	MILP	Heuristic Path Search	BF Search	Mininimal MILP
model	$N[-K]$ #states #transitions	$\|S'\|$ time (seconds) memory (MB)	$\|S'\|$ time (seconds) memory (MB)	$\|S'\|$ time (seconds) memory (MB)	$\|S'\|$ time (seconds) memory (MB)	$\|S'\|$ / $\|S_R\|$ time (seconds) memory (MB)
crowds	10-3 6 563 15 143	109 13.38 48	**109** ≤1 24	161 **0.091** **9**	292 0.16 **9**	26 / 1 560 0.25 16
	10-6 352 535 833 015	972* TO (25.30 %) 1 678	**1 293** 36 819	2 447 79.44 **246**	3 780 **2.47** **246**	229 / 87 360 238.72 439
	15-6 2 464 168 7 347 928	1 820* TO (41.30 %) 4 662	**2 478** 241 4 793	5 208 1 573.16 1 783	10 578 **10.35** **1 782**	424 / 610 470 3 270.84 3 181
	20-6 10 633 591 38 261 191	MO	MO	TO	**23 386** **194.72** **5 567.24**	MO
herman	7 128 2 188	25 0.39 9	**25** ≤1 9	31 **0.004** **5**	45 **0.003** **5**	14 / 128 0.06 8
	13 8 192 1 594 324	228* TO (15.1 %) 655	292 4 **103**	**230** 1.59 104	231 **1.48** 104	109 / 8 192 1.65 132
	15 32 768 14 348 908	360* TO (16.2 %) 1 177	415 22 **831**	**362** 20.27 832	381 **19.26** 832	167 / 32 768 20.38 1 057
	17 131 072 129 140 164	542* TO (19.8 %) 5 267	550 333 **5 506**	**546** **237.63** 5 623	572 245.48 5 542	248 / 131 072 280.65 5 466
egl	4-8 31 486 31 741	1 319 7.34 32.6	**1 319** 2 28	1 407 **0.15** **25**	1 606 1.33 **25**	330 / 668 0.2 31
	5-2 33 790 34 813	2 353 375.93 58	**2 353** 4 33	2 481 3.42 **26**	2 848 **2.74** **26**	574 / 1 163 0.16 33
	7-4 1 654 782 1 671 165	86 943* TO (0.01 %) 1 448	**87 016** **45** **1 033**	106 538 3 504.7 **1 033**	93 681 82.06 **1 033**	9 462 / 18 987 9.18 1 273
	7-8 3 489 790 3 506 173	126 716* TO (0.06 %) 2 172	**126 732** 126 2 172	TO	134 383 **120.13** **2 171**	11 240 / 22 543 23.41 2 686

The *self-stabilization protocol* (herman) [23] considers a ring of N identical processes. A configuration is called stable if there is exactly one designated process. The purpose of this protocol is to transform the system from an arbitrary configuration into a stable one. We are interested in *the expected number of steps until the system reaches a stable configuration.*

The *contract signing protocol* (egl) [24] is dedicated to fairly exchange commitments to a contract between two parties A and B. It is assumed that both parties have N pairs of secrets of length L which will be exchanged. A party has committed to a contract whenever both secrets of one of its pairs are known by the other party. We investigate the *expected number of messages* that A needs to receive in order to know a pair of B where only the messages after B knows a pair of A are considered.

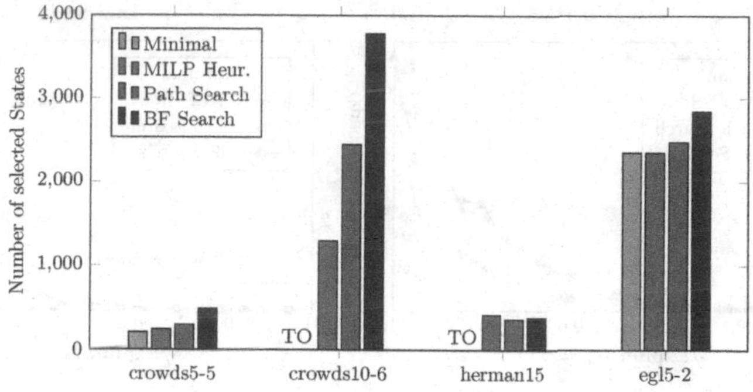

Fig. 3. Sizes of the critical subsystems generated by the different approaches

The results for all benchmarks are depicted in Table 1. First, we computed critical subsystems using the MILP approach (see Equations 2a–2d) and the heuristic approaches (Path search and BF Search, see Sections 4.2 and 4.3). For all approaches we give the *size of the selection*, the *computation time in seconds* and the *memory consumption in MB*. The reward thresholds were set to half of the expected reward in the original system. Minimal MILP refers to the minimization including the proof of minimality. Whenever we reached the time limit, we depict the smallest critical subsystem found until that point (*) as well as the gap to the lower bound.

We also made use of the nature of MILP solving. Iteratively, an intermediate solution is compared w. r. t. its minimality to a certain lower bound on the optimal solution. This intermediate solution satisfies all conditions for a critical subsystem while minimality is not yet proven. We basically aborted the computation of GUROBI after roughly the same time as was consumed for the heuristic approaches and refer to this intermediate result as *MILP as heuristic approach*. This demonstrates the practical use of this approach as a heuristic method. The optimal results, excluding the minimization, are always depicted boldfaced.

We first observe that for the heuristic MILP a very small subsystem which is near the actual minimum is often found after a few seconds. This justifies the MILP approach also as a heuristic method, as benchmarks with millions of states and transitions are possible. Note that the herman benchmark is strongly connected having a large number of transitions. The heuristic approaches perform well for large benchmarks while the BF search is even able to compute results for over 10^7 states and 10^8 transitions. Note that the methods were not able to handle larger systems because this was the threshold for explicit storing.

We tested all value functions explained above where for Path search V_2 and for BF search f_2 performed best. For these approaches, the memory consumption is rather high due to the initial model checking that we perform. For the MILP approaches it is even higher due to the nature of the solving process.

Results for minimal critical reward subsystems as in Definition 8 depict both the size of the selection, i. e., the number of states having a positive reward in the subsystem as well as the original number of such states. We observe that in

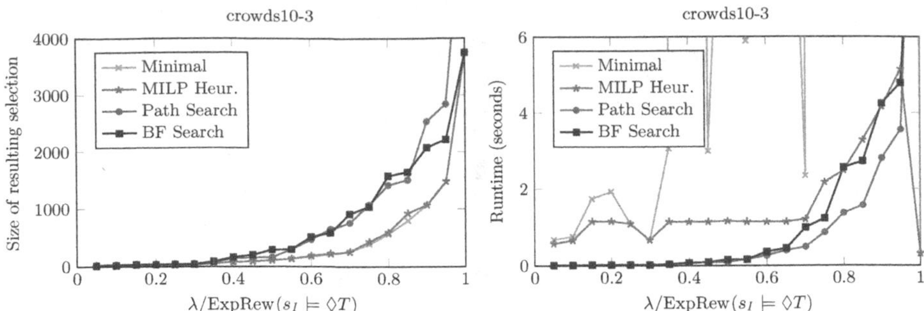

Fig. 4. Results of the different approaches plotted against different reward bounds λ

a relatively small amount of time the number of states having positive reward can drastically be reduced; in some cases even by three orders of magnitude.

For a better overview, Figure 3 shows the sizes for different benchmarks for all approaches. In general, the path search computes smaller subsystems than the BF search. Figure 4 depicts results for a specific benchmark and different reward bounds in terms of the size of the subsystem and the running time. The nearer the reward bound is to the actual expected reward of the original system, the larger the size of the subsystems becomes. Similarly, the times required by the Path search and the BF search increase if the bound is high. The running times for computing minimal critical subsystems do not exhibit such a monotony. For certain reward bounds, the MILP solver is able to find a solution and proof its minimality comparatively fast. A notable example is the case where the ratio between the reward threshold and the actual expected reward is nearly one. Here, the MILP approaches only select the set of contributing states and therefore take nearly no time.

Summary. Using the MILP approaches we are able to compute *optimal* results for both types of critical subsystems. We note that computing critical reward subsystems is more efficient. This is due to the fact that the number of possible solutions is smaller. However, it might be beneficial to compute small counterexamples, in which case this approach is not feasible as the original system's size is not reduced. The path search yields smaller subsystems than the BF search. For very large benchmarks, BF is the only method that can compute results within the time limit.

6 Conclusion and Future Work

In this paper we thoroughly investigated different notions and methods to compute counterexamples in the form of critical system parts for Markov reward models. The experiments were very promising and showed the applicability for rather large benchmark instances. In the future, we will adapt the heuristic methods to symbolic data structures such as binary decision diagrams to enable the treatment of significantly larger systems.

References

1. Clarke, E.M.: The birth of model checking. In: Grumberg, O., Veith, H. (eds.) 25MC Festschrift 2008. LNCS, vol. 5000, pp. 1–26. Springer, Heidelberg (2008)
2. Kwiatkowska, M., Norman, G., Parker, D.: PRISM 4.0: Verification of probabilistic real-time systems. In: Gopalakrishnan, G., Qadeer, S. (eds.) CAV 2011. LNCS, vol. 6806, pp. 585–591. Springer, Heidelberg (2011)
3. Norman, G., Parker, D., Kwiatkowska, M.Z., Shukla, S.K.: Evaluating the reliability of NAND multiplexing with PRISM. IEEE Trans. on CAD of Integrated Circuits and Systems 24(10), 1629–1637 (2005)
4. Norman, G., Shmatikov, V.: Analysis of probabilistic contract signing. Journal of Computer Security 14(6), 561–589 (2006)
5. Kwiatkowska, M.Z., Norman, G., Parker, D.: Using probabilistic model checking in systems biology. SIGMETRICS Performance Evaluation Review 35(4), 14–21 (2008)
6. Alur, R., Henzinger, T., Vardi, M.: Theory in practice for system design and verification. ACM Siglog News 2(1), 46–51 (2015)
7. Behrmann, G., Larsen, K.G., Rasmussen, J.I.: Priced timed automata: Algorithms and applications. In: de Boer, F.S., Bonsangue, M.M., Graf, S., de Roever, W.-P. (eds.) FMCO 2004. LNCS, vol. 3657, pp. 162–182. Springer, Heidelberg (2005)
8. Chatterjee, K., Doyen, L., Henzinger, T.A., Raskin, J.F.: Generalized Mean-payoff and Energy Games. In: Proc. of FSTTCS. LIPIcs, vol. 8, pp. 505–516. Schloss Dagstuhl–Leibniz-Zentrum fuer Informatik (2010)
9. Boker, U., Henzinger, T.A., Radhakrishna, A.: Battery transition systems. In: Proc. of POPL, pp. 595–606. ACM Press (2014)
10. Howard, R.A.: Dynamic Probabilistic Systems; Volume I: Markov models. John Wiley & Sons (1971)
11. Baier, C., Hahn, E.M., Haverkort, B.R., Hermanns, H., Katoen, J.P.: Model checking for performability. Mathematical Structures in Computer Science 23(4), 751–795 (2013)
12. Andova, S., Hermanns, H., Katoen, J.P.: Discrete-time rewards model-checked. In: Larsen, K.G., Niebert, P. (eds.) FORMATS 2003. LNCS, vol. 2791, pp. 88–104. Springer, Heidelberg (2004)
13. Ábrahám, E., Becker, B., Dehnert, C., Jansen, N., Katoen, J.-P., Wimmer, R.: Counterexample generation for discrete-time Markov models: An introductory survey. In: Bernardo, M., Damiani, F., Hähnle, R., Johnsen, E.B., Schaefer, I. (eds.) SFM 2014. LNCS, vol. 8483, pp. 65–121. Springer, Heidelberg (2014)
14. Aljazzar, H., Leue, S.: Directed explicit state-space search in the generation of counterexamples for stochastic model checking. IEEE Trans. on Software Engineering 36(1), 37–60 (2010)
15. Jansen, N., Ábrahám, E., Katelaan, J., Wimmer, R., Katoen, J.-P., Becker, B.: Hierarchical counterexamples for discrete-time Markov chains. In: Bultan, T., Hsiung, P.-A. (eds.) ATVA 2011. LNCS, vol. 6996, pp. 443–452. Springer, Heidelberg (2011)
16. Gurobi Optimization, Inc.: Gurobi optimizer reference manual (2013), http://www.gurobi.com
17. Baier, C., Katoen, J.P.: Principles of Model Checking. The MIT Press (2008)
18. Garey, M.R., Johnson, D.S.: Computers and Intractability: A Guide to the Theory of NP-Completeness. W. H. Freeman & Co Ltd. (1979)
19. Schrijver, A.: Theory of Linear and Integer Programming. Wiley (1986)

20. Han, T., Katoen, J.P., Damman, B.: Counterexample generation in probabilistic model checking. IEEE Trans. on Software Engineering 35(2), 241–257 (2009)
21. Wimmer, R., Jansen, N., Ábrahám, E., Katoen, J.P., Becker, B.: Minimal counterexamples for linear-time probabilistic verification. Theoretical Computer Science 549, 61–100 (2014)
22. Reiter, M.K., Rubin, A.D.: Crowds: Anonymity for web transactions. ACM Trans. on Information and System Security 1(1), 66–92 (1998)
23. Herman, T.: Probabilistic self-stabilization. Information Processing Letters 35(2), 63–67 (1990)
24. Even, S., Goldreich, O., Lempel, A.: A randomized protocol for signing contracts. Communications of the ACM 28(6), 637–647 (1985)

The Semantics of Cardinality-Based Feature Models via Formal Languages

Aliakbar Safilian[1], Tom Maibaum[1(✉)], and Zinovy Diskin[1,2]

[1] Department of Computing and Software, McMaster University, Hamilton, Canada
{safiliaa,maibaum,disnkinz}@mcmaster.ca

[2] Department of Elecetrical and Computer Engineering, University of Waterloo, Waterloo, Canada
zdiskin@gsd.uwaterloo.ca

Abstract. Cardinality-based feature models provide the most expressive language among the existing feature modeling languages. We provide a reduction process, which allows us to transform a cardinality-based feature diagram to an appropriate regular expression. As for crosscutting constraints, we propose a formal language interpretation of them. In this way, we provide a formal language-based semantics for cardinality-based feature models. Accordingly, we describe a computational hierarchy of feature models, which guides us in how feature models can be constructively analyzed. We also characterize some existing analysis operations over feature models in terms of languages and discuss the corresponding decidability problems.

1 Introduction

Product line engineering [14] is a well-known industrial approach to software design. A *product* is a set of *features*, where "a feature is a system property that is relevant to some stakeholders" [6]. A *product line* (PL) is a set of products that share some common features. The main advantage of this approach to software production is a reduction in cost and development time [14], since the common core of a PL is produced, leaving a much smaller task to be completed, namely the adaptation of the core to a concrete application requirement.

Feature modeling is the most common approach for modeling PLs. A feature model (FM) is a tree presenting a hierarchical decomposition of features, called a *feature diagram* (FD), with some possible *crosscutting constraints* (CCs) between them. FMs are grouped into *basic* and *cardinality-based* FMs. Basic FMs represent product variability and commonality in terms of optional/mandatory features, and OR/XOR decomposition operations. In cardinality-based FMs (CFMs), UML-like multiplicities are used in place of annotations, which make them much more expressive than basic ones.

The common understanding of the semantics of an FM in the literature is its PL [17]. This semantics does not capture all essential and practically important information of FMs. This is mainly because an FM provides a hierarchical structure for features, which is forgotten in its PL [11,18]. For a very simple example,

N. Bjørner and F. de Boer (Eds.): FM 2015, LNCS 9109, pp. 453–469, 2015.
DOI: 10.1007/978-3-319-19249-9_28

consider two FMs $\mathbb{M}_1$ (a is the root and b is the only mandatory child of a) and $\mathbb{M}_2$ (b is the root and a is the only mandatory child of b). $\mathbb{M}_1$ and $\mathbb{M}_2$ represent the same PL consisting of the only product $\{a, b\}$, but their hierarchical structures are different. Capturing hierarchical structure of FMs is important for several analysis operations over FMs. Indeed, any analysis operation relying on the hierarchical structure of a given FM cannot be addressed using its PL semantics. Such analysis operations, including *least common ancestor* of a given set of features, *root feature*, *subfeatures* of a given feature were explicitly characterized in the literature as necessarily relying on this information [3]. Also, another deficiency of the PL semantics is relevant to reverse engineering of FMs. Indeed, the main reason making the current state of the art approach [18] heuristic is mainly caused by using such a poor abstract view of FMs.

In [11], in order to adequately represent the hierarchical structure of basic FMs semantically, we introduced a Kripke semantics for basic FMs, and showed that basic feature modeling needs a modal rather than Boolean logic. In the present paper, we invoke formal language (FL) theory to approach building a semantics for cardinality-based feature modeling, which is a more challenging area of feature modeling. This method allows us to approach FM problems by translating them into FL-theory problems that could be managed by well-elaborated FL-theory methods and tools. Indeed, we provide an FL interpretation $\mathcal{L}_{\mathbb{M}}$ for a given FM $\mathbb{M}$. To consider $\mathcal{L}_{\mathbb{M}}$ as a faithful semantics for the FM, $\mathcal{L}_{\mathbb{M}}$ must satisfy the following two fundamental properties:

P-1: "*The multi-set interpretation of* $\mathcal{L}_{\mathbb{M}}$ *is equal to the PL of* $\mathbb{M}$".

P-2: "$\mathcal{L}_{\mathbb{M}}$ *preserves the hierarchical structure of* $\mathbb{M}$".

The meaning of **P-1** is clear. **P-2** says that the hierarchical structure of $\mathbb{M}$ can be extracted from $\mathcal{L}_{\mathbb{M}}$. This property is formalized in Definition 13. Later we will show that our FL semantics does satisfy these two requirements.

Industrial FMs may have thousands of features, and their PLs can be complex [13]. Hence, analysis operations on FMs need automated support. Automated analysis of CFMs is a challenging and open issue [3,15]. We address this problem by employing FL-based tools. We also show that not all of the proposed analysis operations are decidable when applied to all kinds of FMs. The most important contributions of the paper are summarized as follows:

- A set theoretic definition of valid products of given *cardinality-based feature diagrams* (CFDs): see Sect. 3.
- Two levels of generalizations for CFDs: see Sect. 3 and Sect. 4.
- A reduction procedure going from a given CFD to an appropriate regular expression (RE): see Sect. 4.
- FL interpretation of CCs and a computational hierarchy of CFMs: see Sect. 5.
- Discussing the decidability problems of some analysis operations over CFMs: see Sect. 6.
- Discussion of tool support for analysis operations on CFMs: see Sect. 6.

The plan for this paper is as follows. Sect. 2 gives a background on feature modeling. In Sect. 3, we provide a formal syntax for CFDs and a set theoretic definition of their valid products. In Sect. 4, we describe an important generalization of CFDs, called *cardinality-based regular expression diagrams* (CRDs) in which labelling of nodes can be any REs built over an alphabet. Then we show how to translate CRDs to REs. Also, we prove that the RE generated in this way for a given CFD satisfies **P-1** and **P-2**. In Sect. 5, we show how to interperet CCs in FL. In Sect. 6, we investigate the decidability problems of some analysis operations on CFMs. Also, we show how to use some off-the-shelf FL tools to deal with analysis operations on CFMs. Related work is discussed in Sect. 7. Sect. 8 discusses the conclusions and some interesting open problems.

Below we present the notations used throughout the paper. Some further notations are introduced where they are used.

Notations. For a given set A, $|A|$ denotes its cardinality. The notation $f|_A$ for a function f means the restriction of the function f to the subdomain A. For a given set $X = \{x_1, \ldots, x_n\} \subset \mathbb{N}$ ($\mathbb{N}$ denotes the set of natural numbers), $+\, X = x_1 + \ldots + x_n$.

Let S be a sequence or multi-set, U_S denotes the set of elements included in S. By $s \in S$, we mean $s \in U_S$ and $\#_S(s)$ denotes the number of instances (occurrences) of s in S. For a set X, $S \cap X$ means $U_S \cap X$. If S is a sequence, we also consider a partial order $\sqsubseteq_S \;\; \subseteq U_S \times U_S$ defined as follows: $\forall s, s' \in S$, $s \sqsubseteq_S s'$ iff any instance of s' is preceded by some instances of s in S.

The multi-set interpretation of a sequence S (a formal language $\mathcal{L}$, respectively) is denoted by S^{bag} ($\mathcal{L}^{\text{bag}}$, respectively).

Let *Gra*, *Reg* and *Aut* be a formal grammar, regular expression and automaton over an alphabet Σ, respectively. Then $\mathcal{L}(Gra), \mathcal{L}(Reg), \mathcal{L}(Aut)$ denote their corresponding languages, respectively. Let Σ' be another alphabet with a bijection $f : \Sigma \to \Sigma'$. Then $Reg[f]$ ($Gra[f]$ and $Aut[f]$, respectively) is a regular expression (grammar, automaton, respectively) built over Σ' using *Reg* (*Gra* and *Aut*, respectively) by substituting any element $\sigma \in \Sigma$ with $f(\sigma)$. To make the regular expressions more readable, we use the notation f^n to show n repetitions of a letter f. Let $\mathbf{RE}(\Sigma)$ denote the class of all regular expressions built over Σ.

2 Background

Feature modeling languages are grouped into *basic* and *cardinality-based* FMs. We describe them using a small part of the student awards system as an example.

Fig. 1(a) is a basic FD of the system. It is a tree of features, where the edges exhibit the relationships between features. An edge with a black bullet shows a *mandatory* feature: every application must include a ref (reference), and the hollow-ended one shows an *optional* feature: an application can optionally be equipped with citizen (confirming that the applicant is a citizen). These two types of edges (mandatory and optional) are called *solitary*, while other edges are *grouped*, with two variants OR (the black angle) and XOR (the hollow angle). The XOR group {NSERC, GB, IE} shows that the student can apply for at most one and only one of the awards NSERC (Natural Sciences and Engineering

Research Council), GB (Graham Bell) and IE (International Excellence). The OR group {markA, publication} indicates that to apply for the IE award, the student must have either a grade markA, or a publication, or both, in his record.

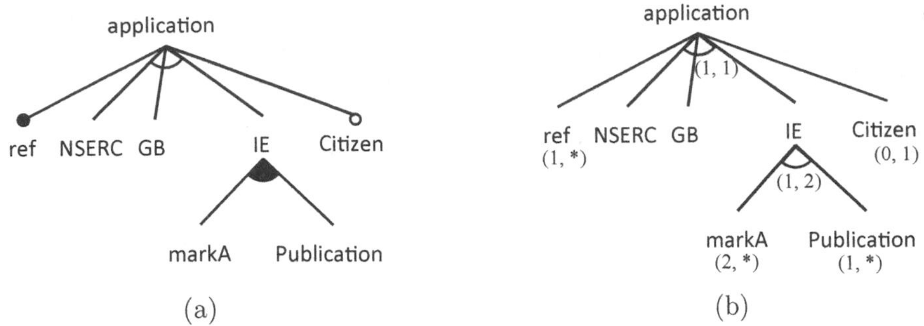

Fig. 1. (a) a basic FD (b) a cardinality-based FD

The set of valid products of a basic FD can be translated into a propositional logic formula generated over the set of features [13]. In this sense, any logical formula can be seen as a CC [8]. Let us have cc_1: "citizen $\longrightarrow \neg$IE" and cc_2: "NSERC $\vee$ GB $\longrightarrow$ citizen" as the CCs stating that a "citizen student cannot apply for the IE award" and "one of the requirements for the NSERC and GB awards is to be a citizen", respectively. cc_1 and cc_2 are called an *exclusive* and an *inclusive* CC, respectively. This FM represents six valid products. $\mathcal{PL}(\mathbb{M})$ denotes the set of valid products of a given FM $\mathbb{M}$.

Now suppose that we need to specify some requirements regarding the number of feature instances. For example, consider the following requirements: (i) There is no upper bound on the number of instances of the features ref, markA, and publication. (ii) If the student applies for the IE award by providing A-marks, the number of markA in his record must be more than two. Clearly, basic FMs like in Fig. 1(a) cannot model such requirements, since they do not manage the number of instances. To address such system requirements, Czarnecki et al. proposed CFMs [5,6,7], where *cardinalities*, are used in place of traditional edge types. A CFD is a labeled tree of features. There are two types of cardinalities: *feature* and *group* cardinalities. Fig. 1(b) provides a CFD for the awards system including the requirements (i) and (ii). The group cardinalities $(1, 1)$ and $(1, n)$ model XOR and OR groups with n elements in terms of cardinalities. The cardinality $(0, 1)$ on citizen models its optional presence in an application. The cardinalities $(1, *)$ on ref and publication, and $(2, *)$ on markA together satisfy the requirements (i) and (ii). If no cardinality was specified on a node, then the cardinality $(1, 1)$ is assumed: the cardinalities on NSERC, GB and IE are $(1, 1)$.

CCs in a CFM can refer to feature instances. Take, for example, the constraint: cc_3: "The number of instances of ref must be even". A product of a CFM is a multi-set of features satisfying the constraints. For an example, the multi-set {application, IE, markA^3, ref^4} is a product of this model. Note that the PL of this model is an infinite set. Obviously, CFMs subsume basic FMs [6].

3 CFDs: Formal Definitions

We use the CFD in Fig. 2 as an example to illustrate the definitions. The feature label of each node is represented in parenthesis next to the node and G denotes the grouped nodes {e, f, g }. To formalize the syntax of CFDs, we will first need the following notion.

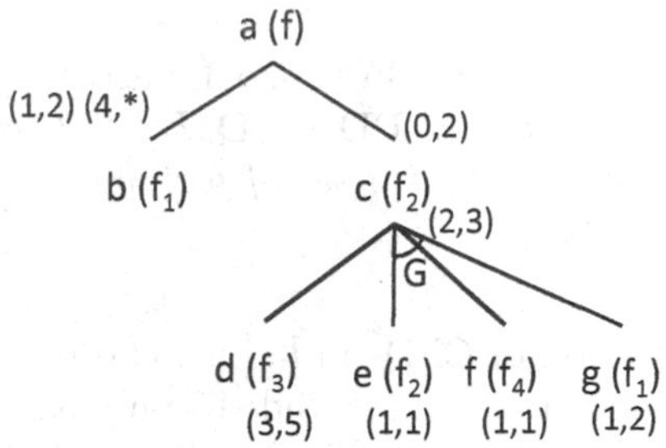

Fig. 2. A CFD

Definition 1 (Cardinalities).
(i) The cardinality-set *is the set* $\mathfrak{C} = \{(k,m) \in \mathbb{N}\times(\mathbb{N}\uplus\{*\}) : (k \leq_* m)\wedge(m \neq 0)\}$, *where* $\leq_*$: $(\mathbb{N} \uplus \{*\}) \times (\mathbb{N} \uplus \{*\})$ *is a reflexive transitive relation defined as follows:* $\forall k,m \in \mathbb{N}$, $k \leq_* m$ *iff* $k \leq m$ *and* $\forall k \in \mathbb{N}$, $k \leq_* *$.

(ii) An element $c = (k,m) \in \mathfrak{C}$ *is called a cardinality. We call* k *and* m *the lower-bound, denoted by* $low(c)$*, and upper-bound, denoted by* $up(c)$*, of* c*, respectively.*

(iii) A subset $C \subseteq \mathfrak{C}$ *is called a cardinality interval if there exists* $I = \{1,\ldots,n\} \subset \mathbb{N}$ *such that* $C = \{(k_i,m_i) : i \in I\}$ *in which* $m_i \leq_* k_{i+1}$*, for all* $i, i+1 \in I$*. We call* k_1 *and* m_n *the lower-bound, denoted by* $low(C)$*, and* upper-bound*, denoted by* $up(C)$*, of* C*, respectively.* □

Consider the CFD in Fig. 2 and ignore the feature labels on nodes (i.e., f, f_1, f_2, f_3 and f_4). We call such a tree a *cardinality-based diagram* (CD). A CD is an unlabelled tree where some subsets of non-root nodes are grouped (e.g., G = {e, f, g} in Fig. 2) and other nodes are called solitary (the nodes b, c, and d in Fig. 2). In addition, non-root nodes and groups are equipped with some cardinality intervals (e.g., $\{(1,2),(4,*)\}$ on the node b and $\{(1,2)\}$ on G).

Definition 2 (Cardinality-based Diagrams).
A cardinality-based diagram (CD) is a 3-tuple $\mathbf{D} = (T, \mathcal{G}, \mathcal{C})$ *consisting of the following components.*

(i) $T = (N, r, \_^{\uparrow})$ *is a* tree *with set* N *of nodes,* $r \in N$ *is the root, and function* $\_^{\uparrow}$ *maps each non-root node* $n \in N_{-r} \stackrel{\text{def}}{=} N \setminus r$ *to its parent* $n^{\uparrow}$*. The inverse function that assigns to each node* n *the set of its children is denoted by* $n_{\downarrow}$*. The set of all descendants of* n *is denoted by* $n_{\downarrow\downarrow}$*.*

(ii) $\mathcal{G} \subseteq 2^{N_{-r}}$ *is a set of* grouped *nodes. For all* $G \in \mathcal{G}$, $|G| > 1$*, and all nodes in* G *have the same parent, denoted by* $G^{\uparrow}$*. All groups in* $\mathcal{G}$ *are disjoint, i.e.,* $\forall G, G' \in \mathcal{G}.\ (G \neq G') \Rightarrow (G \cap G' = \varnothing)$*. The nodes that are not in a group are called solitary nodes. Let* $\mathcal{S}$ *denote the solitary nodes, i.e.,* $\mathcal{S} = N_{-r} - \bigcup_{G \in \mathcal{G}} G$*.*

(iii) $\mathcal{C} \subseteq (N_{-r} \uplus \mathcal{G}) \times \mathfrak{C}$ *is a left-total relation called the* cardinality relation*. For any element* $e \in N_{-r} \uplus \mathcal{G}$*,* $\mathcal{C}(e)$ *is a cardinality interval as defined in Definition 1(iii). In addition, for all* $G \in \mathcal{G}$*,* $up(\mathcal{C}(G)) \leq |G|$*.* □

Definition 3 (Cardinality-based Feature Diagrams). *A cardinality-based feature diagram (CFD) is a 3-tuple* $\mathbf{FD} = (\mathbf{D}, F, l)$ *where* $\mathbf{D} = (T, \mathcal{G}, \mathcal{C})$ *is an CD, as defined in Definition 2,* F *is a set of features, and function* $l : N \rightarrow F$ *labels each node with a feature.* □

Note. The original definition of CFDs in [6] has two restrictions: (i) the cardinality of a grouped node is always $(1, 1)$ and (ii) only one cardinality interval is assigned to a group. However, we generalized CFDs in the above definition without essentially complicating the framework and enabling useful generalizations in feature modeling.

Now we want to formally define a valid product of a given CFD. First, we give a definition of a valid product of its underlying CD. Note that a CD can be seen as a CFD in which the labelling is an inclusion function from nodes to nodes. We call a valid product of the CD a *bare product* of the CFD. To obtain the valid products of the CFD, we just need to apply the labelling function on the bare products. A bare product is a multi-set of nodes satisfying the following membership and arity requirements.

(*membership requirements*): The root is included. If a non-root node is included then its parent must also be included, e.g., the presence of the node d in Fig. 2 implies the presence of the node c. If the parent of a mandatory node (a solitary node with lower bound cardinality greater than 0) is included then it must be included too, e.g., the presence of the node c implies the presence of the node d. If a parent of a grouped set of nodes is included then the presence of the grouped nodes must satisfy the associated group cardinalities, e.g., the presence of the node c implies the presence of two or three of the nodes e, f, and g.

(*arity requirements*): The arity of the root node is always 1. The number of instances of a non-root node is verified by the cardinality interval associated with it and the number of instances of its parent node, e.g., if the number of instances of the node c in Fig. 2 is two, then the number of instances of the node d must be at least six and at most ten. In general, for non-root nodes n included in the bare product, there must be a cardinality c associated with n such that its arity is less (greater, respectively) than the multiplication of its parent's ($n^{\uparrow}$) arity and c's upper bound (lower bound, respectively).

Definition 4 (Product). *Let* $\mathbf{FD} = (\mathbf{D}, F, l)$ *be a CFD with* $\mathbf{D} = (T, \mathcal{G}, \mathcal{C})$ *and* $T = (N, r, \_^{\uparrow})$.

Bare Product: *A multi-set* BP *over the set of nodes* N *is called a bare product if: (i to iv correspond to the membership requirements and the rest correspond to the arity requirements)*

membership:

(i) $r \in BP$,

(ii) $\forall n \in N_{-r} : n \in BP \Rightarrow n^{\uparrow} \in BP$,

(iii) $\forall n \in BP, \forall n' \in \mathcal{S} : [(n'^{\uparrow} = n) \wedge (low(\mathcal{C}(n')) > 0)] \Rightarrow (n' \in BP)$,

(iv) $\forall n \in BP, \forall G \in \mathcal{G} : (G^{\uparrow} = n) \Rightarrow [\exists c \in \mathcal{C}(G) : low(c) \leq |BP \cap G| \leq up(c)]$,

arities:

(v) $\#_{BP}(r) = 1$,

(vi) $\forall n \in N_{-r}, \exists c \in \mathcal{C}(n) : (\#_{BP}(n^{\uparrow}) \times low(c)) \leq \#_{BP}(n) \leq (\#_{BP}(n^{\uparrow}) \times up(c))$

Product: *A multi-set* P *over* F *is called a product if there exists a bare product* BP *of* $\mathbf{FD}$ *such that* P *is the result of applying the labelling function* l *on the elements of* BP, *i.e., for all features* $f \in F$,

(i) $(f \in P) \Leftrightarrow (l^{-1}(f) \cap BP \neq \varnothing)$,

(ii) $\#_P(f) = +_{n \in l^{-1}(f)} \#_{BP}(n)$

The product family of $\mathbf{FD}$ *is denoted by* $\mathcal{PL}(\mathbf{FD})$. □

4 CFDs to Regular Expressions

In this section, we first define a generalization of CFDs called *Cardinality-based Regular-expression Diagrams* (CRDs). Subsequently, we give a procedure to translate a given CRD to a regular expression (RE). This provides a semantics for CRDs by using regular languages as the semantic domain. We also prove that the REs generated for a given CFD and its underlying CD satisfy the properties **P-1** and **P-2**, respectively.

Definition 5 (Cardinality-based Regular-expression Diagrams). *A cardinality-based regular-expression diagram (CRD) over an alphabet* Σ *is a 3-tuple* $\mathbf{RD} = (LT_{re}, \mathcal{G}, \mathcal{C})$ *of the following components:*

(i) $LT_{re} = (N, r, \_^{\uparrow}, \Sigma, l_{re})$ *is a* labeled tree *where* N, r, $\_^{\uparrow}$, *are as defined in Definition 2(i),* Σ *is a finite set (the alphabet), and* $l_{re} : N \rightarrow \boldsymbol{RE}(\Sigma)$ *is a function that labels each node with a regular expression built over* Σ.

(ii) $\mathcal{G} \subseteq 2^{N_{-r}}$ *is a set of* grouped *nodes, as defined in Definition 2(ii).*

(iii) $\mathcal{C} \subseteq (N_{-r} \uplus \mathcal{G}) \times \mathfrak{C}$ *is called the* cardinality relation, *as defined in Definition 2(iii).*

The class of all CRDs over the same alphabet Σ *will be denoted by* $\mathcal{RD}(\Sigma)$. □

CRDs subsume CFDs: A CFD is a CRD in which Σ is the set of features and labels are primitive non-empty REs.

Notation. Given a CRD **RD**, we will need the following notations:

(i) $lev(\mathbf{RD})$ denotes the set of leaf nodes, i.e., $lev(\mathbf{RD}) = \{n \in N : n_{\downarrow} = \varnothing\}$.

(ii) $glev(\mathbf{RD})$ denotes the set of the grouped leaves, i.e., $glev(\mathbf{RD}) = \{G \in \mathcal{G} : \forall n \in G.\ n_{\downarrow} = \varnothing\}$.
(iii) $plev(\mathbf{RD})$ denotes the set of non-leaf nodes all of whose children are leaves, i.e., $plev(\mathbf{RD}) = \{n \in N : n_{\downarrow} \subseteq lev(\mathbf{RD})\}$.
(iv) $cplev(\mathbf{RD})$ denotes the leaves all of whose siblings are leaves, i.e., $cplev(\mathbf{RD}) = \{c \in n_{\downarrow} : n \in plev(\mathbf{RD})\}$.

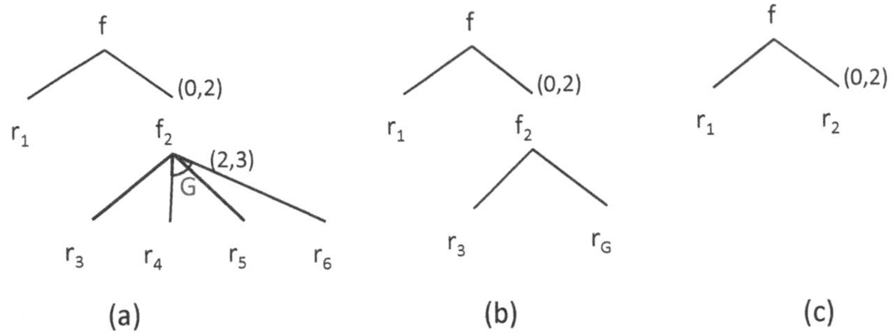

Fig. 3. RCD to RE: Shrinking Procedure on Fig. 2

The translation of a CRD to an RE is a bottom-up procedure and includes a finite number of steps (equal to the depth of the CRD's tree) called *shrinking steps*. Each shrinking step takes a CRD and returns another CRD such that the depth of the output's tree is less than that of the input. The output of the last step is a CRD with the singleton tree (a tree consisting of a single isolated node) whose root is labeled with an RE. A shrinking step includes three stages: (1) *Eliminating cardinalities from leaves*, (2) *Eliminating grouped leaves*, and (3) *Depth reduction*. We will use the CFD in Fig. 2 as a running example to illustrate the translation procedure.

Stage 1: Eliminating Cardinalities from Leaves. At this stage, the REs corresponding to leaf nodes are computed and their cardinalities changed to $(1, 1)$. For an example, the RE corresponding to the node b (Fig. 2) would be $f_1 + f_1^2 + f_1^4 f_1^*$. This RE represents the cardinality constraint on this node properly, as it says that the number of instances of the feature f_1 on this node must be one or two or more than three. Then, the label of the leaves are replaced by their REs, computed in the above way, and their associated cardinalities change to $(1, 1)$. Fig. 3(a) represents the result of this stage applied to the CFD in Fig. 2, where $r_1 = f_1 + f_1^2 + f_1^4 f_1^*$, $r_3 = f_3^3 + f_3^4 + f_3^5$, $r_4 = f_2$, $r_5 = f_4$, and $r_6 = f_1 + f_1^2$.

Definition 6. *Given a CRD* $\mathbf{RD} = (LT_{re}, \mathcal{G}, \mathcal{C})$ *with* $LT_{re} = (N, r, \_^{\uparrow}, \Sigma, l_{re})$, $lex_{\mathbf{RD}} : lev(\mathbf{RD}) \to \boldsymbol{RE}(\Sigma)$ *is a total function which maps a leaf node in* $\mathbf{RD}$ *to an RE built over* Σ. *For a given node* $n \in lev(\mathbf{RD})$ *with* $\mathcal{C}(n) = \{(k_i, m_i)\}_{1 \le i \le j}$ *(for some* $j \in \mathbb{N}$*),* $lex_{\mathbf{RD}}(n) = r_1 + \ldots + r_j$*, where*

$$r_i = \begin{cases} l_{re}(n)^{k_i} + \ldots + l_{re}(n)^{m_i} & \textit{if } m_i \neq * \\ l_{re}(n)^{k_i}\left(l_{re}(n)\right)^* & o.w. \end{cases}$$

□

Definition 7 (Eliminating cardinalities from leaves Stage). *The function cel* : $\mathcal{RD}(\Sigma) \to \mathcal{RD}(\Sigma)$ *is called the cardinality eliminator function and for a given CRD* $\mathbf{RD} = (LT_{re}, \mathcal{G}, \mathcal{C})$ *with* $LT_{re} = (N, r, \_^{\uparrow}, \Sigma, l_{re})$, $cel(\mathbf{RD}) = (LT'_{re}, \mathcal{G}, \mathcal{C}')$ *where* $LT'_{re} = (N, r, \_^{\uparrow}, \Sigma, l'_{re})$ *and*

$$\mathcal{C}'(e) = \begin{cases} \{(1,1)\} & \textit{if } e \in lev(\mathbf{RD}) \\ \mathcal{C}(e) & o.w. \end{cases} \qquad l'_{re}(n) = \begin{cases} lex_{\mathbf{RD}}(n) & \textit{if } n \in lev(\mathbf{RD}) \\ l_{re}(n) & o.w. \end{cases}$$ □

Stage 2: Eliminating the Grouped Leaves. At this stage, grouped leaf nodes are replaced by new nodes with proper REs. The input of this stage is the output of the first stage. For an example, consider the grouped leaves G in Fig. 3(a). The group cardinality $(2, 3)$ says that at least two and at most three of the nodes involved in the group (i.e., the nodes e, f, and g) must be included in a valid product for each instance of their parent (i.e., the node c) in the product. The following REs r'_G and r''_G represent the lower and upper bounds of the cardinality, respectively: $r'_G = r_4r_5 + r_5r_4 + r_5r_6 + r_6r_5 + r_4r_6 + r_6r_4$, $r''_G = r_4r_5r_6 + r_4r_6r_5 + r_5r_4r_6 + r_5r_6r_4 + r_6r_4r_5 + r_6r_5r_4$. Thus, the RE corresponding to the group would be $r_G = r'_G + r''_G$. Then, each grouped leaf is replaced by a new node with a cardinality $(1, 1)$ and is labeled with the computed RE. Fig. 3(b) represents the result of applying this stage to Fig. 3(a).

Notation. Let $Per^k_m(X)$ denote the set of all concatenation permutations S with length between k and m ($k \leq |S| \leq m$) of X. For an example, $Per^1_2(\{r_1, r_2, r_3\})$ would be the following set of expressions: $\{r_1,\ r_2,\ r_3\} \cup \{r_1r_2,\ r_2r_1,\ r_1r_3,\ r_2r_3,\ r_3r_2\}$. Therefore, we mean a sequence $x_1 \cdots x_n$ with $\bigcup_{1\leq i\leq n}\{x_i\} = X$ by a concatenation permutation S of a finite set X with $|X| = n$.

Definition 8. *Given a CRD* $\mathbf{RD} = (LT_{re}, \mathcal{G}, \mathcal{C})$ *with* $LT_{re} = (N, r, \_^{\uparrow}, \Sigma, l_{re})$, $gex_{\mathbf{RD}} : glev(\mathbf{RD}) \to \boldsymbol{RE}(\Sigma)$ *is a total function. For a given group* $G \in glev(\mathbf{RD})$ *with* $\mathcal{C}(G) = \{(k_i, m_i)\}_{1\leq i\leq j}$ *(for some* $j \in \mathbb{N}$*),* $gex_{\mathbf{RD}}(G) = r_1 + \ldots + r_j$ *where for all* $1 \leq i \leq j$*:* $r_i = +\ X_i$*, and* $X_i = Per^{k_i}_{m_i}(E)$ *with* $E = \{l_{re}(n) : n \in G\}$. □

Definition 9 (Eliminating grouped leaves Stage). *The function gle* : $\mathcal{RD}(\Sigma) \to \mathcal{RD}(\Sigma)$ *is called the grouped leaves eliminator. For a given CRD* $\mathbf{RD} = (LT_{re}, \mathcal{G}, \mathcal{C})$ *with* $LT_{re} = (N, r, \_^{\uparrow}, \Sigma, l_{re})$, $gle(\mathbf{RD})$ *is defined as follows:*

For each group node $G \in glev(\mathbf{RD})$*, a node identifier* n_G *is assigned. Let* N_G *denote the set of these node identifiers. In other words, we have a bijection gid* : $N_G \to glev(\mathbf{RD})$ *which assigns each grouped node in* $glev(\mathbf{RD})$ *to a unique node identifier in* N_G*. Then,* $gle(\mathbf{RD}) = (LT'_{re}, \mathcal{G}', \mathcal{C}')$ *with* $LT'_{re} = (N', r, \_^{\uparrow'}, \Sigma, l'_{re})$*, where* $N' = (N - glev(\mathbf{RD})) \uplus N_G$, $\mathcal{G}' = \mathcal{G} - glev(\mathbf{RD})$*, and*

$$\mathcal{C}'(e) = \begin{cases} \{(1,1)\} & \textit{if } e \in N_G \\ \mathcal{C}(e) & o.w. \end{cases}$$

$$n^{\uparrow'} = \begin{cases} gid(n)^{\uparrow} & \textit{if } n \in N_G \\ n^{\uparrow} & o.w. \end{cases}, \quad l'_{re}(n) = \begin{cases} gex_{\mathbf{RD}}(gid(n)), & \textit{if } n \in N_G \\ l_{re}(n) & o.w. \end{cases} \square$$

Stage 3: Depth Reduction. This stage takes the output of the second stage and returns a CRD whose depth is less than that of the input. To this end, the REs corresponding to the nodes all of whose child nodes are leaves are computed. Then, the label of such nodes are replaced by the corresponding computed REs and their child nodes are eliminated from the given CRD. Let us see what the result of this stage applied to the CRD in Fig. 3(b) would be. There is only one node, labeled by f_2, all of whose child nodes are leaf nodes. Fig. 3(c) shows the result, where $r_2 = f_2(r_3 r_G + r_G r_3)$.

Definition 10. *Given a CRD* $\mathbf{RD} = (LT_{re}, \mathcal{G}, \mathcal{C})$ *with* $LT_{re} = (N, r, \_^{\uparrow}, \Sigma, l_{re})$, $pex_{\mathbf{RD}} : plev(\mathbf{RD}) \to \boldsymbol{RE}(\Sigma)$ *is a total function. For a given node* $n \in plev(\mathbf{RD})$, $pex_{\mathbf{RD}}(n) = l_{re}(n)(+\ X)$, *where* $X = Per^j_j(E)$ *and* $j = |n_{\downarrow}|$, *and* $E = \{l_{re}(n') : n' \in n_{\downarrow}\}$. □

Definition 11 (Depth Reduction Stage). *The function* $dre : \mathcal{RD}(\Sigma) \to \mathcal{RD}(\Sigma)$ *is called the depth reducer function. For a given CRD* $\mathbf{RD} = (LT_{re}, \mathcal{G}, \mathcal{C})$ *with* $LT_{re} = (N, r, \_^{\uparrow}, \Sigma, l_{re})$, $dre(\mathbf{RD})$ *is a CRD* $\mathbf{RD}' = (LT'_{re}, \mathcal{G}, \mathcal{C}')$ *with* $LT'_{re} = (N', r, \_^{\uparrow'}, \Sigma, l'_{re})$ *where* $N' = N - cplev(\mathbf{RD})$, $\_^{\uparrow'} = \_^{\uparrow}|_{N'}$, $\mathcal{C}' = \mathcal{C}|_{N' \cup \mathcal{G}}$, *and*

$$l'_{re}(n) = \begin{cases} pex_{\mathbf{RD}}(n) & \textit{if } n \in plev(\mathbf{RD}) \\ l_{re}(n) & o.w. \end{cases}$$

Definition 12 (Shrinking Step). *The function* $shr : \mathcal{RD}(\Sigma) \to \mathcal{RD}(\Sigma)$ *is called the shrinking function and is defined as* $shr = dre \circ gel \circ cel$. *(*$\circ$ *denotes composition.)* □

We keep doing the shrinking steps until we get a CRD which is a singleton tree. In the running example, we need to do the shrinking step once more. The final result would be the expression $r = f(r_1 r'_2 + r'_2 r_1)$, where $r'_2 = \varepsilon + r_2 + r_2^2$. The notation $\mathcal{E}_{\mathbf{RD}}$ is used to denote the regular expression generated for a given CRD **RD**. The following proposition follows obviously.

Proposition 1. *Let* $\mathbf{FD} = (\mathbf{D}, F, l)$ *be a CFD with* $\mathbf{D} = (T, \mathcal{G}, \mathcal{C})$ *and* $T = (N, r, \_^{\uparrow})$. *Then,* $\mathcal{E}_{\mathbf{FD}} = \mathcal{E}_{\mathbf{D}}[l]$. □

Now we are at the point where we can prove that the regular expression interpretation of a given CFD **FD** with **D** as its underlying CD satisfies the properties **P-1** and **P-2**. Note that two different nodes in **FD** can be labeled with the same feature. Thus, to prove the property **P-2** (formalized in Definition 13) of the generative language, we need to work on **D**, i.e., we prove that $\mathcal{L}(\mathcal{E}_{\mathbf{D}})$ satisfies **P-2**. We refer the reader to [16] to see the proofs of the theorems.

Theorem 1 (Satisfying P-1). *For a given CFD* **FD**, $\mathcal{L}(\mathcal{E}_{\mathbf{FD}})^{\mathrm{bag}} = \mathcal{PL}(\mathbf{FD})$.

Definition 13 (Formalizing P-2). *Consider a CD* $\mathbf{D} = (T, \mathcal{G}, \mathcal{C})$ *with* $T = (N, r, \_^{\uparrow})$ *and let* $\mathcal{L}$ *be a language built over* N*. We say* $\mathcal{L}$ *preserves the* hierarchical structure *of* $\mathbf{D}$ *(or simply satisfies* **P-2** *for* $\mathbf{D}$*) if* $\forall n, n' \in N : (n' \in n_{\downarrow\downarrow}) \iff (\forall w \in \mathcal{L}(\mathcal{E}_{\mathbf{D}}) : (n' \in w) \Rightarrow (n \sqsubseteq_w n'))$. □

Theorem 2 (Satisfying P-2). *For a given CD* $\mathbf{D}$, $\mathcal{L}(\mathcal{E}_{\mathbf{D}})$ *satisfies* **P-2** *for* $\mathbf{D}$.

5 CCs and CFMs

CCs only make sense with respect to a given CFD. We formalized the semantics of CFDs using FLs (more precisely, regular languages). Hence, it makes sense to use the same framework to express CCs. This will allow us to integrate the semantics of CCs and CFDs. In the following, we show how to translate the most common CCs using FLs. Assume a CFD with a set of features F including three features f_1, f_2, and f_3. Several interesting CCs applied to a CFM are as follows:

(cc_1) f_1 requires f_2
(in other words: If the number of instances of f_1 is greater than 0, then the number of instances of f_2 must be greater than 0).

(cc_2) f_1 excludes f_2
(in other words: If the number of instances of f_1 is greater than 0, then the number of instances of f_2 must be 0).

(cc_3) If the number of instances of f_1 is even, then the number of instances of f_2 must be odd.

(cc_4) The number of instances of f_1 and f_2 are equal.

(cc_5) The number of instances of f_1, f_2, and f_3 are equal.

The first two CCs are traditional inclusive and exclusive CCs. However, they can be expressed in terms of feature instances, as we see in the parenthetical remarks above. In our approach, the set of features is considered as the alphabet of a language. The FL interpretation of the above CCs are as follows:

$\mathcal{L}(cc_1) = \{w \in F^* : (\#_{f_1}(w) > 0) \Rightarrow (\#_{f_2}(w) > 0)\}$.
$\mathcal{L}(cc_2) = \{w \in F^* : (\#_{f_1}(w) > 0) \Rightarrow (\#_{f_2}(w) = 0)\}$.
$\mathcal{L}(cc_3) = \{w \in F^* : (\exists n \in \mathbb{N}. \#_{f_1}(w) = 2n) \Rightarrow (\exists n \in \mathbb{N}. \#_{f_1}(w) = 2n + 1)\}$.
$\mathcal{L}(cc_4) = \{w \in F^* : \#_{f_1}(w) = \#_{f_2}(w)\}$.
$\mathcal{L}(cc_5) = \{w \in F^* : \#_{f_1}(w) = \#_{f_2}(w) = \#_{f_3}(w)\}$.

Proposition 2. $\mathcal{L}(cc_1)$*,* $\mathcal{L}(cc_2)$*, and* $\mathcal{L}(cc_3)$ *are regular,* $\mathcal{L}(cc_4)$ *is context-free, and* $\mathcal{L}(cc_5)$ *is context-sensitive.* □

Hence, a CFM is a CFD plus a set of languages expressing the CCs. In fact, a set of CCs can be seen as the intersection of the languages expressing the CCs.

Definition 14 (Cardinality-based Feature Models). *A cardinality-based feature model (CFM) is a pair* $\mathbb{M} = (\mathbf{FD}, \mathcal{L}_{cc})$ *with* $\mathbf{FD}$ *a CFD and* $\mathcal{L}_{cc}$ *a language built over* F *(the set of features) expressing the CCs.* □

Thus, a CFM is basically a tuple $\mathbb{M} = (\mathcal{L}_{\mathbf{FD}}, \mathcal{L}_{cc})$ with $\mathcal{L}_{\mathbf{FD}}$ and $\mathcal{L}_{cc}$ denoting the FLs of the CFD **FD** and CCs, respectively. The FL associated with the whole model is denoted by $\mathcal{L}_{\mathbb{M}}$ and is equal to $\mathcal{L}_{\mathbf{FD}} \cap \mathcal{L}_{cc}$. Since any class of languages is closed under intersection with regular languages [9] and $\mathcal{L}_{\mathbf{FD}}$ is regular, the type of $\mathcal{L}_{\mathbb{M}}$ is given by the type of $\mathcal{L}_{cc}$. Hence, CFMs can be grouped based on the types of their languages, say regular and context-free FMs. This grouping is important because it guides us in how FMs can be constructively analyzed.

Definition 15 (Dynamic & Static Semantics). *For a given FM* $\mathbb{M}$,

(i) $\mathcal{L}_{\mathbb{M}}$ *is called the* dynamic semantics *of* $\mathbb{M}$. *Any word* $w \in \mathcal{L}_{\mathbb{M}}$ *is called a dynamic product. We then write* $w \models_{\boldsymbol{DY}} \mathbb{M}$.

Two models $\mathbb{M}$ *and* $\mathbb{M}'$ *are called dynamic equivalent, denoted by* $\mathbb{M} \equiv_{\boldsymbol{DY}} \mathbb{M}'$, *if and only if* $\mathcal{L}_{\mathbb{M}} = \mathcal{L}_{\mathbb{M}'}$.

(ii) The multi-set interpretation of $\mathcal{L}_{\mathbb{M}}$, $\mathcal{L}_{\mathbb{M}}^{\text{bag}}$, *is called the* static semantics *of* $\mathbb{M}$. *Any element* P *of* $\mathcal{L}_{\mathbb{M}}^{\text{bag}}$ *is called a* static product. *We then write* $P \models_{\boldsymbol{ST}} \mathbb{M}$.

Two models $\mathbb{M}$ *and* $\mathbb{M}'$ *are called static equivalent, denoted by* $\mathbb{M} \equiv_{\boldsymbol{ST}} \mathbb{M}'$, *if and only if* $\mathcal{PL}(\mathbb{M}) = \mathcal{PL}(\mathbb{M}')$. □

As an example, consider the three models $\mathbb{M}$, $\mathbb{M}'$, and $\mathbb{M}''$ in Fig. 4(a), (b), (c), respectively. The regular expression encoding of $\mathbb{M}$ is $\mathcal{E}_{\mathbb{M}} = f.(f_2.f_2.(f_2)^* + f_1.f_1.(\varepsilon + f_1).(\varepsilon + f_3 + f_4))$. The regular expression encoding of $\mathbb{M}'$ is $\mathcal{E}_{\mathbb{M}'} = f.(f_2.(f_2)^*.f_2.(f_2)^* + f_1.f_1.(\varepsilon + f_1).(\varepsilon + f_3 + f_4))$. It is obvious that $\mathcal{L}(\mathcal{E}_{\mathbb{M}}) = \mathcal{L}(\mathcal{E}_{\mathbb{M}'})$, which means $\mathbb{M} \equiv_{\mathbf{DY}} \mathbb{M}'$. On the other hand, $\mathbb{M}''$ is not dynamic equivalent to $\mathbb{M}$. $\mathbb{M}''$ and $\mathbb{M}$ are static equivalent, i.e., $\mathbb{M}'' \equiv_{\mathbf{ST}} \mathbb{M}$.

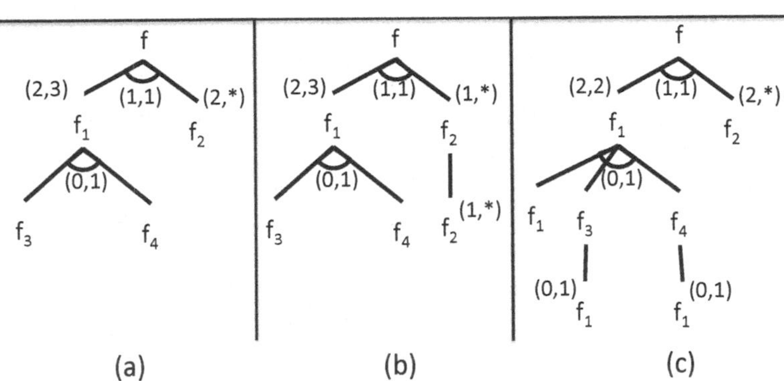

Fig. 4. (a) $\mathbb{M}$, (b) $\mathbb{M}'$ ($\equiv_{\mathbf{DY}} \mathbb{M}$) , (c) $\mathbb{M}''$ ($\equiv_{\mathbf{ST}} \mathbb{M}$)

The above example shows obviously that static semantics (PL) is a poor abstract view for CFMs, while the dynamic semantics (FL) extracts a much greater part of CFMs' intuitive semantics.

6 Analysis Operations

In this section, we investigate the decidability problem for some well-known analysis operations. We refer the interested reader to [16] to see the proofs of the theorems. Some operations take only one FM (along with another potential input that is not an FM) as input and perform some analysis on the FM. Below is a sample list of such operations:

Valid Product: takes an FM and a multi-set of features as inputs and decides whether it is a valid product of the FM or not.

Core Features: takes an FM and returns the set of features that are included in all the products.

Void Feature Model: takes an FM as input and decides whether its PL is empty or not.

Dead Feature: takes an FM and a feature and decides whether the feature is *dead* in the FM or not. A feature f in an FM $\mathbb{M}$ is called dead if $\nexists P \in \mathcal{PL}(\mathbb{M})$ such that $f \in P$.

Least Common Ancestor: takes an FD and a set of features and returns their lowest common ancestor feature.

Theorem 3. *Given a context-free FM* $\mathbb{M}$, *the operations Void Feature Models, Dead Features, Valid Product, Core Features, and Least Common Ancestor are decidable.* □

Note. Since the class of regular languages is a subclass of context-free languages, the above theorem holds for regular FMs too. Note that some analysis operations are not decidable in other classes of CFMs. For example, the Void Feature Model operation is not decidable in the class of context-sensitive CFMs, since the emptiness problem is not decidable in this class.

Some other operations deal with two FMs. Such operations answer some questions about the relationships between the FMs.

Refactoring: takes two FMs and decides whether their PL are equal or not.

Specialization: takes two FMs $\mathbb{M}_1$ and $\mathbb{M}_2$ as inputs and decides whether the PL of $\mathbb{M}_1$ is a subset of the PL of $\mathbb{M}_2$ or not.

Theorem 4. *Given two FMs* $\mathbb{M}_1$ *and* $\mathbb{M}_2$, *the following statements hold:*

(i) If both are regular, then the Refactoring problem between them is decidable.

(ii) If $\mathbb{M}_1$ *and* $\mathbb{M}_2$ *are regular and context-free, respectively, then the Refactoring problem is decidable iff* $\mathbb{M}_1$ *is bounded regular.* □

Note. In general, the equality problem in the class of context-free languages is undecidable. Therefore, the Refactoring problem is not decidable in this class.

Theorem 5. *Given two FMs* $\mathbb{M}_1$ *and* $\mathbb{M}_2$, *the following statements hold:*

(i) If both are regular, the Specialization problem between them is decidable.

(ii) If $\mathbb{M}_1$ *and* $\mathbb{M}_2$ *are regular and context-free, respectively, then the Specialization problem* $\mathcal{PL}(\mathbb{M}_2) \subseteq \mathcal{PL}(\mathbb{M}_1)$ *is decidable.* □

Tool Support:

As discussed above, the class of regular CFMs is the only class over which all the analysis operations are decidable. Thus, we take into account only regular CFMs.

most of the existing tools take finite state automata (FSA) as inputs, we first need to translate a given RE to an FSA. Some tools such as FSA6.2xx [19] can be used in this regard.

Since CFDs and their CCs are translated to different languages, we also need to compute their intersection. FSA6.2xx supports the intersection problem between two FSA.

To reduce the computational complexity in executing the analysis operations, we may prefer to work on minimal automata [12]. The minimization problem is supported by FSA6.2xx.

The valid product problem on a CFM is reduced to the membership problem on the CFM's language interpretation. FSA6.2xx addresses this problem.

The void feature model problem is reduced to the emptiness problem on languages. The emptiness problem for a given language $\mathcal{L}$ can be seen as the equality problem between $\mathcal{L}$ and the empty language. The equality problem over FSA is supported by HKC [4].

The dead feature problem for a given CFM $\mathbb{M}$ and a feature f, can be reduced to the decision problem $\mathcal{L}(\mathbb{M}) \cap \mathcal{L}(F^* f F^*) = \varnothing$. Thus, the problem is the composition of intersection and emptiness problems, which are supported by FSA6.2xx and HKC, respectively.

The refactoring (specialization, respectively) problem between two CFMs is simply reduced to the equality (inclusion, respectively) problem between their languages. The equality (inclusion, respectively) problem between FSA is supported by HKC.

To implement the core features problem, we would need a tool addressing the emptiness problem over context-free languages.

7 Related Work

In this section, we survey the literature relevant to the connection between FMs and FLs. Indeed, it is directly related to what we have done in this paper. We refer the reader to [16] for a more complete review of related work.

de Jong/Visser in [10] and Batory in [2] connected basic FDs to context-free grammars. The translation procedures in both works are essentially the same. Table 1 gives some basic examples showing how Batory's encoding works. Terminal symbols are denoted by italic letters. If a feature is optional, it is surrounded by brackets. In [10] and [2], the set of features that appear in leaf

Table 1. basic FDs to grammars

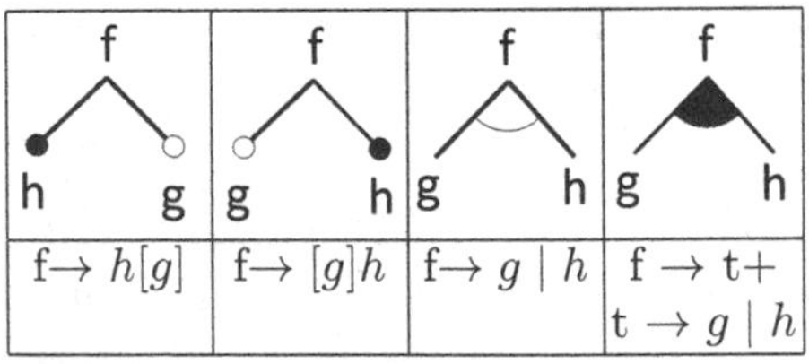

f (h mandatory, g optional)	f (g optional, h mandatory)	f (g, h alternative)	f (g, h or)
f→ $h[g]$	f→ $[g]h$	f→ $g \mid h$	f → t+ t → $g \mid h$

nodes is considered as the set of terminals and other features as the variables (non-terminals). Thus, the corresponding generative grammar for a given FD does not represent the PL of the FD. In other words, they do not satisfy the property **P-1**.

Another property of the above procedures is that they give a left-to-right ordering on siblings (the nodes with the same parent). As the left-most column in Table 1 shows, this may create problems: the left-most feature, h, precedes the right-most feature, g. Such an ordering forces two syntactically equivalent FDs to have different semantics: the grammars of the two FDs in the first and the second columns in Table 1 have different associated languages. In addition, such an ordering on siblings forces the generative grammars to not satisfy the property **P-2**.

Czarnecki et al, in [6], formalize the semantics of CFDs using context-free grammars. Unlike in [2] and [10], this work considers the set of terminals to be equal to the set of all features for a given CFD and generative grammars satisfy the property **P-1**. However, it gives a left-to-right ordering on siblings. Thus, this method does not satisfy the property **P-2** and there are syntactically equivalent CFDs with non-equal generative grammars.

All the above approaches may result in ambiguous grammars, which makes them bad candidates for the semantics of FDs. Also they do not consider CCs in the proposed semantics. This is a very important deficiency, since CCs have a central role to play in feature modeling.

8 Conclusions and Open Problems

Conclusion. We have provided a formal definition of CFDs and also their valid products in a set theoretic way. We have proposed two levels of generalization for CFDs. In the first generalization, we have relaxed some constraints on group cardinalities. We believe that this very simple generalization provides a more succinct and expressive tool for system modeling. The second generalization are CRDs in which the labels of nodes can be any regular expression built over the set of features. We believe that CRDs are a means to move us to modeling much more complicated systems, in which we need to deal with structural (non-atomic) features, e.g., programming codes, etc.

We have provided a reduction process, which allows us to go from a CFD to an RE. The procedure works for the class of CRDs. The generative expression for a given CFD has two main properties: it captures the hierarchical structure of the CFD; it also captures the PL of the CFD. These properties allow us to confidently claim that this translation faithfully captures the semantics of CFDs.

Regular languages have some nice computational properties. These properties, such as the decidability of the emptiness, inclusion, and equality problems, help us to propose algorithmic solutions for analysis operations over CFDs. In addition, the complexity class of all regular languages is SPACE(O(1)), i.e., the decision problems can be solved in constant space. Due to these nice computational properties, we can also claim that regular expressions provide a nice computable framework for reasoning about CFDs.

As for CCs, we have proposed a formal language interpretation of them. In this way, we could integrate the formal semantics of CFDs and CCs. Also, it allows us to group CFMs based on their semantics, which guides us in how to constructively analyze them.

Based on this FL interpretation of CFMs, we have provided two kinds of semantics, called dynamic and static. The dynamic semantics of a given model is equal to the FL of the whole model. The dynamic semantics of CFMs is a new concept, but the static one is, indeed, equivalent to the semantics captured in [6].

We also have characterized some existing analysis operations over CFMs in terms of the FL framework. This allows us to use some off-the-shelf language tools to do analysis on CFMs. Note that automated support for analysis operations over CFMs is a challenging issue. We also have investigated the decidability problems of the introduced analysis operations for different kinds of CFMs. We noted that some analysis operations are not decidable in all classes of CFMs.

Open Problems/Future Work. Based on the closure properties of regular languages, say closure under intersection, union, complement, etc., we believe that our framework is a very good candidate for managing multiple product lines [1]. Indeed, in a forthcoming paper, we will discuss how to manage CFDs using the FL-framework.

The computational complexity problem of analysis operations would be a crucial issue in implementing them for CFMs, and this needs to be investigated.

Sect. 5 needs to be developed more deeply. In the literature, the object-constraint language (OCL) has been proposed for expressing CCs in CFMs [7]. Our next mission is to discover the OCL-definable languages. It can be also fruitful for the model driven engineering (MDE) area, since the MDE community uses mainly OCL to express constraints. This way, we can investigate the expressiveness of OCL in terms of languages. Our conjecture is that there should be some practical CCs that cannot be expressed in OCL (see [16]).

The tool support part discussed in Sect. 6 needs to be deeply developed. Also, we need to find/implement some tools supporting other kinds of formal languages, specially context-free ones.

Acknowledgement. We thank three anonymous reviewers for valuable comments, and Krzysztof Czarnecki and Shoham Ben-David for several valuable discussions. Special thanks go to the authors of papers [2,6,10] for relating the domains of FM and FL. The first author would like to express his sincere gratefulness to Ridha Khedri who introduced FM area to him. The third author is grateful to Martin Erwig for insightful discussions about FM, which resulted in the idea of dynamic semantics. Financial support was provided by NSERC and APC.

References

1. Acher, M., Collet, P., Lahire, P., France, R.: Managing multiple software product lines using merging techniques. France: UniversityofNiceSophiaAntipolis. TechnicalReport, ISRN I3S/RR, vol. 6 (2010)

2. Batory, D.: Feature models, grammars, and propositional formulas. In: Obbink, H., Pohl, K. (eds.) SPLC 2005. LNCS, vol. 3714, pp. 7–20. Springer, Heidelberg (2005)
3. Benavides, D., Segura, S., Ruiz-Cortés, A.: Automated analysis of feature models 20 years later: A literature review. Information Systems 35(6), 615–636 (2010)
4. Bonchi, F., Pous, D.: Checking nfa equivalence with bisimulations up to congruence. ACM SIGPLAN Notices 48(1), 457–468 (2013)
5. Czarnecki, K., Bednasch, T., Unger, P., Eisenecker, U.: Generative programming for embedded software: An industrial experience report. In: Batory, D., Blum, A., Taha, W. (eds.) GPCE 2002. LNCS, vol. 2487, pp. 156–172. Springer, Heidelberg (2002)
6. Czarnecki, K., Helsen, S., Eisenecker, U.: Formalizing cardinality-based feature models and their specialization. Software Process: Improvement and Practice 10(1), 7–29 (2005)
7. Czarnecki, K., Kim, C.H.P.: Cardinality-based feature modeling and constraints: A progress report. In: International Workshop on Software Factories, pp. 16–20 (2005)
8. Czarnecki, K., Wasowski, A.: Feature diagrams and logics: There and back again. In: 11th International on Software Product Line Conference, SPLC 2007, pp. 23–34. IEEE (2007)
9. Davis, M.: Computability, complexity, and languages: fundamentals of theoretical computer science. Academic Press (1994)
10. de Jonge, M., Visser, J.: Grammars as feature diagrams. In: ICSR7 Workshop on Generative Programming, pp. 23–24. Citeseer (2002)
11. Diskin, Z., Safilian, A., Maibaum, T., Ben-David, S.: Modeling product lines with kripke structures and modal logic (GSDLab TR 2014-08-01) (August 2014)
12. Linz, P.: An introduction to formal languages and automata. Jones & Bartlett Publishers (2011)
13. Mannion, M.: Using first-order logic for product line model validation. In: Chastek, G.J. (ed.) SPLC 2002. LNCS, vol. 2379, pp. 176–187. Springer, Heidelberg (2002)
14. Pohl, K., Böckle, G., Van Der Linden, F.: Software product line engineering: foundations, principles, and techniques. Springer (2005)
15. Quinton, C., Romero, D., Duchien, L.: Cardinality-based feature models with constraints: a pragmatic approach. In: Proceedings of the 17th International Software Product Line Conference, pp. 162–166. ACM (2013)
16. Safilian, A., Maibaum, T., Diskin, Z.: The semantics of feature models via formal languages (extended version) (GSDLab TR 2014-08-02) (August 2014)
17. Schobbens, P.-Y., Heymans, P., Trigaux, J.-C., Bontemps, Y.: Generic semantics of feature diagrams. Computer Networks 51(2), 456–479 (2007)
18. She, S., Lotufo, R., Berger, T., Wasowski, A., Czarnecki, K.: Reverse engineering feature models. In: ICSE 2011, pp. 461–470. IEEE (2011)
19. van Noord, G.: Fsa6. 2xx: Finite state automata utilities. http://odur.let.rug.nl/vannoord/Fsa/fsa.html, 3(10), 2003 (2002) (accessed)

Axiomatization of Typed First-Order Logic

Peter H. Schmitt(✉) and Mattias Ulbrich

Karlsruhe Institute of Technology (KIT), Department of Informatics,
Am Fasanengarten 5, 76131, Karlsruhe, Germany
pschmitt@ira.uka.de

Abstract. This paper contributes to the theory of typed first-order logic. We present a sound and complete axiomatization for a basic typed logic lifting restrictions imposed by previous results. As a second contribution, this paper provides complete axiomatizations for the type predicates $instance_T$, $exactInstance_T$, and functions $cast_T$ indispensable for reasoning about object-oriented programming languages.

1 Introduction

Typed first-order logics with sophisticated type systems are by now a tried-and-tested basis for program verification systems. The most common route to proof support for these logics is by translation to simply sorted or unsorted logics for which SMT solvers are available. Typical representatives of this approach are the translation of the Boogie type system explained in [7] and the translation of the type system used in the Why verification tool described in [3]. The alternative approach to implement provers for such typed first-order logics directly is less common, e.g., the prover integrated in the KeY system [1] and the Alt-Ergo SMT solver [2].

In this paper we present a logical framework for a hierarchically typed first order logic and a sound and complete calculus. This paper furthermore addresses an issue with the coincidence lemma that is folklore knowledge in the community though we could not find a published reference. Let $\mathcal{T}_1 = \{A, B\}$ be an example type hierarchy containing the two types A, B with $A \not\sqsubseteq B$ and $B \not\sqsubseteq A$. Let x be a variable of type A and y be a variable of type B. Then the formula $\neg\exists x.\exists y.(x \doteq y)$ is a tautology. If we extend $\mathcal{T}_1$ to the type hierarchy $\mathcal{T}_2 = (\{A, B, C\}, \sqsubseteq)$ with $C \sqsubseteq A$ and $C \sqsubseteq B$, the very same formula is no longer a tautology in the logic using $\mathcal{T}_2$. This phenomenon that universal validity of a formula depends on symbols not occurring in it, is highly undesirable. We adapt the notion of universal validity to exclude this deficiency in Definition 8 below.

There is a rich body of recent literature on the translation approach investigating various variations, optimizations, and tunings directly geared towards program verification, see again [7,3] for references. Typed, or many-sorted, calculi have a long tradition in mathematical logic, [8] may be counted among the earliest contributions in this line. More recently there was a short-lived flurry on order-sorted logic programming and resolution calculi, as witnessed e.g., by [10]. Despite this history there are not many recent papers on implemented calculi

N. Bjørner and F. de Boer (Eds.): FM 2015, LNCS 9109, pp. 470–486, 2015.
DOI: 10.1007/978-3-319-19249-9_29

of typed first-order logic, let along contributions aimed at program verification. This paper falls into this category. The contribution closest to ours is [6] that presents a sound and complete sequent calculus under the restriction that the type hierarchy is closed under greatest lower bounds. An extended version has been published as [1, Chapter 2]. We improve on this by 1) lifting the restriction on the type hierarchy and 2) reducing the logic to a minimal predefined vocabulary, where equality $\doteq$ is the only built-in predicate, and defining the desired vocabulary axiomatically.

Plan of the Paper: The main part of Section 2, after introducing the basic typed logic, is taken up by the proof of the soundness and completeness theorem, Theorem 1. In Section 3, an example of a theory in the basic typed logic is presented axiomatizing $instance_T$, $exactInstance_T$, and $cast_T$ culminating again in a soundness and completeness proof, Theorem 3. Section 4 contains a few hints how some Java-specific notions could be axiomatized. We close with concluding remarks in Section 5.

We thank an anonymous reviewer for the thorough reading of the first version of this paper and his or her expert and useful comments.

2 The Basic Typed Logic

2.1 Syntax

Definition 1. *a* type hierarchy $\mathcal{T} = (\mathrm{TSym}, \sqsubseteq)$ *consists of*

1. *a non-empty set* TSym *of type symbols,*
2. *a partial order relation* $\sqsubseteq$ *on* TSym *called the subtype relation,*
3. *the designated symbols* $\bot \in \mathrm{TSym}$ *for the* empty *type and* $\top \in \mathrm{TSym}$ *for the* universal *type,*
4. $\bot \sqsubseteq A \sqsubseteq \top$ *for all* $A \in \mathrm{TSym}$.

We point out that no further restrictions are placed on type hierarchies in contrast to other approaches requiring the existence of greatest lower bounds. The empty type $\bot$ only plays an *ornamental* role in this paper. We nevertheless kept it in the hope that it may find its uses in future developments.

Definition 2. *A* signature $\Sigma = (\mathrm{FSym}, \mathrm{PSym}, \mathrm{VSym})$ *for a given type hierarchy* $\mathcal{T}$ *is made up of*

1. *a set* FSym *of typed function symbols,*
   by $f : A_1, \ldots, A_n \to A$ *we declare the argument types of* $f \in \mathrm{FSym}$ *to be* $A_1, \ldots, A_n$ *in the given order and its result type to be* A*,*
2. *a set* PSym *of typed predicate symbols,*
   by $p : A_1, \ldots, A_n$ *we declare the argument types of* $p \in \mathrm{PSym}$ *to be* $A_1, \ldots, A_n$ *in the given order,*
3. *a set* VSym *of typed variable symbols,*
   by $v : A$ *for* $v \in \mathrm{VSym}$ *we declare* v *to be a variable of type* A.

4. PSym *contains the dedicated symbol* $\doteq : \top, \top$ *for equality.*

In the above all $A, A_1, \ldots, A_n$ *in* TSym *are required to be different from* $\bot$*. We do not allow overloading: The same symbol may not occur in* FSym$\cup$PSym$\cup$VSym *with different typing.*

The next two definitions define the syntactic categories of terms and formulas of typed first-order logic, as usual.

Definition 3. *Let* $\mathcal{T}$ *be a type hierarchy, and* Σ *a signature for* $\mathcal{T}$*. The set* Trm_A *of terms of type* $A \neq \bot$ *is inductively defined such that*

1. $v \in \mathrm{Trm}_A$ *for each variable symbol* $v : A \in \mathrm{VSym}$ *of type* A*.*
2. $f(t_1, \ldots, t_n) \in \mathrm{Trm}_A$ *for each* $f : A_1, \ldots, A_n \to A \in \mathrm{FSym}$*, and terms* $t_i \in \mathrm{Trm}_{B_i}$ *with* $B_i \sqsubseteq A_i$ *for all* $1 \leq i \leq n$*.*

If $t \in \mathrm{Trm}_A$*, we say that* t *is of (static) type* A *and write* $\sigma(t) = A$*.*

Definition 4. *The set* Fml *is inductively defined as:*

1. $p(t_1, \ldots, t_n) \in \mathrm{Fml}$
   for $p : A_1, \ldots, A_n \in \mathrm{PSym}$*, and* $t_i \in \mathrm{Trm}_{B_i}$ *with* $B_i \sqsubseteq A_i$ *for all* $1 \leq i \leq n$*.*
   In particular $t_1 \doteq t_2 \in \mathrm{Fml}$ *for arbitrary terms* t_i*.*
2. *true, false* $\in$ Fml
3. $\neg\phi$, $\phi \wedge \psi$, $\phi \vee \psi$, $\phi \to \psi$ *are in* Fml *for arbitrary* $\phi, \psi \in \mathrm{Fml}$*.*
4. $\forall v.\phi$, $\exists v.\phi$ *are in* Fml *for* $\phi \in \mathrm{Fml}$ *and* $v : A \in \mathrm{VSym}$*.*

If need arises, we will make dependence of these definitions on Σ *and* $\mathcal{T}$ *explicit by writing* $\mathrm{Trm}_{A,\Sigma}$*,* Fml_Σ *or* $\mathrm{Trm}_{A,\mathcal{T},\Sigma}$*,* $\mathrm{Fml}_{\mathcal{T},\Sigma}$*. When convenient, we will also use the redundant notation* $\forall\, v{:}A.\phi$*,* $\exists\, v{:}A.\phi$ *for a variable* $v : A \in \mathrm{VSym}$*.*

Free and bound variables are defined as usual as well as typed substitutions that allow one to replace a variable of type A by a term of type B if $B \sqsubseteq A$.

2.2 Semantics

Definition 5. *A* universe *or* domain *for a given type hierarchy* $\mathcal{T}$ *and signature* Σ *consists of*

1. *a non-empty set* D*,*
2. *a typing function* $\delta : D \to \mathrm{TSym} \setminus \{\bot\}$*.*

The sets $D^A = \{d \in D \mid \delta(d) \sqsubseteq A\}$ *for* $A \in \mathrm{TSym}$ *are called type universe or type domain for* A*. We require that* $D^A \neq \emptyset$ *for each* $A \in \mathrm{TSym}$ *with* $A \neq \bot$*.*

The typing function δ assigns to every element $o \in D$ of the universe its *dynamic type* $\delta(o)$ and the type domain D^A of a type A contains all elements of dynamic type A or of a dynamic type which is a subtype of A. Definition 5 implies that for different types A, $B \in \mathrm{TSym} \setminus \{\bot\}$, there is $o \in D^A \cap D^B$ only if there exists $C \in \mathrm{TSym}$, $C \neq \bot$ with $C \sqsubseteq A$ and $C \sqsubseteq B$.

Lemma 1. *The type domains for a universe (D, δ) share the following properties:*

1. $D^{\perp} = \emptyset$, $D^{\top} = D$,
2. $D^A \subseteq D^B$ *if* $A \sqsubseteq B$,
3. $D^C = D^A \cap D^B$ *in case the greatest lower bound* C *of* A *and* B *exists.*

Definition 6. *A first-order* structure $\mathcal{M}$ *for a given type hierarchy* $\mathcal{T}$ *and signature* Σ *consists of a domain* (D, δ) *and an interpretation* I *such that*

1. $I(f)$ *is a function from* $D^{A_1} \times \ldots \times D^{A_n}$ *into* D^A *for* $f : A_1, \ldots, A_n \to A$ *in* FSym,
2. $I(p)$ *is a subset of* $D^{A_1} \times \ldots \times D^{A_n}$ *for* $p : A_1, \ldots, A_n$ *in* PSym,
3. $I(\doteq) = \{(d, d) \mid d \in D\}$.

For a first-order structure $\mathcal{M}$ and variable assignment β the evaluation $\text{val}_{\mathcal{M},\beta}(t)$ of a term t and the semantic truth relation $(\mathcal{M}, \beta) \models \phi$ for formulas ϕ are defined as usual.

2.3 Calculus

The following definition formalizes our concept of enlarging a type hierarchy: new types and subtype relations between old and new types may be added without adding new relations among the old types. This can be guaranteed by the restriction that new types can only be declared to be subtypes of old types, never supertypes.

Definition 7. *A type hierarchy* $\mathcal{T}_2 = (\text{TSym}_2, \sqsubseteq_2)$ *is an* extension *of a type hierarchy* $\mathcal{T}_1 = (\text{TSym}_1, \sqsubseteq_1)$*, in symbols* $\mathcal{T}_1 \sqsubseteq \mathcal{T}_2$*, if*

1. $\text{TSym}_1 \subseteq \text{TSym}_2$
2. $\sqsubseteq_2$ *is the smallest subtype relation containing* $\sqsubseteq_1 \cup \Delta$ *where* Δ *is a set of relations* (S, T) *with* $T \in \text{TSym}_1$ *and* $S \in \text{TSym}_2 \setminus \text{TSym}_1$.

Note, that this definitions entails , $\perp \sqsubseteq_2 A \sqsubseteq_2 \top$ for all new types A. For later reference, we note the following lemma.

Lemma 2. *Let* $\mathcal{T}_2 = (\text{TSym}_2, \sqsubseteq_2)$ *be an extension of* $\mathcal{T}_1 = (\text{TSym}_1, \sqsubseteq_1)$ *with* $\sqsubseteq_2$ *being the smallest subtype relation containing* $\sqsubseteq_1 \cup \Delta$*, for some* $\Delta \subseteq (\text{TSym}_2 \setminus \text{TSym}_1) \times \text{TSym}_1$. *Then for* $A, B \in \text{TSym}_1$, $C \in \text{TSym}_2 \setminus \text{TSym}_1$, $D \in \text{TSym}_2$:

1. $A \sqsubseteq_2 B \Leftrightarrow A \sqsubseteq_1 B$
2. $C \sqsubseteq_2 A \Leftrightarrow T \sqsubseteq_1 A$ *for some* $(C, T) \in \Delta$
3. $D \sqsubseteq_2 C \Leftrightarrow D = C$ *or* $D = \perp$.

Proof. This follows easily from the fact that no supertype relations of the form $A \sqsubseteq_2 C$ for new type symbols C are stipulated. □

The following adapted definition of universal validity resolves the undesirable phenomenon, already referred to in the introduction, that validity of a formula depends on symbols not occurring in it.

$$\text{andLeft}\ \frac{\Gamma, \phi, \psi \Longrightarrow \Delta}{\Gamma, \phi \wedge \psi \Longrightarrow \Delta} \qquad \text{andRight}\ \frac{\Gamma \Longrightarrow \phi, \Delta \qquad \Gamma \Longrightarrow \psi, \Delta}{\Gamma \Longrightarrow \phi \wedge \psi, \Delta}$$

$$\text{orRight}\ \frac{\Gamma \Longrightarrow \phi, \psi, \Delta}{\Gamma \Longrightarrow \phi \vee \psi, \Delta} \qquad \text{orLeft}\ \frac{\Gamma, \phi \Longrightarrow \Delta \qquad \Gamma, \psi \Longrightarrow \Delta}{\Gamma, \phi \vee \psi \Longrightarrow \Delta}$$

$$\text{impRight}\ \frac{\Gamma, \phi \Longrightarrow \psi, \Delta}{\Gamma \Longrightarrow \phi \to \psi, \Delta} \qquad \text{impLeft}\ \frac{\Gamma \Longrightarrow \phi, \Delta \qquad \Gamma, \psi \Longrightarrow \Delta}{\Gamma, \phi \to \psi \Longrightarrow \Delta}$$

$$\text{notLeft}\ \frac{\Gamma \Longrightarrow \phi, \Delta}{\Gamma, \neg\phi \Longrightarrow \Delta} \qquad \text{notRight}\ \frac{\Gamma, \phi \Longrightarrow \Delta}{\Gamma \Longrightarrow \neg\phi, \Delta}$$

$$\text{allRight}\ \frac{\Gamma \Longrightarrow [x/c](\phi), \Delta}{\Gamma \Longrightarrow \forall\, x{:}A.\phi, \Delta} \qquad \text{allLeft}\ \frac{\Gamma, \forall\, x{:}A.\phi, [x/t](\phi) \Longrightarrow \Delta}{\Gamma, \forall\, x{:}A.\phi \Longrightarrow \Delta}$$

$c : \to A$ a new constant $\qquad$ $t \in \mathrm{Trm}_{A'}$ ground, $A' \sqsubseteq A$

$$\text{exLeft}\ \frac{\Gamma, [x/c](\phi) \Longrightarrow \Delta}{\Gamma, \exists\, x{:}A.\phi \Longrightarrow \Delta} \qquad \text{exRight}\ \frac{\Gamma \Longrightarrow \exists\, x{:}A.\phi, [x/t](\phi), \Delta}{\Gamma \Longrightarrow \exists\, x{:}A.\phi, \Delta}$$

$c : \to A$ a new constant $\qquad$ $t \in \mathrm{Trm}_{A'}$ ground, $A' \sqsubseteq A$

$$\text{close}\ \frac{}{\Gamma, \phi \Longrightarrow \phi, \Delta}$$

$$\text{closeFalse}\ \frac{}{\Gamma, \text{false} \Longrightarrow \Delta} \qquad \text{closeTrue}\ \frac{}{\Gamma \Longrightarrow \text{true}, \Delta}$$

Fig. 1. First-order rules

Definition 8. *Let $\mathcal{T}$ be a type hierarchy and Σ a signature, $\phi \in \mathrm{Fml}_{\mathcal{T},\Sigma}$ a formula without free variables, and $\Phi \subseteq \mathrm{Fml}_{\mathcal{T},\Sigma}$ a set of formulas without free variables.*

1. *ϕ is a* logical consequence *of Φ, in symbols $\Phi \vdash \phi$, if for all type hierarchies $\mathcal{T}'$ with $\mathcal{T} \sqsubseteq \mathcal{T}'$, and all $\mathcal{T}'$-Σ-structures $\mathcal{M}$ such that $\mathcal{M} \models \Phi$ also $\mathcal{M} \models \phi$ holds.*
2. *ϕ is* universally valid *if it is a logical consequence of the empty set, i.e. $\emptyset \vdash \phi$.*
3. *ϕ is satisfiable if there is a type hierarchy $\mathcal{T}'$, with $\mathcal{T} \sqsubseteq \mathcal{T}'$ and a $\mathcal{T}'$-Σ-structure $\mathcal{M}$ with $\mathcal{M} \models \phi$.*

The notion of *logical consequence* from Definition 8 may be called *super logical consequence* to distinguish it from the concept $\Phi \vdash_{\mathcal{T},\Sigma} \phi$ that is true when for any $\mathcal{T}$-Σ-structure $\mathcal{M}$ with $\mathcal{M} \models \Phi$ also $\mathcal{M} \models \phi$ is true. For the above example type hierarchy $\mathcal{T}_1 = \{A, B\}$ which had unrelated types A and B ($A \not\sqsubseteq B, B \not\sqsubseteq A$), we obtain $\not\vdash \neg\exists\, x{:}A.\exists\, y{:}B.(x \doteq y)$, but $\vdash_{\mathcal{T}_1,\emptyset} \neg\exists\, x{:}A.\exists\, y{:}B.(x \doteq y)$.

Definition 7 forbids the introduction of subtype chains like $A \sqsubseteq B \sqsubseteq T$ into the type hierarchy. However, it can be shown that relaxing the definition in that respect results in an equivalent notion of logical consequence. We keep the restriction here since it simplifies reasoning about type hierarchy extensions.

$$\text{eqLeft}\ \frac{\Gamma, t_1 \doteq t_2, [z/t_1](\phi), [z/t_2](\phi) \Longrightarrow \Delta}{\Gamma, t_1 \doteq t_2, [z/t_1](\phi) \Longrightarrow \Delta}$$
if $\sigma(t_2) \sqsubseteq \sigma(t_1)$

$$\text{eqRight}\ \frac{\Gamma, t_1 \doteq t_2 \Longrightarrow [z/t_2](\phi), [z/t_1](\phi), \Delta}{\Gamma, t_1 \doteq t_2 \Longrightarrow [z/t_1](\phi), \Delta}$$
if $\sigma(t_2) \sqsubseteq \sigma(t_1)$

$$\text{eqSymmLeft}\ \frac{\Gamma, t_2 \doteq t_1 \Longrightarrow \Delta}{\Gamma, t_1 \doteq t_2 \Longrightarrow \Delta} \qquad \text{eqReflLeft}\ \frac{\Gamma, t \doteq t \Longrightarrow \Delta}{\Gamma \Longrightarrow \Delta}$$

$$\text{eqDynamicSort}\ \frac{\Gamma, t_1 \doteq t_2, \exists x.(x \doteq t_1 \wedge x \doteq t_2) \Longrightarrow \Delta}{\Gamma, t_1 \doteq t_2 \Longrightarrow \Delta}$$
if $\sigma(t_1)$ and $\sigma(t_2)$ are incomparable,
the sort C of x is new and satisfies $C \sqsubset \sigma(t_1)$ and $C \sqsubset \sigma(t_2)$

Fig. 2. Equality rules

The calculus of our choice is the *sequent calculus.* The basic data that is manipulated by the rules of the sequent calculus are *sequents.* These are of the form $\phi_1, \ldots, \phi_n \Longrightarrow \psi_1, \ldots, \psi_m$ The formulas $\phi_1, \ldots, \phi_n$ at the left-hand side of the sequent separator, $\Longrightarrow$, are the premises or the antecedent of the sequent, the formulas $\psi_1, \ldots, \psi_m$ on the right are the conclusions or the succedent. The intended meaning of a sequent is that the premises together imply at least one conclusion. In other words, a sequent $\phi_1, \ldots, \phi_n \Longrightarrow \psi_1, \ldots, \psi_m$ is valid iff the formula $\bigwedge_{1 \le i \le n} \phi_i \to \bigvee_{1 \le j \le m} \psi_j$ is valid.

Figures 1 and 2 show the usual set of rules of the sequent calculus with equality as it can be found in many text books, e.g. [5, Section 5.4]. The only exception is rule eqDynamicSort, which is the main innovation of our approach. Here, $[z/t_2](\phi)$ is used to denote the application of the substitution t_2 for free occurrences of variable z in ϕ. Note that the rules contain the schematic variables Γ, Δ for set of formulas, ψ, ϕ for formulas and t, c for terms and constants.

The rule eqDynamicSort is different than the other rules in that it introduces a new type. In that sense it is similar to the rules forallRight and exLeft that introduce new constant symbols. These constants are used to denote an unknown value whose existence is guaranteed. The rationale behind the new type C in eqDynamicSort is the same: Since the equality $t_1 \doteq t_2$ in the antecedent requires that the types $\sigma(t_1)$ and $\sigma(t_2)$ have a common element, there must also be a type to accommodate that value. In the rule that type is made explicit and named C.

Theorem 1 (Soundness and Completeness Theorem).
Let $\mathcal{T}$ = (TSym, $\sqsubseteq$) be a type hierarchy and Σ a signature, $\Gamma, \Delta \subset \mathrm{Fml}_{\mathcal{T},\Sigma}$ without free variables. Assume that for every $A \in \mathrm{TSym} \setminus \{\bot\}$ there is a constant symbol of type A. Then:

$\Gamma \Longrightarrow \Delta$ is universally valid iff there is a closed proof tree for the $\Gamma \Longrightarrow \Delta$.

Proof. Soundness. We only present the proof for the new rule eqDynamicSort, the remaining cases follow the usual pattern.

To prove soundness of eqDynamicSort we assume that $\bigwedge \Gamma \wedge t_1 \doteq t_2 \wedge \exists x.(x \doteq t_1 \wedge x \doteq t_2) \rightarrow \bigvee \Delta$ is universally valid for type hierarchy $\mathcal{T}_C$ and need to show that $\bigwedge \Gamma \wedge t_1 \doteq t_2 \rightarrow \bigvee \Delta$ is universally valid for the hierarchy $\mathcal{T}$.

The type hierarchy $\mathcal{T}_C = (\text{TSym} \cup \{C\}, \sqsubseteq_C)$ is an extension of the hierarchy $\mathcal{T} = (\text{TSym}, \sqsubseteq)$ in the sense of Definition 7 , with $\sqsubseteq_C$ the least subtype relation containing $\sqsubseteq \cup \{(C, \sigma(t_1)), (C, \sigma(t_2))\}$.

Assume that $\bigwedge \Gamma \wedge t_1 \doteq t_2 \wedge \exists x.(x \doteq t_1 \wedge x \doteq t_2) \rightarrow \bigvee \Delta$ is universally valid for type hierarchy $\mathcal{T}_C$. To prove universal validity of $\bigwedge \Gamma \wedge t_1 \doteq t_2 \rightarrow \bigvee \Delta$ we need to consider a type hierarchy $\mathcal{T}^1 = (\text{TSym}^1, \sqsubseteq^1)$ that is an arbitrary extension of $\mathcal{T} = (\text{TSym}, \sqsubseteq)$ and an arbitrary $(\mathcal{T}^1, \Sigma)$-structure $\mathcal{M} = (M, \delta, I)$ satisfying $\mathcal{M} \models \Gamma \wedge t_1 \doteq t_2$ with the aim of showing $\mathcal{M} \models \bigvee \Delta$. Let T be the dynamic type of $t_1^{\mathcal{M}} = t_2^{\mathcal{M}}$, i.e., $\delta(t_1^{\mathcal{M}}) = \delta(t_2^{\mathcal{M}}) = T$, which obviously satisfies $T \sqsubseteq \sigma(t_1)$ and $T \sqsubseteq \sigma(t_2)$. Set $\mathcal{T}_C^1 = (\text{TSym}^1 \cup \{C\}, \sqsubseteq_C^1)$ with $\sqsubseteq_C^1$ being the smallest subtype relation containing $\sqsubseteq^1 \cup \{(C, \sigma(t_1)), (C, \sigma(t_2))\}$. We need a further extension $\mathcal{T}^2 = (\text{TSym}^1 \cup \{C, C^2\}, \sqsubseteq^2)$ of $\mathcal{T}_C^1$, where $\sqsubseteq^2$ is the smallest subtype relation containing $\sqsubseteq_C^1 \cup \Delta$ with $\Delta = \{(C^2, C), (C^2, T)\}$.

We proceed in the main proof by constructing a $(\mathcal{T}^2, \Sigma)$-structure $\mathcal{M}^2 = (M, \delta^2, I)$ that differs from $\mathcal{M}$ only in δ^2 which is given by

$$\delta^2(o) = \begin{cases} C^2 & \text{if } o = t_1^{\mathcal{M}} = t_2^{\mathcal{M}} \\ \delta(o) & \text{otherwise} . \end{cases}$$

This leads to $\mathcal{M}^2 \models \exists x.(x \doteq t_1 \wedge x \doteq t_2)$ – if we remember that x is a variable of the type C and $C^2 \sqsubseteq C$.

The crucial property of the type hierarchy $\mathcal{T}^2$ is

$$\text{for any } o \in M \text{ and any } A \in \text{TSym}^1 \quad \delta(o) \sqsubseteq^1 A \Leftrightarrow \delta^2(o) \sqsubseteq^2 A . \tag{1}$$

Here are the arguments why (1) is true: In case $o \neq t_1^{\mathcal{M}}$ we have $\delta^2(o) = \delta(o) \in \text{TSym}^1$ and $\delta(o) \sqsubseteq^1 A \Leftrightarrow \delta(o) \sqsubseteq^2 A$ by item 1 of Lemma 2. In case $o = t_1^{\mathcal{M}} = t_2^{\mathcal{M}}$ we have $\delta(o) = T$ and $\delta^2(o) = C^2$. By item 2 of Lemma 2, $C^2 \sqsubseteq^2 A$ is equivalent to the disjunction of $T \sqsubseteq_C^1 A$ or $C \sqsubseteq_C^1 A$. Again by Lemma 2, this is equivalent to $T \sqsubseteq^1 A$ or $\sigma(t_1) \sqsubseteq^1 A$ or $\sigma(t_2) \sqsubseteq^1 A$. Since $T \sqsubseteq \sigma(t_1), \sigma(t_2)$, this is equivalent to $T \sqsubseteq^1 A$. In total, we have shown (1) by proving that $C^2 \sqsubseteq^2 A$ is equivalent to $T \sqsubseteq^1 A$.

We need to convince ourselves that $\mathcal{M}^2 \models \bigwedge \Gamma \wedge t_1 \doteq t_2$ is still true. We will prove the following auxiliary statement:

$$\begin{array}{c}\text{Let } \phi \text{ be an arbitrary } (\mathcal{T}, \Sigma)\text{-formula, } \beta \text{ a variable assignment, then} \\ (\mathcal{M}, \beta) \models \phi \quad \Leftrightarrow \quad (\mathcal{M}^2, \beta) \models \phi \end{array} \tag{2}$$

The proof of (2) proceeds by induction on the complexity of ϕ. The only non-trivial steps are the induction steps for quantifiers. So assume that the claim is true for $\phi(x_1, \ldots, x_n)$[1] and we try to establish it for $(\exists x_1.\phi)(x_2, \ldots, x_n)$, with

[1] i.e., a formula with at most the free variables $x_1, \ldots, x_n$.

x_1 a variable of type A. By choice of ϕ, the type A is different from C and C^2.

$$\begin{aligned}(\mathcal{M},\beta) \models \exists x_1.\phi &\Leftrightarrow (\mathcal{M},\beta^{o}_{x_1}) \models \phi(x_1) && \text{for } o \in M \text{ with } \delta(o) \sqsubseteq A \\ &\Leftrightarrow (\mathcal{M}^2,\beta^{o}_{x_1}) \models \phi(x_1) && \text{induction hypothesis} \\ &\Leftrightarrow (\mathcal{M}^2,\beta) \models \exists x_1.\phi && \text{by (1)}\end{aligned}$$

Now, we have established $\mathcal{M}^2 \models \bigwedge \Gamma \wedge t_1 \doteq t_2$. From the assumption we obtain $\mathcal{M}^2 \models \bigvee \Delta$, which entails $\mathcal{M} \models \bigvee \Delta$ by another appeal to (2), as desired.

Completeness. The completeness part of the proof proceeds by contradiction. Assume there is no closed proof tree with root labeled by $\Gamma \Longrightarrow \Delta$. We will eventually construct a $(\mathcal{T}',\Sigma)$-structure $\mathcal{M} = (H,\delta,I)$ that is a counterexample to the universal validity of $\Gamma \Longrightarrow \Delta$.

Let T be a proof tree with root labeled by $\Gamma \Longrightarrow \Delta$ such that all rules have been exhaustively applied, but T is not closed. Because of the rules allLeft and exRight, T is necessarily infinite. By an appeal to König's Lemma there is an infinite branch B of T that is not closed.

Let H_0 be the set of all ground terms. We define the relation $\sim_B$ on H_0 by

$$\begin{aligned}t_1 \sim_B t_2 \text{ iff } & t_1 = t_2 \text{ or} \\ & \text{there is a sequent } \Gamma \Longrightarrow \Delta \text{ in } B \text{ with } t_1 \doteq t_2 \in \Gamma\end{aligned}$$

The relation $\sim_B$ is an equivalence relation. Reflexivity is assured by definition. If $t_1 \sim_B t_2$ with $t_1 \doteq t_2 \in \Gamma$ and $\Gamma \Longrightarrow \Delta \in B$, then somewhere in B the rule eqSymmLeft must have been applied since we assume exhaustive rule application. Thus there will be a sequent $\Gamma' \Longrightarrow \Delta' \in B$ with $t_2 \doteq t_1 \in \Gamma'$ and we arrive at $t_2 \sim_B t_1$. It remains to show transitivity. We start from $t_1 \sim_B t_2$ and $t_2 \sim_B t_3$. By definition of $\sim_B$ there are sequents $\Gamma_1 \Longrightarrow \Delta_1$ and $\Gamma_2 \Longrightarrow \Delta_2$ in B with $t_1 \doteq t_2 \in \Gamma_1$ and $t_2 \doteq t_3 \in \Gamma_2$. Since there is no rule that drops an equality in the antecedent, only the arguments may be swapped, there will be a sequent $\Gamma' \Longrightarrow \Delta'$ in B such that $t_1 \doteq t_2$ or $t_2 \doteq t_1$ and at the same time $t_2 \doteq t_3$ or $t_3 \doteq t_2$ occur in Γ'. We consider each case separately.

1. $t_1 \doteq t_2$ and $t_2 \doteq t_3$
2. $t_1 \doteq t_2$ and $t_3 \doteq t_2$
3. $t_2 \doteq t_1$ and $t_2 \doteq t_3$
4. $t_2 \doteq t_1$ and $t_3 \doteq t_2$

In case (1) we use eqLeft to replace the left-hand side t_2 of the second equation by its right-hand side in the first equation and obtain $t_1 \doteq t_3$.

In case (3) we replace, using eqLeft, the left-hand side t_2 of the first equation by its right-hand side in the second equation and obtain $t_1 \doteq t_3$.

In case (4) replace the left-hand side t_2 of the first equation by its right-hand side in the second equation and obtain $t_3 \doteq t_1$. Another application of eqSymmLeft yields $t_1 \doteq t_3$.

Case (2) is the most involved. By exhaustiveness of B we know that eqSymmLeft will be applied again to both equations in focus. If it is first applied to the first equation, we obtain the situation in case (4). If it is first applied to the second equation, we obtain case (1).

Thus in any case $t_1 \sim_B t_3$ follows and transitivity is established. In total we know now that $\sim_B$ is an equivalence relation.

Next we aim to show that $\sim_B$ is also a congruence relation. This requires first to show that $t_i \sim_B t'_i$ for $1 \leq i \leq n$ implies $f(t_1, \ldots, t_n) \sim_B f(t'_1, \ldots, t'_n)$ for any n-place function symbol f. For simplicity we only present that case of a unary function symbol f. We need to show $f(t) \sim_B f(t')$ from $t \sim_B t'$. We first take on the case that $\sigma(t)$ and $\sigma(t')$ are comparable, e.g., $\sigma(t') \sqsubseteq \sigma(t)$. By assumption there is a sequent $\Gamma \Longrightarrow \Delta$ in branch B with $t \doteq t' \in \Gamma$. From the argument given above, we know that there is also sequent $\Gamma_1 \Longrightarrow \Delta_1$ on B with $f(t) \doteq f(t) \in \Gamma_1$ and $t \doteq t' \in \Gamma_1$. By rule eqLeft we obtain a sequent $\Gamma_2 \Longrightarrow \Delta_2$ on B with $f(t) \doteq f(t') \in \Gamma_2$, and thus $f(t) \sim_B f(t')$. It remains to deal with the case that $\sigma(t)$ and $\sigma(t')$ are incomparable. Then rule eqDynamicSort applies and yields a sequent $\Gamma_3 \Longrightarrow \Delta_3$ on B with $t \doteq t' \in \Gamma_3$ and also $\exists x.(x \doteq t \wedge x \doteq t') \in \Gamma_3$ with x a variable of the new type C, with $C \sqsubseteq \sigma(t)$ and $C \sqsubseteq \sigma(t')$. By exLeft there is a Skolem symbol sk of type C with $sk \sim_B t$ and $sk \sim_B t'$. By the comparable types case of the congruence property already established we obtain $f(sk) \sim_B f(t)$ and $f(sk) \sim_B f(t')$. In total $f(t) \sim_B f(t')$ as desired. The case of arbitrary n-place function symbols is only marginally more complicated.

To show that $\sim_B$ is a congruence relation requires to verify the second claim for any n-place predicate symbol q: if $t_i \sim_B t'_i$ for $1 \leq i \leq n$ and $q(t_1, \ldots, t_n) \in \Gamma$ for some $\Gamma \Longrightarrow \Delta$ in B then also $q(t'_1, \ldots, t'_n) \in \Gamma'$ for some $\Gamma' \Longrightarrow \Delta'$ in B. This follows easily from repeated application of the eqLeft rule.

By $[t]_B$ for $t \in H_0$ we denote the equivalence class of t with respect to $\sim_B$, i.e., $[t]_B = \{s \in H_0 \mid t \sim_B s\}$. The universe of the intended counterexample can be stated as:

$$H = \{[t]_B \mid t \in H_0\}$$

Next we need to decide what (dynamic) type an element $[t]_B$ should have in the structure to be constructed. We call an equivalence class $[t]_B$ *typed* if there is a type $T_0 \in \mathcal{T}$ such that there is an term $t_0 \in [t]_B$ with $\sigma(t_0) = T_0$ and for all $t' \in [t]_B$ the subtype relation $T_0 \sqsubseteq \sigma(t')$ holds true. For every equivalence class $[t]_B$ that is not typed, we introduce a new type constant $T_{[t]}$ and set

$$\begin{aligned} \Delta &= \{T_{[t]} \mid [t]_B \in H \text{ is not typed}\} \\ \Delta_R &= \{T_{[t]} \sqsubseteq \sigma(t') \mid t' \in [t]_B \text{ and } T_{[t]} \in \Delta\} \end{aligned}$$

The type hierarchy $\mathcal{T}' = (\mathrm{TSym}', \sqsubseteq')$ extending $\mathcal{T} = (\mathrm{TSym}, \sqsubseteq)$ is given by $\mathrm{TSym}' = \mathrm{TSym} \cup \Delta$ and $\sqsubseteq'$ the least subtype relation containing $\sqsubseteq \cup \Delta_R$. Obviously, $\mathcal{T} \sqsubseteq \mathcal{T}'$.

We are now ready to define a first-order $(\mathcal{T}', \Sigma)$-structure $\mathcal{M} = (H, \delta, I)$.

The (dynamic) typing function is given by

$$\delta([t]_B) = \begin{cases} T_0 & \text{if } [t]_B \text{ is typed by } T_0 \\ T_{[t]} & \text{the new type constant, otherwise} \end{cases}$$

For any n-place function symbol f, we set $I(f)([t_1]_B, \ldots, [t_n]_B) = [f(t_1, \ldots, t_n)]_B$. Since $\sim_B$ is a congruence relation this is an unambiguous definition.

For any n-place predicate symbol p we set

$$I(p) = \{([t_1]_B, \dots, [t_n]_B) \mid \text{ a sequent } \Gamma, p(t_1, \dots, t_n) \Longrightarrow \Delta \text{ occurs in } B\}$$

Again we have to argue that this definition is unambiguous. We do this again for the special case $n = 1$. The generalization to arbitrary n is left as an easy exercise to the reader. If $\Gamma, p(t) \Longrightarrow \Delta$ occurs in B and $t \sim_B s$ we need to show that also a sequent $\Gamma', p(s) \Longrightarrow \Delta'$ occurs in B. We observe first that there is no rule that removes or changes an atomic formula occurring in a sequent. Even in eqLeft and eqRight the substituted formula is added. Therefore we will have a sequent $\Gamma'', t \doteq s, p(t) \Longrightarrow \Delta''$ in B. An application of eqLeft now completes the argument.

This completes the definition of the structure $\mathcal{M} = (H, \delta, I)$.

$$I(t) = [t]_b \text{ for every ground term } t. \tag{3}$$

For 0-place function symbols c claim (3) is just the definition of $I(c)$. The rest of the claim follows by an easy induction on the structural complexity of t.

The next phase in the proof consists in the verification of the claim

$$\mathcal{M} \models \bigwedge \Gamma \wedge \neg \bigvee \Delta \text{ for all sequents } s = \Gamma \Longrightarrow \Delta \text{ in } B \tag{4}$$

The proof of claim (4) is reduced to the following

$$\begin{array}{l} \text{For every formula } \phi \\ \text{if there is } \Gamma \Longrightarrow \Delta \in B \text{ with } \phi \in \Gamma \text{ then } \mathcal{M} \models \phi \\ \text{if there is } \Gamma \Longrightarrow \Delta \in B \text{ with } \phi \in \Delta \text{ then } \mathcal{M} \not\models \phi \end{array} \tag{5}$$

Claim (5) is proved by induction on the structural complexity $n(\phi)$ of ϕ. If $n(\phi) = 0$ then ϕ is an atomic formula or an equation.

For an atomic formula $p(\bar{t}) \in \Gamma$ we know by definition of $\mathcal{M}$ that $\mathcal{M} \models p(\bar{t})$. Now, consider $p(\bar{t}) \in \Delta$. If $\mathcal{M} \models p(\bar{t})$ then there must by definition of $\mathcal{M}$ be a sequent $\Gamma' \Longrightarrow \Delta'$ in B with $p(\bar{t}) \in \Gamma'$. Since atomic formulas never get removed, we must have either $p(\bar{t}) \in \Delta$ and $p(\bar{t}) \in \Gamma$ or $p(\bar{t}) \in \Delta'$ and $p(\bar{t}) \in \Gamma'$. In both cases the branch B could be closed, contrary to assumption. Thus we must have $\mathcal{M} \models \neg p(\bar{t})$ for all $p(\bar{t}) \in \Delta$.

For $t_1 \doteq t_2 \in \Gamma$ we get $t_1 \sim_B t_2$ by definition of $\sim_B$. Thus $[t_1]_B = [t_2]_B$ which directly yields $\mathcal{M} \models t_1 \doteq t_2$.

For $t_1 \doteq t_2 \in \Delta$ we need to show $t_1 \not\sim_B t_2$. But, if $t_1 \sim_B t_2$ were true, there would by definition of $\sim_B$ be a sequent $\Gamma \Longrightarrow \Delta$ in branch B with $t_1 \doteq t_2 \in \Gamma$. Since atomic formulas never get erased there would also be a sequent $\Gamma' \Longrightarrow \Delta'$ with $t_1 \doteq t_2 \in \Gamma'$ and $t_1 \doteq t_2 \in \Delta'$ and the branch could be closed contrary to assumption.

The inductive step $n(\phi) > 0$ is split into a total of 12 cases. Since this part of the proof follows a well established pattern, we restrict our presentation to two exemplary cases.

Case A $\phi_1 \wedge \phi_2$ in Γ.
Since branch B is assumed to be *exhausted*, rule andLeft will have been applied. There is thus a sequent $\Gamma' \Longrightarrow \Delta'$ in B with $\phi_1, \phi_2 \in \Gamma'$. By induction hypothesis we know $\mathcal{M} \models \phi_1$ and $\mathcal{M} \models \phi_2$ thus $\mathcal{M} \models \phi_1 \wedge \phi_2$.

Case B $\exists x.\phi$ in Γ.
Since branch B is assumed to be *exhausted* rule exLeft will have been applied. There is thus a sequent $\Gamma' \Longrightarrow \Delta'$ in B with $[x/c]\phi \in \Gamma'$. By induction hypothesis we know $\mathcal{M} \models [x/c]\phi$ and thus also $\mathcal{M} \models \exists x.\phi$. □

3 A Basic Theory in Typed Logic

In this section, we introduce the concept of a *basic theory* that may be useful in many application contexts.

Definition 9. *Let $\mathcal{T}$ be a type hierarchy, Σ a signature. A $(\mathcal{T}, \Sigma)$ theory T is called a* basic theory *if*

- *Σ contains at least for each $A \in \mathcal{T}$, $A \neq \top, \bot$*
  - *The unary predicate symbols $instance_A : \top$ and $exactInstance_A : \top$*
  - *The function symbol $cast_A : \top \to A$*
  - *The constant symbol $default_A : A$.*

  Such Σ will be called a basic signature.
- *T contains at least the following axiom schemes $T^{base}_{\mathcal{T}}$*

1. $\forall x.(instance_A(x) \leftrightarrow \exists y.(y \doteq x))$ *with* $y : A$ (Ax-I)

2a. $\forall x.(exactInstance_A(x) \to instance_A(x))$ (Ax-E$_1$)

2b. $\forall x.(exactInstance_A(x) \to \neg instance_B(x))$ *with* $A \not\sqsubseteq B$ (Ax-E$_2$)

3. $\forall x.(\ (\ instance_A(x) \to cast_A(x) \doteq x) \wedge (\neg instance_A(x) \to cast_A(x) \doteq default_A))$ (Ax-C)

A, B range over TSym $\setminus \{\bot\}$ *and $x : \top$ is a variable of the universal sort $\top$.*

Definition 10. *Let Σ be a basic signature. A $(\mathcal{T}, \Sigma)$-structure $\mathcal{M} = (M, \delta, I)$ is called a* standard *structure if*

$$
\begin{array}{lll}
1. & instance^{\mathcal{M}}_A & = \{o \in M \mid \delta(o) \sqsubseteq A\} = M^A \\
2. & exactInstance^{\mathcal{M}}_A & = \{o \in M \mid \delta(o) = A\} \\
3. & cast^{\mathcal{M}}_A(o) & = \begin{cases} o & \text{if } o \in M^A \\ default^{\mathcal{M}}_A & \text{otherwise} \end{cases}
\end{array}
$$

There are at this point no restrictions on $default^{\mathcal{M}}_A$ except, of course, that it be an element of M^A.

Theorem 2.

1. *Let $\mathcal{M}$ be a standard $(\mathcal{T}, \Sigma)$-structure for basic signature Σ. Then $\mathcal{M} \models T^{base}_{\mathcal{T}}$.*

2. *Let $\mathcal{M}$ be a $(\mathcal{T}, \Sigma)$-structure for basic signature Σ and $\mathcal{M} \models T_{\mathcal{T}}^{base}$. Then $o \in exactInstance_A^{\mathcal{M}} \implies \delta(o) = A$.*

Proof. **ad 1**
Parts (1) and (3) of Definition 9 are direct formalization of the definitions of $instance_A$ and $cast_A$ in standard structures in Definition 10. Part (2a) is also an obvious consequence of the semantics of $exactInstance_A$. So let us turn to part (2b) and consider $o \in exactInstance_A^{\mathcal{M}}$ and a type B with $A \not\sqsubseteq B$. By the standard semantics definition this says $\delta(o) = A$ and $\delta(o) \not\sqsubseteq B$ and thus $o \notin instance_B^{\mathcal{M}}$. This proves $\mathcal{M} \models (2b)$.
ad 2
Since the first part of axiom (2) in $T_{\mathcal{T}}^{base}$ entails $exactInstance_A^{\mathcal{M}} \subseteq instance_A^{\mathcal{M}}$, we obtain $\delta(o) \sqsubseteq A$ from the definition of $instance_A$ in $T_{\mathcal{T}}^{base}$. If $\delta(o) \neq A$ axiom (2b) would yield $o \notin exactInstance_{\delta(o)}^{\mathcal{M}}$ contradicting (2) of Definition 10. □

If a $(\mathcal{T}, \Sigma)$-structure $\mathcal{M}$ satisfies $\mathcal{M} \models T_{\mathcal{T}}^{base}$, then it need not be a standard structure, i.e., the reverse implication in Proposition 2 (2) need not hold. The axioms would, e.g., be true if $exactInstance_A^{\mathcal{M}} = \emptyset$ for all A. We will nevertheless be able to prove that the sentences derivable from $T_{\mathcal{T}}^{base}$ are exactly those universally valid in all standard structures. This needs the following preparatory definitions and lemma.

For an arbitrary extension $\mathcal{T}^* = (\text{TSym}^*, \sqsubseteq^*)$ of $\mathcal{T} = (\text{TSym}, \sqsubseteq)$ and signature Σ for the hierarchy $\mathcal{T}$ we construct for any $(\mathcal{T}^*, \Sigma^*)$-structure $\mathcal{M}$ with $\mathcal{M} \models T_{\mathcal{T}}^{base}$ an adapted structure $\mathcal{M}^a$ that is standard and not too far away from $\mathcal{M}$. $\mathcal{M}^a$ will be a $(\mathcal{T}^a, \Sigma^a)$ structure for an extension $\mathcal{T}^a$ of the hierarchy $\mathcal{T}^*$. The signatures Σ^* and Σ^a will at least contain all the symbols from Definition 9 relating to the new types not contained in TSym. In passing from $\mathcal{M}$ to $\mathcal{M}^a$ some elements of the universe need to be "relocated" into different types. We will do this using a partial type projection $\pi_{\mathcal{M},\mathcal{T}} : M \nrightarrow \text{TSym}$ which is characterized by

$$\pi_{\mathcal{M},\mathcal{T}}(o) = A \iff \begin{array}{l} o \in exactInstance_A^{\mathcal{M}} \\ \text{and } \delta(o) \sqsubseteq A \\ \text{and } (\delta(o) \sqsubseteq B \implies A \sqsubseteq B) \text{ for all } B \in \text{TSym}. \end{array} \tag{6}$$

Function π is well-defined: Assume there are two $A, A' \in \text{TSym}$ for which the right-hand side of the above definition is true. By the third condition we have that $A \sqsubseteq A'$ and $A' \sqsubseteq A$, hence, ($\mathcal{T}$ is a poset) $A = A'$.

The idea behind it is that π maps element o to the type it appears to live in ($o \in exactInstance_A^{\mathcal{M}}$) when looking at it from the perspective of $\mathcal{T}$ only. The additional conditions make this well-defined and ensure that domains in the adapted structure remain the same.

Definition 11. *Let $\mathcal{T}^* = (\text{TSym}^*, \sqsubseteq^*)$ be an extension of the type hierarchy $\mathcal{T} = (\text{TSym}, \sqsubseteq)$, Σ a basic signature for hierarchy $\mathcal{T}$, and $\mathcal{M} = (M, \delta, I)$ a $(\mathcal{T}^*, \Sigma^*)$-structure.*
The adapted structure *$\mathcal{M}^a = (M, \delta^a, I^a)$ for $\mathcal{M}$ is the $(\mathcal{T}^a, \Sigma^a)$ structure with*

$$\mathcal{T}^a = (\text{TSym}^a, \sqsubseteq^a)$$

$$\begin{aligned}
\mathrm{TSym}^a &= \mathrm{TSym} \cup \{T_o \mid o \notin \mathrm{dom}\, \pi_{\mathcal{M},\mathcal{T}}\} \textit{ for new symbols } T_o \\
\sqsubseteq^a &= \textit{transitive closure of } \sqsubseteq_{\mathcal{T}} \cup \\
&\qquad \{(T_o, A) \mid o \notin \mathrm{dom}\, \pi_{\mathcal{M},\mathcal{T}}, A \in \mathrm{TSym}, \delta(o) \sqsubseteq A\} \\
\Sigma^a &= \Sigma^* \cup \{\mathit{instance}_C, \mathit{exactInstance}_C, \mathit{cast}_C, \mathit{default}_C \mid \\
&\qquad C \in \mathrm{TSym}^a \setminus \mathrm{TSym}^*\} \\
\delta^a(o) &= \begin{cases} A & \textit{if } \pi_{\mathcal{M},\mathcal{T}}(o) = A \\ T_o & \textit{if } o \notin \mathrm{dom}\, \pi_{\mathcal{M},\mathcal{T}} \end{cases} \\
I^a(f) &= I(f) \textit{ for symbols } f \in \Sigma \\
I^a(\mathit{instance}_{T_o}) &= I^a(\mathit{exactInstance}_{T_o}) = \{o\} \textit{ for all } o \notin \mathrm{dom}\, \pi_{\mathcal{M},\mathcal{T}} \\
I^a(\mathit{cast}_{T_o})(x) &= I^a(\mathit{default}_{T_o}) = o \textit{ for all } o \notin \mathrm{dom}\, \pi_{\mathcal{M},\mathcal{T}}
\end{aligned}$$

Lemma 3.

1. $A^{\mathcal{M}^a} = A^{\mathcal{M}}$ *for* $A \in \mathrm{TSym}$.
2. *If* $\mathcal{M} \models T_{\mathcal{T}}^{base}$ *then* $(\pi_{\mathcal{M},\mathcal{T}}(o) = A \iff o \in \mathit{exactInstance}_A^{\mathcal{M}})$

Property 1 is necessary for the construction of $\mathcal{M}^a$ to be well-defined. If domains had changed, e.g., $A^{\mathcal{M}^a} \neq A^{\mathcal{M}}$, the definition $I^a(f) = I(f)$ would not make sense.

Proof. **ad 1**

- $\subseteq$ Assume $o \in A^{\mathcal{M}^a}$, that is $\delta^a(o) = B \sqsubseteq^a A$ for some $B \in \mathrm{TSym}^a$. If $B = T_o$, then $T_o \sqsubseteq^a A$ implies by the definition of $\sqsubseteq^a$ (see part (2) of Lemma 2) that there must be a type $C \in \mathrm{TSym}$ with $\delta(o) \sqsubseteq C$ and $C \sqsubseteq A$. Hence, also $\delta(o) \sqsubseteq A$, i.e., $o \in A^{\mathcal{M}}$. If $B = \pi_{\mathcal{M},\mathcal{T}}(o)$, then $\delta(o) \sqsubseteq A$ by definition of $\pi_{\mathcal{M},\mathcal{T}}$.
- $\supseteq$ Assume $o \in A^{\mathcal{M}}$, that is $\delta(o) = B \sqsubseteq A$ for some $B \in \mathrm{TSym}^*$. If $o \in \mathrm{dom}\, \pi_{\mathcal{M},\mathcal{T}}$, then $\pi_{\mathcal{M},\mathcal{T}}(o)$ is the $\sqsubseteq$-smallest supertype in TSym covering B. Hence, $\delta^a(o) = \pi_{\mathcal{M},\mathcal{T}}(o) \sqsubseteq A$. Part (1) of Lemma 2 yields $\delta^a(o) \sqsubseteq^a A$ and so $o \in A^{\mathcal{M}^a}$. On the other hand, if $o \notin \mathrm{dom}\, \pi_{\mathcal{M},\mathcal{T}}$, then $\delta^a(o) = T_o$ and $T_o \sqsubseteq^a A$ (by definition of $\sqsubseteq^a$). Again, $\delta^a(o) \sqsubseteq^a A$ and $o \in A^{\mathcal{M}^a}$.

ad 2
We show that under the assumption of the axioms, the first condition in (6) implies the other two. Choose $o \in \mathit{exactInstance}_A^{\mathcal{M}}$ in the following.

Axiom (Ax-E$_1$) ensures that $o \in \mathit{instance}_A^{\mathcal{M}}$, and axiom (Ax-I) that $\delta(o) \sqsubseteq A$. (see later more details...)

Assume that the third condition were violated, that is, there is $B \in \mathrm{TSym}$ with $\delta(o) \sqsubseteq B$ and $A \not\sqsubseteq B$. But this allows us to use axiom (Ax-E$_2$) to obtain $o \notin \mathit{instance}_B^{\mathcal{M}}$ and (again by axiom (Ax-I)) that $\delta(o) \not\sqsubseteq B$. Contradiction. □

Lemma 4. *Let* $\Sigma, \mathcal{T}, \mathcal{T}^*, \mathcal{T}^a$ *be as in Definition 11 and* $\mathcal{M}$ *a* $(\mathcal{T}^*, \Sigma^*)$*-structure satisfying* $\mathcal{M} \models T_{\mathcal{T}}^{base}$.

1. The adapted *structure $\mathcal{M}^a$ of $\mathcal{M}$ is a standard structure and*
2. $\mathcal{M} \models \varphi \iff \mathcal{M}^a \models \varphi$ for all $(\mathcal{T}, \Sigma)$-formulas φ.

Proof.
ad 1. To argue that $\mathcal{M}^a$ is a standard structure we look separately at the three conditions of Definition 10, where A ranges of all type symbols in TSym^a.

1. $instance_A^{\mathcal{M}^a} = \{o \in M \mid \delta^a(o) \sqsubseteq^a A\}$
   We have already observed that we have for all $A \in \mathrm{TSym}$
   $$A^{\mathcal{M}^a} = \{o \in M \mid \delta^a(o) \sqsubseteq^a A\} = \{o \in M \mid \delta(o) \sqsubseteq A\} = A^{\mathcal{M}}.$$
   For $A \in \mathrm{TSym}$ we know $\mathcal{M} \models \forall x(instance_A(x) \leftrightarrow \exists y.(y \doteq x))$ from axiom (Ax-I). Thus $instance_A^{\mathcal{M}} = \{o \in M \mid \delta(o) \sqsubseteq A\}$. By definition of $\mathcal{M}^a$ we have $instance_A^{\mathcal{M}^a} = instance_A^{\mathcal{M}}$. Together with the initial observation this proves what we want.
   It remains to consider types T_o for $o \notin \mathrm{dom}\,\pi_{\mathcal{M},\mathcal{T}}$. By definition $instance_{T_o}^{\mathcal{M}^a} = \{o\}$.
   $$\begin{aligned}\{o' \in M \mid \delta^a(o') \sqsubseteq^a T_o\} &= \{o' \in M \mid \delta^a(o') = T_o\} && \text{Lemma 2(3)}\\ &= \{o' \in M \mid o' = o\} && \text{Def. of } \delta^a\end{aligned}$$
2. $exactInstance_A^{\mathcal{M}^a} = \{o \in M \mid \delta^a(o) = A\}$
   For $A \in \mathrm{TSym}$ the valuation $exactInstance_A^{\mathcal{M}^a}$ is the same as $exactInstance_A^{\mathcal{M}}$ From Lemma 3(2), we obtained that $\pi_{\mathcal{M},\mathcal{T}}(o) = A \iff o \in exactInstance_A^{\mathcal{M}^a}$.
   Let $o \in exactInstance_A^{\mathcal{M}^a}$ be given. The implication from right to left gives us that $\pi_{\mathcal{M},\mathcal{T}}(o) = A$ and also $\delta^a(o) = A$ (since $o \in \mathrm{dom}\,\pi_{\mathcal{M},\mathcal{T}}$).
   For the opposite direction, assume now that $\delta^a(o) = A$. Since $A \in \mathrm{TSym}$, it must be that $o \in \mathrm{dom}\,\pi_{\mathcal{M},\mathcal{T}}$ and $\pi_{\mathcal{M},\mathcal{T}}(o) = A$. The implication from right to left entails $o \in exactInstance_A^{\mathcal{M}^a}$.
   Finally, if $T_o \in \mathrm{TSym}^a \setminus \mathrm{TSym}$ is a type introduced in the adapted type system for $o \notin \mathrm{dom}\,\pi_{\mathcal{M},\mathcal{T}}$, then (by definition of δ^a) o is the only element of that type, and $I^a(exactInstance)$ is defined accordingly.
3. $cast_A^{\mathcal{M}^a}(o) = \begin{cases} o & \text{if } o \in A^{\mathcal{M}^a} \\ default_A^{\mathcal{M}^a} & \text{otherwise} \end{cases}$
   For a type $A \in \mathrm{TSym}$, the domain $A^{\mathcal{M}^a} = A^{\mathcal{M}}$ has *not* changed; the definition of δ^a reveals that some elements o may now have a new dynamic type T_o which is a subtype of A, but this does not modify the extension of the type. We can use axiom (Ax-C) to show that the semantics of the cast is precisely the required. We can use the fact that $A^{\mathcal{M}} = instance_A^{\mathcal{M}^a}$ established in item 1 and leave the proof as an easy exercise.
   Again for the types not already present in TSym, the definition of I^a fixes the semantics of the cast symbols correctly.

ad 2.
For the evaluation of a formula, the adaptation $\mathcal{M}^a$ is indistinguishable from the original $\mathcal{M}$. Keep in mind that the syntactical material for φ is that of $(\mathcal{T}, \Sigma)$, i.e., neither the types in $\mathrm{TSym}^* \setminus \mathrm{TSym}$, $\mathrm{TSym}^a \setminus \mathrm{TSym}$ nor the corresponding function and predicate symbols will appear in φ.
Proof by structural induction over quantifications:

- For any quantifier-free φ we have that $\mathcal{M}, \beta \models \varphi \iff \mathcal{M}^a, \beta \models \varphi$. This is a direct consequence of the fact that functions and predicates in Σ are interpreted identically in $\mathcal{M}$ and $\mathcal{M}^a$.
- Let $\forall x{:}A.\ \varphi$ be a universally quantified formula for $A \in \mathrm{TSym}$. We have:

$$\begin{aligned}
&\mathcal{M}, \beta \models \forall x.\ \varphi \\
\iff\ & \mathcal{M}, \beta_x^o \models \varphi \text{ for all } o \in A^{\mathcal{M}} \\
\iff\ & \mathcal{M}^a, \beta_x^o \models \varphi \text{ for all } o \in A^{\mathcal{M}} \quad \text{(induction hypothesis)} \\
\overset{(*)}{\iff}\ & \mathcal{M}^a, \beta_x^o \models \varphi \text{ for all } o \in A^{\mathcal{M}^a} \\
\iff\ & \mathcal{M}^a, \beta \models \forall x.\ \varphi
\end{aligned}$$

  The essential point is $(*)$ relying upon that quantifiers range over the same domains in $\mathcal{M}$ and $\mathcal{M}^a$. We have observed this already in the proof of the first point of this proposition.
  The case for the existential quantifier is completely analogous.

The next lemma claims that $T_{\mathcal{T}}^{base}$ is a complete axiomatization of standard structures.

Theorem 3. *Let Σ be a basic signature, $\mathcal{T}$ an arbitrary type hierarchy, and ϕ a $(\mathcal{T}, \Sigma)$ sentence. Then*

$$T_{\mathcal{T}}^{base} \models \phi \Leftrightarrow \textit{for all extensions } \mathcal{T}^* \sqsupseteq \mathcal{T} \textit{ and } (\mathcal{T}^*, \Sigma) \textit{ standard structures } \mathcal{M} \\ \mathcal{M} \models \phi$$

Proof. For the implication $\Rightarrow$ from left to right we assume $T_{\mathcal{T}}^{base} \models \phi$ and fix an extension hierarchy $\mathcal{T}^* \sqsupseteq \mathcal{T}$ and a $(\mathcal{T}^*, \Sigma)$ standard structure $\mathcal{M}$ with the aim of showing $\mathcal{M} \models \phi$. We will succeed if we can show $\mathcal{M} \models T_{\mathcal{T}}^{base}$, which is Theorem 2(1)).

For the reverse implication, $\Leftarrow$, we assume the right-hand condition and fix an extension $\mathcal{T}^* \sqsupseteq \mathcal{T}$ and a $(\mathcal{T}^*, \Sigma)$-structure $\mathcal{M}$ with $\mathcal{M} \models T_{\mathcal{T}}^{base}$. We want to arrive at $\mathcal{M} \models \phi$. Let $\mathcal{M}^a$ be the adapted structure for $\mathcal{M}$ as in Definition 11. By the first part of Proposition 4 we know that $\mathcal{M}^a$ is a standard structure. By assumption this implies $\mathcal{M}^a \models \phi$. By the second part of Proposition 4, we get $\mathcal{M} \models \phi$. □

4 Towards a Java Theory

In this section we provide a few hints how theory $T_{\mathcal{T}}^{base}$ can be instantiated and extended to a theory T_J suitable for reasoning about a real Java program Π. The type hierarchy $\mathcal{T}_J$ will consist of the classes occurring in Π with the subclass ordering plus possibly some abstract data types. One might wish to fix certain default elements by adding e.g., $\mathit{default}_{Object} = \mathit{null}$ and $\mathit{default}_{boolean} = \mathit{false}$ to the theory.

It will also be useful to fix certain properties of the type hierarchy, e.g., that *int* and *Object* are disjoint types. This can be done by adding $\neg\exists x.(instance_{int}(x) \wedge instance_{Object}(x))$ to T_J. As another example, one may want to formalize that *int* has no strict subtype. This is achieved by adding $\forall x.(instance_{int}(x) \rightarrow exactInstance_{int}(x))$ to T_J.

Martin Giese in [1, Chapter 2]. included from the start a distinction between abstract and non-abstract types, that he called dynamic types. In our setup we can define a type T to be abstract by the formula $\neg\exists x.(exactInstance_T(x))$, with x a variable of type *Object*.

5 Concluding Remarks

We point out that finiteness of TSym is not assumed for the completeness proof.

One might sum up the distinctive feature of our approach by noting that it allows us to convey typing information firstly in the way of syntax declarations. Thus, associating a unique static type with every term with the usual benefits. Secondly, typing information can be stated freely as axioms. Other approaches, e.g. [11] only offer the second possibility

A first-order theory for Java along the lines sketched in Section 4 but more expressive language has been implemented and used in the KeY system. This theory is, in fact, based on a logic that is richer than the one introduced in Section 2, contains e.g. conditional terms (if ϕ then t_1 else t_2) $\in \mathrm{Trm}_A$ for $\phi \in \mathrm{Fml}$ and $t_i \in \mathrm{Trm}_{A_i}$ such that $A_2 \sqsubseteq A_1 = A$ or $A_1 \sqsubseteq A_2 = A$.

References

1. Beckert, B., Hähnle, R., Schmitt, P.H. (eds.): Verification of Object-Oriented Software. LNCS (LNAI), vol. 4334. Springer, Heidelberg (2007)
2. Bobot, F., Conchon, S., Contejean, E., Lescuyer, S.: Implementing polymorphism in smt solvers. In: Proceedings of the Joint Workshops of the 6th International Workshop on Satisfiability Modulo Theories and 1st International Workshop on Bit-Precise Reasoning, SMT 2008/BPR 2008, pp. 1–5. ACM, New York (2008)
3. Bobot, F., Paskevich, A.: Expressing Polymorphic Types in a Many-Sorted Language. In: Tinelli and Sofronie-Stokkermans [9], pp. 87–102
4. Esparza, J., Majumdar, R. (eds.): TACAS 2010. LNCS, vol. 6015. Springer, Heidelberg (2010)
5. Gallier, J.H.: Logic for Computer Science: Foundations of Automatic Theorem Proving. Wiley (1987)
6. Giese, M.A.: A calculus for type predicates and type coercion. In: Beckert, B. (ed.) TABLEAUX 2005. LNCS (LNAI), vol. 3702, pp. 123–137. Springer, Heidelberg (2005)
7. Leino, K.R.M., Rümmer, P.: A polymorphic intermediate verification language: Design and logical encoding. In: Esparza and Majumdar [4], pp. 312–327
8. Schmidt, A.: Über deduktive Theorien mit mehreren Sorten von Grunddingen. Math. Annalen 115, 485–506 (1938)

9. Tinelli, C., Sofronie-Stokkermans, V. (eds.): FroCoS 2011. LNCS, vol. 6989. Springer, Heidelberg (2011)
10. Walther, C.: A Many-Sorted Calculus Based on Resolution and Paramodulation. Pitman / Morgan Kaufmann (1987)
11. Weidenbach, C.: First-order tableaux with sorts. Logic Journal of the IGPL 3(6), 887–906 (1995)

Model-Based Problem Solving for University Timetable Validation and Improvement

David Schneider(✉), Michael Leuschel, and Tobias Witt

Institut für Informatik, Heinrich Heine University Düsseldorf, Germany
{david.schneider,tobias.witt}@hhu.de, leuschel@cs.uni-duesseldorf.de

Abstract. Constraint satisfaction problems can be expressed very elegantly in state-based formal methods such as B. However, can such specifications be directly used for solving real-life problems? We will try and answer this question in the present paper with regard to the university timetabling problem. We report on an ongoing project to build a formal model-based curriculum timetable validation tool where we use a formal specification as the basis to validate timetables from a student's perspective and to support incremental modification of timetables. In this article we focus on expressing the problem domain, the formalization in B and our approach to execute the formal model in a production system using ProB.

Keywords: B-method · Constraint programming · Timetabling · Scheduling

1 Introduction

Motivation State-based formal methods enable elegant and succinct encodings of constraint satisfaction problems [17], but solving constraints in such high-level formalisms is a major challenge. In [17] we have shown that ProB can be used to effectively solve some interesting constraint programming benchmarks expressed in the B language [2] and have successfully solved a challenge set out by Shapiro [26]. The company ClearSy has successfully used ProB in a similar way to reverse engineer an application binary.[1]

The main question pursued in this paper is whether one can already use this model-based approach to constraint solving in a production system, or whether further research and development is required. In other words, is it possible to completely express a non-trivial constraint satisfaction problem in B (or some other state-based formal method), and to use this formal model in a real production system without manual code-generation? The benefits would be considerable: expressing the constraints (correctly) would be considerably less difficult, modifying the constraints could be done declaratively within the formal model, with all the aid provided by formal methods and their tools. However, to be successful, the constraint solving capabilities need to scale to the real-life problem, they

[1] See `http://www.data-validation.fr/data-validation-reverse-engineering/`.

N. Bjørner and F. de Boer (Eds.): FM 2015, LNCS 9109, pp. 487–495, 2015.
DOI: 10.1007/978-3-319-19249-9_30

need to be robust and predictable, and one needs to be able to link the model with the graphical user interface in particular and the computing architecture in general.

The — maybe surprising — answer to this important question turns out to be positive. In this paper, we show how we have successfully expressed a challenging timetabling problem at our university in B, and have developed a system which executes this formal model in real-time using the ProB constraint solver and provides a web-based graphical interface using a new API. The tools can be used to detect minimal conflict sets efficiently, providing the user with valuable feedback. Data is automatically imported from external sources and high-level constraints can be added or modified simply by editing the formal model.

University Timetabling Problem. In cooperation with the faculty of arts and humanities and the faculty of business administration and economics at the Heinrich Heine University in Düsseldorf we are working on a timetabling application to validate the feasibility of the offered curricula. The central goal of the project is to validate existing and future timetables of all programs to ensure that it is possible for students to attend all required classes to finish their studies in the standard time defined by their chosen curriculum. Secondary goals are to provide assistance to resolve conflicts in the timetables by computing conflict sets and feasible alternative timeslots. The data provided by the faculties consists of a) 249 scheduled events organized in 128 units in 67 different programs with 1751 different links between units and programs, as well as b) 338 events in 222 units and 6 programs with 991 links between units and programs, respectively. Validating this data requires to detect scheduling conflicts, which would require a student, at any point in their studies, to attend two sessions at the same time. The complexity arises from the number of available combinations that need to be validated and the number of possible choices for students: some units are available in more than one semester and students can choose when to attend them. Units might be divided in sections or groups, offered on different days and times, where students have to choose one group and attend all sessions that are part of that group. Programs are often combinations of subjects and thus many programs share teaching units. This needs to be considered when searching for alternative timeslots and modifying timetables.

Figure 1 shows a screenshot of the user interface of our application, which is divided into three components. We have a browser based user interface for interacting with the timetables, a server component built using Groovy that embeds the models using the ProB Java API [4] and exposes them to the frontend using a REST based HTTP API, and finally the model layer, which is built using classical B and evaluated using the ProB. An online version of the tool and further information can be accessed at: http://stups.hhu.de/w/Pub:FM2015.

2 Background

Timetabling is a family of scheduling or resource allocation problems where the goal is to assign events to a limited number of timeslots. Each event might be associated to arbitrary constraints regarding relationships among events, additional resources allocations (e.g. rooms, materials), etc. Corne et al. [7] categorize simple timetabling constraints, as unary, binary, capacity, event spread and agent constraints. In the context of educational institutions the problem is about assigning classes, e.g., lectures and seminars, to timeslots. The fundamental binary constraint is that no person should have to attend two events relevant for them at the same time; other constraints might regard room assignment, teacher workload, etc. The timetable *construction* problem is an NP-complete

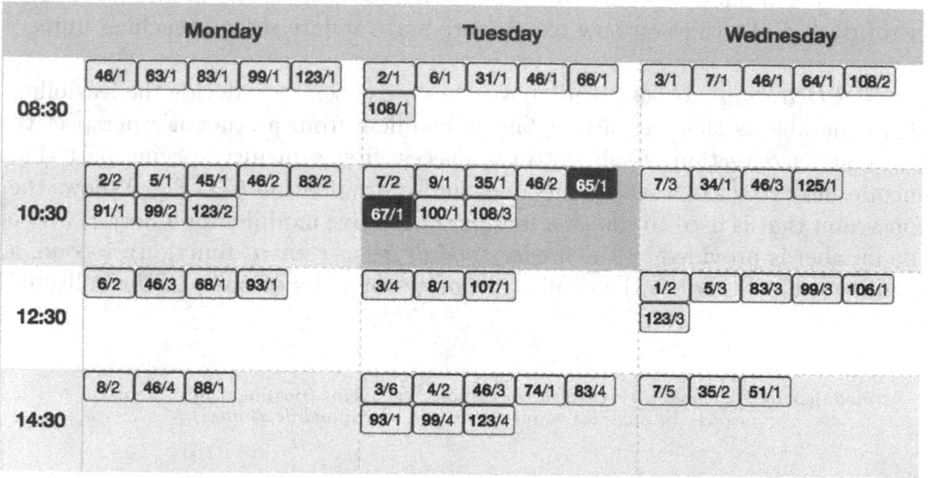

Fig. 1. UI representation of a semester week highlighting a detected scheduling conflict. Each numbered box represents an event, the numbers represent the teaching units and groups the events are associated to. The two highlighted units (65 and 67) are in conflict because they are assigned to the same curriculum while their sessions share a timeslot on Tuesday at 10:30.

problem [6] where the goal is to find a timetable for a set of events that satisfies a set of given constraints (completely or as many as possible). Timetable *validation* can be understood as a similar problem, where the goal is to decide if a given timetable is feasible with regard to different constraints. In this sense, from a student's perspective a timetable in a curriculum is feasible if he or she can attend all units as prescribed by the curriculum in such a way that no constraints are violated and that the degree is finished within the legal timeframe.

In order to validate a timetable for a specific semester or for a complete curriculum it is necessary to verify if it is possible to choose the number of elective classes as required by the curriculum, the semester in which to attend each chosen elective and all mandatory classes and for all sectioned classes the group and thus sessions to attend.

3 Modelling Curricula and Timetables in B

Some of the central and non-trivial features of our application, that have been modelled in B are described below. The modelling of the curricula and timetables is split into several parts. B machines that hold the data (2247 lines for the faculty of humanities and 1724 lines for the faculty of economics) for each faculty are generated from CSV or Excel documents. There are faculty specific machines that model the curricula and validation rules that are distinct for each faculty (377 lines for the faculty of humanities and 734 lines for the faculty economics), e.g. describing mandatory parts and how to select units for the different forms of validation. Common aspects and rules are shared between the models (301 lines in total), e.g. the rules on how to compare and validate sets of teaching units.

Conflict Detection. As described above, the core criterion to decide the feasibility of a timetable is the presence of binary conflicts from a student's perspective. The conflict detection is split into two pieces, first a faculty specific part that encodes how to select a set of units relevant for a validation (e.g. Fig. 2 shows the constraint that is used to choose a number of elective modules for a major, where the number is provided by the $major\_module\_requirement$ function); second, a predicate that describes the conflict property for pairs of units in the collected set.

$$module\_choice \subseteq modules \wedge card(module\_choice) = major\_module\_requirement(cc) \wedge$$
$$units\_in\_modules = union(module\_units[module\_choice])$$

Fig. 2. Simplified selection of elective modules in a given curriculum (cc)

A simplified version of the conflict detection is shown in Fig. 3. The conflict-property of a set of units can be expressed in B as a (nested) universally quantified predicate over the set of pairs of these units. Conflicts are based on the sessions of a unit, which have a slot field that represents the assigned day and time. Two sessions are in conflict if the sessions are scheduled on an interfering rhythm (at least one weekly or both on the same biweekly rhythm) and both sessions are assigned to the same slot. Related sessions form a group; a group is not in conflict with another group if all sessions are pairwise not in conflict. A teaching unit is not in conflict with a second one if they are either assigned to different semesters or if it is possible to choose a group in each such that the groups are not in conflict. In case of sectioning there can be more than one group, such that there are no conflicts among the sessions in those groups. A set of units is conflict free, if it is possible to globally assign a semester and a group to each unit such that all units are pairwise not in conflict. The choice of semester and group is expressed in B using total functions as shown in Fig. 4, that map from a unit to the chosen semester or group respectively. These functions are described only by constraining the range of the functions according to

$$
\begin{array}{ll}
\forall(u1,u2).((u1,u2) \in conflict\_set \Rightarrow (semesterChoice(u1) = semesterChoice(u2) \Rightarrow & \\
\quad \exists(group1, group2).(& \texttt{/* LET */} \\
\quad\quad group1 = unit\_group(u1, groupChoice(u1)) \wedge & \\
\quad\quad group2 = unit\_group(u2, groupChoice(u2)) \wedge & \\
\quad\quad \forall(s1,s2).(s1 \in group1'sessions \wedge s2 \in group2'sessions \Rightarrow & \\
\quad\quad\quad (s1'rhythm = s2'rhythm & \texttt{/* both in the same rhythm */} \\
\quad\quad\quad \vee\ s1'rhythm = weekly & \texttt{/* first weekly */} \\
\quad\quad\quad \vee\ s2'rhythm = weekly) & \texttt{/* second weekly */} \\
\quad\quad\quad\quad \Rightarrow s1'slot \neq s2'slot)))) &
\end{array}
$$

Fig. 3. Simplified conflict detection logic for a set of pairs of teaching units (*conflict_set*)

the curriculum data and chosen by the ProB constraint solver. When validating the units selected, the instantiated functions are used to retrieve the chosen semester and group for a unit.

The formula in Fig. 3 is only true if functions `semesterChoice` and `groupChoice` can be found that satisfy their constraints and lead to no binary conflicts among sessions. If the validation fails ProB will try a different instantiation of the functions that satisfies the provided constraints until the validation succeeds or there are no further possible choices.

$$
\begin{array}{c}
groupChoice \in Units \rightarrow min\_group..max\_group \wedge \\
\forall(u).(u \in Units \Rightarrow groupChoice(u) \in unit\_min\_group(u)..unit\_max\_group(u))
\end{array}
$$

Fig. 4. Defining the choice of group constraint using a total function (*groupChoice*)

Computing Conflict Sources. If no conflicts are detected, the process described above will generate an assignment to the `semesterChoice` and `groupChoice` functions which together represent one of possibly many feasible timetables for the curriculum being validated. In case no assignment can be found it is necessary to find and resolve any scheduling conflicts among the units of the curriculum before generating a viable timetable.

To identify which units cause a conflict we compute a *minimal unsatisfiable core* (UC) [27] of the units used in the validation. This is expressed in B as a recursive function that minimizes the set of units by stepwise removing units, calling the conflict detection logic and pruning units that have no effect on the outcome of the validation. The result is one of potentially many sets of teaching units that are in conflict, i.e. units that can not be attended as recommended by the curriculum. Having computed an UC of units that lead to a conflict, we additionally compute the set of sessions in those units that are actually in conflict, as shown in Fig. 1. Due to sectioning and multi-session groups, the sessions actually in conflict are often only a small subset of all the sessions associated to the units in conflict. The UC of the sessions is computed similarly to the UC of units, by stepwise removing sessions from the units in a computed

UC that do not affect the unsatisfiability of the validation. If a unit is known to have only one session it is never removed, as it must be part of the core.

Computing Alternatives. In case there are conflicts in a timetable, or just to satisfy changed requirements it is often necessary to move a single session to a different timeslot. To avoid creating new conflicts by moving a session to an arbitrary slot we provide a method to compute viable alternatives for a given session, which do not introduce new conflicts.

4 Related Work

Time-Tabling There is plenty of research on automatic timetabling, more than can be covered here. This area has seen interest from different research communities, as it presents a challenging problem with real world applications for a variety of approaches. There is research based on metaheuristics and genetic algorithms, that aim to improve timetables through mutation [7], [18]. There is research on this problem using SAT techniques, such as [1], Answer Set Programming [3], Integer Linear Programming [25] and based on constraints [10], [20], [21], [24]. There has been a timetabling competition ITC 2002, 2007 [11] and 2011 [23], which provides a set of benchmarks to drive and compare research [16].

Could Other Approaches Have Been Used ? Our formal B model could probably just as well have been expressed in another state-based formal method; we return to this issue in the conclusion. The constraint solving capabilities are crucial for our application. Hence tools like the model checker TLC [29] or the animators coreASM [13] or AnimB [19] cannot be used for (variations of) our present model.

ProB relies on constraint logic programming [15]. Other successful approaches to constraint solving in the context of formal methods are SAT and SMT solving [12]. Indeed, in [22] we have presented an alternate constraint solving backend for ProB, which uses the Kodkod library [28], translating first-order relational logic into SAT problems. Unfortunately, we were unable to use this backend here, due to fundamental performance issues for relations over large domains.[2]

Another promising technology is SMT, where one can circumvent the above SAT issue of dealing with large domains by using theories. A translation of Event-B formulas into SMTlib format is available [9], and has proven very successful for proof. For constraint solving (aka model finding) the issue is somewhat different [22]. For example, even the simple n-queens problem for n=4 cannot be solved by current SMT solvers such as Z3 [8] or CVC4 on the translation of [9].[3]

In conclusion, while ProB's constraint solving based on constraint logic programming has some drawbacks over SAT or SMT based approaches (no learning

---

[2] In our experiments, Kodkod was either orders of magnitude slower at various tasks (such as determining programs with units in common), or was unable to achieve the SAT translation (`CapacityExceededException`).

[3] A fundamental issue seems to be that the current SMTlib translation sometimes encodes finite B relations and B sets as infinite functions.

for example), its ability to deal well with large relations, integer values and symbolically with infinite or recursive function make it well suited for the timetabling application described in this paper.

5 Future Work and Conclusion

In this article we have presented the application of formal methods to a novel domain. We have succesfully modelled university curricula and timetables validation in B in a way that captures the domain constraints and can be executed using ProB. Our models scale well within the scope of real-world data we have used in our project, e.g., we are able to validate the timetables for *all* semesters of *all* the programs offered by the faculty of arts and humanities in less than 5 seconds and to compute a minimal unsat core of sessions for each of the 12 infeasible programs in the first semester in 4 seconds. The use of a high level language to model this problem allowed us to decouple the model from the solving strategy and thus permitted us to easily evolve the models during the process of capturing all the domain information.

Modelling this problem and creating the application on top of it has served as a driver for ProB and its related tools. It has been useful to uncover bugs and performance problems and the ongoing project will contribute to evolve ProB and possibly also the B language.

We are aware that a high-level model of a constraint problem cannot compete with either low-level solutions or dedicated solvers specialised for this class of scheduling problems. We want to improve the capabilities of ProB in this regard and we intend to perform an extensive evaluation and compare our approach to other solutions written directly in more tractable formal methods, such as Alloy [14], SAT and SMT encodings, as well as a lower-level Prolog encoding using clp(FD) [5]. We will evaluate the performance aspects, but also compare the complexity of the models, the complexity of validating and modifying the models, and the ease of embedding the model in a production system. Indeed, we believe that developing and adapting a high-level model is considerably easier, and that formal method tooling can help in validating the model. Our goal is to move formal models from design documents to artefacts embedded in running systems. In this paper we have already shown that such formal model-based problem solving is starting to become practically feasible.

References

1. Asín Achá, R., Nieuwenhuis, R.: Curriculum-based course timetabling with SAT and MaxSAT. Annals of Operations Research 218(1), 71–91 (2012)
2. Abrial, J.-R.: The B-Book. Assigning Programs to Meanings. Cambridge University Press (November 2005)
3. Banbara, M., Soh, T., Tamura, N., Inoue, K., Schaub, T.: Answer Set Programming as a Modeling Language for Course Timetabling. Theory and Practice of Logic Programming 13(4-5), 783–798 (2013)

4. Bendisposto, J., Clark, J., Dobrikov, I., Krner, P., Krings, S., Ladenberger, L., Leuschel, M., Plagge, D.: ProB 2.0 Tutorial. In: Proceedings of the 4th Rodin User and Developer Workshop. TUCS Lecture Notes. TUCS (2013)
5. Carlsson, M., Ottosson, G.: An Open-Ended Finite Domain Constraint Solver. In: Hartel, P.H., Kuchen, H. (eds.) PLILP 1997. LNCS, vol. 1292, pp. 191–206. Springer, Heidelberg (1997)
6. Cooper, T.B., Kingston, J.H.: The complexity of timetable construction problems. In: Burke, E.K., Ross, P. (eds.) PATAT 1995. LNCS, vol. 1153, pp. 281–295. Springer, Heidelberg (1996)
7. Corne, D., Ross, P., Fang, H.: Evolving Timetables. Practical Handbook of Genetic Algorithms: Applications 1, 219–276 (1995)
8. de Moura, L., Bjørner, N.S.: Z3: An Efficient SMT Solver. In: Ramakrishnan, C.R., Rehof, J. (eds.) TACAS 2008. LNCS, vol. 4963, pp. 337–340. Springer, Heidelberg (2008)
9. Déharbe, D., Fontaine, P., Guyot, Y., Voisin, L.: SMT solvers for Rodin. In: Derrick, J., Fitzgerald, J., Gnesi, S., Khurshid, S., Leuschel, M., Reeves, S., Riccobene, E. (eds.) ABZ 2012. LNCS, vol. 7316, pp. 194–207. Springer, Heidelberg (2012)
10. Deris, S., Omatu, S., Ohta, H.: Timetable planning using the constraint-based reasoning. Computers & Operations Research 27(9), 819–840 (2000)
11. Di Gaspero, L., McCollum, B., Schaerf, A.: The Second International Timetabling Competition (ITC-2007): Curriculum-based Course Timetabling (Track 3). In: Proceedings of the 14th RCRA Workshop on Experimental Evaluation of Algorithms for Solving Problems with Combinatorial Explosion, Rome (2007)
12. Dutertre, B., de Moura, L.: A fast linear-arithmetic solver for DPLL(T). In: Ball, T., Jones, R.B. (eds.) CAV 2006. LNCS, vol. 4144, pp. 81–94. Springer, Heidelberg (2006)
13. Farahbod, R., Gervasi, V., Glässer, U.: CoreASM: An extensible ASM execution engine. Fundam. Inform. 77(1-2), 71–103 (2007)
14. Jackson, D.: Alloy: A lightweight object modelling notation. ACM Transactions on Software Engineering and Methodology 11, 256–290 (2002)
15. Jaffar, J., Maher, M.J.: Constraint logic programming: A survey. The Journal of Logic Programming 19(20), 503–581 (1994)
16. Lach, G., Lübbecke, M.E.: Curriculum based course timetabling: new solutions to Udine benchmark instances. Annals of Operations Research 194(1), 255–272 (2010)
17. Leuschel, M., Schneider, D.: Towards B as a High-Level Constraint Modelling Language. In: Ait Ameur, Y., Schewe, K.-D. (eds.) ABZ 2014. LNCS, vol. 8477, pp. 101–116. Springer, Heidelberg (2014)
18. Lewis, R.: A survey of metaheuristic-based techniques for University Timetabling problems. OR Spectrum 30(1), 167–190 (2008)
19. Métayer, C.: AnimB 0.1.1 (2010), http://wiki.event-b.org/index.php/AnimB
20. Müller, T., Rudová, H.: Real-life Curriculum-based Timetabling. PATAT (June 2012)
21. Müller, T., Rudová, H.: Real-life curriculum-based timetabling with elective courses and course sections. Annals of Operations Research, 1–18 (June 2014)
22. Plagge, D., Leuschel, M.: Validating B, Z and TLA+ using ProB and kodkod. In: Giannakopoulou, D., Méry, D. (eds.) FM 2012. LNCS, vol. 7436, pp. 372–386. Springer, Heidelberg (2012)
23. Post, G., Di Gaspero, L., Kingston, J.H., McCollum, B.: The Third International Timetabling Competition. Annals of Operations Research (February 2013)

24. Rudová, H., Murray, K.: University Course Timetabling with Soft Constraints. In: Burke, E.K., De Causmaecker, P. (eds.) PATAT 2002. LNCS, vol. 2740, pp. 310–328. Springer, Heidelberg (2003)
25. Schimmelpfeng, K., Helber, S.: Application of a real-world university-course timetabling model solved by integer programming. OR Spectrum 29(4), 783–803 (2006)
26. Shapiro, S.C.: The Jobs Puzzle: A Challenge for Logical Expressibility and Automated Reasoning. In: AAAI Spring Symposium: Logical Formalizations of Commonsense Reasoning (2011)
27. Torlak, E., Chang, F.S., Jackson, D.: Finding minimal unsatisfiable cores of declarative specifications. In: Cuellar, J., Sere, K. (eds.) FM 2008. LNCS, vol. 5014, pp. 326–341. Springer, Heidelberg (2008)
28. Torlak, E., Jackson, D.: Kodkod: A relational model finder. In: Grumberg, O., Huth, M. (eds.) TACAS 2007. LNCS, vol. 4424, pp. 632–647. Springer, Heidelberg (2007)
29. Yu, Y., Manolios, P., Lamport, L.: Model checking TLA^{+} specifications. In: Pierre, L., Kropf, T. (eds.) Proceedings CHARME'99, pp. 54–66. Springer, Heidelberg (1999)

Certified Reasoning with Infinity

Asankhaya Sharma[1(✉)], Shengyi Wang[1], Andreea Costea[1], Aquinas Hobor[2,1], and Wei-Ngan Chin[1]

School of Computing, Yale-NUS College, National University of Singapore, Singapore, Singapore
{asankhs, shengyi, andreeac, hobor, chinwn}@comp.nus.edu.sg

Abstract. We demonstrate how infinities improve the expressivity, power, readability, conciseness, and compositionality of a program logic. We prove that adding infinities to Presburger arithmetic enables these improvements without sacrificing decidability. We develop Omega++, a Coq-certified decision procedure for Presburger arithmetic with infinity and benchmark its performance. Both the program and proof of Omega++ are parameterized over user-selected semantics for the indeterminate terms (such as $0 * \infty$).

1 Introduction

Formal software analysis and verification frameworks benefit from expressive, compositional, decidable, and readable specification mechanisms. Of course, these goals often conflict with each other: for example, it is easy to add expressivity if one is willing to give up decidability! Happily, we have found a free lunch: by adding the notion of "infinity" to the specification language we can usefully add to the expressivity, readability, and compositionality of our specifications while maintaining their decidability.

Specifically, we start from the well-established domains of separation logic [25] and Presburger arithmetic [24] and add two abstract/fictitious/ghost symbols ∞ and $-\infty$, for which we support a precise, well-defined semantics. Although a seeming-minor addition, these symbols add significantly to the expressivity and power of our logic.

In section 2.3, we use infinities to increase the compositionality of our logic by showing that "lists" and "bounded lists" are equivalent when the bound is ∞. Moreover, in section 2.4, we use ∞ to mix notions of partial and total correctness within a logic.

Infinities also add to our specification framework's readability and conciseness. For example, we will see in section 2.2 that ∞ allows us to drop disjuncts in the specification for code that manipulates a sorted linked list.

Finally, infinities enable some interesting applications. In section 2.5, we apply the notion of quantifier elimination in Presburger arithmetic with infinities to infer pure (non-heap) properties of programs.

All of the previous gains are worthy in their own right, but our major technical advance is the development of Omega++, a sound and complete decision procedure for Presburger arithmetic with infinities (including arbitrary quantifier use). In other words, we do not sacrifice any of the computational advantage normally gained by restricting ourselves to Presburger arithmetic, despite the addition of infinities. We call our tool "Omega++" both to acknowledge the importance of the underlying Presburger solver Omega [9] and because we believe we have modestly incremented its utility.

N. Bjørner and F. de Boer (Eds.): FM 2015, LNCS 9109, pp. 496–513, 2015.
DOI: 10.1007/978-3-319-19249-9_31

Omega++ is written in Gallina, the specification language of Coq [1], allowing us to formally certify it (modulo the correctness of Omega itself, which we utilize as our backend). We extract our performance-tuned Gallina into OCaml and package it as a library, which we have benchmarked using the HIP/SLEEK verification toolset [5].

One notable technical feature of Omega++ is that it can handle several semantic variants of Presburger arithmetic with infinity. For example, Presburger arithmetic usually admits multiplication by a constant as a notational convenience, *e.g.* $3 \cdot x \stackrel{\text{def}}{=} x + x + x$. This obvious-seeming convenience becomes a little less obvious when one adds infinities: what is $0 \cdot \infty$? Mathematical sophisticates can—*and do*—disagree: some prefer 0 as a convention in certain contexts (including, reasonably, ours) [19], while others prefer the result to be undefined due to the indeterminate status of the corresponding limit forms [10]. When possible, Omega++ takes an agnostic approach to such disagreements by allowing the user to specify the semantics of some subtle cases. Omega++ is thus a certified compiler from a *set* of related source languages (Presburger arithmetics with infinities) to a fixed, well-understood target (vanilla Presburger).

Omega++ is available for download and experimentation here:

http://loris-7.ddns.comp.nus.edu.sg/~project/SLPAInf/

2 Motivation

In this section, we highlight the benefits of augmenting a specification logic with infinities. For consistency we focus on separation logic [6,25] but other specification mechanisms which rely on Presburger arithmetic can enjoy similar benefits.

2.1 Orientation

Our flavor of separation logic has its grounds in the HIP/SLEEK system [5], thus offering the convenience to test and benchmark with a state-of-the-art verification toolchain. Methods are specified with a pair of pre- and postcondition (Φ_{pr}, Φ_{po}), with the keyword `res` consistently used in the Φ_{po} to refer to the return value. We have enhanced the logic to allow the symbols ∞ and $-\infty$ where it would normally require integers; we also allow quantification over infinities.

From a systems perspective, our setup is sketched in figure 1. First, entailment between separation logic formulae with infinities in HIP/SLEEK is reduced (*à la* Chin *et al.* [5]) to entailment between numeric formulae in Presburger arithmetic with infinities (PAInf). Next, we translate PAInf to vanilla Presburger arithmetic (PA). We emphasize on this phase as being our main contribution and detail it in section 4.

Finally, we discharge PA proof obligations with Omega. There are other combinations of separation logic with extensions of PA (such as sets/multisets) that can be used to enhance the specification. We discuss them in section 7 as related work.

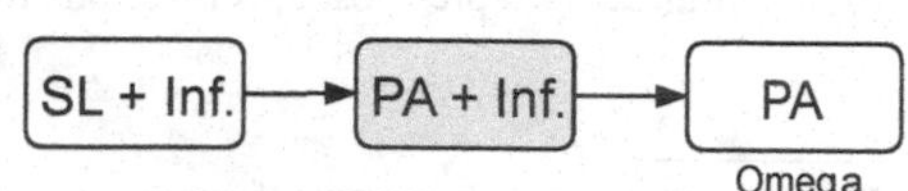

Fig. 1. Our setup: SL + Inf to PA

2.2 Infinities enable Concise Specifications

Let's start to see what infinities can buy us! Consider a simple program which inserts a new node into a sorted linked list, whose nodes are defined as follows:

$$\texttt{data node } \{\texttt{int val; node next;}\}$$

The data field `val` stores numerical information and the pointer field `next` points to the subsequent node in the structure. Consider the next two alternative inductive predicates which characterize sortedness using only a single numeric parameter[1] describing the list's minimum value:

Scenario 1 - no infinity enhancement:

$$\begin{aligned}&\texttt{sorted\_ll}\langle\texttt{root},\texttt{min}\rangle \equiv \texttt{root}{\mapsto}\texttt{node}\langle\texttt{min},\texttt{null}\rangle\\ &\quad\vee\ \exists\,\texttt{q},\ \texttt{mtail}\cdot(\texttt{root}{\mapsto}\texttt{node}\langle\texttt{min},\texttt{q}\rangle * \texttt{sorted\_ll}\langle\texttt{q},\texttt{mtail}\rangle \wedge \texttt{min}{\leq}\texttt{mtail})\end{aligned}$$

Scenario 2 - with infinity enhancement:

$$\begin{aligned}&\texttt{sorted\_ll}\langle\texttt{root},\texttt{min}\rangle \equiv (\texttt{root}{=}\texttt{null} \wedge \texttt{min}{=}\infty)\\ &\quad\vee\ \exists\,\texttt{q},\ \texttt{mtail}\cdot(\texttt{root}{\mapsto}\texttt{node}\langle\texttt{min},\texttt{q}\rangle * \texttt{sorted\_ll}\langle\texttt{q},\texttt{mtail}\rangle \wedge \texttt{min}{\leq}\texttt{mtail})\end{aligned}$$

The base case of *Scenario 1* denotes a singleton, while its inductive case describes a linked list of length at least two. Though useable, this definition has a frustrating shortcoming: it cannot handle empty linked lists, since such lists do not have a finite minimum value. In contrast, *Scenario 2* handles the empty list gracefully since the minimum of an empty list can be defined to be just ∞! We could similarly use $-\infty$ to build a predicate which captures the maximum property of a linked list.

The code for `insert` is in figure 2. Parameter `x` points to a sorted linked list, while `y` is the data node we wish to insert (preserving sortedness). Notice that the pre/post specifications in Scenario 1 require disjunctions to separate the cases when `x` is empty and nonempty, whereas Scenario 2 handles both cases uniformly. Infinities thus enable more *concise* and *readable* (easy to maintain) specifications.

```
node insert(node x, node y){
  if (x == null) return y;
  else {
    if (y.val <= x.val){
      y.next = x;
      return y;
    } else {
      x.next = insert(x.next, y);
      return x;
}}}
```

Scenario 1 :

Φ_{pr} : $\texttt{y}{\mapsto}\texttt{node}\langle\texttt{v},\texttt{null}\rangle \wedge \texttt{x}{=}\texttt{null} \vee \texttt{sorted\_ll}\langle\texttt{x},\texttt{a}\rangle * \texttt{y}{\mapsto}\texttt{node}\langle\texttt{v},\texttt{null}\rangle$

Φ_{po} : $\texttt{sorted\_ll}\langle\texttt{res},\texttt{b}\rangle \wedge \texttt{x}{=}\texttt{null} \wedge \texttt{b}{=}\texttt{v} \vee \texttt{sorted\_ll}\langle\texttt{res},\texttt{b}\rangle \wedge \texttt{b}{=}\texttt{min}(\texttt{a},\texttt{v})$

Scenario 2 :

Φ_{pr} : $\texttt{sorted\_ll}\langle\texttt{x},\texttt{a}\rangle * \texttt{y}{\mapsto}\texttt{node}\langle\texttt{v},\texttt{null}\rangle$

Φ_{po} : $\texttt{sorted\_ll}\langle\texttt{res},\texttt{b}\rangle \wedge \texttt{b}{=}\texttt{min}(\texttt{a},\texttt{v})$

Fig. 2. Two pre-/post-specifications for insertion into a sorted linked list .

[1] Note that there are other ways of specifying sortedness, such as through the use of multi-set, that may also capture stronger properties, such as content preservation. However, they may require more complex provers in their reasoning.

2.3 Infinities Increase Compositionality

Consider this definition for an n-node linked list whose values are bounded by b:

$$\begin{aligned}\mathtt{llB}\langle \mathtt{root}, \mathtt{n}, \mathtt{b}\rangle \equiv\ & (\mathtt{root}{=}\mathtt{null} \wedge \mathtt{n} = 0)\\ & \vee(\exists\, \mathtt{q}, \mathtt{v}\cdot \mathtt{root}{\mapsto}\mathtt{node}\langle \mathtt{v}, \mathtt{q}\rangle * \mathtt{llB}\langle \mathtt{q}, \mathtt{n}-1, \mathtt{b}\rangle \wedge \mathtt{v} \le \mathtt{b})\end{aligned}$$

Suppose we have a function f which uses this definition in its precondition:

$$\Phi_{pr}: \mathtt{llB}\langle \mathtt{x}, \mathtt{n}, \mathtt{m}\rangle * \ldots$$

where x points to a linked list bounded by m. Next, suppose we call f from a program point where the only available information involves the shape and length of a linked list x (that is, we have no information about its bound), *e.g.* we satisfy the predicate $\mathtt{ll}\langle \mathtt{x}, \mathtt{n}\rangle$ as defined below:

$$\mathtt{ll}\langle \mathtt{root}, \mathtt{n}\rangle \equiv (\mathtt{root}{=}\mathtt{null} \wedge \mathtt{n}{=}0) \vee \exists\, \mathtt{q}\cdot (\mathtt{root}{\mapsto}\mathtt{node}\langle \_, \mathtt{q}\rangle * \mathtt{ll}\langle \mathtt{q}, \mathtt{n}-1\rangle)$$

With infinities this is easy: just instantiate m to ∞ since

$$\mathtt{ll}\langle \mathtt{x}, \mathtt{n}\rangle \leftrightarrow \mathtt{llB}\langle \mathtt{x}, \mathtt{n}, \infty\rangle$$

Without infinities, however, this is not so easy since we must first determine an appropriate bound for x's values. Thus, infinities increase the *compositionality* of our logic, which in turn improves the reusability and conciseness of our specifications.

2.4 Infinities Support Termination and Non-Termination Reasoning

Le *et al.* developed a technique to reason about termination and non-termination with a resource constraint $\mathtt{RC}\langle \mathtt{min}, \mathtt{max}\rangle$ that tracks the minimum and maximum permitted execution steps [14]. Using Presburger arithmetic with infinity, terminating programs are modeled by $\mathtt{RC}\langle \_, \mathtt{max}\rangle \wedge \mathtt{max}{<}\infty$, while non-terminating programs are captured by $\mathtt{RC}\langle \infty, \infty\rangle$. Le *et al.* use Omega++ to discharge the associated proof obligations.

```
int length(node x){
  if (x == null)
    return 0;
  else
    return (1 + length(x.next));
}
```

Termination Spec :

$\Phi_{pr}: \mathtt{ls}\langle \mathtt{x}, \mathtt{null}, \mathtt{n}\rangle * \mathtt{RC}\langle \_, \mathtt{M}\rangle \wedge \mathtt{n}{<}\mathtt{M} \wedge \mathtt{M}{<}\infty$

$\Phi_{po}: \mathtt{ls}\langle \mathtt{x}, \mathtt{null}, \mathtt{n}\rangle * \mathtt{RC}\langle \_, \mathtt{M}-(\mathtt{n}+1)\rangle \wedge \mathtt{res}{=}\mathtt{n}$

Non-Termination Spec :

$\Phi_{pr}: \mathtt{cll}\langle \mathtt{x}, \mathtt{n}\rangle * \mathtt{RC}\langle \infty, \infty\rangle$

$\Phi_{po}: \mathtt{false}$

Fig. 3. Example 4: `length` terminates on proper lists and diverges on cyclic lists

Figure 3 demonstrates these resource constraints on a `length` function for linked lists. We show two specifications: the first shows that `length` terminates on finite lists `ls`, and the second shows that `length` diverges on circular lists `cll`, where `ls` and `cll` are defined as below:

$$\begin{aligned}\mathtt{ls}\langle \mathtt{root}, \mathtt{p}, \mathtt{n}\rangle &\equiv (\mathtt{root}{=}\mathtt{p} \wedge \mathtt{n}{=}0)\\ &\quad \vee \exists\, \mathtt{q}\cdot (\mathtt{root}{\mapsto}\mathtt{node}\langle \_, \mathtt{q}\rangle * \mathtt{ls}\langle \mathtt{q}, \mathtt{p}, \mathtt{n}-1\rangle \wedge \mathtt{root}{\neq}\mathtt{p})\\ \mathtt{cll}\langle \mathtt{root}, \mathtt{n}\rangle &\equiv \exists\, \mathtt{q}\cdot (\mathtt{root}{\mapsto}\mathtt{node}\langle \_, \mathtt{q}\rangle * \mathtt{ls}\langle \mathtt{q}, \mathtt{root}, \mathtt{n}-1\rangle)\end{aligned}$$

2.5 Infinities Support Analysis via Quantifier Elimination

Algorithmic quantifier elimination (QE) is a powerful technique for decision procedures in symbolic logic [8]. Kapur *et al.* highlight the importance of geometric QE heuristics for the case of generating program invariants [7]. While they exploit the structure of verification conditions generated from numerical programs, our PAInf-based QE allows us to generate inductive invariants (e.g. using octagonal constraints with infinity: $-\infty \leq \pm x \pm y \leq \infty$) for programs manipulating dynamically allocated data structures.

```
void append(node x, int a){
  if (x.next == null)
    x.next = new node(a, null);
  else
    insert(x.next, a);
}
```

Shape Spec :
Φ_{pr} : $\texttt{ll}\langle\texttt{x}, \_\rangle \wedge \texttt{x} \neq \texttt{null}$
Φ_{po} : $\texttt{ll}\langle\texttt{x}, \_\rangle \wedge \texttt{x} \neq \texttt{null}$

Spec with Inferred Pure :
Φ_{pr} : $\texttt{ll}\langle\texttt{x},\texttt{n}\rangle \wedge \texttt{n}>0$
Φ_{po} : $\texttt{ll}\langle\texttt{x},\texttt{n}+1\rangle \wedge \texttt{n}>0$

Fig. 4. Pure Specification Inferred from PAInf QE

Consider for example the code in figure 4, which appends a node to the end of an acyclic linked list. The Shape Spec does not express the strongest verifiable post-condition as it does not account for the newly inserted node. It would be thus useful to infer size properties as well. We can do so if the verification's relational obligations are discharged by QE over PAInf, leading to the specification with numeric properties.

3 Syntax and Parameterized Semantics

There are several benefits of adding the notion of infinity to a program logic. However, due to the presence of certain terms like $(\infty - \infty)$, it is an interesting problem to define the correct (or rather desired) semantics. We will now proceed to a formal discussion of Presburger arithmetic with infinity.

Our constraint language extends Presburger arithmetic with two abstract symbols designating positive (∞) infinity and negative ($-\infty$) infinity. The language is detailed in figure 5. However, we would like to make some extra notes. First, we use a type based approach to distinguish between the domain of variables. The notation $w : \tau$ denotes that the variable w is of type τ; thus there is a clear distinction between the domain of variables. Second, for performance reasons that are explained in section 5 we do not aim for a minimal input constraint language. That is the reason why the input language also supports min and max constraints over expressions. The min and max constraints in the input language are translated to $\min_=$ and $\max_=$ (using $\pi \rightsquigarrow [v/\max(a_1,a_2)]\pi \wedge \max_=(v, a_1, a_2)$ and $\pi \rightsquigarrow [v/\min(a_1,a_2)]\pi \wedge \min_=(v, a_1, a_2)$).

Next, we present the parameterized semantic model for PAInf and establish theorems and lemmas that show the correctness of our decision procedure. All theorems and lemmas in this paper are machine checked in Coq. Parameters are introduced to adapt different possible ways of handling tricky parts of PAInf such as the terms $(\infty - \infty)$ and $(0 \times \infty)$. Since our semantics is parameterized, all procedures, theorems and lemmas based on the semantics are also parameterized. We start by defining an *environment* to map variables to values.

$$\begin{aligned}
\pi &::= \beta \mid \neg\pi \mid \pi_1 \wedge \pi_2 \mid \pi_1 \vee \pi_2 \mid \pi_1 \rightarrow \pi_2 \mid \exists(w:\tau)\cdot\pi \mid \forall(w:\tau)\cdot\pi \\
\beta &::= \texttt{true} \mid \texttt{false} \mid a_1 < a_2 \mid a_1 \leq a_2 \mid a_1 = a_2 \mid a_1 \neq a_2 \\
&\quad\mid a_1 \geq a_2 \mid a_1 > a_2 \\
a &::= k \mid v \mid c \times a \mid a_1 + a_2 \mid -a \mid a_1 - a_2 \mid \max(a_1,a_2) \mid \min(a_1,a_2) \\
k &::= c \mid \infty \mid -\infty
\end{aligned}$$

where v, w are variable names; c is an integer constant

Fig. 5. PAInf: Input Constraint Language

Definition 1 *An environment for a universe τ of concrete values is a function $\phi_\tau : V \rightarrow \tau$ from the set of variables V to τ. For such a ϕ_τ, we denote by $\phi_\tau[x \mapsto a]$ the function which maps x to a and any other variable y to $\phi_\tau(y)$.*

We define the semantics of arithmetic operations and relations for PAInf formally in figure 6, denoted by $[\![\beta]\!]_{\mathbb{Z}_\infty}$. The subscript of $[\![]\!]$ denotes the domain of constants. $\mathbb{Z}_\infty$ means $\mathbb{Z} \cup \{\infty, -\infty\}$. By analogy, $[\![\beta]\!]_{\mathbb{Z}}$ means the domain is $\mathbb{Z}$. With these definitions one can compute every atomic term into a truth value with respect to an environment ϕ_τ and domain of constants η as described in figure 7, and denoted by $\text{E}\small{\text{VAL}}^{\eta}_{\phi_\tau}$.

We define the satisfaction relation $\phi_\tau \models^{\text{sat}}_{\eta} \pi$ and dissatisfaction relation $\phi_\tau \models^{\text{dst}}_{\eta} \pi$ (in figure 8) for each logical formula π over the environment ϕ_τ and domain of constants η by structural induction on π. Sometimes, a formula π can neither be satisfied nor be dissatisfied. In that case, we say π is undetermined, which can be presented as $\phi_\tau \models^{\text{udt}}_{\eta} \pi$. We define two distinct relations for satisfaction and dissatisfaction as we support both two-valued and three-valued logic. In case of three-valued logic a formula can be neither satisfied nor dissatisfied (undetermined).

Much of the semantics for PAInf is "as you might expect". For example, when all the values are finite, all of the operations and relations behave the same way they would in PA. On the other hand, any finite value plus ∞ equals ∞ and any finite value plus $-\infty$ equals $-\infty$. It is trickier to figure out what to do with the sum of ∞ and $-\infty$; we treat this as a meaningless value (much like the "value" of $\frac{0}{0}$ in the reals) denoted by "$\perp$". If ∞ and $-\infty$ were actually inverses, we would need to admit the following whopper:

$$0 = \infty + -\infty = \infty + (-\infty + 1) = (\infty + -\infty) + 1 = 1$$

In fact there is no perfect solution, since it is impossible to add a finite number of symbols to $\mathbb{Z}$ while remaining a group. Lasaruk and Sturm [13] propose dodging part of this problem by using only a single value for both positive and negative infinity, which is both greater than *and* less than all finite values. This approach ensures that every sum is defined, although ∞ still does not have an inverse and you lose antisymmetry for $\leq$. We find the notion of a single infinity to be too restrictive as it prohibits us from expressing some of the motivating examples from section 2.

In addition to the issues encountered while using a single infinity symbol, handling comparisons with $\perp$ is another challenge. A possible solution is treating all comparisons with $\perp$ as false. This is reasonable but not perfect. For example, in this context, it is not the case that $x > y$ is equivalent to $\neg(x \leq y)$ when x or y are $\perp$. Interestingly, this is the choice made by IEEE floating point standard [2]. Another possibility is to use a three-valued logic and treat any comparison with $\perp$ as the "third unknown value". There are several three-valued logics studied in the literature [3]. We use Kleene's weak three-valued logic which interprets the unknown value as "Error" and propagates it to the

[ADDITION]

$$[\![k_1 + k_2]\!]_{\mathbb{Z}_\infty} \stackrel{\text{def}}{=} \begin{cases} \bot & k_1 \text{ or } k_2 \text{ is } \bot \\ \bot & k_1 = \infty, k_2 = -\infty \\ \bot & k_1 = -\infty, k_2 = \infty \\ \infty & k_1 \text{ or } k_2 \text{ is } \infty\text{, and neither is } -\infty \\ -\infty & k_2 \text{ or } k_2 \text{ is } -\infty\text{, and neither is } \infty \\ [\![k_1 + k_2]\!]_{\mathbb{Z}} & k_1 \text{ and } k_2 \text{ are finite} \end{cases}$$

[LESS−THAN−EQ]

$$[\![k_1 \leq k_2]\!]_{\mathbb{Z}_\infty} \stackrel{\text{def}}{=} \begin{cases} \mathtt{F/U} & k_1 \text{ or } k_2 \text{ is } \bot \\ \mathtt{T} & k_2 = \infty \\ \mathtt{T} & k_1 = -\infty \\ \mathtt{T} & k_1 = k_2 = \infty \\ \mathtt{T} & k_1 = k_2 = -\infty \\ \mathtt{F} & k_1 = \infty, k_2 \neq \infty \\ \mathtt{F} & k_1 \neq -\infty, k_2 = -\infty \\ [\![k_1 \leq k_2]\!]_{\mathbb{Z}} & k_1 \text{ and } k_2 \text{ are finite} \end{cases}$$

[IDENTITY]

$$[\![k]\!]_{\mathbb{Z}_\infty} \stackrel{\text{def}}{=} k$$

[NEGATION]

$$[\![-k]\!]_{\mathbb{Z}_\infty} \stackrel{\text{def}}{=} \begin{cases} \bot & k = \bot \\ \infty & k = -\infty \\ -\infty & k = \infty \\ [\![-k]\!]_{\mathbb{Z}} & k \text{ is finite} \end{cases}$$

[OTHER−OPERATIONS−AND−RELATIONS]

$$[\![0 \times k]\!]_{\mathbb{Z}_\infty} \stackrel{\text{def}}{=} \begin{cases} 0 & k \text{ is finite} \\ 0/\bot/k & k \text{ is not finite} \end{cases} \qquad [\![c \times k]\!]_{\mathbb{Z}_\infty} \stackrel{\text{def}}{=} \begin{cases} [\![0 \times k]\!]_{\mathbb{Z}_\infty} & c = 0 \\ k & c = 1 \\ [\![k + (c-1) \times k]\!]_{\mathbb{Z}_\infty} & c > 1 \\ [\![-((-c) \times k)]\!]_{\mathbb{Z}_\infty} & c < 0 \end{cases}$$

$$[\![k_1 \geq k_2]\!]_{\mathbb{Z}_\infty} \stackrel{\text{def}}{=} [\![k_2 \leq k_1]\!]_{\mathbb{Z}_\infty} \qquad [\![k_1 > k_2]\!]_{\mathbb{Z}_\infty} \stackrel{\text{def}}{=} [\![k_1 \geq k_2]\!]_{\mathbb{Z}_\infty} \wedge [\![k_1 \neq k_2]\!]_{\mathbb{Z}_\infty}$$

$$[\![k_1 \neq k_2]\!]_{\mathbb{Z}_\infty} \stackrel{\text{def}}{=} \neg[\![k_1 = k_2]\!]_{\mathbb{Z}_\infty} \qquad [\![k_1 = k_2]\!]_{\mathbb{Z}_\infty} \stackrel{\text{def}}{=} [\![k_1 \leq k_2]\!]_{\mathbb{Z}_\infty} \wedge [\![k_2 \leq k_1]\!]_{\mathbb{Z}_\infty}$$

$$[\![k_1 - k_2]\!]_{\mathbb{Z}_\infty} \stackrel{\text{def}}{=} [\![k_1 + (-k_2)]\!]_{\mathbb{Z}_\infty} \qquad [\![k_1 < k_2]\!]_{\mathbb{Z}_\infty} \stackrel{\text{def}}{=} [\![k_1 \leq k_2]\!]_{\mathbb{Z}_\infty} \wedge [\![k_1 \neq k_2]\!]_{\mathbb{Z}_\infty}$$

$$[\![\max_{=}(k_1, k_2, k_3)]\!]_{\mathbb{Z}_\infty} \stackrel{\text{def}}{=} ([\![k_1 = k_2]\!]_{\mathbb{Z}_\infty} \wedge [\![k_3 \leq k_2]\!]_{\mathbb{Z}_\infty}) \vee ([\![k_1 = k_3]\!]_{\mathbb{Z}_\infty} \wedge [\![k_2 \leq k_3]\!]_{\mathbb{Z}_\infty})$$

$$[\![\min_{=}(k_1, k_2, k_3)]\!]_{\mathbb{Z}_\infty} \stackrel{\text{def}}{=} ([\![k_1 = k_2]\!]_{\mathbb{Z}_\infty} \wedge [\![k_2 \leq k_3]\!]_{\mathbb{Z}_\infty}) \vee ([\![k_1 = k_3]\!]_{\mathbb{Z}_\infty} \wedge [\![k_3 \leq k_2]\!]_{\mathbb{Z}_\infty})$$

Fig. 6. Operations and Relations in $\mathbb{Z}_\infty$

entire formula. In three-valued logic, when x or y are $\bot$, $x > y$ and $\neg(x \leq y)$ are equivalent. In Omega++, user can choose between a two-valued or three-valued logic, which is indicated in [LESS−THAN−EQ] of figure 6. Note that in three-valued logic, according to the relation definition in figure 8, formulae like $\bot < 0$ are neither satisfied nor dissatisfied.

The definition of multiplication in the presence of infinities $(0 \times \infty)$ can also be selected by the user as shown in figure 6. There are three possible choices for defining $0 \times \infty : 0$, $\bot$ and ∞. For each of these options we can choose a two-valued or three-valued logic, thus Omega++ supports six different customized semantics in total. As described in section 6, for our experiments we use the semantics with three-valued logic and $0 \times \infty \stackrel{\text{def}}{=} 0$. However, in general any of the six customized semantics can be used as the decision procedure is parameterized over these choices and our certified proof guarantees that all choices are sound, complete and decidable.

In order to match the intuition of user, by design, most valid formulae in PA remain so in our semantics for PAInf, just as most invalid formulae in PA are still invalid in

[ARITH−EVAL]

$$\textsc{Eval}^{\eta}_{\phi_\tau}(k) \stackrel{\text{def}}{=} [\![k]\!]_\eta \qquad \textsc{Eval}^{\eta}_{\phi_\tau}(v) \stackrel{\text{def}}{=} [\![\phi_\tau(v)]\!]_\eta$$
$$\textsc{Eval}^{\eta}_{\phi_\tau}(c \times a) \stackrel{\text{def}}{=} [\![\textsc{Eval}^{\eta}_{\phi_\tau}(c) \times \textsc{Eval}^{\eta}_{\phi_\tau}(a)]\!]_\eta$$
$$\textsc{Eval}^{\eta}_{\phi_\tau}(a_1 + a_2) \stackrel{\text{def}}{=} [\![\textsc{Eval}^{\eta}_{\phi_\tau}(a_1) + \textsc{Eval}^{\eta}_{\phi_\tau}(a_2)]\!]_\eta$$
$$\textsc{Eval}^{\eta}_{\phi_\tau}(a_1 - a_2) \stackrel{\text{def}}{=} [\![\textsc{Eval}^{\eta}_{\phi_\tau}(a_1) - \textsc{Eval}^{\eta}_{\phi_\tau}(a_2)]\!]_\eta$$
$$\textsc{Eval}^{\eta}_{\phi_\tau}(-a) \stackrel{\text{def}}{=} [\![-\textsc{Eval}^{\eta}_{\phi_\tau}(a)]\!]_\eta$$

[BOOLEAN−EVAL]

$$\textsc{Eval}^{\eta}_{\phi_\tau}(\texttt{true}) \stackrel{\text{def}}{=} \mathtt{T} \qquad \textsc{Eval}^{\eta}_{\phi_\tau}(\texttt{false}) \stackrel{\text{def}}{=} \mathtt{F} \qquad \textsc{Eval}^{\eta}_{\phi_\tau}(\texttt{undefined}) \stackrel{\text{def}}{=} \mathtt{U}$$
$$\textsc{Eval}^{\eta}_{\phi_\tau}(a_1 \circ a_2) \stackrel{\text{def}}{=} [\![\textsc{Eval}^{\eta}_{\phi_\tau}(a_1) \circ \textsc{Eval}^{\eta}_{\phi_\tau}(a_2)]\!]_\eta$$
$$\textsc{Eval}^{\eta}_{\phi_\tau}(\max_{=}(a_1, a_2, a_3)) \stackrel{\text{def}}{=} [\![\max_{=}(\textsc{Eval}^{\eta}_{\phi_\tau}(a_1), \textsc{Eval}^{\eta}_{\phi_\tau}(a_2), \textsc{Eval}^{\eta}_{\phi_\tau}(a_2))]\!]_\eta$$
$$\textsc{Eval}^{\eta}_{\phi_\tau}(\min_{=}(a_1, a_2, a_3)) \stackrel{\text{def}}{=} [\![\min_{=}(\textsc{Eval}^{\eta}_{\phi_\tau}(a_1), \textsc{Eval}^{\eta}_{\phi_\tau}(a_2), \textsc{Eval}^{\eta}_{\phi_\tau}(a_2))]\!]_\eta$$

where $\circ$ above means one of $\leq, \geq, <, >, =, \neq$.

Fig. 7. Evaluations on atomic terms

PAInf. Here are two short examples that are valid in both (if you drop the universe of quantification as you move from PAInf to PA):

$$\forall(x : \mathbb{Z}_\infty) \cdot \exists(y : \mathbb{Z}_\infty) \cdot x \leq y \qquad \forall(x : \mathbb{Z}_\infty) \cdot \forall(y : \mathbb{Z}_\infty) \cdot x + 1 = y + 1 \rightarrow x = y$$

However, there are differences. This formula is valid in PA but invalid in PAInf:

$$\forall(x : \mathbb{Z}_\infty) \cdot \exists(y : \mathbb{Z}_\infty) \cdot x + y = 0$$

The previous formula is false in PAInf when $x = \infty$. More generally, although $\mathbb{Z}_\infty$ is not a group, it still has many useful algebraic properties, such as the following.

Lemma 1. + is Associative *$[\![(a + b) + c]\!]_{\mathbb{Z}_\infty}$ and $[\![a + (b + c)]\!]_{\mathbb{Z}_\infty}$ are equal or both undefined.*

Lemma 2. + is Commutative *$[\![a + b]\!]_{\mathbb{Z}_\infty}$ and $[\![b + a]\!]_{\mathbb{Z}_\infty}$ are equal or both undefined.*

Lemma 3. 0 is the Additive Identity *$[\![a + 0]\!]_{\mathbb{Z}_\infty}$ and a are equal for all defined a.*

Lemma 4. + is Monotonic *If $[\![a \leq b]\!]_{\mathbb{Z}_\infty}$ is* T *and if both $[\![a + c]\!]_{\mathbb{Z}_\infty}$ and $[\![b + c]\!]_{\mathbb{Z}_\infty}$ are defined, then $[\![a + c \leq b + c]\!]_{\mathbb{Z}_\infty}$ is also* T.

4 Reasoning with Infinity

For the following discussion we assume the existence of a solver for Presburger arithmetic (such as Omega [9]). Our focus is to automate the reasoning of ghost infinities by leveraging on existing solvers. Note that $v \in \mathbb{Z}_\infty$, is the same as, $v \in \mathbb{Z} \vee v = \infty \vee v = -\infty$. This fact can be used to give a quantifier elimination procedure for PAInf as shown in figure 9. However, using this approach naively leads to an explosion in the size of formulae to be checked. As an example, consider the following formula,

$$\forall \mathtt{x}, \mathtt{y}, \mathtt{z} \cdot (\mathtt{z}{=}\infty \wedge \mathtt{y}{=}\mathtt{x} + \mathtt{z} \wedge \mathtt{x}{<}\infty)$$

$\phi_\tau \models^{\text{sat}}_{\eta} \beta$	iff $\text{EVAL}^{\eta}_{\phi_\tau}(\beta)$ is T.
$\phi_\tau \models^{\text{sat}}_{\eta} \neg\pi$	iff $\phi_\tau \models^{\text{dst}}_{\eta} \pi$ holds.
$\phi_\tau \models^{\text{sat}}_{\eta} \pi_1 \wedge \pi_2$	iff both $\phi_\tau \models^{\text{sat}}_{\eta} \pi_1$ and $\phi_\tau \models^{\text{sat}}_{\eta} \pi_2$ holds.
$\phi_\tau \models^{\text{sat}}_{\eta} \pi_1 \vee \pi_2$	iff both $\phi_\tau \models^{\text{sat}}_{\eta} \pi_1$ and $\phi_\tau \models^{\text{sat}}_{\eta} \pi_2$ holds, or both $\phi_\tau \models^{\text{dst}}_{\eta} \pi_1$ and $\phi_\tau \models^{\text{sat}}_{\eta} \pi_2$ holds, or both $\phi_\tau \models^{\text{sat}}_{\eta} \pi_1$ and $\phi_\tau \models^{\text{dst}}_{\eta} \pi_2$ holds.
$\phi_\tau \models^{\text{sat}}_{\eta} \pi_1 \rightarrow \pi_2$	iff both $\phi_\tau \models^{\text{sat}}_{\eta} \pi_1$ and $\phi_\tau \models^{\text{sat}}_{\eta} \pi_2$ holds, or both $\phi_\tau \models^{\text{dst}}_{\eta} \pi_1$ and $\phi_\tau \models^{\text{sat}}_{\eta} \pi_2$ holds, or both $\phi_\tau \models^{\text{dst}}_{\eta} \pi_1$ and $\phi_\tau \models^{\text{sat}}_{\eta} \pi_2$ holds.
$\phi_\tau \models^{\text{sat}}_{\eta} \exists(w:\tau)\cdot\pi$	iff $\phi_\tau[w \mapsto k] \models^{\text{sat}}_{\eta} \pi$ holds for some $k \in \tau$, and forall all $k \in \tau$, either $\phi_\tau[w \mapsto k] \models^{\text{sat}}_{\eta} \pi$ or $\phi_\tau[w \mapsto k] \models^{\text{dst}}_{\eta} \pi$ holds.
$\phi_\tau \models^{\text{sat}}_{\eta} \forall(w:\tau)\cdot\pi$	iff $\phi_\tau[w \mapsto k] \models^{\text{sat}}_{\eta} \pi$ holds for all $k \in \tau$
$\phi_\tau \models^{\text{dst}}_{\eta} \beta$	iff $\text{EVAL}^{\eta}_{\phi_\tau}(\beta)$ is F.
$\phi_\tau \models^{\text{dst}}_{\eta} \neg\pi$	iff $\phi_\tau \models^{\text{sat}}_{\eta} \pi$ holds.
$\phi_\tau \models^{\text{dst}}_{\eta} \pi_1 \wedge \pi_2$	iff both $\phi_\tau \models^{\text{dst}}_{\eta} \pi_1$ and $\phi_\tau \models^{\text{dst}}_{\eta} \pi_2$ holds, or both $\phi_\tau \models^{\text{sat}}_{\eta} \pi_1$ and $\phi_\tau \models^{\text{dst}}_{\eta} \pi_2$ holds, or both $\phi_\tau \models^{\text{dst}}_{\eta} \pi_1$ and $\phi_\tau \models^{\text{sat}}_{\eta} \pi_2$ holds.
$\phi_\tau \models^{\text{dst}}_{\eta} \pi_1 \vee \pi_2$	iff both $\phi_\tau \models^{\text{dst}}_{\eta} \pi_1$ and $\phi_\tau \models^{\text{dst}}_{\eta} \pi_2$ holds.
$\phi_\tau \models^{\text{dst}}_{\eta} \pi_1 \rightarrow \pi_2$	iff both $\phi_\tau \models^{\text{sat}}_{\eta} \pi_1$ and $\phi_\tau \models^{\text{dst}}_{\eta} \pi_2$ holds.
$\phi_\tau \models^{\text{dst}}_{\eta} \exists(w:\tau)\cdot\pi$	iff $\phi_\tau[w \mapsto k] \models^{\text{dst}}_{\eta} \pi$ holds for all $k \in \tau$
$\phi_\tau \models^{\text{dst}}_{\eta} \forall(w:\tau)\cdot\pi$	iff $\phi_\tau[w \mapsto k] \models^{\text{dst}}_{\eta} \pi$ holds for some $k \in \tau$, and forall all $k \in \tau$, either $\phi_\tau[w \mapsto k] \models^{\text{sat}}_{\eta} \pi$ or $\phi_\tau[w \mapsto k] \models^{\text{dst}}_{\eta} \pi$ holds.
$\phi_\tau \models^{\text{udt}}_{\eta} \pi$	iff neither $\phi_\tau \models^{\text{sat}}_{\eta} \pi$ or $\phi_\tau \models^{\text{dst}}_{\eta} \pi$ holds.

Fig. 8. Definition of satisfaction relation

Using the [FORALL−INF] rule to eliminate the three quantified variables (x, y and z), leads to 3^3 (= 27) constraints. To avoid this problem, we support both kinds of quantifiers ($\exists(w:\mathbb{Z})$ and $\exists(w:\mathbb{Z}_\infty)$) in the implementation. This allows for a more efficient quantifier elimination as variables with finite domain do not give rise to new disjunctions in formulae. Since, infinity is added as a ghost constant only in the specification logic, all program variables are still in finite domain. Supporting two kinds of quantifiers matches nicely with the distinction between the domain of specification variables ($\mathbb{Z}_\infty$) and program variables ($\mathbb{Z}$). In section 6 we compare our system with an implementation of PAI from [13] and demonstrate the effectiveness of using our procedure.

[EXISTS−INF]	[FORALL−INF]
$\exists(w:\mathbb{Z}_\infty)\cdot\pi \rightsquigarrow \exists(w:\mathbb{Z})\cdot\pi$ $\vee[\infty/w]\pi$ $\vee[-\infty/w]\pi$	$\forall(w:\mathbb{Z}_\infty)\cdot\pi \rightsquigarrow \forall(w:\mathbb{Z})\cdot\pi$ $\wedge[\infty/w]\pi$ $\wedge[-\infty/w]\pi$

Fig. 9. PAInf: Quantifier Elimination (INF-TRANS)

For checking satisfiability in the PAInf we use the algorithm shown in figure 10. We denote the procedure for satisfiability checking as $SAT(\pi)$. The algorithm has four steps: (i) first we eliminate the quantifiers starting with the innermost quantifier, (ii) next we apply a normalization which detects tautologies and contradictions in constraints using infinity, (iii) then we eliminate min-max and constant constraints and (iv) finally we solve the resulting formula using an existing PA solver Omega.

$SAT(\pi)$	$\pi_F = \text{INF-TRANS}(\pi)$	*(1) Quantifier Elimination*
$\Longrightarrow SAT(\pi_F)$	$\pi_N = \text{INT-TRANS}(\pi_F)$	*(2) Normalization*
$\Longrightarrow SAT(\pi_N)$	$\pi_G = \text{SIMP}(\pi_N)$	*(3) Simplification*
$\Longrightarrow SAT(\pi_G)$		*(4) Omega*

Fig. 10. PAInf: SAT Checking

At a high level the intuition behind the SAT checking algorithm is as follows: after quantifier elimination, the π_F formula has quantifiers only on the finite domain variables. The normalization and simplification eliminate all the infinite constants from the formula. The resulting formula (π_G) is in PA and its satisfiability can be checked using Omega. Next we describe the steps in the SAT checking algorithm in detail.

[EVAL−FIN]	[EVAL−INF]	[EVAL−BOT]
$v \leadsto Z$	$\infty + \infty \leadsto \infty$	$\infty + (-\infty) \leadsto \bot$
$c \leadsto Z$	$-\infty + (-\infty) \leadsto -\infty$	$-\infty + \infty \leadsto \bot$
$-Z \leadsto Z$	$-\infty + Z \leadsto -\infty$	$\bot + Z \leadsto \bot$
$Z + Z \leadsto Z$	$Z + (-\infty) \leadsto -\infty$	$Z + \bot \leadsto \bot$
$Z - Z \leadsto Z$	$\infty + Z \leadsto \infty$	$\bot + \bot \leadsto \bot$
$c \times Z \leadsto Z$	$Z + \infty \leadsto \infty$	$-\bot \leadsto \bot$

Fig. 11. PAInf: Evaluation Check

4.1 Normalization and Simplification

We define a set of rewriting rules based on the semantics of formulae in PAInf. We work only with closed-form formulae, thus after applying the quantifier elimination given in figure 9, all the remaining variables are in the finite domain ($\mathbb{Z}$). It is possible to compare the variables with infinities by evaluating their values (as they are all finite) using the semantics given in the section 3. This is performed by the `Evaluation Check` function in figure 11 which reduces each expression to a finite value (denoted by Z). Thus, for the normalization rules in figure 12 we only need to consider the integer values (Z) and the infinity constants. Note that, the `Evaluation Check` is only applied for the purpose of checking the finiteness and eliminating infinity, the actual formula is not evaluated.

The normalization process uses the rewriting rules given in figure 12 (rules for $\neq, \geq, <$ and $\min_=$ are similar and omitted for brevity). These rules detect the tautologies and contradictions in the usage of ∞ and $-\infty$, and the constraints involving ∞ and $-\infty$ are eliminated. After the application of these rules the given formula is reduced to a form which can be solved by existing PA solvers like Omega.

We also proved the following theorems and lemmas about quantifier elimination INF-TRANS and normalization INT-TRANS. These theorems and lemmas hold for both two-valued/three-valued logics and all choices of $(0 \times \infty)$. Hence, the Coq certified proof of these theorems and lemmas is also parameterized. Note that for quantifier elimination the universe of environment τ and the domain of constants η are both instantiated to $\mathbb{Z}_\infty$.

[NORM-INF-EQ]	[NORM-INF-LEQ]	[NORM-INF-LT]
$\bot = \_ \leadsto$ `error`	$\bot \leq \_ \leadsto$ `error`	$\bot < \_ \leadsto$ `error`
$\_ = \bot \leadsto$ `error`	$\_ \leq \bot \leadsto$ `error`	$\_ < \bot \leadsto$ `error`
$Z = \infty \leadsto$ `false`	$Z \leq \infty \leadsto$ `true`	$Z < \infty \leadsto$ `true`
$\infty = \infty \leadsto$ `true`	$\infty \leq \infty \leadsto$ `true`	$\infty < \infty \leadsto$ `false`
$-\infty = \infty \leadsto$ `false`	$-\infty \leq \infty \leadsto$ `true`	$-\infty < \infty \leadsto$ `true`
$-\infty = Z \leadsto$ `false`	$-\infty \leq Z \leadsto$ `true`	$-\infty < Z \leadsto$ `true`
$-\infty = -\infty \leadsto$ `true`	$-\infty \leq -\infty \leadsto$ `true`	$-\infty < -\infty \leadsto$ `false`
$\infty = Z \leadsto$ `false`	$\infty \leq Z \leadsto$ `false`	$\infty < Z \leadsto$ `false`
$\infty = -\infty \leadsto$ `false`	$\infty \leq -\infty \leadsto$ `false`	$\infty < -\infty \leadsto$ `false`
$Z = -\infty \leadsto$ `false`	$Z \leq -\infty \leadsto$ `false`	$Z < -\infty \leadsto$ `false`

[NORM-EQ-MAX]

$\max_=(\infty,\infty,\infty) \leadsto$ `true`	$\max_=(-\infty,Z,Z) \leadsto$ `false`	$\max_=(\_,\_,\bot) \leadsto$ `error`
$\max_=(-\infty,-\infty,-\infty) \leadsto$ `true`	$\max_=(\infty,Z,-\infty) \leadsto$ `false`	$\max_=(\infty,Z,Z) \leadsto$ `false`
$\max_=(-\infty,Z,-\infty) \leadsto$ `false`	$\max_=(\infty,-\infty,\infty) \leadsto$ `true`	$\max_=(\infty,\infty,Z) \leadsto$ `true`
$\max_=(-\infty,\infty,-\infty) \leadsto$ `false`	$\max_=(-\infty,\infty,Z) \leadsto$ `false`	$\max_=(Z,\infty,Z) \leadsto$ `false`
$\max_=(\infty,-\infty,-\infty) \leadsto$ `false`	$\max_=(\infty,-\infty,Z) \leadsto$ `false`	$\max_=(\_,\bot,\_) \leadsto$ `error`
$\max_=(-\infty,-\infty,Z) \leadsto$ `false`	$\max_=(Z,\infty,-\infty) \leadsto$ `false`	$\max_=(\infty,Z,\infty) \leadsto$ `true`
$\max_=(\infty,\infty,-\infty) \leadsto$ `true`	$\max_=(-\infty,Z,\infty) \leadsto$ `false`	$\max_=(\bot,\_,\_) \leadsto$ `error`
$\max_=(Z,-\infty,-\infty) \leadsto$ `false`	$\max_=(Z,-\infty,\infty) \leadsto$ `false`	$\max_=(Z,Z,\infty) \leadsto$ `false`
$\max_=(-\infty,-\infty,\infty) \leadsto$ `false`	$\max_=(-\infty,\infty,\infty) \leadsto$ `false`	$\max_=(Z,\infty,\infty) \leadsto$ `false`

[NORM-INF-ERR]

`error` $\leadsto$ `false` (two-valued logic)

`error` $\leadsto$ `undefined` (three-valued logic)

Fig. 12. PAInf: Normalization (INT-TRANS)

Lemma 5. Quantifier Elimination $\phi_{\mathbb{Z}_\infty} \models^{sat}_{\mathbb{Z}_\infty} \pi$ *if and only if* $\phi_{\mathbb{Z}} \models^{sat}_{\mathbb{Z}_\infty}$ INF-TRANS(π), $\phi_{\mathbb{Z}_\infty} \models^{dst}_{\mathbb{Z}_\infty} \pi$ *if and only if* $\phi_{\mathbb{Z}} \models^{dst}_{\mathbb{Z}_\infty}$ INF-TRANS(π),

For infinity elimination τ is $\mathbb{Z}_\infty$ and η is $\mathbb{Z}$. This is due to the fact that after quantifier elimination the domain of all the variables is finite.

Lemma 6. Infinity Elimination $\phi_{\mathbb{Z}} \models^{sat}_{\mathbb{Z}_\infty} \pi$ *if and only if* $\phi_{\mathbb{Z}} \models^{sat}_{\mathbb{Z}}$ INT-TRANS(π), $\phi_{\mathbb{Z}} \models^{dst}_{\mathbb{Z}_\infty} \pi$ *if and only if* $\phi_{\mathbb{Z}} \models^{dst}_{\mathbb{Z}}$ INT-TRANS(π).

So for the total transformation TRANS(π) = INT-TRANS(INF-TRANS(π)) used in satisfiability checking, we have the following theorem:

Theorem 1. Satisfiability Checking $\phi_{\mathbb{Z}_\infty} \models^{sat}_{\mathbb{Z}_\infty} \pi$ *if and only if* $\phi_{\mathbb{Z}} \models^{sat}_{\mathbb{Z}}$ TRANS(π), $\phi_{\mathbb{Z}_\infty} \models^{dst}_{\mathbb{Z}_\infty} \pi$ *if and only if* $\phi_{\mathbb{Z}} \models^{dst}_{\mathbb{Z}}$ TRANS(π),

Gallina, the internal functional language of Coq is strongly normalizing. Thus, all functions written in Coq must terminate.

Theorem 2. Termination *Satisfiability checking in PAInf (figure 10) terminates.*

The quantifier elimination with infinity expands the logical formula π and the normalization introduces many logical constants. We introduce a simplification function SIMP which recursively eliminates logical constants according to the rules in figure 13 in order to reduce the length of a formula. As Omega doesn't support $\max_=$ or $\min_=$

[ELIM]

$$\max_{=}(a_1, a_2, a_3) \leadsto (a_1 = a_2 \wedge a_3 \leq a_2) \vee (a_1 = a_3 \wedge a_2 \leq a_3)$$
$$\min_{=}(a_1, a_2, a_3) \leadsto (a_1 = a_2 \wedge a_2 \leq a_3) \vee (a_1 = a_3 \wedge a_3 \leq a_2)$$

[SIMP]

$\beta \leadsto \text{ELIM}(\beta)$	$\neg\texttt{undefined} \leadsto \texttt{undefined}$
$\texttt{undefined} \wedge \pi \leadsto \texttt{undefined}$	$\pi \wedge \texttt{undefined} \leadsto \texttt{undefined}$
$\texttt{true} \wedge \pi \leadsto \pi$	$\pi \wedge \texttt{true} \leadsto \pi$
$\texttt{false} \wedge \pi \leadsto \texttt{false}$	$\pi \wedge \texttt{false} \leadsto \texttt{false}$
$\texttt{undefined} \vee \pi \leadsto \texttt{undefined}$	$\pi \vee \texttt{undefined} \leadsto \texttt{undefined}$
$\texttt{true} \vee \pi \leadsto \texttt{true}$	$\pi \vee \texttt{true} \leadsto \texttt{true}$
$\texttt{false} \vee \pi \leadsto \pi$	$\pi \vee \texttt{false} \leadsto \pi$
$\texttt{undefined} \rightarrow \pi \leadsto \texttt{undefined}$	$\pi \rightarrow \texttt{undefined} \leadsto \texttt{undefined}$
$\texttt{false} \rightarrow \pi \leadsto \texttt{true}$	$\pi \rightarrow \texttt{true} \leadsto \texttt{true}$
$\texttt{true} \rightarrow \pi \leadsto \pi$	$\pi \rightarrow \texttt{false} \leadsto \neg\pi$
$\neg\texttt{true} \leadsto \texttt{false}$	$\neg\texttt{false} \leadsto \texttt{true}$
$\forall(w : \tau) \cdot \texttt{undefined} \leadsto \texttt{undefined}$	$\exists(w : \tau) \cdot \texttt{undefined} \leadsto \texttt{undefined}$
$\forall(w : \tau) \cdot \texttt{true} \leadsto \texttt{true}$	$\exists(w : \tau) \cdot \texttt{true} \leadsto \texttt{true}$
$\forall(w : \tau) \cdot \texttt{false} \leadsto \texttt{false}$	$\exists(w : \tau) \cdot \texttt{false} \leadsto \texttt{false}$

Fig. 13. Definition of Simplification

we also include the elimination of $\max_{=}$ and $\min_{=}$ in SIMP. Note that for three-valued logic, the logical constants contain a third value: `undefined` which is not supported by Omega. Our SIMP function propagates `undefined` to the whole formula such that we know if a formula is undetermined before calling Omega due of the following theorem:

Theorem 3. Decide Undetermined $\phi_{\mathbb{Z}} \models_{\mathbb{Z}}^{\text{udt}} \pi$ *if and only if* SIMP(π)=`undefined`

Thus, we do not need to extend Omega to support `undefined`. SIMP also preserves the validity of formulae:

Theorem 4. Simplification $\phi_{\mathbb{Z}} \models_{\mathbb{Z}}^{\text{sat}} \pi$ *if and only if* $\phi_{\mathbb{Z}} \models_{\mathbb{Z}}^{\text{sat}}$ SIMP(π), $\phi_{\mathbb{Z}} \models_{\mathbb{Z}}^{\text{dst}} \pi$ *if and only if* $\phi_{\mathbb{Z}} \models_{\mathbb{Z}}^{\text{dst}}$ SIMP(π).

5 Implementation

We gain a number of benefits in exchange for implementing Omega++ in Coq. We get proof of termination for free since Gallina (the extractable pure functional language of Coq) is strongly normalizing. More importantly, we get full machine-checked formal correctness proofs for our source code with respect to a well defined semantics for Presburger arithmetic with infinity. Coq's extraction facility then transforms the Gallina program into OCaml (or Haskell or Scheme), which we then compile and run as normal.

The following table presents some statistics for our Coq development of Omega++. The first column shows the file name, while the second and third columns are the number of lines in the file taken by the program and its soundness proof, respectively. Our total development is a modest 3,988 lines and the ratio of proof to program is 2.35. The fourth column gives the time taken by Coq to verify the file (*i.e.*, proof/type checking), using a 2.6 GHz Intel Core i7 with 16 GB of DDR3 RAM.

Coq File	*Program*	*Proof*	*Time (s)*	*Description*
`Theory.v`	585	737	20.68	*Syntax and Semantics;* SIMP
`Transformation.v`	350	1,203	31.07	INF-TRANS, INT-TRANS
`Simplification.v`	0	856	338.96	*Tactics/lemmas for* SIMP
`Extraction.v`	257	0	1.27	*Module to extract OCaml code*
	1,192	2,796	391.98	*Total Coq*

Note that type checking times have very little to do with file length. For example `Transformation.v` has 1,553 lines (combined program and proof), but takes less than 32 seconds to verify. On the other hand, verifying the 44 lines of the SIMP procedure, whose code is contained in `Theory.v`, takes more than five minutes! We also used one engineering trick to boost the performance of the extracted code. The code uses strings to represent both variables and (arbitrary-sized) integers, but Coq's encoding of strings is less efficient than OCaml's. We therefore usually treat strings as an abstract type within Coq and manipulate them via an interface to OCaml's string functions, passed in using a functor.

We will next highlight the key optimizations we used to get good performance and discuss how the program affected the proof—and vice versa. In the implementation we directly handle all of the logical operators and min-max constraints of the constraint language (figure 5), even though the "obvious" strategy would be to desugar aggressively. Unfortunately, sugar-free formulae are actually quite a bit larger than their svelter sugared cousins, resulting in a significant performance penalty. Working with fully-sugared formulae has a significant impact on the proofs because we must handle more cases.

Similarly, we allow the input formulae to specify, for each quantifier, whether the domain of quantification is over $\mathbb{Z}$ or over $\mathbb{Z}_\infty$. Quantifier elimination is expensive, and our "user"—the HIP/SLEEK verification toolset—often knows when a variable must be finite: in particular, program variables must be finite, whereas specification variables need not be. Communicating this fact to Omega++ resulted in significant performance gains, but again increased the proof effort due to the necessity of handling more cases.

To enable min/max, reduce the length of the output, eliminate redundant clauses, and propagate the `undefined` value, we implemented some basic simplifications (figure 13). The SIMP procedure was easy to implement but very painful to verify due to the vast number of cases we need to consider. In the end we wrote some custom proof tactics in Ltac (Coq's proof tactic language) which crunched through the tedium.

The previous examples all trade one-time verification effort for a better-performing algorithm. On the other hand, sometimes the proof improves the program. Before we started on our Coq implementation, we did a OCaml prototype for the quantifier-free fragment of the problem. That prototype's version of normalization did additional case analysis. Due to our careful treatment of quantifier elimination we were able to prove that much of this case analysis was unnecessary in our Coq tool. Moreover, the Coq development identified a soundness bug in the OCaml prototype, which allowed the invalid transformation $x \geq y \leadsto x+1 > y$, which is false when $x = y = \infty$.

Overall, Omega++ is far better than our previous OCaml prototype. Consider:

Tool	*Sound*	*Complete*	*Termination*	*Semantics*	*Verified*
OCaml Prototype	*No*	*No*	*Unclear*	*Unclear*	*No*
Omega++	*Yes*	*Yes*	*Guaranteed*	*Precise*	*in Coq*

Of course, our OCaml prototype is a bit of a straw man, but we have been quite convinced that the substantial effort that it took to write Omega++ in Coq was well-rewarded. Moreover, as we will soon see, Omega++ has comparable performance to our OCaml prototype, despite solving a trickier problem in a much more through way.

6 Experiments

To benchmark Omega++ we integrated it into the HIP/SLEEK verification toolset [5] and developed a suite of tests (mostly searching and sorting programs) whose specifications use ∞ in interesting ways. The source code for each of these programs can be investigated in detail and tested with Omega++ [29] on our web site. In all the experiments we selected three-valued logic in Omega++ and used $0 \cdot \infty \stackrel{\text{def}}{=} 0$ as these are the appropriate choices for program verification. We used a 3.20GHz Intel Core i7-960 processor with 16GB memory running Ubuntu Linux 10.04 for our benchmarks, the first set of which are detailed in the table below.

Benchmark	*LOC*	*Disjuncts* ($\mathbb{Z}$)	*Time* (Ω)	*Disjuncts* ($\mathbb{Z}_\infty$)	*Time* (Ω++)
Insertion Sort	30	4	0.14	2	0.15
Selection Sort	69	14	0.36	7	0.35
Binary Search Tree	105	12	0.43	6	0.35
Bubble Sort	110	12	0.29	9	0.50
Merge Sort	91	6	0.32	4	1.81
Priority Queue	207	16	0.84	10	2.73
Total Correctness	21	-	-	2	0.21
Sorting with Min and Max	79	-	-	7	1.82

The first column lists the test name and the second gives its lines of code. The third and fifth columns show that $\mathbb{Z}_\infty$ enables more readable and concise specifications. Specifically, the third column gives the number of disjunctions required to express the test's specifications using $\mathbb{Z}$, whereas the fifth column expresses the same properties using $\mathbb{Z}_\infty$. For each test in the first group (top six), $\mathbb{Z}_\infty$ requires fewer disjunctions. We do need to be a bit careful: although the specifications are informally for the same property (*e.g.*, "sortedness"), typically the specifications in $\mathbb{Z}_\infty$ are formally stronger since the embedded quantification occurs over larger sets. Note that we do not claim that Omega++ eliminates the disjunctions from reasoning since the quantifiers over infinities hide the disjunctions inside them. However, using infinities provides a useful abstraction to express the same property as the given specification is more concise. The difference in formal strength is the fundamental reason why the times given in columns four and six differ. Column four gives the time (including all of HIP/SLEEK) using Omega, whereas column six gives the time using Omega++. For the first four examples Omega++ is comparable to Omega, but in the final two of the first group of tests we believe the difference in the domain of quantification results in a significantly harder theorem in $\mathbb{Z}_\infty$, and thus, a noticeably longer runtime.

Comparison with Similar Tools. Lasaruk and Sturm [13] also propose extending Presburger arithmetic with infinity. Their work differs from ours in several respects. First, they only add a single infinity value, thus dodging any thorny—but in our view, important—semantic issues involving $\infty - \infty$. More importantly, Lasaruk and Sturm describe an algorithm but do not provide an implementation. For benchmarking purposes, we implemented their algorithm and tested it using the constraints generated from our test suite. We also compared our previous OCaml prototype as shown below:

Benchmark	*Calls*	*Time (PAI)*	*Time (Proto)*	*Time (Ω++)*
Insertion Sort	100	4.58	0.78	0.39
Selection Sort	245	>600.00	0.62	0.78
Binary Search Tree	116	150.00	0.48	0.50
Bubble Sort	336	>600.00	1.25	1.34
Merge Sort	155	>600.00	1.05	1.92
Priority Queue	778	>600.00	FAIL	1.20
Total Correctness	120	>600.00	0.31	0.16
Sorting with Min and Max	376	>600.00	0.29	0.19
Entailment Examples	124	1.89	FAIL	1.42
Lemma Examples	35	1.88	1.27	1.65
Total (except PQ and EE)	1,824	>3,862.14	7.21	8.11

The second column gives the number of times the associated decision procedure was called for each test. The third column gives the times for Lasaruk and Sturm's "PAI" algorithm; many of the tests timed out after 10 minutes. The fourth column gives the times for our OCaml prototype "Proto"; notice that for two of the tests Proto failed (completeness holes). The fifth column gives the times for Omega++.

It is obvious that PAI, at least when implemented directly as given by Lasaruk and Sturm [13], is uncompetitive. Thus, Omega++ is always faster than PAI. When comparing Proto to Omega++, recall that Proto is only trying to solve the simpler problem of quantifier-free formulae. Despite this, for many of our tests the tools perform similarly. For a few tests, some of Proto's heuristics result in appreciably better times; we plan to study these tests in more detail in the future to try to improve Omega++. Overall, Omega++'s performance is competitive.

Inference. As described in section 2.5, quantifier elimination in Presburger arithmetic with infinity can help with invariant generation of octagonal constraints. The table below benchmarks using Omega++ for this analysis technique.

Method	*Pre*	*Post*	*Inferred*	*Time (Omega++)*
Create	true	$\mathtt{ll}\langle\mathtt{res},\mathtt{m}\rangle$	m=n	0.13
Delete	$\mathtt{ll}\langle\mathtt{x},\mathtt{n}\rangle$	$\mathtt{ll}\langle\mathtt{res},\mathtt{m}\rangle$	$\mathtt{n}-1\leq\mathtt{m}$	0.17
Insert	$\mathtt{ll}\langle\mathtt{x},\mathtt{n}\rangle\wedge\mathtt{x}\neq\mathtt{null}$	$\mathtt{ll}\langle\mathtt{x},\mathtt{m}\rangle$	$\mathtt{n}=\mathtt{m}-1$	0.13
Copy	$\mathtt{ll}\langle\mathtt{x},\mathtt{n}\rangle * \mathtt{ll}\langle\mathtt{res},\mathtt{m}\rangle$	$\mathtt{ll}\langle\mathtt{x},\mathtt{m}\rangle$	m=n	0.16
Remove	$\mathtt{ll}\langle\mathtt{x},\mathtt{n}\rangle\wedge\mathtt{x}\neq\mathtt{null}$	$\mathtt{ll}\langle\mathtt{x},\mathtt{m}\rangle$	$\mathtt{n}-1\leq\mathtt{m}\wedge\mathtt{m}\leq\mathtt{n}$	0.19
Return	$\mathtt{ll}\langle\mathtt{x},\mathtt{n}\rangle$	$\mathtt{ll}\langle\mathtt{x},\mathtt{m}\rangle$	$\mathtt{m}=\mathtt{n}\wedge 0\leq\mathtt{m}$	0.07
Traverse	$\mathtt{ll}\langle\mathtt{x},\mathtt{n}\rangle$	$\mathtt{ll}\langle\mathtt{x},\mathtt{m}\rangle$	m=n	0.12
Get	$\mathtt{ll}\langle\mathtt{x},\mathtt{n}\rangle\wedge\mathtt{x}\neq\mathtt{null}$	$\mathtt{ll}\langle\mathtt{res},\mathtt{m}\rangle$	$\mathtt{m}=\mathtt{n}-2\wedge 2\leq\mathtt{n}$	0.11
Head	$\mathtt{ll}\langle\mathtt{x},\mathtt{n}\rangle*\mathtt{ll}\langle\mathtt{y},\mathtt{m}\rangle$	$\mathtt{ll}\langle\mathtt{res},\mathtt{n}+\mathtt{m}-1\rangle$	$1=\mathtt{min}(\mathtt{n},\mathtt{m})$	0.21

The first column gives the test name. The second and third columns give the user-provided spatial pre- and postconditions in separation logic. The fourth column gives the inferred pure specification, while the last column gives the time used by Omega++. The final test is noteworthy because the inferred invariant uses min/max constraints.

7 Related Work and Conclusion

Reynolds demonstrated that *ghost variables* [26] were useful for verifying sequential programs. Their importance is highlighted when proving program, object or loop invariants [18], refining between two transition systems [17] or when considering program's security aspects [16]. Our work enriches specifications by extending the domain of ghost values with the mathematical concepts of positive and negative infinity.

Presburger arithmetic [24] is one of the canonical examples of an important decidable problem. Kuncak *et al.* [11,12] presented a decision procedure for a quantifier-free fragment of Boolean Algebra with Presburger arithmetic which can be used to prove a mixed set-based constraint with symbolic cardinality and linear arithmetic. QFBAPA was later extended to the more challenging case of multisets [22] and proved to be NP-complete [23]. The VCDryad [21] framework combines separation logic with decision procedures for sets and multi sets to verify programs with natural proofs. The combination of set/multi-sets with separation logic even though quite useful requires complex provers that can reason over the domain of sets/muti-sets.

Lasaruk and Sturm [13] were the first to tackle the problem of extending PA with infinity, proving completeness and decidability. Our work differs from theirs as we allow two distinct values for positive and negative infinities and provide a implementation. Our decision procedure is built on top of Omega calculator [9], and certified in Coq [1]. The general problem of adding infinities to the set of reals was addressed by Weispfenning [27]. This was later extended to mixed real and integer quantifier elimination in [28]. Another interesting extension of decision procedures for real arithmetic is the addition of infinitesimals. The proof assistant Isabelle/HOL [20] has support for infinitesimals. Loos and Weispfenning [15] first proposed a virtual substitution approach for quantifier elimination of infinitesimals. We also use a similar virtual substitution to eliminate infinities as part of the decision procedure. Chaieb and Nipkow [4] present a reflective implementation of Cooper's algorithm for quantifier elimination in PA. Their work complements our approach as we reduce from PA extended with infinities to PA.

Conclusion. We presented Omega++, a decision procedure for Presburger arithmetic with infinity $\mathbb{Z}_\infty$. Infinity is a useful abstraction, increasing a program logic's ability to reason about termination and compose more elegantly. Moreover, specifications with infinity are often more concise. Omega++ has been Coq-certified to respect a precise formal semantics for $\mathbb{Z}_\infty$. We integrated Omega++ into an existing verifier and evaluated it on a benchmark of small programs, demonstrating that it can perform well in practice. Omega++ demonstrates that we can develop useful, efficient, and certified programs for program verification and analysis.

Acknowlegement. This work is supported by MoE Tier-1 NUS research project R-252-000-525-112 and Yale-NUS College R-607-265-045-121.

References

1. The Coq Proof Assistant, http://coq.inria.fr/
2. IEEE Standard for Floating-Point Arithmetic. IEEE Std 754-2008, pp. 1–70 (August 2008)
3. Bergmann, M.: An introduction to many-valued and fuzzy logic: semantics, algebras, and derivation systems. Cambridge University Press (2008)
4. Chaieb, A., Nipkow, T.: Verifying and reflecting quantifier elimination for presburger arithmetic. In: Sutcliffe, G., Voronkov, A. (eds.) LPAR 2005. LNCS (LNAI), vol. 3835, pp. 367–380. Springer, Heidelberg (2005)
5. Chin, W.-N., David, C., Nguyen, H.H., Qin, S.: Automated verification of shape, size and bag properties via user-defined predicates in separation logic. Sci. Comput. Program. 77(9), 1006–1036 (2012)
6. Ishtiaq, S., O'Hearn, P.W.: BI as an assertion language for mutable data structures. In: ACM POPL (January 2001)
7. Kapur, D., Zhang, Z., Horbach, M., Zhao, H., Lu, Q., Nguyen, T.: Geometric Quantifier Elimination Heuristics for Automatically Generating Octagonal and Max-plus Invariants. In: Bonacina, M.P., Stickel, M.E. (eds.) McCune Festschrift 2013. LNCS (LNAI), vol. 7788, pp. 189–228. Springer, Heidelberg (2013)
8. Kapur, D.: Automatically generating loop invariants using quantifier elimination. In: Deduction and Applications (2005)
9. Kelly, P., Maslov, V., Pugh, W.: The Omega Library Version 1.1.0 Interface Guide (1996)
10. Kolmogorov, N.A.: "Infinity". Encyclopaedia of Mathematics: An Updated and Annotated Translation of the Soviet "Mathematical Encyclopaedia," vol. 3. Reidel (1995)
11. Kuncak, V., Nguyen, H.H., Rinard, M.: An algorithm for deciding BAPA: Boolean algebra with Presburger arithmetic. In: Nieuwenhuis, R. (ed.) CADE 2005. LNCS (LNAI), vol. 3632, pp. 260–277. Springer, Heidelberg (2005)
12. Kuncak, V., Rinard, M.: Towards efficient satisfiability checking for boolean algebra with Presburger arithmetic. In: Pfenning, F. (ed.) CADE 2007. LNCS (LNAI), vol. 4603, pp. 215–230. Springer, Heidelberg (2007)
13. Lasaruk, A., Sturm, T.: Effective quantifier elimination for Presburger arithmetic with infinity. In: Gerdt, V.P., Mayr, E.W., Vorozhtsov, E.V. (eds.) CASC 2009. LNCS, vol. 5743, pp. 195–212. Springer, Heidelberg (2009)
14. Le, T.C., Gherghina, C., Hobor, A., Chin, W.-N.: A Resource-Based Logic for Termination and Non-Termination Proofs. In: Merz, S., Pang, J. (eds.) ICFEM 2014. LNCS, vol. 8829, pp. 267–283. Springer, Heidelberg (2014)
15. Loos, R., Weispfenning, V.: Applying linear quantifier elimination. Comput. J. 36(5), 450–462 (1993)
16. Mai, H., Pek, E., Xue, H., King, S.T., Madhusudan, P.: Verifying security invariants in expressos. In: ASPLOS (2013)
17. Marcus, M., Pnueli, A.: Using ghost variables to prove refinement. In: AMST (1996)
18. McPeak, S., Necula, G.C.: Data structure specifications via local equality axioms. In: Etessami, K., Rajamani, S.K. (eds.) CAV 2005. LNCS, vol. 3576, pp. 476–490. Springer, Heidelberg (2005)
19. McShane, E.J.: Unified integration, vol. 107. Academic Press (1983)
20. Nipkow, T., Paulson, L.C., Wenzel, M.: Isabelle/HOL. LNCS, vol. 2283. Springer, Heidelberg (2002)
21. Pek, E., Qiu, X., Madhusudan, P.: Natural proofs for data structure manipulation in c using separation logic. In: Proceedings of the 35th ACM SIGPLAN Conference on Programming Language Design and Implementation, p. 46. ACM (2014)

22. Piskac, R., Kuncak, V.: Decision procedures for multisets with cardinality constraints. In: Logozzo, F., Peled, D.A., Zuck, L.D. (eds.) VMCAI 2008. LNCS, vol. 4905, pp. 218–232. Springer, Heidelberg (2008)
23. Piskac, R., Kuncak, V.: Linear arithmetic with stars. In: Gupta, A., Malik, S. (eds.) CAV 2008. LNCS, vol. 5123, pp. 268–280. Springer, Heidelberg (2008)
24. Presburger, M.: Über die Vollständigkeit eines gewissen Systems der Arithmetik ganzer Zahlen, in welchen die Addition als einzige Operation hervortritt (1929)
25. Reynolds, J.: Separation Logic: A Logic for Shared Mutable Data Structures. In: LICS (2002)
26. Reynolds, J.C.: The craft of programming. Prentice Hall International series in computer science. Prentice Hall (1981)
27. Weispfenning, V.: Quantifier elimination for real algebra - the quadratic case and beyond. Appl. Algebra Eng. Commun. Comput. 8(2), 85–101 (1997)
28. Weispfenning, V.: Mixed real-integer linear quantifier elimination. In: Proceedings of the 1999 International Symposium on Symbolic and Algebraic Computation, ISSAC 1999, Vancouver, B.C., Canada, July 29-31, pp. 129–136 (1999)
29. Omega++ with HIP/SLEEK. Source and binaries available at, http://loris-7.ddns.comp.nus.edu.sg/~project/SLPAInf/ (October 2014.)

Direct Formal Verification of Liveness Properties in Continuous and Hybrid Dynamical Systems

Andrew Sogokon(✉) and Paul B. Jackson

LFCS, School of Informatics, University of Edinburgh, Edinburgh, UK
a.sogokon@sms.ed.ac.uk, pbj@inf.ed.ac.uk

Abstract This paper is concerned with proof methods for the temporal property of eventuality (a type of liveness) in systems of polynomial ordinary differential equations (ODEs) evolving under constraints. This problem is of a more general interest to hybrid system verification, where reasoning about temporal properties in the continuous fragment is often a bottleneck. Much of the difficulty in handling continuous systems stems from the fact that closed-form solutions to non-linear ODEs are rarely available. We present a general method for proving eventuality properties that works with the differential equations directly, without the need to compute their solutions. Our method is intuitively simple, yet much less conservative than previously reported approaches, making it highly amenable to use as a rule of inference in a formal proof calculus for hybrid systems.

1 Introduction

In computer science, by *liveness* one informally understands the property of something "good" happening along the execution paths in a program. Thus, in stating that a program is *live* one asserts that some desirable property will hold true as the program runs. Liveness properties of discrete programs were studied by Lamport and Owicki in [16,23] and formally defined by Alpern and Schneider in [1]. In this paper we will be concerned with a particular type of liveness known as *eventuality*, which requires that some *target* set of states is eventually attained. Furthermore, instead of discrete computer programs, we will be working with continuous systems that are governed by ordinary differential equations and have an uncountably infinite number of states.

Continuous systems have generated significant interest among computer science and formal verification researchers over the past years as they form an important part of a broader class of dynamical systems known as *hybrid* (or *cyber-physical*) systems. Hybrid systems combine discrete and continuous behaviour; they are interesting because they provide the most general framework for modelling and verifying properties of dynamic phenomena. To give but a few examples, hybrid systems have found application in verifying safety of aircraft collision avoidance protocols [26], train control systems [25,17], simulating control systems for oil drills working with discontinuous friction [21] and many more.

This material is based upon work supported by the UK Engineering and Physical Sciences Research Council (EPSRC) under grant EP/I010335/1.

N. Bjørner and F. de Boer (Eds.): FM 2015, LNCS 9109, pp. 514–531, 2015.
DOI: 10.1007/978-3-319-19249-9_32

Formally verifying temporal properties of hybrid systems is no easy enterprise [11], in no small part due to their expressiveness, which makes most interesting questions about their behaviour inherently undecidable [13]. However, this does not mean that hybrid system verification is impossible and thus futile. On the contrary, formal verification tools have already been successfully applied in some impressive case studies, but it is also true that there is great scope for improvement in what verification tools are capable of. This is especially true of methods for verifying liveness properties, which are typically more difficult to prove than safety. In this paper we seek to partially remedy this by proposing a new deductive verification method for proving eventuality properties in continuous systems that can be implemented as a rule of inference in a theorem prover for hybrid systems.

The method we propose is able to work directly with initial states and target regions given by arbitrary semi-algebraic sets (that is, sets given by finite boolean combinations of polynomial equalities and inequalities) and generalizes previously reported approaches reported in [30,31,33,26]. Our approach is not restricted to bounded evolution domains (as e.g. [31]) and is able to prove eventuality properties for target regions described by formulas featuring equations (unlike [26,30]). Finally, the presence of system equilibria outside the target region presents an insurmountable obstacle for approaches reported in [30,31,26] and requires the user to manually remove them from the evolution domain [30]. We work with weaker conditions that only require a semi-algebraic over-approximation of the reachable set, which can be used to avoid equilibria without the need to manually alter the system. The conditions we give are much more general than in [33] and may be checked automatically using a decision procedure.

1.1 Contributions

In this paper we (**I**) describe a necessary condition for eventuality – the existence of what we call a *staging set* – and use it to (**II**) formulate conditions for proving eventuality properties in systems of polynomial ODEs without computing their solutions. (**III**) We illustrate the proof principle using some basic examples and (**IV**) describe how our approach can be used to construct formal proofs of certain liveness properties in a deductive verification tool for hybrid systems. Lastly, we (**V**) generalize total derivatives for formulas introduced in [26] by exploiting directional differentiability properties of the min max function.

2 Preliminaries

In what follows, we will work with autonomous [1] systems of ordinary differential equations defined on $\mathbb{R}^n$ and evolving under constraints, i.e.

$$\dot{x}_i = f_i(\boldsymbol{x}), \quad 1 \leq i \leq n,$$
$$\boldsymbol{x} \in H \subseteq \mathbb{R}^n.$$

[1] By this we mean that our ODEs have no *explicit* dependence on the time variable t. No generality is lost because any system with explicit time dependence can be turned into an autonomous system by adding a new 'clock' variable to model time evolution, e.g. if we let $\dot{x}_{n+1} = 1$ and replace every instance of t in the system with x_{n+1}.

We will write this more concisely as $\dot{\boldsymbol{x}} = f(\boldsymbol{x})\ \&\ H$. We will be interested in verifying properties of evolutions that lie within the constraints H, though in doing so we consider evolutions that might go outside of H. Furthermore, we will only work with polynomial systems, i.e. $f \in \mathbb{R}[\boldsymbol{x}]^n$, under evolution constraints H that are semi-algebraic sets.

Remark 1. To simplify our presentation we will interchangeably use the notation for sets and formulas characterizing those sets. Thus, H will denote both a semi-algebraic set $H \subseteq \mathbb{R}^n$ and a quantifier-free formula H of real arithmetic with free variables in $x_1, \ldots, x_n$ that characterizes the set H.

A *solution* to the initial value problem $(\dot{\boldsymbol{x}} = f(\boldsymbol{x}),\ \boldsymbol{x}_0)$ is a function $\varphi : (a, b) \rightarrow \mathbb{R}^n$ such that $\varphi(t)|_{t=0} = \boldsymbol{x}_0$ and $\frac{d}{dt}\varphi(t)|_{t=\tau} = f(\varphi(\tau))$ for all τ in some non-empty extended real interval (a, b) including 0. We will denote solutions to the initial value problem at time $t \in (a, b)$ by $\varphi_t(\boldsymbol{x}_0)$, where $\boldsymbol{x}_0$ is the initial value. The interval (a, b) is known as the *interval of existence* of a given solution; in what follows we will always consider the largest such interval, i.e. the *maximal* interval of existence.

In general, solutions to initial value problems need not be unique or even exist for all time $t \geq 0$, i.e. the maximal interval of existence need not be of the form (a, ∞). For instance, solutions to simple non-linear systems, such as $\dot{x} = x^2$, already exhibit *finite time blow-up*, i.e. diverge to infinity in finite time. In this paper we will work with differential equations whose solutions are unique and of sufficient duration to allow us to prove properties of interest. For simplicity we sometimes assume that solutions exist for all $t \geq 0$. In such cases, refinements of the arguments are needed if the solutions are of sufficient duration but do not exist for all $t \geq 0$. To remove this problem entirely, it is common (but not necessary) to require the system of ODEs to be Lipschitz continuous. Under these assumptions, we will refer to the solution φ as the *flow* of the system.

If the solution is available in *closed-form*, by which we informally understand a *finite* expression in terms of polynomials or elementary functions, then one can answer questions pertaining to the temporal behaviour of the system by working with the closed-form expression. In practice, however, closed-form solutions to non-linear ODEs are rarely available; even when they are, their form is often much more involved than the differential equations themselves. For instance, transcendental functions, such as sin, cos, exp, log, etc., frequently occur in solutions to very simple polynomial ODEs. This introduces a source of undecidability [32], which further undermines approaches to formal verification that rely on the knowledge of closed-form solutions.

Rather than working with the solution, it is sometimes possible to prove properties of interest by working with the differential equations *directly*[2]. This approach has been applied to formal safety verification (e.g. in [29,27,34]) and verification of progress and eventuality properties (e.g. see [33,30,26,31]). *Direct methods* for proving eventuality properties in ODEs have to date been rather conservative, i.e. they often fail even if the property is indeed true in a given system. Our interest in this paper is in exploring a direct verification approach that generalizes those previously reported and is at the same time less conservative.

[2] This idea is at the heart of the *qualitative theory* of differential equations and has its intellectual origins in the late nineteenth-century work of Henri Poincaré, published in [28].

In what follows, we will often write temporal properties as formulas of differential dynamic logic ($d\mathcal{L}$) [25], which provides a specification and verification language for hybrid systems, using hybrid programs [25] as operational models. The logic $d\mathcal{L}$ extends first-order logic with modalities $\langle\ \rangle$ and $[\ ]$ for hybrid programs. We will only be concerned with hybrid programs that define continuous systems; these are always of the form $\dot{\boldsymbol{x}} = f(\boldsymbol{x})\ \&\ H$. To a significant extent, our work will build upon results about invariant sets, which we discuss next.

2.1 Continuous Invariants

A fundamental property that provides the foundation for reasoning about safety in dynamical systems (be they discrete, continuous or hybrid) is that of set invariance. For continuous dynamical systems, by invariants we understand sets of states that remain invariant under the flow $\varphi_t(\cdot)$ for all $t \geq 0$. *Flow-invariant* (or *positively invariant*) sets are a very well-established concept in control and dynamical systems (see e.g. [4,3]) and can be used to prove safety properties for flows in a way analogous to program invariants in discrete programs. Platzer and Clarke in [27] generalized flow-invariant sets to *continuous invariants* for verifying safety of continuous systems under evolution constraints.

Definition 2. *A semi-algebraic set $I \subseteq \mathbb{R}^n$ is a continuous invariant for $\dot{\boldsymbol{x}} = f(\boldsymbol{x})\ \&\ H$ if and only if*

$$\forall\, \boldsymbol{x} \in I.\, \forall\, t \geq 0.\, (\forall\, \tau \in [0,t].\, \varphi_\tau(\boldsymbol{x}) \in H) \rightarrow (\forall\, \tau \in [0,t].\, \varphi_\tau(\boldsymbol{x}) \in I).$$

We may write a continuous invariance assertion as a formula in $d\mathcal{L}$ as follows:

$$I \rightarrow [\dot{\boldsymbol{x}} = f(\boldsymbol{x})\ \&\ H]\, I.$$

This formula asserts that if evolution starts anywhere inside I, then by following any solution *(box modality $[\ ]$) to the system $\dot{\boldsymbol{x}} = f(\boldsymbol{x})\ \&\ H$ for any length of time, the system* always *remains inside I.*

One useful way of thinking about continuous invariants (this will become apparent later) is as sets that "can only be left by entering $\neg H$ first".

Liu, Zhan and Zhao in [18] reported necessary and sufficient conditions for checking whether a given semi-algebraic set is a continuous invariant; their conditions are *direct*, i.e. do not require explicit knowledge of the solutions, and *decidable* if the system of ODEs is polynomial and H is semi-algebraic. This result leads to a *decision procedure* for semi-algebraic continuous invariant assertions. The decision procedure described in [18] involves computing a finite number of higher-order *Lie derivatives* and exploits the ascending chain condition in Noetherian rings; see [18] for details and also [12] for related work on algebraic invariants. A Lie derivative of a real-valued differentiable function is the directional derivative of that function in the direction of the vector field induced by the system of ODEs. We denote the first-order Lie derivative of a function $p : \mathbb{R}^n \rightarrow \mathbb{R}$ with respect to the vector field $f : \mathbb{R}^n \rightarrow \mathbb{R}^n$ as $\mathfrak{L}_f(p)$. Formally, the first Lie derivative is defined as

$$\mathfrak{L}_f(p) \equiv \sum_{i=1}^{n} \frac{\partial p}{\partial x_i} f_i \equiv \nabla p \cdot f.$$

Higher-order Lie derivatives are defined inductively, i.e. $\mathfrak{L}_f^k(p) = \mathfrak{L}_f(\mathfrak{L}_f^{k-1}p)$ for $k > 0$ and $\mathfrak{L}_f^0(p) = p$. Note also that in vector fields generated by ODEs, since $f_i = \dot{x}_i = \frac{dx_i}{dt}$, we have $\mathfrak{L}_f(p) = \sum_{i=1}^n \frac{\partial p}{\partial x_i}\frac{dx_i}{dt} = \frac{dp}{dt}$, i.e. the Lie derivative gives the *total derivative* of p with respect to time t. We will be using Lie derivatives in this capacity in the following sections.

3 Direct Method for Eventuality Verification

As a first attempt, one may define eventuality for continuous systems as follows:

$$\forall\, \boldsymbol{x}_0 \in X_0.\, \exists\, t \geq 0.\, \big(\varphi_t(\boldsymbol{x}_0) \in X_T\big),$$

where $X_0 \subseteq \mathbb{R}^n$ is the set of initial states and $X_T \subseteq \mathbb{R}^n$ is the target set. As with invariants, because continuous systems we consider may impose evolution domain constraints $H \subseteq \mathbb{R}^n$, the formal definition of eventuality needs an additional clause stipulating that continuous evolutions remain within the constraint until the target set is attained. Below we give a general definition of eventuality for continuous systems.

Definition 3. *Given a system $\dot{\boldsymbol{x}} = f(\boldsymbol{x})\ \&\ H$, where $H \subseteq \mathbb{R}^n$ is the evolution constraint, $X_0 \subseteq H$ is the set of initial states from which solutions are unique and of sufficient duration and $X_T \subseteq \mathbb{R}^n$ is the target set of states that we wish the system to attain by starting anywhere inside X_0, then the eventuality property holds if and only if*

$$\forall\, \boldsymbol{x}_0 \in X_0.\, \exists\, t \geq 0.\, \big((\forall \tau \in [0,t].\, \varphi_\tau(\boldsymbol{x}_0) \in H)\ \wedge\ \varphi_t(\boldsymbol{x}_0) \in X_T\big),$$

By solutions of sufficient duration we understand solutions that may blow up in finite positive time, but only after reaching X_T (finite time blow up in negative time is innocuous for showing eventuality).

We may phrase the eventuality property using a $d\mathcal{L}$ formula as follows:

$$X_0 \rightarrow \langle \dot{\boldsymbol{x}} = f(\boldsymbol{x})\ \&\ H\rangle\, X_T.$$

The above formula asserts that if we start anywhere inside X_0, then by following the *solution* to the system $\dot{\boldsymbol{x}} = f(\boldsymbol{x})\ \&\ H$, we *eventually* (diamond modality $\langle\ \rangle$) reach a state which lies inside X_T. In using the above formula, we assume that each of the sets H, X_0 and X_T is semi-algebraic and is thus characterized by a quantifier-free formula in the theory of real arithmetic.

3.1 Staging Sets

We now introduce *staging sets*, which are a particular kind of continuous invariants that we use to give an over-approximation of the continuous behaviour in a system with a view to proving eventuality properties without computing solutions to ODEs.

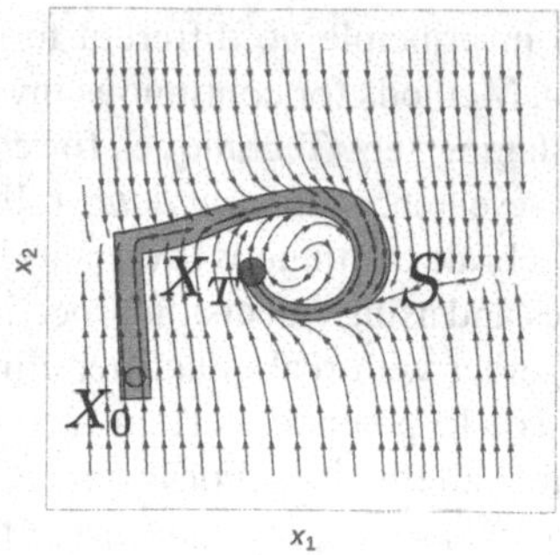

Fig. 1. Staging set (intuitively). Initial set of states X_0 is shown in green, the target set X_T in red and a possible choice for a staging set S in grey; H is taken to be $\mathbb{R}^2$.

Definition 4. *Given a system $\dot{\boldsymbol{x}} = f(\boldsymbol{x})$ & H, a set of initial states $X_0 \subseteq H$ and a target set of states $X_T \subseteq \mathbb{R}^n$, we say that a set $S \subseteq \mathbb{R}^n$ is a* ***staging set*** *if we have $S \subseteq H$, $X_0 \setminus X_T \subseteq S$ and*

$$\forall\, \boldsymbol{x}_0 \in S.\, \forall\, t \geq 0.\, (\forall \tau \in [0,t].\, \varphi_\tau(\boldsymbol{x}_0) \notin X_T \cap H) \;\rightarrow\; (\forall \tau \in [0,t].\, \varphi_\tau(\boldsymbol{x}_0) \in S).$$

One could write this formally using $d\mathcal{L}$ as

$$\big(X_0 \wedge \neg X_T \rightarrow S\big) \wedge \big(S \rightarrow [\dot{\boldsymbol{x}} = f(\boldsymbol{x}) \;\&\; \neg(X_T \wedge H)]\, S\big) \wedge \big(X_0 \vee S \rightarrow H\big).$$

Intuitively, a staging set is any set within the evolution constraint H that includes the non-trivial initial states $X_0 \setminus X_T$ and that "can only be left by entering the target region X_T within the constraint H", or provides a "continuous exit window into X_T within H". Fig. 1 illustrates this intuition. Let us remark that staging sets are very natural because their existence is a necessary pre-requisite for the eventuality property to hold.

Proposition 5. *If the eventuality property holds for $\dot{\boldsymbol{x}} = f(\boldsymbol{x})$ & H with initial and target sets $X_0 \subseteq H$, $X_T \subseteq \mathbb{R}^n$ as before, then there exists a staging set for the system.*

Proof. Assuming the eventuality property holds true in the system, we have $X_0 \subseteq H$ and for each $\boldsymbol{x}_0 \in X_0 \setminus X_T$ there exists some $t > 0$ such that $\varphi_t(\boldsymbol{x}_0) \in X_T$ and $\forall \tau \in [0,t].\, \varphi_\tau(\boldsymbol{x}_0) \in H$. Now define $\gamma(\boldsymbol{x}_0) \equiv \{\varphi_{t'}(\boldsymbol{x}_0) \mid t' \in [0,t)\}$ to construct a staging set $S \equiv \bigcup_{\boldsymbol{x}_0 \in X_0} \gamma(\boldsymbol{x}_0)$. □

Remark 6. The construction in the proof above gives a staging set which may not possess a closed-form description. In practice, by restricting attention to semi-algebraic sets, one can *decide* whether a given candidate set constitutes a staging set for the system at hand. Also, note that if S is a staging set, then $S' \equiv S \setminus X_T$ is also a staging set.

Searching for a staging set is in principle no different to searching for a continuous invariant for safety verification. Methods for continuous invariant generation can therefore be applied to search for staging sets. Techniques for continuous invariant generation are still an active area of research, with *complete*[3] (albeit intractable) procedures available to search for semi-algebraic continuous invariants based on enumerating parametric semi-algebraic templates and using a decision procedure for continuous invariant checking described in [18] together with real quantifier elimination [35] (see [9] for a survey of more recent methods). In practice, certain incomplete invariant generation methods may offer more scalable alternatives. For instance, sum-of-squares techniques for computing polynomial sub-level set approximations of the finite-time reachable set due to Wang, Lall & West [36] are promising in this regard.

3.2 Progress Functions

The existence of a staging set only provides a *necessary condition* for eventuality. In this section we will give a *sufficient condition* that will allow us to soundly conclude the eventuality property. Because we already require the sets we work with to be semi-algebraic, we can invoke the following lemma.

Lemma 7. *If $H, I \subseteq \mathbb{R}^n$ are semi-algebraic and I is a continuous invariant for the system $\dot{\boldsymbol{x}} = f(\boldsymbol{x})\ \&\ H$ then any solution that starts in $I \cap H$ and subsequently leaves I either* **(i)** *leaves H while still in I or* **(ii)** *has a non-empty segment immediately on leaving I that is wholly contained in $\mathbb{R}^n \setminus H$ (i.e. $\neg H$).*

Proof (sketch). Case (i) is obvious and follows from the definition of continuous invariants. For case (ii) we need to show that if I and H are left at the same time, then $\neg H$ is sustained for some non-empty time interval. If there is a time t' such that $\forall\, \tau \in [0, t').\ \varphi_\tau(\boldsymbol{x}_0) \in H \cap I$ and $\varphi_{t'}(\boldsymbol{x}_0) \notin H \cup I$, then $\neg H$ is sustained for $[t', t']$ immediately upon leaving I. If no such t' exists, consider a point $\boldsymbol{x}_1 \in I \cap H$ from which the system can no longer evolve inside I without violating the constraint H. It is necessarily the case that $\forall\, \epsilon > 0.\ \exists\, t \in (0, \epsilon).\varphi_t(\boldsymbol{x}_1) \notin H$ holds, i.e. no further motion of the system can sustain the constraint. We need to show the stronger property $\exists\, \epsilon > 0.\, \forall\, t \in (0, \epsilon).\varphi_t(\boldsymbol{x}_1) \notin H$. For any semi-algebraic set, let $P \subset \mathbb{R}[\boldsymbol{x}]$ be the collection of polynomials appearing in its description. At the point $\boldsymbol{x}_1$ for each $p_i \in P$ we have that $p_i(\boldsymbol{x}_1) \sim 0$, where $\sim \in \{<, =, >\}$. For those $p_i \in P$ such that $p_i(\boldsymbol{x}_1) > 0$ or $p_i(\boldsymbol{x}_1) < 0$, there is guaranteed to be an open neighbourhood U_i around $\boldsymbol{x}_1$ for which $p_i(U_i) > 0$ or $p_i(U_i) < 0$ holds (since polynomials are continuous functions). Therefore, there is some non-empty time neighbourhood $(0, \epsilon)$ for which the solution will sustain the strict sign conditions. When $p_i(\boldsymbol{x}_1) = 0$, one either has $\mathfrak{L}_f^k(p_i(\boldsymbol{x}_1)) = 0$ for infinitely many orders k, or there exists an $k \geq 1$ such that $\mathfrak{L}_f^k(p_i(\boldsymbol{x}_1)) \neq 0$. Since polynomials and solutions to polynomial ODEs are analytic functions, there is some open time neighbourhood $(0, \epsilon)$ where the sign condition on the polynomial p_i is sustained under the solution (see e.g. [18, Proposition 9]). Thus, if a semi-algebraic set cannot be sustained, then its semi-algebraic complement is sustained for some non-empty open time interval following the solution. □

[3] In the sense that an appropriate continuous invariant (if it exists) will always be found.

If one can show that any trajectory starting inside a staging set S eventually leaves S, one can use Lemma 7 to conclude the eventuality property. An obvious way of showing that S is eventually left (without computing the solution to the system of ODEs) is to search for an appropriate function, whose derivative can be used as a measure of "progress in leaving S".

Proposition 8. *Given a staging set S for some polynomial system $\dot{\boldsymbol{x}} = f(\boldsymbol{x})$ & H with initial and target sets $X_0 \subseteq H$, $X_T \subseteq \mathbb{R}^n$ respectively and whose* solutions are of sufficient duration, *if there exists a continuously differentiable function $P : \mathbb{R}^n \to \mathbb{R}$ such that*

$$\exists\, \varepsilon > 0.\, \forall\, \boldsymbol{x} \in S.\quad \mathfrak{L}_f(P(\boldsymbol{x})) \leq -\varepsilon \wedge P(\boldsymbol{x}) \geq 0,$$

then, provided the sets are semi-algebraic, the eventuality property holds and P is known as a ***progress function*** *for S.*

Proof. Fix a start point $\boldsymbol{x}_0 \in X_0 \setminus X_T$ from which we want to argue there is a finite flow with end point in X_T and which is fully contained in H. First we show that there is a finite flow from $\boldsymbol{x}_0$ with end point outside of S. Assume that the solution with initial condition $\boldsymbol{x}_0$ is of sufficient duration such that either **(i)** the trajectory exits S at some point or **(ii)** the trajectory is inside S up to and including at least some time $\tau > P(\boldsymbol{x}_0)/\varepsilon$. In case **(ii)**, a simple application of the fundamental theorem of calculus yields

$$\begin{aligned} P(\varphi_\tau(\boldsymbol{x}_0)) - P(\varphi_0(\boldsymbol{x}_0)) &= \int_0^\tau \frac{d}{dt} P(\varphi_t(\boldsymbol{x}_0))\, dt = \int_0^\tau \mathfrak{L}_f(P(\varphi_t(\boldsymbol{x}_0)))\, dt \\ &\leq \int_0^\tau -\varepsilon\, dt \\ &= -\varepsilon\tau. \end{aligned}$$

Given $P(\varphi_0(\boldsymbol{x}_0)) = P(\boldsymbol{x}_0)$ we have that $P(\varphi_\tau(\boldsymbol{x}_0)) < 0$ which is impossible since $P(\boldsymbol{x}_0) \geq 0$ for all $\boldsymbol{x}_0 \in S$. Hence case **(i)** must hold. Using case **(i)**, we now apply Lemma 3 to the invariance property of the staging set S. We have that either the trajectory reaches $X_T \cap H$ within S and the eventuality property obviously holds, or, on exiting S we immediately have a non-empty segment of the trajectory contained in $X_T \cap H$ and the eventuality property holds too. □

Remark 9. Of course, given some set $\hat{S}$ such that $S \subseteq \hat{S}$, where S is a staging set, if one shows that $\hat{S}$ is left in finite time by following the solutions, then one can also conclude that X_T is eventually attained. This may seem like a complete waste of effort, but methods developed for *verified integration* of ODEs [2,22] can compute *enclosures* of finite-time reachable sets where the enclosure itself is *not* a staging set but is guaranteed to enclose one; in this case, the enclosure can act as $\hat{S}$. Formally verified implementations of enclosure construction algorithms have been reported by Immler [14,15].

Polynomial progress functions may be generated automatically using pre-defined polynomial *templates* of bounded degree with parametric coefficients. The templates can be enumerated (e.g. by successively increasing the polynomial degree) and checked using a real quantifier elimination procedure (such as e.g. CAD [6]), leaving the parameters as free variables. The result is a semi-algebraic constraint on the coefficients that will yield a progress function. Of course, the computational complexity of real quantifier elimination [7] makes this approach infeasible and therefore practically uninteresting; however, theoretically, one has a *semi-decision procedure* for checking whether a polynomial progress function exists for a given semi-algebraic staging set and a polynomial ODE. Methods based on sum-of-squares techniques (e.g. [30]) may offer more practical (albeit incomplete) alternatives for finding progress functions.

4 Proof Rule for Eventuality in ODEs

We are now ready to formalize the proof method for eventuality properties using staging sets and progress functions, as described in the previous section, into a rule of inference.

Proposition 10. *The rule of inference given below (with four premises) is sound with the proviso that solutions are of sufficient duration.*

$$\text{(SP)}\ \frac{\vdash \exists\, \varepsilon > 0.\, \forall\, \boldsymbol{x}.\ \ S \to \left(P \geq 0\ \wedge\ \mathfrak{L}_f(P) \leq -\varepsilon\right) \qquad X_0, \neg X_T \vdash S \qquad \vdash S \to [\dot{\boldsymbol{x}} = f(\boldsymbol{x})\ \&\ \neg(H \wedge X_T)]\ S \qquad X_0 \vee S \vdash H}{\vdash X_0 \to \langle \dot{\boldsymbol{x}} = f(\boldsymbol{x})\ \&\ H \rangle\ X_T}.$$

Proof. Corollary to Prop. 8. The sufficient duration proviso is soundness-critical (see [26, Counterexample 9] for an example of why this is important). A stronger requirement, e.g. Lipschitz continuity of f (if not globally, then within some compact subset of $\mathbb{R}^n$ containing X_T and S) may be used to give a formal criterion for ensuring the proviso holds, but this can be restrictive in practice. □

Example 11 (System with limit cycle and equilibrium). Consider the system of ODEs with an equilibrium and a limit cycle

$$\dot{x}_1 = x_2 - x_1\left(x_1^2 + x_2^2 - 1\right), \quad \dot{x}_2 = -x_1 - x_2\left(x_1^2 + x_2^2 - 1\right),$$

with $H \equiv x_1 \leq 2 \wedge x_1 \geq -2 \wedge x_2 \leq 2 \wedge x_2 \geq -2$ and let the initial set of states and the target region be as follows:

$$X_0 \equiv x_2 > 0 \wedge x_1 \geq -\frac{1}{4} \wedge x_1 \leq \frac{1}{4} \wedge (x_1^2 + x_2^2 - 1)^2 \leq \frac{1}{30},$$
$$X_T \equiv x_2 < 0 \wedge x_1 \geq -\frac{1}{4} \wedge x_1 \leq \frac{1}{4} \wedge (x_1^2 + x_2^2 - 1)^2 \leq \frac{1}{30}.$$

Consider also the following sets (depicted in Fig. 2):

$$S_1 \equiv \neg X_T \wedge x_1 \geq -\frac{1}{4} \wedge (x_1^2 + x_2^2 - 1)^2 \leq \frac{1}{30},$$
$$S_2 \equiv \neg X_0 \wedge x_1 \leq \frac{1}{4} \wedge (x_1^2 + x_2^2 - 1)^2 \leq \frac{1}{30}.$$

One may check using a decision procedure that S_1 is indeed a staging set for this system.

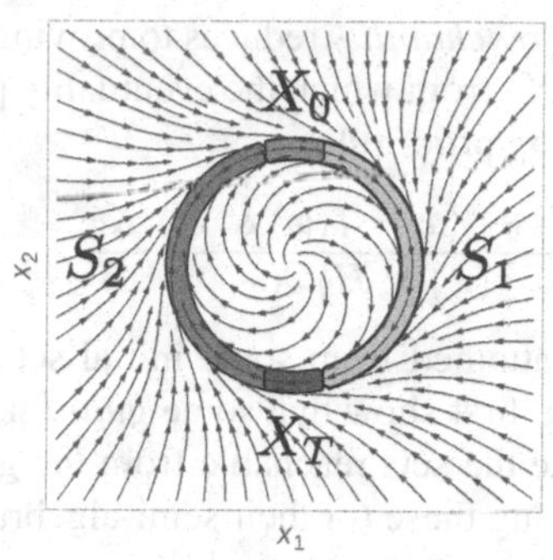

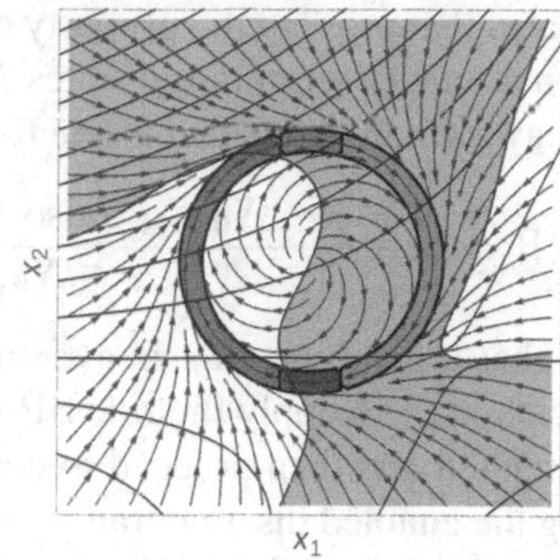

Fig. 2. **(left)** Initial states X_0 (in green), target region X_T (in red) and staging sets S_1 (in grey and green, i.e. S_1 includes X_0) and S_2 (dark grey and red, i.e. S_2 includes X_T). **(right)** Level sets of the progress function P_1 for showing eventual exit out of S_1 and the region where $\exists\, \varepsilon > 0.\ \mathfrak{L}_f(P_1) \le -\varepsilon$ holds (includes S_1; shaded in blue).

A possible progress function for S_1 is $P_1(\boldsymbol{x}) = -\left(x_1 - \frac{6}{5}\right)^2 + (x_1 - x_2 - 2)^2 + 10$. Computing the total derivative of P_1 (i.e. Lie derivative with respect to the vector field) we obtain $\mathfrak{L}_f(P_1(\boldsymbol{x})) =$

$$2\,(x_1 - x_2 - 2)\left(x_2^3 + x_1^2 x_2 - x_2 + x_1\right) + \frac{2}{5}\,(5x_2 + 4)\left(x_1^3 + \left(x_2^2 - 1\right)x_1 - x_2\right).$$

Using a decision procedure for real arithmetic to check that the sentence

$$\exists\, \varepsilon > 0.\ \forall\, \boldsymbol{x} \in S_1. \quad \mathfrak{L}_f(P_1(\boldsymbol{x})) \le -\varepsilon \ \wedge\ P_1(\boldsymbol{x}) \ge 0$$

is true is sufficient to conclude the eventuality property

$$X_0 \to \langle \dot{x}_1 = x_2 - x_1\left(x_1^2 + x_2^2 - 1\right),\, \dot{x}_2 = -x_1 - x_2\left(x_1^2 + x_2^2 - 1\right)\ \&\ H\rangle\, X_T$$

using the proof rule SP with S_1 as the staging set and P_1 acting as the progress function. Similarly, one may instead take X_T to be the initial set of states and X_0 to be the target region. By using S_2 as a staging set and taking the progress function

$$P_2(\boldsymbol{x}) = -\left(-x_1 - \frac{6}{5}\right)^2 + (-x_1 + x_2 - 2)^2 + 10$$

one may use the proof rule SP, instantiating S_2 and P_2 appropriately, to prove

$$X_T \to \langle \dot{x}_1 = x_2 - x_1\left(x_1^2 + x_2^2 - 1\right),\, \dot{x}_2 = -x_1 - x_2\left(x_1^2 + x_2^2 - 1\right)\ \&\ H\rangle\, X_0.$$

The proof rule SP can be used as part of a formal verification calculus in which liveness properties of hybrid systems are reduced using rules of inference to proving liveness properties for discrete and continuous sub-components. When working in a proof calculus, the following proof rule, formalizing the transitivity of the eventuality relation between sets of states, is often convenient:

$$(\langle\rangle\ \text{Trans})\ \frac{\vdash X_0 \to \langle \dot{\boldsymbol{x}} = f(\boldsymbol{x})\ \&\ H\rangle\, T \qquad \vdash T \to \langle \dot{\boldsymbol{x}} = f(\boldsymbol{x})\ \&\ H\rangle\, X_T}{\vdash X_0 \to \langle \dot{\boldsymbol{x}} = f(\boldsymbol{x})\ \&\ H\rangle\, X_T}.$$

Let us note also that proving the property of *set reachability* reduces to proving the existence of a non-empty set of initial states $R \subseteq X_0$ from which the eventuality property holds. We may formalize this fact in the following proof rule:

$$\text{(Reach)}\ \frac{\vdash R \wedge X_0 \not\equiv_{\mathbb{R}} \text{False} \quad \vdash R \rightarrow \langle \dot{\boldsymbol{x}} = f(\boldsymbol{x})\ \&\ H\rangle\ X_T}{\vdash \exists\, \boldsymbol{x} \in X_0.\ \langle \dot{\boldsymbol{x}} = f(\boldsymbol{x})\ \&\ H\rangle\ X_T}.$$

To show that a given set X_T is eventually attained from some initial set X_0 in a hybrid system, one can apply the rule SP to e.g. first show that some *guard set* within a mode is attained and then proceed to compute the sets reachable from the guard set by following the enabled discrete transitions, using these (or their semi-algebraic over-approximation) as the new initial sets in subsequent applications of SP.

The next section will discuss the relationship between SP and an existing proof method called *differential induction* using *differential variants* [26] that is part of the logic $d\mathcal{L}$ and has been applied to hybrid system liveness verification problems.

5 Non-differentiable Progress Functions

In this section we will use directional differentiability properties of the min max functional with differentiable arguments [8,10] to broaden the class of progress functions at our disposal and discuss how this generalizes the definition of total derivative for *formulas* that was used for *differential variants* in [26]. We will also show how the proof rule SP serves to remove certain limitations inherent in differential variants.

5.1 Derivatives of Formulas and Differential Variants

Differential induction using differential variants (and differential invariants) is a direct proof method introduced by Platzer in [26] for proving eventuality (invariance) properties in ODEs, as part of a verification calculus for hybrid systems. The method allows one to work with arbitrary semi-algebraic sets represented by quantifier-free formulas. In order to work in this general setting, differential induction requires the notion of total derivative to be lifted to formulas, which is achieved through the use of the derivation operator D (see [26, Def. 13]); it is given as follows: $D(r) = 0$ for numbers, $D(x) = \dot{x}$ for variables, $D(a + b) = D(a) + D(b)$, where a, b stand for numbers or variables, $D(a \cdot b) = D(a) \cdot b + a \cdot D(b)$ (product rule), $D\left(\frac{a}{b}\right) = \frac{D(a) \cdot b - a \cdot D(b)}{b^2}$ (quotient rule),

$$\begin{aligned} D(F \wedge G) &\equiv D(F) \wedge D(G), && \text{for quantifier-free formulas } F \text{ and } G,\\ D(F \vee G) &\equiv D(F) \wedge D(G), && \wedge \text{ needed for soundness in proving invariance [26]}\\ D(a \le b) &\equiv D(a) \le D(b), && \text{accordingly for } \ge, >, <, = . \end{aligned}$$

The formula $(D(F) \geq \varepsilon)_{\dot{\boldsymbol{x}}}^{f(\boldsymbol{x})}$ is obtained by applying the derivation operator to formula F, performing a substitution where each $\dot{x}_i$ in $D(F)$ is replaced with the corresponding right-hand side in the differential equation and replacing all inequalities $a \geq b$ by $a \geq b + \varepsilon$ (accordingly for $<, \leq, >$; see [26, Section 4.6]).

$$\text{(DV)}\ \frac{\vdash \exists\, \varepsilon > 0 (\neg X_T \wedge H \rightarrow (D(X_T) \geq \varepsilon)_{\dot{\boldsymbol{x}}}^{f(\boldsymbol{x})})}{[\dot{\boldsymbol{x}} = f(\boldsymbol{x})\ \&\ {\sim} X_T] H \vdash \langle \dot{\boldsymbol{x}} = f(\boldsymbol{x})\ \&\ H\rangle X_T}$$

The formula $\sim X_T$ is the *weak negation* of X_T [26, Section 4.6] defined by the negation of X_T in which every strict inequality is made non-strict. Formulas X_T provable using the rule DV [4] are called differential variants. Like our proof rule SP, the rule DV may be applied under the proviso that solutions are of sufficient duration (see [26, Section 4.7]).

In practice, DV is rather conservative because it is incapable of proving eventuality properties for target regions described by equations [26, Counterexample 7]. In Example 12 we demonstrate a simple proof of such a property using staging sets and progress functions.

Example 12 (Target region with equational description). Let the dynamics be given by the non-linear system $\dot{x}_1 = -1, \dot{x}_2 = (x_2 - x_1)^2$, $H = \mathbb{R}^2$ and consider a target region described an equation $X_T \equiv x_2 - x_1 = 0$ (see Fig. 3).

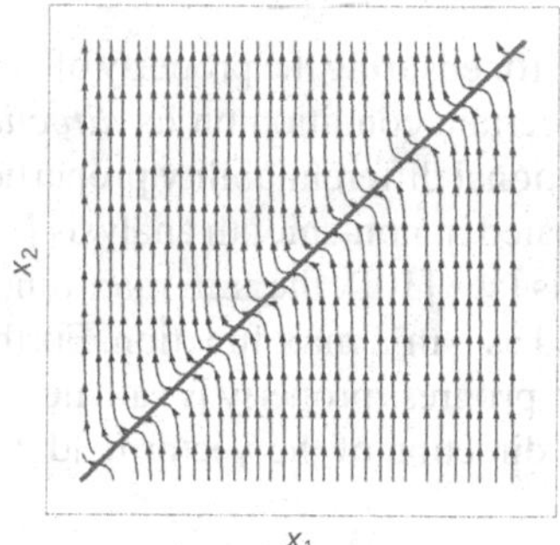

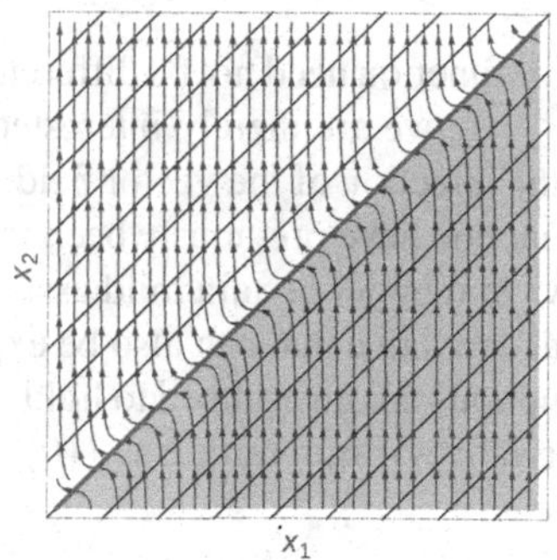

Fig. 3. (left) Target region $X_T \equiv x_2 - x_1 = 0$ (in red) and any initial set such that $X_0 \rightarrow x_2 - x_1 < 0$ (anywhere below the red line, not shown). **(right)** Staging set $S \equiv x_2 - x_1 < 0$ (in grey) and level sets of the progress function $P(\boldsymbol{x}) = -(x_2 - x_1)$.

Suppose the initial set of states X_0 is any subset of $\{\boldsymbol{x} \in \mathbb{R}^2 \mid x_2 - x_1 < 0\}$. To show the eventuality property let us take $S \equiv x_2 - x_1 < 0$, which can be easily shown to be a staging set, and use $P(\boldsymbol{x}) = -(x_2 - x_1)$ as a progress function. The total derivative of P is given by $\mathfrak{L}_f(P(\boldsymbol{x})) = -(x_2 - x_1)^2 - 1$, which satisfies the ε-progress property inside the staging set S. An application of the rule SP proves the property $X_0 \rightarrow \langle \dot{x}_1 = -1, \dot{x}_2 = (x_2 - x_1)^2 \;\&\; H \rangle X_T$.

In general, finding an appropriate progress function P for use with the rule SP can be rather non-trivial; however, sometimes the description of the target region itself may suggest a progress function. Indeed, this is how the rule DV checks the ε-progress property towards the target region: by considering the total derivative of the formula giving the target region itself. This is not guaranteed to work even if the eventuality property is true, but one may think of DV as generating a "progress formula" from the description of the target region. Because DV relies on the derivation operator D for its notion of ε-progress for formulas, the resulting conditions are very strong. In what follows, we will seek to relax them, while still using the description of the target region to suggest a progress function that can be used with our proof method.

[4] Note that X_T is required to define a closed set for the rule DV to be sound.

5.2 Non-differentiable Progress Functions

Given a quantifier-free formula X_T characterizing a semi-algebraic set, the weak negation of its negation, $\sim\neg X_T$ ($\sim$ defined as for DV), gives a formula characterizing a *closed* semi-algebraic set that over-approximates the closure of X_T. Note that any closed semi-algebraic set can always be put into the form

$$\bigvee_{i=1}^{n} \bigwedge_{j=1}^{m(i)} p_{ij} \leq 0,$$

where p_{ij} are polynomials. The set of states satisfying such a formula can equivalently be expressed as a sub-level set of a continuous function, i.e.

$$\min_{i \in [1,n]} \max_{j \in [1,m(i)]} p_{ij} \leq 0.$$

Although this function need not be differentiable, for ensuring the property of ε-progress, viz. $\mathfrak{L}_f(\cdot) \leq -\varepsilon$, we are merely interested in a certain condition on its *directional derivative* in the direction of the vector field. Directional differentiability properties of the min max function have previously been investigated in non-smooth analysis [10,8] and it was shown that under certain mild assumptions (see [10]), the min max function has a directional derivative that can also be expressed as a min max function. Furthermore, these assumptions are guaranteed to hold if the ε-progress property is satisfied. The directional derivative of min max (see [10]) in the direction of the vector field f, may be used to define

$$\mathfrak{L}_f(\min_{i \in [1,n]} \max_{j \in [1,m(i)]} p_{ij}) = \min_{i \in I_*} \max_{j \in J_*} \left(\mathfrak{L}_f(p_{ij})\right),$$

where p_{ij} are differentiable real-valued functions and

$$J_* = \{j_* \in [1, m(i)] \mid p_{ij_*} = \max_{j \in [1,m(i)]} (p_{ij})\},$$

$$I_* = \{i_* \in [1, n] \mid p_{i_* j} = \min_{i \in [1,n]} \max_{j \in [1,m(i)]} (p_{ij})\}.$$

The above definition may at first sight appear rather opaque; the following illustrative example is useful in exposing some of the intuition.

Example 13. Suppose that we have a formula $F \equiv p_1 \leq 0 \wedge p_2 \leq 0$. Then we have $F \equiv_{\mathbb{R}} \max(p_1, p_2) \leq 0$ and the directional derivative along f given by

$$\mathfrak{L}_f \max(p_1, p_2) = \begin{cases} \mathfrak{L}_f(p_1) & p_1 > p_2 \\ \mathfrak{L}_f(p_2) & p_2 > p_1 \\ \max(\mathfrak{L}_f(p_1), \mathfrak{L}_f(p_2)) & p_1 = p_2 \end{cases}$$

Intuitively, when there is only one differentiable "active component" (i.e. a function p_j which evaluates to the same value as the whole max function), the directional derivative is simply given by $\mathfrak{L}_f(p_j)$; however, when there are many, the index set J_* contains more than one element and the directional derivative is given by $\max_{j \in J_*} \mathfrak{L}_f(p_j)$

where all p_j are currently active. More generally, once the directional derivative of $\min\max p_{ij}$ is computed and an ε-progress condition is imposed, the resulting expression will feature conditionals involving min, max, ε and p_{ij}s and can thus be converted back into a formula giving precisely the conditions for the ε-progress of the min max function. The resulting formulas will often be long and unwieldy, but for this simple example we can write the condition in full:

$$\begin{aligned}\mathfrak{L}_f \max(p_1, p_2) \leq -\varepsilon \equiv\ & (p_1 > p_2 \rightarrow \mathfrak{L}_f(p_1) \leq -\varepsilon) \\ \wedge\ & (p_2 > p_1 \rightarrow \mathfrak{L}_f(p_2) \leq -\varepsilon) \\ \wedge\ & (p_1 = p_2 \rightarrow \\ & \quad (\mathfrak{L}_f(p_1) \geq \mathfrak{L}_f(p_2) \rightarrow \mathfrak{L}_f(p_1) \leq -\varepsilon) \wedge \\ & \quad (\mathfrak{L}_f(p_1) < \mathfrak{L}_f(p_2) \rightarrow \mathfrak{L}_f(p_2) \leq -\varepsilon)\ ).\end{aligned}$$

Similarly, if one wanted to impose the ε-progress property towards the formula $F \equiv p_1 \leq 0 \vee p_2 \leq 0$, encoded as $F \equiv_{\mathbb{R}} \min(p_1, p_2) \leq 0$, one would obtain

$$\begin{aligned}\mathfrak{L}_f \min(p_1, p_2) \leq -\varepsilon \equiv\ & (p_1 < p_2 \rightarrow \mathfrak{L}_f(p_1) \leq -\varepsilon) \\ \wedge\ & (p_2 < p_1 \rightarrow \mathfrak{L}_f(p_2) \leq -\varepsilon) \\ \wedge\ & (p_1 = p_2 \rightarrow \\ & \quad (\mathfrak{L}_f(p_1) \leq \mathfrak{L}_f(p_2) \rightarrow \mathfrak{L}_f(p_1) \leq -\varepsilon) \wedge \\ & \quad (\mathfrak{L}_f(p_1) > \mathfrak{L}_f(p_2) \rightarrow \mathfrak{L}_f(p_2) \leq -\varepsilon)\ ).\end{aligned}$$

By nesting these definitions appropriately, using facts such as e.g. $\min(p_1, p_2, p_3) = \min(p_1, \min(p_2, p_3))$, one can arrive at ε-progress conditions for more complicated closed semi-algebraic sets.

Remark 14. Similar tools and ideas have been employed in sufficient conditions for positive invariance of certain sets with non-smooth boundaries (e.g. *practical sets* in [5] and closed semi-algebraic sets [34]). These approaches are based on Nagumo's theorem [20] and require computing/under-approximating the *contingent cone*, which can be defined in terms of limits of directional derivatives. The interested reader is invited to consult [10] for a more detailed exposition of the technical assumptions used in formulating the directional derivative of min max.

Example 15 (Non-differentiable progress function). Consider the continuous system $\dot{x}_1 = -x_1, \dot{x}_2 = -x_2, H = \mathbb{R}^2$ and let the target set of states correspond to a 2×2 box centred at the origin, i.e. $X_T \equiv x_1 \leq 1 \wedge x_1 \geq -1 \wedge x_2 \leq 1 \wedge x_2 \geq -1$. From the phase portrait in Fig. 4 (left) it is clear that the eventuality property is true, i.e. by starting the system outside the box, we are guaranteed to eventually enter the box by following the flow.

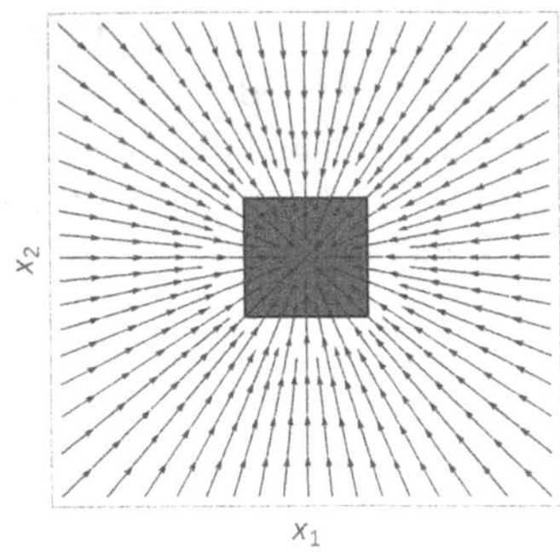

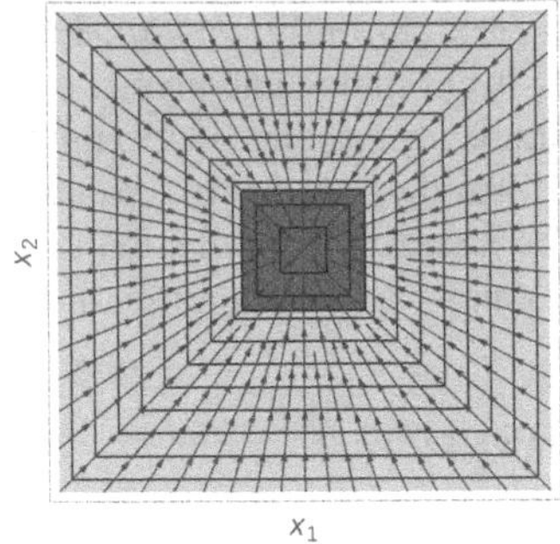

Fig. 4. (**left**) Phase portrait, target set X_T (in red). (**right**) Level curves of a non-differentiable progress function (black) and a staging set $S \equiv \neg X_T$ (grey).

This property cannot be proved directly using the rule DV because the definition of the derivation operator for formulas requires one to show that *each* conjunct is a differential variant. In this case,

$$D(X_T) \geq \varepsilon \equiv \dot{x}_1 \leq \varepsilon \wedge \dot{x}_1 \geq \varepsilon \wedge \dot{x}_2 \leq \varepsilon \wedge \dot{x}_2 \geq \varepsilon.$$

Upon substituting the dynamics, this leads to unsatisfiable conditions (since $\varepsilon > 0$):

$$(D(X_T) \geq \varepsilon)_{\dot{\boldsymbol{x}}}^{f(\boldsymbol{x})} \equiv -x_1 \leq \varepsilon \wedge -x_1 \geq \varepsilon \wedge -x_2 \leq \varepsilon \wedge -x_2 \geq \varepsilon \equiv_{\mathbb{R}} \text{False}.$$

Instead, one may write down the formula for the box as a sub-level set, i.e.

$$X_T \equiv \max(x_1 - 1, -x_1 - 1, x_2 - 1, -x_2 - 1) \leq 0$$

and taking the complement of X_T to be the staging set, i.e. $S \equiv \neg X_T$, check that

$$\exists\, \varepsilon > 0.\, \forall \boldsymbol{x} \in S. \big(\max(x_1 - 1, -x_1 - 1, x_2 - 1, -x_2 - 1) \geq 0 \\ \wedge\ \mathfrak{L}_f \max(x_1 - 1, -x_1 - 1, x_2 - 1, -x_2 - 1) \leq -\varepsilon \big)$$

is valid, which is sufficient to conclude the eventuality property for any $X_0 \subseteq S$.

6 Related Work

Prajna and Rantzer investigated automatic verification of eventuality properties for ODEs in [30]; their approach ensures that evolution occurs within the domain constraint by imposing extra constraints on the function used to demonstrate progress along the solutions. Furthermore, the ε-progress property is required to hold everywhere outside the target region. System equilibria lying outside the target region present a problem for this approach and need to be manually removed from the evolution domain. Ratschan and She introduced set-Lyapunov functions to study attraction to target regions in [31], considering only bounded domains and also imposing conditions for ensuring progress along the solutions everywhere outside the target region, which suffers from the same problem. The proof method we have proposed works with a more general class of eventuality verification problems (as it makes fewer assumptions about the problem statement and the nature of the system) and can handle systems with equilibria outside the target region by appropriately over-approximating the reachable set using staging sets.

Our approach is fundamentally different from that used by Platzer in [26], e.g. allowing target regions with equational descriptions (among other things; see Section 5).

Ideas broadly similar to staging sets were explored by Stiver et al. in [33] using *common flow regions*. Informally, common flow regions are sets bounded by invariant manifolds and an "exit boundary". The conditions given in [33] require the target and the common flow regions to be given by a conjunction of sub-level sets of smooth functions and the defining polynomials (except the exit boundary) to be conserved quantities of the system. Conditions for staging sets are more general and less conservative.

Lastly, unlike previous approaches, we completely decouple the progress property (using progress functions) from conditions for over-approximating the reachable set of the system (using staging sets).

7 Conclusion

In this paper we have presented a very general proof principle for eventuality properties of continuous systems governed by polynomial ODEs under semi-algebraic evolution constraints that works without computing the solutions and can be shown to both extend and generalize previous approaches in [30,31,26,33]. We have presented a formalization of our method in a proof rule (SP) which is very well suited for use as part of a formal verification calculus for hybrid systems.

Our work addressed some important theoretical limitations inherent in available methods for eventuality verification; however, much future work remains before scalable formal verification tools can emerge and be applied in practice to large, industrially relevant verification problems. The two most important practical obstacles are manifested in the current dearth of scalable methods for continuous invariant (staging set) generation and limited tool support for searching for progress functions. As we have discussed, searching for staging sets is no different to generating continuous invariants, so improved invariant generation tools developed for safety verification of continuous systems can be applied to search for staging sets. Automatically generating progress functions is likewise a difficult problem and would greatly benefit from improved tools for non-linear optimization. We should note that these problems are pervasive in direct methods and are not limited to safety and liveness verification. In the control and dynamical systems community, direct methods for proving the property of *stability* [19] are considered standard, but do not provide the means of computing the stability-proving (Lyapunov) function; this task is delegated to the user and is the focus of much ongoing work to facilitate their automatic discovery (see e.g. [24]).

Acknowledgements. The authors would like to thank Dr. Khalil Ghorbal at Carnegie Mellon University for his detailed technical scrutiny and suggestions for improving an early version of this work, Dr. André Platzer at the same institution for kindly responding to our query concerning the method of differential variants and extend special thanks to the anonymous reviewers for their diligent reading and valuable feedback.

References

1. Alpern, B., Schneider, F.B.: Defining liveness. Information Processing Letters 21(4), 181–185 (1985)
2. Berz, M., Makino, K.: Verified integration of ODEs and flows using differential algebraic methods on high-order Taylor models. Reliable Computing 4(4), 361–369 (1998)
3. Bhatia, N.P., Szegő, G.P.: Stability Theory of Dynamical Systems. Die Grundlehren der mathematischen Wissenschaften in Einzeldarstellungen mit besonderer Berücksichtigung der Anwendungsgebiete, vol. 161. Springer (1970)
4. Blanchini, F.: Set invariance in control. Automatica 35(11), 1747–1767 (1999)
5. Blanchini, F., Miani, S.: Set-Theoretic Methods in Control. Systems & Control: Foundations & Applications. Birkhäuser (2008)
6. Collins, G.E.: Hauptvortrag: Quantifier elimination for real closed fields by cylindrical algebraic decomposition. In: Brakhage, H. (ed.) GI-Fachtagung 1975. LNCS, vol. 33, pp. 134–183. Springer, Heidelberg (1975)
7. Davenport, J.H., Heintz, J.: Real quantifier elimination is doubly exponential. J. Symb. Comput. 5(1/2), 29–35 (1988)
8. Demyanov, V.F.: The solution of minimaximin problems. USSR Computational Mathematics and Mathematical Physics 10(3), 44–55 (1970)
9. Dolzmann, A., Sturm, T., Weispfenning, V.: Real Quantifier Elimination in Practice. In: Algorithmic Algebra and Number Theory, pp. 221–247 (1998)
10. Ekici, E.: On the directional differentiability properties of the max-min function. Boletín de la Asociación Matemática Venezolana X(1), 35–42 (2003)
11. Fehnker, A., Krogh, B.H.: Hybrid system verification is not a sinecure. In: Wang, F. (ed.) ATVA 2004. LNCS, vol. 3299, pp. 263–277. Springer, Heidelberg (2004)
12. Ghorbal, K., Platzer, A.: Characterizing algebraic invariants by differential radical invariants. In: Ábrahám, E., Havelund, K. (eds.) TACAS 2014. LNCS, vol. 8413, pp. 279–294. Springer, Heidelberg (2014)
13. Henzinger, T.A.: The theory of hybrid automata. In: Proceedings, 11th Annual IEEE Symposium on Logic in Computer Science, pp. 278–292 (1996)
14. Immler, F.: Formally verified computation of enclosures of solutions of ordinary differential equations. In: Badger, J.M., Rozier, K.Y. (eds.) NFM 2014. LNCS, vol. 8430, pp. 113–127. Springer, Heidelberg (2014)
15. Immler, F.: Verified reachability analysis of continuous systems. In: Baier, C., Tinelli, C. (eds.) TACAS 2015. LNCS, vol. 9035, pp. 37–51. Springer, Heidelberg (2015)
16. Lamport, L.: Proving the correctness of multiprocess programs. IEEE Transactions on Software Engineering 3(2), 125–143 (1977)
17. Liu, J., Lv, J., Quan, Z., Zhan, N., Zhao, H., Zhou, C., Zou, L.: A calculus for hybrid CSP. In: Ueda, K. (ed.) APLAS 2010. LNCS, vol. 6461, pp. 1–15. Springer, Heidelberg (2010)
18. Liu, J., Zhan, N., Zhao, H.: Computing semi-algebraic invariants for polynomial dynamical systems. In: Chakraborty, S., Jerraya, A., Baruah, S.K., Fischmeister, S. (eds.) EMSOFT, pp. 97–106. ACM (2011)
19. Lyapunov, A.M.: The general problem of stability of motion. Kharkov Mathematical Society, Kharkov (1892)
20. Nagumo, M.: Über die Lage der Integralkurven gewöhnlicher Differentialgleichungen. In: Proceedings of the Physico-Mathematical Society of Japan, vol. 24, pp. 551–559 (May 1942)
21. Navarro-López, E.M., Carter, R.: Hybrid automata: an insight into the discrete abstraction of discontinuous systems. International Journal of Systems Science 42(11), 1883–1898 (2011)
22. Neher, M., Jackson, K.R., Nedialkov, N.S.: On Taylor model based integration of ODEs. SIAM Journal on Numerical Analysis 45(1), 236–262 (2007)

23. Owicki, S., Lamport, L.: Proving liveness properties of concurrent programs. ACM Transactions on Programming Languages and Systems (TOPLAS) 4(3), 455–495 (1982)
24. Parrilo, P.A.: Structured semidefinite programs and semialgebraic geometry methods in robustness and optimization. Engineering and applied science, control and dynamical systems, California Institute of Technology (May 2000)
25. Platzer, A.: Differential dynamic logic for hybrid systems. J. Autom. Reasoning 41(2), 143–189 (2008)
26. Platzer, A.: Differential-algebraic dynamic logic for differential-algebraic programs. J. Log. Comput. 20(1), 309–352 (2010)
27. Platzer, A., Clarke, E.M.: Computing differential invariants of hybrid systems as fixedpoints. In: Gupta, A., Malik, S. (eds.) CAV 2008. LNCS, vol. 5123, pp. 176–189. Springer, Heidelberg (2008)
28. Poincaré, H.: Mémoire sur les courbes définies par une équation différentielle. Journal de Mathématiques Pures et Appliquées 7, 3, 4, 375–422, 251–296, 167–224 (1881, 1882, 1885)
29. Prajna, S., Jadbabaie, A.: Safety verification of hybrid systems using barrier certificates. In: Alur, R., Pappas, G.J. (eds.) HSCC 2004. LNCS, vol. 2993, pp. 477–492. Springer, Heidelberg (2004)
30. Prajna, S., Rantzer, A.: Primal–dual tests for safety and reachability. In: Morari, M., Thiele, L. (eds.) HSCC 2005. LNCS, vol. 3414, pp. 542–556. Springer, Heidelberg (2005)
31. Ratschan, S., She, Z.: Providing a basin of attraction to a target region of polynomial systems by computation of Lyapunov-like functions. SIAM J. Control Optim. 48(7), 4377–4394 (2010)
32. Richardson, D.: Some undecidable problems involving elementary functions of a real variable. Journal of Symbolic Logic 33(4), 514–520 (1968)
33. Stiver, J.A., Koutsoukos, X.D., Antsaklis, P.J.: An invariant-based approach to the design of hybrid control systems. International Journal of Robust and Nonlinear Control 11(5), 453–478 (2001)
34. Taly, A., Tiwari, A.: Deductive verification of continuous dynamical systems. In: Kannan, R., Kumar, K.N. (eds.) FSTTCS. LIPIcs, vol. 4, pp. 383–394. Schloss Dagstuhl - Leibniz-Zentrum für Informatik (2009)
35. Tarski, A.: A decision method for elementary algebra and geometry. Bulletin of the American Mathematical Society 59 (1951)
36. Wang, T.C., Lall, S., West, M.: Polynomial level-set method for polynomial system reachable set estimation. IEEE Transactions on Automatic Control 58(10), 2508–2521 (2013)

Rigorous Estimation of Floating-Point Round-off Errors with Symbolic Taylor Expansions

Alexey Solovyev(✉), Charles Jacobsen,
Zvonimir Rakamarić, and Ganesh Gopalakrishnan

School of Computing, University of Utah, Salt Lake City, UT, 84112, USA
{monad,charlesj,zvonimir,ganesh}@cs.utah.edu

Abstract. Rigorous estimation of maximum floating-point round-off errors is an important capability central to many formal verification tools. Unfortunately, available techniques for this task often provide overestimates. Also, there are no available rigorous approaches that handle transcendental functions. We have developed a new approach called *Symbolic Taylor Expansions* that avoids this difficulty, and implemented a new tool called FPTaylor embodying this approach. Key to our approach is the use of rigorous global optimization, instead of the more familiar interval arithmetic, affine arithmetic, and/or SMT solvers. In addition to providing far tighter upper bounds of round-off error in a vast majority of cases, FPTaylor also emits analysis certificates in the form of HOL Light proofs. We release FPTaylor along with our benchmarks for evaluation.

Keywords: Floating-point · Round-off error analysis · Global optimization

1 Introduction

Many algorithms are conceived (and even formally verified) in real numbers, but ultimately deployed using floating-point numbers. Unfortunately, the finitary nature of floating-point, along with its uneven distribution of representable numbers introduces round-off errors, as well as does not preserve many familiar laws (e.g., associativity of +) [22]. This mismatch often necessitates re-verification using tools that precisely compute round-off error bounds (e.g., as illustrated in [21]). While SMT solvers can be used for small problems [52,24], the need to scale necessitates the use of various abstract interpretation methods [11], the most popular choices being interval [41] or affine arithmetic [55]. However, these tools very often generate pessimistic error bounds, especially when nonlinear functions are involved. No tool that is currently maintained rigorously handles transcendental functions that arise in problems such as the safe separation of aircraft [20].

Key to Our Approach. In a nutshell, the aforesaid difficulties arise because of a tool's attempt to abstract the "difficult" (nonlinear or transcendental) functions. Our new approach called *Symbolic Taylor Expansions* (realized in a tool

N. Bjørner and F. de Boer (Eds.): FM 2015, LNCS 9109, pp. 532–550, 2015.
DOI: 10.1007/978-3-319-19249-9_33

FPTaylor) side-steps these issues entirely as follows. (1) We view round-off errors as "noise," and compute Taylor expansions in a symbolic form. (2) In these symbolic Taylor forms, all difficult functional expressions appear as symbolic coefficients; they do not need to be abstracted. (3) We then apply a *rigorous* global maximization method that has no trouble handling the difficult functions and can be executed sufficiently fast thanks to the ability to trade off accuracy for performance.

Let us illustrate these ideas using a simple example. First, we define *absolute round-off error* as $err_{\mathsf{abs}} = |\tilde{v} - v|$, where $\tilde{v}$ is the result of floating-point computations and v is the result of corresponding exact mathematical computations. Now, consider the estimation of worst case absolute round-off error in $t/(t+1)$ computed with floating-point arithmetic where $t \in [0, 999]$ is a floating-point number. (Our goal here is to demonstrate basic ideas of our method; pertinent background is in Sect. 2.) Let $\oslash$ and $\oplus$ denote floating-point operations corresponding to / and +.

Suppose interval abstraction were used to analyze this example. The round-off error of $t \oplus 1$ can be estimated by 512ϵ where ϵ is the machine epsilon (which bounds the maximum relative error of basic floating-point operations such as $\oplus$ and $\oslash$) and the number $512 = 2^9$ is the largest power of 2 which is less than $1000 = 999 + 1$. Interval abstraction replaces the expression $d = t \oplus 1$ with the abstract pair $([1, 1000], 512\epsilon)$ where the first component is the interval of all possible values of d and 512ϵ is the associated round-off error. Now we need to calculate the round-off error of $t \oslash d$. It can be shown that one of the primary sources of errors in this expression is attributable to the propagation of error in $t \oplus 1$ into the division operator. The propagated error is computed by multiplying the error in $t \oplus 1$ by $\frac{t}{d^2}$.[1] At this point, interval abstraction does not yield a satisfactory result since it computes $\frac{t}{d^2}$ by setting the numerator t to 999 and the denominator d to 1. Therefore, the total error bound is computed as $999 \times 512\epsilon \approx 512000\epsilon$.

The main weakness of the interval abstraction is that it does not preserve variable relationships (e.g., the two t's may be independently set to 999 and 0). In the example above, the abstract representation of d was too coarse to yield a good final error bound (we suffer from eager composition of abstractions). While affine arithmetic is more precise since it remembers linear dependencies between variables, it still does not handle our example well as it contains division, a nonlinear operator (for which affine arithmetic is known to be a poor fit).

A better approach is to *model the error at each subexpression position* and *globally solve for maximal error*—as opposed to merging the worst-cases of local abstractions, as happens in the interval abstraction usage above. Following this approach, a simple way to get a much better error estimate is the following. Consider a simple model for floating-point arithmetic. Write $t \oplus 1 = (t+1)(1+\epsilon_1)$ and $t \oslash (t \oplus 1) = (t/(t \oplus 1))(1 + \epsilon_2)$ with $|\epsilon_1| \le \epsilon$ and $|\epsilon_2| \le \epsilon$. Now, compute

[1] Ignoring the round-off division error, one can view $t \oslash d$ as $t/(d_{\mathsf{exact}} + \delta)$ where δ is the round-off error in d. Apply Taylor approximation which yields as the first two terms $(t/d_{\mathsf{exact}}) - (t/(d^2_{\mathsf{exact}}))\delta$.

the first order Taylor approximation of our expression with respect to ϵ_1 and ϵ_2 by taking ϵ_1 and ϵ_2 as the perturbations around t, and computing partial derivatives with respect to them (see (4) and (5) for a recap):

$$t \oslash (t \oplus 1) = \frac{t(1+\epsilon_2)}{(t+1)(1+\epsilon_1)} = \frac{t}{t+1} - \frac{t}{t+1}\epsilon_1 + \frac{t}{t+1}\epsilon_2 + O(\epsilon^2) \ .$$

(Here $t \in [0, 999]$ is fixed and hence we do not divide by zero.) It is important to keep all coefficients in the above Taylor expansion as symbolic expressions depending on the input variable t. The difference between $t/(t+1)$ and $t \oslash (t \oplus 1)$ can be easily estimated (we ignore the term $O(\epsilon^2)$ in this motivating example but later in Sect. 3 we demonstrate how rigorous upper bounds are derived for all error terms):

$$\left| -\frac{t}{t+1}\epsilon_1 + \frac{t}{t+1}\epsilon_2 \right| \le \left|\frac{t}{t+1}\right||\epsilon_1| + \left|\frac{t}{t+1}\right||\epsilon_2| \le 2\left|\frac{t}{t+1}\right|\epsilon \ .$$

The only remaining task now is finding a bound for the expression $t/(t+1)$ for all $t \in [0, 999]$. Simple interval computations as above yield $t/(t+1) \in [0, 999]$. The error can now be estimated by 1998ϵ, which is already a much better bound than before. We go even further and apply a global optimization procedure to maximize $t/(t+1)$ and compute an even better bound, i.e., $t/(t+1) \le 1$ for all $t \in [0, 999]$. Thus, the error is bounded by 2ϵ.

Our combination of Taylor expansion with symbolic coefficients and global optimization yields an error bound which is $512000/2 = 256000$ times better than a naïve error estimation technique implemented in many other tools for floating-point analysis. Our approach never had to examine the inner details of / and + in our example (these could well be replaced by "difficult" functions; our technique would work the same way). The same cannot be said of SMT or interval/affine arithmetic. The key enabler is that most rigorous global optimizers deal with a very large class of functions smoothly.

Our Key Contributions:

• We describe all the details of our global optimization approach, as there seems to be a lack of awareness (even misinformation) among some researchers.

• We release an open source version of our tool FPTaylor.[2] FPTaylor handles all basic floating-point operations and all the binary floating-point formats defined in IEEE 754. It is the only tool we know providing guaranteed bounds for transcendental expressions. It handles uncertainties in input variables, supports estimation of relative and absolute round-off errors, provides a rigorous treatment of subnormal numbers, and handles mixed precision.

• For the same problem complexity (i.e., number of input variables and expression size), FPTaylor obtains tighter bounds than state-of-the-art tools in most cases, while incurring comparable runtimes. We also empirically verify that our overapproximations are within a factor of 3.5 of the corresponding underapproximations computed using a recent tool [7].

[2] Available at https://github.com/soarlab/FPTaylor

• FPTaylor has a mode in which it produces HOL Light proof scripts. *This facility actually helped us find a bug in our initial tool version.* It therefore promises to offer a similar safeguard for its future users.

2 Background

Floating-Point Arithmetic. The IEEE 754 standard [28] concisely formalized in (e.g.) [22] defines a binary floating-point number as a triple of sign (0 or 1), significand, and exponent, i.e., (sgn, sig, exp), with numerical value $(-1)^{sgn} \times sig \times 2^{exp}$. The standard defines three general binary formats with sizes of 32, 64, and 128 bits, varying in constraints on the sizes of *sig* and *exp*. The standard also defines special values such as infinities and NaN (not a number). We do not distinguish these values in our work and report them as potential errors.

Rounding plays a central role in defining the semantics of floating-point arithmetic. Denote the set of floating-point numbers (in some fixed format) as $\mathbb{F}$. A rounding operator $\mathrm{rnd} : \mathbb{R} \to \mathbb{F}$ is a function which takes a real number and returns a floating-point number which is closest to the input real number and has some special properties defined by the rounding operator. Common rounding operators are rounding to nearest (ties to even), toward zero, and toward $\pm\infty$. A simple model of rounding is given by the following formula [22]

$$\mathrm{rnd}(x) = x(1 + e) + d \tag{1}$$

where $|e| \leq \epsilon$, $|d| \leq \delta$, and $e \times d = 0$. If x is a symbolic expression, then exact numerical values of e and d are not explicitly defined in most cases. (Values of e and d may be known in some cases; for instance, if we know that x is a sufficiently small integer then $\mathrm{rnd}(x) = x$ and thus $e = d = 0$.) The parameter ϵ specifies the maximal relative error introduced by the given rounding operator. The parameter δ gives the maximal *absolute* error for numbers which are very close to zero (relative error estimation does not work for these small numbers called subnormals). Table 1 shows values of ϵ and δ for the rounding to nearest operator of different floating-point formats. Parameters for other rounding operators can be obtained from Table 1 by multiplying all entries by 2, and (1) does not distinguish between rounding operators toward zero and infinities.

Table 1. Rounding to nearest operator parameters

Precision (bits)	ϵ	δ
single (32)	2^{-24}	2^{-150}
double (64)	2^{-53}	2^{-1075}
quad. (128)	2^{-113}	2^{-16495}

The standard precisely defines the behavior of several basic floating-point arithmetic operations. Suppose $op : \mathbb{R}^k \to \mathbb{R}$ is an operation. Let op_{fp} be the corresponding floating-point operation. Then the operation op_{fp} is exactly rounded if the following equation holds for all floating-point values $x_1, \ldots, x_k$:

$$op_{\mathrm{fp}}(x_1, \ldots, x_k) = \mathrm{rnd}\big(op(x_1, \ldots, x_k)\big) \ . \tag{2}$$

The following operations must be exactly rounded according to the standard: $+, -, \times, /, \sqrt{}, \text{fma}$. (Here, $\text{fma}(a, b, c)$ is a ternary *fused multiply-add* operation that computes $a \times b + c$ with a single rounding.)

Combining (1) and (2), we get a simple model of floating-point arithmetic which is valid in the absence of overflows and invalid operations:

$$op_{\text{fp}}(x_1, \dots, x_k) = op(x_1, \dots, x_k)(1 + e) + d \ . \tag{3}$$

There are some special cases where the model given by (3) can be improved. For instance, if *op* is $-$ or $+$ then $d = 0$ [22]. Also, if *op* is $\times$ and one of the arguments is a nonnegative power of two then $e = d = 0$. These and several other special cases are implemented in FPTaylor to improve the quality of the error analysis.

Equation (3) can be used even with operations that are not exactly rounded. For example, most implementations of floating-point transcendental functions are not exactly rounded but they yield results which are very close to exactly rounded results [25]. The technique introduced by Bingham et al. [3] can verify relative error bounds of hardware implementations of transcendental functions. So we can still use (3) to model transcendental functions but we need to increase values of ϵ and δ appropriately. There exist software libraries that exactly compute rounded values of transcendental functions [12,17]. For such libraries, (3) can be applied without any changes.

Taylor Expansion. A Taylor expansion is a well-known formula for approximating an arbitrary sufficiently smooth function with a polynomial expression. In this work, we use the first order Taylor approximation with the second order error term. Higher order Taylor approximations are possible but they lead to complex expressions for second and higher order derivatives and do not give much better approximation results [44]. Suppose $f(x_1, \dots, x_k)$ is a twice continuously differentiable multivariate function on an open convex domain $D \subset \mathbb{R}^k$. For any fixed point $\mathbf{a} \in D$ (we use bold symbols to represent vectors) the following formula holds (for example, see Theorem 3.3.1 in [39])

$$f(\mathbf{x}) = f(\mathbf{a}) + \sum_{i=1}^{k} \frac{\partial f}{\partial x_i}(\mathbf{a})(x_i - a_i) + \frac{1}{2} \sum_{i,j=1}^{k} \frac{\partial^2 f}{\partial x_i \partial x_j}(\mathbf{p})(x_i - a_i)(x_j - a_j) \ . \tag{4}$$

Here, $\mathbf{p} \in D$ is a point which depends on $\mathbf{x}$ and $\mathbf{a}$.

Later we will consider functions with arguments $\mathbf{x}$ and $\mathbf{e}$ defined by $f(\mathbf{x}, \mathbf{e}) = f(x_1, \dots, x_n, e_1, \dots, e_k)$. We will derive Taylor expansions of these functions with respect to variables $e_1, \dots, e_k$:

$$f(\mathbf{x}, \mathbf{e}) = f(\mathbf{x}, \mathbf{a}) + \sum_{i=1}^{k} \frac{\partial f}{\partial e_i}(\mathbf{x}, \mathbf{a})(e_i - a_i) + R_2(\mathbf{x}, \mathbf{e}) \ . \tag{5}$$

In this expansion, variables $x_1, \dots, x_n$ appear in coefficients $\frac{\partial f}{\partial e_i}$ thereby producing Taylor expansions with symbolic coefficients.

3 Symbolic Taylor Expansions

Given a function $f\colon \mathbb{R}^n \to \mathbb{R}$, the goal of the Symbolic Taylor Expansions approach is to estimate the round-off error when f is realized in floating-point. We assume that the arguments of the function belong to a bounded domain I, i.e., $\mathbf{x} \in I$. The domain I can be quite arbitrary. The only requirement is that it is bounded and the function f is twice differentiable in some open neighborhood of I. In FPTaylor, the domain I is defined with inequalities over input variables. In the benchmarks presented later, we have $a_i \leq x_i \leq b_i$ for all $i = 1, \ldots, n$. In this case, $I = [a_1, b_1] \times \ldots \times [a_n, b_n]$ is a product of intervals.

Let $\mathrm{fp}(f)\colon \mathbb{R}^n \to \mathbb{F}$ be a function derived from f where all operations, variables, and constants are replaced with the corresponding floating-point operations, variables, and constants. Our goal is to compute the following round-off error:

$$\mathrm{err}_{\mathrm{fp}}(f, I) = \max_{\mathbf{x} \in I} |\mathrm{fp}(f)(\mathbf{x}) - f(\mathbf{x})| \ . \tag{6}$$

The optimization problem (6) is computationally hard and not supported by most classical optimization methods as it involves a highly irregular and discontinuous function $\mathrm{fp}(f)$. The most common way of overcoming such difficulties is to consider abstract models of floating-point arithmetic that approximate floating-point results with real numbers. Section 2 presented the following model of floating-point arithmetic (see (3)):

$$op_{\mathrm{fp}}(x_1, \ldots, x_n) = op(x_1, \ldots, x_n)(1 + e) + d \ .$$

Values of e and d depend on the rounding mode and the operation itself. Special care must be taken in case of exceptions (overflows or invalid operations). Our tool can detect and report such exceptions.

First, we replace all floating-point operations in the function $\mathrm{fp}(f)$ with the right hand side of (3). Constants and variables also need to be replaced with rounded values, unless they can be exactly represented with floating-point numbers. We get a new function $\tilde{f}(\mathbf{x}, \mathbf{e}, \mathbf{d})$ which has all the original arguments $\mathbf{x} = (x_1, \ldots, x_n) \in I$, but also the additional arguments $\mathbf{e} = (e_1, \ldots, e_k)$ and $\mathbf{d} = (d_1, \ldots, d_k)$ where k is the number of potentially inexact floating-point operations (plus constants and variables) in $\mathrm{fp}(f)$. Note that $\tilde{f}(\mathbf{x}, \mathbf{0}, \mathbf{0}) = f(\mathbf{x})$. Also, $\tilde{f}(\mathbf{x}, \mathbf{e}, \mathbf{d}) = \mathrm{fp}(f)(\mathbf{x})$ for some choice of $\mathbf{e}$ and $\mathbf{d}$. Now, the difficult optimization problem (6) can be replaced with the following simpler optimization problem that overapproximates it:

$$\mathrm{err}_{\mathrm{overapprox}}(\tilde{f}, I) = \max_{\mathbf{x} \in I, |e_i| \leq \epsilon, |d_i| \leq \delta} |\tilde{f}(\mathbf{x}, \mathbf{e}, \mathbf{d}) - f(\mathbf{x})| \ . \tag{7}$$

Note that for any I, $\mathrm{err}_{\mathrm{fp}}(f, I) \leq \mathrm{err}_{\mathrm{overapprox}}(\tilde{f}, I)$. However, even this optimization problem is still hard because we have $2k$ new variables e_i and d_i for (inexact) floating-point operations in $\mathrm{fp}(f)$. We further simplify the optimization problem using Taylor expansion.

We know that $|e_i| \le \epsilon$, $|d_i| \le \delta$, and ϵ, δ are small. Define $y_1 = e_1, \dots, y_k = e_k, y_{k+1} = d_1, \dots, y_{2k} = d_k$. Consider the Taylor formula with the second order error term (5) of $\tilde{f}(\mathbf{x}, \mathbf{e}, \mathbf{d})$ with respect to $e_1, \dots, e_k, d_1, \dots, d_k$.

$$\tilde{f}(\mathbf{x}, \mathbf{e}, \mathbf{d}) = \tilde{f}(\mathbf{x}, \mathbf{0}, \mathbf{0}) + \sum_{i=1}^{k} \frac{\partial \tilde{f}}{\partial e_i}(\mathbf{x}, \mathbf{0}, \mathbf{0}) e_i + R_2(\mathbf{x}, \mathbf{e}, \mathbf{d}) \tag{8}$$

with

$$R_2(\mathbf{x}, \mathbf{e}, \mathbf{d}) = \frac{1}{2} \sum_{i,j=1}^{2k} \frac{\partial^2 \tilde{f}}{\partial y_i \partial y_j}(\mathbf{x}, \mathbf{p}) y_i y_j + \sum_{i=1}^{k} \frac{\partial \tilde{f}}{\partial d_i}(\mathbf{x}, \mathbf{0}, \mathbf{0}) d_i$$

for some $\mathbf{p} \in \mathbb{R}^{2k}$ such that $|p_i| \le \epsilon$ for $i = 1, \dots, k$ and $|p_i| \le \delta$ for $i = k+1, \dots, 2k$. Note that we added first order terms $\frac{\partial \tilde{f}}{\partial d_i}(\mathbf{x}, \mathbf{0}, \mathbf{0}) d_i$ to the error term R_2 because $\delta = O(\epsilon^2)$ (see Table 1; in fact, δ is much smaller than ϵ^2).

We have $\tilde{f}(\mathbf{x}, \mathbf{0}, \mathbf{0}) = f(\mathbf{x})$ and hence the error (7) can be estimated as follows:

$$\mathrm{err}_{\mathrm{overapprox}}(\tilde{f}, I) \le \max_{\mathbf{x} \in I, |e_i| \le \epsilon} \left| \sum_{i=1}^{k} \frac{\partial \tilde{f}}{\partial e_i}(\mathbf{x}, \mathbf{0}, \mathbf{0}) e_i \right| + M_2 \tag{9}$$

where M_2 is an upper bound for the error term $R_2(\mathbf{x}, \mathbf{e}, \mathbf{d})$. In our work, we use simple methods to estimate the value of M_2, such as interval arithmetic or several iterations of a global optimization algorithm. We always derive a rigorous bound of $R_2(\mathbf{x}, \mathbf{e}, \mathbf{d})$ and this bound is small in general since it contains an ϵ^2 factor. Large values of M_2 may indicate serious stability problems—for instance, the denominator of some expression is very close to zero. Our tool issues a warning if the computed value of M_2 is large.

Next, we note that in (9) the maximized expression depends on e_i linearly and it achieves its maximum value when $e_i = \pm\epsilon$. Therefore, the expression attains its maximum when the sign of e_i is the same as the sign of the corresponding partial derivative, and we transform the maximized expression into the sum of absolute values of partial derivatives. Finally, we get the following optimization problem:

$$\mathrm{err}_{\mathrm{fp}}(f, I) \le \mathrm{err}_{\mathrm{overapprox}}(\tilde{f}, I) \le M_2 + \epsilon \max_{\mathbf{x} \in I} \sum_{i=1}^{k} \left| \frac{\partial \tilde{f}}{\partial e_i}(\mathbf{x}, \mathbf{0}, \mathbf{0}) \right| . \tag{10}$$

The solution of our original, almost intractable problem (i.e., estimation of the floating-point error $\mathrm{err}_{\mathrm{fp}}(f, I)$) is reduced to the following two much simpler subproblems: (i) compute all expressions and constants involved in the optimization problem (10) (see our technical report [54] for details), and (ii) solve the optimization problem (10).

3.1 Solving Optimization Problems

We compute error bounds using rigorous global optimization techniques [45]. In general, it is not possible to find an exact optimal value of a given real-valued function. The main property of rigorous global optimization methods is that they always return a rigorous bound for a given optimization problem (some conditions on the optimized function are necessary such as continuity or differentiability). These methods can also balance between accuracy and performance. They can either return an estimation of the optimal value with the given tolerance or return a rigorous upper bound after a specific amount of time (iterations). It is also important that we are optimizing real-valued expressions, not floating-point ones. A particular global optimizer can work with floating-point numbers internally but it must return a rigorous result. For instance, the optimal maximal floating-point value of the function $f(x) = 0.3$ is the smallest floating-point number r which is greater than 0.3. It is known that global optimization is a hard problem. But note that abstraction techniques based on interval or affine arithmetic can be considered as primitive (and generally inaccurate) global optimization methods. FPTaylor can use any existing global optimization method to derive rigorous bounds of error expressions, and hence it is possible to run it with an inaccurate but fast global optimization technique if necessary.

The optimization problem (10) depends only on input variables of the function f, but it also contains a sum of absolute values of functions. Hence, it is not trivial—some global optimization solvers may not accept absolute values since they are not smooth functions. In addition, even if a solver accepts absolute values, they make the optimization problem considerably harder.

There is a naïve approach to simplify and solve this optimization problem. Find minimum (y_i) and maximum (z_i) values for each term $s_i(\mathbf{x}) = \frac{\partial \tilde{f}}{\partial e_i}(\mathbf{x}, \mathbf{0}, \mathbf{0})$ separately and then compute

$$\max_{\mathbf{x} \in I} \sum_{i=1}^{k} |s_i(\mathbf{x})| \le \sum_{i=1}^{k} \max_{\mathbf{x} \in I} |s_i(\mathbf{x})| = \sum_{i=1}^{k} \max\{-y_i, z_i\} \ . \tag{11}$$

This result can be inaccurate, but in many cases it is close to the optimal result as our experimental results demonstrate (see Sect. 4.2).

We also apply global optimization to compute a range of the expression for which we estimate the round-off error (i.e., the range of the function f). By combining this range information with the bound of the absolute round-off error computed from (10), we can get a rigorous estimation of the range of $\mathrm{fp}(f)$. The range of $\mathrm{fp}(f)$ is useful for verification of program assertions and proving the absence of floating-point exceptions such as overflows or divisions by zero.

3.2 Improved Rounding Model

The rounding model described by (1) and (3) is imprecise. For example, if we round a real number $x \in [8, 16]$ then (1) yields $\mathrm{rnd}(x) = x + xe$ with $|e| \le \epsilon$. A more precise bound for the same e would be $\mathrm{rnd}(x) = x + 8e$. This more precise rounding model follows from the fact that floating-point numbers have the same distance between each other in the interval $[2^n, 2^{n+1}]$ for integer n.

We define $p_2(x) = \max_{n \in \mathbb{Z}}\{2^n \mid 2^n < x\}$ and rewrite (1) and (3) as

$$\begin{aligned} \mathrm{rnd}(x) &= x + p_2(x)e + d, \\ op_{\mathrm{fp}}(x_1, \ldots, x_k) &= op(x_1, \ldots, x_k) + p_2\big(op(x_1, \ldots, x_k)\big)e + d \ . \end{aligned} \tag{12}$$

The function p_2 is piecewise constant. The improved model yields optimization problems with discontinuous functions p_2. These problems are harder than optimization problems for the original rounding model and can be solved with branch and bound algorithms based on rigorous interval arithmetic (see Sect. 4.2).

3.3 Formal Verification of FPTaylor Results in HOL Light

We formalized error estimation with the simplified optimization problem (11) in HOL Light [27]. In our formalization we do not prove that the implementation of FPTaylor satisfies a given specification. Instead, we formalized theorems necessary for validating results produced by FPTaylor. The validity of results is checked against specifications of floating-point rounding operations given by (1) and (12). We chose HOL Light as the tool for our formalization because it is the only proof assistant for which there exists a tool for formal verification of nonlinear inequalities (including inequalities with transcendental functions) [53]. Verification of nonlinear inequalities is necessary since the validity of results of global optimization procedures can be proved with nonlinear inequalities.

The validation of FPTaylor results is done as follows. First, FPTaylor is executed on a given problem with a special proof saving flag turned on. In this way, FPTaylor computes the round-off errors and produces a proof certificate and saves it in a file. Then a special procedure is executed in HOL Light which reads the produced proof certificate and formally verifies that all steps in this certificate are correct. The final theorem has the following form (for an error bound e computed by FPTaylor):

$$\vdash \forall \mathbf{x} \in I,\ |\mathrm{fp}(f)(\mathbf{x}) - f(\mathbf{x})| \le e\ .$$

Here, the function $\mathrm{fp}(f)$ is a function where a rounding operator is applied to all operations, variables, and constants. As mentioned above, in our current formalization we define such a rounding operator as any operator satisfying (1) and (12). We also implemented a comprehensive formalization of floating-point arithmetic in HOL Light (our floating-point formalization is available in the HOL Light distribution). Combining this formalization with theorems produced from FPTaylor certificates, we can get theorems about floating-point computations which do not explicitly contain references to rounding models (1) and (12).

The formalization of FPTaylor helped us to find a subtle bug in our implementation. We use an external tool for algebraic simplifications of internal expressions in FPTaylor (see Sect. 4.1 for more details). All expressions are passed as strings to this tool. Constants in FPTaylor are represented with rational numbers and they are printed as fractions. We forgot to put parentheses around these fractions and in some rare cases it resulted in wrong expressions passed to and from the simplification tool. For instance, if $c = 111/100$ and we had the expression $1/c$ then it would be given to the simplification tool as $1/111/100$. We discovered this associativity-related bug when formal validation failed on one of our test examples.

All limitations of our current formalization are limitations of the tool for verification of nonlinear inequalities in HOL Light. In order to get a verification of all features of FPTaylor, it is necessary to be able to verify nonlinear inequalities containing absolute values and the discontinuous function $p_2(x)$ defined in Sect. 3.2. We are working on improvements of the inequality verification tool which will include these functions. Nevertheless, we already can automatically verify interesting results which are much better than results produced by Gappa, another tool which can produce formal proofs in the Coq proof assistant [9].

4 Implementation and Evaluation

4.1 Implementation

We implemented a prototype tool called FPTaylor for estimating round-off errors in floating-point computations based on our method described in Sect. 3. The tool implements several additional features we did not describe, such as estimation of relative errors and support for transcendental functions and mixed precision floating-point computations.

FPTaylor is implemented in OCaml and uses several third-party tools and libraries. An interval arithmetic library [1] is used for rigorous estimations of floating-point constants and second order error terms in Taylor expansions. Internally, FPTaylor implements a very simple branch and bound global optimization technique based on interval arithmetic. The main advantage of this simple optimization method is that it can work even with discontinuous functions which are required by the improved rounding model described in Sect. 3.2. Our current implementation of the branch and bound method supports only simple interval constraints for input domain specification. FPTaylor also works with several external global optimization tools and libraries, such as NLopt optimization library [29] that implements various global optimization algorithms. Algorithms in NLopt are not rigorous and may produce incorrect results, but they are fast and can be used for obtaining solid preliminary results before applying slower rigorous optimization techniques. Z3 SMT solver [42] can also be used as an optimization backend by employing a simple binary search algorithm similar to the one described in related work [14]. Z3-based optimization supports any inequality constraints but it does not work with transcendental or discontinuous functions. We also plan to support other free global optimization tools and libraries in FPTaylor such as ICOS [31], GlobSol [30], and OpenOpt [46]. We rely on Maxima computer algebra system [37] for performing symbolic simplifications. Using Maxima is optional but it can significantly improve performance of optimization tools by simplifying symbolic expressions beforehand.

```
Variables
  float64 x in [1.001, 2.0],
  float64 y in [1.001, 2.0];
Definitions
  t rnd64= x * y;
// Constraints
//   x + y <= 2;
Expressions
  r rnd64= (t-1)/(t*t-1);
```

Fig. 1. FPTaylor input file example

As input FPTaylor takes a text file describing floating-point computations, and prints out the computed floating-point error bounds as output. Figure 1 demonstrates an example FPTaylor input file. Each input file contains several sections which define variables, constraints (in Fig. 1 constraints are not used and commented out), and expressions. FPTaylor analyses all expressions in an input file. All operations are assumed to be over real numbers. Floating-point arithmetic is modeled with rounding operators and with initial types of variables. The operator `rnd64=` in the example means that the rounding operator `rnd64` is applied to all operations, variables, and constants on the right hand side (this notation is borrowed from Gappa [15]). See the FPTaylor user manual distributed with the tool for all usage details.

4.2 Experimental Results

We compared FPTaylor with Gappa (version 1.1.2) [15], the Rosa real compiler (version from May 2014) [14], and Fluctuat (version 3.1071) [16] (see Sect. 5 for more information on these tools). We tested our tool on all benchmarks from the Rosa paper [14] and on three simple benchmarks with transcendental functions.[3] We also tried SMT tools which support floating-point reasoning [8,42] but they were not able to produce any results even on simple examples in a reasonable time (we ran them with a 30-minute timeout).

Table 2 presents our experimental results. In the table, column *FPTaylor(a)* shows results computed using the simplified optimization problem (11), column *FPTaylor(b)* using the full optimization problem (10) and the improved rounding model (12). Columns *Gappa (hints)* and *Fluctuat (subdivisions)* present results of Gappa and Fluctuat with manually provided subdivision hints. More precisely, in these experiments Gappa and Fluctuat were instructed to subdivide intervals of input variables into a given number of smaller pieces. The main drawback of these manually provided hints is that it is not always clear which variable intervals should be subdivided and how many pieces are required. It is very easy to make Gappa and Fluctuat very slow by subdividing intervals into too many pieces (even 100 pieces are enough in some cases).

Benchmarks *sine*, *sqroot*, and *sineOrder3* are different polynomial approximations of sine and square root. Benchmarks *carbonGas*, *rigidBody1*, *rigidBody2*, *doppler1*, *doppler2*, and *doppler3* are nonlinear expressions used in physics. Benchmarks *verhulst* and *predatorPrey* are from biological modeling. Benchmarks *turbine1*, *turbine2*, *turbine3*, and *jetEngine* are from control theory. Benchmark *logExp* is from Gappa++ paper [33] and it estimates the error in $log(1+exp(x))$ for $x \in [-8, 8]$. Benchmarks *sphere* and *azimuth* are taken from NASA World Wind Java SDK [57], which is a popular open-source 3D interactive world viewer with many users ranging from US Army and Air Force to European Space Agency. An example application that leverages World Wind is a critical component of the Next Generation Air Transportation System (NextGen) called AutoResolver, whose task is to provide separation assurance for airplanes [20].

[3] Our benchmarks are available at https://github.com/soarlab/FPTaylor

Table 2. Experimental results for absolute round-off error bounds (**bold font** marks the best results for each benchmark; *italic font* marks pessimistic results)

Benchmark	Gappa	Gappa (hints)	Fluctuat	Fluctuat (subdiv.)	Rosa	FPT.(a)	FPT.(b)
Univariate polynomial approximations							
sine	*1.46*	*5.17e-09*	7.97e-16	6.86e-16	9.56e-16	6.71e-16	**4.43e-16**
sqroot	5.71e-16	**5.37e-16**	6.84e-16	6.84e-16	8.41e-16	7.87e-16	5.78e-16
sineOrder3	8.89e-16	**6.50e-16**	1.16e-15	1.03e-15	1.11e-15	9.96e-16	7.95e-16
Rational functions with 1, 2, and 3 variables							
carbonGas	2.62e-08	**6.00e-09**	4.52e-08	8.88e-09	4.64e-08	1.25e-08	9.99e-09
verhulst	5.41e-16	2.84e-16	5.52e-16	4.78e-16	6.82e-16	3.50e-16	**2.50e-16**
predPrey	2.44e-16	1.66e-16	2.50e-16	2.35e-16	2.94e-16	1.87e-16	**1.59e-16**
rigidBody1	3.22e-13	**2.95e-13**	3.22e-13	3.22e-13	5.08e-13	3.87e-13	**2.95e-13**
rigidBody2	3.65e-11	**3.61e-11**	3.65e-11	3.65e-11	6.48e-11	5.24e-11	**3.61e-11**
doppler1	2.03e-13	1.61e-13	3.91e-13	1.40e-13	4.92e-13	1.57e-13	**1.35e-13**
doppler2	3.92e-13	2.86e-13	9.76e-13	2.59e-13	1.29e-12	2.87e-13	**2.44e-13**
doppler3	1.08e-13	8.70e-14	1.57e-13	7.63e-14	2.03e-13	8.16e-14	**6.97e-14**
turbine1	9.51e-14	2.63e-14	9.21e-14	8.31e-14	1.25e-13	2.50e-14	**1.86e-14**
turbine2	1.38e-13	3.54e-14	1.30e-13	1.10e-13	1.76e-13	3.34e-14	**2.15e-14**
turbine3	*39.91*	*0.35*	6.99e-14	5.94e-14	8.50e-14	1.80e-14	**1.07e-14**
jetEngine	*8.24e+06*	*4426.37*	*4.08e-08*	1.82e-11	*1.62e-08*	1.49e-11	**1.03e-11**
Transcendental functions with 1 and 4 variables							
logExp	–	–	–	–	–	1.71e-15	**1.53e-15**
sphere	–	–	–	–	–	1.29e-14	**8.08e-15**
azimuth	–	–	–	–	–	1.41e-14	**8.78e-15**

Table 3 contains additional information about benchmarks. Columns *Vars*, *Ops*, and *Trans* show the number of variables, the total number of floating-point operations, and the total number of transcendental operations in each benchmark. The column *FPTaylor(b)* repeats results of FPTaylor from Table 2. The column *s3fp* shows lower bounds of errors estimated with the underapproximation tool s3fp [7]. The column *Ratio* gives ratios of overapproximations computed with FPTaylor(b) and underapproximations computed with s3fp.

For all these benchmarks, input values are assumed to be real numbers, which is how Rosa treats input values, and hence we always need to consider uncertainties in inputs. All results are given for double precision floating-point numbers and we ran Gappa, Fluctuat, and Rosa with standard settings. We used a simple branch and bound optimization method in FPTaylor since it works better than a Z3-based optimization on most benchmarks. For transcendental functions, we used increased values of ϵ and δ: $\epsilon = 1.5 \cdot 2^{-53}$ and $\delta = 1.5 \cdot 2^{-1075}$.

Table 3. Additional benchmark information

Benchmark	Vars	Ops	Trans	FPTaylor(b)	s3fp	Ratio
Univariate polynomial approximations						
sine	1	18	0	4.43e-16	2.85e-16	1.6
sqroot	1	14	0	5.78e-16	4.57e-16	1.3
sineOrder3	1	5	0	7.95e-16	3.84e-16	2.1
Rational functions with 1, 2, and 3 variables						
carbonGas	1	11	0	9.99e-09	4.11e-09	2.4
verhulst	1	4	0	2.50e-16	2.40e-16	1.1
predPrey	1	7	0	1.59e-16	1.47e-16	1.1
rigidBody1	3	7	0	2.95e-13	2.47e-13	1.2
rigidBody2	3	14	0	3.61e-11	2.88e-11	1.3
doppler1	3	8	0	1.35e-13	8.01e-14	1.7
doppler2	3	8	0	2.44e-13	1.54e-13	1.6
doppler3	3	8	0	6.97e-14	4.54e-14	1.5
turbine1	3	14	0	1.86e-14	1.01e-14	1.8
turbine2	3	10	0	2.15e-14	1.20e-14	1.8
turbine3	3	14	0	1.07e-14	5.04e-15	2.1
jetEngine	2	48	0	1.03e-11	6.37e-12	1.6
Transcendental functions with 1 and 4 variables						
logExp	1	3	2	1.53e-15	1.19e-15	1.3
sphere	4	5	2	8.08e-15	5.05e-15	1.6
azimuth	4	14	7	8.78e-15	2.53e-15	3.5

Gappa with user provided hints computed best results in 5 out of 15 benchmarks (we do not count last 3 benchmarks with transcendental functions). FPTaylor computed best results in 12 benchmarks.[4] Gappa without hints was able to find a better result than FPTaylor only in the *sqroot* benchmark. On the other hand, in several benchmarks (*sine*, *jetEngine*, and *turbine3*), Gappa (even with hints) computed very pessimistic results. Rosa consistently computed decent error bounds, with one exception being *jetEngine*. FPTaylor outperformed Rosa on all benchmarks even with the simplified rounding model and optimization problem. Fluctuat results without subdivisions are similar to Rosa's results. Fluctuat results with subdivisions are good but they were obtained with carefully chosen subdivisions. FPTaylor with the improved rounding model outperformed Fluctuat with subdivisions on all but one benchmark (*carbonGas*). Only FPTaylor and Fluctuat with subdivisions found good error bounds for the *jetEngine* benchmark.

[4] While the absolute error changing from (e.g.) 10^{-8} to 10^{-10} does not appear to be significant, it is a significant two-order of magnitude difference; for instance, imagine these differences accumulating over 10^4 iterations in a loop.

FPTaylor yields best results with the full optimization problem (10) and with the improved rounding model (12). But these results are at most 2 times better (and even less in most cases) than results computed with the simple rounding model (3) and the simplified optimization problem (11). The main advantage of the simplified optimization problem is that it can be applied to more complex problems. Finally, we compared results of FPTaylor with lower bounds of errors estimated with a state-of-the-art underapproximation tool s3fp [7]. All FPTaylor results are only 1.1–2.4 times worse than the estimated lower bounds for polynomial and rational benchmarks and 1.3–3.5 times worse for transcendental tests.

Table 4 compares performance results of different tools on first 15 benchmarks (the results for the *jetEngine* benchmark and the total time for all 15 benchmarks are shown; FPTaylor takes about 33 seconds on three transcendental benchmarks). Gappa and Fluctuat (without hints and subdivisions) are considerably faster than both Rosa and FPTaylor. But Gappa often fails on nonlinear examples as Table 2 demonstrated. Fluctuat without subdivisions is also not as good as FPTaylor. All other tools (including FPTaylor) have roughly the same performance. Rosa is slower than FPTaylor because it relies on an inefficient optimization algorithm implemented with Z3.

Table 4. Performance results on an Intel Core i7 2.8GHz machine (in seconds)

Tool	jetEng.	Total
Gappa	0.02	0.38
Gappa(hints)	21.47	80.27
Fluctuat	0.01	0.75
Fluct.(div.)	23.00	228.36
Rosa	129.63	205.14
FPTaylor(a)	14.73	86.92
FPTaylor(b)	16.63	102.23

We also formally verified all results in the column *FPTaylor(a)* of Table 2. For all these results, corresponding HOL Light theorems were automatically produced using our formalization of FPTaylor described in Sect. 3.3. The total verification time of all results without the *azimuth* benchmark was 48 minutes on an Intel Core i7 2.8GHz machine. Verification of the *azimuth* benchmark took 261 minutes. Such performance figures match up with the state of the art, considering that even results pertaining to basic arithmetic operations must be formally derived from primitive definitions.

5 Related Work

Taylor Series. Method based on Taylor series have a rich history in floating-point reasoning, including algorithms for constructing symbolic Taylor series expansions for round-off errors [40,56,19,43], and stability analysis. These works do not cover round-off error estimation. Our key innovations include computation of the second order error term in Taylor expansions and global optimization of symbolic first order terms. Taylor expansions are also used to strictly enclose values of floating-point computations [51]. Note that in this case round-off errors are not computed directly and cannot be extracted from computed enclosures without large overestimations.

Abstract Interpretation. Abstract interpretation [11] is widely used for analysis of floating-point computations. Abstract domains for floating-point values include intervals [41], affine forms [55], and general polyhedra [6]. There exist different tools based on these abstract domains. Gappa [15] is a tool for checking different aspects of floating-point programs, and is used in the Frama-C verifier [18]. Gappa works with interval abstractions of floating-point numbers and applies rewriting rules for improving computed results. Gappa++ [33] is an improvement of Gappa that extends it with affine arithmetic [55]. It also provides definitions and rules for some transcendental functions. Gappa++ is currently not supported and does not run on modern operating systems. SmartFloat [13] is a Scala library which provides an interface for computing with floating-point numbers and for tracking accumulated round-off. It uses affine arithmetic for measuring errors. Fluctuat [16] is a tool for static analysis of floating-point programs written in C. Internally, Fluctuat uses a floating-point abstract domain based on affine arithmetic [23]. Astrée [10] is another static analysis tool which can compute ranges of floating-point expressions and detect floating-point exceptions. A general abstract domain for floating-point computations is described in [34]. Based on this work, a tool called RangeLab is implemented [36] and a technique for improving accuracy of floating-point computations is presented [35]. Ponsini et al. [49] propose constraint solving techniques for improving the precision of floating-point abstractions. Our results show that interval abstractions and affine arithmetic can yield pessimistic error bounds for nonlinear computations.

The work closest to ours is Rosa [14] in which they combine affine arithmetic and an optimization method based on an SMT solver for estimating round-off errors. Their tool Rosa keeps the result of a computation in a symbolic form and uses an SMT solver for finding accurate bounds of computed expressions. The main difference from our work is representation of round-off errors with numerical (not symbolic) affine forms in Rosa. For nonlinear arithmetic, this representation leads to overapproximation of error, as it loses vital dependency information between the error terms. Our method keeps track of these dependencies by maintaining symbolic representation of all first order error terms in the corresponding Taylor series expansion. Another difference is our usage of rigorous global optimization which is more efficient than using SMT-based binary search for optimization.

SMT. While abstract interpretation techniques are not designed to prove general bit-precise results, the use of bit-blasting combined with SMT solving is pursued by [5]. Recently, a preliminary standard for floating-point arithmetic in SMT solvers was developed [52]. Z3 [42] and MathSAT 5 [8] SMT solvers partially support this standard. There exist several other tools which use SMT solvers for reasoning about floating-point numbers. FPhile [47] verifies stability properties of simple floating-point programs. It translates a program into an SMT formula encoding low- and high-precision versions, and containing an assertion that the two are close enough. FPhile uses Z3 as its backend SMT solver. Leeser et al. [32] translate a given floating-point formula into a corresponding formula for real numbers with appropriately defined rounding operators. Ariadne [2] relies on SMT solving for detecting floating-point exceptions. Haller et al. [24] lift the conflict analysis algorithm of SMT solvers to abstract domains to improve their efficacy of floating-point reasoning.

In general, the lack of scalability of SMT solvers used by themselves has been observed in other works [14]. Since existing SMT solvers do not directly support mixed real/floating-point reasoning, one must often resort to non-standard approaches for encoding properties of round-off errors in computations (e.g., using low- and high-precision versions of the same computation).

Proof Assistants. An ultimate way to verify floating-point programs is to give a formal proof of their correctness. To achieve this goal, there exist several formalizations of the floating-point standard in proof assistants [38,26]. Boldo et al. [4] formalized a non-trivial floating-point program for solving a wave equation. This work partially relies on Gappa, which can also produce formal certificates for verifying floating-point properties in the Coq proof assistant [9].

6 Conclusions and Future Work

We presented a new method to estimate round-off errors of floating-point computations called Symbolic Taylor Expansions. We support our work through rigorous formal proofs, and also present a tool FPTaylor that implements our method. FPTaylor is the only tool we know that rigorously handles transcendental functions. It achieves tight overapproximation estimates of errors—especially for nonlinear expressions.

FPTaylor is not designed to be a tool for complete analysis of floating-point programs. It cannot handle conditionals and loops directly; instead, it can be used as an external decision procedure for program verification tools such as [18,50]. Conditional expressions can be verified in FPTaylor in the same way as it is done in Rosa [14] (see our technical report [54] for details).

In addition to experimenting with more examples, a promising application of FPTaylor is in error analysis of algorithms that can benefit from reduced or mixed precision computations. Another potential application of FPTaylor is its integration with a recently released tool Herbie [48] which improves the accuracy of numerical programs. Herbie relies on testing for round-off error estimations. FPTaylor can provide strong guarantees for results produced by Herbie.

We also plan to improve the performance of FPTaylor by parallelizing its global optimization algorithms, thus paving the way to analyze larger problems.

Ideas presented in this paper can be directly incorporated into existing tools. For instance, an implementation similar to Gappa++ [33] can be achieved by incorporating our error estimation method inside Gappa [15]; the Rosa compiler [14] can be easily extended with our technique.

Acknowledgments. We would like to thank Nelson Beebe, Wei-Fan Chiang, John Harrison, and Madan Musuvathi for their feedback and encouragement. This work is supported in part by NSF CCF 1421726.

References

1. Alliot, J.M., Durand, N., Gianazza, D., Gotteland, J.B.: Implementing an interval computation library for OCaml on x86/amd64 architectures (short paper). In: ICFP 2012. ACM (2012)
2. Barr, E.T., Vo, T., Le, V., Su, Z.: Automatic Detection of Floating-point Exceptions. In: POPL 2013, pp. 549–560. ACM, New York (2013)
3. Bingham, J., Leslie-Hurd, J.: Verifying Relative Error Bounds Using Symbolic Simulation. In: Biere, A., Bloem, R. (eds.) CAV 2014. LNCS, vol. 8559, pp. 277–292. Springer, Heidelberg (2014)
4. Boldo, S., Clément, F., Filliâtre, J.C., Mayero, M., Melquiond, G., Weis, P.: Wave Equation Numerical Resolution: A Comprehensive Mechanized Proof of a C Program. Journal of Automated Reasoning 50(4), 423–456 (2013)
5. Brillout, A., Kroening, D., Wahl, T.: Mixed abstractions for floating-point arithmetic. In: FMCAD 2009, pp. 69–76 (2009)
6. Chen, L., Miné, A., Cousot, P.: A Sound Floating-Point Polyhedra Abstract Domain. In: Ramalingam, G. (ed.) APLAS 2008. LNCS, vol. 5356, pp. 3–18. Springer, Heidelberg (2008)
7. Chiang, W.F., Gopalakrishnan, G., Rakamarić, Z., Solovyev, A.: Efficient Search for Inputs Causing High Floating-point Errors. In: PPoPP 2014, pp. 43–52. ACM, New York (2014)
8. Cimatti, A., Griggio, A., Schaafsma, B.J., Sebastiani, R.: The MathSAT5 SMT Solver. In: Piterman, N., Smolka, S.A. (eds.) TACAS 2013. LNCS, vol. 7795, pp. 93–107. Springer, Heidelberg (2013)
9. The Coq Proof Assistant, http://coq.inria.fr/
10. Cousot, P., Cousot, R., Feret, J., Mauborgne, L., Miné, A., Monniaux, D., Rival, X.: The ASTREÉ Analyzer. In: Sagiv, M. (ed.) ESOP 2005. LNCS, vol. 3444, pp. 21–30. Springer, Heidelberg (2005)
11. Cousot, P., Cousot, R.: Abstract Interpretation: A Unified Lattice Model for Static Analysis of Programs by Construction or Approximation of Fixpoints. In: POPL 1977, pp. 238–252. ACM, New York (1977)
12. Daramy, C., Defour, D., de Dinechin, F., Muller, J.M.: CR-LIBM: a correctly rounded elementary function library. Proc. SPIE 5205, 458–464 (2003)
13. Darulova, E., Kuncak, V.: Trustworthy Numerical Computation in Scala. In: OOPSLA 2011, pp. 325–344. ACM, New York (2011)
14. Darulova, E., Kuncak, V.: Sound Compilation of Reals. In: POPL 2014, pp. 235–248. ACM, New York (2014)
15. Daumas, M., Melquiond, G.: Certification of Bounds on Expressions Involving Rounded Operators. ACM Trans. Math. Softw. 37(1), 2:1–2:20 (2010)
16. Delmas, D., Goubault, E., Putot, S., Souyris, J., Tekkal, K., Védrine, F.: Towards an Industrial Use of FLUCTUAT on Safety-Critical Avionics Software. In: Alpuente, M., Cook, B., Joubert, C. (eds.) FMICS 2009. LNCS, vol. 5825, pp. 53–69. Springer, Heidelberg (2009)
17. Fousse, L., Hanrot, G., Lefèvre, V., Pélissier, P., Zimmermann, P.: MPFR: A Multiple-precision Binary Floating-point Library with Correct Rounding. ACM Trans. Math. Softw. 33(2) (2007)
18. Frama-C Software Analyzers, http://frama-c.com/
19. Gáti, A.: Miller Analyzer for Matlab: A Matlab Package for Automatic Roundoff Analysis. Computing and Informatics 31(4), 713– (2012)

20. Giannakopoulou, D., Howar, F., Isberner, M., Lauderdale, T., Rakamarić, Z., Raman, V.: Taming Test Inputs for Separation Assurance. In: ASE 2014, pp. 373–384. ACM, New York (2014)
21. Goodloe, A.E., Muñoz, C., Kirchner, F., Correnson, L.: Verification of Numerical Programs: From Real Numbers to Floating Point Numbers. In: Brat, G., Rungta, N., Venet, A. (eds.) NFM 2013. LNCS, vol. 7871, pp. 441–446. Springer, Heidelberg (2013)
22. Goualard, F.: How Do You Compute the Midpoint of an Interval? ACM Trans. Math. Softw., 40(2) 11:1–11:25 (2014)
23. Goubault, E., Putot, S.: Static Analysis of Finite Precision Computations. In: Jhala, R., Schmidt, D. (eds.) VMCAI 2011. LNCS, vol. 6538, pp. 232–247. Springer, Heidelberg (2011)
24. Haller, L., Griggio, A., Brain, M., Kroening, D.: Deciding floating-point logic with systematic abstraction. In: FMCAD 2012, pp. 131–140 (2012)
25. Harrison, J.V.: Formal Verification of Floating Point Trigonometric Functions. In: Hunt Jr., W.A., Johnson, S.D. (eds.) FMCAD 2000. LNCS, vol. 1954, pp. 217–233. Springer, Heidelberg (2000)
26. Harrison, J.: Floating-Point Verification Using Theorem Proving. In: Bernardo, M., Cimatti, A. (eds.) SFM 2006. LNCS, vol. 3965, pp. 211–242. Springer, Heidelberg (2006)
27. Harrison, J.: HOL Light: An Overview. In: Berghofer, S., Nipkow, T., Urban, C., Wenzel, M. (eds.) TPHOLs 2009. LNCS, vol. 5674, pp. 60–66. Springer, Heidelberg (2009)
28. IEEE Standard for Floating-point Arithmetic. IEEE Std 754-2008, pp. 1–70 (2008)
29. Johnson, S.G.: The NLopt nonlinear-optimization package, http://ab-initio.mit.edu/nlopt
30. Kearfott, R.B.: GlobSol User Guide. Optimization Methods Software 24(4-5), 687–708 (2009)
31. Lebbah, Y.: ICOS: A Branch and Bound Based Solver for Rigorous Global Optimization. Optimization Methods Software 24(4-5), 709–726 (2009)
32. Leeser, M., Mukherjee, S., Ramachandran, J., Wahl, T.: Make it real: Effective floating-point reasoning via exact arithmetic. In: DATE 2014, pp. 1–4 (2014)
33. Linderman, M.D., Ho, M., Dill, D.L., Meng, T.H., Nolan, G.P.: Towards Program Optimization Through Automated Analysis of Numerical Precision. In: CGO 2010, pp. 230–237. ACM, New York (2010)
34. Martel, M.: Semantics of roundoff error propagation in finite precision calculations. Higher-Order and Symbolic Computation 19(1), 7–30 (2006)
35. Martel, M.: Program Transformation for Numerical Precision. In: PEPM 2009, pp. 101–110. ACM, New York (2009)
36. Martel, M.: RangeLab: A Static-Analyzer to Bound the Accuracy of Finite-Precision Computations. In: SYNASC 2011, pp. 118–122. IEEE Computer Society, Washington, DC (2011)
37. Maxima: Maxima, a Computer Algebra System. Version 5.30.0 (2013), http://maxima.sourceforge.net/
38. Melquiond, G.: Floating-point arithmetic in the Coq system. Information and Computation 216(0), 14–23 (2012)
39. Mikusinski, P., Taylor, M.: An Introduction to Multivariable Analysis from Vector to Manifold. Birkhäuser Boston (2002)
40. Miller, W.: Software for Roundoff Analysis. ACM Trans. Math. Softw. 1(2), 108–128 (1975)

41. Moore, R.: Interval analysis. Prentice-Hall series in automatic computation, Prentice-Hall (1966)
42. de Moura, L., Bjørner, N.S.: Z3: An Efficient SMT Solver. In: Ramakrishnan, C.R., Rehof, J. (eds.) TACAS 2008. LNCS, vol. 4963, pp. 337–340. Springer, Heidelberg (2008)
43. Mutrie, M.P.W., Bartels, R.H., Char, B.W.: An Approach for Floating-point Error Analysis Using Computer Algebra. In: ISSAC 1992, pp. 284–293. ACM, New York (1992)
44. Neumaier, A.: Taylor Forms - Use and Limits. Reliable Computing 2003, 9–43 (2002)
45. Neumaier, A.: Complete search in continuous global optimization and constraint satisfaction. Acta Numerica 13, 271–369 (2004)
46. OpenOpt: universal numerical optimization package, http://openopt.org
47. Paganelli, G., Ahrendt, W.: Verifying (In-)Stability in Floating-Point Programs by Increasing Precision, Using SMT Solving. In: SYNASC, 2013, pp. 209–216 (2013)
48. Panchekha, P., Sanchez-Stern, A., Wilcox, J.R., Tatlock, Z.: Automatically Improving Accuracy for Floating Point Expressions. In: PLDI 2015. ACM (2015)
49. Ponsini, O., Michel, C., Rueher, M.: Verifying floating-point programs with constraint programming and abstract interpretation techniques. Automated Software Engineering, 1–27 (2014)
50. Rakamarić, Z., Emmi, M.: SMACK: Decoupling Source Language Details from Verifier Implementations. In: Biere, A., Bloem, R. (eds.) CAV 2014. LNCS, vol. 8559, pp. 106–113. Springer, Heidelberg (2014)
51. Revol, N., Makino, K., Berz, M.: Taylor models and floating-point arithmetic: proof that arithmetic operations are validated in COSY. The Journal of Logic and Algebraic Programming 64(1), 135–154 (2005)
52. Rümmer, P., Wahl, T.: An SMT-LIB Theory of Binary Floating-Point Arithmetic. In: SMT Workshop 2010 (2010)
53. Solovyev, A., Hales, T.C.: Formal verification of nonlinear inequalities with taylor interval approximations. In: Brat, G., Rungta, N., Venet, A. (eds.) NFM 2013. LNCS, vol. 7871, pp. 383–397. Springer, Heidelberg (2013)
54. Solovyev, A., Jacobsen, C., Rakamarić, Z., Gopalakrishnan, G.: Rigorous Estimation of Floating-Point Round-off Errors with Symbolic Taylor Expansions. Tech. Rep. UUCS-15-001, School of Computing, University of Utah (2015)
55. Stolfi, J., de Figueiredo, L.: An Introduction to Affine Arithmetic. TEMA Tend. Mat. Apl. Comput. 4(3), 297–312 (2003)
56. Stoutemyer, D.R.: Automatic Error Analysis Using Computer Algebraic Manipulation. ACM Trans. Math. Softw. 3(1), 26–43 (1977)
57. NASA World Wind Java SDK, http://worldwind.arc.nasa.gov/java/

Static Optimal Scheduling for Synchronous Data Flow Graphs with Model Checking

Xue-Yang Zhu[1(✉)], Rongjie Yan[1], Yu-Lei Gu[1,2], Jian Zhang[1], Wenhui Zhang[1], and Guangquan Zhang[2]

[1] State Key Laboratory of Computer Science, Institute of Software, Chinese Academy of Sciences, Beijing, China

[2] School of Computer Science and Technology, Soochow University, Suzhou, China

{zxy,yrj,guyl,zj,zwh}@ios.ac.cn, gqzhang@suda.edu.cn

Abstract. Synchronous data flow graphs (SDFGs) are widely used to model digital signal processing and streaming media applications. In this paper, we present exact methods for static optimal scheduling and mapping of SDFGs on a heterogenous multiprocessor platform. The optimization criteria we consider are throughput and energy consumption, taking into account the combination of various constraints such as auto-concurrency and buffer sizes. We present a concise and flexible (priced) timed automata semantics of system models, which include an SDFG and a multiprocessor platform, and formulate the optimization goals as temporal logic formulas. The optimization and scheduling problems are then transformed to model checking problems, which are solved by UPPAAL (CORA). Thanks to the exhaustive exploration nature of model checking and the facility of the tools, we obtain two pareto-optimal schedules, one with an optimal throughput and a best energy consumption and another with an optimal energy consumption and a best throughput. The approach is applied to two real applications with different parameters. The case studies show that our approach can deal with moderate models within reasonable execution time and reveal the impacts of different constraints on optimization goals.

Keywords: Data Flow Graphs · Throughput · Energy Consumption · Multi-constraint · Timed Automata · UPPAAL

1 Introduction

Synchronous data flow graphs (SDFGs) [16] are widely used to represent DSP and streaming media applications, such as a spectrum analyzer [25] and an MPEG-4 decoder [23]. Such applications are usually operated on multiprocessor platforms and under real-time and resource constraints. In this paper, we are concerned with constructing efficient static (compile-time) schedules of SDFGs on a heterogeneous multiprocessor platform.

This work is partially supported by National Key Basic Research Program of China (973 program) (No. 2014CB340701) and the National Natural Science Foundation of China (Nos. 61472406, 61472474, 61272135, 61361136002 and U1435220).

N. Bjørner and F. de Boer (Eds.): FM 2015, LNCS 9109, pp. 551–569, 2015.
DOI: 10.1007/978-3-319-19249-9_34

Each node (also called actor) in an SDFG represents a computation and each edge models a FIFO channel; the sample rates of actors may differ. *Homogenous synchronous data flow graphs* (HSDFGs) are a special type of SDFGs, of which all sample rates of actors are set to 1. A *static schedule* arranges the actors of an SDFG to be executed repeatedly, also called a *periodic schedule.* Execution of all the actors for the required number of times is referred to as an *iteration*, which may include more than one execution, also called a *firing*, of an actor. Different actors may fire a different number of firings. Actor B in SDFG G_1, shown in Fig. 1(a), for example, fires twice in an iteration, while A fires once. The average computation time per iteration is called *iteration period* (IP). The IP is the reciprocal of the *throughput*. We use IP and throughput alternatively in the remainder of the paper. The *iteration energy consumption* (IEC) is the average energy consumption per iteration.

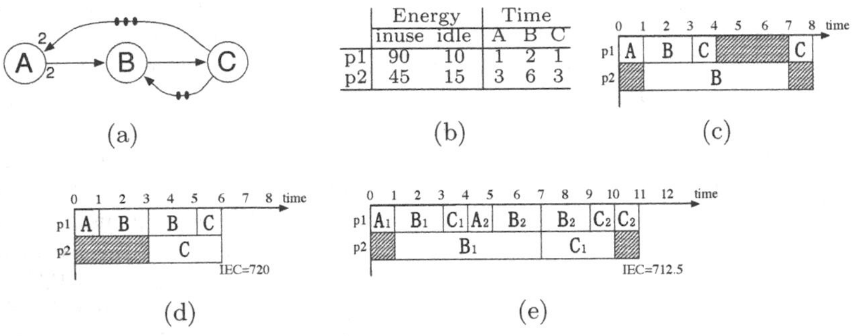

Fig. 1. The system model $\mathcal{M}_1$ and its schedules. (a) The SDFG G_1; (b) the execution platform P_1 and the execution time of actors in G_1 on different processors; (c) an ASAP periodic schedule of G_1 with IP=8; (d) a periodic schedule of G_1 with IP=6; (e) an unfolding schedule of G_1 with IP=$\frac{11}{2}$. The sample rates in the SDFG are omitted when they are 1; black dots on edges represent initial tokens on the edges.

For homogeneous multiprocessor scheduling of SDFGs, an *as soon as possible* (ASAP) execution can be used to find schedules with minimal IP [24]. For heterogeneous multiprocessor scheduling, however, an ASAP schedule is not necessarily throughput-optimal. The ASAP schedule shown in Fig. 1(c), for example, arranges executions of actors of G_1 on a platform including two heterogeneous processors as shown in Fig. 1(b). It has an IP larger than the IP of another schedule shown in Fig. 1(d), which is not ASAP.

Scheduling f iterations as one *schedule cycle* may lead to more options for parallel execution and therefore may reduce the IP and the IEC of a schedule. This is *unfolding* scheduling [19] and f is called *unfolding factor.* See Fig. 1(e) for example. The IP of a periodic schedule of G_1 with unfolding factor 2 is $\frac{11}{2}$, smaller than that of the schedule shown in Fig. 1(d). The IEC is also improved.

In this paper, we present exact methods to schedule and map an SDFG on a heterogeneous multiprocessor platform. The schedules are pareto-optimal. That is, they are either throughput-optimal with a best energy consumption or energy consumption-optimal with a best throughput. Other kinds of constraints, e.g. buffer size constraints, are also considered and integrated into the framework of the proposed methods.

For a given platform and a given unfolding factor, even if we consider only one optimization criterion, e.g. throughput, the scheduling and mapping problem is already NP-complete [20]. For solving the multi-constraint and multi-criterion problems we are considering, we use model checking, which is widely acknowledged to be a powerful tool for such problems.

Actors of an SDFG can fire concurrently if the tokens and other required resources are available. For the analysis of the time and resource constraints, it is appropriate to model the behavior of SDFGs as networks of (priced) timed automata [3] [4], and we choose the real-time model checking tools UPPAAL (CORA) [15] [4] as the back-end solvers. Our contributions are as follows.

1. We present a concise (priced) timed automata (TA) semantics of system models, which include an SDFG and a multiprocessor platform. Various constraints can be integrated flexibly.
2. Based on the semantics, we present two novel exact methods: one for finding static schedules with an optimal throughput and a best energy consumption, and the other for finding static schedules with an optimal energy consumption and a best throughput for SDFGs on heterogenous multiprocessor platforms. Optimal solutions under various constraints are guaranteed.
3. We implement the methods and apply it to two real applications. Although state explosion is inevitable as the models become larger (for checking NP-complete problems), the experimental results show that our methods can deal with moderate models within reasonable time and reveal the impacts of different constraints on optimization goals.

The remainder of this paper is organized as follows. We introduce related work in Section 2. The input models and the problems addressed are formulated in Section 3 and (priced) timed automata are introduced in Section 4. Our main contributions are illustrated in Sections 5, 6 and 7. Section 8 provides case studies. Section 9 concludes and discusses future work.

2 Related Work

Scheduling SDFGs according to different optimization goals have been studied extensively [16], [13], [21], and there are also many studies on real-time schedulability analysis using model checking [11] [8] [1] [17] [5]. Here we review those works most related to our methods, which solve scheduling problems of SDFGs via model checking.

Using model checking to schedule SDFGs according to a particular optimization goal was first presented by Geilen et al. [9]. They focus on buffer minimization problem on a single processor with model checker SPIN [14]. [10] and [12] solve the same problem with NuSMV [6] and SPIN, respectively.

The closest works to our methods are [7] and [18]. Both use UPPAAL as a solver to analyze or schedule SDFGs on a heterogeneous platform. The main differences between them and our methods are summarized as follows.

1. The problems addressed are different. [7] analyzes the schedulability for a given timing constraint, [18] schedules an SDFG to achieve a minimal makespan (i.e. the IP of 1-schedule in this paper), while we consider multiple optimization goals and constraints.
2. The input models are different. In [7], actors of SDFGs are binding to some core and edges to memories, while in our methods, no binding are considered. On the contrary, we try to find bindings according to the optimization goals. In [18], besides data dependencies between actors, task parallelism is explicitly denoted by split and join nodes. In our methods, only data dependencies available in the models, task parallelism needs to be explored to decide whether two tasks can be executed concurrently.
3. The transformations are different. [7] transforms each actor to a TA and each processor to an NTA. In [18], each possible allocation is represented by a TA and each possible communication is also represented by a TA. In our methods, we combine the behavior of actors on processors. The conciseness makes our methods easy to be extended to deal with additional constraints.

3 Model Description and Problem Formulation

An *execution platform* P is a set of heterogeneous processors. A computation may require different amounts of running time if it is executed on different processors. The energy consumption for each processor p is defined by $uEC(p)$ and $iEC(p)$, indicating the energy consumption per unit time when p is used and when p is idle, respectively.

A *synchronous dataflow graph* (SDFG) is a finite directed graph $G = \langle V, E\rangle$, where V is the set of actors, modeling the computations of the system; E is the set of directed edges, modeling interconnections between computations. Each edge e is weighted with three properties, $d(e)$, $prd(e)$ and $cns(e)$, where $d(e)$ is the number of initial tokens on e, $prd(e)$ is the number of tokens produced onto e by each firing of the source of e, and $cns(e)$ is the number of tokens consumed from e by each firing of the sink actor of e. These numbers are also called the *delay*, *production rate* and *consumption rate*, respectively. The source actor and sink actor of e are denoted by $src(e)$ and $snk(e)$, respectively. The set of incoming edges to actor α is denoted by $InE(\alpha)$, and the set of outgoing edges from α by $OutE(\alpha)$. If $prd(e) = cns(e) = 1$ for each $e \in E$, G is a *homogeneous SDFG* (HSDFG).

If execution platform P is considered, each actor α is weighted with computation times $t(\alpha, p)$, for all $p \in P$. Normally, $t(\alpha, p)$ is a positive integer. For technical reason, we also allow $t(\alpha, p)$ to be 0 or -1. The former is used for some dummy actors; the latter is used when α is not allowed to run on p.

An SDFG G is *sample rate consistent* [16] if and only if there exists a positive integer vector $q(V)$ satisfying *balance equations*, $q(src(e)) \times prd(e) = q(snk(e)) \times$

$cns(e)$ for all $e \in E$. The smallest such q is called the *repetition vector.* We use q to represent the repetition vector directly. For example, a balance equation can be constructed for each edge of G_1 in Fig. 1 (a). By solving the equations, we have G_1's repetition vector $q = [1, 2, 2]$. An *iteration* is a firing sequence in which each actor α occurs exactly $q(\alpha)$ times. Only sample rate consistent and deadlock-free SDFGs are meaningful in practice. We consider only such SDFGs, which can be verified efficiently [16].

Definition 1 (System model). *A* system model *includes an SDFG G and its execution platform P, denoted by* $\mathcal{M} = (G, P)$.

A *static schedule* arranges computations of an algorithm to be executed repeatedly. An *unfolding schedule* of system model $\mathcal{M} = (G, P)$ is a static schedule arranging f consecutive iterations of G running on P. The number f is called *unfolding factor* and the f iterations form a *schedule cycle.*

Definition 2 (f-schedule). *An* f-schedule *of system model* $\mathcal{M} = (G, P)$ *is a function* $S : V \times \mathbb{N} \to \mathbb{N} \times P$*, where* $\mathbb{N}$ *is the set of non-negative integers, defining the time arrangement and the processor allocation of firings of actors in G. Schedule S with a cycle period (CP) T is defined as follows. For the* i^{th} *firing of actor* α*, denoted by* (α, i)*,* $i \in [1, \infty)$*:*

1. $S(\alpha, i).st$ *is* (α, i)*'s start time, when there are sufficient tokens on each* $e \in InE(\alpha)$ *for a firing of* α*;*
2. $S(\alpha, i).pa$ *is the processor assigned to* (α, i)*, which is available at the moment* $S(\alpha, i).st$*;*
3. $S(\alpha, i + f \cdot q(\alpha)).st = S(\alpha, i).st + T$*;*
4. $S(\alpha, i + f \cdot q(\alpha)).pa = S(\alpha, i).pa$

Such a schedule can be represented by the first f iterations and period T. It is the part of the schedule defined by $S(\alpha, i)$ with $1 \le i \le f \cdot q(\alpha)$ for all α. From now on, we only consider the finite part of f-schedules.

The *iteration period* (IP) of S is the average computation time of an iteration, that is, $IP = \frac{T}{f}$.

The energy consumption of f-schedule S can be computed as follows. For conciseness, we omit parameters S and f when it is clear in context. Denote the set of all firings assigned on processor p by $AonP(p)$.

$$AonP(p) \equiv_{def} \{(\alpha, i) | S(\alpha, i).pa = p \wedge i \in [1, f \cdot q(\alpha)] \wedge \alpha \in V\}.$$

The total time p occupied in S is

$$occT(p) = \sum_{(\alpha,i) \in AonP(p)} t((\alpha, i), p), \text{ where } t((\alpha, i), p) = t(\alpha, p). \tag{1}$$

Then the energy consumption of S is

$$EC = \sum_{p \in P} occT(p) \cdot uEC(p) + [T - occT(p)] \cdot iEC(p). \tag{2}$$

The *iteration energy consumption* (IEC) of S is the average energy consumption per iteration, that is, $IEC = \frac{EC}{f}$.

Given a system model $\mathcal{M} = (G, P)$ and an unfolding factor f, suppose the set of all f-schedules of $\mathcal{M}$ is $\mathbf{S}$, the problems we address are:

1. how to find an f-schedule S_{optP} such that

$$IP(S_{optP}) = \min\{IP(S) | S \in \mathbf{S}\}, \text{ and}$$
$$IEC(S_{optP}) = \min\{IEC(S) | S \in \mathbf{S} \wedge IP(S) = IP(S_{optP})\}$$

2. how to find an f-schedule S_{optE} such that

$$IEC(S_{optE}) = \min\{IEC(S) | S \in \mathbf{S}\}, \text{ and}$$
$$IP(S_{optE}) = \min\{IP(S) | S \in \mathbf{S} \wedge IEC(S) = IEC(S_{optE})\}$$

4 Introduction to Timed Automata

In this section we recap the concepts of syntax and semantics of timed automata (TA) [3] and its extension with cost [4]. Let X be a set of clocks, $\mathcal{V}$ be a set of bounded integer variables. We use $C(X, \mathcal{V})$ and $U(X, \mathcal{V})$, respectively, to denote the set of linear constraints and the set of updates over clocks and integer variables, where updates on clocks are restricted to resetting clock variables to zero.

A TA is a tuple $(L, X, \mathcal{V}, \mathcal{E}, Inv, l_0)$, where L is a set of locations, $\mathcal{E} \subseteq L \times C(X, \mathcal{V}) \times U(X, \mathcal{V}) \times L$ is a set of edges, $Inv : L \rightarrow C(X, \mathcal{V})$ assigns invariants to locations, and l_0 is the initial location. A network of n timed automata (NTA) is a tuple of timed automata $A_1 || \cdots || A_n$ over X, $\mathcal{V}$. A clock valuation γ for a set X is a mapping from X to $\mathbb{R}^+$, where $\mathbb{R}^+$ is the set of non-negative real numbers. A variable valuation u is a function from $\mathcal{V}$ to $\mathbb{Z}$, where $\mathbb{Z}$ is the set of integers. A pair of valuation (γ, u) satisfies a constraint ϕ over X and $\mathcal{V}$, denoted by $(\gamma, u) \models \phi$, if and only if ϕ evaluates to *true* with the valuations γ and u. Let $\gamma_0(x) = 0$ for all $x \in X$. For $\delta \in \mathbb{R}^+$, $\gamma + \delta$ denotes the clock valuation that maps every clock x to the value $\gamma(x) + \delta$. For an update $\eta(Y, \mathcal{V}')$ over a pair of (γ, u), where $Y \subseteq X$ and $\mathcal{V}' \subseteq \mathcal{V}$, $(\gamma, u)[\eta(Y, \mathcal{V}')]$ denotes the clock valuation that maps all clocks in Y to zero and agrees with γ for all clocks in $X \setminus Y$, and the variable valuation that maps all integer variables in $\mathcal{V}'$ according to the update expression in η and agrees with u in $\mathcal{V} \setminus \mathcal{V}'$.

Definition 3 (Semantics of timed automata). *The semantics of a timed automaton* $A = (L, X, \mathcal{V}, \mathcal{E}, Inv, l_0)$ *is a timed transition system* $\mathcal{T} = \langle \mathcal{S}, s_0, \rightarrow \rangle$ *where* $\mathcal{S} \subseteq L \times \mathbb{R}^+ \times \mathbb{Z}$ *is the set of states,* $s_0 = (l_0, \gamma_0, u_0)$ *is the initial state and* $\rightarrow$ *is the transition relation such that*

- $(l, \gamma, u) \xrightarrow{\delta} (l, \gamma + \delta, u)$ *if* $\forall \delta' : 0 \leq \delta' \leq \delta \Rightarrow (\gamma + \delta', u) \models Inv(l)$ *where* $\delta \in \mathbb{R}^+$, *and*
- $(l, \gamma, u) \rightarrow (l', \gamma', u')$ *if there exists* $e = (l, g, \eta(Y, \mathcal{V}'), l') \in \mathcal{E}$ *such that* $(\gamma, u) \models g$, $(\gamma', u') = (\gamma, u)[\eta(Y, \mathcal{V}')]$, *and* $(\gamma', u') \models Inv(l')$.

The former is called delay transition and the latter is called discrete transition.

The trace of a timed automaton is a finite or infinite sequence $(l_0, \gamma_0, u_0) \rightarrow (l_1, \gamma_1, u_1) \rightarrow \ldots$, where $\rightarrow$ is either a delay transition or a discrete transition. For an NTA, the discrete transitions are executed interleavingly.

Priced timed automata (PTA) [4] is an extension of TA to allow the accumulation of costs during behaviour. The extension from timed automata is $A_c = (L, X, \mathcal{V}, \mathcal{E}, Inv, l_0, \mathcal{P})$, where $\mathcal{P} : L \cup \mathcal{E} \rightarrow \mathbb{N}$ assigns cost rates and costs to locations and edges, resp. The semantics of priced timed automata is similar to the version without price, except that the cost in a delay transition is in direct proportion to the time elapsed, and the cost in a discrete transition is the cost of the edge. For a network of PTAs, which is defined similarly to an NTA, we use vectors of locations and the cost rate of a vector of locations is the sum of cost rates in the locations of the vector. For a finite trace of a PTA, the cost is the sum of the costs for all discrete and delay transitions.

5 A Timed Automata Semantics of System Models

The behavior of an SDFG consists of a sequence of *firings*. We use updates $sFiring(\alpha)$ and $eFiring(\alpha)$ to encode the start and the end of a firing of α, and use $readyS(\alpha)$ to describe the enabling condition of $sFiring(\alpha)$. Additionally, we introduce sets of variables $tn(E) = \{tn(e) | e \in E\}$ and $numF(V) = \{numF(v) | v \in V\}$, to record the current number of tokens on edges in E and the firing times of actors in V, respectively. Testing and updating the value of $numF(V)$ are not really a part of the behavior of SDFGs, which are used to facilitate the construction of an f-schedule.

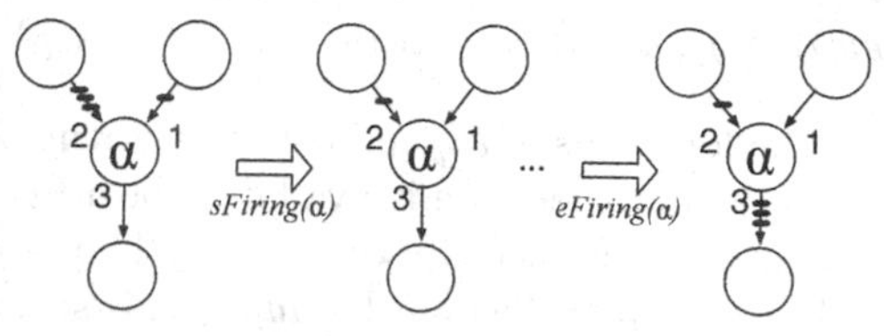

Fig. 2. The effect of *sFiring* and *eFiring*

Guard $readyS(\alpha)$ tests if there are sufficient tokens on the incoming edges of actor α to enable a firing. If the firing number of α reaches $f \cdot q(\alpha)$, no new firing of α is allowed, because α has finished its firings in f iterations.

$$readyS(\alpha) \equiv_{def} \forall e \in InE(\alpha) : tn(e) \geq cns(e) \wedge numF(\alpha) < f \cdot q(\alpha).$$

When a firing of α starts, it reduces the number of tokens of its incoming edges according to the consumption rates.

$$sFiring(\alpha) \equiv_{def} \forall e \in InE(\alpha) : tn'(e) = tn(e) - cns(e) \wedge numF'(\alpha) = numF(\alpha) + 1,$$

where x' refers to the value of x in the new state. For conciseness, we omit the elements of states if their values remain unchanged.

If a firing of α runs on processor p, it will finish after $t(\alpha, p)$ units of time. And update $eFiring(\alpha)$ increases tokens of α 's outgoing edges according to their production rates.

$$eFiring(\alpha) \equiv_{def} \quad \forall e \in OutE(\alpha) : tn'(e) = tn(e) + prd(e)$$

The effects of *sFiring* and *eFiring* are demonstrated in Fig. 2.

At a first glance, it seems natural to model each actor as a TA with status *idle* and *firing*, and each processors as a TA with status *idle* and *running* and then to model the allocation as synchronization between these TAs to form an NTA. Having a closer look, however, we observe that once an actor is firing, it must be running on some processor. Hence, we can represent the behavior of the system model only by the behavior of processors.

The behavior of actor α running on processor p can be modeled in a TA $ta_p(\alpha)$; and the behavior of p can be modeled by $ta_p(\alpha)$ with non-deterministically selecting actor α from V.

Definition 4 (TA of the behavior of processors). *A TA of the behavior of processor p is* $ta_p = \exists \alpha \in V : ta_p(\alpha)$*, and* $ta_p(\alpha) = (L, X, \mathcal{V}, \mathcal{E}, Inv, l_0)$*, where* $L = \{idle, running\}$*,* $X = \{x\}$*,* $\mathcal{V} = tn(E) \cup numF(V)$*,* $l_0 = idle$*,* $Inv = \{running : x \leq t(a,p)\}$*, and* $\mathcal{E} = \{ir, ri\}$*, where* $ir = (idle, readyS, \{sFiring(\alpha), x := 0\}, running)$*, and* $ri = (running, x == t(\alpha, p), eFiring(\alpha), idle)$*.*

The locations of ta_p indicate the status of processor p. That is, $ta_p.idle$ means p is idle and therefore is available for a firing of actors to run, and $ta_p.running$ means p is occupied by some firing. The graphical representation of ta_p is shown in Fig. 3. When the guard $readyS(\alpha)$ is satisfied, the transition from location *idle* to *running* is enabled. Once the transition is triggered, updates on clock $x := 0$ and other integer variables in $sFiring(\alpha)$ are executed. The invariant $x \leq t(\alpha, p)$ of location *running* restricts the allowed maximal delay.

Actors of SDFG G can fire in parallel only if they are ready and there are available processors. Subsequently, system model $\mathcal{M}$ can be modeled in an NTA $nta_{\mathcal{M}}$, which has $|P|$ concurrent processes and a global clock, where $|P|$ is the size of P. The global clock is used to measure the execution time of the system.

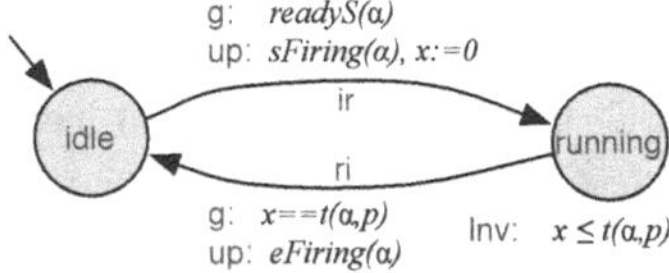

Fig. 3. The timed automaton ta_p.

Definition 5 (NTA of the behavior of system models). *The behavior of system model* $\mathcal{M} = (G, P)$ *is an NTA* $nta_{\mathcal{M}} = ||_{p \in P} ta_p$ *with a global clock* $glbClk$*.*

The above-mentioned semantics are the standard timed automata description, which can be translated into the input of UPPAAL straightforwardly. Quantification $\exists \alpha \in V$ can be implemented by the 'Selections' feature of UPPAAL.

The above defined ta_p and $nta_{\mathcal{M}}$ implicatively include f as a parameter. We omit it in the notations for conciseness. The semantics we present is much more concise than those in related works. For example, [7] transforms a system model to an NTA with more than $|V| + 3|P|$ TAs, and [18] more than $|V| \cdot |P| + |E|$ TAs, while our methods use $|P|$ TAs. This provides our methods the flexibility to deal with various constraints as shown in Section 7.

Algorithm 1. Sch($\mathcal{M}$,σ)

Input: A trace σ of $nta_{\mathcal{M}}$
Output: An f-schedule of $\mathcal{M}$, S

```
for all e ∈ E_σ do
    if ∃α ∈ V : e == p.sf(α) then
        S(α, s_{p,α}.numF(α)).st = s_{p,α}.glbClk
        S(α, s_{p,α}.numF(α)).pa = p
    end if
end for
return S
```

6 Static Optimal Scheduling and Mapping

6.1 Traces and Schedules

An f-schedule of $\mathcal{M}$ can be constructed from a trace of $nta_{\mathcal{M}}$ as follows.

Let $p.sf(\alpha)$ and $p.ef(\alpha)$ be discrete transitions, representing the transition caused by update $sFiring(\alpha)$ of edge ir of ta_p and the transition caused by $eFiring(\alpha)$ of edge ri. The use of $numF(\alpha) < f \cdot q(\alpha)$ as a guard in $readyS(\alpha)$ will force $nta_{\mathcal{M}}$ to be deadlocked after the firings of f-iterations of G are finished. Therefore a trace of $nta_{\mathcal{M}}$ includes finitely many discrete transitions.

Hence we consider only the finite part of a trace that includes all finite discrete transitions. Denote the set of transitions of trace σ as $\mathcal{E}_\sigma$ and the state caused by $p.sf(\alpha)$ as $s_{p,\alpha}$.

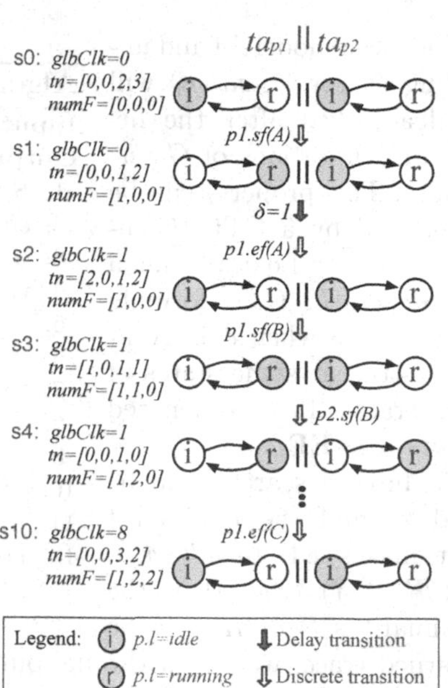

Fig. 4. A part of a trace of system model $\mathcal{M}_1$ shown in Fig. 1, where circles in blue show the current location.

Theorem 1. *In a trace σ of $nta_{\mathcal{M}}$, for each actor α:*

1. *$\nexists s_{p,\alpha}$ such that $s_{p,\alpha}.numF(\alpha) > f \cdot q(\alpha)$;*
2. *$\forall i \in [1, f \cdot q(\alpha)]$, there is a unique $s_{p,\alpha}$ such that $s_{p,\alpha}.numF(\alpha) = i$;*
3. *when $p.sf(\alpha)$ occurs, there are sufficient tokens on each $e \in InE(\alpha)$ for one firing of α and processor p is available.*

Proof. 1) is guaranteed by $readyS(\alpha)$; 2) is guaranteed by $sFiring(\alpha)$; according to the definition of ta_p, only when $ta_p.idle$ and $readyS(\alpha)$ are satisfied, p may select α to fire and therefore 3) is guaranteed.

Algorithm 1 presents the procedure of finding an f-schedule from a trace. Its correctness is ensured by Theorem 1. The schedule in Fig. 1(c), for example, is a 1-schedule of system model $\mathcal{M}_1$. It can be found in a trace of $nta_{\mathcal{M}_1}$, part of which is shown in Fig. 4.

6.2 Throughput-Optimal Solution

We denote the f-schedule derived by trace σ as S_σ. The cycle period of S_σ is the time when the last firing terminates, that is:

$$CP(S_\sigma) = \max\{s_{p,\alpha}.glbClk + t(\alpha, p) | s_{p,\alpha} \in \sigma\}.$$

Suppose the set of traces of $nta_{\mathcal{M}}$ is Σ, the optimal IP of f-schedules of $\mathcal{M}$ is

$$optIP(\mathcal{M}) = \min\left\{\frac{CP(S_\sigma)}{f}\Big|\sigma \in \Sigma\right\}$$

For given model $\mathcal{M}$ and unfolding factor f, $nta_{\mathcal{M}}$ will be deadlocked after the firings of f-iterations of G terminate. This property can be formalized by a CTL (Computation Tree Logic) formula **EF** *deadlock*. CTL formula **EF**ϕ is true when ϕ is eventually true at some states of some traces of $nta_{\mathcal{M}}$, denoted by $nta_{\mathcal{M}} \models$ **EF**ϕ.

A binary search can be used to find the minimal t that makes **EF** (*deadlock* $\wedge$ *glbClk* $\leq t$) true; then the minimal t is $f \cdot optIP$. By the returned trace, we find a throughput-optimal f-schedule. Even better, we can ask UPPAAL to check **EF** *deadlock* and to return a *fastest* trace, which is a trace with the shortest accumulated time delay. The latter way returns the same results as the binary search but only checks the property once. In the following discussion, we always apply UPPAAL to return a fastest trace, implemented by function $trace(nta_{\mathcal{M}}, \psi)$. From the trace returned by $trace(nta_{\mathcal{M}}$, **EF** *deadlock*), we obtain a throughput-optimal f-schedule of $\mathcal{M}$, denoted by S_{optIP}, i.e.,

$$S_{optIP} = Sch(\mathcal{M}, trace(nta_{\mathcal{M}}, \textbf{EF}\ deadlock)).$$

Algorithm 2. optPSch($\mathcal{M}$)

Input: $\mathcal{M}$
Output: An f-schedule S_{optP} of $\mathcal{M}$

```
S_optIP = Sch(M, trace(nta_M, EF deadlock))
ec = EC(S_optIP)
S_optP = S_optIP
repeat
   φ = EF deadlock ∧ con(ec − 1)
   S_IP = Sch(M, trace(nta_M', φ))
   if IP == optIP then
      ec = EC(S_IP)
      S_optP = S_IP
   end if
until IP > optIP
return S_optP
```

The energy consumption of the schedule, $EC(S_{optIP})$, can be computed according to Eqn. (2).

To find an f-schedule with *optIP* and a best energy consumption, we need to add a constraint on energy consumption. Therefore, we add an update $occT(p) = occT(p) + t(\alpha, p)$ to edge ri in ta_p, and the subsequent model is $nta_{\mathcal{M}'}$. When *deadlock* occurs, *glbClk* is the CP of the schedule. Then according to Eqn. (2), the property that the energy consumption at time *glbClk* is no more than a given ec is defined as

$$con(ec) \equiv_{def} glbClk \leq \frac{ec - \sum_{p\in P} occT(p) \cdot [uEC(p) - iEC(p)]}{\sum_{p\in P} iEC(p)}$$

With $con(ec)$ as the additional constraint, we decrease ec gradually to check whether we can reach a smaller energy consumption with *optIP*. The details on computing an f-schedule S_{optP} with *optIP* and a best energy consumption are explained in Algorithm 2.

6.3 Energy-Optimal Solution

Decreasing ec in Algorithm 2 until ϕ is not satisfied, we can obtain an f-schedule with an optimal energy consumption and a best throughput. We can answer our second problem formulated in Section 3 by this way. The experiments we performed reveal that this method is inefficient, however. A more efficient way is to integrate the use of PTA.

By adding cost $iEC(p)$ and $uEC(p)$ to locations *idle* and *running* of ta_p, respectively, we obtain a priced timed automaton pta_p for processor p. Consequently, we use $npta_{\mathcal{M}} = ||_{p\in P} pta_p$ with a global clock *glbClk* to describe system model $\mathcal{M}$. With this formalization, by applying UPPAAL CORA to check $npta_{\mathcal{M}} \models \mathbf{EF}\ deadlock$, we obtain an energy consumption-optimal f-schedule of $\mathcal{M}$ with *optEC*, denoted by S_{optEC}. Taking $con(optEC)$ as the additional constraint, we can apply UPPAAL to check $nta_{\mathcal{M}} \models \mathbf{EF}\ (deadlock \wedge con(optEC))$, and obtain an f-schedule S_{optE} with an optimal energy consumption and a best throughput.

7 Dealing with More Constraints

In this section, we show how various kinds of constraints can be integrated into our methods. We first introduce the general framework of our methods, then discuss the details of the three kinds of constraints, auto-concurrency constraints, buffer size constraints and processor constraints.

The effects of constraints on the behavior of an SDFG are summarized in Table 1. The first column lists the corresponding names of *readyS*, *sFiring* and *eFiring* for constraint *con*. The second column includes guard and updates we defined before. The 3-5 columns give the extra guard and updates for different constraints, auto-concurrency (ac), buffer size (bs) and both of them, respectively. Combining any of them with the second column forms the corresponding $readyS_{con}$, $sFiring_{con}$ and $eFiring_{con}$. For example, the enable condition of starting firing for an auto-concurrency constraint is represented as:

$$readyS_{ac} \equiv_{def} readyS \wedge hasF.$$

Table 1. Constrained Behavior of actor α

Constrained Behavior of α	NO Con.	Constraints (con)		
		auto-conc. (ac)	buffer size (bs)	both
$readyS_{con}$	$readyS$	$hasF$	$sufB$	$hasF \wedge sufB$
$sFiring_{con}$	$sFiring$	$addF$	$claB$	$addF \wedge claB$
$eFiring_{con}$	$eFiring$	$delF$	$relB$	$delF \wedge relB$

Replacing $readyS$, $sFiring$ and $eFiring$ in ta_p and pta_p defined in Section 5 with $readyS_{con}$, $sFiring_{con}$ and $eFiring_{con}$, respectively, we get NTA and NPTA of a system model with constraint con. The ways to find f-schedules S_{optP} and S_{optE} are the same as the system without these constraints.

7.1 Auto-concurrency constraints

When there are no limitation on auto-concurrency, at the same time, there can be unlimited number of concurrent firings of the same actor. Suppose the number of auto-concurrent actors is limited to $conN$. At each moment, only $conN$ firings allowed for each actor. We use a set $conC(V)$ to control the number of concurrent firings of each actor $\alpha \in V$. The extra condition for $readyS$, updates for $sFiring$ and $eFiring$ are formulated as $hasF(\alpha)$, $addF(\alpha)$ and $delF(\alpha)$, respectively.

$$\begin{aligned} hasF(\alpha) &\equiv_{def} \quad conC(\alpha) \leq conN \\ addF(\alpha) &\equiv_{def} \quad conC'(\alpha) = conC(\alpha) + 1 \\ delF(\alpha) &\equiv_{def} \quad conC'(\alpha) = conC(\alpha) - 1 \end{aligned}$$

Non-auto-concurrency, which can be used to model stateful actor [18], is a special case, which can be specified by $conN = 1$. Our method can also be used in a generalized case in which there is a constraint for each actor. For the generalized case, a set $conN(V)$ is used and above $conN$ are replace by $conN(\alpha)$.

7.2 Buffer size constraints

In practice, the storage space of a system must be bounded. The storage used by edges may be shared or separate. Firstly, we consider a relatively conservative separate buffer storage abstraction. That is, when an actor starts firing, it claims the space of the tokens it will produce, and it releases the space of the tokens it consumes only when the firing ends. A set $tnb(E)$ is added to capture the buffer space used by each $e \in E$.

Suppose a schedule is constrained by a set $B(E)$, which limits the buffer usage of each edge, an enabled firing can not start when there is no sufficient space on its outgoing edges. The extra condition for *readyS* is formulated as $sufB(\alpha)$. When an actor starts a firing, it claims the required space on its outgoing edges. The update is formulated as $claB(\alpha)$. Only when a firing ends, it releases the space of its incoming edges. The update is formulated as $relB(\alpha)$.

$$sufB(\alpha) \equiv_{def} \quad \forall e \in OutE(\alpha) : prd(e) \leq B(e) - tnb(e)$$
$$claB(\alpha) \equiv_{def} \quad \forall e \in OutE(\alpha) : tnb'(e) = tnb(e) + prd(e)$$
$$relB(\alpha) \equiv_{def} \quad \forall e \in InE(\alpha) : tnb'(e) = tnb(e) - cns(e)$$

A separate storage with other abstraction is even easier to be integrated. For example, suppose an actor releases the space of its incoming edges when it starts a firing and claims and occupies the space of its outgoing edges only when it ends a firing, we do not need the extra set $tnb(E)$ and updates *claB* and *relB*. In $sufB(\alpha)$, $tnb(e)$ is simply replaced by $tn(e)$.

A shared memory usage can be easily integrated in the framework by modifying $sufB(\alpha)$ as $\sum_{e \in OutE(\alpha)} prd(e) \leq sM - \sum_{e \in E} tnb(e)$, where sM is the bound of the shared memory.

7.3 Constraints on processors

The situation that an actor is not allowed to be allocated on some processors can be modeled by adding extra condition $t(\alpha, p) \geq 0$ to the enable condition of starting firing. That is, $readyS(\alpha) \wedge t(\alpha, p) \geq 0$. The constraint that actor α is not allowed to run on processor p can be represented by $t(\alpha, p) = -1$.

The constraint that a processor has a higher priority than another can be modeled by the 'Priorities' feature of UPPAAL.

8 Case Studies

We have implemented the translation from system models with different constraints to input models of UPPAAL and UPPAAL CORA and the procedure to extract f-schedules from the returned traces. The approach has been applied to two practical applications with different parameters, running on a 2.90GHz CPU with 24M Cache and 384GB RAM. If not marked specially, the units of execution time and memory in performance evaluation are in second (s) and megabyte (MB), respectively.

The execution platforms for all SDFGs includes two types of processors, PT1 with $uEC = 90$W and $iEC = 10$W and PT2 with $uEC = 30$W and $iEC = 20$W. PT1 is faster than PT2. We consider 2 processors, including one PT1 processor and one PT2 processor, and 4 processors, including two PT1 processors and two PT2 processors. We use the first buffer storage abstraction described in Section 7.2. The units of time and energy consumption used in system models are in picosecond and nanojoule, respectively.

8.1 MPEG-4 Decoder

The first case is an MPEG-4 decoder [23] with different parameters. The MPEG-4 decoder supports various kinds of frames. It is modeled as a Scenario-aware dataflow (SADF) model in [23]. Each scenario in an SADF model is actually an SDFG. We consider three scenarios, P30, P70 and P99. The system models of the MPEG-4 decoder are shown in Fig. 5. The parameterized SDFG is shown in Fig. 5 (a), the value of x corresponding to Px. The repetition vector and the sum of its elements (nQ) of each Px and the execution times of actors on different processors are shown in Fig. 5 (b). This case is used to evaluate our methods when different parameters are considered: the sum of the repetition vector, the unfolding factor, the number of processors, and the buffer size constraints. Auto-concurrency are not allowed in all models.

To evaluate the impact of the buffer size constraints, we consider two cases: a model with a low buffer size bound and a high bound. The low bound is computed according to the method described in [2] to guarantee deadlock-freeness of an SDFG. The high bound is a minimal buffer size requirement to guarantee throughput-optimal of an SDFG when it is scheduled in an infinite number of homogeneous processors [22]. The sum of buffer size bounds of all edges of Px are shown in the last two columns of Fig. 5 (b).

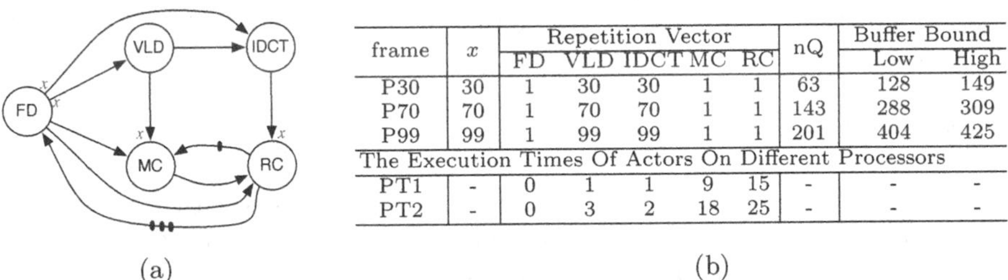

(a)

frame	x	Repetition Vector FD	VLD	IDCT	MC	RC	nQ	Buffer Bound Low	High
P30	30	1	30	30	1	1	63	128	149
P70	70	1	70	70	1	1	143	288	309
P99	99	1	99	99	1	1	201	404	425
The Execution Times Of Actors On Different Processors									
PT1	-	0	1	1	9	15	-	-	-
PT2	-	0	3	2	18	25	-	-	-

(b)

Fig. 5. System models of the MPEG-4 decoder. (a) Its SDFG; (b) the repetition vector of each Px, the sums of the vectors, the considered bound of buffer size, and the execution times of actors on different processors.

We show the experimental results for the MPEG-4 decoder in Table 2, in which the parameters are shown in the first two rows and the first two columns. The others are the results. The first column is the unfolding factor f. We consider 1-schedule and 2-schedule of models. The second column is the number of processors $\#P$. The other 6 columns are the results for SDFG Px under a low buffer size bound and a high buffer size bound. The results include three parts. The first part shows the optimal iteration period (optIP) and the best iteration energy consumption under optIP (bestIEC). The second part is the optimal iteration energy consumption (optIEC) and the best IP under optIEC (bestIP). The third part shows the execution times and memory consumptions of the procedure finding optIP.

Table 2. Experimental results for MPEG-4 Decoder

info		Low Bound			High Bound		
		P30	P70	P99	P30	P70	P99
f	$\#P$	optIP/bestIEC					
1	2	83/9.2	163/18.0	221/24.3	82/7.4	162/13.8	220/18.4
	4	83/11.6	163/N	221/N	54/N	94/N	123/N
2	2	83/9.2	163/18.0	221/24.3	74/7.0	154/13.4	212/18.0
	4	83/N	163/N	221/N	48/N	88/N	117/N
		optIEC/bestIP					
1	2	7.4/131	15.0/251	20.5/338	6.6/102	13.0/182	17.6/240
	4	11.3/93	22.5/N	30.6/N	9.5/64	18.3/N	24.7/N
2	2	7.4/131	15.0/251	20.5/338	6.5/89.5	12.9/169.5	17.6/227.5
	4	11.3/N	22.5/N	30.6/N	8.6/N	17.4/N	23.8/N
		Execution Time (s)/Memory Consumed (MB) of optIP					
1	2	0.0/4.7	0.0/4.8	0.0/4.9	0.0/4.8	0.0/5.0	0.0/5.2
	4	0.1/5.6	0.1/6.8	0.2/7.7	0.2/7.1	0.5/10.6	0.6/13.7
2	2	0.0/4.9	0.0/5.2	0.1/5.5	0.1/5.6	0.1/6.3	0.2/7.0
	4	0.3/11.9	0.8/18.8	0.9/26.8	2.8/34.3	3.9/54.0	4.3/70.8

* N: not finished after 3 hours or running out of memory.

When a low buffer size bound is used, the increase of unfolding factor and number of processors have no improvement on the four values we have evaluated. Therefore, small unfolding factor and a few of processors are good enough for an optimal schedule of Px with a low buffer size constraint. A high bound provides more room for the improvement of iteration period and energy consumption at the cost of longer execution time and larger memory consumption.

When two processors are considered, our methods perform well on all cases. When four processors, 2-schedule and IEC are considered, state explosion occurs and hence our methods perform poorly. Another reason is that we only find 32bit version of UPPAAL CORA, which uses no more than 4GB memory. Besides the number of processors, the nQ seems affecting the performance of our methods mostly. Note that nQ is also the number of actors of the equivalent HSDFG of an SDFG, or the number of jobs in a task graph [1]. It is an important factor affecting the performance of almost all algorithms on SDFGs.

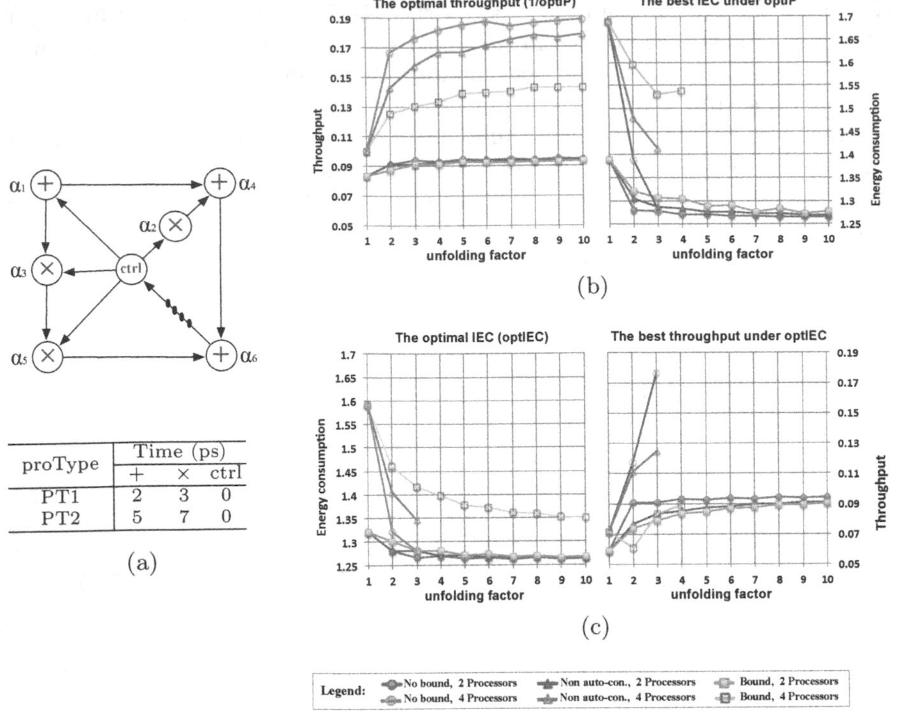

proType	Time (ps)		
	+	×	ctrl
PT1	2	3	0
PT2	5	7	0

Fig. 6. (a) System model of the computation example; (b) the optimal throughput and the best energy consumption under the optimal throughput; (c) the optimal energy consumption and the best throughput under the optimal energy consumption.

8.2 Computation Example

The second case study is mainly used to measure the impact of the unfolding factor. We consider a computation example, which is described in a task graph in [5]. Its system model is shown in Fig. 6(a). Actor *ctrl* connecting with original source and sink actors is added to limit the total latency. We have computed the results of unfolding factor from 1 to 10, and taken into account different combinations of values of three parameters: with and without a buffer bound, with and without auto-concurrency, 2 processors and 4 processors.

The experimental results are illustrated in Fig. 6 (b) and (c). The throughput and energy consumption of schedules are improved by increasing unfolding factor; the degree of improvement decreasing accordingly. The buffer size bound and auto-concurrency constraints have larger impact on the cases with 4 processors than that with 2 processors. Some lines stop at the point that unfolding factor reaches 4 or 5, because the corresponding procedures for larger unfolding factors run out of memory.

9 Conclusion

In this paper, we have presented exact methods for scheduling SDFGs on heterogenous multiprocessor platforms considering both throughput and energy consumption. Various parameters, including unfolding factors, constraints on auto-concurrency, buffer sizes and processors, can be integrated into the methods. Our experimental results show that our methods can deal with moderate scale models within reasonable execution time, and can find how different parameters impact on the results of different optimization goals.

We have used model checking as backend technique to solve the scheduling problems. While enjoying the benefits it provides, we encountered state explosion inevitably. As a future work, we will explore further the features of the considered models to reduce the state space. On the one hand, we will try to provide more domain insight when encoding the considered problems to model checking problems; on the other hand, we may tailor model checking techniques to deal with specialized tasks, instead of using a model checker directly. We have not considered the communications between processors based on the assumption that its cost is much smaller than the execution times of actors. In practical designs, the cost may be large in some situations. Then the communication needs to be taken into account. This can be integrated into our approach straightforwardly by modeling communications as actors that use special processors which model the connections between processors. But this method enlarges the scale of system models accordingly. A more efficient way to deal with communications is also an interesting topic for our further study.

References

1. Abdeddaïm, Y., Asarin, E., Maler, O., et al.: Scheduling with timed automata. Theor. Comput. Sci. 354(2), 272–300 (2006)
2. Adé, M., Lauwereins, R., Peperstraete, J.: Data memory minimisation for synchronous data flow graphs emulated on DSP-FPGA targets. In: Proc. of the 34th Ann. Design Automation Conf (DAC), pp. 64–69 (1997)
3. Alur, R., Dill, D.L.: A theory of timed automata. Theor. Comput. Sci. 126(2), 183–235 (1994)
4. Behrmann, G., Larsen, K.G., Rasmussen, J.I.: Priced timed automata: Algorithms and applications. In: de Boer, F.S., Bonsangue, M.M., Graf, S., de Roever, W.-P. (eds.) FMCO 2004. LNCS, vol. 3657, pp. 162–182. Springer, Heidelberg (2005)
5. Bouyer, P., Fahrenberg, U., Larsen, K.G., Markey, N.: Quantitative analysis of real-time systems using priced timed automata. Comm. of the ACM 54(9), 78–87 (2011)

6. Cimatti, A., Clarke, E., Giunchiglia, F., Roveri, M.: NuSMV: a new symbolic model checker. International Journal on Software Tools for Technology Transfer 2(4), 410–425 (2000)
7. Fakih, M., Grüttner, K., Fränzle, M., Rettberg, A.: Towards performance analysis of SDFGs mapped to shared-bus architectures using model-checking. In: Proc. of the Conference on Design, Automation and Test in Europe, pp. 1167–1172 (2013)
8. Fersman, E., Mokrushin, L., Pettersson, P., Yi, W.: Schedulability analysis of fixed-priority systems using timed automata. Theor. Comput. Sci. 354(2), 301 (2006)
9. Geilen, M., Basten, T., Stuijk, S.: Minimising buffer requirements of synchronous dataflow graphs with model checking. In: Proc. of the 42nd Annu. Design Automation Conf. (DAC) (2005)
10. Gu, Z., Yuan, M., Guan, N., Lv, M., He, X., Deng, Q., Yu, G.: Static scheduling and software synthesis for dataflow graphs with symbolic model-checking. In: Proc. of 28th International Real-Time Systems Symposium (RTSS), pp. 353–364 (2007)
11. Harbour, M.G., Klein, M.H., Lehoczky, J.P.: Timing analysis for fixed-priority scheduling of hard real-time systems. IEEE Trans. on Soft. Eng. 20(1), 13–28 (1994)
12. Hartel, P.H., Ruys, T.C., Geilen, M.C.: Scheduling optimisations for SPIN to minimise buffer requirements in synchronous data flow. In: Proc of the International Conference on Formal Methods in Computer-Aided Design, p. 21 (2008)
13. Hirzel, M., Soulé, R., Schneider, S., Gedik, B., Grimm, R.: A catalog of stream processing optimizations. ACM Comput. Surv. 46(4), 46:1–46:34 (2014)
14. Holzmann, G.J.: The model checker SPIN. IEEE Transactions on Software Engineering 23(5), 279–295 (1997)
15. Larsen, K.G., Pettersson, P., Yi, W.: UPPAAL in a nutshell. International Journal on Software Tools for Technology Transfer (STTT) 1(1), 134–152 (1997)
16. Lee, E., Messerschmitt, D.: Static scheduling of synchronous data flow programs for digital signal processing. IEEE Trans. Comput. 36(1), 24–35 (1987)
17. Madsen, J., Hansen, M.R., Knudsen, K.S., Nielsen, J.E., Brekling, A.W.: System-level verification of multi-core embedded systems using timed-automata. In: Proc. of the 17th World Congress International Federation of Automatic Control, Seoul, Korea, pp. 9302–9307 (2008)
18. Malik, A., Gregg, D.: Orchestrating stream graphs using model checking. ACM Trans. Archit. Code Optim. 10(3), 19:1–19:25 (2013)
19. Parhi, K.K., Messerschmitt, D.G.: Static rate-optimal scheduling of iterative dataflow programs via optimum unfolding. IEEE Trans. Comput. 40(2), 178–195 (1991)
20. Singh, A.K., Shafique, M., Kumar, A., Henkel, J.: Mapping on multi/many-core systems: Survey of current and emerging trends. In: Proc. of the 50th Ann. Design Automation Conf. (DAC), p. 1 (2013)
21. Sriram, S., Bhattacharyya, S.S.: Embedded multiprocessors: scheduling and synchronization. CRC Press (2009)
22. Stuijk, S., Geilen, M., Basten, T.: Throughput-buffering trade-off exploration for cyclo-static and synchronous dataflow graphs. IEEE Trans. Comput. 57(10), 1331–1345 (2008)
23. Theelen, B., Katoen, J.P., Wu, H.: Model checking of scenario-aware dataflow with CADP. In: Proceedings of the Conference on Design, Automation and Test in Europe, pp. 653–658 (2012)

24. Zhu, X.-Y., Geilen, M., Basten, T., Stuijk, S.: Static rate-optimal scheduling of multirate DSP algorithms via retiming and unfolding. In: Proc. of the 18th Real-Time and Embedded Technology and Applications Symposium (RTAS), pp. 109–118 (2012)
25. Zivojnovic, V., Ritz, S., Meyr, H.: Optimizing DSP programs using the multirate retiming transformation. Proc. EUSIPCO Signal Process. VII, Theories Applicat. (1994)

Industry Track

Eliminating Static Analysis False Positives Using Loop Abstraction and Bounded Model Checking

Bharti Chimdyalwar(✉), Priyanka Darke, Anooj Chavda, Sagar Vaghani, and Avriti Chauhan

Tata Research Development and Design Center, Pune, India
bharti.c@tcs.com

Abstract. Sound static analyzers over-approximate the input program behaviour and thus imprecisely report many correct properties as potential errors (false warnings). Manual investigation of these warnings is cost intensive and error prone. To get an insight into the causes and explore the effectiveness of current solutions, we analyzed the code structure associated with warnings reported by sound state of the art static analyzers: Polyspace and TCS Embedded Code Analyzer, over six industrial embedded applications. We observed that most of the warnings were due to variables modified inside loops with large or unknown bounds.

While earlier techniques have suggested the use of program slicing, abstraction, Iterative Context Extension (ICE) with Bounded Model Checking (BMC) to eliminate false warnings automatically, more recently an effective approach has been proposed called loop abstraction for BMC (LABMC), aimed specially at proving properties using BMC in the presence of loops with large and unknown bounds. Therefore, we experimentally evaluated a combination of program slicing, ICE and LABMC to enable practitioners to eliminate false warnings automatically. This combination successfully identified more than 70% of the static analysis warnings on the applications as false positives. We share the details of our approach and experimentation in this paper.

1 Introduction

Static analysis is the most scalable formal verification technique, widely used in the industry to detect standard run-time errors. However, all static analyzers implement abstractions which lead to an imprecise analysis [8]. Thus they report many warnings, most of which are not actual errors and are termed as *false positives*. These false positives have to be weeded out manually. But on real world applications manual analysis is time consuming and error prone. Thus there is a need for precise and automatic false positive elimination. Towards this, we first consolidated warnings generated by practitioners over six embedded applications. The practitioners had used either of the two sound static analyzers, Polyspace [6] or TCS Embedded Code Analyzer (TCS ECA) [1]. Then we analyzed the code structure corresponding to the warnings. We observed that 71% of the warnings were due to variables modified in complex loops (loop outputs). Such loops had a large or unknown bound or several branching conditions, and in most

N. Bjørner and F. de Boer (Eds.): FM 2015, LNCS 9109, pp. 573–576, 2015.
DOI: 10.1007/978-3-319-19249-9_35

cases, the loop variable on which the warning depended was modified using linear recurrence along some branches of the loop body. Sound static analyzers over-approximate such loops, hence report several false positives.

To improve precision, techniques have been presented in [7], [5] and [3]. They use BMC to verify programs post static analysis and have been proved to be useful. Additionally, the technique presented in [9] combines static analysis and model checking to find bugs, but it may miss out actual errors. The authors of [7] and [3] present the use of Iterative Context Extension (ICE), while the authors of [3] and [5] additionally reduce the input program before applying BMC. However, these techniques have their limitations. The technique presented in [5] converts the input program into a model, optimizes it using static analysis and verifies the optimized model using BMC. Hence its precision is limited to static analysis. The technique presented in [7] is partly automated and in the presence of large or unknown bounded loops, its scalability is limited because BMC can verify programs up to a bounded execution length. The authors of [3] present a loop abstraction technique to overcome limitations of BMC. But recently, an effective technique has been presented with a more precise loop abstraction called LABMC [4]. It aims to scale up BMC for proving program properties in the presence of large or unknown bounded loops by abstracting each loop using a combination of output abstraction, abstract acceleration and induction. It replaces loops in programs with abstract loops having a small known bound so that all the loop outputs are over-approximated [4]. However LABMC did not abstract loops which modified array contents or aliases. So we extended it to abstract those loops by providing non deterministic values throughout the program to all the array elements and aliases modified in loops. Also, in [4], the authors show that LABMC could verify properties of a large industrial automotive system which many other tools and techniques could not.

In this paper, we experimentally evaluate a combination of program slicing, ICE and LABMC to automatically eliminate false positives generated by sound static analyzers. Our experiments identified, on an average, 57% and 77% warnings reported by Polyspace and TCS ECA respectively as false positives, thus helping practitioners by reducing the chances of errors and effort involved in the analysis of critical systems.

The key contributions of this paper are: (a) an evaluation of the applicability of combining program slicing, ICE and LABMC to eliminate false positives automatically over multiple industrial applications (b) highlighting the key areas of improvement to researchers.

2 Experimentation

Fig.1 presents the experimental setup. Assert Annotator first annotates each warning as an assertion in the input program. Then Slicer slices annotated program with respect to the assertion and feed it to LABMC for loop abstraction. This abstract program is then passed to the ICE module which further abstracts this program by selecting the function f containing the assertion, assigning non deterministic values to inputs of f, and specifying f as the analysis function to the C Bounded Model Checker (CBMC) [2]. If the assertion is proved to be valid for f, then the analysis stops, proving the property to be valid and eliminate the corresponding warning. But if CBMC generates

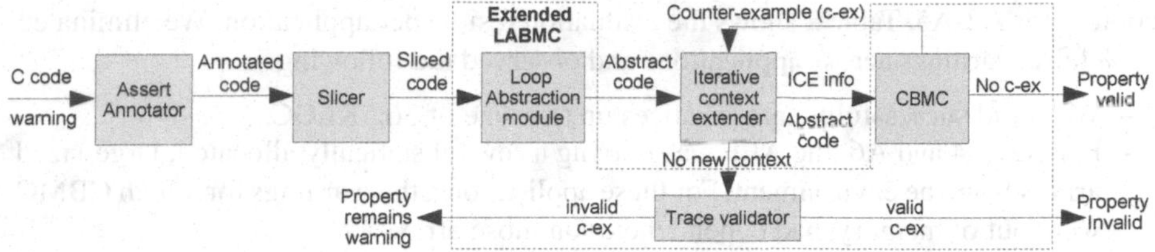

Fig. 1. Experimental Setup

a counter-example (c-ex), the ICE module extends the context to the functions calling f and invokes CBMC with respect to all the callers of f. This process of ICE is repeated till either the property is proved to be valid for all callers, or a valid c-ex is generated at the Application Entry Function (AEF) showing the warning to be an actual error, or the warning is retained if CBMC runs out of resources or generates an invalid c-ex with respect to the original program at AEF.

We conducted experiments on six real-life embedded applications using a desktop with a 3.0 GHz Intel processor, 2 GB of RAM and 32 bit Windows OS. The applications A1, A2, A4, A5 and A6 implement the car alarm, battery controller, navigation, protocol stack, and breaking control applications of a vehicle respectively. A3 implements a smart-card functionality. These applications were developed (in the C language) by six different development teams, and also verified by them for the array index out of bounds (AIOB) property using either Polyspace or TCS ECA. They shared with us the warnings report generated by the respective static analyzer. We analyzed the code structure corresponding to the warnings of each application. Our observations are presented in Table 1. As seen, around 71% of the warnings had a dependency on variables modified inside loops of large or unknown bound. These loops had several branching conditions, and the variables which caused the warning were modified using linear recurrences along different branches of the loops.

We verified the assertion corresponding to each warning, as explained in Fig. 1. For A1 and A6, we set a CBMC time out of 30 minutes per context, and 17 minutes per

Table 1. Warnings Analysis

Metrics	Values
Total warnings (warns.)	134
% Warns. due to loop outputs	71
% Warns. due to function return values	1
% Warns. due to branching conditions over environment variables (outside loops)	28

Table 2. Experimental Results

Metrics	Application					
	A1	A2	A3	A4	A5	A6
Application size (KLOC)	0.98	60	4.6	230	8	33.8
Average (Avg.) slice size (KLOC)	0.98	16	1.3	1.5	1.9	6
Avg. known-bound loops in a slice	2	25	2	60	0	53
Avg. unknown-bound loops in a slice	1	25	2	76	2	11
Static Analyzer	P	P	P	T	T	T
Number of (NO.) warns.	2	44	3	32	30	23
NO. warns. reduced	2	23	3	30	21	15
NO. warns. CBMC went OOM	0	21	0	2	0	7
NO. warns. with invalid c-ex	0	0	0	0	9	1
% Warns. reduced	100	52	100	93	70	65
Largest validated slice size (KLOC)	0.98	36.5	1.9	29.7	2.1	6.3
P - Polyspace, T - TCS ECA, OOM - Out of memory						

context for A2-A5. Table 2 shows the evaluation results per application. We eliminated 70% false warnings across applications and observed the following:

- We could successfully analyze slices up to a size of 36.5KLOC.
- For A2, A4 and A6, the AEF was reading a several statically allocated, large-sized arrays from the environment. For these applications, the warnings for which CBMC went out of memory, had dependencies on those arrays.
- For A2, one warning (of slice size 36.5KLOC) was eliminated at the AEF, but it did not depend on arrays from the environment.
- For A5, CBMC generated invalid counter-examples at the AEF due to imprecision of LABMC abstraction caused by array contents being read in loop conditions.
- For A6, CBMC generated an invalid counter-example at the AEF due to imprecision in the points-to-analysis used by LABMC while abstracting loops.
- The average number of context extensions needed to eliminate warnings was 1.

3 Conclusion

For the given set of applications, we showed the practicality of combining static analysis, slicing, ICE and LABMC for precise industrial code analysis through our experiments. This combination of techniques ensured a sound and automatic elimination of false positives, reducing manual effort of practitioners to a large extent, and minimizing chances of error in critical software systems. Our experiments highlight to the researchers that (a) During BMC, arrays are the main contributors of state space explosion. (b) LABMC abstraction needs improvement when arrays are read in loop conditions and pointers are modified in loops.

References

1. TCS Embedded Code Analyzer (TECA).http://www.tcs.com/offerings/engineering_services/Pages/TCS-Embedded-Code-Analyzer.aspx
2. Clarke, E., Kroening, D., Lerda, F.: A Tool for Checking ANSI-C Programs. In: Jensen, K., Podelski, A. (eds.) TACAS 2004. LNCS, vol. 2988, pp. 168–176. Springer, Heidelberg (2004)
3. Darke, P., Khanzode, M., Nair, A., Shrotri, U., Venkatesh, R.: Precise analysis of large industry code. In: Asia Pacific Software Engineering Conference, pp. 306–309 (2012)
4. Darke, P., Chimdyalwar, B., Venkatesh, R., Shrotri, U., Metta, R.: Over-approximating loops to prove properties using bounded model checking. In: DATE (2015)
5. Ganai, M., Gupta, A., Ivani, F., Kahlon, V., Li, W., Papakonstantinou, N., Sankaranarayanan, S., Wang, C.: Towards precise and scalable verification of embedded software. In: DVCon (2008)
6. MathWorks. Polyspace Embedded Software Verification, http://www.mathworks.in/products/polyspace/
7. Post, H., Sinz, C., Kaiser, A., Gorges, T.: Reducing false positives by combining abstract interpretation and bounded model checking. In: ASE (2008)
8. Rival, X.: Understanding the origin of alarms in ASTRÉE. In: Hankin, C., Siveroni, I. (eds.) SAS 2005. LNCS, vol. 3672, pp. 303–319. Springer, Heidelberg (2005)
9. Valdiviezo, M., Cifuentes, C., Krishnan, P.: A method for scalable and precise bug finding using program analysis and model checking. In: Garrigue, J. (ed.) APLAS 2014. LNCS, vol. 8858, pp. 196–215. Springer, Heidelberg (2014)

Autofunk: An Inference-Based Formal Model Generation Framework for Production Systems

William Durand[1](✉) and Sébastien Salva[2]

[1] Michelin, Clermont-Ferrand, France
william.durand@fr.michelin.com
[2] Auvergne University, Clermont-Ferrand, France
sebastien.salva@udamail.fr

Abstract. In this paper, we present *Autofunk*, a fast and scalable framework designed at Michelin to automatically build formal models (Symbolic Transition Systems) based on production messages gathered from production systems themselves. Our approach combines model-driven engineering with rule-based expert systems and human knowledge.

Keywords: Model inference · Symbolic transition system · Expert system · Production system · Regression testing

1 Introduction

Michelin is a worldwide tire manufacturer which designs all its factories, production systems, and software by itself. Like many other industrial companies, Michelin follows the Computer Integrated Manufacturing approach, using computers and software to control the entire manufacturing process. Michelin Level 2 applications are often deployed for 20 years, and are very important for its business. Maintaining these software is inevitable, but due to their importance, this is risky. That is why Michelin puts a lot of efforts in documenting how these applications behave. Unfortunately, keeping such knowledge up to date is difficult, and it often implies under-specified or not documented legacy systems that no one wants to maintain because of lack of understanding.

In this paper, we focus on this problem for legacy systems in an industrial context. Model inference is a recent research field that addresses this issue. Models are here built from execution traces (i.e. sequences of observed actions of an application). Several approaches have been proposed for different types of systems, usually GUI applications [4,5,3]. However, our experience shows that these approaches are not tailored to support running production systems that are complex and distributed over several devices. From the literature, we deduced the following key observations:

- Model inference approaches learn approximate models capturing the behaviours of a system and more. In our context, we want exact models that could be used for regression test case generation,

N. Bjørner and F. de Boer (Eds.): FM 2015, LNCS 9109, pp. 577–580, 2015.
DOI: 10.1007/978-3-319-19249-9_36

- Some approaches perform active testing on the systems to learn models. Applying active testing on running systems is not possible since these must not be disrupted,
- Production systems exchange thousands and thousands of messages a day. Most of the model inference approaches cannot take such a huge amount of information to build models.

That is why we have developed *Autofunk*, our fast and scalable framework to infer both exact and formal models from production messages, using expert systems and inference rules to emulate human knowledge, and transition systems to embrace formal tools.

2 Framework

Figure 1 depicts the architecture of our framework. It contains five modules (in grey in the figure), the first four modules aim at building models and the last one (which will not be described in the paper) is used to generate test cases. *Autofunk* is developed in Java and relies on *Drools* [1], a powerful Java rule-based expert system engine which supports knowledge bases with facts given as Java objects.

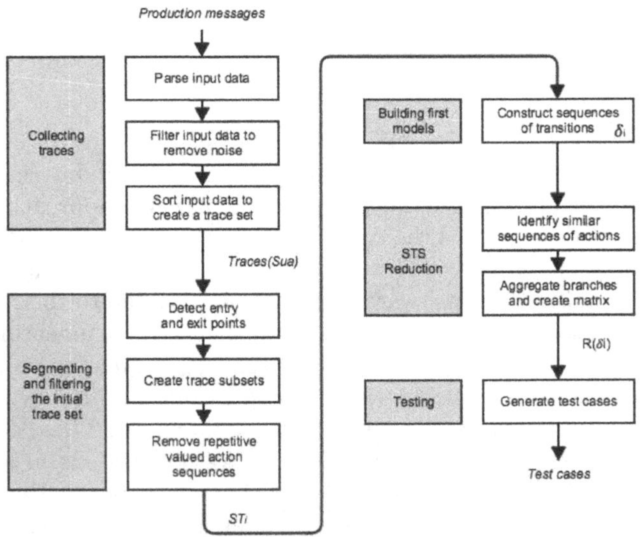

Fig. 1. Autofunk's architecture

We consider Symbolic Transition Systems (STS) [2] as models for representing production system behaviours. STSs are state machines incorporating actions, labelled on transitions, that show what can be observed on a system. In addition, actions are tied to an explicit notion of data.

[1] http://www.drools.org/

2.1 Production Messages and Traces

Autofunk takes production messages as input from a (running) system under analysis Sua. A production message can be either a stimulus or a response, owns a timestamp defined by a global clock, and contains variable data. These messages are formatted no matter their initial source (e.g. a logging system in our case), so that it is possible to use messages from different providers. We call *valued actions* the resulting set of messages.

Some of these actions are not part of the functioning of the system (logging information for instance), and thus must be removed. Filtering is achieved by Drools expert system and a few inference rules given by a domain expert. The remaining actions are sorted to produce an initial set of traces denoted $Traces(Sua)$.

2.2 Trace Segmentation and STSs

We define a complete trace as a trace containing all actions expressing the path taken by a product in a production system, from one of its entry points to one of its exit points. In the trace set $Traces(Sua)$, we do not want to keep incomplete traces. *Autofunk* performs a statistical analysis on $Traces(Sua)$ and computes two ratios for the first and last valued actions of every trace in order to automatically find the entry and exit points of Sua.

$Traces(Sua)$ is then split into subsets ST_i, one for each entry point of Sua. Every trace set ST_i will give birth to one model, describing all possible behaviours starting from its corresponding entry point. Here we obtain the set $ST = \{ST_1, ..., ST_N\}$ such that each $ST_i \subseteq Traces(Sua)$.

Given a subset ST_i in ST, a first STS denoted $\mathcal{S}$ is built by relying on the LTS semantics [2] transformation applied in a backward manner. This model has a tree structure and its traces are equivalent to those of ST_i.

2.3 STS Reduction

The previous model $\mathcal{S}$ is often too large, and thus cannot be beneficial as is. Using such a model for testing purpose would lead to too many test cases for instance. That is why *Autofunk* performs a reduction step, aiming at diminishing the first model into a second one, denoted $R(\mathcal{S})$ that will be more usable.

Most of the existing approaches propose two solutions. Models can directly be inferred with high levels of abstraction but it implies not exact models. The second solution is to apply a minimisation technique [1] which guarantees trace equivalence, but it is costly and highly time consuming on large models. As a result, we chose a simpler approach which consists in combining branches that have the same sequences of actions so that we still obtain a model having a tree structure. *Autofunk* generates a signature for each branch b, i.e. a hash (SHA1 algorithm) of the concatenation of the signatures of the actions of b. This gives good results in terms of STS reduction and requires low processing time, even with millions of actions.

3 Evaluation

We conducted several experiments with real sets of production messages, recorded in one of Michelin's factories. The most significant one ran with a month of data. *Autofunk* handled 10 million production messages in 5 minutes to build two models including around 1,600 branches (parsing step put aside). The framework revealed 120,000 complete traces, which represents 78% of the initial trace set, and reduced the models by 97%. More results can be found in [6].

4 Conclusion

We built a fast and scalable framework combining model inference, expert systems and statistical analyses to derive STSs models based on production traces, i.e. generating formal models from running production systems.

We focused on reducing the models while keeping them exact thanks to trace equivalence preservation, and also because we considered complete branches only. We would like to investigate partial branch concatenation to reduce generated models because we believe that models could be even more reduced. However, this would probably affect performance as partial branch concatenation is time consuming, and we don't want to sacrify speed.

This framework is part of a regression testing system we are working on. In the future, we plan to work on passive testing by applying our framework for different versions of a system and draw conclusions based on the generated models. This will be part of a newer testing module.

References

1. Abdulla, P.A., Kaati, L., Högberg, J.: Bisimulation minimization of tree automata. In: Ibarra, O.H., Yen, H.-C. (eds.) CIAA 2006. LNCS, vol. 4094, pp. 173–185. Springer, Heidelberg (2006)
2. Frantzen, L., Tretmans, J., Willemse, T.A.C.: Test Generation Based on Symbolic Specifications. In: Grabowski, J., Nielsen, B. (eds.) FATES 2004. LNCS, vol. 3395, pp. 1–15. Springer, Heidelberg (2005)
3. Mariani, L., Pezze, M.: Dynamic detection of cots component incompatibility. IEEE Software 24(5), 76–85 (2007)
4. Memon, A., Banerjee, I., Nagarajan, A.: Gui ripping: Reverse engineering of graphical user interfaces for testing. In: Proceedings of the 10th Working Conference on Reverse Engineering, WCRE 2003, p. 260. IEEE Computer Society, Washington, DC (2003), http://dl.acm.org/citation.cfm?id=950792.951350
5. Mesbah, A., van Deursen, A., Lenselink, S.: Crawling Ajax-based web applications through dynamic analysis of user interface state changes. ACM Transactions on the Web (TWEB) 6(1), 3:1–3:30 (2012)
6. Salva, S., Durand, W.: Inferring formal models from production systems. Tech. rep., LIMOS, LIMOS Research Report RR-15-02 (2015), http://sebastien.salva.free.fr/RR-15-02.pdf

Software Development and Authentication for Arms Control Information Barriers

Neil Evans(✉)

AWE Aldermaston, Aldermaston, UK
neil.evans@awe.co.uk

Abstract. The UK-Norway initiative [1] is a joint project to investigate the technologies available for monitoring future arms control agreements. This paper describes one way in which formal methods can assist in the verification of software that is used for such a purpose.

Keywords: Arms control challenges · SPARK · MALPAS · SMT

1 Introduction

In a future verification regime for nuclear warhead dismantlement, inspecting parties are likely to request measurements on warheads and warhead components to ensure that the items presented are consistent with the declarations made by a host party. Such measurements are likely to be based on radiation signatures, and would be used to confirm physical attributes of the fissile material present within the system. Almost any measurement of this type, which would be of use for inspection purposes, would be likely to contain sensitive or proliferative information. It will therefore be essential for such measurements to be performed behind an information barrier (IB) which, while protecting the sensitive information, will reveal a pass/fail to an agreed attribute threshold. It will be crucial that the IB design process builds in mechanisms whereby both parties can have high confidence in the validity and veracity of any result obtained.

This paper presents an overview of the challenges and the use of formal methods to develop and verify (authenticate) the software aspects of an envisaged IB system so that measurements on warheads or warhead components can be taken with confidence, but without an excessive dependency on trust by either party. Of course there are many other important aspects to the development and verification of such a system, such as the hardware and the deployment processes, but these are outside the scope of this paper.

The development concept of an IB system is a difficult one because it involves parties with a mutual distrust of each other. The principles that have been derived from consideration of this difficult situation are summarised as *design-driven challenges* and *challenges in use*.

Design-Driven Challenges. A good IB design gives confidence to both parties. The following four points explore how the design concept can be used to incorporate features that will assist with this.

N. Bjørner and F. de Boer (Eds.): FM 2015, LNCS 9109, pp. 581–584, 2015.
DOI: 10.1007/978-3-319-19249-9_37

1) Joint (agreed) design. All aspects of the design and construction should be agreed by both parties. This gives more trust in the system, but also allows verification of the design by either party prior to any measurements.
2) Simplicity. A simple design reduces the complexity of hardware and software verification tasks.
3) Modularity. This allows easy interchange of modules, such as electronic circuit boards, and enables a greater degree of random selection (see below) at any stage. Modules that the host is confident cannot retain information can be given to the inspectors after use. Being able to check the equipment after measurements is a powerful confidence builder for the inspecting party.
4) Low cost. This will be essential if the equipment can only be used once or a limited number of times. Modularity helps by allowing reuse of components.

Challenges in Use. An IB must provide confidence when in use, as well as in design. Features of the modes of operation, many of which are obvious but are frequently overlooked, should allow for reliable and repeatable operation.

5) Simple to deploy and operate. Confusion over results or procedure could adversely affect the verification process.
6) Robust. The system needs to be reliable, work in a variety of environments, and be able to withstand standard transportation.
7) Portable and self-powered. The system must be portable, fast to set up, and preferably does not rely on host-supplied power or other utilities to function.
8) Use of random selection. This allows the inspectors to choose from multiple copies of (modules of) the equipment provided by the host. For example, they could choose which items to use for measurement and which to take away for further analysis. This is particularly relevant for any items or modules that inspectors are unable to check after measurements have been taken.

2 Software Aspects of an Information Barrier

Information barriers usually involves a considerable software aspect (see, for example, [2]). What has been lacking previously, however, is any extensive use of formal methods to specify and verify the intent of IB software which, due to its simplicity and modularity, is amenable to such analysis.

Formal software development has focused largely on the pre-compilation phases. This is a problem because, in a context where mistrust arises at all levels, it is difficult to argue the veracity of generated object code based on verified source code (without subjecting the compiler to extensive scrutiny.) The approach taken assesses the merits of software development at two different levels (each of which was based on an agreed design): a high level version in SPARK [3] (which has mature tool support for formal verification of source code but requires a compilation phase), and a low level version in 8-bit AVR assembler code (with no dedicated formal methods support but eliminates the compilation phase).

SPARK Ada. Each module (or *package*) consists of two objects: a specification and a body. A specification contains information about the functions and procedures that are implemented in the body, i.e. names, parameters and types. However, the specification allows declarations of more intent-like information about the functions and procedures via preconditions, postconditions and, in the case of functions, *return* annotations. Further intent-like information can be included via *assertions* within the body of the code itself.

Design processes, such as Altran's (previously Praxis') Informed process, allow users to go from high level intent to annotated SPARK code. A good example of this is the Tokeneer system [4]. The SPARK tools are used to check that the code is well-formed. Rudimentary checks are made to make sure the code is syntactically correct but, more importantly from a verification perspective, the SPARK Examiner will generate verification conditions that are required to be proven to ensure that the package is well-typed and fulfils all assertions and annotations. The SPARK Simplifier proves as many of the verification conditions as it can automatically. After simplification, the SPARK Proof Checker is available to assist the manual proof of the remaining verification conditions.

AVR Assembler Code. The simplicity demanded in Section 1 makes it feasible to write the IB software directly in assembler code. The resulting code is of course far less readable than the corresponding SPARK and lacks dedicated tool support for verification. Of the general-purpose tools that have maturity, MALPAS [5] was chosen as a way to analyse the assembler code. Coincidentally MALPAS and SPARK have common ancestry but diverged when MALPAS was developed at RSRE Malvern to target the analysis of existing (legacy/COTS) software, whereas SPARK evolved as a means of software development from inception.

The MALPAS Static Code Analysis tool has been used to analyse safety-critical assembly code for in-service systems (such as nuclear power stations). The analysers determine various properties of the code ranging from basic topology to detailed mathematical functionality. They operate on a modelling language called Intermediate Language (IL) which resembles a simple high-level programming language with additional mathematical constructs. Hence the first stage of analysis is to translate the assembler code and the AVR instruction set into IL.

Like SPARK, MALPAS IL allows assertions to declare intent-like information. The Compliance Analysis tool generates (and tries to discharge) so-called *threats* from the embedded assertions. They are called threats because they are (simplified) negations of the assertions that must be shown to be false. Initially, high-level assertions were used to declare the intent of the low-level IB software. Unfortunately the semantic gap separating these from the assembler code was too wide for the compliance analyser so an alternative approach has been taken: as a stepping stone from the high level assertions to the assembler code, the SPARK source code itself is used to specify the 'intent' of the assembler code.

Since MALPAS IL resembles a high-level programming language it is easy to represent SPARK source code in IL. The MALPAS tools can show compliance between the SPARK code and the assembler code by embedding assertions that, for example, relate bit-vector registers in the assembler code with (representations of) SPARK variables. In this manner relationships between the assembler code and the SPARK code can be proven and, by transitivity, a relationship between the assembler code and the high-level intent can be established. Unfortunately the MALPAS tools also struggled with the complexity of this task, so additional measures were sought.

Satisfiability Modulo Theories (SMT). SMT [6] tools have matured to the extent that they are now being used to support formal method development and analysis. After translating (by hand) the threats generated by MALPAS into the SMT-LIB language, CVC4 [7] is being used to prove their unsatisfiability. This has been extremely successful and is testament to the evolution of these tools over recent years. In addition to threat generation, MALPAS still makes an important contribution to the analysis of the code because it compensates for some of the things that are missing from SMT. Examples of this are the handling of non-linear expressions and looping constructs.

3 Conclusion

This paper has given a brief overview of the use of formal methods to verify the correctness of the software for an arms control application. This is a very important part of the development and deployment of equipment in an arms control regime because of the potential risks (and rewards) of using malicious code to subvert a disarmament process. Of course all of the tools used, in their current configurations, demand an element of trust but it is hoped that in the future these will have the ability to generate proofs that can be verified independently.

References

1. The United Kingdom Norway Initiative: Research into the verification of nuclear warhead dismantlement. Working paper to the Non-Proliferation Treaty Review Conference, NPT/CONF2010/WP.41 (May 2010)
2. MacArthur, D.W., Wolford Jr., J.K.: Information barriers and authentication. In: INMM 42nd Annual Meeting, Indian Wells, CA, USA, July 15-19 (2001)
3. Barnes, J.: High integrity software - The SPARK approach to safety and security. Pearson Education (2003)
4. Barnes, J., Chapman, R., Johnson, R., Widmaier, J., Cooper, D., Everett, W.: Engineering the Tokeneer enclave protection software. In: 1st IEEE International Symposium on Secure Software Engineering (March 2006)
5. Webb, J.T.: MALPAS, an automatic static analysis tool for software validation and verification. In: 1st International Conference on Reliability and Robustness of Engineering Software. Elsevier (1987)
6. Nieuwenhuis, R., Oliveras, A., Tinelli, C.: Solving SAT and SAT Modulo Theories: From an Abstract Davis-Putnam-Logemann-Loveland Procedure to DPLL(T). Journal of the ACM 53(6) (2006)
7. Barrett, C., Conway, C.L., Deters, M., Hadarean, L., Jovanović, D., King, T., Reynolds, A., Tinelli, C.: CVC4. In: Gopalakrishnan, G., Qadeer, S. (eds.) CAV 2011. LNCS, vol. 6806, pp. 171–177. Springer, Heidelberg (2011)

Analyzing the Restart Behavior of Industrial Control Applications

Stefan Hauck-Stattelmann[1(✉)], Sebastian Biallas[2], Bastian Schlich[1], Stefan Kowalewski[2], and Raoul Jetley[3]

[1] ABB Corporate Research Germany, Research Area Software, Ladenburg, Germany
stefan.hauck-stattelmann@de.abb.com

[2] Embedded Software Laboratory, RWTH Aachen University, Aachen, Germany

[3] ABB Corporate Research India, Research Area Software, Bangalore, India

Abstract. Critical infrastructure such as chemical plants, manufacturing facilities or tidal barrages are usually operated using specialized control devices. These devices are programmed using domain-specific programming languages for which static code analysis techniques are not widely used yet. This paper compares a sophisticated academic tool to a lightweight compliance check approach regarding the detection of programming errors that only occur after program restart. As this is a common problem in industrial control code, the paper proposes a way to improve the accuracy of analyses for this class of errors.

Keywords: Static Analysis · Abstract Interpretation · Programmable Logic Controllers

1 Introduction

Programmable Logic Controllers (PLCs) are widely used for industrial automation tasks, e. g., for controlling equipment or supervising production processes. Most PLC programs are written in programming languages defined in the IEC 61131-3 standard [1]. As these languages are rarely used in other domains, the number of available tools for static code analysis is quite limited in comparison to other languages. The authors previously investigated the use of static code analysis for PLC programs using abstract interpretation [2] and more lightweight techniques [3]. This work discusses the detection of problems that are only triggered after a PLC restart and proposes a way to improve this detection.

PLC programs have several interesting properties distinguishing them from standard applications. PLC programs are always executed cyclically, i. e., they are executed over and over again as long as the PLC is running. From an analysis perspective, this means that there is an implicit loop around the entry and exit point of a program. Interaction with the environment, e. g., sensors and actuators interfacing with machinery, is cleanly separated from program execution through the runtime system. Additionally, many PLCs have battery-backed memory regions, which means that certain program variables can *retain* their

N. Bjørner and F. de Boer (Eds.): FM 2015, LNCS 9109, pp. 585–588, 2015.
DOI: 10.1007/978-3-319-19249-9_38

values even after the PLC is restarted. This is a very important capability of a PLC and required, e. g., to document the operating hours of machinery.

While **retain** variables are often necessary to implement the required functionality, they are also the source of problems in the code that are hard to detect. The reason for this is that the interaction between variables with and without the **retain** attribute is sometimes difficult to understand and even harder to test. A simplified example of this kind of problem is shown in Fig. 1. The variable **fs** is erroneously marked with the **retain** attribute and thus is only set to the initial value when the program is started the first time. All other variables are set to the value specified in their declaration whenever the PLC is restarted. This leads to a division by zero in the last assignment of the program after a restart, yielding unexpected results.

2 Comparison of Available Analysis Tools

To the best of our knowledge, Bornot et al. [4] were the first to describe static analysis of PLC programs based on abstract interpretation. More recently, Prahofer et al. [5] discuss the applicability of static code analysis for IEC 61131-3 languages and also assess the available commercial tools in this area. Existing commercial tools focus on syntactic checks, e. g., enforcing naming conventions for variables or looking for error-prone code patterns such as dividing by a variable that has not been compared to zero.

```
PROGRAM Program1
VAR RETAIN
   fs : BOOL := TRUE;
END_VAR
VAR
   a : INT := 0;
   b : INT := 0;
END_VAR
   IF fs THEN
      b := 2;
   END_IF;
   fs := FALSE;
   a := 1234 / b;
END_PROGRAM
```

Fig. 1. Example Program

The authors were involved in the development of different research tools for the static analysis of PLC programs. The ARCADE.PLC tool[1] developed by RWTH Aachen University focuses on formal methods. A prototype tool developed by ABB corporate research [3] is a hybrid analysis combining abstract interpretation and syntactic checks. The example from Fig. 1 will be used to discuss the different approaches regarding **retain** variables.

ARCADE.PLC can detect the division by zero problem shown in the example by first performing a value-set analysis and then using this information to perform further checks, e. g., detecting divisions where zero is part of the potential value range of the divisor. Since the value-set analysis is based on abstract interpretation, it can calculate a sound over-approximation of the value ranges without considering the semantics of the **retain** attribute. The analysis will simply deduce that **fs** can have the value *true* or *false* while **b** can have the value *0* or *2* at program entry. Thus, the division by zero cannot be ruled out and a warning is issued.

The ABB tool supports data flow analyses, but also can check purely syntactic compliance rules. One such rule, which is already used by ABB business units

[1] http://arcade.embedded.rwth-aachen.de, example can be tested there

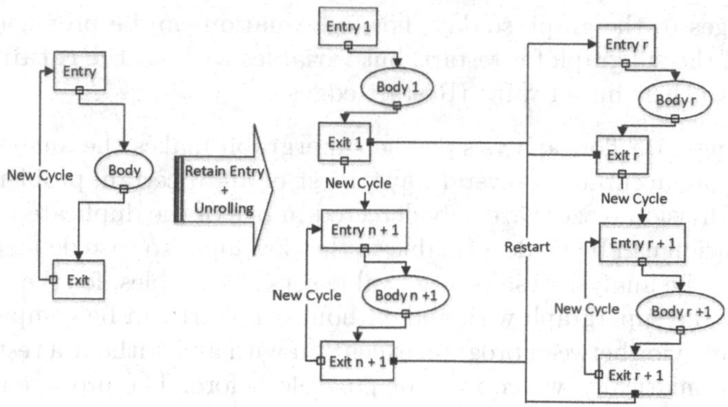

Fig. 2. Proposed Inlining and Unrolling of the Control Flow Graph for a PLC Program

for *manual* code reviews, is that every variable declaration has to specify the **retain** attribute (or a similar one). Applying this rule on the example program yields warnings for the variables **a** and **b**. Automating this check can help in detecting problematic statements in control code, in particular when combined with checks for programming errors like a potential division by zero. While the latter is also supported by the tool, the correlation between a potential error and the missing **retain** attribute still has to be done manually.

Neither of these tools cannot provide a developer with the information that certain problems are only triggered when a program has been running for some time and the PLC is restarted. Unexpected behavior due to incorrectly specified **retain** attributes, however, is a common problem in PLC programs. Detecting these errors manually is very difficult, in particular if the behavior of a program relates to certain characteristics of the equipment it is controlling.

3 Improving Accuracy Through Context Information

Detecting problems during restart can be automated by making the restart explicit during analysis. To achieve this, the analysis has to be made context-sensitive with respect to PLC restart behavior by adding disjoint analysis contexts for the execution cycles after a restart. This technique allows detecting initialization problems and problems that only manifest themselves after a restart. It is similar to the VIVU (Virtual Inlining and Virtual Unrolling) approach proposed in [6] which aims at improving the results for cache modeling.

Improved analysis accuracy can be achieved by building a supergraph from the regular control flow graph (CFG) of the program, as illustrated in Fig. 2. This is achieved through the following steps:

- Unroll the implicit loop around the program once (left hand side of the supergraph).
- Duplicate the unrolled CFG to consider the restart context (right hand side of the supergraph).

– Add edges to the graph so data flow information can be propagated to the entry of the subgraph for restart, but variables without the **retain** attribute are set to their initial value (Restart edges).

Performing data flow analysis on the supergraph makes the analysis of PLC programs more accurate in several ways. First of all, if certain problems such as a potential division by zero are only detected in one of the duplicated subgraphs, this information can be made available to the developer to ease debugging. Most importantly, the analysis results, e. g., value sets of variables, for the corresponding parts of the supergraph with and without a restart can be compared. Thus, divergent behavior between program execution with and without a restart can be detected automatically, which was not possible before. The proposed technique is applicable to all forms of data flow analysis.

4 Conclusion

This paper discussed the capabilities of formal static code analysis based on abstract interpretation and lightweight analysis using code compliance checks regarding errors in PLC programs rooted in PLC restart behavior. Both approaches can detect code smells hinting at these problems, but directly presenting this information to the developer has not been possible so far. To overcome this issue, this paper proposed handling the PLC restart in a separate analysis context by virtual inlining of the restart entry and virtual unrolling of the cyclic code execution. Considering the restart behavior of PLC in the analysis enables the automatic detection of divergent program behavior after a restart. This improvement has already been integrated into Arcade.PLC with little development effort and without significantly impacting the runtime of the analysis.

References

1. International Electrotechnical Commission, IEC 61131-3 Programmable Controllers Part 3: Programming languages (2003)
2. Stattelmann, S., Biallas, S., Schlich, B., Kowalewski, S.: Applying Static Code Analysis on Industrial Controller Code. In: Emerging Technology and Factory Automation (2014)
3. Nair. S., Jetley, R., Nair, A., Hauck-Stattelmann, S.: A Static Code Analysis Tool for Control System Software. In: 22nd IEEE International Conference on Software Analysis, Evolution, and Reengineering (2015)
4. Bornot, S., Huuck, R., Lakhnech, Y., Lukoschus, B.: Utilizing Static Analysis for Programmable Logic Controllers. In: 4th International Conference on Automation of Mixed Processes (2000)
5. Prahofer, H., Angerer, F., Ramler, R., Lacheiner, H., Grillenberger, F.: Opportunities and Challenges of Static Code Analysis of IEC 61131-3 programs. In: Emerging Technology and Factory Automation (2012)
6. Martin, F., Alt, M., Wilhelm, R., Ferdinand, C.: Analysis of Loops. In: Koskimies, K. (ed.) CC 1998. LNCS, vol. 1383, pp. 80–94. Springer, Heidelberg (1998)

Case Study: Static Security Analysis of the Android Goldfish Kernel

Tao Liu[1](✉) and Ralf Huuck[2]

[1] University of New South Wales, Sydney, Australia
tao.liu4@unsw.edu.au

[2] NICTA and Red Lizard Software, Sydney, Australia
ralf.huuck@nicta.com

Abstract. In this work we present an industry-driven case study of applying static program analysis to the Android kernel. In particular, we investigate the ability of open source tools as represented by *Cppcheck* and of commercial tools as represented by *Goanna* to detect security vulnerabilities. In our case study, we explore static security checking along the dimensions of setup effort, run time, quality of results and usability for large code bases. We present the results we obtained from analyzing the Android Goldfish kernel module of around 740 kLoC of C/C++ code. Moreover, we highlight some lessons learned that might serve as a guidance for future applications.

1 Introduction

The Android operating system as developed by Google has reached universal prominence as the most popular OS for mobile devices. More recently Android is advancing into adjacent domains including automotive, medical devices and home automation systems.

Given Android's ubiquitous presence the operating system's overall security is deemed to be paramount. However, while the design of Android has been relatively stable over time, firmware and drivers are constantly changing leading to different software versions on almost a monthly schedule. Given the size of the Android OS with millions of lines of code spread over 10, 000 files, managing the security implications manually is a arduous task. As such, many organizations either trust new updates and hope to detect any anomalies during integration or system testing, or they rely on complimentary automated tools such a *static program analysis* [1] to achieve a minimum level of assurance.

This work is a case study of using static program analysis tools for security checking of the Android kernel. It was developed in conjunction with the static analysis tools company Red Lizard Software and driven by their customers in the telecommunication and entertainment devices market. The goal of the case

NICTA is funded by the Australian Government through the Department of Communications and the Australian Research Council through the ICT Centre of Excellence Program.

N. Bjørner and F. de Boer (Eds.): FM 2015, LNCS 9109, pp. 589–592, 2015.
DOI: 10.1007/978-3-319-19249-9_39

study was to evaluate the overall lifecycle effort and benefits of using static analysis tools for security checking. This includes: setup and integration effort, run time and analysis bottlenecks, ease of evaluating the results and quality of the results. Moreover, the case study involved Red Lizard Software's own tool *Goanna* [2] as well as the popular open source tool *Cppcheck*[1].

In the following we give an introduction to the tools and environments used, explain the results we obtained and give a summary of our observations that might be helpful for others in similar circumstances.

2 Experimental Setup and Evaluation

Tools. We choose two static analysis tools for our case study representing two different classes of software checking tools: *Cppcheck,* a free GPL licensed tool for checking generic problems in C/C++ code including memory leaks, out of bounds arrays, and null pointer dereferences. Cppcheck aims at having zero false positives. The second tool, *Goanna*, is a commercial static analysis tool developed around software verification techniques such as model checking, SMT solving and abstract interpretation. Its aims at deep analysis that is scalable to large code bases.

The purpose of this evaluation is not to decide on a better tool, but to explore differences and strengths of each tool. Moreover, the tools where chosen based on their availability to the authors and the good reputation of Cppcheck. While Goanna is representing the commercial tool space, we would not expect fundamental differences from similar commercial tools. Further comparisons can be found in the NIST SAMATE program [3] and earlier evaluations [4].

Android Kernel. As a test bed the Android Goldfish 3.4 kernel was chosen. This is a generic kernel for software emulation of various hardware platforms of interest to Red Lizard Sofwtare's customers. The Goldfish kernel contains the essence of the recent Android releases KitKat and Lollipop and has around 740k lines of code.

Configuration. The analysis was run using Goanna 3.4.1 and Cppcheck 1.68. We focused on the security relevant checks for each tool including buffer overflows, null pointer issues or tainted data. This resulted in 27 specific categories for Cppcheck and 46 for Goanna. All experiments were run on a quadcore Dell PowerEdge 1950 2.66GHz with 16 GB of RAM running Ubuntu 12.10.

2.1 Evaluation Results

Installation and Configuration. Both Cppcheck and Goanna have been straight forward to install. Cppcheck comes as a drop-in binary and Goanna has an installer file. Configuring Cppcheck required running all check with subsequent filtering results as there is no method to select individual checks. For Goanna the defaults of the security package were selected.

[1] http://cppcheck.sourceforge.net/

Running the Analysis. Goanna parses the source code and does handle includes, preprocessing and macro expansion. It gets the necessary information after monitoring the native build process for relevant compiler and linker calls. In contrast, Cppcheck does not fully parse the code, but scans the actual text of the source files. As a result it be run on any file or from a directory. We used the Goanna facility to determine the relevant set of files in the build and passed those files to Cppcheck. The overall run time for Cppcheck on the Android Goldfish 3.4 kernel was just under 10 minutes, while the same run took 75 minutes for Goanna. Compilation itself is slightly over 8 minutes.

Quantitative Results. Goanna reported 279 potential issues from 14 categories out of the total 46 security checks[2]. Cppcheck reported 37 potential issues in 3 categories (`Null Pointer` *warnings* and *errors*, and `Memory Leaks`) for the same code base. Additionally we made use of Cppchecks ability to run over any file even if not in the build to include all driver files for all platforms in a second experiment. For the latter Cppcheck reported 755 issues in 10 categories.

We manually evaluated how many of the reported issues are false positives, i.e., where the tool spuriously warns, to determine the actual true positive (TP) rate. We used a random sample size of 20 for each category of each tool. Only 4 categories in of each tool had more than 20 warnings. Only 1 category more than 100 warning and was as such under-sampled. We did not have any means to determine the false negative rate, i.e., the number of issues that are in the code and are missed.

Firstly, for the 37 issues Cppcheck detected in the actual build the `Null Pointer` errors had a 67% TP rate, while the weaker `Null Pointer` warnings had a 21% TP rate. The `Memory Leak` issues were all false positives. Only about one third of all reported issues were true positives. However, for the second experiment scanning all remaining kernel files Cppcheck had a much better TP rate of 76% when averaging out over the reported 10 categories. Only only 2 categories had less than 50% TP rates and 6 categories at TP rates of 90% or higher.

Secondly, for Goanna's 279 reported issues in 14 categories the lowest TP rate was of any category was 67% (two of three bugs were correct) and 11 categories had a TP rate of 90% or higher. Averaged out over the 14 categories Goanna's TP rate was 94%. We were advised by Red Lizard Software, however, that this TP rate was better than what usually should be expected from such a tool.

Thirdly, we examined the overlap between Goanna's 279 reported issues and Cppcheck's 37. Only a combined 23 issues were in files, where both tools reported a warning. For those files Cppcheck reported 11 warnings with 9 false positives and Goanna 12 warnings with 3 false positives. No two of the same false positives were reported by both tools, but all true positives of Cppcheck in the overlap were also correctly reported by Goanna. Outside the files where both tools reported and issue there were 8 TPs by Cppcheck not reported by Goanna, the remaining Goanna TPs were not reported by Cppcheck.

[2] all raw data available at http://www.cse.unsw.edu.au/~rhuuck/fm15

Qualitative Results. Generally, the cause of bugs differed a lot between the two tools. Cppcheck's bugs tend to be patterns such as a constant 0 that is used later as a divisor or an explicit Null pointer being referenced close by. The Goanna bugs tended to be much deeper involving computation of data or passing of values between functions. At the same time it took the evaluator much longer to determine the truth of a Cppcheck warning as the tool outputs a line number with a rather simple message. Goanna additionally provided a compact trace through the program with explanatory text, making an assessment easier. One of the easier to rectify drawbacks of Cppcheck was the absence of a reference manual, leading to some steep learning curve and a degree of guesswork for causes of claimed errors.

3 Lessons

There are a few key observation from our case study: Both tools where simple to setup, had reasonable sets of security checks and had no problems scaling to the Android kernel as such. Also, both tools had medium to very low rates of false positives rates making them applicable in practice. We suspect that the Android code's maturity makes it easier to understand for tools as well.

Major differences are: The Cppcheck issues were much shallower than the Goanna issues, although still relevant. A cause is Cppcheck's absence of full parsing and reliance on pattern matching instead. This has the advantage though of easy applicability and the ability to scan all files even outside the build. In contrast, Goanna analyzes what is being build, which has its pros and cons.

As a summary, we believe that Cppcheck is a useful first line of defense with very low run time overhead. Its key role is quick scanning of code under development. Goanna or similar commercial tools appear much more comprehensive in its analysis suitable for higher levels of assurance, while also requiring slightly more run time.

While we were able to asses the check results for both tools, we do not know the implications of the bugs we found. Currently, we are in the process of feeding our findings back to both the Android developers as well as Red Lizard Software and its customers.

References

1. Nielson, F., Nielson, H.R., Hankin, C.L.: Principles of Program Analysis. Springer (1999)
2. Fehnker, A., Huuck, R., Jayet, P., Lussenburg, M., Rauch, F.: Model checking software at compile time. In: Proceedings of the First Joint IEEE/IFIP Symposium on Theoretical Aspects of Software Engineering, TASE 2007, pp. 45–56. IEEE Computer Society, Washington, DC (2007)
3. Okun, V., Delaitre, A., Black, P.E.: Report on the Third Static Analysis Tool Exposition, SATE 2010, Technical report, NIST, Special Report 500-283 (2010)
4. Emanuelsson, P., Nilsson, U.: A comparative study of industrial static analysis tools. Electron. Notes Theor. Comput. Sci. 217, 5–21 (2008)

Practices for Formal Models as Documents: Evolution of VDM Application to "Mobile FeliCa" IC Chip Firmware

Taro Kurita[1], Fuyuki Ishikawa[2(✉)], and Keijiro Araki[3]

[1] Sony Corporation, Tokyo, Japan
taro.kurita@jp.sony.com

[2] National Institute of Informatics, Tokyo, Japan
f-ishikawa@nii.ac.jp

[3] Kyushu University, Fukuoka, Japan
araki@csce.kyushu-u.ac.jp

Abstract. This paper reports on the application of VDM to the development of the third generation of firmware for the Mobile FeliCa IC chip. The practices of VDM were improved by incorporating the experience gained in the previous development. The primary focus was maintainability and understandability, as the VDM specification was used as the sole reference document for various development activities. The resulting improvements eliminated deficiencies caused by misunderstandings, while keeping costs similar to before.

Keywords: Formal Specification · VDM · Industrial Application

1 Introduction

"FeliCa" is a contactless IC card technology developed by the Sony Corporation and is widely used in Japan. In particular, Mobile FeliCa IC chips are embedded in over 250 million mobile phones. Their applications, including electronic money, train tickets, identifications, door keys, and so on, form an essential foundation for business and daily activities in Japan. These chips interact with other components, including server-side applications and reader/writer equipment. Their core functions consist of a secure file system and communication protocols, as well as firewall functions to enable multiple services on the chip.

Given the significance of the system, it was decided that VDM, a formal specification method [2], be applied to the development of the second generation of its firmware [3,4]. The objective was to resolve problems in the early phases, such as vagueness in the specification. A process was established that uses the VDM specification as the key artifact, through interactions among three teams performing specification, design implementation, and testing tasks. The benefits were primarily in terms of when and what deficiencies were detected.

The engineers involved in this first application of VDM did not have any knowledge or experience in the practices of formal specification. Not only was the

N. Bjørner and F. de Boer (Eds.): FM 2015, LNCS 9109, pp. 593–596, 2015.
DOI: 10.1007/978-3-319-19249-9_40

language new to them (with a syntax based on sets and predicates), there were issues about how to determine the right abstraction level, how to use declarative or functional styles of description effectively, how to position natural language as well as formal language, how to define specification conventions, and so on.

This paper reports on the evolution of the VDM application in the following third generation of Mobile FeliCa IC chip firmware. The key point is the improvement demonstrated by the engineers as to maintainability and understandability in the use of the VDM model as the main reference document.

2 Development of the Second-Generation

This section first provides an overview of the development of the second generation of Mobile FeliCa IC chip firmware. VDM was used for the specification of the external interface functions to interact with the server and the reader/writer equipment. The VDM++ language was used with VDMTools [1] for Object-Oriented modeling and validation by specification animation, i.e., testing.

The specification was constructed by the specification team and passed to the design-implementation team for the firmware as well as the testing team. Thus, the VDM model was used not only for validation of the specification, but also directly for a number of activities, including communications among the teams. Nevertheless, a natural-language (Japanese) specification was also used as a "familiar" description especially for the external partners.

Testing was the primary means of quality assurance. In addition to the unit testing of the VDM specification, intensive black-box tests (over 7,000) were carried out. These tests were shared for the VDM specification and for the different implementations. Over 100 million random tests on the implementations were also conducted using scripts constructed from the VDM specification.

As a result of the VDM application, deficiencies were discovered in the early stages, e.g., when constructing and testing the formal specification. Though, there were deficiencies that were caused by issues relevant to the specification and detected in the implementation. Deficiencies caused by the description (missing, erroneous or unclear statements) were amounted to only 2% of the total number of deficiencies detected in the implementation. On the other hand, deficiencies caused by the comprehension (oversights or insufficient understanding) were amounted to 16.3%. The primary causes of the latter type of deficiencies were about maintainability and understandability and found to be as follows.

1. The VDM model was a mixture of "specification" descriptions and "mock-up" descriptions to make the model executable for validation. The engineers needed to understand and follow the former precisely, but not the latter. The mixture was confusing and led to misunderstandings.
2. The comments allowed to "imagine" the meanings, but possibly imprecisely. It was also easy to forget to update the comments when the VDM specification was updated. ASCII names were used for identifiers, and they followed popular naming conventions for programming languages. However, ASCII

names are not natural for the non-ASCII Japanese language, and this resulted in many comments that give translation or link to corresponding names in the Japanese version.

3. The same issue existed at the document level. Referring to the Japanese version of the specification led to misunderstandings. In addition, the maintenance of both the VDM and Japanese versions was costly and error-prone.

3 Evolution in Development of the Third Generation

The development of the third generation started in 2007 and involved many features, such as enhancement of the encryption mechanisms and adaptation of the global standard of Near Field Communication (NFC). The implementation code was three times the LOC of the second-generation.

Given the three issues described in Section 2, the usage of the VDM specification was changed in the third generation of development.

Regarding issue 1, the specification convention was defined to separate the specification part and mock-up part in the VDM model. VDM languages allow for a mixture of declarative description using pre- and post-conditions, and imperative behavior description. The specification part was completely described in a declarative way. As the behavior was not the specification, or decisions for the implementations, it was separated into subclasses for the executable mock-up.

For example, it is typical to use set variables to denote data held by the target system. Then the behavior of operations is defined by set operators such as union and difference. Such mock-up part of the model was put in subclasses, while the specification part only gives pre- and post-conditions by using not the set variables but auxiliary functions that represent addition, deletion, and so on.

Regarding issue 2, the Japanese language was used for the identifiers in the VDM model. This eliminated the necessity of duplicate translation comments. The ratio of comments in the VDM specification was 7%, and this compares with 27% in the second generation. This does not mean exclusion of natural language: Japanese documents could be also used, but warnings were given about possible imprecision and that they should not be used as references.

Regarding issue 3, the VDM specification was the sole specification document that worked as the reference for various development activities. External partners, e.g., the development team of the server-side applications, also read the VDM specification.

Note that the practices for issues 1 and 2 included new specification conventions different from coding conventions. For example, the naming rules in Japanese were completely new, as non-ASCII Japanese names are not usually used in programming languages. The auxiliary functions support a new kind of specification pattern, which allows for specifications without defining data types or structures. This is quite different from the abstract classes in programming languages because we still need to mention data additions, deletions, etc., in order to define the pre- and post-conditions.

Table 1 shows comparison of the second and third generations. Increase of the specification lines was moderate by declarative description, even with the large

Table 1. Comparison of the Second and Third Generations

Generation	C Implementation [LOC]	VDM Specification [LOC]
Second	40,876	39,315
Third	126,944	55,400

Generation	Deficiencies by description	Deficiencies by comprehension	Productivity [LOC/Man-month]	Debug density [errors/kLOC]
Second	2%	16.3%	1,000	11
Third	0%	10.9%	1,000	11

increase of the implementation lines[1]. Deficiencies caused by the description and the comprehension were both decreased, while the productivity and debug density were kept to a similar level.

4 Summary

This paper reported on the latest application of VDM to the development of third-generation firmware for Mobile FeliCa IC chip. Practices for maintainability and understandability were investigated by the practitioners, and this resulted in improvements to the specification. We believe this unique industrial experience, a evolution from the first application of formal methods, has provided us with a lot of insights. The fourth generation of development is now benefitting from this valuable experience in reported practices.

Acknowledgments. We would like to thank Professor Peter Gorm Larsen of Aarhus University, Shin Sahara of Hosei University and Hiroshi Sako of Designers' Den Corporation for their great assistance in the application of VDM.

References

1. VDM information web site. http://vdmtools.jp/en/
2. Fitzgerald, J., Larsen, P.G., Mukherjee, P., Plat, N., Verhoef, M.: Validated Designs for Object-oriented Systems. Springer (2005)
3. Kurita, T., Chiba, M., Nakatsugawa, Y.: Application of a formal specification language in the development of the "Mobile FeliCa" IC chip firmware for embedding in mobile phone. In: The 15th International Symposium on Formal Methods (FM 2008). pp. 425–429 (2008)
4. Kurita, T., Nakatsugawa, Y.: The application of VDM to the industrial development of firmware for a smart card IC chip. International Journal of Software and Informatics 3(2-3), pp. 343–355 (2009)

[1] LOC excludes comments and blank lines

Formal Virtual Modelling and Data Verification for Supervision Systems

Thierry Lecomte(✉)

ClearSy, 320 avenue Archimède,
13857 Aix en Provence, France
thierry.lecomte@clearsy.com

Abstract. This paper reports on the use of formal techniques to ensure as far as possible a safe decommissioning of a plant several decades after it was designed and built. Combination of supervised learning, formal modelling, model animation and model checking enabled the recovery of an almost lost specification and the design of a virtual supervision system that could be checked against recorded plant data.

Keywords: B Method · Safety critical system · Event-B · Model animation · Model checking

1 Introduction

Industry plants that were built in the 60s or 70s (nuclear plants for example) usually have their design documentation far from current standards, some could be handwritten or referring to punch-card-based programs. In any case, initial designers cannot be asked as they are now retired or dead. As such, any modification to existing installation (decommissioning) is a real engineering challenge and requires cautious investigation and experiments before the deployment on the real plant, especially when it fulfills a safety critical mission.

Recovering the original specification of the plant, as a virtual model that could be checked against recorded data during the lifetime of the plant, would constitute a good starting point prior to any functional modification of such a plant.

Formal methods [1] enable to obtain precise specification document, as all ambiguities are removed due to the semantics of the formal language used for the modelling [4]. Such a model is then likely to be animated [2] (i.e. virtually executed) through a number of scenarios elaborated from real life. The construction of scenarios is tough work as the recorded data are interleaved and not tagged: some pattern recognition is required to sort out the data.

The objectives are to recover the system specification, to design a supervision system that can bootstrap the existing one and to ensure forthcoming functional evolution.

2 The Supervision System

The supervision system (Fig 1) described in this article does not control directly the plant. Instead it is in charge of surveying actions issued by other systems, displaying

N. Bjørner and F. de Boer (Eds.): FM 2015, LNCS 9109, pp. 597–600, 2015.
DOI: 10.1007/978-3-319-19249-9_41

information (messages) when an action has been completed successfully or not. Its mission is to assist human operators to make sure that the different actions carried out complete successfully or to provide a negative feedback. For example, when a pump is switched on or when a valve is open, it may result in the increase of a level in a tank, measured by a sensor after some time. When the threshold level is reached, the system may display a successful message. In case the level is not reached after a certain period, an error message may be displayed. This survey is performed through a number of programs, each program being in charge of one particular sequence of actions.

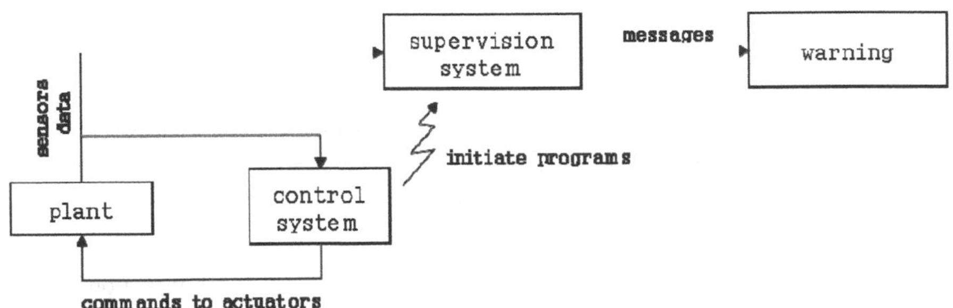

Fig. 1. Architecture of the industrial plant: the supervision system provides feedback for the human operators

These programs (Fig 2) are directly triggered by control & command systems that require their execution to be followed-up. Basically these programs set up predicate listeners and watchdogs, start other programs and then go to sleep. Their execution is resumed when, following the update of a variable, a predicate state changes to TRUE, or when a timer elapses. Execution, sleep and resume actions are managed through an execution queue: the program on top of the queue is the only program executed, the others are waiting to be executed or are sleeping. A program entering a sleep period is moved at the end of the queue. A program resuming its execution is put on top of the execution queue. Executed program is also able to generate messages (on various displays, on printers, etc.).

In practice, this supervision system is made up of several execution queues: one with few programs able to be executed and hence able to take into account events (inputs) more quickly, others with potentially more programs in the queue (then with slower response time). There are some constraints like the impossibility for a program to be executed at the same time on different execution queues. Such system has to deal with a lot of asynchronous events ranging from milliseconds to half-an-hour periods, with an avalanche effect leading to more than 10,000 events to process, when the plant meets a functional transition that affects most sensors.

3 Formal Techniques in Action

Several formal techniques are used in combination in order to address all engineering problems that has appeared during the ongoing project, namely: recovering the

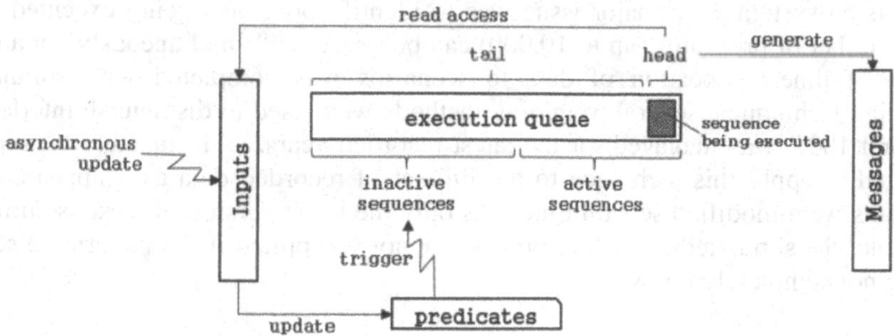

Fig. 2. Architecture of the interpreter in charge of executing sequences of instructions (i.e. programs). The real interpreter is made of several execution queues with different priorities. A sequence can only be executed in a single execution queue.

specification of the supervision system and checking it against real data to ensure a high level of confidence.

3.1 Recovering the System Level Specification

The specification was entirely modelled with Event-B and animated with the ProB model-checker. The plan was first to mimic the behavior briefly described in various technical documents available: events were added first, then some scenarios were designed by-hand and replayed. Preconditions for events were completed to ensure that only regular scenarios to occur. Invariants (other than typing) were then added to add some guarantees to the model. Finally the model was proved against these invariant properties. This modelling was iterated several times, by including larger parts of the specification. If the core specification was quite easy to complete, the introduction of exploitation modes was trickier; for example the fact that the supervision system cannot be shut down at any time. So the upload of new programs has to be done on-the-fly and some new properties emerged (never upload a new version of a program that is being executed) and the model had to be slightly refactored to integrate these new features.

3.2 Checking Against Decades of Recorded Data

The formal model obtained previously has been checked against our understanding of the natural language specification documents. It constitutes a good starting point but we had no idea how close our model was from the real system. The documents may not correspond to the system being executed – remember that documents are hand-written and some of these might have not been updated. Hopefully decades of recorded data are available even if they are stored on very old medium. Recorded data include timed inputs (sensors), commands (actuators) and messages identifiers emitted by the supervision system. The objective of this phase was to extract real scenarios in order to check if they can be replayed with our formal model of the supervision system. The major issue was to identify programs being executed, as a huge number of programs (up to 10,000) can be executed "simultaneously" in a short period of time. Allocation of data to scenarios was completed with simulated-annealing techniques: several weighting methods were used to distinguish interleaved data and 100% was managed for the latest recorded years. Unfortunately we did not managed to apply this technique to the full set of recorded data as it appeared that programs were modified several times. As only the latest version of these is currently available, the simulated-annealing process cannot be applied if the patterns to search for are not completely known.

4 Experience Gained and Conclusion

We have been able to reverse-engineer the specification of the supervision system with a help of formal modelling and animation in Event-B, by using Atelier B and ProB tools, which enabled us to make a number of "wise guesses" and to slightly improve the correctness of the model. This specification has then been checked with success against some scenarios extracted from real recorded data. Indeed the behavior exhibited by our virtual animation seems to comply with the existing supervision plant. The next step would be to connect the software model to a virtual model of the plant, and to obtain a co-simulation that would allow to check timing behavior especially when a large number of events has to be taken into account. Forthcoming investigations will be linked to the H2020 Into-CPS project. Another issue is the coupling of the interpreter with its virtual model to check at runtime discrepancies between the real plant and its model. Formal data validation [3][5] will also be used for checking parameters and programs correctness.

This way of reverse-engineering old systems seems promising, as formal techniques and tools are now mature enough to be applied to real industry-strength systems.

References

1. Abrial, J.R.: The B-Book: Assigning Programs to Meanings. Cambridge University Press (2005)
2. Hallerstede, S., Leuschel, M., Plagge, D.: Validation of Formal Models by Refinement Animation, Science of Computer Programming (March 2013)
3. Lecomte, T., Burdy, L., Leuschel, M.: Formally Checking Large Data Sets in the Railways. In: Proceedings of DS-Event-B 2012: Workshop on the Experience of and Advances in Developing Dependable Systems in Event-B, in Conjunction with ICFEM 2012, Kyoto, Japan, November 13 (2012)
4. Lecomte, T.: Safe and Reliable Metro Platform Screen Doors Control/Command Systems. In: Cuellar, J., Sere, K. (eds.) FM 2008. LNCS, vol. 5014, pp. 430–434. Springer, Heidelberg (2008)
5. Leuschel, M., Falampin, J., Fritz, F., Plagge, D.: Automated Property Verification for Large Scale B Models with ProB. Formal Aspects of Computing, 683–709 (November 2011)

Using Simulink Design Verifier for Automatic Generation of Requirements-Based Tests

Bruno Miranda, Henrique Masini, and Rodrigo Reis(✉)

EMBRAER S.A, Belo Horizonte, Brazil
{bruno.miranda,henrique.masini,rodrigo.pimenta}@embraer.com.br

Abstract. In general, creating requirements-based tests that comply with standards is a time-consuming activity, especially in safety critical systems, where standards can be very strict. In this paper we present a methodology for generating requirements-based tests using Simulink Design Verifier, by representing requirements as models. With this methodology we estimate a considerable reduction of effort for creating requirements based tests that satisfy the DO-178C standard.

Keywords: Model-based testing · Software verification · Requirements-based testing · RBT

1 Introduction

Embedded systems are becoming increasingly common in the aerospace industry, including in safety critical systems, such as avionics and flight controls. Therefore, a robust verification and validation process is necessary in order to minimize the risks.

The document DO-178C *Software Considerations in Airborne Systems and Equipment Certification* [1] has been accepted by the FAA and many other aviation authorities as a mean of compliance with certification requirements of airborne computer software. This document enumerates a set of objectives for software life cycle processes. The number of objectives that the software developers need to satisfy varies according to the level of criticality assigned to the software during the evaluation of the effects of a failure condition in the system.

Some of the activities to comply with the verification objectives that are listed in tables A-6 and A-7 of the DO-178C consists in creating and executing requirements-based tests (RBT), as specified in section 6.4 [1]. Such requirements can be represented with the use of models, which has the advantage of being easier to simulate and manipulate with scripts.

In addition, a test standard can be created in order to increase the rigorousness that the tests will achieve. A test standard can define how to test commonly used blocks, the type of coverage, and provide definitions. For example, a test standard can define that every instance of a Saturation block must be tested as follows:

1. The input shall be greater than the upper limit;
2. The input shall be less than the lower limit;
3. The input shall be between the lower and upper limit.

N. Bjørner and F. de Boer (Eds.): FM 2015, LNCS 9109, pp. 601–604, 2015.
DOI: 10.1007/978-3-319-19249-9_42

Considering that the requirement is represented by a Simulink model, it should be simple to create a RBT for an instance of a Saturation block. However, in practice, the Saturation block will almost never represent the full functionality and it will be connected to other blocks with different degrees of complexity. Figure 1 illustrates such situation. In this example, calculation inside "Actuator" subsystem can be very complex.

Therefore, in order to comply with the test standard, the verification engineer must manually calculate the inputs to the Saturation block that will satisfy the three criteria specified in the test standard. Nonetheless, this method proves to be very time-consuming and not scalable. For example, if a given block is changed and the Saturation block depends on its outputs, not only the test for the block that has changed will need to be redone, but also the test for the Saturation block should change since its input signals will be affected, as well as every other block that depends on the first one.

In this paper, we describe a methodology of automatic RBT generation based on the Simulink Design Verifier.

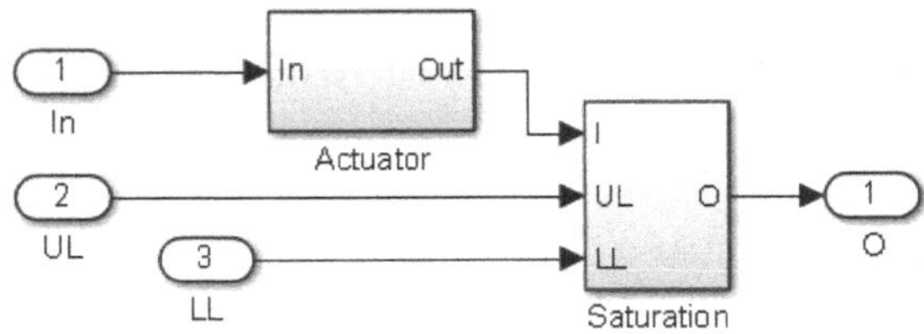

Fig. 1. Tested block example

2 Methodology

The Simulink Design Verifier [2] is a toolbox created by Mathworks and it uses formal methods in order to detect design error in Simulink models. The main functionalities of this toolbox are finding divisions by zero, dead code, and other common design errors, prove properties, and test generation.

In this paper, we will only discuss the test generation functionality. In order to create tests, the Design Verifier offers a test objective block, which is graphically represented by the letter 'O'. The Design Verifier will try to create a test that makes the expression connected to this block equal to true in one of the execution cycles. Each test objective block corresponds to a test criterion in the test standard.

The toolbox also offers a test condition block, which is graphically represented by the letter 'C'. The Design Verifier will try to create a test that makes the expression connected to this block equal to true in every execution cycle. Figure 2 illustrates how to generate two tests for the Saturation block. The test objective block connected to R1 will result in a test in which the input 'I' is greater the upper limit 'UL'; the test objective block connected to R2 will result in a test in which the input 'I' is less than the lower limit 'LL'. These two tests will always obey the condition in which 'UL' is greater than 'LL'.

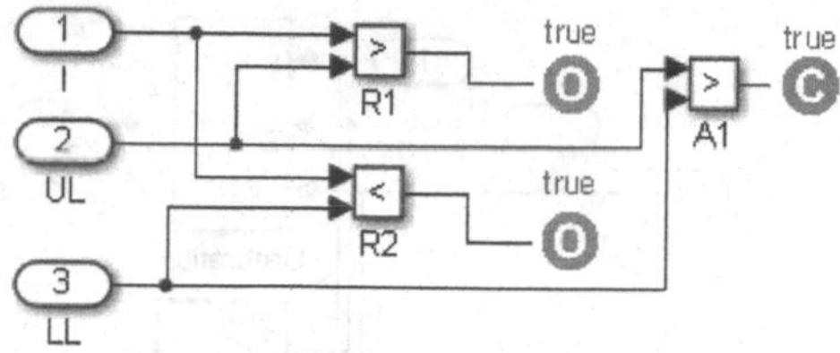

Fig. 2. Using Simulink Design Verifier for test generation

The test standard is also useful in automating the generation of tests using the Simulink Design Verifier. The fact that each block has its established way of testing, allows the creation of a verification subsystem with the implementation of each test criteria for each block.

A script automatically navigates through the model, and each time it finds a specific block, its corresponding verification subsystem is attached to the tested block. The script also captures the block and criteria identification and writes them in the test case, resulting in an easily traceable RBT. By tracing the criteria and blocks to the tests, the test review, which is one of the objectives of the DO-178C, is less laborious. Figure 3 shows the results of automatically connecting a verification subsystem to the tested block.

The Simulink Design Verifier, however, has limitations that make it impossible to achieve some criteria. One of the main limitation occurs when using non-linear arithmetic, such as multiplication and division with unbounded inputs. We addressed this problem by using Condition blocks, avoiding non-linear calculations. Another problem is creating long tests. For example, a Filter block should be tested by applying a step signal in its input. If the filter has a low response frequency it will take a very long time to generate a test that will correctly test the block. We tackled this issue by processing the resulting test and increasing its duration. During the execution, the scripts simplify the model in order to reduce its complexity so that the processing time is decreased. The simplification starts from a given signal to be tested for each requirement and navigates through the model until all the external outputs are reached. The blocks that do not belong to the simplification path are then temporarily removed from the model.

In summary, our test generation application automates the following methodology, for each output or internal signal:

- Simplify the model, removing all calculation that do not affect that signal;
- Deal with non-linear algebra, imposing constraints or approximations;
- Identify instances of blocks previously defined in test standard and connect modeled test objectives (as showed in Figure 3);
- Extend input cycles for objectives involving temporal logic;
- Consolidate generated tests information in a report, including tests description and traceability.

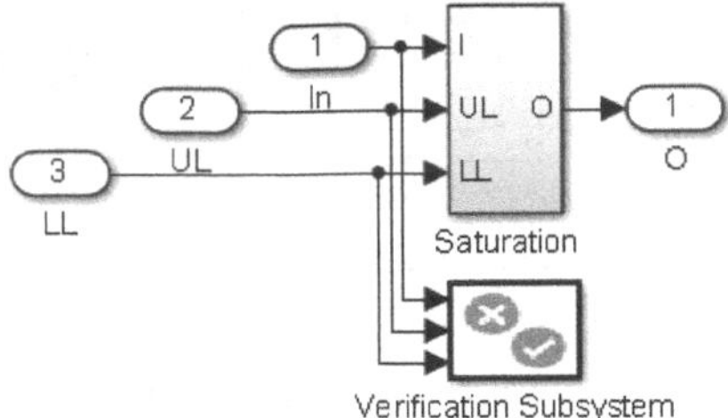

Fig. 3. Automatic connection of the verification subsystem to the tested block

3 Results

The methodology was implemented in a prototype and it was used to generate tests for 90 Simulink models that varied from very simple to very complex ones, with thousands of blocks. Therefore, we could extend Simulink Design Verifier functionality and generate custom types of tests automatically. We also addressed three limitations of the Simulink Design Verifier: creating tests for large models, non-linear calculations and long tests. On average, more than half of the tests were successfully generated taking less than a week to generate them. The prototype worked completely automatically, therefore reducing the required effort for this task.

4 Conclusions

We presented a methodology for generating RBT using Simulink Design Verifier, complying with applicable standards, which proved to be satisfactory. However, the methodology does not exclude the need to review the tests in order to verify if it complies with the standards and DO-178C.

In general, during software development the requirements change frequently, and a change in one requirement can impact on tests of other requirements. Therefore, the use of this methodology would also reduce the rework needed. However, it is not in the scope of this paper to measure how frequent the requirements change during a project and the impact of such changes in the tests creation using the methodology proposed.

References

1. RTCA/DO-178C.Software Considerations in Airborne Systems and Equipment Certification (2012)
2. MATHWORKS. Simulink Design Verifier™ User Guide (2010)

Formalizing the Concept Phase of Product Development

Mathijs Schuts[1(✉)] and Jozef Hooman[2,3]

[1] Philips Healthcare, Best, The Netherlands
mathijs.schuts@philips.com
[2] Embedded Systems Innovation by TNO, Eindhoven, The Netherlands
[3] Radboud University, Nijmegen, The Netherlands

Abstract. We discuss the use of formal techniques to improve the concept phase of product realisation. As an industrial application, a new concept of interventional X-ray systems has been formalized, using model checking techniques and the simulation of formal models.

1 Introduction

Traditionally, during the concept phase an informal document is being created with a high level description of the concept. This document consists of a decomposition of the product to be developed, the different hardware and software components it consists of, the responsibilities per component, and the interaction between the components. From the concept description, different development groups concurrently start developing the component they are responsible for.

A frequently occurring problem in industry is that the integration and validation phase takes a large amount of time and is rather uncontrollable because many problems are detected in this phase. An important reason for these problems is the informal nature of the concept phase. This leads to ambiguities, inconsistencies, and omissions. Typically, a large part of system behaviour is implicitly defined during the implementation phase. If multiple development groups work in parallel in realizing the concept, the integration phase can take a lot of time because the independently developed components do not work together seamlessly. Moreover, during the integration phase sometimes issues are found in which hardware is involved. Then it is usually too late to change the hardware and a workaround in software has to be found and implemented.

To prevent these types of problems, we investigate the use of formal modelling techniques in the concepts phase, because all consecutive phases can benefit from an improved concept description. We report about our experiences with model checking and simulation of formal models in a real development project concerning the start-up and shut-down of interventional X-ray systems of Philips.

2 Industrial Application

The interventional X-ray systems of Philips are intended for minimally invasive treatment of mainly cardiac and vascular diseases. For a new product release,

This research was supported by the Dutch national program COMMIT.

N. Bjørner and F. de Boer (Eds.): FM 2015, LNCS 9109, pp. 605–608, 2015.
DOI: 10.1007/978-3-319-19249-9_43

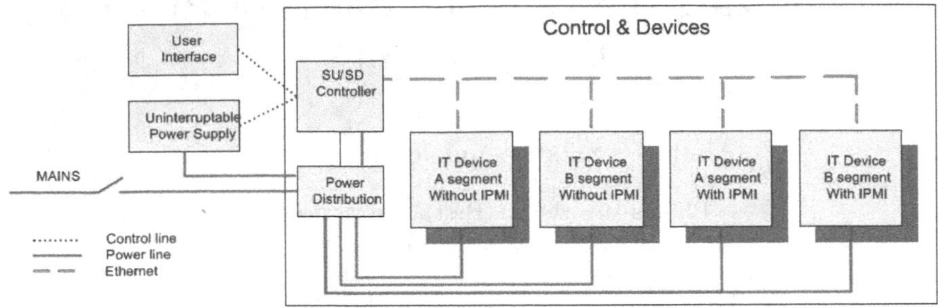

Fig. 1. System overview

we had to create a new concept for starting up and shutting down the system. This new start-up/shut-down (SU/SD) behaviour includes power failure scenarios where graceful degradation mechanisms should ensure that crucial functionality remains operational.

An interventional X-ray system contains a number of IT devices such as computers and touch screen modules. All IT devices can communicate with each other via an internal Ethernet control network. There is a central SU/SD controller which coordinates SU/SD scenarios. A user of the system can initiate a SU/SD scenario by pressing a button on the User Interface (UI). Another scenario can be initiated by the Uninterruptable Power Supply (UPS), for instance, when mains power source fails or when mains power recovers.

The system is partitioned into two segments: A and B[1]. This partitioning is mainly used in the case of a power failure. When all segments are powered and the mains power is lost, the UPS takes over. Once this happens, the A segment is shut down in a controlled way, leaving the B segment powered by the battery of the UPS. If the battery energy level of the UPS becomes critical, also the B segment is shut down in a controlled way.

The new SU/SD concept uses the Intelligent Platform Management Interface (IPMI), a standard interface to manage and monitor IT devices in a network. The IT devices in our system are either IPMI enabled or IPMI disabled. Combined with the two types of segments, this leads to four types of IT devices, as depicted in Figure 1. This figure also shows that there are several communication mechanisms; the internal Ethernet network, power lines for turning the power on and off, and control lines to connect the controller to the UI and the UPS.

3 Formal Techniques Applied

3.1 Model Checking Using mCRL2

We made an abstract model of the SU/SD concept using the mCRL2 model checker[2]. Making the model was very useful to clarify the main concepts and

[1] For reasons of confidentiality, some aspects have been renamed

[2] www.mcrl2.org

remove ambiguities. To allow model checking, this model does not include IPMI and the segments. Also timing aspects and error scenarios are ignored. Nevertheless, model checking such a model (78,088,550 states and 122,354,296 transitions) easily takes hours. The full concept is far more complex because of the many IT devices that all exhibit different behaviour and might fail to start-up or shut down. Moreover, these components are loosely coupled using asynchronous communication mechanisms, leading to a large number of message queues. Hence, we did not see a possibility to check the full model.

3.2 Simulation of POOSL Models

As an alternative to increase the confidence in the concept, we used simulation using formal models expressed in the Parallel Object Oriented Specification Language (POOSL) [3]. POOSL is a modelling language for systems that include both software and digital hardware. It is an object-oriented language with concurrent parallel processes. Processes communicate by synchronous message passing along ports, similar to CS and CCS. Progress of time can be represented and also stochastic distribution functions are supported.

The formal semantics of POOSL has been defined in [4] by means of a probabilistic structural operational semantics for the process layer and a probabilistic denotational semantics for the data layer. This semantics has been implemented in a high-speed simulation engine called Rotalumis. Recently, a modern Eclipse IDE has been developed on top of an improved Rotalumis simulation engine. The Eclipse IDE is free available[3] and supports advanced textual editing with early validation and extensive model debugging possibilities.

Application of POOSL

The aim was to model the Control & Devices part of Figure 1 in POOSL. Besides the SU/SD Controller and the Power Distribution, the model should contain all four types of IT devices, i.e., all combinations of segments (A and B) and IPMI support. Moreover, to capture as much as possible of the timing and ordering behaviour, we decided to include two instances of each type.

To be able to discuss the main concepts with stakeholders, we connect the POOSL model by means of a socket to a simulation environment of the Control & Devices part. The simulator allows sending commands from the User Interface and power components to the model and displaying information received from the model. Additionally, one can observe the status of IT devices and even influence the behaviour of these devices, e.g., to validate scenarios in which one or more IT devices do not start-up or shut down properly.

The simulator has been used to align the behaviour with stakeholders and to get confidence in the correctness of the behaviour. To increase the confidence without the need of many manual mouse clicks, we created a separate test environment in POOSL. It contains stubs which randomly decide if a device fails

[3] poosl.esi.nl

to start-up or shut-down. Moreover, observers are added to check conformance to component interfaces. The test environment leads to a deadlock when the SU/SD controller or the IT devices do not behave as intended. Already during the first simulation run we experienced such a deadlock. The cause of the problem was easily found using the debug possibilities of the new POOSL IDE.

4 Concluding Remarks

Our experiences with the use of model-checking and formal simulation are similar to the observations of [1] on the application of formal methods early in the development process. They propose a rapid prototyping approach, where prototypes are tested against high level objectives. The difficulty to use formal methods early in the development process, when there are many uncertainties and information changes rapidly, is also observed in [2]. They investigated the use of formal simulations based on rewriting logic.

In our case, we successfully used a formal system description in POOSL in combination with a graphical user interface to align stakeholders and get confidence in the behaviour of the system. To increase the confidence in the concept, we created an automated test environment for the system with stubs that exhibit random behaviour and random timing.

While modelling, we found several issues that were not foreseen in the draft concept. We had to address issues that would otherwise have been postponed to the implementation phase and which might easily lead to integration problems. We observed that the definition of a formal executable model of the SU/SD system required a number of design choices.

In addition, the model triggered many discussions about the combined behaviour of the hardware and software involved in start-up and shut-down. This resulted in a clear description of responsibilities in the final concept. Also the exceptional system behaviour when errors occur has been elaborated much more compared to the traditional approach. Note that the modelling approach required a relatively small investment. The main POOSL model and the simulator were made in 40 hours by the first author, starting with very limited POOSL experience; the tester and the stubs required another 10 hours.

References

1. Easterbrook, S.M., Lutz, R.R., Covington, R., Kelly, J., Ampo, Y., Hamilton, D.: Experiences using lightweight formal methods for requirements modeling. IEEE Trans. Software Eng. 24(1), 4–14 (1998)
2. Goodloe, A., Gunter, C.A., Stehr, M.-O.: Formal prototyping in early stages of protocol design. In: WITS 2005, pp. 67–80. ACM (2005)
3. Theelen, B.D., Florescu, O., Geilen, M., Huang, J., van der Putten, P.H.A., Voeten, J.: Software/Hardware Engineering with the Parallel Object-Oriented Specification Language. In: Proc. of MEMOCODE 2007, pp. 139–148. IEEE (2007)
4. van Bokhoven, L.J.: Constructive tool design for formal languages; from semantics to executing models. Phd thesis, Eindhoven Univ. of Tech., The Netherlands (2004)

Author Index

Printed in the United States
By Bookmasters